Parkdale School
1 Parkdale West
Tettenhall Road
W'ton WV1 4TE

INDEPENDENT SCHOOLS OF THE UNITED KINGDOM

1993

E.J.BURROWS
NORTHCOTE HOUSE

JOANELLA SLATTERY ASSOCIATES

EDUCATIONAL CONSULTANTS AND GUARDIANSHIP SERVICES

SIX OF THE BEST
REASONS FOR CONSULTING JSA

1. We are a small firm of educational consultants advising UK, ex-patriate and overseas parents and students.
2. Our services are individual and personal.
3. We only recommend educational establishments which fulfil the specific requirements of the student.
4. Our counselling service encompasses preparatory and secondary boarding schools, secretarial colleges, exclusive English tuition, school holiday courses as well as a wide variety of further educational opportunities.
5. An educational psychologist is available for assessment and advice.
6. We appoint carefully selected 'guardian families' to care for children from overseas who need a 'home' for half-terms, free weekends (and some long holidays if required).

OUR ADVICE IS FREE

Please write or telephone for further information.
Mrs J. Slattery, 63 Grosvenor Road, Tunbridge Wells, Kent TN1 2AY
Tel: 0892 515875   Fax: 0892 520825

HOW THE BLAZES TO KEEP THEM IN BLAZERS

If your children are at an independent school – or soon will be – the ISIS School Fees Special Reserve Plan can give you access to money to help you pay the fees.

It provides a flexible cash fund which you can use to pay all or part of the fees due through each school year. Or simply as a safety net – just in case.

This really is a quick and easy way to take the sting out of school fees.

For the full facts, complete and return the coupon – today.

The School Fees Special Reserve Plan has been designed by financial consultants Claremont Savile jointly with ISIS (the Independent Schools Information Service).

SCHOOL FEES SPECIAL RESERVE PLAN

Advice on School Fees? 'phone HELPLINE 0344 873 377

To: The ISIS Manager, Claremont, Savile, FREEPOST, Ascot, Berks SL5 0YZ
Mr/Mrs/Miss_____ Address_____
_____ Post Code_____ Tel:_____

ISIS
INDEPENDENT SCHOOLS INFORMATION SERVICE

Applicants must be 18 years old or older. Loans subject to status and conditions. Security and insurance will be required. Claremont Savile is a licensed credit broker and a FIMBRA member. Not all the products/services advertised here are regulated by the Financial Services Act 1986 and the rules made for the protection of investors by that Act will not apply to them.

CONTENTS

SCHOOLS OF THE UNITED KINGDOM
an introduction to the directory   Page 5

WHAT IS AN INDEPENDENT SCHOOL?   Page 6
the advantages of an independent
education for all kinds of children

CHOOSING THE RIGHT SCHOOL - WHERE DO I START?
how to begin narrowing down your options   Page 10

VISITING THE SCHOOL OF YOUR CHOICE
contacting schools and planning a visit,
plus a checklist of questions to ask   Page 15

HOW DO I ENTER MY CHILD?
a guide to entry procedures and the interview   Page 20

HOW MUCH WILL IT COST?
school fees and different ways to pay them   Page 22

SCHOLARSHIPS AND GRANTS
an explanation of some of the scholarships,
grants and bursaries available as well as
the Government's Assisted Places Scheme   Page 24

WHAT DO I DO IF I LIVE OVERSEAS?
ways to find the right school for your
child while living abroad   Page 26

USEFUL SOURCES OF FURTHER INFORMATION
addresses and phone numbers of
useful organisations   Page 30

GLOSSARY   Page 33

HOW DO I USE THE DIRECTORY?
a step-by-step guide to using the directory
and the Schools Profile section   Page 34

DIRECTORY   Page 35

SCHOOL PROFILES   Page 653

PROFILES OF FURTHER EDUCATION & TUTORIAL COLLEGES   Page 728

SCHOLARSHIP ANNOUNCEMENTS   Page 736

ALPHABETICAL LIST OF SCHOOLS   Page 753

SCHOOLS OF THE UNITED KINGDOM

Welcome to the 82nd edition of The Schools of the United Kingdom, the most comprehensive guide to Independent schools in Britain and one of the longest-established.

The aim of the DIRECTORY is to help make the whole process of choosing the right school for your child as simple and as easy as possible.

With up-to-date information, clear presentation and geographical and alphabetical listings, The Schools of the United Kingdom offers you a step-by-step guide to help you narrow down your options and then make a firm choice – what to do, where to go for more information, what to ask and what to look for when you visit the school of your choice.

The Schools of the United Kingdom is designed with you in mind.

1 What is an Independent School?

Independent schools offer a choice to all parents who care about their childrens' education.

They are not maintained by local or national government and are financed instead by endowments and the fees they charge to parents. As a result they have remained a stable force unaffected by ever-changing political and bureaucratic influence.

So, while the state maintained sector has been suffering uncertainty and confusion, Independent schools have kept a clear identity in their pursuit of academic excellence and broad cultural and social awareness.

There are three major changes currently affecting the state sector: the establishment of a National Curriculum (a minimum standard for most Independent schools), the Parents' Charter making schools more accountable and the Conservative Government's encouragement to grant maintained schools to opt out of local government control towards a system of independently managed schools operating to a clearly-defined budget – a system more responsive to the wishes of parents and the needs of children.

Meanwhile, Independent schools which include so-called "public" schools and "private" schools – some with histories stretching back to the 14th and 15th centuries – remain freer to decide their own policies and priorities.

Unlike the state maintained schools, the proven independent school system offers parents the widest possible variety of schools to choose from to satisfy the individual needs of their children – both academically and in terms of the cultural and sporting resources and facilities parents want for their children.

It is now generally accepted that Independent schools are not the exclusive preserve of rich or privately-educated parents. Today's Independent school pupils come from all walks of life and every background: what they share in common is parents who are firmly committed to the importance of their child's education and to the principal of freedom of choice.

The most quoted advantages of an Independent school are high standards of education, a well-disciplined environment and smaller classes offering more individual attention.

From an academic point of view, the performance of children at Independent schools is reassuring to parents who accept that academic qualifications still count towards a successful career.

Parents, too, because they are paying for their child's education, are kept more involved. Independent schools have to be seen to be offering value for money and that makes them more accountable.

Equally important, parents – precisely because they are committed enough to pay for their child's education - are keen to encourage their children to do well.

The traditionally smaller classes mean greater individual attention to develop a child's potential to the full, across the complete range of subjects – artistic, practical, physical as well as academic.

Independent schools also cater for those children with special needs - deafness, blindness, epilepsy, dyslexia, and many others including the gifted, the slow-to-learn, those with strong religious beliefs, boarders and those who will benefit most from a single-sex school environment. (see page 31).

For all these reasons, the independent sector continues to attract parents who value the standards of excellence set by Independent schools in all their activities.

Schools for all ages

Independent schools offer an education for children of almost all ages, from two to eighteen-years-old.

England and Wales

Pre-preparatory departments catering for children between the ages of two and seven are becoming more popular. They're equivalent to the infants and nursery stages in the state maintained sector.

These pre-prep departments (also called nursery schools or kindergartens) are usually attached to junior schools. Children normally follow through to junior level but there is no obligation to do so.

Preparatory Schools take children from between the ages of seven and thirteen. Often called prep schools or junior schools, they prepare children for the Common Entrance Examination into senior school but some pupils leave at 11 or later to go on to state maintained secondary schools.

For more information about the Common Entrance Examination, see the section on "How Do I Enter My Child?" on page 20. Some senior schools have their own exam or admit on the basis of an interview only.

Senior Schools cater for pupils between the ages of 11 and 13 to 18-years old. They can be boarding schools or day schools or a mixture of the two; they can be single-sex or co-educational or single-sex but with a mixed sixth form.

Senior schools prepare pupils for General Certificate of Secondary Education (GCSE) examinations at 16 and "A" levels at 18 in the sixth form. The National Curriculum, introduced into state maintained schools, is regarded as a minimum requirement by most Independent schools.

Scotland

Preparatory Schools in Scotland take pupils from four to 13 and prepare them for the Common Entrance Examination. They are largely boys schools but many of them take girls.

Junior Schools take pupils between eight and 13 and tend to be smaller junior departments of senior schools.

Senior Schools take pupils from between 10 and 13 to 18 and prepare them for Scottish examinations.

In most Scottish schools, pupils study for the Scottish Certificate of Education (SCE) Ordinary and Higher Grade examinations. Ordinary Grade is taken at 15 and is roughly equivalent to GCSE. There is also a Scottish Certificate of Sixth Year Studies and some Independent Scottish schools also do "A"levels.

For more information about Scotland, contact Scottish ISIS at: Floor 2/1, Castle Street, Edinburgh EH2 3AH. Tel: 031 220 2106.

Choosing the right school – where do I start?

With more than 2,000 Independent schools to choose from – and every one of them claiming to be a little different to the rest – the task ahead may seem a daunting one.

Asking yourself three basic questions will help you to see the wood from the trees so that you can narrow down your choices to just a few. Once you've decided, make a list of the three or so you'd like to know more about.

The three questions are: boarding or day school? Single sex or mixed? Junior or senior school? As much as possible, try to involve your child from the very start of the process. The process of adjustment to a new school really does start here.

Question One

Is it to be a boarding or a day school? Boarding is less popular than it used to be and the majority of children at Independent schools are day pupils. Weekly boarding where the child comes home at weekends is a more popular compromise and, in future, more schools are likely to offer it.

The vast majority of Independent schools have a combination of day and boarding pupils with the emphasis either one way or the other.

If you feel a day school would best suit your child, then you will immediately be narrowing down your choice of school to those within convenient travelling distance of your home.

Generally, pupils at Independent schools come from a much wider catchment area than those attending local authority schools. Take a look at rail and bus links. Some schools even run their own bus service and there may be parents near you with children already at the school who could share car journeys. Schools will be happy to put you in touch.

One of the principal advantages of boarding schools is that it offers you a much wider choice of schools outside your own area.

Most people seem to pick schools within reasonable driving distance. If you're going to be working abroad or if the school has to be further away, try and choose one near close relatives, such as grandparents, or close friends so that there's someone your child knows near at hand.

Above all, make sure your child is happy with the idea. Some independent children flourish in such an environment, others definitely don't. You know best if your child would benefit from or cope with being away from you for long periods. If you find the choice a difficult one, discuss it with a close friend who knows you and your child and can give an objective view.

Question Two

Will your child do better at a single sex or mixed school? There are advantages and disadvantages to single sex and co-educational schools and opinions vary a great deal about which is best.

Most preparatory or junior schools are co-educational. Not surprisingly, a mixed environment tends to become more of an issue the older the child gets. Again, what works for one may not work for another.

You may feel your son or daughter would make better progress without the distraction of the opposite sex but, if there is a trend, it is towards the co-educational school. Those who support it, talk about the need for the school to reflect the real world outside by educating for life and not for some artificial single sex environment.

Once more, you are probably the best judge of which environment will suit your child best and your child's view is also important.

You may, however, need to be on your guard if the co-educational school you are choosing used to be a single-sex school. While many have integrated well, some schools may still be dominated by that sex and by the ethos which went with it. You should learn something of the school's history and investigate how well the second sex has been integrated.

Question Three

Do you want your child to start as a junior or a senior? Here, the choice is relatively straightforward. Do you want to give your child an independent education throughout his or her school life, or will you be choosing a good maintained school for part of that period, either at the junior or senior stage?

Some Independent schools educate all ages from five to 18 to avoid any break in continuity. Others are entered between the ages of 11 and 13 after preparatory school and the sitting of the Common Entrance Examination, though this is not always necessary. Lots of schools have their own entrance tests. Check what's required by the schools on your shortlist.

An increasing number of parents are prepared to combine an independent and state education, depending on how good their local maintained school is at secondary and primary level.

It is perfectly possible to take advantage of the best of both school systems in your area and Independent schools can accommodate this flexible approach.

Question Four

Once you have got this far, one further fundamental question suggests itself: what kind of school environment will best suit your child? It's not easy matching a school to the individual needs of your child. There is no such thing as a school that suits every type of pupil and the trick is to find a school to which your child will be able to adapt most easily.

Few parents are very objective when it comes to assessing their child's abilities but it pays to be so. Too academic and your child will feel swamped and inferior, too far the other way and he or she will be bored and demotivated. The best environment is where your child is slightly above average.

Choose the school which you feel is able to develop your child's potential to the full and where the range of subjects can broadly match your child's own interests, whilst still leaving scope to develop others. Don't lose sight of other subjects such as music, drama and other activities which can contribute to a rounded, well-balanced education.

If your child is less academically able, look for the benefit of smaller classes where your child will receive more individual attention.

Drawing-up your short list
By now you should be in a position to identify the type of independent school you are looking for. The next step is to use the directory on pages 35 to 652 to select your short list of schools worthy of closer examination.

Additional information about many of the schools in the Directory, often with accompanying photographs is contained in our special School Profiles section and these are cross-referenced for your convenience.

Approaching the School
Once you have made your choice of three or four possibilities, you will need to approach each one to ask for a prospectus.

At this stage, you should mention your child's age, sex and intended year of entry as well as any special requirements.

The prospectus will give you a more detailed impression of the school, its ethos and aims as well as more practical information about the curriculum, facilities and fees etc.

Regard them as an additional source of information about the school to be used in combination with a visit. With that in mind, you can use the prospectus to arm yourself with a list of worthwhile questions to ask when you get there (see the following chapter).

■

3 Visiting the school of your choice

There are two things to say here. First of all, make sure you visit the school during term time so you can see it in action and secondly, prepare a list of questions beforehand. We show you how on page 17.

By now a shortlist of three or four schools should be enough.

When you arrive, sum up your first impressions. You can learn a lot from looking at the pupils and the staff. What impression do they give of a lively, well-motivated school?

Noticeboards and classroom displays all have a story to tell and you can ask to see examples of work. Don't attach too much importance to buildings: they won't tell you whether the teaching is good. Pay more attention to the equipment available to pupils in labs and classrooms. How well run is the library?

Check the size of classes – one of the most quoted advantages over local maintained schools. Ask about the curriculum. Is it well balanced or weighted towards the arts or sciences and will this suit your child? Ask about homework and how much pupils are given.

Try to assess the pupil/staff relationship. How interested are staff in your child and whether their school will be right for your child?

Try to arrange your visit so that you can meet the Head as well as other staff. Ask about discipline. Does it offer the right balanced atmosphere to suit your child? Ask about rules and the usual punishments and satisfy yourself that they're based on responsible common sense and are not too rigid or too petty.

How well does the school involve parents? How often are parents' evenings held to discuss pupils' work? How easily can you gain access to teachers to discuss progress or problems with them?

Ask about the school's examination performance in comparison to the national average but don't regard it as the 'be all and end all'. Make sure you know what figures they are giving you. High percentage passes may refer only to those pupils submitted for exams because they were likely to pass.

Some schools may have a lower pass rate because they are more willing to spend time with less academic pupils bringing out the best in them. This may be a much more suitable school for your child than one with, for instance, a high Oxbridge intake.

Ask whether they have good contacts with outside companies; what is the standard of their careers support and advice?

Last year, under the Parents' Charter provisions, all state schools were forced to disclose examination results and such things as truancy rates and the destinations of their final year pupils. From this summer, disclosure is compulsory for Independent schools, too.

If you're considering a boarding school for your child, there are a number of additional questions to consider on your visit.

What happens after classes have finished for the day? How is the rest of the day planned? What extra-curricular activities are there? How much privacy does a pupil have? Are they allowed out? When do they have to go to bed? Do they have any duties to perform? What happens at weekends?

Evenings and weekends at school will effectively replace the home environment and you should take particular care to identify what your child will be doing and whether he or she will adapt well to that school's regime.

Who does a pupil go to for personal rather than academic advice? Housemasters or housemistresses are just as important as the head of the school and you should feel comfortable with them. Also, what medical facilities are available?

Above all, take your child with you, if you can. It's important that he or she should be involved in your ultimate decision.

Ask the school for the phone numbers of any parents who may live near you. Their opinions of the school my help you to make up your own mind.

YOUR QUESTIONS CHECK LIST

The following is a checklist of possible questions that will give you a fuller picture of the school you are visiting to help you make the best possible choice.

The list is by no means a comprehensive one. Each of the main topics for investigation is covered but you will want to expand some sections with additional questions to suit your child's own individual needs.

1. How big is the school?

- [ ] Number of Boys. [ ] Girls [ ] Boarders [ ] Day pupils

- [ ] Number of Teachers [ ] Size of classes

2. Does it have comprehensive resources and facilities?

- [ ] Academic
- [ ] Sports
- [ ] Music
- [ ] Art
- [ ] Others (clubs, societies and extra curricular activities)

3. How academic is the school?

- [ ] Exam results in comparison to national average
- [ ] Academic standards **a.** high **b.** low
- [ ] School's attitude to less academic children
- [ ] School's streaming system
- [ ] Amount of homework: **a.** How much? **b.** How is it monitored?
- [ ] Subjects available at GCSE level or Scottish equivalent
- [ ] Subjects available at A level or Scottish equivalent

4. How well-qualified and experienced are the teachers?

- [ ] Number of graduate teachers
- [ ] Number qualified in the subjects they're teaching

5. How disciplined is the school?

- [ ] The level of discipline **a.** high **b.** low
- [ ] Type of punishments **a.** responsible **b.** rigid **c.** petty

6. Does the school involve parents?

- [ ] Number of parents evenings
- [ ] Is there a PTA?
- [ ] Access to teachers **a.** good **b.** bad

7. How much will it cost?

- [ ] Fees per term
- [ ] Methods of payment
- [ ] Any extra charges

8. Available scholarships, grants, bursaries

9. Are there any parents from the area?

☐ Telephone number of parents willing to discuss the school and possible travel arrangements

10. Admission procedures?

☐ Examination, tests or interviews required
☐ Anything else taken into account

11. What's special about this school?

☐ Level of interest shown in my child   **a.** A lot   **b.** A little

12. Does the school cater for pupils with particular special needs?

13. Boarding Schools?

Some additional points to consider if your child will be boarding: standard of accommodation and facilities. An example of a typical school day:

☐ Amount of free time, privacy, freedom
☐ Level of supervision
☐ Organised activities after school hours/ at weekends
☐ Role of housemaster/mistress
☐ Medical and pastoral facilities

How do I enter my child?

The first thing to do is to register your child's name as soon as you can. Many schools, particularly those which are better-known and those in major cities, have waiting lists of two years and more. Others will choose on a first come, first served formula.

Entry Requirements
Pre-Prep schools for children between 5 and 8 years old require little more than a simple interview and some indication of your child's verbal skill level. Most of the time, entry has more to do with the number of places available.

Prep Schools for entry at 8 years old usually have some form of competitive examination in the three "R"s as well as an interview.

At senior level, the procedures for admission may vary from the Common Entrance Examination, a school's own test, or an interview to a combination of all three. Find out which applies to your school and begin preparing your child. You should be able to get hold of some old exam papers from the school.

Those schools which do use the Common Entrance Examination will have separate exams for state pupils or pupils above or below the standard age for entry into senior school. Exams are usually held in the year prior to entry so it is important to approach the school early.

The Common Entrance Examination is taken by boys at 13 for entry into senior school and between 11 and 13 by girls. The exam is set centrally and you can get copies from the Common Entrance Board, Ashley Lane, Lymington, Hants SO41 9YR. Tel: 0590 675947.

Each school marks the papers themselves and has its own pass mark. The exam is normally held in February, June and November. If your child is currently in a state primary school, ISIS can advise you about tutors and tutorial colleges, if necessary. (see page 30)

The Interview

The dreaded interview is in fact a constructive two-way process for both you and the school to find out more about each other. Between you, you ought to be able to decide whether you have found the right school for your child. So you should be doing just as much of the interviewing.

The more relaxed you appear, the more comfortable your child will be about the interview, particularly once he or she is left alone with the head.

It's always rather dangerous to rehearse for interviews. More often than not, they're not what you expected. However, one or two sensible questions your child can ask the Head can help create a good impression.

From your point of view, it works both ways. It is just as important that the Head makes a good impression and shows the proper level of interest in your child.

All Heads will have witnessed creeping paralysis descending upon even the most self-confident child so don't worry if it happens to yours. Any Head will have seen it all before and your child will become more relaxed once you're out the room.

It's at this stage that involving your child, from the start, in the process of choosing the right school may well pay dividends. Instead of being thrust into some terrifying abyss, they'll understand what's happening and why.

How much will it cost?

Fees vary from around £700 to £2,500 a term for a senior day pupil and from around £1,900 to £3,000 and above for a boarder. Fees for junior day pupils vary between £600 and £1,700 and for junior boarders from about £1,300 to £2,500. Most schools charge by the term.

Banks, insurance companies, other financial institutions and some schools offer different schemes to help parents pay school fees.

Planning early is by far the best way to reduce the burden of fees. The more you can put down as a lump sum in advance, the bigger the potential savings. Up to 40% is possible if you put down a lump sum to cover all of your child's education at least four years in advance. A 15% saving is possible by paying at the time of your child's entry.

There are a variety of ways of financing school fees.

Taking out an insurance policy before your child's first birthday (so that it matures near the start of your child's entry to senior school) and then one every subsequent year, is still seen as one of the less risky ways of saving for school fees.

Other savings schemes which may offer a greater return on your investment, include unit trust savings schemes, PEPs and personal pension plans. In every case, you should discuss all these options with a school fees expert. For more information see the advertisements on pages 653 to 752.

Relatives, such as grandparents, are another option – either as providers of a lump sum or regular contributions to help you pay for a policy.

If you own your own home, equity release plans or a second mortgage are other ways to release capital tied up in your home. Again, seek expert advice.

Bank loans or overdrafts are expensive ways to raise school fees and National Westminster and the Midland Banks are more than willing to tailor loan plans or savings plans to meet your particular financial circumstances.

Lloyds Bank, offer an educational option as part of a secured loan. There's a preferential rate for money borrowed to pay school fees and the repayment period can be extended to 30 years. They also offer parents a monthly savings plan to build up a substantial sum over 10 years or more.

The Barclays School Fees Plan offers an immediate fees option and a savings option for parents planning ahead. SFIA, the School Fees Insurance Agency is an independent financial adviser set up in 1952 to help parents meet the cost of school fees. Their address is in the glossary on page 33.

Understandably the majority of parents have not been able to save in advance for school fees; if you don't have the luxury of being able to draw on capital and need help now, ISIS (The Independent Schools Information Service) has, together with their Advisers, Claremont Savile devised a new Plan to make school fees manageable.

The ISIS School Fees Special Reserve Plan creates a borrowing facility, secured on your home for you to use as and when required, interest is only charged on the monies borrowed (at competitive Building Society rates) and the repayment of capital is arranged via Claremont Savile in the most tax-efficient and cost-effective manner possible.

A brochure describing the scheme is available from ISIS at 56 Buckingham Gate, London SW1E 6AG. Tel 071 630 8793 or, alternatively should you wish to discuss your own situation in detail the Helpline number is 0344 873377.

There are also special schemes run by schools in co-operation with insurance companies to pay back fees in the event of your child being off school due to illness. Others guarantee the continued payment of fees in the event of your illness, redundancy or death. It's one of the things to ask the school you visit.

You should be able to determine the most efficient payment strategy to suit your pocket. ISIS is a good starting point for your enquiries.

Scholarships and Grants

Scholarships are a way of helping parents to pay the fees. Most schools offer them. They're awarded on the strength of a pupil's potential – either academic, musical, artistic or sporting - and are usually decided by competitive examination or test.

They can cover all or part of a pupil's school fees and sometimes the parent's income is taken into account, sometimes not. It's just possible that you're less than objective about your child's abilities so discuss the chances of success with the Head of his or her existing school.

Bursaries are normally grants made by schools to parents who can't afford to pay full fees. They're usually awarded after a means test of family income and, more often than not, go to the parents of children already at the school who have fallen on hard times.

Grants are offered by some schools to children of clergymen, teachers, service personnel, the children of former pupils or of single parent families and orphans. If any of these apply, ask the school of your choice for more details.

The Ministry of Defence gives grants to the children of parents in all ranks of the armed forces. You can get more information from your local Service Education Unit or the Service Children's Education Authority at Court Road, Eltham, SE9 5NR. Tel: 081 781 4277/9.

Many boarding schools offer concessions to service children. Grants can also be given by some Education Authorities and Social Services Departments to help children who need to board, either because their parents have to go abroad, the family have to move frequently or because travelling to the nearest maintained school is difficult. Ask the Education

Department of your local authority for details.

Certain trusts will also award grants to help with school fees in special circumstances and will consider applications from anyone who genuinely needs help with a child's education.

National ISIS runs a grant advisory service and can provide further details on request. (see page 30.)

Assisted Places Scheme – Parents unable to afford to send gifted children to Independent schools can get help from the Government under its Assisted Places Scheme.

The scheme applies to children of 11 and above and the amount of financial assistance depends on parental income. Altogether the government contributes towards 36,000 assisted places at about 350 participating schools in England, Wales and Scotland.

Though they don't include boarding fees, some schools offer boarding bursaries to children who win Assisted Places under the scheme. Each school uses its own selection procedures.

The DIRECTORY section identifies which schools participate in the scheme. A full list of participating schools is also available from ISIS at 56 Buckingham Gate, London SW1 6AG. Tel: 071 630 8793/4.

Further details of the scheme are available from the Department for Education, Mowden Hall, Staindrop Road, Darlington, County Durham DL3 9BG. Tel: 0325 392158.

Or: The Welsh Office Education Department (SAD3), Phase II Government Buildings, Ty Glas Road, Llanishen, Cardiff CF4 5WE. Tel: 0222 761456 ext 5362.

There is a separate Assisted Places Scheme in Scotland. To find out more, contact: Scottish ISIS, Floor 2/1, 11 Castle Street, Edinburgh EH2 3AH. Tel: 031 220 2106.

What do I do, if I live overseas?

The two best pieces of advice to overseas parents are not to leave choosing a school until the last minute and not to insist upon a school near London. There are many first class schools throughout the UK. The education and facilities offered by these schools are just as good as those near London and many of the buildings and countryside surrounding these schools cannot be bettered.

Overseas parents tend to look for a school near Heathrow and Gatwick. This is not necessary. There are many good airports throughout the UK and parents should ask for information from travel agents in their own country.

Overseas parents can find the task of trying to choose a school a daunting one. Prospectuses give an overall picture of a school but it is not always possible to get the "feel" of the school from them. Many questions remain unanswered. When parents have little or no knowledge of the British education system, it is advisable to approach an Educational Consultant for advice. These consultants are experienced, have expert knowledge of a variety of schools and can help parents to identify "the right school" for their child. Appointments can be made for parents and child to be interviewed at one or more schools before a final decision is taken.

When applying initially, parents should send the child's details: full name, date of birth, nationality, religion, interests, as well as (if possible) copies of recent school reports. Heads are reluctant to offer a place unless they have some idea of a child's academic ability. If this is done at the very beginning it avoids unnecessary delay.

Parents should make every effort to visit at least two or three schools with their child before making a decision. This can be difficult for some parents but it can make the experience easier for their child. To have seen the school and met the staff and other students beforehand, can help make the first few weeks of school life less stressful. It is important to visit the school during the term when the school is functioning.

English language
An important consideration is the child's level of spoken and written English. Some schools will be able to offer extra English lessons and help the child, but children are not suitable for secondary school unless they can understand the spoken word and read English text books.

It is wise to send the child to the UK for a few weeks before term starts. A good time is during the long summer holidays in July and August. Summer courses are available every year, especially for overseas students.

Guardianship
Most schools and colleges now insist that parents nominate a "Guardian". Some overseas parents have friends and/or relatives in the UK who are happy to undertake this responsibility. Others do not.

For this reason there are companies which run a guardianship service which should cover every possible aspect of an overseas student's needs.

Guardians should be expected to perform the usual duties of a parent - arrange travel to and from school, send presents and cards on birthdays, attend parents' day and speech days, and have the child home for holidays, if necessary.

It is a wise precaution for overseas parents to check with a company, before paying the registration fee or signing an agreement, to make certain that it does fulfil their requirements.

The most important part of the service should be the provision of a responsible, caring and committed "guardian family" who will look after the child exactly like one of their own children. They will have the child to stay with them during half-terms, exeat weekends and at the beginning and end of terms, if flights do not coincide with term dates. They will also be available for some long school holidays if required, as well as in an emergency such as illness. The family should be prepared to visit the school, take an interest in the student's progress and welfare as well as school functions when parents are unable to do so. Overseas children should be given their own bedroom where they can leave their belongings, where they can go if they need to work quietly, or if they just need to be alone.

A guardianship service should include the care and commitment normally given by parents and should provide full administrative responsibility. The service should include general liaison with the school, parents and the appointed "guardian family", responsibility for arranging a reliable escort service for the child to and from the airport, holiday arrangements, booking and confirmation of flights, renewal of passports, advice about visas, inoculations and vaccinations etc.

Companies charge a fee for their guardianship service and may run their services differently from one another. It would be wise to check exactly what the company charges as fees vary. Above all it would be wise to obtain a written estimate of the overall annual cost and to ask whether a detailed statement of account is submitted periodically so that expenditure can be checked and thus enable parents to budget in advance.

The Service Children's Education Authority
The Service Children's Education Authority offers advice about boarding schools to the armed forces and civilians attached to the Ministry of Defence. You should contact: SCEA, HQ Director of Army Education, Court Road, Eltham, London SE9 5NR. Tel: 081 781 4277/9.

For foreign parents living abroad and sending their children to a British school, command of English becomes more important the older a child becomes. As work becomes more advanced, fluent English reading is necessary to keep up. ISIS International can arrange for children to attend additional English Language courses.

ISIS International

ISIS International helps parents living overseas to find places for their children in British Independent schools. It offers three principal services:

A Placement Scheme – Once it has details of your child, ISIS International will provide a shortlist of suitable schools prepared to accept your child, subject to any relevant entry requirements. It will co-ordinate visit arrangements, advise on guardians and oversee all administrative arrangements until a school is finally selected.

A Consultancy Service – This provides detailed personal advice about suitable schools but leaves parents to apply to schools themselves.

A Clearing House – The ISIS International clearing house passes your details on to schools who then make their offers of a place direct to parents.

A National ISIS consultancy service for UK parents is also available via ISIS International. (see page 30).

School Fees Service

BDO Binder Hamlyn is an international accounting organisation with offices in 61 countries. It offers a school fees planning service for clients overseas as well as in the UK and invests their money with offshore institutions to avoid unnecessary taxation.

You can contact them at: 17 Lansdowne Road, Croydon CR9 2PL. Tel: 081 688 4422. Fax: 081 0315. Telex: 917857. Ask for Peter Lewiston.

Useful sources of further information

National ISIS

The Independent Schools Information Service exists to promote its 1300 Independent schools and answers 30,000 enquiries a year on all aspects of an Independent education. It also runs eight regional offices around the UK. Contact them at: 56 Buckingham Gate, London SW1E 6AG. Tel: 071 630 8793/4.

ISIS International helps parents living abroad to find suitable British schools for their children. Their address is the same as above but you can telephone them direct on: 071 630 8790 or by fax on: 071 630 5013.

Religious Schools

For more information about schools which meet specific religious needs contact the following organisations.

Church of England. The Woodard Corporation, 1 The Sanctuary, London SW1P 3JT. Tel: 071 222 5381.
The Allied Schools, 42 South Bar Street, Banbury, Oxon OX16 9XL. Tel: 0295 56441.

Roman Catholic. The Catholic Education Service for England and Wales, 41 Cromwell Road, London SW7 2DJ. Tel: 071 584 7491.

Methodist. The Methodist Church Division of Education and Youth, 25 Marylebone Road, London NW1 5JP. Tel: 071 935 3723.

Quaker. The Friends' Schools Joint Council, Friends' House, Euston Road, London NW1 2BJ. Tel: 071 387 3601.

Jewish. The Jewish Board of Deputies, Woburn House, Tavistock Square, London WC1H 0EP. Tel: 071 387 3952.

Choir Schools. Mr H. Moore, Secretary of the Choir Schools Association and Headmaster of The Cathedral Choir School, Whitcliff Ripon, North Yorkshire H94 2LA Tel: 0765 602134.

Gifted children. The National Association for Gifted Children, Park Campus, Boughton Green Road, Northampton NN2 7AL. Tel: 0604 792300.

Special Needs
Some schools provide for children with special needs. These may range from mild handicap and learning or language difficulties to epilepsy, blindness, deafness and a whole range of other special needs. To find out which schools cater for a special need relevant to your child contact the following:

England
Department of Education and Science, Schools Branch 2, Division B (Special Education), Elizabeth House, 39 York Road, London SE1 7PH. Tel: 071 934 9000.

Wales
Welsh Office of Education Department, Schools Administration Branch 3, Phase 2 Government Buildings, Ty Glas Road, Llanishen, Cardiff CF4 5WE. Tel: 0222 761456.

Scotland

Scottish Education Department (Special Schools), New St Andrew's House, St James Centre, Edinburgh EH1 35Y. Tel: 031 556 8400.

Northern Ireland

Department of Education for Northern Ireland, Schools 1 Division, Rathgael House, Balloo Road, Bangor, Northern Ireland BT 19 2PR. Tel: 0247 270077.

Common Entrance Examination

Common Entrance Board, Ashley Lane, Lymington, Hants SO41 9YR. Tel: 0590 675947

Glossary

SFIA – The School Fees Insurance Agency Ltd, SFIA House, 15 Forlease Road, Maidenhead, Berks SL6 IJA. Tel: 0628 34291.

GPDST – The Girls' Public Day School Trust. Founded in 1872 it currently has 26 member schools providing education for day girls between the ages of 5 and 18.

GSA – Girls' Schools Association. An association of independent girls' school Heads which furthers the interests and standards of girls' education.

HMC – The Headmasters' Conference has a membership limited to 240 Heads of Independent schools with a small additional number of members from voluntary and state schools. Membership is a good indication of the academic standards of a member headmaster's school.

IAPS – The Incorporated Association of Preparatory Schools. This is the professional association of the Heads of preparatory schools.

ISJC – The Independent Schools Joint Council. In conjunction with ISIS, the Council represents the collective views of the leading associations of Independent schools and has its own system for accrediting the member schools of those associations.

9 How do I use this directory?

The Schools of the United Kingdom offers you two ways to find the school of your choice.

1. If your shortlist provides you with a specific geographical area, you will find schools listed under each County in Britain in the DIRECTORY which starts on the following page

The DIRECTORY is part of a full information profile of each school. Each entry contains important details and a brief description of the school.

2. Schools are also listed alphabetically in the index on page 753.

Make sure you see all the information about your chosen schools. Each DIRECTORY entry will also guide you to where else the school is mentioned - most importantly in the SCHOOLS PROFILE section, which will contain additional information and perhaps a photograph to give you a visual impression of the school. The school may also be one of those in the SCHOLARSHIPS AND GRANTS section.

To make sure you take full advantage of every mention, the ALPHABETICAL INDEX also lists every page where a school is mentioned so that you can begin building the fullest possible picture of those schools which interest you most.

N.B. * *Indicates that the school participates in the Assisted Places Scheme.*
† *Indicates Special School.*

AVON

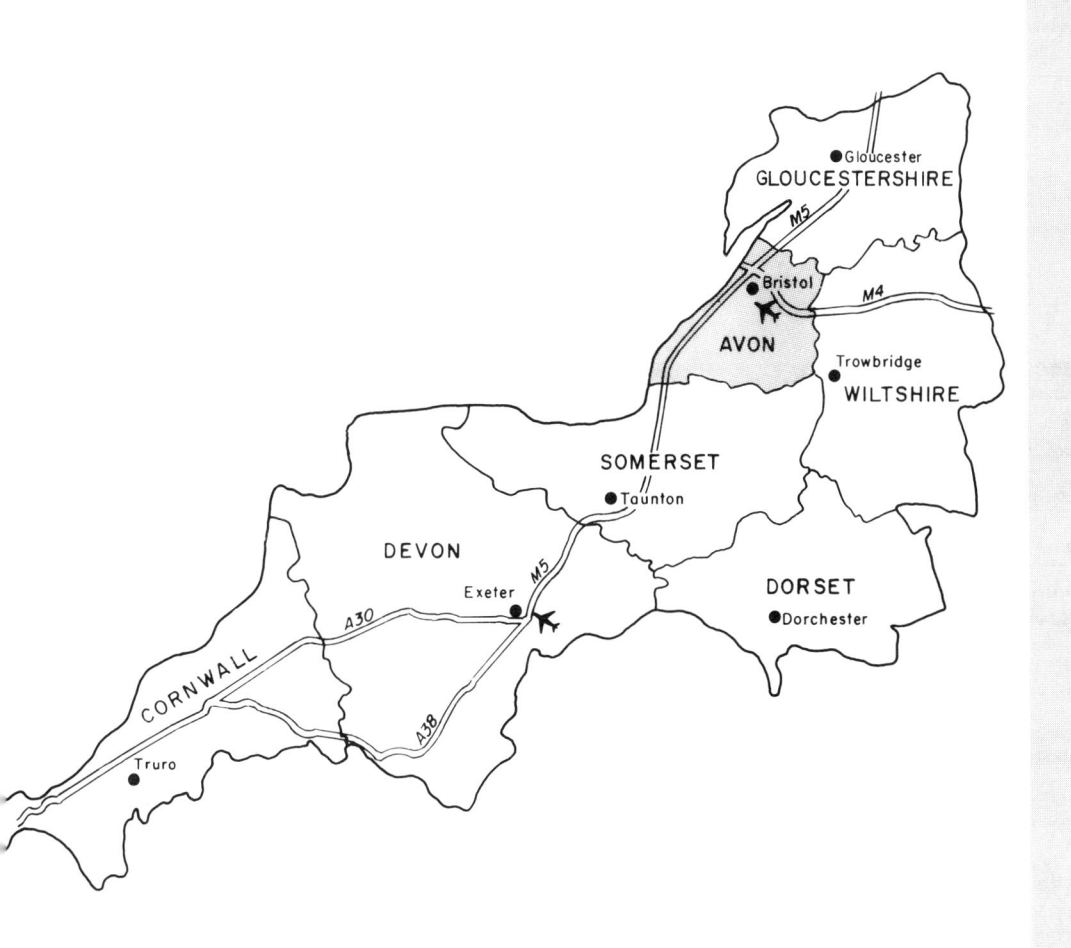

Amberley House

Address: 42 Apsley Road, Clifton, Bristol, Avon BS8 2SU

Telephone: 0272 735515

Head: Mrs M Lenko

Age range: 0-11
No. of pupils: 220
Scholarships:
Religion: Non-denominational

Fees per term
Day: £230-£690
Weekly board: -
Full board: -

Boy ○ Girl ○ Co-ed ●
Day ● Week ○ Board ○

A baby nursery from one month to two years leading into a preparatory school for girls and boys from two to eleven plus. Open all year except bank holidays and until 6pm each day. Pupils are prepared for the independent schools of Bristol. The school is staffed by teachers who consider the needs of every individual pupil.

Ashbrooke House Preparatory School

Address: 9 Ellenborough Park North, Weston-super-Mare, Avon BS23 1XH

Telephone: 0934 629515

Heads: Mr D C M Atkinson Mr A J Counsell

Age range: 4-13
No. of pupils: 66
Scholarships:
Religion: Non-denominational

Fees per term
Day: £479-£566
Weekly board: -
Full board: -

Boy ○ Girl ○ Co-ed ●
Day ● Week ○ Board ○

Ashbrooke House Preparatory School offers existing and prospective parents a formal and traditional style of education for children aged 5-13 years. Besides offering all National Curriculum subjects the school incorporates the teaching of computers, French and German into the timetable. The primary function of the school is to 'prepare' children for transition to senior school.

Badminton

Address: Westbury-on-Trym, Bristol, Avon BS9 3BA

Telephone: 0272 623141

Head: Mr C J J Gould

Age range: 7-18
No. of pupils: 360
Scholarships: Yes
Religion: Non-denominational

Fees per term
Day: £965-£1680
Weekly board: -
Full board: £2310-£3075

Boy ○ Girl ● Co-ed ○
Day ● Week ○ Board ●

Badminton regularly achieves a more than 90% pass rate in its A levels, and all leavers go on to higher education. The style of the school is to develop motivation and self-discipline to a high level without cramming, so that the school can excel not only in its academic results (98% GCSE pass rate A to C) but also boast outstanding music, art and sport. Badminton is not a narrowly selective school.

Badminton Junior School

Address: Westbury-on-Trym, Bristol, Avon BS9 3BA
Telephone: 0272 624733

Head: Mrs A Lloyd

Age range: 7-11
No. of pupils: 60
Scholarships: Yes
Religion: Non-denominational

Fees per term
Day: £1035-£1250
Weekly board: -
Full board: £2480-£2480

Boy ○ Girl ● Co-ed ○
Day ● Week ○ Board ●

Badminton has a friendly and welcoming atmosphere with high standards expected for both work and behaviour. There is automatic entry to the senior school at 11+ with academic and music scholarships available. Bristol is blessed with good transport links.

Bath High School ✻

Address: Hope House,
Lansdown, Bath, Avon
BA1 5ES
Telephone: 0225 422931

Age range: 4-18
No. of pupils: 636
Scholarships: Yes
Religion: Non-denominational

Fees per term
Day: £880-£1148
Weekly board: -
Full board: -

○ ● ○
Boy Girl Co-ed
● ○ ○
Day Week Board

Head: Miss M A Winfield BA

Bath High School, founded in 1875, is one of 26 schools administered by the Girls' Public Day School Trust. Six hundred and thirty girls aged between 4-18 presently attend, 104 of these being in the sixth form. The school has a reputation for high academic achievement, whilst maintaining numerous extra-curricular activities. Plans to massively develop the school's facilities will be implemented during 1992-1994.

Bristol Cathedral School ✻

Address: College Square,
Bristol, Avon BS1 5TS

Telephone: 0272 291872

Age range: 11-18
No. of pupils: 470
Scholarships: Yes
Religion: Church of England

Fees per term
Day: £1226-£1226
Weekly board: -
Full board: -

● ● ○
Boy Girl Co-ed
● ○ ○
Day Week Board

Head: Mr R A Collard MA

For further details and a prospectus, please contact the school. Girls accepted in sixth form.

Bristol Grammar School ✻

Address: University Road,
Bristol, Avon BS8 1SR

Telephone: 0272 736006

Age range: 7-18
No. of pupils: 1000
Scholarships: Yes
Religion: Non-denominational

Fees per term
Day: £676-£1179
Weekly board: -
Full board: -

○ ○ ●
Boy Girl Co-ed
● ○ ○
Day Week Board

Head: Mr C E Martin MA

The school is a co-educational day school with approximately 1,000 pupils from age 11 to age 18, the different age groups being housed in separate, self-contained buildings. Entry to the school is normally in September at age 11+ following a satisfactory performance in the entrance examination held in the previous spring, but some places become available each year at ages 13+ and 16+.

Bristol Waldorf School

Address: Park Place, Clifton,
Bristol, Avon BS8 1JR

Telephone: 0272 260440

Age range: 3-14
No. of pupils: 250
Scholarships:
Religion: Rudolph Steiner

Fees per term
Day: -
Weekly board: -
Full board: -

○ ○ ●
Boy Girl Co-ed
● ○ ○
Day Week Board

Head: See Below

Bristol Waldorf School, founded in 1973, is open to all children of whatever social, racial, religious or financial background. The school is co-educational, independent and offers a comprehensive Waldorf education to children from 3-14 years. There are no set fees, but the school operates a guided contribution system based on net income. The school is run by two chair persons elected annually.

Clark's Grammar School

Address: 21 Alma Road,
Clifton, Bristol, Avon BS8 2BZ

Telephone: 0272 735404

Head: Mr M J Barber

Age range: 9-16
No. of pupils: 176
Scholarships:
Religion:

Fees per term
Day: £575-£695
Weekly board: -
Full board: -

Boy ○　Girl ○　Co-ed ●
Day ●　Week ○　Board ○

Clark's is a small day school in the heart of Clifton. The school caters for boys and girls of a wide ability range in a caring community. Class sizes are small and attention is given to the needs of each pupil.

Cleve House School

Address: 245 Wells Road,
Bristol, Avon BS4 2PN

Telephone: 0272 777218

Heads: Mr D Lawson BA(Hons) MA, Mrs F E Lawson BEd MA

Age range: 2-11
No. of pupils: 200
Scholarships:
Religion: Non-denominational

Fees per term
Day: £550-£575
Weekly board: -
Full board: -

Boy ○　Girl ○　Co-ed ●
Day ●　Week ○　Board ○

Cleve House School was established on its present site in 1948. Classes are small in a caring and friendly environment. High academic standards. Separate nursery and kindergarten departments. Our aim is to educate children to be useful and compassionate members of society as well as emphasising high standards of literacy and numeracy.

Clifton College *

Address: Bristol, Avon
BS8 3JH

Telephone: 0272 739187
Headmaster: Mr A H Monro

Age range: 13-18
No. of pupils: 670
Scholarships: Yes
Religion: Church of England

Fees per term
Day: £2590-
Weekly board: -
Full board: £3695-

Boy ○　Girl ○　Co-ed ●
Day ●　Week ○　Board ●

Founded in 1862 the school has produced three Nobel prizewinners, and nationally known figures in many walks of life. Music and drama play a major part in the life of the school, while a great range of sport is available. Excellent academic, sporting and cultural facilities are available, and the school is fully co-educational. There is one Jewish house within the school.

Clifton College Preparatory School

Address: The Avenue, Clifton,
Bristol, Avon BS8 3HE

Telephone: 0272 737264

Head: Mr R S Trafford

Age range: 3-13
No. of pupils: 525
Scholarships: Yes
Religion: Church of England

Fees per term
Day: £750-£1995
Weekly board: -
Full board: £2760-£2760

Boy ○　Girl ○　Co-ed ●
Day ●　Week ○　Board ●

A big school with a staff of 50 and extensive facilities, including sports centre, two astroturf pitches, art and resource centres, with specialist teaching leading to 17/18 scholarships a year. Children divided into pre-preparatory (3-7) and small pastoral units, each with house master/mistress and other staff.

Clifton High School for Girls *

Address: College Road, Clifton, Bristol, Avon BS8 3JD

Telephone: 0272 730201

Head: Mrs J D Walters

Age range: 3-18
No. of pupils: 785
Scholarships: Yes
Religion: Non-denominational

Fees per term
Day: £550-£1425
Weekly board: £2350-£2560
Full board: £2470-£2690

Boy / Girl / Co-ed
Day / Week / Board

Clifton High School, situated in one of the most beautiful areas of Bristol, prepares girls for GCSE, A Level and university entrance. In addition to the broad curriculum, there is a wide range of extra-curricular activities. The school also has a fine sporting and music tradition. There are excellent facilities, including an indoor heated swimming pool, a new library and sixth form centre, and an art and design complex.

Colston's Colegiate Lower School

Address: Stapleton, Bristol, Avon BS16 1BA

Telephone: 0272 655297

Head: Mr J A Aveyard

Age range: 3-13
No. of pupils: 300
Scholarships: Yes
Religion: Church of England

Fees per term
Day: £790-£1505
Weekly board: £2190-£2405
Full board: £2290-£2505

Boy / Girl / Co-ed
Day / Week / Board

The school seeks to develop the potential of each individual. Pupils are encouraged to aim for excellence, whether it be academic, cultural or sporting. The school's guiding philosophy is the Christian ideal of consideration for others; high standards of behaviour and demeanour are expected. The school is within easy reach of the centre of Bristol, yet in an almost rural setting.

Colston's Collegiate School *

Address: Stapleton, Bristol, Avon BS16 1BJ

Telephone: 0272 655207

Head: Mr S B Howarth MA(Oxon)

Age range: 3-18
No. of pupils: 700
Scholarships: Yes
Religion: Church of England

Fees per term
Day: £1190-£1635
Weekly board: £1975-£2560
Full board: £2075-£2710

Boy / Girl / Co-ed
Day / Week / Board

Standing in 30 acres of grounds on the northern outskirts of Bristol, Colston's Collegiate forms a close and happy community. It has an excellent academic record with small classes and high pass rates in GCSE and A Level examinations, most sixth formers proceeding to university and other colleges of higher education. There is a strong sporting tradition, whilst pupils' talents in drama, music and the visual arts are also encouraged.

Colston's Girls' School *

Address: Cheltenham Road, Bristol, Avon B56 5RD

Telephone: 0272 424328

Head: Mrs J P Franklin BA(Hons)

Age range: 10-18
No. of pupils: 580
Scholarships: Yes
Religion: Church of England

Fees per term
Day: £750-£1053
Weekly board: -
Full board: -

Boy / Girl / Co-ed
Day / Week / Board

Colston's Girls' School is a selective girls school, 10-18, near the centre of the city of Bristol with its excellent transport links. All girls are prepared for 9 GCSE's and the majority enter the sixth form where there is a choice of 22 A Level subjects. Great importance is attached to extra-curricular pursuits as well as academic excellence.

The Downs School

Address: Wraxall, Bristol, Avon BS19 1PF

Telephone: 0275 852008

Head: Mr J K MacPherson

Age range: 3-14
No. of pupils: 315
Scholarships:
Religion: Non-denominational

Fees per term
Day: £485-£1495
Weekly board: £2080-
Full board: £2080-

Boy ○ Girl ○ Co-ed ●
Day ● Week ● Board ●

Independent preparatory school for boys and girls aged 3-14. Day places as well as boarding and weekly boarding. Well known locally for achievement in work, sport, music and many other activities.

Well-mannered, cheerful, confident children.

Downside School

Address: Stratton-on-the-Fosse, Bath, Avon BA3 4RJ

Telephone: 0761 232206

Head: Dom Aidan Bellenger MA PhD FRHistS FRSA

Age range: 11-18
No. of pupils: 396
Scholarships: Yes
Religion: Roman Catholic

Fees per term
Day: -£2120
Weekly board: -
Full board: -£3306

Boy ● Girl ○ Co-ed ○
Day ● Week ○ Board ●

Roman Catholic boarding school for boys under the care of the Benedictine monks of Downside Abbey, near Bath. Strong academic, musical, sporting and drama traditions. Pupils of 11 to 18 are educated for Christian life. GCSEs, A Levels and Oxbridge examinations. Scholarships available at 11, 13 or when starting at sixth form level: academic, art and musical.

Fairfield PNEU School

Address: Fairfield Way, Farleigh Road, Backwell, Bristol, Avon BS19 3PD

Telephone: 0275 462743

Head: Mrs K D Wedd

Age range: 3-11
No. of pupils: 120
Scholarships:
Religion: Non-denominational

Fees per term
Day: £300-£835
Weekly board: -
Full board: -

Boy ○ Girl ○ Co-ed ●
Day ● Week ○ Board ○

For further information and a prospectus, please contact the school.

Gracefield Preparatory School

Address: 266 Overndale Road, Fishponds, Bristol, Avon BS16 2RG

Telephone: 0272 567977

Head: Mrs M Garman

Age range: 4-11
No. of pupils: 90
Scholarships:
Religion: Christian

Fees per term
Day: £483-£535
Weekly board: -
Full board: -

Boy ○ Girl ○ Co-ed ●
Day ● Week ○ Board ○

Long established preparatory school. Small classes (max. 16) individual attention. Concerned with high academic and social standards. Excellent eleven plus results. All qualified long serving staff, total caring environment.

The Hall, Sidcot

Address: Sidcot, Winscombe, Avon BS25 9PD

Telephone: 0934 844118

Head: Ms W Wardman

Age range: 3-8
No. of pupils: 40
Scholarships:
Religion: Quaker

Fees per term
Day: £450-£860
Weekly board: -
Full board: -

Boy ○ Girl ○ Co-ed ●
Day ● Week ○ Board ○

A small encouraging environment in which to start an educational career. Small class groups, well qualified staff and a well-resourced learning environment in a superb location with our own playing fields. High academic standards, but full support for those with modest gifts.

King Edward's Junior School

Address: North Road, Bath, Avon BA2 6JA

Telephone: 0225 463218

Head: Mr P M Garner

Age range: 7-11
No. of pupils: 176
Scholarships:
Religion: Christian Based

Fees per term
Day: -£842
Weekly board: -
Full board: -

Boy ● Girl ○ Co-ed ○
Day ● Week ○ Board ○

King Edward's Junior School is located in brand new premises on the site of the Senior School, overlooking the city from the south. The school has a tradition of academic excellence, coupled with an outstanding range of activities including music, art, drama, mountain biking, pottery, outdoor pursuits and the regular sporting challenges. Entrance is by examination and interview.

King Edward's School *

Address: North Road, Bath, Avon BA2 6HU

Telephone: 0225 464313

Head: Dr J P Wroughton

Age range: 7-18
No. of pupils: 860
Scholarships: Yes
Religion: Non-denominational

Fees per term
Day: £842-£1200
Weekly board: -
Full board: -

Boy ● Girl ● Co-ed ○
Day ● Week ○ Board ○

King Edward's School, Bath, has a reputation for academic excellence. It offers a wide range of extra-curricular activities which enrich personality and develop character. With a strong cultural tradition, the school has modern facilities and teaching methods. There is a friendly and caring atmosphere, a disciplined environment, and an excellent rapport between pupils and staff. Girls are accepted in the sixth form.

Kingswood Day Preparatory School

Address: 4/5 Portland Place, Bath, Avon BA1 2RU

Telephone: 0225 310468

Head: Mrs M Newberry BA

Age range: 3-11
No. of pupils: 90
Scholarships: Yes
Religion: Christian

Fees per term
Day: £406-£998
Weekly board: -
Full board: -

Boy ○ Girl ○ Co-ed ●
Day ● Week ○ Board ○

Kingswood Day Preparatory School is a small friendly school with a Christian ethos. It aims to give children the opportunity to achieve high standards in both social and academic life, and to develop self-confidence and self-respect. The school has a broadly based curriculum with a particular strength in music and a large number of extra-curricular activities.

Kingswood School *

Address: Lansdown, Bath, Avon BA1 5RG

Telephone: 0225 311627

Head: Mr G M Best MA

Age range: 11-18
No. of pupils: 483
Scholarships: Yes
Religion: Methodist

Fees per term
Day: £1550-£1980
Weekly board: £2400-£3045
Full board: £2400-£3045

	Boy	Girl	Co-ed
	○	○	●
	●	●	●
	Day	Week	Board

Kingswood occupies a superb site overlooking the City of Bath, is within easy reach of the M4 and M5 motorways, rail and air links, and offers academic excellence, a wide range of extra-curricular activities, excellent facilities and a concern for the development of each individual's talents. Kingswood has two prep schools, Prior's Court at Newbury and Hermitage House in Bath.

Lancaster House School

Address: 38 Hill Road, Weston-super-Mare, Avon BS23 2RY

Telephone: 0934 624116

Head: Mrs S Lewis

Age range: 4-11
No. of pupils: 65
Scholarships:
Religion: Non-denominational

Fees per term
Day: £265-£285
Weekly board: -
Full board: -

	Boy	Girl	Co-ed
	○	○	●
	●	○	○
	Day	Week	Board

Lancaster House School caters for boys and girls up to the age of eleven. The curriculum is broad-based but maintains the best of the traditional approach while also emphasising social skills, good manners, self-discipline and consideration for others. Children are prepared for entrance examinations to senior schools and the school has an enviable record of success in this respect.

Mander Portman Woodward School

Address: 10 Elmdale Road, Tyndalls Park, Clifton, Avon BS8 1SL

Telephone: 0272 255688

Head: Miss F A Eldridge

Age range: 13-18+
No. of pupils: 80
Scholarships: Yes
Religion: Non-denominational

Fees per term
Day: -
Weekly board: -
Full board: -

	Boy	Girl	Co-ed
	○	○	●
	●	○	○
	Day	Week	Board

For further information and a prospectus, please contact the school.

Monkton Combe Junior School

Address: Combe Down, Bath, Avon BA2 7ET

Telephone: 0225 837912

Head: Mr P J Le Roy

Age range: 3-13
No. of pupils: 275
Scholarships:
Religion: Church of England

Fees per term
Day: £965-£1845
Weekly board: -
Full board: -£2585

	Boy	Girl	Co-ed
	○	○	●
	●	○	●
	Day	Week	Board

For further information and a prospectus, please contact the school.

Monkton Combe School *

Address: Bath, Avon
BA2 7HG

Telephone: 0225 721102

Head: Mr M J Cuthbertson MA

Age range: 11-18
No. of pupils: 340
Scholarships: Yes
Religion: Church of England

Fees per term
Day: £2095-£2565
Weekly board: -
Full board: £2895-£3485

Boy ○ Girl ○ Co-ed ●
Day ● Week ○ Board ●

Monkton Combe combines high academic standards with a wide range of cultural and sporting activities. Now merged with Clarendon School, its distinctiveness rests in its active Christian tradition, its pastoral care and its beautiful setting close to Bath. The school encourages the fulfilment of the talents of each individual, while inculcating moral values and a sense of service.

Oak Hill First School

Address: Okebourne Road,
Brentry, Bristol, Avon
BS10 6QY
Telephone: 0272 591083

Principal: Mrs R Deakin *Head:* Dr A Jones

Age range: 4-9
No. of pupils: 76
Scholarships:
Religion: Christian

Fees per term
Day: -
Weekly board: -
Full board: -

Boy ○ Girl ○ Co-ed ●
Day ● Week ○ Board ○

For further information and a prospectus, please contact the school.

Overndale School

Address: Chapel Lane, Old
Sodbury, Bristol, Avon
BS17 6NQ
Telephone: 0454 310332

Head: Mr A J Wallis Eade

Age range: 3-11
No. of pupils: 100
Scholarships:
Religion: Non-denominational

Fees per term
Day: -£560
Weekly board: -
Full board: -

Boy ○ Girl ○ Co-ed ●
Day ● Week ○ Board ○

For further information and a prospectus, please contact the school.

The Paragon School

Address: Lyncombe House,
Lyncombe Vale, Bath, Avon
BA2 4LT
Telephone: 0225 310837

Head: Mrs M J Trimby

Age range: 3-11
No. of pupils: 300
Scholarships:
Religion: Non-denominational

Fees per term
Day: £660-£725
Weekly board: -
Full board: -

Boy ○ Girl ○ Co-ed ●
Day ● Week ○ Board ○

The school is housed in a beautiful Georgian building set in 7 acres of grounds and woodlands about a mile from Bath City centre. The best of modern and traditional ideas and equipment are used throughout the school and the need for training in discipline and courtesy is not forgotten.

The Park School

Address: Weston Lane, Bath, Avon BA1 4AQ
Telephone: 0225 421681
Head: Mr R E J Chambers

Age range: 3-13
No. of pupils: 163
Scholarships: Yes
Religion: Non-denominational

Fees per term
Day: £760-£1145
Weekly board: -
Full board: -

● Boy ○ Girl ○ Co-ed
● Day ○ Week ○ Board

The only preparatory school in the City of Bath. Aims enhancement of the individual child. Prospectus on application. Parental visit is vital.

Prior Park College

Address: Bath, Avon BA2 5AH
Telephone: 0225 835353
Head: Mr J W R Goulding

Age range: 11-18
No. of pupils: 445
Scholarships: Yes
Religion: Roman Catholic

Fees per term
Day: £1607-£1678
Weekly board: -
Full board: -£3035

○ Boy ○ Girl ● Co-ed
● Day ○ Week ● Board

Prior Park is a co-educational community built around the family lives of committed and talented lay teachers. The school programme is fundamentally that of the boarding school, so that every pupil, day or boarding, takes full advantage of the whole range of educational activities. The broad curriculum is well supplemented by many activities.

Queen Elizabeth Hospital *

Address: Berkeley Place, Clifton, Bristol, Avon BS8 2AY
Telephone: 0272 291856
Head: Dr R Gliddon

Age range: 11-18
No. of pupils: 490
Scholarships: Yes
Religion:

Fees per term
Day: £1173-
Weekly board: -
Full board: £2059-

● Boy ○ Girl ○ Co-ed
● Day ○ Week ● Board

Queen Elizabeth's Hospital has 490 boys, aged between 11 and 18, 80 of whom are boarders. Entry is by selective examination at 11 and 13 and approximately half the pupils hold Assisted Places. The school has a tradition of academic excellence, combined with high standards in games, music and drama. Facilities include a new theatre and recently opened technology centre.

The Red Maids' School *

Address: Westbury-on-Trym, Bristol, Avon BS9 3AW
Telephone: 0272 622641
Head: Miss S Hampton

Age range: 11-18
No. of pupils: 500
Scholarships: Yes
Religion: Non-denominational

Fees per term
Day: £1140-
Weekly board: -
Full board: £2260-

○ Boy ● Girl ○ Co-ed
● Day ○ Week ● Board

Founded in 1634 Red Maids' is the oldest surviving girls' school in the country. The atmosphere is friendly and purposeful. The curriculum is broad and well balanced. The majority of girls stay on into the sixth form where a very flexible choice of A Level subjects is provided. There are excellent recreational facilities.

AVON 45

Redland High School *

Address: Redland Court,
Redland, Bristol, Avon
BS6 7EH
Telephone: 0272 245796

Head: Mrs C Lear

Age range: 4-18
No. of pupils: 660
Scholarships: Yes
Religion: Non-denominational

Fees per term
Day: £564-£1155
Weekly board: -
Full board: -

○ ● ○
Boy Girl Co-ed
● ○ ○
Day Week Board

The school is a friendly, caring and purposeful community with high academic achievement. Girls are encouraged to realise their potential and develop their talents. We provide a full and balanced education which will help them to form happy relationships, equip them to feel of value and capable of assuming responsibility.

The Royal School

Address: Lansdown Road,
Bath, Avon BA1 5SZ

Telephone: 0225 313877

Head: Dr J McClure MA DPhil

Age range: Boys 3-18
No. of pupils: 390
Scholarships: Yes
Religion: Anglican

Fees per term
Day: £1085-£2120
Weekly board: -
Full board: £2910-£3324

● ● ○
Boy Girl Co-ed
● ○ ○
Day Week Board

It is an old and distinguished school set in extensive grounds on the north side of Bath. It is a happy, caring community which offers students a rich, broad and balanced education. Academic achievement is high and standards of behaviour reflect the warm, friendly atmosphere within the school where respect for others within and outside the community, and happy relationships are paramount.

Rydal School

Address: 11 Albert Road,
Clevedon, Avon BS21 7RP

Telephone: 0275 874127

Head: Mrs E A Humby

Age range: 4-8
No. of pupils: 21
Scholarships:
Religion:

Fees per term
Day: £625-
Weekly board: -
Full board: -

○ ○ ●
Boy Girl Co-ed
● ○ ○
Day Week Board

Rydal School is a small pre-preparatory school. We have small classes of around ten pupils, ensuring much idivdual attention and the continuation of a close 'family' atmosphere. We regularly win scholarships to Bristol Grammar School. We encourage boys and girls to thoroughly enjoy work and to love books.

Sacred Heart Preparatory

Address: Chew Magna, Bristol,
Avon BS18 8PT

Telephone: 0275 332470

Headmistress: Ms V M Hogan

Age range: 3-11
No. of pupils: 170
Scholarships:
Religion: Roman Catholic

Fees per term
Day: £545-
Weekly board: -
Full board: -

● ● ●
Boy Girl Co-ed
● ○ ○
Day Week Board

The Sacred Heart Preparatory School is conducted by the Srs of Our Lady of the Missions. Its reputation is founded on its interest and care of the pupil and on the Christian and moral training it provides. It is based on purposeful teaching and the encouragement of sound standards particularly in literacy and numeracy. The curriculum includes RE, Social Studies, Music, PE, Drama, etc.

Sheiling School Camphill Community

Address: Thornbury Park, Park Road, Thornbury, Bristol, Avon BS12 1HP
Telephone: 0454 412194
Head:

Age range: 6-16
No. of pupils: 50+
Scholarships:
Religion: Christian

Fees per term
Day: -
Weekly board: -
Full board: -£4722

Boy ○ Girl ○ Co-ed ●
Day ○ Week ○ Board ●

This school provides a caring residential environment for boys and girls who have a wide range of learning difficulties and behaviour problems arising from organic disorders and/or emotional disturbances. Schooling (based on the Rudolf Steiner School Curriculum), home-life and therapies are afforded equal importance in this School. There is a rich and varied cultural life.

Sidcot School

Address: Sidcot, Winscombe, Avon BS25 9PD
Telephone: 0934 843102
Head: Mr C Greenfield

Age range: 9-18
No. of pupils: 325
Scholarships: Yes
Religion: Quaker

Fees per term
Day: £1265-£1715
Weekly board: £2860-£2960
Full board: £2860-£2960

Boy ○ Girl ○ Co-ed ●
Day ● Week ● Board ●

Small community run on Quaker principles offering a broad education within an ethical and spiritual framework. Dating to 1699 the school has modern facilties including library opened in 1990, sports complex opened in 1992 and stables due to be opened shortly. Pupil ratio 1:10 with excellent examination results. Sidcot provides horse riding, drama, music, pottery and outdoor pursuits.

Silverhill School

Address: Winterbourne House, Winterbourne, Bristol, Avon
Telephone:
Head: Mr G J Clewer

Age range: 2-16
No. of pupils: 300
Scholarships:
Religion: Church of England

Fees per term
Day: £325-£880
Weekly board: £1480-
Full board: -

Boy ○ Girl ○ Co-ed ●
Day ● Week ● Board ○

A very happy Christian family school. Bilingual teaching from age 7 (English am, French pm). Specialist dyslexia department. Very strong music/drama. Very high academic standards. Well worth a visit.

St Brandon's School

Address: Clevedon, Avon BS21 7SD
Telephone: 0275 875042
Head: Mrs S Vesey

Age range: 3-11
No. of pupils: 140
Scholarships:
Religion: Christian

Fees per term
Day: £595-£795
Weekly board: -
Full board: -

Boy ○ Girl ○ Co-ed ●
Day ● Week ○ Board ○

St Brandon's aims to be Clevedon's first independent day school, offering a first class education for children aged 3-11. The modern, purpose built school, set in 5 acres, has excellent facilities, including a sports complex, and superb teaching and pupil resources. The National Curriculum study programme is followed, but in the more thorough way traditionally associated with private education.

St Christopher's School †

Address: 1/2 Carisbrooke Lodge, Westbury Park, Bristol, Avon BS6 7JE
Telephone: 0272 736875

Age range: 6-19
No. of pupils: 55
Scholarships:
Religion: Non-denominational

Fees per term
Day: -
Weekly board: -
Full board: -

○ ○ ● Boy Girl Co-ed
● ○ ● Day Week Board

Head of Education: Miss O Matz

This is a Steiner special training school. For fees, further information and a prospectus, please contact the school.

St Ursula's High School

Address: Brecon Road, Westbury-on-Trym, Bristol, Avon BS9 4DT
Telephone: 0272 622616

Age range: 3-18
No. of pupils: 410
Scholarships: Yes
Religion: Roman Catholic

Fees per term
Day: £481-£810
Weekly board: -
Full board: -

● ● ○ Boy Girl Co-ed
● ○ ○ Day Week Board

Head: Mrs M A Macnaughton

St Ursula's High School is a lay Catholic independent school for boys 3-11 years and girls 3-18 years organised in junior and senior departments and set in its own extensive grounds on the outskirts of Bristol. In partnership with parents, we offer a sound and varied education, in a happy atmosphere based upon the Christian values of care and respect for the individual pupil.

Tockington Manor

Address: Tockington, Bristol, Avon BS12 4NY
Telephone: 0454 613229

Age range: 3-13
No. of pupils: 213
Scholarships:
Religion: Church of England

Fees per term
Day: £360-£1850
Weekly board: £2650-£2650
Full board: £2650-£2650

○ ○ ● Boy Girl Co-ed
● ● ● Day Week Board

Head: Mr R G Tovey

Tockington Manor School is a family school with traditional values set in a country situation of 28 acres of lovely grounds with good facilities. Close to M4/M5 motorways thus providing excellent road, rail and air links. Pupils from overseas welcome and specialist EFL teaching available. Good academic, sporting and musical records.

Torwood House School

Address: 29 Durdham Park Road, Redland, Bristol, Avon
Telephone: 0272 735620

Age range: 2-8
No. of pupils: 170
Scholarships:
Religion: Non-denominational

Fees per term
Day: £170-£620
Weekly board: -
Full board: -

○ ○ ● Boy Girl Co-ed
● ○ ○ Day Week Board

Head: Mrs S Sheppard

Torwood House School overlooks Durdham Downs. We are a modern progressive school of over 50 years experience. We aim to provide the best possible education throughout the National Curriculum and beyond. We have a dedicated staff, and all our children benefit from good organisation and motivation. This is reflected in the undoubted success of our pupils past and present.

Westwing School

Address: Kyneton House,
Thornbury, Bristol, Avon
BS12 2JZ
Telephone: 0454 412311

Head: Mrs A Rispin

Age range: 4-18
No. of pupils: 110
Scholarships:
Religion:

Fees per term
Day: -
Weekly board: -
Full board: -

○ ● ○
Boy Girl Co-ed
● ● ●
Day Week Board

For further information and a prospectus, please contact the school.

BEDFORDSHIRE

Bedford High School * p653

Address: Bromham Road,
Bedford, Bedfordshire
MK40 2BS
Telephone: 0234 360221

Head: Mrs B M Willis

Age range: 7-18
No. of pupils: 1013
Scholarships:
Religion: Non-denominational

Fees per term
Day: £1114-£1383
Weekly board: -
Full board: -£2584

Boy ○ | Girl ● | Co-ed ○
Day ● | Week ● | Board ●

Sited in the centre of Bedford the school has well equipped buildings generously equipped to meet the demands of modern education. Academic standards are high and a wide range of subjects is offered.

Extra-curricular activities are many and varied. The 21 acres of playing fields, swimming pool, gymnasium and boathouse offer excellent games facilities. The music, drama, dance departments are thriving.

Bedford Modern School *

Address: Manton Lane,
Bedford, Bedfordshire
MK41 7NT
Telephone: 0234 364331

Head: Mr P J Squire MA

Age range: 7-18
No. of pupils: 1250
Scholarships: Yes
Religion: Church of England

Fees per term
Day: £924-£1268
Weekly board: -
Full board: -£3315

Boy ● | Girl ○ | Co-ed ○
Day ● | Week ● | Board ●

Bedford Modern School is an independent day and boarding school for boys aged 7-18 years. The results at GCSE and A Level are outstanding. It has first class modern facilities including a magnificent technology centre. There is a fine sporting tradition and particular strengths in music, art and drama. A high proportion of students go on to university.

Bedford Preparatory School

Address: Burnaby Road,
Bedford, Bedfordshire
MK40 2TU
Telephone: 0234 360221

Head: Mr E James

Age range: 7-11
No. of pupils: 220
Scholarships:
Religion:

Fees per term
Day: -
Weekly board: -
Full board: -

Boy ● | Girl ○ | Co-ed ○
Day ● | Week ○ | Board ●

For further information and a prospectus, please contact the school.

Bedford School *

Address: Burnaby Road,
Bedford, Bedfordshire
MK40 2TU
Telephone: 0234 340444

Head: Dr I P Evans

Age range: 7-18
No. of pupils: 1120
Scholarships:
Religion:

Fees per term
Day: -
Weekly board: -
Full board: -

Boy ● | Girl ○ | Co-ed ○
Day ● | Week ○ | Board ●

For further information and a prospectus, please contact the school.

BEDFORDSHIRE 51

Broadmead School

Address: 117 Tennyson Road, Luton, Bedfordshire LU1 3RR

Telephone: 0582 22570

Head: Mr A F Compton

Age range: 3-11
No. of pupils: 130
Scholarships:
Religion: Non-denominational

Fees per term
Day: £600-£600
Weekly board: -
Full board: -

Boy ○ Girl ○ Co-ed ●
Day ● Week ○ Board ○

Broadmead School is a small caring environment for children aged 3 to 11 years. We have year groups and cater for gifted, normal and some dyslexic children in our family atmosphere. We have a happy mixture of creed, religion and ability. Children leave at 11 years to go on to senior independent schools in the area.

Bury Lawn School

Address: Soskin Drive, Stantonbury Fields, Milton Keynes, Bucks. MK14 6DP
Telephone: 0908 220345

Head: Mrs H W Kiff

Age range: 3-18
No. of pupils: 420
Scholarships:
Religion: Non-denominational

Fees per term
Day: £1055-£1460
Weekly board: -
Full board: -

Boy ○ Girl ○ Co-ed ●
Day ● Week ○ Board ○

Non-selective day school catering for all-ability range with small classes not exceeding 18 pupils. Purpose built school founded in 1970 but moved to new premises in 1988. Special needs department.

Known for excellent results and speech, drama and music.

Dame Alice Harpur *

Address: Cardington Road, Bedford, Bedfordshire MK42 0BX
Telephone: 0234 340871

Head: Mrs R Randle

Age range: 7-18
No. of pupils: 983
Scholarships: Yes
Religion: Christian

Fees per term
Day: £858-£1185
Weekly board: -
Full board: -

Boy ○ Girl ● Co-ed ○
Day ● Week ○ Board ○

For further information and a prospectus, please contact the school.

Moorlands School

Address: Leagrave Hall, Luton, Bedfordshire LU4 9LE

Telephone: 0582 573376

Senior Master: Mr A Cook, *Senior Mistress:* Mrs J Jacobs

Age range: 2-13
No. of pupils: 150
Scholarships:
Religion: Church of England

Fees per term
Day: -£875
Weekly board: -
Full board: -

Boy ○ Girl ○ Co-ed ●
Day ● Week ○ Board ○

Moorlands School was founded in 1891, and has grown up around 19th Century Leagrave Hall. It is a happy and friendly school of 150 boys and girls. Within a family atmosphere we offer a traditionally-based education to meet the needs of children whose ages range from 2 to 13. We strongly believe that all pupils should be given the opportunity to reach their full potential.

Parkside Preparatory School

Address: 41-43 Grove Road,
Leighton Buzzard,
Bedfordshire LU7 8SF
Telephone: 0525 379293

Head: Mrs M S Fuller

Age range: 1-8
No. of pupils: 20
Scholarships:
Religion: Non-denominational

Fees per term
Day: -
Weekly board: -
Full board: -

Boy ○ Girl ○ Co-ed ●
Day ● Week ○ Board ○

For further information and a prospectus, please contact the school.

Polam School

Address: 45 Lansdowne Road,
Bedford, Bedfordshire
MK40 2BY
Telephone: 0234 261864

Head: Mr A R Brown

Age range: 3-9
No. of pupils: 242
Scholarships:
Religion: Non-denominational

Fees per term
Day: £405-£703
Weekly board: -
Full board: -

Boy ○ Girl ○ Co-ed ●
Day ● Week ○ Board ○

Polam School believes strongly in providing a happy, stimulating environment in which to live and learn. A sound traditionally based education is supplemented by a wide ranging, forward looking curriculum. On site facilities are excellent and, with specialist teaching, give every opportunity for the maximisation of potential in all subjects.

Rushmoor School

Address: 58/60 Shakespeare Road, Bedford, Bedfordshire
MK40 2DL
Telephone: 0234 352031

Head: Mr P J Owen MA

Age range: 4-16
No. of pupils: 267
Scholarships:
Religion: Non-denominational

Fees per term
Day: £585-£1135
Weekly board: -
Full board: -

Boy ● Girl ○ Co-ed ○
Day ● Week ○ Board ○

For further information and a prospectus, please contact the school.

St Andrew's School

Address: Kimbolton Road,
Bedford, Bedfordshire
MK40 2PA
Telephone: 0234 267272

Head: Mrs J E Stephen

Age range: 3-16
No. of pupils: 360
Scholarships:
Religion: Non-denominational

Fees per term
Day: £592-£960
Weekly board: -
Full board: -

Boy ○ Girl ● Co-ed ○
Day ● Week ○ Board ○

Situated in the heart of Bedford, St Andrew's has provided parents in Bedford with choice in education for their girls for a hundred years. It offers continuity, challenge and care in equal measure, with full access to the magnificent educational facilities of Bedford and outstanding results at all ability levels. St Andrew's stands for individual care, achievement and for excellence.

St George's School

Address: 28 Priory Road,
Dunstable, Bedfordshire
LU5 4HR
Telephone: 0582 661471

Head: Mrs P Plater

Age range: 3-11
No. of pupils: 60
Scholarships:
Religion: Non-denominational

Fees per term
Day: £270-£625
Weekly board: -
Full board: -

Boy ○ Girl ○ Co-ed ●
Day ● Week ○ Board ○

For further information and a prospectus, please contact the school.

Sutherlands School

Address: Stoke Road, Linslade,
Leighton Buzzard,
Bedfordshire LU7 7SR
Telephone: 0525 373360

Head: Mrs K Goulding

Age range: 4-10
No. of pupils: 50
Scholarships:
Religion:

Fees per term
Day: -
Weekly board: -
Full board: -

Boy ○ Girl ○ Co-ed ●
Day ● Week ○ Board ○

For further information and a prospectus, please contact the school.

Walmsley House School

Address: 23 Kimbolton Road,
Bedford, Bedfordshire
MK40 2NY
Telephone: 0234 59686

Head: Mr W Anderson

Age range: 3-9
No. of pupils: 240
Scholarships:
Religion:

Fees per term
Day: -
Weekly board: -
Full board: -

Boy ○ Girl ○ Co-ed ●
Day ● Week ○ Board ○

For further information and a prospectus, please contact the school.

BERKSHIRE

BERKSHIRE 55

The Abbey School *

Address: 17 Kendrick Road, Reading, Berkshire RG1 5DZ

Telephone: 0734 872256

Head: Miss B C L Sheldon

Age range: 4-18
No. of pupils: 1050
Scholarships: Yes
Religion: Church of England

Fees per term
Day: £960-£1210
Weekly board: -
Full board: -

○ ● ○
Boy Girl Co-ed
● ○ ○
Day Week Board

The Abbey School, Reading provides education for girls to the highest academic standards. Most students proceed to university—many to Oxford and Cambridge. Extra-curricular activities flourish, including music, drama and sports. The school has excellent facilities including modern science laboratories, networked computers, a large indoor swimming pool, and a fine stage.

Bearwood College

Address: Wokingham, Berkshire RG11 5BG

Telephone: 0734 786915

Head: The Hon M C Penney

Age range: 11-18
No. of pupils: 300
Scholarships: Yes
Religion: Church of England

Fees per term
Day: £1675-
Weekly board: £2950-
Full board: £2950-

● ○ ○
Boy Girl Co-ed
● ● ●
Day Week Board

An independent boys boarding and day school for ages 11-18 for 300 pupils. Set in 500 acres of Berkshire woodland and close to excellent road, rail and air communications. A full curriculum leads to placement at university or polytechnic. A balanced education is enhanced by the modern art, drama and music facilities. Please telephone or write for a prospectus.

Bracknell Montessori School

Address: Windlesham Centre, Priestwood, Bracknell, Berkshire RG12 1UD
Telephone: 0344 50922

Head: Mrs E R M Ashcroft

Age range: 2-6
No. of pupils: 60
Scholarships:
Religion: Non-denominational

Fees per term
Day: £320-£750
Weekly board: -
Full board: -

○ ○ ●
Boy Girl Co-ed
● ○ ○
Day Week Board

Founded in 1972, we are a private nursery school offering a broad-based curriculum including French, music, dancing and swimming. The aim of the school is to help every pupil to achieve their full potential.

Bradfield College *

Address: Reading, Berkshire RG7 6AR

Telephone: 0734 744203

Head: Mr P B Smith

Age range: 13-18
No. of pupils: 590
Scholarships: Yes
Religion: Church of England

Fees per term
Day: £2775-
Weekly board: -
Full board: £3700-

● ● ○
Boy Girl Co-ed
● ○ ●
Day Week Board

For further information and a prospectus, please contact the school.

The Brigidine School

Address: King's Road,
Windsor, Berkshire SL4 2AX

Telephone: 0753 863779

Head: Mrs M B Cairns

Age range: 4-18
No. of pupils: 453
Scholarships:
Religion: Roman Catholic

Fees per term
Day: £872-£1273
Weekly board: -
Full board: -

● ● ○
Boy Girl Co-ed
● ○ ○
Day Week Board

The aim of the school is to give the pupils a careful, moral, intellectual and physical training based on sound Christian principles, which will fit them for future responsibilities and enable them to take their place in the world, confident and fully equipped. Close and continuous co-operation between school and parents is encouraged. Boys 4-7; Girls 4-18.

Brockhurst

Address: Hermitage,
Newbury, Berkshire RG16 9UL

Telephone: 0635 200293

Head: Mr A J Pudden

Age range: 3-13
No. of pupils: 176
Scholarships: Yes
Religion: Church of England

Fees per term
Day: £550-£1890
Weekly board: -£2450
Full board: -£2450

● ○ ○
Boy Girl Co-ed
● ● ●
Day Week Board

Boarding and day school for boys. High academic and sporting reputation; prepares boys for all major schools. Sixty acres of own grounds in countryside of outstanding natural beauty. Excellent facilities including recently completed hall for indoor sports, drama and music. Riding taught as an optional extra using school ponies. Junior school age range rising 3 to 7 years. Boys and girls.

Cheam School

Address: Headley, Newbury,
Berkshire RG15 8LD

Telephone: 0635 268242

Head: Mr C C Evers

Age range: 7-13
No. of pupils: 130
Scholarships:
Religion: Church of England

Fees per term
Day: £1990-
Weekly board: -
Full board: £2725-

● ○ ○
Boy Girl Co-ed
● ○ ●
Day Week Board

Cheam School for boys 7-13, boarding and day, with 80 acres of grounds on the Hampshire/Berkshire border, provides the ideal setting for growing boys. Founded in 1645, we provide a broad, sound education within a caring family environment. Success in academics, sport, music, drama or art is achieved through encouragement and reward. Boys may start at 7 either as day boys or in our new junior boarding house.

Claires Court School

Address: Ray Mill Road East,
Maidenhead, Berkshire
SL6 8TE

Telephone: 0628 23069

Head: Mr J T Wilding BSc

Age range: 10-16
No. of pupils: 260
Scholarships: Yes
Religion: Catholic

Fees per term
Day: £1010-£1535
Weekly board: -
Full board: -

● ○ ○
Boy Girl Co-ed
● ○ ○
Day Week Board

Claires Court & Ridgeway is an independent day school for boys aged 4+ to 17 with 450 boys on the school roll. The school offers a full education in the broadest sense for all ages of the National Curriculum. Sound academic results, excellent sporting and a wide range of extra-curricular provision have underpinned the school's successful expansion in recent years.

Crosfields

Address: Shinfield, Reading, Berkshire RG2 9BL

Telephone: 0734 871810

Head: Mr F G Skipwith

Age range: 5-13
No. of pupils: 320
Scholarships:
Religion: Non-denominational

Fees per term
Day: £1050-£1525
Weekly board: -
Full board: -

● Boy   ○ Girl   ○ Co-ed
● Day   ○ Week   ○ Board

Day preparatory school with pre-preparatory department for boys 5-14. Close to Lower Earley and M4. Extensive parkland grounds with good games playing facilities including a gymnasium and a 25m indoor pool. Individual potential and happiness is developed and fostered. From a three form entry boys are taught in small ability sets.

Dolphin School

Address: Hurst, Reading, Berkshire RG10 0BP

Telephone: 0734 341277

Head: Dr N Follett

Age range: 3-13
No. of pupils: 240
Scholarships:
Religion: Non-denominational

Fees per term
Day: £645-£1260
Weekly board: -
Full board: -

○ Boy   ○ Girl   ● Co-ed
● Day   ○ Week   ○ Board

The Dolphin School curriculum is designed for bright or gifted children; from age 6 all classes (maximum 14 children) are taught in separate subjects by qualified graduate specialists. Scholarships from 10 years in art, music, drama and creative writing. Entry at any age. Preparation for Common Entrance or public school scholarship. Notable scholarship success at top public schools in recent years.

Douai School * p654

Address: Upper Woolhampton, Reading, Berkshire RG7 5TH
Telephone: 0734 713114

Head: Fr G Scott

Age range: 10-18
No. of pupils: 242
Scholarships: Yes
Religion: Roman Catholic

Fees per term
Day: £546-£670
Weekly board: £733-£1006
Full board: £833-£1040

● Boy   ○ Girl   ○ Co-ed
● Day   ● Week   ● Board

Douai is an HMC boarding and day school, becoming co-educational in 1993, set in 150 acres of attractive Berkshire countryside and possessing excellent facilities. Pupils are prepared for a full range of GCSE and A level examinations and the majority go on to higher education. Excellence is our keynote, in academic work, sporting and creative activities.

Downe House * p741

Address: Cold Ash, Newbury, Berkshire RG16 9JJ

Telephone: 0635 200286

Head: Miss S R Cameron

Age range: 11-18
No. of pupils: 478
Scholarships: Yes
Religion: Church of England

Fees per term
Day: -£2630
Weekly board: -
Full board: -£3630

○ Boy   ● Girl   ○ Co-ed
● Day   ○ Week   ● Board

The school has an excellent academic record and offers many additional activities. A great majority of girls go on to higher education from the sixth form, which has exceptional facilities. The school offers various scholarships—for further details please contact the registrar.

Elstree School

Address: Woolhampton, Reading, Berkshire RG7 5TD
Telephone: 0734 713302
Head: Mr T B McMullen

Age range: 4-13
No. of pupils: 150
Scholarships:
Religion: Church of England

Fees per term
Day: -£1991
Weekly board: -
Full board: -£2745

● ○ ○
Boy Girl Co-ed
● ○ ●
Day Week Board

Elstree, a traditional country boarding and day school, aims to develop each boy's ability and character in a well ordered, friendly, Christian environment. The extensive facilities, dedicated staff, magnificent buildings and grounds all contribute. Boys are encouraged to work hard, behave well and fully enjoy life. The school, founded in 1848 at Elstree, Hertfordshire, moved to Woolhampton, Berkshire in 1939.

Eton College

Address: Windsor, Berkshire SL4 6DW
Telephone: 0753 671000
Head: Dr W.E.K. Anderson

Age range: 13-18
No. of pupils: 1270
Scholarships: Yes
Religion: Church of England

Fees per term
Day: -
Weekly board: -
Full board: £3870-

● ○ ○
Boy Girl Co-ed
○ ○ ●
Day Week Board

Founded by Henry VI in 1440. Entrance is via Common Entrance examination at 13 and King's Scholarship examination. Almost all Etonians take 'A' levels and go on to university. Unique feature is tutorial system known as 'Private Business'. All usual games offered. Musical and artistic life of the school is vigorous and more than a dozen full-length plays are performed annually.

Eton End PNEU

Address: 35 Eton Road, Datchet, Slough, Berkshire SL3 9AX
Telephone: 0753 541075
Head: Mrs B E Ottley

Age range: 3-11
No. of pupils: 210
Scholarships:
Religion: Church of England

Fees per term
Day: £582-£916
Weekly board: -
Full board: -

○ ○ ●
Boy Girl Co-ed
● ○ ○
Day Week Board

Eton End School is situated in six acres of rural countryside on the outskirts of Datchet village with Windsor Castle on the skyline. The school is a family school which strives to cater for each individual, where each child is encouraged to be creative, confident and caring. Boys 3-7, girls 3-11.

Falkland St Gabriel's

Address: Sandleford Priory, Newbury, Berkshire RG15 9BB
Telephone: 0635 40054
Head: Mrs J H Felton

Age range: 3-16
No. of pupils: 397
Scholarships:
Religion:

Fees per term
Day: -
Weekly board: -
Full board: -

● ● ○
Boy Girl Co-ed
● ○ ○
Day Week Board

For further information and a prospectus, please contact the school. Boys 3-11, girls 3-16.

BERKSHIRE 59

Foxley PNEU School

Address: Manor Drive, Shurlock Road, Reading, Berkshire RG10 0PS
Telephone: 0734 343578

Head: Miss M J Fallon

Age range: 4-7
No. of pupils: 35
Scholarships:
Religion: Church of England

Fees per term
Day: £50-£484
Weekly board: -
Full board: -

● Boy ○ Girl ○ Co-ed
● Day ○ Week ○ Board

Foxley offers children of ages 4 to 7 years an education based on traditional methods but with modern ideas covering all topics in the National Curriculum. Children aged 4 years may attend on a part-time or full-time basis. All children are prepared for entry into preparatory schools.

Haileybury Junior School

Address: Imperial Raod, Windsor, Berkshire SL4 3RS
Telephone: 0753 866330

Head: Mr B J Hare

Age range: 7-13
No. of pupils: 185
Scholarships:
Religion: Church of England

Fees per term
Day: £1775-£1775
Weekly board: -
Full board: £2300-£2300

● Boy ○ Girl ○ Co-ed
● Day ○ Week ● Board

Haileybury Junior School is a boys' preparatory school preparing boys for Haileybury, Hertford, and other senior independent schools. There is a full programme of out of school activities involving games, music, art and numerous other opportunities. About 40% of the boys go on to Haileybury and the school is ideally situated near motorways and airports.

Heathfield School

Address: London Road, Ascot, Berkshire SL5 8BQ
Telephone: 0344 882955

Head: Mrs J M Benammar

Age range: 11-18
No. of pupils: 210
Scholarships: Yes
Religion: Church of England

Fees per term
Day: -
Weekly board: -
Full board: -£3590

○ Boy ● Girl ○ Co-ed
○ Day ○ Week ● Board

Founded in 1899, the school buildings consist of a late Georgian house in 34 acres with modern extensions housing a science block, an art studio and a sports hall. Teaching and pastoral care are of a high standard, more than half the school having single bedrooms and emphasis generally on individual achievement and depth. The school is comfortable and competitive, with every pupil committed to hard work.

Hemdean House School

Address: Hemdean Road, Caversham, Reading, Berkshire RG4 7SD
Telephone: 0734 472590

Head: Dr M J Marwick

Age range: 3-16
No. of pupils: 180
Scholarships: Yes
Religion: Church of England

Fees per term
Day: £625-£915
Weekly board: -
Full board: -

● Boy ● Girl ○ Co-ed
● Day ○ Week ○ Board

Founded in 1859, Hemdean House is a school where traditional educational concepts are still valued. An emphasis on study being well organised and enjoyable allows children's natural curiosity to be encouraged and directed into orderly learning. Classes are small, with special emphasis upon the needs of each pupil. Examination results including National Curriculum Key Stage Assessments are excellent.

Herries School

Address: Dean Lane,
Cookham Dean, Berkshire
SL6 9BD
Telephone: 0628 483350

Head: Mrs W A Spicer

Age range: 4-12
No. of pupils: 101
Scholarships: Yes
Religion: Christian

Fees per term
Day: £406-£1027
Weekly board: -
Full board: -

Boy ○ Girl ○ Co-ed ●
Day ● Week ○ Board ○

Herries is an independent day school for boys aged 4-7 and girls aged 4-12. We offer a wide curriculum culminating in 11+ Common Entrance or 12+ Grammar School Entry. It is a small friendly school which combines academic achievement and excellent pastoral care. The school is renowned for its drama department.

Highfield PNEU School

Address: West Road,
Maidenhead, Berkshire
SL6 1PD
Telephone: 0628 24918

Head: Mrs P Rowe

Age range: 3-11
No. of pupils: 210
Scholarships:
Religion: Non-denominational

Fees per term
Day: £100-£995
Weekly board: -
Full board: -

Boy ○ Girl ○ Co-ed ●
Day ● Week ○ Board ○

Highfield PNEU School was founded in 1918. The aim of the school is to provide an all-round education while maximizing potential, and to engender in each pupil a love of learning which will endure for a lifetime. Preparation for Common Entrance and other entry tests. Supervision available from 8.00am. Voluntary after school activities, tea and prep. until 6.00pm.

The Highlands School

Address: Wardle Avenue,
Tilehurst, Reading, Berkshire
RG3 6JR
Telephone: 0734 427186

Head: Miss E D Lind-Smith

Age range: 3-11
No. of pupils: 183
Scholarships:
Religion: Non-denominational

Fees per term
Day: £595-£950
Weekly board: -
Full board: -

Boy ● Girl ● Co-ed ○
Day ● Week ○ Board ○

The well established school is situated in a quiet residential area of Reading. The excellent student teacher ratio ensures a happy, caring atmosphere encouraging the children to reach their full potential. All areas of the National Curriculum are covered including French. Other facilities: lively PE department, central library and computer room, individual music and special needs tuition, educational visits and speakers.

Holme Grange School

Address: Easthampstead Road,
Wokingham, Berkshire
RG11 3AL
Telephone: 0734 781566

Head: Mr N J Brodrick BEd

Age range: 4-13
No. of pupils: 227
Scholarships:
Religion: Church of England

Fees per term
Day: £1048-£1344
Weekly board: -
Full board: -

Boy ● Girl ● Co-ed ○
Day ● Week ○ Board ○

A family school employing only qualified teachers. A broad curriculum is followed, embracing both the full National Curriculum and the requirements for both 11+ and 13+ Common Entrance Examinations. Excellent facilities include a new technology block and a large sports hall with staging. The 21 acres of grounds contain 3 playing fields, 4 tennis courts and a heated swimming pool. Boys 4-13, girls 4-11.

Horris Hill

Address: Newtown, Newbury, Berkshire

Telephone: 0635 40594

Head: Mr M J Innes

Age range: 8-13
No. of pupils: 160
Scholarships:
Religion: Church of England

Fees per term
Day: -
Weekly board: -
Full board: £2710-

● Boy ○ Girl ○ Co-ed
○ Day ○ Week ● Board

Horris Hill is a traditional boys boarding preparatory school set in over 80 acres south of Newbury. Many pupils go on to Eton and Winchester. A wide variety of games and activities is available including golf, squash, fives, badminton and tennis and a new courtyard of art and crafts is under construction.

Hurst Lodge School

Address: Charters Road, Sunningdale, Berkshire SL5 9QG
Telephone: 0344 22154

Head: Mrs A M Smit

Age range: 2-18
No. of pupils: 200
Scholarships: Yes
Religion: Non-denominational

Fees per term
Day: £510-£1700
Weekly board: -£2850
Full board: -£2995

● Boy ● Girl ○ Co-ed
● Day ● Week ● Board

Hurst Lodge is a small, friendly school taking children of all abilities aged two and a half to eighteen. A broad general education is provided in sciences, humanities and languages. There are special facilities for studying dance, drama, music and art. Classes are very small with 2-16 girls per class. There is a good dyslexia department. Children are fully integrated with their peers. Boys 2-7, girls 2-18.

Lambrook School

Address: Winkfield Row, Bracknell, Berkshire RG12 6LU
Telephone: 0344 882717

Head: Mr I M A Stewart

Age range: 7-13
No. of pupils: 95
Scholarships:
Religion: Church of England

Fees per term
Day: -£1875
Weekly board: -
Full board: -£2675

● Boy ○ Girl ○ Co-ed
● Day ○ Week ● Board

Extremely accessible from the M3, M4 and Heathrow, Lambrook is situated in 70 acres of magnificent grounds. The curriculum embraces the requirements of Common Entrance and scholarship to senior schools. The school has a fine record of academic and sporting achievement, and offers many extra-curricular activities. Children are educated in a friendly, disciplined atmosphere.

Langley Manor School

Address: St. Marys Road, Langley, Slough, Berkshire SL3 6BZ
Telephone: 0753 577005

Head: Mrs S Eaton

Age range: 3-11
No. of pupils: 230
Scholarships:
Religion: Non-denominational

Fees per term
Day: £844-£878
Weekly board: -
Full board: -

○ Boy ○ Girl ● Co-ed
● Day ○ Week ○ Board

The Langley Manor School caters for children aged 3-12 years. We provide a good traditional education, encourage children to enjoy learning and achieve basic skills early. It is important that children become independent, self motivated and enquiring. We aim to educate the complete child, keeping in balance creativity and control, discipline and freedom. French and swimming are taught from the age of three.

Leighton Park School *

Address: Shinfield Road,
Reading, Berkshire RG2 7DH

Telephone: 0734 872065

Head: Mr J A Chapman

Age range: 11-18
No. of pupils: 350
Scholarships: Yes
Religion: Quaker

Fees per term
Day: £2037-£2430
Weekly board: -
Full board: £2754-£3240

Boy ○   Girl ○   Co-ed ●
Day ●   Week ○   Board ●

Leighton Park School has a strong academic record with a great majority of upper sixth students leaving to read for a degree. Music, drama and the arts play an important part in the life of the school. The school intends to implement full co-education from September 1993. Leighton Park is a Quaker foundation with a community based on trust, respect and tolerance and which is an enriching environment in which to learn.

Licensed Victuallers' School p654

Address: London Road, Ascot,
Berkshire SL5 8DR

Telephone: 0344 882770

Head: Mrs P Cowley

Age range: 5-18
No. of pupils: 700
Scholarships: Yes
Religion: Church of England

Fees per term
Day: £1080-£1485
Weekly board: £2475-£2583
Full board: £2520-£2628

Boy ○   Girl ○   Co-ed ●
Day ●   Week ●   Board ●

A 700 pupil co-educational school for pupils aged 5 to 18, offering day, weekly- and full-boarding places. The school offers high standards of education reflecting modern curriculum changes and an excellent pastoral care structure within a purpose-built complex (completed in 1989) and equipped to the highest standards.

Long Close

Address: Upton Court Road,
Slough, Berkshire SL3 7LU

Telephone: 0753 520095

Headmaster: Mr M H Kneath

Age range: 7-13
No. of pupils: 180
Scholarships: Yes
Religion: Church of England

Fees per term
Day: £1365-£1465
Weekly board: -
Full board: -

Boy ○   Girl ○   Co-ed ●
Day ●   Week ○   Board ○

Long Close is an IAPS co-educational preparatory school 7-13+. Children are prepared for a wide range of day and boarding senior independent schools, and for grammar schools situated in Buckinghamshire and Berkshire. Children with specific learning difficulties are well catered for. There is a supervised Club Hour after school followed by a supervised prep hour as required.

Luckley Oakfield School

Address: Wokingham,
Berkshire RG11 3EU

Telephone: 0734 784175

Head: Mr R C Blake

Age range: 11-18
No. of pupils: 300
Scholarships: Yes
Religion: Church of England

Fees per term
Day: £1490-
Weekly board: £2350-
Full board: £2395-

Boy ○   Girl ●   Co-ed ○
Day ●   Week ●   Board ●

The school is set in 22 acres of pleasant grounds on the edge of the M3, M4 and Heathrow. Luckley Oakfield is proud of its academic standards and of the high quality of pastoral care which springs directly from its Christian tradition.

BERKSHIRE 63

Ludgrove School

Address: Wixenford,
Wokingham, Berkshire
RG11 3AB
Telephone: 0734 789881

Age range: 8-13
No. of pupils: 189
Scholarships:
Religion: Church of England

Fees per term
Day: -
Weekly board: -
Full board: -£2675

● Boy ○ Girl ○ Co-ed
○ Day ○ Week ● Board

Heads: Mr G W P Barber Mr C N J Marston

Ludgrove is situated just outside Wokingham with an easy access to London and the airports. The school stands in grounds of 130 acres, with extensive playing fields and a nine hole golf course. There is a wealth of other sport facilities including an indoor swimming pool. There is a well equipped science laboratory, art and design centre, music school and computer room.

Maidenhead College for Girls

Address: 1 College Avenue,
Maidenhead, Berkshire
SL6 6AW
Telephone: 0628 28225

Age range: 3-16
No. of pupils: 225
Scholarships: Yes
Religion: Roman Catholic

Fees per term
Day: £352-£1320
Weekly board: -
Full board: -

● Boy ● Girl ○ Co-ed
● Day ○ Week ○ Board

Head: Mrs A P Doherty

Energetic pursuit of each pupil's personal best in a warm, friendly atmosphere. Intake is comprehensive, but good examination results are achieved. Small classes provide scope for individual attention throughout the school. Extra-curricular activities until 5.00pm. Admission to the lower school by interview. Entry to the upper school is automatic for lower school girls: outside candidates sit an entrance test.

Marist Convent Senior School ✱

Address: Sunninghill, Ascot,
Berkshire SL5 7PS

Telephone: 0344 24291

Age range: 11-18
No. of pupils: 450
Scholarships:
Religion: Roman Catholic

Fees per term
Day: £805-£1160
Weekly board: -
Full board: -

○ Boy ● Girl ○ Co-ed
● Day ○ Week ○ Board

Head: Sister M Gaffney

The school enjoys a good academic record achieving an excellent pass rate in examinations. It offers a balanced relevant curriculum broader than National Curriculum requirements. Music and drama play an important part in the life of the school and students are given opportunity to develop creative and artisitic gifts and skills. A wide variety of sport is played. Thesixth form offers a good range of courses at A level.

Mary Hare Grammar School for the Deaf †

Address: Arlington Manor,
Newbury, Berkshire
RG16 9BQ
Telephone: 0635 248303

Age range: 11-19
No. of pupils: 200
Scholarships:
Religion: Non-denominational

Fees per term
Day: -
Weekly board: -
Full board: -£4946

○ Boy ○ Girl ● Co-ed
○ Day ○ Week ● Board

Head: Dr I Tucker

For further information and a prospectus, please contact the school.

Newbold School

Address: Popeswood Road, Binfield, Bracknell, Berkshire RG12 5AH
Telephone: 0344 421088

Head: Mr M Brooks

Age range: 3-11
No. of pupils: 100
Scholarships:
Religion:

Fees per term
Day: £360-£470
Weekly board: -
Full board: -

Boy ○ Girl ○ Co-ed ●
Day ● Week ○ Board ○

A small school set in the rural village of Binfield, Berkshire. Children are admitted from the age of three and a half into the pre-school and start school full time as rising fives. All areas of the curriculum are taught — with special emphasis on mathematics, English and science. There is no provision for special needs children. Newbold School is a Christian school and focusses on these values.

The Oratory Preparatory School *p747*

Address: Great Oaks, Goring Heath, Reading, Berkshire RG8 7SF
Telephone: 0734 844511

Head: Mr D L Sexon

Age range: 4-13
No. of pupils: 240
Scholarships:
Religion: Roman Catholic

Fees per term
Day: £473-£1715
Weekly board: -
Full board: -£2443

Boy ● Girl ● Co-ed ○
Day ● Week ○ Board ●

The Oratory Preparatory School aims to provide a broadly based education in homely surroundings to equip children with the necessary self-confidence, development and academic foundations in preparation for senior school life.

The Oratory School

Address: Woodcote, Reading, Berkshire RG8 0PJ
Telephone: 0491 680207

Head: Mr S W Barrow

Age range: 11-18
No. of pupils: 360
Scholarships: Yes
Religion: Roman Catholic

Fees per term
Day: £1995-£2459
Weekly board: -
Full board: £2769-£3519

Boy ● Girl ○ Co-ed ○
Day ● Week ○ Board ●

The Oratory School was founded by Cardinal Newman in 1859 and is run by the laity. Entry is at 11, 13 or 16, with academic, music, art and sports scholarships available at all entry levels. The school has an outstanding academic record and a very wide range of sporting and extra-curricular facilities.

Padworth College

Address: Padworth, Reading, Berkshire RG7 4NR
Telephone: 0734 832644

Principal: Doctor S Villazon

Age range: 14-20
No. of pupils: 220
Scholarships: Yes
Religion: Non-denominational

Fees per term
Day: -£1575
Weekly board: -
Full board: -£3150

Boy ○ Girl ● Co-ed ○
Day ● Week ○ Board ●

In addition to a wide range of GCSE, A level and EFL courses, Padworth offers the BTEC National and First Diplomas in Business, Finance and Hotel Studies. These courses which stress practical application of knowledge are fully established as qualifications for entry into University and are also well regarded by employers. The international character of Padworth provides a challenging and interesting environment.

Pangbourne College * p747

Address: Pangbourne, Berkshire RG8 8LA

Telephone: 0734 842101

Head: Mr A B E Hudson

Age range: 11-18
No. of pupils: 410
Scholarships: Yes
Religion: Church of England

Fees per term
Day: £1580-£2175
Weekly board: -
Full board: £2275-£3100

● ○ ○
Boy Girl Co-ed
● ○ ●
Day Week Board

There is emphasis on character development, leadership and a sense of responsibility to the community. Courteous caring and comitted schoolboys constitute the typical Pangbourne product. All rounders by instinct, the sixth formers are increasingly gaining places in good universities. Few join the Forces but all benefit from the structure, the uniform and advantages of a genuine boarding school.

Papplewick

Address: Windsor Road, Ascot, Berkshire SL5 7LH

Telephone: 0344 21488

Head: Mr D R Llewellyn BA DipEd

Age range: 7-13
No. of pupils: 200
Scholarships:
Religion: Church of England

Fees per term
Day: -£1989
Weekly board: -
Full board: -£2806

● ○ ○
Boy Girl Co-ed
● ○ ●
Day Week Board

Papplewick enjoys exceptional facilities within a spacious location on the edge of Windsor Great Park. Convenient links exist with the M4, M3, M24, Heathrow and Gatwick airports. The quality of care provided and the dedication of staff are outstanding and remain Papplewick's proud hallmark: a visit is essential to absorb its special atmosphere. All boarders from 11.

The Preparatory School

Address: 84 Enborne Road, Newbury, Berkshire RG14 6AN

Telephone: 0635 41638

Head: Mr B.A. Freer

Age range: 3-11
No. of pupils: 120
Scholarships:
Religion: Christian

Fees per term
Day: £630-£860
Weekly board: -
Full board: -

○ ○ ●
Boy Girl Co-ed
● ○ ○
Day Week Board

The school, established in 1946, is an independent day school. Its motto, 'ad astra', symbolises its spirit. Children are encouraged to aim high and to give of their best. In this they are guided by an experienced and effective staff. We aim to create a caring environment, and an atmosphere of truth and harmony. Emphasis is placed upon courtesy and consideration for others.

Presentation College

Address: 63 Bath Road, Reading, Berkshire RG3 2BB

Telephone: 0734 572861

Head: Revd Brother J Bell

Age range: 7-18
No. of pupils: 460
Scholarships:
Religion: Roman Catholic

Fees per term
Day: £800-£900
Weekly board: -
Full board: -

● ○ ○
Boy Girl Co-ed
● ○ ○
Day Week Board

The college was founded in 1931 by the Presentation Brothers, and ever since it has aimed at achieving academic distinction in a friendly, happy environment of faith, expectation and excellence. Christian values and standards are promoted: each pupil is cherished and helped to develop into a mature, independent and well rounded young man.

Prior's Court Preparatory

Address: Chieveley, Newbury, Berkshire

Telephone: 0635 248209

Head: Mr P High MA

Age range: 4-13
No. of pupils: 200
Scholarships: Yes
Religion: Christian

Fees per term
Day: £912-£1727
Weekly board: -
Full board: £2467-

Boy ○ Girl ○ Co-ed ●
Day ● Week ○ Board ●

Traditional preparatory education to Common Entrance and scholarship level. Pre-preparatory from 4. Automatic progression to our senior school, Kingswood, Bath. International community. ESL. Special needs. Escorted travel to airports and London. Activities: scouts, guides, judo, drama, golf. Sports hall and fields, swimming pool, pony club. Superb teaching facilities. Fifty acres estate. Near J13 on M4/A34.

Queen Anne's School

Address: 6 Henley Road, Caversham, Reading, Berkshire RG4 0DX

Telephone: 0734 471582

Head: Miss A M Scott

Age range: 11-18
No. of pupils: 400
Scholarships: Yes
Religion: Anglican

Fees per term
Day: £2058-
Weekly board: -
Full board: £3290-

Boy ○ Girl ● Co-ed ○
Day ● Week ○ Board ●

Situated in large grounds on the edge of town and country and within easy reach of Heathrow and Gatwick airports. 300 boarders, 100 day girls aged 11-18 with 120 in the sixth form. 90% continue to higher education. Outstanding facilities for art, design and technology, computing, languages and science. Future plans include new music school and sports hall for centenary year in 1994.

Reading Blue Coat School

Address: Holme Park, Sonning-on-Thames, Berks RG4 0SU

Telephone: 0734 441005

Head: Rev A C E Saunders

Age range: 11-18
No. of pupils: 560
Scholarships: Yes
Religion: Church of England

Fees per term
Day: £1478-
Weekly board: £2617-
Full board: £2696-

Boy ● Girl ○ Co-ed ●
Day ● Week ● Board ●

The School, founded in 1646, is situated in 46 acres alongside the River Thames. Has fine facilities for high academic standards, games and activities, including CCF. Sixty weekly and full boarders live in the main house. Aim is to provide stimulating and friendly atmosphere which develop full potential of each pupil. Easily accessible from motorways and Heathrow.

Reading School

Address: Erleigh Road, Reading, Berkshire RG1 5LW

Telephone: 0734 261406

Head: Dr P R Mason

Age range: 11-18
No. of pupils: 669
Scholarships: Yes
Religion: Non-denominational

Fees per term
Day: -
Weekly board: -
Full board: £1100-

Boy ● Girl ○ Co-ed ○
Day ● Week ○ Board ●

Reading School is a grant-maintained selective grammar school for boys. Catering for both day and boarding pupils. The school has a strong academic record (in 1991, 57.3% grade A and B at advanced level), with all students obtaining 5 or more passes (grade C and above) at GCSE, the vast majority achieving 9 subjects at this level. A wide variety of sports available, music and drama flourish.

BERKSHIRE 67

The Ridge House School

Address: Cold Ash, Newbury, Berkshire

Telephone: 0635 63259

Head: Mrs R A Fleming

Age range: 3-6
No. of pupils: 53
Scholarships:
Religion:

Fees per term
Day: -
Weekly board: -
Full board: -

○ ○ ● Boy Girl Co-ed
● ○ ○ Day Week Board

For further information and a prospectus, please contact the school.

Ridgeway School (Claires Court Junior School)

Address: Maidenhead Thicket, Berkshire SL6 3QE

Telephone: 062 882 2609

Head: Mrs K M Boyd BEd

Age range: 4-10
No. of pupils: 192
Scholarships:
Religion: Roman Catholic

Fees per term
Day: £1010-£1175
Weekly board: -
Full board: -

● ○ ○ Boy Girl Co-ed
● ○ ○ Day Week Board

For further information and a prospectus, please contact the school.

Silchester House School

Address: Bath Road, Maidenhead, Berkshire SL6 0AP

Telephone: 0628 20549

Head: Mrs D J Austen

Age range: 3-12
No. of pupils: 110
Scholarships:
Religion: Church of England

Fees per term
Day: £540-£995
Weekly board: -
Full board: -

○ ○ ● Boy Girl Co-ed
● ○ ○ Day Week Board

Silchester House stands in three acres of grounds on the outskirts of Maidenhead. The nursery offers either termly places on a full or part-time basis or an extended day scheme from 8.00am to 5.30pm, 50 weeks a year. The main school offers a wide range of subjects with a firm grounding in the basic skills, achieving an excellent academic record.

St Andrew's School p655

Address: Buckhold, Pangbourne, Reading, Berkshire RG8 8QA

Telephone: 0734 744276

Head: Dr R J Acheson

Age range: 4-13
No. of pupils: 280
Scholarships:
Religion: Church of England

Fees per term
Day: £1695-
Weekly board: -
Full board: £2365-

○ ○ ● Boy Girl Co-ed
● ● ● Day Week Board

The school is set in magnificent woodlands but conveniently situated near the M4. The curriculum offers a broad range of subjects including modern, technology-related ones. Small classes ensure individual attention.

St Bernard's Preparatory School

Address: Hawtrey Close, Slough, Berkshire SL1 1TB

Telephone: 0753 521821

Head: Sister Francis Mary

Age range: 3-12
No. of pupils: 240
Scholarships:
Religion: Roman Catholic

Fees per term
Day: £775-£815
Weekly board: -
Full board: -

● Boy ● Girl ○ Co-ed
● Day ○ Week ○ Board

The school aims to provide a good primary education based on sound Christian principles, in a lively atmosphere. Children are assessed individually, and offer of places follow this procedure.

St Edward's School

Address: 64 Tilehurst Road, Reading, Berkshire RG3 2JH

Telephone: 0734 574342

Head: Mr J Wall BA

Age range: 7-13
No. of pupils: 114
Scholarships:
Religion: Non-denominational

Fees per term
Day: £910-£960
Weekly board: -
Full board: -

● Boy ○ Girl ○ Co-ed
● Day ○ Week ○ Board

For further information and a prospectus, please contact the school.

St Gabriel's School

Address: Sandleford Priory, Newbury, Berkshire RG15 9BB

Telephone: 0635 40663

Head: Mr D J Cobb

Age range: 3-16
No. of pupils: 400
Scholarships: Yes
Religion: Church of England

Fees per term
Day: £575-£1450
Weekly board: -
Full board: -

● Boy ● Girl ○ Co-ed
● Day ○ Week ○ Board

We open our own sixth form in 1998. With the excellent GCSE results we obtain it seemed foolish not to. There are new technology facilities, a modern science building, over 50 acres of grounds, a Grade I listed building and a staff that cares - about excellence, fostering the self confidence of all our children, about a total quality education. Boys 3-8.

St George's School

Address: Ascot, Berkshire RG12 3TA

Telephone: 0344 20273

Head: Mrs A M Griggs

Age range: 11-18
No. of pupils: 290
Scholarships:
Religion: Church of England

Fees per term
Day: £1850-
Weekly board: -
Full board: £3300-

○ Boy ● Girl ○ Co-ed
● Day ○ Week ● Board

St George's School, Ascot is an independent girls' secondary school. It is an Educational Trust administered by a Board of Governors and is a member of the Governing Bodies of Girls' School asssociation and is ISJC accredited. The School has approximately 285 girls aged from 11 to 18, two thirds of whom are boarders and a Sixth Form of approximately 65 girls.

BERKSHIRE 69

St George's School

Address: Windsor Castle, Windsor, Berkshire SL4 1QF

Telephone: 0753 865553

Head: Mr B C Biggs

Age range: 7-13
No. of pupils: 100
Scholarships: Yes
Religion:

Fees per term
Day: £1750-
Weekly board: £2430-
Full board: £2460-

● Boy ○ Girl ○ Co-ed
● Day ● Week ● Board

For further information and a prospectus, please contact the school.

St John's Beaumont

Address: Old Windsor, Berkshire SL4 2JN

Telephone: 0784 432428

Head: Mr D St J Gogarty

Age range: 4-13
No. of pupils: 175
Scholarships:
Religion: Jesuit

Fees per term
Day: £950-£1641
Weekly board: £2374-
Full board: £2734-

● Boy ○ Girl ○ Co-ed
● Day ○ Week ○ Board

An IAPS school situation in beautiful surroundings close to Heathrow and London. Boys are prepared for common entrance and scholarship examinations for entry to public schools, with notable academic success. The school aims to provide an environment in which the boys will learn their faith and see daily prayers and a happy Christian concern for one another as a natural way of life.

St Joseph's Convent Preparatory School

Address: 66 Upper Redlands Road, Reading, Berkshire RG1 5JT

Telephone: 0734 351717

Head: Sister Helen Marie

Age range: 3-11
No. of pupils: 180
Scholarships:
Religion: Roman Catholic

Fees per term
Day: -
Weekly board: -
Full board: -

● Boy ● Girl ○ Co-ed
● Day ○ Week ○ Board

For further information and a prospectus, please contact the school.

St Joseph's Convent School *

Address: 64 Upper Redlands Road, Reading, Berkshire RG1 5JT

Telephone: 0734 661000

Head: Mrs V Brookes

Age range: 11-18
No. of pupils: 500
Scholarships:
Religion: Roman Catholic

Fees per term
Day: -
Weekly board: -
Full board: -

○ Boy ● Girl ○ Co-ed
● Day ○ Week ○ Board

For further information and a prospectus, please contact the school.

St Mary's School

Address: Ascot, Berkshire SL5 9JF

Telephone: 0344 23721

Head: Sister M Mark Orchard IBVM

Age range: 10-18
No. of pupils: 330
Scholarships: Yes
Religion: Roman Catholic

Fees per term
Day: £1967-
Weekly board: -
Full board: £3278-£3606

Boy ○ Girl ● Co-ed ○
Day ○ Week ○ Board ●

St Mary's is a selective independent Roman Catholic boarding school for girls aged 10-18. The School is situated in 44 acres of green belt close to the M3, M4 and M25 motorways and within easy access of London and the airports. Entry at 10+, 11+, and 16+ is subject to the school's own entry procedure. Facilities are excellent as are examination results. The majority of pupils stay on for the Sixth Form and 90% go on to University.

St Piran's

Address: Gringer Hill, Maidenhead, Berkshire SL6 7LZ

Telephone: 0628 27316

Head: Mr A P Blumer

Age range: 7-13
No. of pupils: 175
Scholarships:
Religion: Christian

Fees per term
Day: £1495-£1940
Weekly board: £2465-
Full board: -

Boy ● Girl ○ Co-ed ○
Day ● Week ● Board ○

St Piran's is an independent day and weekly boarding school for boys aged 7-13. In September 1993 the school will become an all day school and a pre-preparatory department will be opening subject to planning permission. The first girls will arrive aged 3 and 4.

Stubbington House

Address: Earlywood, Bagshot Road, Ascot, Berkshire SL5 9JU

Telephone: 0344 20257

Head: Mr B M Allen

Age range: 3-13
No. of pupils: 130
Scholarships:
Religion:

Fees per term
Day: -
Weekly board: -
Full board: -

Boy ○ Girl ○ Co-ed ●
Day ● Week ● Board ●

For further information and a prospectus, please contact the school.

Sunningdale

Address: Sunningdale, Berkshire SL5 9PY

Telephone: 0344 20159

Headmasters: Mr A J N Dawson, Mr T M E Dawson

Age range: 8-13
No. of pupils: 120
Scholarships:
Religion: Church of England

Fees per term
Day: -
Weekly board: -
Full board: £2075-

Boy ● Girl ○ Co-ed ○
Day ○ Week ○ Board ●

Founded in 1874 Sunningdale is set in 23 acres of grounds with extensive games fields and woodland. The majority of boys go on to Eton. A new classroom block, changing rooms, computer design and woodwork rooms as well as a new music school have been built in the last two years. The school is kept at 120 boarders to preserve the friendly family atmosphere.

BERKSHIRE 71

Upton House School

Address: St Leonard's Road, Windsor, Berkshire SL4 3DF

Telephone: 0753 862610

Head: Mrs J G Woodley

Age range: 3-11
No. of pupils: 210
Scholarships:
Religion: Church of England

Fees per term
Day: £450-£1040
Weekly board: -
Full board: -

● Boy   ● Girl   ○ Co-ed
● Day   ○ Week ○ Board

Upton House is a day school, accredited by the ISJC whose Head is a member of the IAPS. Our aim is to motivate each child to achieve his/her personal best in a happy, caring environment. Our objectives are to offer a rich academic and cultural environment within which each child may develop his/her potential to the full.

Waverley School

Address: Ravenswood Avenue, Crowthorne, Berkshire RG11 6AY
Telephone: 0344 772379

Head: Mr S G Melton BSc

Age range: 3-11
No. of pupils: 160
Scholarships:
Religion: Christian

Fees per term
Day: £422-£892
Weekly board: -
Full board: -

○ Boy   ○ Girl   ● Co-ed
● Day   ○ Week ○ Board

Waverley is a co-educational day school for children age 3 to 11. Normal entry is at age 3 into the nursery department, although later entry is possible by arrangement. Emphasis is placed on enabling individuals to achieve their full potential. Pupils are successfully prepared for entry to senior independent schools by examination at 11+.

Wellington College ✻

Address: Crowthorne, Berkshire RG11 7PU

Telephone: 0344 772261

Head: Mr C J Driver

Age range: 13-18
No. of pupils: 829
Scholarships:
Religion:

Fees per term
Day: -
Weekly board: -
Full board: -

● Boy   ● Girl   ○ Co-ed
● Day   ○ Week ● Board

Girls accepted in sixth form. For further information and a prospectus, please contact the school.

White House

Address: Wokingham, Berkshire RG11 3HD

Telephone: 0734 785151

Head: Mrs B M Collins

Age range: 3-11
No. of pupils: 120
Scholarships:
Religion: Christian

Fees per term
Day: £410-£870
Weekly board: -
Full board: -

○ Boy   ○ Girl   ● Co-ed
● Day   ○ Week ○ Board

The school aims to provide a good all-round education in a happy atmosphere, where all the children are able to achieve their full potential. Entry is by interview with the headteacher. Girls aged 3-11, boys aged 3-7 years.

Winbury School

Address: Hibbert Road, Bray,
Maidenhead, Berkshire
SL6 1UU
Telephone: 0628 27412

Head: Mr G R Graham

Age range: 3-8
No. of pupils: 107
Scholarships:
Religion:

Fees per term
Day: -
Weekly board: -
Full board: -

Boy ○ Girl ○ Co-ed ●
Day ● Week ○ Board ○

For further information and a prospectus, please contact the school.

BUCKINGHAMSHIRE

Akeley Wood Junior School

Address: Wicken Park, Wicken, Milton Keynes, Buckinghamshire MK17 6DA
Telephone: 0908 57231

Head: Mr J C Lovelock

Age range: 3-10
No. of pupils: 300
Scholarships:
Religion: Non-denominational

Fees per term
Day: £475-£1180
Weekly board: -
Full board: -

Boy ○ Girl ○ Co-ed ●
Day ● Week ○ Board ○

Situated between Milton Keynes and Buckingham, the school occupies an imposing Georgian mansion set in eleven acres of parkland. There is a happy and caring atmosphere. The very full curriculum strikes a balance between sound teaching of the basic skills and the fostering of creative, musical, artistic and sporting talent. Pupils move to the senior school after their tenth birthday.

Akeley Wood School

Address: Buckingham, Buckinghamshire MK18 5AE
Telephone:

Head: Mr J C Lovelock

Age range: 10-18
No. of pupils: 375
Scholarships:
Religion: Non-denominational

Fees per term
Day: £1180-£1365
Weekly board: -
Full board: -

Boy ○ Girl ○ Co-ed ●
Day ● Week ○ Board ○

The school lies in twenty three acres of park and woodland to the north of Buckingham. There is a happy and caring atmosphere. Outstanding results are achieved at both GCSE and A Level — and there are strengths in music, drama and sport. Specialist teaching is available for dyslexic pupils.

Ashfold

Address: Dorton, Aylesbury, Buckinghamshire HP18 9NG
Telephone: 0844 238237

Head: Mr D H M Dalrymple MA(Oxon)

Age range: 4-13
No. of pupils: 190
Scholarships: Yes
Religion: Christian

Fees per term
Day: £670-£1920
Weekly board: £2525-
Full board: £2525-

Boy ○ Girl ○ Co-ed ●
Day ● Week ● Board ●

Ashfold is a busy and lively school where children are offered opportunities and challenged on a wide front - academic, sporting, musical, artistic and dramatic. The facilities have been much extended and improved over recent years - and now include a music school and an art and CDT block, as well as a sports hall and external play areas.

The Beacon School and Winterbourn

Address: Chessam Bois, Amersham, Buckinghamshire HP6 5PF
Telephone: 0494 433654
Head: Mr J V Cross

Age range: 3-13
No. of pupils: 320
Scholarships:
Religion: Church of England

Fees per term
Day: £550-£1576
Weekly board: -
Full board: -

Boy ● Girl ○ Co-ed ○
Day ● Week ○ Board ○

For further information and a prospectus, please contact the school.

Bury Lawn School

Address: Soskin Drive, Stantonbury Fields, Milton Keynes, Bucks. MK14 6DP
Telephone: 0908 220345

Head: Mrs H W Kiff

Age range: 3-18
No. of pupils: 420
Scholarships:
Religion: Non-denominational

Fees per term
Day: £1055-£1460
Weekly board: -
Full board: -

Boy ○ Girl ○ Co-ed ●
Day ● Week ○ Board ○

Non-selective day school catering for all-ability range with small classes not exceeding 18 pupils. Purpose built school founded in 1970 but moved to new premises in 1988. Special needs department.

Known for excellent results and speech, drama and music.

Caldicott School

Address: Farnham Royal, Buckinghamshire SL2 3SL

Telephone: 0753 644457

Head: Mr R P Wright

Age range: 7-13
No. of pupils: 244
Scholarships:
Religion: Christian

Fees per term
Day: -£1945
Weekly board: -
Full board: -£2665

Boy ● Girl ○ Co-ed ○
Day ● Week ○ Board ●

Caldicott is a flourishing IAPS day/boarding preparatory school for boys 8-13, beside Burnham Beeches, close to Heathrow and 20 miles from London. Excellent academic/sporting record, preparing boys for scholarship and Common Entrance to the better known public schools. Superb facilities, within a traditional, caring, homely environment. The building of a new music school is nearing completion.

Chesham Preparatory School

Address: Orchard Leigh, Chesham, Buckinghamshire HP5 3QF
Telephone: 0494 782619

Head: Mr R J H Ford

Age range: 5-13
No. of pupils: 286
Scholarships:
Religion: Non-denominational

Fees per term
Day: £840-£1060
Weekly board: -
Full board: -

Boy ○ Girl ○ Co-ed ●
Day ● Week ○ Board ○

The aim of the school is to introduce young children to education in a happy and sympathetic atmosphere so as to engender a desire to learn. The school has always maintained a high academic standard with good speech and behaviour expected from pupils. Skill in art, craft, music, drama, design and technology are equally encouraged; thereby children may be helped to develop each aspect of their personality and ability.

Crown House

Address: 19 London Road, High Wycombe, Buckinghamshire HP11 1BJ
Telephone: 0494 529927

Head: Mr L Clark

Age range: 4-12
No. of pupils: 150
Scholarships:
Religion: Non-denominational

Fees per term
Day: £840-£840
Weekly board: -
Full board: -

Boy ○ Girl ○ Co-ed ●
Day ● Week ○ Board ○

The school's greatest resource is its caring, family atmosphere and small class size, ensuring that each child receives the individual attention and encouragement necessary for effective learning and the growth of self-confidence. We aim to promote a sense of purpose and pride in achievement and we regard the enjoyment of learning as essential to the realisation of personal potentials.

Dair House School Trust Ltd.

Address: Bishops Blake, Beaconsfield Road, Farnham Royal, Slough, Bucks SL2 3BY
Telephone: 0753 643964

Age range: 3-8
No. of pupils: 150
Scholarships:
Religion: Church of England

Fees per term
Day: £450-£930
Weekly board: -
Full board: -

Boy ○ Girl ○ Co-ed ●
Day ● Week ○ Board ○

Head: Mrs T A Devonside

The school is a charitable trust founded in 1932. The nursery department provides a purposeful, carefully constructed introduction to school life, and children in the upper school are successfully prepared for entrance examinations to local preparatory schools. The school is accredited by ISJC.

Davenies School p655

Address: Station Road, Beaconsfield, Buckinghamshire HP9 1AA
Telephone: 0494 674169

Age range: 4-13
No. of pupils: 172
Scholarships:
Religion: Non-denominational

Fees per term
Day: £1170-£1260
Weekly board: -
Full board: -

Boy ● Girl ○ Co-ed ○
Day ● Week ○ Board ○

Head: Mr J R Jones BEd (Oxon)

All traditional core subjects are taught in line with the requirements of the National Curriculum. Extra subjects include information and design technology, drama, music, art and Latin. Some boys leave at 12+ for the Buckinghamshire grammar schools; the rest continue in independent education. Entry up to the age of 7 years is by interview, thereafter by a combination of interview and academic tests. Davenies School is a member of IAPS.

Gateway School

Address: High Street, Great Missenden, Buckinghamshire HP16 9AA
Telephone: 02406 2407

Age range: 2-13
No. of pupils: 350
Scholarships:
Religion: Non-denominational

Fees per term
Day: £246-£1090
Weekly board: -
Full board: -

Boy ○ Girl ○ Co-ed ●
Day ● Week ○ Board ○

Heads: Mr J L Wade Mrs J H Wade

For further information and a prospectus, please contact the school.

Gayhurst School

Address: Bull Lane, Gerrards Cross, Buckinghamshire SL9 8RJ
Telephone: 0753 882690

Age range: 5-13
No. of pupils: 250
Scholarships:
Religion: Christian

Fees per term
Day: £1050-£1350
Weekly board: -
Full board: -

Boy ● Girl ○ Co-ed ○
Day ● Week ○ Board ○

Head: Mr R F Eglin

Gayhurst School offers basic subjects taught by formal methods but embracing the requirements of modern educational practices, in a non-pressurised atmosphere which results in a boy being prepared academically, socially and culturally for secondary education. Each boy is able to find his own level and a large range of extra-curricular activities enables him to develop interests outside the classroom.

BUCKINGHAMSHIRE 77

Godstowe School

Address: Shrubbery Road, High Wycombe, Buckinghamshire HP13 6PR
Telephone: 0494 529273

Head: Mrs F J Henson

Age range: 4-13
No. of pupils: 360
Scholarships:
Religion: Church of England

Fees per term
Day: £625-£1300
Weekly board: -
Full board: £2465-£2465

○ ● ●
Boy Girl Co-ed
● ○ ●
Day Week Board

Godstowe School was founded in 1900 and is one of the largest girls' boarding and day preparatory schools in the country. With excellent facilities and small classes we are able to offer a vibrant and diverse range of activities, within a secure and caring environment. The pre-preparatory department is co-educational; the preparatory school from 8 to 18 has an equal balance between boarding and day places.

Gyosei International School UK

Address: Japonica Lane, V10 Brickhill Street, Milton Keynes, Bucks MK15 9JX
Telephone: 0908 690100

Head: Mr T Ochis

Age range: 9-18
No. of pupils: 283
Scholarships:
Religion: Roman Catholic

Fees per term
Day: £1400-£2410
Weekly board: -
Full board: £2100-£4010

○ ○ ●
Boy Girl Co-ed
● ○ ●
Day Week Board

We are a boarding school for Japanese children, but we are prepared to accept pupils from other nationalities. We think it important for our students to be as good at speaking English as possible. We often exchange classes and teachers with local schools.

Hampden Manor

Address: Little Hampden, Great Missenden, Buckinghamshire HP16 9PS
Telephone: 0296 622101

Head: Mr N H Lloyd-Webb

Age range: 4-13
No. of pupils: 100
Scholarships: Yes
Religion: Church of England

Fees per term
Day: £850-£1220
Weekly board: £1650-
Full board: -

● ○ ○
Boy Girl Co-ed
● ● ○
Day Week Board

Hampden Manor is set in the Chilterns, but within easy reach of Aylesbury, High Wycombe and Thame. A small school with a friendly atmosphere, we specialise in looking after the 'whole child' in small classes. Discipline is firm but kind, reinforced by a strong house system. Half the staff, including the Headmaster and his family live on the estate.

Heatherton House School

Address: 10 Copperkins Lane, Amersham, Buckinghamshire HP6 5QB
Telephone: 0494 726433

Head: Mrs J Burrell

Age range: 3-12
No. of pupils: 150
Scholarships:
Religion: Non-denominational

Fees per term
Day: £400-£1020
Weekly board: -
Full board: -

● ● ○
Boy Girl Co-ed
● ○ ○
Day Week Board

To the staff at Heatherton House School each child is an individual with their own particular requirements. It has always been our concern to provide encouragement, opportunity and support for every pupil so that each may flourish and develop to the best of their own abilities. We are justifiably proud of the pupils whom we send on to senior schools. Boys 3-5, girls 3-12.

High March

Address: Beaconsfield, Buckinghamshire HP9 2PZ
Telephone: 0494 675186

Head: Mrs P A Forsyth

Age range: 3-13
No. of pupils: 300
Scholarships: Yes
Religion: Non-denominational

Fees per term
Day: £400-£1240
Weekly board: -
Full board: -

○ ● ●
Boy Girl Co-ed
● ○ ○
Day Week Board

High March is a long established happy school founded in 1926. It is situated in its own grounds in a pleasant residential area. Active membership of IAPS and ISIS in maintained. The school has a separate junior house and nursery under its own head of department. Co-educational up to 7 years.

Holy Cross Convent

Address: The Grange, Chalfont St Peter, Buckinghamshire SL9 9DW
Telephone: 0753 882583

Head: Sister Kevin

Age range: 4-18
No. of pupils: 450
Scholarships:
Religion: Roman Catholic

Fees per term
Day: £900-
Weekly board: -
Full board: £2500-

○ ● ○
Boy Girl Co-ed
● ● ●
Day Week Board

For further information and a prospectus, please contact the school.

Kingscote Pre-preparatory School

Address: Oval Way, Gerrards Cross, Buckinghamshire SL9 8PZ
Telephone: 0753 885535

Head: Mrs S A Tunstall CertEd

Age range: 4-7
No. of pupils: 108
Scholarships:
Religion: Non-denominational

Fees per term
Day: -
Weekly board: -
Full board: -

● ○ ○
Boy Girl Co-ed
● ○ ○
Day Week Board

For further information and a prospectus, please contact the school.

Ladymede p656

Address: Little Kimble, Aylesbury, Buckinghamshire
Telephone: 08444 6154

Head: Mrs P A Hollis

Age range: 3-12
No. of pupils: 130
Scholarships:
Religion: Non-denominational

Fees per term
Day: £450-£1030
Weekly board: -£1895
Full board: -£1895

○ ● ●
Boy Girl Co-ed
● ● ●
Day Week Board

Girls' preparatory and co-educational pre-preparatory school situated in beautiful countryside. The interest of the staff is to provide a happy family atmosphere and first-class education, 11+, 12+ and Common Entrance, in small classes. Swimming is available throughout the year. Escorted transport to and from London and airports.

BUCKINGHAMSHIRE 79

Maltman's Green Preparatory School for Girls p656

Address: Gerrards Cross, Buckinghamshire SL9 8RR

Telephone: 0753 883022

Head: Mrs M Evans BA

Age range: 4-13
No. of pupils: 330
Scholarships:
Religion: Non-denominational

Fees per term
Day: £900-£1366
Weekly board: £2100-
Full board: £2400-

○ ● ○
Boy Girl Co-ed
● ● ●
Day Week Board

Each of our 330 pupils is encouraged to strive for excellence in a happy and caring environment with good, constantly up-dated facilities for work and play. Established in 1918, the school is set in rural surroundings within easy reach of London, close to M1, M4 and M40 and a short journey from Heathrow, Stansted and Luton airports.

Milton Keynes Preparatory School

Address: Tattenhoe Lane, Milton Keynes, Buckinghamshire MK3 7EG
Telephone: 0908 642111

Head: Mrs H Pauley

Age range: 0-13
No. of pupils: 420
Scholarships: Yes
Religion: Non-denominational

Fees per term
Day: £1135-£1250
Weekly board: -
Full board: -

○ ○ ●
Boy Girl Co-ed
● ○ ○
Day Week Board

As the only selective IAPS preparatory school in the city Milton Keynes Preparatory School has a solid reputation for academic excellence within its total concept of caring for children from the age of two months to 13 years and offering extended hours and holidays for the professional parent. Steady and sustained growth has brought the school close to capacity with waiting lists in several departments.

Pipers Corner School

Address: Great Kingshill, High Wycombe, Buckinghamshire HP15 6LP
Telephone: 0494 718255

Head: Dr M M Wilson

Age range: 8-18
No. of pupils: 380
Scholarships: Yes
Religion: Church of England

Fees per term
Day: £1310-£1545
Weekly board: £2465-£2670
Full board: £2505-£2710

○ ● ○
Boy Girl Co-ed
● ● ●
Day Week Board

For further information and a prospectus, please contact the school.

St Mary's

Address: Packhorse Road, Gerrards Cross, Bucks SL9 8JQ
Telephone: 0753 883370

Head: Mrs J P G Smith

Age range: 3-18
No. of pupils: 350
Scholarships: Yes
Religion: Church of England

Fees per term
Day: £750-£1435
Weekly board: -
Full board: -

○ ● ○
Boy Girl Co-ed
● ○ ○
Day Week Board

At St Mary's a caring, disciplined environment and an excellent pupil teacher ratio mean that every girl is personally encouraged to achieve her best. Academic standards are excellent while sport, drama, art, music are all encouraged. Careers advice is available for all senior pupils and particularly for sixth formers choosing their university courses.

St Teresa's Catholic School

Address: Aylesbury Road, Princes Risborough, Buckinghamshire HP27 0JW
Telephone: 084 44 5005

Age range: 3-12
No. of pupils: 174
Scholarships:
Religion: Roman Catholic

Fees per term
Day: £216-£660
Weekly board: -
Full board: -

Boy ○ Girl ○ Co-ed ●
Day ● Week ○ Board ○

Head: Mrs C M Sparkes

St Terea's School is situated in the rural town of Princes Risborough, Buckinghamshire, close to the Oxfordshire border and equidistant to Aylesbury and High Wycombe. Though primarily Catholic, the school is open to boys and girls (3-12 years) of any or no religion. National Curriculm subjects are taught as well as drama, ballet and swimming. Children are prepared for the twelve plus and any entrance examinations required.

Stowe School *

Address: Stowe, Buckingham, Buckinghamshire MK18 5EH
Telephone: 0280 813164

Age range: 13-18
No. of pupils: 583
Scholarships:
Religion:

Fees per term
Day: -
Weekly board: -
Full board: -

Boy ● Girl ● Co-ed ○
Day ● Week ○ Board ●

Head: Mr J G L Nichols

For further information and a prospectus, please contact the school. Co-ed sixth form.

Swanbourne House

Address: Swanbourne, Milton Keynes, Buckinghamshire

Telephone: 0296 720264

Age range: 3-13
No. of pupils: 300
Scholarships: Yes
Religion: Church of England

Fees per term
Day: £1030-£1800
Weekly board: -£2400
Full board: -£2400

Boy ○ Girl ○ Co-ed ●
Day ● Week ● Board ●

Head: Mr T V More

The school provides a continuous, structured education for children aged 3-13 years. The school is run on family lines: the friendly and caring atmosphere that prevails can only be fully appreciated at first hand - a visit to the school is essential. The school stands in 25 acres of grounds. Recent developments include a multi purpose hall and design technology centre.

Thornton College

Address: Thornton, Milton Keynes, Buckinghamshire MK17 0HJ
Telephone: 0280 812610

Age range: 5-16
No. of pupils: 300
Scholarships: Yes
Religion: None

Fees per term
Day: £1160-£1460
Weekly board: -£1900-£1900
Full board: £2070-£2380

Boy ○ Girl ● Co-ed ○
Day ● Week ● Board ●

Head: Mrs E Speddy

Founded in 1917 by the Sisters of Jesus and Mary, Thornton College is set in 25 acres of parkland in rural Buckinghamshire. Modern teaching techniques combine with traditional values within a firmly Christian ethos. Classes are small with high academic achievement; girls are encouraged to develop their own optimum potential. Convenient to motorway network. Milton Keynes is 35 minutes from Euston.

BUCKINGHAMSHIRE 81

Thorpe House School

Address: Oval Way, Gerrards Cross, Buckinghamshire SL9 8PZ
Telephone: 0753 882474

Head: Mr J M Snow

Age range: 7-13
No. of pupils: 210
Scholarships:
Religion: Church of England

Fees per term
Day: £1190-£1240
Weekly board: -
Full board: -

● Boy ○ Girl ○ Co-ed
● Day ○ Week ○ Board

Thorpe House prepares boys for the Common Entrance and scholarship examinations to senior independent schools, and also for Buckinghamshire Grammar School. There is a pre-preparatory school, Kingscote, for boys aged 4-7.

The Vale School

Address: Peverel Court, Portway Road, Stone, Aylesbury, Buckinghamshire
Telephone: 0296 748786

Head: Mr D A Heffer

Age range: 10-16
No. of pupils: 146
Scholarships:
Religion:

Fees per term
Day: -£780
Weekly board: -
Full board: -

● Boy ● Girl ○ Co-ed
● Day ○ Week ○ Board

An independent school for boys and girls from 10-16. Pupils are prepared for GCSE examinations. Small classes, qualified staff, sound discipline and a happy purposeful atmosphere all combine to produce good examination results.

Wicken Park School

Address: Wicken, Milton Keynes, Buckinghamshire MK19 6DA
Telephone:

Head:

Age range: 9-13
No. of pupils:
Scholarships:
Religion:

Fees per term
Day: -
Weekly board: -
Full board: -

● Boy ○ Girl ○ Co-ed
○ Day ○ Week ● Board

For further information and a prospectus, please contact the school.

Wycombe Abbey School

Address: High Wycombe, Buckinghamshire HP11 1PE
Telephone: 0494 520381

Head: Mrs J M Goodland

Age range: 11-18
No. of pupils: 500
Scholarships: Yes
Religion: Church of England

Fees per term
Day: -
Weekly board: -
Full board: £3696-£3696

○ Boy ● Girl ○ Co-ed
○ Day ○ Week ● Board

Wycombe Abbey is a highly academic boarding school for girls. All the buildings are within extensive and beautiful grounds. Pupils follow a broad curriculum to GCSE and A level, and all continue to univeristy, many to Oxbridge. A wide variety of extra-curricular activities are provided. Music, drama, art and sport play an important part in school life.

CAMBRIDGESHIRE

CAMBRIDGESHIRE 83

Cambridge Centre for Sixth Form Studies

Address: 1 Salisbury Villas, Station Road, Cambridge, Cambridgeshire CB1 2JF
Telephone:

Age range: 15-19
No. of pupils: 220
Scholarships: Yes
Religion:

Fees per term
Day: £1777-£2793
Weekly board: -
Full board: £2772-£4153

○ ○ ● Boy Girl Co-ed
● ○ ● Day Week Board

Heads: Mr P C Redhead, Dr A M Dawson

CCSS is a co-educational 6th form college offering a new environment to 6th form entrants and final year GCSE pupils. With an average class size of 6, integral individual teaching and a highly qualified staff, the college has a strong academic reputation. The college has an active sports/extra-curricular programme and boarding places for 130 of its 225 pupils.

Dean Grange Preparatory School

Address: Upper Dean, Huntingdon, Cambridgeshire PE18 0LT
Telephone: 0234 708243

Age range: 2-13
No. of pupils: 130
Scholarships:
Religion: Inter denominational

Fees per term
Day: £490-£800
Weekly board: £1435-£1745
Full board: £1540-£1850

○ ○ ● Boy Girl Co-ed
● ● ● Day Week Board

Head: Mr D Roach

Dean Grange Preparatory School is situated in rural north Bedfordshire. Small happy classes ensure that pupils obtain their true academic potential. A full curriculum, including sport, prepares pupils for 7+ and 13+ entrance examinations. The boarding house philosophy is to provide a 'home from home'. The school has a special needs unit. Extra-curricular activities include horse riding and ballet.

Kimbolton School *

Address: Kimbolton, Huntingdon, Cambridgeshire PE18 0EA
Telephone: 0480 860505

Age range: 7-18
No. of pupils: 714
Scholarships: Yes
Religion: Non-denominational

Fees per term
Day: £1267-£1520
Weekly board: -
Full board: £2620-

○ ○ ● Boy Girl Co-ed
● ○ ● Day Week Board

Head: Mr R V Peel

The school aims to provide, within a disciplined and caring framework, a balanced education and to encourage pupils to develop their individual personalities, interests and potential to the full. In addition to the sports complex, the school has recently added to its facilities with a physical science laboratory complex and a computer centre. Boarding facilities are for senior school only.

King's College School

Address: West Road, Cambridge, Cambridgeshire CB3 9DN
Telephone: 0223 65814

Age range: 4-13
No. of pupils: 270
Scholarships: Yes
Religion: Church of England

Fees per term
Day: £1150-£1575
Weekly board: £816-£2430
Full board: £816-£2430

● ○ ● Boy Girl Co-ed
● ● ● Day Week Board

Head: Mr G S P Peacocke

The school is located on a pleasant site in west Cambridge and educates the choristers of the world-famous King's College Choir and some 250 other pupils. It has undertaken a major development programme, with new facilities for boarders, technology, science, computers, music, library, and a new pre-preparatory department from the age of 4, open in September 1992.

The King's School p744

Address: Ely, Cambridgeshire CB7 4DB

Telephone: 0353 662824

Head: Mr R H Youdale

Age range: 4-18
No. of pupils: 800
Scholarships: Yes
Religion: Church of England

Fees per term
Day: £551-£2213
Weekly board: £2015-£3383
Full board: £2085-£3471

Boy ○ Girl ○ Co-ed ●
Day ● Week ● Board ●

The school traces its origins to the Benedictine Monastery in 970 AD and continues to provide an excellent modern education within an environment of medieval buildings. A long programme of building, rebuilding and modernising the academic, residential and sporting facilities is almost complete. The school is well-equipped for all academic subjects including the sciences, and for a wide range of activities.

Kirkstone House School

Address: Main Street, Baston, Peterborough, Cambridgeshire PE6 9NU
Telephone: 0778 560350

Head: Mrs P M J Little

Age range: 3-16
No. of pupils: 270
Scholarships: Yes
Religion: Church of England

Fees per term
Day: £718-£1139
Weekly board: -
Full board: -

Boy ○ Girl ○ Co-ed ●
Day ● Week ○ Board ○

Kirkstone House School is an ISAI accredited co-educational day school situated in beautiful surroundings 4 miles north of Market Deeping. Pupils learn and progress in small classes following a broad, academic curriculum. There are flourishing music, art and drama schools and 60 acres of natural woodland and lakes provide opportunity for outdoor education.

The Leys *

Address: Cambridge, Cambridgeshire CB2 2AD

Telephone: 0223 355426

Head: Revd J C A Barrelt

Age range: 13-18
No. of pupils: 400
Scholarships: Yes
Religion: Methodist

Fees per term
Day: £2650-
Weekly board: -
Full board: £3580-

Boy ○ Girl ○ Co-ed ●
Day ● Week ○ Board ●

The Leys maintains a liberal Christian tradition, encouraging high personal standards academically, culturally, intellectually and on the games field. The school is small enough to enjoy a friendly atmosphere, but large enough to offer a wide range of activities of all kinds. It is situated on an attractive site on the edge of the university city of Cambridge.

Madingley School

Address: Cambridge Road, Madingley, Cambridge, Cambridgeshire CB3 8AH
Telephone: 0954 210309

Head: Mrs J West

Age range: 3-11
No. of pupils: 60
Scholarships:
Religion: Non-denominational

Fees per term
Day: £675-£775
Weekly board: -
Full board: -

Boy ○ Girl ○ Co-ed ●
Day ● Week ○ Board ○

Madingley is a small community of about 60 pupils. Personal attention is given through small classes. There is a real concern for each child's welfare and every child has the opportunity to develop his talents.

CAMBRIDGESHIRE 85

The Perse *

Address: Hills Road,
Cambridge, Cambridgeshire
CB2 2QF
Telephone: 0223 248127

Head: Dr G M Stephen

Age range: 11-18
No. of pupils: 490
Scholarships: Yes
Religion: Anglican

Fees per term
Day: £1226-
Weekly board: -
Full board: -

● ○ ○
Boy Girl Co-ed
● ○ ○
Day Week Board

The Perse School was founded in 1615 by Stephen Perse, a Fellow of Caius College. As a doctor and benefactor he showed compassion and wisdom. As a University member he believed in scholarship and the excitement of learning. The Perse School aims to live up to these high ideals and to provide the widest possible education for children in Cambridge and its surrounding areas.

The Perse School for Girls *

Address: Union Road,
Cambridge, Cambridgeshire
CB2 1HF
Telephone: 0223 359589

Head: Miss H Smith

Age range: 7-18
No. of pupils: 700
Scholarships:
Religion: Non-denominational

Fees per term
Day: £1124-£1291
Weekly board: -
Full board: -

○ ● ○
Boy Girl Co-ed
● ○ ○
Day Week Board

The Perse takes pride in a strong tradition of academic excellence. All pupils take three sciences and two languages (French and one of German, Italian, Russian or Spanish). The broad and balanced curriculum also includes technological, creative and classical subjects. Excellent teaching is provided with emphasis on individual attention. A wide range of extra curricular activities supports the academic programme.

Peterborough High School p657

Address: Westwood House,
Thorpe Road, Peterborough,
Cambridgeshire PE3 6JF
Telephone: 0733 343357

Head: Mrs A J V Storey

Age range: 4-18
No. of pupils: 370
Scholarships: Yes
Religion: Church of England

Fees per term
Day: £590-£1195
Weekly board: £2205-£2400
Full board: £2205-£2400

● ● ○
Boy Girl Co-ed
● ● ●
Day Week Board

Peterborough High School provides a sound academic education in a well-disciplined environment. Through a wide curriculum and a variety of extra-curricular activities, individual interests are recognised and fostered. In addition to all academic subjects which are catered for, the school enjoys an excellent reputation for its pupils' achievements in art, drama, music and sport. Boys 4-8 years.

Sancton Wood School

Address: 2 St. Pauls Road,
Cambridge, Cambridgeshire
CA1 2EZ
Telephone: 0223 359488

Head: Mrs J Sturdy

Age range: 3-16
No. of pupils: 200
Scholarships:
Religion: Anglican

Fees per term
Day: £450-£1050
Weekly board: -
Full board: -

○ ○ ●
Boy Girl Co-ed
● ○ ○
Day Week Board

For further information and a prospectus, please contact the school.

St Audrey's Convent

Address: Alexandra Road, Wisbech, Cambridgeshire PE13 1HW
Telephone: 0945 583465

Age range: 3-11
No. of pupils: 130
Scholarships:
Religion: Roman Catholic

Fees per term
Day: £539-£704
Weekly board: -
Full board: -

Boy ○ Girl ○ Co-ed ●
Day ● Week ○ Board ○

Head: Sister Mary Assunta O'Shea

For further information and a prospectus, please contact the school.

St Faith's School

Address: Trumpington Road, Cambridge, Cambridgeshire CB2 2AG
Telephone: 0223 352073

Age range: 4-13
No. of pupils: 450
Scholarships:
Religion: Non-denominational

Fees per term
Day: £1115-£1440
Weekly board: -
Full board: -

Boy ● Girl ○ Co-ed ○
Day ● Week ○ Board ○

Head: Mr R A Dyson

For further information and a prospectus, please contact the school.

St John's College School

Address: 73 Grange Road, Cambridge, Cambridgeshire
Telephone: 0223 353532

Age range: 4-13
No. of pupils: 435
Scholarships:
Religion: Church of England

Fees per term
Day: £789-£1578
Weekly board: £2448-£2448
Full board: -

Boy ● Girl ● Co-ed ○
Day ● Week ● Board ●

Head: Mr K L Jones

St John's prides itself on the quality of academic and pastoral care it provides for each child. Through relaxed and friendly relations with children in a well-structured environment rich with opportunity; through expert staffing and, above all, through a sense of community that cares for the strengths and weaknesses of each of its members, St John's has consistently achieved outstanding results.

St Mary's School *

Address: Bateman Street, Cambridge, Cambridgeshire
Telephone:

Age range: 11-18
No. of pupils: 575
Scholarships:
Religion: Roman Catholic

Fees per term
Day: £1100-
Weekly board: -
Full board: -

Boy ○ Girl ● Co-ed ○
Day ● Week ● Board ○

Head: Ms M Conway

St Mary's offers girls the opportunity to develop their talents within a Christian community where high standards of both work and behaviour are expected. Academic standards are high and an awareness of the needs of others is encouraged. Charity work and fund-raising form an important part of school life. The school is well situated, backing onto the University Botanic Gardens with public transport nearby.

Stonely Grange School

Address: Easter Road, Stonely, Huntingdon, Cambridgeshire PE18 0EL
Telephone: 0480 860295

Head: Mrs J T Larter

Age range: 4-16
No. of pupils: 80
Scholarships:
Religion:

Fees per term
Day: -
Weekly board: -
Full board: -

Boy ○ Girl ○ Co-ed ●
Day ● Week ○ Board ●

For further information and a prospectus, please contact the school.

Wisbech Grammar School ✶

Address: North Brink, Wisbech, Cambridgeshire PE13 1JX
Telephone: 0945 583631

Head: Mr R S Repper

Age range: 11-18
No. of pupils: 620
Scholarships:
Religion: Church of England

Fees per term
Day: £1340-
Weekly board: -
Full board: -

Boy ○ Girl ○ Co-ed ●
Day ● Week ○ Board ○

The School was founded in 1379 in the Church of St Peter & Paul, Wisbech. Since 1970 the School has become fully co-educational. In 1983 full independence was regained and the numbers in the School have grown by a further 200 since then, giving 630 in all; 140 in the Sixth Form.

CHESHIRE

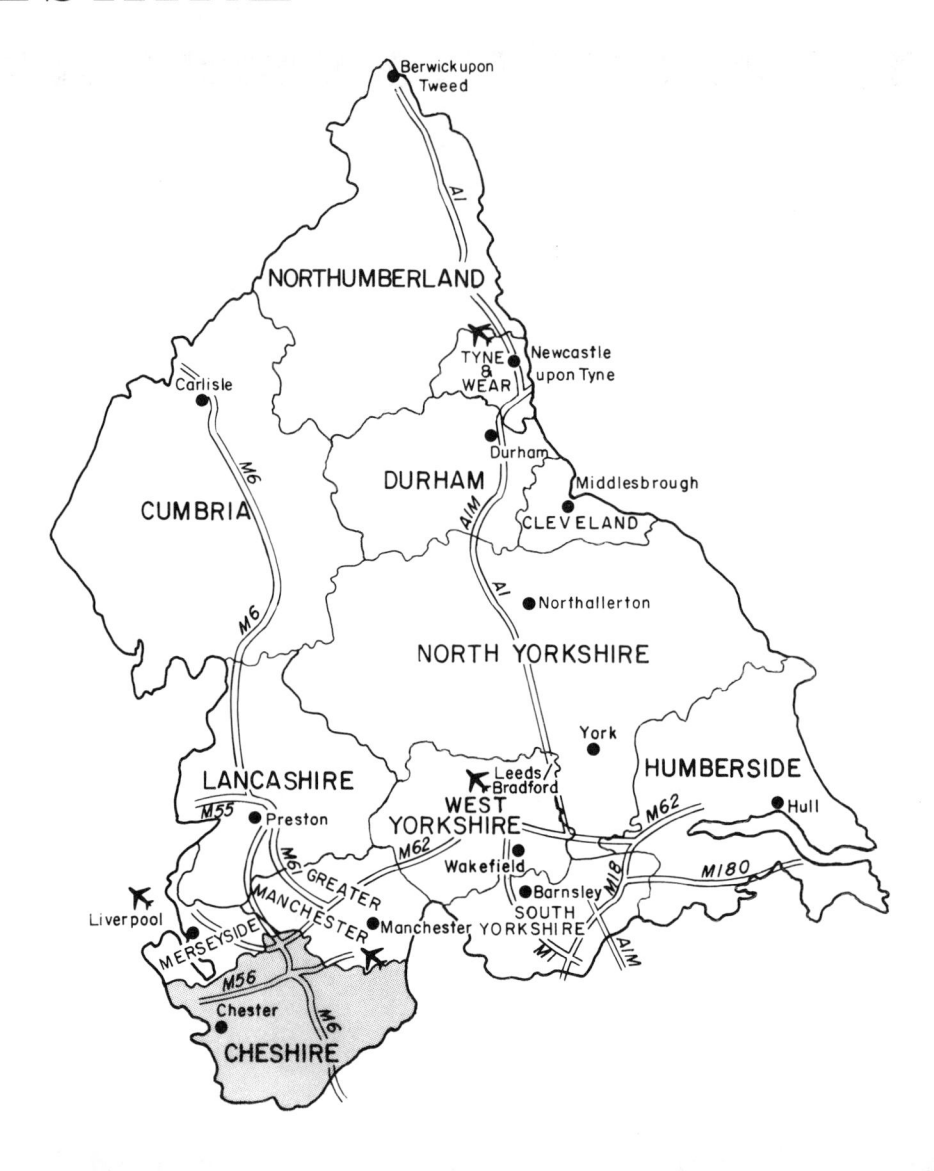

CHESHIRE 89

Abbey Gate College p657

Address: Saighton Grange, Saighton, Chester, Cheshire
Telephone: 0244 332077

Age range: 11-18
No. of pupils: 300
Scholarships: Yes
Religion: Church of England

Fees per term
Day: £1100-
Weekly board: -
Full board: -

Boy ○ | Girl ○ | Co-ed ●
Day ● | Week ○ | Board ○

Head: Mr E W Mitchell

Abbey Gate College is a co-educational independent school set in beautiful surroundings south of Chester. Academic results are outstanding, but the College is proud of its ability to educate children in an all-round way, encouraging each to achieve his/her potential. Strong music department (chapel choir, dance band etc.), drama and sport in abundance.

Abbey Gate School p658

Address: Victoria Road, Chester, Cheshire CH2 2AY

Telephone: 0824 702833

Age range: 3-11
No. of pupils: 180
Scholarships:
Religion: Church of England

Fees per term
Day: £480-£540
Weekly board: -
Full board: -

Boy ○ | Girl ○ | Co-ed ●
Day ● | Week ○ | Board ○

Head: Mrs M Ford

Abbey Gate School, founded in 1910 is a co-educational day school 240 children aged three and a half to eleven years. The school has a tradition of academic success preparing children for entrance to senior school locally and nationally. The curiculum is varied and well balanced with opportunities in art, music, sport and drama plus all academic subjects. Children benefit from the well disciplined, caring atmosphere.

Altrincham Preparatory School for Boys

Address: Highbury, West Road, Bowden, Altrincham, Cheshire WA14 2LE
Telephone: 061 928 3366

Age range: 4-12
No. of pupils: 320
Scholarships:
Religion: Non-denominational

Fees per term
Day: £725-£870
Weekly board: -
Full board: -

Boy ● | Girl ○ | Co-ed ○
Day ● | Week ○ | Board ○

Head: Mr R J McCay MA

Altrincham Preparatory School has a high reputation for academic and sporting achievements. The school has a constant programme of improvement and development. The curriculum offers a wide range of subjects with emphasis on English, mathematics and science. The school has a good pupil/teacher ratio and an excellent record for entry to Manchester Grammar School and other public schools.

Beech Hall School

Address: Beech Hall Drive, Tythelington, Macclesfield, Cheshire SK10 2EG
Telephone: 0625 422192

Age range: 4-13
No. of pupils: 200
Scholarships:
Religion: Church of England

Fees per term
Day: £870-£1375
Weekly board: £1795-
Full board: £2070-

Boy ○ | Girl ○ | Co-ed ●
Day ● | Week ● | Board ●

Head: Mr J S Fitzgerald

Beech Hall School was established in 1926 and since then has continued to give high quality education to girls and boys from the age of four to thirteen. We aim to develop each child to full potential whatever the ability or interest. Rugby, football, hockey, cricket, athletics, rounders, tennis and swimming are taught. Activities include squash, shooting, riding, archery, ju-jitsu and cooking.

Bowden Preparatory School

Address: 48 Stamford Road, Bowden, Altrincham, Cheshire WA14 2JP
Telephone: 061 928 0678

Head: Mrs J H Tan

Age range: 2-11
No. of pupils: 180
Scholarships:
Religion: Non-denominational

Fees per term
Day: -
Weekly board: -
Full board: -

Girl — Day

For further information and a prospectus, please contact the school.

Brabyns School

Address: 34/36 Arkwright Road, Marple, Stockport, Cheshire SK6 7DB
Telephone: 061 427 2395

Head: Mrs A D Briggs

Age range: 2-11
No. of pupils: 182
Scholarships:
Religion: Non-denominational

Fees per term
Day: £232-£685
Weekly board: -
Full board: -

Co-ed — Day

Brabyns caters for the education of children from a wide catchment area. It responds to the National Curriculum with small classes and a staff dedicated to high educational and social standards with an excellent success rate into senior grammar schools. The school's philosophy is to provide a stimulating and caring environment where children flourish and fulfil their potential.

Cheadle Hulme School ✱ *p739*

Address: Claremont Road, Cheadle Hulme, Cheshire SK8 6EF
Telephone: 061 485 4142

Head: Mr D J Wilkinson

Age range: 7-18
No. of pupils: 1110
Scholarships: Yes
Religion: Non-denominational

Fees per term
Day: £980-£1220
Weekly board: -
Full board: £2395-£2635

Co-ed — Day, Board

Entry: At 7 and 11 by competitive examination in the Spring, and at 16 with six good GCSE passes. GCSE: A wide range of subjects is offered. A levels: Nearly all pupils stay for A levels, which are offered in most GCSE subjects, plus business studies, economics and politics. Minority courses are also available. Careers: Some 80% go to university. Boarding ceases July 1993.

Cheadle Preparatory School

Address: Matlock Road, Heald Green, Cheadle, Cheshire SK8 3BU
Telephone: 061-437-4956

Head: Mrs L Simmons

Age range: 3-11
No. of pupils: 140
Scholarships:
Religion: Non-Denominational

Fees per term
Day: -
Weekly board: -
Full board: -

Co-ed — Day

For further information and costs contact the school.

Cransley School

Address: Belmont Hall, Great Budworth, Northwich, Cheshire CW9 6NQ
Telephone: 0606 891717

Head: Mr M A Eagar MA

Age range: 3-16
No. of pupils: 215
Scholarships: Yes
Religion: Non-denominational

Fees per term
Day: £485-£1173
Weekly board: -
Full board: -

● Boy ● Girl ○ Co-ed
● Day ○ Week ○ Board

This excellent school situated in secluded and beautiful surroundings, has a unique atmosphere. Pupils maximise their potential, taught in small classes by highly qualified and fully experienced staff. Education is based on traditional moral and social values, whilst still developing lively and enquiring minds. The firm foundations laid in junior school are consolidated in senior school, leading to excellent achievements.

Culcheth Hall School

Address: Ashley Road, Altrincham, Cheshire WA14 2LT
Telephone: 061 928 1862

Head: Mr C D Taylor

Age range: 3-18
No. of pupils: 400
Scholarships: Yes
Religion: Non-Denominational

Fees per term
Day: £470-£985
Weekly board: -
Full board: -

○ Boy ● Girl ● Co-ed
● Day ○ Week ○ Board

Culcheth Hall is a small, friendly school, where girls are encouraged to work to the best of their ability in a secure and happy environment. Although academic success is a primary aim, girls join in a wide range of sporting, dramatic and nusical activities in order to fulfil their potential in all areas and to develop a sense of responsibility and service to others. Expeditions and theatre visits take place throughout the year.

The Firs School

Address: 45 Newton Lane, Chester, Cheshire CH2 1HB
Telephone: 0244 322443

Head: Mr M Ellis

Age range: 4-11
No. of pupils: 230
Scholarships:
Religion: Church of England

Fees per term
Day: £585-£635
Weekly board: --
Full board: -

○ Boy ○ Girl ● Co-ed
● Day ○ Week ○ Board

The Firs School is a caring community in pleasant surroundings founded over forty years ago. A qualified and experienced staff seek to meet the varying needs of all pupils and also prepare them for entrance to independent schools. The school has a definite christian ethos which is open to children of other faiths and which respects their traditions and beliefs.

Forest Park School

Address: Lauriston House, 27 Oakfield, Sale, Cheshire M33 1NB
Telephone: 061 973 4835

Head: Mrs R Smart

Age range: 3-11
No. of pupils: 115
Scholarships:
Religion: Non-denominational

Fees per term
Day: £700-£790
Weekly board: -
Full board: -

○ Boy ○ Girl ● Co-ed
● Day ○ Week ○ Board

Your child will be assured of a first class education in an excellent teaching and caring environment. Small classes ensure individual attention. Pupils are prepared for independent grammar school entry. Early morning, late stay and holiday care facilities are available.

Forest School

Address: Moss Lane,
Timperley, Cheshire WA15 6LJ

Telephone: 061 980 4075

Age range: 3-11
No. of pupils: 160
Scholarships:
Religion: Non-denominational

Fees per term
Day: £430-£790
Weekly board: -
Full board: -

Boy ○ Girl ○ Co-ed ●
Day ● Week ○ Board ○

Head: Mrs J Quest CertEd FCollP

Set in spacious grounds, with high academic standards and enviable reputation for its care. Working within a happy environment, the children experience a traditional approach to education both in the subject disciplines and high expextations of good behaviour. Small classes, a friendly atmosphere and extra-curricular activities ensure children achieve their full potential and are well prepared for future schooling.

The Grange School

Address: Bradburns Lane,
Hartford, Northwich, Cheshire
CW8 1LU

Telephone: 0606 74007

Age range: 4-18
No. of pupils: 980
Scholarships: Yes
Religion:

Fees per term
Day: £690-£980
Weekly board: -
Full board: -

Boy ○ Girl ○ Co-ed ●
Day ● Week ○ Board ○

Head: Mr E S Marshall

The dramatic rise of the Grange School as a leading school in the north of England has been acclaimed both regionally and nationally. Pupils are educated in the preparatory school (4+ - 10+), senior school (11 - 16) and sixth form (17 -18). Results at both GCSE and A level of over 95% success explain the demand for places with sport, music and drama given prominence in an extensive curriculum.

Greenbank School

Address: Heathbank Road,
Cheadle Hulme, Cheadle,
Cheshire SK8 6HU

Telephone: 061 485 3724

Age range: 3-11
No. of pupils: 200
Scholarships:
Religion: Non-Denominational

Fees per term
Day: £456-£788
Weekly board: -
Full board: -

Boy ○ Girl ○ Co-ed ●
Day ● Week ○ Board ○

Head: Mr N Brown

Greenbank provides sound, all-round education at the primary stage, combining the best of traditional and modern teaching, in a caring and disciplined environment. It has excellent facilities, full or part-time for children from 3 years of age. The junior department has outstanding results in the independent grammar school examinations.

Hale Preparatory School

Address: Broomfield Lane,
Hale, Altrincham, Cheshire
WA15 6AS

Telephone: 061 928 2386

Age range: 4-11
No. of pupils: 170
Scholarships:
Religion: Non-denominational

Fees per term
Day: £705-
Weekly board: -
Full board: -

Boy ○ Girl ○ Co-ed ●
Day ● Week ○ Board ○

Head: Mr J Connor

For further information and a prospectus, please contact the school.

Hammond School

Address: Hoole Bank House, Mannings Lane, Chester, Cheshire CH2 2PB
Telephone: 0244 323542

Head: Mrs P Dangerfield

Age range: 11-16
No. of pupils: 145
Scholarships: Yes
Religion: Church of England

Fees per term
Day: -£960
Weekly board: -
Full board: -£2750

● Boy ● Girl ○ Co-ed
● Day ○ Week ○ Board

The Hammond School provides full vocational training in ballet, modern theatre and related dance forms. The Junior Dance School caters for girls and boys between the ages of 11-16. Entry is normally at the age of 11, but children may join the school at a later age. A specialised training in dance and the allied arts and a general education is given.

Hillcrest Grammar School

Address: Beech Avenue, Stockport, Cheshire SK3 8HB

Telephone: 061 480 0329

Head: Mr D K Blackburn

Age range: 2-16
No. of pupils: 314
Scholarships: Yes
Religion:

Fees per term
Day: £660-£857
Weekly board: -
Full board: -

○ Boy ○ Girl ● Co-ed
● Day ○ Week ○ Board

Hillcrest is a charitable educational trust and comprises senior, preparatory and nursery departments. Pupils are encouraged to fulfill their academic potential and high standards of courtesy, behaviour and effort are expected. Within a disciplined framework there is a friendly family atmosphere. Classes are small (average 18). At 16+ most pupils progress to sixth form courses.

Holly Bank School

Address: 1 Abbot's Heyes, Liverpool Road, Chester, Cheshire CH2 1AB
Telephone: 0244 390434

Head: Mrs T Gabriel

Age range: 2-16
No. of pupils: 130
Scholarships:
Religion: Non-denominational

Fees per term
Day: £400-£650
Weekly board: -
Full board: -

○ Boy ○ Girl ● Co-ed
● Day ○ Week ○ Board

For further information and a prospectus, please contact the school.

Hulme Hall Schools

Address: 75 Hulme Hall Road, Cheadle Hulme, Stockport, Cheshire SK8 6LA
Telephone: 061 485 4638

Head: Mr G Kellock

Age range: 11-16
No. of pupils: 350
Scholarships:
Religion: Non-denominational

Fees per term
Day: -£3270
Weekly board: -
Full board: -

○ Boy ○ Girl ● Co-ed
● Day ○ Week ○ Board

This 4 form entry, co-educational school provides a positive, encouraging regime, a teacher/pupil ratio of 1:10, a broad curriculum and a wide range of GCSE courses (currently 28 subject options). Given the support of firm but caring teachers, pupils can build up their self-confidence and develop the study disciplines essential for GCSE success.

Hulme Hall Schools Junior Section

Address: Swann Lane,
Cheadle Hulme, Stockport,
Cheshire SK8 7HU
Telephone: 061 486 9970

Head: Mrs J.K. Carr

Age range: 3-11
No. of pupils: 200
Scholarships:
Religion: Non-denominational

Fees per term
Day: £545-£780
Weekly board: -
Full board: -

○ ○ ● Boy Girl Co-ed
● ○ ○ Day Week Board

Parents who enter children at Hulme Hall are attracted by our controlled class size and caring approach. The children will recieve sympathetic treatment and encouragement to forge ahead when ready. There is no conflict seen, between a sound education and the fostering of self expression through music, speech, drama, art and physical activities.

The King's School *

Address: Wrexham Road,
Chester, Cheshire CH4 7QL

Telephone: 0244 680026

Head: Mr A R D Wickson

Age range: 8-18
No. of pupils: 612
Scholarships: Yes
Religion: Church of England

Fees per term
Day: £920-£1215
Weekly board: -
Full board: -

● ○ ○ Boy Girl Co-ed
● ○ ○ Day Week Board

The King's School has a reputation for being one of the leading academic schools in the country. It is also very well known for its rowing, soccer, cricket and other sporting activities. Drama and music thrive. Boys are encouraged to develop their talents in a caring and friendly atmosphere. Founded in 1541 the school values its relationship with the cathedral which was founded at the same time. Boys are admitted at 8, 9, 11 and 16.

The King's School *

Address: Macclesfield,
Cheshire SK10 1DA

Telephone: 0625 618586

Head: Mr A G Silcock

Age range: 7-18
No. of pupils: 1030
Scholarships: Yes
Religion: Church of England

Fees per term
Day: £1000-£1275
Weekly board: -
Full board: -

○ ○ ● Boy Girl Co-ed
● ○ ○ Day Week Board

The King's School, Macclesfield, which is an independent day school for pupils aged 7-18, is taking girls all through from September 1993. It has an outstanding reputation not only for excellent academic results, but also for the high quality and variety of its extra-curricular activities. Its pupils benefit from fine teaching, small class sizes, modern facilities and a broad and balanced curriculum.

Lady Barn House School

Address: Schools Hill,
Cheadle, Cheshire SK8 1JE

Telephone: 061 428 2912

Head: Mr E J Bonner

Age range: 3-11
No. of pupils: 420
Scholarships: Yes
Religion: Non-denominational

Fees per term
Day: £705-£800
Weekly board: -
Full board: -

○ ○ ● Boy Girl Co-ed
● ○ ○ Day Week Board

Fully qualified and experienced staff. The aim of the school is to provide the preparatory stage of a good general education and to lay a sound foundation for the future. Small classes ensure individual attention. Music, art and drama play an important role and excellent facilities exist for physical education, games and athletics. Educational visits are arranged throughout the year.

CHESHIRE 95

Loreto Convent Grammar School *

Address: Dunham Road,
Altrincham, Cheshire

Telephone: 061 928 3703

Head: Sister A McEvoy

Age range: 11-18
No. of pupils: 820
Scholarships: Yes
Religion: Catholic

Fees per term
Day: £820-
Weekly board: -
Full board: -

○ ● ○
Boy Girl Co-ed

● ○ ○
Day Week Board

In a Christian, caring atmosphere, each girl is encouraged to appreciate herself as a unique person and make her personal response to the Christian values presented to her and to develop to her full potential in every field: academic, aesthetic, physical, emotional and personal; and thus be people able to take full responsibility for shaping the world.

Macclesfield Preparatory School

Address: Chester Road,
Macclesfield, Cheshire
SK11 8PX

Telephone: 0625 422315

Principal: Mrs D E Copley

Age range: 3-11
No. of pupils: 60
Scholarships:
Religion: Non-Denominational

Fees per term
Day: £540-£630
Weekly board: -
Full board: -

○ ○ ●
Boy Girl Co-ed

● ○ ○
Day Week Board

Boys and girls are prepared for entry into a wide variety of independent schools. Classes are kept small, 10 pupils to a class allowing individual attention. There is a popular pre-preparatory department giving a good grounding in reading, writing and arithmetic. Extended hours and holiday care available.

Merton House School

Address: 27 Liverpool Road,
Chester, Cheshire CH2 1AB

Telephone: 0244 377165

Head: Mr P J Watts

Age range: 4-11
No. of pupils: 120
Scholarships:
Religion: Church of England

Fees per term
Day: £500-£600
Weekly board: -
Full board: -

● ● ○
Boy Girl Co-ed

● ○ ○
Day Week Board

Merton House School is a co-educational day preparatory school catering for pupils in the age range 4+ to 11+ years. Pupils are accepted as soon as possible after their fourth birthday. At the age of eleven the pupils are carefully prepared for all public and independent schools, wherever they might be or whatever their entrance requirements call for.

Mount Carmel School *

Address: Alderley Edge,
Cheshire SK9 7QB

Telephone: 0625 583028

Head: Mrs M Moss

Age range: 5-18
No. of pupils: 600
Scholarships: Yes
Religion: Roman Catholic

Fees per term
Day: £660-£1040
Weekly board: -
Full board: -

○ ● ○
Boy Girl Co-ed

● ○ ○
Day Week Board

Mount Carmel School aims to provide the very best facilities for the pursuit of a rigorous academic education within a community which is caring, happy and above all informed by Christian principles. Pupils are encouraged to set high standards for themselves in behaviour and attainment, and to view the pursuit of excellence in the context of commitment to the service of others.

North Cestrian Grammar

Address: Dunham Road,
Altrincham, Cheshire
WA14 4AJ
Telephone: 061 928 1856

Head: Mr P F Morton

Age range: 11-18
No. of pupils: 450
Scholarships:
Religion: Non-denominational

Fees per term
Day: £1020-
Weekly board: -
Full board: -

● Boy ○ Girl ○ Co-ed
● Day ○ Week ○ Board

A grammar school for boys firmly based on traditional grammar school principles of industry, discipline and good manners, with a lively and friendly community spirit and strong links between home and school. Excellent teaching accommodation includes five laboratories and a computer room, with special facilities for art, ceramics, photography and music. There is a strong sporting tradition.

Pownhall Hall School

Address: Carrwood Road,
Wilmslow, Cheshire SK9 5DW
Telephone: 0625 523141

Head: Mr J J Meadmore

Age range: 3-13
No. of pupils: 220
Scholarships:
Religion: Non-denominational

Fees per term
Day: £475-£1360
Weekly board: -
Full board: -

● Boy ○ Girl ○ Co-ed
● Day ○ Week ○ Board

Boys at Pownall Hall are taught in a happy yet hardworking environment, with excellent facilities. They are prepared for entry to the independent day schools at 11+ and also for the day and boarding schools at 13+ via Common Entrance or scholarhip examination. The curriculum follows the National Curriculum without jeopardy to external examination work.

The Preparatory School

Address: Daintry Hall, North Road, Congleton, Cheshire CW12 2PF
Telephone: 0260 223568

Head: Mrs M Leyland

Age range: 3-11
No. of pupils: 50
Scholarships:
Religion: Non-denominational

Fees per term
Day: £625-£655
Weekly board: -
Full board: -

○ Boy ○ Girl ● Co-ed
● Day ○ Week ○ Board

Established in 1981, the school in North Rode village aims to provide relaxed yet disciplined atmosphere where children develop their potentials at own individual rate, using traditional and modern methods with firm grounding in basic subjects. Children are prepared for entrance to independent schools ar any school of the parents' choice. Staff are fully experienced, teaching age for which qaulified.

The Queen's School *

Address: City Walls Road,
Chester, Cheshire CH1 2NN
Telephone: 0244 312078

Head: Miss D M Skilbeck

Age range: 4-18
No. of pupils: 614
Scholarships:
Religion: Church of England

Fees per term
Day: £555-£1010
Weekly board: -
Full board: -

● Boy ● Girl ○ Co-ed
● Day ○ Week ○ Board

The Queen's School provides a stimulating educational experience for pupils from 4-18 years. In the Preparatory and Junior Departments, attention is given to basic skills and varied experiences in art, music, science, craft and P.E. are provided. The Senior School offers an academic education leading to Higher Education. A wide and varied programme of extra-curricular activities is available.

CHESHIRE 97

Ramillies Hall

Address: Cheadle Hulme, Cheshire SK8 7AJ

Telephone: 061 485 3804

Head: Mr M F Brown

Age range: 2-13
No. of pupils: 210
Scholarships:
Religion: Non-denominational

Fees per term
Day: £747-£1105
Weekly board: £1700-£2180
Full board: £1870-£2180

Boy ○ Girl ○ Co-ed ●
Day ● Week ● Board ●

A family run preparatory school in the best tradition. A high academic standard in small classes. Plenty of games and many active outdoor pursuits.

The Ryleys

Address: Alderley Edge, Cheshire SK9 7UY

Telephone: 0625 583241

Head: Mr H†J C Mackay

Age range: 3-13
No. of pupils: 230
Scholarships:
Religion: Non-denominational

Fees per term
Day: £380-£1235
Weekly board: £1630-
Full board: -

Boy ● Girl ○ Co-ed ○
Day ● Week ● Board ○

The school is situated on the edge of the village in rural surroundings. 7 acres of playing fields. Purpose built classrooms. Sports Hall, theatre, heated outdoor pool, modern science and technology lab. All sports and various clubs and activities available. Full balanced curriculum.

S Hillary's School

Address: Alderley Edge, Cheshire SK9 7AG

Telephone: 0625 583532

Head: Mrs J Tracey

Age range: 4-18
No. of pupils: 310
Scholarships: Yes
Religion: Church of England

Fees per term
Day: £745-£1210
Weekly board: -
Full board: -

Boy ○ Girl ● Co-ed ○
Day ● Week ○ Board ○

S Hilary's offers its pupils an education designed to be distinct and individual. We seek at all times to recognise and develop the potential of our pupils to the full. Examination results are fundamental in the assessment of any school and we are proud of our record. Visitors are most welcome.

Sandbach School

Address: Crewe Road, Sandbach, Cheshire CW11 0NT

Telephone: 0270 767321

Head: Mr C R Brown

Age range: 11-18
No. of pupils: 900
Scholarships:
Religion: Anglican

Fees per term
Day: £850-£900
Weekly board: -
Full board: -

Boy ● Girl ○ Co-ed ○
Day ● Week ○ Board ○

Sandbach School is an independent comprehensive school. It follows the National Curriculum to KS4 with academic and vocational courses at 16+ (A, A/S, NVQ). Sixth form roll 210 including co-educational youth training. Strong music, drama, sport and societies. Excellent facilities: music centre, laboratories, IT, technology, observatory, chapel, sports hall, pool, 40 acres of fields.

Southfields School

Address: Raglan Road, Sale, Cheshire M33 4AN

Telephone: 061 973 7223

Head: Mrs J Fildes

Age range: 3-11
No. of pupils: 100
Scholarships:
Religion: Non-denominational

Fees per term
Day: -£520
Weekly board: -
Full board: -

Boy ○ Girl ○ Co-ed ●
Day ● Week ○ Board ○

Southfields, founded in 1950 and registered with DES, enjoys a caring atmosphere, small classes, individual attention, a well-structured discipline and teaching development through the National Curriculum. Preparation for independent schools is given to those suited for this level of education. Sporting activities include football, netball, swimming, athletics and cross country running.

St Ambrose College *

Address: Hale Barns, Altrincham, Cheshire WA15 0HF

Telephone: 061 980 2711

Head: Mr G E Hester

Age range: 4-18
No. of pupils: 782
Scholarships: Yes
Religion: Roman Catholic

Fees per term
Day: £533-£839
Weekly board: -
Full board: -

Boy ● Girl ○ Co-ed ○
Day ● Week ○ Board ○

St Ambrose College Altrincham, is one of England's leading Catholic independent HMC boys' day schools. Situated in peaceful parkland, it has very modern facilities. Its A Level results and Oxbridge entrance are most impressive. The preparatory school, in splendid new buildings, takes boys from 4+. There are bursaries, assisted places and, in some cases, local authority support.

St Bride's School

Address: 154 Cumberland Street, Macclesfield, Cheshire SK10 1BP

Telephone: 0625 423255

Head: Mrs H Clayton

Age range: 3-8
No. of pupils: 62
Scholarships:
Religion: Non-denominational

Fees per term
Day: £480-£640
Weekly board: -
Full board: -

Boy ○ Girl ○ Co-ed ●
Day ● Week ○ Board ○

For further information and a prospectus, please contact the school.

St Catherine's Preparatory School

Address: Hollins Lane, Marple Bridge, Stockport, Cheshire SK6 5BB

Telephone: 061 449 8800

Head: Mrs M A Sidwell

Age range: 3-11
No. of pupils: 160
Scholarships:
Religion: Roman Catholic

Fees per term
Day: £369-£650
Weekly board: -
Full board: -

Boy ○ Girl ○ Co-ed ●
Day ● Week ○ Board ○

For further information and a prospectus, please contact the school.

CHESHIRE 99

St Peter's Preparatory School

Address: Chapel Street, Congleton, Cheshire CW12 4AB
Telephone: 0260 276085

Head:

Age range:
No. of pupils:
Scholarships:
Religion:

Fees per term
Day: -
Weekly board: -
Full board: -

○ Boy ○ Girl ○ Co-ed
○ Day ○ Week ○ Board

For further information and a prospectus, please contact the school.

Stella Maris Junior School

Address: St Johns Road, Heaton Mersey, Stockport, Cheshire SK4 3BR
Telephone: 061 432 0522

Head: Mrs I L Gannon

Age range: 4-11
No. of pupils: 100
Scholarships:
Religion: Roman Catholic

Fees per term
Day: £535-
Weekly board: -
Full board: -

○ Boy ○ Girl ● Co-ed
● Day ○ Week ○ Board

With a dedicated staff of fully qualified teachers our aim is to establish a thorough and firm basis to ensure a powerful foundation for success and achievement in the later years of a child's academic career. In a happy atmosphere all children are encouraged to work to their maximum potential. The school follows the Department of Education's guidelines with a full curriculum of subjects augmented by computers, music and sport.

Stockport Grammar School *

Address: Buxton Road, Stockport, Cheshire SK2 7AF
Telephone: 061 456 9000

Head: Mr D R J Bird

Age range: 11-18
No. of pupils: 1005
Scholarships:
Religion: Non-denominational

Fees per term
Day: £1086-
Weekly board: -
Full board: -

○ Boy ○ Girl ● Co-ed
● Day ○ Week ○ Board

Stockport Grammar School is a fully co-educational day school which serves a wide area of south Manchester. The aim is to enable 510 boys and 495 girls to achieve the best possible education in a caring, friendly family atmosphere. The junior school has 260 boys and girls between 4 and 11.

Stretton House PNEU School

Address: Thorneyholme Drive, Knutsford, Cheshire WA16 8BT
Telephone: 0565 63010

Head: Miss H F Barton

Age range: 3-7
No. of pupils: 30
Scholarships:
Religion:

Fees per term
Day: -
Weekly board: -
Full board: -

○ Boy ○ Girl ● Co-ed
● Day ○ Week ○ Board

For further information and a prospectus, please contact the school.

Syddal Park School

Address: 33 Syddal Road, Bramhall, Stockport, Cheshire SK7 1AB
Telephone: 061 439 1751

Head: Mrs P Hamel

Age range: 3-7+
No. of pupils: 85
Scholarships:
Religion: Non-denominational

Fees per term
Day: £340-£660
Weekly board: -
Full board: -

● Boy ● Girl ○ Co-ed
● Day ○ Week ○ Board

Syddal Park School is a long established school for boys and girls up to the age of 7. The school offers a sound education in small classes ensuring the individual attention so necessary in the early stages.

The accent is on 'learning by doing'. Many children continue their education at the local independent grammar schools.

Tabley House School

Address: Knutsford, Cheshire

Telephone:

Head:

Age range: 11-18
No. of pupils:
Scholarships:
Religion: Church of England

Fees per term
Day: -
Weekly board: -
Full board: -

● Boy ○ Girl ○ Co-ed
● Day ○ Week ● Board

For further information and a prospectus, please contact the school.

Terra Nova School

Address: Jodrell Bank, Holmes Chapel, Cheshire CW4 8BT
Telephone: 0477 71251

Head: Mr J D Eadie

Age range: 4-13
No. of pupils: 210
Scholarships: Yes
Religion: Non-denominational

Fees per term
Day: £900-£1850
Weekly board: £2275-£2275
Full board: £2275-£2275

○ Boy ○ Girl ● Co-ed
● Day ● Week ● Board

Terra Nova is a co-educational boarding and day school taking children from 4 to 13 years of age set in 35 acres of Cheshire countryside. There is a new block housing technology, library and English departments.

Facilities for creative and physical activities are comprehensive, and there is a highly qualified staff caring for and educating each individual child.

Wilmslow Preparatory School

Address: Grove Avenue, Wilmslow, Cheshire SK9 5EG
Telephone: 0625 524246

Head: Mr J J Meadmore

Age range: 3-11
No. of pupils: 180
Scholarships:
Religion:

Fees per term
Day: -
Weekly board: -
Full board: -

○ Boy ● Girl ○ Co-ed
● Day ○ Week ○ Board

For further information and a prospectus, please contact the school.

Yorston Lodge

Address: St John's Road, Knutsford, Cheshire WA16 0DP

Telephone: 0565 633177

Head: Mr I N Cumpsty

Age range: 4-11
No. of pupils: 120
Scholarships:
Religion: Church of England

Fees per term
Day: £520-£520
Weekly board: -
Full board: -

○ ○ ● Boy Girl Co-ed
● ○ ○ Day Week Board

Yorston Lodge is an independent primary school. There are usually about 120 boys and girls in the school with an average class size of 17. Teaching methods are essentially traditional with homework in the junior school. The top juniors are prepared for the entrance examinations to all local independent secondary schools. There is an active PTA and close links between home and school.

CLEVELAND

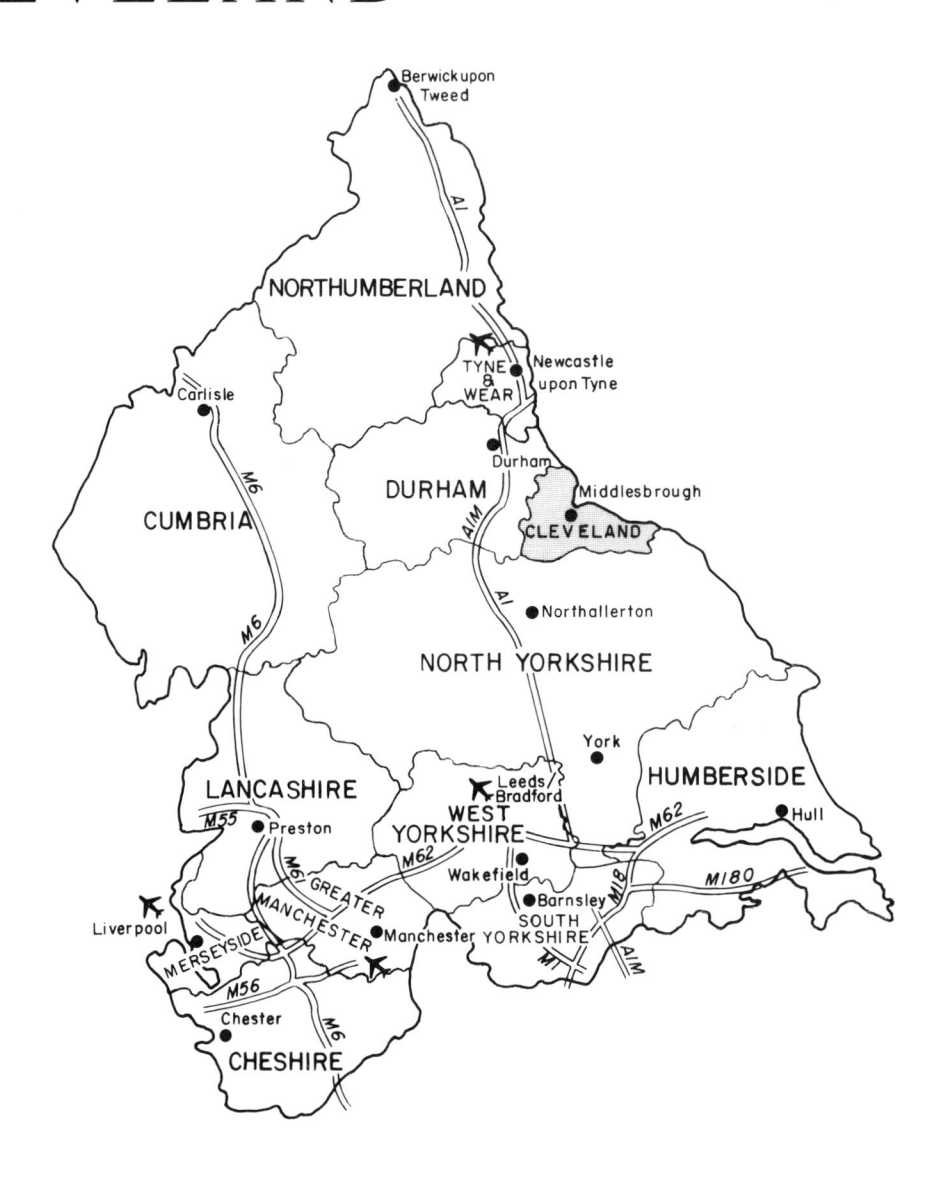

Mill Hill School

Address: Green Lane,
Middlesborough, Cleveland
TS5 7RY
Telephone: 0642 816875

Age range: 3-16
No. of pupils: 120
Scholarships: Yes
Religion: Non-denominational

Fees per term
Day: £660-£815
Weekly board: -
Full board: -

Boy ○ Girl ○ Co-ed ●
Day ● Week ○ Board ○

Head: Mr T M Duncanson

The school was founded in 1952 and completed, as is seen today in 1959. Since the beginning, the school has provided first class education at a sensible cost. Small class sizes mean that each child can develop its full potential and be treated as an individual. There is a wide range of sporting activities as well as opportunities to develop music and art talents.

Red House School

Address: 36 The Green,
Norton, Stockton on Tees,
Cleveland TS20 1DX
Telephone: 0642 553370

Age range: 4-16
No. of pupils: 410
Scholarships: Yes
Religion: Non-denominational

Fees per term
Day: £731-£816
Weekly board: -
Full board: -

Boy ○ Girl ○ Co-ed ●
Day ● Week ○ Board ○

Head: Mr M England

The School is set in a conservation area with excellent road communications. Boys and girls are accepted from the age of four up to sixteen. Results in both Common Entrance and GCSE are very good with any pupils winning scholarships at both 13 and 16.

The Sheila Bruce Community Arts Establishment

Address: Wilton Grange,
Grange Road, Hartlepool,
Cleveland TS26 8LX
Telephone: 0429 264976

Age range: 0-16
No. of pupils: 75
Scholarships: Yes
Religion: Non-denominational

Fees per term
Day: £300-£450
Weekly board: -
Full board: -

Boy ○ Girl ○ Co-ed ●
Day ● Week ○ Board ○

Head: Mrs S Bruce

Day care/education combined, ages 0-16, open 7.30am-6pm all year. Holly Mount Baby Unit 0-2 years; Nursery School 2-5 years; Wilton Grange Primary and Senior Schools 5-16 years. Free entry to school for nursery school pupils on reaching school age. Holly Mount children pay for attendances only. Pupils may attend between 7.30am and 6.00pm all year or school hours and terms.

Teesside High School ✱

Address: The Avenue,
Eaglescliffe, Stockton-on-Tees,
Cleveland TS16 9AT
Telephone: 0642 782095

Age range: 4-18
No. of pupils: 554
Scholarships:
Religion: Non-denominational

Fees per term
Day: £772-£1090
Weekly board: -
Full board: -

Boy ○ Girl ● Co-ed ○
Day ● Week ○ Board ○

Head: Mrs H Coles

Teesside High School set in 20 acres was founded in 1970 from the amalgamation of Queen Victoria School, Stockton and Cleveland Independent School. Facilities comprise a kindergarten/junior department for girls 4-10 years, and a senior school for 11-18 years. The school has well-equipped laboratories, computer room, gymnasium, sports hall, pupose built music and technology facilities.

Yarm School

Address: The Friarage, Yarm, Cleveland TS15 9EJ

Telephone:

Head: Mr R Neville-Tate

Age range: 7-18
No. of pupils: 620
Scholarships: Yes
Religion: Christian

Fees per term
Day: £890-£1405
Weekly board: -
Full board: -

● Boy ● Girl ○ Co-ed
● Day ○ Week ○ Board

Yarm School is a day grammar school having a high academic reputation, over 90% of the sixth form (120 pupils) moving on to take university degree courses. The average sixth former passes 3.9 A Levels. There is a separate junior department of 170 boys. The school is situated within an attractive and extensive campus. Girls accepted in the sixth form.

CORNWALL

Duchy Grammar

Address: Tregye, Carnon Downs, Truro, Cornwall TR3 6JH
Telephone: 0872 862289

Head: Mr M L Fuller

Age range: 7-18
No. of pupils: 170
Scholarships: Yes
Religion: Church of England

Fees per term
Day: £1018-£1263
Weekly board: £2032-£2277
Full board: £2112-£2357

Boy ○ Girl ○ Co-ed ●
Day ● Week ● Board ●

The school pursues a course of excellence towards such goals as academic success, courtesy, self-discipline and consideration of others. A broad curriculum and wide range of extra-curricular activities are provided for all pupils in an environment which is stimulating, ordered and happy. The low pupil teacher ratio and frequent assessment of progress enables a close appraisal of interests and development.

Polwhele House Pre-Preparatory School

Address: Newquay Road, Truro, Cornwall TR4 9AE
Telephone: 0872 73011

Head: Mrs R A White

Age range: 3-7
No. of pupils: 70
Scholarships:
Religion: Non-denominational

Fees per term
Day: £690-£930
Weekly board: -
Full board: -

Boy ○ Girl ○ Co-ed ●
Day ● Week ○ Board ○

National Curriculum mathematics, English and science are taught. We also include good manners, imaginative play, creative art work, gymnastics and outdoor physical activities, swimming, music, technology, computing and French. We have our own riding school. Each class is carefully geared to the needs of the children at each stage. We offer an exceptional environment and a highly motivated and caring staff.

Polwhele House Preparatory School

Address: Newquay Road, Truro, Cornwall TR4 9AE
Telephone: 0872 73011

Head: Mr R I White

Age range: 7-13
No. of pupils: 120
Scholarships:
Religion: Non-denominational

Fees per term
Day: £1140-£1260
Weekly board: £2080-£2256
Full board: -

Boy ○ Girl ○ Co-ed ●
Day ● Week ● Board ○

The preparatory school is organised on traditional lines and prepares children for the Common Entrance examination to public schools as well as the 11+ examination to local schools. The normal wide range of subjects is taught by specialists, when appropriate. A wide variety of sporting and extra-curricular activities is offered. Assessments of the childrens' work are sent home two or three times a term.

Roselyon School

Address: St Blazey Road, Par, Cornwall PL24 2HZ
Telephone: 0726 812110

Head: Mr A J H Stone

Age range: 3-13
No. of pupils: 105
Scholarships:
Religion: Church of England

Fees per term
Day: £240-£800
Weekly board: -
Full board: -

Boy ○ Girl ○ Co-ed ●
Day ● Week ○ Board ○

Roselyon School has an overall teacher-pupil ratio of 1:10. Small classes and individual attention help to ensure each child receives an excellent education for life. Academic standards are high within a friendly but disciplined atmosphere. Roselyon strives to develop full potential, initiative, good manners and a sense of responsibility. Many extra-curricular activities are offered, maximising opportunity.

The School of St Clare

Address: Polwithen, Penzance, Cornwall

Telephone: 0736 63271

Head: Mr I Halford

Age range: 3-18
No. of pupils: 220
Scholarships: Yes
Religion: Church of England

Fees per term
Day: £275-£1193
Weekly board: £2060-£2120
Full board: £2153-£2255

Boy ● Girl ● Co-ed ○
Day ● Week ● Board ●

Boarding can begin at the age of 7 for boys and girls. Wide choice of GCSE and A Level subjects together with various secretarial courses. Strong emphasis on music, drama and dance. Many extra-curricular activities. A member of the Woodard Corporation. Boys 3-11, girls 3-18.

St Joseph's School

Address: St Stephens Hill, Launceston, Cornwall PL15 8HN

Telephone: 0566 772988

Head: Mr A G Taylor

Age range: Boys 4-16
No. of pupils: 240
Scholarships:
Religion: Roman Catholic

Fees per term
Day: £700-£980
Weekly board: £1680-£1870
Full board: £2017-£2207

Boy ● Girl ● Co-ed ○
Day ● Week ● Board ●

The DFE's publication show St Joseph's top of the Cornish GCSE league table, with 81% of candidates achieving 5 or more GCSE passes at Grade C or above. This reflects the dedication and hard work of the teaching staff, and enthusiasm and effort of the girls. Academic excellence is only one aspect of school life. St. Joseph's is also proud of its musical, sporting and dramatic traditions. Boys 4-11

St Petroc's School

Address: Ocean View Road, Bude, Cornwall EX23 8NJ

Telephone: 0288 352876

Head: Mr P W Blundell

Age range: 3-13
No. of pupils: 116
Scholarships:
Religion:

Fees per term
Day: -
Weekly board: -
Full board: -

Boy ○ Girl ○ Co-ed ●
Day ● Week ● Board ●

For further information and a prospectus, please contact the school.

Treliske School

Address: Truro, Cornwall TR1 3QN

Telephone: 0872 72616

Head: Mr R L Hollins

Age range: 3-11
No. of pupils: 172
Scholarships:
Religion:

Fees per term
Day: -
Weekly board: -
Full board: -

Boy ○ Girl ○ Co-ed ●
Day ● Week ○ Board ●

For further information and a prospectus, please contact the school.

Tremore Christian School

Address: Tremore Manor, Lanivet, Bodmin, Cornwall PL30 5JT
Telephone: 0208 831713

Head: Miss A Whitaker

Age range: 3-16
No. of pupils: 38
Scholarships:
Religion:

Fees per term
Day: -
Weekly board: -
Full board: -

○ ○ ● Boy Girl Co-ed
● ○ ○ Day Week Board

For further information and a prospectus, please contact the school.

Tremough Convent School p658

Address: Penryn, Cornwall TR10 9EZ
Telephone: 0326 372226

Head: Sister Maria

Age range: 3-18
No. of pupils: 300
Scholarships: Yes
Religion: Roman Catholic

Fees per term
Day: -£800
Weekly board: £1200-£1200
Full board: -

● ● ○ Boy Girl Co-ed
● ● ○ Day Week Board

Tremough Convent is an independent day and weekly boarding school established in 1943 by the Daughters of the Cross of Plymouth. The school is set around a historic house and gardens and comprises senior, junior and nursery departments. Tremough is a Catholic school with about one third Catholic pupils, the rest from other denominations. All pupils attend religious services. Boys 3-11.

Trescol Vean

Address: Baldhu, Truro, Cornwall TR3 6EG
Telephone: 0872 560788

Head: Mrs S M Baron

Age range: 3-7
No. of pupils: 60
Scholarships:
Religion: Church of England

Fees per term
Day: £198-£660
Weekly board: -
Full board: -

○ ○ ● Boy Girl Co-ed
● ○ ○ Day Week Board

A co-educational pre-preparatory day school, in a rural environment, within easy reach of the major Cornish towns. Strong traditional values. National Curriculum. Swimming, ballet, gymnastics, French. Established 1972. Close links with local preparatory schools.

Truro High School for Girls *

Address: Falmouth Road, Truro, Cornwall TR1 2HU
Telephone: 0872 72830

Head: Mr J Graham Brown

Age range: 3-18
No. of pupils: 350
Scholarships: Yes
Religion: Church of England

Fees per term
Day: £1005-£1210
Weekly board: £1971-£2176
Full board: £2004-£2209

○ ● ○ Boy Girl Co-ed
● ● ● Day Week Board

The High School, set on an elevated site on the outskirts of the City of Truro, has over 100 years' experience in girls' education. Academic results are outstanding and there is a long tradition of excellence in sports, music and drama. A wide range of extra-curricular activities is offered including year-round swimming.

Truro School ✱

Address: Trennick Lane,
Truro, Cornwall TR1 1TH

Telephone: 0872 72763

Head: Mr B K Hobbs

Age range: 11-18
No. of pupils: 924
Scholarships:
Religion:

Fees per term
Day: -
Weekly board: -
Full board: -

● Boy ● Girl ○ Co-ed
● Day ○ Week ● Board

For further information and a prospectus, please contact the school. Girls accepted in the sixth form.

CUMBRIA

CUMBRIA 111

Austin Friars School *

Address: St Ann's Hill, Carlisle, Cumbria CA3 9PB

Telephone: 0228 28042

Head: Rev T Lyons

Age range: 11-18
No. of pupils: 300
Scholarships: Yes
Religion: Roman Catholic

Fees per term
Day: £1255-£1309
Weekly board: £2140-
Full board: £2195-£2272

○ ○ ● Boy Girl Co-ed
● ● ● Day Week Board

The school was founded in 1952 by the Augustinian Order. The staff consists of members of the order and lay staff. Teacher pupil ration is 1:10 ensuring that teaching and pastoral care are personal in nature.

Harecroft Hall

Address: Gosforth Seascale, Cumbria

Telephone: 09467 25220

Head: Mr T D Penrice

Age range: 5-13
No. of pupils: 90
Scholarships: Yes
Religion: Non-denominational

Fees per term
Day: £990-£1210
Weekly board: -£1914
Full board: -£2000

○ ○ ● Boy Girl Co-ed
● ● ● Day Week Board

Harecroft Hall is a co-educational preparatory school within the Lake District National Park. Children are taught in classes of about twelve by staff of thirteen well-qualified men and women.

The usual team games are played and because of the school's location there are exceptional opportunities for sailing, canoeing, fell-walking, orienteering etc.

Holme Park Preparatory School

Address: Hill Top, Kendal, Cumbria LA8 0AH

Telephone: 0539 721245

Head: Mr N J V Curry

Age range: 3-13
No. of pupils: 93
Scholarships:
Religion: Church of England

Fees per term
Day: £950-£1260
Weekly board: -£1600
Full board: -

○ ○ ● Boy Girl Co-ed
● ● ○ Day Week Board

In 1960 the school moved to the current premises, a Georgian country house which stands in nine acres of grounds. Well protected by woodland, this Webster building commands a superb view of the Kent valley and its estuary. Here the Curry family run a small, friendly and very personal type of preparatory school, fostering academic attainment, the development of individual qualities and traditional moral values.

Hunter Hall School

Address: Frenchfield Farm, Carleton, Penrith, Cumbria CA11 8UA
Telephone: 0768 891291

Head: Mr J A F Warlow

Age range: 7-11
No. of pupils: 60
Scholarships:
Religion: Non-denominational

Fees per term
Day: -£740
Weekly board: -
Full board: -

○ ○ ● Boy Girl Co-ed
● ○ ○ Day Week Board

For further information and a prospectus, please contact the school.

Lime House School

Address: Holm Hill, Dalston, Carlisle, Cumbria CA5 7BX
Telephone: 0228 710225
Head: Mr N A Rice BA

Age range: 4-18
No. of pupils: 318
Scholarships:
Religion: Non-denominational

Fees per term
Day: -£950
Weekly board: -£1600
Full board: -£2300

Boy ○ Girl ○ Co-ed ●
Day ● Week ● Board ●

Throughout the school classes are small, and all subjects are taught by experienced and qualified teachers. Great attention is given to the preparation of each child's timetable and there is a regular assessment of their progress by their tutor so that weaknesses can be corrected before they become serious and special abilities can be strengthened and encouraged. There is a trained remedial teacher on the staff.

Riverside School

Address: Whasset, Milnthorpe, Cumbria LA7 7DN
Telephone:
Head:

Age range:
No. of pupils:
Scholarships:
Religion:

Fees per term
Day: -
Weekly board: -
Full board: -

Boy ○ Girl ○ Co-ed ●
Day ○ Week ○ Board ○

For further information and a prospectus, please contact the school.

Sedbergh School ✻

Address: Sedbergh, Cumbria LA10 5HG
Telephone: 05396 20535
Head: Dr R G Baxter

Age range: 11-18
No. of pupils: 450
Scholarships: Yes
Religion: Church of England

Fees per term
Day: £1750-£2470
Weekly board: -
Full board: £2500-£3520

Boy ● Girl ○ Co-ed ○
Day ● Week ○ Board ●

An HMC boarding school for boys aged 11-18, situated in a spectacular rural environment between the Yorkshire Dales and the Lake District (and only 5 miles from the M6 motorway). Clean air and clear skies, coupled with a keen academic environment, modern facilities and scope for a variety of outdoor pursuits, music and sport, Sedbergh offers an excellent educational opportunity for its 460 boys.

St Annes School for Girls p659 *p750*

Address: Browhead, Windermere, Cumbria LA23 1NW
Telephone: 0539 446264
Head: Mr M P Hawkins MA

Age range: 3-18
No. of pupils: 400
Scholarships: Yes
Religion: Non-denominational

Fees per term
Day: -
Weekly board: -
Full board: -

Boy ○ Girl ● Co-ed ○
Day ● Week ○ Board ●

Situated in the heart of the Lake District National Park, and within easy reach of the M6, rail links and Manchester Airport, the school is ideally positioned, giving its pupils an outstanding environment to live and work in. The senior and junior departments are strongly linked giving a continuous and progressive education.

St Bees School ✳

Address: The School House,
St Bees, Cumbria CA27 0DU

Telephone: 0946 822263

Head: Mr P A Chamberlain

Age range: 11-18
No. of pupils: 300
Scholarships: Yes
Religion: Church of England

Fees per term
Day: £1752-£2160
Weekly board: £2158-£3050
Full board: £2274-£3109

Boy ○ Girl ○ Co-ed ●
Day ● Week ● Board ●

St Bees became co-educational in 1976 and boarders now comprise about 50% of the total. Weekly boarding is an increasingly popular option. The School has excellent sports facilities, including a 9-hole golf course, indoor swimming pool, indoor shooting range and a large multi-purpose sports hall. The Lake District is very close at hand and outdoor pursuits form an integral part of the curriculum.

DERBYSHIRE

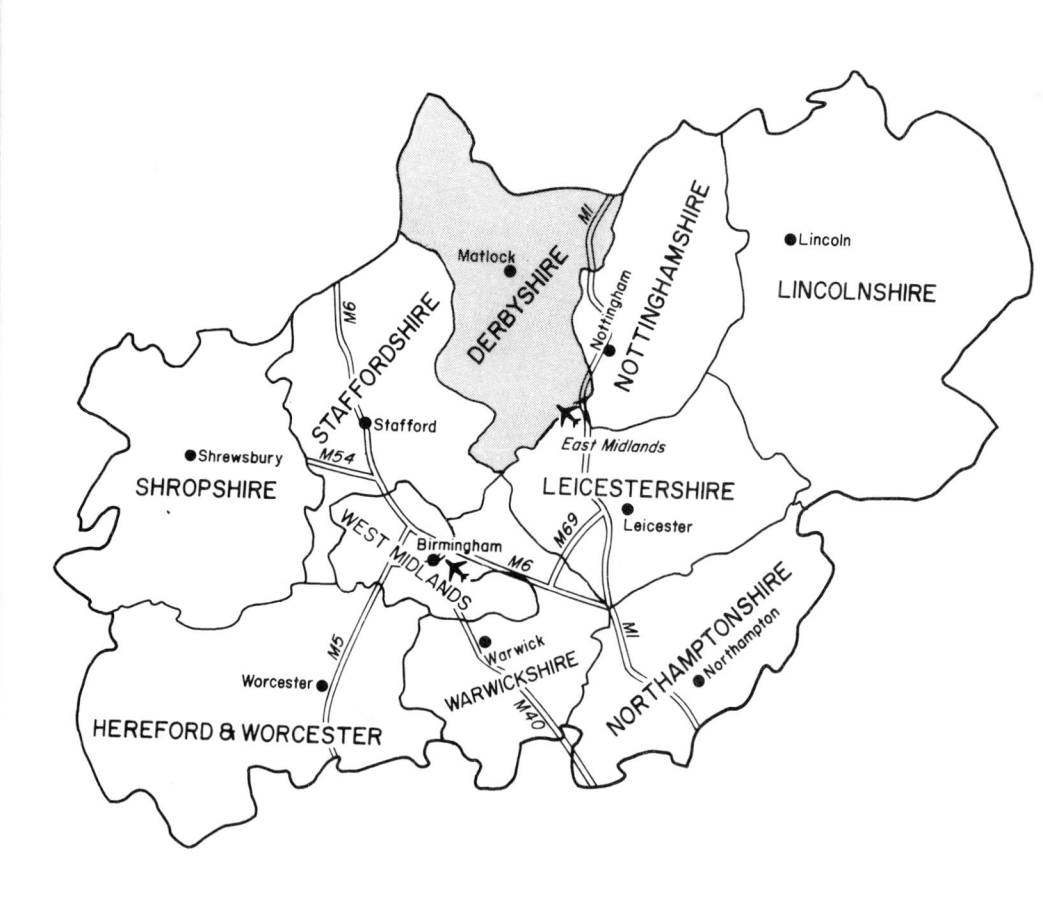

Ashbourne PNEU School

Address: St Monica's House, Windmill Lane, Ashbourne, Derbyshire
Telephone: 0335 43294

Head: Mr H G Broadbent

Age range: 3-13
No. of pupils: 120
Scholarships:
Religion: Church of England

Fees per term
Day: £500-£900
Weekly board: -
Full board: -

Boy ○ Girl ○ Co-ed ●
Day ● Week ○ Board ○

The school is an independent co-educational day school serving the needs of children and parents from Ashbourne and the surrounding communities in Derbyshire and Staffordshire. We educate in small classes across a wide ability range and at different rates of progress matching the capabilities of individual pupils. Our wide curriculum maintains a proper balance between academic, recreational and cultural activities.

Barlborough Hall School

Address: Barlborough, Chesterfield, Derbyshire S43 4TJ
Telephone: 0246 810511

Head: Rev A Forrester SJ

Age range: 4-13
No. of pupils: 185
Scholarships: Yes
Religion: Roman Catholic

Fees per term
Day: £734-£1313
Weekly board: -
Full board: £1844-

Boy ○ Girl ○ Co-ed ●
Day ● Week ● Board ●

Barlborough Hall School is an independent Jesuit day and boarding preparatory school, (linked to Mount St Mary's College), near junction 30 of the M1. Housed in a beautiful Elizabethan mansion with many acres of playing fields, the school is famous for its caring environment and good academic results.

Brocksford Hall

Address: Doveridge, Derbyshire DE6 5PA
Telephone: 0889 562809

Head: Revd R M Clarke

Age range: 3-13
No. of pupils: 94
Scholarships: Yes
Religion: Church of England

Fees per term
Day: £520-£1735
Weekly board: £2235-£2235
Full board: £2235-£2235

Boy ○ Girl ○ Co-ed ●
Day ● Week ● Board ●

Fully co-educational preparatory school including nursery and pre-preparatory departments. Situated in rural south west Derbyshire but easily accessible from most airports. A school with a long tradition of academic purpose and an atmosphere of tolerance. Bursaries available for Service children.

Derby High School *

Address: Hillsway, Littleover, Derby, Derbyshire DE3 7DT
Telephone: 0332 514267

Head: Dr G H Goddard

Age range: 3-18
No. of pupils: 512
Scholarships: Yes
Religion: Church of England

Fees per term
Day: £875-£1270
Weekly board: -
Full board: -

Boy ● Girl ● Co-ed ○
Day ● Week ○ Board ○

For further information and a prospectus, please contact the school. Boys 3-11, girls 3-18.

Friar Gate House School

Address: 65 Friar Gate, Derby, Derby, Derbyshire DE1 1DJ

Telephone: 0332-42765

Principal:

Age range: 3-16
No. of pupils: 250
Scholarships:
Religion: Non-denominational

Fees per term
Day: -
Weekly board: -
Full board: -

Boy ○ Girl ○ Co-ed ●
Day ● Week ○ Board ○

For further information, please contact the school.

Michael House School

Address: The Field, Shipley, Heanor, Derbyshire DE7 7JH

Telephone: 0773 718050

Head: Mr A Peacock

Age range: 4-16
No. of pupils: 180
Scholarships:
Religion: Non-denominational

Fees per term
Day: £332-£784
Weekly board: -
Full board: -

Boy ○ Girl ○ Co-ed ●
Day ● Week ○ Board ○

Rudolf Steiner (Waldorf) education is concerned with developing all faculties of the human being as a necessary means of support for the modern intellect. In the kindergarten, the main educational medium is 'activity' - the element in which the pre-school abounds. In the lower school, the emphasis shifts to the education of the imaginative, rythmical and emotional faculties. In the senior school, on clear integrated thinking.

Normanton School

Address: St John's Road, Buxton, Derbyshire SK17 6SJ

Telephone: 0298 22745

Head: Mr D M Sanderson

Age range: 10-18
No. of pupils: 90
Scholarships: Yes
Religion: Non-denominational

Fees per term
Day: -
Weekly board: -
Full board: -£2500

Boy ○ Girl ○ Co-ed ●
Day ○ Week ○ Board ●

Normanton School can trace its history back to 1877, and has occupied its present site since 1948. Situated in the heart of the Peak District, yet only 45 minutes drive from Manchester Airport and linked by rail to all major Inter-City routes, the location of the school offers a pleasant balance of scenic attraction and good accessibility.

Ockbrook School

Address: The Settlement, Ockbrook, Derby, Derbyshire DE7 3RJ

Telephone: 0332 673532

Head: Dr M Rennie

Age range: 3-18
No. of pupils: 380
Scholarships: Yes
Religion: Moravian

Fees per term
Day: £740-£1052
Weekly board: £1622-£1934
Full board: £1622-£1934

Boy ● Girl ● Co-ed ○
Day ● Week ● Board ●

Our education is based on Christian principles. All are encouraged to enjoy working hard to achieve their best in GCSE examinations, A Levels and in the wide range of extra-curricular activities available. The school has strong musical and sports traditions. Set in beautiful grounds near M1 (J25), East Midlands Airport and Derby Station. Girls 3-18. Boys 3-7. Boarding 8-18.

DERBYSHIRE 117

Repton Preparatory

Address: Foremarke Hall, Milton, Derbyshire DE6 6EJ

Telephone: 0283 703269

Head: Mr R C Theobald

Age range: 7-13
No. of pupils: 353
Scholarships: Yes
Religion: Church of England

Fees per term
Day: -
Weekly board: -
Full board: -

Boy ○ Girl ○ Co-ed ●
Day ● Week ● Board ●

Repton Preparatory is directly under the control of the Governors of Repton School. Pupils are prepared for all independent schools but the majority go to Repton. The school occupies a fine Georgian mansion with 40 acres of woods, lake and playing fields. The facilities include a competition size swimming bath, gymnasium, tennis court, three science laboratories, a computer room and an excellent library.

Repton School * p748

Address: The Hall, Repton, Derbyshire DE6 6FH

Telephone: 0283 702375

Head: Mr G E Jones MA

Age range: 13-18
No. of pupils: 580
Scholarships: Yes
Religion: Church of England

Fees per term
Day: -£2610
Weekly board: -
Full board: -£3480

Boy ○ Girl ○ Co-ed ●
Day ● Week ○ Board ●

Repton School, founded in 1557, is the oldest public school in the area and combines a high academic standard with first class extra-curricular facilities. The school is fully co-educational and takes pupils at 13 and into the sixth form. Its preparatory school is nearby at Foremarke and takes pupils up to the age of 13.

St Anselm's School

Address: Bakewell, Derbyshire DE45 1DP

Telephone: 062 981 2734

Head: Mr T S H Piper

Age range: 3-13
No. of pupils: 155
Scholarships:
Religion: Non-denominational

Fees per term
Day: £905-£2000
Weekly board: -
Full board: -£2615

Boy ○ Girl ○ Co-ed ●
Day ● Week ○ Board ●

An education at St Anselm's is an education for life. High standards are every bit as important outside the classroom as in it; so attention is given to the development of good manners, self-discipline and kindness. The school installs friendliness, enthusiasm and happy self-confidence of the children. It strives to find aspects of school life at which every child may excel.

St Elphin's School p659

Address: Darley Dale, Matlock, Derbyshire DE4 2HA

Telephone: 0629 732687

Head: Mr A P C Pollard BA

Age range: 3-18
No. of pupils: 330
Scholarships: Yes
Religion: Church of England

Fees per term
Day: £690-£1717
Weekly board: £2526-£2802
Full board: £2659-£2949

Boy ○ Girl ● Co-ed ○
Day ● Week ● Board ●

St Elphin's is a Church of England boarding and day school for girls, aged 3-18. Its situation in the Derbyshire Dales, alongside the A6, makes it easy to reach from Derby, Manchester, Nottingham, Sheffield and from the M1. The school has excellent academic, music and sports facilities and is noted for its friendliness and the care and concern shown to all its pupils.

St Joseph's Convent School

Address: 42 Newbold Road, Chesterfield, Derbyshire S41 7PL
Telephone: 0246 232392

Age range: 3-11
No. of pupils: 200
Scholarships:
Religion:

Fees per term
Day: -
Weekly board: -
Full board: -

Boy / Girl / **Co-ed**
Day / Week / Board

Head: Sister M Carolan

For further information and a prospectus, please contact the school.

St Peter and St Paul's School

Address: Penmore House, Hasland Road, Chesterfield, Derbyshire S41 0SY
Telephone: 0246 278522

Age range: 3-11
No. of pupils: 170
Scholarships:
Religion:

Fees per term
Day: £400-£475
Weekly board: -
Full board: -

Boy / Girl / **Co-ed**
Day / Week / Board

Head: Mrs B Beet

In small classes (maximum 16), our qualified teachers provide a caring, traditional education. High educational standards are maintained; and subjects taught include computer studies, swimming, ballet, music and French. Each child is encouraged to attain his or her full potential, building self-confidence and preparing the pupil for any type of secondary education which the parents may choose.

St Wystan's

Address: 11A High Street, Repton, Derby, Derbyshire
Telephone: 0283 703258

Age range: 2-11
No. of pupils: 120
Scholarships:
Religion: Church of England

Fees per term
Day: £330-£770
Weekly board: -
Full board: -

Boy / Girl / **Co-ed**
Day / Week / Board

Head: Mrs J Roberts

In the village of Repton in South Derbyshire, St Wystan's encourages children to achieve their potential in a disciplined, caring environment. Traditional methods are used alongside modern aids. Music, sport and drama are enjoyed by all. Children join the school at any age, but obtain maximum benefit by entering at Nursery level and progressing through to secondary school entry.

Stancliffe Hall

Address: Darley Dale, Matlock, Derbyshire DE4 2HJ
Telephone: 0629 732310

Age range: 3-13
No. of pupils:
Scholarships: Yes
Religion: Non-denominational

Fees per term
Day: £780-£1850
Weekly board: £2300-£2300
Full board: £2300-£2300

Boy / Girl / **Co-ed**
Day / **Week** / **Board**

Head: Mr A R R Wareham

The school is set in 34 acres of beautiful park, woodlands and playing fields. There is a good academic standard with sport, drama, art, design technology, outdoor pursuits and a wide variety of our own facilities. We are keen to encourage the all-round development of our children in a caring, busy, family atmosphere.

DEVON

The Abbey School

Address: Saint Marychurch, Torquay, Devon TQ1 4PR

Telephone: 0803 327868

Head Teacher: Mrs S J Greinig

Age range: 2-11
No. of pupils: 250
Scholarships:
Religion: Non-denominational

Fees per term
Day: £325-£850
Weekly board: -
Full board: -

Boy ○ Girl ○ Co-ed ●
Day ● Week ○ Board ○

The Abbey School aims to provide a sound primary education for children in a happy environment where individual potential may develop to the full under the guidance of a fully qualified and experienced staff. Children participate in many and varied extra-curricular activities including skiing, windsurfing and sailing.

Bendarroch School

Address: West Hill, Ottery St. Mary, Devon EX11 1JY

Telephone: 040 481 4422

Head: Mr N R Home MA

Age range: 4-13
No. of pupils: 40
Scholarships:
Religion: Non-denominational

Fees per term
Day: £600-£750
Weekly board: -
Full board: -

Boy ○ Girl ○ Co-ed ●
Day ● Week ○ Board ○

Bendarroch was established in 1978 to provide for up to 40 children an academic curriculum in caring, non-institutionalised surroundings. The school is therefore run as part of a large family home set in beautiful grounds. Children's confidence and self-esteem is developed in a happy, hard-working environment where the quality of classroom teaching is regarded as the schools most important asset.

Blundell's School

Address: Tiverton, Devon EX16 4DN

Telephone: 0884 252543

Head: Mr J Leigh MA

Age range: 13-18
No. of pupils: 430
Scholarships: Yes
Religion: Church of England

Fees per term
Day: £2160-
Weekly board: -
Full board: £3500-

Boy ● Girl ● Co-ed ○
Day ● Week ○ Board ●

Blundell's expectation is that all pupils will proceed to A Level via GCSE. It provides a wide ranging education incorporating the National Curriculum and much more. 95% of higher education applicants were successful in 1992 ranging from Oxford and Cambridge places to polytechnics. Emphasis is placed on pastoral care and Blundell's is strong in music, drama and sport. Girls accepted in the sixth form.

Bramdean Independent Preparatory and Grammar School

Address: Richmond Lodge, Homefield Road, Exeter, Devon EX1 2QR

Telephone: 0392 73387

Head: Mr T Connett

Age range: 7-18
No. of pupils: 190
Scholarships: Yes
Religion: Non-denominational

Fees per term
Day: £1055-£1160
Weekly board: £1826-£1826
Full board: -

Boy ● Girl ● Co-ed ○
Day ● Week ● Board ○

For further details and a prospectus, please contact the headmaster. Boys 7-18, girls 7-11.

Buckfast Abbey School

Address: Buckfastleigh, Devon TQ11 0EQ

Telephone: 0364 42310

Head: Dom G Miller OSB

Age range: 7-13
No. of pupils: 125
Scholarships:
Religion: Roman Catholic

Fees per term
Day: £1490-
Weekly board: £2100-
Full board: £2100-

Boy ○   Girl ○   Co-ed ●
Day ●   Week ●   Board ●

A Catholic preparatory school for children 7 to 13, boarding and day, conducted by the Benedictines of Buckfast Abbey. Children of other denominations welcome. A purpose-built school with all modern facilities set in the superb Dart Valley. High reputation for academic excellence - 35 scholarships in the past five years. Excellent sporting facilities and a full range of outdoor activities and hobbies.

The Dolphin School

Address: Raddenstile Lane, Exmouth, Devon EX8 2JH

Telephone: 0395 272418

Head: Mr R J S Higgins

Age range: 3-13
No. of pupils: 55
Scholarships: Yes
Religion: Church of England

Fees per term
Day: £250-£556
Weekly board: -
Full board: -

Boy ○   Girl ○   Co-ed ●
Day ●   Week ○   Board ○

The Dolphin School is a non-denominational pre-preparatory and preparatory school for boys and girls between the ages of three and thirteen. We are a tangibly happy school with a wide variety of extra-curricular activities ranging from horse riding to chess and modelling. All National Curriculum subjects catered for in our exciting yet homely atmosphere.

Edgehill College *

Address: Northdown Road, Bideford, Devon

Telephone: 02374 71701

Head: Mrs E M Burton

Age range: 3-18
No. of pupils: 510
Scholarships: Yes
Religion: Methodist

Fees per term
Day: £845-£1375
Weekly board: £1880-£2270
Full board: £2060-£2515

Boy ○   Girl ○   Co-ed ○
Day ●   Week ●   Board ●

Edgehill is a friendly, caring and purposeful community with a reputation for high academic standards. The co-educational junior department specialises in small classes: care is taken to give a good grounding in the basic subjects. There is a large sixth form, most students studying 3 or 4 A or AS Levels from a choice of 19 subjects which includes music, theatre studies and psychology.

Elm Grove School

Address: Elm Grove Road, Topsham, Exeter, Devon EX3 0EQ

Telephone: 0392 873031

Heads: Mr B E Parsons, Mrs K M Parsons

Age range: 3-8
No. of pupils: 60
Scholarships:
Religion: Church of England

Fees per term
Day: -£510
Weekly board: -
Full board: -

Boy ○   Girl ○   Co-ed ●
Day ●   Week ○   Board ○

For further information and a prospectus, please contact the school.

Exeter Cathedral School

Address: Palace Gate, Exeter, Devon EX1 1HX

Telephone: 0392 55298

Head: Mr R A C Hay

Age range: 7-13
No. of pupils: 167
Scholarships: Yes
Religion: Church of England

Fees per term
Day: £1160-
Weekly board: £1860-
Full board: £1870-

● ○ ○
Boy Girl Co-ed
● ● ●
Day Week Board

The school is very lively, encouraging boys to extend their talents in all areas. Discipline is firmly set in the context of a caring Christian community, with emphasis placed on high standards and consideration of others. The school has excellent facilities for the visual and creative arts. Forty music awards have been won in the last six years, and 36 academic awards. There is an outstanding newly purpose-built art and CDT centre.

Exeter Preparatory School

Address: Victoria Park Road, Exeter, Devon EX2 4NS

Telephone: 0392 58712

Head: Mr J B D Lawford

Age range: 7-11
No. of pupils: 100
Scholarships:
Religion: Church of England

Fees per term
Day: £1026-£1122
Weekly board: -
Full board: -

● ○ ○
Boy Girl Co-ed
● ○ ○
Day Week Board

Exeter Preparatory School is the junior partner of Exeter School, and shares campus and all facilities with the senior school. Entrance at 7 is by examination and interview, and almost all pupils take the entrance examination to Exeter School at the age of 11.

Exeter School ✻

Address: Exeter, Devon EX2 4NS

Telephone: 0392 73679

Head: Mr G T Goodall

Age range: 11-19
No. of pupils: 722
Scholarships: Yes
Religion: Christian

Fees per term
Day: £1094-
Weekly board: £2049-
Full board: £2049-

● ● ○
Boy Girl Co-ed
● ● ●
Day Week Board

This former direct grant school is an academically selective school. 90% of 6th form (265 pupils) went on to degree courses in 1991. In 1992 25 pupils received Oxbridge offers. The arts, music and drama especially are strong, as is sport and service. (Girls 6th form only).

Fletewood School

Address: 88 North Road East, North Hill, Plymouth, Devon PL4 6AN

Telephone: 0752 663782

Head: Mr J Martin

Age range: 3-11
No. of pupils: 58
Scholarships:
Religion: 7th Day Adventist

Fees per term
Day: £400-
Weekly board: -
Full board: -

○ ○ ●
Boy Girl Co-ed
● ○ ○
Day Week Board

Small classes, individual attention. For further information and a prospectus, please contact the school.

Gramercy Hall School

Address: Churston Ferrers, Brixham, Devon TQ5 0HR

Telephone: 0803 844338

Head: Mr R W R Purdom

Age range: 3-16
No. of pupils: 160
Scholarships: Yes
Religion: Non-denominational

Fees per term
Day: £400-£1295
Weekly board: -
Full board: -

Boy ○ Girl ○ Co-ed ●
Day ● Week ○ Board ○

We are an independent, co-educational day school for pupils aged 3-16. The school is set in 10 acres of magnificent Devon countryside. We follow the recommendations of the National Curriculum. We prepare pupils for the 11+, 13+, Common Entrance and scholarship examinations to independent schools. We also prepare pupils for the GCSE examinations.

Grenville College p743

Address: Bideford, Devon EX39 3JR

Telephone: 0237 472212

Head: Dr M C V Cane BSc PhD MRSC

Age range: 10-18
No. of pupils: 330
Scholarships: Yes
Religion: Church of England

Fees per term
Day: £1302-£1302
Weekly board: -
Full board: £2618-£2655

Boy ● Girl ○ Co-ed ○
Day ● Week ○ Board ●

This Woodard School on the Torridge Estuary (Atlantic Coast) is small enough to offer the benefits of a varied curriculum to boys of differing needs and abilities, and a broad range of clubs and activities taking full advantage of its unique setting. Self-confidence and individuality thrive in a friendly community in which there is also a well staffed special English unit for intelligent dyslexic boys.

Greylands Preparatory School

Address: 9 Belle Vue Road, Paignton, Devon TQ4 6ES

Telephone: 0803 557298

Head: Mrs P M Adams

Age range: 3-11
No. of pupils: 65
Scholarships:
Religion: Non-denominational

Fees per term
Day: £575-£575
Weekly board: -
Full board: -

Boy ○ Girl ○ Co-ed ●
Day ● Week ○ Board ○

For further information and a prospectus, please contact the school.

Hylton Pre-Preparatory School

Address: 13a Lyndhurst Road, Exeter, Devon EX 2 4PA

Telephone: 0392 54755

Head: Mrs B J Glass

Age range: 4-8
No. of pupils: 60
Scholarships:
Religion: Non-denominational

Fees per term
Day: £437-£640
Weekly board: -
Full board: -

Boy ○ Girl ○ Co-ed ●
Day ● Week ○ Board ○

The happiness of the children is of primary importance. In an atmosphere of friendliness and co-operation, the fully qualified staff aim to maintain a high standard of behaviour and scholastic achievement. The centrally heated classrooms are light and spacious. There is an asphaled playground and a large grassed area for outside activities.

Kelly College

Address: Tavistock, Devon PL19 0HZ

Telephone: 0822 613005

Head: Mr C H Hirst

Age range: 11-18
No. of pupils: 320
Scholarships: Yes
Religion: Church of England

Fees per term
Day: £1425-£2250
Weekly board: £3370-
Full board: £3370-

○ Boy ○ Girl ● Co-ed
● Day ● Week ● Board

Kelly College is an HMC co-educational boarding and day school set in magnificent Dartmoor countryside outside the ancient market town of Tavistock. Academic standards are high and there is a strong tradition of excellence both in sport (especially swimming, rugby and adventure training), music and the creative arts.

Kingsbridge Preparatory School

Address: Embankment Road, Kingsbridge, Devon

Telephone: 0548 2703

Head: Mr J C Johnson

Age range: 2-11
No. of pupils: 60
Scholarships: Yes
Religion:

Fees per term
Day: £698-£768
Weekly board: -
Full board: -

○ Boy ○ Girl ● Co-ed
● Day ○ Week ○ Board

A country day school: small, vital, productive of the 3Rs as nucleii embracing a full range of studies old and new. Full outdoor activities ensure well balanced, alert and happy pupils.

Manor House School

Address: Springfield House, Honiton, Devon EX14 8TL

Telephone: 0404 42026

Head: Mr P A Eyles

Age range: 3-13
No. of pupils: 210
Scholarships:
Religion: Church of England

Fees per term
Day: £630-£800
Weekly board: £1390-£1390
Full board: -

○ Boy ○ Girl ● Co-ed
● Day ● Week ○ Board

At Manor House we believe that children need a happy, relaxed, yet well structured and disciplined enivironment in which to achieve their best. We think this is crucial, and indeed it is the starting point for our entire approach to your child's education. A dedicated staff, small classes, wide ranging curriculum, excellent academic and sporting facilities. This is Manor House.

Margaret McMillan Nursery School

Address: 24 Hoe Street, Plymouth, Devon PL1 2JA

Telephone: 0752 664884

Head: Mrs A Ackford

Age range: 3-5
No. of pupils: 50
Scholarships:
Religion: Non-denominational

Fees per term
Day: -£600
Weekly board: -
Full board: -

○ Boy ○ Girl ● Co-ed
● Day ○ Week ○ Board

For further information and a prospectus, please contact the school.

Marist Convent Nursery School

Address: Broad Street, Ottery St Mary, Devon EX11 1BZ

Telephone: 0404 812833

Head: Sister Margaret

Age range: 3-5
No. of pupils: 34
Scholarships:
Religion: Roman Catholic

Fees per term
Day: £300-£600
Weekly board: -
Full board: -

Boy ○ Girl ○ Co-ed ●
Day ● Week ○ Board ○

For further information and a prospectus, please contact the school.

Marland School †

Address: Petersmarland, Torrington, Devon EX38 8QQ

Telephone: 0805 5324

Head: Mr W K Gerrish

Age range: 11-16
No. of pupils: 32
Scholarships:
Religion: Non-denominational

Fees per term
Day: -
Weekly board: -
Full board: -

Boy ● Girl ○ Co-ed ○
Day ○ Week ○ Board ●

Caring school for 36 boys aged 10 to 16, with statements of special educational need because of behavioural and emotional disabilities. Termly boarding - normal school holidays. Very experienced teaching and care staff. Small classes. Wide subject range. Remedial teaching. Many activities, spacious grounds. DFE recognised. Social Service inspected and approved. Highly placed in league tables for EDB schools.

Maynard School ✱

Address: Denmark Road, Exeter, Devon EX1 1SJ

Telephone: 0392 73417

Head: Miss F Murdin MA(Oxon)

Age range: 7-18
No. of pupils: 567
Scholarships: Yes
Religion: Non-denominational

Fees per term
Day: £910-£1168
Weekly board: -
Full board: -

Boy ○ Girl ● Co-ed ○
Day ● Week ○ Board ○

The Maynard School, set in attractive grounds five minutes' walk from the cathedral, has a wide catchment area well served by public and private transport. Its academic reputation is phenomenal; sport and the creative arts also flourish. Students are encouraged to develop as individuals. Assisted Places ensure up to total fee remission for one-third of the pupils.

Mount House

Address: Tavistock, Devon PL19 9JL

Telephone: 0822 612244

Head: Mr C D Price

Age range: 7-14
No. of pupils: 180
Scholarships: Yes
Religion: Church of England

Fees per term
Day: £1755-£1755
Weekly board: -
Full board: £2420-£2420

Boy ● Girl ○ Co-ed ○
Day ● Week ○ Board ●

A traditional boys' boarding preparatory school with some day boys, set in superb grounds of playing fields, woodland, lakes and rivers. Excellent facilities and outstanding academic results with good sport, music, art and outward bound.

Mount St Mary's Convent School

Address: Wonford Road, Exeter, Devon EX2 4PF

Telephone: 0392 436770

Head: Sister E Delaney

Age range: 11-18
No. of pupils: 320
Scholarships:
Religion: Roman Catholic

Fees per term
Day: -£950
Weekly board: -
Full board: -

○ ● ○
Boy Girl Co-ed
● ○ ○
Day Week Board

The aim of the school is to promote Gospel values and to provide an education which is both academically challenging yet sensitive to the particlar needs of each pupil. We recognise that each pupil is gifted in a unique way; therefore we judge our success as a school not only on academic results important though these are, but on the ability of our pupils to be positive about themselves and their future.

Netherton Hall †

Address: Farway, Colyton, Devon EX13 6EB

Telephone: 0404 87261

Head: Mr J Hooper

Age range: 10-16
No. of pupils: 47
Scholarships:
Religion: Mixed

Fees per term
Day: -
Weekly board: -
Full board: £24000-£30000

○ ○ ○
Boy Girl Co-ed
○ ○ ○
Day Week Board

Netherton Hall is a special school catering for students with emotional/behavioural problems. School video is available upon request.

Plymouth College *

Address: Ford Park, Plymouth, Devon PL4 6RN

Telephone: 0752 228596

Head: Mr A J Morsley

Age range: 11-18
No. of pupils: 640
Scholarships: Yes
Religion: Non-Denominational

Fees per term
Day: £1275-
Weekly board: £2445-
Full board: £2465-

● ● ○
Boy Girl Co-ed
● ● ●
Day Week Board

Top academic results of South West Independent Schools. Outward bound; music; art; drama; international games reputation. Traditional values in first class modern facilities. Caring, happy ethos; individual attention. Boys 11-18. Girls in Sixth Form.

Plymouth College Preparatory School

Address: Hartley Road, Plymouth, Devon PL3 5LW

Telephone: 0752 772283

Head: Mr A Hudson

Age range: 4-11
No. of pupils: 250
Scholarships:
Religion: Church of England

Fees per term
Day: £650-£935
Weekly board: -£2105
Full board: -£2135

● ○ ○
Boy Girl Co-ed
● ● ●
Day Week Board

For further information an a prospectus, please contact the school.

Presentation of Mary Convent School

Address: Palace Gate, Exeter, Devon EX1 1JA

Telephone: 0392 72395

Head: Mrs J M Hunt

Age range: 3-11
No. of pupils: 130
Scholarships:
Religion: Roman Catholic

Fees per term
Day: £450-£690
Weekly board: -
Full board: -

● Boy   ● Girl   ○ Co-ed
● Day   ○ Week   ○ Board

Presentation of Mary School was founded in 1896. The sisters from Bourg St. Andeol arrived in April of that year. Since then the school has grown steadily to the point where today it has 130 pupils aged between 3 and 11 years of age. Boys 3-7, girls 3-11.

Rudolf Steiner School

Address: Hood Manor, Dartington, Devon TQ9 6AB

Telephone: 080 426 528

Administrator: Mr C Cooper

Age range: 4-16
No. of pupils: 240
Scholarships:
Religion: Christian

Fees per term
Day: £380-£710
Weekly board: -
Full board: -

○ Boy   ○ Girl   ● Co-ed
● Day   ○ Week   ○ Board

The school has been established in Devon for the past thirteen years and is part of the world-wide organisation of some 500 Steiner schools. It caters for children from 4-16 in a beautiful environment with 20 trained teachers who work creatively with the Steiner Curriculum.

Sands School

Address: Greylands, 48 East Street, Ashburton, Devon TQ13 7AX
Telephone: 0364 53666

Head: Mr S Bellamy

Age range: 11-16
No. of pupils: 30
Scholarships: Yes
Religion: Non-denominational

Fees per term
Day: -£890
Weekly board: -
Full board: -

○ Boy   ○ Girl   ● Co-ed
● Day   ○ Week   ○ Board

Policy is made at the school meeting, where children and teachers have one vote each. The school meeting also appoints new teachers, admits new pupils and takes all the important decisions usually taken by the head teacher. Sands gives its pupils the best possible opportunity to develop their own natural self-confidence, self respect and sense of responsibility without losing sight of conventional academic objectives.

Shebbear College *p749*

Address: Shebbear, Devon EX21 5HJ

Telephone: 0409 281228

Head: Mr R J Buley

Age range: 5-18
No. of pupils: 315
Scholarships: Yes
Religion: Methodist

Fees per term
Day: £750-£1470
Weekly board: -
Full board: £1998-£2680

● Boy   ○ Girl   ● Co-ed
● Day   ○ Week   ● Board

Co-educational day school with boys boarding. Junior school with kindergarten for boys and girls to 11 is separately organised but uses extensive facilities of Senior school on the same site. Senior school has two day and two boarding houses for pupils 11 to 18. Flourishing extra-curricular programme using the environment of rural Devon.

Shobrooke House School

Address: Shobrooke, Crediton, Devon
Telephone: 0363 772715
Head: P G Spencer MA

Age range: 3-9
No. of pupils: 60
Scholarships:
Religion: Christian

Fees per term
Day: £180-£530
Weekly board: -
Full board: -

○ ○ ● Boy Girl Co-ed
● ○ ○ Day Week Board

A small pre-preparatory school, the only private school in the area. Forms average only 10 children, so much individual attention is possible. Traditional methods and outlook, with emphasis on discipline, manners and effort. Exceptional record (100% most years) of success in entrance examinations to senior and preparatory schools.

St Aubyn's School

Address: Howden Court, Tiverton, Devon EX16 5PB
Telephone: 0884 252393
Head: Mr A C C Herniman

Age range: 3-13
No. of pupils: 275
Scholarships: Yes
Religion: Christian

Fees per term
Day: £140-£1255
Weekly board: -
Full board: £2065-£2175

○ ○ ● Boy Girl Co-ed
● ○ ● Day Week Board

Set in 14 acres of secluded woodland, St Aubyn's offers a very broad curriculum taught in the caring atmosphere of small classes. As well as academic excellence, with first rate exam and scholarship results, we strive for the highest standards outside the classroom. Excellent sport and music, design technology and drama help fulfil the 'whole person' philosophy. All within a caring, Christian community.

St Bernard's School

Address: Courtnay Road, Newton Abbot, Devon TQ12 1HP
Telephone: 0626 65424
Head: Mr R Dudley-Cooke

Age range: 3-11
No. of pupils: 120
Scholarships:
Religion: Non-denominational

Fees per term
Day: £485-£795
Weekly board: -
Full board: -

● ● ○ Boy Girl Co-ed
● ○ ○ Day Week Board

The school prepares girls for the entrance examinations of the secondary school of their choice with an excellent record in that respect. Boys go mainly to the local preparatory schools. The curriculum is broadly based and designed to provide a good all-round education. The school has a fine music tradition and children are encouraged to participate in games and swimming. Boys 3-7.

St Dunstan's Abbey

Address: North Road West, Plymouth, Devon PL1 5DH
Telephone: 0752 663998
Head: Mr R A Bye MA

Age range: 11-18
No. of pupils: 220
Scholarships: Yes
Religion: Church of England

Fees per term
Day: -£1250
Weekly board: -£2020
Full board: -

○ ● ○ Boy Girl Co-ed
● ● ○ Day Week Board

The school has a high academic standard but is also proud of its caring atmosphere and record of helping girls realise their full potential. Traditional values are maintained with smart dress, courtesy, consideration and good manners. As well as receiving an excellent education, the girls leaving St Dunstan's are articulate, knowledgeable and able to hold their own in any company.

St Dunstan's Abbey

Address: North Road West, Plymouth, Devon PL1 5DH

Telephone:

Head: Mrs A J Bailey

Age range: 4-11
No. of pupils: 100
Scholarships:
Religion: Church of England

Fees per term
Day: £715-£1045
Weekly board: -£1815
Full board: -

● Boy ● Girl ○ Co-ed
● Day ● Week ○ Board

Our prime concern is to help each child achieve their full potential in a happy and supportive environment so that they develop fully as a person within the community by showing sensitivity to the needs of others, acquire a sense of personal responsibility and initiative and develop their own natural talents. Boys 4 to 7.

St Johns School

Address: The Broadway, Sidmouth, Devon EX10 8RG

Telephone: 0395 513984

Head: Mr N R Pocket

Age range: 3-13
No. of pupils: 250
Scholarships:
Religion: Church of England

Fees per term
Day: £650-£1095
Weekly board: £1835-
Full board: £1835-

○ Boy ○ Girl ● Co-ed
● Day ● Week ● Board

The headmaster and his wife believes that the best results are achieved by children who are able to relate to a happy family community. Good facilities and a strong team of caring staff mean that each child is treated as an individual and with understanding so that they have the confidence to share any problem should the need arrive.

St Joseph's Roman Catholic School

Address: The Strand, Bideford, Devon EX39 2PW

Telephone:

Head:

Age range: 3-11
No. of pupils:
Scholarships:
Religion: Roman Catholic

Fees per term
Day: -
Weekly board: -
Full board: -

○ Boy ○ Girl ● Co-ed
● Day ○ Week ● Board

For further information and a prospectus, please contact the school.

St Luke's School †

Address: Exeter Road, Teignmouth, Devon TQ14 9JG

Telephone: 0626 778328

Head: Mr J Brandwood

Age range: 11-18
No. of pupils: 18
Scholarships:
Religion: Non-denominational

Fees per term
Day: -
Weekly board: -
Full board: -

○ Boy ○ Girl ● Co-ed
○ Day ○ Week ● Board

For fees, further information and a prospectus, please contact the school.

St Margaret's Exeter * p660

Address: Magdalen Road, Exeter, Devon

Telephone: 0392 73197

Head: Mrs J M Giddings

Age range: 7-18
No. of pupils: 460
Scholarships: Yes
Religion: Church of England

Fees per term
Day: £894-£1032
Weekly board: £1557-£1695
Full board: -

○ ● ○
Boy Girl Co-ed
● ● ○
Day Week Board

Independent school convenient to the city centre. Well equipped for modern studies, emphasis given to music and drama, wide range of extra-curricular activities. All denominations welcome.

St Michael's School

Address: Tawstock Court, Barnstaple, Devon

Telephone: 0271 43242

Head: Mr J M Batten

Age range: 3-13
No. of pupils: 215
Scholarships: Yes
Religion: Church of England

Fees per term
Day: £620-£1485
Weekly board: £1655-£2280
Full board: £1655-£2410

● ● ●
Boy Girl Co-ed
● ● ●
Day Week Board

St Michael's incorporates a pre-prep department for children between 3 and 7 and a first form centre for an easy introduction to the prep school. The aim of the school is to give every child an opportunity to reach his or her highest potential in both academic subjects and a wide variety of sports and activities as well as encouraging them to become kind and responsible members of the community.

St Michael's - Kelly College Junior School

Address: Hazledon, Parkwood Road, Tavistock, Devon PL19 0JS

Telephone: 0822 612244

Head: Mr M J Nicholls

Age range: 4-12
No. of pupils: 120
Scholarships:
Religion: Church of England

Fees per term
Day: -
Weekly board: -
Full board: -

○ ○ ●
Boy Girl Co-ed
● ○ ○
Day Week Board

For further information and a prospectus, please contact the school.

St Michaels School PNEU

Address: Hazledon House, Parkwood Road, Tavistock, Devon PL19 0JS

Telephone: 0822 612919

Head:

Age range:
No. of pupils:
Scholarships:
Religion:

Fees per term
Day: -
Weekly board: -
Full board: -

○ ○ ○
Boy Girl Co-ed
○ ○ ○
Day Week Board

For further information and a prospectus, please contact the school.

St Peter's School

Address: Harefield,
Lympstone, Devon EX8 5AU

Telephone:

Head:

Age range:
No. of pupils:
Scholarships:
Religion:

Fees per term
Day: -
Weekly board: -
Full board: -

○ ○ ○
Boy Girl Co-ed
○ ○ ○
Day Week Board

For further information and a prospectus, please contact the school.

St Thomas More's School

Address: East Allington,
Totnes, Devon

Telephone:

Head:

Age range: 8-16
No. of pupils:
Scholarships:
Religion:

Fees per term
Day: -
Weekly board: -
Full board: -

● ○ ○
Boy Girl Co-ed
○ ○ ○
Day Week Board

For further information and a prospectus, please contact the school.

St Wilfrid's Junior School

Address: 33 St David's Hill,
Exeter, Devon EX4 4DA

Telephone: 0392 55047

Head: Mrs M J Bews

Age range: 3-11
No. of pupils: 100
Scholarships:
Religion:

Fees per term
Day: -
Weekly board: -
Full board: -

○ ○ ●
Boy Girl Co-ed
● ○ ○
Day Week Board

For further information and a prospectus, please contact the school.

St Wilfrid's School

Address: 25 St David's Hill,
Exeter, Devon EX4 4DA

Telephone: 0392 76171

Head: Mr J G Buckrod

Age range: 11-16
No. of pupils: 120
Scholarships:
Religion:

Fees per term
Day: -
Weekly board: -
Full board: -

○ ○ ●
Boy Girl Co-ed
● ○ ○
Day Week Board

For further information and a prospectus, please contact the school.

Stella Maris School p660

Address: Bideford, Devon EX39 2PW

Telephone: 0237 472208

Head: Mr T H Andrew

Age range: 3-18
No. of pupils: 373
Scholarships: Yes
Religion: Non-denominational

Fees per term
Day: £725-£935
Weekly board: £1625-£1790
Full board: £1825-£1990

Boy ○ Girl ● Co-ed ○
Day ● Week ● Board ●

Stella Maris provides high educational standards in a caring environment. It is a Christian school with committed, well-qualified staff. Laboratories and classrooms are well-equipped, and sports facilities include a heated, indoor swimming pool. Drama, art, music and outdoor activities flourish throughout the school. Bursaries for girls of good academic ability are awarded annually.

Stonelands School of Dance and Drama

Address: Ashcombe Road, Dawlish, Devon

Telephone: 0626 866708

Director: Mrs I Z Filpi

Age range: 5-16
No. of pupils: 50
Scholarships: Yes
Religion: Church of England

Fees per term
Day: £1045-
Weekly board: £1518-£1900
Full board: £1793-£2200

Boy ○ Girl ● Co-ed ○
Day ● Week ● Board ●

Stonelands is a small boarding and day school for gifted girls in an idyllic county setting close to the sea. Whilst specializing in dance, drama, music and related subjects it is proud of its high academic standards with preparation for GCSE examinations at an early age and emphasis on individual needs in all subjects. Entrance by audition and written assessment.

Stoodley Knowle Convent School

Address: Ansteys Cove Road, Torquay, Devon TQ1 2JB

Telephone: 0803 293160

Head: Sister Perpetua

Age range: 7-18
No. of pupils: 220
Scholarships:
Religion: Catholic

Fees per term
Day: £775-£850
Weekly board: £1231-£1364
Full board: -

Boy ○ Girl ● Co-ed ○
Day ● Week ● Board ○

Our pupils are prepared for the GCSE and A Level Oxford Board. We seek to provide a cultured, well balanced education, based on sound Christian principles. Special importance is given to religious instruction, the sciences, as well as sport and other outdoor activities - the DOE Award Scheme. Music and drama are very much a part of the school curriculum and Stoodley Knowle has a sound musical tradition.

Stover School

Address: Newton Abbot, Devon TQ12 6QG

Telephone: 0626 54505

Head: Mrs W Lunel

Age range: 11-18
No. of pupils: 250
Scholarships: Yes
Religion: Church of England

Fees per term
Day: £1275-
Weekly board: £2370-
Full board: £2430-

Boy ○ Girl ● Co-ed ○
Day ● Week ● Board ●

Stover School, set in a Georgian mansion with extensive grounds and specialist facilities offers a full range of subjects at GCSE and A Level. We aim to provide a high quality education in a Christian environment which enables girls to acquire the confidence, skills, qualifications and attitude to fulfil varied and demanding roles in the 21st century.

DEVON 133

Tower House School

Address: Fisher Street, Paignton, Devon

Telephone: 0803 557077

Head: Dr D J Samworth

Age range: 3-16
No. of pupils: 200
Scholarships: Yes
Religion: Christian

Fees per term
Day: £675-£995
Weekly board: -
Full board: -

○ ○ ● Boy Girl Co-ed
● ○ ○ Day Week Board

Our principal aim is to enable each child to achieve a good academic standard whilst developing the necessary skills to become a useful adult member of the community. The school follows the National Curriculum and offers a full range of GCSE subjects.

Trengweath School †

Address: Hartley Road, Plymouth, Devon PL3 5LP

Telephone:

Head:

Age range: 2-12
No. of pupils:
Scholarships:
Religion:

Fees per term
Day: -
Weekly board: -
Full board: -

○ ○ ● Boy Girl Co-ed
○ ○ ○ Day Week Board

For further information and a prospectus, please contact the school.

Trinity School

Address: Buckeridge Road, Teignmouth, Devon TQ14 8LY

Telephone: 0626 774138

Head: Mr C J Ashby

Age range: 3-18
No. of pupils:
Scholarships: Yes
Religion: Catholic/Anglican

Fees per term
Day: £1205-
Weekly board: £2210-
Full board: £2270-

○ ○ ● Boy Girl Co-ed
● ● ● Day Week Board

Trinity combines a strong academic reputation with high standards of discipline, communication skills and courtesy. Small class sizes and a dedicated teaching staff ensure excellent results. With a beautiful setting overlooking Lyme Bay on the South Devon coast, the school has excellent facilities. Boarders are cared for in a warm, friendly environment and many extra-curricular activities are offered.

West Buckland School * p752

Address: Barnstaple, Devon EX32 0SX
Telephone: 0598 760281

Head: Mr M Downward

Age range: 5-18
No. of pupils: 573
Scholarships: Yes
Religion: Anglican

Fees per term
Day: £720-£1392
Weekly board: -
Full board: £1980-£2567

○ ○ ● Boy Girl Co-ed
● ○ ● Day Week Board

West Buckland's rural setting fosters a happy community spirit. An essential element is the encouragement of individuals to succeed to the best of their ability, both academically and in a wide range of sports and activities. The school offers continuity of education for all the family, with the opportunity to board for all or part of the time.

Western College Preparatory School

Address: Seymour Road, Plymouth, Devon PL3 5AS

Telephone: 0752 668558

Head: Mrs M A Knaggs

Age range: 4-11
No. of pupils: 125
Scholarships:
Religion: Non-denominational

Fees per term
Day: £600-£642
Weekly board: -
Full board: -

Boy ○ Girl ● Co-ed ○
Day ● Week ○ Board ○

This lovely, girls only preparatory school is placed in the centre of Plymouth. The homely atmosphere is just one of the delights about this school. The staff are just like family and with being a small school you get plenty of your form teacher's time and efforts. It has wonderful facilties especially if you are keen on art.
Antonia Thomson, age 10

White House School

Address: Old Beer Road, Seaton, Devon EX12 2PX

Telephone: 0297 20614

Head: Mr H R Doran

Age range: 4-11
No. of pupils: 100
Scholarships:
Religion: Non-denominational

Fees per term
Day: £490-£610
Weekly board: -
Full board: -

Boy ○ Girl ○ Co-ed ●
Day ● Week ○ Board ○

The school is situated in a beautiful area on the western side of Seaton near the sea. It is a small caring school with an excellent academic record. A full curriculum includes science, French and Latin. It is a private school owned by the four principals. The teachers are highly qualified. Each has responsibility for a form and additionally specialises in a particular area.

Wolborough Hill School

Address: South Road, Newton Abbot, Devon TQ12 1HH

Telephone:

Head: Mr S J G Day

Age range: 7-13
No. of pupils: 200
Scholarships: Yes
Religion: Church of England

Fees per term
Day: £1250-
Weekly board: £1860-
Full board: -

Boy ○ Girl ○ Co-ed ●
Day ● Week ● Board ○

The school has been established for 114 years. It has a strong sporting and musical tradition, and over half the pupils learn a musical instrument. Scholarships have been won to many major public schools. Facilities include design technology studio, heated swimming pool, 3 tennis courts, purpose built library and multi-purpose hall.

DORSET

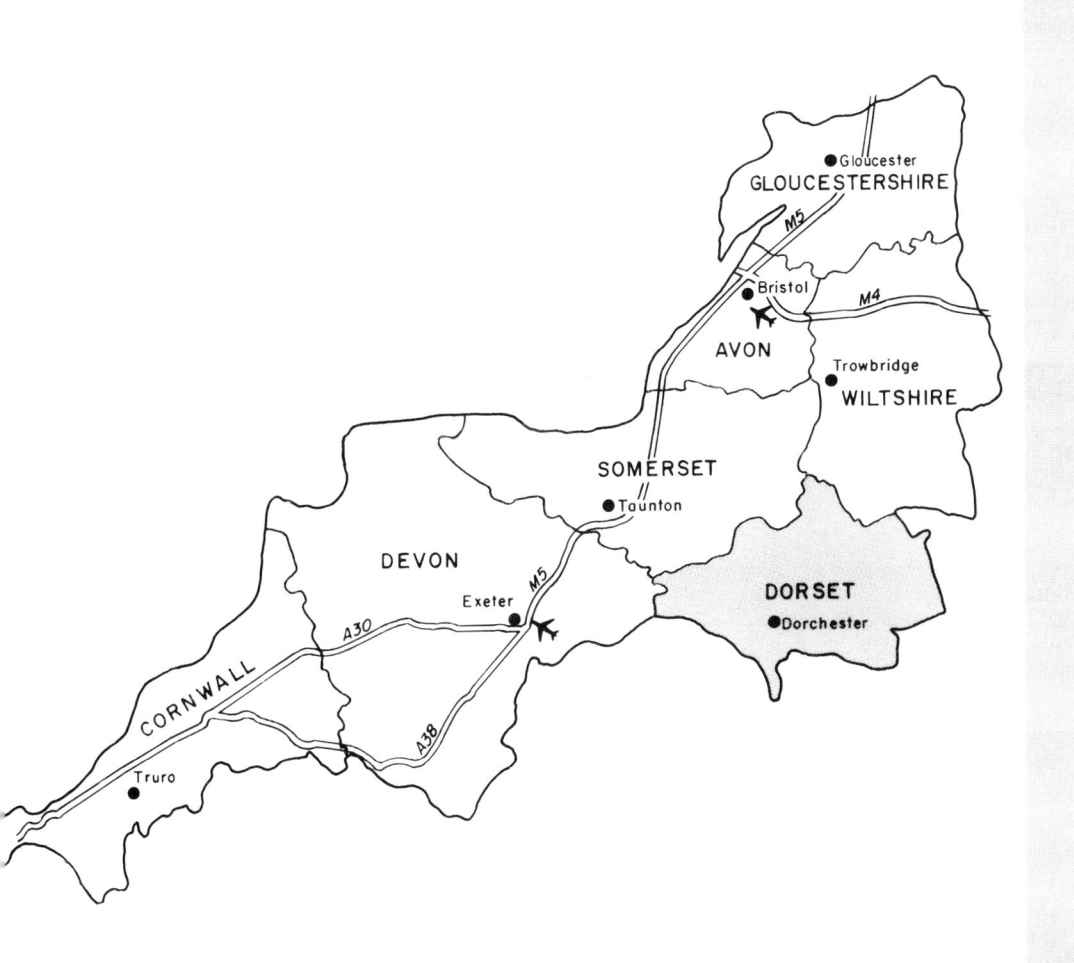

Allhallows School

Address: Rousdon, Lyme Regis, Dorset DT7 3RA

Telephone: 0297 20444

Head: Mr P S Larkman LVO MA(Cantab)

Age range: 11-18
No. of pupils: 250
Scholarships: Yes
Religion: Church of England

Fees per term
Day: £1200-£1704
Weekly board: -
Full board: £3408-

Boy ○ Girl ○ Co-ed ●
Day ● Week ○ Board ●

Allhallows School is an independent co-educational boarding and day school for 300 pupils between the ages of 11 and 18. The school's situation is unique. It occupies a 140 HT site combining playing fields, agricultural land, nature reserve, cliffs and beach, set in an important geological area of the south coast of England. The school is committed to developing each individual's potential by a balanced education.

Bryanston School

Address: Blandford, Dorset DT11 0PX

Telephone: 0258 452411

Head: Mr T D Wheare MA (Cantab)

Age range: 13-18
No. of pupils: 660
Scholarships: Yes
Religion: Church of England

Fees per term
Day: -
Weekly board: -
Full board: -£3890

Boy ○ Girl ○ Co-ed ●
Day ○ Week ○ Board ●

Bryanston School has an excellent academic record at both GCSE and A Level, and more than 90% of pupils continue to higher education. The school's tutorial and pastoral arrangements keep pupils, teachers and parents in regular contact, whilst the modified Dalton Plan with its assignment system allows pupils to proceed at their own pace and make the best of their talents in extra-curricular as well as academic matters.

Buckholme Towers School

Address: 18 Commercial Road, Parkstone, Poole, Dorset BH14 0JW

Telephone: 0202 742871

Head: Mrs D V Stacey

Age range: 3-12
No. of pupils: 156
Scholarships:
Religion: Non-denominational

Fees per term
Day: £290-£710
Weekly board: -
Full board: -

Boy ○ Girl ○ Co-ed ●
Day ● Week ○ Board ○

A co-educational day school for 3 to 12 year olds, established for over 50 years. The school aims for a high academic standard within a caring atmosphere allowing individual pupils to develop to their full potential. Children are prepared for Common Entrance examinations and 11+ or 12+ entry to local grammar schools.

Canford School * p739

Address: Wimborne, Dorset BH21 3AD

Telephone: 0202 841254

Head: Mr J D Lever

Age range: 13-18
No. of pupils: 520
Scholarships: Yes
Religion: Church of England

Fees per term
Day: £2615-£2915
Weekly board: -
Full board: £3580-£3580

Boy ● Girl ● Co-ed ○
Day ● Week ○ Board ●

An independent secondary boarding school with 520 pupils of whom 100 are day boys and 60 are girls in the sixth form. Situated in 300 acres of beautiful Dorset Parkland. Scholarships, bursaries and Assisted Places are offered each year. The school has an excellent academic record, extensive modern facilities and a wide range of cultural, sporting and out-of-doors activities.

DORSET 137

Castle Court Preparatory

Address: The Knoll House,
Knoll Lane, Corfe Mullen,
Wimborne, Dorset
Telephone: 0202 694438

Headmaster: Mr R E T Nicholl

Age range: 4-13
No. of pupils: 250
Scholarships: Yes
Religion: Non-denominational

Fees per term
Day: £940-£1940
Weekly board: -
Full board: -

○ ○ ● Boy Girl Co-ed
● ○ ○ Day Week Board

Castle Court is a superbly equipped day-school, set in beautiful grounds within 20 minutes of Bournemouth, Poole, Wimborne and Blandford, providing excellence in all-round education from 4-13 years. Strengths lie in music, sport and art, and many children win academic scholarships to their senior schools. Recent building includes science, technology and art block, computer room and school library.

Clayesmore

Address: Iwerne Minster,
Blandford Forum, Dorset
DT11 8LL
Telephone: 0747 812122

Head: Mr D J Beeby MA

Age range: 13-18
No. of pupils: 300
Scholarships: Yes
Religion: Church of England

Fees per term
Day: £2336-
Weekly board: -
Full board: £3380-

○ ○ ● Boy Girl Co-ed
● ○ ● Day Week Board

Clayesmore aims to treat pupils as individuals and to develop their talents to the full extent. The school believes it is important to encourage them to aim for standards of excellence. The wide range of opportunities on offer at Clayesmore makes it possible for every pupil to achieve success and self-confidence in one field or another.

Clayesmore Preparatory School

Address: Iwerne Minster,
Blandford, Dorset DT11 8PH

Telephone: 0747 811707

Head: Mr H D Watson MA(Oxon)

Age range: 4-13
No. of pupils: 275
Scholarships: Yes
Religion: Church of England

Fees per term
Day: £863-£1808
Weekly board: -£2549
Full board: -£2549

○ ○ ● Boy Girl Co-ed
● ● ● Day Week Board

Clayesmore Preparatory School shares a beautiful 60 acre campus in Dorset with its senior school, offering continuity from 4-18. The Preparatory School also has a fine CE and scholarship record to other senior schools. Music, drama and the arts are held in high esteem. The school also has outstanding sporting facilities. Above all, we seek to uphold traditional values.

Croft House School

Address: Shillingstone,
Blandford, Dorset DT11 0QS

Telephone: 0258 860295

Head: Mrs S Rawlinson

Age range: 11-18
No. of pupils: 150
Scholarships: Yes
Religion: Church of England

Fees per term
Day: -£2025
Weekly board: -£2870
Full board: -£2870

○ ● ○ Boy Girl Co-ed
● ● ● Day Week Board

Croft House lies on the edge of the beautiful Blackmore Vale and the grounds include excellent sports and riding facilities. New science laboratories have been built in 1992. Our aim is to develop the individual talents of each girl within a Christian community and to equip them with personal values and a love of learning which will last a lifetime.

Dewlish House

Address: 30-32 Howard Road, Bournemouth, Dorset

Telephone: 0202 528872

Head: Mrs B H F Dunfold

Age range: 4-8
No. of pupils: 32
Scholarships:
Religion: Christian

Fees per term
Day: £400-
Weekly board: -
Full board: -

○ Boy ○ Girl ● Co-ed
● Day ○ Week ○ Board

We are a long established pre-preparatory school.

Dorchester Preparatory School

Address: 25-26 Icen Way, Dorchester, Dorset DT1 1EP

Telephone: 0305 264925

Head: Mr J Rose

Age range: 3-13
No. of pupils: 200
Scholarships:
Religion: Non-denominational

Fees per term
Day: £290-£755
Weekly board: -
Full board: -

○ Boy ○ Girl ● Co-ed
● Day ○ Week ○ Board

For further information and a prospectus, please contact the school.

Dumpton School

Address: Deans Grove House, Wimborne, Dorset BH21 7AF

Telephone: 0202 883818

Head: Mr A G M Watson

Age range: 4-13
No. of pupils: 220
Scholarships:
Religion: Church of England

Fees per term
Day: £600-£1785
Weekly board: -£2310
Full board: -

● Boy ● Girl ○ Co-ed
● Day ● Week ○ Board

Founded in 1903, the school is housed in a lovely Victorian manor with 15 acres of grounds. The aim of the school is to prepare boys both academically and socially for their public school. Classes are small and are not streamed. Games play an important part in school life. Boys are given every opportunity to pursue their own hobbies. Girls are welcome in the pre-preparatory school up to the age of 7 years

Forres School

Address: Northbrook Road, Swanage, Dorset BH19 1PR

Telephone: 0929 422760

Head: Mr R P J Moore BA

Age range: 4-13
No. of pupils: 100
Scholarships: Yes
Religion: Non-denominational

Fees per term
Day: £715-£1940
Weekly board: -
Full board: -£2515

○ Boy ○ Girl ● Co-ed
● Day ○ Week ● Board

Forres is a school for boys and girls aged 4-13. Situated beside the sea and surrounded by the beautiful countryside of the Isle of Purbeck, the school prides itself on offering an extraordinary range of extra-curricular activities in addition to a rigorous but progressive academic education. Forres children are relaxed, polite and, above all, happy.

Grangewood Hall School †

Address: 24 St John's Hill, Wimborne, Dorset BH21 1BZ
Telephone: 0202 883954

Age range: 6-13
No. of pupils: 32
Scholarships:
Religion: Non-denominational

Fees per term
Day: -
Weekly board: -
Full board: £4360-

Boy ○ Girl ○ Co-ed ●
Day ○ Week ○ Board ●

Heads: Mrs S Jee Mr M G Jee

We are a small mixed boarding school for children with emotional and behavioural difficulties and/or moderate learning difficulties. We cater for a maximum of 32 pupils and our age range is 6-12+. The staff work as a dedicated team to develop the children's confidence and maturity. We encourage close links with family. We are proud of our warm and loving environment which promotes the children's happiness.

Hanford School

Address: Childe Okeford, Blandford Forum, Dorset DT11 8HL
Telephone: 0258 860219

Age range: 7-13
No. of pupils: 155
Scholarships:
Religion: Church of England

Fees per term
Day: -
Weekly board: -
Full board: -£2390

Boy ○ Girl ● Co-ed ○
Day ○ Week ○ Board ●

Heads: Mr & Mrs M E Sharp Miss S Canning

Hanford School aims at combining the best teaching with the fullest opportunity for self expression. Each child is encouraged to develop her personality and to exercise self-discipline as a happy member of a large family; above all, she is taught to look upon true values as the centre of life.

Homefield School

Address: Salisbury Road, Winkton, Christchurch, Dorset BH23 7AR
Telephone: 0202 476644

Age range: 3-16
No. of pupils: 450
Scholarships: Yes
Religion: Non-denominational

Fees per term
Day: £650-£1030
Weekly board: -
Full board: -£2630

Boy ○ Girl ○ Co-ed ●
Day ● Week ○ Board ●

Head: Mr A C Partridge

Homefield enjoys an excellent reputation with strong emphasis on traditional methods of teaching. The school aims to produce well educated, responsible individuals able to play useful roles in society, leading by example. Homefield offers a wide curriculum and achieves a high level of pass rates. It boasts good sporting and extra-curricular activities and has an orchestra of international recognition.

Knighton House School

Address: Durweston, Blandford, Dorset DT11 0PY
Telephone: 0258 452065

Age range: 4-13
No. of pupils: 185
Scholarships:
Religion: Church of England

Fees per term
Day: £650-£1830
Weekly board: £2535-
Full board: £2535-

Boy ● Girl ● Co-ed ○
Day ● Week ● Board ●

Head: Mr R P Weatherly

The school community is friendly, cohesive, civilised and supportive. 80% of girls aged over seven are boarders. The many extra-curricular activities include riding from our stables. Discipline is firm but flexible reflecting Christian principles. The staff is highly qualified and dedicated. The eight scholarships won during 1991-92 have rewarded academic, musical, artistic, riding and 'all-rounder' prowess. Please register early!

Milton Abbey School p746

Address: Blandford Form, Dorset
Telephone: 0258 880484
Head: Mr R H Hardy

Age range: 13-18
No. of pupils: 270
Scholarships: Yes
Religion: Church of England

Fees per term
Day: £2359-
Weekly board: -
Full board: £3370-

● Boy   ○ Girl   ○ Co-ed
● Day   ○ Week   ● Board

Milton Abbey has added modern academic, creative and recreational facilities (computer/technology block; theatre; music and art studios; heated indoor pool; golf course) to its exquisite historic buildings. The flexible, wide-ranging curriculum, small classes, close individual monitoring, and atmosphere of disciplined informality enable each boy to make his mark fostering greater confidence and a positive attitude to life.

Motcombe Grange School

Address: Motcombe, Shaftsbury, Dorset SP7 9HJ
Telephone: 0747 52426
Head: Mrs M.R. Williams

Age range: 3-11
No. of pupils: 95
Scholarships:
Religion: Non-denominational

Fees per term
Day: £365-£730
Weekly board: -
Full board: -

○ Boy   ○ Girl   ● Co-ed
● Day   ○ Week   ○ Board

In a happy atmosphere, all the children are well motivated to fulfill their potential and develop confidence. They are encouraged to pursue individual interests, as well as group activities, at every age level. All classes are small in number to ensure a high standard of work and conduct. Good manners and thoughtfulness for others are important. The school endeavours to nurture a spirit of unity and Christian fellowship.

Newell House School

Address: Cornhill, Sherborne, Dorset DT9 3PL
Telephone: 0935 812584
Head: Mr P J R Dale BSc CertEd

Age range: 2-11
No. of pupils: 56
Scholarships: Yes
Religion: Non-denominational

Fees per term
Day: £395-£2925
Weekly board: -
Full board: -

○ Boy   ○ Girl   ● Co-ed
● Day   ○ Week   ○ Board

Newell House is a small preparatory and nursery school, where children are taught in small classes, allowing them much individual attention, which helps them to develop their potential with confidence and self-motivation. The school promotes traditional educational values and standards and is very much a 'family' school, with a caring atmosphere for all its pupils. It is set within spacious, attractive and historic buildings.

The Old Malthouse

Address: Langton Matravers, Swanage, Dorset BH19 3HB
Telephone: 0929 422302
Head: Mr J H L Phillips

Age range: 8-13
No. of pupils: 95
Scholarships: Yes
Religion: Church of England

Fees per term
Day: £1900-
Weekly board: £2535-
Full board: £2535-

● Boy   ○ Girl   ○ Co-ed
● Day   ● Week   ● Board

OMH is one of the best-known small boarding schools in the country because the school enjoys a good reputation for academic achievement together with a high standard of manners in a relaxed and uniquely friendly atmosphere. The boys work hard, but are encouraged to develop their natural talents as individuals; each boy succeeds at his own level.

Port Regis

Address: Motcombe Park, Shaftesbury, Dorset

Telephone: 0747 52566

Head: Mr D C M Prichard

Age range: 7-13
No. of pupils: 280
Scholarships: Yes
Religion: Church of England

Fees per term
Day: £2275-
Weekly board: £3115-
Full board: £3115-

Boy ○ Girl ○ Co-ed ●
Day ● Week ● Board ●

A magical school in 150 acres with extensive facilities; golf course, covered pool; sports halls, £1m technology building, 400 seater theatre; 15 sports; 50 hobbies. The Port Regis experience is unique so demand for places is high. With 60% boarding and numbers rising, parents value high calibre staff, brilliant food, fear free environment and academic track record.

Sherborne Preparatory School

Address: Acreman Street, Sherborne, Dorset DT9 3NY

Telephone: 0935 812097

Head: Mr R T M Lindsay

Age range: 7-13
No. of pupils: 167
Scholarships:
Religion: Church of England

Fees per term
Day: £1470-
Weekly board: £2205-
Full board: £2205-

Boy ○ Girl ○ Co-ed ●
Day ● Week ● Board ●

The school stands in its own grounds and though not part of Sherborne, pupils use its many facilities. Many go on to the senior school. Rugger and hockey are played in the winter terms, cricket, athletics and tennis in the summer. A wide variety of musical instruments are learnt and there is a good school orchestra.

Sherborne School

Address: Abbey Road, Sherborne, Dorset DT9 3AP

Telephone: 0935 812646

Head: Mr P H Lapping MA

Age range: 13-18
No. of pupils: 652
Scholarships: Yes
Religion: Anglican

Fees per term
Day: £2875-
Weekly board: -
Full board: £3775-

Boy ● Girl ○ Co-ed ○
Day ● Week ○ Board ●

Sherborne School is an independent boarding and day school for boys aged 13-18 and offers the highest standards of academic education. A traditional curriculum plus superb facilities for sport, drama, art, design technology and an innovative careers department combine to prepare today's young men for tomorrow's world.

Sherborne School for Girls *p749*

Address: Sherborne, Dorset DT9 3QN

Telephone: 0935 812245

Head: Miss J M Taylor

Age range: 12-18
No. of pupils: 456
Scholarships: Yes
Religion: Church of England

Fees per term
Day: £2210-
Weekly board: -
Full board: £3320-

Boy ○ Girl ● Co-ed ○
Day ● Week ○ Board ●

Entry by scholarship, 12+ or 13+ Common Entrance. Entry into sixth form is competitive. The school offers an all-round education to girls who have the ability to do three A Levels. All the usual subjects are offered up to GCSE and A Level; 25 subjects offered at A Level including Russian, Italian, history of art and social biology. The school is situated on the edge of Sherborne with a train service to Waterloo and Exeter.

St Anthony's Convent Preparatory School

Address: Westbury, Sherborne, Dorset DT9 3EW
Telephone: 0935 812117
Head: Mrs P MacDonald

Age range: Boys 3-11
No. of pupils: 160
Scholarships:
Religion: Roman Catholic

Fees per term
Day: £480-£1140
Weekly board: -
Full board: -£2025

Boy ● Girl ● Co-ed ○
Day ● Week ○ Board ●

For further information and a prospectus, please contact the school.

St Antony's-Leweston School

Address: Sherborne, Dorset DT9 6EN
Telephone: 0963 210691
Head: Mrs P Cartwright

Age range: 11-18
No. of pupils: 380
Scholarships: Yes
Religion: Roman Catholic

Fees per term
Day: £1975-
Weekly board: -
Full board: £3030-

Boy ○ Girl ● Co-ed ○
Day ● Week ○ Board ●

Leweston combines an old and well-tried tradition with a contemporary approach to the education of girls. While maintaining commitment to the arts, we are building new science facilities, following major investment in our new Norfolk Centre for Design & Technology. We believe in effective pastoral care, expressing our moral and religious beliefs. We are building for the future upon an historic past.

St Genevieve's Convent

Address: South Walks, Dorchester, Dorset DT1 1EB
Telephone: 0305 264898
Head: Mrs B A Beakes BA

Age range: 4-16
No. of pupils: 280
Scholarships:
Religion: Roman Catholic

Fees per term
Day: £600-£700
Weekly board: £1000-£1000
Full board: -

Boy ● Girl ● Co-ed ○
Day ● Week ● Board ○

St Genevieve's Convent is an independent day and weekly boarding school for girls age 4-16 and junior boys. Pleasantly situated in the centre of Dorchester, the school offers a liberal and cultural education to pupils of all denominations based on sound religious principles in a caring and disciplined environment. Girls are prepared for GCSE and separate sciences are taught.

St Martins'

Address: 15 Stokewood Road, Bournemouth, Dorset BH3 7NA
Telephone: 0202 554483
Head: Mr T Shenton

Age range: 4-12
No. of pupils: 100
Scholarships: Yes
Religion: Church of England

Fees per term
Day: £495-£650
Weekly board: -
Full board: -

Boy ○ Girl ○ Co-ed ●
Day ● Week ○ Board ○

Founded 1914. Science laboratory, new library, playing field, swimming.

St Mary's School

Address: Shaftesbury, Dorset SP7 9LP

Telephone: 0747 54005

Head: Sister M Campion Livesey IBVM

Age range: 10-18
No. of pupils: 310
Scholarships: Yes
Religion: Roman Catholic

Fees per term
Day: £1635-£1720
Weekly board: -
Full board: £2555-£2690

Boy ○ Girl ● Co-ed ○
Day ● Week ○ Board ●

The school aims to educate girls of all Christian denominations but primarily Roman Catholics, in an environment which both makes explicit and inculcates Christian values and prepares them for any walk of life.

St Monica's

Address: The Yarrels, Upton, Poole, Dorset BH16 5EU
Telephone: 0202 622229

Head: Mrs N.A. Covell

Age range: 3-12
No. of pupils: 167
Scholarships: Yes
Religion: Church of England

Fees per term
Day: £398-£1246
Weekly board: -
Full board: -

Boy ○ Girl ● Co-ed ●
Day ● Week ○ Board ○

A friendly, dynamic school set in wooded grounds and gardens. Small classes, enthusiastic, well-qualified staff and carefully designed programmes of study ensure appropiate provisions across the ability range with excellent results. The curriculum is enhanced by many after-school activities and study trips. Every child is encouraged to contribute to the vibrant intellectual sporting and artistic life of the school.

St Peter's School

Address: Bournemouth, Dorset

Telephone:

Head:

Age range:
No. of pupils:
Scholarships:
Religion:

Fees per term
Day: -
Weekly board: -
Full board: -

Boy ○ Girl ○ Co-ed ○
Day ○ Week ○ Board ○

For further information and a prospectus, please contact the school.

St Ronan's School

Address: Asker Mead, Bridport, Dorset DT6 4DA
Telephone: 0308 22128

Teacher In Charge: Mrs J A Fairbrother

Age range: 3-11
No. of pupils: 60
Scholarships:
Religion:

Fees per term
Day: -
Weekly board: -
Full board: -

Boy ○ Girl ○ Co-ed ●
Day ● Week ○ Board ○

For further information and a prospectus, please contact the school.

St Thomas Garnet's School

Address: Parkwood Road,
Boscombe, Bournemouth,
Dorset BH5 2DE
Telephone: 0202 420172

Age range: 3-11
No. of pupils: 175
Scholarships:
Religion: Roman Catholic

Fees per term
Day: £750-
Weekly board: -
Full board: -

● Boy ● Girl ● Co-ed
● Day ○ Week ○ Board

Head: Mr P R Gillings

We aim to provide a happy environment suitable for the all round development of children from 3+ to 11+ years of age. We teach the skills which we consider essential for the development of the children - the fundamental skils of reading and writing, the formation of mathematical concepts and the development of self expression in words, music, movement, art and craft.

Sunninghill Preparatory School

Address: 6 Herringston Road,
Dorchester, Dorset DT1 2BS

Telephone: 0305 262306

Age range: 3-13
No. of pupils: 179
Scholarships:
Religion: Christian

Fees per term
Day: £365-£835
Weekly board: -
Full board: -

○ Boy ○ Girl ● Co-ed
● Day ○ Week ○ Board

Head: Mr C S Pring

Sunninghill was founded in 1939 and caters for children aged 3-13. The school is fully co-educational and we believe this provides the most natural framework in which a young child can be educated, and also encourages our distinctive family atmosphere. Sunninghill School is a charitable trust administered by a board of governors and the headmaster, who is a member of IAPS.

Talbot Heath School ✱ p661

Address: Rothesay Road,
Bournemouth, Dorset
BH4 9NJ
Telephone: 0202 761881

Age range: 7-18
No. of pupils: 600
Scholarships: Yes
Religion: Church of England

Fees per term
Day: £1107-£1405
Weekly board: -£1003
Full board: -£1070

○ Boy ● Girl ○ Co-ed
● Day ● Week ● Board

Head: Mrs C Dipple BA Mies L

Talbot Heath is an independent day and flexible boarding school for 600 girls aged 7-18. The school has an outstanding academic record, a well integrated junior school, extensive modern buildings and grounds with excellent facilities for music and sport. A lively, caring environment exists with high personal standards. Scholarships, Assisted Places and bursaries are available.

Talbot House Preparatory School

Address: 8 Firs Glen Road,
Bournemouth, Dorset BH9 2LR
Telephone: 0202 510348

Age range: 3-12
No. of pupils: 168
Scholarships:
Religion: Non-denominational

Fees per term
Day: £515-£552
Weekly board: -
Full board: -

○ Boy ○ Girl ● Co-ed
● Day ○ Week ○ Board

Head: Mrs E H Stevenson

The subjects studied are those required for all examinations up to 12 years of age. In addition, special attention is given to art, music, French, physical education, games and swimming; all of which are considered of vital importance to the all round development of the child. German and elocution, ballet and karate are offered as extra subjects.

DORSET 145

Thornlow Junior School

Address: Connaught Road, Weymouth, Dorset DT4 0SA

Telephone: 0305 785703

Head: Mrs J D Crocker

Age range: 3-11
No. of pupils: 60
Scholarships:
Religion: Non-denominational

Fees per term
Day: £600-£700
Weekly board: £1885-£1885
Full board: £2065-£2065

● Boy ● Girl ● Co-ed
● Day ● Week ● Board

At Thurnlow Junior School we view the early years as crucial to a child's happiness and development. Pupils are offered a sound, basic curriculum which broadens as they progress through the school. Our teachers are experienced and enthusiastic. They treat children as individuals and develop their potential through a blend of the best of traditional and modern methods.

Thornlow Senior School

Address: 101 Buxton Road, Weymouth, Dorset DT4 9PR
Telephone: 0305 782977

Head: Mr D H Crocker

Age range: 11-16
No. of pupils: 160
Scholarships: Yes
Religion: Non-denominational

Fees per term
Day: £905-£1015
Weekly board: £1980-£1980
Full board: £2175-£2175

● Boy ● Girl ● Co-ed
● Day ● Week ● Board

Thornlow is a small independent co-educational school set in seven acres of grounds overlooking Portland Harbour. We offer a small friendly environment where staff, pupils and parents work together to achieve not only the best academic results for each pupil but also to prepare your child to be articulate and confident.

Uplands School

Address: 40 St Osmund's Road, Parkstone, Poole, Dorset BH14 9JY
Telephone: 0202 742626

Head: Miss E Kirkpatrick

Age range: 3-18
No. of pupils: 290
Scholarships:
Religion:

Fees per term
Day: -
Weekly board: -
Full board: -

○ Boy ○ Girl ● Co-ed
● Day ○ Week ○ Board

For further information and a prospectus, please contact the school.

Victoria School for Physically Handicapped Children †

Address: 12 Lindsay Road, Branksome Park, Poole, Dorset
Telephone:

Head:

Age range: 2-16
No. of pupils:
Scholarships:
Religion:

Fees per term
Day: -
Weekly board: -
Full board: -

○ Boy ○ Girl ● Co-ed
● Day ○ Week ● Board

For further information and a prospectus, please contact the school.

Wentworth Milton Mount

Address: College Road,
Bournemouth, Dorset
BH5 2DY
Telephone: 0202 423266

Head: Miss S Coe

Age range: 11-18
No. of pupils: 320
Scholarships:
Religion:

Fees per term
Day: -
Weekly board: -
Full board: -

○ ● ○
Boy Girl Co-ed
● ● ●
Day Week Board

For further information and a prospectus, please contact the school.

Woodsford House School †

Address: Woodsford,
Dorchester, Dorset DT2 8AT

Telephone: 0305 848202

Head: Mr R S R Mileham

Age range: 7-13
No. of pupils: 35
Scholarships:
Religion: Non-denominational

Fees per term
Day: £2000-
Weekly board: £3000-
Full board: £3000-

○ ○ ●
Boy Girl Co-ed
● ● ●
Day Week Board

Woodsford House aims to provide an all-round education for boys and girls, 25 boarders and 10 day pupils, with specific learning difficulties (dyslexia) and mild language disorders. The school, housed in a fine old rectory, is also the Mileham's family home: they have four children and many animals, including dogs and horses. Our primary task is to teach children how to learn.

DURHAM

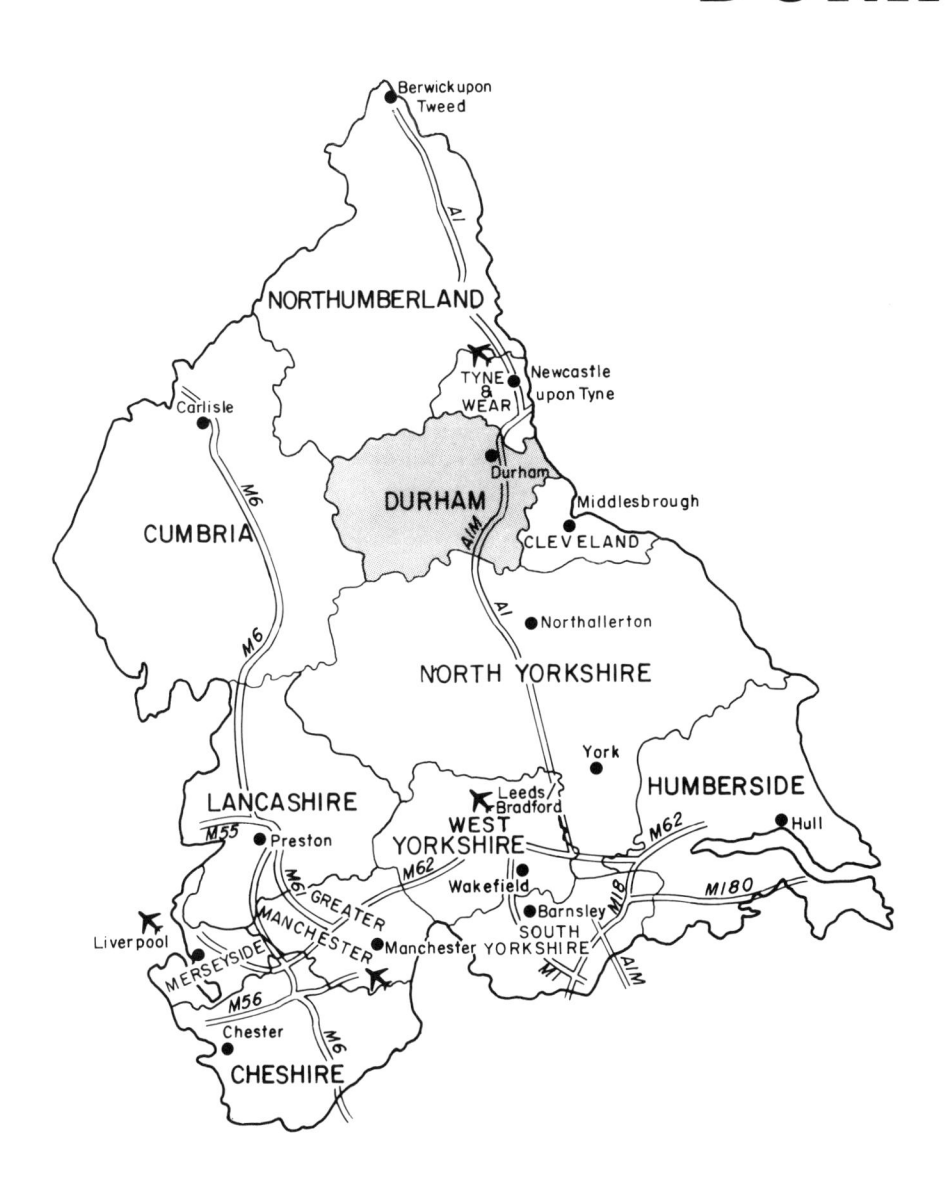

Barnard Castle School *

Address: Barnard Castle, Co Durham DL12 8UN

Telephone: 0833 690222

Head: Mr F S McNamara

Age range: 7-18
No. of pupils: 580
Scholarships: Yes
Religion: Non-denominational

Fees per term
Day: £1009-£1451
Weekly board: -
Full board: £1879-£2452

Boy ● Girl ● Co-ed ○
Day ● Week ○ Board ●

The school is situated on the outskirts of Barnard Castle within its own spacious grounds and offers excellent opportunities for a wide range of sporting, recreational, artistic and cultural activities. The school provides comprehensive careers advice and the majority of pupils continue on to the sixth form and hence into higher education, mostly to degree courses studied at universities. Girls accepeted in the sixth form.

Bow School

Address: South Road, Durham, Co. Durham DH1 3LS

Telephone: 091 384 8233

Headmaster: Mr C R F Paterson

Age range: 4-13
No. of pupils: 115
Scholarships:
Religion: Church of England

Fees per term
Day: -£1452
Weekly board: -
Full board: -£2104

Boy ● Girl ○ Co-ed ○
Day ● Week ○ Board ●

Beautifully situated on the edge of Durham City, Bow School offers to its boys a care and concern over their individual development that would be hard to match. We will ensure that your son's potential is explored to the full in a stable, disciplined and happy atmosphere.

The Chorister School

Address: Durham, Co Durham DH1 3EL

Telephone: 091 384 2935

Head: Mr R G Lawrence

Age range: 5-13
No. of pupils: 170
Scholarships: Yes
Religion: Anglican

Fees per term
Day: £850-£1221
Weekly board: £1820-
Full board: £1820-

Boy ● Girl ○ Co-ed ○
Day ● Week ● Board ●

Entrants do not have to be musical unless they want to be Durham Cathedral Choristers! We aim to encourage all talents - academic, artistic, musical and sporting - to help boys reach their potential.

Durham High School

Address: Farewell Hall, Durham, Co Durham DH1 3TB

Telephone: 091 384 3226

Head: Miss M L Walters BA

Age range: 4-18
No. of pupils: 251
Scholarships: Yes
Religion: Church of England

Fees per term
Day: £688-£1105
Weekly board: -
Full board: -

Boy ● Girl ● Co-ed ○
Day ● Week ○ Board ○

The school aims to give a sound broad education within a Christian framework; its atmosphere is friendly. An excellent and caring staff is its strongest asset. The buildings are modern and well-equipped and situated in pleasant, semi-rural surroundings. Boys 4-7 years, girls 4-18 years.

Durham School * p741

Address: Durham, Co Durham
Telephone: 091 384 7977
Head: Mr M A Lang

Age range: 11-18
No. of pupils: 374
Scholarships: Yes
Religion: Church of England

Fees per term
Day: £1841-£2165
Weekly board: -
Full board: £2762-£3248

Boy ● Girl ● Co-ed ○
Day ● Week ○ Board ●

Durham School, a traditional school founded in 1414, is magnificently situated above the River Wear overlooked by Durham Cathedral and aims at all-round excellence. Facilities for both work and play are first rate. Since 1977 a physics block, sports centre, theatre, classroom block, a new girls' house and a CDT centre have been built leading to considerable success, both academic and sporting. Girls accepted in sixth form.

Hurworth House School

Address: The Green, Hurworth on Tees, Darlington, Co Durham DL2 2AD
Telephone: 0325 620745
Head: Mr G.N. Burgess

Age range: 4-13
No. of pupils: 130
Scholarships:
Religion: Non-denominational

Fees per term
Day: £810-£1370
Weekly board: -
Full board: -

Boy ● Girl ○ Co-ed ○
Day ● Week ○ Board ○

Hurworth House is now a day-only school operating on a full five day per week basis. Hurworth House serves the Darlington-Teesside area and is delightfully situated in the village of Hurworth. Its premises combine the charm of a Georgian domestic building with the educational efficiency of modern teaching buildings and ample sports fielsd and facilities.

Polam House School *

Address: Grange Road, Darlington, Co Durham DL1 5PA
Telephone: 0325 463383
Head: Mrs H C Hamilton

Age range: 3-18
No. of pupils: 500
Scholarships: Yes
Religion: Non-denominational

Fees per term
Day: £241-£1277
Weekly board: -
Full board: £2110-£2610

Boy ○ Girl ○ Co-ed ●
Day ● Week ○ Board ●

For further information and a prospectus, please contact the school.

St Anne's High School

Address: Wolsingham, Bishop Aukland, Durham DL13 3AL
Telephone: 0388 527298
Head: Sister M Michael

Age range: Boys 4-16
No. of pupils: 220
Scholarships:
Religion: Roman Catholic

Fees per term
Day: £700-£735
Weekly board: -
Full board: -

Boy ● Girl ● Co-ed ○
Day ● Week ○ Board ○

For further information and a prospectus, please contact the school. Boys 4-11, girls 4-16.

ESSEX

ESSEX 151

Alleyn Court Preparatory School

Address: 3 Imperial Avenue,
Westcliff-on-Sea, Essex
SS0 8ND
Telephone: 0702 343702

Heads: Mr S Bishop, Mr P Green

Age range: 3-13
No. of pupils: 299
Scholarships: Yes
Religion: Church of England

Fees per term
Day: £495-£1370
Weekly board: -
Full board: -

● ○ ○
Boy Girl Co-ed
● ○ ○
Day Week Board

Throughout the school pupils learn to live as members of a community while developing their individual personalities in a happy and structured enivironment. Old boys make an outstanding contribution to local and national life: there are two present M.P.s, a member of the House of Lords, a novelist of international renown, a prize winning playwrite and internationals in rugby, soccer, hockey and cricket.

Avon House

Address: 490 High Road,
Woodford Green, Essex
IG8 0PN
Telephone: 081 504 1749

Principal: Mrs S Ferrari

Age range: 3-11
No. of pupils: 300
Scholarships:
Religion: Non-denominational

Fees per term
Day: -£696
Weekly board: -
Full board: -

○ ○ ●
Boy Girl Co-ed
● ○ ○
Day Week Board

Further information available from the school.

Bancroft's *

Address: Woodford Green,
Essex IG8 0RF

Telephone: 081 505 4821

Head: Dr P C D Southern

Age range: 7-18
No. of pupils: 900
Scholarships: Yes
Religion: Church of England

Fees per term
Day: £1230-£1640
Weekly board: -
Full board: -

○ ○ ●
Boy Girl Co-ed
● ○ ○
Day Week Board

Bancroft's is a fully co-educational day school taking pupils from 7 through to A Level and university entrance. Its academic standards are high with generous provision of scholarships and other awards. About 80 per cent of pupils proceed to degree courses and most others enter employment in the City or other professional openings. The programme of extra-curricular activities is exceptional.

Beehive Preparatory School

Address: 233 Beehive Lane,
Redbridge, Ilford, Essex
IG4 5ED
Telephone: 081 550 3224

Head: Mr C Beasant

Age range: 4-11
No. of pupils: 85
Scholarships:
Religion: Non-denominational

Fees per term
Day: -£440
Weekly board: -
Full board: -

○ ○ ●
Boy Girl Co-ed
● ○ ○
Day Week Board

The Beehive Preparatory School offers a traditional academic curriculum to a small annual intake to ensure individual attention and a quality education in classes averaging 17-18 children. The morning session, from 9.00am to 1.00pm, is devoted entirely to academic work concentrating on mathematics and English. The afternoon offers optional activities including art/craft, football, multisports, design technology etc.

Bell House School

Address: Brizes Park, Ongar Road, Kelvedon Hatch, Brentwood, Essex CM15 0DG
Telephone: 0277 373613

Head: Mrs B J Morton

Age range: 3-16
No. of pupils: 275
Scholarships: Yes
Religion: Non-denominational

Fees per term
Day: £575-£1427
Weekly board: -
Full board: -

● Boy ● Girl ○ Co-ed
● Day ○ Week ○ Board

For further details please contact the school.

Braeside School

Address: 130 High Road, Buckhurst Hill, Essex IG9 5SD
Telephone: 081 504 1133

Head: Mrs C Naismith

Age range: 4-16
No. of pupils: 250
Scholarships:
Religion: Non-denominational

Fees per term
Day: £720-£955
Weekly board: -
Full board: -

○ Boy ● Girl ○ Co-ed
● Day ○ Week ○ Board

Braeside is an independent day school for girls aged 4 to 16. The senior school which has a large wooded garden and tennis court is adjacent to Epping Forest. The majority of its leavers continue their studies on A Level courses at local sixth forms. The junior school is on a separate site, providing classes from kindergarten to 10 years.

Brentwood School * p738

Address: Ingrove Road, Brentwood, Essex CM15 8AS
Telephone: 0277 212271

Head: Mr J A E Evans MA

Age range: 7-18
No. of pupils: 1100
Scholarships: Yes
Religion: Church of England

Fees per term
Day: £1658-
Weekly board: -
Full board: £2904-

● Boy ● Girl ○ Co-ed
● Day ○ Week ● Board

The school takes boys (boarding and day) from 7-19. Day girls are accepted at 11, (there is a separate girls' section up to GCSE) and at sixth form co-educational.

Chigwell School *

Address: High Road, Chigwell, Essex IG7 6QF
Telephone: 081 500 1396

Head: Mr A R M Little

Age range: 7-18
No. of pupils: 630
Scholarships: Yes
Religion: Church of England

Fees per term
Day: £1255-£1873
Weekly board: £1868-£2696
Full board: £1912-£2848

● Boy ● Girl ○ Co-ed
● Day ● Week ● Board

The school grounds extend to some 70 acres of fields and woodlands and the combination of space, attractive buildings and grounds all help to create high standards of self discipline and a happy atmosphere. The standard of work is notably high and this is shown by the consistently high pass rates in excess of 90% obtained at GCSE and A Level over a number of years. Girls are accepted in the sixth form.

ESSEX 153

Colchester Boys' High School

Address: Wellesley Road, Colchester, Essex
Telephone: 0206 573389

Age range: 4-16
No. of pupils: 400
Scholarships: Yes
Religion: Church of England

Fees per term
Day: £810-£990
Weekly board: -
Full board: -

● Boy ○ Girl ○ Co-ed
● Day ○ Week ○ Board

Head: Mr A L Moore

Founded in 1882 this ISAI accredited school prepares boys for GCSE from a broad-based and varied curriculum. A wide range of academic subjects is covered in the preparatory and junior departments, and throughout the school there are small class sizes, an excellent staffing ratio and a full selection of sporting and extra-curricular activities.

College St Pierre

Address: 16 Leigh Road, Leigh-on-Sea, Essex
Telephone: 0702 74164

Age range: 3-11
No. of pupils: 100
Scholarships:
Religion:

Fees per term
Day: £360-£635
Weekly board: -
Full board: -

○ Boy ○ Girl ● Co-ed
● Day ○ Week ○ Board

Head: Mr G E F Bragard

Preparation in small classes for the selective test at 11+. French taught in all classes. Sports: football, netball, cricket, tennis and swimming.

Coopersale Hall School

Address: Flux's Lane, Off Stewarts Green Road, Epping, Essex CM16 7PE
Telephone: 0992 577133

Age range: 3-11
No. of pupils: 190+
Scholarships:
Religion: Non-denominational

Fees per term
Day: £550-£690
Weekly board: -
Full board: -

○ Boy ○ Girl ● Co-ed
● Day ○ Week ○ Board

Principal: Mr N Hagger MA

For further information please contact the school.

Cranbrook College

Address: Mansfield Road, Ilford, Essex IG1 3BD
Telephone: 081 554 1757

Age range: 4-18
No. of pupils: 230
Scholarships:
Religion: Non-denominational

Fees per term
Day: £720-£820
Weekly board: -
Full board: -

● Boy ○ Girl ○ Co-ed
● Day ○ Week ○ Board

Head: Mr G T Reading

A primary and secondary day-school for boys, founded in 1896. The main entry age is 4, and there are a few places every year at 11. Boys are admitted at other ages if and when vacancies exist. Admission is subject to an entrance test.

Crowstone School p662

Address: 121/123 Crowstone Road, Westcliff-on-Sea, Essex SS0 8LH
Telephone: 0702 346758

Head: Mr J P Thayer

Age range: 3-16
No. of pupils: 300
Scholarships:
Religion: Non-denominational

Fees per term
Day: £550-£1075
Weekly board: -
Full board: -

○ ○ ● Boy Girl Co-ed
● ○ ○ Day Week Board

An independent day school (mixed) 3-16 years. Offers a thorough grounding in mathematics, English and reading, forming the base of a wide curriculum. Plus, (optional) a revolutionary new education system, exclusive to Crowstone: EDUFAX - worksheets by fax, (various subjects) for 'extra homework,' school holidays etc., available every day of the year. (On offer to non-pupils also).

Daiglen School

Address: 68 Palmerston Road, Buckhurst Hill, Essex IG9 5LG
Telephone: 081 504 7108

Head: Mr D Wood

Age range: 4-11
No. of pupils: 148
Scholarships:
Religion: Christian

Fees per term
Day: £720-£720
Weekly board: -
Full board: -

● ○ ○ Boy Girl Co-ed
● ○ ○ Day Week Board

The school aims to provide a good traditional education for boys between the ages of 4+ and 11+ and to develop each boy to the full extent of his ability. The curriculum is arranged to meet the requirements of the County and various entrance examinations to public schools at the age of 11 years.

Dame Johane Bradbury's School

Address: Ashdon Road, Saffron Walden, Essex CB10 2AL
Telephone: 0799 522348

Head: Mrs R M Rainey

Age range: 4-11
No. of pupils: 262
Scholarships:
Religion: Non-denominational

Fees per term
Day: £670-£890
Weekly board: -
Full board: -

○ ○ ● Boy Girl Co-ed
● ○ ○ Day Week Board

A high teacher/pupil ratio is maintained and the fully qualified staff, augmented by ancilliary helpers work as a team to provide a stimulating, educational environment. The curriculum is designed to give a broad, general education of a high standard. Creative potential is encouraged in a wide variety of areas and the school has a successful programme for sports.

Eastcourt Independent School

Address: 1 Eastwood Road, Goodmayes, Essex IG3 8UW
Telephone: 081 590 5472

Head: Mrs C Redgrave

Age range: 4-11
No. of pupils: 300
Scholarships:
Religion:

Fees per term
Day: £550-
Weekly board: -
Full board: -

○ ○ ● Boy Girl Co-ed
● ○ ○ Day Week Board

Co-educational day school (4-11 years). Entry at 4+ follows informal screening; at all other ages by entrance tests (Maths, English, Reasoning). We aim to provide an education whereby each child reaches his/her full potential. Children prepare for entrance examinations to a variety of schools. Details of recent results available on request.

ESSEX 155

Elm Green Preparatory School

Address: Parsonage Lane,
Little Baddow, Chelmsford,
Essex CM3 4SU
Telephone: 0245 225230

Age range: 4-11
No. of pupils: 200
Scholarships:
Religion: Non-denominational

Fees per term
Day: -£890
Weekly board: -
Full board: -

○ ○ ● Boy Girl Co-ed
● ○ ○ Day Week Board

Headmistress: Mrs E L Mimpriss CertEd

For further information and prospectus please contact the headmistress, Mrs E L Mimpriss at the address above.

Eton House School

Address: Southchurch Lawn,
Wakering Road,
Southend-on-Sea, Essex
Telephone: 0702 582553

Age range: 6-16
No. of pupils: 110
Scholarships:
Religion: Christian

Fees per term
Day: £830-£1049
Weekly board: -
Full board: -

● ○ ○ Boy Girl Co-ed
● ○ ○ Day Week Board

Head: Mr R N Slocombe

Set in 15 acres of parkland with sports field. Day school for boys up to GCSE level. Established 1898. The school will be merging with Alleyn Court Preparatory School in late 1993 on its present site.

New facilities include technology and computing suite. Sports hall ready in late 1993.

Felsted Preparatory School

Address: Felsted, Dunmow,
Essex CM6 3JL

Telephone: 0371 820252

Age range: 4-13
No. of pupils: 170
Scholarships: Yes
Religion: Church of England

Fees per term
Day: £750-£2000
Weekly board: -
Full board: -£2730

○ ○ ● Boy Girl Co-ed
● ○ ● Day Week Board

Head: Mr P Pomphrey

Curriculum: Common Entrance and public school scholarships, with strong music, art, CDT and computing departments. Wide range of sporting and out-of-class activities. Entry requirements: By school report and individual assessment. Guaranteed entry to the senior school available for 11+ candidates. Felsted is a day and boarding preparatory school set in rural Essex, but within easy reach of several large towns

Felsted School *

Address: Dunmow, Essex
CM6 3LL

Telephone: 0371 820258

Age range: 4-18
No. of pupils: 600
Scholarships: Yes
Religion: Church of England

Fees per term
Day: £750-£2675
Weekly board: -
Full board: £2530-£3390

● ● ● Boy Girl Co-ed
● ○ ● Day Week Board

Head: Mr E J H Gould

Established in 1564, this HMC and IAPS affiliated school for boys, which introduced girls into the VIth Form in 1972, will be opening a co-educational pre-preparatory department in Autumn 1992, followed by the admission of girls from the ages of 8-13 from Autumn 1993. In Autumn 1994 girls will be introduced below the Sixth Form in the Senior School.

Friends' School *

Address: Saffron Walden, Essex CB11 3FB

Telephone: 0799 25351

Head: Mr S H Evans

Age range: 7-18
No. of pupils: 280
Scholarships: Yes
Religion: Quaker

Fees per term
Day: £1070-£1790
Weekly board: -
Full board: £2830-£2830

○ Boy ○ Girl ● Co-ed
● Day ● Week ● Board

Friends' School offers a well balanced education for the individual child. Founded in 1702 by the Religious Society of Friends (Quakers) the school aims to offer opportunities for intellectual, aesthetic, physical and moral development within a cohesive and supportive community.

Gidea Park College

Address: 2 Balgores Lane, Gidea Park, Romford, Essex RM2 5JR
Telephone: 0708 740381

Head: Mr M Powell

Age range: 3-11
No. of pupils: 185
Scholarships:
Religion: Church of England

Fees per term
Day: £817-
Weekly board: -
Full board: -

○ Boy ○ Girl ● Co-ed
● Day ○ Week ○ Board

Established 70 years ago, standing in almost an acre of its own grounds, the co-educational school for 3 to 11 year olds has an excellent reputation for its high levels of academic attainment. Traditional and dedicated teaching methods, together with a friendly caring and disciplined atmosphere, combine to ensure the continuation of those high academic standards.

Glenarm College

Address: 20 Coventry Road, Ilford, Essex IG1 4QR
Telephone: 081 554 1760

Head: Mrs V Mullooly

Age range: 4-11
No. of pupils: 130
Scholarships:
Religion: Non-denominational

Fees per term
Day: £730-£730
Weekly board: -
Full board: -

● Boy ● Girl ○ Co-ed
● Day ○ Week ○ Board

For further information and a prospectus, please contact the school.

Gosfield School

Address: Halstead Road, Gosfield, Halstead, Essex CO9 1PF
Telephone: 0787 474040

Head: Mr R Boyd

Age range: 4-18
No. of pupils: 130
Scholarships:
Religion: Church of England

Fees per term
Day: £915-£1315
Weekly board: -
Full board: £1915-£2355

○ Boy ○ Girl ● Co-ed
● Day ○ Week ● Board

A co-educational boarding and day school for pupils from 4-18 in a 100 acre rural setting. Gosfield is run on family lines, with strong pastoral care and a good range of weekend and evening activities and sports. A positive caring atmosphere and understanding teaching produces personable adolescents with excellent academic results.

Heathcote School

Address: Eves Corner, Danbury, Chelmsford, Essex CM3 4QB
Telephone: 0245 223131

Head: Mr R H Greenland

Age range: 3-11
No. of pupils: 220
Scholarships:
Religion: Non-denominational

Fees per term
Day: -£825
Weekly board: -
Full board: -

Boy ○ Girl ○ Co-ed ●
Day ● Week ○ Board ○

Heathcote School was established in 1935 and is situated in the centre of Danbury, opposite the village green. A member of ISAI and accredited by the ISJC, the school, which offers a pre-school teaching nursery, provides a well rounded education of a high academic standard whilst also fostering the virtues of courtesy, consideration and self discipline. Children are successfully prepared for public school.

Herington House School

Address: Mount Avenue, Hutton, Brentwood, Essex CM13 2NS
Telephone: 0277 211595

Head: Mrs A Wiseall

Age range: 3-11
No. of pupils: 150
Scholarships:
Religion: Non-denominational

Fees per term
Day: £460-£980
Weekly board: -
Full board: -

Boy ● Girl ● Co-ed ○
Day ● Week ○ Board ○

The school was founded in 1936 as a private day school, and after full inspection by the Independent Schools Joint Committee was awarded accreditation in 1984. Most children enter the school at three and three quarters. The school aims to give its pupils a good all-round education, firmly based on a core curriuclum but as diverse in subject matter as can be reasonably expected in a primary school. Boys 3-7, girls 3-11.

Holmwood House School

Address: Lexden, Colchester, Essex CO3 5ST
Telephone: 0206 574305

Head: Mr H S Thackray

Age range: 4-14
No. of pupils: 350
Scholarships: Yes
Religion: Non-denominational

Fees per term
Day: £1158-£2047
Weekly board: -
Full board: £2360-£2640

Boy ○ Girl ○ Co-ed ●
Day ● Week ○ Board ●

Holmwood House, founded 1922, provides a secure, closeknit and active background in which boys and girls work, play games, develop responsibility and pursue hobbies. Facilities include 25 acres of sports fields, 5 squash courts, 2 covered tennis courts, indoor swimming pool, large music school, stage with computerised lighting/sound systems, library/resource centre and computer room. Range of scholarships.

Ilford Usuline High School

Address: Moorland Road, Ilford, Essex IG1 4QS
Telephone: 081 554 1995

Head: Miss J Reddington

Age range: 11-18
No. of pupils: 400
Scholarships: Yes
Religion: Roman Catholic

Fees per term
Day: -£1293
Weekly board: -
Full board: -

Boy ○ Girl ● Co-ed ○
Day ● Week ○ Board ○

The school sees each student as an individual with her own strengths and potential and given every opportunity to develop these to the full. A broad and balanced curriculum including the National Curriculum is offered leading to a wide range of subjects at GCSE and Advanced Level. Academic results are excellent with many students going on to higher education.

Jacques Hall Foundation

Address: Harwich Road, Bradfield, Manningtree, Essex CO11 2XW
Telephone: 0255 870311

Head: Mr T Lee

Age range: 11-18
No. of pupils: 19
Scholarships:
Religion: Church of England

Fees per term
Day: -
Weekly board: -
Full board: £12922-

Boy ○ Girl ○ Co-ed ●
Day ○ Week ○ Board ●

An independent therapeutic community for emotionally damaged adolescents who have experienced emotional deprivation, physical and sexual abuse, compounded by failed foster family placements and mainstream education. The educational programme adheres to the National Curriculum, with small tutorial groups of 4 or 5 students added to which are individual therapeutic programmes.

Landry School

Address: Whites Hill, Stock, Ingatestone, Essex CM4 9QD
Telephone: 0277 840338

Head: Miss E Prior

Age range: 4-8
No. of pupils: 10
Scholarships:
Religion: Non-denominational

Fees per term
Day: £350-
Weekly board: -
Full board: -

Boy ○ Girl ○ Co-ed ●
Day ● Week ○ Board ○

For further information and a prospectus, please contact the school.

Littlegarth School

Address: Dedham, Colchester, Essex CO7 6HJ
Telephone: 0206 323196

Head: Mrs ML Harvey

Age range: 2-11
No. of pupils: 130
Scholarships:
Religion: Non-denominational

Fees per term
Day: £250-£805
Weekly board: -
Full board: -

Boy ○ Girl ○ Co-ed ●
Day ● Week ○ Board ○

Formal teaching and careful discipline within a structured syllabus ensure excellent standards of achievement, including French and computers from 4 and a half. Pupils are well prepared for entry into senior schools of all types. Many musical, sporting and recreational activities are available during and after school and pupils perform in termly concerts and plays. Children with learning difficulties recieve extra tuition.

Loyola Preparatory School

Address: 103 Palmerston Road, Buckhurst Hill, Essex IG9 5NH
Telephone: 081 504 7372

Head: Mr P G M Nicholson

Age range: 4-11
No. of pupils: 180
Scholarships:
Religion: Roman Catholic

Fees per term
Day: -£875
Weekly board: -
Full board: -

Boy ● Girl ○ Co-ed ○
Day ● Week ○ Board ○

Loyola caters for boys from the ages of 4-11. It aims at realising each students potential whether at scholarship level, entrance to senior independent school level or at a level consistent with the successful transfer into the maintained sector either through the 11+ or otherwise. Each class of twenty five boys will have its own class teacher back up with ancillary help.

ESSEX 159

Maldon Court Preparatory School

Address: Silver Street, Maldon, Essex CM9

Telephone: 0621 853529

Head: Mr A G Sutton

Age range: 4-11
No. of pupils: 126
Scholarships:
Religion: Non-denominational

Fees per term
Day: £835-
Weekly board: -
Full board: -

Boy ○ Girl ○ Co-ed ●
Day ● Week ○ Board ○

Maldon Court prepares children for independent and maintained schools. It works to the National Curriculum and independent schools' entrance requirements. Games played are association football, hockey, netball, squash, racquet ball and swimming (all year). There is an active parent's association, separately constituted and registered as a charity.

New Hall School

Address: Chelmsford, Essex CM3 3HT

Telephone: 0245 467588

Head: Sister Margaret Mary

Age range: 11-18
No. of pupils: 490
Scholarships: Yes
Religion: Roman Catholic

Fees per term
Day: £2054-
Weekly board: £3207-
Full board: £3207-

Boy ○ Girl ● Co-ed ○
Day ● Week ● Board ●

An independent catholic school for girls aged 11-18 which welcomes girls of other traditions. Entrance is by interview, exam and report. Scholarships and awards available. Facilities include a new preforming arts centre, 6 science laboratories, new business studies, new home economics area, arts and crafts, spacious grounds and playing fields.

Oaklands School

Address: 8 Albion Hill, Loughton, Essex IG10 4RA

Telephone: 081 508 3517

Head: Mrs M A Hagger

Age range: 3-11
No. of pupils: 235
Scholarships:
Religion: Anglican

Fees per term
Day: £695-£918
Weekly board: -
Full board: -

Boy ○ Girl ○ Co-ed ●
Day ● Week ○ Board ○

For further information and a prospectus, please contact the school. Boys 3-7, girls 3-11.

Oxford House

Address: 2-4 Lexden Road, Colchester, Essex CO3 3NE

Telephone: 0206 576686

Head: Mr R P Spendlove

Age range: 2-11
No. of pupils: 125
Scholarships:
Religion: Non-denominational

Fees per term
Day: £450-£895
Weekly board: -
Full board: -

Boy ○ Girl ○ Co-ed ●
Day ● Week ○ Board ○

Founded in 1959, Oxford House is accredited by the ISJC. The school aims to help children to develop their full potential in readiness for senior schools, encouraging high standards in behaviour and manners as well as in academic achievement. The atmosphere is very happy and friendly - 'Joy in Achievement' - is the school motto.

Park School for Girls

Address: 20 Park Avenue, Ilford, Essex IG1 4RS

Telephone: 081 554 2466

Head: Mrs N E O'Brien

Age range: 7-18
No. of pupils: 226
Scholarships: Yes
Religion: Non-denominational

Fees per term
Day: £765-£995
Weekly board: -
Full board: -

○ ● ○
Boy Girl Co-ed
● ○ ○
Day Week Board

For further information and a prospectus, please contact the school.

Queensland Preparatory School

Address: 100 Crowstone Road, Westcliffe-on-Sea, Essex SS0 8LQ

Telephone: 0702 340664

Principal: Miss R G Waltham

Age range: 4-11
No. of pupils: 47
Scholarships:
Religion: Non-denominational

Fees per term
Day: £400-
Weekly board: -
Full board: -

○ ○ ●
Boy Girl Co-ed
● ○ ○
Day Week Board

For further information and a prospectus, please contact the school.

Raphael

Address: 35 Junction Road, Romford, Essex RM1 3QS

Telephone: 0708 741262

Head: Mr P A Roberts BSc(Hons)

Age range: 4-16
No. of pupils: 140
Scholarships: Yes
Religion: Christian

Fees per term
Day: £965-£1180
Weekly board: -
Full board: -

○ ○ ●
Boy Girl Co-ed
● ○ ○
Day Week Board

Raphael School is a co-educational day school for pupils aged 4-16. Situated in central Romford, easily accessible by public transport, Raphael offers small class sizes and individual attention. From Infants to GCSE students, an atmosphere of care and community exists, allied with firm but fair discipline and academic and sporting competition.

Springfield PNEU

Address: Stondon Road, Ongar, Essex CM5 9RG

Telephone: 0277 362945

Head: Mrs S G M Jeans-Jakobson

Age range: 3-13
No. of pupils: 152
Scholarships:
Religion: Non-denominational

Fees per term
Day: £500-£1100
Weekly board: -
Full board: -

○ ○ ●
Boy Girl Co-ed
● ○ ○
Day Week Board

Springfield was founded by the principal in 1956. It is affiliated to the Parents National Education Union which was founded by Charlotte Mason. Reading is the first priority, and training is given in all other subjects including English grammar and spelling, traditional and modern mathematics, appreciation of art and music, science and computer studies, French and German.

ESSEX 161

St Anne's School

Address: 154 New London Road, Chelmsford, Essex CM2 0AW
Telephone: 0245 353488

Head: Mrs G Healey

Age range: 4-11
No. of pupils: 140
Scholarships:
Religion:

Fees per term
Day: £640-£780
Weekly board: -
Full board: -

● Boy ● Girl ● Co-ed
● Day ○ Week ○ Board

The curriculum is designed to meet the needs of young children, providing them with the means to develop their mental and physical skills, creative ability and confidence. The children's intellectual progress is balanced by musical, artistic and cultural learning.

St Aubyn's (Woodford Green) School Ltd

Address: Bunces Lane, Woodford Green, Essex IG8 9DU
Telephone: 081 504 1577

Head: Mr H H Colley

Age range: 4-13
No. of pupils: 230
Scholarships:
Religion: Non-denominational

Fees per term
Day: £1044-£1187
Weekly board: -
Full board: -

● Boy ○ Girl ○ Co-ed
● Day ○ Week ○ Board

For further information and a prospectus, please contact the school.

St Cedd's School

Address: Maltese Road, Chelmsford, Essex CM1 2PB
Telephone: 0245 354380

Head: Dr S A Foster

Age range: 4-11
No. of pupils: 333
Scholarships:
Religion: Non-denominational

Fees per term
Day: £760-£875
Weekly board: -
Full board: -

○ Boy ○ Girl ● Co-ed
● Day ○ Week ○ Board

St Cedd's Educational Trust Ltd has a sound academic reputation obtaining scholarships and bursaries to senior independent schools and also preparing candidates for the 11+ and the Essex grammar schools with commendable success each year. A wide curriculum is followed and the school is well equipped for art, French, science, drama, music, computer studies and physical activities.

St Hilda's School p662

Address: 15 Imperial Avenue, Westcliffe-on-Sea, Essex SS0 8NE
Telephone: 0702 344542

Head: Mrs V M Tunnicliffe

Age range: 3-16
No. of pupils: 260
Scholarships:
Religion: Non-denominational

Fees per term
Day: £682-£838
Weekly board: -
Full board: -

○ Boy ● Girl ○ Co-ed
● Day ○ Week ○ Board

St Hilda's is situated in a large Edwardian building in a quiet residential area of the town within easy walking distance of the buses and trains. The school attaches great importance to offering a caring environment and is renowned for its academic excellence and sporting achievements as well as its reputation in music and the arts.

St John's School

Address: Stock Road,
Billericay, Essex CM12 0AR

Telephone: 0277 623070

Head: Mr R C Woods

Age range: 4-16
No. of pupils: 380
Scholarships: Yes
Religion: Church of England

Fees per term
Day: £815-£1123
Weekly board: -
Full board: -

Boy ○ Girl ○ Co-ed ●
Day ● Week ○ Board ○

The School is situated in eight acres of grounds overlooking parkland which includes extra sports fields and an indoor swimming pool. The School provides a traditional education encompassing firm discipline and academic excellence.

St Margaret's Preparatory School

Address: Gosfield Hall Park,
Gosfield, Essex CO9 1SE

Telephone: 0787 472134

Head: Mr G R Williams

Age range: 4-13
No. of pupils: 155
Scholarships:
Religion: Non-denominational

Fees per term
Day: £765-£920
Weekly board: -
Full board: -

Boy ○ Girl ○ Co-ed ●
Day ● Week ○ Board ○

Pupils are taught in small classes according to their ability and age. The basic 3Rs predominate for the first years. A full range of subjects begins around 7; French (including time spent in France) around 8 and Latin around 10. Drama, music, art and sport are encouraged throughout the school. Common Entrance is taken at the appropriate ages.

St Mary's Hare Park School

Address: South Drive, Gidea
Park, Romford, Essex
RM2 6HH

Telephone: 0708 761220

Head: Mrs J Guilford

Age range: 3-11
No. of pupils: 180
Scholarships:
Religion: Catholic

Fees per term
Day: £635-
Weekly board: -
Full board: -

Boy ○ Girl ○ Co-ed ●
Day ● Week ○ Board ○

St Mary's Hare Park School is run on traditional lines for girls to age 11 and boys to age 7. The school curriculum concentrates on the basics of language development, mathematics, art and craft, physical education, music, French and religious education. There is a fully equipped computer room and pupils are able to acquire keyboard skills and benefit from computer-based tuition in several subjects.

St Mary's School p663

Address: Lexden Road,
Colchester, Essex CO3 3RB

Telephone: 0206 572544

Head: Mrs G M G Mouser MPhil

Age range: 4-16
No. of pupils: 600
Scholarships:
Religion: Non-denominational

Fees per term
Day: £765-£1075
Weekly board: -
Full board: -

Boy ○ Girl ● Co-ed ○
Day ● Week ○ Board ○

Throughout the school each girl is encouraged to develop her personality and academic potential as fully as possible, and a broadly based curriculum is followed until the 4th year seniors, when a little more specialisation is necessary, to cater for GCSE courses. The forms are not streamed: setting is arranged as necessary. Optional extras include lessons in woodwind, brass, violin, piano, and speech and drama.

St Michael's School

Address: 198 Hadleigh Road, Leigh-on-Sea, Essex SS9 2LP

Telephone: 0702 78719

Head: Mrs S V Stokes

Age range: 3-11
No. of pupils: 270
Scholarships:
Religion: Church of England

Fees per term
Day: £665-£700
Weekly board: -
Full board: -

Boy ○ Girl ○ Co-ed ●
Day ● Week ○ Board ○

St Michael's is a happy, Christian school where children are encouraged to develop as individuals, with a responsibility to the community. We follow the National Curriculum and also prepare pupils for scholarship, Common Entrance, the County 11+ etc. French is taught from age 5. We have a strong orchestra. Facilities include a chapel, swimming pool, gym and computer area.

St Nicholas

Address: Hillingdon House, Old Harlow, Essex CM17 0NJ

Telephone: 0279 429910

Head: Mr G W Brant

Age range: 4-16
No. of pupils: 280
Scholarships: Yes
Religion: Christian

Fees per term
Day: £595-£1225
Weekly board: -
Full board: -

Boy ○ Girl ○ Co-ed ●
Day ● Week ○ Board ○

St Nicholas is an independent co-educational day school providing excellent facilities for 280 pupils from 4-16 years. Situated in a delightful rural location in Old Harlow, St Nicholas is committed to retaining the best traditions of a small caring school setting the highest standards in academic, sporting and creative endeavour, whilst encouraging personal achievement and responsibility in all pupils.

St Phillip's Priory New School

Address: 178 New London Road, Chelmsford, Essex CM2 0AR
Telephone: 0245 284907

Head: Sister Elizabeth OSM

Age range: 4-11
No. of pupils: 190
Scholarships:
Religion:

Fees per term
Day: -
Weekly board: -
Full board: -

Boy ○ Girl ○ Co-ed ●
Day ● Week ○ Board ○

For further information and a prospectus, please contact the school.

St Philomena's School

Address: Hadleigh Road, Frinton-on-Sea, Essex CO13 9HQ
Telephone: 0255 674492

Head: Mrs B Buck CertEd

Age range: 4-11
No. of pupils: 100
Scholarships:
Religion: Roman Catholic

Fees per term
Day: £440-£440
Weekly board: -
Full board: -

Boy ● Girl ● Co-ed ○
Day ● Week ○ Board ○

St Philomena's is a Catholic independent day school open to children of all denominations from the age of 4 to 11. With a small pupil-to-teacher ratio, every endeavour is made in developing a sense of self-discipline, courtesy and individuality whilst steering each child's gifts and skills towards academic successes so necessary for today's secondary education.

Thorpe Hall School

Address: Thorpe Hall Avenue, Thorpe Bay, Essex SS1 3RD

Telephone:

Head:

Age range: 3-16
No. of pupils: 340
Scholarships:
Religion:

Fees per term
Day: -
Weekly board: -
Full board: -

Boy ○ / Girl ○ / Co-ed ●
Day ● / Week ○ / Board ○

For further information and a prospectus, please contact the school.

Ursuline Preparatory School

Address: Belmont House, Rose Bank, Rose Valley, Brentwood, Essex CM14 4HX

Telephone: 0277 227152

Head: Mrs H Brown

Age range: 3-11
No. of pupils: 90
Scholarships:
Religion: Roman Catholic

Fees per term
Day: £450-£775
Weekly board: -
Full board: -

Boy ○ / Girl ● / Co-ed ○
Day ● / Week ○ / Board ○

The Ursuline Preparatory School is a small Independent Day School for girls providing a sound Catholic, social and academic education. It stands in its own spacious grounds and is in close proximity to Brentwood Town Centre and Railway Station. Girls are prepared for public examinations. A full extra-curricular programme is available.

Widford Lodge

Address: Widford Road, Chelmsford, Essex CM2 9AN

Telephone: 0245 352581

Head: Mr H C Witham

Age range: 4-13
No. of pupils: 180
Scholarships:
Religion:

Fees per term
Day: -
Weekly board: -
Full board: -

Boy ● / Girl ○ / Co-ed ○
Day ● / Week ● / Board ○

For further information and a prospectus, please contact the school.

Woodcroft School †

Address: Whitakers Way, Loughton, Essex IG10 1SQ

Telephone:

Principal:

Age range: 2-11
No. of pupils: 18
Scholarships:
Religion:

Fees per term
Day: -
Weekly board: -
Full board: -

Boy ○ / Girl ○ / Co-ed ●
Day ● / Week ○ / Board ○

For further information and a prospectus, please contact the school.

Woodford Green Preparatory School

Address: Glengall Road,
Snakes Lane, Woodford
Green, Essex IG8 0BQ
Telephone: 081 504 5045

Age range: 3-11
No. of pupils: 400
Scholarships:
Religion:

Fees per term
Day: -
Weekly board: -
Full board: -

Boy ○ Girl ○ Co-ed ●
Day ● Week ○ Board ○

Head: Mr D G Kidd

For further information and a prospectus, please contact the school.

GLOUCESTERSHIRE

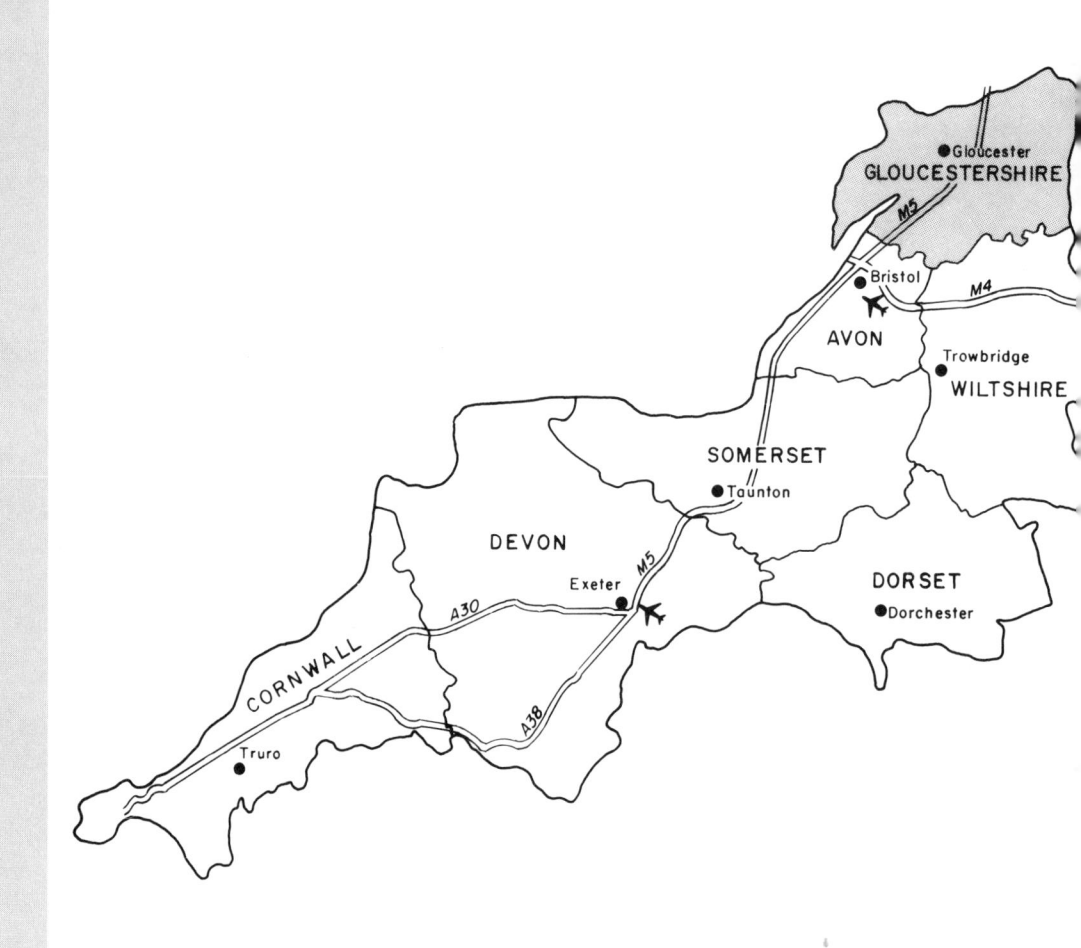

The Abbey School

Address: Church Street,
Tewkesbury, Gloucestershire
GL20 5PD
Telephone: 0684 294460

Head: Mr J H Milton

Age range: 4-13
No. of pupils: 100
Scholarships: Yes
Religion: Church of England

Fees per term
Day: £795-£1595
Weekly board: £1910-£2245
Full board: -

Boy ○ Girl ○ Co-ed ●
Day ● Week ● Board ○

Day and weekly boarding preparatory school for boys and girls aged 4-13 set in the heart of Tewkesbury. Small classes, well qualified staff and individual attention ensure happy children and high standards. Particularly strong music and art departments. Chorister scholarships for boys aged 8+. Choristers have no weekend or holiday commitments.

Airthrie School with Hillfield Dyslexia Trust

Address: 27/29 Christchurch Road, Cheltenham, Gloucestershire
Telephone: 0242 512837

Head: Mrs A E Sullivan

Age range: 3-11
No. of pupils: 185
Scholarships:
Religion: Church of England

Fees per term
Day: £674-£791
Weekly board: -
Full board: -

Boy ○ Girl ○ Co-ed ●
Day ● Week ○ Board ○

Airthrie is a long established preparatory school for children aged 3-11 years. It has an excellent reputation for high academic standards and successful application to senior schools after Common Entrance and similar examinations. Groups are small and a very friendly, homely atmosphere pervades. Every pupil receives attention and is encouraged to achieve excellence in all aspects of a very broad curriculum.

Beaudesert Park p663

Address: Minchinhampton, Gloucestershire GL6 9AF

Telephone: 0453 832072

Head: Mr J C P Keyte

Age range: 4-13
No. of pupils: 240
Scholarships:
Religion: Church of England

Fees per term
Day: £890-£1782
Weekly board: £2422-
Full board: £2422-

Boy ○ Girl ○ Co-ed ●
Day ● Week ● Board ●

The school is set in beautiful grounds. Classes are small and staff are concerned with the all-round development of each child, balancing academic achievement with artistic and cultural accomplishments and outdoor pursuits. Facilities include an indoor heated swimming pool, large sports hall and an information technology department. An extremely wide range of clubs and activities are available.

Berkhampstead School

Address: Pittville Circus Road, Cheltenham, Gloucestershire GL52 2PZ
Telephone: 0242 523263

Head: Mr W R Marsh

Age range: 3-11
No. of pupils: 270
Scholarships: Yes
Religion: Church of England

Fees per term
Day: £610-£1010
Weekly board: -
Full board: -

Boy ○ Girl ○ Co-ed ●
Day ● Week ○ Board ○

This school has long had an outstanding reputation for academic and musical success, winning many scholarships. Many children also move forward each year to the grammar schools.

Bredon School

Address: Pull Court, Bushley, Tewkesbury, Gloucestershire GL20 6AH
Telephone: 0684 293156

Head: Mr M Caplin

Age range: 5-18
No. of pupils: 310
Scholarships:
Religion: Church of England

Fees per term
Day: £920-£2000
Weekly board: £2460-£3440
Full board: £2520-£3500

Boy ○ Girl ○ Co-ed ●
Day ● Week ● Board ●

The National Curriculum is offered at all key stages, from 5 to 16. Post-16 education, comprising both academic (A, A/S Level) and vocational (BTEC 1st and National Diplomas, NCVQ Agriculture, etc.).

Teacher/pupil ratio is 1:7 with small classes (10-12). Selection according to potential, not just attainment, with learning support available if required. A sound reputation and outstanding achievements.

Brightlands School

Address: Church Road, Newnham-on-Severn, Gloucestershire GL14 1AS
Telephone: 0594 516210

Head: Mr P L Gray

Age range: 3-13
No. of pupils: 120
Scholarships: Yes
Religion: Church of England

Fees per term
Day: £795-£1610
Weekly board: £1595-£1895
Full board: -

Boy ○ Girl ○ Co-ed ●
Day ● Week ● Board ○

Brightlands is situated in the attractive town of Newnham-on-Severn on the edge of the beautiful Royal Forest of Dean, overlooking the River Severn. We have a first class academic, music and artistic record, with small classes and a warm, family atmosphere together with strong links with the local church. The excellent facilities include a heated swimming pool, squash courts and many sporting outlets.

Cheltenham College

Address: Bath Road, Cheltenham, Gloucestershire GL53 7LD
Telephone: 0242 513540

Head: Mr P D V Wilkes

Age range: 13-18
No. of pupils: 557
Scholarships: Yes
Religion: Church of England

Fees per term
Day: £2755-
Weekly board: -
Full board: £3645-

Boy ● Girl ● Co-ed ○
Day ● Week ○ Board ●

Cheltenham College is a boarding and day school for boys, with one hundred girls in the sixth form. It enjoys an outstanding reputation in the fields of science, technology, sport and music, and is fortunate to be situated in the most beautiful town in England. For details of scholarships, which are awarded to outstanding candidates in academic, musical, artistic and sporting fields, please contact the headmaster's secretary.

Cheltenham College Junior School p664

Address: Thirlestaine Road, Cheltenham, Gloucestershire GL53 7AB
Telephone: 0242 522697

Head: Mr N I Archdale

Age range: 7-13
No. of pupils: 270
Scholarships: Yes
Religion: Church of England

Fees per term
Day: £1995-
Weekly board: -
Full board: £2575-

Boy ● Girl ○ Co-ed ○
Day ● Week ○ Board ●

Cheltenham College Junior School is set in fine grounds on its own site adjacent to Cheltenham College. The boys follow a very full and well resourced curriculum leading to CE and PSS examinations. The boys also achieve an extremely high standard in all aspects of music as well as partaking in a wide range of sports. Both boarders and day boys are also provided with a great range of after school activities.

The Cheltenham Ladies' College * p740

Address: Bayshill Road, Cheltenham, Gloucestershire GL50 3EP
Telephone: 0242 520691

Age range: 11-18
No. of pupils: 849
Scholarships: Yes
Religion: Christian

Fees per term
Day: £2140-£2140
Weekly board: -
Full board: £3370-£3370

○ Boy ● Girl ○ Co-ed
● Day ○ Week ● Board

Head: Miss E Castle

Cheltenham Ladies' College was founded in 1853 and provides an education for girls on Christian lines. There has been a continuing programme of development and modernisation and there are excellent facilities for music, art, drama and sport as well as a very broad curriculum. There are 11 boarding houses and 3 daygirl houses.

Cotswold Chine Home School †

Address: Stroud, Gloucestershire GL6 9AG
Telephone: 0453 832398

Age range: 10-16
No. of pupils: 42
Scholarships:
Religion: Christian

Fees per term
Day: -
Weekly board: -
Full board: -

○ Boy ○ Girl ● Co-ed
○ Day ○ Week ● Board

Head: Mr C Troy

A Rudolf Steiner special school catering for children with EBD and MLD. For further deails please contact the school.

Dean Close Junior School

Address: Lansdown Road, Cheltenham, Gloucestershire GL51 6QS
Telephone: 0242 512217

Age range: 4-13
No. of pupils: 250
Scholarships: Yes
Religion: Church of England

Fees per term
Day: £750-£1765
Weekly board: -
Full board: -£2580

○ Boy ○ Girl ● Co-ed
● Day ○ Week ● Board

Head: Mr I Ferguson

Dean Close Junior School (IAPS) is an independent co-educational boarding/day school of 235 pupils for 4+ to 13+. Most of the pupils move on to Dean Close School for their secondary education after taking scholarships or Common Entrance. A caring, sharing community with a family atmosphere in the firmly based Christian school, having ample facilities for all forms of physical and cultural recreation.

Dean Close School

Address: Shelbourne Road, Cheltenham, Gloucestershire GL51 6HE
Telephone: 0242 522640

Age range: 13-18
No. of pupils: 440
Scholarships: Yes
Religion: Church of England

Fees per term
Day: -£2450
Weekly board: -
Full board: -£3500

○ Boy ○ Girl ● Co-ed
● Day ○ Week ● Board

Head: Mr C J Bacon

Strong emphasis is placed on personal faith, mutual respect, service, integrity, friendship and the need to discover and develop individual talents. We endeavour to find and enhance these talents, whether they are creative, intellectual or athletic, employing the skills of a versatile and professional staff and our extensive facitlities. We expect to see self-discipline, leadership and use of personal initiative.

The Dormer House PNEU School

Address: High Street, Moreton-in-Marsh, Gloucestershire GL56 0AD
Telephone: 0608 50758

Head: Ms D A A Trembath

Age range: 2-11
No. of pupils: 167
Scholarships:
Religion:

Fees per term
Day: -
Weekly board: -
Full board: -

- Co-ed
- Day

For further information and a prospectus, please contact the school.

Hatherop Castle School

Address: Cirencester, Gloucestershire GL7 3NB

Telephone: 0285 750206

Head: Mr P Easterbrook BEd

Age range: 2-18
No. of pupils: 200
Scholarships: Yes
Religion: Church of England

Fees per term
Day: £700-£1200
Weekly board: -£2100
Full board: -£2200

- Boy, Girl
- Day, Week, Board

For further information and a prospectus, please contact the school. Boys 2-18, girls 2-13

Hopelands

Address: 38 Regent Street, Stonehouse, Gloucestershire GL10 2AO
Telephone: 0453 822164

Head: Mrs B J Janes

Age range: 3-11
No. of pupils: 55
Scholarships:
Religion:

Fees per term
Day: £485-£725
Weekly board: -
Full board: -

- Co-ed
- Day

A well established small independent day school with a friendly family atmosphere and excellent academic record; catering for boys and girls from nursery through to 11+, Common Entrance and entry to competitive state schools.

Ingleside PNEU School

Address: The Beeches, Cirencester, Gloucestershire

Telephone: 0285 654046

Head: Mrs M L Selby

Age range: 4-11
No. of pupils: 90
Scholarships:
Religion: Non-denominational

Fees per term
Day: £540-£600
Weekly board: -
Full board: -

- Co-ed
- Day

The school is co-educational preparing pupils for Common Entrance at 11+. Children are encouraged to work hard and behave well.

GLOUCESTERSHIRE 171

The King's School

Address: Pitt Street,
Gloucester, Gloucestershire
GL1 2BG
Telephone: 0452 521251

Head: Mr P R Lacey

Age range: 4-18
No. of pupils: 584
Scholarships: Yes
Religion: Church of England

Fees per term
Day: £442-
Weekly board: -
Full board: -£1068

○ ○ ●
Boy Girl Co-ed
● ○ ●
Day Week Board

Throughout its history the school has produced leaders in church, state and county affairs and has sought to provide a first class liberal education within the context of the Christian faith, although people of all faiths are equally welcomed and valued. The curriculum is very broad and there is a wealth of extra-curricualr activities, clubs and societies to join.

Kitebrook House School

Address: Moreton-in-Marsh,
Gloucestershire GL56 0RP

Telephone: 060 874350

Head: Mrs A McDermott

Age range:
No. of pupils: 180
Scholarships:
Religion: Non-denominational

Fees per term
Day: £450-£920
Weekly board: -£2060
Full board: -

○ ○ ○
Boy Girl Co-ed
● ● ○
Day Week Board

Schools aim has always been to make school a vital part of a child's ordinary life - not a strange and a separate world. The main aim is to provide a happy and secure environment in which each individual child may flourish. Secure and confident children are able - given skilled help and high expectations - to fulfil their potential.

New Barns School †

Address: Church Lane,
Toddington, Gloucestershire
GL54 5DH
Telephone: 0242 621200

Head:

Age range: 7-13
No. of pupils: 28
Scholarships:
Religion: Non-denominational

Fees per term
Day: -
Weekly board: -
Full board: -

○ ○ ●
Boy Girl Co-ed
○ ○ ●
Day Week Board

For details of fees, further information and a prospectus, please contact the school.

Oakley Hall

Address: Cirencester,
Gloucestershire GL7 1TU

Telephone: 0285 653891

Head: Mr R F B Letts

Age range: 7-14
No. of pupils: 100
Scholarships: Yes
Religion: Church of England

Fees per term
Day: £1725-£1725
Weekly board: -
Full board: £2275-£2275

● ● ○
Boy Girl Co-ed
● ○ ●
Day Week Board

A family school in 17 acres of well-equipped grounds on the outskirts of Cirencester offering excellent academic and extra-curricular standards and individual attention.

Querns School

Address: Querns Lane,
Cirencester, Gloucestershire
GL7 1RL
Telephone: 0285 652953

Age range: 4-11
No. of pupils: 115
Scholarships:
Religion: Church of England

Fees per term
Day: £500-£700
Weekly board: -
Full board: -

Boy ○ Girl ○ Co-ed ●
Day ● Week ○ Board ○

Head: Mrs M Paine

Querns School is situated in its own beautiful grounds in the heart of the Cotswold town of Cirencester. We prepare all children for entrance examinations to both independent senior schools and local secondary schools. We pay great attention to good manners and self discipline and encourage self motivation in learning whilst keeping a happy family atmosphere.

Rendcomb College *

Address: Cirencester,
Gloucestershire GL7 7HA

Telephone: 0285 831213

Age range: 11-18
No. of pupils: 250
Scholarships: Yes
Religion: Church of England

Fees per term
Day: £2082-£2526
Weekly board: -
Full board: £2634-£3192

Boy ○ Girl ○ Co-ed ●
Day ● Week ○ Board ●

Head: Mr J N Tolputt

In its beautiful Cotswold setting, Rendcomb combines the friendliness of a small school with excellent academic standards. Boarding accommodation is superb; every pupil from the fifth form upwards has a single, spacious study bedroom. Pupils gifted in sport and the creative arts are especially welcome; the atmosphere is one of care and encouragement.

Richard Pate School

Address: Southern Road,
Leckhampton, Gloucester,
Gloucestershire GL53 9RP
Telephone: 0242 522086

Age range: 3-11
No. of pupils: 280
Scholarships:
Religion: Christian

Fees per term
Day: £388-£896
Weekly board: -
Full board: -

Boy ○ Girl ○ Co-ed ●
Day ● Week ○ Board ○

Head: Mr E L Rowland

The Richard Pate School has a fine academic record and fully prepares children in a happy, caring environment for whatever secondary schools are ultimately chosen for them. Although the school began in 1946, it has occupied an eleven and a half acre semi-rural site, on the southern outskirts of Cheltenham, since 1987.

Rose Hill

Address: Alderley,
Wotton-under-Edge,
Gloucestershire GL12 7QT
Telephone: 0453 843196

Age range: 3-13
No. of pupils: 140
Scholarships: Yes
Religion: Church of England

Fees per term
Day: £780-£1840
Weekly board: £1840-£2440
Full board: £1840-£2440

Boy ○ Girl ○ Co-ed ●
Day ● Week ● Board ●

Head: Mr R C G Lyne-Pirkis

Situated in the glorious Cotswold countryside, Rose Hill School exists to provide the highest level of educational care and development possible for our children. We believe in the pursuit of excellence, in fair discipline, good manners and, above all, in making school fun. We pride ourselves in having the most flexible approach to boarding that you will find anywhere in the UK. Come and see us soon.

GLOUCESTERSHIRE 173

Selwyn p665

Address: Matson House,
Matson Lane, Gloucester,
Gloucestershire GL4 9DY
Telephone: 0452 305663

Head: Mr A J Beatson

Age range: 3-18
No. of pupils: 370
Scholarships: Yes
Religion: Church of England

Fees per term
Day: £650-£1525
Weekly board: £1675-£2525
Full board: £1825-£2675

● Boy ● Girl ○ Co-ed
● Day ● Week ● Board

Selwyn — a small friendly school with co-educational nursery and junior department (3-11). Senior school for girls (11-18) day pupils and boarders. Academic reputation with emphasis on individual all-round development. Recent major developments include a new junior department, music rooms, re-sited extended library, enhanced PE facilities, greatly increased investment in science and computing.

St Anthony's Convent School

Address: 93 Belle Vue Road,
Cinderford, Gloucestershire
GL14 2AA
Telephone: 0594 823558

Head: Sister M Celestine

Age range: 3-11
No. of pupils: 120
Scholarships:
Religion: Roman Catholic

Fees per term
Day: £450-£600
Weekly board: -
Full board: -

● Boy ● Girl ○ Co-ed
● Day ○ Week ○ Board

St Anthony's is an independent day school for girls and boys. It has high academic standards with 100% pass rate for grammar and other independent schools and scholarship examinations.

It also has a thriving nursery.

St Clotilde's School

Address: Lechlade Manor,
Lechlade, Gloucestershire
GL7 3BB
Telephone: 0367 52259

Head: Sister M Dominic Mazure

Age range: 3-18
No. of pupils: 195
Scholarships:
Religion: Roman Catholic

Fees per term
Day: £300-£1250
Weekly board: £1930-£2090
Full board: -

● Boy ● Girl ○ Co-ed
● Day ● Week ○ Board

St Clotilde's takes day boys from 3-8, day girls from 3-18 and weekly boarding girls from 9-18. Bright girls, girls whose first language is not English as well as those with learning difficulties, receive individual attention. We offer traditional values, friendly encouragement, small classes and excellent results in a tranquil country setting - a sound education from sandpit to university.

St Edward's School

Address: Ashley Road,
Charlton Kings, Cheltenham,
Gloucestershire GL52 6NT
Telephone: 0242 526697

Head: Mr A J Martin

Age range: 2-18
No. of pupils: 833
Scholarships: Yes
Religion: Roman Catholic

Fees per term
Day: £871-£1567
Weekly board: -
Full board: -

○ Boy ○ Girl ● Co-ed
● Day ○ Week ○ Board

St Edward's provides an excellent all-round education for pupils from kindergarten to A level. There is a Christian family atmosphere with the emphasis on developing each child's individual talents. The depth and breadth of the curriculum, with a high succes rate in external examinations, is complemented by a wide range of facilities in sports, creative arts and many after-school clubs.

St Joseph's School

Address: Nympsfield, Gloucestershire
Telephone:
Head:

Age range:
No. of pupils:
Scholarships:
Religion: Roman Catholic

Fees per term
Day: -
Weekly board: -
Full board: -

○ ○ ● Boy Girl Co-ed
● ○ ○ Day Week Board

For further information and a prospectus, please contact the school.

Upfield Preparatory School Ltd

Address: Upfield House, Paganhill, Stroud, Gloucestershire GL5 4AY
Telephone: 0453 764820
Head: Mr P S Harris

Age range: 3-14
No. of pupils: 100
Scholarships:
Religion: Church of England

Fees per term
Day: £345-£600
Weekly board: -
Full board: -

○ ○ ● Boy Girl Co-ed
● ○ ○ Day Week Board

Recently celebrating its 50th year the school offers remarkable value. It has excellent wide-ranging facilities and pupils prosper in small classes in a friendly, caring environment. In addition to a broad well structured curriculum the school provides a variety of extra subjects to interest today's child. Traditional methods are used and aims are clear. Academic expectations are high.

Westonbirt School p666

Address: Tetbury, Gloucestershire GL8 8QT
Telephone: 0666 880333
Head: Mrs G J Hylson-Smith

Age range: 11-18
No. of pupils: 280
Scholarships: Yes
Religion: Church of England

Fees per term
Day: £1905-
Weekly board: -
Full board: £2960-

○ ● ○ Boy Girl Co-ed
● ○ ● Day Week Board

Westonbirt is set in glorious surroundings in the Gloucestershire countryside, but close to motorways and easy access to Bath, Bristol, Cheltenham and airports. It caters for about 280 girls aged 11-18 and is fortunate to be able to offer small classes and careful fostering of individual talents. Both day girls and boarders are equally welcome.

Wycliffe College Junior School *

Address: Stonehouse, Gloucestershire GL10 2LD
Telephone: 0453 823233
Head: Mr M J Thompson

Age range: 4-13
No. of pupils: 300
Scholarships: Yes
Religion: Non-denominational

Fees per term
Day: £730-£1785
Weekly board: £1910-£2435
Full board: £1990-£2515

○ ○ ● Boy Girl Co-ed
● ● ● Day Week Board

The school combines a high academic standard with a broad spectrum approach involving pupils in art, drama, music and games. Individual achievement is fostered by a strong pastoral system. The school is set at the foot of the Cotswolds with easy access to major road and rail services.

Wynstones p666

Address: Church Lane,
Whaddon, Gloucester,
Gloucestershire GL4 0UF
Telephone: 0452 522475

Age range: 3-18
No. of pupils: 290
Scholarships:
Religion: Christian

Fees per term
Day: £760-£1070
Weekly board: £1403-£1713
Full board: £1660-£1970

Boy ○ Girl ○ Co-ed ●
Day ● Week ● Board ●

Wystones offers an education for life. It is part of a worldwide network - more than 500 strong and growing. Common to them all is Rudolf Steiner's approach to education: to awaken the potential of each child and to nourish the whole personality. A full range of GCSEs is offered, with A Levels for those going on to further education.

HAMPSHIRE

HAMPSHIRE 177

The Atherley School

Address: Hill Lane,
Southampton, Hampshire
SO9 1GR
Telephone: 0703 772898

Head: Mrs M E Williams BD

Age range: 4-18
No. of pupils: 440
Scholarships:
Religion: Non-denominational

Fees per term
Day: £425-£1248
Weekly board: -
Full board: -

○ ● ○
Boy Girl Co-ed
● ○ ○
Day Week Board

The school is situated near enough to the station and bus routes for children to travel from a distance. It belongs to the Church Schools Company and aims to develop every aspect of a girl's intellectual, physical, social and spiritual potential. The curriculum is broad based and academic so that most girls proceed to higher education. Sixth form bursaries.

Avonlea School

Address: 8 Broadshard Lane,
Ringwood, Hampshire
BH24 1RR
Telephone: 0425 473994

Head: Mrs C M Palomo

Age range: 3-11
No. of pupils: 85
Scholarships:
Religion: Non-denominational

Fees per term
Day: £380-£525
Weekly board: -
Full board: -

○ ○ ●
Boy Girl Co-ed
● ○ ○
Day Week Board

The aim of the school is to provide a sound and systematic education for all children, in a happy and caring environment. Development of each child's potential is fostered by the small classes and individual attention. All children are prepared for the relevant examinations to senior schools.

Bedales School * p738

Address: Petersfield,
Hampshire GU32 2DG

Telephone: 0730 263286

Head: Mr R E I Newton

Age range: 3-18
No. of pupils: 632
Scholarships: Yes
Religion: Non-denominational

Fees per term
Day: £582-£2708
Weekly board: -
Full board: £2797-£3778

○ ○ ●
Boy Girl Co-ed
● ○ ●
Day Week Board

Bedales was described in this year's 'Daily Telegraph' Schools' Guide as an 'exceptional co-educational school which is to be recommended for bright and motivated children of talent, who will flourish in its unusually happy atmosphere.'

Boundary Oak School

Address: Roche Court,
Fareham, Hampshire
PO17 5BL
Telephone: 0329 280955

Head: Mr R B Bliss

Age range: 3-13
No. of pupils: 220
Scholarships: Yes
Religion: Non-denominational

Fees per term
Day: £425-£1560
Weekly board: £1725-£2350
Full board: £1725-£2350

○ ○ ●
Boy Girl Co-ed
● ● ●
Day Week Board

Situated close by Junction 10 on the M26, Boundary Oak is an independent school accredited by ISJC. The grounds cover 22 acres which include tennis courts, games pitches, woodland, heated swimming pool and full facilities for a caring and friendly school environment. Children are prepared for entry to senior school by way of Common Entrance and scholarship.

Churcher's College *

Address: Petersfield, Hampshire GU31 4AS
Telephone: 0730 263033
Head: Mr G W Buttle MA

Age range: 11-18
No. of pupils: 572
Scholarships: Yes
Religion: Non-denominational

Fees per term
Day: £1480-
Weekly board: £2690-
Full board: £2740-

Boy ○ Girl ○ Co-ed ●
Day ● Week ● Board ○

Churcher's College is an independent, co-educational day and boarding school. The college offers a wide range of extra-curricular activities including a strong sporting element. A new classroom block, including a language laboratory, was completed in June 1990 and a new sports hall was opened in January 1992. Churcher's prides itself on its caring attitude to its pupils.

Convent of Our Lady of Providence School

Address: Anstey Lane, Alton, Hampshire GU34 2NG
Telephone: 0420 82070
Head: Mr F A Martin BA *Principal:* Rev Mother Madeleine de Jesus BA

Age range: 11-18
No. of pupils: 273
Scholarships:
Religion: Roman Catholic

Fees per term
Day: -£860
Weekly board: -
Full board: -

Boy ○ Girl ● Co-ed ○
Day ● Week ○ Board ○

One mile from Alton town centre and set in 18 acres, shared with the junior department, the senior school has 300 girls aged 11-19 and enjoys a reputation for academic excellence, regularly achieving a 90+% success rate at GCSE grades A-C and 100% with the small sixth form. Emphasis is placed on team sports, music and drama. Visitors to view this Christian school are very welcome.

Coxlease School †

Address: High Coxlease House, Clay Hill, Lyndhurst, Hampshire SO43 7DE
Telephone: 0703 283633
Head: Mr D G Hendley

Age range: 9-17
No. of pupils: 49
Scholarships:
Religion:

Fees per term
Day: -
Weekly board: -
Full board: £7800-

Boy ● Girl ○ Co-ed ○
Day ○ Week ○ Board ●

Residential special school providing for boys with educational, behavioural and emotional problems.

Daneshill School

Address: Stratfield Turgis, Basingstoke, Hampshire RG27 0AR
Telephone: 0256 882707
Head: Mr S V Spencer

Age range: 3-11
No. of pupils: 300
Scholarships:
Religion: Church of England

Fees per term
Day: £450-£1150
Weekly board: -
Full board: -

Boy ○ Girl ○ Co-ed ●
Day ● Week ○ Board ○

Daneshill is an IAPS co-educational school for pupils aged three to eleven years. Our aim is to give children every opportunity to develop their potential amidst a stimulating and friendly atmosphere. Whilst aiming to produce well-rounded individuals we are ever aware that we are laying both the moral and educational foundations that will equip our pupils for the future.

Ditcham Park School

Address: Petersfield, Hampshire GU31 5RN

Telephone: 0730 825659

Head: Mrs P M Holmes

Age range: 4-16
No. of pupils: 320
Scholarships: Yes
Religion: Non-denominational

Fees per term
Day: £955-£1535
Weekly board: -
Full board: -

○ Boy ○ Girl ● Co-ed
● Day ○ Week ○ Board

Ditcham Park has a reputation for being a friendly, purposeful school where children achieve excellent results and where individuals' needs and talents are considered important. It is in an outstandingly beautiful position on the South Downs.

Dunhurst School

Address: Alton Road, Petersfield, Hampshire GU32 2DP
Telephone: 0730 262984

Heads: Mr & Mrs M L Heslop

Age range: 8-13
No. of pupils: 175
Scholarships:
Religion: Non-denominational

Fees per term
Day: £1887-£2070
Weekly board: -
Full board: £2797-£3032

○ Boy ○ Girl ● Co-ed
● Day ○ Week ● Board

As the junior school to Bedales, Dunhurst has very different aims and objectives to most other preparatory schools. It is properly co-educational and has a relaxed and friendly atmosphere. Pupils do not sit Common Entrance examination. The curriculum is broad with considerable emphasis on creative studies, music and drama. Sound teaching of 'core' subjects is also a priority.

Durlston Court School

Address: Becton Lane, Barton on Sea, Hampshire BH25 7AQ
Telephone: 0425 610010

Head: Mr J T Seddon

Age range: 3-14
No. of pupils: 256
Scholarships: Yes
Religion: Church of England

Fees per term
Day: £400-£1720
Weekly board: -
Full board: £2430-

○ Boy ○ Girl ● Co-ed
● Day ○ Week ● Board

Durlston Court is situated in 26 acres of grounds, 800 metres from the sea and two miles from the beautiful New Forest. A happy caring atmosphere with strong traditions in music, art and sport combine with high academic results achieved in both open scholarships and Common Entrance each year. Bursaries available to Forces children.

Edinburgh House School

Address: Fernhill Lane, New Milton, Hampshire BH25 5SU
Telephone: 0425 611153

Head: Mr A R Leighton

Age range: 3-14
No. of pupils: 165
Scholarships: Yes
Religion: Non-denominational

Fees per term
Day: £910-£1760
Weekly board: -
Full board: -£2430

● Boy ○ Girl ○ Co-ed
● Day ○ Week ● Board

The school's philosophy is that learning should be fun and thus we aim to make lessons purposeful and enjoyable. Academic work comes first, but there are plenty of opportunities for art, music, drama, sport and other hobbies. We are a caring school-all members of staff are involved with the welfare of the boys, and the value of hard work and good behaviour are instilled at an early age.

Embley Park School

Address: Romsey, Hampshire SO51 6ZE

Telephone: 0794 512206

Head: Mr D F Chapman BA

Age range: 11-18
No. of pupils: 220
Scholarships: Yes
Religion: Church of England

Fees per term
Day: £1730-£1830
Weekly board: -
Full board: -£2995

Boy ● Girl ● Co-ed ○
Day ● Week ○ Board ●

A small school with small teaching groups in a magnificent rural setting with a large boarding element; a system of weekly tutorial supervision and a strong tradition of games and activities. 80% upper sixth entry to degree courses in 1992. Embley is an educational charity, its governors members of GBA and its head of SHMIS. Boys 11-18, girls 16-18.

Farleigh School

Address: Red Rice, Andover, Hampshire SP11 7PW

Telephone: 0264 710766

Head: Mr Murphy JE

Age range: 3-13
No. of pupils: 250
Scholarships:
Religion: Roman Catholic

Fees per term
Day: £370-£1710
Weekly board: £2442-£2442
Full board: £2442-£2442

Boy ○ Girl ○ Co-ed ●
Day ● Week ● Board ●

Children are successfully prepared for Common Entrance and for scholarships, where appropriate, in the usual subjects. Wide range of sports coached and many hobbies on offer. This is a very happy school. It prides itself on turning out well-adjusted children, making the fullest use of their talents without undue pressure.

Farnborough Hill *

Address: Farnborough, Hampshire GU14 8AT

Telephone: 0252 545197

Head: Sister E McCormack

Age range: 11-18
No. of pupils: 490
Scholarships: Yes
Religion: Roman Catholic

Fees per term
Day: £1256-
Weekly board: -
Full board: -

Boy ○ Girl ● Co-ed ○
Day ● Week ○ Board ○

The school is established in the beautiful home of the late Empress Eugénie of France to which the architect Adrian Gilbert Scott added a chapel and three school wings. Each pupil is valued for herself and helped to develop her gifts in the friendly, stable atmosphere of the school which is large enough to offer good educational facilities yet small enough to provide a sense of community.

Fernhill Manor School

Address: Fernhill Lane, New Milton, Hampshire BH25 5JL

Telephone: 0425 611090

Head Senior School: Rev A J Folks *Head Junior School:* Miss G Morris

Age range: 3-18
No. of pupils: 270
Scholarships: Yes
Religion: Church of England

Fees per term
Day: £380-£1545
Weekly board: £2020-£2315
Full board: £2245-£2425

Boy ○ Girl ● Co-ed ○
Day ● Week ● Board ●

Fernhill offers a broad and balanced modern curriculum. The Junior School prepares girls for Common Entrance and scholarships at 11+, whilst the Senior School prepeares girls for GCSE. English, French and mathematics are core subjects at GCSE and girls can take up to nine subjects. A full range of subjects is offered at GCSE and A Level courses are provided in most subjects.

Glenhurst School

Address: 16 Beechworth Road, Havant, Hampshire PO9 1AX
Telephone: 0705 484054

Head: Mrs E A Newman

Age range: 3-9
No. of pupils: 115
Scholarships:
Religion: Non-denominational

Fees per term
Day: £310-£415
Weekly board: -
Full board: -

○ Boy ○ Girl ● Co-ed
● Day ○ Week ○ Board

Co-educational pre-preparatory day school catering for children aged 3+ in kindergarten (mornings only in Autumn and Spring terms; full-time in Summer term) through to 9 years. Emphasis on small classes with attention to individual needs. Traditional approach to teaching within a happy, but disciplined environment. Modest fees. Prospectus available on request.

The Gregg School

Address: 13-19 Winn Road, Southampton, Hampshire SO2 1EJ
Telephone: 0703 671676

Head: Mr R D Hart

Age range: 11-16
No. of pupils: 250
Scholarships: Yes
Religion: Non-denominational

Fees per term
Day: -£1190
Weekly board: -
Full board: -

○ Boy ○ Girl ● Co-ed
● Day ○ Week ○ Board

The Gregg School is a co-educational school for pupils 11-16. Pupils are taught in small groups and enjoy studying in a friendly, happy atmosphere. A challenging range of extra-curricular activities develops resourcefulness, initiative and confidence.

The Grey House School

Address: Mount Pleasant, Hartley Wintney, Hampshire RG27 8PW
Telephone: 0252 842353

Head: Mrs E M Purse

Age range: 4-11
No. of pupils: 150
Scholarships:
Religion: Church of England

Fees per term
Day: £784-£995
Weekly board: -
Full board: -

○ Boy ○ Girl ● Co-ed
● Day ○ Week ○ Board

The school aims to give a broad balanced academic education within a happy atmosphere. An emphasis is also placed on courtesy and concern for others. Full opportunities are given for creative work, self-expression and individual development.

Highfield School

Address: Liphook, Hampshire GU30 7LQ
Telephone: 0428 722228

Head: Mr R M M Orr

Age range: 7-13
No. of pupils: 170
Scholarships:
Religion: Church of England

Fees per term
Day: £1675-£2025
Weekly board: -
Full board: £2650-

○ Boy ○ Girl ● Co-ed
● Day ○ Week ● Board

Highfield is a boarding school in an exceptionally beautiful area (and having an estate of 170 acres) where a limited number of local children may be day pupils to start with, but primarily boarding. Boys 7-9 years, girls 7-13. Full boarding from 7 years.

Holy Cross Junior School

Address: Stakes Hill,
Waterlooville, Portsmouth,
Hampshire PO7 7BP
Telephone: 0705 262352

Head: Mrs E Sweeney

Age range: 4-11
No. of pupils: 158
Scholarships:
Religion: Roman Catholic

Fees per term
Day: -£660
Weekly board: -
Full board: -

Boy ○ Girl ○ Co-ed ●
Day ● Week ○ Board ○

Pupils at Holy Cross receive careful religious and moral training, giving special attention to the development of personality and formation of character. The education received builds a solid foundation for secondary level study, covering all aspects of the National Curriculum with specialisation in music, PE, French and drama.

Hordle House School

Address: Cliff Road, Milford
on Sea, Lymington,
Hampshire SO41 0NW
Telephone: 0590 642104

Head: Mr J J Vernon

Age range: 3-13
No. of pupils: 211
Scholarships:
Religion: Non-denominational

Fees per term
Day: £450-£1860
Weekly board: -
Full board: -£2475

Boy ○ Girl ○ Co-ed ●
Day ● Week ● Board ●

The school is an educational trust with a board of governors. The school's freehold is owned by the trust. There are 17 acres, close to the sea, and within 3 miles of the New Forest. Additions to the buildings since 1981 include particularly good music, art and technology facilities. The school runs a minibus to and from Heathrow, Gatwick and Luton.

Inhurst House School

Address: Baughurst,
Basingstoke, Hampshire
RG26 5JJ
Telephone: 0734 813388

Head: Mrs A P Burnett

Age range: 3-11
No. of pupils: 100
Scholarships:
Religion: Non-denominational

Fees per term
Day: £480-£995
Weekly board: -
Full board: -

Boy ● Girl ● Co-ed ○
Day ● Week ○ Board ○

A small academically flourishing school with an excellent staff providing a strong all-round preparatory education. French is taught from the nursery upwards, computer instruction throughout the main school and a variety of instruments may be learned. Confident and well-mannered children go on to do well at their senior schools. Boys 3-8, girls 3-11.

King Edward VI School *

Address: Kellett Road,
Southampton, Hampshire

Telephone: 0703 704561

Head: Mr T R Cookson

Age range: 11-18
No. of pupils: 950
Scholarships: Yes
Religion: Non-denominational

Fees per term
Day: £1373-£1373
Weekly board: -
Full board: -

Boy ● Girl ● Co-ed ○
Day ● Week ○ Board ○

King Edward's is an independent day school for boys which takes girls in the sixth form. The school prepares pupils for university entrance and the professions. There is a wide range of cultural and sporting activities. 85% of pupils go on to degree courses at universities and polytechnics. Assisted places are available under the Government scheme.

La Sagesse Convent School

Address: Abbey House, Romsey, Hampshire SO51 8YB
Telephone: 0794 522320

Age range: 3-16
No. of pupils: 300
Scholarships: Yes
Religion: Roman Catholic

Fees per term
Day: £320-£865
Weekly board: -
Full board: -

● Boy ● Girl ○ Co-ed
● Day ○ Week ○ Board

Head: Sister T Cox

A small, friendly, caring community for pupils from 3 to 16. Pupils are encouraged to develop self-reliance as well as achieving their maximum potential at academic studies. Small numbers in classes ensure that each pupil is well known to every member of staff who can consequently give appropriate encouragement to students to give of their best. Boys 3-8, girls 3-16.

The Loddon †

Address: Wildmoor Lane, Sherfield-on-Loddon, Basingstoke, Hampshire RG27 0JD
Telephone:
Head:

Age range: 7-19
No. of pupils: 16
Scholarships:
Religion:

Fees per term
Day: -
Weekly board: -
Full board: -

○ Boy ○ Girl ● Co-ed
○ Day ○ Week ● Board

For further information and a prospectus, please contact the school.

Lord Wandsworth College *

Address: Long Sutton, Basingstoke, Hampshire RG25 1TB
Telephone:

Age range: 11-18
No. of pupils: 440
Scholarships: Yes
Religion: Non-Denominational

Fees per term
Day: £2000-
Weekly board: £2650-
Full board: £2650-

● Boy ○ Girl ● Co-ed
● Day ● Week ● Board

Head: Mr G A G Dodd

Lord Wandsworth College is an independenet school - for boys up to GCSE, thereafter for boys and girls. The school occupies a very attractive campus in north east Hampshire. Academic success is considered important as is involvement in a wide variety of other activities both cultural and athletic. Bursaries available for sons/daughters of widows, widowers and single parents.

Marycourt School

Address: 27 Crescent Road, Alverstoke, Gosport, Hampshire PO12 2DJ
Telephone: 0705 581766

Age range: 3-11
No. of pupils: 130
Scholarships:
Religion: Non-denominational

Fees per term
Day: £451-£544
Weekly board: -
Full board: -

○ Boy ○ Girl ● Co-ed
● Day ○ Week ○ Board

Head: Mrs M Crane

For further information and a prospectus, please contact the school.

Mayfield School

Address: 103 Anstey Road, Alton, Hampshire

Telephone: 0420 83105

Head: Mr T T Incles

Age range: 4-11
No. of pupils: 130
Scholarships: Yes
Religion: Non-denominational

Fees per term
Day: £803-£823
Weekly board: -
Full board: -

Boy ○ Girl ○ Co-ed ●
Day ● Week ○ Board ○

The basic aim of Mayfield School is solidly academic, set in a happy, friendly and busy atmosphere. The school's philosophy includes the pursuit of excellence and the development of the child's full potential. We have an excellent academic record, with an extremely high pupil success rate in all entrance examinations.

Mayville High School

Address: Kenilworth Lodge, St Simon's Road, Southsea, Hampshire PO5 2PE

Telephone: 0705 734847

Head: Mrs L M March

Age range: 3-16
No. of pupils: 250
Scholarships: Yes
Religion: Church of England

Fees per term
Day: £650-950
Weekly board: -
Full board: -

Boy ○ Girl ● Co-ed ○
Day ● Week ○ Board ○

We pride ourselves on our caring family atmosphere, believing that this is the environment in which children are most likely to fulfil their potential. Mayville offers small classes, a broad curriculum, French and Computers from age 4. An After School Service is available and from September 1992 our Dyslexic Unit will provide help for children with learning difficulties.

Meoncross Pre-school

Address: Burnt House, Stubbington, Fareham, Hampshire PO14 2EF

Telephone: 0329 668888

Head: Mrs P Bate BA

Age range: 3-5
No. of pupils: 52
Scholarships:
Religion: Non-denominational

Fees per term
Day: £528-1020
Weekly board: -
Full board: -

Boy ○ Girl ○ Co-ed ●
Day ● Week ○ Board ○

Hours: 8.00am to 6.00pm Monday to Friday. 50 weeks a year. Meoncross Pre-school provides a safe and happy learning environment for children aged 3-5 years, with access to the best facilities, resources and a qualified, caring staff. Children are encouraged in all aspects of reading, writing and number skills and also a wide range of structured curriculum activities.

Meoncross School (Infant & Junior Department)

Address: Burnt House, Stubbington, Fareham, Hampshire PO17 5AV

Telephone: 0329 662182

Head: Mr C Ford BEd

Age range: 4-11
No. of pupils: 260
Scholarships:
Religion: Non-denominational

Fees per term
Day: £800-£884
Weekly board: -
Full board: -

Boy ○ Girl ○ Co-ed ●
Day ● Week ○ Board ○

Entry: interview and test. Curriculum: the usual junior school subjects are taught plus French, science, art and craft, health education, nutrition and an introduction to information technology. After school activities: junior choir, ensemble, swim club, netball, football and rounders. Within a caring family school children are treated as individuals and provided with a sound education enabling them to use their abilities.

Meoncross Senior School

Address: Burnt House, Stubbington, Fareham, Hampshire PO14 2EF
Telephone: 0329 662182

Head: Mr C Ford BEd

Age range: 11-16
No. of pupils: 170
Scholarships: Yes
Religion: Non-denominational

Fees per term
Day: £1107-£1107
Weekly board: -
Full board: -

Co-ed
Day

Meoncross is a caring, family school with a strong emphasis on self-discipline. Academic standards are high and each pupil is treated as an individual. GCSEs are taken in 16 subjects. Pupils are encouraged to take full responsibility for their actions and to be aware of the needs of others. Sports taught include: athletics, basketball, cricket, cross-country, hockey, netball, lacrosse, squash, swimming, skiing and tennis.

Moreton House School

Address: The Spain, Petersfield, Hampshire
Telephone: 0730 263724

Head: Mr D Wolfe

Age range: 4-11
No. of pupils: 131
Scholarships:
Religion:

Fees per term
Day: £709-£746
Weekly board: -
Full board: -

Boy Girl Co-ed
Day

Moreton House is a co-educational day preparatory school situated close to the centre of Petersfield. It offers a broad but well structured and wide-ranging syllabus based on the national curriculum, and including French for the older children. Children are prepared for entrance examinations at 11+. There is a simple and practical school uniform.

Moyles Court School

Address: Moyles Court, Ringwood, Hampshire BH24 3NF
Telephone: 0425 472856

Head: Mr C A Coghill

Age range: 4-16
No. of pupils: 187
Scholarships: Yes
Religion: Church of England

Fees per term
Day: £690-£1325
Weekly board: £1825-£1825
Full board: £1950-£1950

Co-ed
Day Week Board

Moyles Court is a co-educational day/boarding school for children aged between 4 and 16. It is situated in lovely New Forest surroundings and is well equipped to educate pupils to a high standard. The dedicated and qualified staff ensure academic success and small classes mean that every child can be treated as an individual. The general atmosphere is friendly and conducive to learning and personal achievement.

Nethercliffe School

Address: Hatherley Road, Winchester, Hampshire
Telephone: 0962 854570

Head: Mr R F G Whitfield

Age range: 3-11
No. of pupils: 130
Scholarships:
Religion: Church of England

Fees per term
Day: £387-£992
Weekly board: -
Full board: -

Co-ed
Day

Nethercliffe is a friendly, caring school where boys and girls work together in small classes under experienced qualified staff. Pupils are prepared for entrance exams at 11+. We have a very high success rate. Academic, physical and personal development is encouraged through a balanced and stimulating curriculum, giving each child a chance to shine.

North Foreland Ladge p667

Address: Sherfield-on-Loddon, Basingstoke, Hampshire
Telephone: 0256 882431

Head: Miss D L Matthews

Age range: 11-18
No. of pupils: 189
Scholarships: Yes
Religion: Church of England

Fees per term
Day: -
Weekly board: -
Full board: £3200-£3200

Boy ● Girl ○ Co-ed ○
Day ○ Week ○ Board ●

The school is set in 90 acres of Parkland with easy access to the M4 and M3. Teaching groups are usually 12-16 and years are streamed. Girls take between 8-10 GCSE subjects and 3-4 A Levels. A large number continue on to university. The girls benefit from a happy and friendly environment, in which each girl is encouraged to achieve her full potential. A wide range of extra-curricular activities arranged for weekends and evenings.

Northcliffe School

Address: Grove Place, Nursling, Southampton, Hampshire SO1 9YL
Telephone: 0703 732406

Head: Mrs D P Duff-Mitchell

Age range: 3-11
No. of pupils: 220
Scholarships:
Religion: Church of England

Fees per term
Day: £545-£1690
Weekly board: -
Full board: -£2365

Boy ○ Girl ○ Co-ed ●
Day ● Week ○ Board ●

Traditional, co-educational, day and boarding school, 3-13 years. 40-50 boarders run as a large, happy familiy. Excellent academic results. Many and varied facilities include - two modern teaching blocks, new science laboratory, sports hall, all-weather playing surfaces. Discount on boarding fees for service families.

The Pilgrim's School

Address: 3 The Close, Winchester, Hampshire SO23 9LT
Telephone: 0962 854189

Head: Mr M E K Kefford MA DipEd

Age range: 8-13
No. of pupils: 180
Scholarships: Yes
Religion: Church of England

Fees per term
Day: -£1730
Weekly board: -
Full board: -£2360

Boy ● Girl ○ Co-ed ○
Day ● Week ○ Board ●

Boys' preparatory school (IAPS) for boarders and dayboys, incorporating the Choristers of Winchester Cathedral and the Quiristers of Winchester College, who receive choral scholarships to the value of half the boarding fee. Boys are prepared for the Common Entrance Examination and scholarships to senior independent schools and the Entrance Examination to Winchester College. Excellent facilities for music.

The Portsmouth Grammar School *

Address: High Street, Portsmouth, Hampshire PO1 2LN
Telephone: 0705 819125

Head: Mr A C V Evans

Age range: 5-18
No. of pupils: 1070
Scholarships: Yes
Religion: Non-denominational

Fees per term
Day: £805-£1270
Weekly board: -
Full board: -

Boy ○ Girl ○ Co-ed ●
Day ● Week ○ Board ○

The Portsmouth Grammar School is an independent co-educational school for pupils between the ages of 5 and 18. The Headmaster is a member of the Headmasters' Conference. The school enjoys an excellent academic reputation and offers a broad and flexible curriculum. At the same time it encourages pupils to participate in a wide range of sport and extra-curricular activities.

Portsmouth High School *

Address: 25 Kent Road,
Southsea, Hampshire PO5 3EG

Telephone: 0705 826714

Head: Mrs J M Dawtrey BA

Age range: 4-18
No. of pupils: 710
Scholarships:
Religion: Non-denominational

Fees per term
Day: £880-£1148
Weekly board: -
Full board: -

○ ● ○
Boy Girl Co-ed
● ○ ○
Day Week Board

For over a century this school has provided a broad education for girls. It attracts girls of ability from all backgrounds in a wide catchment area. Its ethos encourages hard work at all levels and its academic record is outstanding. Girls display their various talents in music, drama and sport. They benefit from an atmosphere in which they are stimulated by a highly qualified staff who ensure that each is valued as an individual.

Prince's Mead School

Address: 43 Edgar Road,
Winchester, Hampshire
SO23 9TN
Telephone: 0962 853416

Head: Mrs D Moore

Age range: 3-8
No. of pupils: 246
Scholarships: Yes
Religion: Church of England

Fees per term
Day: £400-£1395
Weekly board: -
Full board: -

● ● ○
Boy Girl Co-ed
● ○ ○
Day Week Board

The children are encouraged to develop their ability to the maximum in a friendly, lively atmosphere. Emphasis is placed on helping them acquire sound working habits and an enthusiastic enquiring approach, in preparation for their senior schools. The school has its own netball court and the playing field is nearby. Two scholarships may be awarded annually. Boys 3-8 years.

Ringwood Waldorf School

Address: Folly Farm Lane,
Pohley, Ringwood,
Hampshire BH24 2NN
Telephone: 0425 472664

Head: Chairman College of Teachers

Age range: 3-16
No. of pupils: 123
Scholarships:
Religion: Christian

Fees per term
Day: -
Weekly board: -
Full board: -

○ ○ ●
Boy Girl Co-ed
● ○ ○
Day Week Board

For further information and a prospectus, please contact the school.

Rockwood School

Address: Weyhill Road,
Andover, Hampshire
SP10 3AL

Telephone: 0264 352855
Head: Mrs S Hindle

Age range: 3-16
No. of pupils: 260
Scholarships: Yes
Religion: Church of England

Fees per term
Day: £700-£1200
Weekly board: -
Full board: £1925-£2170

● ● ○
Boy Girl Co-ed
● ○ ●
Day Week Board

Rockwood offers a broad, balanced education to day girls of 3-16, boarders from 7-16 and day boys to 11. Computers and modern languages are introduced from four years, eight acres of grounds give ample space for sport and the stimulating environment provides encouragement for each child to develop academic and creative strengths and fulfil his or her potential.

Rookesbury Park School

Address: Wickham, Hampshire PO17 6HT

Telephone: 0329 833108

Head: Miss L A Appleyard

Age range: 3-13
No. of pupils: 150
Scholarships:
Religion: Church of England

Fees per term
Day: £475-£1656
Weekly board: -
Full board: £2052-£2408

Boy ○ Girl ● Co-ed ○
Day ● Week ○ Board ●

An unrivalled setting with 14 acres overlooking farmland in the village of Wickham. A friendly and flourishing school with a newly established nursery department offering small classes and a balanced curriculum. Well equipped with science laboratory, swimming pool, tennis courts, athletics field, computer and technology rooms. Good preparation is provided for Common Entrance to all independent schools.

Rushmoor Independent School

Address: 40 Reading Road, Farnborough, Hampshire GU14 6NB

Telephone: 0252 544738

Head: Mrs J M Morrish BEd

Age range: 5-16
No. of pupils: 52
Scholarships:
Religion: Non-denominational

Fees per term
Day: £665-£835
Weekly board: -
Full board: -

Boy ○ Girl ○ Co-ed ●
Day ● Week ○ Board ○

For further information and a prospectus, please contact the school.

Rushmore Independent Nursery School

Address: 59 Southampton Street, Farnborough, Hampshire GU14 6BG

Telephone: 0252 541804

Head: Mrs I Paterson

Age range: 3-5
No. of pupils: 73
Scholarships:
Religion: Non-denominational

Fees per term
Day: £375-
Weekly board: -
Full board: -

Boy ○ Girl ○ Co-ed ●
Day ● Week ○ Board ○

For further information and a prospectus, please contact the school.

Salesian College *

Address: Reading Road, Farnborough, Hampshire GU14 6PA

Telephone: 0252 542919

Head: Rev Bro M Delmer

Age range: 11-18
No. of pupils: 510
Scholarships:
Religion: Roman Catholic

Fees per term
Day: £765-
Weekly board: -
Full board: -

Boy ● Girl ○ Co-ed ○
Day ● Week ○ Board ○

Founded in 1901, the aim of Salesian College is to form young people academically, culturally, physically and spiritually. To achieve this a friendly and respectful attitude exists between staff and pupils, providing an atmosphere conducive to good order, scholarship and self assurance. The pupils are encouraged to develop a strong sense of responsibility and a caring attitude.

Sandle Manor

Address: Fordingbridge, Hampshire

Telephone: 0425 653181

Head: Mr M D Barton

Age range: 3-13
No. of pupils: 230
Scholarships: Yes
Religion: Anglican

Fees per term
Day: -
Weekly board: -
Full board: -

Boy ○ Girl ○ Co-ed ●
Day ● Week ● Board ●

Sandle Manor School is an I.A.P.S. school, a charitable trust and owning its own freehold of thirty five acres, with over ten acres of level playing fields. Emphasis is given to traditional standards of honesty and good manners within a happy disciplined environment based on Christian ideals. Children go to leading independent schools.

Seafield School

Address: Westlands Grove, Portchester, Fareham, Hampshire PO16 9AA
Telephone: 0705 377158

Head: Mrs E G Jones

Age range: 3-7
No. of pupils: 60
Scholarships:
Religion: Non-denominational

Fees per term
Day: £380-£475
Weekly board: -
Full board: -

Boy ○ Girl ○ Co-ed ●
Day ● Week ○ Board ○

We are a small friendly co-educational day school in a village in Hampshire, serving the area between Portsmouth and Southampton. Established in 1954, six fully qualified staff provide a warm and caring environment. Good teaching practice and discipline ensure pupils easily achieve entrance to public schools. German, French and Spanish spoken to aid children of foreign nationals. Admission at pre-school stage.

The Sheiling School

Address: Ashley, Ringwood, Hampshire BH24 2EB

Telephone:

Head:

Age range: 6-19
No. of pupils:
Scholarships:
Religion:

Fees per term
Day: -
Weekly board: -
Full board: -

Boy ○ Girl ○ Co-ed ●
Day ○ Week ○ Board ○

A Camphill Rudolf Steiner for children in need of special care and understanding. For further information and a prospectus, please contact the school.

Sherborne House School

Address: Lakewood Road, Chandlers' Ford, Hampshire SO5 1EU
Telephone: 0703 252440

Head: Mrs S M Warner

Age range: 3-11
No. of pupils: 180
Scholarships:
Religion: Non-denominational

Fees per term
Day: £660-£800
Weekly board: -
Full board: -

Boy ○ Girl ● Co-ed ○
Day ● Week ○ Board ○

An independent girls' day preparatory school of about 170 acres with a co-educational pre-preparatory department and nursery. In four acres of wooded grounds between Winchester and Romsey. The school has high academic standards and the girls have won many scholarships to senior schools in recent years. Purpose built classrooms, computacabin, sports hall, art studio.

St Anne's

Address: 13 Milvil Road,
Lee-on-the-Solent, Hampshire

Telephone: 0705 550820

Head: Mrs J G Bottomley

Age range: 3-8
No. of pupils: 45
Scholarships:
Religion: All

Fees per term
Day: £380-£480
Weekly board: -
Full board: -

Boy ○ Girl ○ Co-ed ●
Day ● Week ○ Board ○

St Anne's is a well established pre-prep school where the expertise of the staff is directed exclusively towards children of primary age. Small classes permit individual attention by qualified and experienced staff.

St Benedict's Convent School p667

Address: Penton Lodge,
Andover, Hampshire SP11 0RD

Telephone: 0264 772291

Head: Sister Scholastica

Age range: 3-16
No. of pupils: 84
Scholarships: Yes
Religion: Roman Catholic

Fees per term
Day: £460-£900
Weekly board: -
Full board: £1700-£1900

Boy ● Girl ● Co-ed ○
Day ● Week ○ Board ●

Pupils are prepared for GCSE and Common Entrance examinations. Over 95% of our pupils go to further education. The well-being and happiness of our pupils is our primary cancern. Emphasis is placed on good manners, courtesy and consideration; we endeavour to educate in the true sense of the word, enabling each to reach their full potential. Children of all denominations are welcomed.

St John's College *

Address: Grove Road South,
Southsea, Portsmouth,
Hampshire PO6 3QN
Telephone:

Head: Rev Brother Cyril FSC

Age range: 8-18
No. of pupils:
Scholarships:
Religion: Roman Catholic

Fees per term
Day: -
Weekly board: -
Full board: -

Boy ● Girl ○ Co-ed ○
Day ● Week ○ Board ●

For further information and a prospectus, please contact the school.

St Mary's College

Address: 57 Midanbury Lane,
Bitterne Park, Southampton,
Hampshire SO9 4TE
Telephone: 0703 671267

Head: Rev Br Paul

Age range: 4-18
No. of pupils: 620
Scholarships:
Religion: Roman Catholic

Fees per term
Day: -
Weekly board: -
Full board: -

Boy ● Girl ○ Co-ed ○
Day ● Week ○ Board ○

For further information and a prospectus, please contact the school.

HAMPSHIRE 191

St Neot's School

Address: Eversley, Basingstoke, Hampshire RG27 0PN
Telephone: 0734 732118

Head: Mr R J Thorpe

Age range: 4-13
No. of pupils: 120
Scholarships:
Religion: Church of England

Fees per term
Day: -
Weekly board: -
Full board: -

○ ○ ● Boy Girl Co-ed
● ● ○ Day Week Board

For further information and a prospectus, please contact the school.

St Nicholas's School p668

Address: Branksomewood Road, Fleet, Hampshire GU13 8JT
Telephone: 0252 614864

Head: Mrs L G Smith

Age range: 4-18
No. of pupils: 440
Scholarships:
Religion: Church of England

Fees per term
Day: £470-£975
Weekly board: -
Full board: -

● ● ○ Boy Girl Co-ed
● ○ ○ Day Week Board

The school admits both girls and boys at 4 years - girls progress to senior house at 12. Boys are prepared for preparatory school and leave at 7. Senior house girls are prepared for GCSEA, A level and Scholarship Level and for entrance to universities and colleges of higher education. There is a wide range of optional, extra-curricular activities.

St Swithun's Junior School

Address: Winchester, Hampshire SO21 1HA
Telephone: 0962 852634

Head: Mrs V Lewis

Age range: 3-11
No. of pupils: 200
Scholarships:
Religion: Church of England

Fees per term
Day: £490-£1250
Weekly board: -
Full board: -

○ ○ ● Boy Girl Co-ed
● ○ ○ Day Week Board

Children are accepted into the nursery from the age of three years. Girls remain until they are eleven, and are prepared for entrance examinations, including Common Entrance, to independent senior schools. Boys stay with us until the ages of seven or eight and are prepared for entrance to preparatory schools.

St Swithun's School * p668, p751

Address: Winchester, Hampshire SO21 1HA
Telephone: 0962 861316

Head: Miss J E Jefferson

Age range: 11-18
No. of pupils: 440
Scholarships: Yes
Religion: Church of England

Fees per term
Day: £2000-
Weekly board: £3310-
Full board: £3310-

○ ● ○ Boy Girl Co-ed
● ● ● Day Week Board

The School occupies a fine site on the Downs to the east of Winchester, a mile from the centre of the city. A flexible, broadly-based, academic education is offered enabling girls to develop their potential. Entry is by Common Entrance or Scholarship examination in January and February. Details, including that of Sixth Form entry, are available from the school.

St Winifrid's School

Address: 50 Westwood Road, Southampton, Hampshire SO2 1DP
Telephone: 0703 557352

Age range: 4-11
No. of pupils: 148
Scholarships:
Religion:

Fees per term
Day: -
Weekly board: -
Full board: -

Boy ○ Girl ○ Co-ed ●
Day ● Week ○ Board ○

Head: Mr B Smith

For further information and a prospectus, please contact the school.

Stanbridge Earls School

Address: Stanbridge Lane, Romsey, Hampshire SO51 0ZS
Telephone: 0794 516777

Age range: 11-18
No. of pupils: 170
Scholarships:
Religion:

Fees per term
Day: -
Weekly board: -
Full board: -

Boy ○ Girl ○ Co-ed ●
Day ● Week ○ Board ●

Head: Mr H Moxon

For further information and a prospectus, please contact the school.

Stanley House School

Address: 108 St Michaels Road, Aldershot, Hampshire GU12 4JW
Telephone: 0252 23425

Age range: 3-7
No. of pupils: 30
Scholarships:
Religion:

Fees per term
Day: -
Weekly board: -
Full board: -

Boy ○ Girl ○ Co-ed ●
Day ● Week ○ Board ○

Head: Mrs J A Emberson

For further information and a prospectus, please contact the school.

The Stroud School

Address: Highwood House, Romsey, Hampshire
Telephone: 0794 513231

Age range: 3-13
No. of pupils: 330
Scholarships:
Religion: Church of England

Fees per term
Day: £390-£1550
Weekly board: -
Full board: -

Boy ○ Girl ○ Co-ed ●
Day ● Week ○ Board ○

Head: Mrs E Sanger-Davies

Stroud stands on the outskirts of Romsey in its own grounds of 20 acres, including playing fields, solar heated swimming pool, tennis courts, lawns and gardens. Main team games for boys are cricket, rugger and soccer, and girls cricket and netball. Both play hockey and tennis. Music and drama play an important part in the school, including a musical production annually.

HAMPSHIRE 193

Twyford School

Address: Twyford, Winchester, Hampshire SO21 1NW

Telephone: 0962 712269

Head: Mr P R D Gould

Age range: 3-13
No. of pupils: 250
Scholarships: Yes
Religion: Church of England

Fees per term
Day: £510-£1825
Weekly board: -
Full board: £2510-

Boy ○ Girl ○ Co-ed ●
Day ● Week ○ Board ●

This long established preparatory school lies in a delightful setting just south of Winchester. Fine modern facilities include ten classrooms and a superb combined sports hall and indoor heated swimming pool. A music school will be built shortly. Thanks to excellent staff, the school is happy and the academic record good; many sports and activities enjoyed. Good road and rail links.

Walhampton School *p752*

Address: Lymington, Hampshire SO41 5ZG

Telephone: 0590 672013

Head: Mr A W S Robinson

Age range: 4-13
No. of pupils:
Scholarships: Yes
Religion: Christian

Fees per term
Day: £930-£1970
Weekly board: -
Full board: £2580-£2580

Boy ○ Girl ○ Co-ed ●
Day ● Week ○ Board ●

Situated in spacious grounds overlooking the Solent and with excellent facilities, Walthampton aims to provide all children with a real breadth of education both in and out of the classroom. A lively, exciting boarding school education for boys and girls with limited places for day children.

West Downs School

Address: 54 Romsey Road, Winchester, Hampshire SO22 5DQ
Telephone:

Head:

Age range: 4-13
No. of pupils:
Scholarships:
Religion:

Fees per term
Day: -
Weekly board: -
Full board: -

Boy ○ Girl ○ Co-ed ●
Day ● Week ○ Board ●

For further information and a prospectus, please contact the school.

West Hill Park

Address: Titchfield, Fareham, Hampshire PO14 4BS

Telephone: 0329 842356

Head: Mr M A Elmitt

Age range: 3-13
No. of pupils: 250
Scholarships:
Religion: Church of England

Fees per term
Day: £420-£1720
Weekly board: -
Full board: -£2330

Boy ○ Girl ○ Co-ed ●
Day ● Week ○ Board ●

West Hill provides a continuous education from 3 to 13 years. Set in 30 acres, the school enjoys excellent facilities in a lively, vigorous, happy and caring community. Education is a three-way partnership, involving child, school and parents, and one of the strengths of West Hill is the interest, involvement and support that the parents show in the school.

Winchester College *

Address: College Street, Winchester, Hampshire SO23 9NA
Telephone: 0962 854328

Age range: 13-18
No. of pupils: 659
Scholarships:
Religion:

Fees per term
Day: -
Weekly board: -
Full board: -

● Boy ○ Girl ○ Co-ed
● Day ○ Week ● Board

Head: Mr J P Sabben-Clare

For further information and a prospectus, please contact the school.

Woodhill Preparatory School

Address: Brook Lane, Botley, Southampton, Hampshire SO3 2ER
Telephone: 0489 781112

Age range: 3-11
No. of pupils: 140
Scholarships:
Religion:

Fees per term
Day: -
Weekly board: -
Full board: -

○ Boy ○ Girl ● Co-ed
● Day ○ Week ○ Board

Head: Mr R Medway

For further information and a prospectus, please contact the school.

Woodhill School

Address: 61 Brownhill Road, Chandlers Ford, Hampshire SO5 2EH
Telephone: 0703 268012

Age range: 3-11
No. of pupils: 120
Scholarships:
Religion:

Fees per term
Day: -
Weekly board: -
Full board: -

○ Boy ○ Girl ● Co-ed
● Day ○ Week ○ Board

Head: Mrs M Dacombe

For further information and a prospectus, please contact the school.

Wykeham House p669

Address: East Street, Fareham, Hampshire PO16 0BW
Telephone: 0329 280178

Age range: 4-16
No. of pupils: 370
Scholarships: Yes
Religion: Anglican

Fees per term
Day: £459-£1131
Weekly board: -
Full board: -

○ Boy ● Girl ○ Co-ed
● Day ○ Week ○ Board

Head: Mrs C M Moore

Wykeham House seeks to encourage a high academic achievement by giving its pupils a sense of purpose and an appreciation of the value of sound and thorough work in a friendly, caring environment. A secure background is provided with attention being paid to the individual needs of each pupil.

HEREFORD AND WORCESTER

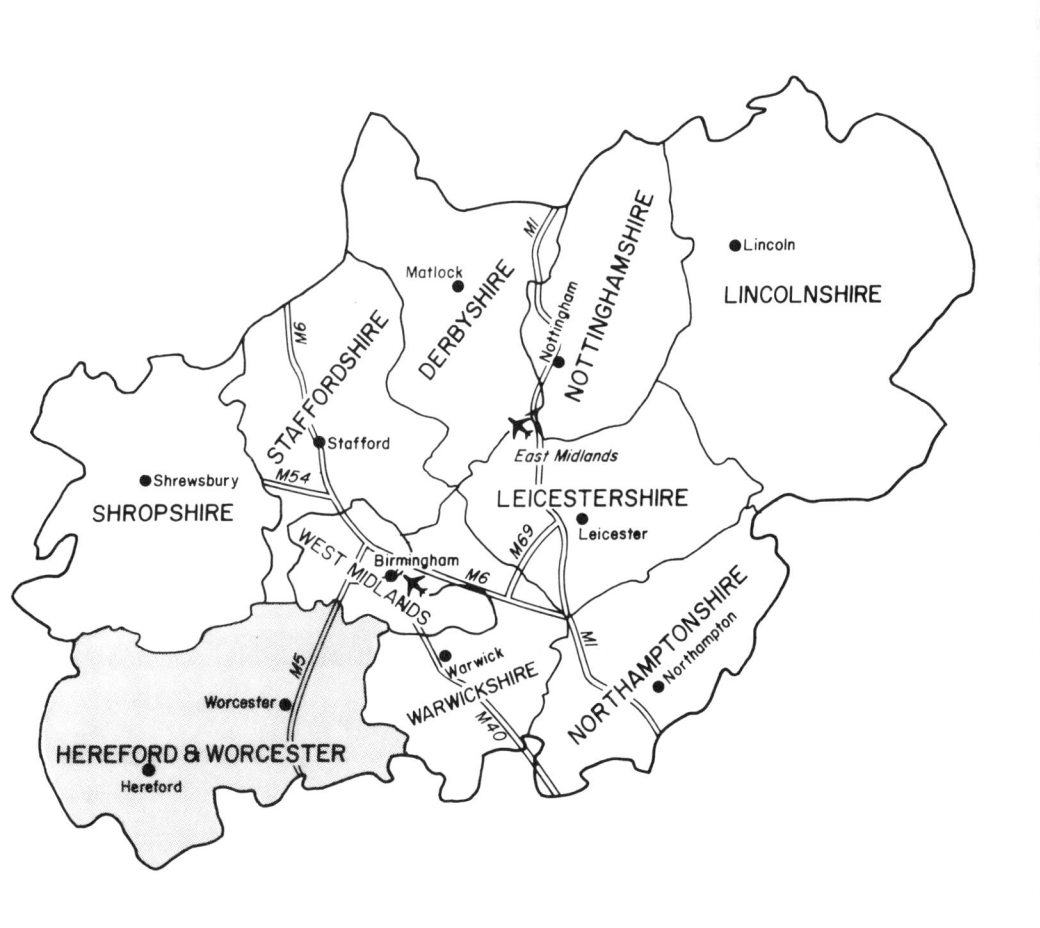

Abberley Hall

Address: Worcester, Hereford and Worcester WR6 6DD

Telephone: 0299 896275

Head: Mr M V D Haggard

Age range: 8-13
No. of pupils: 195
Scholarships: Yes
Religion: Church of England

Fees per term
Day: £1850-£1850
Weekly board: -
Full board: £2465-£2465

● Boy ○ Girl ○ Co-ed
● Day ○ Week ● Board

Abberley Hall is a boys' boarding school set in 90 acres of wooded grounds. There is no entry examination, but tuition in small classes (average size 12 pupils) enables most boys to pass into the top academic public schools. There are excellent specialist facilities for arts, crafts, design and music - which the boys enjoy in the notably happy atmosphere.

The Abbey College p669

Address: 253 Wells Road, Malvern Wells, Hereford and Worcester WR14 4JF

Telephone:

Head: Mr R Bellerby

Age range: 13-18
No. of pupils: 120
Scholarships: Yes
Religion: Mixed

Fees per term
Day: £1350-£1800
Weekly board: £2000-£2600
Full board: £3000-£3600

○ Boy ○ Girl ● Co-ed
● Day ● Week ● Board

Established as a school in the last century Abbey College provides pre GCSE, A Levels and university access courses. Set on the beautiful Malvern Hills, the College occupies 70 acres of grounds with extensive facilities and experienced, caring staff. Excellent results obtained.

The Alice Ottley School *

Address: Britannia House, Upper Tything, Hereford and Worcester

Telephone: 0905 27061

Head: Miss C Sibbit

Age range: 3-19
No. of pupils: 700
Scholarships: Yes
Religion: Church of England

Fees per term
Day: £472-£1358
Weekly board: -
Full board: -

○ Boy ● Girl ○ Co-ed
● Day ○ Week ○ Board

Founded in 1883, the school provides a high standard of education, both academic and cultural, in a disciplined and happy environment. The attractive Georgian buildings have been extensively modernised. There is a separate sixth form centre and junior school. The school has excellent examination results, an impressive record of entries to universites and offers a wide range of extra mural activities.

Aymestrey School

Address: Crown East, Worcester, Hereford and Worcester WR2 5TR

Telephone: 0905 425 619

Head: Mr D H Griffith

Age range: 8-13
No. of pupils: 45
Scholarships:
Religion: Church of England

Fees per term
Day: -1130
Weekly board: -
Full board: £1500-

● Boy ○ Girl ○ Co-ed
○ Day ○ Week ● Board

Aymestrey is three miles from Worcester in 30 acres including woods, lakes and an assault course. Classes are small; the school achieves a 100% pass rate at Common Entrance and scholarships have been won at several leading schools. Aymestrey gives boys a broad education; music, art, sport, chess and computing form an important part of school life.

Belmont Abbey School

Address: Hereford, Hereford and Worcester HR2 9RZ

Telephone: 0432 277362

Head: Revd D C Jenkins

Age range: 11-18
No. of pupils: 190
Scholarships: Yes
Religion: Roman Catholic

Fees per term
Day: £1500-
Weekly board: -
Full board: £2600-

● ○ ○
Boy Girl Co-ed
● ○ ●
Day Week Board

Spacious rural setting in Wye Valley. Small and intimate family size, 8 monks and 20 lay staff, natural and genuine relationship between staff and boys, a friendly and sensible school. 15 A Level and GCSE subjects offered. 120 boarders, 70 day boys; 110 Roman Catholics, 80 non Catholics.

Bowbrook House School

Address: Peopleton, Pershore, Hereford and Worcester WR10 2EE

Telephone: 0905 841242

Head: Mr S W Jackson

Age range: 3-16
No. of pupils: 143
Scholarships:
Religion: Non-denominational

Fees per term
Day: £600-£1065
Weekly board: -
Full board: -

○ ○ ●
Boy Girl Co-ed
● ○ ○
Day Week Board

Bowbrook House is set in 14 acres of picturesque Worcestershire countryside yet within easy reach of Worcester, Pershore and Evesham. The school caters for the academic child and also those of average ability, who can benefit from the small classes. All pupils are able to take advantage of the opportunities offered and are encouraged to participate in all activities. The school has a flourishing art and textiles department.

Bowbrook School

Address: Hartlebury, Kidderminster, Hereford and Worcester DY11 7TE

Telephone: 0299 250258

Head: Mr J Styler

Age range: 3-16
No. of pupils:
Scholarships:
Religion: Non-denominational

Fees per term
Day: £595-£1395
Weekly board: -
Full board: -

○ ○ ●
Boy Girl Co-ed
● ○ ○
Day Week Board

Bowbrook at Hartlebury has been operating since 1977 and in a short time has established itself as one or the most attractive educational prospects to many families; indeed, we are known as a family school to which many members of the same family come and with which whole families can identify. Pupils are taught to their potential ability, not their age.

Bromsgrove Lower School

Address: Conway Road, Bromsgrove, Hereford and Worcester B60 2AD

Telephone: 0527 579600

Head: Mr E J Omerod BEd

Age range: 7-13
No. of pupils: 440
Scholarships: Yes
Religion: Church of England

Fees per term
Day: £1095-£1830
Weekly board: -
Full board: £2095-£2770

○ ○ ●
Boy Girl Co-ed
● ○ ●
Day Week Board

The school is administered by the Governors and Headmaster of Bromsgrove School but it is an independent unit having its own headmaster, staff, buildings and playing fields. The proximity of the Upper School is such that the Lower School can use the Chapel, all the year round indoor swimming pool, squash courts, sports hall and music school. Pupils are accepted from the age seven.

Bromsgrove Pre-Preparatory School

Address: 28-30 College Road, Bromsgrove, Hereford and Worcester B60 2NF
Telephone: 0527 73007

Head: Mrs S Pickering

Age range: 3-7
No. of pupils: 145
Scholarships:
Religion: Non-denominational

Fees per term
Day: £404-£832
Weekly board: -
Full board: -

Boy ○ Girl ○ Co-ed ●
Day ● Week ○ Board ○

Bromsgrove Pre-Preparatory School (Ottilie Hild House) for children between the ages of 3 and 7 years has a team of dedicated, professional and highly qualified staff. High academic achievement, cosideration for others, good manners and self reliance are expected throughout school. We hope to imbue our children with a love for learning and confidence in the basic skills which will stand them in good stead.

Bromsgrove School *

Address: Worcester Road, Bromsgrove, Hereford and Worcester B61 7DU
Telephone: 0527 579679

Head: Mr T M Taylor MA Dip Ed

Age range: 13-18
No. of pupils: 610
Scholarships: Yes
Religion: Anglican

Fees per term
Day: £1890-
Weekly board: -
Full board: -£3020

Boy ○ Girl ○ Co-ed ●
Day ● Week ○ Board ●

A leading Midlands co-educational boarding and day school. Upper school (13+): 610 pupils. Lower school (7-13): 430 pupils. Pre-preparatory (3-6+): 170 pupils. Excellent facilities in 100 acre grounds. High academic standard. Wide range of activities, games, music and drama. Scholarships, exhibitions, bursaries and Government Assisted Places available. Good access by road, rail and air. Visitors welcome.

Croftdown School

Address: Abbey Road, Great Malvern, Hereford and Worcester WR14 3HE
Telephone: 0684 575083

Head: Miss E Curtis Roper

Age range: 3-12
No. of pupils: 84
Scholarships:
Religion: Church of England

Fees per term
Day: £425-£1270
Weekly board: -£1840
Full board: -£1840

Boy ○ Girl ● Co-ed ○
Day ● Week ● Board ●

Croftdown, an all girls' boarding and day school. Classes offer traditional methods in harmony with modern technology; high teacher-pupil ratios produce excellent results. Plentiful, healthy activity provides the ideal learning environment. Dedicated, caring staff, good discipline and a happy relaxed atmosphere promotes confidence and community spirit.

Dodderhill

Address: Droitwich, Hereford and Worcester WR9 0BE
Telephone: 0905 778290

Head: Mrs M Maybee

Age range: 9-16
No. of pupils: 125
Scholarships: Yes
Religion: Church of England

Fees per term
Day: £1160-£1310
Weekly board: -
Full board: -

Boy ○ Girl ○ Co-ed ●
Day ● Week ○ Board ○

Academic results are good. All senior girls take 8 or more GCSE subjects and gain entry to a wide range of sixth forms and colleges. Small classes enable them to receive individual attention and thus gain in confidence. There is a flourishing junior department (9-11). Fees are inclusive of a wide range of extra-curricular activities.

HEREFORD AND WORCESTER 199

The Downs School

Address: Brockhill Road, Colwall, Malvern, Hereford and Worcester WR13 6EY
Telephone: 0684 40277

Age range: 4-13
No. of pupils: 162
Scholarships:
Religion:

Fees per term
Day: -
Weekly board: -
Full board: -

Boy ○ Girl ○ Co-ed ●
Day ● Week ● Board ●

Head: Mr A H Auster

For further information and a prospectus, please contact the school.

The Elms School

Address: Colwall, Malvern, Hereford and Worcester WR1 6EF
Telephone: 0684 40344

Age range: 3-13
No. of pupils: 165
Scholarships: Yes
Religion: Church of England

Fees per term
Day: £440-£2085
Weekly board: -
Full board: -£2485

Boy ○ Girl ○ Co-ed ●
Day ● Week ○ Board ●

Head: Mr L A C Ashby

The Elms is a family based preparatory school in a village setting at the foot of the Malvern Hills with regular trains to London and close to Birmingham Airport. Scholarships are regularly attained to leading public schools. The school has excellent academic and sporting facilities, and prides itself on being a caring community.

Green Hill School

Address: Evesham, Hereford and Worcester WR11 4NG
Telephone: 0386 442364

Age range: 2-16
No. of pupils: 130
Scholarships: Yes
Religion: Non-denominational

Fees per term
Day: £295-£795
Weekly board: -
Full board: -£1900

Boy ○ Girl ○ Co-ed ●
Day ● Week ○ Board ●

Head: Mrs V Pate

Housed in an attractive Edwardian building in pleasant grounds and established for over a hundred years. A sound, traditional approach to education. Small teaching groups enable teachers to give close attention. Varied syllabus in line with the National Curriculum. Ten subjects offered at GCSE. Family boarding from seven years old. Secure, happy atmosphere. Reasonable fees and convenient geographic situation.

Hawforth Lodge School

Address: Worcester, Hereford and Worcester WR3 7SE
Telephone: 0905 51292

Age range: 3-13
No. of pupils: 170
Scholarships: Yes
Religion: Church of England

Fees per term
Day: £300-£1446
Weekly board: -
Full board: -

Boy ○ Girl ○ Co-ed ●
Day ● Week ○ Board ○

Head: Mr A Race

For further information and a prospectus, please contact the school.

Heathfield School

Address: Wolverley, Kidderminster, Hereford and Worcester DY10 3QE
Telephone: 0562 850204

Age range: 3-16
No. of pupils: 260
Scholarships: Yes
Religion: Non-denominational

Fees per term
Day: £550-£1175
Weekly board: -
Full board: -

Boy ○ Girl ○ Co-ed ●
Day ● Week ○ Board ○

Head: Mr G L Sinton BA MD

Heathfield is a small co-educational school where a wide curriculum is followed in small teaching groups. Children are accepted from three years and are prepared for CEE at 11 and 13. The senior school prepares children for GCSE. Heathfield has a rural situation with playing fields, sports hall, tennis courts and swimming pool. There is an art studio, well stocked library and science laboratories.

The Hereford Cathedral Junior School

Address: 28 Castle Street, Hereford, Hereford and Worcester HR1 2NW
Telephone: 0432 353726

Age range: 4-11
No. of pupils: 170
Scholarships:
Religion:

Fees per term
Day: -
Weekly board: -
Full board: -

Boy ○ Girl ○ Co-ed ●
Day ● Week ● Board ●

Head: Mr S A Sides

For further information and a prospectus, please contact the school.

Hereford Cathedral School *

Address: 29 Castle Street, Hereford, Hereford and Worcester HR1 2NN
Telephone: 0432 273757

Age range: 3-18
No. of pupils: 820
Scholarships: Yes
Religion: Church of England

Fees per term
Day: £680-£1330
Weekly board: £1640-£2290
Full board: £1640-£2290

Boy ○ Girl ○ Co-ed ●
Day ● Week ○ Board ●

Head: Dr H C Tomlinson

Hereford Cathedral School sets out to be a community that encourages the establishment of good personal relationships, in which the pupils may develop their academic, cultural and athletic talents. We set high standards and achieve excellent results at all levels. Most pupils progress to higher education.

Hereford Waldorf School

Address: Much Dewchurch, Hereford, Hereford and Worcester HR2 8DE
Telephone: 0981 540221

Age range: 3-15
No. of pupils: 180
Scholarships:
Religion: Rudolf Steiner

Fees per term
Day: -
Weekly board: -
Full board: -

Boy ○ Girl ○ Co-ed ●
Day ● Week ○ Board ○

Head: Chairman College of Yearchesrs

Hereford Waldorf School's curriculum is based on the work of Rudolf Steiner. The school is independent, comprehensive and co-educational. The curriculum respects a child's right to childhood and is designed to meet the academic, physical and spiritual needs of the children at each stage of their development. Fees according to means.

Holy Trinity School

Address: Birmingham Road, Kidderminster, Hereford and Worcester DY10 2BY
Telephone: 0562 822929

Head: Mrs S M Bell

Age range: 3-18
No. of pupils: 400
Scholarships: Yes
Religion: Roman Catholic

Fees per term
Day: £300-£980
Weekly board: -
Full board: -

● Boy ● Girl ○ Co-ed
● Day ○ Week ○ Board

We aim to enable all pupils to fulfil their academic potential, to make the most of their talents, and to develop their personality. We aim to create a positive, caring atmosphere in which pupils are encouraged to develop self-discipline, high personal standards and to grow morally and socially in a Christian setting. We warmly welcome pupils who are members of other religious persuasions. Boys 3-8, girls 3-18.

Kinloss School

Address: Martley, Worcester, Hereford and Worcester WR6 6QB
Telephone: 0886 888 223

Head: Mr D Tuohy

Age Range: 11-17
No. of pupils: 60
Scholarships:
Religion: Non-denominational

Fees per term
Day: -
Weekly board: -
Full board: -

● Boy ○ Girl ○ Co-ed
● Day ○ Week ● Board

Kinloss is a secondary school for bright boys with dyslexia. We have a very high staff : pupil ratio, small classes and individual tuition. Boys follow the full National Curriculum and take a wide range of GCSE examinations. Boys with behaviour problems are not accepted so we have a pleasant, well-motivated community in which boys can flourish and succeed.

The King's School * p744

Address: Worcester, Hereford and Worcester
Telephone: 0905 23016

Head: Dr J M Moore

Age range: 7-18
No. of pupils: 907
Scholarships: Yes
Religion: Church of England

Fees per term
Day: £3072-£4752
Weekly board: £6273-£7953
Full board: £6273-£7953

○ Boy ○ Girl ● Co-ed
● Day ● Week ● Board

The school is situated in the heart of Worcester, next to the Cathedral. It has a mixture of fine old buildings and modern purpose-built teaching facilities. We are determined to identify the potential of all pupils wherever it may lie, and to give them the chance to explore their talents to the full.

The Knoll School

Address: 33 Manor Avenue, Kidderminster, Hereford and Worcester DY11 6EA
Telephone: 0562 822622

Head: Mrs L Maggs-Wellings

Age range: 3-11
No. of pupils: 125
Scholarships:
Religion: Church of England

Fees per term
Day: £177-£650
Weekly board: -
Full board: -

○ Boy ○ Girl ● Co-ed
● Day ○ Week ○ Board

For further information and a prospectus, please contact the school.

Lawnside School p745

Address: Great Malvern, Hereford and Worcester WR14 3AJ
Telephone: 0684 575504

Head: Miss J A Harvey

Age range: 11-18
No. of pupils: 100
Scholarships: Yes
Religion: Church of England

Fees per term
Day: -
Weekly board: -
Full board: -

Boy ○ Girl ● Co-ed ○
Day ● Week ● Board ●

Lawnside combines traditional teaching values with modern technology. Wide range of GCSE subjects including theory and practice of physical education and design technology. One and two year sixth form courses. Day girls and boarders. A small community where everyone's contribution is significant and no-one is overlooked. Lawnside aims to encourage its students to gain self-confidence and self-reliance.

Lea House School

Address: The Lea, Bewdley Hill, Kidderminster, Hereford and Worcester DY11 6PR
Telephone: 0562 822376

Head: Mrs B A Bartter

Age range: 3-11
No. of pupils: 110
Scholarships:
Religion: Church of England

Fees per term
Day: £575-£745
Weekly board: -
Full board: -

Boy ○ Girl ○ Co-ed ●
Day ● Week ○ Board ○

We have a very low pupil/teacher ratio, good sports facilities, flourishing music and drama department, and French from the age of four years. We have a high record of achievement to senior schools. Our nursery prepares the three year olds for entry into the main school at the age of four.

Lucton School

Address: Near Leominster, Hereford and Worcester HR6 9PN
Telephone: 056 885 686

Head: Mr P H Moody

Age range: 11-16
No. of pupils: 30
Scholarships:
Religion: Church of England

Fees per term
Day: -£995
Weekly board: -£1700
Full board: -£1850

Boy ○ Girl ○ Co-ed ●
Day ● Week ● Board ●

Entry at 8+ (from September 1993) and 11+. Co-educational day and boarding. Spacious accommodation for all the pupils in family atmosphere. Wide curriculum taught in good facilities which leads to all types of futher education. Healthy range of extra activity. School is set in beautiful rural setting.

Malvern College * p745

Address: Malvern, Hereford and Worcester WR14 3DF
Telephone: 0684 892333

Head: Mr R DE C Chapman

Age range: 13-18
No. of pupils: 700
Scholarships: Yes
Religion: Church of England

Fees per term
Day: £2490-
Weekly board: -
Full board: £3420-

Boy ○ Girl ○ Co-ed ●
Day ● Week ○ Board ●

Malvern College is an independent, co-educational school which aims to identify and nurture the individual talents of its pupils through participation in the life of a boarding community. Building on its traditional excellence in the areas of Academic Scholarship and Games the school also enjoys an outstanding reputation in the Arts. In recent years it has pioneered developments in pastoral care.

Malvern Girls' College

Address: 15 Avenue Road, Great Malvern, Hereford and Worcester
Telephone: 0684 892288

Head: Dr V B Payne

Age range: 11-18
No. of pupils: 520
Scholarships: Yes
Religion: Church of England

Fees per term
Day: £2104-
Weekly board: -
Full board: £3156-

Boy / **Girl** / Co-ed
Day / Week / **Board**

Malvern Girls' College is an academic school with a long tradition of excellence in music and in sport. For further details please contact the Registrar.

Margaret Allen Preparatory School

Address: 32 Broomy Hill, Hereford and Worcester HR4 0LH
Telephone: 0432 273594

Head: Mrs J Rees BEd (Wales)

Age range: 4-11
No. of pupils: 119
Scholarships:
Religion: Non-denominational

Fees per term
Day: £685.50-£910
Weekly Board: -
Board: -

Boys / **Girls** / Co-ed
Day / Week / Board

The Margaret Allen Preparatory School is the only girls' preparatory school within a 30 mile radius of Hereford. Girls are prepared in small classes for all senior school examinations. The school has a fine tradition of excellent examination results. Music and drama are an important feature of the school curriculum. Additional help is available for children with learning difficulties.

Moffats

Address: Kinlet Hall, Bewdly, Hereford and Worcester DY12 3AY
Telephone: 029 924 230

Heads: J & D Engleheart

Age range: 7-13
No. of pupils: 90
Scholarships: Yes
Religion: Church of England

Fees per term
Day: £1075-£1075
Weekly board: £1775-£1775
Full board: £1775-£1775

Boy / Girl / **Co-ed**
Day / **Week** / **Board**

A country boarding school owned and run by the same family for over 50 years. Historic mansion and 100 acres of grounds. Speciality is the care of children whose parents are overseas. High standards in academic work, music, art and sport. Own riding stables.

Mount School

Address: Birmingham Road, Bromsgrove, Hereford and Worcester B61 0EP
Telephone: 0527 77772

Head: Mr B J Maybee

Age range: 3-13
No. of pupils: 130
Scholarships:
Religion: Non-denominational

Fees per term
Day: £615-£993
Weekly board: -
Full board: -

Boy / **Girl** / Co-ed
Day / Week / Board

The school now over 50 years old, stands in quiet elevated grounds of nearly two acres on the northern outskirts of Bromsgrove, by the A38. The purpose-built school accomodation gives a modern, light and attractive environment. The National Curriculum is implemented throughout the school together with additional activities. The needs of each child are very carefully considered.

The River School

Address: Droitwich Road, Worcester, Hereford and Worcester WR3 7ST
Telephone: 0905 57047

Head: Mr T M D Crow

Age range: 5-16
No. of pupils: 160
Scholarships:
Religion: Evangelical Christian

Fees per term
Day: -£500
Weekly board: -
Full board: -

Co-ed / Day

Member of Christian Schools Trust. A non-denominational school set in extensive grounds. Established 1985. Small classes (max 20). Caring atmosphere. Strong home/school links. Good academic record.

RNIB New College † p670

Address: Whittington Road, Worcester, Hereford and Worcester
Telephone: 0905 763933

Head: Revd B R Manthorp

Age range: 10-19
No. of pupils: 122
Scholarships:
Religion: Church of England

Fees per term
Day: -
Weekly board: -
Full board: -

Co-ed / Day / Board

Fees paid by the LGA. A co-educational, residential, secondary school for the visually impaired who are able to follow a full academic education of GCSE and 'A' Level courses. After school hours the academic staff are ably replaced by the pastoral staff who encourage the pupils in independence skills and leisure activities both so important for a full and fulfilled life.

Royal Grammar School *

Address: Upper Tything, Worcester, Hereford and Worcester WR1 1HP
Telephone: 0905 613391

Head: Mr T E Savage

Age range: 7-18
No. of pupils: 900
Scholarships: Yes
Religion: Non-denominational

Fees per term
Day: £1020-£1314
Weekly board: £1929-£2223
Full board: -

Boy / Day / Week

Royal Grammar School Worcester is a well established boys' grammar school (ante 1291) with an excellent local reputation. The school aims to offer a challenging and balanced education, preparing its pupils for adult responsibility in the modern world. The curriculum looks forward to the future and includes information technology, electronics, design technology, three modern languages, and strong international links.

Somerleaze Preparatory School

Address: Lucton, Leominster, Hereford and Worcester HR6 9PJ
Telephone: 0568 85473

Head: Mrs J A Hurst

Age range: 3-11
No. of pupils: 100
Scholarships:
Religion: Church of England

Fees per term
Day: £175-£830
Weekly board: -
Full board: -

Co-ed / Day

For further information and a prospectus, please contact the school.

St James' and The Abbey School

Address: West Malvern, Great Malvern, Hereford and Worcester WR14 4DF
Telephone:

Principal:

Age range: 3-13
No. of pupils:
Scholarships:
Religion:

Fees per term
Day: -
Weekly board: -
Full board: -

○ ○ ●
Boy Girl Co-ed
● ○ ●
Day Week Board

For further information and a prospectus, please contact the school.

St Mary's Convent School

Address: Mount Battenhall, Worcester, Hereford and Worcester
Telephone: 0905 357786

Head: Mrs M Kilbride

Age range: 3-18
No. of pupils: 420
Scholarships: Yes
Religion: Roman Catholic

Fees per term
Day: £650-£975
Weekly board: -
Full board: -

○ ● ○
Boy Girl Co-ed
● ○ ○
Day Week Board

Set in attractive grounds, a mile from the centre of Worcester, St Mary's is a Catholic school which warmly welcomes those of other faiths. It offers an excellent academic education, first class facilities for sport and music and a warm caring atmosphere.

St Michael's College

Address: Tenbury Wells, Hereford and Worcester

Telephone:

Head:

Age range:
No. of pupils:
Scholarships:
Religion:

Fees per term
Day: -
Weekly board: -
Full board: -

○ ○ ○
Boy Girl Co-ed
○ ○ ○
Day Week Board

For further information and a prospectus, please contact the school.

St Richard's

Address: Bredenbury Court, Bromyard, Hereford and Worcester HR7 4TD
Telephone: 0885 482491

Head: Mr R E H Coghlan

Age range: 4-13
No. of pupils: 108
Scholarships:
Religion:

Fees per term
Day: -
Weekly board: -
Full board: -

○ ○ ●
Boy Girl Co-ed
● ● ●
Day Week Board

For further information and a prospectus, please contact the school.

Sunfield †

Address: Clent, Stourbridge, Hereford and Worcester DY9 9PB
Telephone: 0562 882253

Headteacher: Mr P M Cummings

Age range: 6-19
No. of pupils: 105
Scholarships:
Religion: All

Fees per term
Day: -
Weekly board: -
Full board: £8700-

Boy ○ Girl ○ Co-ed ●
Day ○ Week ○ Board ●

Sunfield is an independent charity registered and approved under the 1981 Education Act residential school (52 week boarding). Pupils have severe learning difficulties, many with additional complex learning difficulties including autism, delayed language, emotional disturbance etc.

Sunnyside School

Address: Barbourne Terrace, Worcester, Hereford and Worcester
Telephone: 0905 23973

Head: Mrs J M Douglas-Pennant

Age range: 3-9
No. of pupils: 150
Scholarships:
Religion:

Fees per term
Day: -
Weekly board: -
Full board: -

Boy ○ Girl ○ Co-ed ●
Day ● Week ○ Board ○

For further information and a prospectus, please contact the school.

Wells House School

Address: Malvern Wells, Hereford and Worcester WR14 4LH
Telephone:

Head:

Age range: 3-13
No. of pupils:
Scholarships:
Religion:

Fees per term
Day: -
Weekly board: -
Full board: -

Boy ○ Girl ○ Co-ed ●
Day ● Week ○ Board ●

For further information and a prospectus, please contact the school.

Whitford Hall School

Address: Kidderminster Road, Bromsgrove, Hereford and Worcester B61 7LB
Telephone: 0527 31631

Head: Mr G Lumsdon

Age range: 3-13
No. of pupils: 220
Scholarships:
Religion:

Fees per term
Day: -
Weekly board: -
Full board: -

Boy ○ Girl ○ Co-ed ●
Day ● Week ○ Board ○

For further information and a prospectus, please contact the school. Boys 3-9.

Winterfold House School

Address: Chaddesley Corbett, Kidderminster, Hereford and Worcester DY10 4PL
Telephone: 0562 83234

Age range:
No. of pupils:
Scholarships:
Religion:

Fees per term
Day: -
Weekly board: -
Full board: -

○ Boy ○ Girl ○ Co-ed
○ Day ○ Week ○ Board

Head: Mr S D Arbuthnott

For further information and a prospectus, please contact the school.

HERTFORDSHIRE

Abbots Hill School p670

Address: Bunkers Lane, Hemel Hempstead, Hertfordshire HP3 8RP
Telephone: 0442 240333

Age range: 11-16
No. of pupils: 170
Scholarships: Yes
Religion: Church of England

Fees per term
Day: £1660-
Weekly board: £2790-
Full board: £2815-

Boy ○ Girl ● Co-ed ○
Day ● Week ● Board ●

Head: Mrs J S Kingsley MA(Cantab)

Abbot's Hill is set in 70 acres of parkland, 25 minutes by train from Euston, 3 miles from M1 and M25. There are boarders, weekly boarders and day girls. The wide number of extra curricular activities means that weekly boarders can develop interests within the school without time spent travelling, and full boarders are ensure of an energetic and enjoyable weekend.

Aldenham School *

Address: Elstree, Hertfordshire WD6 3AJ
Telephone: 0923 858122

Age range: 11-18
No. of pupils: 335
Scholarships: Yes
Religion: Church of England

Fees per term
Day: £2300-£2700
Weekly board: £2700-£2900
Full board: £3300-£3495

Boy ● Girl ● Co-ed ○
Day ● Week ● Board ●

Head: Mr M Higginbottom MA SM

A small boarding and day school for boys aged 11-18 with girls in the co-educational sixth form. Aldenham offers excellent facilities in a picturesque setting with first class travel communications. The homely, friendly environment ensures individual development and success in all areas: academic, technical, sporting, musical. Admission by examination/interview with emphasis on the interview.

Al dwickbury School

Address: Wheathampstead Road, Harpenden, Hertfordshire AL5 1AE
Telephone: 0582 713022

Age range: 4-13
No. of pupils: 270
Scholarships: Yes
Religion: Church of England

Fees per term
Day: -
Weekly board: -
Full board: -

Boy ● Girl ● Co-ed ○
Day ● Week ● Board ○

Head: Mr P H Jeffery

For fees and further information contact the headmaster. Boys 4-13, girls 4-6.

The Arts Educational School

Address: Tring Park, Tring, Hertfordshire HP23 5LX
Telephone: 0442 824255

Age range: 10-18
No. of pupils: 280
Scholarships:
Religion:

Fees per term
Day: -
Weekly board: -
Full board: -

Boy ○ Girl ● Co-ed ○
Day ● Week ○ Board ●

Head: Mrs M A Sweet

For further information and a prospectus, please contact the school.

The Barn School

Address: Much Hadham, Ware, Hertfordshire SG10 6DL
Telephone: 0279 842502

Head: Mrs M Renny

Age range: 3-11
No. of pupils: 87
Scholarships:
Religion: Non-denominational

Fees per term
Day: £600-£1020
Weekly board: -
Full board: -

● ○ ● Boy Girl Co-ed
● ○ ○ Day Week Board

For further information and a prospectus, please contact the school.

Beechwood Park School

Address: Markyate, St Albans, Hertfordshire AL3 8AW
Telephone: 0582 840333

Head: Mr D S MacPherson MA

Age range: 4-13
No. of pupils: 315
Scholarships:
Religion: Church of England

Fees per term
Day: £1122-£1532
Weekly board: -£1842
Full board: -£2218

● ● ○ Boy Girl Co-ed
● ● ● Day Week Board

Beechwood Park School occupies a former stately home with considerable modern additions including sports hall and music school, and is set in beautiful countryside and enjoys extensive playing fields. Music features strongly and the choir won the 1991/2 National Choral Competition. The broad academic curriculum and wide range of additional activities are conducted in a disciplined, secure and happy environment.

Berkhamsted School *

Address: Berkhamsted, Hertfordshire HP4 2BB
Telephone: 0442 863236

Head: Revd K H Wilkinson

Age range: 7-18
No. of pupils: 775
Scholarships: Yes
Religion: Christian

Fees per term
Day: £1139-£1791
Weekly board: £2624-£3140
Full board: £2624-£3140

● ○ ○ Boy Girl Co-ed
● ● ● Day Week Board

Founded in 1541. All-round education and high academic standards. Wide curriculum and vigorous extra-curricular programme: Duke of Edinburgh, sports, CCCF, music, art etc. Preparatory school 7-10 years, junior school 10-13 years. Own entrance tests. 90%+ pass rate at GCSE and 'A' levels. Large university entrance. Former pupils: Robin Knox-Johnson (explorer), Anthony Hopkins (musician), Graham Greene (author).

Berkhamsted School for Girls *

Address: King's Road, Berkhamsted, Hertfordshire HP4 3BG
Telephone: 0442 862168

Headmistress: Miss V E M Shepherd

Age range: 3-18
No. of pupils: 600
Scholarships: Yes
Religion: Non-denominational

Fees per term
Day: £308-£1481
Weekly board: -£1206
Full board: -£1206

● ● ○ Boy Girl Co-ed
● ● ● Day Week Board

Berkhamsted School for Girls offers high academic standards with excellent examination results up to and including university entrance. In addition it has good all-round facilities in music, drama, sport and many other extra-curricular activities. Government Assisted Places are available for day girls: the school also has its own academic and music awards open to both day girls and boarders. Boys 3 to 7 years.

HERTFORDSHIRE 211

Bishop's Stortford College *

Address: 10 Maze Green Road,
Bishop's Stortford,
Hertfordshire CM23 2QZ
Telephone: 0279 758575

Age range: 7-18
No. of pupils: 650
Scholarships: Yes
Religion: Non-denominational

Fees per term
Day: £1570-£2200
Weekly board: -
Full board: £2120-£3040

Boy ● Girl ● Co-ed ○
Day ● Week ○ Board ●

Head: Mr S G G Benson MA

Bishop's Stortford College provides a balanced education incorporating sport, music, drama, a wide range of activities and a curriculum which provides breadth and depth through the age range 7-18. Continuity of education is a keynote, and academic results have received national recognition. Stortford sets great store by its pastoral care, its emphasis on the developing of self-reliance and confidence.

Bishop's Stortford College Junior School p671

Address: Maze Green Road,
Bishop's Stortford,
Hertfordshire CM23 2PH
Telephone: 0279 653616

Age range: 7-13
No. of pupils: 240
Scholarships: Yes
Religion: Non-denominational

Fees per term
Day: £1670-£1870
Weekly board: -
Full board: £2260-£2470

Boy ● Girl ○ Co-ed ○
Day ● Week ○ Board ●

Head: Mr D J Defoe

Situated in 130 acres of countryside, yet only half a mile from the town of Bishop's Stortford and next to the M11 and Stansted Airport. The school provides continuity of education from age 7 to 18 via the senior school. The college prides itself on being a small, friendly and caring community.

Convent of St Francis de Sales p671

Address: Aylesbury Road,
Tring, Hertfordshire HP23 4DL
Telephone: 0442 822315

Age range: 2-17
No. of pupils: 178
Scholarships:
Religion: Roman Catholic

Fees per term
Day: £830-£1000
Weekly board: -
Full board: -

Boy ● Girl ● Co-ed ○
Day ● Week ○ Board ○

Head: Sister Miriam Elizabeth BA DipEd DipRel

The school is conducted by the Oblate Sisters of Saint Francis de Sales, aided by highly qualified teachers whose aim is to give their pupils a solid foundation through religious and moral training in the gentle spirit of Saint Francis de Sales, strengthening their character for their future lives. Pupils are prepared for GCSE examinations and also for examinations in music theory and pianoforte. Junior boys accepted.

Duncombe School

Address: 4 Warren Park Road,
Bengeo, Hertford,
Hertfordshire SG14 3JA
Telephone: 0992 582653

Age range: 4-11
No. of pupils: 200
Scholarships:
Religion: Church of England

Fees per term
Day: £426-£1198
Weekly board: -
Full board: -

Boy ○ Girl ○ Co-ed ●
Day ● Week ○ Board ○

Head: Miss R M Martin

The school is well known for its academic success and our aim is that the children will pass competently to the senior schools of their choice. Along with academic success, the children are encouraged to be well behaved and we teach the need for tolerance and compassion and the fact that privileges and responsibility go together.

Edge Grove Preparatory School for Boys p672

Address: Aldenham, Hertfordshire WD2 8BL
Telephone: 0923 855724

Age range: 7-13
No. of pupils: 162
Scholarships: Yes
Religion: Church of England

Fees per term
Day: £1800-
Weekly board: £2400-
Full board: £2500-

● Boy ○ Girl ○ Co-ed
● Day ● Week ● Board

Head: Mr K J Waterfield CertEd

We believe a family atmosphere fosters happiness, promoting self-confidence and achievement. We have an excellent academic, music and sporting tradition with a high scholarship record. Founded in 1935, the school is situated in 25 acres of beautiful grounds 15 miles from central London, close to M1, M25 and A1 and within easy access of Heathrow and Stansted airports.

Egerton-Rothesay School p672

Address: Durrants Lane, Berkhamsted, Hertfordshire HP4 3UJ
Telephone: 0442 866305

Age range: 2-18
No. of pupils: 652
Scholarships:
Religion: Non-denominational

Fees per term
Day: £155-£1595
Weekly board: -
Full board: -

○ Boy ○ Girl ● Co-ed
● Day ○ Week ○ Board

Head: Mr J R Adkins

Egerton-Rothesay School in Berkhamsted, Hertfordshire provides a caring community atmosphere where the pupils learn happily from good teaching. Children are encouraged to practice self control and acquire a concern for others that will help them to gain maximum benefit from the School, and allow their fellow pupils the opportunity to do likewise.

The Haberdashers' Aske's School *

Address: Butterfly Lane, Elstree, Hertfordshire WD6 3AF
Telephone: 081 207 4323

Age range: 7-18
No. of pupils: 1300
Scholarships: Yes
Religion: Church of England

Fees per term
Day: £1429-£1559
Weekly board: -
Full board: -

● Boy ○ Girl ○ Co-ed
● Day ○ Week ○ Board

Head: Mr A K Dawson

All boys follow a broad, balanced and demanding academic curriculum which encourages independent thought but also fosters teamwork. In addition, sports, drama and music flourish at all levels in the school, which enjoys excellent facilities for all these activities. Community service and a strong careers and work experience programme develop links with the surrounding community.

Haberdashers' Aske's School for Girls *

Address: Aldenham Road, Elstree, Hertfordshire WD6 3BT
Telephone: 081 953 4261

Age range: 5-18
No. of pupils: 1122
Scholarships:
Religion: Christian

Fees per term
Day: £915-£1110
Weekly board: -
Full board: -

○ Boy ● Girl ○ Co-ed
● Day ○ Week ○ Board

Head: Mrs A P Penney

An outstanding academic school with a reputation for intellectual challenge. Exceptional facilities, in 52 acres of land. A school which gives high value to the individual.

Haileybury * p743

Address: Hertford, Hertfordshire SG13 7NU

Telephone: 0994 463353

Head: Mr D J Jewell

Age range: 11-18
No. of pupils: 640
Scholarships: Yes
Religion: Church of England

Fees per term
Day: £1664-£2460
Weekly board: -
Full board: £3515-

● Boy ○ Girl ● Co-ed
● Day ○ Week ● Board

Traditional boys' boarding-school, 13-18. 100 girls in VI Form of 300, 20% day pupils, small 11+ intake. Academically strong, majority proceeding to GCSEs, 3 A-Levels and University. Classical buildings and Chapel grouped round Quadrangle in beautiful countryside. 600-acre campus, 20 miles from central London. Strong sport, music, art, drama, technology, popular CCF. Full community life.

Haresfoot School

Address: Chesham Road, Berkhamsted, Hertfordshire HP4 2SZ

Telephone: 0442 872742

Head: Mrs G R Waterhouse

Age range: 2-12
No. of pupils: 200
Scholarships: Yes
Religion: Non-denominational

Fees per term
Day: £170-£995
Weekly board: -
Full board: -

○ Boy ○ Girl ● Co-ed
● Day ○ Week ○ Board

Haresfoot preparatory and senior schools Berkhamsted provide continuing broad based co-education from the age of 3 to 18. The philosophy of the happy development of the whole person within a caring environment exists along with the expectation of high standards of work and behaviour. Excellent teacher/pupil ratio ensures access to a wide range and choice of GCSE and A Levels for all.

Haresfoot Senior School

Address: Amersfort, The Common, Berhamsted, Hertfordshire HP4 2QF

Telephone: 0442 377215

Head: Mr D L Davies

Age range: 11-18
No. of pupils: 40
Scholarships: Yes
Religion: Non-denominational

Fees per term
Day: £1340-£1640
Weekly board: -
Full board: -

○ Boy ○ Girl ○ Co-ed
○ Day ○ Week ○ Board

See Haresfoot School for further details.

Heath Mount School

Address: Woodhall Park, Watton-at-Stone, Hertford, Hertfordshire SG14 3NG

Telephone: 0920 830230

Head: Rev H J Matthews

Age range: 3-13
No. of pupils: 340
Scholarships: Yes
Religion: Church of England

Fees per term
Day: £378-£1808
Weekly board: -
Full board: -£2527

○ Boy ○ Girl ● Co-ed
● Day ○ Week ● Board

Now 175 years old and boarding famous old boys like Evelyn Waugh and Cecil Beaton, Heath Mount offers both strong tradition and a forward-looking approach to education. Oral French begins at 6 years whilst 13 year olds run their own business from a flourishing sixth form centre. A full programme of activities for boarders ensures happy after-school hours.

Homewood Independent

Address: Hazel Road, Park Street, St Albans, Hertfordshire AL2 2AH
Telephone: 0727 873542

Age range: 3-11
No. of pupils: 75
Scholarships:
Religion: Non-Denominational

Fees per term
Day: £490-£840
Weekly board: -
Full board: -

○ Boy ○ Girl ● Co-ed
● Day ○ Week ○ Board

Head: Mr B H Cooper

Homewood was established in 1949. It is purpose-built and set in peaceful and attractive woodland. The school is small and friendly. It has a tradition of high academic standards, as well as caring for a small number of children with special needs. The school has a highly qualified and committed staff.

Kingshott School

Address: St Ippolyts, Hitchin, Hertfordshire SG4 7JX
Telephone: 0462 432009

Age range: 4-13
No. of pupils: 300
Scholarships: Yes
Religion: Non-denominational

Fees per term
Day: £920-£1230
Weekly board: -
Full board: -

○ Boy ○ Girl ● Co-ed
● Day ○ Week ○ Board

Head: Rev D Highton BA Hons

For further information and a prospectus, please contact the school.

The Little Folks Lab

Address: 22 North Road, Stevenage, Hertfordshire SG1 4AJ
Telephone: 0438 351220

Age range: 2-7
No. of pupils: 160
Scholarships:
Religion:

Fees per term
Day: -
Weekly board: -
Full board: -

○ Boy ○ Girl ● Co-ed
● Day ○ Week ○ Board

Heads: Mr H V Howe, Mrs J E Howe

For further information and a prospectus, please contact the school.

Lochinver House School

Address: Heath Road, Potters Bar, Hertfordshire EN6 1LW
Telephone: 0707 53064

Age range: 4-13
No. of pupils: 300
Scholarships:
Religion: Church of England

Fees per term
Day: £1290-£1465
Weekly board: -
Full board: -

● Boy ○ Girl ○ Co-ed
● Day ○ Week ○ Board

Head: Mr P.C.E. Atkinson

Lochinver House is a Preparatory School for boys providing a broad, balanced curriculum. We aim to enable each child to achieve his full potential in a happy atmosphere full of useful and varied activities. The school is well equipped with purpose built, modern, bright, spacious classrooms, a sports hall, gymnasium, a music department and 8 acres of playing fields.

Lockers Park School

Address: Lockers Park Lane, Hemel Hempstead, Hertfordshire HP1 1TL
Telephone: 0442 251712

Heads: Mr N J Chapman BA, Mr C R Stephens

Age range: 7-13
No. of pupils: 120
Scholarships: Yes
Religion: Non-denominational

Fees per term
Day: -£1820
Weekly board: -
Full board: -£2520

● Boy ○ Girl ○ Co-ed
● Day ○ Week ● Board

The school is a happy community in which boys can take their work seriously and develop their individual talents. We set out to provide opportunities, encourage initiative and to foster positive and caring attitudes. The boys are prepared for entry to many top public schools. The school also provides additional educational help for boys who need it.

Lyndale

Address: 3 and 5 Hillside Road, St Albans, Hertfordshire AL1 3QR
Telephone: 0727 53939

Head: Mrs C J F Tubby

Age range: 3-16
No. of pupils: 120
Scholarships:
Religion: Non-denominational

Fees per term
Day: £400-£760
Weekly board: -
Full board: -

● Boy ● Girl ○ Co-ed
● Day ○ Week ○ Board

Lyndale is a small traditional school in the centre of St Albans. Boys leave at 7 to go to preparatory schools, girls may remain to 16. Girls take GCSE subjects and AEB basic tests, Highly qualified and long serving staff help to crate a happy and hard working environment.

Lyonsdown School

Address: 3 Richmond Road, New Barnet, Hertfordshire EN5 1SA
Telephone: 081 449 0225

Head: Mrs R Miller BA

Age range: Boys 4-11
No. of pupils: 182
Scholarships:
Religion: Christian

Fees per term
Day: £900-£950
Weekly board: -
Full board: -

● Boy ● Girl ○ Co-ed
● Day ○ Week ○ Board

The School has a tradition of high academic standards and achievements. The experienced, qualified staff follow a varied curriculum which is under continual evaluation and review. Other activities include recorders, country dancing, diction, netball and choir. A number of outings to places of interest are offered. A five day field trip fro the eleven year old girls is arranged. Boys 4-7.

Marlin Montessori School

Address: 1 Park View Road, Berkhamsted, Hertfordshire HP4 3EY
Telephone: 0442 866290

Head: Mrs S O'Neill

Age range: 1-7
No. of pupils: 50
Scholarships:
Religion: Non-denominational

Fees per term
Day: £465-£773
Weekly board: -
Full board: -

○ Boy ○ Girl ● Co-ed
● Day ○ Week ○ Board

For further information and a prospectus, please contact the school.

Moreton End School

Address: 53 Luton Road, Harpenden, Hertfordshire AL5 2UE
Telephone: 0582 712361

Head: Mrs A E Clements

Age range: 2-11
No. of pupils: 90
Scholarships:
Religion: Non-denominational

Fees per term
Day: £313-£860
Weekly board: -
Full board: -

Boy ○ / Girl ○ / Co-ed ●
Day ● / Week ○ / Board ○

Moreton End School provides a caring environment in which we aim to bring out the full potential of every pupil. Progress through the school depends on ability and social factors, not just age. Our curriculum is wide and well balanced. We specialise in preparing pupils for transfer to public schools at 11 years of age and our examination success is first rate.

Northfield School

Address: Church Road, Watford, Hertfordshire WD1 3QB
Telephone: 0923 229758

Head: Mrs P Hargreaves

Age range: 3-18
No. of pupils: 185
Scholarships:
Religion: Non-denominational

Fees per term
Day: £401-£1253
Weekly board: -
Full board: -

Boy ○ / Girl ● / Co-ed ●
Day ● / Week ○ / Board ○

Northfield is a well established school, set in 6.5 acres of lovely grounds. A wide range of subjects for GCSE and Advanced Level is offered and girls are taught in small groups. Design and information technology are taught throughout the school in newly equipped premises. Northfield gives high priority to the pastoral care of its girls, and the development of personal skills and leadership qualitites. Boys 3-7 years.

Northwood Preparatory School

Address: Moor Farm, Sandy Lodge Road, Rickmansworth, Hertfordshire WD3 1LW
Telephone: 0923 825648

Acting Head: Mr N D Flynn

Age range: 4-13
No. of pupils: 190
Scholarships:
Religion: Christian

Fees per term
Day: £1125-£1325
Weekly board: -
Full board: -

Boy ● / Girl ○ / Co-ed ○
Day ● / Week ○ / Board ○

Northwood Preparatory School is an independent schhool for boys between the ages of 4 and 13. It is divided into three sections: the junior, middle and senior school. The school is located amidst 14 acres on a former farm, in an enviable park and woodland setting. The Grade II listed buildings have been skilfully converted for school use.

The Princess Helena College

Address: Preston, Hitchin, Hertfordshire SG4 7RT
Telephone: 0462 432100

Head: Miss H Davidson-Wall

Age range: 11-18
No. of pupils: 150
Scholarships: Yes
Religion: Church of England

Fees per term
Day: £1960-£1960
Weekly board: £2780-£2780
Full board: £2780-£2780

Boy ○ / Girl ● / Co-ed ○
Day ● / Week ● / Board ●

The Princess Helena College is a small school with much emphasis on individual attention. It occupies magnificent Lutyens buildings in 183 acres of parkland. Academic standards are high and most girls go on to higher education. A new sixth form house was opened in January 1992 and a new design technology centre will open in September 1992.

Queenswood

Address: Shepherd's Way, Brookman's Park, Hatfield, Hertfordshire AL9 6NS
Telephone: 0707 52262

Head: Mrs A M B Butler

Age range: 11-18
No. of pupils: 410
Scholarships: Yes
Religion: Non-denominational

Fees per term
Day: £2025-£2112
Weekly board: -
Full board: £3285-£3424

Girl, Day

Beautifully situated amidst 420 acres of farmland, woodland and sports fields, Queenswood is an independent school for over 400 girls aged 11-18. Facilities include a new education centre, a large science building, a fine arts centre, a music block, a magnificent library and first class sports facilities. A broad and balanced education is offered together with a wide range of extra-curricular activities.

Radlett Preparatory School

Address: Kendal Hall, Watling Street, Radlett, Hertfordshire WD7 7LY
Telephone: 0923 856812

Head: Mrs D A Smith

Age range: 4-11
No. of pupils: 450
Scholarships:
Religion: Christian

Fees per term
Day: £880-
Weekly board: -
Full board: -

Co-ed, Day

For further information and a prospectus, please contact the school.

Rickmansworth Masonic School p674

Address: Rickmansworth Park, Rickmansworth, Hertfordshire WD3 4HF
Telephone: 0923 773168

Head: Mrs I M Andrews

Age range: 7-18
No. of pupils: 650
Scholarships: Yes
Religion: Church of England

Fees per term
Day: £824-£1424
Weekly board: £1438-£2459
Full board: £1438-£2484

Girl, Day, Week, Board

A superb site on 315 acres within easy reach of M25. Excellent facilities and a variety of educational opportunities, in a caring and friendly atmosphere. A wide range of A Levels in flexible combinations. Secretarial and business studies in the sixth form. Scholarships available at 7, 11 and 16+.

Rickmansworth PNEU School

Address: 88 The Drive, Rickmansworth, Hertfordshire WD3 4DU
Telephone: 0923 772101

Head: Miss M I MacLeod

Age range: 4-11
No. of pupils: 175
Scholarships:
Religion:

Fees per term
Day: £517-£891
Weekly board: -
Full board: -

Boy, Girl, Day

The Rickmansworth PNEU School offers high educational standards within the framework of a caring family environment. The curriculum is broad-based and the teaching staff are well qualified and class sizes and experienced assistants enable full attention to be given to the needs of the child as an individual. Girls 4-11, boys 4-7.

Royal Caledonian Schools

Address: Aldenham Road, Bushey, Watford, Hertfordshire WD2 3TS
Telephone: 0923 226642

Age range: 5-18
No. of pupils: 80
Scholarships:
Religion: Non-denominational

Fees per term
Day: -
Weekly board: -
Full board: £1525-£1850

Boy ○ Girl ○ Co-ed ●
Day ○ Week ○ Board ●

The Master: Capt D F Wates RN

Founded in 1815 to educate the children of Scottish servicemen, today the 'Caley' aims to provide continuity of education for those children to enable them to achieve their full potential in a homely, family environment. By using seven local day schools and colleges, a wide curriculum is achieved to suit all children's requirements. Accommodation standards and amenities are well above average.

Rudolf Steiner School

Address: Langley Hill, Kings Langley, Hertfordshire WD4 9HG
Telephone: 0923 262505

Age range: 3-18
No. of pupils: 420
Scholarships:
Religion: Non-denominational

Fees per term
Day: £350-£1095
Weekly board: -
Full board: -

Boy ○ Girl ○ Co-ed ●
Day ● Week ○ Board ○

Head: Chairman of College of Teachers.

For further information and a prospectus, please contact the school.

Sherrardswood School

Address: Welwyn Garden City, Hertfordshire AL8 7JN
Telephone: 0707 322281

Age range: 4-18
No. of pupils: 285
Scholarships: Yes
Religion: Church of England

Fees per term
Day: £775-£1225
Weekly board: £1970-£2310
Full board: £1970-£2310

Boy ○ Girl ○ Co-ed ●
Day ● Week ● Board ●

Head: Mr T M Ham

Sherrardswood, founded in 1928 is divided into Junior (4-11) and Senior (11-18) Schools. The Junior School, housed in fine 18th century building set in 25 acres of attractive grounds, is two miles north of Welwyn Garden City and provides games fields, tennis courts and pool for both schools. The Senior School is conveniently situated near the centre of the town, a few minutes' walk from the station and bus stops.

South Lodge School

Address: High Street, Baldock, Hertfordshire SG7 6BX
Telephone:

Age range: 12-18
No. of pupils: 30
Scholarships:
Religion:

Fees per term
Day: -
Weekly board: -
Full board: -

Boy ○ Girl ● Co-ed ○
Day ○ Week ○ Board ●

Head: Mrs R Kirkwood BSc(Hons) MSc DipSpEd

For further information and a prospectus, please contact the school.

HERTFORDSHIRE 219

St Albans High School for Girls *

Address: Townsend Avenue, St Albans, Hertfordshire AL1 3SJ
Telephone: 0727 53800

Head: Miss E M Diggory

Age range: 7-18
No. of pupils: 680
Scholarships: Yes
Religion: Anglican

Fees per term
Day: £1183-£1366
Weekly board: -
Full board: -

Boy ○ Girl ● Co-ed ○
Day ● Week ○ Board ○

Founded in 1889 the school is situated on a pleasant urban site and seeks to uphold its Christian foundation as a caring community. The buildings are mainly purpose built with some modern additions. A broad academic education is provided and public examination results are of a high standard. Girls go on to a wide variety of careers, most via degree courses. Extra-curricular activities are plentiful and varied.

St Albans School *

Address: Abbey Gateway, St Albans, Hertfordshire AL3 4HB
Telephone: 0727 55521

Head: Mr S C Wilkinson

Age range: 11-18
No. of pupils: 665
Scholarships: Yes
Religion: Undenominational

Fees per term
Day: £1435-£1570
Weekly board: -
Full board: -

Boy ● Girl ● Co-ed ○
Day ● Week ○ Board ○

St Albans is a day school with a high academic standards. Over 640 boys were joined by girls in the sixth form in September 1991. It has a unique atmosphere and ethos which are enhanced by the school's position in the centre of the city, near the Abbey and overlooking the site of the Roman City of Verulamium.

St Andrew's Independent Montessori Preparatory School

Address: Royal Caledonian Schools, Aldenham Road, Bushey, Hertfordshire
Telephone: 0923 212875

Head: Mrs S R M O'Neill DipArts, AMIDip, Teacher's Cert

Age range: 3-12
No. of pupils: 150
Scholarships:
Religion: Christian/Jewish

Fees per term
Day: £450-£1120
Weekly board: -
Full board: -

Boy ○ Girl ○ Co-ed ●
Day ● Week ○ Board ○

After school care and boarding available. Pick up points: Harrow, Rickmansworth, Kings Langley, St Albans. Seventeen acres, indoor heated swimming pool, tennis courts, playing fields. Vegetarian meal option. French, German And Spanish.

St Christopher School p675

Address: Barrington Road, Letchworth, Hertfordshire SG6 3JZ
Telephone: 0462 679301

Head: Mr C Reid

Age range: 3-18
No. of pupils: 500
Scholarships:
Religion: Non-denominational

Fees per term
Day: £634-£1860
Weekly board: -
Full board: £2628-£3284

Boy ○ Girl ○ Co-ed ●
Day ● Week ○ Board ●

St Christopher provides for children from average to outstanding ability, complementing academic study with learning through experience with strong drama and outdoor pursuits, vegetarian diet, a vigorous exchange programme and pupil involvement in self-government. Fully co-educational from 1915, the school has always been noted for its friendly informality, breadth of educational vision and success.

St Christopher's School

Address: 17 Watford Road, Radlett, Hertfordshire WF7 8LF

Telephone: 0923 855745

Head: Mrs E Cornelisson

Age range: 3-7
No. of pupils: 97
Scholarships:
Religion: Church of England

Fees per term
Day: -
Weekly board: -
Full board: -

○ Boy ○ Girl ● Co-ed
● Day ○ Week ○ Board

For further information and a prospectus, please contact the school.

St Columba's College

Address: King Harry Lane, St Albans, Hertfordshire AL3 4AW

Telephone: 0727 55185

Head: Br Adrian Gaudin

Age range: 11-18
No. of pupils: 550
Scholarships: Yes
Religion: Roman Catholic

Fees per term
Day: -£985
Weekly board: -
Full board: -

● Boy ○ Girl ○ Co-ed
● Day ○ Week ○ Board

Under the direction of the Brothers of the Sacred Heart, St Columba's College prepares its students for modern society by nurturing the growth of the whole individual within a framework of the Roman Catholic Faith tradition. A healthy partnership exists among parents, students and staff, evident in a pastoral system balancing concerned care with firmness. Excellence is encouraged throughout the school.

St Edmund's College *

Address: Old Hall Green, Ware, Hertfordshire SG11 1DS

Telephone: 0920 821504

Head: Mr D J McEwen

Age range: 7-18
No. of pupils: 620
Scholarships: Yes
Religion: Roman Catholic

Fees per term
Day: £1353-£1625
Weekly board: £1926-£2351
Full board: £2048-£2536

○ Boy ○ Girl ● Co-ed
● Day ● Week ● Board

St Edmund's College is an independent HMC Catholic school which offers the National Curriculum plus additional optional courses; examination results are above average. Boys and girls enter either as day pupils, weekly boarders or full boarders at age 7, 11, 13 or 16. Scholarships are awarded; the College participates in the Assisted Places Scheme.

St Francis' College p676

Address: Letchworth, Hertfordshire SG6 3PY

Telephone: 0462 670511

Head: Mrs J Frith

Age range: 3-18
No. of pupils: 400
Scholarships: Yes
Religion: Catholic

Fees per term
Day: £900-£1450
Weekly board: £2440-£2810
Full board: £2440-£2810

○ Boy ● Girl ○ Co-ed
● Day ● Week ● Board

The college has a strongly academic and broad curriculum, extensive science facilities as well as excellent sport facilities. There is also a 600 seat theatre, heated swimming pool and a 12 room music wing.

St Hilda's School

Address: 28 Douglas Road, Harpenden, Hertfordshire AL5 2ES
Telephone: 0582 712307

Head: Mrs M Piachaud

Age range: 3-11
No. of pupils: 156
Scholarships:
Religion: Church of England

Fees per term
Day: £585-£935
Weekly board: -
Full board: -

○ ● ○
Boy Girl Co-ed
● ○ ○
Day Week Board

The academic courses are set to the requirements of the Common Entrance examination, and entrance examinations to senior independent schools. The usual subjects are taught, also science, environmental studies, French, Latin, art, craft and drama. Sports include athletics, netball, rounders, tennis and swimming, the school having a large playing field, a hard court and a pool. Piano and elocution are available.

St Hilda's School

Address: High Street, Bushey, Hertfordshire
Telephone: 081 950 1751

Head: Mrs M Simmons

Age range: 3-11
No. of pupils: 160
Scholarships:
Religion:

Fees per term
Day: £755-£1190
Weekly board: -
Full board: -

○ ● ○
Boy Girl Co-ed
● ○ ○
Day Week Board

St Hilda's provides a secure and happy environment in which every pupil can develop her academic and personal potential. Art, drama and music play an important role. French is taught from the age of five, and there is a wide range of extra-curricular activities. The 4 acre grounds include tennis courts, sports hall and a covered heated swimming pool.

St Hugh's Preparatory School

Address: Old Hall Green, Ware, Hertfordshire SG11 1DS
Telephone:

Principal:

Age range:
No. of pupils:
Scholarships:
Religion:

Fees per term
Day: -
Weekly board: -
Full board: -

○ ○ ●
Boy Girl Co-ed
○ ○ ○
Day Week Board

For further information and a prospectus, please contact the school.

St John's Preparatory School

Address: Brownloes, The Ridgeway, Potters Bar, Hertfordshire EN6 5QT
Telephone: 0707 657294

Head: Mr and Mrs A Tardios

Age range: 4-13
No. of pupils: 160
Scholarships:
Religion: Non-denominational

Fees per term
Day: £855-£910
Weekly board: -
Full board: -

○ ○ ●
Boy Girl Co-ed
● ○ ○
Day Week Board

Established in 1987 and set in 4 and a half acres of green belt, the school has approximately 180 pupils, co-educational, (5-16 years old). Curriculum: whole range of subjects, maths, English, biology, physics, chemistry, history, geography, R.E., Latin, French and German. Art, craft games and PE, computer studies, music and drama. Chess competitions emphasized.

St Joseph's School

Address: The Park, Hertingfordbury, Hertfordshire SG14 2LX
Telephone: 0992 581378

Head: Mr B C Buckley

Age range: 3-11
No. of pupils:
Scholarships:
Religion: Roman Catholic

Fees per term
Day: £460-£995
Weekly board: -
Full board: -

Boy ○ Girl ○ Co-ed ●
Day ○ Week ○ Board ○

Situated in parkland about one mile outside Hertford, the school's aim is to provide a good wide primary education based on sound Christian principles and to develop in the children a social sense and due consideration for others, thus laying the foundation for correct behaviour and good manners.

St Margaret's School *

Address: Merryhill Road, Bushey, Hertfordshire WD2 1DT
Telephone: 081 950 1548

Head: Miss M de Villiers

Age range: 7-18
No. of pupils: 450
Scholarships: Yes
Religion: Anglican

Fees per term
Day: £1460-£1630
Weekly board: £2245-£2575
Full board: £2245-£2575

Boy ○ Girl ● Co-ed ○
Day ● Week ● Board ●

Established in 1749 St Margaret's School is an Anglican foundation for girls ideally situated in 60 acres of green belt within easy access of central London. We have a fine reputation as a caring and supportive community with a good record of success at GCSE, A level and Oxbridge Entrance. Scholarships, bursaries and assisted places offered.

St Martha's Junior School

Address: 22 Wood Street, Barnet, Hertfordshire EN5 4BW
Telephone: 081 441 8017

Head: Sister C O'Dwyer

Age range: 4-11
No. of pupils: 165
Scholarships:
Religion: Roman Catholic

Fees per term
Day: £400-
Weekly board: -
Full board: -

Boy ● Girl ● Co-ed ○
Day ● Week ○ Board ○

For further information and a prospectus, please contact the school. Boys 4-7

St Martha's Senior School p676

Address: Camlet Way, Hadley, Barnet, Hertfordshire EN5 5PX
Telephone: 081 449 6889

Head: Sister M C Archer

Age range: 11-18
No. of pupils: 300
Scholarships:
Religion: Roman Catholic

Fees per term
Day: £850-£850
Weekly board: -
Full board: -

Boy ○ Girl ● Co-ed ○
Day ● Week ○ Board ○

The Mount House (18th century) has become the centre of a large complex - class rooms, science laboratories, music/drama studio, dining hall gymnasium, home economics, art and crafts and CDT centres. The old house has become the VIth form centre. We offer a wide range of subjects to GCSE and A levels and university entrance.

St Mary's Catholic School

Address: Bishops Stortford, Hertfordshire CM23 2NQ

Telephone:

Principal

Age range: 11-18
No. of pupils: 680
Scholarships:
Religion: Roman Catholic

Fees per term
Day: -
Weekly board: -
Full board: -

○ Boy　○ Girl　● Co-ed
● Day　○ Week　○ Board

For further information and a prospectus, please contact the school.

St Nicholas House

Address: Bunkers Lane, Hemel Hempstead, Hertfordshire HP3 8RP
Telephone: 0442 211156

Head: Mrs D A Harrison

Age range: 4-11
No. of pupils: 130
Scholarships:
Religion: Church of England

Fees per term
Day: -
Weekly board: -
Full board: -

● Boy　● Girl　○ Co-ed
● Day　○ Week　○ Board

For further information and a prospectus, please contact the school. Boys 4-7, girls 4-11.

Stanborough School

Address: Stanborough Park, Watford, Hertfordshire WD2 6JT
Telephone: 0923 673268

Head: Mr I J Margerison

Age range: 11-18
No. of pupils: 113
Scholarships:
Religion:

Fees per term
Day: -
Weekly board: -
Full board: -

○ Boy　○ Girl　● Co-ed
● Day　● Week　● Board

For further information and a prospectus, please contact the school.

Stormont

Address: The Causeway, Potters Bar, Hertfordshire EN6 5HA
Telephone: 0707 54037

Head: Miss F R Pearson

Age range: 4-11
No. of pupils: 175
Scholarships: Yes
Religion: Non-denominational

Fees per term
Day: £560-£1210
Weekly board: -
Full board: -

○ Boy　● Girl　○ Co-ed
● Day　○ Week　○ Board

Stormont is a day preparatory school for girls on the edge of a residential area with easy access to both London and the countryside. The education offered is both broadly-based and well-structured providing a firm foundation for entry to day and boarding schools at 11 years of age.

Waterside School

Address: Hazel End, Bishop's Stortford, Hertfordshire CM23 1HE
Telephone: 0279 814071

Head: Mr P F McGowan

Age range: 4-18
No. of pupils: 200
Scholarships: Yes
Religion: Non-Denominational

Fees per term
Day: -
Weekly board: -
Full board: -

○ ● ●
Boy Girl Co-ed
● ○ ○
Day Week Board

Waterside has one of the most attractive sites of any day school and boasts exceedingly good facilities. Operating a co-educational junior school, it has a commitment to provide a quality education for girls only in the senior school.

Watford Grammar School

Address: Rickmansworth Road, Watford, Hertfordshire
Telephone:

Head:

Age range: 11-18
No. of pupils:
Scholarships:
Religion:

Fees per term
Day: -
Weekly board: -
Full board: -

● ○ ○
Boy Girl Co-ed
● ○ ○
Day Week Board

For further information and a prospectus, please contact the school.

Westbrook Hay School

Address: Bourne End, London Road, Hemel Hempstead, Hertfordshire HP1 2RF
Telephone: 0442 256143

Head: Mr J A Allen

Age range: 4-13
No. of pupils: 156
Scholarships:
Religion:

Fees per term
Day: -
Weekly board: -
Full board: -

○ ○ ●
Boy Girl Co-ed
● ○ ●
Day Week Board

For further information and a prospectus, please contact the school.

Westwood School

Address: 6 Hartsbourne Road, Bushey, Hertfordshire WD2 3DA
Telephone: 081 950 1751

Head: Mrs M Simmons

Age range: 4-8
No. of pupils: 65
Scholarships:
Religion:

Fees per term
Day: -
Weekly board: -
Full board: -

○ ○ ●
Boy Girl Co-ed
● ○ ○
Day Week Board

For further information and a prospectus, please contact the school.

York House School

Address: Redheath, Croxley Green, Rickmansworth, Hertfordshire WD3 4LW
Telephone: 0923 772395

Age range: 4-13
No. of pupils: 260
Scholarships:
Religion:

Fees per term
Day: -
Weekly board: -
Full board: -

● Boy ○ Girl ○ Co-ed
● Day ○ Week ○ Board

Head: Mr P B Moore

For further information and a prospectus, please contact the school.

HUMBERSIDE

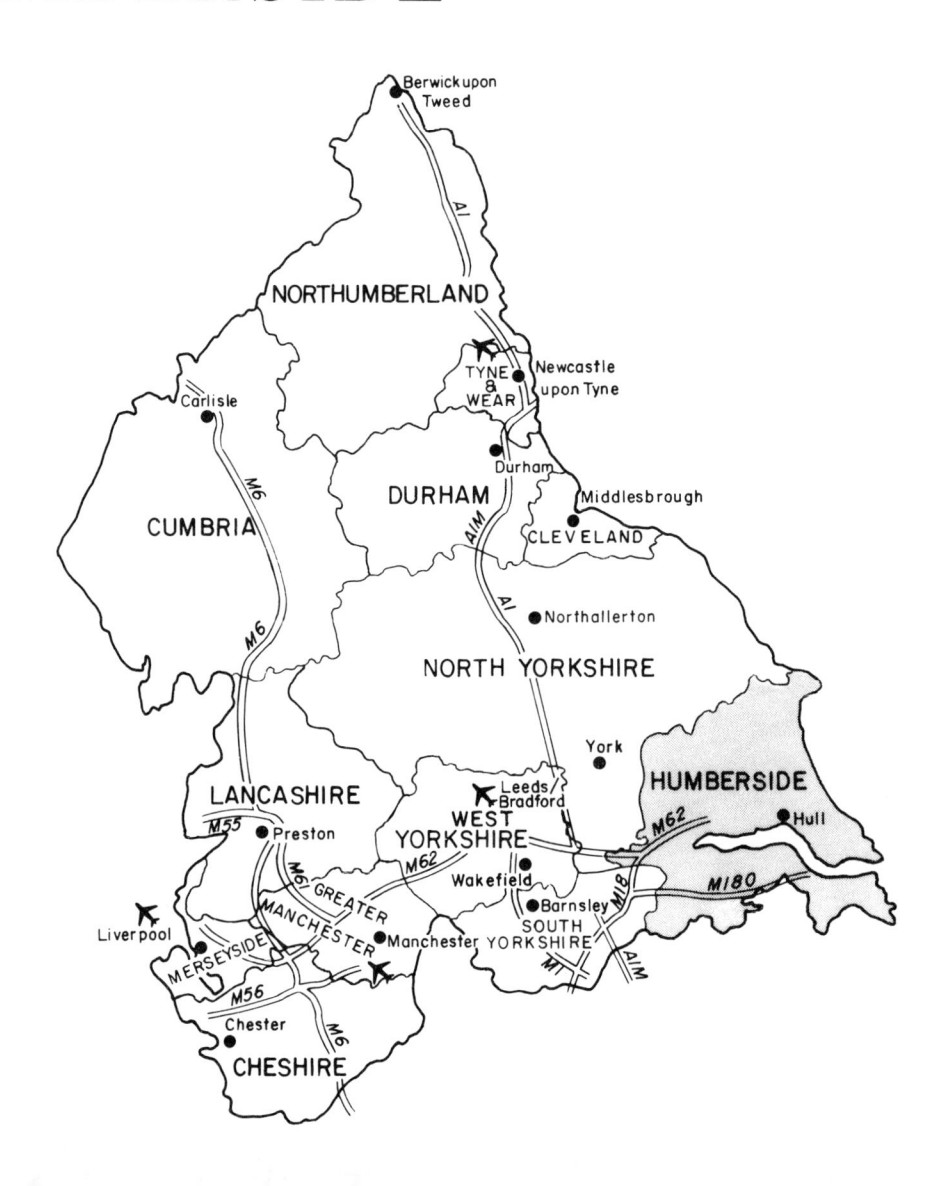

Brigg Preparatory School

Address: Bigby Street, Brigg, Humberside DN20 8EF

Telephone: 0652 653237

Head: Mr L J Shephard

Age range: 3-11
No. of pupils: 192
Scholarships:
Religion: Church of England

Fees per term
Day: £533-£556
Weekly board: -
Full board: -

Boy ○ Girl ○ Co-ed ●
Day ● Week ○ Board ○

The school is situated in pleasant walled grounds in Brigg. A nursery class for children of 3+ is run in the purpose built infant block. Children are admitted into the main school from the age of 4+ and are prepared for entry to independent senior schools and grammar schools at 11+.

Hull High School for Girls

Address: Tranby Croft, Anlaby, Kingston-upon-Hull, Humberside HU10 7EH
Telephone: 0482 657016

Head: Miss C M B Radcliffe

Age range: 3-18
No. of pupils: 380
Scholarships: Yes
Religion: Church of England

Fees per term
Day: £399-£1160
Weekly board: -£1840
Full board: -

Boy ● Girl ● Co-ed ○
Day ● Week ● Board ○

For further information and a prospectus, please contact the school. Boys 3-8, girls 3-18.

Hymers College *

Address: Hymers Avenue, Hull, Humberside HU3 1LW

Telephone: 0482 43555

Head: Mr J C Morris

Age range: 8-18
No. of pupils: 920
Scholarships:
Religion: Non-denominational

Fees per term
Day: £880-£1020
Weekly board: -
Full board: -

Boy ○ Girl ○ Co-ed ●
Day ● Week ○ Board ○

Hymers College is a selective co-educational school providing a wide range of academic and extra-curricular opportunities. High standards are expected from pupils in work, play, conduct and appearance, and considerable success is achieved each year in public eaxaminations and in sport, music and drama. Nearly all pupils qualify for higher education. The school has a stable and well-qualified staff.

Lynton Preparatory School

Address: 250 Froddingham Road, Scunthorpe, Humberside DN15 7NW
Telephone: 0724 850881

Head: Mrs E J Broadbent

Age range: 3-11
No. of pupils: 100
Scholarships:
Religion: Non-denominational

Fees per term
Day: £380-400
Weekly board: -
Full board: -

Boy ○ Girl ○ Co-ed ●
Day ● Week ○ Board ○

For further information and a prospectus, please contact the school.

St James' School

Address: 24 Bargate, Grimsby,
Humberside DN34 3SY

Telephone:

Principal:

Age range:
No. of pupils:
Scholarships:
Religion:

Fees per term
Day: -
Weekly board: -
Full board: -

○ ○ ●
Boy Girl Co-ed

● ○ ●
Day Week Board

For further information and a prospectus, please contact the school.

St Martin's Preparatory School

Address: 63 Bargate, Bargate,
Grimsby, Humberside
DN34 5AA
Telephone: 0472 78907

Head: Mrs M Hardy

Age range: 3-11
No. of pupils: 236
Scholarships:
Religion:

Fees per term
Day: -
Weekly board: -
Full board: -

○ ○ ●
Boy Girl Co-ed

● ○ ○
Day Week Board

For further information and a prospectus, please contact the school.

ISLE OF WIGHT

Bembridge School

Address: Isle of Wight
PO35 5PH

Telephone: 0983 872101

Head: Mr J High

Age range: 7-18
No. of pupils: 290
Scholarships: Yes
Religion: Non-denominational

Fees per term
Day: £1295-£1340
Weekly board: £2335-£2660
Full board: £2370-£2695

Boy ○ Girl ○ Co-ed ●
Day ● Week ● Board ●

The school enjoys a magnificent coastal setting and the grounds provide excellent sports pitches, a 9 hole golf course, woods and shoreline for field studies, sea bathing and watersports. Drama and music are popular in a wide range of extra-curricular activities. The non-denominational chapel has a flourishing choir. Highly successful dyslexia department.

Ryde *

Address: Queen's Road, Ryde,
Isle of Wight

Telephone: 0983 62229

Head: Mr M D Featherstone

Age range: 3-18
No. of pupils: 620
Scholarships: Yes
Religion: Non-denominational

Fees per term
Day: £601-£1198
Weekly board: £2277-£2277
Full board: £2392-£2392

Boy ○ Girl ○ Co-ed ●
Day ● Week ● Board ●

The school aims to provide a good all-round education based upon Christian principles, and enjoys an enviable reputation on the island for high standards both inside and outside the classroom. The school offers excellent facilities on an attractive site overlooking the Solent and promotes the traditional values of discipline and good manners whilst encouraging all pupils to have high expectations of themselves.

St Therese Presentation Convent

Address: 55 High Street, Ryde,
Isle of Wight

Telephone:

Head: Sister S J Ryan

Age range: 3-16
No. of pupils: 185
Scholarships:
Religion:

Fees per term
Day: -
Weekly board: -
Full board: -

Boy ○ Girl ● Co-ed ○
Day ● Week ○ Board ○

For further information and a prospectus, please contact the school.

Upper Chine School

Address: 22 Church Road,
Shanklin, Isle of Wight
PO37 6QU
Telephone: 0983 862208

Head: Dr H L Harvey

Age range: 3-18
No. of pupils: 279
Scholarships:
Religion:

Fees per term
Day: -
Weekly board: -
Full board: -

Boy ○ Girl ● Co-ed ○
Day ● Week ○ Board ●

For further information and a prospectus, please contact the school.

Westmont School

Address: 84-86 Carisbrooke Road, Newport, Isle of Wight PO30 1BY
Telephone: 0983 523051

Age range: 3-13
No. of pupils: 140
Scholarships:
Religion: Non-denominational

Fees per term
Day: £86-£595
Weekly board: -
Full board: -

Boy ○ Girl ○ Co-ed ●
Day ● Week ○ Board ○

Head: Mrs J S Maclean

Westmont was established over 100 years ago. It is situated in the centre of Newport, the Island Country Town. It is a family school for boys and girls aged 3-13 years, run on traditional lines with small classes. It has a fine record of academic achievement. Westmont specialises in music and regularly produces outstanding shows. Parents appreciate the happy, disciplined atmosphere.

KENT

The Abbey School

Address: 125 Canterbury Road, Westgate-on-Sea, Kent CT8 8NL
Telephone: 0843 832441

Head: Rev B A Coyle OSB

Age range: 7-13
No. of pupils: 110
Scholarships: Yes
Religion: Roman Catholic

Fees per term
Day: £1250-£1385
Weekly board: £2195-£2370
Full board: £2195-£2370

Boy ● Girl ○ Co-ed ○
Day ● Week ● Board ●

The course of studies, incorporating National Cuurriculum developments and ability ranges, is designed to meet the requirements of the Common Entrance Examination. The school is situated close to the major London airports and Channel ports and is 90 minutes by road or rail from London. Assistance is given with travelling arrangements and close links with parents are encouraged.

Ashford School *

Address: East Hill, Ashford, Kent TN24 8PB
Telephone: 0233 625171

Headmistress: Mrs P Metham

Age range: 3-18
No. of pupils: 652
Scholarships: Yes
Religion: Non-denominational

Fees per term
Day: £245-£1455
Weekly board: £2129-£2493
Full board: £2159-£2523

Boy ○ Girl ● Co-ed ○
Day ● Week ● Board ●

Ashford School encourages every girl to gain the self-confidence to develop her full potential. Small classes and effective teaching. Escorted travel and full programme of activities for boarders. Music and academic scholarships, assisted places.

Babington House School

Address: Grange Drive, Chiselhurst, Kent BR7 5ES
Telephone: 081 467 5537

Head: Mrs E V Walter

Age range: 3-16
No. of pupils: 200
Scholarships: Yes
Religion: Non-denominational

Fees per term
Day: £660-£1060
Weekly board: -
Full board: -

Boy ● Girl ● Co-ed ○
Day ● Week ○ Board ○

Babington House has stayed determinedly small for over a 100 years. The excellent staff/pupil ratio and happy atmosphere ensures potential is maximised. Most boys leave at 7+ for the major independent/public boys' schools. Girls are geared for transfer at 16 to mixed sixth form colleges now promoted by many of the above schools and for colleges for specific training. Boys 3-8, girls 3-16.

Baston School

Address: Baston Road, Hayes, Bromley, Kent BR2 7AB
Telephone: 081 462 1010

Head: Mr C R C Wimble MA(Cantab)

Age range: 3-18
No. of pupils: 360
Scholarships: Yes
Religion: Non-denominational

Fees per term
Day: £430-£1299
Weekly board: -£2469
Full board: -£2499

Boy ○ Girl ● Co-ed ○
Day ● Week ● Board ●

Baston School has demonstrated once again that success in public examinations is achieved by having highly qualified staff with small teaching groups. This summer's GCSE result produced 83% A-C grades with almost 40% at grade A. Following the A Level results 83% of the upper sixth have gone into degree courses or nursing. In addition to academic work, the girls are offered many opportunities to enjoy the school's facilities.

Bedgebury School p677, p738

Address: Bedgebury,
Goudhurst, Kent TN17 2SH

Telephone: 0580 211221

Head: Mrs M E Anne Kaye

Age range: 3-18
No. of pupils: 430
Scholarships: Yes
Religion: Church of England

Fees per term
Day: £460-£1960
Weekly board: £2542-£3166
Full board: £2542-£3166

○ ● ○
Boy Girl Co-ed
● ● ●
Day Week Board

Bedgebury School is an independent school for girls. In Hawkhurst, we offer weekly/full boarding from 8 years old and day places from 5 with a kindergarten half days or full, for rising 3 year olds. At Bedgebury, we have all the teenagers - day, weekly or full boarding. The sixth form offers a full range of A levels, academic, practical, artisitic and vocational subjects.

Beechwood School Sacred Heart

Address: Beechwood,
12 Pembury Road, Tunbridge
Wells, Kent TN2 3QD
Telephone: 0892 529193

Head: Dr J A Fallon

Age range: 4-18
No. of pupils: 210
Scholarships: Yes
Religion: Roman Catholic

Fees per term
Day: £725-£1925
Weekly board: £1698-£2548
Full board: £2420-£3270

● ● ○
Boy Girl Co-ed
● ● ●
Day Week Board

The Sacred Heart is characterised by the friendly atmosphere which pervades it and by a genuine concern for each individual girl. Full range of GCSE and A Level subjects, including law, theatre and business studies. Wide programme of sport, music, drama, public speaking and the DOE Award Scheme. Extensive facilities include computer centre, three science laboratories and spacious art department.

Benenden School

Address: Cranbrook, Kent
TN17 4AA

Telephone: 0580 240592

Head: Mrs G D du Charme MA (Cantab)

Age range: 11-18
No. of pupils: 420
Scholarships: Yes
Religion: Christian

Fees per term
Day: -
Weekly board: -
Full board: -£3760

○ ● ○
Boy Girl Co-ed
○ ○ ●
Day Week Board

Benenden is a fully residential school for 420 girls. Academic excellence is central, but we aim to develop talent of all kinds; to teach girls to take responsibility and to show initiative; and to leave us as confident, committed and caring young women. Our facilities are excellent, and will shortly be further enhanced by the addition of a new fully integrated sixth form centre.

Bethany

Address: Curtisden Green,
Goudhurst, Cranbrook, Kent
TN17 1LB
Telephone: 0580 211273

Head: Mr W M Harvey

Age range: 11-18
No. of pupils: 270
Scholarships: Yes
Religion: Church of England

Fees per term
Day: £1790-£1790
Weekly board: -
Full board: £2798-£2798

○ ○ ●
Boy Girl Co-ed
● ○ ●
Day Week Board

Bethany is a well-established school in the Weald of Kent, within easy reach of the Channel ports, Gatwick and Heathrow. Our classes are small and we desire to see each pupil fulfil his or her potential. The school has outstanding facilities, especially for sport, music and art. Entry at 11+, 12+ and 13+ and other year groups, including sixth form.

Bickley Park School

Address: 2 Southborough Raod, Bickley, Bromley, Kent BR1 2DY
Telephone: 081 467 2195

Head: Mr B O Hunt BA

Age range: 3-13
No. of pupils: 360
Scholarships:
Religion: Non-denominational

Fees per term
Day: £320-£1480
Weekly board: -
Full board: -

Boy ● Girl ● Co-ed ○
Day ● Week ○ Board ○

The aim of the school is to develop each boy through a broad, balanced and well defined curriculum, enabling him to move forward with confidence and self discipline to the next phase of education. The school was founded in 1918 and since 1962 it has been a charitable trust controlled by a board of governors. Girls 3 to 5 years.

Bickley Parva School

Address: 14 Page Heath Lane, Bickley, Bromley, Kent BR1 2DS
Telephone: 081 460 9800

Head: Mrs M P Dorning

Age range: 3-8
No. of pupils: 200
Scholarships:
Religion: Non-denominational

Fees per term
Day: £350-£920
Weekly board: -
Full board: -

Boy ● Girl ● Co-ed ○
Day ● Week ○ Board ○

For further details and a prospectus, please contact the school. Boys 3-8, girls 3-5.

Bishop Challoner School

Address: 228 Bromley Road, Shortlands, Bromley, Kent BR2 0BS
Telephone: 081 460 3546

Head: Mr T Robinson MSc

Age range: 2-18
No. of pupils: 310
Scholarships: Yes
Religion: Roman Catholic

Fees per term
Day: £370-£1055
Weekly board: -
Full board: -

Boy ○ Girl ○ Co-ed ●
Day ● Week ○ Board ○

In the school environment, Catholic pupils are joined by other Christians and those of other faiths in creating a community of understanding and learning. The mixed nursery and junior school lay an excellent foundation for the seniors where two small forms per year work to successful GCSE results. The sixth form (mixed) mostly proceed to degree courses in universities countrywide.

Bramble Wood School

Address: 22 The Glen, Farnborough Park, Orpington, Kent
Telephone: 0689 852682

Head: Mrs P.N. Prynne

Age range: 3-5
No. of pupils: 19
Scholarships:
Religion: Non-denominational

Fees per term
Day: £400-
Weekly board: -
Full board: -

Boy ○ Girl ○ Co-ed ●
Day ● Week ○ Board ○

For further details please contact the headmistress.

Breaside Preparatory School

Address: 41 Orchard Road,
Bromley, Kent BR1 2PR

Telephone: 081 460 0916

Head: Mr J S Hartley

Age range: 3-11
No. of pupils: 155
Scholarships:
Religion: Non-denominational

Fees per term
Day: £380-£795
Weekly board: -
Full board: -

Boy ○ Girl ○ Co-ed ●
Day ● Week ○ Board ○

Breaside Preparatory School offers its children a friendly, hard-working start to school life. Classes are small and taught by experienced teachers. Pupils are prepared for all senior schools in the area. Recent major improvements have been made to the school. There is also, on site, a pre-school for 3-5 year olds open 50 weeks of the year.

Bromley High School GPDST *

Address: Blackbrook Lane,
Bickley, Bromley, Kent
BR1 2TW
Telephone: 081 468 7981

Head: Mrs E W Hancock

Age range: 4-18
No. of pupils: 700+
Scholarships: Yes
Religion: Christian

Fees per term
Day: £1036-£1340
Weekly board: -
Full board: -

Boy ○ Girl ● Co-ed ○
Day ● Week ○ Board ○

Founded in 1883 and now situated in splendid accommodation in 24 acres of parkland, BHS combines the best of academic tradition (including Oxbridge) with modern cross-curricular subjects and IT. Sports and cultural interests enhance the broad curriculum. Excellent facilities, a friendly atmosphere and strong pastoral systems produce a warm, lively environment in which every individual is valued.

Bronte

Address: 5-7 Parrock Road,
Gravesend, Kent

Telephone: 0474 533805

Head: Mrs J Gibson

Age range: 4-11
No. of pupils: 90
Scholarships:
Religion: Church of England

Fees per term
Day: £850-
Weekly board: -
Full board: -

Boy ○ Girl ○ Co-ed ●
Day ● Week ○ Board ○

Bronte School, established in 1905, is a small school with a family atmosphere. It is a member of ISAI. Children are prepared for all types of secondary education in both independent and state sectors.

Bryony

Address: Marshall Road,
Rainham, Gillingham, Kent
ME8 0AJ
Telephone: 0634 231511

Principals: D E & M P Edmunds

Age range: 2-11
No. of pupils: 250
Scholarships:
Religion:

Fees per term
Day: £581-£673
Weekly board: -
Full board: -

Boy ○ Girl ○ Co-ed ●
Day ● Week ○ Board ○

Founded in 1956, giving individual attention and high academic standards in small classes. Pupils are entered for Common Entrance and 11 plus examinations. Traditional, specialised schooling combined with an up-to-date approach including information technology, science, French etc., with a strong musical tradition. The school caters for all abilities, specialist help available with dyslexia.

Cannock School

Address: Hawstead Lane, Chelsfield, Orpington, Kent BR6 7PH
Telephone: 0689 828096

Head: Mr K Lawrey

Age range: 7-16
No. of pupils: 124
Scholarships:
Religion: Church of England

Fees per term
Day: £860-£1170
Weekly board: £1680-£1990
Full board: £1730-£2040

● Boy ○ Girl ○ Co-ed
● Day ● Week ● Board

Cannock School, situated in fourteen acres of parkland, is an independent day and boarding school providing nursery (co-educational), junior (boys), senior (boys) and (proposed) sixth form (co-educational) classes. Facilities include library, gymnasium, covered swimming pool, science laboratories, art, DT, computer, AV, music and games rooms. The school is busy and happy.

Chartfield School

Address: 45 Minster Road, Westgate-on-Sea, Kent CT8 8DA
Telephone: 0483 831716

Head: Mrs J L Prebble

Age range: 4-11
No. of pupils: 72
Scholarships:
Religion:

Fees per term
Day: -
Weekly board: -
Full board: -

○ Boy ○ Girl ● Co-ed
● Day ○ Week ○ Board

For further information and a prospectus, please contact the school.

Cobham Hall p678

Address: Cobham, Kent DA12 3BL
Telephone: 0474 823371

Head: Mrs R McCarthy

Age range: 11-18
No. of pupils: 300
Scholarships: Yes
Religion: Non-denominational

Fees per term
Day: £2397-
Weekly board: -
Full board: £3573-

○ Boy ● Girl ○ Co-ed
● Day ● Week ● Board

One of the leading girls' schools in Britain. Situated close to the M25 within easy reach of Heathrow and Gatwick. 300 girls, mostly boarders aged from 11-18 years. Wide curriculum, promoting academic excellence in a friendly atmosphere. High teacher pupil ratio of 1:6. Sixth form scholarships. Dyslexia centre for selected pupils of high ability. EFL centre/introductory language week. Interested parents are always welcome.

Combe Bank School

Address: Sundridge, Sevenoaks, Kent TN14 6AE
Telephone: 0959 563720

Head: Mrs A J K Austin

Age range: 3-18
No. of pupils: 445
Scholarships: Yes
Religion: Non-Denominational

Fees per term
Day: £512-£1600
Weekly board: -
Full board: -

○ Boy ● Girl ○ Co-ed
● Day ○ Week ○ Board

Combe Bank is a school where everyone has a chance of real achievement. Small classes allow us to match teaching to intellect, with excellent results. Sports, the arts, service to the community, spiritual and personal development are considered important. Girls work in exceptionally happy and beautiful surroundings, enjoy a full range of afternoon activities and have a sound and interesting programme of study.

Coney Hill School and Nash House †

Address: The Shaftesbury Society, Croydon Rd, Hayes, Bromley, Kent BR2 7AG
Telephone: 081 462 7419

Head: Mrs D E Hobbs

Age range: 5-19
No. of pupils: 50
Scholarships:
Religion: Non-denominational

Fees per term
Day: -
Weekly board: -
Full board: -

Boy ○ Girl ○ Co-ed ●
Day ● Week ○ Board ●

For pupils with special educational needs, associated with physical disability and/or speech/language disorder. Coney Hill School: Daily structured intensive therapy and a balanced curriculum. Nash House: 'Learning for Living', social, health and personal education and core subjects leading to the Diploma of Vacational Education. 'Communication' includes switch access to synthesisers and computers.

Convent Preparatory School

Address: 46 Old Road East, Gravesend, Kent DA12 1NR
Telephone: 0474 533012

Head: Sister D M Day BA

Age range: 3-11
No. of pupils: 310
Scholarships:
Religion: Roman Catholic

Fees per term
Day: £590-
Weekly board: -
Full board: -

Boy ○ Girl ○ Co-ed ●
Day ● Week ○ Board ○

The usual primary school subjects are taught, plus French, and the National Curriculum is followed. Twice yearly reports are issued and the first is followed by a parents' open evening. Sports facilities provide for gymnastics, netball, badminton, hockey, rounders, swimming and short tennis. Recorder is taught. There are two school choirs and assemblies are held twice weekly.

Cranbrook School

Address: Cranbrook, Kent TN17 3JD
Telephone: 0580 712163

Head: Mr P A Close

Age range: 13-18
No. of pupils:
Scholarships:
Religion: Non-denominational

Fees per term
Day: -
Weekly board: -
Full board: -£1450

Boy ○ Girl ○ Co-ed ○
Day ● Week ○ Board ●

Cranbrook seeks to realise the following educational aims: To maintain and develop in pupils lively enquiring minds; to promote the ability to question and argue rationally; to encourage pupils to apply themselves to a range of tasks and skills. To foster attitudes which will instil self-confidence in pupils, and help them aquire knowledge and skills relevant to life and work in a fast changing world.

Derwent Lodge

Address: 1 Lansdowne Road, Tunbridge Wells, Kent TN1 2NG
Telephone: 0892 525839

Head: Mrs C M York

Age range: 3-11
No. of pupils: 140
Scholarships: Yes
Religion: Christian

Fees per term
Day: £795-£1040
Weekly board: -
Full board: -

Boy ○ Girl ● Co-ed ●
Day ● Week ○ Board ○

Derwent Lodge is an independent preparatory school for girls aged 7-11+, with a co-educational nursery/preparatory department. The school is noted for its strong academic tradition and caring, happy atmosphere. Girls can enter Kent's Selection Procedure for grammar schools or 11+ Common Entrance. Scholarships and exhibition places are regularly achieved.

KENT 239

Dover College * p740

Address: Dover, Kent
CT17 9RH

Telephone: 0304 205969

Head: Mr M P G Wright JP BA

Age range: 11-18
No. of pupils: 280
Scholarships: Yes
Religion: Church of England

Fees per term
Day: £1600-£1990
Weekly board: -£3300
Full board: -£3500

Boy ○ Girl ○ Co-ed ●
Day ● Week ● Board ●

Dover College occupies the grounds of the Priory of St Martin in central Dover. Medieval buildings surround the picturesque close where there has been a centre of learning for 800 years. A small, successful family school, Dover enjoys its opportunities to bring the best out of every individual child from whichever part of the world they come.

Dover College Preparatory School

Address: Westbrook House, Shorncliffe Road, Folkestone, Kent CT20 2NQ
Telephone: 0303 851222

Head: Mr N J Brodrick

Age range: 2-13
No. of pupils: 316
Scholarships: Yes
Religion: Church of England

Fees per term
Day: £325-£1480
Weekly board: -$2100-£2100
Full board: £2100-£2200

Boy ○ Girl ○ Co-ed ●
Day ● Week ● Board ●

Dover College Preparatory School is fully co-educational taking children from 2 years old in a pre-nursery group up to Common Entrance and Scholarship level. There are separate boarding houses.

The school boasts many fine facilities including the Queen Elizabeth The Queen Mother Music School. The Senior School is eight miles away in Dover.

Duke of York's Royal Military School

Address: Dover, Kent
CT15 5EQ

Telephone: 0304 241549

Head: Lieutenant Colonel G H Wilson

Age range: 11-18
No. of pupils: 450
Scholarships: Yes
Religion: Church of England

Fees per term
Day: -£236
Weekly board: -
Full board: -

Boy ● Girl ○ Co-ed ○
Day ● Week ○ Board ●

At the present moment the school admits boys only. Parents of all candidates must be serving or retired officers, warrant officers, NCO's or soldiers, male or female, who have completed a minimum of four years' service on a regular engagement in the armed forces. There are no school fees but parents are required to make a home savings contribution towards the cost of clothing.

Dulwich College Preparatory School

Address: Coursehorn, Cranbrook, Kent TN17 3NP

Telephone: 0580 712179

Head: Mr M C Wagstaffe

Age range: 3-13
No. of pupils: 540
Scholarships:
Religion: Church of England

Fees per term
Day: £480-£1475
Weekly board: £2220-
Full board: £2265-

Boy ○ Girl ○ Co-ed ●
Day ● Week ● Board ●

The school aims to provide the best co-educational opportunities for the children both day and boarding. There is a strong emphasis on up to date teaching and the school has achieved notable successes in academic subjects, music and art. Set in attractive Kentish countryside, 40 acres of gardens, playing field, swimming pools, new sports hall and all weather tennis courts.

East Court School †

Address: Victoria Parade, Ramsgate, Kent CT11 8ED

Telephone: 0843 592077

Heads: Dr M E Thomson, Mr E J Watkins

Age range: 8-13
No. of pupils: 66
Scholarships:
Religion: Non-denominational

Fees per term
Day: -£2750
Weekly board: -£4070
Full board: -£4180

○ ○ ●
Boy Girl Co-ed
● ● ●
Day Week Board

East Court is a residential and day school for 8-13 year old boys and girls who have dyslexia (specific learning difficulties). It is ideally situated in an attractive residential area on the cliff tops, with views over the Channel. A small group, multi-sensory teaching approach enables dyslexic children to develop and re-enter mainstream education as equals.

Eden Park School

Address: 204 Upper Elmers End Road, Beckenham, Kent BR3 3HE

Telephone: 081 650 0365

Principal: Mr N O Malleson *Head:* Mrs A Marshallsa

Age range: 4-11
No. of pupils: 170
Scholarships:
Religion: Non-denominational

Fees per term
Day: £430-£650
Weekly board: -
Full board: -

○ ○ ●
Boy Girl Co-ed
● ○ ○
Day Week Board

For further details and a prospectus, please contact the school.

Elliott Park School

Address: Marina Drive, Minster, Sheppey, Kent ME12 2DP

Telephone: 0795 873372

Head: Mr C G Hudson

Age range: 4-13
No. of pupils: 95
Scholarships: Yes
Religion: Christian

Fees per term
Day: £540-£580
Weekly board: -
Full board: -

○ ○ ●
Boy Girl Co-ed
● ○ ○
Day Week Board

A traditional 3 Rs, disciplined school; uniform is worn; civility and good order maintained; small clases (16) max; the School has good success at Grammar and Public School entry.

Eylesden Court Preparatory School

Address: Bearsted House, Bearsted, Maidstone, Kent ME14 4EB

Telephone: 0622 37845

Head: Mr R G Dean-Hughes

Age range: 4-13
No. of pupils: 160
Scholarships:
Religion: Non-denominational

Fees per term
Day: £800-£1155
Weekly board: -
Full board: -

● ○ ○
Boy Girl Co-ed
● ○ ○
Day Week Board

For further information and a prospectus, please contact the school.

KENT 241

Farringtons School p678, p742

Address: Perry Stret, Chislehurst, Kent BR7 6LR

Telephone: 081 467 0256

Head: Mrs B J Stock BA Hons

Age range: 4-18
No. of pupils: 450
Scholarships: Yes
Religion: Methodist Affiliated but all are wel

Fees per term
Day: £1021-£1456
Weekly board: £2289-£2557
Full board: £2396-£2660

● Boy ● Girl ○ Co-ed
● Day ● Week ● Board

Farringtons is a broad ability intake day, weekly and full boarding school for girls with on site kindergarten and junior school. It is situated in 25 acres of parkland, but is only 25 minutes from Central London.

Academic results are excellent with A-C GCSE passes running at 82% and 88% of our leavers continuing on to their chosen degree courses in 1992. Classes are small, the teacher/pupil ratio is 1:10 and facilities are excellent.

Fosse Bank Preparatory School

Address: Quarry Hill, Tonbridge, Kent TN9 2NT

Telephone: 0732 353820

Head: Mrs J A Mills

Age range: 2-11
No. of pupils: 65
Scholarships:
Religion: Church of England

Fees per term
Day: £562-£895
Weekly board: -
Full board: -

○ Boy ○ Girl ● Co-ed
● Day ○ Week ○ Board

Fosse Bank is a small friendly school, where every child is known individually and encouraged to develop their talents with a happy, meaningful and purposeful approach to both work and recreation.

The basic curriculum places a strong emphasis on the sound foundations of literacy, oracy and numeracy. Science, history, geography, religious and physical education and creative activities are all taught.

Friars School

Address: Great Chart, Ashford, Kent TN23 3DJ

Telephone: 0233 620493

Head: Mr J M Stevens

Age range: 3-13
No. of pupils: 139
Scholarships: Yes
Religion: Non-denominational

Fees per term
Day: £350-£1600
Weekly board: -£2240
Full board: -

● Boy ● Girl ○ Co-ed
● Day ● Week ○ Board

Friars School, co-educational 2-6, boys only 7-13, caters for all educational needs of children in a caring and well disciplined atmosphere. Excellent Common Entrance and scholarship results at 13. Numerous extra-curricular and sporting facilities in 10 acres. Sports include soccer, rugby, hockey, cricket, tennis and athletics. Scholarships available to pupils under 9. Music and drama are important. Three new buildings recently.

Gad's Hill School

Address: Higham-by-Rochester, Kent ME3 7PA

Telephone: 0474 822366

Head: Mrs A P N Everitt

Age range: 3-18
No. of pupils: 160
Scholarships:
Religion:

Fees per term
Day: £367-£735
Weekly board: -
Full board: -

○ Boy ● Girl ○ Co-ed
● Day ○ Week ○ Board

Gad's Hill School, a day school for girls of all ages and kindergarten boys, occupies Charles Dickens' former home, is set in eleven acres of beautiful grounds. Excellent education in small classes is provided at all levels at reasonable cost. There is a wide range of extra-curricular activities. Above all, Gad's is notable for its happy family atmosphere.

The Granville School

Address: 2 Bradbourne Park Road, Sevenoaks, Kent

Telephone: 0732 453039

Head: Mrs J Evans

Age range: 3-11
No. of pupils: 202
Scholarships:
Religion: Non-Denominational

Fees per term
Day: £415-£1000
Weekly board: -
Full board: -

● Boy ● Girl ○ Co-ed
● Day ○ Week ○ Board

We present a happy, caring environment based on a combination of tradition and the best of modern teaching. We are proud of our ability to provide a varied curriculum which equips our girls to be able to attend the secondary school of their choice. Particular strengths include music and drama.

Greenhayes School for Boys

Address: Corkscrew Hill, West Wickham, Kent BR4 9BA

Telephone: 081 777 2093

Head: Mr D J Cozens

Age range: 4-11
No. of pupils: 100
Scholarships:
Religion: Non-denominational

Fees per term
Day: £650-£700
Weekly board: -
Full board: -

● Boy ○ Girl ○ Co-ed
● Day ○ Week ○ Board

A firm grounding in reading, language and mathematics is provided, together with all other core subjects, including French, music and games. Music includes singing and recorder tuition, while games includes gymnastics, swimming, football, cricket and cross-country running. After school activities include chess, tennis and table tennis. Boys are prepared for entrance examinations at 11 only.

Haddon Dene School

Address: 57 Gladstone Road, Broadstairs, Kent CT10 2HY

Telephone: 0843 61176

Head: Mr W N Warren

Age range: 3-11
No. of pupils: 200
Scholarships:
Religion: Non-denominational

Fees per term
Day: £490-£610
Weekly board: -
Full board: -

○ Boy ○ Girl ● Co-ed
● Day ○ Week ○ Board

The school was established in 1929 and is situated in a quiet but central position in Broadstairs. Within a happy, caring environment a stable educational framework is established, that fosters qualities of honesty, self-confidence and consideration for others - while children's potentials are developed to the full.

Harenc Preparatory School

Address: Church House, 167 Rectory Lane, Footscray, Kent DA14 5BU

Telephone: 081 309 0619

Head: Mr S H D Cassidy

Age range: 3-11
No. of pupils: 140
Scholarships:
Religion: Non-denominational

Fees per term
Day: £750-£850
Weekly board: -
Full board: -

○ Boy ○ Girl ● Co-ed
● Day ○ Week ○ Board

Harenc is a home-from-home. We want our children to be happy and productive and to achieve a high degree of personal success. Situated on the boarder of NW Kent and SE London, the school is widely known as 'The small school with the huge reputation'.

Hilden Grange School

Address: 62 Dry Hill Park Road, Tonbridge, Kent TN10 3BX
Telephone: 0732 352706

Heads: Mr J A Stewart Mr J Withers

Age range: 4-13
No. of pupils: 272
Scholarships: Yes
Religion: Church of England

Fees per term
Day: £835-£1435
Weekly board: -
Full board: -

Co-ed
Day

As a preparatory school our main aims are to prepare our children for entrance, by the Common Entrance or scholarship or 13+ examinations, to the senior school (independent or grammar) most suited to develop their individual talents and personalities, and beyond that we endeavour to teach them the basic skills and social attitudes which will prepare them to continue their education through life.

Hilden Oaks School

Address: 38 Dry Hill Park Road, Tonbridge, Kent TN10 3BU
Telephone: 0732 353941

Head: Mrs H J Bacon

Age range: 3-11
No. of pupils: 150
Scholarships:
Religion: Non-denominational

Fees per term
Day: £440-£920
Weekly board: -
Full board: -

Co-ed
Day

For further information and a prospectus, please contact the school. Boys 3-7, girls 3-11.

The Hill School

Address: Pilgrim's Way, Westerham, Kent TN16 2DU
Telephone: 0959 563381

Head: Mr N Sanceau

Age range: 3-13
No. of pupils: 100
Scholarships: Yes
Religion: Non-denominational

Fees per term
Day: £475-£1165
Weekly board: -
Full board: -

Co-ed
Day

The Hill is a co-educational day school for children aged 7 to 13. Croft Hall is its associated pre-preparatory department, and this serves boys and girls aged from 3 to 7. Learning and teaching takes place in small classes (the pupil-teacher ratio is 1:14) and this enables each child to achieve academic competence and confidence.

Hollington School

Address: Hollington Place, Ashford, Kent TN24 8UN
Telephone: 0233 621000

Head: Mrs M J Cox BA (hons)

Age range: 2-11
No. of pupils: 70
Scholarships:
Religion: Non-denominational

Fees per term
Day: £755-£845
Weekly board: -
Full board: -

Co-ed
Day

Hollington aims to provide a broadly based education of high standards to children of all denominations. Children with dyslexia, moderate learning difficulties and partial sight are also catered for. As well as a nursery where reading, writing and number work are introduced, Hollington has a playgroup catering for children from two years encouraging development through play and purposeful activities.

Holmewood House

Address: Langton Green,
Tunbridge Wells, Kent
TN3 0EB
Telephone: 0892 862088

Head: Mr D G Ives

Age range: 3-13
No. of pupils:
Scholarships: Yes
Religion: Non-denominational

Fees per term
Day: £560-£2059
Weekly board: -£3073
Full board: -£3073

○ ○ ● Boy Girl Co-ed
● ● ● Day Week Board

Set in beautiful grounds near Tunbridge Wells, Holmewood House is an IAPS boarding and day preparatory school for boys and girls aged 3-13. The school offers an excellent academic edcucation, outstanding sports facilities and strong music, art and drama departments. The school prepares its boys and girls for the top independent senior schools. Academic and music scholarships offered annually.

Holy Trinity Convent School

Address: 81 Plaistow Lane,
Bromley, Kent BR1 3LL
Telephone: 081 313 0399

Head: Sr B Wetz

Age range: 3-18
No. of pupils: 580
Scholarships: Yes
Religion: Roman Catholic

Fees per term
Day: £852-£1257
Weekly board: -
Full board: -

● ● ○ Boy Girl Co-ed
● ○ ○ Day Week Board

Holy Trinity is an independent day school for girls offering a total education programme from the nursery to university. A Christian school in the Catholic tradition which welcomes members of other faiths. High academic standards, small teaching groups - girls are encouraged to make full use of the school's extensive creative technology and sporting facilities and to join in the many extra-curricular activities on offer.

Kent College

Address: Pembury, Tunbridge
Wells, Kent TN2 4AX
Telephone: 0892 822006

Head: Miss B J Crompton

Age range: 4-18
No. of pupils: 375
Scholarships: Yes
Religion: Methodist

Fees per term
Day: £1260-£1865
Weekly board: £2100-£2930
Full board: £2400-£3155

○ ● ○ Boy Girl Co-ed
● ● ● Day Week Board

Kent College, Pembury has a strong Christian tradition and a reputation for being an active school. Standards are high; girls are encouraged to work hard and achieve. Through an extensive extra-curricular programme girls can discover their strengths and develop their potential. They learn to accept responsibility and take decisions and are expected to contribute to the life of the community.

Kent College *

Address: Canterbury, Kent
CT2 9DT
Telephone: 0227 763231

Head: Mr R J Wicks

Age range: 11-18
No. of pupils: 550
Scholarships:
Religion: Methodist

Fees per term
Day: -£1610
Weekly board: -
Full board: -£2874

○ ○ ● Boy Girl Co-ed
● ○ ● Day Week Board

Very high standards are achieved across a wide range of GCSE and A Level subjects. The reputation for sport, music and drama is excellent. There are many fine facilities and a special unit which gives support to dyslexic children. We seek to provide a broad-based education within the framework of a supportive, Christian ethos.

KENT   245

Kent College Junior School

Address: Aultmore House, Old Church Road, Pembury, Kent TN2 4AX
Telephone: 0892 824986

Head: Mrs D C Dunham

Age range: 4-11
No. of pupils: 120
Scholarships:
Religion: Methodist

Fees per term
Day: £1260-£1260
Weekly board: £2100-£2100
Full board: £2400-£2400

○ ● ○ Boy Girl Co-ed
● ● ● Day Week Board

Kent College Junior School is a boarding and day school for girls from 4-11. It is a new building, situated in beautiful Kent countryside, but with easy access to Gatwick and Heathrow. Our excellent games facilities include a heated indoor swimming pool. Girls are prepared for external examinations, including CE, but most go on to our senior school.

The King's School

Address: Canterbury, Kent CT1 2ES

Telephone: 0227 475501

Head: Rev Cannon A C J Phillips

Age range: 13-18
No. of pupils: 711
Scholarships: Yes
Religion: Church of England

Fees per term
Day: -£2625
Weekly board: -
Full board: -£3750

○ ○ ● Boy Girl Co-ed
● ○ ● Day Week Board

Set in the superb surroundings of Canterbury Cathedral Precincts, The King's School traces its origins back to the 6th Century. However, whilst retaining a formal uniform and a strong academic tradition, the school is noted for its friendly atmosphere and its commitment to music, drama and sport. The school has recently made a highly successful transition to full co-education.

King's School Rochester * p679

Address: Satis House, Boley Hill, Rochester, Kent ME1 1TE

Telephone: 0634 843913

Head: Dr I R Walker

Age range: 4-18
No. of pupils: 650
Scholarships: Yes
Religion: Church of England

Fees per term
Day: £824-£1914
Weekly board: £3059-£3257
Full board: £3059-£3257

○ ○ ● Boy Girl Co-ed
● ● ● Day Week Board

An independent, co-educational day and boarding school of some 650 pupils located on a beautiful site in the conservation area of central Rochester. HMC and IAPS. It offers a full extra-curricular and community life coupled with excellent entrance numbers to higher education including Oxbridge.

Knowle Court

Address: Langton Green, Tunbridge Wells, Kent TN3 0EA
Telephone: 0892 862050

Head: Mr D Ives

Age range: 3-5
No. of pupils: 48
Scholarships:
Religion: Non-denominational

Fees per term
Day: £560-£1254
Weekly board: -
Full board: -

○ ○ ● Boy Girl Co-ed
● ○ ○ Day Week Board

For further details contact the school - see also entry for Holmewood House School. For which Knowle Court is the pre-preparatory and nursery school.

Margaret May Schools Ltd. Appletree Cottage School

Address: Seal Chart, Sevenoaks, Kent TN15 0ES

Telephone: 0732 61095

Head: Mrs M May

Age range: 3-8
No. of pupils: 35
Scholarships:
Religion: Non-denominational

Fees per term
Day: £300-£300
Weekly board: -
Full board: -

Co-ed / Day

Appletree Cottage School has an excellent reputation for its individual attention to children to help them attain a high standard in basic subjects. Speech and drama are taught to encourage children to develop their personalities and to become extrovert. Children compete in the local Three Arts Festival with excellent results.

Marlborough House School

Address: Hawkhurst, Cranbrook, Kent TN18 4PY

Telephone: 0580 75355

Head: Mr D R Lees-Jones

Age range: 3-13
No. of pupils: 220
Scholarships:
Religion: Church of England

Fees per term
Day: £845-£1915
Weekly board: £2555-
Full board: £2615-

Co-ed / Day / Week / Board

The school's function is to educate the children academically, so that they can make the most of their mental abilities socially, and morally, so that they become upright, well mannered, and aware of the community around them. The school aims to ensure that the children will pass the entrance examination into their parents' elected school, and for some the target may well be scholarship.

The Mead School

Address: 16 Frant Road, Tunbridge Wells, Kent TN2 5SN

Telephone: 0892 525837

Head: Mrs A Culley

Age range: 3-11
No. of pupils: 130
Scholarships:
Religion: Non-Denominational

Fees per term
Day: £430-£995
Weekly board: -
Full board: -

Co-ed / Day

The Mead is situated in the centre of Tunbridge Wells and prepares children for Kent selection and for Common Entrance to a wide variety of independent schools. We aim to create a happy, secure and enthusiastic atmosphere in which every individual can develop their all round potential. Broad range of extra-curricular activities, sport, drama, music, ballet, judo, swimming.

Merton Court Preparatory School

Address: 38 Knoll Road, Sidcup, Kent DA14 4QU

Telephone: 081 300 2122

Head: Mrs E Price

Age range: 2-11
No. of pupils: 250
Scholarships:
Religion: Non-denominational

Fees per term
Day: £330-£850
Weekly board: -
Full board: -

Co-ed / Day

For further information and a prospectus, please contact the school.

KENT 247

Nativity School

Address: West Street,
Sittingbourne, Kent ME10 1XJ

Telephone: 0795 423713

Head: Mr G T Tierney

Age range: 3-18
No. of pupils: 302
Scholarships: Yes
Religion: Roman Catholic

Fees per term
Day: £750-£1145
Weekly board: -
Full board: -

● Boy   ● Girl   ○ Co-ed
● Day   ○ Week   ○ Board

Nativity School provides a broad-based and challenging education in a caring and supportive family atmosphere. Pupils are valued as individuals and encouraged to develop both academic and non-academic skills. Emphasis is placed on the importance of establishing confidence, self-discipline and motivation, so enabling children to learn and progress quickly. Close co-operation with parents is encouraged.

New Beacon School

Address: Brittains Lane,
Sevenoaks, Kent TN13 2PB

Telephone: 0732 452131

Head: Mr R Constantine

Age range: 5-13
No. of pupils: 357
Scholarships:
Religion: Church of England

Fees per term
Day: £725-£1300
Weekly board: -£2060
Full board: -

● Boy   ○ Girl   ○ Co-ed
● Day   ● Week   ○ Board

Boys are prepared for all independent schools with considerable success in both CE and scholarship. The forms are divided into senior, middle and junior school and boys placed according to ability. Initiative is encouraged by organising the school into 4 houses or companies. The school is complemented by many modern facilities.

Northbourne Park School

Address: Betteshanger, Deal,
Kent CT14 0NW

Telephone: 0304 611215

Head: Mr T R Lewis

Age range: 3-13
No. of pupils: 220
Scholarships: Yes
Religion: Non-denominational

Fees per term
Day: £940-£1700
Weekly board: -
Full board: -£2350

○ Boy   ○ Girl   ● Co-ed
● Day   ○ Week   ● Board

For further information and a prospectus, please contact the school.

Perry Court Rudolf Steiner School

Address: Garlinge Green,
Chartham, Canterbury, Kent
CT4 5RU

Telephone: 0227 738285

Head: Chairman of the College of Teachers

Age range: 3-17
No. of pupils: 204
Scholarships:
Religion: Non-denominational

Fees per term
Day: £780-£910
Weekly board: -
Full board: -

○ Boy   ○ Girl   ● Co-ed
● Day   ○ Week   ○ Board

Perry Court is part of a worldwide fellowship of Rudolf Steiner Schools. It treats each child as an individual, offering a full education through GCSE with no early specialization. It aims to develop responsible young people capable of clear though, keen imagination and decisive action. Languages and foreign exchanges are emphasized. The school is set in beautiful countryside south west of Canterbury.

Rose Hill School

Address: Culverden Down, Tunbridge Wells, Kent TN4 9SY
Telephone: 0892 525591

Head: Mr J G L Parker

Age range: 3-13
No. of pupils: 185
Scholarships: Yes
Religion: Church of England

Fees per term
Day: £465-£1540
Weekly board: -
Full board: -

Boy ○ Girl ○ Co-ed ●
Day ● Week ○ Board ○

IAPS day preparatory school (founded 1832), 180 boys and girls 3-13. Superb new pre-preparatory department and art design technology centre. Preparation for scholarship and Common Entrance to independent schools and for 11+ and 13+ entry to grammar school. Strong on mathematics, science, computing, languages and arts subjects. Full range of individual and team sports including hockey and golf.

Russell House

Address: Station Road, Otford, Sevenoaks, Kent TN14 5QU
Telephone: 0959 522352

Head: Mrs E Lindsay

Age range: 3-11
No. of pupils: 190
Scholarships:
Religion: Non-denominational

Fees per term
Day: £595-£1085
Weekly board: -
Full board: -

Boy ○ Girl ○ Co-ed ●
Day ● Week ○ Board ○

The school occupies seven acres of attractive land in village setting. Boys and girls carefully prepared for transfer at 11 to wide range of grammar and independent schools. The school has a well qualified professional staff, excellent record in examinations. Strong music department. Full range of sports - football, netball, tennis, cricket, swimming, athletics, judo, ballet.

Sackville

Address: Tonbridge Road, Hildenborough, Kent TN11 9HN
Telephone: 0732 838888

Head: Mr J G Langdale BA

Age range: 11-16
No. of pupils: 125
Scholarships: Yes
Religion: Church of England

Fees per term
Day: £1345-£1690
Weekly board: -
Full board: -

Boy ○ Girl ○ Co-ed ●
Day ● Week ○ Board ○

Established in 1987, Sackville enables day education in a numerically small school for academically 'good average' pupils, taking 8 GCSEs before entering a wide range of independent and grammar school sixth forms, and FE colleges. The school has made a name for itself in sports and games, is rapidly increasing its musical and dramatic commitment and offers an extensive range of other activities.

Sevenoaks Preparatory School

Address: Godden Green, Sevenoaks, Kent TN15 0JU
Telephone: 0732 62336

Head: Mr E H Oatley

Age range: 3-13
No. of pupils: 252
Scholarships:
Religion: Non-denominational

Fees per term
Day: £800-£1250
Weekly board: -
Full board: -

Boy ○ Girl ○ Co-ed ●
Day ● Week ○ Board ○

For further information and a prospectus, please contact the school. Boys 3-13, girls 3-6.

KENT 249

Sevenoaks School * p749

Address: Sevenoaks, Kent
TN13 1HU

Telephone: 0732 455133

Head: Mr R P Barker

Age range: 11-18
No. of pupils: 920
Scholarships: Yes
Religion: Non-denominational

Fees per term
Day: £1953-£2178
Weekly board: -
Full board: £3213-£3438

○ ○ ● Boy Girl Co-ed
● ○ ○ Day Week Board

Sevenoaks is a co-educational, independent, HMC, day/boarding school, near to London and to Heathrow and Gatwick Airports. Pupils worldwide enter at 11, 13 or 16, taking GCSE's and 'A' Levels or the International Baccalaureate. High academic standards, plus wide sporting and cultural activities, ensure that 90% go on to degree courses.

Shernold School

Address: Hill Place, Queen's Avenue, Maidstone, Kent ME16 0ER
Telephone: 0622 752868

Head: Mrs E C Drewe

Age range: 4-13
No. of pupils: 140
Scholarships: Yes
Religion: Non-denominational

Fees per term
Day: £429-£880
Weekly board: -
Full board: -

○ ● ○ Boy Girl Co-ed
● ○ ○ Day Week Board

For further information and a prospectus, please contact the school.

Sibton Park Girls' Preparatory School

Address: Sibton Park, Lyminge, Folkestone, Kent CT18 8HA
Telephone: 0303 862284

Heads: Mr & Mrs C Blackwell

Age range: 3-13
No. of pupils: 130
Scholarships: Yes
Religion: Church of England

Fees per term
Day: £590-£1792
Weekly board: -
Full board: £2095-£2743

○ ● ○ Boy Girl Co-ed
● ○ ● Day Week Board

Created in 1948 in the Founder's own home, Sibton Park combines the highest academic standards with excellent facilities, including a science and technology wing. Sibton girls are welcomed at all the major senior schools. The caring family atmosphere, with evening and week-end activities, stables, pet area, and home-like bedrooms, ensure a full and happy life at Sibton.

Sir Roger Manwood's

Address: Sandwich, Kent
CT13 9JX

Telephone: 0304 613286

Head: Mr I Mellor

Age range: 11-18
No. of pupils: 650
Scholarships:
Religion: Non-Denominational

Fees per term
Day: -
Weekly board: -
Full board: -£1450

○ ○ ● Boy Girl Co-ed
○ ○ ● Day Week Board

Manwood's is a mixed selective 11-18 school, taking Grant Maintained Status in September 1992. It has a long tradition of academic success and a wide range of extra-curricular activities. Three boarding houses accommodate up to 100 boarding pupils.

Solefield

Address: Solefields Road, Sevenoaks, Kent TN13 1PH
Telephone: 0732 452142
Head: Mr J R Baugh

Age range: 5-13
No. of pupils: 180
Scholarships:
Religion: Church of England

Fees per term
Day: £825-£1205
Weekly board: -
Full board: -

Boy ● / Girl ○ / Co-ed ○
Day ● / Week ○ / Board ○

A day preparatory school for boys founded in 1948. Facilities include everything necessary for complete coverage of the curriculum. Has a strong tradition of academic excellence and a caring well-structured atmosphere.

Spring Grove School

Address: Harville Road, Wye, Ashford, Kent TN25 5EX
Telephone: 0233 812337
Head: Mr N Washington-Jones

Age range: 3-11
No. of pupils: 160
Scholarships:
Religion: Non-denominational

Fees per term
Day: £400-£1020
Weekly board: -
Full board: -

Boy ○ / Girl ○ / Co-ed ●
Day ● / Week ○ / Board ○

For further information and the prospectus please contact the school.

St Andrew's Preparatory School

Address: Eden Hall, Stick Hill, Edenbridge, Kent TN8 5NN
Telephone: 0342 850388
Head: Mrs S J Brown

Age range: 3-11
No. of pupils: 105
Scholarships:
Religion: Roman Catholic

Fees per term
Day: £550-£650
Weekly board: -
Full board: -

Boy ○ / Girl ○ / Co-ed ●
Day ● / Week ○ / Board ○

For further information and a prospectus, please contact the school.

St Andrew's School

Address: 24-28 Watts Avenue, Rochester, Kent ME1 1SA
Telephone: 0634 843479
Head: Mr D McKenna

Age range: 4-11
No. of pupils: 250
Scholarships:
Religion: Church of England

Fees per term
Day: £675-£700
Weekly board: -
Full board: -

Boy ○ / Girl ○ / Co-ed ●
Day ● / Week ○ / Board ○

St Andrew's School prepares pupils for preparatory schools, public schools and for the Kent County Council Selection Procedure (11+). It is a co-educational independent day school with 250 pupils in the age range of 4-11. It has an excellent academic record with high rates of achievement in examinations.

St Augustine's College

Address: 125 Canterbury Road, Westgate on Sea, Kent CT8 8NL
Telephone: 0843 832441

Head: Mr K Doherty BA

Age range: 13-18
No. of pupils: 129
Scholarships: Yes
Religion: Roman Catholic

Fees per term
Day: -£1570
Weekly board: -
Full board: -£2750

Boy ● / Girl ○ / Co-ed ○
Day ● / Week ○ / Board ●

The college accepts boys from thirteen years of age and takes them through their teenage years to A level and university entrance. During this period of their lives boys need guidance and support; they need to feel cared for while learning to develop their independence and their sense of responsibility. The college has a well deserved reputation for this important task of guiding boys through these sometimes difficult years.

St Christopher's School

Address: 49 Bromley Road, Beckenham, Kent BR3 2PA
Telephone: 081 650 2200

Head: Mrs G M Scales

Age range: 3-11
No. of pupils: 220
Scholarships:
Religion: Non-denominational

Fees per term
Day: £275-£900
Weekly board: -
Full board: -

Boy ○ / Girl ○ / Co-ed ●
Day ● / Week ○ / Board ○

St Christopher's is a thriving preparatory school for children aged 3 to 11. Situated in its own attractive grounds close to the centre of Beckenham, the school successfully prepares children for the major independent schools in the area. As well as the kindergarten classes there is a nursery on site for children aged 3 to 5.

St David's College

Address: Beckenham Road, West Wickham, Kent BR4 0QS
Telephone: 081 777 5852

Head: Mrs P A Johnson

Age range: 4-11
No. of pupils: 196
Scholarships:
Religion: Non-denominational

Fees per term
Day: £695-£745
Weekly board: -
Full board: -

Boy ○ / Girl ○ / Co-ed ●
Day ● / Week ○ / Board ○

A fully qualified staff of class teachers supplemented by qualified peripatetic teachers. Entry by interview and test. Children are prepared for entrance to local independent boys and girls schools. Many awards are gained every year including places at the local super selective schools. Speech and drama, music, ballet, piano, violin, clarinet are available. The usual curriculum is followed for basic subjects.

St Edmund's School

Address: Canterbury, Kent CT2 8HB
Telephone: 0227 454575

Head: Mr J V Tyson MA(Cantab)

Age range: 4-18
No. of pupils: 560
Scholarships: Yes
Religion: Church of England

Fees per term
Day: £907-£2275
Weekly board: -
Full board: £2431-£3715

Boy ○ / Girl ○ / Co-ed ●
Day ● / Week ○ / Board ●

St Edmund's School has been on its magnificent site overlooking historic Canterbury since 1854. Pupils, who include the choristers of Canterbury Cathedral, enjoy a wide range of subjects and activities as well as excellent facilites and pastoral care. Easy access to London and the Channel ports. Academic and music scholarships. Nine former pupils gained first class honours degrees in 1990/91.

St Faith's School

Address: 5 The Street, Ash, Kent CT3 2HH
Telephone: 0304 813409
Head: Mr P J Wrathall BEd

Age range: 3-11
No. of pupils: 160
Scholarships:
Religion: Non-denominational

Fees per term
Day: £300-£680
Weekly board: -
Full board: -

○ ○ ● Boy Girl Co-ed
● ○ ○ Day Week Board

For further information and a prospectus, please contact the school.

St Joseph's Convent School

Address: 53 St Peter's Park Road, Broadstairs, Kent CT10 2BA
Telephone: 0843 61738
Head: Sister Mary Ita Ryan

Age range: 3-11
No. of pupils: 160
Scholarships:
Religion:

Fees per term
Day: -
Weekly board: -
Full board: -

○ ○ ● Boy Girl Co-ed
● ○ ○ Day Week Board

For further information and a prospectus, please contact the school.

St Lawrence College *

Address: Thanet, Ramsgate, Kent CT11 7AE
Telephone: 0843 592680
Head: Mr J H Binfield

Age range: 5-18
No. of pupils: 580
Scholarships: Yes
Religion: Church of England

Fees per term
Day: £1620-£2180
Weekly board: -
Full board: £2440-£3250

○ ○ ● Boy Girl Co-ed
● ○ ● Day Week Board

St Lawrence College (a christian foundation, 1879) is a family school with a preparatory (220) and senior school (360) on a campus of 160 acres. Structured on a tutor and house system, it has high examination pass rates with most leavers taking degree courses. Significant recent investment includes information and design technology, new science facilities and language laboratory.

St Lawrence College Junior School

Address: Ramsgate, Kent CT11 7AP
Telephone: 0843 591 788
Head: Mr R I H Gollop

Age range: 4-13
No. of pupils: 220
Scholarships: Yes
Religion: Church of England

Fees per term
Day: £990-£1620
Weekly board: -
Full board: -£2440

○ ○ ● Boy Girl Co-ed
● ○ ● Day Week Board

For further information and a prospectus, please contact the school, also see entry for St Lawrence College.

St Mary's Convent School

Address: Ravenlea Road, Folkestone, Kent CT20 2JU

Telephone: 0303 851363

Head: Miss J Skinner

Age range: 4-16
No. of pupils: 250
Scholarships:
Religion: Roman Catholic

Fees per term
Day: -
Weekly board: -
Full board: -

Boy ○ Girl ○ Co-ed ●
Day ● Week ○ Board ○

For further information and a prospectus, please contact the school.

St Michaels Preparatory School

Address: Otford Court, Otford, Sevenoaks, Kent TN14 5SA

Telephone: 0959 22137

Head: Mr S Cummins

Age range:
No. of pupils:
Scholarships:
Religion:

Fees per term
Day: -
Weekly board: -
Full board: -

Boy ○ Girl ○ Co-ed ●
Day ● Week ● Board ●

For further information and a prospectus, please contact the school.

St Nicholas Nursery and Preparatory

Address: 18 Wiltie Gardens, Folkestone, Kent CT19 5AX

Telephone: 0303 254578

Head: Mrs C F Carlile

Age range: 2-7
No. of pupils: 20
Scholarships:
Religion: Non-denominational

Fees per term
Day: £585-£650
Weekly board: -
Full board: -

Boy ○ Girl ○ Co-ed ●
Day ● Week ○ Board ○

Saint Nicholas is a small, non-denominational private school. Children are accepted from the age of 2 until 7. To ensure individual attention, classes are limited to 12, which enables us to properly assist the pupils in achieving their full potential.

St Ronans

Address: Hawkhurst, Kent TN18 5DJ

Telephone: 0580 752271

Head: Mr J R Vassar-Smith

Age range: 5-13
No. of pupils: 90
Scholarships:
Religion: Church of England

Fees per term
Day: £825-£1654
Weekly board: £2137-£2137
Full board: £2137-£2137

Boy ● Girl ○ Co-ed ○
Day ● Week ● Board ●

Founded in 1883 the school has always been family run and greatly relies on the support of its old boys and friends. Set within 245 acres in the Weald of Kent, it is a Victorian style country house and is within sixty miles of London, down the A21.

Stratford House p679

Address: 8/10 Southborough Road, Bromley, Kent BR1 2EB
Telephone: 081 467 3580
Head: Mrs A Williamson

Age range: 3-18
No. of pupils: 400
Scholarships: Yes
Religion: Non-denominational

Fees per term
Day: £335-£1420
Weekly board: -
Full board: -

Boy ○ Girl ● Co-ed ○
Day ● Week ○ Board ○

Stratford House aims to fully develop the academic and practical student by providing a wide curriculum and small groups. We are noted for our ability to build confidence and provide a caring environment.

Business courses provide a firm foundation for careers in industry, whilst a pass rate at A Level of between 95-100% means that girls enter all major universities and professions, including music, drama and art.

Sunrise Independent

Address: Sutton Road, Langley, Maidstone, Kent
Telephone: 0622 861325
Head: Mrs M Murray

Age range: 2-8
No. of pupils: 100
Scholarships:
Religion: Church of England

Fees per term
Day: £335-£675
Weekly board: -
Full board: -

Boy ○ Girl ○ Co-ed ●
Day ● Week ○ Board ○

A school where caring and learning work side by side. Excellent ratio of 10 children to 1 adult.

Sutton Valence School * p751

Address: Sutton Valence, Maidstone, Kent ME17 3HL
Telephone: 0622 842281
Head: Mr M R Haywood

Age range: 11-18
No. of pupils: 390
Scholarships: Yes
Religion: Church of England

Fees per term
Day: £2200-£2200
Weekly board: £3450-£3450
Full board: £3450-£3450

Boy ○ Girl ○ Co-ed ●
Day ● Week ● Board ●

A safe, secure and beautiful environment. Small enough to be a genuine, caring community but large enough to provide full range of academic and extra-curricular activities. Wide ability range, but tough academic and personal expectations of all. Very strong music, drama, sport, art and technology.

Tonbridge School * p751

Address: Tonbridge, Kent TN9 1JP
Telephone: 0732 365555
Head: Mr J M Hammond

Age range:
No. of pupils: 650
Scholarships: Yes
Religion: Church of England

Fees per term
Day: £2450-
Weekly board: -
Full board: £3475-

Boy ● Girl ○ Co-ed ○
Day ● Week ○ Board ●

HMC boarding and day school for boys, 13-18 (440 boarders, 210 day boys). Outstanding academic record (1991 A Level pass-rate 99%, 65% A and B grades). First-class sporting facilities. Entry at 13 by Common Entrance or Tonbridge Scholarship examination (about 25 scholarships - academic, music and art - offered each year). Small sixth form entry (including Assisted Places).

Underhill Preparatory School

Address: Church Road, Chart Sutton, Maidstone, Kent ME17 3RF
Telephone: 0622 842117

Head: Mr I C Stainton-James

Age range: 3-13
No. of pupils: 348
Scholarships: Yes
Religion: Non-denominational

Fees per term
Day: £895-£1265
Weekly board: -
Full board: -

Boy ○ Girl ○ Co-ed ●
Day ● Week ○ Board ○

A co-educational all day preparatory school situated in eighteen acres, Underhill aims to provide a happy environment for all children and to fully prepare them for transfer to senior independent schools or the maintained sector. Classes are small, with a large, well qualified staff and the school's excellent facilities enables a full range of extra-curricular activities to be offered.

Ursuline Convent School *

Address: 225 Canterbury Road, Westgate-on-Sea, Kent CT8 8LN
Telephone: 0843 34431

Head: Sister Mary Murphy

Age range: 10-19
No. of pupils: 300
Scholarships:
Religion:

Fees per term
Day: -
Weekly board: -
Full board: -

Boy ○ Girl ● Co-ed ○
Day ● Week ○ Board ●

For further information and a prospectus, please contact the school.

Vernon Holme

Address: Harbledown, Canterbury, Kent CT2 9AQ
Telephone: 0227 762436

Head: Mr T J Smith

Age range: 4-11
No. of pupils: 150
Scholarships:
Religion: Methodist

Fees per term
Day: £1093-£1610
Weekly board: -£2315
Full board: -£2315

Boy ○ Girl ○ Co-ed ●
Day ● Week ● Board ●

Vernon Holme is the junior school of Kent College. Although just off the A2 and only 1.5 miles from Canterbury, we are set in orchards and have 12 acres of our own beautiful grounds. We are a warm and happy school where all children matter, whatever their ability. We have high academic standards and follow the National Curriculum.

Walthamstow Hall *

Address: Sevenoaks, Kent TN13 3UL
Telephone: 0732 451334

Head: Mrs J S Lang

Age range: 5-18
No. of pupils: 532
Scholarships: Yes
Religion: Non-denominational

Fees per term
Day: £1025-£1555
Weekly board: £2318-£2870
Full board: £2318-£2870

Boy ○ Girl ● Co-ed ○
Day ● Week ● Board ●

Walthamstow Hall offers a sound, broad academic programme to able girls from all backgrounds, and achieves notable success in public examinations and university entrance. The range of extra-curricular activities is wide. Set on the edge of Sevenoaks, the school has excellent access to London, Heathrow and Gatwick airports and the English Channel ports. We warmly encourage you to visit us.

Wellesley House

Address: Ramsgate Road, Broadstairs, Kent CT10 2DG

Telephone: 0843 862991

Head: Mr R R Steel BSc

Age range: 8-13
No. of pupils: 197
Scholarships:
Religion: Church of England

Fees per term
Day: £2300-
Weekly board: £2600-
Full board: £2700-

Boy ○ Girl ○ Co-ed ●
Day ● Week ● Board ●

Wellesley House is situated in 16 acres of grounds. Pupils spend their first year in the junior wing linked to the main school. The Orchard is a large house in the grounds that accommodates girl boarders. The school has its own chapel. Wellesley has a sound record of scholarships. A disciplined yet caring community encourages children to become self-reliant.

West Heath School

Address: Ashgrove Road, Sevenoaks, Kent TN13 1SR

Telephone: 07332 452541

Head: Mrs L Cohn-Sherbok

Age range: 11-18
No. of pupils: 166
Scholarships:
Religion:

Fees per term
Day: -
Weekly board: -
Full board: -

Boy ○ Girl ● Co-ed ○
Day ● Week ○ Board ●

For further information and a prospectus, please contact the school.

West Lodge School Ltd

Address: 36 Station Road, Sidcup, Kent DA15 7DU

Telephone: 081 300 2489

Head: Mrs J U Barrett

Age range: 3-11
No. of pupils: 150
Scholarships:
Religion:

Fees per term
Day: £450-£760
Weekly board: -
Full board: -

Boy ○ Girl ○ Co-ed ●
Day ● Week ○ Board ○

An independent day school for girls aged 3-11 and boys 3-7. The school covers a wide range of academic subjects as well as art, games, dancing, music and drama. The school is situated in a large walled garden and has a friendly relaxed atmosphere whilst achieving high academic standards.

Yardley Court

Address: Somerhill, Five Oak Green Road, Tonbridge, Kent TN11 0NJ

Telephone: 0732 352124

Head: Mr J D Barber

Age range: 3-13
No. of pupils: 303
Scholarships:
Religion: Church of England

Fees per term
Day: £510-£1695
Weekly board: -£2380
Full board: -£2430

Boy ● Girl ○ Co-ed ○
Day ● Week ● Board ●

The school prepares boys for Common Entrance to senior schools particularly Tonbridge. Sound foundations are essential to all academic teaching. Excellent music traditions, all major sports coached, superb sports grounds of 145 acres, five tennis courts and wide range of activities. Marvellous 'home' for boarders to enjoy.

LANCASHIRE

Arnold School *

Address: Lytham Road, Blackpool, Lancashire FY4 2HF
Telephone: 0253 46391

Head: Mr J A B Kelsall

Age range: 11-18
No. of pupils: 820
Scholarships: Yes
Religion: Non-denominational

Fees per term
Day: £1086-
Weekly board: £2145-
Full board: £2193-

Boy ○ Girl ○ Co-ed ●
Day ● Week ● Board ●

The school has an enviable academic record at both GCSE and A Level, but prides itself on its broad, educational provision. Facilities, including a new design centre and an all-weather pitch, are being continually up-dated. Visitors are most welcome.

Beech House School

Address: 184 Manchester Road, Rochdale, Lancashire OL11 4JQ
Telephone: 0706 46309

Head: Mr I R Barber

Age range: 3-16
No. of pupils: 198
Scholarships:
Religion: Non-denominational

Fees per term
Day: -
Weekly board: -
Full board: -

Boy ○ Girl ○ Co-ed ●
Day ● Week ○ Board ○

The aim of the school is to blend the best of traditional education with the skills and resources of the modern system to ensure that pupil's talents are exercised to the full. The class sizes are kept small with 20 or fewer pupils per form at preparatory level and approximately 15 pupils in each secondary class. The school achieves considerable success at all levels and in particular at GCSE and 11+.

Bentham School

Address: Bentham, Lancaster, Lancashire LA2 7DB
Telephone: 05242 61275

Head: Mr N K D Ward

Age range: 3-18
No. of pupils: 300
Scholarships: Yes
Religion: Church of England

Fees per term
Day: £740-£1190
Weekly board: £2125-£2405
Full board: £2125-£2405

Boy ○ Girl ○ Co-ed ●
Day ● Week ● Board ●

A friendly yet disciplined and caring community where the full development potential and needs of the individual are of utmost importance. We are proud of our traditions yet have a forward looking approach to the education of boys and girls in the 1990's. Full use is made of the magnificent rural setting on the edge of the Yorkshire Dales.

Bolton School (Boy's Division) *

Address: Chorley New Road, Bolton, Lancashire BL1 4PA
Telephone: 0204 840201

Head: Mr A W Wright

Age range: 8-18
No. of pupils: 1000
Scholarships: Yes
Religion: Non-denominational

Fees per term
Day: £959-£1332
Weekly board: -
Full board: -

Boy ● Girl ○ Co-ed ○
Day ● Week ○ Board ○

Bolton School has a long standing tradition of academic excellence. A stimulating environment is provided for pupils who enjoy challenges of an intellectual nature, the broad in-depth curriculum being balanced by a vigorous extra-curricular programme. A substantial number of Assisted Places are available. Entry by examination at 8,9,11; by interview at 16.

Bolton School (Girls School) *

Address: Chorley New Road, Bolton, Lancashire BL1 4PB

Telephone: 0204 840201

Head: Mrs M A Spurr BA FRSA

Age range: 4-18
No. of pupils: 1141
Scholarships: Yes
Religion: Non-denomination

Fees per term
Day: £959-£1332
Weekly board: -
Full board: -

Boy ○ Girl ● Co-ed ○
Day ● Week ○ Board ○

For further information and a prospectus, please contact the school

Bury Catholic Preparatory School

Address: Arden House, Manchester Road, Bury, Lancashire BL9 9BH

Telephone: 061 764 2346

Head: Mrs S F Entwistle

Age range: 4-11
No. of pupils: 140
Scholarships:
Religion: Catholic

Fees per term
Day: £600-£600
Weekly board: -
Full board: -

Boy ○ Girl ○ Co-ed ●
Day ● Week ○ Board ○

The school provides a caring, friendly environment in small classes for children rising 4 to 11 years. Entrance is by interview with the head teacher at all ages. Children of other denominations are welcome. Emphasis is placed on numeracy and literacy and all National Curriuclum subjects are taught. Children prepared for entrance to senior schools at 10+. Active PTA.

Bury Grammar School (Girls) *

Address: Bridge Road, Bury, Lancashire BL9 0HH

Telephone: 061 797 2808

Head: Miss J M Lawley

Age range:
No. of pupils:
Scholarships: Yes
Religion: Non-denominational

Fees per term
Day: £1100-£1100
Weekly board: -
Full board: -

Boy ○ Girl ● Co-ed ○
Day ● Week ○ Board ○

The Girls' School seeks to provide a broad and balanced education in a lively environment. Each girl is encouraged to develop her indivdual talents and abilities as far as she can in a community which strives to respond to the challenge of change whilst retaining traditional grammar school virtues - sound learning, sensible discipline and good manners.

Bury Grammar School *

Address: Tenterden Street, Bury, Lancashire BL9 0HN

Telephone: 061 797 2700

Head: Mr K Richards MA

Age range: 8-18
No. of pupils: 791
Scholarships: Yes
Religion: Non-denominational

Fees per term
Day: £783-£1100
Weekly board: -
Full board: -

Boy ● Girl ○ Co-ed ○
Day ● Week ○ Board ○

Junior School (7+) 110 boys, Senior School (11+) 680 boys. The school is housed in modern buildings close to the Girl's School and within easy reach of the centre of Bury. The school aims to provide a broad and balanced education in a lively environment. Expansion of its facilities is continuing with the construction of additional senior classrooms and a relocated and extended Junior School.

Casterton School * p680

Address: Kirkby Lonsdale, Carnforth, Lancashire LA6 2SG
Telephone: 05242 71202

Head: Mr A F Thomas

Age range: 8-18
No. of pupils: 330
Scholarships: Yes
Religion: Church of England

Fees per term
Day: £1416-£1626
Weekly board: £2196-£2196
Full board: £2106-£2640

○ ● ○
Boy Girl Co-ed

● ● ●
Day Week Board

Situated amidst delightful rural scenery, between the Yorkshire Dales and the Lake District, Casterton is a boarding and day school for girls aged 8-18, with first class teaching and sports facilities and outstanding academic results. Activities include riding, outdoor pursuits, music, drama and full use is made of the school's unique environment. Recent developments include a new creative arts block.

Chorcliffe School

Address: The Old Manse, Park Street, Chorley, Lancashire PR7 1ER
Telephone: 0257 268807
Head: Miss H Mayer

Age range: 3-9
No. of pupils: 50
Scholarships:
Religion: Non-denominational

Fees per term
Day: £600-£1190
Weekly board: -
Full board: -

○ ○ ○
Boy Girl Co-ed

○ ○ ○
Day Week Board

Pre-Prep 3-8 years. Preparation for Grammar Schools of 8+; (From 1992) Prep 8-13 years. Preparation for Public Schools at 13+ via Common Entrance, Senior 13-16 years, Preparation for GCSE.

Small classes, individual attention, homely atmosphere, emphasis on good speech and manners and all-round excellence.

Clevelands Preparatory School

Address: 349 Chorley New Road, Bolton, Lancashire BL1 5DA
Telephone: 0204 843898

Head: Mr G Hart

Age range: 4-11
No. of pupils: 182
Scholarships:
Religion: Non-denominational

Fees per term
Day: -£729
Weekly board: -
Full board: -

○ ○ ●
Boy Girl Co-ed

● ○ ○
Day Week Board

Clevelands Preparatory School is an independent day school for boys and girls. The school caters for children aged 4-11 years, and is non-denominational. The school offers a unique course with regard to the basic subjects, in that the majority of textbooks in use in the school have been specifically written for the pupils of Clevelands by the original headmaster and his deputy. The information subjects are also treated unusually.

Convent Primary School

Address: Beechwood, Manchester Road, Rochdale, Lancashire OL11 4LU
Telephone: 0706 46627

Head: Sister Rosemarie Steinbach

Age range: 3-11
No. of pupils: 203
Scholarships:
Religion: Roman Catholic

Fees per term
Day: £490-£550
Weekly board: -
Full board: -

○ ○ ●
Boy Girl Co-ed

● ○ ○
Day Week Board

Beechwood Convent Primary School is a Catholic independent mixed primary school for children from three to eleven years of age. The school's basic aims are to develop the full potential of each child in a Christian environment and set and maintain high standards of behaviour.

Elmslie Girls' School

Address: 194 Whitegate Drive, Blackpool, Lancashire FY3 9HL
Telephone: 0253 763775

Head: Miss E M Smithies

Age range: 3-18
No. of pupils: 400
Scholarships: Yes
Religion: Church of England

Fees per term
Day: £650-£1085
Weekly board: -
Full board: -

Boy ○ Girl ● Co-ed ○
Day ● Week ○ Board ○

For further information and a prospectus, please contact the school.

Emmanuel Christian School p681

Address: Elm Street, Fleetwood, Lancashire
Telephone: 0253 770646

Principal: Dr N B Smith

Age range: 3-16
No. of pupils: 80
Scholarships:
Religion: Christian

Fees per term
Day: £314-£420
Weekly board: -
Full board: -

Boy ○ Girl ○ Co-ed ●
Day ● Week ○ Board ○

Emmanuel Christian School is a small, independent day school for boys and girls aged 3 to 16. It provides a Christian education in a caring, family atmosphere with the emphasis on the individual progress of the student. Courses are provided in the Upper School leading to GCSE.

Fleetwood Preparatory School

Address: Fleetwood, Lancashire FY7 8JW
Telephone: 0253 774222

Head: Mr A N Rostron

Age range: 7-13
No. of pupils: 183
Scholarships:
Religion: Church of England but all denominati

Fees per term
Day: £970-£1570
Weekly board: -£2365
Full board: -£2365

Boy ○ Girl ○ Co-ed ●
Day ● Week ● Board ●

For further information and a prospectus, please contact the school.

Glebe House School

Address: Broadfield Stile, Rochdale, Lancashire OL16 1UT
Telephone: 0706 45985

Head: Mr K Bayliss

Age range: 3-7
No. of pupils: 80
Scholarships:
Religion: Non-denominational

Fees per term
Day: £565-£565
Weekly board: -
Full board: -

Boy ○ Girl ○ Co-ed ●
Day ● Week ○ Board ○

For further information and a prospectus, please contact the school.

Heathfield School

Address: 16 East Park Road,
Blackburn, Lancashire
BB1 8AT
Telephone: 0254 56923

Head: Mr P Martin

Age range: 2-16
No. of pupils: 230
Scholarships:
Religion: Non-denominational

Fees per term
Day: £400-£990
Weekly board: -
Full board: -

Boy ○ Girl ○ Co-ed ●
Day ● Week ○ Board ○

Heathfield School offers quality and continuity in education in modern buildings with a traditional environment. We have newly refurbished facilities and well qualified, enthusiastic staff. With small classes and academic record, Heathfield ensures that your child's ability is brought out through encouragement and close, constant monitoring.

Highfield Priory School

Address: Fullwood Row,
Fullwood, Preston, Lancashire
PR2 6SL
Telephone: 0772 709624

Headmaster: Mr B C Duckett

Age range: 3-11
No. of pupils: 320
Scholarships: Yes
Religion: Non-denominational

Fees per term
Day: £725-£725
Weekly board: -
Full board: -

Boy ○ Girl ○ Co-ed ●
Day ● Week ○ Board ○

Highfield is set in 4 acres of landscaped gardens and is a co-educational preparatory school for children aged 3 to 11+ years. It is fully equipped with its own well established nursery and prepares children for all independent grammar and public schools in Lancashire. Extra-curricular activities include ballet, swimming, gymnastics, badminton, table tennis, modelling, chess and instrument tuition.

King Edward VII School *

Address: Lytham, Lancashire
FY8 1DT

Telephone: 0253 736459

Head: Mr D Heap

Age range: 7-18
No. of pupils: 630
Scholarships: Yes
Religion: Non-denominational

Fees per term
Day: £664-£996
Weekly board: -
Full board: -

Boy ● Girl ○ Co-ed ○
Day ● Week ○ Board ○

King Edward's is an ex-direct grant grammar school, with its own junior department. It strives to achieve high academic standards while offering a broad education to serve the needs of individual boys. Sport and a wide variety of activities are strongly devloped.

Kirkham Grammar School *

Address: Ribby Road,
Kirkham, Preston, Lancashire
PR4 2BH
Telephone: 0772 671079

Head: Mr B Stacey

Age range: 6-18
No. of pupils: 650
Scholarships: Yes
Religion: Non-denominational

Fees per term
Day: £1026-
Weekly board: £1881-
Full board: £1926-

Boy ○ Girl ○ Co-ed ●
Day ● Week ● Board ●

The school is attractively situated in more than 20 acres of its own grounds in a semi-rural area midway between Preston and Blackpool. Its unique ethos exudes warmth, friendship and a sense of 'one-family.' Generations of families continue to send their children to this traditional, highly esteemed grammar school where academic standards are high and the breadth of educational experience is impressive.

Lawrence House School

Address: Beauclerk Road, St. Annes-on-Sea, Lytham St. Annes, Lancashire FY8 3LJ
Telephone: 0253 722178

Head: Mr G N Phillips BEd

Age range: 3-13
No. of pupils: 160
Scholarships: Yes
Religion: Church of England

Fees per term
Day: £450-£950
Weekly board: -
Full board: £1650-£2050

Boy ○ Girl ○ Co-ed ●
Day ● Week ○ Board ●

Co-educational day and boarding school for children aged 3 to 14. In its own grounds overlooking The Royal Lytham an St. Annes Golf Course, the school provides a standard of schooling in a caring but disciplined environment. An excellent pupil/teacher ratio ensures maximum individual attention; a very extensive programme of extra-curricular activities caters for the need of every child.

Lord's College

Address: 53 Manchester Road, Bolton, Lancashire BL2 1ES
Telephone: 0204 23731

Head: Mr A Thomas

Age range: 11-17
No. of pupils: 70
Scholarships:
Religion: Non-denominational

Fees per term
Day: -£415
Weekly board: -
Full board: -

Boy ○ Girl ○ Co-ed ●
Day ● Week ○ Board ○

For further information and a prospectus, please contact the school.

Moorland School

Address: Ribblesdale Avenue, Clitheroe, Lancashire BB7 2JA
Telephone: 0200 23833

Head: Mrs J Harrison BA Hons.

Age range: 2-18
No. of pupils: 205
Scholarships:
Religion: Church of England

Fees per term
Day: £537-£935
Weekly board: -
Full board: £1971-£2073

Boy ○ Girl ○ Co-ed ●
Day ● Week ○ Board ●

Moorland School is a selective school set in 15 acre grounds. We promote traditional educational and social values within a happy and caring environment with a fundamental aim of helping each child to fulfil its individual potential. This does not only mean the acquisition of good examination results but also the development of physical fitness and sporting skills. The small classes enable the staff to give each pupil attention.

Nugent House School †

Address: Carr Mill Road, Billinge, Wigan, Lancashire WN5 7TT
Telephone: 0744 892551

Head: Mr C G Mills

Age range: 8-17
No. of pupils: 75
Scholarships:
Religion: Non-denominational

Fees per term
Day: -
Weekly board: -
Full board: -

Boy ● Girl ○ Co-ed ○
Day ● Week ○ Board ●

For fees, further information and a prospectus, please contact the school.

Oakhill College

Address: Wiswell Lane, Whalley, Lancashire BB6 9AF

Telephone: 0254 823546

Head: Mrs C A Finlay

Age range: 3-16
No. of pupils: 210
Scholarships: Yes
Religion: Roman Catholic

Fees per term
Day: £709-£1146
Weekly board: -
Full board: -

Boy ○ Girl ○ Co-ed ●
Day ● Week ○ Board ○

For further information and a prospectus, please contact the school.

Queen Elizabeth's Grammar School *

Address: Blackburn, Lancashire BB2 6DF

Telephone: 0254 59911

Head: Mr P F Johnson

Age range: 8-18
No. of pupils: 1223
Scholarships: Yes
Religion: Non-denominational

Fees per term
Day: £1155-£917
Weekly board: -
Full board: -

Boy ● Girl ● Co-ed ○
Day ● Week ○ Board ○

Queen Elizabeth's Grammar School has 1100 boys with 100 sixth form girls and 140 in the junior department serving a very large catchment area of north-east Lancashire. Academically orientated with 25 annual places at Oxford and Cambridge, it has a wide range of extra-curricular activities, being particularly noted for its prowess at soccer and swimming.

Queen Mary School *

Address: Lytham, Lancashire FY8 1DS

Telephone: 0253 723246

Head: Miss M C Ritchie

Age range: 6-18
No. of pupils: 630
Scholarships: Yes
Religion:

Fees per term
Day: £682-£1023
Weekly board: -
Full board: -

Boy ○ Girl ● Co-ed ○
Day ● Week ○ Board ○

Queen Mary School is an independent girls' grammar school with entry by examination. The school provides a balanced education combining traditional academic curriculum with modern educational developments, achieving very good examination results at advanced level and GCSE. With excellent facilities, friendly atmosphere and caring pastoral system.

Rossall Pre-Preparatory School

Address: Fleetwood, Lancashire FY7 8JW

Telephone: 0253 774222

Head: Mr A N Rostron

Age range: 3-7
No. of pupils: 100
Scholarships:
Religion: Church of England

Fees per term
Day: £220-£810
Weekly board: -
Full board: -

Boy ○ Girl ○ Co-ed ●
Day ● Week ○ Board ○

For further information and a prospectus, please contact the school.

Rossall Preparatory School

Address: Fleetwood,
Lancashire FY7 8JW
Telephone: 0253 774 222

Age range:
No. of pupils:
Scholarships:
Religion:

Fees per term
Day: -
Weekly board: -
Full board: -

○ ○ ●
Boy Girl Co-ed
● ● ●
Day Week Board

Head: Mr A N Rostron

For further information and a prospectus, please contact the school.

Rossall School *

Address: Fleetwood,
Lancashire

Telephone: 0253 774247

Age range: 7-18
No. of pupils: 810
Scholarships: Yes
Religion: Church of England

Fees per term
Day: £1120-£2270
Weekly board: -
Full board: £2200-£3255

○ ○ ●
Boy Girl Co-ed
● ○ ●
Day Week Board

Head: Mr R D W Rhodes

Rossall, founded in 1844, is co-educational and predominantly boarding. Situated on the Lancashire coast, the M6 and M55 motorways provide fast access by road while Manchester Airport is just one hour away. The School provides a Christian-based education based upon the principles of honesty, intergrity and hard work. A strong house system and a wide range of extra-curricular activities.

Scarisbrick Hall School

Address: Scarisbrick,
Ormskirk, Lancashire
L40 9RQ
Telephone: 0704 880200

Age range: 3-18
No. of pupils: 450
Scholarships: Yes
Religion: Non-Denominational

Fees per term
Day: £440-£735
Weekly board: -
Full board: -

○ ○ ●
Boy Girl Co-ed
● ○ ○
Day Week Board

Head: Mr D M Raynor BA DipEd

For further information and a prospectus, please contact the school.

St Anne's College Grammar School and Junior School

Address: 293 Clifton Drive
South, Lytham St Annes,
Lancashire FY8 1HN
Telephone: 0253 725815

Age range: 2
No. of pupils: 180
Scholarships: Yes
Religion: Christian

Fees per term
Day: £570-£750
Weekly board: -
Full board: -

○ ○ ●
Boy Girl Co-ed
● ○ ○
Day Week Board

Head: Mr S R Welsby

For further information and a prospectus, please contact the school.

St Joseph's Convent School

Address: Park Hill, Padiham Road, Burnley, Lancashire BB12 6TG
Telephone: 0282 55622

Age range: 4-11
No. of pupils: 204
Scholarships:
Religion:

Fees per term
Day: -
Weekly board: -
Full board: -

● Boy ○ Girl ○ Co-ed (Co-ed filled)
● Day ○ Week ○ Board

Head: Sister Mary Clement

For further information and a prospectus, please contact the school.

St Mary's Hall

Address: Stonyhurst, Lancashire BB6 9PU
Telephone: 0254 826 242

Age range: 7-13
No. of pupils: 185
Scholarships: Yes
Religion: Roman Catholic

Fees per term
Day: £1103-£1593
Weekly board: -
Full board: £2246-£2246

● Boy ○ Girl ○ Co-ed
● Day ○ Week ● Board

Head: Mr R F O'Brien

Set in our own grounds close to Stonyhurst College in beautiful Ribble Valley. Easy access to M6, Preston Station (30 minutes), Manchester Airport (1 hour), boys escorted. Common Entrance syllabus spiced with computer and environmental studies (own rare breed centre), theatre workshop, music, extensive indoor activities, excellent games tradition-own sports hall, swimming pool, tennis courts and theatre.

St Pius X Preparatory School

Address: 200 Garstane Road, Fulwood, Preston, Lancashire PR2 4JR
Telephone: 0772 719937

Age range: 2-11
No. of pupils: 320
Scholarships:
Religion: Roman Catholic

Fees per term
Day: £610-£710
Weekly board: -
Full board: -

○ Boy ○ Girl ● Co-ed
● Day ○ Week ○ Board

Head: Miss B M Banks

Co-educational, Roman Catholic, independent day school. All denominations welcome. Kindergarten from 2 and a half years (morning, afternoon or full day sessions). Preparatory division from 4-11 years. Excellent examination results to senior school. Extensive time table encompassing many subjects. Excellent on-site sporting facilities.

Stonyhurst College ✻

Address: Stonyhurst, Lancashire BB6 9PZ
Telephone: 0254 826345

Age range: 13-18
No. of pupils: 425
Scholarships: Yes
Religion: Roman Catholic

Fees per term
Day: £1954-
Weekly board: -
Full board: £3396-

● Boy ● Girl ○ Co-ed
● Day ○ Week ● Board

Head: Dr R G G Mercer

Stonyhurst College is an independent (HMC) school offering boarding and day places to boys at all age levels up to 18 and day places to girls in the sixth form. Excellent academic and extra-curricular facilities and results. Outstanding higher education and careers department. High staff-pupil ratio and extensive pastoral system. All students live in the college which is set in an estate of great natural beauty.

Sunnybank Preparatory School

Address: 171-173 Manchester Road, Burnley, Lancashire BB11 4HR
Telephone: 0282 21336

Head: Mrs J M M Taylor

Age range: 3-11
No. of pupils: 100
Scholarships:
Religion:

Fees per term
Day: -
Weekly board: -
Full board: -

Boy ○ Girl ○ Co-ed ●
Day ● Week ○ Board ○

For further information and a prospectus, please contact the school.

Westholme *

Address: Meins Road, Blackburn, Lancashire BB2 6QU
Telephone: 0254 53447

Head: Mrs L Croston

Age range: 4-18
No. of pupils: 1000
Scholarships: Yes
Religion: Christian

Fees per term
Day: £695-£975
Weekly board: -
Full board: -

Boy ● Girl ● Co-ed ○
Day ● Week ○ Board ○

Westholme is organised into three departments; lower school, 4-8 years, co-educational; middle school, 8-11 years, girls; upper school, 11-18 years, girls. Our aim is to provide pupils with a liberal and sound academic education based on christian principles. Pupils are treated as individuals in an ordered, purposeful and happy environment.

The William Skurr School

Address: 184 Manchester Road, Rochdale, Manchester OL11 4LU
Telephone: 0706 46309

Principals: I R Barber BEd H Barber CertEd

Age range: 3-16
No. of pupils: 185
Scholarships:
Religion:

Fees per term
Day: -
Weekly board: -
Full board: -

Boy ○ Girl ○ Co-ed ●
Day ● Week ○ Board ○

For further information and a prospectus, please contact the school.

Woodlands School

Address: 162 Ribbleton Avenue, Preston, Lancashire
Telephone: 0772 792484

Head: Mrs J G Hirst

Age range: 2-11
No. of pupils: 120
Scholarships:
Religion: Non-Denominational

Fees per term
Day: £485-£645
Weekly board: -
Full board: -

Boy ○ Girl ○ Co-ed ●
Day ● Week ○ Board ○

A small school. Preparation for Grammar School. Small classes (average 16). French is taught. Swimming. Supervised daily transport from many areas.

LEICESTERSHIRE

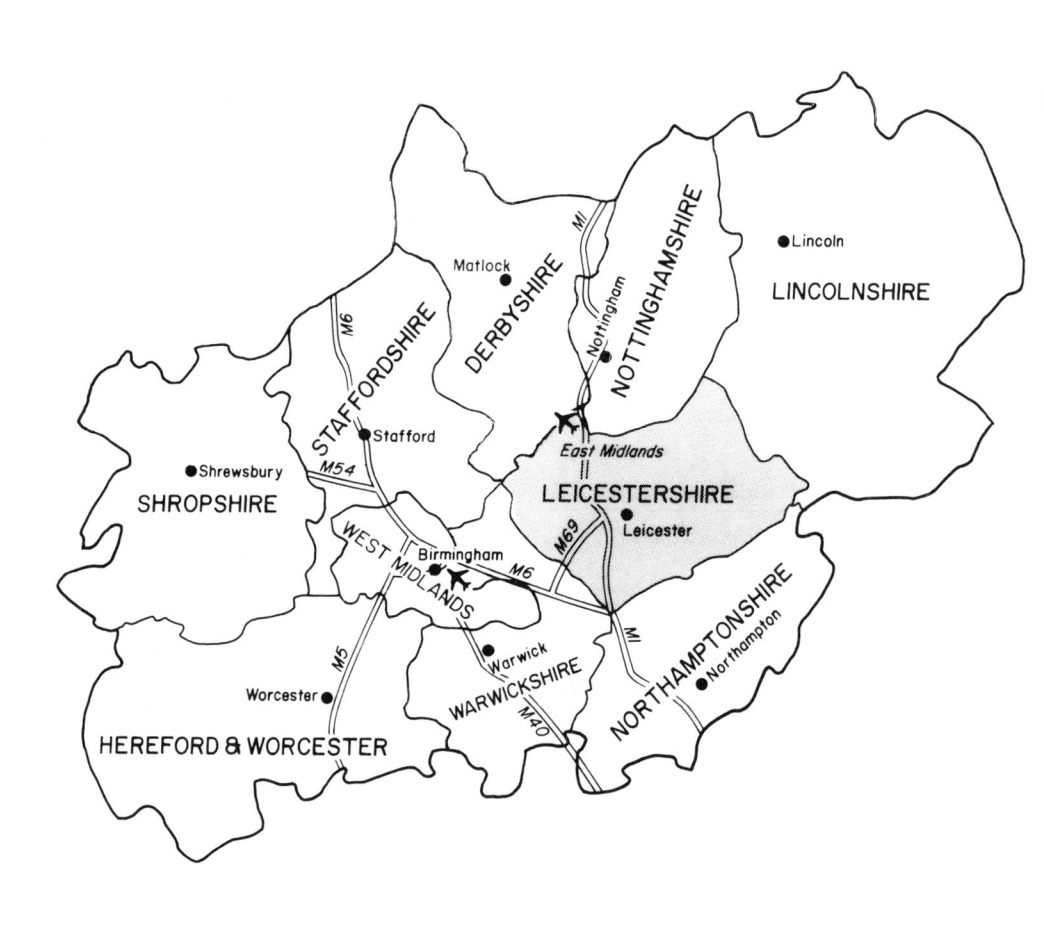

Brooke Priory

Address: Brooke Oakham, Rutland, Leicestershire LE15 8DG
Telephone: 0572 724778

Headmistress: Mrs S Allen

Age range: 4-11
No. of pupils: 102
Scholarships:
Religion: Church of England

Fees per term
Day: £586-£790
Weekly board: -
Full board: -

Boy ○ Girl ○ Co-ed ●
Day ● Week ○ Board ○

Brooke is a country school within the grounds of the Old Priory. The classes are small allowing for excellent pupil teacher relationship. Children are encouraged to develop both socially and academically, and a good work talent is developed from an early age. The school has an excellent record of pupils gaining entry to a wide range of senior schools.

Fairfield School

Address: Leicester Road, Loughborough, Leicestershire LE11 2AE
Telephone: 0509 215172

Head: Mr T A Eadon

Age range: 4-11
No. of pupils: 466
Scholarships:
Religion: Non-denominational

Fees per term
Day: -£897
Weekly board: -
Full board: -

Boy ○ Girl ○ Co-ed ●
Day ● Week ○ Board ○

Fairfield aims to give a broad based education appropriate for the needs of the children in our care. Many of our children go on to Loughborough Grammar School or High School. The school aims for standards of excellence in all that it does whilst at the same time providing a wide range of activities for all children.

Fosse Way School

Address: 72 Fosse Road South, Leicester, Leicestershire LE3 0QD
Telephone: 0533 541115

Head: Mrs S J Cooper

Age range: 3-11
No. of pupils: 65
Scholarships:
Religion: Christian

Fees per term
Day: £462-£660
Weekly board: -
Full board: -

Boy ○ Girl ○ Co-ed ●
Day ● Week ○ Board ○

We aim to provide a sound, high standard of education, and to develop a sense of reliability and social responsibility in each pupil. Within a wide curriculum the emphasis in on the basic skills of reading, writing and numeracy. Importance is attached to pupils being happy in an organised, disciplined environment as well as to character training and good manners.

Glenn Preparatory School

Address: Great Glen, Leicester, Leicestershire LE8 0DJ
Telephone: 0533 592282

Head: Mrs J M Josephs

Age range: 3-11
No. of pupils: 175
Scholarships:
Religion: Non-denominational

Fees per term
Day: £415-£1050
Weekly board: -
Full board: -

Boy ○ Girl ○ Co-ed ●
Day ● Week ○ Board ○

For further information and a prospectus, please contact the school.

Grace Dieu Manor School

Address: Grace Dieu,
Coalville, Leicestershire
LE67 5UE
Telephone: 0530 222 276

Head: Fr G J Duffy

Age range: 4-13
No. of pupils: 350
Scholarships: Yes
Religion: Roman Catholic

Fees per term
Day: £866-£1347
Weekly board: -
Full board: -£2022

Co-ed / Day / Board

Grace Dieu Manor is a preparatory school run by the Institute of Charity with the assistance of fully qualified lay staff. The school is set in 90 acres at the edge of Charnwood Forest. Its aim is to foster the development of the whole child academically, socially and spiritually in a family atmosphere with the best facilities available.

Leicester Grammar School

Address: 8 Peacock Lane,
Leicester, Leicestershire
LE1 5PX
Telephone: 0533 621221

Head: Mr J B Sugden

Age range: 10-18
No. of pupils: 570
Scholarships: Yes
Religion: Church of England

Fees per term
Day: £1075-
Weekly board: -
Full board: -

Co-ed / Day

Leicester Grammar School offers a first-class academic education (A Level: 95%; GCSE A to C: 96%). A Christian foundation, it lays equal stress on moral and spiritual awareness, on a high standard of all-round education and on nurturing each individual personality in a friendly, disciplined, family environment. Good staff, pupil ratio 1:11. Wide range of musical, dramatic, creative, sporting and charity activities.

Leicester High School Charitable Trust Limited p682

Address: 454 London Road,
Leicester, Leicestershire
LE2 2PP
Telephone: 0533 705338

Head: Mrs P A Watson

Age range: 3-18
No. of pupils: 430
Scholarships: Yes
Religion: Church of England

Fees per term
Day: £690-£1170
Weekly board: -
Full board: -

Girl / Day

Leicester High School for Girls stands in pleasant wooded grounds about three miles south of the city centre. It offers an academic education within a very caring environment. Class size is kept small to enable girls to reach their full potential. The school aims to encourage social conscience within a community while developing self-discipline and self confidence in the girls.

Loughborough Grammar School *

Address: 6 Burton Walks,
Loughborough, Leicestershire
LE11 2DU
Telephone: 0509 233233

Head: Mr D N Ireland

Age range: 10-18
No. of pupils: 920
Scholarships: Yes
Religion: Non-denominational

Fees per term
Day: £1260-£1344
Weekly board: £2082-£2202
Full board: £2364-£2496

Boy / Day / Week / Board

Loughborough Grammar School is part of an ancient family of schools occupying a large and attractive campus on the outskirts of Loughborough. Buildings and facilities are first class. Although academically amongst the strongest in the country, the school seeks education in its widest sense and sport, music and drama are pursued to a very high level.

Loughborough High School *

Address: Burton Walks, Loughborough, Leicestershire LE11 2DU
Telephone: 0509 212348

Head: Miss J E L Harvatt

Age range: 11-18
No. of pupils: 530
Scholarships: Yes
Religion: Non-Denominational

Fees per term
Day: £1098-
Weekly board: £1753-
Full board: -

Boy ○ Girl ● Co-ed ○
Day ● Week ● Board ○

Loughborough High School, the first girls' grammar school in England, has excellent facilities, which are being added to and improved all the time. We share a site with our brother school, Loughborough Grammar and the co-educational junior school, Fairfield. School offers a wide range of cultural, recreational and sporting opportunities and aims to provide an excellent education in a caring atmosphere.

Manor House School

Address: South Street, Ashby-de-la-Zouch, Leicestershire
Telephone: 0530 412932

Head: Mr R J Sill

Age range: 4-14
No. of pupils: 150
Scholarships:
Religion: Non-denominational

Fees per term
Day: £785-£1240
Weekly board: -
Full board: -

Boy ○ Girl ○ Co-ed ●
Day ● Week ○ Board ○

Manor House School caters for mixed ability children and prepares them for entry to the local senior schools at 11 and 13, or to local state schools at 14. The pre-preparatory department has its own self-contained facilities. Children are taught French by French born teachers from the age of 5. German is taught from the age of 11, while Latin is taught to more able children.

Nevill Holt p682

Address: Market Harborough, Leicestershire LE16 8EG
Telephone: 085 883 234

Head: Mr C M Woolley

Age range: 4-13
No. of pupils: 145
Scholarships: Yes
Religion: Church of England

Fees per term
Day: £675-£1500
Weekly board: -£1950
Full board: -£2050

Boy ○ Girl ○ Co-ed ●
Day ● Week ● Board ●

Nevill Holt is a preparatory school, originally founded as the Lower School for Uppingham in 1868, but housed in its present site, a grade 1 listed building, since 1920. The school, situated in an unspoilt rural area, has excellent facilities and a fine academic and sporting track record. Many children move on to Uppingham, Rugby, Oundle or Oakham.

Oakham School * p683

Address: Chapel Close, Oakham, Leicestershire LE15 6DT
Telephone: 0572 722487

Head: Mr G Smallbone

Age range: 11-18
No. of pupils: 1000
Scholarships: Yes
Religion: Church of England

Fees per term
Day: £1855-
Weekly board: -
Full board: £3355-

Boy ○ Girl ○ Co-ed ●
Day ● Week ○ Board ●

Oakham has been wholly committed to co-education for more than twenty years and there are equal numbers of boys and girls, boarding and day, at every level in the school. High standards are maintained in both traditional and modern areas of education.

Our Lady's Convent School

Address: Burton Street, Loughborough, Leicestershire LE11 2DT
Telephone: 0509 263901

Head: Sister Mary Fynn

Age range: 3-18
No. of pupils: 654
Scholarships:
Religion: Roman Catholic

Fees per term
Day: £530-£890
Weekly board: -
Full board: -

Boy ○ / Girl ● / Co-ed ○
Day ● / Week ○ / Board ○

Pleasant convent grounds within residential area. Religious and secular influences combined create a warm and loving environment. Consideration for others, courtesy and discipline are valued. Christian principles are the basis of daily life, wherein the individual is important and the realities of the world fully appreciated. Within a wide ability range most pupils achieve excellent results.

PNEU School

Address: 8 Station Road, East Leake, Loughborough, Leicestershire LE12 6LQ
Telephone: 0509 852229

Head: Mrs B G Warder

Age range: 3-11
No. of pupils: 90
Scholarships:
Religion: Non-denominational

Fees per term
Day: £687-£760
Weekly board: -
Full board: -

Boy ○ / Girl ○ / Co-ed ●
Day ● / Week ○ / Board ○

A day school for boys and girls from 3 to 11 years of age. Situated in pleasant grounds providing facilities for all games. Classes are small and the staff are well qualified and experienced. School life is based upon the principles of Charlotte Mason, founder of the PNEU, and attention is paid to the needs of every individual pupil.

PNEU School

Address: 22 Stockerston Road, Uppingham, Leicestershire LE15 9UD
Telephone: 0572 823593

Head: Mrs J Taylor

Age range: 4-11
No. of pupils: 86
Scholarships:
Religion: Non-denominational

Fees per term
Day: -
Weekly board: -
Full board: -

Boy ○ / Girl ○ / Co-ed ●
Day ● / Week ○ / Board ○

For further information and a prospectus, please contact the school.

Portland House School

Address: 454 London Road, Leicester, Leicestershire LE2 2PP
Telephone: 0533 705338

Head: Mrs D Buchan

Age range: 3-9
No. of pupils: 120
Scholarships:
Religion:

Fees per term
Day: -
Weekly board: -
Full board: -

Boy ○ / Girl ● / Co-ed ○
Day ● / Week ○ / Board ○

For further information and a prospectus, please contact the school.

LEICESTERSHIRE 273

Ratcliffe College *

Address: Fossway, Ratcliffe on the Wreake, Leicestershire LE7 4SG
Telephone: 0509 812221

Head: Rev L G Hurdidge

Age range: 11-18
No. of pupils: 462
Scholarships: Yes
Religion: Roman Catholic

Fees per term
Day: £1415-£1780
Weekly board: £2123-£2669
Full board: £2669-£2669

Co-ed / Day / Week / Board

The school aims to keep up with the latest and best developments in the world of education, without ever losing sight of the ultimate objective, to induce young men and women whose Christian ideals fit them to take proper place in society. The college has an excellent academic record.

St Crispin's

Address: St Mary's Road, Leicester, Leicestershire LE2 1XA
Telephone: 0533 707648

Head: Mr B Harrild

Age range: 4-13
No. of pupils: 165
Scholarships:
Religion: Non-denominational

Fees per term
Day: £530-£985
Weekly board: -
Full board: -

Boy / Day

St Crispin's is a day preparatory and pre-preparatory school for boys aged four to thirteen. Individual attention is given in classes of 18 boys and there is a wide range of extra-curricular activities. Admission is by interview rather than by examination.

St Paul's Primary Independent School

Address: Evington Hall Convent, Spencefield Lane, Leicester, Leicestershire LE5 6HN
Telephone: 0533 412000
Head: Sister Clare Aspinwall

Age range: 2-11
No. of pupils: 156
Scholarships:
Religion:

Fees per term
Day: -
Weekly board: -
Full board: -

Co-ed / Day

For further information and a prospectus, please contact the school.

Stoneygate School

Address: 254 London Road, Leicester, Leicestershire LE2 1RP
Telephone: 0533 707536

Head: Mr J B Josephs

Age range: 4-13
No. of pupils: 260
Scholarships:
Religion:

Fees per term
Day: -
Weekly board: -
Full board: -

Boy / Girl / Day

For further information and a prospectus, please contact the school. Girls 7-13.

Uppingham *p752*

Address: Uppingham, Leicestershire LE15 9QU

Telephone: 0572 822216

Head: Dr S C Winkley

Age range: 13-18
No. of pupils: 650
Scholarships: Yes
Religion: Christian

Fees per term
Day: £2142-
Weekly board: -
Full board: £3570-

● Boy ● Girl ○ Co-ed
● Day ○ Week ● Board

Uppingham is a boarding school with girls in the sixth form, set in a beautiful market town in Rutland. Approximatley 14% of sixth form go on to Oxbridge, nearly all to higher education. Especially noted for magnificent games facilities and outstanding music. Academic, music, art and CDT scholarships available.

Woodbank Grammar School

Address: 320 London Road, Leicester, Leicestershire LE2 2PJ
Telephone: 0533 703287

Head: Mr R C Rayner

Age range: 8-16
No. of pupils: 213
Scholarships:
Religion:

Fees per term
Day: -
Weekly board: -
Full board: -

○ Boy ○ Girl ● Co-ed
● Day ○ Week ○ Board

For further information and a prospectus, please contact the school.

LINCOLNSHIRE

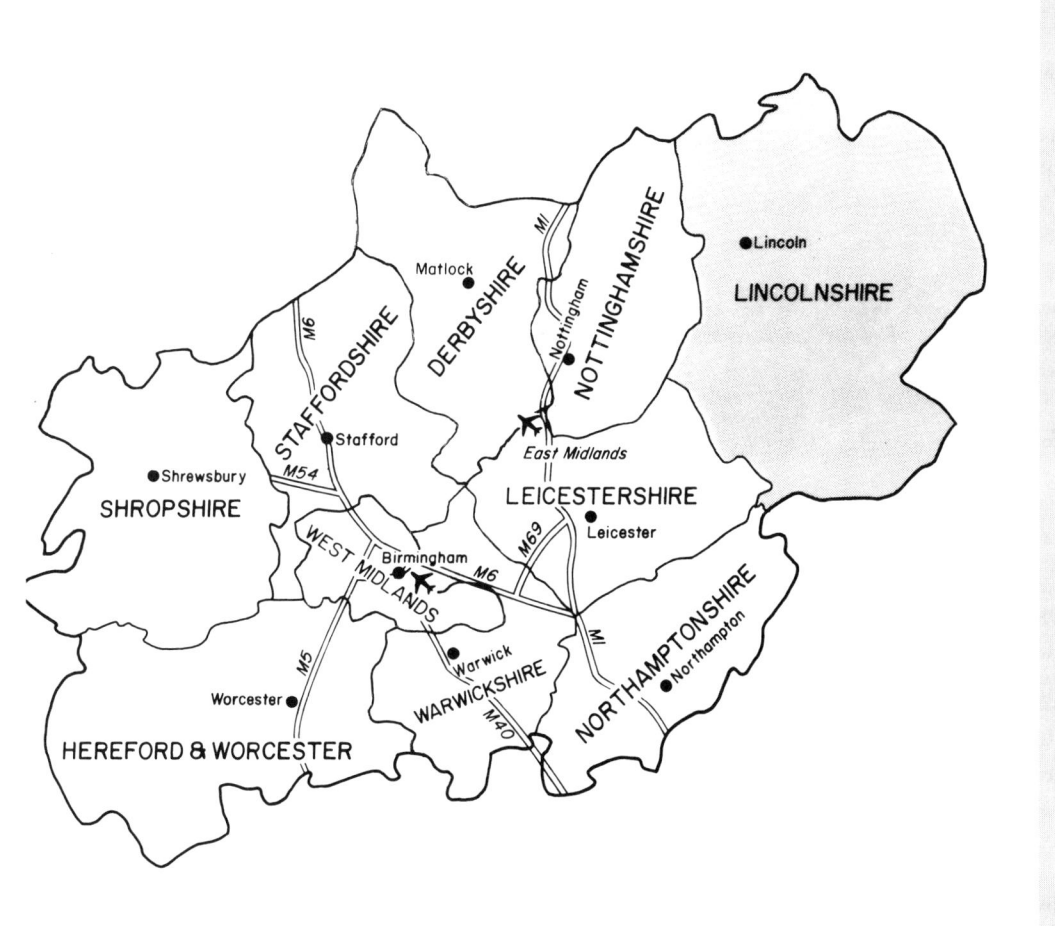

Ayscoughfee Hall School

Address: Church Street,
Spalding, Lincolnshire
PE11 2PB
Telephone: 0775 724733

Head: Mr B G Chittick

Age range: 3-11
No. of pupils: 150
Scholarships:
Religion: Non-denominational

Fees per term
Day: £438-£525
Weekly board: -
Full board: -

○ ○ ● Boy Girl Co-ed
● ○ ○ Day Week Board

Ayscoughfee Hall is an independent day school which prepares children for senior schooling at a wide range of public, as well as local selective secondary, schools. Education is traditional in content incorporating the best elements of, but going beyond, the National Curriculum. A small school, Ayscoughfee Hall embraces the concept of an enlarged family, emphasising care and individual attention.

The Cathedral School

Address: Eastgate, Lincoln,
Lincolnshire LN2 1QE
Telephone: 0522 523769

Head: Revd Canon R G Western

Age range: 2-13
No. of pupils: 108
Scholarships: Yes
Religion: Church of England

Fees per term
Day: £325-£1057
Weekly board: £1937-
Full board: £1937-

● ● ○ Boy Girl Co-ed
● ● ● Day Week Board

The school, in the close of Lincoln Minster, has a friendly, family atmosphere. Good facilities make the early years of schooling happy, challenging and satisfying. It is a Christian foundation where a warm welcome is given to children of other faiths. A wide range of facilities for extra-curricular activities include particular opportunities for budding musicians.

Conway School

Address: Tunnard Street,
Boston, Lincolnshire PE21 6PL
Telephone: 0205 363150

Head: Mrs J E Nyman

Age range: 3-11
No. of pupils: 180
Scholarships:
Religion: Church of England

Fees per term
Day: £190-£430
Weekly board: -
Full board: -

○ ○ ● Boy Girl Co-ed
● ○ ○ Day Week Board

Conway School is a co-educational primary school--age range from 3-11. Entry via nursery or school test or assessment. All subjects are offered with emphasis on mathematics, English and science. Extra-curricular activities include cookery, first aid and music. Sporting activities include football, netball, rounders, running and athletics in summer term. Pupils are prepared for Common Entrance examinations.

Handel House Preparatory School

Address: Northolme,
Gainsborough, Lincolnshire
DN21 2JB
Telephone: 0427 612426

Head: Mrs M Hornsey

Age range: 3-13
No. of pupils: 60
Scholarships:
Religion: Non-Denominational

Fees per term
Day: £360-£520
Weekly board: -
Full board: -

○ ○ ● Boy Girl Co-ed
● ○ ○ Day Week Board

Handel House, a small family school established in 1850, in the market town of Gainsborough. The aim of the school is to provide a safe and happy environment in which the young can develop sound personalities, firm academic foundations, inner strength and a sense of security.

Heathlands Preparatory School

Address: Gorse Lane,
Grantham, Lincolnshire
NG31 7UF
Telephone: 0476 593293

Head: Mrs P A Anderson

Age range: 3-11
No. of pupils: 134
Scholarships:
Religion: Non-denominational

Fees per term
Day: £820-
Weekly board: -
Full board: -

Boy ○ Girl ○ Co-ed ●
Day ● Week ○ Board ○

High individual standards achieved in small classes. A wide stimulating curriculum providing an excellent basis for future public or state secondary education.

Maypole House

Address: Horncastle,
Lincolnshire

Telephone: 0507 462764

Heads: Mr & Mrs M G White

Age range: 3-16
No. of pupils: 130
Scholarships:
Religion: Non-denominational

Fees per term
Day: £510-£625
Weekly board: -
Full board: -

Boy ○ Girl ○ Co-ed ●
Day ● Week ○ Board ○

Maypole House is an independent co-educational day school for pupils 3-16 years. The school is situated in beautiful grounds within a 2000 acre estate. Classes are small (average 12), examination results at GCSE excellent. Superb sporting facilities and opportunities. A friendly, family atmosphere with firm discipline.

Priory College

Address: St Martin's Without,
Stamford, Lincolnshire
PE9 3JW
Telephone: 0780 65900

Acting Headmistress: Mrs A Cutforth

Age range: 11-18
No. of pupils: 130
Scholarships:
Religion: Church of England

Fees per term
Day: £1250-£1350
Weekly board: £2450-£2650
Full board: £2450-£2650

Boy ○ Girl ○ Co-ed ●
Day ● Week ● Board ●

Priory College (co-educational day and boarding places age 11 to 18) provides the foundation for the future, in a caring, friendly atmosphere, where traditional values are a priority for a complete education. Each child is important as an individual. All pupils are provided with a wealth of experiences including a wide range of academic, cultural, sporting and recreational activities.

Priory Preparatory School

Address: Brownlow Terrace,
Stamford, Lincolnshire
PE9 2EH
Telephone: 0780 63214

Head: Ms E T Teall

Age range: 4-11
No. of pupils: 50
Scholarships:
Religion: Christian

Fees per term
Day: £485-£802
Weekly board: -
Full board: £1393-£1617

Boy ○ Girl ○ Co-ed ●
Day ● Week ○ Board ●

The school offers individual attention in small classes. There is a happy family atmosphere, with firm, but fair discipline. The stress is put on importance of reading, good grounding in English and mathematics. There is also a number of extra-curricular activities as well as the help of Stamford Dyslexia Institute, which is situated within the school building.

St Hugh's School

Address: Cromwell Avenue, Woodhall Spa, Lincolnshire LN10 6TQ
Telephone:

Head: Mr M W Kelham

Age range: 4-13
No. of pupils:
Scholarships:
Religion:

Fees per term
Day: -
Weekly board: -
Full board: -

○ ○ ● Boy Girl Co-ed
● ○ ● Day Week Board

For further information and a prospectus, please contact the school.

St Joseph's School

Address: Upper Lindum Street, Lincoln, Lincolnshire
Telephone: 0522 543764

Head: Mrs A Scott

Age range: 7-18
No. of pupils: 270
Scholarships:
Religion: Christian

Fees per term
Day: £730-£1080
Weekly board: £1795-£1980
Full board: £1895-£2080

○ ● ○ Boy Girl Co-ed
● ● ● Day Week Board

Each child matters at St Joseph's, Lincoln, a small school where girls are encouraged to develop their talents, not only in the academic field, but in the arts, music, drama, sport and leadership. At GCSE 78% passes are at grades A-C, and the tutorial nature of the sixth form helps girls gain places at the universities of their choice.

St Mary's School

Address: 5 Pottergate, Lincoln, Lincolnshire LN2 1PH
Telephone: 0522 524622

Head: Mr C Gough

Age range: 2-13
No. of pupils: 140
Scholarships:
Religion:

Fees per term
Day: -
Weekly board: -
Full board: -

○ ○ ● Boy Girl Co-ed
● ○ ○ Day Week Board

For further information and a prospectus, please contact the school.

Stamford High School *

Address: St Martin's, Stamford, Lincolnshire PE9 2LJ
Telephone: 0780 62330

Head: Miss G K Bland

Age range: 4-18
No. of pupils: 1012
Scholarships:
Religion:

Fees per term
Day: -
Weekly board: -
Full board: -

● ● ○ Boy Girl Co-ed
● ● ● Day Week Board

For further information and a prospectus, please contact the school. Boys 4-8, girls 4-18.

LINCOLNSHIRE 279

Stamford School ✴

Address: St Paul's Street,
Stamford, Lincolnshire
PE9 2BS
Telephone: 0780 62171

Head: Mr G J Timm

Age range: 8-18
No. of pupils: 950
Scholarships:
Religion:

Fees per term
Day: -
Weekly board: -
Full board: -

● ○ ○
Boy Girl Co-ed
● ○ ●
Day Week Board

For further information and a prospectus, please contact the school.

Stonefield House School

Address: Church Lane,
Lincoln, LN2 1QR

Telephone: 0522 541741

Head: Mr I S T Welham BSc

Age range: 4-16
No. of pupils: 175
Scholarships: Yes
Religion: Christian

Fees per term
Day: £820-£1380
Weekly board: -
Full board: -

○ ○ ●
Boy Girl Co-ed
● ○ ○
Day Week Board

Stonefield House School is an independent mixed day school, taking children from 4 to 16. Classs are small and the GCSE results are impressive. A full range of sporting and extra-mural activities is provided, with numerous inter-school fixtures at all age groups. Most children leave at 16 to study ALlevels at other schools, either state or independent.

White House School

Address: Stamford Road,
Easton-on-the-Hill, Stamford,
Lincolnshire PE9 3NU
Telephone: 0780 53405

Head: Mrs C M Coleman

Age range: 2-9
No. of pupils: 64
Scholarships:
Religion:

Fees per term
Day: -
Weekly board: -
Full board: -

○ ○ ●
Boy Girl Co-ed
● ○ ○
Day Week Board

For further information and a prospectus, please contact the school.

Witham Hall School

Address: Witham-on-the-Hill,
Bourne, Lincolnshire PE10 0JJ

Telephone: 0778 33222

Head: Mr D H Burston

Age range: 7-13
No. of pupils: 136
Scholarships: Yes
Religion: Church of England

Fees per term
Day: -£1640
Weekly board: -£2260
Full board: -£2260

○ ○ ●
Boy Girl Co-ed
● ● ●
Day Week Board

The school is situated in a country house setting. There is a teaching staff of 14 and no class is larger than 16. The music is strong, over half the children learning one or more musical instruments. There is a multi-purpose sports hall and recently a CDT centre was set up.

LONDON

Abercorn Place School

Address: 28 Abercorn Place, London NW8 9XP

Telephone: 071 286 4785

Head: Mrs A Greystock

Age range: 3-13
No. of pupils: 200
Scholarships:
Religion: Non-denominational

Fees per term
Day: £965-£1660
Weekly board: -
Full board: -

Boy ○ Girl ○ Co-ed ●
Day ● Week ○ Board ○

Traditional values taught by modern methods in a gracious Grade II listed building. Children participate in computing, design technology, and a full sporting programme. Excellent entrance results to further schools.

Akiva School

Address: The Manor House, 80 East End Road, London N3 2SY

Telephone: 081 349 4980

Head: Mrs J Roback

Age range: 4-11
No. of pupils: 140
Scholarships:
Religion: Jewish

Fees per term
Day: -£950
Weekly board: -
Full board: -

Boy ○ Girl ○ Co-ed ●
Day ● Week ○ Board ○

Akiva School is a progressive Jewish day school offering a primary education to the highest standards - secular studies and Jewish living and learning are not kept separate - they are brought together in a curriculum which covers the full range of primary subjects. The school is set in beautiful grounds adding an additional dimension to a town school.

The Albany College

Address: 23/24 Queens Road, London NW4 2TL

Telephone: 081 202 9748

Head: Mr R J Arthy

Age range: 14-19
No. of pupils: 200
Scholarships: Yes
Religion:

Fees per term
Day: £2200-
Weekly board: -
Full board: -

Boy ○ Girl ○ Co-ed ●
Day ● Week ○ Board ○

The Albany College has long enjoyed a well earned reputation for excellence and consistently maintains a high grade pass rate. Our college enjoys a happy, caring purposeful teaching atmosphere with individual counselling for each student. Of 115 students who sat for A Levels this year, no less than 105 achieved places at universities and polytechnics.

Allendale Preparatory School

Address: Allen Street, Kensington, London W8 6BL

Telephone: 071 937 3593

Head: Mrs M E Peake

Age range: 4-11
No. of pupils: 80
Scholarships:
Religion: Non-denominational

Fees per term
Day: -
Weekly board: -
Full board: -

Boy ● Girl ● Co-ed ○
Day ● Week ○ Board ○

Fees on application. For further details and a prospectus, please contact the school. Boys 4-9, girls 4-11.

Alleyn's School * p736

Address: Townley Road,
London SE22 8SU

Telephone: 081 693 3422

Head: Dr C H R Niven

Age range: 11-18
No. of pupils: 930
Scholarships: Yes
Religion: Church of England

Fees per term
Day: -£1735
Weekly board: -
Full board: -

Boy ○   Girl ○   Co-ed ●
Day ●   Week ○   Board ○

Alleyn's School is a selective, co-educational day school, with a 6th Form of over 250 pupils. The school provides an excellent all-round academic education, but at the same time places great emphasis on such extra-curricular activities as music, drama and a wide range of sports. There are flourishing Duke of Edinburgh and CCF organisations.

The American School in London

Address: 2-8 London Road,
London NW8 0NP

Telephone: 071 722 0101

Head: Dr J Glickman

Age range: 4-18
No. of pupils: 1240
Scholarships:
Religion: Non-denominational

Fees per term
Day: -
Weekly board: -
Full board: -

Boy ○   Girl ○   Co-ed ●
Day ●   Week ○   Board ○

A private, non-profit institution, the school offers a challenging curriculum for students from pre-kindergarten through grade twelve. English, math, science and history form the core of the academic program for all students, which is enriched by a selection of required and elective courses from the foreign language, fine arts, and physical education departments. The school provides a nurturing environment.

Annemount School

Address: 18 Holne Chase,
London N2 0QN

Telephone: 081 455 2132

Head: Miss E J Jamaiker

Age range: 3-7
No. of pupils: 50
Scholarships:
Religion: Non-denominational

Fees per term
Day: £550-£700
Weekly board: -
Full board: -

Boy ○   Girl ○   Co-ed ●
Day ●   Week ○   Board ○

Annemount was established in 1936 by Miss E J Jamaiker. The school offers a full primary education for children between the ages of 3 to 7 years. Annemount is a small school with a friendly environment. The classes are small and well staffed. Subjects cover English, reading, maths, science, French and art and craft.

Arnold House School

Address: 3 Loudon Road, St
John's Wood, London
NW8 0LH

Telephone: 071 286 1100

Head: Mr J Clegg MA

Age range: 5-13
No. of pupils: 250
Scholarships:
Religion: Church of England

Fees per term
Day: £1640-£1640
Weekly board: -
Full board: -

Boy ●   Girl ○   Co-ed ○
Day ●   Week ○   Board ○

The school incorporates a pre-preparatory department. A traditional London day school with a good academic record. It aims to provide a happy, caring environment where the joy and excitement of learning is more important than learning for learning's sake, where music, art and caring for the body through exercise have their proper place and where the individuality and sensitivity of each boy is encouraged.

The Arts Educational London Schools

Address: Cone Ripman House, 14 Bath Road, Chiswick, London W4 1LY
Telephone: 081 994 9366

Age range: 11-16
No. of pupils: 270
Scholarships: Yes
Religion: Non-denominational

Fees per term
Day: £1731-
Weekly board: £2030-£2236
Full board: -

○ Boy   ○ Girl   ● Co-ed
● Day   ○ Week   ○ Board

Head: Mr P A Fowler

The Arts Educational London Schools have a long history as centres of excellence in the training of talented pupils and students in dance, drama and musical theatre. The School provides high quality training in the performing arts and a sound academic education to GCSE levels for pupils 11-16. Student courses: The Dance School and The Musical Theatre School (16+) and The Drama School (18+).

Ashbourne Independent School

Address: 17 Old Court Place, London W8 4PL
Telephone: 071 937 3858

Age range: 11-19
No. of pupils: 150
Scholarships: Yes
Religion: Non-denominational

Fees per term
Day: £2150-£2650
Weekly board: -
Full board: -

○ Boy   ○ Girl   ● Co-ed
● Day   ○ Week   ○ Board

Head: Mr M Hatchard-Kirby

Ashbourne Independent School was founded in 1981 and is now two schools based at separate sites in Kensington. Ashbourne Middle School is a co-educational day school offering Common Entrance and foundation GCSE courses for 10-15 year olds. The sixth form college caters for 16-19 year olds and offers 2 year, 1 year and resit courses at GCSE and A Level. Both schools offer a strict academic programme.

Barbara Speake Stage School

Address: East Acton Lane, East Acton, London W3 7EG
Telephone: 081 743 2746

Age range: 4-16
No. of pupils: 150
Scholarships:
Religion: Non-denominational

Fees per term
Day: £494-£552
Weekly board: -
Full board: -

○ Boy   ○ Girl   ● Co-ed
● Day   ○ Week   ○ Board

Head: Miss B M Speake

The school prides itself on creating a happy learning atmosphere with friendly, helpful staff who love their work. The school is recognised by the Associated Examining Board as a centre for taking GCSE examinations in nine subjects. A thorough training for the entertainment industry is given with opportunities for professional experience in all areas by the agency which is under the direction of Mrs June Collins.

Bassett House School

Address: 60 Bassett Road, London W10 6JP
Telephone: 081 969 0313

Age range: 3-8
No. of pupils: 120
Scholarships:
Religion: Non-denominational

Fees per term
Day: £550-£1080
Weekly board: -
Full board: -

○ Boy   ○ Girl   ● Co-ed
● Day   ○ Week   ○ Board

Head: Mrs D M Ritchie

Bassett House School is a mixed, independent school of approximately 120 children between 3 and 8 years. Founded in 1947, the school is situated in a large Victorian house in Kensington. Teaching is primarily Montessori based although more formal methods are introduced in the final year when children are prepared for entrance to leading London and country preparatory schools.

Battersea Montessori Schools

Address: Bridge Lane and Cabul Road, London SW11

Telephone: 071 622 7658

Head: Mrs E A Hood

Age range: 1-6
No. of pupils: 100
Scholarships:
Religion: Non-denominational

Fees per term
Day: £500-£700
Weekly board: -
Full board: -

Boy ○ Girl ○ Co-ed ●
Day ● Week ○ Board ○

The Montessori Society AMI (UK) Registered Schools List includes both schools which have been established since 1960. The Montessori Directresses hold AMI Diplomas and the full range of teaching materials are available to the children. French and colour-strings music are offered in addition to all the areas covered in the Montessori Approach.

Beacon House School

Address: 15 Gunnersbury Avenue, Ealing, London W5 3XD

Telephone: 081-992-5189

Head: Mrs M Milner

Age range: 3-11
No. of pupils: 140
Scholarships:
Religion: Non-denominational

Fees per term
Day: £395-£880
Weekly board: -
Full board: -

Boy ○ Girl ○ Co-ed ●
Day ● Week ○ Board ○

For further information please contact the school.

Belmont School p684

Address: The Ridgeway, Mill Hill, London NW7 4ED

Telephone: 081 959 1431

Head: Mr J R Hawkins BA CertEd

Age range: 7-13
No. of pupils: 300
Scholarships: Yes
Religion: Christian

Fees per term
Day: £1690-£1740
Weekly board: -
Full board: -

Boy ● Girl ○ Co-ed ○
Day ● Week ○ Board ○

Belmont combines proximity to London's cultural facilities with a semi-rural position in 35 acres of its own grounds on the Mill Hill Ridgeway. Sports, music, clubs and activities all flourish. Entry to Belmont's adjacent senior school (Mill Hill) is by interview and report, but pupils are also prepared for scholarship and Common Entrance examinations to other schools, if so desired.

Blackheath High School GPDST ✽

Address: Wemyss Road, Blackheath, London SE3 0TF

Telephone: 081 852 1537

Head: Miss R K Musgrave

Age range: 4-18
No. of pupils: 550
Scholarships: Yes
Religion: Non-denominational

Fees per term
Day: £1036-£1340
Weekly board: -
Full board: -

Boy ○ Girl ● Co-ed ○
Day ● Week ○ Board ○

Founded in 1880 and a member of the Girls' Public Day School Trust, the school is non-denominational, and academically selective. Almost all pupils progress to higher education. The curriculum is broad and includes a strong cross-curricular element. The sense of community is strong and the school serves a wide area including Lewisham, Greenwich, Docklands and beyond. The school is popular and visitors are always welcome.

LONDON 285

Bloomsbury College

Address: 8 Herbrand Street, London WC1N 1HZ

Telephone: 071 837 3864

Head: Mr I D Dawbarn

Age range: 16-18
No. of pupils: 100
Scholarships: Yes
Religion: Non-denominational

Fees per term
Day: £560-£1600
Weekly board: -
Full board: -

Boy ○   Girl ○   Co-ed ●
Day ●   Week ○   Board ○

Students are prepared for A Level and GCSE examinations by experienced and well qualified teachers and are given the attention and guidance needed to fulfil their potential. Each year a large proportion of students gain entry to university. The college, with about 120 students from the age of 15 upwards, is small enough to encourage a relatively informal yet academically disciplined atmosphere.

Broomwood Hall Preparatory School

Address: 74 Nightingale Lane, London SW12 8NR

Telephone: 081 673 1616

Head: Mrs K A H Calquhoun

Age range: 4-12
No. of pupils: 260
Scholarships:
Religion: Church of England

Fees per term
Day: £1200-£1450
Weekly board: -
Full board: -

Boy ○   Girl ○   Co-ed ●
Day ●   Week ○   Board ○

Broomwood Hall is a pre-preparatory school for boys and girls from the ages of 4-8 (boys) and 4-12 (girls). Boys are prepared for preparatory (often boarding schools) and girls for London day school examinations and Common Entrance at 11+ and 12+. Children must live within the school's catchment area - roughly, a one mile radius from the school.

Calder House School †

Address: Mandeville Courtyard, 142 Battersea Park Road, London SW11 4NB
Telephone: 071 720 8783

Head: Mrs L Robertson

Age range: 6-13
No. of pupils: 30
Scholarships:
Religion: Non-denominational

Fees per term
Day: £2600-
Weekly board: -
Full board: -

Boy ○   Girl ○   Co-ed ●
Day ●   Week ○   Board ○

We are a small school and admit only children who are underachieving because of specific learning difficulties (dyslexia). We have a 'whole school' rather than a 'unit' approach and teach to a full curriculum. Each pupil's remedial programme is specific to need and progress, and we liase closely with parents. We are DES registered and SENIC approved Category A.

Cameron House

Address: 4 The Vale, Chelsea, London SW3 4AH

Telephone: 071 352 4040

Principal: Mrs J M Ashcroft BSc   *Head:* Mrs J M Emme

Age range: 5-11
No. of pupils: 90
Scholarships:
Religion: Non-denominational

Fees per term
Day: £1695-
Weekly board: -
Full board: -

Boy ○   Girl ○   Co-ed ●
Day ●   Week ○   Board ○

Independent London day school for boys and girls, 5-11 years, entry generally at 5 or 8 years. A small friendly school (approximately 90 pupils), exceptionally high teacher pupil ratio and small classes. The broad and balanced curriculum, with a wide range of optional after-school clubs, seeks to develop independent thinking individuals who appreciate hard work, good manners and kindness.

The Cavendish School

Address: 179 Arlington Road, Camden, London NW1 7EY

Telephone: 071 485 1958

Head: Mrs L J Harris BA

Age range: 4-11
No. of pupils: 150
Scholarships:
Religion: Roman Catholic

Fees per term
Day: £945-£1025
Weekly board: -
Full board: -

Boy ● Girl ● Co-ed ○
Day ● Week ○ Board ○

Parents seeking a happy academic girl's preparatory school should consider The Cavendish School - an IAPS Catholic preparatory school housed in a spacious Victorian school building, with a secluded playground. With a broad range of subjects, the school aims to stimulate the children's attainment of sound academic standards whilst also encouraging the development of creative skills, confidence and happiness.

Channing School

Address: Highgate, London N6 5HF

Telephone: 081 340 2328

Head: Mrs I R Raphael

Age range: 5-18
No. of pupils: 455
Scholarships: Yes
Religion: Non-denominational

Fees per term
Day: £1160-£1670
Weekly board: -
Full board: -

Boy ○ Girl ● Co-ed ○
Day ● Week ○ Board ○

Channing is a day school for girls 5-18. It offers a balanced education, combining a traditional academic curriculum with modern educational developments. Channing has been in the forefront of women's education for more than 199 years, preparing girls for university, the professions and training of every kind, and helping them to be independent, caring people with wide interests.

The Charterhouse Square School

Address: 40 Charterhouse Square, London EC1M 6EA

Telephone: 071 600 3805

Head: Miss J Malden MA BEd(Hons)

Age range: 4-11
No. of pupils: 150
Scholarships:
Religion: Non-denominational

Fees per term
Day: £1200-
Weekly board: -
Full board: -

Boy ○ Girl ○ Co-ed ●
Day ● Week ○ Board ○

We offer a broad, well balanced, stimulating curriculum with the ultimate aim of bringing out the very best in each individual child. We would wish our children to remember their school days with fondness.

The Chelsea Kindergarten

Address: St Andrews Church, Chelsea Park Walk, London SW10

Telephone: 235 1237

Head: Mr J Ewing-Hoy

Age range: 2-5
No. of pupils: 40
Scholarships:
Religion:

Fees per term
Day: £650-
Weekly board: -
Full board: -

Boy ○ Girl ○ Co-ed ●
Day ● Week ○ Board ○

The kindergarten provides an all round education with an interest in the child as an individual. Emphasis is on encouragement in a happy and secure environment. We offer French conversation, ballet, music, singing, art, craft, simple gymnastics as well as teaching children to read, write and learn about numbers. (Every morning 9-12 plus 2 afternoons for those who wish).

The Chelsea Nursery School

Address: The Chelsea Centre, King's Road, London SW10 0DR
Telephone: 071 351 0993

Head: Mrs N Issa

Age range: 2-5
No. of pupils: 30
Scholarships:
Religion: Church of England

Fees per term
Day: -
Weekly board: -
Full board: -

● Boy   ● Girl   ○ Co-ed
● Day   ○ Week   ○ Board

Our school provides a secure, well supervised, happy environment in which your child can develop the confidence, love of learning and discovery essential to life. Our teaching staff are fully qualified and are always ready to listen to parents' concerns and questions. Our teaching methods are based on the philosophy of Dr Maria Montessori.

The Children's House Montessori Nursery School

Address: St Mary's Church Hall, 46 Wimbledon Road, London SW18 5NZ
Telephone: 081 947 7359

Head: Mrs C Narain

Age range: 2-5
No. of pupils: 48
Scholarships:
Religion:

Fees per term
Day: -
Weekly board: -
Full board: -

○ Boy   ○ Girl   ● Co-ed
● Day   ○ Week   ○ Board

For further information and a prospectus, please contact the school.

Chiswick and Bedford Park Preparatory School

Address: Priory House, Priory Avenue, Bedford Park, London W4 1TX
Telephone: 081 994 1804

Head: Mrs M B Morrow

Age range: 4-11
No. of pupils: 195
Scholarships:
Religion: Non-denominational

Fees per term
Day: £780-£970
Weekly board: -
Full board: -

○ Boy   ○ Girl   ● Co-ed
● Day   ○ Week   ○ Board

Established in 1915, the school provides a high standard of education using traditional and modern methods in a friendly environment. The staff seek to ensure that each child achieves its full potential, while allowances and recommendations are made for children with learning difficulties. The school enjoys a high success rate for entry to top day and boarding schools.

Christ's College

Address: 4 St German's Place, Blackheath, London SE3 0NJ
Telephone: 081 858 0692

Head: Mr T Barclay

Age range: 4-18
No. of pupils: 200
Scholarships:
Religion: Non-denominational

Fees per term
Day: £775-£1180
Weekly board: £1940-
Full board: £2155-

● Boy   ○ Girl   ○ Co-ed
● Day   ● Week   ● Board

Christ's College, founded in 1823, has a reputation for providing a sound, traditional education in a disciplined but caring and happy environment. Classes are small and our excellent facilities include 5 acres of playing fields and a new science and computing block. Future re-development is envisaged. More than 80% of our pupils leave for some form of Higher Education.

City of London School *

Address: Queen Victoria Street, London EC4V 3AL

Telephone: 071-489 0291

Head: Mr B G Bass

Age range: 10-18
No. of pupils: 850
Scholarships: Yes
Religion: Non-denominational

Fees per term
Day: -£1734
Weekly board: -
Full board: -

● Boy ○ Girl ○ Co-ed
● Day ○ Week ○ Board

The school occupies magnificent premises on a riverside site in the City of London, only a short walk from several underground stations. The school has a long-standing record of high academic achievement. Pass-rates 1992: A Level 99% (67% grade A/B), GCSE 97% (84% grades A/B). Most boys proceed to higher education, many at Oxford and Cambridge.

City of London School for Girls *

Address: The Barbican, London EC2Y 8BB

Telephone: 071 628 0841

Head: Lady V E France

Age range: 7-18
No. of pupils: 650
Scholarships: Yes
Religion: Non-denominational

Fees per term
Day: -£1491
Weekly board: -
Full board: -

○ Boy ● Girl ○ Co-ed
● Day ○ Week ○ Board

The school is centrally situated on the splendid Barbican site and has an enviable record of academic success. The majority of sixth formers go on to university, medicine being a popular choice. A superb swimming pool helps to keep the girls fit and the cultural life is enriched by a variety of musical activities and other societies. There is also a new purpose built design and technology suite.

Clifton Lodge Boys Preparatory School p684

Address: 9 Florence Road, Ealing, London W5 3TU

Telephone: 081 579 3662

Head: Mr D A P Blumlein

Age range: 4-13
No. of pupils: 140
Scholarships:
Religion: Christian

Fees per term
Day: £1004-£1113
Weekly board: -
Full board: -

● Boy ○ Girl ○ Co-ed
● Day ○ Week ○ Board

At Clifton Lodge we regard each boy as an individual, and our aim is to enable him to realise his full potential in all aspects of school life. We seek to nurture a spirit of self-disciplie from which a boy can aquire a sense of self-confidence. We want him to leave the school a well mannered, honest citizen, having achieved his best academically.

Colf's School *

Address: Horn Park Lane, London SE12 8AW

Telephone: 081 852 2283

Head: Dr D J Richardson

Age range: 3-18
No. of pupils: 901
Scholarships: Yes
Religion: Church of England

Fees per term
Day: £1065-£1415
Weekly board: -
Full board: -

● Boy ● Girl ○ Co-ed
● Day ○ Week ○ Board

Colf's School is a selective independent school, which accepts girls in the sixth form. It is proud of its academic record and maintains a wide range of extra-curricular activities including music, games, drama and outdoor pursuits. Colf's pupils come from a wide area of south east London using the excellent public transport facilities and the school's own coaches. Generous scholarships and bursaries are available.

Collingham

Address: 23 Collingham Gardens, London SW5 0HL

Telephone: 071 244 7414

Head: Mrs G M Green

Age range: 14
No. of pupils: 300
Scholarships: Yes
Religion: Non-denominational

Fees per term
Day: £890-£2310
Weekly board: -
Full board: -

○ ○ ● Boy Girl Co-ed
● ○ ○ Day Week Board

A sixth from college with a specialist GCSE department. Tutorials are given in small groups. All tutors and graduates are specialists in their subjects. A strict academic discipline is maintained to enable students to achieve their full potential. Set in a quiet garden square in Kensington, Collingham offers 3 science laboratories, art studio, computer room and a large library. 1 year, 2 year and short revision courses.

Connaught House School

Address: 47 Connaught Square, London W2 2HL

Telephone: 071 262 8830

Head: Mrs J A Hampton

Age range: 4-11
No. of pupils: 80
Scholarships:
Religion: Non-denomintional

Fees per term
Day: -£1445
Weekly board: -
Full board: -

○ ○ ● Boy Girl Co-ed
● ○ ○ Day Week Board

The school was established in 1953 and has occupied its present site since 1956. There are about 17 pupils in each of the first three forms and less in older forms. Boys are prepared for entry at 8 years or for senior school entry up to 11 years. Girls are prepared for Common Entrance or public school entry at 11 years.

Corfton Hill Educational Establishment †

Address: Corfton Hill, 35 Corfton Road, Ealing, London W5 2HP

Telephone: 081 998 4175

Head: Mrs G Levitt

Age range: 6-11
No. of pupils: 12
Scholarships:
Religion: Non-denominational

Fees per term
Day: -£940
Weekly board: -
Full board: -

○ ○ ● Boy Girl Co-ed
● ○ ○ Day Week Board

Corfton Hill Educational Establishment specialises in the one to one tuition for intelligent children who have special educational needs. Children are prepared for public school entrance after learning all basic subjects to a very high standard. Sport, swimming and visits to places of historical and educational interest are regular features of the timetable.

Dallington

Address: 8 Dallington Street, London EC1V 0BQ

Telephone: 071 251 2284

Head: Mrs M Hercules

Age range: 3-11
No. of pupils: 170
Scholarships: Yes
Religion: Non-denominational

Fees per term
Day: £772-£1078
Weekly board: -
Full board: -

○ ○ ● Boy Girl Co-ed
● ○ ○ Day Week Board

Non-selective 'family' school, all have siblings somewhere in school. Aim - non-competitive - but highest possible standards. All very successfully transfer to all London public day schools. Entry requires very early registration.

Devonshire House Preparatory and Pre-Preparatory School p685

Address: 69 Fitzjohn's Avenue, Hampstead, London NW3 6PB

Telephone: 071 435 1916

Age range: 3-13
No. of pupils: 398
Scholarships:
Religion: Non-Denominational

Fees per term
Day: £1150-£1290
Weekly board: -
Full board: -

Boy ○ Girl ○ Co-ed ●
Day ● Week ○ Board ○

Head: Mr B G Wigglesworth BEd(Hons) CertEd

Devonshire House provides education and individual attention for boys and girls, from three in the Pre-Preparatory School and from five to thirteen in the Main School. The traditional subjects are important and talents and individual personalities are encouraged so that children can enjoy school and reach their potential. The school provides academic standards whilst developing enthusiasm, initiative and responsibility.

Dr Rolfe's Montessori School

Address: 10 Pembridge Square, London W2 4ED

Telephone: 071 727 8300

Age range: 2-5
No. of pupils: 50
Scholarships:
Religion: Non-denominational

Fees per term
Day: £565-£1130
Weekly board: -
Full board: -

Boy ○ Girl ○ Co-ed ●
Day ● Week ○ Board ○

Head: Miss A Arnold

Our aim is to give your child the best possible start to the most important school years. We want the children to progress at their own pace without pressure and most importantly to enjoy their days at school as much as we do. Maria Montessori wanted children to be independent, to share, to have freedom within structure and to learn to take care and help each other.

Dulwich College *

Address: Dulwich, London SE21 7LD

Telephone: 081 693 3601

Age range: 7-18
No. of pupils: 1400
Scholarships: Yes
Religion: Church of England

Fees per term
Day: £1795-£1895
Weekly board: £3540-
Full board: £3690-

Boy ● Girl ○ Co-ed ○
Day ● Week ● Board ●

Head: Mr A C F Verity

Dulwich College is situated in a leafy suburb of South London. Pupils enjoy a broad academic education with excellent facilities, a dedicated and skilful staff in a disciplined day-to-day framework. An unusually wide range of games and extra-curricular opportunities is available to all. Flexibility is offered to parents by the boarding element.

Dulwich College Preparatory School

Address: 42 Alleyn Park, London SE21 7AA

Telephone: 081 670 3217

Age range: 3-13
No. of pupils: 746
Scholarships:
Religion: Church of England

Fees per term
Day: £985-£1590
Weekly board: £2260-
Full board: -

Boy ● Girl ● Co-ed ○
Day ● Week ● Board ○

Head: Mr G Marsh

DCPS is a selective boys' Preparatory school which has a national reputation for its academic record. The boys are offered a broad based education in which music and art play a prominent role. There are a wide variety of clubs, activities and sport to help boys gain a varied experience and to challenge them in different areas. (Co-ed in Nursery)

Durston House

Address: 12 Castlebar Road, Ealing, London W5 2DR

Telephone: 081 997 0511

Head: Mr P D Craze

Age range: 4-13
No. of pupils: 334
Scholarships: Yes
Religion: Non-denominational

Fees per term
Day: £1390-£1565
Weekly board: -
Full board: -

● Boy ○ Girl ○ Co-ed
● Day ○ Week ○ Board

Durston House is an IAPS day school expanding to 430 boys by 1996. An outstanding academic record continues alongside a rich diversity of sporting, cultural and extra-curricular activities to help boys develop a sense of communal responsibility, strong minds and bodies and a positive attitude. They transfer to the top senior schools at 13 plus.

Ealing College Upper School

Address: 83 The Avenue, Ealing, London W13 8JS

Telephone: 081 997 4346

Head: Mr B Webb

Age range: 11-18
No. of pupils: 250
Scholarships: Yes
Religion: Non-denominational

Fees per term
Day: £1200-£1200
Weekly board: -
Full board: -

● Boy ● Girl ○ Co-ed
● Day ○ Week ○ Board

Ealing College Upper School is a small independent grammar school which takes pride in its happy and caring atmosphere. It caters for boys from 11-18 and takes girls in the sixth form. Examination results, both GCSE and A Level, are generally well above the national average in most subjects. About 90% of sixth form leavers move on to degree courses at universities or colleges of higher education.

The Ealing Dean Anglo-French School

Address: 8 Mattock Lane, Ealing, London W5 5BG

Telephone: 081 567 1294

Head: Madame R Peret

Age range: 3-11
No. of pupils: 170
Scholarships:
Religion: Non-denominational

Fees per term
Day: £1030-£1140
Weekly board: -
Full board: -

○ Boy ○ Girl ● Co-ed
● Day ○ Week ○ Board

The school admits children between three and eight years, from English or French speaking backgrounds. The aim is to provide a warm and stimulating environment, designed to produce, happy, disciplined and educationally rounded, bi-lingual children. These results are produced by the eclectic use of the best in both the British and French education systems.

Eaton House School

Address: 3-5 Eaton Gate, London SW1

Telephone: 071 730 9343

Head: Mrs H Harper

Age range: 4-8
No. of pupils: 250
Scholarships:
Religion: Non-denominational

Fees per term
Day: £1200-
Weekly board: -
Full board: -

● Boy ○ Girl ○ Co-ed
● Day ○ Week ○ Board

Eaton House was founded in 1897. The premises have light airy classrooms, a library, science lab and computer room. The aim of the school is to provide the boys with a good academic and social base and to develop their understanding and self-reliance. The staff are widely experienced in preparing children for London Day School examinations and entrance to boarding schools.

Eaton Square Nursery & Pre-Preparatory School

Address: 30 Eccleston Street, London SW1W 9PY

Telephone: 071 823 4525

Principal: Miss Y Cuthberth

Age range: 2-9
No. of pupils: 156
Scholarships:
Religion: Non-denominational

Fees per term
Day: £625-£1632
Weekly board: -
Full board: -

Boy ○ Girl ○ Co-ed ●
Day ● Week ○ Board ○

Eaton Square School is situated in Belgravia and is housed in a building modernised to provide light, airy classrooms, a library, gymnasium and facilities for music, drama and computer studies. The reputation of the school is founded on care, enthusiasm and small classes, fostered by well qualified and dedicated staff.

Elmwood Montessori School

Address: St. Michael's Church Hall, Elmwood Road, London W4 3DY

Telephone: 081 994 8177

Head: Mrs S Herbert

Age range: 2-5
No. of pupils: 38
Scholarships:
Religion: Non-denominational

Fees per term
Day: -£550
Weekly board: -
Full board: -

Boy ○ Girl ○ Co-ed ●
Day ● Week ○ Board ○

An independently-run Montessori nursery school, Elmwod offers young children a secure, happy and rich environment in which to follow their desire to discover new things, and to develop to their own social, personal and academic potentials. Individual activity is balanced with project work and group activities such as music, drama and cookery. The emphasis is on happy, active children.

Eltham College

Address: London SE9 4QF

Telephone: 081 857 1455

Head: Mr D M Green MA(Cantab)

Age range: 7-18
No. of pupils: 730
Scholarships: Yes
Religion: Non-denominational

Fees per term
Day: £1081-£1470
Weekly board: £3105-
Full board: £3105-

Boy ● Girl ● Co-ed ○
Day ● Week ● Board ●

Eltham College, founded in 1841, is an independent HMC day school with a small boarding house. An outstanding academic tradition with a broad and balanced curriculum. Girls in the 6th form. Very strong drama, music, art, technology and sport. In 25 acres, excellent modern facilities and a highly professional staff.

Emanuel School *

Address: Battersea Rise, London SW11 1HS

Telephone: 081 870 4171

Head: Mr P F Thomson

Age range: 10-19
No. of pupils: 760
Scholarships: Yes
Religion: Church of England

Fees per term
Day: £1270-£1370
Weekly board: -
Full board: -

Boy ● Girl ○ Co-ed ○
Day ● Week ○ Board ○

For further information and a prospectus, please contact the school.

Fairley House School †

Address: 44 Bark Place, London W2 4AT

Telephone: 071 229 0977

Head: Mrs P Thomson

Age range: 5-12
No. of pupils: 90
Scholarships:
Religion: Non-denominational

Fees per term
Day: £3550-
Weekly board: -
Full board: -

○ ○ ● Boy Girl Co-ed
● ○ ○ Day Week Board

Fairley House provides intensive remediation in basic literacy and numeracy skills on an individual or small group basis. Pupil/staff ratio is 3:1. Concurrently the full National Curriculum is followed with minor adaptations to meet the needs of SLD children. Particular emphasis is laid on IT. The eventual aim, wherever possible, is successful reintegration into a mainstream environment.

The Falcons Pre-Preparatory School

Address: 2 Burnaby Gardens, Chiswick, London W4

Telephone: 081 747 8393

Head: Miss J F Baker

Age range: 3-8
No. of pupils: 170
Scholarships:
Religion:

Fees per term
Day: -
Weekly board: -
Full board: -

● ○ ○ Boy Girl Co-ed
● ○ ○ Day Week Board

For further information and a prospectus, please contact the school.

Falkner House Girls' Preparatory School

Address: 19 Brechin Place, London SW7 4QB

Telephone: 071 373 4501

Head: Mrs J Bird

Age range: 4-11
No. of pupils: 136
Scholarships:
Religion: Christian

Fees per term
Day: -£1525
Weekly board: -
Full board: -

○ ● ○ Boy Girl Co-ed
● ○ ○ Day Week Board

Falkner House exists as a partnership between staff and parents, to ensure the happiness and success of each child. Pupils are prepared for the entrance and scholarship examinations for the leading academic boarding and day schools. The abilities and needs of each child are carefully and continuously assessed. The girls are taken frequently to the neighbouring museums, art galleries and places of interest.

Finton House School

Address: 171 Trinity Road, London SW17 7HL

Telephone: 081 682 0921

Head: Miss T O'Neil

Age range: 4-11
No. of pupils: 180
Scholarships: Yes
Religion: Non-denominational

Fees per term
Day: £930-£1550
Weekly board: -
Full board: -

○ ○ ● Boy Girl Co-ed
● ○ ○ Day Week Board

Finton House is a mainstream co-educational school integrated with a percentage of special needs children. We offer places to children between the age of 4 and 11 years on a first-come first-served basis. There is no testing to enter at any age. Finton House offers an environment where children of mixed ability are taught individually in small classes. We are very keen for the pupil to be given an all round education.

Forest Girls' School

Address: College Place, Snaresbrook, London E17 3PY
Telephone: 081 521 7477
Head: Mrs C Y Daly

Age range: 11-18
No. of pupils: 360
Scholarships: Yes
Religion: Church of England

Fees per term
Day: £1617-
Weekly board: -
Full board: -

Boy ○ / Girl ● / Co-ed ●
Day ● / Week ○ / Board ○

Girls aged 11 to 16 follow a broad balanced curriculum, culminating in GCSE. Most girls go on to study for A Levels in our co-educational Sixth Form and then to Higher Education. The numbers opting for arts and sciences are approximately equal. The school shares the campus with the senior boys and juniors schools, providing excellent sports, drama and computer facilities.

Forest Junior School p742

Address: College Place, Nr Snaresbrook, London E17 3PY
Telephone: 081 520 1744
Head: Mr R T Cryer

Age range: 7-13
No. of pupils: 377
Scholarships: Yes
Religion: Church of England

Fees per term
Day: £1106-£1617
Weekly board: £1494-£1691
Full board: £1778-£2539

Boy ● / Girl ● / Co-ed ○
Day ● / Week ● / Board ●

The Junior School serves as a Preparatory Department for Forest School. It has its own separate buildings including science laboratory but uses the school chapel, swimming pool, squash courts, theatre, computer centre, cricket pavilion and playing fields. The main sports are football, hockey and cricket. Entry is by examination and interview. A prospectus is available on request.

Forest Senior School * p742

Address: College Place, Nr Snaresbrook, London E17 3PY
Telephone: 081 520 1744
Head: Dr C Barker

Age range: 13-18
No. of pupils: 450
Scholarships: Yes
Religion: Church of England

Fees per term
Day: £1617-
Weekly board: -
Full board: £2539-

Boy ● / Girl ● / Co-ed ○
Day ● / Week ● / Board ●

Forest Senior School is an independent day and boarding school for boys aged 13 to 18, situated on the edge of Epping Forest. Boys are taught separately to GCSE and then co-educationally for A Level. The school has excellent facilities and enjoys an enviable academic reputation. A balanced approach to life is encouraged and sport, music and drama flourish.

Francis Holland School *

Address: Clarence Gate, London NW1 6XR
Telephone: 071 723 0176
Head: Mrs P H Parsonson

Age range: 11-18
No. of pupils: 360
Scholarships: Yes
Religion: Church of England

Fees per term
Day: £1470-£1510
Weekly board: -
Full board: -

Boy ○ / Girl ● / Co-ed ○
Day ● / Week ○ / Board ○

The School is adjacent to Regent's Park, used for games, and three minutes walk from Baker Street Station. Girls are encouraged to develop as individuals and to pursue excellence in any undertaking, intellectual, creative or sporting. Nearly all girls take 9 GCSE subjects and go on into sixth form to study subjects for A Levels before going on to University.

The French Institute

Address: 14 Cromwell Place, London SW7 2JR

Telephone: 071 581 2701

Head: Mlle B Freyche

Age range: 18-30
No. of pupils: 65
Scholarships:
Religion:

Fees per term
Day: £800-£867
Weekly board: -
Full board: -

○ ○ ● Boy Girl Co-ed
● ○ ○ Day Week Board

Bilingual careers start here, with the coming of the Single European Market the outlook has never been better. The Collège de Secrétariat Bilingue of the Institut Français has been training top-level bilingual secretaries and administrators for over 50 years. Many of our students go on to executive positions with the EEC, the UN and Nato. So if you're looking for a career rather than a job, start here!

Garden House School

Address: 53 Sloane Gardens, London SW1W 8ED

Telephone: 071 730 1652

Head: Mrs K Pringle

Age range: 3-11
No. of pupils: 308
Scholarships:
Religion: Church of England

Fees per term
Day: £805-£1710
Weekly board: -
Full board: -

● ● ○ Boy Girl Co-ed
● ○ ○ Day Week Board

Garden House offers a thorough education in a lively and alert atmosphere and high academic results are achieved with pupils going on to top day and boarding schools. There is a strong emphasis on ballet, art, drama, music and computers. Garden House also offers good recreational facilities: netball, rounders, fencing and swimming. Boys 3-8, girls 3-11.

Gatehouse School

Address: Sewardstone Road, Bethnal Green, London E2 9JG

Telephone: 081 980 2978

Head: Mr P J Faupel

Age range: 4-18
No. of pupils: 200
Scholarships:
Religion: Non-denominational

Fees per term
Day: £1000-£1450
Weekly board: -
Full board: -

○ ○ ● Boy Girl Co-ed
● ○ ○ Day Week Board

A small, friendly school, we concentrate on the academic and social development of individuals. We follow the National Curriculum to GCSE but expand its range and scope. Physical and aesthetic education is also important here. Facilities are as good as many larger schools, with two computer and technology rooms, language lab. etc. A Levels will be available from September 1993.

Glendower School

Address: 87 Queens Gate, London SW7 5JX

Telephone: 071 370 1927

Head: Mrs B Humber

Age range: 4-11
No. of pupils: 186
Scholarships:
Religion: Non-denominational

Fees per term
Day: -£1415
Weekly board: -
Full board: -

○ ● ○ Boy Girl Co-ed
● ○ ○ Day Week Board

For further information and a prospectus, please contact the school.

The Godolphin and Latymer School *

Address: Iffley Road,
Hammersmith, London
W6 0PG
Telephone: 081 741 1936

Head: Miss M F Rudland

Age range: 11-18
No. of pupils: 700
Scholarships: Yes
Religion: Non-denominational

Fees per term
Day: £1610-
Weekly board: -
Full board: -

Boy ○ Girl ● Co-ed ○
Day ● Week ○ Board ○

Godolphin and Latymer is a day school for 700 girls aged between 11 and 18. It stands on a four acre site with its own playing fields. Several additions have been made to the original Victorian building. The most recent were opened in March 1991 and the school now has excellent facilities for its needs during the coming years.

Golders Hill School

Address: 666 Finchley Road,
Barnet, London NW11 7NT
Telephone: 081 455 2589

Head: Mr A T Eglash

Age range: 3-8
No. of pupils: 100
Scholarships:
Religion:

Fees per term
Day: -£995
Weekly board: -
Full board: -

Boy ○ Girl ○ Co-ed ●
Day ● Week ○ Board ○

For further information and a prospectus, please contact the school.

Goodwyn School

Address: Hammers Lane, Mill
Hill, London NW7 4DB
Telephone: 081 959 3756

Head: Mr S W E Robertson

Age range: 3-7
No. of pupils: 214
Scholarships:
Religion: Non-denominational

Fees per term
Day: £1150-£1150
Weekly board: -
Full board: -

Boy ○ Girl ○ Co-ed ●
Day ● Week ○ Board ○

The school provides both well-balanced and forward looking education in a friendly atmosphere with a staff who aim at encouraging effort, experiment and satisfaction in work. Various activities are organised to provide the opportunity for each child to develop under guidance on lines appropriate to his or her own bent. Entry is conditional upon interview.

Grange Park Preparatory School

Address: 13 The Chine,
Grange Park, Enfield, London
N21 2EA
Telephone: 081 360 1469

Head: Mrs R J Jeans

Age range: 3-11
No. of pupils: 105
Scholarships:
Religion: Christian

Fees per term
Day: £418-£706
Weekly board: -
Full board: -

Boy ○ Girl ● Co-ed ○
Day ● Week ○ Board ○

For further information and a prospectus, please contact the school.

Great Beginnings Montessori School

Address: 82a Chiltern Street, London W1M 1PS

Telephone: 071 486 2276

Head: Mrs W Innes

Age range: 2-6
No. of pupils: 35
Scholarships:
Religion: Non-denominational

Fees per term
Day: £650-£950
Weekly board: -
Full board: -

○ Boy   ○ Girl   ● Co-ed
● Day   ○ Week   ○ Board

For further information and a prospectus, please contact the school.

The Hall

Address: 23 Crossfield Road, London NW3 4NV

Telephone: 071 722 1700

Head: Mr R Dawe

Age range: 5-13
No. of pupils: 385
Scholarships:
Religion: Church of England

Fees per term
Day: £1555-£1655
Weekly board: -
Full board: -

● Boy   ○ Girl   ○ Co-ed
● Day   ○ Week   ○ Board

The Hall has a non-competitive entry at 5; boys normally continue until they are 13. The school is on two sites close to each other; boys spend four years in each; they are cheerfully noisy, work hard and proceed to a vast variety of secondary schools.

The Hampshire School (Kensington Gardens)

Address: 9 Queensborough Terrace, London W2 3TB

Telephone: 071 229 7065

Head: Mr A G Bray

Age range: 3-13
No. of pupils: 105
Scholarships:
Religion:

Fees per term
Day: -
Weekly board: -
Full board: -

○ Boy   ○ Girl   ● Co-ed
● Day   ○ Week   ○ Board

For further information and a prospectus, please contact the school.

The Hampshire School (Knightsbridge)

Address: 63 Ennismore Gardens, London SW7 1NH

Telephone: 071 584 3297

Head: Mr A G Bray

Age range: 4-13
No. of pupils: 165
Scholarships:
Religion:

Fees per term
Day: -
Weekly board: -
Full board: -

○ Boy   ○ Girl   ● Co-ed
● Day   ○ Week   ○ Board

For further information and a prospectus, please contact the school. Boys 4-8, girls 4-13.

Hampstead Hill Pre-Preparatory and Nursery School

Address: St Stephen's Hall,
Pond Street, London NW3 2PP

Telephone: 071 435 6262

Head: Mrs A Taylor

Age range: 3-8
No. of pupils: 210
Scholarships:
Religion: Non-denominational

Fees per term
Day: £780-£1380
Weekly board: -
Full board: -

Boy ○ | Girl ○ | Co-ed ●
Day ● | Week ○ | Board ○

Hampstead Hill Pre-Preparatory and Nursery School gives all pupils from 3 to 8+ years old a sound academic education and full development of each child's personality and talents. Children leave us at 5+, 7+ or 8+, the older ones well prepared for entrance examinations to junior public schools. The Nursery School is open 52 weeks a year-extended hours service-holiday group for over 5s.

Harvington School

Address: 20 Castlebar Road,
Ealing, London W5 2DS

Telephone: 081 997 1583

Head: Mrs A Fookes BA

Age range: 3-16
No. of pupils: 230
Scholarships:
Religion: Non-denominational

Fees per term
Day: £440-£1057
Weekly board: -
Full board: -

Boy ● | Girl ● | Co-ed ○
Day ● | Week ○ | Board ○

For further information and a prospectus, please contact the school. Boys 3-5, girls 3-16.

Hazelhurst School For Girls

Address: 17 The Downs,
Wimbledon, London
SW20 8HF

Telephone: 081-946 1704

Head: Mrs C W M Milner-Williams

Age range: 5-16
No. of pupils: 150
Scholarships: Yes
Religion: Non-denominational

Fees per term
Day: £980-£1080
Weekly board: -
Full board: -

Boy ○ | Girl ● | Co-ed ○
Day ● | Week ○ | Board ○

Hazelhurst is a small independent day school for girls aged 5-16 and boys aged 5-7. Excellent facilities and individual attention ensure good results in Common Entrance and GCSE. All girls take 9-11 subjects achieving 70% A-C grades and proceed to A-levels and FE courses.

The Hellenic College of London

Address: 67 Pont Street,
London SW1X 0BD

Telephone: 071 581 5044

Head: Mr J W Wardrobe MA

Age range: 2-18
No. of pupils: 210
Scholarships: Yes
Religion: Greek Orthodox

Fees per term
Day: £1055-£1365
Weekly board: -
Full board: -

Boy ○ | Girl ○ | Co-ed ●
Day ● | Week ○ | Board ○

The Hellenic College was founded in 1980 by prominent members of the Greek community in London and offers an integrated curriculum of subjects in Greek and English throughout the nursery, primary and secondary age range. The principal aim of the college is to give all pupils a first class British education to GCSE and A Level standard, coupled with fluency in the Greek language and tradition.

Hendon Preparatory School

Address: 20 Tenterden Grove, Hendon, London NW4 1TD

Telephone: 081 203 7727

Head: Mr T D Lee

Age range: 3-13
No. of pupils: 182
Scholarships:
Religion: Non-denominational

Fees per term
Day: £1548-
Weekly board: -
Full board: -

Boy ○ Girl ○ Co-ed ●
Day ● Week ○ Board ○

In this IAPS approved co-educational school, quality education is our prime objective. Hendon Preparatory is well known for its happy, friendly, family atmosphere as well as for its stimulating academic programme which enables young people to identify, strive for and achieve their full intellectual, social and physical potential.

Hereward House School

Address: 14 Strathray Gardens, London NW3 4NY

Telephone: 071 794 4820

Head: Mrs L Sampson

Age range: 5-13
No. of pupils: 180
Scholarships:
Religion: Non-denominational

Fees per term
Day: £1295-£1485
Weekly board: -
Full board: -

Boy ● Girl ○ Co-ed ○
Day ● Week ○ Board ○

The school's aim is to provide a lively, stimulating environment in which boys receive a thorough grounding in the basic skills. Modern teaching methods, computers and other audio visual aids are employed alongside those traditional methods that have proved their worth. Art, music, drama, handicraft, games and swimming are integral part of the curriculum.

Highfield School

Address: 1 Bloomfield, Highgate, London N6 4ET

Telephone: 081 340 5981

Head: Mrs L Hayes

Age range: 3-11
No. of pupils: 150
Scholarships:
Religion: Non-denominational

Fees per term
Day: £600-£1100
Weekly board: -
Full board: -

Boy ● Girl ● Co-ed ○
Day ● Week ○ Board ○

For further information and a prospectus, please contact the school. Boys 3-7, girls 3-11.

Highfield School

Address: 256 Trinity Raod, Wandsworth Common, London SW18 3RQ
Telephone: 081 874 2778

Head: Mrs V-J F Lowe

Age range: 2-11
No. of pupils: 125
Scholarships:
Religion: Non-denominational

Fees per term
Day: £820-£950
Weekly board: -
Full board: -

Boy ○ Girl ○ Co-ed ●
Day ● Week ○ Board ○

Established in 1894, Highfield consists of three departments - nursery, infants and junior. The school teaches a full range of academic subjects as well as a range of activities exploring the creative talents of the children.

Highgate Junior School

Address: Cholmeley House, 3 Bishopswood Road, London N6 4PL
Telephone: 081 340 9193

Head: Mr H S Evers

Age range: 7-13
No. of pupils: 345
Scholarships:
Religion: Church of England

Fees per term
Day: -£1875
Weekly board: -
Full board: -

● Boy ○ Girl ○ Co-ed
● Day ○ Week ○ Board

Highgate Junior School prepares boys solely for entrance to the senior school. A broad and balanced curriculum is followed, and standards are high. Entry tests are held annually in January. A new pre-preparatory school opens in September 1993.

Highgate School

Address: North Road, London N6 4NY
Telephone: 081 340 1524

Head: Mr R P Kennedy

Age range: 7-18
No. of pupils: 950
Scholarships: Yes
Religion: Church of England

Fees per term
Day: £1875-£2095
Weekly board: £3402-
Full board: -

● Boy ○ Girl ○ Co-ed
● Day ● Week ○ Board

Marvellously situated next to Hampstead Heath, Highgate School offers the best features of a traditional independent school within an up-to-date curriculum. Very high academic standards are coupled with a particular emphasis on sport, the arts and other extra-curricular activities. Highgate Junior School (boys 7-13) and our Pre-Preparatory School (boys and girls 3-7) ensure continuity of education.

Hill House International Junior School p687

Address: Hans Place, London SW1X 0EP
Telephone: 071 584 1331

Head: Lt Col H S Townend OBE MA(Oxon)

Age range: 3-14
No. of pupils: 1050
Scholarships:
Religion: All religions

Fees per term
Day: £1200-£1500
Weekly board: -
Full board: -

○ Boy ○ Girl ● Co-ed
● Day ○ Week ○ Board

Hill House is a private day school, in the centre of London, for boys and girls aged 3 to 14, preparing them for entry into English public schools and schools overseas. It has 120 full-time teachers plus 15 part-time music teachers. For the last 42 years it has had a permanent annexe in Switzerland.

Hornsby House School

Address: Broomwood Methodist Hall, Kyrle Road, London SW11 6JX
Telephone: 071 924 3521

Head: Mrs E Nightingale

Age range: 4-11
No. of pupils: 150
Scholarships:
Religion: Non-denominational

Fees per term
Day: £1235-£1375
Weekly board: -
Full board: -

○ Boy ○ Girl ● Co-ed
● Day ○ Week ○ Board

Hornsby House School accepts children from 4-11 years and follows a broad range of subjects using a structured approach. Reading and spelling are taught by a multisensory method. We are a caring school which prepares children for entrance tests to leading day and boarding schools. It was founded by Dr Beve Hornsby whose work is in the field of learning difficulties.

Hurlingham Private School

Address: 94-97 Deodar Road, Putney, London SW15 2NU

Telephone: 081 874 1673

Principal: Miss R Whitehead *Head:* Mrs M Hamilton

Age range: 4-11
No. of pupils: 90
Scholarships:
Religion: Non-denominational

Fees per term
Day: £700-£800
Weekly board: -
Full board: -

● Boy ● Girl ○ Co-ed
● Day ○ Week ○ Board

Hurlingham Private School was founded 40 years ago by Miss Whitehead and continues as a small, friendly school. Children are taught in small classes with individual tuition to encourage their own talents and prepared for preparatory and senior schools. Boys 4-8, girls 4-11.

Hyland House

Address: 896 Forest Road, Walthamstow, London E17 8AE

Telephone: 081 520 4186

Head: Mrs J Thorpe

Age range: 3-11
No. of pupils:
Scholarships:
Religion: Non-denominational

Fees per term
Day: £430-£430
Weekly board: -
Full board: -

○ Boy ○ Girl ● Co-ed
● Day ○ Week ○ Board

For further information and a prospectus, please contact the school.

Ibstock Place School

Address: Clarence Lane, Roehampton, London SW15 5PY

Telephone: 081 876 9991

Head: Mrs F Bayliss

Age range: 3-16
No. of pupils: 450
Scholarships: Yes
Religion: Non-denominational

Fees per term
Day: £433-£1602
Weekly board: -
Full board: -

○ Boy ○ Girl ● Co-ed
● Day ○ Week ○ Board

Ibstock Place, The Froebel School is a co-educational day school for 450 children aged 3-16. A former country house on the edge of Richmond Park, the school now has many fine additions including a new library and a science and technology centre. Information about open days and entry can be obtained from the Admissions Secretary.

International School of London

Address: 139 Gunnersbury Avenue, London W3 8LG

Telephone: 081 992 5823

Head: Dr R S Ghusayni

Age range: 4-18
No. of pupils: 210
Scholarships: Yes
Religion: Non-sectarian

Fees per term
Day: £1050-£2410
Weekly board: -
Full board: -

○ Boy ○ Girl ● Co-ed
● Day ○ Week ○ Board

In 20 years the school has helped children of over 70 nationalities. It gives an English education up to GCSE, and access to universities through its long-established International Baccalaureate course. A door-to-door bus service covers Central and West London. If necessary English as a second language and several mother-tongues are available. Some bursaries for local families.

Islamia Primary School

Address: 129 Salisbury Road, London NW6 6RG

Telephone: 071 372 2532

Head: Dr A Baig

Age range: 4-11
No. of pupils: 180
Scholarships: Yes
Religion: Islam

Fees per term
Day: £1100-
Weekly board: -
Full board: -

Boy ○ Girl ○ Co-ed ●
Day ● Week ○ Board ○

Islamia Primary follows National Curriculum and Islamic education. Quran, Arabic and Islamic Studies are the prominent features of education. Pupils are encouraged to practice Islam and be proud of their Islamic identity.

Islamic College

Address: 16 Settles Street, London E1 1JP

Telephone: 377 1595

Head: Mr A Sayeed

Age range: 11-16
No. of pupils: 60
Scholarships:
Religion: Islam

Fees per term
Day: £166-£250
Weekly board: -
Full board: -

Boy ● Girl ○ Co-ed ○
Day ● Week ○ Board ○

Subjects taught: English, mathematics, science, geography, Bengali, Arabic, Islamic Studies, technology and physical education. Classes start at 8.15am. Education provided in a sound, moral atmosphere, based on the guidance of the teachings of Islam.

Italia Conti Academy of Theatre Arts

Address: Italia Conti House, 23 Goswell Road, London EC1M 7AJ

Telephone: 071 608 0044

Head: Mr C K Vote

Age range: 11-21
No. of pupils: 40
Scholarships: Yes
Religion: Non-denominational

Fees per term
Day: £1355-£1855
Weekly board: -
Full board: -

Boy ○ Girl ○ Co-ed ●
Day ● Week ○ Board ○

Pupils are accepted for entry to the academy by audition. Once enrolled, they embark on an exciting educational career which encourages effort by frequent achievement of personal success. Pupils under fourteen spend the mornings on vocational subjects and the afternoons on academic curriculum. Pupils preparing for GCSEs have their academic lessons in the mornings, the emphasis being more scholastic.

James Allen's Girls' School *

Address: East Dulwich Grove, London SE22 8TE

Telephone: 081 693 1181

Head: Mrs B C Davies

Age range: 11-18
No. of pupils: 725
Scholarships: Yes
Religion: Church of England

Fees per term
Day: £1675-£1730
Weekly board: -
Full board: -

Boy ○ Girl ● Co-ed ○
Day ● Week ○ Board ○

JAGS occupies a twenty two acre site with a range of first class facilities. The school firmly believes that the girls deserve nothing but the best. There are three sections, with new privileges at each stage so that the girls can feel that their growing maturity is recognised. The forms are of mixed ability with plenty of individual attention given to each girl.

LONDON 303

James Allen's Preparatory School

Address: East Dulwich Grove, London SE22 8TE

Telephone: 081 693 0374

Head: Mr P Heyworth

Age range: 4-11
No. of pupils: 200
Scholarships: Yes
Religion: Church of England

Fees per term
Day: £1290-£1350
Weekly board: -
Full board: -

○ ● ○
Boy Girl Co-ed
● ○ ○
Day Week Board

The school sees primary education as a fundamental basis where children learn the pleasure of finding out new things. They are taught to work together in a group rather than always striving to be the best. The school believes in hard work and high endeavour which will give children a greater personal satisfaction in later life. All children are preparerd to take an 11+ entrance examination to senior schools.

Jewish Preparatory School

Address: 2 Andover Place, London NW6 5ED

Telephone: 071 328 2802

Head: Mr I Benyunes

Age range: 3-11
No. of pupils: 120
Scholarships: Yes
Religion: Jewish

Fees per term
Day: £891-£1042
Weekly board: -
Full board: -

○ ○ ●
Boy Girl Co-ed
● ○ ○
Day Week Board

The Jewish Preparatory School is a small, caring school for children aged 3-11 years which offers a broad, secular curriculum alongside a rich programme of Jewish Studies. We cater for children of all abilities, providing for each child's needs. Prospective parents are welcome to visit the school.

The John Loughborough School

Address: Holcombe Road, Tottenham, London N17 9AD

Telephone: 081 808 7837

Head: Mr K Davidson

Age range: 9-16
No. of pupils: 250
Scholarships:
Religion: 7th Day Adventist

Fees per term
Day: £400-£650
Weekly board: -
Full board: -

○ ○ ●
Boy Girl Co-ed
● ○ ○
Day Week Board

The John Loughborough School operates a system to ensure that its youth may receive a balanced physical, mental, moral, social and vocational education in harmony with Seventh-day Adventist standards and ideals, with God as the Source of all moral value and truth. Our students are encouraged to aim at the great ideals of spiritual maturity, mental excellence and physical well-being.

Keble Preparatory School

Address: Wades Hill, London N21 1BG

Telephone: 081 360 3359

Head: Mr G C Waite BEd(Hons)

Age range: 4-13
No. of pupils: 200
Scholarships:
Religion: Non-denominational

Fees per term
Day: £1075-£1250
Weekly board: -
Full board: -

● ○ ○
Boy Girl Co-ed
● ○ ○
Day Week Board

Keble School, founded in 1929, seeks to encourage personal development by offering a broad education in a friendly environment. It provides excellent academic and sporting opportunities. It is consistently successful in preparing boys for Scholarship and Common Entrance examinations to senior schools at 13+. In addition to a science laboratory and gymnasium, specialist rooms are provided for other subjects.

Kenley Montessori School

Address: Kenley Walk, Notting Hill, London W11 4BA
Telephone: 071 229 2740
Head: Mrs I Altovin

Age range: 2-5
No. of pupils: 20
Scholarships:
Religion: Non-denominational

Fees per term
Day: £425-£545
Weekly board: -
Full board: -

Boy ○ Girl ○ Co-ed ●
Day ● Week ○ Board ○

For further information and a prospectus, please contact the school.

Kensington Park p688

Address: 10 Pembridge Square, London W2 4ED
Telephone: 071 221 5748
Head: Dr M Calcraft

Age range: 11-16
No. of pupils: 60
Scholarships:
Religion: Non-denominational

Fees per term
Day: £1800-£2500
Weekly board: -
Full board: -

Boy ○ Girl ○ Co-ed ●
Day ● Week ○ Board ○

Kensington Park combines the best of a tutorial college with the organization of a small secondary school. Our small group intensive tuition allows us to cater for a small proportion of pupils with special needs.

Kensington Preparatory School For Girls

Address: 17 Upper Phillimore Gardens, Kensington, London W8 7HF
Telephone: 071 937 0108
Head: Miss M J Nelson

Age range: 5-11
No. of pupils: 200
Scholarships:
Religion: Non-denominational

Fees per term
Day: £1320-
Weekly board: -
Full board: -

Boy ○ Girl ● Co-ed ○
Day ● Week ○ Board ○

For further details please contact the school.

Kerem House

Address: 18 Kingsley Way, London NR2 0ER
Telephone: 081 455 7524
Head: Mrs A Kennard

Age range: 3-5
No. of pupils: 90
Scholarships:
Religion: Jewish Orthodox

Fees per term
Day: £787-
Weekly board: -
Full board: -

Boy ○ Girl ○ Co-ed ●
Day ● Week ○ Board ○

For further details please contact the school.

Kerem School

Address: Norrice Lea, London N2 0RE

Telephone: 081 455 0909

Head: Mrs R Goulden

Age range: 4-11
No. of pupils: 145
Scholarships:
Religion: Jewish Orthodox

Fees per term
Day: £970-
Weekly board: -
Full board: -

○ ○ ● Boy Girl Co-ed
● ○ ○ Day Week Board

For further details please contact the school.

The King Alfred School

Address: North End Road, London NW11 7HY

Telephone: 081 905 5599

Head: Mr F P Moran

Age range: 4-18
No. of pupils: 468
Scholarships:
Religion: Non-denominational

Fees per term
Day: £995-£1695
Weekly board: -
Full board: -

○ ○ ● Boy Girl Co-ed
● ○ ○ Day Week Board

This well-established (1898) north London independent day school is unique; ahead of its time at its foundation (it was and is co-educational, all-age, secular, wide ability-range). KAS still maintains an unusually relaxed atmosphere, friendly staff-student relations, a pupil-teacher ratio of 9:1, good GCSE and A level results. Subjects include drama, photography and computing.

The King Fahad Academy

Address: Bromyard Avenue, London W3 7HD

Telephone: 081 743 0131

Head: Dr I Al-Bassam

Age range: 4-19
No. of pupils: 1000
Scholarships: Yes
Religion: Islamic

Fees per term
Day: -
Weekly board: -
Full board: -

○ ○ ● Boy Girl Co-ed
● ○ ○ Day Week Board

The academy opened in 1985 and is following a gradual and planned programme of expansion. The kindergarten's premises are new, purpose built and self contained. The lower schools have well-equipped classrooms, each with a BBC microcomputer. The upper schools have tutorial rooms, science laboratories, gymnasiums, computer rooms, specialist art, music and home economic areas, language laboratories and a CDT suite.

King's College School * p744

Address: Wimbledon Common, London SW19 4TT

Telephone: 081 947 9311

Head: Mr R M Reeve MA

Age range: 13-18
No. of pupils: 670
Scholarships: Yes
Religion: Anglican

Fees per term
Day: £1690-£1690
Weekly board: -
Full board: -

● ○ ○ Boy Girl Co-ed
● ○ ○ Day Week Board

KCS has long been recognised for its high level of academic achievement. A tutorial system provides careful personal guidance for all pupils. There is a full and varied programme of sport, music, drama and other extra-curricular activities. The sixth form is housed in new accommodation specially designed for the student aspirations of older boys over 95% of whom continue into higher education.

Kings College Junior School

Address: Southside,
Wimbledon Common, London
SW19 4TT
Telephone: 081 946 2503

Age range: 7-13
No. of pupils: 411
Scholarships: Yes
Religion: Church of England

Fees per term
Day: £1710-£1810
Weekly board: -
Full board: -

● Boy ○ Girl ○ Co-ed
● Day ○ Week ○ Board

Head: Mr C Holloway

School has two related aims: to provide a full and rounded education for boys who show an aptitude for study, and to prepare them for continuing their education in the senior school. The school encourages boys to acquire high standards in achievement and attitude, to explore new subjects and activities, to recognise and develop their own abilities and to respect those of others.

Kingston Vale Montessori School

Address: St. John The Baptist
Church Hall, Robin Hood
Lane, Kingston Vale SW15
Telephone: 081 944 8584

Age range: 2-5
No. of pupils: 28
Scholarships:
Religion: Non-denominational

Fees per term
Day: £410-
Weekly board: -
Full board: -

○ Boy ○ Girl ● Co-ed
● Day ○ Week ○ Board

Head: Mrs V Wilberforce-Ritchie

Kingston Vale is a small friendly local nursery school. Our philosophy is to produce a happy and stimulating environment, where your children can develop at their own pace discovering their abilities with our guidance. We encourage the children to be creative through dance, painting, enabling them to enjoy their first years at school, and therefore be ready for their next stage of life.

The Knightsbridge and Chelsea Kindergarten

Address: 77 Kinnerton St,
Knightsbridge, London
SW1X 8ED
Telephone: 351 0368

Age range: 2-5
No. of pupils: 20
Scholarships:
Religion:

Fees per term
Day: £650-
Weekly board: -
Full board: -

○ Boy ○ Girl ● Co-ed
● Day ○ Week ○ Board

Head: Mr J Ewing-Hoy

The Kindergarten provides an all round education with an interest in the child as an individual. Emphasis is on encouragement in a happy and secure environment. We offer French conversation, ballet, music, singing, art, craft, simple gymnastics as well as teaching children to read, write and learn about numbers. (Every morning 9-12 plus 2 afternoons for those who wish).

Ladbrooke Square Montessori School

Address: 43 Ladbroke Square,
London W11 3ND
Telephone: 071 229 0125

Age range: 3-5
No. of pupils: 100
Scholarships:
Religion: Non-denominational

Fees per term
Day: £540-£595
Weekly board: -
Full board: -

○ Boy ○ Girl ● Co-ed
● Day ○ Week ○ Board

Joint Head: Mrs P Drinkwater, Mrs S Russel-Cobb

The school occupies four floors of a large Victorian house. We have our own private garden and access to the extensive square gardens, one minute's walk away. Children start in the afternoon session (1.30-4pm) and move to the mornings (9am-12.15) for their second year. Full days are optional for four year olds. All teachers are qualified in the Montessori method.

Lady Eden's School

Address: 41 Victoria Road, London W8 5RJ

Telephone: 071 937 0583

Head: Mrs G A Wayne

Age range: 3-11
No. of pupils: 150
Scholarships:
Religion: Non-denominational

Fees per term
Day: £795-£1695
Weekly board: -
Full board: -

○ ● ○
Boy Girl Co-ed
● ○ ○
Day Week Board

For further information and a prospectus, please contact the school.

Latymer Upper * p688

Address: King Street, Hammersmith, London W6 9LR
Telephone: 081 741 1851

Head: Mr C Diggory

Age range: 9-18
No. of pupils: 1060
Scholarships: Yes
Religion: Non-denominational

Fees per term
Day: £1300-£1600
Weekly board: -
Full board: -

● ○ ○
Boy Girl Co-ed
● ○ ○
Day Week Board

Latymer Upper is a leading London grammar school open to all able boys. Strong academic traditions are supported by a wide and active extra-curricular programme and good pastoral care. Most boys proceed onto university, some to Oxbridge. The school has strong links with the Godolphin and Latymer Girls School, eg. joint orchestra, and German exchange.

Lilliput Nursery School

Address: St. Augustine's Church Hall, 250 Lillie Road, Fulham, London SW6 7PX
Telephone: 071 385 3888

Head: Miss A Uden

Age range: 2-5
No. of pupils: 24
Scholarships:
Religion: Non-denominational

Fees per term
Day: £430-
Weekly board: -
Full board: -

○ ○ ●
Boy Girl Co-ed
● ○ ○
Day Week Board

Lilliput is a happy, friendly school. Offering an all round education suited suited to the individual child's needs. As well as developing learning skills we ensure the child's social skills are not overlooked, so that when the children leave to further their education they are happy confident individuals.

London Montessori Centre Ltd.

Address: 18 Balderton Street, London W1Y 1TG

Telephone: 071 493 0165

Head: Miss M Furness

Age range: 2-5
No. of pupils: 30
Scholarships:
Religion: Non-denominational

Fees per term
Day: £1200-
Weekly board: -
Full board: -

○ ○ ●
Boy Girl Co-ed
● ○ ○
Day Week Board

Nursery School established over 20 years, part of the London Montessori College. In the heart of Mayfair with exceptional model Montessori facilities. Indoor and outdoor garden area. Full day 9-3.30pm only, a cooked lunch is provided. Ballet and swimming offered as extra curricular activities, also regular outings. Summer and easter holiday playscheme for children aged between 2-8 years.

Lubavitch House Grammar School for Boys

Address: 3-5 Kingsley Way, East Finchley, London N2 0EH
Telephone: 081 458 2312
Head: Rabbi T M Hertz

Age range:
No. of pupils:
Scholarships:
Religion:

Fees per term
Day: -
Weekly board: -
Full board: -

Boy ○ Girl ○ Co-ed ○
Day ○ Week ○ Board ○

For further information and a prospectus, please contact the school.

Lubavitch House Primary School

Address: 135 Clapton Common, London E5 5RR
Telephone: 081 800 1044
Head: Rabbi D Karnowski

Age range: 4-11
No. of pupils: 125
Scholarships:
Religion: Jewish

Fees per term
Day: -
Weekly board: -
Full board: -

Boy ○ Girl ○ Co-ed ●
Day ● Week ○ Board ○

For further information and a prospectus, please contact the school. Fees on application.

Lycee Francais Charles De Gaulle

Address: 35 Cromwell Road, London SW7 2DG
Telephone: 071 584 6322
Head: Mr H L Brusa

Age range: 4-18
No. of pupils: 2500
Scholarships:
Religion: Non-denominational

Fees per term
Day: £523-£639
Weekly board: -
Full board: -

Boy ○ Girl ○ Co-ed ●
Day ● Week ○ Board ○

English speaking pupils may join the Lycée at the age of 4. They may join the GCSE class at 14 or the A level courses at 16. These classes are taught by fully qualified graduate staff. In 1992 all our pupils gained 5 or more (usually 9) grade C or better GCSEs. The average A-level points score was 23.

Lyndhurst House Preparatory School

Address: 24 Lyndhurst Gardens, Hampstead, London NW3 5NW
Telephone: 071 435 4936
Head: Mr M O Spilberg

Age range: 7-13
No. of pupils: 140
Scholarships:
Religion: Non-denominational

Fees per term
Day: £1520-£1520
Weekly board: -
Full board: -

Boy ● Girl ○ Co-ed ○
Day ● Week ○ Board ○

Lyndhurst House in an entirely independent preparatory school feeding all the major London public schools, and boarding schools beyond. High achievement in Common Entrance and Scolarship is mirrored on the sports side, in a small, friendly and cheerful environment.

Manor House School

Address: 16 Golden Manor, Hanwell, London W7 3EG

Telephone: 081 567 4101

Head: Mr J Carpenter

Age range: 3-12
No. of pupils: 150
Scholarships:
Religion: Non-denominational

Fees per term
Day: £870-£930
Weekly board: -
Full board: -

○ Boy ○ Girl ● Co-ed
● Day ○ Week ○ Board

For further information and a prospectus, please contact the school.

Maria Montessori Children's House

Address: 26 Lyndhurst Gardens, London NW3 5NW

Telephone: 071 435 3646

Head: Miss J Cavanagh

Age range: 2-6
No. of pupils: 30
Scholarships: Yes
Religion: All/None

Fees per term
Day: £365-£750
Weekly board: -
Full board: -

○ Boy ○ Girl ● Co-ed
● Day ○ Week ○ Board

The Children's House was established in 1963. The rooms used by the school are large and bright and open onto a lovely mature garden which is put to full use by the children. The aim of the school is to provide a secure and happy environment for the children within which they can fulfil their development potential and become independent.

Marist Convent Junior School

Address: 596 Fulham Road, London SW6 5NU

Telephone: 071 731 3672

Head: Sister Evelyn Kearns MA

Age Range: 5-11
No. of Pupils: 125
Scholarships:
Religion: Roman Catholic

Fees per term
Day: -£650
Weekly Board: -
Full Board: -

○ Boy ● Girl ○ Co-ed
● Day ○ Week ○ Board

For further information contact the school - see also the entry for the Marist Convent Senior School.

Marist Convent Senior School

Address: 596 Fulham Road, London SW6 5NU

Telephone: 071 731 3258

Head: Sister Evelyn Kearns MA

Age range: 11-16
No. of pupils: 165
Scholarships:
Religion: Roman Catholic

Fees per term
Day: £790-
Weekly board: -
Full board: -

○ Boy ● Girl ○ Co-ed
● Day ○ Week ○ Board

The School promotes in its students a personal spiritual life, a sense of moral values and social responsibility, and an enthusiasm for academic achievement. A broadly based curriculum includes the study of French And German, science and technology, enabling girls to take 9-10 subjects for GCSE, thus preparing them for their sixth form studies, to which 100 per cent of students progress.

Merlin School

Address: 4 Carlton Drive, Putney Hill, Wandsworth, London SW15 2BZ
Telephone: 081 788 2769

Head: Mrs J Addis

Age range: 4-8
No. of pupils: 200
Scholarships:
Religion: Anglican

Fees per term
Day: -£1500
Weekly board: -
Full board: -

○ Boy ○ Girl ● Co-ed
● Day ○ Week ○ Board

Merlin School has an unsurpassed reputation for its academic results and gives children an excellent grounding for their future education. Children receive individual attention from staff who are 1st class degree graduates and who make their subject come alive and inspire the children to strive for excellence.

Milestone College

Address: 85 Cromwell Road, London SW7 5BW

Telephone: 071 373 4956

Head: Mr R Smart

Age range: 12-19
No. of pupils: 100
Scholarships:
Religion:

Fees per term
Day: -
Weekly board: -
Full board: -

○ Boy ○ Girl ● Co-ed
● Day ○ Week ○ Board

For further information and a prospectus, please contact the college.

Mill Hill School ✶ p689

Address: Mill Hill Village, The Ridgeway, Mill Hill, London NW7 1QS
Telephone: 081 959 1176

Head: Mr E A M MacAlpine

Age range: 13-18
No. of pupils: 560
Scholarships: Yes
Religion: Non-denominational

Fees per term
Day: £2250-
Weekly board: £3395-
Full board: £3395-

● Boy ● Girl ○ Co-ed
● Day ● Week ● Board

Mill Hill seeks to develop the individual talents of its pupils and to qualify them to take a responsible place in Society. To this end it provides a full academic curriculum and extensive sporting and cultural facilities within the secure structure of a well-disciplined community life. (Girls VI Form only).

Miss Morley's Nursery School

Address: Fountain Court Club Room, Edbury Road, London SW1
Telephone: 071 730 5797

Head: Mrs C Spence

Age range: 2-5
No. of pupils: 45
Scholarships:
Religion: Non-denominational

Fees per term
Day: £425-£550
Weekly board: -
Full board: -

○ Boy ○ Girl ● Co-ed
● Day ○ Week ○ Board

Miss Morley's Nursery School gives children a good basic grounding in the three Rs in small groups with individual attention. Emphasis is also placed on music and children are encouraged to share and to help one another.

Montessori 3-5 Nursery Wimbledon p690

Address: 58 Queen's Road, Wimbledon, London SW19 8LR
Telephone: 081 946 8139

Head: Mrs I Hodgson

Age range: 3-6
No. of pupils: 100
Scholarships:
Religion: All denominations

Fees per term
Day: £450-£850
Weekly board: -
Full board: -

○ Boy ○ Girl ● Co-ed
● Day ○ Week ○ Board

A purpose-built fully-equipped Montessori school in central Wimbledon, established in 1977. Small classes of 8-9 children per trained Montessori teacher. Although Montessori teaching is structured, it allows the child to be free to choose within the prepared environment. It is essential for our teachers to have love, respect and understanding of young children. We welcome parents to visit and observe their children in class.

Montessori St Nicholas School

Address: 23/24 Princes Gate, Kensington, London SW7 1PT
Telephone: 071 589 3095

Acting Head: Miss Z Dharas

Age range: 3-7
No. of pupils: 80
Scholarships:
Religion: Non-denominational

Fees per term
Day: £577-£875
Weekly board: -
Full board: -

○ Boy ○ Girl ● Co-ed
● Day ○ Week ○ Board

For further information and a prospectus, please contact the school.

More House

Address: 22-24 Pont Street, London SW1X 0AA
Telephone: 071 235 2855

Head: Miss M M Connell

Age range: 11-18
No. of pupils: 230
Scholarships: Yes
Religion: Roman Catholic

Fees per term
Day: £1545-
Weekly board: -
Full board: -

○ Boy ● Girl ○ Co-ed
● Day ○ Week ○ Board

More House is a day school with a Catholic foundation, but serving a variety of other faiths, situated in the heart of London within range of museums, art galleries and theatres. The curriculum is wide, classes are small and girls are prepared for GCSE, Advanced level and higher education in arts, science and humanities.

Mount School p690

Address: Milespit Hill, Mill Hill, London NW7 2RX
Telephone: 081 959 3403

Head: Mrs M Pond

Age range: 7-18
No. of pupils: 419
Scholarships: Yes
Religion: Non-denominational

Fees per term
Day: £990-£885
Weekly board: -
Full board: -

○ Boy ● Girl ○ Co-ed
● Day ○ Week ○ Board

Founded in 1925, the Mount offers a wide range of GCSE and A level subjects in a caring and supportive environment, situated in 5 acres within the Green Belt. Entrance is by examination and interview. There is an English as a foreign language department. The school has good facilities for art, CDT, music, information technology, business studies and a variety of sports.

Nightingale Montessori School Beck Kindergartens Ltd.

Address: Summit House, 40 Highgate West Hill, London N6 6LS
Telephone: 081 675 4387

Age range: 2-5
No. of pupils: 48
Scholarships:
Religion: Non-denominational

Fees per term
Day: £375-£440
Weekly board: -
Full board: -

○ Boy ○ Girl ● Co-ed
● Day ○ Week ○ Board

Head: Mrs T Earp

For further information and a prospectus, please contact the school.

Norfolk House School

Address: 10 Muswell Avenue, Muswell Hall, London N10 2EG
Telephone: 081 883 4584

Age range: 4-11
No. of pupils: 100
Scholarships:
Religion: Church of England

Fees per term
Day: £975-
Weekly board: -
Full board: -

● Boy ○ Girl ○ Co-ed
● Day ○ Week ○ Board

Head: Mr R Howat

Modest, moderate, disciplined and unpretentious, acieving good results whilst maintaining a balanced outlook. Pupils tend to be happy, honest and supportive; further encouraged by the house system, group activities, teams and small classes. Available are trained remedial support, a modernized library and well equipped computer room, with P.C.'s. Full range of inside and outside sports are offered. Enquiries welcomed.

Norland Place School

Address: 162-166 Holland Avenue, Kensington, London W11 4UH
Telephone: 071 603 9103

Age range: 4-11
No. of pupils: 240
Scholarships:
Religion: Non-denominational

Fees per term
Day: £930-£1400
Weekly board: -
Full board: -

○ Boy ○ Girl ● Co-ed
● Day ○ Week ○ Board

Head: Mrs S J Garner

Norland Place School was founded in 1876. The children are prepared for entry into preparatory schools at 8 (boys) and CE and Independent School Entry at 11+ (girls). Music and French are taught throughout the school. Individual music tuition can be arranged in piano and flute. Sports include football, netball, rounders, tennis and swimming. Boys 4-8, girls 4-11.

Normanhurst School

Address: 68/72 Station Road, Chingford, London E4 7BA
Telephone: 081 529 4307

Age range: 4-18
No. of pupils: 160
Scholarships:
Religion: Non-denominational

Fees per term
Day: £1084-£1342
Weekly board: -
Full board: -

○ Boy ○ Girl ● Co-ed
● Day ○ Week ○ Board

Head: Mr R C Holt

For further information and a prospectus, please contact the school.

Northbridge House Junior School

Address: 1 Gloucester Avenue, London NW1 7AB

Telephone: 071 485 0661

Head: Miss J Battye

Age range: 8-10
No. of pupils: 242
Scholarships:
Religion: Non-denominational

Fees per term
Day: -£1555
Weekly board: -
Full board: -

Boy ○ Girl ○ Co-ed ●
Day ● Week ○ Board ○

For further information and a prospectus, please contact the school.

Northbridge House Senior School

Address: 1 Gloucester Avenue, London NW1 7AB

Telephone: 071 485 0661

Head: Mr R Shaw

Age range: 10-16
No. of pupils: 220
Scholarships:
Religion: Non-denominational

Fees per term
Day: £1555-
Weekly board: -
Full board: -

Boy ○ Girl ○ Co-ed ●
Day ● Week ○ Board ○

For further information and a prospectus, please contact the school.

The Norwegian School

Address: 28 Arteberry Road, Wimbledon, London SW20 8AH

Telephone: 081 947 6617

Head: Mr J Furumo

Age range: 3-16
No. of pupils: 104
Scholarships:
Religion:

Fees per term
Day: -
Weekly board: -
Full board: -

Boy ○ Girl ○ Co-ed ●
Day ● Week ○ Board ○

For further information and a prospectus, please contact the school.

Notting Hill and Ealing High School, GPDST *

Address: 2 Cleveland Road, London W13 8AX

Telephone: 081 997 5744

Head: Mrs S M Whitfield

Age range: 5-18
No. of pupils: 835
Scholarships: Yes
Religion: Non-denominational

Fees per term
Day: £1036-£1340
Weekly board: -
Full board: -

Boy ○ Girl ● Co-ed ○
Day ● Week ○ Board ○

Founded in 1873, a full and academic education is provided to girls within a happy and caring environment. Sport, music, drama, art and public speaking are some of the other specialities of the school. There is an effective pastoral system and girls progress to the universities and colleges of their choice with well-founded confidence in themselves and their futures.

Oakfield Preparatory School

Address: 125-128 Thurlow Park Road, Dulwich, London SE21 8HP
Telephone: 081 670 4206

Head: Mrs A Tomkins

Age range: 2-11
No. of pupils: 490
Scholarships:
Religion: Non-denominational

Fees per term
Day: £990-£1040
Weekly board: -
Full board: -

○ ○ ● Boy Girl Co-ed
● ○ ○ Day Week Board

Founded in 1887 Oakfield is today a modern co-ed prep school preparing children for entry to senior school at 11+. The core subjects - English and maths form the basis of the curriculum but not to the exclusion of French, science, the humanities, computing and the arts. The school site of nearly 3 acres allows ample room for sport and play. Entry is by informal assessment, or formal test for older children.

Paint Pots Montessori School

Address: Bayswater United Reformed Church, Newton Road, London W5 5LS
Telephone: 071 792 0433

Head: Miss G Hood

Age range: 2-5
No. of pupils: 36
Scholarships:
Religion: Non-denominational

Fees per term
Day: £540-£940
Weekly board: -
Full board: -

○ ○ ● Boy Girl Co-ed
● ○ ○ Day Week Board

For further information and a prospectus, please contact the school.

Palmers Green High School

Address: Hoppers Road, London, N21 3LJ

Telephone: 081 886 1135

Head: Mrs S Grant

Age range: 3-16
No. of pupils: 320
Scholarships: Yes
Religion: Non-denominational

Fees per term
Day: £460-£1150
Weekly board: -
Full board: -

○ ● ○ Boy Girl Co-ed
● ○ ○ Day Week Board

Academic school with a caring environment. Small senior school classes, broad curriculum, including strong emphasis on the arts - visual and performing. One computer per child in all IT classes, whole school linked on an Econet network. Continuity of education between 3 and 16 years combining with a close school parent relationship leading to success and fulfilment.

The Paragon Hill School

Address: 84a Heath Road, Hampstead, London NW3

Telephone: 071 794 5857

Head: Mr R Wade

Age range: 3-13
No. of pupils: 120
Scholarships: Yes
Religion:

Fees per term
Day: £600-£1950
Weekly board: -
Full board: -

○ ○ ● Boy Girl Co-ed
● ○ ○ Day Week Board

For further information and a prospectus, please contact the school. See also Paragon Hill at 16 New End.

The Paragon Hill School

Address: 16 New End, London NW3
Telephone: 071 794 5857

Age range: 3-13
No. of pupils: 120
Scholarships: Yes
Religion:

Fees per term
Day: £600-£1950
Weekly board: -
Full board: -

○ Boy ○ Girl ● Co-ed
● Day ○ Week ○ Board

Head: Mr R Wade

Small distinctive school set in the centre of Old Hampstead. The school offers small classes, a broad curriculum and specialist teaching for children with learning difficulties.

Parayhouse School †

Address: St John's, World's End, King's Road, Chelsea, London SW10 0LU
Telephone: 071 352 2882

Age range: 5-17
No. of pupils: 50
Scholarships:
Religion: Non-denominational

Fees per term
Day: £2475-£2475
Weekly board: -
Full board: -

○ Boy ○ Girl ● Co-ed
● Day ○ Week ○ Board

Head: Mrs S L Jackson

For further information and a prospectus, please contact the school.

Pardes House School Ltd

Address: Hendon Lane, London N3 1SA
Telephone: 081 343 3568

Age range: 4-17
No. of pupils: 440
Scholarships:
Religion: Jewish

Fees per term
Day: £750-£1566
Weekly board: -
Full board: -

● Boy ○ Girl ○ Co-ed
● Day ○ Week ○ Board

Head: Mr C M King BA

For further information and a prospectus, please contact the school.

Pembridge Hall School

Address: 18 Pembridge Square, London W2 4EH
Telephone: 071 229 0121

Age range: 4-11
No. of pupils: 250
Scholarships:
Religion: Non-denominational

Fees per term
Day: £1375-
Weekly board: -
Full board: -

○ Boy ● Girl ○ Co-ed
● Day ○ Week ○ Board

Head: Mrs E M Collison

For further information and a prospectus, please contact the school.

The Pointer School

Address: 19 Stratheden Road, Blackheath, London
Telephone: 081 858 5524
Head: Mr B W Newcombe

Age range: 3-11
No. of pupils: 140
Scholarships:
Religion: Non-denominational

Fees per term
Day: £550-£1070
Weekly board: -
Full board: -

Boy ○ Girl ○ Co-ed ●
Day ● Week ○ Board ○

Pointers is a small school which endeavours to create a well motivated pupil who is working to the best of his/her ability.

The Pre-Preparatory School

Address: 16 Highbury Road, Wimbledon, London SW19
Telephone:
Head:

Age range:
No. of pupils:
Scholarships:
Religion:

Fees per term
Day: -
Weekly board: -
Full board: -

Boy ○ Girl ○ Co-ed ○
Day ○ Week ○ Board ○

For further information and a prospectus, please contact the school.

Putney High School *

Address: 35 Putney Hill, London SW15 6BH
Telephone: 081 788 4886
Head: Mrs E Merchant

Age range: 5-18
No. of pupils: 830
Scholarships: Yes
Religion: Church of England

Fees per term
Day: £1036-£1340
Weekly board: -
Full board: -

Boy ○ Girl ● Co-ed ○
Day ● Week ○ Board ○

Putney provides an all round education in a lively and friendly atmosphere which encourages creativity and confidence. The school places great emphasis on the development of the individual and is strong in many extra-curricular activities. It is academically selective with entry by examination and interview. Most girls go on to higher education.

Putney Park School

Address: 11 Woodborough Road, Putney, London SW15 6PY
Telephone: 081 788 8316
Head: Miss J Tweedie-Smith

Age range: 4-16
No. of pupils: 380
Scholarships:
Religion: Non-denominational

Fees per term
Day: -
Weekly board: -
Full board: -

Boy ○ Girl ○ Co-ed ●
Day ● Week ○ Board ○

For further information and a prospectus, please contact the school. Boys 4-8, girls 4-16.

Queen's College *

Address: 43-49 Harley Street, London W1N 2BT

Telephone: 071 636 2446

Head: The Hon Lady Goodhart

Age range: 11-18
No. of pupils: 400
Scholarships:
Religion: Church of England

Fees per term
Day: £1725-
Weekly board: £1200-
Full board: -

Boy ○ | Girl ● | Co-ed ○
Day ● | Week ○ | Board ○

Queen's College, founded in 1848, was the first establishment to provide academic qualifications for women and in 1853 received the first every Royal charter for the furtherance of women's education. We provide a wide-ranging curriculum, aiming for academic excellence in a friendly atmosphere.

Queens' Gate School

Address: 131-133 Queens Gate, London SW7 5LE

Telephone: 071 589 3597

Principal: Mrs A M Holyoak

Age range: 4-18
No. of pupils: 350
Scholarships:
Religion: Non-denominational

Fees per term
Day: £990-£1695
Weekly board: -
Full board: -

Boy ○ | Girl ● | Co-ed ○
Day ● | Week ○ | Board ○

The aim of the school is to create a secure and happy environment in which each girl can realise her academic and personal potential. The schools expectations of our pupils are high, whether they are exceptionally able or of an average ability. The school seeks to inspire a love of learning, to extend individual talents and to encourage the development of self discipline.

Rainbow Montessori School

Address: Highgate U R C, Pond Square, Highgate, London N6 6BA
Telephone: 081 348 2434

Head: Mrs L C Madden

Age range: 2-8
No. of pupils: 35
Scholarships:
Religion:

Fees per term
Day: £450-£800
Weekly board: -
Full board: -

Boy ○ | Girl ○ | Co-ed ●
Day ● | Week ○ | Board ○

A happy environment that adheres strictly to the Montessori Method. Extra-curricular activities include dance, French, music and piano. We cover a wide range of subjects all with individual attention.

Rainbow Montessori School

Address: St James's Hall, Sherriff Road, London NW6 2AP
Telephone: 071 328 8986

Head: Mrs L C Madden

Age range: 2-8
No. of pupils: 35
Scholarships:
Religion:

Fees per term
Day: £450-£800
Weekly board: -
Full board: -

Boy ○ | Girl ○ | Co-ed ●
Day ● | Week ○ | Board ○

A happy environment that adheres strictly to the Montessori Method. Extra-curricular activities include dance, French, music and piano. We cover a wide range of subjects all with individual attention.

Ravenscourt Theatre School

Address: London House, 271-273 King Street, London W6 9LZ
Telephone: 081 741 0707

Head: Rev R Blakeley

Age range: 6-16
No. of pupils: 84
Scholarships: Yes
Religion: Church of England

Fees per term
Day: £860-
Weekly board: -
Full board: -

Boy ○ / Girl ○ / Co-ed ●
Day ● / Week ○ / Board ○

The school specialises in forms of theatrical training including ballet, jazz and tap dance. Television and audition techniques are also catered for. The academic side of the school takes children to GCSE standard in all the basic subjects.

Ravenstone House

Address: The Long Garden, Albion Street, Marble Arch, London W2 2AX
Telephone: 071 262 1190

Head: Mrs A J Saunders

Age range: 1-7
No. of pupils: 100
Scholarships:
Religion: Non-denominational

Fees per term
Day: £670-£1200
Weekly board: -
Full board: -

Boy ○ / Girl ○ / Co-ed ●
Day ● / Week ○ / Board ○

For further information and a prospectus, please contact the school.

Redcliffe School

Address: 47 Redcliffe Gardens, London SW10 9JH
Telephone: 071 352 9247

Head: Miss R E Cunnah

Age range: 4-11
No. of pupils: 96
Scholarships:
Religion: Christian

Fees per term
Day: £1325-
Weekly board: -
Full board: -

Boy ● / Girl ● / Co-ed ○
Day ● / Week ○ / Board ○

Redcliffe School is a small, friendly school. It caters for a range of abilities and enables children to reach a high academic standard whilst developing the potential of each individual. Basic skills are accentuated within a broad and balanced curriculum incorporating creative and practical activities. Boys 4-8, girls 4-11.

Riverston School

Address: 63-69 Eltham Road, Lee Green, London SE12 8UF
Telephone: 081 318 4327

Head: Mr D M Lewis

Age range: 2-16
No. of pupils: 600
Scholarships: Yes
Religion: Non-denominational

Fees per term
Day: £825-£1100
Weekly board: -
Full board: -

Boy ○ / Girl ○ / Co-ed ●
Day ● / Week ○ / Board ○

Riverston is a privately owned co-educational day school which has been serving south-east London since 1923. It is a traditional school with a strong emphasis in developing the full potential of each pupil, in a caring and secure manner. Pupils are prepared for a wide ranging number of public examinations and have use of the school's own château in France.

The Roche School

Address: 11 Frogmore, Wandsworth, London SW18 1HW
Telephone: 081 877 0823

Age range: 8-13
No. of pupils: 100
Scholarships:
Religion:

Fees per term
Day: -
Weekly board: -
Full board: -

○ ○ ●
Boy Girl Co-ed
● ○ ○
Day Week Board

Head: Mrs C Roche

For further information and a prospectus, please contact the school.

The Rose Montessori School

Address: St Alban's Church Hall, Margravine Road, London W6
Telephone: 071 381 6002

Age range: 3-5
No. of pupils: 24
Scholarships:
Religion:

Fees per term
Day: -
Weekly board: -
Full board: -

○ ○ ●
Boy Girl Co-ed
● ○ ○
Day Week Board

Head: Miss K Gould

For further information and a prospectus, please contact the school.

Rosemead Preparatory School

Address: 70 Thurlow Park Road, Dulwich, London SE21 8GZ
Telephone: 081 670 5865

Age range: 3-11
No. of pupils: 260
Scholarships: Yes
Religion: Non-denominational

Fees per term
Day: £912-£1072
Weekly board: -
Full board: -

○ ○ ●
Boy Girl Co-ed
● ○ ○
Day Week Board

Head: Mrs R Lait

For further information and a prospectus, please contact the school.

Rowens School

Address: 17 Drax Avenue, Wimbledon, London SW20 0EG
Telephone: 081 946 8220

Age range: 3-8
No. of pupils: 120
Scholarships:
Religion: Non-denomintional

Fees per term
Day: £460-£860
Weekly board: -
Full board: -

○ ○ ●
Boy Girl Co-ed
● ○ ○
Day Week Board

Head: Mrs J Anderson

For further information and a prospectus, please contact the school.

Royal School

Address: 65 Rosslyn Hill,
Hampstead, London NW3 5UD

Telephone: 071 794 7708

Head: Mrs C A Sibson

Age range: 4-18
No. of pupils: 185
Scholarships: Yes
Religion: Non-denominational

Fees per term
Day: £855-£1001
Weekly board: -
Full board: £2020-£2480

○ ● ○
Boy Girl Co-ed

● ○ ●
Day Week Board

The school was founded on its present site in 1855. It has been priveleged to enjoy Royal Patronage since its formation and the present patron is Her Royal Highness Princess Alexandra, The Hon. Lady Ogilvy, GCVO. Today the school is a small independent boarding and day school for girls. It is open to the daughters of servicemen, ex-servicemen and of civilians.

Salcombe Preparatory School

Address: 224/226 Chase Side,
Southgate, London N14 4PL

Telephone: 081 441 5282

Head: Mr A J Blackhurst

Age range: 4-11
No. of pupils:
Scholarships:
Religion: Non-denominational

Fees per term
Day: -
Weekly board: -
Full board: -

○ ○ ●
Boy Girl Co-ed

● ○ ○
Day Week Board

For further information and a prospectus, please contact the school.

Sarum Hall School

Address: 51 Eaton Avenue,
Camden, London NW3 3EP

Telephone: 071 794 2261

Head: Lady Smith-Gordon

Age range: 5-11
No. of pupils: 127
Scholarships:
Religion: Church of England

Fees per term
Day: -£1350
Weekly board: -
Full board: -

○ ● ○
Boy Girl Co-ed

● ○ ○
Day Week Board

For further information and a prospectus, please contact the school.

The Shepherd's Bush Day Nursery

Address: 101 Ferthville
Gardens, London W12 7JQ

Telephone: 081 749 1256

Head: Ms E Harvey

Age range: 1-5
No. of pupils: 35
Scholarships:
Religion: Non-denominational

Fee per term
Day: -
Weekly board: -
Full Board: -

○ ○ ●
Boy Girl Co-ed

● ○ ○
Day Week Board

The Sheperds Bush Day Nursery provides high quality day care n beautifully designed premises in West London. The strong education programme to their age and ability. The curriculum includes French, music, swimming, cookery and gardening as well as lots of art and craft activities and regular outings (educational and social).

Sinclair House School

Address: 159 Munster Road, Fulham, London SW6 2DA

Telephone: 071 736 9182

Head: Miss T Ashley

Age range: 2-8
No. of pupils: 50
Scholarships: Yes
Religion: Non-denominational

Fees per term
Day: £500-£1000
Weekly board: -
Full board: -

○ ○ ● Boy Girl Co-ed
● ○ ○ Day Week Board

Sinclair House is a small school offering individual attention to each child. It combines traditional 3 Rs with history, geography, french, science, music, pottery, painting, swimming, tennis, hockey, cricket, basketball, trampolining, gymnastics and athletics. To create a vibrant, happy, disciplined environment to maximise each child's potential.

Snaresbrook College

Address: 75 Woodford Road, South Woodford, London E18 2EA

Telephone: 081 989 2394

Head: Mrs L J Chiverrell

Age range: 3-11
No. of pupils: 155
Scholarships:
Religion: Christian

Fees per term
Day: £710-£944
Weekly board: -
Full board: -

○ ○ ● Boy Girl Co-ed
● ○ ○ Day Week Board

For further details and a prospectus, please contact the school.

Somerville School

Address: 12 Wavetree Road, London SW2 3SJ

Telephone: 081 674 5495

Head: Mrs E A Tye

Age range: 3-7
No. of pupils: 70
Scholarships:
Religion:

Fees per term
Day: -
Weekly board: -
Full board: -

○ ○ ● Boy Girl Co-ed
● ○ ○ Day Week Board

For further information and a prospectus, please contact the school.

South Hamstead High School

Address: 3 Maresfield Gardens, London NW3 5SS

Telephone: 071 435 2899

Head: Mrs D A Burgess BA(Hons)

Age range: 5-18
No. of pupils: 740
Scholarships: Yes
Religion: Non-denominational

Fees per term
Day: £1036-£1340
Weekly board: -
Full board: -

○ ● ○ Boy Girl Co-ed
● ○ ○ Day Week Board

For further information and a prospectus, please contact the school.

South Hamstead High School

Address: 3 Maresfield Gardens, London NW3 5SS

Telephone: 071 435 2899

Head: Mrs D A Burgess BA(Hons)

Age range: 5-18
No. of pupils: 740
Scholarships: Yes
Religion: Non-denominational

Fees per term
Day: £1036-£1340
Weekly board: -
Full board: -

○ ● ○
Boy Girl Co-ed

● ○ ○
Day Week Board

For further information and a prospectus, please contact the school.

St Angelo Preparatory School

Address: 10 Montpelier Road, Ealing, London W5 2QP

Telephone: 081 997 3209

Head: Mr D G A Cattini

Age range: 5-13+
No. of pupils: 95
Scholarships:
Religion: Non-denominational

Fees per term
Day: £975-
Weekly board: -
Full board: -

● ○ ○
Boy Girl Co-ed

● ○ ○
Day Week Board

The primary purpose of this small, intimate community is to prepare candidates for entry to the Public Schools. This is achieved within the context of a disciplined teaching and learning environment in which all pupils are encouraged to achieve their optimum potential in all areas of the curriculum and to develop a positive attitude towards all aspects of school life.

St Anthony's School

Address: 90 Fitzjohn's Avenue, Camden, London NW3 6NP

Telephone: 071 435 0316

Head: Mr T W Patton

Age range: 6-13
No. of pupils: 270
Scholarships:
Religion: Roman Catholic

Fees per term
Day: £1430-£1465
Weekly board: -
Full board: -

● ○ ○
Boy Girl Co-ed

● ○ ○
Day Week Board

For further information an a prospectus, please contact the school.

St Augustine's Priory

Address: Hillcrest Road, Ealing, London W5 2JL

Telephone: 081 997 2022

Mother: MARY Gabriel

Age range: 4-18
No. of pupils: 425
Scholarships:
Religion: Roman Catholic

Fees per term
Day: £610-£925
Weekly board: -
Full board: -

○ ● ○
Boy Girl Co-ed

● ○ ○
Day Week Board

St Augustine's Priory is an independent grammar day school for girls from 4-18 year. The school provides a full course GCSE, 'A' Level and University Entrance. The grounds provide ten hard tennis courts, and a full sized astroturf hockey pitch. A prospectus and further details may be obtained from the Headmistress.

St Benedict's Junior School

Address: 5 Montpelier Avenue, Ealing, London W5 2XP

Telephone: 081 997 9800

Head: Revd M Shipperlee OSB

Age range: 4-11
No. of pupils: 265
Scholarships:
Religion: Roman Catholic

Fees per term
Day: £900-£1025
Weekly board: -
Full board: -

● Boy ○ Girl ○ Co-ed
● Day ○ Week ○ Board

A relatively small Catholic school which aims to give boys a thorough grounding using traditional and modern methods, preparing them for transfer to the Senior School - all in a happy yet disciplined atmosphere. A Benedictine Headmaster leads a lay staff of qualified teachers in providing a full academic and sporting curriculum.

St Benedict's School *

Address: 54 Eaton Rise, Ealing, London W5 2ES

Telephone: 081 997 9828

Head: Dr A J Dachs

Age range: 11-18
No. of pupils: 600
Scholarships:
Religion: Roman Catholic

Fees per term
Day: -£4260
Weekly board: -
Full board: -

● Boy ● Girl ○ Co-ed
● Day ○ Week ○ Board

St Benedict's, managed by the Benedictine monks of Ealing Abbey, is the only Catholic Independent School for boys in Greater London. Pupils follow a broad range of academic subjects, as well as Art, Design Technology, Drama, Music and Sport. Admissions at 11+ and 13+. Girls are welcomed to the Sixth Form dependent on Public Examination results.

St Christina's Roman Catholic Preparatory School

Address: 25 St Edmund's Terrace, Regents Park, London NW8 7PY
Telephone: 071 722 8784

Head: Sister Mary Corr

Age range: 3-11
No. of pupils: 230
Scholarships:
Religion: Roman Catholic

Fees per term
Day: £800-
Weekly board: -
Full board: -

○ Boy ○ Girl ● Co-ed
● Day ○ Week ○ Board

For further information and a prospectus, please contact the school.

St Christopher's School

Address: 32 Belsize Lane, London NW3 5AE

Telephone: 071 435 1521

Head: Miss J M Anderson

Age range: 5-11
No. of pupils: 235
Scholarships:
Religion: Non-Denominational

Fees per term
Day: £1355-£1430
Weekly board: -
Full board: -

○ Boy ● Girl ○ Co-ed
● Day ○ Week ○ Board

For further information and a prospectus, please contact the school.

St Dunstan's College *

Address: Stanstead Road, Catford, London SE6 4TY

Telephone: 081 690 1274

Head: Mr B D Dance MA

Age range: 7-18
No. of pupils: 750
Scholarships: Yes
Religion: Church of England

Fees per term
Day: -£1479
Weekly board: -
Full board: -

● Boy ○ Girl ○ Co-ed
● Day ○ Week ○ Board

For further information and a prospectus, please contact the school.

St Godric's College

Address: 2 Arkwright Road, Hampstead, London NW3 6AD

Telephone: 071 4359831

Head: Sir J Loveridge

Age range:
No. of pupils:
Scholarships:
Religion:

Fees per term
Day: -
Weekly board: -
Full board: -

○ Boy ○ Girl ○ Co-ed
○ Day ○ Week ○ Board

For further information and a prospectus, please contact the school.

St James Independent School for Boys

Address: 91 Queen's Gate, London SW7 5AB

Telephone: 071 373 5638

Head: Mr N Debenham

Age range: 4-10
No. of pupils: 145
Scholarships:
Religion: Non-denominational

Fees per term
Day: £900-£1030
Weekly board: -
Full board: -

● Boy ○ Girl ○ Co-ed
● Day ○ Week ○ Board

Curriculum combines traditional features with unusual features of our own. Reading is taught phonetically; any writing is beautiful; boys learn their table by heart. There is generous provision for music, art, drama and speech; there is daily physical training. In addition classical languages have been reintroduced as the foundation of all learning: Sanskrit and Greek are taught to all pupils.

St James Independent School for Boys

Address: 61 Eccleston Square, London SW1V 1PH

Telephone: 071 834 0471

Head: Mr N Debenham

Age range: 10-18
No. of pupils: 200
Scholarships:
Religion: Non-denominational

Fees per term
Day: £1270-£1300
Weekly board: -
Full board: -

● Boy ○ Girl ○ Co-ed
● Day ○ Week ○ Board

Entry direct from Junior school or by interview and test. Curriculum gives broad range of traditional subjects including Classical Languages, English, Mathematics, French, all three Sciences, History and Geography. Most boys take 8-10 GCSEs. Compulsory games for all. Art, music and drama are specialities. Sailing, climbing, cadets, DofE, strongly encouraged. Strong sixth form with wide base of A Levels.

St James Independent School for Girls

Address: 91 Queen's Gate,
London SW7 5AB

Telephone: 071 373 5638

Head: Miss S M Caldwell

Age range: 4-10
No. of pupils: 139
Scholarships:
Religion: Non-denominational

Fees per term
Day: £900-£1030
Weekly board: -
Full board: -

○ ● ○
Boy Girl Co-ed
● ○ ○
Day Week Board

The school sets out to provide a finely balanced education that will encourage the unfolding and development of the whole person. Reading, writing and mathematics are taught by traditional methods and much attention is given to the ancient scriptures, to art, singing and to fine calligraphy. There is daily physical exercise. At 10 girls move to the senior school.

St James Independent School for Girls

Address: 19 Pembridge Villas,
London W11 3EP

Telephone: 071 229 2253

Head: Miss S M Caldwell

Age range: 10-18
No. of pupils: 142
Scholarships:
Religion: Non-denominational

Fees per term
Day: £1270-£1300
Weekly board: -
Full board: -

○ ● ○
Boy Girl Co-ed
● ○ ○
Day Week Board

Entry direct from junior school or by interview. A wide range of GCSE and A Level subjects is provided. Curriculum also includes philosophy and Sanskrit. Music plays an important part and there are regular dramatic productions. Sports: athletics, lacrosse, tennis, swimming. Regular school holidays in Britain and abroad. Most girls proceed after A Levels to university or professional training.

St John's Wood

Address: Lord's Roundabout,
St John's Wood, London
NW8 7NE
Telephone: 071 722 7149

Head: Mrs S Segal MSc

Age range: 3-11
No. of pupils: 150
Scholarships:
Religion: Non-denominational

Fees per term
Day: £550-£1075
Weekly board: -
Full board: -

○ ○ ●
Boy Girl Co-ed
● ○ ○
Day Week Board

For further information and a prospectus, please contact the school. Boys 3-8, girls 3-11.

St Joseph's Academy

Address: 5 Lee Terrace,
Blackheath, Lewisham,
London SE3 9TY
Telephone:

Principal:

Age range:
No. of pupils:
Scholarships:
Religion: Roman Catholic

Fees per term
Day: -
Weeklyboard: -
Full board: -

● ○ ○
Boy Girl Co-ed
● ○ ○
Day Week Board

For further information and a prospectus, please contact the school.

St Joseph's Convent

Address: Watford Way, Barnet, London NW4

Telephone:

Principal:

Age range:
No: of pupils:
Scholarships:
Religion:

Fees per term
Day: -
Weekly board: -
Full board: -

Boy ○ Girl ○ Co-ed ●
Day ● Week ○ Board ○

For further information and a prospectus, please contact the school.

St Joseph's Convent School

Address: 59 Cambridge Park, Wanstead, London E11 2PR

Telephone: 081 989 4700

Head: Mrs C Youle

Age range: 4-11
No: of pupils: 195
Scholarships:
Religion: Roman Catholic

Fees per term
Day: £530-£530
Weekly board: -
Full board: -

Boy ○ Girl ● Co-ed ○
Day ● Week ○ Board ○

St Joseph's is a convent school offering education to girls aged 4 to 11 years. The school is owned by the Sisters of Mercy and is conducted by the Sisters and a dedicated lay staff. There are seven classes, three infant classes and four junior classes.

St Margeret's School

Address: 18 Kidderpore Gardens, London NW3 7SR

Telephone: 071 435 2439

Head: Mrs S J Meaden

Age range: 5-16
No: of pupils: 140
Scholarships:
Religion: Church of England

Fees per term
Day: £960-£1145
Weekly board: -
Full board: -

Boy ○ Girl ● Co-ed ○
Day ● Week ○ Board ○

St Margeret's aims to provide a sound education based on the National Curriculum. Classes are small, attention is given to each girl's individual need. We aim to achieve high standards in work and discipline while fostering a happy atmosphere. Extra-curricular activities include ski-trips, visits abroad and weekly events. Girls are prepared for speech and drama and instrumental examinations.

St Martin's School

Address: 22 Goodwyn Avenue, Barnet, London NW7 2TL

Telephone:

Head: Mrs G A Murray

Age range: 4-7
No: of pupils: 115
Scholarships:
Religion: Roman Catholic

Fees per term
Day: -
Weekly board: -
Full board: -

Boy ○ Girl ○ Co-ed ●
Day ● Week ○ Board ○

For further information and a prospectus, please contact the school.

St Mary's Convent

Address: 47 Fitzjohn's Avenue, Camden, London NW3 6PG

Telephone: 071 435 1868

Age range: 4-11
No. of pupils: 165
Scholarships:
Religion: Roman Catholic

Fees per term
Day: -
Weekly board: -
Full board: -

○ ○ ●
Boy Girl Co-ed
● ○ ○
Day Week Board

Head: Sister M Richard Prendergast

For further information and a prospectus, please contact the school. Boys 4-7, girls 4-11.

St Olave's Preparatory School

Address: 106-110 Southwood Road, Greenwich, London SE9 3QS

Telephone:

Age range: 3-11
No: of pupils: 218
Scholarships:
Religion: Roman Catholic

Fees per term
Day: -
Weekly board: -
Full board: -

○ ○ ●
Boy Girl Co-ed
● ○ ○
Day Week Board

Head: Mr N Stuttle

For further information and a prospectus, please contact the school.

St Paul's Cathedral Choir School

Address: 2 New Change, London EC4M 9AD

Telephone:

Age range: 8-13
No: of pupils: 80
Scholarships:
Religion: Church of England

Fees per term
Day: -
Weekly board: -
Full board: -

● ○ ○
Boy Girl Co-ed
● ○ ●
Day Week Board

Head: Rev G Hopley

For further information and a prospectus, please contact the school.

St Paul's Girls' Preparatory School

Address: Bute House, Hammersmith and Fulham, London W6 7EA
Telephone: 071 603 7381

Age range: 5-11
No: of pupils: 260
Scholarships:
Religion:

Fees per term
Day: -
Weekly board: -
Full board: -

○ ● ○
Boy Girl Co-ed
● ○ ○
Day Week Board

Head: Miss J E Lee

For further information and a prospectus, please contact the school.

St Paul's Girls' School

Address: Brook Green,
Hammersmith and Fulham,
London W6 7BS
Telephone: 071 603 2288

Head: Mrs H Williams

Age range: 11-18
No. of pupils: 620
Scholarships:
Religion:

Fees per term
Day: -
Weekly board: -
Full board: -

○ ● ○
Boy Girl Co-ed
● ○ ○
Day Week Board

For further information and a prospectus, please contact the school.

St Paul's Preparatory School

Address: Lonsdale Road,
Barnes, London SW13 9JT
Telephone: 081 748 3461

Head: Mr W N J Howard

Age range: 8-13
No. of pupils: 400
Scholarships:
Religion:

Fees per term
Day: -
Weekly board: -
Full board: -

● ○ ○
Boy Girl Co-ed
● ○ ●
Day Week Board

For further information and a prospectus, please contact the school.

St Paul's School *

Address: Lonsdale Road,
Barnes, London SW13 9JT
Telephone: 081 748 9162

Head: Mr R S Baldock

Age range: 13-18
No. of pupils: 750
Scholarships: Yes
Religion: Church of England

Fees per term
Day: £2400-
Weekly board: £3800-
Full board: £3800-

● ○ ○
Boy Girl Co-ed
● ● ●
Day Week Board

Founded in 1509, the school moved to new buildings, south of the Thames at Hammersmith Bridge and has its own preparatory school, Colet Court, on the same 40 acre site. With a new art school and technology centre opened in 1991, the facilities are impressive, and the school's excellent academic record is complemented by an equally high standard in games, music, art and drama.

St Philip's p691

Address: 6 Wetherby Place,
London SW7 4NE
Telephone: 071 373 3944

Head: Mr H Biggs-Davison

Age range: 7-13
No. of pupils: 100
Scholarships: Yes
Religion: Roman Catholic

Fees per term
Day: £1365-£1365
Weekly board: -
Full board: -

● ○ ○
Boy Girl Co-ed
● ○ ○
Day Week Board

St Philip's is the Roman Catholic Preparatory School which, since 1934, has served the south west part of central London. The school has an exceptionally high Common Entrance success rate, but aims to provide a wide curriculum with a range of sports, art, CDT, music, poetry and drama. A large number of extra-curricular clubs offer fencing, judo, chess, computers, gymnastics, etc.

St Vedast Independent School for Boys

Address: 23 West Heath Road, Camden, London N12 8SY
Telephone:
Head:
Age range: 10-18
No. of pupils:
Scholarships:
Religion:
Fees per term
Day: -
Weekly board: -
Full board: -

● Boy ○ Girl ○ Co-ed
● Day ○ Week ○ Board

For further information and a prospectus, please contact the school.

Streatham Hill and Clapham High School *

Address: Wavetree Road, London SW2 3SR
Telephone: 081 674 6912
Head: Miss G M Ellis
Age range: 5-18
No. of pupils: 530
Scholarships:
Religion:
Fees per term
Day: -
Weekly board: -
Full board: -

○ Boy ● Girl ○ Co-ed
● Day ○ Week ○ Board

For further information and a prospectus, please contact the school.

Streatham Modern School

Address: 508 Streatham High Road, London SW16 3QB
Telephone: 081 764 7232
Head: Mr B Russell-Owen
Age range: 3-12
No. of pupils: 110
Scholarships:
Religion: Mixed
Fees per term
Day: £685-
Weekly board: -
Full board: -

● Boy ○ Girl ○ Co-ed
● Day ○ Week ○ Board

We are an independent preparatory school for boys. The school was founded in 1908 and still believes in the traditional values of education. The school is small and each pupil is treated as an individual by a caring, dedicated staff. A prospectus and further details can be obtained from the school.

The Study Preparatory School

Address: Wilberforce House, Camp Road, Wimbledon Common, London SW19 5ER
Telephone: 081 947 6969
Head: Mrs L Bond
Age range: 4-11
No. of pupils: 240
Scholarships: Yes
Religion: Non-denominational
Fees per term
Day: £1155-£1310
Weekly board: -
Full board: -

○ Boy ● Girl ○ Co-ed
● Day ○ Week ○ Board

The Study is a happy, friendly and informal school on two sites next to Wimbledon Common, both of which are spacious, light, bright and very well equipped. Girls receive a sound foundation in basic subjects within a wide and stimulating curriculum. All girls are prepared for entrance into day and boarding schools at 11+.

Sussex House Preparatory School

Address: 68 Cadogan Square, Kensington and Chelsea, London SW1X 0EA
Telephone: 071 584 1741

Head: Mr J H E Whittaker

Age range: 8-13
No. of pupils: 172
Scholarships:
Religion:

Fees per term
Day: -
Weekly board: -
Full board: -

● Boy ○ Girl ○ Co-ed
● Day ○ Week ○ Board

For further information and a prospectus, please contact the school.

Sydenham High School GPDST ✻ p691

Address: 19 Westwood Hill, London SE26 6BL
Telephone: 081 778 8737

Head: Mrs G Baker BSc

Age range: 4-18
No. of pupils: 706
Scholarships: Yes
Religion: Non-denominational

Fees per term
Day: £1036-£1340
Weekly board: -
Full board: -

○ Boy ● Girl ○ Co-ed
● Day ○ Week ○ Board

The school is an attractive blend of Victorian buildings and modern accommodation including technology and sixth form centre. Sydenham High School is an individual-orientated school that retains a balance between the traditions it embodies whilst developing in line with the best of current educational thinking. The school's broad, balanced education fosters confidence through success. A happy, lively school.

Sylvia Young Theatre School

Address: Rossmore Road, Marylebone, London NW1 6NJ
Telephone: 071 402 0673

Headteacher: Miss M Melville

Age range: 7-16
No. of pupils: 132
Scholarships:
Religion: Non-denominational

Fees per term
Day: £825-£1000
Weekly board: -
Full board: -

○ Boy ○ Girl ● Co-ed
● Day ○ Week ○ Board

The Sylvia Young Theatre School is an independent theatre school emphasizing drama, ballet, jazz, tap, speech and music along with academics. All students are prepared for GCSE and several pupils leave to perform or work in the theatrical field or go to study A Levels at other schools.

Talmud Torah School

Address: 112-114 Bethune Road, London N16 5DU
Telephone: 081 802 2512

Head: Mr S Harris

Age range: 4-11
No. of pupils: 100
Scholarships:
Religion: Jewish

Fees per term
Day: -
Weekly board: -
Full board: -

● Boy ○ Girl ○ Co-ed
● Day ○ Week ○ Board

For further information and a prospectus, please contact the school.

Thomas's Preparatory School, Battersea

Address: 28-40 Battersea High Street, London SW11 3JB

Telephone: 071 978 4224

Head: Mr P Moss

Age Range: 4-13
No. of pupils: 372
Scholarships:
Religion: Church of England

Fees per term
Day: £1510-£1810
Weekly board: -
Full board: -

Boy ○ Girl ○ Co-ed ●
Day ● Week ○ Board ○

An independent London Day School providing a fine education in appropriate surroundings. The facilities are second to none and the school has a large playground, gymnasium, science labs., hall and extensive music and drama facilities. It prepares children for entry to boarding and day schools at 11+, 12+ and 13+. The academic results are excellent and the children are happy, well motivated and enthusistic.

Thomas's Preparatory School, Kensington

Address: 17-19 Cottesmore Gardens, London W8 5PR

Telephone: 071 938 1931

Head: Miss J Kelham

Age range: 4-13
No. of pupils: 211
Scholarships:
Religion: Church of England

Fees per term
Day: £1510-£1810
Weekly board: -
Full board: -

Boy ○ Girl ○ Co-ed ●
Day ● Week ○ Board ○

Thomas's provides a broad, well balanced curriculum. We aim to achieve high academic standards through providing the finest example and materials and a stimulating, encouraging atmosphere Pupils take part in a wide range of sports and arts activities and are given ample opportunity to discover areas of skill, talent and enjoyment in a wide variety of academic and non-academic subjects.

Toad Hall Nursery School

Address: 37 St Mary's Gardens, Kennington, London SE11 4UF

Telephone: 071 735 5087

Head: Mrs V K Rees

Age range: 2-5
No. of pupils: 40
Scholarships:
Religion: Non-denominational

Fees per term
Day: -£535
Weekly board: -
Full board: -

Boy ○ Girl ○ Co-ed ●
Day ● Week ○ Board ○

Small nursery situated in basement of owner's house in quiet gardens. Follows the Montessori method.

Tower House

Address: 188 Sheen Lane, London SW14 8LF

Telephone: 081 876 3323

Head: Mr A J Beale

Age range: 5-13
No. of pupils: 178
Scholarships:
Religion: Non-denominational

Fees per term
Day: £1325-£1325
Weekly board: -
Full board: -

Boy ● Girl ○ Co-ed ○
Day ● Week ○ Board ○

Tower House is an IAPS school which accepts boys from the age of 5 with a wide range of ability. There are no selection tests, and all pupils stay to the age of 13, when they transfer to independent day or boarding secondary schools.

Trinity Catholic High School

Address: Mornington Road, Woodford Green, Redbridge, London
Telephone:
Head:

Age range: 11-18
No. of pupils:
Scholarships:
Religion: Roman Catholic

Fees per term
Day: -
Weekly board: -
Full board: -

Boy ○ Girl ○ Co-ed ●
Day ● Week ○ Board ○

For further information and a prospectus, please contact the school.

Twice Times Montessori Nursery School

Address: The Cricket Pavilion, South Park, London SW6
Telephone: 071 731 4929
Head: Mrs S Henderson

Age range: 2-5
No. of pupils: 50
Scholarships:
Religion:

Fees per term
Day: -
Weekly board: -
Full board: -

Boy ○ Girl ○ Co-ed ●
Day ● Week ○ Board ○

For further information and a prospectus, please contact the school.

University College School *

Address: Frognal, Hampstead, London NW3 6XH
Telephone: 071 435 2215
Head: Mr G D Slaughter

Age range: 8-18
No. of pupils: 750
Scholarships: Yes
Religion: Non-denominational

Fees per term
Day: £1850-£1975
Weekly board: -
Full board: -

Boy ● Girl ○ Co-ed ○
Day ● Week ○ Board ○

Established as part of University College, London, in 1830 UCS has remained true to the aims of its founders: the pursuit of academic excellence, a respect for, and encouragement of, independent thought and individual judgement, a broad curriculum and finally, the lack of any religious barriers. These beliefs have ensured the encouragement of diversity and talent for over 150 years.

University College School Junior Branch

Address: 11 Holly Hill, London NW3 6QN
Telephone: 071 435 3068
Head: Mr J F Hubbard

Age range: 7-13
No. of pupils: 250
Scholarships:
Religion:

Fees per term
Day: -
Weekly board: -
Full board: -

Boy ● Girl ○ Co-ed ○
Day ● Week ○ Board ○

For further information and a prospectus, please contact the school.

Upper Tooting Independent High School

Address: 169 Trinity Road,
London SW17 7HL

Telephone:

Head: Mrs A Abbott

Age range: 4-16
No. of pupils: 170
Scholarships:
Religion:

Fees per term
Day: -
Weekly board: -
Full board: -

Boy ○ Girl ○ Co-ed ●
Day ● Week ○ Board ○

For further information and a prospectus, please contact the school.

The Urdang Academy of Ballet

Address: 20-22 Shelton Street,
London WC2H 9JJ

Telephone: 071 836 5709

Head: Miss L Urdang

Age range: 10-16
No. of pupils:
Scholarships:
Religion:

Fees per term
Day: -
Weekly board: -
Full board: -

Boy ○ Girl ○ Co-ed ●
Day ● Week ○ Board ○

For further information and a prospectus, please contact the school.

Ursuline Convent Preparatory School

Address: 18 The Downs,
Wimbledon, London
SW20 8HR

Telephone: 081 947 0859

Head: Sister B Perrott

Age range: 4-13
No. of pupils: 250
Scholarships:
Religion: Roman Catholic

Fees per term
Day: £680-£680
Weekly board: -
Full board: -

Boy ○ Girl ● Co-ed ○
Day ● Week ○ Board ○

The preparatory school is for Catholic girls most of whom will continue their education at the Ursuline High School. We aim for a friendly and kind ethos and a relaxed and polite atmosphere which will be conducive to learning and high standards of achievement. Religion plays an important part in the life of the school.

Ursuline High School *

Address: Morland Road, Ilford,
London IG1 4QS

Telephone:

Head:

Age range: 11-18
No. of pupils:
Scholarships:
Religion:

Fees per term
Day: -
Weekly board: -
Full board: -

Boy ○ Girl ● Co-ed ○
Day ● Week ○ Board ○

For further information and a prospectus, please contact the school.

The Vale

Address: 2 Elvaston Place, London SW7 5QH

Telephone: 071 730 9343

Head: Miss S Calder

Age range: 4-11
No. of pupils: 100
Scholarships:
Religion: Non-denominational

Fees per term
Day: £1200-
Weekly board: -
Full board: -

○ ○ ● Boy Girl Co-ed
● ○ ○ Day Week Board

The Vale is a co-educational school which has been established for over 40 years. The children are prepared for London Day School examinations and entrance to boarding school. The aim of the school is to provide the children with a sound academic and social base in small classes with plenty of individual attention.

The Village School

Address: 81-89 Fortress Road, London NW5 1AG

Telephone: 071 267 5439

Head: Mrs F M Prior

Age range: 4-11
No. of pupils: 108
Scholarships:
Religion:

Fees per term
Day: -
Weekly board: -
Full board: -

○ ● ○ Boy Girl Co-ed
● ○ ○ Day Week Board

For further information and a prospectus, please contact the school.

Virgo Fidelis Convent

Address: Central Hill, Upper Norwood, London SE19 1RS

Telephone: 081 670 6917

Head: Sister Madeleine

Age range: 3-18
No. of pupils: 430
Scholarships:
Religion:

Fees per term
Day: -
Weekly board: -
Full board: -

● ● ○ Boy Girl Co-ed
● ○ ○ Day Week Board

For further information and a prospectus, please contact the school. Boys 3-7.

Vita et Pax Convent School

Address: Priory Close, Green Road, Southgate, London N14 4AT

Telephone: 081 449 8336

Head: Mr P M Condon

Age range: 4-11
No. of pupils: 180
Scholarships:
Religion:

Fees per term
Day: -
Weekly board: -
Full board: -

○ ○ ● Boy Girl Co-ed
● ○ ○ Day Week Board

For further information and a prospectus, please contact the school.

Waldorf School of South West London

Address: 12 Balham Park Road, London SW12 8PR

Telephone: 081 677 1763

Head: The College of Teachers

Age range: 3-11
No. of pupils: 75
Scholarships: Yes
Religion: Non-denominational

Fees per term
Day: £500-£700
Weekly board: -
Full board: -

Boy ○ Girl ○ Co-ed ●
Day ● Week ○ Board ○

As Waldorf teachers we endeavour to bring an artistic and imaginative approach to what might become dry subjects, encouraging children to express themselves in a creative and harmonious way. We strive to nourish the sense of reverence that children bring with them into life as well as high standards of work and behaviour.

Welsh School of London

Address: 265 Willesden Lane, London NW2 5JG

Telephone: 081 459 2690

Head: Mrs S Edwards

Age range: 4-11
No. of pupils: 28
Scholarships:
Religion:

Fees per term
Day: -
Weekly board: -
Full board: -

Boy ○ Girl ○ Co-ed ●
Day ● Week ○ Board ○

For further information and a prospectus, please contact the school.

Westminster Abbey Choir School

Address: Dean's Yard, London SW1P 3NY

Telephone: 071 222 6151

Head: Mr G Rowland-Adams BMsc CertEd

Age range: 7-13
No. of pupils: 36
Scholarships: Yes
Religion: Church of England

Fees per term
Day: -
Weekly board: -
Full board: £762-

Boy ● Girl ○ Co-ed ○
Day ○ Week ○ Board ●

A unique school in the shadow of Westminster Abbey where all the boys hold choral scholarships worth about £8,000 per annum. Entry is by voice trial and academic test and in recent years the record of music scholarships to secondary independent schools has been exceptional. The headmaster welcomes enquiries, however tentative, from parents of potential choristers.

Westminster Cathedral Choir School

Address: Ambrosden Avenue, London SW1P 1QH

Telephone: 071 834 9247

Head: Mr P Hannigan

Age range: 8-13
No. of pupils: 90
Scholarships: Yes
Religion: Roman Catholic

Fees per term
Day: £1825-
Weekly board: -
Full board: £900-£1010

Boy ● Girl ○ Co-ed ○
Day ● Week ○ Board ●

For further information and a prospectus, please contact the school.

Westminster School *

Address: 17 Dean's Yard, London SW1P 3PF

Telephone: 071 222 5516

Head: Mr D M Summerscale

Age range: 13-18
No. of pupils: 610
Scholarships: Yes
Religion: Church of England

Fees per term
Day: £2300-£2625
Weekly board: £3475-£3850
Full board: -

Boy ○ Girl ○ Co-ed ●
Day ● Week ● Board ●

Situated on its original site next to the Abbey, Westminster is a school of high academic standard, but with excellent achievement too in drama, music and sport. Admission for boys at 13+ by CE or scholarship, and for girls and boys at Sixth Form by competitive examination.

Westminster Tutors

Address: 5 Wetherby Place, London SW7 4NX

Telephone: 071 373 6327

Head: Miss K A Buckley

Age range: 15-19
No. of pupils: 90
Scholarships: Yes
Religion:

Fees per term
Day: £2530-
Weekly board: -
Full board: -

Boy ○ Girl ○ Co-ed ●
Day ● Week ○ Board ○

Westminster Tutors prepares students for A Level, GCSE and Oxbridge entrance. Classes are small and taught by experienced graduates, with the focus on lively discussion, essay-writing and examination technique. A personal tutor supervises each student's academic progress and gives comprehensive guidance on University and Polytechnic Entrance. Short retake, intensive one-year and two-year courses are available.

Westminster Under School

Address: 27 Vincent Square, London SW1P 2NN

Telephone: 071 821 5788

Head: Mr G Ashton

Age range: 8-13
No. of pupils: 260
Scholarships: Yes
Religion:

Fees per term
Day: -£1800
Weekly board: -
Full board: -

Boy ● Girl ○ Co-ed ○
Day ● Week ○ Board ○

The Under School has close connections with Westminster School and shares governors. Games are played at Westminster School's grounds at Vincent Square. Boys are prepared for senior schools through Common Entrance and scholarships, and although most boys proceed to Westminster, many go eslewhere. Entry is by examination. Forty boys enter at age 8, and 20 at age 10, the latter being mostly from primary schools.

Whittingham School

Address: 206-208 Muswell Hill Road, London N10 3NH

Telephone: 081 883 2247

Head: Mrs R Beumer

Age range: 3-11
No. of pupils: 170
Scholarships:
Religion:

Fees per term
Day: -
Weekly board: -
Full board: -

Boy ○ Girl ○ Co-ed ●
Day ● Week ○ Board ○

For further information and a prospectus, please contact the school.

Willington School

Address: Worcester Road, Wimbledon, London SW19 7QQ
Telephone: 081 944 7020

Heads: Mr K Marx Mr J A C Hey

Age range: 4-13
No. of pupils: 195
Scholarships:
Religion:

Fees per term
Day: -
Weekly board: -
Full board: -

● Boy ○ Girl ○ Co-ed
● Day ○ Week ○ Board

For further information and a prospectus, please contact the school.

Willoughby Hall School

Address: 1 Willoughby Road, Hampstead, London NW3 1RP
Telephone: 071 794 3538

Head: Mrs G M McAndrew

Age range: 4-11
No. of pupils: 125
Scholarships:
Religion: Christian

Fees per term
Day: £1120-£1250
Weekly board: -
Full board: -

● Boy ● Girl ○ Co-ed
● Day ○ Week ○ Board

Boys prepared for entry to schools with starting age 7-8, - U.C.S., Westminster Under, St Paul's, Colet Court etc. Girls - Common Entrance and entry to London day schools. Boys 4-8, girls 4-11.

Wimbledon College Preparatory School

Address: Donhead Lodge, 33 Edge Hill, Wimbledon, London SW19 4NP
Telephone: 081 946 7000

Head: Mr D J O'Leary

Age range: 7-13
No. of pupils: 300
Scholarships:
Religion:

Fees per term
Day: -
Weekly board: -
Full board: -

● Boy ○ Girl ○ Co-ed
● Day ○ Week ○ Board

For further information and a prospectus, please contact the school.

Wimbledon Common Preparatory School

Address: 113 Ridgway, Merton, London SW19 4TA
Telephone:

Head:

Age range: 4-9
No. of pupils:
Scholarships:
Religion:

Fees per term
Day: -
Weekly board: -
Full board: -

● Boy ○ Girl ○ Co-ed
● Day ○ Week ○ Board

For further information and a prospectus, please contact the school.

Wimbledon High School GPDST *

Address: Mansel Road,
Wimbledon, London
SW19 4AB
Telephone: 081 946 1756

Head: Mrs E Baker

Age range: 5-18
No. of pupils: 800
Scholarships: Yes
Religion: Non-denominational

Fees per term
Day: £1036-£1340
Weekly board: -
Full board: -

Boy ○ | Girl ● | Co-ed ○
Day ● | Week ○ | Board ○

Wimbledon High School is conveniently situated in the centre of Wimbledon. The aim of the school is to give every girl a broad academic education and to help each person to fulfil her talents. The school encourages full involvement in extra-curricular activities in such areas as music, drama, art, sport, community service and debating.

Wimbledon Park Montessori School

Address: 170 Arthur Road,
Wimbledon, London
SW19 8AQ
Telephone: 081 944 8584

Head: Mrs V Wilberforce-Ritchie

Age range: 2-5
No. of pupils: 48
Scholarships:
Religion: Non-denominational

Fees per term
Day: £440-
Weekly board: -
Full board: -

Boy ○ | Girl ○ | Co-ed ●
Day ● | Week ○ | Board ○

Wimbledon Park is a small friendly local nursery school. Our philosophy is to produce a happy and stimulating environment, where your children can develop at their own pace discovering their abilities with our guidance. We encourage the children to be creative through painting and dance enabling them to enjoy their first years at school and therefore be ready for their next stage in life.

Wood Tutorial College

Address: 25-27 Heath Street,
Camden, London NW3 6TR

Telephone:

Head:

Age range: 4-18
No. of pupils:
Scholarships:
Religion:

Fees per term
Day: -
Weekly board: -
Full board: -

Boy ○ | Girl ○ | Co-ed ●
Day ● | Week ○ | Board ○

For further information and a prospectus, please contact the college.

Woodside Park School

Address: Woodside Lane,
London N12 8SY

Telephone: 081 445 2333

Head: Mr R F Metters

Age range: 3-13
No. of pupils: 350
Scholarships:
Religion:

Fees per term
Day: -
Weekly board: -
Full board: -

Boy ○ | Girl ○ | Co-ed ●
Day ● | Week ○ | Board ○

For further information and a prospectus, please contact the school. Boys 3-13, girls 3-11.

Yesodey Hatorah Jewish School

Address: 2-4 Amhurst Park, London N16 5AE

Telephone: 081 800 8612

Head: Rabbi Pinter

Age range: 11-16
No. of pupils: 270
Scholarships:
Religion:

Fees per term
Day: -
Weekly board: -
Full board: -

Boy ○ Girl ○ Co-ed ●
Day ● Week ○ Board ○

For further information and a prospectus, please contact the school.

Yetev Lev Day School for Boys

Address: 111-115 Cazenove Road, London N16 6AX

Telephone: 081 806 3834

Head: Mr I Greenbaum

Age range: 3-13
No. of pupils: 240
Scholarships:
Religion:

Fees per term
Day: -
Weekly board: -
Full board: -

Boy ● Girl ○ Co-ed ○
Day ● Week ○ Board ○

For further information and a prospectus, please contact the school.

Young England Kindergarten

Address: St Saviours Hall, St Georges Square, London SW1V 2HP

Telephone: 071 834 3171

Head: Mrs K C King

Age range: 2-5
No. of pupils: 75
Scholarships:
Religion: Non-denominational

Fees per term
Day: £390-£635
Weekly board: -
Full board: -

Boy ○ Girl ○ Co-ed ●
Day ● Week ○ Board ○

We are a long established kindergarten with teaching methods based on the Montessori method. We cater for children from two and a half to five years and have stimulating and varied curriculum with an emphasis on learning through play.

MANCHESTER

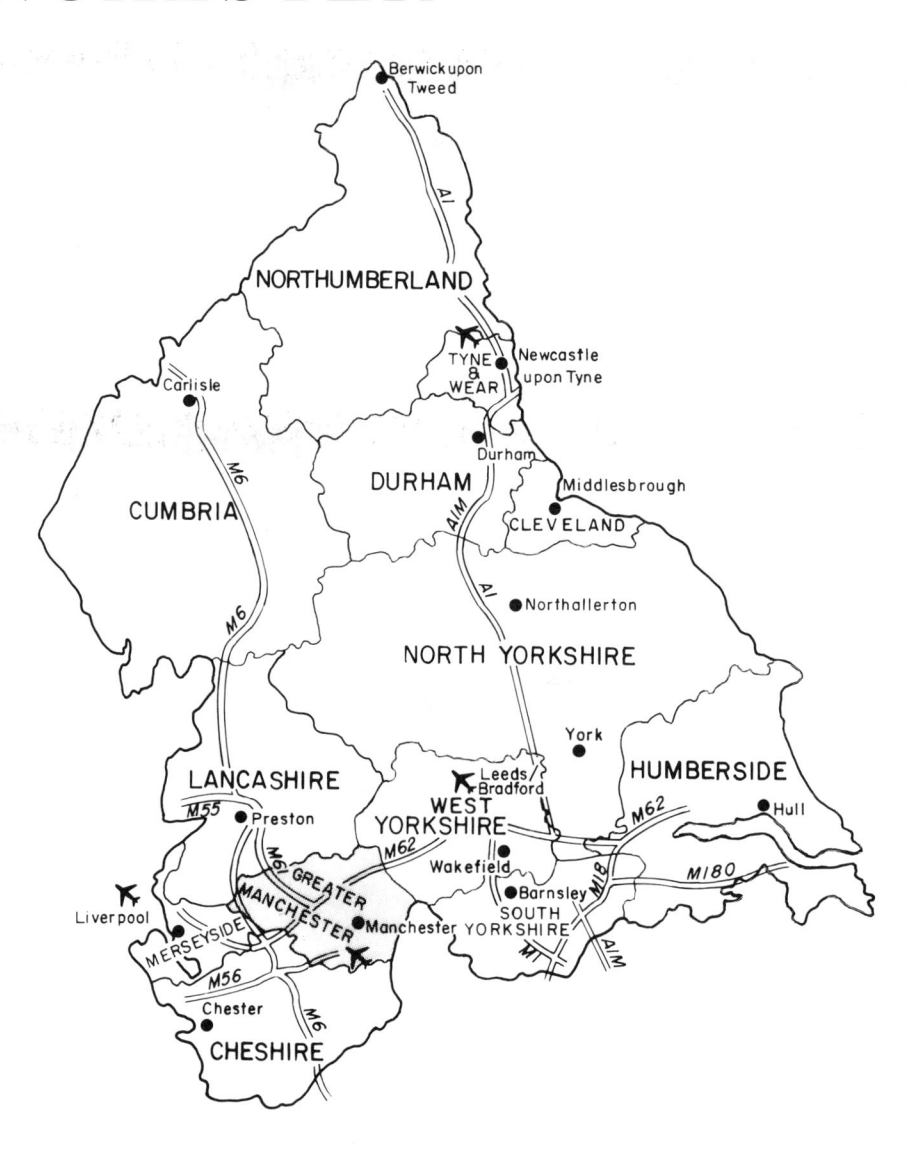

Amberleigh Preparatory School

Address: 398 Wilbraham Road, Chorlton-cum-Hardy, Manchester M21 1UH
Telephone: 061 881 1593

Head: Mr P F Hayden

Age range: 4-11
No. of pupils: 130
Scholarships:
Religion: Non-denominational

Fees per term
Day: £372-£552
Weekly board: -
Full board: -

Co-ed / Day

Accredited to the ISJC and the headmaster is a member of the ISAI. Amberleigh is proud of its reputation for being a friendly, happy school which thrives upon firm discipline and a keen desire to see that our children make the most of their talents. There are seven classes of average size 20 pupils. Preparation for independent and local authority selection procedures form an integral part of the curriculum.

Ash Lea School

Address: 1 Half Edge Lane, Eccles, Manchester M30 9GJ
Telephone: 061 789 3892

Head: Mr J Swift

Age range: 2-16
No. of pupils: 140
Scholarships: Yes
Religion: Non-denominational

Fees per term
Day: £460-£790
Weekly board: -
Full board: -

Co-ed / Day

Ash Lea School has a long-established record of providing children with a happy, friendly environment in which to learn, helped by a caring and dedicated staff. Small class sizes allow individual attention. Pupils are encouraged to take part in extra-curricular activities such as gardening, art craft, computing, science club and CREST awards, as well as PTA and charity events.

Bramwood Preparatory School

Address: Stafford Road, Monton, Eccles, Manchester M30 9HN
Telephone: 061 789 1054

Head: Mr W M Howard

Age range: 3-11
No. of pupils: 180
Scholarships: Yes
Religion: Non-denominational

Fees per term
Day: £340-£568
Weekly board: -
Full board: -

Co-ed / Day

Bramwood specialises in the preparation of boys and girls for the entry examinations at 11 plus to the Greater Manchester area independent secondary schools. Basically its teaching is traditional and there is careful attention to the usual extras that are expected in an independent preparatory school (music, drama etc.).

Bridgewater School p692

Address: Drywood Hall, Worsley Road, Worsley, Manchester M28 4WQ
Telephone: 061 794 1463

Head: Dr B Blundell

Age range: 3-18
No. of pupils: 400
Scholarships: Yes
Religion: Non-denominational

Fees per term
Day: £662-£1166
Weekly board: -
Full board: -

Co-ed / Day

Bridgewater School is a 3-18 co-educational grammar school, which attains academic excellence with small classes ppy purposeful atmosphere. Bridgewater School is in a beautiful setting based in the 16th century listed building Drywood Hall. Phase 1 and 2 of a £1.5 million development programme now complete.

Caius House School

Address: 99 Church Road, Urmston, Manchester M31 1FJ

Telephone: 061 748 3261

Head: Mr N A Ricketts BA

Age range: 3-11
No. of pupils: 120
Scholarships:
Religion: Christian

Fees per term
Day: £560-
Weekly board: -
Full board: -

Boy ○ Girl ○ Co-ed ●
Day ● Week ○ Board ○

Our combination of small classes, well-qualified, experienced teachers and a friendly, family atmosphere ensure success in our emphasis on the early learning of reading and numeracy and the continuation of the excellent record in senior school entrance examinations. We cover the full primary curriculum including science and technology and have a wide range of sporting and extra-curricular activities.

Chetham's School of Music

Address: Long Millgate, Manchester M3 1SB

Telephone: 061 834 9644

Head: Revd P F Hullah

Age range: 8-18
No. of pupils: 270
Scholarships:
Religion: Non-denominational

Fees per term
Day: -£3693
Weekly board: -
Full board: -£4769

Boy ○ Girl ○ Co-ed ●
Day ● Week ○ Board ●

Chetham's provides specialist education for musically gifted children between 8-18. HMC and fully co-educational, the largest school of its kind for boarders and day pupils, its community situated in Central Manchester enjoys close links with the city's musical life. Admission at any age by musical audition. All UK entrants receive Government grants under the Aided Pupil (Music & Ballet) Scheme.

Farrowdale House

Address: Farrow House, Farrow Street, Oldham, Manchester

Telephone: 0706 844533

Head: Mrs A Graydon

Age range: 4-11
No. of pupils: 146
Scholarships:
Religion:

Fees per term
Day: £560-£590
Weekly board: -
Full board: -

Boy ○ Girl ○ Co-ed ●
Day ● Week ○ Board ○

Farrowdale House School is a small, independent co-educational preparatory school, situated close to Shaw town centre. The school offers a full primary education for children 3 years 9 months to 11 years. We offer a full academic curriculum within the framework of traditional values and the expectation of high personal achievement.

Grasscroft Independent School

Address: Stockport Road, Lydgate, Oldham, Manchester OL4 4JJ

Telephone: 0457 820485

Head: Mrs B Donough BEd MEd

Age range: 3-8
No. of pupils: 70
Scholarships:
Religion: Non-denominational

Fees per term
Day: -£506
Weekly board: -
Full board: -

Boy ○ Girl ○ Co-ed ●
Day ● Week ○ Board ○

Grasscroft School is staffed by highly trained and/or well qualified personnel and is organised to provide a sound general education based upon the best of traditional and progressive lines. Each child is treated in a positive way to develop his/her self esteem and independence in a well disciplined small group setting. Every endeavour is made to ensure that your child realises their maximum potential in all areas.

Hulme Grammar School for Boys *

Address: Chamber Road, Oldham, Manchester OL8 4BX

Telephone: 061 624 4497

Age range: 7-19
No. of pupils: 865
Scholarships: Yes
Religion: Non-denominational

Fees per term
Day: £731-£1070
Weekly board: -
Full board: -

● Boy ○ Girl ○ Co-ed
● Day ○ Week ○ Board

Head: Mr G F Dunkin MA(Cantab)

The present foundation dates from 1887 and the buildings occupy an elevated site overlooking the town. Boys are accepted into the school at 7+ and 11+ by entrance examination and interview, and into the sixth form after GCSE results. Entrance at other times is sometimes possible by arrangement with the Headmaster. Thirty Assisted Places are available each year.

The Hulme Grammar School for Girls

Address: Chamber Road, Oldham, Manchester OL8 4BX

Telephone: 061 624 2523

Age range: 7-18
No. of pupils: 640
Scholarships:
Religion: Non-denominational

Fees per term
Day: £995-
Weekly board: -
Full board: -

○ Boy ● Girl ○ Co-ed
● Day ○ Week ○ Board

Head: Miss M S Smolenski

Entry to the school is by examination and 30 Assisted Places are avaialble. The curriculum is broad and the school has a fine record of examination success. Our fundamental aims are to pursue academic excellence and realise potential, to develop attitudes of independent and social behaviour, to encourage participation in a wide range of extra-curricular activities, to develop professional integrity for life.

Jewish High School for Girls

Address: Bethmalkah, Salford, Manchester M7 0NT

Telephone: 061 792 2118

Age range: 11-18
No. of pupils: 160
Scholarships: Yes
Religion: Jewish

Fees per term
Day: -£975
Weekly board: -
Full board: -

○ Boy ● Girl ○ Co-ed
● Day ○ Week ○ Board

Head: Rabbi M I Young

For further information and a prospectus, please contact the school.

Manchester Grammar School *

Address: Old Hall Lane, Manchester M13 0XT

Telephone: 061 224 7201

Age range: 11-18
No. of pupils: 1450
Scholarships:
Religion: Non-denominational

Fees per term
Day: £1214-
Weekly board: -
Full board: -

● Boy ○ Girl ○ Co-ed
● Day ○ Week ○ Board

Head Mr J.G. Parker

Manchester Grammar School has an international reputation for excellence. Boys achieve outstanding examination results and have the advantage of splendid facilities for the widest range of extra-curricular activities. Sport, music, drama and outdoor activities are important in the broad education provided at MGS.

Manchester High School for Girls *

Address: Grangethorpe Road, Manchester M14 6HS

Telephone: 061 224 0447

Head: Miss M M Moon BA MEd

Age range: 4-18
No. of pupils: 960
Scholarships: Yes
Religion: Non-denominational

Fees per term
Day: £765-£1160
Weekly board: -
Full board: -

Boy ○ | Girl ● | Co-ed ○
Day ● | Week ○ | Board ○

The school offers a very strong programme of academic study for girls of good ability, together with a rich variety of artistic, creative, practical and sporting activities to stimulate and develop individual talents. The school has maintained a fine tradition of high academic standards for well over a century. It has a highly qualified and experienced staff and extensive facilities for study in depth.

Manchester Jewish Grammar School

Address: Charleton Avenue, Prestwich, Manchester M25 8PH
Telephone: 061 773 1789

Head: Mr P Pink

Age range: 11-18
No. of pupils: 135
Scholarships: Yes
Religion: Jewish

Fees per term
Day: -£3600
Weekly board: -
Full board: -

Boy ● | Girl ○ | Co-ed ○
Day ● | Week ○ | Board ○

For further information and a prospectus, please contact the school.

Moor Allerton

Address: 131 Barlow Moor Road, West Didsbury, Manchester M20 8PW
Telephone: 061 445 4521

Head: Mr M J Clarke

Age range: 3-11
No. of pupils: 140
Scholarships:
Religion: Non-denominational

Fees per term
Day: £445-£920
Weekly board: -
Full board: -

Boy ○ | Girl ○ | Co-ed ●
Day ● | Week ○ | Board ○

Situated in the pleasant suburb of Didsbury, the school is particularly noted for its high academic standards and achievements and for its caring and happy atmosphere. The children are prepared for entry into the local independent grammar schools. The school has its own choir and orchestra and there is emphasis on Christian standards and principles.

Norman House Preparatory School

Address: 349 Hollinwood Avenue, New Moston, Manchester M10 0JX
Telephone: 061 681 3097

Head: Mr S J Jobling

Age range: 3-11
No. of pupils: 165
Scholarships:
Religion: Non-denominational

Fees per term
Day: £595-£645
Weekly board: -
Full board: -

Boy ○ | Girl ○ | Co-ed ●
Day ● | Week ○ | Board ○

Although Norman House has a strong tradition for its care of the individual, it has an enviable academic reputation. The classes are small so as to enable the staff to care for the needs of each child. The children are happy within a framework of discipline and achieve their full potential through the habit of hard work. Pupils are prepared for Manchester independent grammar schools.

Oaklands Preparatory School

Address: 643 Wilbraham Road, Chorlton, Manchester M21 1JT
Telephone: 061 881 4702

Head: Mr J R Harrity

Age range: 4-11
No. of pupils: 120
Scholarships:
Religion: Non-denominational

Fees per term
Day: £640-
Weekly board: -
Full board: -

Boy ○ Girl ○ Co-ed ●
Day ● Week ○ Board ○

The normal ages of entry are 4+ and 5+. Some places for children of 8+ are available each year subject to assessment. Pupils are prepared chiefly for the 11+ entrance examinations to independent secondary schools in the Greater Manchester area.

Oriel Bank High School

Address: Devonshire Park Road, Davenport, Stockport, Manchester SK2 6JP
Telephone: 061 483 2935

Head: Mrs A Perrett

Age range: 3-16
No. of pupils: 270
Scholarships:
Religion: Church of England

Fees per term
Day: £450-£995
Weekly board: -
Full board: -

Boy ○ Girl ● Co-ed ○
Day ● Week ○ Board ○

High acadmeic achievements are combined with equally high standards of courtesy, appearance and self-discipline. A wide range of extra-curricular activities is offered together with opportunities for leadership and work experience. Our small classes allow individual attention to be given to each girl. The Victorian houses help to create a family atmosphere. An after-school care service operates until 5.30.

Rosecroft Preparatory School

Address: Whitechapel Street, Didsbury, Manchester M20 0TX
Telephone: 061 434 2616

Head: Miss M L Mullins BSc

Age range: 3-12
No. of pupils: 120
Scholarships:
Religion: Roman Catholic

Fees per term
Day: £550-£700
Weekly board: -
Full board: -

Boy ○ Girl ● Co-ed ○
Day ● Week ○ Board ○

Rosecroft is situated on the A34 close to the Mersey Valley on the way into Manchester. It is open to children of all faiths whose parents admire the Catholic ethos in education. Girls are prepared for entrance examinations of secondary schools and have plenty of music, drama, art, sport, french and a good grounding in science. A charitable trust.

St Bede's College *

Address: Alexandra Park, Manchester M16 8HX
Telephone: 061 226 3323

Head: Mr J Byrne

Age range: 11-18
No. of pupils: 900
Scholarships: Yes
Religion: Roman Catholic

Fees per term
Day: £1162-
Weekly board: -
Full board: -

Boy ○ Girl ○ Co-ed ●
Day ● Week ○ Board ○

St Bede's College provides a traditional grammar school education to Catholics from Manchester and from an extensive surrounding area which is served by college bus services. Excellent examination results are obtained in an ordered Catholic atmosphere with almost all students proceding to higher education.

St Bede's College Preparatory School

Address: Alexandra Park, Manchester MI6 8HX

Telephone: 061 226 3323

Head: Mr P Hales

Age range: 7-11
No. of pupils: 180
Scholarships:
Religion: Roman Catholic

Fees per term
Day: -£775
Weekly board: -
Full board: -

Boy ○ Girl ○ Co-ed ●
Day ● Week ○ Board ○

For further information and a prospectus, please contact the school.

Werneth Private Preparatory School

Address: Plum Street, Oldham, Manchester OL8 1TJ

Telephone: 061 624 2947

Head: Mrs M J Press

Age range: 2-11
No. of pupils: 165
Scholarships:
Religion: Christian

Fees per term
Day: £435-£664
Weekly board: -
Full board: -

Boy ○ Girl ○ Co-ed ●
Day ● Week ○ Board ○

The nursery is the first step into Werneth Preparatory, but children should be registered from birth. Our aim is to help each child attain the highest level of personal and scholastic achievement of which they are capable. Examinations twice a year and reports plus homework provide the essential home-school link. Parents are encouraged to involve themselves with the school at all stages.

Whitefield Preparatory School

Address: Holly Bank, Church Lane, Whitefield, Manchester M25 7NF
Telephone: 061 766 2744

Head: Mr J G H Roscoe

Age range: 3-11
No. of pupils: 64
Scholarships:
Religion:

Fees per term
Day: -
Weekly board: -
Full board: -

Boy ○ Girl ○ Co-ed ●
Day ● Week ○ Board ○

For further information and a prospectus, please contact the school.

William Hulme's Grammar School *

Address: Spring Bridge Road, Manchester M16 8PR

Telephone: 061 226 2054

Head: Mr P D Briggs MA

Age range: 11-18
No. of pupils: 790
Scholarships: Yes
Religion: Non-denominational

Fees per term
Day: £1235-
Weekly board: -
Full board: -

Boy ○ Girl ○ Co-ed ●
Day ● Week ○ Board ○

William Hulme's is a co-educational independent day grammar school easily accessible from all areas around Manchester. In a positive environment boys and girls grow up devloping their intellectual, cultural and social skills. Academic rigour and personal and corporate discipline are at the centre of the school's ethos and character.

Withington Girls' School *

Address: Wellington Road, Fallowfield, Manchester M14 6BL
Telephone: 061 224 1077

Head: Mrs M Kenyon

Age range: 7-18
No. of pupils: 570
Scholarships:
Religion: Non-denominational

Fees per term
Day: £765-£1120
Weekly board: -
Full board: -

○ Boy ● Girl ○ Co-ed
● Day ○ Week ○ Board

Withington Girls' School was founded in 1890 and throughout its history has remained relatively small, with about 570 pupils, of whom 100 are in the junior department. The atmosphere is academic, but intimate, and each girl is encouraged to grow both intellectually and in self awareness. Almost all girls go on to higher education. The school is proud of its fine academic and sporting record.

MERSEYSIDE

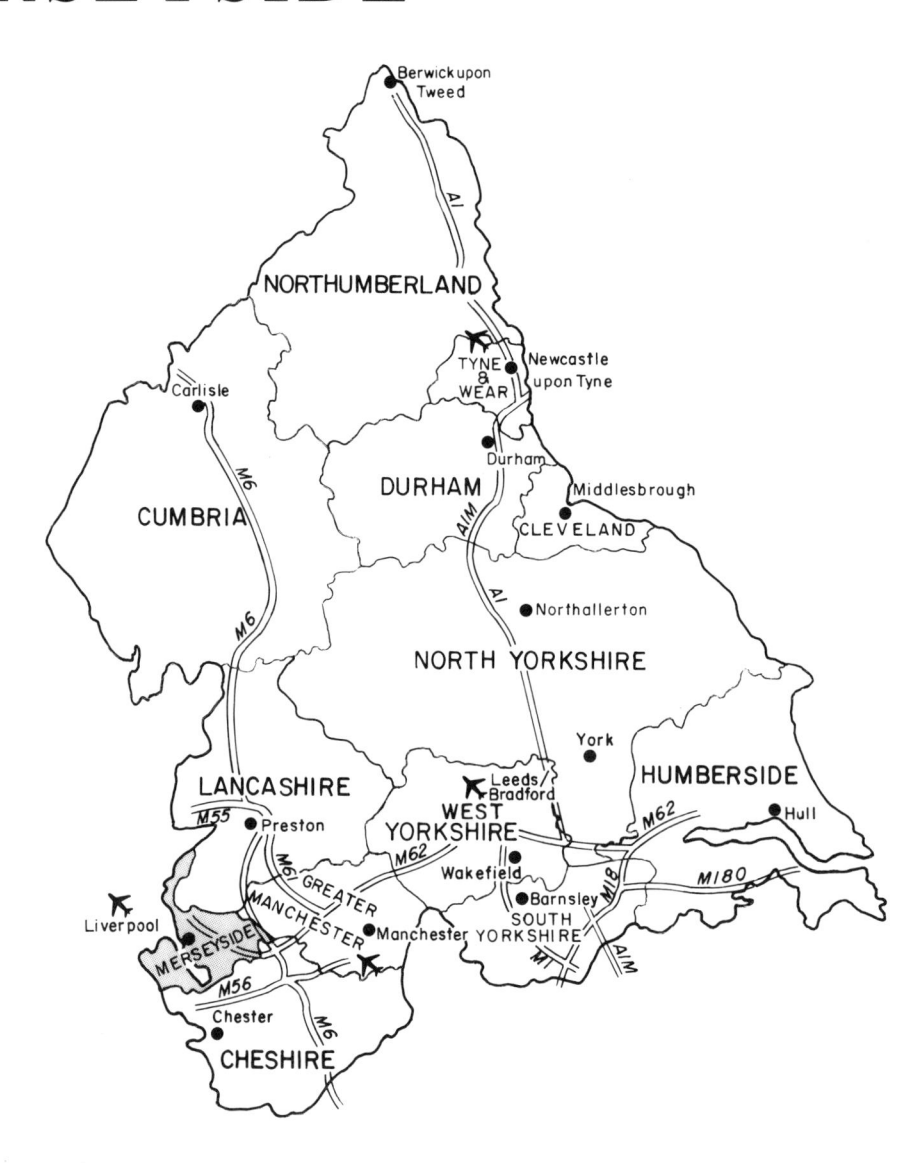

Atherton House

Address: Alexandra Road, Great Crosby, Liverpool, Merseyside L23 7TF
Telephone: 051 924 5578

Head: Mrs B Wooster

Age range: 2-11
No. of pupils: 98
Scholarships:
Religion: Non-denominational

Fees per term
Day: £340-£615
Weekly board: -
Full board: -

Boy ○ Girl ○ Co-ed ●
Day ● Week ○ Board ○

At Atherton House School the pupils work hard in a happy well-disciplined atmosphere to achieve their full potential. Academic standards are high, but the small classes enable us to give help to children of all abilities. Communication between parents and staff is encouraged and all pupils take part in an annual sports day and a spring concert.

Avalon School

Address: Caldy Road, West Kirby, Wirral, Merseyside L48 2HE
Telephone: 051 625 6993

Head: Mr C L Kirch

Age range:
No. of pupils: 135
Scholarships: Yes
Religion: Non-denominational

Fees per term
Day: £175-£710
Weekly board: -
Full board: -

Boy ○ Girl ○ Co-ed ●
Day ● Week ○ Board ○

Avalon School was founded in 1907 and has been a girls only school for 80 years. In September 1991 it went fully co-educational. We believe in good manners, self-discipline, hard work with emphasis on teaching the 3 Rs. We have an outstanding record in getting children into independent secondary schools.

The Belvedere School, GPDST*

Address: 17 Belvedere Road, Liverpool, Merseyside L8 3TF
Telephone: 051 727 1284

Head: Mrs C.H. Evans

Age range: 4-18
No. of pupils: 563
Scholarships: Yes
Religion: Non-denominational

Fees per term
Day: £880-£1148
Weekly board: -
Full board: -

Boy ○ Girl ● Co-ed ○
Day ● Week ○ Board ○

Independent day school for girls aged 4-18. A total of 563 pupils including 93+ in the sixth form. Assisted places, scholarships and bursaries available. Entrance is by assessment at 4+, examination 11+ and interview 16+. High academic standards and a wide range of extra-curricular activities. Excellent facilities. Prospectus available on application from the Headmistress.

Birkenhead High School, G.P.D.S.T. *

Address: 86 Devonshire Place, Birkenhead, Merseyside L43 1TY
Telephone: 051 652 5777

Head: Mrs K Irving

Age range: 4-18
No. of pupils: 1022
Scholarships: Yes
Religion: Non-denominational

Fees per term
Day: £880-£1148
Weekly board: -
Full board: -

Boy ○ Girl ● Co-ed ○
Day ● Week ○ Board ○

We offer girls a stimulating academic education in a friendly and caring atmosphere. Examination results are outstanding and almost all our students go on to higher education. There are opportunities for sport, music, drama, D of E. The junior department which occupies adjoining premises caters for girls aged 4-11 years. Prospectus on application to the headmistress.

Birkenhead School *

Address: 58 Beresford Road,
Oxton, Birkenhead,
Merseyside L43 2JD
Telephone: 051 652 4014

Head: Mr S J Haggett

Age range: 11-18
No. of pupils: 750
Scholarships: Yes
Religion: Non-denominational

Fees per term
Day: £742-£1072
Weekly board: -
Full board: -

● Boy ○ Girl ○ Co-ed
● Day ○ Week ○ Board

Selective boys' independent school in pleasant suburbs of Birkenhead. First-rate examination results and high entry rates to further education, but concentrates also on education of the whole person. Excellent sporting facilities, very strong music and drama. Emphasis on Christian tradition; own chapel and chaplain. Strong links with the local community - potential parents always welcome to visit.

Brighthelmston School

Address: 21 Waterloo Road,
Birkdale, Southport,
Merseyside PR8 2HL
Telephone: 0704 66375

Head: Mrs B J Usher ATD

Age range: 3-16
No. of pupils: 180
Scholarships:
Religion: Non-denominational

Fees per term
Day: £1245-£2175
Weekly board: -
Full board: -

○ Boy ○ Girl ● Co-ed
● Day ○ Week ○ Board

Established in 1861, the school aims for sound education from kindergarten to GCSE at 16 years in small classes, (maximum 16 juniors or 12 seniors). Further education is provided by an excellent local sixth form college to which many of our pupils progress. Good behaviour is insisted upon and emphasis is also placed on pastoral care by a highly professional staff.

Carleton House Preparatory School

Address: Lyndhurst Road,
Mossley Hill, Liverpool,
Merseyside L18 8AQ
Telephone: 051 724 4880

Acting Head: Mrs K Line

Age range: 4-11
No. of pupils: 138
Scholarships:
Religion: Roman Catholic

Fees per term
Day: £640-£640
Weekly board: -
Full board: -

○ Boy ○ Girl ● Co-ed
● Day ○ Week ○ Board

Carleton House is a small, Catholic preparatory school, open to children of all denominations. The class sizes are small and high educational standards are maintained by a well qualified and experienced staff. Pupils receive a thorough grounding in all areas of the curriculum and there are many opportunities for them to take part in extra-curricular activities including football, netball, cricket, swimming, chess, ballet, music.

Christian Fellowship School

Address: 1 Princes Road,
Liverpool, Merseyside L8 1TG
Telephone: 051 709 1642

Head: Mr P R Williamson

Age range: 5-16
No. of pupils: 200
Scholarships: Yes
Religion: Christian Fellowship

Fees per term
Day: -£320
Weekly board: -
Full board: -

○ Boy ○ Girl ● Co-ed
● Day ○ Week ○ Board

For further information and a prospectus, please contact the school.

MERSEYSIDE 351

Elliot Clark School

Address: 63 Rodney Street, Liverpool, Merseyside L1 9ER
Telephone: 051 709 3323
Head: Miss A I Thomas

Age range: 7-16
No. of pupils: 40
Scholarships:
Religion: Non-denominational

Fees per term
Day: £620-£620
Weekly board: -
Full board: -

Boy ○ Girl ○ Co-ed ●
Day ● Week ○ Board ○

For further information and a prospectus, please contact the school.

Highfield School

Address: 96 Bidston Road, Oxton, Birkenhead, Merseyside L43 6TW
Telephone: 051 652 3708
Head: Mrs S Morris

Age range: 3-16
No. of pupils: 130
Scholarships:
Religion: Non-denominational

Fees per term
Day: £350-£795
Weekly board: -
Full board: -

Boy ● Girl ● Co-ed ○
Day ● Week ○ Board ○

For further information and a prospectus, please contact the school. Boys 3-11, girls 3-16.

Huyton College

Address: Huyton, Liverpool, Merseyside L36 5XQ
Telephone: 051 489 4321
Head: Mrs C Bradley

Age range: 2-18
No. of pupils: 350
Scholarships: Yes
Religion: All welcome

Fees per term
Day: £575-£1195
Weekly board: -
Full board: £1965-£2585

Boy ● Girl ● Co-ed ○
Day ● Week ○ Board ●

Huyton College is an independent day and boarding school for girls aged 2-18 years and boys are also accepted in the nursery class (2-6 Years). The school is situated close to Liverpool in attractive spacious grounds with playing fields, sports hall and home economics block. The school encourages personal repsonsibility, serious study and the development of individual talents.

Kingsmead School

Address: Bertram Drive, Hoylake, Merseyside L47 0LL
Telephone: 051 632 3156
Head: Mr E H Bradby

Age range: 3-13
No. of pupils: 209
Scholarships: Yes
Religion: Christian

Fees per term
Day: £415-£1495
Weekly board: £1845-£2045
Full board: £1865-£2075

Boy ○ Girl ○ Co-ed ●
Day ● Week ● Board ●

Kingsmead is an independent boarding and day school for boys and girls aged 3-13. It is situated in 30 acres of grounds in the seaside town of Hoylake. Pupils are prepared for admission to state or independent schools at 11+ or 13+. The school has an excellent academic tradition as well as caring for the needs of each individual.

Kingswood School

Address: 26 Westcliffe Road, Southport, Mersyside PR8 2BU
Telephone: 0704 63211
Head: Mr E J Borowski

Age range: 2-18
No. of pupils: 560
Scholarships: Yes
Religion: Non-denominational

Fees per term
Day: £310-£885
Weekly board: -
Full board: -

Boy ○ Girl ○ Co-ed ●
Day ● Week ○ Board ○

For further information and a prospectus, please contact the school.

Liverpool College *

Address: Mossley Hill, Liverpool, Merseyside L18 8BE
Telephone: 051 724 2359
Head: Mr B.R. Martin

Age range: 5-18
No. of pupils: 662
Scholarships: Yes
Religion: Church of England

Fees per term
Day: £735-£1234
Weekly board: -
Full board: -

Boy ● Girl ● Co-ed ○
Day ● Week ○ Board ○

Organised as four separate departments for the different age ranges, the school occupies a 26-acre campus. Recent buildings include award-winning C D T centre. Excellent academic records; nearly all sixth form progress to degree courses. Strong games tradition; many extra-curricular activities at lunchtime and after school. A friendly sized school with the usual facilities of a much larger one. Girls 16-18.

Marymount Convent School

Address: Love Lane, Wallesey, Merseyside L44 5SB
Telephone: 051 638 8467
Head: Sister C O'Reilley

Age range: 3-11
No. of pupils: 210
Scholarships:
Religion: Roman Catholic

Fees per term
Day: £400-
Weekly board: -
Full board: -

Boy ○ Girl ● Co-ed ○
Day ● Week ○ Board ○

The school, founded in 1878, is an interdenominational school for girls run by the Sisters of the Holy Family of Bordeaux. The school offers an excellent primary education based on the National Curriculum and prepares children for entrance to senior independent schools and the 11+ examination for entrance to local grammar schools. The school offers lessons in French (at junior level).

McKee School of Education, Dance, Drama

Address: 2 Carnforth Road, Liverpool, Merseyside L18 6JS
Telephone: 051 724 1316
Head: Mrs K M McKee

Age range: 3-11
No. of pupils: 70
Scholarships:
Religion: Non-denominational

Fees per term
Day: -£360
Weekly board: -
Full board: -

Boy ○ Girl ○ Co-ed ●
Day ● Week ○ Board ○

For further information and a prospectus, please contact the school.

MERSEYSIDE 353

Merchant Taylors' School *

Address: Crosby, Liverpool, Merseyside L23 0QP

Telephone: 051 928 3308

Head: Mr S J R Dawkins

Age range: 7-18
No. of pupils: 848
Scholarships: Yes
Religion: Non-denominational

Fees per term
Day: £747-£1128
Weekly board: -
Full board: -

● Boy ○ Girl ○ Co-ed
● Day ○ Week ○ Board

Since its foundation in 1620 the School has provided a Christian, academic, disciplined education for local boys from a wide range of backgrounds. It has a reputation for academic excellence (25th in Financial Times Survey of top independent schools) and a strong tradition for sport, music and drama combined with a friendly and caring approach to life. The facilities are excellent.

Merchant Taylors' School for Girls *

Address: Liverpool Road, Crosby, Liverpool, Merseyside L23 5SP

Telephone: 051 924 3140

Head: Miss E J Panton MA(Oxon)

Age range: 4-18
No. of pupils: 906
Scholarships: Yes
Religion: Non-denominational

Fees per term
Day: £720-£1128
Weekly board: -
Full board: -

○ Boy ● Girl ○ Co-ed
● Day ○ Week ○ Board

The School has recently celebrated it's centenary and is proud of it's traditions, particularly of consistently high academic achievement. The facilities are excellent and the staff are highly qualified and caring. Formal discipline is kept to a minimum but order and courtesey are high priorities. The curriculum is wide and full allowing each girl to develop to her full potential.

Mostyn House

Address: Parkgate, Wirral, Merseyside L64 6SG

Telephone: 051 336 1010

Head: Mr A D J Grenfell

Age range: 4-16
No. of pupils: 300
Scholarships: Yes
Religion: Non-denominational

Fees per term
Day: £1080-£1360
Weekly board: -
Full board: -

○ Boy ○ Girl ● Co-ed
● Day ○ Week ○ Board

Mostyn House is a junior and senior co-educational day school for pupils aged 4-16, and we are opening a sixth form in September 1993. Small classes (average 15) and highly qualified staff ensure excellent personal attention. Beautiful old buildings are complemented by up-to-the-minute facilities for teaching a modern curriculum and a wide extra-curricular programme is offered, including many sports.

Newborough School

Address: Quarry Street, Woolton, Liverpool, Merseyside L25 6HD

Telephone: 051 428 1838

Head: Miss D Prior

Age range: 3-16
No. of pupils: 150
Scholarships:
Religion: Non-denominational

Fees per term
Day: £295-£425
Weekly board: -
Full board: -

○ Boy ○ Girl ● Co-ed
● Day ○ Week ○ Board

Newborough School is situated in a very pleasant residential part of Liverpool. The school provides continuous education for girls from 3-16 years, boy 3-11, in a happy family atmosphere. Our policy is to have a well balanced curriculum, together with discipline, moral values and principles. The senior girls are prepared for GCSE, having been advised and assisted in the study of those subjects most beneficial to them.

Pershore House School

Address: Prenton Lane, Birkenhead, Wirral, Merseyside L42 8LA
Telephone: 051 608 1170

Head: Mr D B Winterford

Age range: 2-11
No. of pupils: 94
Scholarships:
Religion: Church of England

Fees per term
Day: £525-£620
Weekly board: -
Full board: -

Boy ○ Girl ○ Co-ed ●
Day ● Week ○ Board ○

Our pupils range from two 1f to eleven+ years and from the start, a disciplined attitude towards work is instilled by a highly motivated and experienced staff. From nursery to the fouth year of the preparatory school, we aim to create a happy and successful young person, ready for any external examination at 11+; the 'professional pupil', in a success rate at 80-100%.

Prenton Preparatory School

Address: Wirral Lodge, Mount Pleasant, Oxton, Birkenhead, Merseyside L43 5SY
Telephone: 051 652 3182

Head: Mrs J B Mounsey

Age range: 3-11
No. of pupils: 160
Scholarships:
Religion: Non-denominational

Fees per term
Day: £510-£670
Weekly board: -
Full board: -

Boy ○ Girl ○ Co-ed ●
Day ● Week ○ Board ○

Prenton Preparatory School aims to provide a sound education and balanced curriculum. We aim to instil good working habits and a thirst for knowledge as the best preparation for life. The development of character is of equal importance to academic achievement, each child is encouraged to develop both to fulfil his or her own potential.

Runnymede Preparatory School

Address: North Drive, Sandfield Park, West Derby, Liverpool, Merseyside
Telephone: 051 220 7775

Head: Mr P Sweeney

Age range: 4-11
No. of pupils: 257
Scholarships:
Religion: Roman Catholic

Fees per term
Day: £650-£683
Weekly board: -
Full board: -

Boy ○ Girl ○ Co-ed ●
Day ● Week ○ Board ○

The college is an independent (HMC) grammar school founded by the Congregation of Christian Brothers. There are 260 children in the preparatory school. The school recognises that every child is an individual. Within a broadly based curriculum every attempt is made to encourage the growth and development of each child's talents. The majority of pupils transfer to the senior school at age eleven.

St Anselm's College *

Address: Manor Hill, Birkenhead, Merseyside L43 1UG
Telephone: 051 652 1408

Head: Rev Brother C J Streenan

Age range: 3-18
No. of pupils: 900
Scholarships: Yes
Religion: Roman Catholic

Fees per term
Day: £525-£942
Weekly board: -
Full board: -

Boy ● Girl ● Co-ed ○
Day ● Week ○ Board ○

For further information and a prospectus, please contact the school. Boys 3-18, girls 3-11.

St Edward's College *

Address: Sandfield Park, West Derby, Liverpool, Merseyside L12 1LF
Telephone: 051 228 3376

Head: Mr J E Waszek BSc, MA

Age range: 11-18
No. of pupils: 676
Scholarships:
Religion: Roman Catholic

Fees per term
Day: £1050-
Weekly board: -
Full board: -

Boy ○ Girl ○ Co-ed ●
Day ● Week ○ Board ○

St Edward's College is an independent, Catholic, HMC School, founded by the Christian Brothers. The College's facilities include 6th Form Centre, CDT block, music centre and sports centre with swimming pool. Students are prepared for GCSE and A Level examinations, with 75% of the Sixth Form going on to degree courses. St Edward's is also the choir school for the Liverpool Metropolitan Cathedral.

St Mary's College *

Address: Crosby, Merseyside L23 3AR

Telephone: 051 924 3926

Head: Mr W Hammond

Age range: 4-18
No. of pupils: 800
Scholarships:
Religion: Roman Catholic

Fees per term
Day: £574-£1055
Weekly board: -
Full board: -

Boy ○ Girl ○ Co-ed ●
Day ● Week ○ Board ○

The School's aim is the development of the whole person within a Christian vision of the person. Committed to acdemic excellence (with some 85% of the pupils proceeding to University and Polytechnics), it provides this within a context of Christian relationships, values, witness, worship and service to others. The curriculum combines breadth and balance with respect of individual talents, and includes values awareness.

St Wyburn School

Address: 26 Westcliffe Road, Southport, Merseyside

Telephone:

Head:

Age range: 11-18
No. of pupils:
Scholarships:
Religion:

Fees per term
Day: -
Weekly board: -
Full board: -

Boy ○ Girl ● Co-ed ○
Day ● Week ○ Board ○

For further information and a prospectus, please contact the school.

Steatham House School

Address: Victoria Road, Blundellsands, Great Crosby, Merseyside L23 8UQ
Telephone: 051 924 1514

Head: Mrs C Baxter

Age range: 2-11
No. of pupils: 190
Scholarships:
Religion:

Fees per term
Day: -
Weekly board: -
Full board: -

Boy ○ Girl ○ Co-ed ●
Day ● Week ○ Board ○

For further information and a prospectus, please contact the school.

Sunnymede School

Address: 4 Westcliffe Road, Birkdale, Southport, Merseyside PR8 2BN
Telephone: 0704 68593

Head: Mr S J Pattinson

Age range: 3-13
No. of pupils: 180
Scholarships:
Religion: Non-denominational

Fees per term
Day: £570-£1170
Weekly board: -
Full board: -

Boy ○ Girl ○ Co-ed ●
Day ● Week ○ Board ○

Sunnymede is a family run IAPS day school serving the local area. There are no entrance requirements and pupils may be registered from birth. Pupils are prepared for both day and boarding senior independent schools by following a full and varied curriculum.

Tower College

Address: Mill Lane, Rainhill, Merseyside L35 6NE

Telephone: 051 426 4333

Head: Mrs M J Oxley

Age range: 4-16
No. of pupils: 433
Scholarships:
Religion:

Fees per term
Day: -
Weekly board: -
Full board: -

Boy ○ Girl ○ Co-ed ●
Day ● Week ○ Board ○

For further information and a prospectus, please contact the school.

Tower Dene Preparatory School

Address: 59-76 Cambridge Road, Southport, Merseyside PR9 9RH
Telephone: 0704 28556

Head: Mrs A Lewin

Age range: 3-11
No. of pupils: 85
Scholarships:
Religion:

Fees per term
Day: -
Weekly board: -
Full board: -

Boy ○ Girl ○ Co-ed ●
Day ● Week ○ Board ○

For further information and a prospectus, please contact the school.

Upton Hall Convent School *

Address: Upton, Wirral, Merseyside L49 6JL

Telephone: 051 677 7696

Head: Sr L Madigan FCJ

Age range: 11-18
No. of pupils: 600
Scholarships:
Religion: Roman Catholic

Fees per term
Day: £806-£806
Weekly board: -
Full board: -

Boy ○ Girl ● Co-ed ○
Day ● Week ○ Board ○

The aim of the school is to enable each girl to realise her full potential. There is a strong emphasis on community spirit. There is a high success rate at all levels of public examination and the majority of girls go on for degree courses. Co-operation of parents on all levels is expected by the school.

Wellington School

Address: Bebbington, Wirral, Merseyside L63 7NG

Telephone: 051 645 2332

Head: Dr B Scott

Age range: 11-18
No. of pupils: 160
Scholarships: Yes
Religion: Non-denominational

Fees per term
Day: £615-£920
Weekly board: -
Full board: -

Boy ○ Girl ○ Co-ed ●
Day ● Week ○ Board ○

Wellington School is an independent day school for boys and girls, aged 11 to 18. The children are prepared for GCSE and A Level. The school has small classes and has a happy family atmosphere. We lay stress on smart appearance, good manners and discipline. We seek to promote a sense of confidence and security.

Westbourne School

Address: 45 Penkett Road, Wallasey, Merseyside

Telephone:

Head: Mr T N Cottram

Age range: 4-11
No. of pupils:
Scholarships:
Religion:

Fees per term
Day: -
Weekly board: -
Full board: -

Boy ○ Girl ○ Co-ed ●
Day ● Week ○ Board ○

For further information and a prospectus, please contact the school.

MIDDLESEX

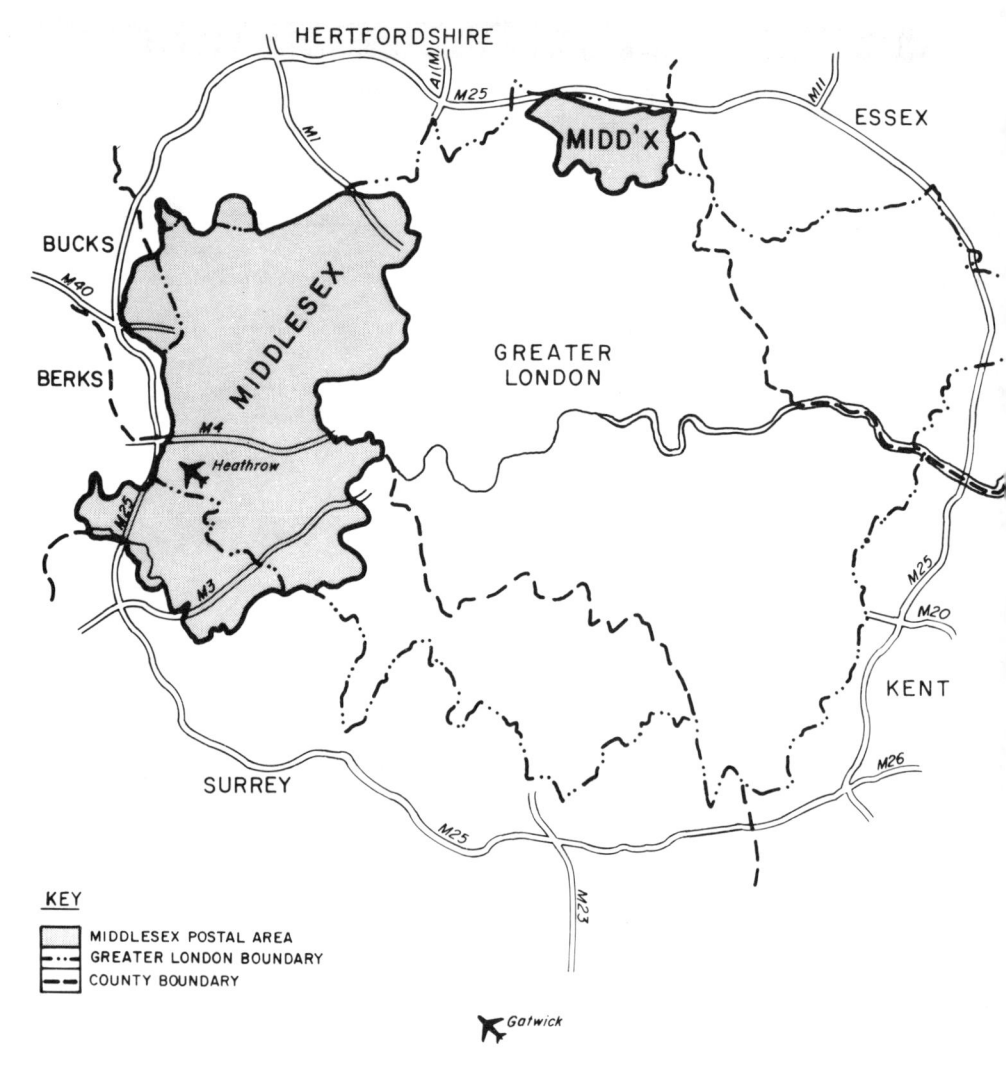

KEY
- MIDDLESEX POSTAL AREA
- GREATER LONDON BOUNDARY
- COUNTY BOUNDARY

NB MIDDLESEX IS NOT AN ADMINISTRATIVE COUNTY – PLEASE USE FOR POSTAL REFERENCE ONLY

Alpha Preparatory School

Address: 21 Hindes Road,
Harrow, Middlesex HA1 1SH

Telephone: 081 427 1471

Head: Mr P J Wylie

Age range: 4-13
No. of pupils: 165
Scholarships:
Religion: Church of England

Fees per term
Day: £420-£1100
Weekly board: -
Full board: -

● Boy ○ Girl ○ Co-ed
● Day ○ Week ○ Board

Alpha is a small, friendly preparatory school of 170 boys aged 4-13 situated in central Harrow. We have enviable class sizes (pupil/teacher ratio 1:11), a good discipline and high academic standards. Although our reception class is heavily over-subscribed, we also take boys at any age from 5-11, providing they satisfy our academic requirements.

The American Community School Ltd

Address: Hillingdon Court,
Vine Lane, Hillingdon,
Middlesex UB19 0BE

Telephone: 0895 259771

Head: Mr B Duncan

Age range: 4-18
No. of pupils: 585
Scholarships:
Religion: Non-denominational

Fees per term
Day: £2290-£3750
Weekly board: -
Full board: -

○ Boy ○ Girl ● Co-ed
● Day ○ Week ○ Board

Spacious campus near to London. Stable environment, high educational standards, happy social life for relocated youngsters. Fully accredited co-educational day school pre-kindergarten to grade 13. Advanced Placement and International Baccalaureate programs additional to curriculum designed to promote acceptance at colleges and universities worldwide. Extensive extra-curricular opportunities.

Ashton House School

Address: 50/52 Eversley
Crescent, Isleworth,
Middlesex TW7 4LW

Telephone: 081 560 3902

Head: Mrs J Bruce

Age range: 3-11
No. of pupils: 160
Scholarships:
Religion: Non-denominational

Fees per term
Day: £962-£994
Weekly board: -
Full board: -

○ Boy ○ Girl ● Co-ed
● Day ○ Week ○ Board

Member of ISAI and ISIS. Excellent record of examination successes. Prospectus sent on request. Entry by interview and assessment.

Athelstan House School

Address: 36 Percy Road,
Hampton, Middlesex
TW12 2LA

Telephone: 081 979 1045

Head: Mrs E Woolf

Age range: 3-7
No. of pupils: 75
Scholarships:
Religion: Non-denominational

Fees per term
Day: £484-£913
Weekly board: -
Full board: -

○ Boy ○ Girl ● Co-ed
● Day ○ Week ○ Board

The school provides a happy, secure family environment, without pressure, where children (16 per class) are encouraged to develop self-discipline, independence and a caring attitude to those around them. The school curriculum is designed to encourage these positive attitudes within a framework of learning and study geared towards the needs of the National Curriculum and entry at seven to local preparatory schools.

Atholl School

Address: 458 Rayners Lane, Pinner, Middlesex HA5 5DT

Telephone: 081 866 0271

Head: Mr C Dodsworth

Age range: 11-16
No. of pupils: 130
Scholarships:
Religion: Non-denominational

Fees per term
Day: £1095-£1230
Weekly board: -
Full board: -

● Boy ○ Girl ○ Co-ed
● Day ○ Week ○ Board

Classes of no more than sixteen ensure that in a small, family community, individual needs are well cared for and although successes in public examinations in an essential target (separate sciences, 3 modern languages, 15 subjects at GCSE) the school provides education in its broadest sense.

Buckingham College Lower School

Address: The Ridgeway, Kenton, Middlesex HA3 0LJ

Telephone: 081 907 1522

Head: Mr N Wilkins

Age range: 4-11
No. of pupils: 120
Scholarships:
Religion: Non-denominational

Fees per term
Day: £850-£1095
Weekly board: -
Full board: -

● Boy ○ Girl ○ Co-ed
● Day ○ Week ○ Board

At Buckingham College Lower School we know that the primary years are the foundation for success. We teach and learn in a friendly and stimulating environment where good manners and courtesy co-exist with the very best of modern professional practice in a thorough wide-ranging curriculum. We have an excellent record of scholarship success. Visits from prospective parents are welcome.

Buckingham College Senior School

Address: 15-17 Hindes Road, Harrow, Middlesex HA1 1SH

Telephone: 081 427 1220

Head: Mr D Bell

Age range: 11-18
No. of pupils: 200
Scholarships: Yes
Religion: Non-denominational

Fees per term
Day: £1095-£1285
Weekly board: -
Full board: -

● Boy ○ Girl ○ Co-ed
● Day ○ Week ○ Board

Founded in 1936, Buckingham College has a tradition of combining academic excellence with high personal standards. Our motto is 'Man know thyself,' and we believe it is vital that every boy becomes self-confident, self-reliant and self-disciplined. Our small classes enable us to give individual attention that leads to success. We offer 24 subjects at GCSE and A Level.

Buxlow Preparatory School

Address: 5/6 Castleton Gardens, Wembley, Middlesex HA9 7QJ

Telephone: 081 904 3615

Head: Mrs B L Lancaster

Age range: 4-11
No. of pupils: 125
Scholarships:
Religion:

Fees per term
Day: £815-£840
Weekly board: -
Full board: -

○ Boy ○ Girl ● Co-ed
● Day ○ Week ○ Board

Founded in 1927, Buxlow Preparatory School is a small and caring school with a far reaching reputation for academic excellence. The school philosophy is based on the premise that every child should be enabled to reach his or her intellectual, physical and emotional potential in a warm, happy and disciplined environment.

Denmead

Address: 41-43 Wensleydale Road, Hampton, Middlesex TW12 2LP
Telephone: 081 979 1844

Age range: 3-13
No. of pupils: 205
Scholarships:
Religion: Church of England

Fees per term
Day: £495-£1180
Weekly board: -
Full board: -

● Boy ○ Girl ○ Co-ed
● Day ○ Week ○ Board

Head: Mr R Millard MA(Oxon)

The aim of the school is to prepare each boy thoroughly for his secondary education at 13+ - sound work habits, a sense of responsibility, a willingness to take part wholeheartedly in music and the arts as well as in games and sport, a sense of duty and respect for one's neighbour, the community and the environment.

Halliford School

Address: Russell Road, Shepperton, Middlesex TW17 9HX
Telephone: 0932 223 593

Age range: 11-18
No. of pupils: 320
Scholarships: Yes
Religion: Non-denominational

Fees per term
Day: -£1300
Weekly board: -
Full board: -

● Boy ○ Girl ○ Co-ed
● Day ○ Week ○ Board

Head: Mr J Crook

Halliford is a two-form entry school, small in numbers but high in aspiration. As the result of consortium arrangements with St David's School for Girls, Ashford, we have co-educational sixth form teaching.

Hampton School *

Address: Hanworth Road, Hampton, Middlesex TW12 3HD
Telephone: 081 979 5526

Age range: 11-18
No. of pupils: 886
Scholarships: Yes
Religion: Non-Denominational

Fees per term
Day: £1350-£1350
Weekly board: -
Full board: -

● Boy ○ Girl ○ Co-ed
● Day ○ Week ○ Board

Head: Mr G G Able MA

The school stands in 26 acres of grounds and games fields. It aims to provide a humane community, tolerant but ordered, where academically promising boys of many different temperaments and backgrounds can all be encouraged to develop their abilities and personalities to the full.

Harrow School p743

Address: Harrow on the Hill, Middlesex HA1 3HW
Telephone: 081 869 1200

Age range: 13-18
No. of pupils: 776
Scholarships: Yes
Religion:

Fees per term
Day: -
Weekly board: -
Full board: £3975-£3975

● Boy ○ Girl ○ Co-ed
○ Day ○ Week ● Board

Head Master: Mr N R Bomford MA FRSA

Entrance scholarships examination in February for boys under 14 on 1st July. Up to 15 scholarships and exhibitions are offered annually, ranging in value from £240 to half of the fees. A percentage of the remaining fee may be remitted in cases of need and having regard to the scholar's ability. Music and art are offered annually; music scholarships of half fees are also supplementable.

Heathfield School

Address: Beaulieu Drive, Pinner, Middlesex HA5 1NB

Telephone: 081 868 2346

Head: Mrs J Merrit

Age range: 4-18
No. of pupils: 500
Scholarships: Yes
Religion: Non-denominational

Fees per term
Day: £1036-£1340
Weekly board: -
Full board: -

● Girl ○ Co-ed ○ Boy
● Day ○ Week ○ Board

For further information and a prospectus, please contact the school.

Holland House School

Address: 1 Broadhurst Avenue, Edgware, Middlesex HA8 8TP

Telephone: 081 958 6979

Head: Mrs I Tyk

Age range: 4-11
No. of pupils: 140
Scholarships:
Religion: Non-denominational

Fees per term
Day: £695-
Weekly board: -
Full board: -

○ Boy ○ Girl ● Co-ed
● Day ○ Week ○ Board

Great emphasis is placed from the beginning on reading, writing, numberwork and clear self-expression. The curriculum is comprehensive and covers academic subjects, music, art, drama and sport.

Children are successfully prepared for various competitive examinations at 11+. Extra curricular activities include judo, tap-dancing and music.

Innellan House

Address: St Andrew's School Group, 44 Love Lane, Pinner, Middlesex HA5 3EX

Telephone: 081 866 1855

Head: Mrs R Edwards

Age range: 3-8
No. of pupils: 105
Scholarships:
Religion: Church of England

Fees per term
Day: £690-£750
Weekly board: -
Full board: -

○ Boy ○ Girl ● Co-ed
● Day ○ Week ○ Board

The school is run on the lines of a large family with a good ratio of staff to pupils. Discipline is firm but kind. Traditional and modern methods in the many subjects covered by the wide curriuclum. Pupils are prepared at 7+ for entry to preparatory schools.

Jack and Jill School

Address: 30 Nightingale Road, Hampton, Middlesex TW12 3HX

Telephone: 081 979 3195

Head: Mrs M Papirnik

Age range: 3-7
No. of pupils: 105
Scholarships:
Religion: Non-denominational

Fees per term
Day: £445-£840
Weekly board: -
Full board: -

● Boy ● Girl ○ Co-ed
● Day ○ Week ○ Board

For further information and a prospectus, please contact the school. Boys 3-5, girls 4-7.

The John Lyon School *

Address: Middle Road, Harrow, Middlesex HA2 0HN

Telephone: 081 422 2046

Head: Revd T J Wright

Age range: 11-18
No. of pupils: 505
Scholarships: Yes
Religion: Non-denominational

Fees per term
Day: £1385-
Weekly board: -
Full board: -

Boy ● Girl ○ Co-ed ○
Day ● Week ○ Board ○

The school shares the same foundation as Harrow School, some of whose facilities it uses. It occupies a site on the hill at Harrow with games fields nearby. Entry at 11 is very competitive and the school has a strong academic tradition as well as excellence in music, games and drama. There are small entries at 13 and 16.

The Lady Eleanor Holles *

Address: Hanworth Road, Hampton, Middlesex TW12 3HF

Telephone: 081 979 1601

Head: Miss E M Candy

Age range: 7-18
No. of pupils: 810
Scholarships: Yes
Religion: Non-denominational

Fees per term
Day: £1250-£1400
Weekly board: -
Full board: -

Boy ○ Girl ● Co-ed ○
Day ● Week ○ Board ○

Set in 30 acres of playing fields and gardens, the school, built in 1936, has had many additions including a swimming pool, art block, music and drama wing, technology suite and sixth form library and class room block. High academic standards at GCSE and A Level. Good sporting record. Large sixth form most of whom go on to university.

The Mall School

Address: 185 Hampton Road, Twickenham, Middlesex TW2 5NQ

Telephone: 081 977 2523

Head: Mr T P A MacDonogh

Age range: 4-13
No. of pupils: 280
Scholarships:
Religion: Church of England

Fees per term
Day: £1015-£1175
Weekly board: -
Full board: -

Boy ● Girl ○ Co-ed ○
Day ● Week ○ Board ○

The Mall, an IAPS preparatory school, combines a relaxed friendly environment and much parental involvement with high academic standards at both Common Entrance and scholarships to local London day schools and a variety of boarding schools. Recent building includes two teaching blocks, whilst amongst extra-curricular activities music, drama and, most recently, rugby, are strongly encouraged.

Merchant Taylor's School *

Address: Sandy Lodge, Northwood, Middlesex HA6 2HT

Telephone: 0923 820644

Head: Mr J.R. Gabitass MA

Age range: 11-18
No. of pupils: 750
Scholarships: Yes
Religion: Church of England

Fees per term
Day: -£1988
Weekly board: -
Full board: -£3238

Boy ● Girl ○ Co-ed ○
Day ● Week ○ Board ●

Balanced all-round education with wide range for extra-curricular activities. Lively boarding house with high standards of care and accommodation. Outstanding record of academic success: 61% AB grades; over 90% of boys each year proceed to degree courses in higher education. Entry at 11+, 13+, 16+. We place great emphasis on knowing each individual boy well (pupil-teacher ratio 1:10:4).

Newland House School

Address: Waldegrave Park, Twickenham, Middlesex
Telephone: 081 892 7479
Head: Mr D K Geddes

Age range: 4-13
No. of pupils: 444
Scholarships: Yes
Religion: Church of England

Fees per term
Day: £472-£1173
Weekly board: -
Full board: -

Boy ○ Girl ○ Co-ed ●
Day ● Week ○ Board ○

Newland House is an IAPS co-educational preparatory school. An extensive building programme has recently been completed. There are excellent facilities for design technology, science, computing, music, PE and games. The school has an excellent academic record. Normal entry is at either age 4 or 7 but there are also occasional vacancies in other age groups. Open afternoons are held regularly.

North London Collegiate School

Address: Canons, Edgeware, Middlesex HA8 7RJ
Telephone: 081 952 0912
Head: Mrs J L Clanchy

Age range: 7-18
No. of pupils: 900
Scholarships: Yes
Religion: Non-denominational

Fees per term
Day: £1119-£1417
Weekly board: -
Full board: -

Boy ○ Girl ● Co-ed ○
Day ● Week ○ Board ○

The school is set in 30 acres of fine grounds, unusual for a city school. It is proud of its tradition of academic excellence and has high expectations of its pupils. Assisted Places and bursaries ensure that pupils come from every walk of life. Practical music is encouraged and the orchestras perform at a high level.

Northwood College

Address: Maxwell Road, Northwood, Middlesex HA6 2YE
Telephone: 0923 825446
Head: Mrs A Mayou MA

Age range: 4-18
No. of pupils: 560
Scholarships: Yes
Religion: Non-denominational

Fees per term
Day: £987-£1419
Weekly board: -
Full board: -

Boy ○ Girl ● Co-ed ○
Day ● Week ○ Board ○

Northwood College was founded in 1876. We provide a sound academic education to girls aged 4-18, with a full range of A Level course in the Sixth Form. We have excellent facilities including a recently completed swimming pool and sports hall. We are a community in which everyone is involved and everyone counts, where the Governors and staff are united in working with parents for the welfare of the girls.

Orley Farm School

Address: South Hill Avenue, Harrow, Middlesex HA1 3NU
Telephone: 081 422 1525
Head: Mr I S Elliott

Age range: 4-13
No. of pupils: 420
Scholarships:
Religion: Church of England

Fees per term
Day: £965-£1420
Weekly board: -
Full board: -

Boy ● Girl ○ Co-ed ○
Day ● Week ○ Board ○

For further information and a prospectus, please contact the school.

Peterborough and St Margaret's High School for Girls

Address: 13-17 Sheepcote Road, Harrow, Middlesex HA1 2JL
Telephone: 081 427 3534

Head: Mrs J M Tomlinson

Age range: 4-16
No. of pupils: 206
Scholarships:
Religion: Church of England

Fees per term
Day: £800-£1175
Weekly board: -
Full board: -

○ ● ○
Boy Girl Co-ed
● ○ ○
Day Week Board

Peterborough and St Margaret's High School aims to provide a well disciplined and happy community. Small classes enable girls to receive individual attention, thus achieving their own potential. Emphasis is placed on courtesy and consideration of others. Professional, dedicated teaching leads towards GCSE results being well above the national average

The Purcell School p692

Address: Mount Park Road, Harrow on the Hill, Middlesex HA1 3JS
Telephone: 081 422 1284

Head: Mr K J Bain MA

Age range: 8-18
No. of pupils: 150
Scholarships: Yes
Religion: Non-Denominational

Fees per term
Day: £1940-£2372
Weekly board: -
Full board: £3540-£4011

○ ○ ●
Boy Girl Co-ed
● ○ ○
Day Week Board

The only specialist music school in Greater London. Outstanding musical opportunities and training, together with an excellent academic education up to A Level in small classes. All orchestral instruments, keyboard, composition, voice, media music. Orchestral and choral training. Regular performing opportunities and some overseas tours. Talented children are selected by musical audition throughout the year.

Quainton Hall

Address: 91 Hindes Road, Harrow, Middlesex HA1 1RX
Telephone: 081 427 1304

Head: Mr P J Milner

Age range: 4-13
No. of pupils: 220
Scholarships:
Religion: Church of England

Fees per term
Day: £935-£1195
Weekly board: -
Full board: -

● ○ ○
Boy Girl Co-ed
● ○ ○
Day Week Board

We are a friendly school community where boys are encouraged to develop all their talents. Considerable emphasis on academic work in addition to art, computing, drama, music, sport, school expeditions and technology. Much rebuilding has recently included swimming pool enclosure and technology centre.

Reddiford School

Address: 38 Cecil Park, Pinner, Middlesex HA5 5HH
Telephone: 081 866 0660

Head: Mr B Hemby

Age range: 4-11
No. of pupils: 140
Scholarships:
Religion: Church of England

Fees per term
Day: £855-
Weekly board: -
Full board: -

○ ○ ●
Boy Girl Co-ed
● ○ ○
Day Week Board

Reddiford School is a co-educational day school for children between the ages of 4 and 11. It is a charitable trust administered by a board of govenors, and is a member of the Independent Schools Association. All pupils are expected to remain at the school until the age of 11, when they are prepared for entry to senior independent schools in the area.

Roxeth Mead School

Address: Buckhold House, 25 Middle Road, Harrow, Middlesex HA2 0HW
Telephone: 081 422 2092

Age range: 4-7
No. of pupils: 70
Scholarships:
Religion: Church of England

Fees per term
Day: £695-
Weekly board: -
Full board: -

Boy ○ Girl ○ Co-ed ●
Day ● Week ○ Board ○

Head: Mrs A Collins

For further information and a prospectus, please contact the school.

St Andrew's Boys' Preparatory School

Address: St George's Hall, Pinner View, North Harrow, Middlesex HA1 4RJ
Telephone: 081 427 0114

Age range: 7-11
No. of pupils: 60
Scholarships:
Religion: Church of England

Fees per term
Day: £790-
Weekly board: -
Full board: -

Boy ● Girl ○ Co-ed ○
Day ● Week ○ Board ○

Head: Mrs P Pugh

A small family school. Small classes with individual attention allows close monitoring of progress and helps each boy to develop to his full potential. Entrance to the school is by interview and examination in mathematics, English and verbal reasoning. Boys progress to local public schools and independent grammar schools.

St Andrew's School

Address: 39, 42, 44 Gloucester Road, Harrow, Middlesex

Telephone: 081 427 0692

Age range: 8-18
No of pupils: 180
Scholarships:
Religion: Church of England

Fees per term
Day: -
Weekly board: -
Full board: -

Boy ○ Girl ● Co-ed ○
Day ● Week ○ Board ○

Head: Mrs M Hudson BA Hons, *Principal:* Miss M Roberts

St Andrew's School was established in September 1923. There is an excellent graduate staff and a wide range of GCSE, A Level and AS Level subjects are offered. Prospectus is enclosed with public examinations results. Buildings include two laboratories and there are good sports facilities. Educational journeys are arranged yearly. We are happy, caring and successful school.

St Andrew's Senior Girls School

Address: 39, 42-44 Gloucester Road, Harrow, Middlesex HA1 4PW
Telephone: 081 427 0692

Age range: 8-18
No. of pupils: 135
Scholarships:
Religion: Non-denominational

Fees per term
Day: £790-£920
Weekly board: -
Full board: -

Boy ○ Girl ● Co-ed ○
Day ● Week ○ Board ○

Head: Mrs M Hudson

For further information and a prospectus, please contact the school.

MIDDLESEX 367

St Catherine's School

Address: Cross Deep,
Twickenham, Middlesex
TW1 4QJ
Telephone: 081 891 2898

Head: Miss J M Thomas

Age range: 3-16
No. of pupils: 300
Scholarships:
Religion: Catholic

Fees per term
Day: £470-£1100
Weekly board: -
Full board: -

Boy ○ Girl ● Co-ed ○
Day ● Week ○ Board ○

St Catherine's School has an excellent range of facilities. There is an indoor swimming pool, fully equipped science laboratories, music, art and technology facilities and a multi-purpose hall. The school promotes high academic standards and in 1991 77% of GCSE results were at grades A-C. Each girl is helped to reach her potential in a supportive and caring environment in which Christian values are shared by all.

St Christopher's School

Address: 71 Wembley Park
Drive, Wembley, Middlesex
HA9 8HE
Telephone: 081 902 5069

Head: Mrs S M Morley

Age range: 4-11
No. of pupils: 112
Scholarships:
Religion: Christian

Fees per term
Day: £731-£863
Weekly board: -
Full board: -

Boy ○ Girl ○ Co-ed ●
Day ● Week ○ Board ○

For further information and a prospectus, please contact the school.

St David's Junior School

Address: Church Road,
Ashford, Middlesex TW15 3DZ
Telephone: 0784 252494

Head: Mrs D Watkins

Age range: 4-11
No. of pupils: 181
Scholarships:
Religion: Church of England

Fees per term
Day: £840-£1145
Weekly board: -
Full board: -

Boy ○ Girl ● Co-ed ○
Day ● Week ● Board ●

The school is 275 years old. Its present community is as rich as its past, with an IAPS junior school on-site and its sixth form girls sharing study and social time with the young men of Halliford's Boys School, Shepperton. Some academic scholarships available on entry at 11. Coveniently located on Waterloo/Staines/Windsor railway close to M4, M25 and Heathrow.

St David's School

Address: Church Road,
Ashford, Middlesex TW15 3DZ
Telephone: 0784 252494

Head: Mrs J G Osbourne BA

Age range: 11-18
No. of pupils: 245
Scholarships: Yes
Religion: Church of England

Fees per term
Day: -£1535
Weekly board: -£2500
Full board: -£2660

Boy ○ Girl ● Co-ed ○
Day ● Week ● Board ●

St David's hopes that it creates among its students a fair balance between freedom and order and between the needs of the individual and those of the community. Throughout the school particular emphasis is placed upon self-discipline and traditional standards of conduct, while avoiding unreasonable restrictions. The school hopes that every student will be maintaining these standards also beyond the school gates.

St Dominic's College

Address: Harrow, Middlesex
Telephone:
Principal: Mr J S Lipscomb MA MSc
Age range: 16-19
No. of pupils: 450
Scholarships:
Religion: Roman Catholic
Fees per term
Day: -
Weekly board: -
Full board: -

Boy ○ Girl ○ Co-ed ●
Day ● Week ○ Board ○

For further information and a prospectus, please contact the school.

St Helen's College

Address: Parkway, Hillingdon, Middlesex UB10 9JX
Telephone: 0895 234371
Head: Mr D A Crehan
Age range: 3-11
No. of pupils: 240
Scholarships:
Religion: Church of England
Fees per term
Day: £615-£695
Weekly board: -
Full board: -

Boy ○ Girl ○ Co-ed ●
Day ● Week ○ Board ○

For further information and a prospectus, please contact the school.

St Helen's School *

Address: Northwood, Middlesex HA6 3AS
Telephone: 0923 828511
Head: Dr Y A Burne
Age range: 4-18
No. of pupils: 920
Scholarships: Yes
Religion: Christian
Fees per term
Day: £855-£1398
Weekly board: £2228-£2539
Full board: £2325-£2636

Boy ○ Girl ● Co-ed ○
Day ● Week ● Board ●

St Helen's is an independent day and boarding school for girls, aged 4-18, situated in 22 acres containing playing fields, tennis courts and covered heated swimming pool. The school has a good record of academic achievement and offers a wide range of extra-curricular acitivities. Each girl is encouraged to live up to the best within herself and developing her talents to the full.

St John's School

Address: Potter Hill, Northwood, Middlesex HA6 3QY
Telephone: 081 866 0067
Head: Mr P F Ramage BA
Age range: 4-13
No. of pupils: 300
Scholarships: Yes
Religion: Church of England
Fees per term
Day: £1025-£1275
Weekly board: -
Full board: -

Boy ● Girl ○ Co-ed ○
Day ● Week ○ Board ○

St John's is an IAPS day school set in 30 acres of playing fields and grounds. Since 1984 it has been owned by the Merchant Taylors' Educational Trust and in that time an expensive programme of development has been under taken with new class rooms, science, CDT, music facilities completed and a purpose built sports hall opened.

St Martin's School

Address: 40 Moor Park Road,
Northwood, Middlesex
HA6 2DJ
Telephone: 0923 824723

Head: Mr M J Hodgson

Age range: 4-13
No. of pupils: 355
Scholarships:
Religion: Church of England

Fees per term
Day: £1095-£1380
Weekly board: -£1995
Full board: -£1995

● ○ ○
Boy Girl Co-ed
● ● ●
Day Week Board

Seventy years of traditional education and equipped with excellent modern resources. Assessment tests at 4 and 7. Preparation for Common Entrance and scholarship entrance to senior school

All-round education involving sport and music. Pastoral system encourages self-reliance and a sense of responsibility in a happy atmosphere.

St Mary's College

Address: Strawberry Hill,
Twickenham, Middlesex
TW1 4SX
Telephone:

Principal:

Age range: 18
No. of pupils:
Scholarships:
Religion:

Fees per term
Day: -
Weekly board: -
Full board: -

○ ○ ●
Boy Girl Co-ed
○ ○ ○
Day Week Board

For further information and a prospectus, please contact the college.

Staines Preparatory School Trust

Address: 3 Gresham Road,
Staines, Middlesex TW18 2BT
Telephone: 0784 450909

Head: Mr P Monger MA

Age range: 4-11
No. of pupils: 400
Scholarships:
Religion: Non-denominational

Fees per term
Day: £736-£840
Weekly board: -
Full board: -

○ ○ ●
Boy Girl Co-ed
● ○ ○
Day Week Board

The school, founded in 1935, prepares pupils for entry to secondary school at the age of 11 years. The school occupies some three acres of grounds and is five minutes walk from Staines station. A new wing was recently completed comprising a large hall, a science laboratory, and an art/design technology room among its facilities.

Twickenham Preparatory School

Address: 'Beveree', 43 High
Street, Hampton, Middlesex
TW12 2SA
Telephone: 081 979 6216

Head: Mr G D Malcolm

Age range: 4-13
No. of pupils: 140
Scholarships:
Religion: Christian

Fees per term
Day: £720-£1145
Weekly board: -
Full board: -

● ● ●
Boy Girl Co-ed
● ○ ○
Day Week Board

A small, happy school with a clear non-sectarian Christian tradition. Pupils of all faiths are accepted. The school is well equipped to cover the full range of subjects. Classes never exceed 18 pupils. The emphasis is on individual attention - boys are prepared for Common Entrance and girls for the 11+ examinations. Music and art are included in the curriculum for all children. There are out of school clubs and activities.

NORFOLK

NORFOLK 371

Beeston Hall School

Address: West Runton, Cromer, Norfolk NR27 9NQ

Telephone: 0263 837 324

Head: Mr J Elder MA, PGCE

Age range: 7-13
No. of pupils: 160
Scholarships:
Religion: Non-denominational

Fees per term
Day: -£1729
Weekly board: -
Full board: -£2037

○ ○ ● Boy Girl Co-ed
● ○ ● Day Week Board

Small, compact traditional boarding school with emphasis on good manners, respect for the community, fostering of confidence and friendship. Excellent record in all areas of academic, music, art, drama and poetry (37 scholarships in the last 6 years, national awards in art and poetry). No cramming at any stage, exams are faced in a relaxed manner. Sporting success in all areas - especially rugby, cricket and hockey.

Bracondale School

Address: 13-15 Bracondale, Norwich, Norfolk NR1 2AL

Telephone: 0603 624042

Head: Mr D M Gaudoin

Age range: 7-17
No. of pupils: 103
Scholarships: Yes
Religion: Non-denominational

Fees per term
Day: £860-£1130
Weekly board: £1510-£1780
Full board: -

● ○ ○ Boy Girl Co-ed
● ● ○ Day Week Board

We are a traditional, caring and well-ordered community in which boys are able to develop happily into self-reliant and considerate young gentlemen and are prepared for GCSE examinations in small classes. Up to 15 examinable subjects are available and boys have no difficulty proceeding to further education elsewhere, our best pupils achieving passes in eight or more subjects at Grade C or better.

Bushey Place School

Address: Cromer Road, Aylsham, Norfolk NR11 6HF

Telephone: 0263 734108

Head: Mr R G Horne

Age range: 7-16
No. of pupils: 76
Scholarships:
Religion: Christian

Fees per term
Day: £645-£695
Weekly board: -£1895
Full board: -£1995

○ ○ ● Boy Girl Co-ed
● ● ● Day Week Board

Bushey Place is a small co-educational day and boarding school situated in the north Norfolk historic market town of Aylsham. There are sixty day places available in the school and sixteen boarding. One of the main aims of the school is to maximise individual attention to pupils in small mixed ability classrooms. There is also special provision for children with learning difficulties of a moderate nature.

Cawston College

Address: Cawston, Norwich, Norfolk NR10 4YD

Telephone: 0603 871204

Head: Mr J Sutton

Age range: 8-17
No. of pupils: 114
Scholarships:
Religion:

Fees per term
Day: £790-£1315
Weekly board: £1745-£2320
Full board: £1790-£2365

○ ○ ● Boy Girl Co-ed
● ● ● Day Week Board

Cawston holds the view that basic literacy and numeracy skills should be mastered before the complexities of modern technology can be appreciated; thus our junior department aims to give a thorough and structured grounding in reading writing and arithmetic. The senior school offers a full academic programme in small classes. There are numerous extra-curricular activities.

Convent of the Sacred Heart

Address: 17 Mangate Street, Swaffam, Norfolk PE37 7QW

Telephone: 0760 721330

Head: Sister F Ridler

Age range: 3-16
No. of pupils: 300
Scholarships:
Religion: Catholic

Fees per term
Day: £600-£860
Weekly board: -£1425
Full board: -

Boy ● Girl ● Co-ed ○
Day ● Week ● Board ○

The primary aim of the Daughters of Divine Charity who conduct the school is to impart to their pupils a moral training combined with an education to fit them for the responsibilities of life based on a sound religious foundation. It is assumed that parents are in sympathy with this, otherwise there can be no true co-operation between parents and staff. Boys from 3-11 years.

Eccles Hall School

Address: Quidenham, Norwich, Norfolk NR16 2NZ

Telephone: 0953 87217

Head: Mr S A Simington

Age range: 10-16
No. of pupils: 160
Scholarships: Yes
Religion: Non-demoninational

Fees per term
Day: -£1400
Weekly board: -
Full board: -£2675

Boy ○ Girl ○ Co-ed ●
Day ● Week ○ Board ●

For further information please contact the headmaster.

Glebe House School

Address: 2 Cromer Road, Hunstanton, Norfolk PE36 6HW

Telephone: 0485 532809

Head: Mr N R Johnson

Age range: 4-13
No. of pupils: 110
Scholarships: Yes
Religion: Church of England

Fees per term
Day: £635-£1740
Weekly board: £2130-£2245
Full board: £2130-£2245

Boy ○ Girl ○ Co-ed ●
Day ● Week ● Board ●

A small, friendly school - ideal for first-time boarders. The school combines an informal atmosphere with a serious, dedicated approach to work in the classroom, play on the sportsfield and artistic pursuits and activities.

Gresham's Preparatory School

Address: Cromer Road, Holt, Norfolk NR25 6EY

Telephone: 0263 712227

Head: Mr A H Cuff

Age range: 8-13
No. of pupils: 250
Scholarships: Yes
Religion: Church of England

Fees per term
Day: £1775-
Weekly board: £2430-
Full board: £2540-

Boy ○ Girl ○ Co-ed ●
Day ● Week ● Board ●

The preparatory school is closely affiliated to the senior school but with its own headmaster and staff. Accomodation is in two well appointed houses. We aim to encourage each child's particular talents and foster informally courtesy and self discipline. Entry at any age up to 11 is by headmaster's report, assessment tests and interview.

NORFOLK 373

Gresham's School *

Address: Holt, Norfolk
NR25 6EA

Telephone: 0263 713271

Head: Mr J H Arkell MA

Age range: 3-18
No. of pupils: 465
Scholarships: Yes
Religion: Church of England

Fees per term
Day: £2262-
Weekly board: -
Full board: £3232-

Boy ○ Girl ○ Co-ed ●
Day ● Week ○ Board ●

Attractive rural setting on the edge of a north Norfolk Georgian town. Fully co-ed. Excellent facilities and opportunities for rural studies. 90% A Level results, 45% A and B grades, 85% to Degree courses. 8.8 average GCSE passes per pupil at C grade and above. Very strong mathematics. Tradition of engineering and arts.

Hethersett Old Hall School

Address: Norwich, Norfolk
NR9 3DW

Telephone: 0603 810390

Head: Mrs V M Reddington

Age range: 8-18
No. of pupils: 245
Scholarships: Yes
Religion: Church of England

Fees per term
Day: £935-£1185
Weekly board: -
Full board: £1920-£2280

Boy ○ Girl ● Co-ed ○
Day ● Week ○ Board ●

An independent boarding and day school for girls aged 8-18. In beautiful grounds, the school provides excellent study facilities, many sports and extra-curricular opportunities. A broad academic curriculum, excellent teaching and small classes ensure that girls reach their potential and achieve pleasing exam results. A carefully structured careers programme ensures entry to appropriate higher education course.

Langley Preparatory School

Address: Beech Hill,
Yarmouth Road, Thorpe,
Norwich, Norfolk NR7 0EA
Telephone: 0603 33861

Head: Doctor J Scaife

Age range: 4-11
No. of pupils: 135
Scholarships:
Religion: Non-denominational

Fees per term
Day: £615-£1205
Weekly board: -
Full board: -

Boy ○ Girl ○ Co-ed ●
Day ● Week ○ Board ○

The curriculum is both balanced and broadly based. It aims to promote the spiritual, moral, cultural, mental and physical developement of each individual pupil. English, mathematics and science form the core curriculum. Particular emphasis is place upon the teaching of science and computer studies, both are taught in well equipped and specialist laboratories. Physical education and music are also fostered.

Langley School

Address: Langley Park,
Norwich, Norfolk NR14 6BJ

Telephone: 0508 20210

Head: Mr S J W McArthur Bsc MA CertEd FGLP

Age range: 11-18
No. of pupils: 234
Scholarships: Yes
Religion: Non-denominational

Fees per term
Day: £1280-£1575
Weekly board: £2110-£2425
Full board: £2465-£2995

Boy ○ Girl ○ Co-ed ●
Day ● Week ● Board ●

At Langley, pupils will be taught to use their gifts and their time wisely. They will be nurtured to acquire the values of honesty, enterprise, independence and good citizenship. It is important that young people grow up in a happy school atmosphere where they will gain in confidence and learn to stand up for what they think is right.

Norwich High School for Girls GPDST *

Address: 95 Newmarket Road, Norwich, Norfolk NR2 2HU

Telephone: 0603 53265

Head: Mrs V C Bidwell

Age range: 5-18
No. of pupils: 850
Scholarships: Yes
Religion: Non-denominational

Fees per term
Day: £880-£1148
Weekly board: -
Full board: -

Boy ○ | Girl ● | Co-ed ○
Day ● | Week ○ | Board ○

Norwich High School is a long established day school offering an academic education and many extra-curricular activities to girls from a wide social background. The atmosphere in the school is friendly and several generations of families have been educated here. The curriculum and buildings are continuously updated. Prospective parents and pupils are invited to open days to meet girls and teachers.

Norwich School *

Address: The Close, Norwich, Norfolk NR1 4DQ

Telephone: 0503 523194

Head: Mr C D Brown

Age range: 8-18
No. of pupils: 750
Scholarships: Yes
Religion: Non-denominational

Fees per term
Day: £1255-£1305
Weekly board: -£2305
Full board: -£2405

Boy ● | Girl ○ | Co-ed ○
Day ● | Week ● | Board ●

Set in the Cathedral Close, Norwich School seeks high academic standards as well as encouraging its pupils to develop in confidence through a wide range of extra-curricular activities. The school also educates the Cathedral choristers.

Notre Dame Preparatory School

Address: 147 Dereham Road, Norwich, Norfolk NR2 3TA

Telephone: 0742 663835

Head: Mrs A E Mancini

Age range: 2-12
No. of pupils: 185
Scholarships:
Religion: Roman Catholic

Fees per term
Day: £200-£510
Weekly board: -
Full board: -

Boy ● | Girl ● | Co-ed ○
Day ● | Week ○ | Board ○

For further information and a prospectus, please contact the school. Boys 2-8, girls 2-12.

Riddlesworth Hall p693

Address: Diss, Norfolk IP22 2TA

Telephone: 095 381246

Head: Miss S A Smith BA

Age range: 4-13
No. of pupils: 140
Scholarships:
Religion: Church of England

Fees per term
Day: £1450-£1450
Weekly board: -
Full board: £2640-£2640

Boy ○ | Girl ● | Co-ed ○
Day ● | Week ○ | Board ●

Riddlesworth Hall is a boarding school for girls aged 7 to 13. Based in a Georgian house in the Norfolk countryside, the school has a happy, homely atmosphere. It caters for girls of all abilities with a new scholarship form for girls planning to join senior schools at 13. Excellent sports facilities: indoor swimming pool, netball, tennis, hockey and venture playground.

Runton and Sutherland School

Address: West Runton, Cromer, Norfolk NR27 9NF

Telephone: 0263 837661

Head: Miss A C Ritchie

Age range: 3-18
No. of pupils: 208
Scholarships: Yes
Religion: Church of England

Fees per term
Day: £726-£1625
Weekly board: -
Full board: £2225-£2800

Boy ● Girl ● Co-ed ○
Day ● Week ○ Board ●

On a healthy coastal site in north Norfolk with fast road and rail connections with London, this girls' boarding and day school (boarders 8-18 years) has lively and articulate youngsters, a happy family-type environment, good academic standards and strong creative arts. Boys from 3-11 years.

Silfield School

Address: 85 Gayton Road, Gaywood, Kings Lynn, Norfolk PE30 4EH
Telephone: 0553 774642

Head: Mr C E A Phillips DFC BA

Age range: 3-11
No. of pupils: 76
Scholarships:
Religion: Non-denominational

Fees per term
Day: £350-£680
Weekly board: -
Full board: -

Boy ○ Girl ○ Co-ed ●
Day ● Week ○ Board ○

For further information and a prospectus, please contact the school.

St Christopher's School

Address: George Hill, Old Catton, Norwich, Norfolk RH6 7DE
Telephone: 0603 425179

Head: Mrs F McGarry BAHons

Age range: 2-12
No. of pupils: 150
Scholarships:
Religion: Non-denominational

Fees per term
Day: £122-£779
Weekly board: -
Full board: -

Boy ○ Girl ○ Co-ed ●
Day ● Week ○ Board ○

We welcome parents who genuinely require a whole education for their child according to his/her individual needs and potential within the framework of a broad, balanced curriculum. Our comprehensive curriculum is underpinned by a thorough basic grounding in reading, writing and mathematics. The children are encouraged to develop as self-disciplined, caring human beings within our friendly, family atmosphere.

St Nicholas Preparatory and Kindergarten School

Address: Yarmouth Road, North Walsham, Norfolk NR28 9AT
Telephone: 0692 403143

Head: Mr P Bonham

Age range: 3-11
No. of pupils: 252
Scholarships:
Religion:

Fees per term
Day: -
Weekly board: -
Full board: -

Boy ○ Girl ○ Co-ed ●
Day ● Week ○ Board ○

For further information and a prospectus, please contact the school.

Sutherland House School

Address: Overstrand Road, Cromer, Norfolk NR27 0AL

Telephone:

Head:

Age range: 2-18
No. of pupils:
Scholarships:
Religion: Church of England

Fees per term
Day: -
Weekly board: -
Full board: -

● Boy ● Girl ○ Co-ed
● Day ○ Week ● Board

For further information and a prospectus, please contact the school. Girls 2-18, boys 2-8.

Taverham Hall

Address: Taverham, Norwich, Norfolk NR8 6HU

Telephone: 0603 868206

Head: Mr W D Lawton

Age range: 4-13
No. of pupils: 200
Scholarships: Yes
Religion: Church of England

Fees per term
Day: £950-£1825
Weekly board: £2460-
Full board: £2460-

○ Boy ○ Girl ● Co-ed
● Day ● Week ● Board

Set in 100 acres of parkland near Norwich, Taverham Hall provides an excellent opportunity for children to succeed in their formative years. Classes are kept small to promote academic success and a wide range of extra-curricular activities are offered along with music, art and games being of particular strength.

Thetford Grammar School

Address: Bridge Street, Thetford, Norfolk IP24 3AF

Telephone: 0842 752840

Head: Mr J R Weeks MA MLitt (Oxon)

Age range: 8-18
No. of pupils: 300
Scholarships: Yes
Religion: Church of England

Fees per term
Day: £1024-£1124
Weekly board: -
Full board: -

○ Boy ○ Girl ● Co-ed
● Day ○ Week ○ Board

Thetford Grammar School provides co-educational independent education 8-18 to a high academic standard in a small school with a tradition of care and support for the individual and commitment to the breadth of educational experience. There is a separate junior department and an active sixth form and the life of the school extends widely into sport, community service and the performing arts.

Thorpe House School

Address: 7 Yarmouth Road, Thorpe St Andrew, Norwich, Norfolk NR7 0EA

Telephone: 0603 33055

Head: Mrs F M Hunt BA

Age range: 4-16
No. of pupils: 365
Scholarships:
Religion: Church of England

Fees per term
Day: £450-£710
Weekly board: -
Full board: -

○ Boy ● Girl ○ Co-ed
● Day ○ Week ○ Board

Thorpe House is situated in ten acres of woodland and gardens. The academic courses lead to GCSE examinations. A second foreign language, Spanish, is being introduced in September 1992. The girls follow courses in dance, speech and drama. They also participate in a wide range of sports. Thorpe House has a covered, heated swimming pool, a sports hall and a gymnasium. There is an orchestra and three choirs.

Town Close House Preparatory School

Address: 14 Ipswich Road, Norwich, Norfolk NR2 2LR

Telephone: 0603 620180

Head: Mr S Higginson

Age range: 3-13
No. of pupils: 330
Scholarships:
Religion: Church of England

Fees per term
Day: £315-£1326
Weekly board: -£1925
Full board: -

Co-ed / Day / Week

A successful and developing school set in beautiful grounds conveniently near the city centre, Town Close enjoys a considerable reputation both academically and in sport. The school is in the process of becoming co-educational with girls now at all levels of the pre-preparatory department. Good facilities are being added to and pupils are prepared for a comprehensive range of independent schools.

Wood Dene School

Address: Aylmerton Hall, Aylmerton, Norwich, Norfolk NR11 8QA
Telephone: 0263 75224

Head: Mrs D M Taylor

Age range: 4-16
No. of pupils: 120
Scholarships:
Religion:

Fees per term
Day: -
Weekly board: -
Full board: -

Boy / Girl / Day

For further information and a prospectus, please contact the school. Boys 4-8.

NORTHAMPTONSHIRE

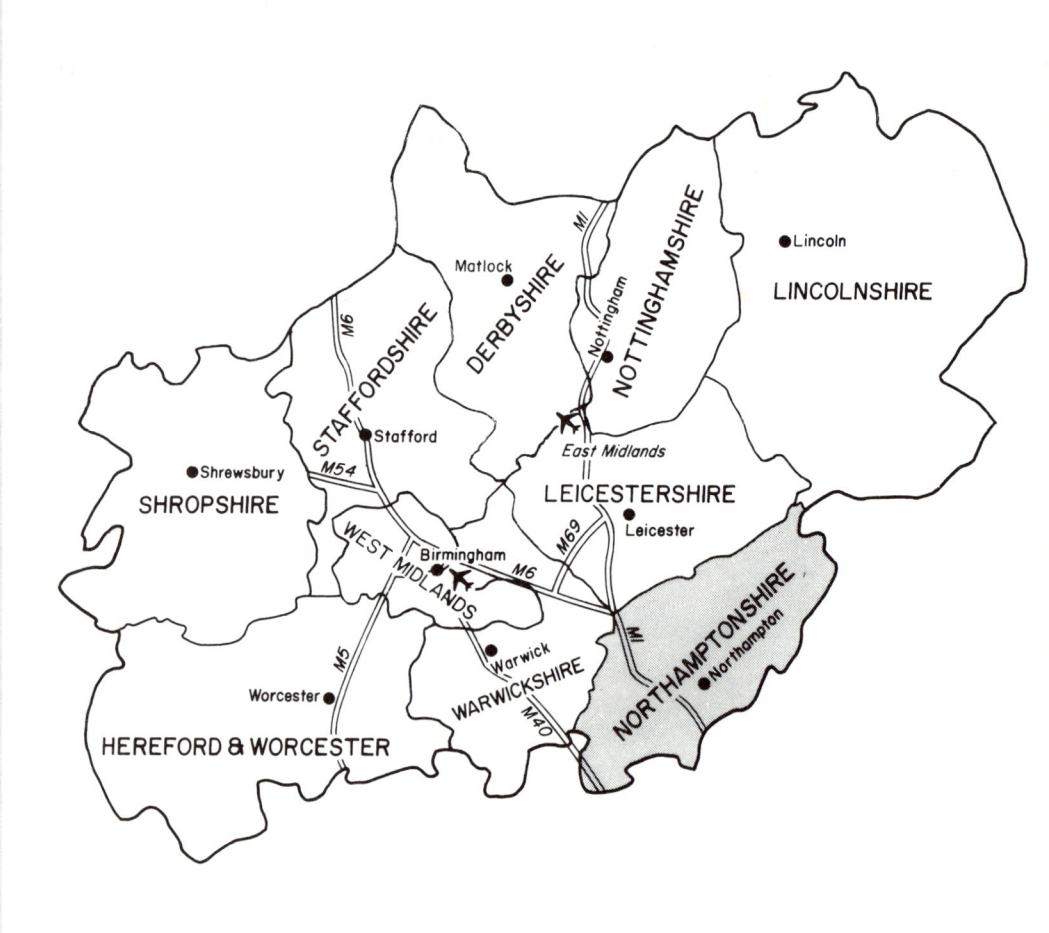

Beachborough

Address: Westbury, Brackley, Northamptonshire NN13 5LB

Telephone: 0280 700071

Head: Mr A J L Boardman

Age range: 3-13
No. of pupils: 190
Scholarships:
Religion: Christian

Fees per term
Day: £1045-£1850
Weekly board: £2465-
Full board: £2465-

Boy / Girl / Co-ed
Day / Week / Board

Beachborough is a co-educational boarding and day school of 200 boys and girls from 3 to 13. Set in a beautiful manor house with 25 acres, it provides a structured family atmosphere within which the children can develop. Self discipline and care for others are stressed. A full curriculum balances academic excellence with a strong emphasis on music, art and sport.

Falcon Manor School

Address: Greens Norton, Towcester, Northamptonshire NN12 8BN

Telephone: 0327 50544

Head: Mr E M Burr

Age range: 9-18
No. of pupils: 130
Scholarships: Yes
Religion: Non-denominational

Fees per term
Day: -£1100
Weekly board: -£2050
Full board: -£2200

Boy / Girl / Co-ed
Day / Week / Board

The aim of Falcon Manor is to provide a small school with a family atmosphere for the boy or girl who would be lost in a larger school. The school sets out to give a sound all-round education, and children are encouraged to realise that at Falcon Manor they are expected to work to achieve their full potential, and to learn to become responsible adults.

Great Houghton Preparatory School

Address: Great Houghton Hall, Northampton, Northamptonshire NN4 0AG

Telephone: 0604 761907

Head: Mr M T E Street

Age range: 4-13
No. of pupils: 260
Scholarships: Yes
Religion: Non-denominational

Fees per term
Day: £720-£1475
Weekly board: -
Full board: -

Boy / Girl / Co-ed
Day / Week / Board

For further information and a prospectus, please contact the school.

Laxton Junior School

Address: North Street, Oundle, Northamptonshire PE8 4AL

Telephone: 0832 273673

Head: Miss S C A Thomas

Age range: 4-11
No. of pupils: 140
Scholarships: Yes
Religion: Church of England

Fees per term
Day: -£855
Weekly board: -
Full board: -

Boy / Girl / Co-ed
Day / Week / Board

For further information and a prospectus, please contact the school.

Laxton School *

Address: North Street, Oundle, Northamptonshire

Telephone: 0832 273569

Head: Mr R I Briggs

Age range: 11-18
No. of pupils: 187
Scholarships: Yes
Religion: Church of England

Fees per term
Day: £1440-
Weekly board: -
Full board: -

○ ○ ● Boy Girl Co-ed
● ○ ○ Day Week Board

Laxton School is linked academically and for sport with Oundle School. There are specialised classroom blocks, libraries, indoor heated swimming pool, sports hall and IT centre. Major school sports are rugby, soccer, hockey, cricket, rowing plus a wide range of minor sports.

Maidwell Hall

Address: Northampton, Northamptonshire NN6 9JG

Telephone: 060 128 234

Head: Mr J H Paul

Age range: 8-13
No. of pupils: 75
Scholarships: Yes
Religion: Church of England

Fees per term
Day: £1795-
Weekly board: -
Full board: £2775-

● ○ ○ Boy Girl Co-ed
● ○ ● Day Week Board

Maidwell Hall is a boys' preparatory school in the rural Midlands which prepares boys for the leading public schools. Small classes ensure individual attention and good academic results. Squash, golf, riding, sailing, climbing, fishing and archery are amongst activities offered to boys. Special emphasis is laid on the teaching of art, music, drama and computer studies.

Northampton High School *

Address: Newport Pagnell Road, Hardinstone, Northamptonshire NN4 0UU
Telephone: 0604 765765

Head: Mrs L A Mayne BSC

Age range: 3-18
No. of pupils: 800
Scholarships: Yes
Religion: Anglican

Fees per term
Day: £565-£1230
Weekly board: -
Full board: -

○ ● ○ Boy Girl Co-ed
● ○ ○ Day Week Board

For further information and a prospectus, please contact the school.

Oundle School

Address: New Street, Oundle, Northamptonshire PE8 4EN

Telephone: 0832 273536

Head: Mr D B McMurray MA

Age range: 11-18
No. of pupils: 800
Scholarships: Yes
Religion: Non-denominational

Fees per term
Day: -
Weekly board: -
Full board: -£3890

● ● ○ Boy Girl Co-ed
○ ○ ● Day Week Board

The school's intention is to create at Oundle an environment in which boys and girls can fulfil their individual talents and respect one another as equals. In common with most school curricular, the Oundle curriculum is complex but flexible. Boys 11-18, girls 13-18.

Our Lady's Convent School

Address: Hall Lane, Kettering, Northamptonshire NN15 7LJ

Telephone: 0536 513882

Head: Mrs L Burgess

Age range: 2-11
No. of pupils: 180
Scholarships:
Religion: Catholic

Fees per term
Day: £325-£610
Weekly board: -
Full board: -

○ ○ ● Boy Girl Co-ed
● ○ ○ Day Week Board

A friendly and happy school where the education is firmly based on Christian teaching and high standards of behaviour are expected. National Curriculum requirements, including French, are met with a combination of traditional and modern methods of teaching resulting in excellent academic success. Visitors are warmly welcomed.

Potterspury Lodge School

Address: Towchester, Northamptonshire NN12 7LL

Telephone: 0980 542912

Head: Miss G Lietz

Age range: 8-16
No. of pupils: 49
Scholarships:
Religion: Non-denominational

Fees per term
Day: -
Weekly board: -
Full board: -

● ○ ○ Boy Girl Co-ed
● ● ● Day Week Board

For further information and a prospectus, please contact the school.

Quinton House School

Address: Upton Hall, Upton, Northampton, Northamptonshire NN5 6UX

Telephone: 0604 752050

Head: Mr G H Griffiths

Age range: 3-18
No. of pupils: 320
Scholarships:
Religion: Non-denominational

Fees per term
Day: £610-£1040
Weekly board: -
Full board: -

○ ○ ● Boy Girl Co-ed
● ○ ○ Day Week Board

Quinton House, beautifully situated on the edge of Northampton, has an excellent reputation as a caring school with academic standards and very pleasing results at GCSE level. The newly established sixth form offers A Level courses in a full range of subjects and the opportunity to develop confidence and responsibility.

Spratton Hall School

Address: Spratton, Northampton, Northamptonshire NN6 8HP

Telephone: 0604 847292

Head: Mr A P Bickley BA DipEd

Age range: 4-13
No. of pupils: 327
Scholarships:
Religion: Non-denominational

Fees per term
Day: £896-£1335
Weekly board: -
Full board: -

○ ○ ● Boy Girl Co-ed
● ○ ○ Day Week Board

For further information and a prospectus, please contact the school.

St Matthews Preparatory School

Address: 100 Park Avenue North, Northampton, Northamptonshire NN3 2JB
Telephone:

Age range: 3-7
No. of pupils:
Scholarships:
Religion:

Fees per term
Day: -
Weekly board: -
Full board: -

Boy ○ Girl ○ Co-ed ●
Day ● Week ○ Board ○

Head:

For further information and a prospectus, please contact the school.

St Peter's Independent School

Address: Lingswood Park, Northampton, Northamptonshire NN3 4TA
Telephone:

Age range: 8-18
No. of pupils:
Scholarships:
Religion: Christian

Fees per term
Day: -
Weekly board: -
Full board: -

Boy ○ Girl ○ Co-ed ●
Day ● Week ○ Board ○

Head:

For further information and a prospectus, please contact the school.

St Peter's School

Address: 52 Headlands, Kettering, Northamptonshire NN15 6DJ
Telephone: 0536 512066

Age range: 3-16
No. of pupils: 268
Scholarships:
Religion:

Fees per term
Day: -
Weekly board: -
Full board: -

Boy ● Girl ● Co-ed ○
Day ● Week ○ Board ○

Head: Mrs B Blakeley

For further information and a prospectus, please contact the school. Boys 3-11, girls 3-16.

Wellingborough School ✻

Address: Wellingborough, Northamptonshire NN8 2BX
Telephone: 0933 222427

Age range: 4-18
No. of pupils: 800
Scholarships: Yes
Religion: Church of England

Fees per term
Day: £1475-£1595
Weekly board: £2500-£2655
Full board: £2500-£2655

Boy ○ Girl ○ Co-ed ●
Day ● Week ● Board ●

Head: Mr G Garrett

Wellingborough School has its 400th anniversary in 1995: senior school ages 13-18, junior school 8-13 and pre-preparatory 4-8. Facilities for all subjects, academic and practical, and for drama, music, sport are excellent. There are 40 acres of first class playing fields. The sixth form numbers 160 most of whom go to university.

Weston Favell School

Address: 473 Wellingborough Road, Northampton, Northamptonshire NN3 3HN
Telephone: 0604 712098

Age range: 4-8
No. of pupils: 80
Scholarships:
Religion:

Fees per term
Day: -
Weekly board: -
Full board: -

Boy ○ Girl ○ Co-ed ●
Day ● Week ○ Board ○

Head: Mrs J Badenoch

For further information and a prospectus, please contact the school.

Winchester House School

Address: 12 Manor Road, Brackley, Northamptonshire NN13 5AZ
Telephone: 0280 702483

Age range: 8-14
No. of pupils: 182
Scholarships:
Religion:

Fees per term
Day: -
Weekly board: -
Full board: -

Boy ○ Girl ○ Co-ed ●
Day ● Week ○ Board ●

Head: Mr D R Speight

For further information and a prospectus, please contact the school.

NORTHUMBERLAND

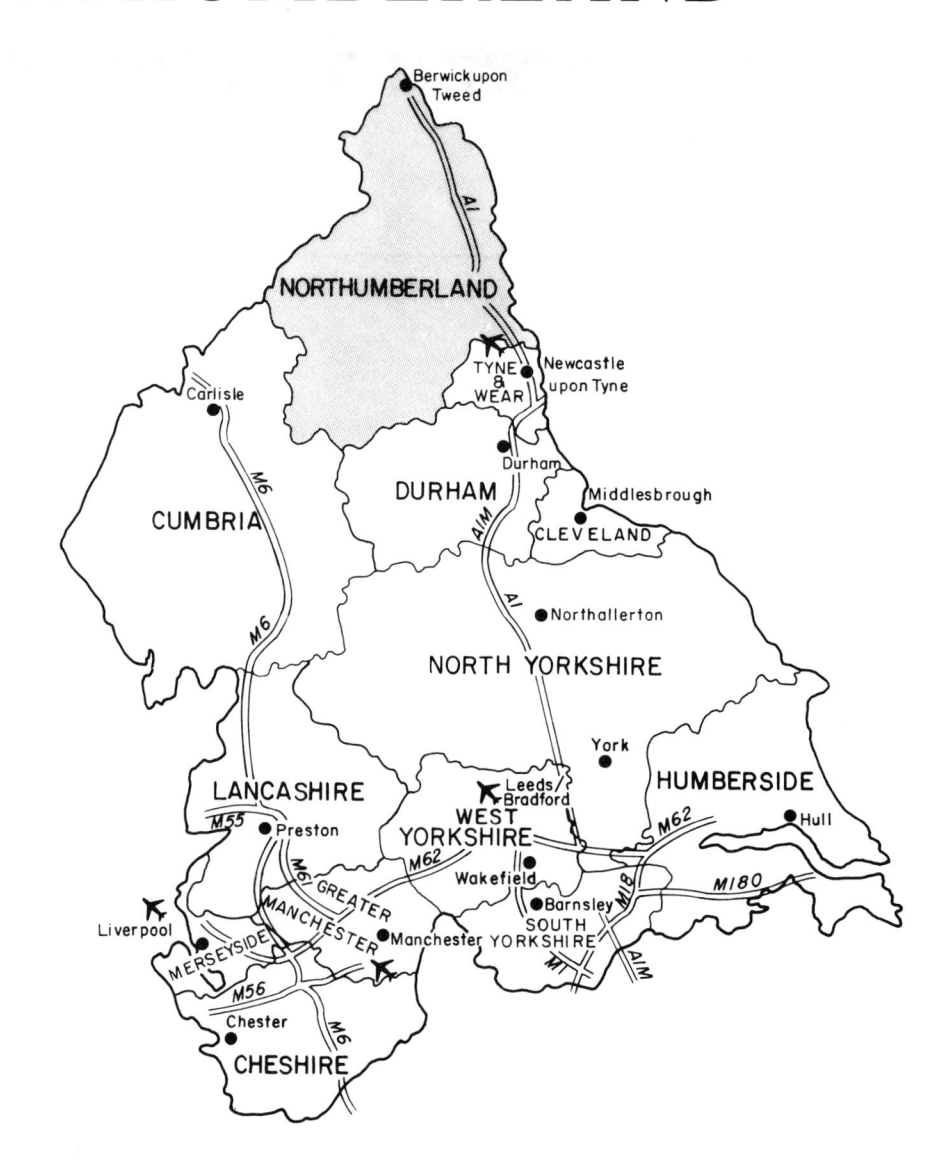

Croft House School

Address: Leazes Lane,
Hexham, Northumberland
NE46 3BB
Telephone: 0434 602082

Head: Mrs J Dudley

Age range: 3-11
No. of pupils: 134
Scholarships:
Religion: Non-denominational

Fees per term
Day: £330-£975
Weekly board: -
Full board: -

○ ○ ● Boy Girl Co-ed
● ○ ○ Day Week Board

For further information and a prospectus, please contact the school. Discount to following children.

Longridge Towers School

Address: Berwick upon
Tweed, Northumberland
TD15 2XH
Telephone: 0289 307584

Head: Dr M J Barron

Age range: 4-18
No. of pupils: 270
Scholarships: Yes
Religion: Non-denominational

Fees per term
Day: £730-£1185
Weekly board: -
Full board: £2060-£2240

○ ○ ● Boy Girl Co-ed
● ○ ● Day Week Board

For further information and a prospectus, please contact the school.

Mowden Hall School

Address: Newton, Stocksfield,
Northumberland NE43 7TP

Telephone: 0661 842147

Head: Mr A P Lewis

Age range: 8-13
No. of pupils: 142
Scholarships:
Religion: Church of England

Fees per term
Day: £1550-
Weekly board: -
Full board: £2300-

○ ○ ● Boy Girl Co-ed
● ○ ● Day Week Board

For further information and a prospectus, please contact the school.

Nunnykirk Hall School †

Address: Netherwitton,
Morpeth, Northumberland
NE61 4PB
Telephone: 067072 685

Head: Mr P R A Booker

Age range: 9-16
No. of pupils: 40
Scholarships:
Religion: Non-denominational

Fees per term
Day: -
Weekly board: -
Full board: -

○ ○ ○ Boy Girl Co-ed
● ○ ● Day Week Board

For fees, further information and a prospectus, please contact the school.

Our Lady's Convent High School

Address: Spring Gardens,
South Road, Alnwick,
Northumberland NE66 1LU
Telephone: 0665 602739

Age range: 4-18
No. of pupils: 160
Scholarships: Yes
Religion: Roman Catholic

Fees per term
Day: £493-£740
Weekly board: -
Full board: -

Boy ● Girl ● Co-ed ○
Day ● Week ○ Board ○

Head: Sister M Brigid

A caring day-school run on Christian principles by the Sisters of Mercy, assisted by highly qualified and experienced lay staff. The school will now provide education for boys, 4-8 years, as well as girls. Pupils are successfully presented for GCSE, Scottish Higher, AS, A level and Oxford Entrance examinations. Music and drama students are entered for LAMDA and Associated Board examinations.

NOTTINGHAMSHIRE

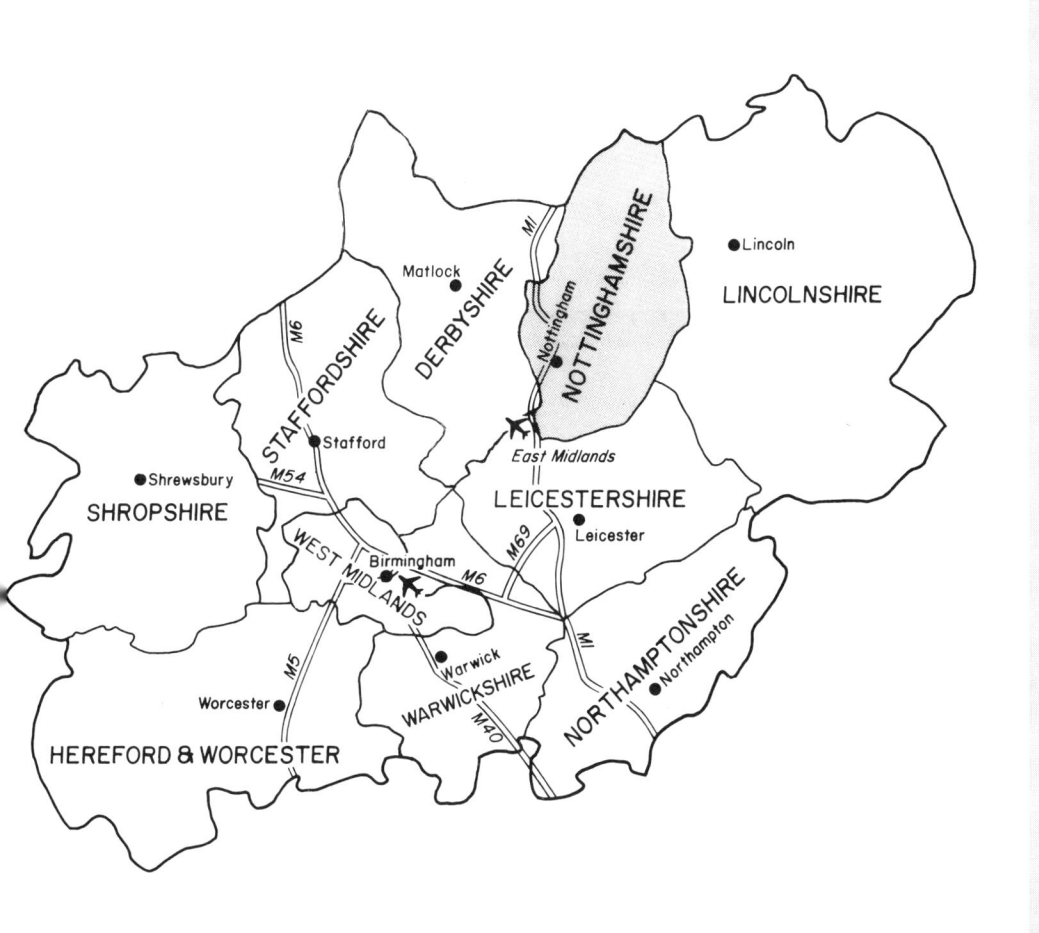

Bramcote School

Address: Gamston, Retford, Nottinghamshire DN22 0QQ

Telephone: 0777 83636

Head: Mr D H Fuller

Age range: 2-13
No. of pupils: 140
Scholarships: Yes
Religion: Non-denominational

Fees per term
Day: £375-£1560
Weekly board: £2054-£2054
Full board: £2054-£2054

Boy ○ Girl ○ Co-ed ●
Day ● Week ● Board ●

A good all-round education and the opportunity for each child to realise their potential, in and out of the classroom. A caring, family atmosphere with a well-qualified and dedicated staff. There is close communication between school and home, to give children the best possible chance of success. The school is set in 20 acres of its own grounds in the pleasant village of Gamston near the A1.

Broadgate School

Address: 1 Western Terrace, The Park, Nottingham, Nottinghamshire NG7 1AF
Telephone: 0602 474275

Head: Mr T Osgerby

Age range: 4-16
No. of pupils: 160
Scholarships:
Religion: Non-denominational

Fees per term
Day: £600-£950
Weekly board: -
Full board: -

Boy ○ Girl ○ Co-ed ●
Day ● Week ○ Board ○

Broadgate School (founded 1900) is a small, co-educational day school which stresses traditional values within a caring structure. Academic results cover a full range of GCSE subjects and have been of good standard.

Cotswold House School

Address: 19 Thackeray's Lane, Woodthorpe, Nottinghamshire NG5 4HT
Telephone: 0602 604818

Head: Miss E Gamble

Age range: 3-11
No. of pupils: 42
Scholarships:
Religion: Non-denominational

Fees per term
Day: £320-£390
Weekly board: -
Full board: -

Boy ○ Girl ○ Co-ed ●
Day ● Week ○ Board ○

Cotswold House School follows traditional teaching methods to give all children a good grounding in the basic subjects, homework is set and parents are asked to check their child's work. Frequent visits are arranged to places of interest and museums. The school encourages children to support various charities by holding collections.

Dagfa House School

Address: Broadgate, Beeston, Nottinghamshire NG9 2FU
Telephone: 0602 254100

Head: Mr A Oatway

Age range: 2-16
No. of pupils: 260
Scholarships: Yes
Religion: Non-denominational

Fees per term
Day: £370-£915
Weekly board: -
Full board: -

Boy ○ Girl ○ Co-ed ●
Day ● Week ○ Board ○

Dagfa House School is situated in pleasant wooded grounds on the western edge of University Park, easily accessible from all areas of city and county. Small classes are taught by caring and dedicated staff, creating a purposeful learning environment where individual talents may flourish. Admission is usually at 2 or 4, or by interview and examination at 11.

NOTTINGHAMSHIRE 389

Edgehill School

Address: Edingley, Newark, Nottinghamshire

Telephone: 0623 882936

Head: Mrs B Rimmer

Age range: 2-11
No. of pupils: 80
Scholarships:
Religion: Christian

Fees per term
Day: -
Weekly board: -
Full board: -

○ Boy ○ Girl ● Co-ed
● Day ○ Week ○ Board

Edgehill School aims to create a happy stimulating environment carefully structured to meet the physical, social, emotional and intellectual needs of each individual. High standards of effort and achievement are expected throughout all aspects of the School's broad curriculum. Small classes of twelve children ensure that each child reaches his or her full potential.

Greenholme School

Address: 392 Derby Road, Nottingham, Nottinghamshire NG7 2DX
Telephone: 0602 787329

Head: Miss P M Breen

Age range: 3-11
No. of pupils: 207
Scholarships:
Religion: Non-denominational

Fees per term
Day: £580-£955
Weekly board: -
Full board: -

○ Boy ○ Girl ● Co-ed
● Day ○ Week ○ Board

Entry is at any age from 3-11 by interview and informal test. Curriculum: The usual Common Entrance subjects are taught plus computer studies, CDT, drama, PE and games, dance and science. Class sizes are small with remedial help for pupils where necessary.

Grosvenor House School

Address: Edwalton Grange, 218 Melton Road, Edwalton, Nottinghamshire NG12 4BS
Telephone: 0602 231184

Heads: Mr R J D Oldershaw, Mr C G J Oldershaw

Age range: 4-13
No. of pupils: 176
Scholarships: Yes
Religion: Non-denominational

Fees per term
Day: £500-£771
Weekly board: -
Full board: -

○ Boy ○ Girl ● Co-ed
● Day ○ Week ○ Board

This family-run preparatory school was founded in 1876 and moved to its present site in 1945. It is situated in a pleasant residential area of Nottingham, south of the river on the A606 (Meton Mowbray Road). The school has some 176 pupils between the ages of 4+ and 13+, about one third of whom are girls. Entrance at 6+ by examination.

Hazel Hurst Preparatory School

Address: 400 Westdale Lane, Mapperley, Nottinghamshire NG3 6DG
Telephone: 0602 606759

Head: Mrs E A Murray

Age range: 3-8
No. of pupils: 72
Scholarships:
Religion: Non-denominational

Fees per term
Day: £560-£630
Weekly board: -
Full board: -

○ Boy ○ Girl ● Co-ed
● Day ○ Week ○ Board

For further information and a prospectus, please contact the school.

Highfields School

Address: London Road, New Balderton, Newark, Nottinghamshire NG24 3AL
Telephone: 0636 704103

Head: Mr P F Smith

Age range: 2-11
No. of pupils: 200
Scholarships:
Religion: Church of England

Fees per term
Day: £660-
Weekly board: -
Full board: -

Boy ○ Girl ○ Co-ed ●
Day ● Week ○ Board ○

Highfields School combines traditional values with a full range of National Curriculum programmes of study. All children are encouraged to be creative and exhibit a delight in learning. There is music, including peripatetic lessons, drama and a wide range of sporting activities for all the pupils. Highfields has an excellent academic record preparing children for senior schools in various sectors. Acredited to ISAI and a member of ISIS.

Hollygirt School

Address: Elm Avenue, Nottingham, Nottinghamshire NG3 4GF
Telephone: 0602 580596

Head: Mrs M R Banks

Age range: 4-16
No. of pupils: 310
Scholarships:
Religion: Non-denominational

Fees per term
Day: £805-£1065
Weekly board: -
Full board: -

Boy ○ Girl ● Co-ed ○
Day ● Week ○ Board ○

Founded in 1877, Hollygirt School provides for 320 girls between the ages of 4-10 years. It occupies three spacious buildings on either side of a tree-lined avenue on the north-east side of the city, four minutes from the Victoria Centre. The school has an excellent academic record with emphasis on the needs and abilities of each individual girl.

Lammas School

Address: Lammas Road, Sutton-in-Ashfield, Nottinghamshire NG17 2AD
Telephone: 0623 516879

Head: Mr H Beldon

Age range: 4-16
No. of pupils: 130
Scholarships:
Religion: Non-denominational

Fees per term
Day: £500-£700
Weekly board: -
Full board: -

Boy ○ Girl ○ Co-ed ●
Day ● Week ○ Board ○

The school is situated 3 miles from Junction 28 of the M1 Motorway, within the delightful surroundings of St Mary's Church, Lammas Road, Sutton-in-Ashfield. The school has a well qualified and experienced staff, with the aim of developing the potential of all pupils, whether highly academic or less academically gifted. The school offers a wide range of sports, which includes football, cricket, netball, hockey, swimming and cross country.

Longacre Preparatory School

Address: 55 Long Acre, Bingham, Nottinghamshire
Telephone: 0949 839242

Head: Mrs G A Robinson

Age range: 4-7
No. of pupils: 14
Scholarships:
Religion:

Fees per term
Day: £1125-
Weekly board: -
Full board: -

Boy ○ Girl ○ Co-ed ●
Day ● Week ○ Board ○

Opening hours 8.00am - 6.00pm, 50 weeks of the year.

Lorne House School

Address: London Road, East Retford, Nottinghamshire DN22 7EB
Telephone: 0777 703434

Head: Mr A N Brownridge

Age range: 2-13
No. of pupils: 135
Scholarships:
Religion: Church of England

Fees per term
Day: £580-£900
Weekly board: -
Full board: -

Boy ○ Girl ○ Co-ed ●
Day ● Week ○ Board ○

For further information and a prospectus, please contact the school.

Mount Day Nursery and Preparatory School

Address: St Ann's Hill, Nottingham, Nottinghamshire NG3 4LA
Telephone: 0602 607439

Head: Mrs Mallen

Age range: 4-8
No. of pupils: 42
Scholarships:
Religion: Non-denominational

Fees per term
Day: -
Weekly board: -
Full board: -

Boy ○ Girl ○ Co-ed ●
Day ● Week ○ Board ○

For further information and a prospectus, please contact the school.

Mountford House School

Address: 373 Mansfield Road, Nottingham, Nottinghamshire NG5 2DA
Telephone: 0602 605676

Head: Miss B M Hartley

Age range: 3-11
No. of pupils: 120
Scholarships:
Religion: Church of England

Fees per term
Day: £490-£794
Weekly board: -
Full board: -

Boy ○ Girl ○ Co-ed ●
Day ● Week ○ Board ○

For further information and a prospectus, please contact the school.

Nottingham High School *

Address: Waverley Mount, Nottingham, Nottinghamshire NG7 4ED
Telephone: 0602 786056

Head: Dr D T Witcombe MA BLit (Oxon)

Age range: 11-18
No. of pupils: 850
Scholarships: Yes
Religion: Non-denominational

Fees per term
Day: £1320-£1380
Weekly board: -
Full board: -

Boy ● Girl ○ Co-ed ○
Day ● Week ○ Board ○

For further information and a prospectus, please contact the school.

Nottingham High School for Girls, GPDST *

Address: 9 Arboretum Street, Nottingham, Nottinghamshire NG1 4JB
Telephone: 0602 260173

Head: Mrs C Bowering

Age range: 4-18
No. of pupils: 1073
Scholarships: Yes
Religion:

Fees per term
Day: £808-£1052
Weekly board: -
Full board: -

Boy ○ Girl ● Co-ed ○
Day ● Week ○ Board ○

The school aims to promote high academic standards within the context of a broad curriculum and stimulate the intellectual and creative needs of pupils. We cater for intelligent girls from a wide variety of backgrounds and endeavour to provide a disciplined, but friendly, environment in which girls are encouraged to contribute fully in the life of school and community.

Orchard School

Address: South Leverton, Retford, Nottinghamshire DN22 0DJ
Telephone: 0427 880395

Principal: Mrs S Winstanley

Age range: 5-16
No. of pupils: 75
Scholarships:
Religion: Non-denominational

Fees per term
Day: £635-£870
Weekly board: -
Full board: -

Boy ○ Girl ○ Co-ed ●
Day ● Week ○ Board ○

For further information and a prospectus, please contact the school.

Orchard School (Nursery Department)

Address: Holly Road, Retford, Nottinghamshire DN22 6BE
Telephone: 0777 700486

Principal: Mrs S Winstanley

Age range: 2-5
No. of pupils: 50
Scholarships:
Religion: Non-denominational

Fees per term
Day: £420-£560
Weekly board: -
Full board: -

Boy ○ Girl ○ Co-ed ●
Day ● Week ○ Board ○

For further details and a prospectus, please contact the school.

PNEU School

Address: 13 Waverley Street, Nottingham, Nottinghamshire NG7 4DX
Telephone: 0602 783230

Head: Mrs R Wood

Age range: 3-11
No. of pupils: 130
Scholarships:
Religion:

Fees per term
Day: £775-£825
Weekly board: -
Full board: -

Boy ○ Girl ○ Co-ed ●
Day ● Week ○ Board ○

Aim - to provide a wide, rounded education bringing out the best of each child as an individual. To teach each child a love of learning for its own sake. Children are prepared for Common Entrance and other schools' entry tests. The school is an educational charitable trust administered by a board of governors.

NOTTINGHAMSHIRE 393

Ranby House

Address: Retford, Nottinghamshire DN22 8HX

Telephone: 0777 703138

Head: Mr D C Wansey

Age range: 3-13
No. of pupils: 250
Scholarships: Yes
Religion: Church of England

Fees per term
Day: £970-£1605
Weekly board: £2175-£2175
Full board: £2175-£2175

Boy ○ Girl ○ Co-ed ●
Day ● Week ● Board ●

Ranby is the preparatory school for Worksop College, and is a Woodard school. There are about 50 boarders. We have 50 acres of beautiful grounds. Excellent facilities and a very happy family atmosphere. The school is 800m from the A1.

Rodney School

Address: Kirklington, Newark, Nottinghamshire NH22 8NB

Telephone: 0636 813281

Head: Miss J G Thomas

Age range: 8-18
No. of pupils: 245
Scholarships:
Religion: Church of England

Fees per term
Day: £610-£760
Weekly board: £1420-£1485
Full board: £1420-£1485

Boy ○ Girl ○ Co-ed ●
Day ● Week ● Board ●

This high achieving and supportive family is small enough for each child to be 'known', with his/her competitive spirit unfettered. They have a surprising impact at National level in sport and the Performing Arts. More than twice as many gain 5 or more top grades at GCSE as the national average.

Salterford House

Address: Salterford Lane, Calverton, Nottinghamshire NG14 6NZ

Telephone: 0602 652127

Head: Mrs M Venables

Age range: 3-11
No. of pupils: 230
Scholarships:
Religion: Church of England

Fees per term
Day: £650-£750
Weekly board: -
Full board: -

Boy ○ Girl ○ Co-ed ●
Day ● Week ○ Board ○

Salterford House is situated in rural Nottingham, in a woodland setting and aims to provide a happy, family atmosphere with small classes, in order to equip children academically and socially to cope with the demands of any type of education which might follow.

Saville House School

Address: Church Street, Mansfield Woodhouse, Nottinghamshire NG19 8AH

Telephone: 0623 25068

Head: Mrs E Bradrury

Age range: 3-11
No. of pupils: 155
Scholarships:
Religion: Non-denominational

Fees per term
Day: £330-£340
Weekly board: -
Full board: -

Boy ○ Girl ○ Co-ed ●
Day ● Week ○ Board ○

For further information and a prospectus, please contact the school.

St Joseph's School

Address: 33 Derby Road, Nottingham, Nottinghamshire NG1 5AW
Telephone: 0602 418356

Head: Miss M McNamara

Age range: 2-11
No. of pupils: 220
Scholarships:
Religion: Roman Catholic

Fees per term
Day: £780-
Weekly board: -
Full board: -

Boy ○ Girl ○ Co-ed ●
Day ● Week ○ Board ○

A co-educational day school combining all that is best in both traditional and more current educational practice. It provides a happy and caring environment in which children are encouraged to develop their full potential both socially and academically.

Trent College *

Address: Long Eaton, Nottinghamshire NG10 4AD
Telephone: 0602 732737

Head: Mr J S Lee

Age range: 11-18
No. of pupils: 625
Scholarships:
Religion:

Fees per term
Day: -
Weekly board: -
Full board: -

Boy ● Girl ● Co-ed ○
Day ● Week ○ Board ●

For further information and a prospectus, please contact the college.

Welbeck College

Address: Worksop, Nottinghamshire S80 3LN
Telephone:

Head:

Age range: 16-19
No. of pupils:
Scholarships:
Religion:

Fees per term
Day: -
Weekly board: -
Full board: -

Boy ● Girl ○ Co-ed ○
Day ○ Week ○ Board ●

For further information and a prospectus, please contact the school.

Wellow House School

Address: Wellow, Newark, Nottinghamshire NG22 0EA
Telephone: 0623 861054

Head: Mr M L Jones

Age range: 3-13
No. of pupils: 165
Scholarships: Yes
Religion: Non-denominational

Fees per term
Day: £675-£1450
Weekly board: £1975-£1975
Full board: -

Boy ○ Girl ○ Co-ed ●
Day ● Week ● Board ○

Wellow House School is a co-educational weekly boarding and day preparatory school for children aged 3 to 13 plus. The friendly yet disciplined atmosphere of the school provides the children with an environment in which they can grow in confidence, develop their individual talents, achieve their academic potential and enjoy their childhood. Staff:pupil ratio is 1:9 and the average class size is 14.

West Bridgford School

Address: 61-63 Musters Road, West Bridgford, Nottingham, Nottinghamshire NG2 7PY
Telephone: 0602 812967

Head: Mr C W Redwood

Age range: 7-18
No. of pupils: 138
Scholarships: Yes
Religion: Christian

Fees per term
Day: £835-£935
Weekly board: -
Full board: -

● ○ ○
Boy Girl Co-ed

● ○ ○
Day Week Board

The only small, day boys' school in Nottingham. Situated in a pleasant suburb to the south of the city it lies on a main bus route from the centre of the city and railway station, close to Trent Bridge, where many country buses call. Average class size is 18, and each pupil is encouraged to utilize the very best of his talents.

Worksop College *

Address: Worksop, Nottinghamshire S80 3AP

Telephone: 0909 472286

Head: Mr R D V Knight

Age range: 13-18
No. of pupils: 380
Scholarships: Yes
Religion: Church of England

Fees per term
Day: £2015-
Weekly board: £2920-
Full board: £2920-

○ ○ ●
Boy Girl Co-ed

● ● ●
Day Week Board

Individuals are enabled to develop in an all round sense in a structured family school. There are excellent facilities for sport, drama, music, art and many other interests in the 310 acres of the college grounds, but, of course, it is the people who provide the right atmosphere for study and all round education.

OXFORDSHIRE

Abingdon School * p736

Address: Park Road, Abingdon, Oxfordshire OX14 1DE
Telephone: 0235 521563

Head: Mr St John Parker

Age range: 11-18
No. of pupils: 750
Scholarships: Yes
Religion: Church of England

Fees per term
Day: £1530-
Weekly board: £2883-
Full board: £2883-

Boy ● Girl ○ Co-ed ○
Day ● Week ● Board ●

Occupying a green site in market town near Oxford, strongly academic school with average ten GCSE passes per boy; broad sixth form studies leading to 85% university entrance. Fine music, arts, technology; many leisure activities, strong fixtures in rowing, rugby, cricket, hockey, other sports. Assisted places, very moderate fees. A school noted for its intellectual and cultural vitality, wide opportunities and friendly atmosphere.

Audley House School

Address: Chesterton, Bicester, Oxfordshire OX6 8UZ
Telephone: 0869 252474

Heads: Dr D G F Flynn, Mr J I M Black

Age range: 5-13
No. of pupils: 96
Scholarships:
Religion: None

Fees per term
Day: £750-£1492
Weekly board: -
Full board: -

Boy ○ Girl ○ Co-ed ●
Day ● Week ○ Board ○

Audley House is a small, friendly school where children are encouraged by much individual attention to do justice to their abilities. Most boys and girls like to stay on after prep. at least one evening in the week to pursue their special interests such as model-making, King Fu, drama or computing.

Bloxham School * p738

Address: Bloxham, Banbury, Oxfordshire OX15 4PE
Telephone: 0295 720222

Head: Mr D K Exham MA

Age range: 13-18
No. of pupils: 365
Scholarships: Yes
Religion: Church of England

Fees per term
Day: -£2540
Weekly board: -
Full board: -£3390

Boy ● Girl ○ Co-ed ○
Day ● Week ○ Board ●

Boarding school close to Oxford; easy acces to Heathrow. Excellent facilities for sporting and cultural activities; high standards of accommodation and pastoral care. Excellent academic results; traditional standards of discipline.

Bruern Abbey School

Address: Bruern, Oxford, Oxfordshire OX7 6PZ
Telephone: 0993 831831

Head: Mr J S Stover

Age range: 7-13
No. of pupils: 44
Scholarships: Yes
Religion: Non-denominational

Fees per term
Day: -£1755
Weekly board: -
Full board: -£2441

Boy ● Girl ○ Co-ed ○
Day ● Week ● Board ●

The pursuit of high academic standards, in preparation for Common Entrance and scholarships, is coupled with an early introduction to subjects such as art, history of music, politics, economics and social studies. A high teacher-to-pupil ratio reflects our emphasis on personal attention to each boy. A caring environment provides the basis for encouraging both individuality and responsibility.

Carmel College *

Address: Mongewell Park, Wallingford, Oxfordshire OX10 8BT
Telephone: 0491 37505

Age range: 11-18
No. of pupils: 333
Scholarships: Yes
Religion: Jewish

Fees per term
Day: £2400-
Weekly board: -
Full board: £3950-

○ ○ ● Boy Girl Co-ed
● ○ Day Week Board

Head: Mr P Skelker

The aim of the college is to educate each pupil in a wide range of secular and religious subjects and to involve them enthusiasticly in sporting and recreational activities, thus ensuring that each individual is able to achieve his or her maximum potential.

The Carrdus School

Address: Overthorpe Hall, Banbury, Oxfordshire OX17 2BS
Telephone: 0295 263733

Age range: 3-11
No. of pupils: 140
Scholarships:
Religion: Non-denominational

Fees per term
Day: £365-£1150
Weekly board: -
Full board: -

○ ○ ● Boy Girl Co-ed
● ○ ○ Day Week Board

Head: Miss S Carrdus BA

Overthorpe Hall is a large house with 11 acres of gardens and excellent sports facilities. It is a happy school, in which hard work, disciplined behaviour and a good standard of manners is both expected and achieved. We aim to produce confident children who reach their own highest standards both socially and academically. Boys 3-7, girls 3-11

Cherwell Tutors p731

Address: Greyfriars, Paradise Street, Oxford, Oxfordshire OX1 1LD
Telephone: 0865 242670

Age range: 15+
No. of pupils: 100
Scholarships: Yes
Religion:

Fees per term
Day: £600-£1800
Weekly board: -
Full board: £1300-£2500

○ ○ ● Boy Girl Co-ed
● ○ ● Day Week Board

Head: Mr P J Gordon

Cherwell Tutors, founded in 1973, is a small semi-residential tutorial establishment situated in the heart of Oxford, specialising in preparing boys and girls under close personal supervision for entrance into higher education. Usually, one hundred pupils join Cherwell each academic year to be prepared for GCSE, A Level and Oxbridge entrance examinations. Accommodation in Halls of Residence. All sports.

Chiltern House School

Address: 30 Queen's Road, Thame, Oxfordshire OX9 3NQ
Telephone: 0844 212932

Age range: 3-7
No. of pupils: 80
Scholarships:
Religion: Un-denominational

Fees per term
Day: £325-£570
Weekly board: -
Full board: -

○ ○ ● Boy Girl Co-ed
● ○ ○ Day Week Board

Head: Mrs J M Dodds

The school has a high academic record and seeks to provide a good standard of behaviour and manners, whilst achieving a happy, relaxed atmosphere created by well qualified and experienced staff. All aspects of the curriculum are studied in order to give an all round education.

OXFORDSHIRE 399

Christ Church Cathedral School

Address: 3 Brewer Street,
Oxford, Oxfordshire
OX1 1QW
Telephone: 0865 242561

Head: Mr A H Mottram

Age range: 4-13
No. of pupils: 130
Scholarships: Yes
Religion: Church of England

Fees per term
Day: £790-£1402
Weekly board: -
Full board: £965-£2139

● ○ ○
Boy Girl Co-ed
● ● ●
Day Week Board

Christ Church Cathedral School is a boarding and day preparatory school for about one hundred boys between the ages of seven and thirteen plus. In addition, there is a small pre-preparatory department of some twenty-five boys between the ages of four and seven. The school provides about forty bursaries for choristers of the choirs of Christchurch Cathedral, Exeter College and Worcester College.

Cokethorpe p693

Address: Witney, Oxfordshire
OX8 7PU
Telephone: 0993 703921

Head: Mr D G Crawford

Age range: 11-18
No. of pupils: 200
Scholarships: Yes
Religion: Anglo Catholic

Fees per term
Day: £1175-£2300
Weekly board: £2800-£3500
Full board: £2800-£3500

○ ○ ●
Boy Girl Co-ed
● ● ●
Day Week Board

Cokethorpe admits children of average to above average ability, providing day places for boys and girls, and full or weekly boarding places for boys only. Class sizes of 16 enable pupils to achieve their full potential with a well developed house and tutorial system providing both academic and pastoral support.

Cothill House

Address: Abingdon,
Oxfordshire OX13 6JL
Telephone: 0865 390800

Head: Mr A D Richardson

Age range: 7-13
No. of pupils: 220
Scholarships:
Religion: Church of England

Fees per term
Day: -£1870
Weekly board: -
Full board: -£2800

● ○ ○
Boy Girl Co-ed
● ○ ●
Day Week Board

Cothill House is a mostly boarding preparatory school. It aims to provide a friendly family atmosphere, yet one in which the boys learn the need for self discipline. The majority of pupils go on to Radley and Eton.

Cranford House School

Address: Moulsford,
Wallingford, Oxfordshire
OX10 9HT
Telephone: 0491 651218

Head: Mrs A B Gray

Age range: 3-16
No. of pupils: 250
Scholarships: Yes
Religion: Non-denominational

Fees per term
Day: £490-£1350
Weekly board: -
Full board: -

● ● ○
Boy Girl Co-ed
● ○ ○
Day Week Board

Cranford House, an independent day school for girls age 3-16 and boys age 3-8, is situated in the village of Moulsford on the A329 Wallingford to Reading road. School transport operates within a 20 mile radius. Cranford is a caring community which aims to strike a balance bewteen a traditional approach and the wider ranging demands of the National Curriculum.

Crescent School

Address: 306 Woodstock Road, Oxford, Oxfordshire OX2 7NL
Telephone: 0865 515183

Head: Mr N G Morris

Age range: 3-13
No. of pupils: 200
Scholarships:
Religion: Non-denominational

Fees per term
Day: £562-£1250
Weekly board: -
Full board: -

Boy ○ Girl ○ Co-ed ●
Day ● Week ○ Board ○

The Crescent School is a day school for boys and girls from 3-13. Teaching is provided in a structured, stimulating and happy environment where individual talents and abilities are encouraged and developed in small classes. Children follow a structured time-table covering a broad curriculum, however, particular attention is paid to work on the 'Three Rs'. Sports offered include football, hockey, cricket, tennis, swimming etc.

Dragon School

Address: Bardwell Road, Oxford, OX2 6SS
Telephone: 0865 311660

Head: Mr N P V Richardson

Age range: 7-13
No. of pupils: 650
Scholarships:
Religion: Church of England

Fees per term
Day: £1265-£1653
Weekly board: -
Full board: £2585-

Boy ○ Girl ○ Co-ed ●
Day ● Week ○ Board ●

Dragon School is situated on the northern edge of Oxford University with playing fields adjoining the River Cherwell. The school regularly wins 16-20 open awards and prepares pupils for entry to senior schools throughout the country. A wide range of sporting and extra-curricular activities includes lectures and debates, termly dramatic productions and two school orchestral concerts annually.

Ferndale School

Address: Faringdon, Oxfordshire SN7 7FE
Telephone: 0367 240618

Head: Mr R S Collinge

Age range: 4-12
No. of pupils: 140
Scholarships:
Religion: Non-denominational

Fees per term
Day: £650-£795
Weekly board: -
Full board: -

Boy ○ Girl ○ Co-ed ●
Day ● Week ○ Board ○

Ferndale offers a broad and enlightened curriculum, while retaining rigorous emphasis on the basic disciplines in language and number. High academic standards are achieved - with a history of outstanding results in a wide variety of entrance examinations to public school at 11+. This is achieved within a caring and disciplined environment where children are encouraged to develop their individual abilities.

Greycotes School

Address: 1 Bardwell Road, Oxford, Oxfordshire OX2 6SU
Telephone: 0865 515647

Head: Mrs S R Hayward

Age range: 3-11
No. of pupils:
Scholarships:
Religion:

Fees per term
Day: -
Weekly board: -
Full board: -

Boy ○ Girl ○ Co-ed ●
Day ● Week ○ Board ○

Fees on application. For further details and a prospectus, please contact the school.

Headington School * p694, p743

Address: Oxford, Oxfordshire OX3 7TD

Telephone: 0865 62711

Head: Miss E M Tucker

Age range: 4-18
No. of pupils: 720
Scholarships: Yes
Religion: Church of England

Fees per term
Day: £540-£1313
Weekly board: £2553-£2553
Full board: £2573-£2573

● Boy ● Girl ○ Co-ed
● Day ● Week ● Board

We offer a broad, balanced education in our junior and senior schools. Oxford attracts boarders from all over the world to join other boarders and day girls from nearby. Our results in public examinations, music and sport are excellent. We are known for thre caring, friendly atmosphere in the school. Boys 4-7 years.

Highlands School

Address: Peppard Common, Henly-on-Thames, Oxfordshire RG9 5JD
Telephone: 0491 628240

Head: Mrs C A Brewer

Age range: 3-11
No. of pupils: 90
Scholarships:
Religion: Anglican

Fees per term
Day: £425-£975
Weekly board: -
Full board: -

● Boy ● Girl ○ Co-ed
● Day ○ Week ○ Board

For further information and a prospectus, please contact the school. Boys 3-8, girls 3-11.

Josca's Preparatory School

Address: Frilford House, Frilford, Abingdon, Oxfordshire OX13 5NY
Telephone: 0865 391570

Head: Mr T Savin MA

Age range: 5-13
No. of pupils: 162
Scholarships: Yes
Religion: Church of England

Fees per term
Day: £920-£1375
Weekly board: -
Full board: -

● Boy ● Girl ○ Co-ed
● Day ○ Week ○ Board

The school was founded in 1956. In addition to preparing boys for Common Entrance and scholarship examinations to independent senior schools, the school offers a broad curriculum to cater for widely differing talents and abilities. Boys are encouraged to pursue hobbies through various clubs. Every summer there is a four day camp on land for older boys. Boys 5-13, girls 5-7.

Kingham Hill School p695

Address: Kingham, Chipping Norton, Oxfordshire OX7 6TH

Telephone: 0608 658999

Head: Mr M H Payne

Age range: 11-18
No. of pupils: 200
Scholarships: Yes
Religion: Church of England

Fees per term
Day: £1545-£1545
Weekly board: £2575-£2575
Full board: £2575-£2575

○ Boy ○ Girl ● Co-ed
● Day ● Week ● Board

Occupying a beautiful 60 acre site in the Cotswolds the school offers a complete range of GCSE and A Level subjects for both able and average ability pupils. Classes are small and facilities excellent, including a very successful dyslexia unit. School boarding houses create a family atmosphere. Kingham Hill is a Christian foundation with bursaries available in cases of need.

Magdalen College School *

Address: Oxford, Oxfordshire OX4 1DZ

Telephone: 0865 242191

Head: Mr P M Tinniswood

Age range: 11-18
No. of pupils: 500
Scholarships: Yes
Religion: Church of England

Fees per term
Day: £1400-
Weekly board: -
Full board: -

● Boy ○ Girl ○ Co-ed
● Day ○ Week ○ Board

Magdalen College School is an Ex-Direct Grant School (500 boys aged 11-18) providing a traditional academic education preparing boys for university. Set in the heart of Oxford, students gain from the proximity of the university city. A wide range of extra-curricular activities provides the opportunity for boys to excel in their chosen field.

The Manor Preparatory School

Address: Faringdon Road, Abingdon, Oxfordshire OX13 6LN

Telephone: 0235 523789

Head: Mrs J Hearnden

Age range: 3-11
No. of pupils: 360
Scholarships:
Religion: Church of England

Fees per term
Day: £474-£1133
Weekly board: -
Full board: -

● Boy ● Girl ○ Co-ed
● Day ○ Week ○ Board

Recently built architect designed classrooms centred round an 18th century house with spacious grounds provide children with excellent working facilities. Well-qualified staff aim to create a happy, stimulating but ordered environment in which to learn and pupils are encouraged to make the most of their potential. The school has a high academic record. Boys to 7+, girls to 11+.

Millbrook House School

Address: Milton, Abingdon, Oxfordshire OX14 4EL

Telephone: 0235 831237

Head: Mr H M Glazebrook

Age range: 9-14
No. of pupils: 42
Scholarships:
Religion: Non-denominational

Fees per term
Day: £2200-
Weekly board: -
Full board: £3200-

○ Boy ○ Girl ● Co-ed
● Day ○ Week ● Board

Specialised tuition for children who recieve help for dyslexia and other learning problems, or those that need that little extra help. High pupil teacher ratio 8:1. Emphasis on personal attention and confidence building. All major sports: cricket, soccer, rugby, tennis and swimming. Continuous success to all principal public schools and, more importantly, finding the right school for the individual.

Moulsford Preparatory School

Address: Moulsford, Wallingford, Oxfordshire OX10 9HR

Telephone: 0491 651438

Head: Mr D R Jarman BA MED FCP

Age range: 7-13
No. of pupils: 176
Scholarships:
Religion: Non-denominational

Fees per term
Day: -£1781
Weekly board: -£2253
Full board: -

● Boy ○ Girl ○ Co-ed
● Day ● Week ○ Board

Moulsford aims to provide each boy with the greatest possible individual attention and involve him in a happy, disciplined community; to enable him to achieve the highest academic standards of which he is capable; to encourage the habits of hard work and unselfishness and to develop a personality enriched by active leisure and imbued with the good manners that 'makyth man'.

New College School

Address: Savile Road, Oxford, Oxfordshire OX1 3UA

Telephone: 0865 243657

Head: Mr J Edmunds

Age range: 7-13
No. of pupils: 130
Scholarships: Yes
Religion: Church of England

Fees per term
Day: £1230-£1355
Weekly board: -
Full board: -

● Boy ○ Girl ○ Co-ed
● Day ○ Week ○ Board

A small city centre day preparatory school for boys with a strong academic and fine musical record; to complement our education of the choristers of New College, Oxford, strong creative arts curriculum a feature.

Our Lady's Convent Junior School

Address: St John's Road, Abingdon, Oxfordshire OX14 2EB

Telephone: 0235 23147

Head: Sister Jean Frances

Age range: 5-11
No. of pupils: 175
Scholarships:
Religion: Roman Catholic

Fees per term
Day: £775-£805
Weekly board: -
Full board: -

○ Boy ○ Girl ● Co-ed
● Day ○ Week ○ Board

The aim of the sisters and the staff is to provide pupils with a thorough religious and moral training together with an efficient and modern education. The children are encouraged to work hard and to develop their special aptitudes and skills. All pupils are prepared for Common Entrance examinations. The school has a swimming pool, good sports facilities and offers a variety of after school clubs for 8-11 year old pupils.

Our Lady's Convent Senior School

Address: Radley Road, Abingdon, Oxfordshire OX14 3PS

Telephone: 0235 524658

Head: Sister Monica Sheehy

Age range: 11-18
No. of pupils: 350
Scholarships: Yes
Religion: Roman Catholic

Fees per term
Day: -£1030
Weekly board: -
Full board: -

○ Boy ● Girl ○ Co-ed
● Day ○ Week ○ Board

For further information and a prospectus, please contact the school.

Oxford High School GPDST *

Address: Belbroughton Road, Oxford, Oxfordshire OX2 6XA

Telephone: 0865 59888

Head: Mrs J Townsend MA MSc

Age range: 9-18
No. of pupils: 650
Scholarships: Yes
Religion: Non-denominational

Fees per term
Day: £880-£1148
Weekly board: -
Full board: -

○ Boy ● Girl ○ Co-ed
● Day ○ Week ○ Board

Life at Oxford High School is never dull! Our aims are realised through energetic infectious enthusiasm resulting in academic excellence, sparkling choirs, orchestras and drama (sometimes in Greek), articulate public speakers, Young Enterprise, chess, bridge and games champions, personal involvement in charities and community service, and ultimately justifiably self-confident adults!

Radley College

Address: Abingdon, Oxfordhsire OX14 2HR

Telephone: 0235 520294

Head: Mr R M Morgan

Age range: 13-18
No. of pupils: 600
Scholarships: Yes
Religion: Church of England

Fees per term
Day: -
Weekly board: -
Full board: -£3675

● Boy ○ Girl ○ Co-ed
○ Day ○ Week ● Board

Radley is both traditional and radical. Its hallmark is warmth and generosity.

Rupert House School

Address: 90 Bell Street, Henley-on-Thames, Oxfordshire RG9 2BN

Telephone: 0491 574263

Head: Mrs S C Salvidant

Age range: 4-12
No. of pupils: 210
Scholarships:
Religion: Non-denominational

Fees per term
Day: £480-£1305
Weekly board: -
Full board: -

● Boy ● Girl ○ Co-ed
● Day ○ Week ○ Board

For further information and a prospectus, please contact the school. Boys 4-8, Girls 4-12.

Rye St Antony

Address: Pullen's Lane, Headington Hill, Oxford, Oxfordshire OX3 0BG

Telephone: 0865 62802

Head: Miss A M Jones

Age range: 8-18
No. of pupils: 400
Scholarships:
Religion: Roman Catholic

Fees per term
Day: £885-£1435
Weekly board: £2295-£2295
Full board: £2395-£2395

○ Boy ● Girl ○ Co-ed
● Day ● Week ● Board

The school aims to provide an environment in which the full potential of each girl can be achieved: girls are helped to understand their strengths and weaknesses; they are encouraged to accept challenges and to learn initiative and independence; and they have many opportunities to contribute to the decision-making and activities of the school community.

S Helen and S Katherine

Address: Abingdon, Oxfordshire OX14 1BE

Telephone: 0235 520173

Head: Miss Y Paterson

Age range: 11-18
No. of pupils: 520
Scholarships: Yes
Religion: Church of England

Fees per term
Day: -£1200
Weekly board: -£2300
Full board: -

○ Boy ○ Girl ● Co-ed
● Day ● Week ○ Board

Church of England academically selective day school (weekly boarding for 32 in sixth form) of 500 girls, with 140 in sixth form. Excellent facilities for academic subjects, drama, art, music and sport. The school combines the highest standards with excellence in all these areas. Entry at 10+, 11+ and 16+. Government assisted places, Governors' scholarships and bursaries available.

Shiplake College

Address: Henley-on-Thames, Oxfordshire RG9 4BW

Telephone: 0734 402455

Head: Mr N V Bevan

Age range: 13-18
No. of pupils: 330
Scholarships: Yes
Religion: Church of England

Fees per term
Day: £2270-
Weekly board: -
Full board: £3390-

● Boy ○ Girl ○ Co-ed
● Day ○ Week ● Board

Situated on the bank of the river two miles up stream of Henley-on-Thames. Close to London and the M3, M4 and M25 motorways and a half hour from Heathrow Airport. Teaching and recreational facilities are excellent with new classrooms, laboratories, workshops and art studio. Recently described in a national newspaper as 'a super confidence building establishment'.

Sibford School

Address: Sibford Ferris, Banbury, Oxfordshire OX15 5QL

Telephone: 0295 78441

Head: Mr J Dunston

Age range: 7-18
No. of pupils: 320
Scholarships: Yes
Religion: Quaker

Fees per term
Day: £875-£1439
Weekly board: £2000-£2826
Full board: £2000-£2826

○ Boy ○ Girl ● Co-ed
● Day ● Week ● Board

Founded 150 years ago, Sibford School is one of eight Quaker schools in England. Sibford draws on this heritage in its co-educational approach to education. Pupils learn to co-operate with others and compete against themselves, seeking high standards in all areas of life. Backed by excellent facilities, Sibford School offers a rich variety of artistic, musical, athletic and creative pursuits.

The Squirrel School

Address: 90 Woodstock Road, Oxford, Oxfordshire

Telephone: 0865 58279

Head: Mrs M Easton

Age range: 3-9
No. of pupils: 155
Scholarships:
Religion: Church of England

Fees per term
Day: £415-£805
Weekly board: -
Full board: -

○ Boy ○ Girl ● Co-ed
● Day ○ Week ○ Board

Situated in North Oxford, the school's aim is to provide a happy, friendly environment for each of its pupils, by specialising in small classes and individualised tuition. Music, art and sport are an important part of the curriculum. Each child is prepared fully for future schools and any entrance examination which may be required.

St Aldates College

Address: Rose Place, Oxford, Oxfordshire OX1 1SB

Telephone: 0865 240963

Head: Mrs J Manasseh

Age range: 16+
No. of pupils: 200
Scholarships:
Religion: Non-denominational

Fees per term
Day: £1100-£1529
Weekly board: -
Full board: -

○ Boy ○ Girl ● Co-ed
○ Day ○ Week ● Board

Situated in the heart of Oxford, St Aldates offers a comprehensive range of business, office and secretarial courses leading to NVQ qualifications. Facilities include two large combined training offices, an experience accommodation department and an extensive career guidance/placement service.

St Andrew's School

Address: Wallingford Street, Wantage, Oxfordshire OX12 8AZ
Telephone: 0235 72345

Age range: 3-11
No. of pupils: 103
Scholarships:
Religion: Non-denominational

Fees per term
Day: £173-£798
Weekly board: -
Full board: -

Boy ○ Girl ○ Co-ed ●
Day ● Week ○ Board ○

Heads: Mrs M Farley, Mrs M MacBeth

St Andrew's provides a caring atmosphere with high academic standards. The timetable has been revised to comply with the National Curriculum and includes French, science and computer studies. Music and drama also figure significantly. Childen are taught in classes of no more than 16 and there are full-time helpers in the lower forms. Lunch is cooked on the premises and is included in the fees.

St Clare's *p750*

Address: 139 Banbury Road, Oxford, Oxfordshire OX2 7AL
Telephone: 0865 52031

Age range: 16+
No. of pupils: 300
Scholarships: Yes
Religion: No affiliation

Fees per term
Day: £2167-£2267
Weekly board: -
Full board: £3532-£3632

Boy ○ Girl ○ Co-ed ●
Day ● Week ○ Board ●

Principal: Mrs M Suarland

St Clare's is an international college for students of sixth form age and above. Sixth form students (16-18 years) follow the broadly based International Baccalaureate programme, acceptable for university entry world-wide, or a pre-18 course. The atmosphere is informal and students take increasing responsibility for themselves. Almost all students proceed to higher education, assisted by a full time careers adviser.

St Edward's School

Address: Oxford, Oxfordshire OX2 7NN
Telephone: 0865 515241

Age range: 13-18
No. of pupils: 580
Scholarships: Yes
Religion: Church of England

Fees per term
Day: £2760-£2760
Weekly board: -
Full board: £3675-£3675

Boy ● Girl ● Co-ed ○
Day ● Week ○ Board ●

Head: Mr D Christie

Situated on a 90 acre site between town and country the school offers high academic standards combined with a friendly, caring atmosphere and strong traditions in music, drama, art and sport. There are eight boarding houses with a residence for sixth form boarding girls. Recent new facilities include the design centre, mathematics building and astroturf.

St Hugh's School

Address: Carswell Manor, Faringdon, Oxfordshire SN7 8PT
Telephone: 0367 87223

Age range: 4-13
No. of pupils: 275
Scholarships: Yes
Religion: Church of England

Fees per term
Day: £860-£1715
Weekly board: -
Full board: -£2365

Boy ○ Girl ○ Co-ed ●
Day ● Week ○ Board ●

Head: Mr D Cannon MA(Oxon)

For further information and a prospectus, please contact the school.

St John's Priory School

Address: St John's Road,
Banbury, Oxfordshire
OX16 8HX
Telephone: 0295 259607

Head: Mrs J M Walker

Age range: 3-11
No. of pupils: 70
Scholarships:
Religion: Non-Denominational

Fees per term
Day: £550-£610
Weekly board: -
Full board: -

Boy ○ | Girl ● | Co-ed ○
Day ● | Week ○ | Board ○

The Priory School provides a happy and productive environment for girls to excel in academic, musical and sporting activities. From the Nursery through to the Upper Fourths, girls are encouraged to be self-motivated and to achieve. The classes are relatively small and the girls receive much individual attention from dedicated and caring staff.

St Mary's School

Address: 13 St Andrew's Road,
Henley-on-Thames,
Oxfordshire RG9 1HS
Telephone:

Head:

Age range: Girls 3-11
No. of pupils: 110
Scholarships:
Religion:

Fees per term
Day: -
Weekly board: -
Full board: -

Boy ○ | Girl ○ | Co-ed ●
Day ○ | Week ○ | Board ○

For further information and a prospectus, please contact the school.

St Mary's School

Address: Wantage,
Oxfordshire OX12 8BZ

Telephone: 02357 3571

Head: Rev P Jones MA

Age range: 11-18
No. of pupils: 280
Scholarships: Yes
Religion: Church of England

Fees per term
Day: -
Weekly board: -
Full board: £3200-

Boy ○ | Girl ● | Co-ed ○
Day ○ | Week ○ | Board ●

Tutorial system; high pass rate in public examinations; wide range of A level subjects offered; careers guidance - all girls take ISCO Morrisby (vocational guidance) Tests; all girls go on to further education; many clubs and other recreational activities; most girls take the Duke of Edinburgh's Bronze Award, and several take the Gold Award. One sixth form and one junior scholarship are awarded annually.

Summer Fields School

Address: Banbury Road,
Oxford, Oxfordshire
OX2 7EN
Telephone: 0865 54433

Head: Mr N Talbot-Rice

Age range: 8-13
No. of pupils: 240
Scholarships:
Religion:

Fees per term
Day: -
Weekly board: -
Full board: -

Boy ● | Girl ○ | Co-ed ○
Day ● | Week ○ | Board ●

For further information and a prospectus, please contact the school.

Tudor Hall

Address: Wykham Park,
Banbury, Oxfordshire
OX16 9UR
Telephone: 0295 263434

Head: Miss M Godfrey

Age range: 11-18
No. of pupils: 250
Scholarships: Yes
Religion: Church of England

Fees per term
Day: £1870-
Weekly board: -
Full board: £2930-

Boy · Girl · Co-ed
Day · Week · Board

Tudor Hall is set in attractive surroundings near Junction 11 on the M40 half way between Oxford and Stratford-on-Avon. It offers a wide curriculum, high academic standards and a busy boarding life style.

Entry is at 11+, 12+ or 13+ Common Entrance. Girls live in age groups. The sixth form is large for the size of school and careers advice is good.

Wychwood School p696

Address: 74 Banbury Road,
Oxford, Oxfordshire
OX2 6JR
Telephone: 0865 57976

Head: Mrs M L Duffill

Age range: 11-18
No. of pupils: 160
Scholarships:
Religion: Church of England

Fees per term
Day: £1280-
Weekly board: £2090-
Full board: £2090-

Boy · Girl · Co-ed
Day · Week · Board

Wychwood School offers a wide education in a very understanding and, for senior members, mature atmosphere. The girls take an active part in the school council where they may put forward ideas of their own and state their opinions on matters raised. There is a natural form of discipline which, balanced between freedom and trust, is appreciated and not resented.

SHROPSHIRE

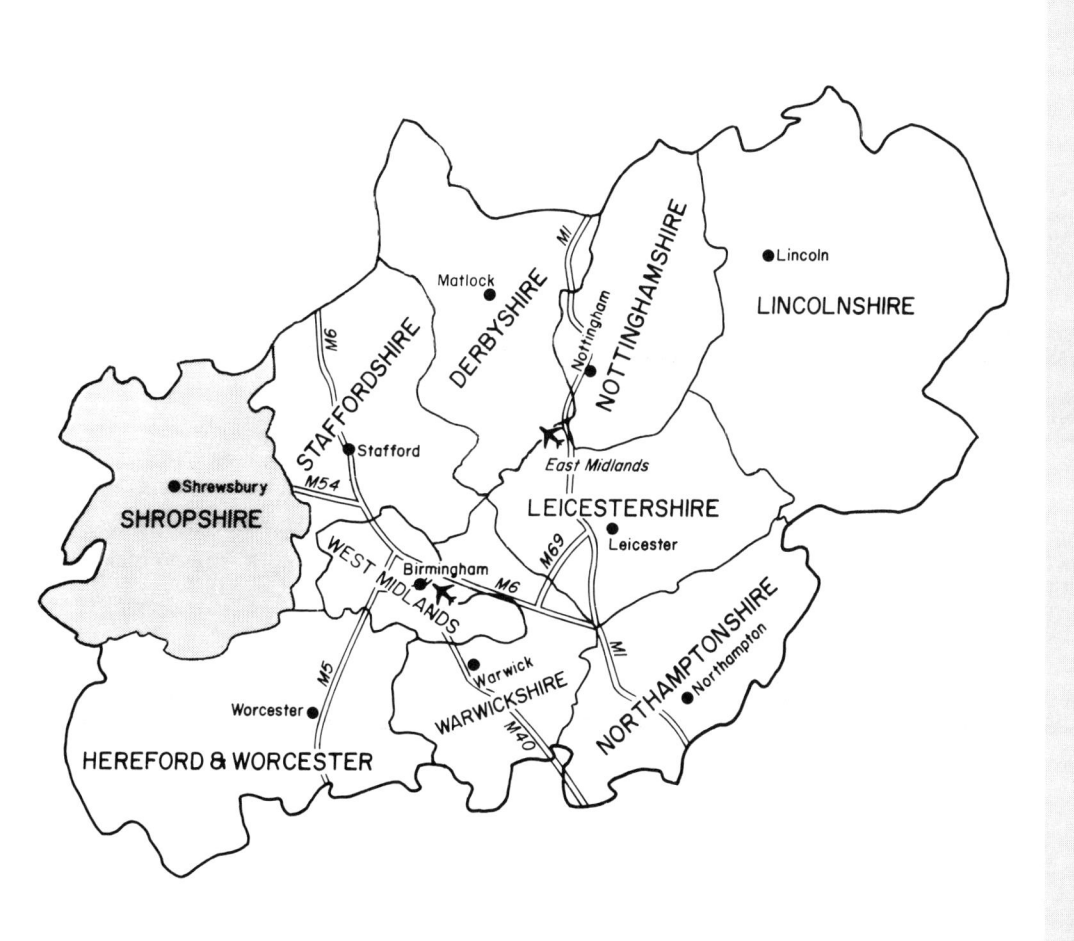

Acton Reynald

Address: Shrewsbury, Shropshire SY4 4DX

Telephone: 093928 365

Head: Mrs D Matthews

Age range: 7-18
No. of pupils: 100
Scholarships: Yes
Religion: Church of England

Fees per term
Day: £690-£850
Weekly board: £1740-£1915
Full board: £1750-£1925

Boy ○ Girl ● Co-ed ○
Day ● Week ● Board ●

A long-established school in historic mansion providing a sound education for girls in a happy family atmosphere. Classes are small and there is much emphasis on careful individual attention and encouragement. There are two well-equipped laboratories, a gymnasium/theatre, indoor heated swimming pool, art studio and pottery, tennis courts, music, modern visual and audio equipment and computers.

Adams Grammar School

Address: Newport, Shropshire TF10 7BD

Telephone: 0952 810698

Head Mr D J Taylor

Age range: 11-18
No. of pupils: 480
Scholarships:
Religion: Non-denominational

Fees per term
Day: -
Weekly board: £1200-
Full board: £1200-

Boy ● Girl ○ Co-ed ○
Day ○ Week ● Board ●

The school is situated in rural surroundings with easy access from Manchester, Birmingham and London. A modern curriculum is designed for 1990's, with strong accent on sporting activities. All staff and boys are enthusiastic and well motivated and the school has a friendly atmosphere with good discipline and manners. Entry at 11, 12, 13 or sixth form.

Adcote School

Address: Little Ness, Shrewsbury, Shropshire SY4 2JY

Telephone: 0939 260202

Head: Mrs S B Cecchet

Age range: 7-18
No. of pupils: 112
Scholarships:
Religion: Church of England

Fees per term
Day: £940-£1515
Weekly board: -
Full board: £1980-£2555

Boy ○ Girl ● Co-ed ○
Day ● Week ● Board ●

Subjects offered to GCSE and A level: English, history, mathematics, geography, religious studies, French, German, biology, chemistry, physics, music, dance, art/design, home economics, computer studies/information technology within core curriculum. Interview and assessment up to 14. At sixth form, interview, report and 5 GCSEs grade C or above. Wide range of extra-curricular activities.

Bedstone College

Address: Bucknell, Shropshire SY7 0BG

Telephone: 054 74 303

Head: M S Synonds

Age range: 8-18
No. of pupils: 207
Scholarships: Yes
Religion: Church of England

Fees per term
Day: £1174-£1644
Weekly board: £1788-£2665
Full board: £1788-£2665

Boy ○ Girl ○ Co-ed ●
Day ● Week ● Board ●

Bedstone College is a fully co-educational, independent boarding and day school covering the entire age range from eight to university entrance - small enough to have a strong family atmosphere, yet large enough to enjoy a full academic and extra-curricular life. Since its foundation in 1948, the college has built up a fine reputation for academic, sporting and cultural achievement.

SHROPSHIRE 411

Bellan House

Address: Church Street, Oswestry, Shropshire SY11 2ST
Telephone: 0691 653453

Head: Mrs L Durham

Age range: 2-9
No. of pupils: 175
Scholarships:
Religion: None

Fees per term
Day: £809-£970
Weekly board: -
Full board: -

○ ○ ● Boy Girl Co-ed
● ○ ○ Day Week Board

Bellan House was built in 1779. It became a school in 1900 and has subsequently become one of the largest pre-preparatory schools in Great Britain with children from two and a half to nine and a half years of age. In 1978 Bellan House School became the preparatory section of Oswestry School which was founded in 1407 and is the second oldest secular school in England. It prides itself on its high academic standards.

Castle House

Address: Chetwynd End, Newport, Shropshire TF10 7JE
Telephone: 0952 811035

Head: Mrs R E Davies

Age range: 3-11
No. of pupils: 130
Scholarships:
Religion:

Fees per term
Day: £370-£740
Weekly board: -
Full board: -

○ ○ ● Boy Girl Co-ed
● ○ ○ Day Week Board

A private day school for girls and boys aged 3 to 11. Teaching by qualified staff on traditional lines, giving sound introduction to formal education, in small classes with emphasis on deportment and good manners. Individual remedial teaching is available where needed, together with sports, music, gym, tennis, swimming and dance.

Concord College

Address: Acton Burnell Hall, Shrewsbury, Shropshire SY5 7PF
Telephone: 0694 731631

Head: Mr A L Morris

Age range: 14+
No. of pupils:
Scholarships:
Religion: Non-denominational

Fees per term
Day: -
Weekly board: -
Full board: -£3465

○ ○ ● Boy Girl Co-ed
○ ○ ● Day Week Board

Colleges' principal aim is to prepare students for entry to degree courses at universities or polytechnics. We consequently offer a range of GCE A level courses and preparatory GCSE courses. Concord is proud of its success in achieving this aim. There is a strong tradition of entry into the more prestigious unversities and college has particular strong links with the University of London.

Cotsbrook Community †

Address: Higford, Shifnal, Shropshire TF11 9ET
Telephone: 0952 87237

Head: Mr J Hughes

Age range: 11-16
No. of pupils: 12
Scholarships:
Religion: Non-denominational

Fees per term
Day: -
Weekly board: -
Full board: -

○ ○ ● Boy Girl Co-ed
○ ○ ● Day Week Board

Fees between £850 and £950 per week, further information and a prospectus available from the school.

Ellesmere College *

Address: Ellesmere,
Shropshire SY12 9AB

Telephone: 0691 622321

Head: Mr D R Du Croz

Age range: 10-18
No. of pupils: 380
Scholarships: Yes
Religion: Church of England

Fees per term
Day: £1400-£2200
Weekly board: -
Full board: -£3200

● Boy ● Girl ○ Co-ed
● Day ○ Week ● Board

Ellesmere College is a medium sized school on a rural campus. It is predominantly a boarding school for boys with girls in the sixth form. Major refurbishment of accommodation has provided the first class facilities for boarders. The education is mainstream academic with many opportunities for developing cultural, sporting and extra-curricular abilities and interests.

Kingsland Grange

Address: Old Roman Road,
Shrewsbury, Shropshire
SY3 9AH
Telephone: 0743 232132

Head: Mr M C James

Age range: 4-13
No. of pupils: 190
Scholarships: Yes
Religion: Non-denominational

Fees per term
Day: £590-£1120
Weekly board: £1390-
Full board: -

● Boy ○ Girl ○ Co-ed
● Day ● Week ○ Board

Set within extensive wooded grounds the school offers a wide variety of academic and extra-curricular activities to boys of all abilities. A happy, family atmosphere aids the maintenance of the highest standards in all aspects of school life. Many scholarships are gained to senior schools, 32 to Shrewsbury School in the past eight years. A traditional experienced school.

Kingsland Grange Junior School

Address: The Rocks, 17
Hereford Road, Shrewsbury,
Shropshire SY3 7QX
Telephone: 0743 353008

Head: Mrs J T Shaw

Age range: 4-7
No. of pupils: 37
Scholarships:
Religion: Church of England

Fees per term
Day: -£590
Weekly board: -
Full board: -

● Boy ○ Girl ○ Co-ed
● Day ○ Week ○ Board

For further details please contact the school - See also entry for Kingsland Grange School.

Moor Park School

Address: Ludlow, Shropshire
SY8 4EA

Telephone: 0584 872342

Head: Mr J R Badham MA

Age range: 3-13 and a
No. of pupils: 215
Scholarships: Yes
Religion: non-denominational

Fees per term
Day: £150-£1650
Weekly board: -
Full board: -£2280

○ Boy ○ Girl ● Co-ed
● Day ○ Week ● Board

Moor Park has a strong academic and sporting tradition. Set in a magnificent 85 acre estate the liberal, christian ethos of the school helps to produce confident children who respect authority and each other. The main house accommodates the boys, while the girls are boarding in the converted coach house. The curriculum is augmented by many activities.

SHROPSHIRE 413

Moreton Hall

Address: Weston Rhyn, Oswestry, Shropshire SY11 6EW
Telephone: 0691 773671

Head: Mr J Forster

Age range: 11-18
No. of pupils: 300
Scholarships: Yes
Religion: Church of England

Fees per term
Day: £2250-
Weekly board: -
Full board: £3250-

Boy ○ Girl ● Co-ed ○
Day ● Week ○ Board ●

Moreton Hall is a modern girls' boarding school in a beautiful setting, with outstanding accommodation and high academic standards. It aims to develop the potential of every girl to the full. Boarding houses are viewed as extended families and twinned with Shrewsbury School for cultural and social functions. We are less than an hour from Manchester Airport.

The Old Hall

Address: Wellington, Telford, Shropshire TF1 2DN
Telephone: 0952 223117

Head: Mr R J Ward MA

Age range: 3-13
No. of pupils: 320
Scholarships: Yes
Religion: Church of England

Fees per term
Day: £825-£1325
Weekly board: -£1705
Full board: -

Boy ○ Girl ○ Co-ed ●
Day ● Week ● Board ○

The buildings stand in 25 acres and include chapel, music and drama studio, science laboratory, design and technology suite, art and pottery department, a new sports and performing arts hall, a new indoor swimming pool and a large library. Care is given to the moral, social, physical and spiritual development of pupils as well as the academic.

Oswestry Junior School

Address: The Quarry, Upper Brook Street, Oswestry, Shropshire SY11 2TJ
Telephone: 0691 653209

Head: Mr J W Potter JP MAE

Age range: 8-13
No. of pupils: 167
Scholarships: Yes
Religion: Non-denominational

Fees per term
Day: £1472-£1607
Weekly board: -
Full board: £2557-£2697

Boy ○ Girl ○ Co-ed ●
Day ● Week ○ Board ●

In a happy, purposeful environment children are encouraged by an excellent staff to give of their best in work and games, in music, drama and clubs. Over fifty pupils have individual instrumental lessons. Emphasis is placed on good manners and courteous consideration for others. Over £5000 has been raised for charities on each of our recent sponsored walks. At 13+ nearly all boys and girls transfer to Oswestry School.

Oswestry School

Address: Bellan House, Church Street, Oswestry, Shropshire SY11 2ST
Telephone: 0691 653453

Head: Mrs S L Durham

Age range: 2-9
No. of pupils: 190
Scholarships:
Religion: Non-denominational

Fees per term
Day: £205-£970
Weekly board: -
Full board: -

Boy ○ Girl ○ Co-ed ●
Day ● Week ○ Board ○

Bellan House was built in 1779 and became a school in 1900. In 1978 Bellan House School became the preparatory section of Oswestry School which was founded in 1407 and is the second oldest secular school in England. It prides itself on its high academic standards and encourages children to become well mannered rounded members of the school. Recently it has become renown for the standard of its French.

Oswestry School

Address: Upper Brook Street, Oswestry, Shropshire SY11 2TL
Telephone: 0691 655711

Head: Mr J V Light

Age range: 13-18
No. of pupils: 300
Scholarships: Yes
Religion: Non-denominational

Fees per term
Day: £1472-£1607
Weekly board: -
Full board: £2557-£2697

Boy ○ Girl ○ Co-ed ●
Day ● Week ○ Board ●

Oswestry is a very old school, founded in 1407. Over the past twenty years or so, it has grown to its present ideal size. With 325 pupils in the senior school and 170 in the junior school, it is large enough to offer the full range of subjects and activities, but small enough for the headmasters to know each child personally, and to be able to take a direct interest in their progress.

Packwood Haugh School

Address: Ruyton-XI-Towns, Shrewsbury, Shropshire SY4 1HX
Telephone: 0939 260217

Head: Mr P J F Jordon

Age range: 7-13
No. of pupils: 246
Scholarships: Yes
Religion: Church of England

Fees per term
Day: £1835-
Weekly board: -
Full board: £2350-

Boy ○ Girl ○ Co-ed ●
Day ● Week ○ Board ●

Packwood Haugh stands in 65 acres of ground just north of Shrewsbury. Teaching staff number 30. The school prides itself on its high standards both on the academic side and on the games field and go on to all the major public schools. We offer a variety of outdoor activities and clubs and plans are going ahead to open a pre-preparatory school in September.

Prestfelde

Address: Shrewsbury, Shropshire SY2 6NZ
Telephone: 0743 356500

Head: Mr R W Trimby

Age range: 3-13
No. of pupils: 275
Scholarships: Yes
Religion: Church of England

Fees per term
Day: £350-£1460
Weekly board: -
Full board: -£1995

Boy ● Girl ○ Co-ed ○
Day ● Week ○ Board ●

A boys' preparatory school with a co-ed pre-preparatory department located on the outskirts of Shrewbury.

Queen's Park School †

Address: Oswestry, Shropshire SY11 2HZ
Telephone: 0691 652416

Director of Education: Mrs D Baur

Age range: 8-16
No. of pupils: 50
Scholarships:
Religion: Non-denominational

Fees per term
Day: £2365-£2450
Weekly board: £3050-£3200
Full board: £3230-£3390

Boy ○ Girl ○ Co-ed ●
Day ● Week ● Board ●

The school specialises in dyslexic children. For further information and a prospectus, please contact the school.

Shotton Hall School †

Address: Harmer Hill,
Shrewsbury, Shropshire
SY4 3DW
Telephone: 0939 290376

Head: Mr J W Parker

Age range: 10-18
No. of pupils: 32
Scholarships:
Religion: Non-denominational

Fees per term
Day: -
Weekly board: -
Full board: -

● Boy ○ Girl ○ Co-ed
○ Day ○ Week ● Board

Shotton Hall is a country house set in rural Shropshire which, over the years, has been adapted and extended to serve the needs of a developing residential community for thirty five emotionally disturbed boys. The rural environment and comparative isolation provides both a degree of sanctuary as well as enabling a concentration of effort within the community without city distractions. Details of fees on application.

Shrewsbury High School *

Address: 32 Town Walls,
Shrewsbury, Shropshire
SY1 1TN
Telephone: 0743 362872

Head: Miss S Gardner MA

Age range: 4-18
No. of pupils: 610
Scholarships: Yes
Religion: Non-denominational

Fees per term
Day: £880-£1148
Weekly board: -
Full board: -

○ Boy ● Girl ○ Co-ed
● Day ○ Week ○ Board

Girls have enjoyed a high quality academic education here for over 100 years. Shrewsbury High School is one of 26 schools of the nationally acclaimed Girls' Public Day School Trust which has an on-going commitment to the all-round education of young women. Girls are admitted to the junior department at 4+, 7+ and 9+. Senior department entry is at 11+ and 6th form.

Shrewsbury School

Address: The Schools,
Shrewsbury, Shropshire
SY3 7BA
Telephone: 0743 344537

Head: Mr F E Maidment

Age range: 13-18
No. of pupils: 670
Scholarships: Yes
Religion: Church of England

Fees per term
Day: £2380-
Weekly board: -
Full board: £3375-

● Boy ○ Girl ○ Co-ed
● Day ○ Week ● Board

Shrewsbury sets out to achieve its aims within the traditional structure of house communities and with a boys-only entry. It offers a combination of different elements - established educational virtues and new ideas, and distinctive geographical position looking both North and South and a unique site combining both town and country. It is both a national and a local school.

St Winefride's

Address: Belmont,
Shrewsbury, Shropshire
SY1 1LS
Telephone: 0743 369883

Head: Sr M Felicity

Age range: 4-11
No. of pupils: 120
Scholarships:
Religion: Roman Catholic

Fees per term
Day: £410-£425
Weekly board: -
Full board: -

○ Boy ○ Girl ● Co-ed
● Day ○ Week ○ Board

Founded 1868. The school has a long tradition of high academic standards. The enthusiastic pursuit of music and drama has always been a feature of the school, which is noted for its friendly and caring atmosphere. The ethos of St Winefride's is summed up in its motto 'Soli Dei'.

White House School

Address: Heath Road,
Whitchurch, Shropshire
SY13 1LE
Telephone: 0948 2730

Head: Mrs E Hall

Age range: 4-11
No. of pupils: 175
Scholarships:
Religion:

Fees per term
Day: £385-£385
Weekly board: -
Full board: -

Boy ○ Girl ○ Co-ed ●
Day ● Week ○ Board ○

Children from 4 to 11 are taught in a warm friendly atmosphere and all abilities are helped to acheive their full potential. Pupils are prepared for scholarship examinations. We have separate art, science laboratory and computer rooms and a gymnasium and assembly hall. High standard in music, art and French. Easy access from Cheshire, Shropshire and Clwyd.

Wrekin College *

Address: Wellington, Telford,
Shropshire TF1 3BG

Telephone: 0952 240131

Head: Mr P M Johnson

Age range: 13-18
No. of pupils: 330
Scholarships: Yes
Religion: Church of England

Fees per term
Day: £2350-
Weekly board: -
Full board: £3355-

Boy ○ Girl ○ Co-ed ●
Day ● Week ○ Board ●

Situated one mile from the M54, Wrekin College stand in over 100 acres. Facilities include sports hall, theatre, art school, business studies and economics block, swimming pool and extensive playing fields.

The VI form numbers 135 and there is also a strong emphasis on games, music, drama and other recreations to ensure the broad development of all pupils.

SOMERSET

Abbey School

Address: Magdalene, Glastonbury, Somerset BA6 9EJ
Telephone: 0458 832902

Head: Mrs K L Cookson

Age range: 3-8
No. of pupils: 170
Scholarships:
Religion: Non-denominational

Fees per term
Day: £590-£780
Weekly board: -
Full board: -

Boy ○ Girl ○ Co-ed ●
Day ● Week ○ Board ○

Abbey School, Millfield Preparatory School. Co-educational school for 3-8 year olds. Maximum class size 15. Abbey School children are encouraged to develop sound working habits in a happy, yet disciplined, environment. A thorough grounding in the core subjects and learning a wide variety of other skills form the basis of a structured programme.

All Hallows

Address: Cranmore Hall, East Cranmore, Shepton Mallet, Somerset BA4 4SF
Telephone: 0749 880227

Head: Mr P F J Ketterer

Age range: 4-14
No. of pupils: 276
Scholarships:
Religion: Roman Catholic

Fees per term
Day: £750-£1500
Weekly board: £2300-£2300
Full board: £2300-£2300

Boy ○ Girl ○ Co-ed ●
Day ● Week ● Board ●

A Catholic co-educational boarding and day school for the 4-14 age range. The timetable for each pupil is arranged individually to extend the academically gifted and to assist the slower learner. All normal common entrance subjects are taught plus religious education, art, music and gymnastics. Set in beautiful Somerset countryside, All Hallows pioneered Catholic boarding co-education for this age group.

Beehive School

Address: 68 Wellington Road, Taunton, Somerset TA1 5AP
Telephone: 0823 333638

Head: Mr J P Garret

Age range: 4-11
No. of pupils: 135
Scholarships:
Religion: Non-denominational

Fees per term
Day: £300-£305
Weekly board: -
Full board: -

Boy ○ Girl ○ Co-ed ●
Day ● Week ○ Board ○

For further information please contact the school.

Bruton School for Girls * p739

Address: Sunny Hill, Bruton, Somerset BA10 0NT
Telephone: 0749 812277

Head: Mrs J M Wade

Age range: 8-18
No. of pupils: 560
Scholarships: Yes
Religion: Non-denominational

Fees per term
Day: £896-£1077
Weekly board: £1720-£1989
Full board: £1720-£1989

Boy ○ Girl ● Co-ed ○
Day ● Week ● Board ●

A friendly school of 560 pupils of whom 250 board. With a strong academic tradition, we offer a balanced curriculum and lively after school activities in extensive specialist accommodation. Our upper sixth proceed to higher education or professional training in a variety of careers.

Chard School

Address: Fore Street, Chard, Somerset

Telephone: 0460 63234

Head: Mr C Organ

Age range: 3-11
No. of pupils: 115
Scholarships:
Religion: Church of England

Fees per term
Day: £600-£650
Weekly board: -
Full board: -

Boy ○ / Girl ○ / Co-ed ●
Day ● / Week ○ / Board ○

A small independent school originally founded in 1671. The school is housed in historic Grade I and II listed buildings. The pupils move at 11 to public, independent and grant maintained sectors.

Childscourt School †

Address: Lattiford House, Wincanton, Somerset BA9 8AH
Telephone: 0963 32213

Head: Mrs T Day

Age range: 9-17
No. of pupils: 45
Scholarships:
Religion:

Fees per term
Day: -
Weekly board: -
Full board: -

Boy ○ / Girl ○ / Co-ed ●
Day ○ / Week ○ / Board ●

Fees on application. For further information and a prospectus, please contact the school.

Chilton Cantelo School

Address: Chilton Cantelo, Yeovil, Somerset BA22 8BG
Telephone: 0935 850555

Principal: Mr D S von Zeffman LLB

Age range: 10-18
No. of pupils: 110
Scholarships:
Religion: Non-denominational

Fees per term
Day: £1080-£1280
Weekly board: £1650-£1850
Full board: £1920-£2315

Boy ○ / Girl ○ / Co-ed ●
Day ● / Week ● / Board ●

Chilton is a small civilised 'family' school set in and around an imposing 18th century manor house and grounds. The school offers a genuine all-round education focussing on individual development. Classes are seldom more than 12. The curriculum consists of a comprehensive range of academic subjects integrated into a balanced programme of activities designed to maximise individual attention.

Edgarley Hall (Millfield Junior School)

Address: Glastonbury, Somerset BA6 8LD
Telephone: 0458 832446

Head: Mr R J Smyth MA CertEd

Age range: 8-13
No. of pupils: 473
Scholarships: Yes
Religion: Non-denominational

Fees per term
Day: -£1820
Weekly board: -
Full board: -£2795

Boy ○ / Girl ○ / Co-ed ●
Day ● / Week ○ / Board ●

Edgarley Hall, which was founded in 1946, is situated on the slopes of Glastonbury Tor, just four miles from Millfield, and links between the two schools are close. Both schools share a commitment to developing the unique talent which they believe each individual possesses. The school strives to discover the aptitudes, build the self-esteem and develop the potential of every one of its children.

Edington † p696

Address: Mark Road, Burtle, Bridgewater, Somerset

Telephone: 0278 722012

Head: Mr G Nickerson

Age range: 8-13
No. of pupils: 122
Scholarships:
Religion: Non-denominational

Fees per term
Day: £1814-£2018
Weekly board: £2873-£2994
Full board: £2873-£2994

Boy ○ Girl ○ Co-ed ●
Day ● Week ● Board ●

Edington is for dyslexic pupils only. The caring and sympathetic environment allows the children to flourish and devlop their confidence and esteem. This co-educational school offers a wide curriculum commensurate with National Curriculum requirements but adapted to the needs of the dyslexic. A full range of sports and outdoor activities is offered. The Headmaster is a member of IAPS.

King's College

Address: South Road, Taunton, Somerset TA1 3DX

Telephone: 0823 272708

Head: Mr R S Funnell

Age range: 13-18
No. of pupils: 475
Scholarships: Yes
Religion: Church of England

Fees per term
Day: £2390-
Weekly board: -
Full board: £3370-

Boy ○ Girl ○ Co-ed ●
Day ● Week ○ Board ●

King's College is a community of 470 pupils and is small enough to ensure that each pupil can feel at home, gain the self-confidence to succeed, and learn qualities of independence, leadership and a concern for others. King's has excellent academic and leisure facilities and an enviable reputation for sport, music and the creative arts.

King's Hall School

Address: Kingston Road, Taunton, Somerset TA2 8AA

Telephone: 0823 272431

Head: Mrs M Willson

Age range: 3-13
No. of pupils: 384
Scholarships: Yes
Religion: Church of England

Fees per term
Day: £500-£1660
Weekly board: £1310-£2270
Full board: £1390-£2350

Boy ○ Girl ○ Co-ed ●
Day ● Week ● Board ●

King's Hall is run as a boarding school, with a high proportion of living in staff. In addition to the excellent education, therefore, day children may also take advantage of all the boarding facilities, including temporary boarding, all daily meals and the evening and weekend activity programme. Music and games are other strengths of a broad curriculum delivered by well qualified enthusiasts.

King's School Bruton

Address: Bruton, Somerset BA10 0ED

Telephone: 0749 813326

Head: Mr R I Smyth

Age range: 13-18
No. of pupils: 325
Scholarships: Yes
Religion: Church of England

Fees per term
Day: £2350-
Weekly board: -
Full board: £3315-

Boy ● Girl ● Co-ed ○
Day ● Week ○ Board ●

King's School is a medium sized boarding school in a small town, but in a rural setting. It offers a sound academic education within a caring and friendly pastoral framework. Five boys' boarding houses and a separate sixth form girls' house provide excellent accommodation.

King's School Bruton Junior *

Address: Hazelgrove House, Sparkford, Yeovil, Somerset BA22 7JA
Telephone: 0963 40314

Head: Mr J A C Cann

Age range: 7-13
No. of pupils: 250
Scholarships: Yes
Religion: Church of England

Fees per term
Day: £1765-£1765
Weekly board: £2525-£2525
Full board: £2525-£2525

● Boy ○ Girl ○ Co-ed
● Day ● Week ● Board

A country preparatory school with three academic streams where boys learn how to work in happy and rewarding surroundings. Strong music and CDT departments, support unit, indoor pool, lovely grounds.

Millfield p697, p746

Address: Street, Somerset BA16 0YD
Telephone: 0458 42291

Head: Mr C S Martin

Age range: 13-18
No. of pupils: 1230
Scholarships: Yes
Religion: Non-denominational

Fees per term
Day: £2385-
Weekly board: -
Full board: £3940-

○ Boy ○ Girl ● Co-ed
● Day ○ Week ● Board

Millfield offers an exceedingly wide range of choice both academic and recreational to boys and girls over a broad spectrum of ability. A large number of scholarships and bursaries is available for pupils with academic, artistic or musical talent, and for those of all-round abilities.

The Park School

Address: Yeovil, Somerset BA20 1DH
Telephone: 0935 23514

Head: Mrs M J Hannon

Age range: 3-16
No. of pupils: 200
Scholarships: Yes
Religion: Non-denomination

Fees per term
Day: £485-£1460
Weekly board: £2055-£2340
Full board: £2265-£2540

○ Boy ○ Girl ● Co-ed
● Day ● Week ● Board

For further information and a prospectus, please contact the school.

Perrott Hill

Address: North Perrott, Crewkerne, Somerset
Telephone: 0460 72051

Head: Mr J E A Barnes

Age range: 7-13
No. of pupils: 85
Scholarships: Yes
Religion: Church of England

Fees per term
Day: £1525-
Weekly board: £2160-
Full board: £2160-

● Boy ● Girl ○ Co-ed
● Day ● Week ● Board

Perrott Hill is a small preparatory school with high standards set in the heart of the countryside. Excellent academic and sporting results are achieved. There is a strong music tradition. Spacious grounds ensure a wide range of extra-curricular activities.

Quantock School

Address: Over Stowey, Bridgwater, Somerset TA5 1HD
Telephone: 0278 732252

Head: Mr D T Peaster

Age range: 8-16
No. of pupils: 150
Scholarships:
Religion: Non-denominational

Fees per term
Day: -
Weekly board: -
Full board: £1600-£1900

	Boy	Girl	Co-ed
Day	○	○	●
Week	○	○	●
Board			

Quantock School came into existence largely to meet a very real need for a small boys' school which could cater for children whose parents have to work abroad, where there are neither no suitable schools, or where to0 frequent changes of school cause considerable hardship and/or backwardness. Parents wanted a school that could be warm and relaxed whilst still meeting high standards of education and maintaining good discipline.

Queens College *

Address: Trull Road, Taunton, Somerset TA1 4QS
Telephone: 0823 272559

Head: Mr C T Brandock MA

Age range: 12-18
No. of pupils: 470
Scholarships: Yes
Religion: Methodist

Fees per term
Day: £1800-
Weekly board: -
Full board: £2755-

	Boy	Girl	Co-ed
Day	○	○	●
Week	●	○	●
Board			

Founded in 1843, a Methodist foundation, Queen's College moved to its present premises in 1846. These are single-site and semi-rural in 30 acres on the southern outskirts of Taunton. Very pleasant buildings and fine playing fields. Junior school and pre-prep combined. Much development in the last 25-30 years including a fine new concert hall/theatre, music school and science labortories.

Queens College Junior School

Address: Trull Road, Taunton, Somerset TA1 4QR
Telephone: 0823 272990

Head: Mr P N Lee-Smith

Age range: 8-12
No. of pupils: 170
Scholarships:
Religion: Methodist

Fees per term
Day: £815-£1535
Weekly board: -
Full board: £1275-£2320

	Boy	Girl	Co-ed
Day	○	○	●
Week	●	○	●
Board			

For further information and a prospectus, please contact the school.

Queens College Pre-Preparatory School

Address: Trull Road, Taunton, Somerset TA1 4QS
Telephone: 0823 272559

Head: Mrs G Gibbs

Age range: 4-8
No. of pupils: 60
Scholarships:
Religion: Methodist

Fees per term
Day: -£555
Weekly board: -
Full board: -

	Boy	Girl	Co-ed
Day	○	○	●
Week	●	○	○
Board			

For further information and a prospectus, please contact the school.

Rossholme School

Address: East Brent,
Highbridge, Somerset
TA9 4JA
Telephone: 0278 760219

Head: Mrs S J B Webb

Age range: 4-16
No. of pupils: 100
Scholarships: Yes
Religion: Non-denominational

Fees per term
Day: £680-£770
Weekly board: £1820-£1905
Full board: £1860-£1945

Boy ○ / Girl ● / Co-ed ○
Day ● / Week ● / Board ●

Rossholme itself is a lovely country house with its own well maintained grounds. Small classes make individual attention possible resulting in a good academic record. Drama and sporting activities reflect the emphasis placed upon confidence building and team spirit which together with self reliance, loyalty and good manners are qualities which Rossholme aims to develop in cooperation with parents.

Shapwick School p698

Address: Shapwick Manor,
Shapwick, Bridgwater,
Somerset TA7 9NJ
Telephone: 0458 210384

Head: Mr D C Walker BA(Hons) CertEd

Age range: 13-17
No. of pupils: 98
Scholarships:
Religion: Non-denominational

Fees per term
Day: -£1982
Weekly board: -
Full board: -£3148

Boy ○ / Girl ○ / Co-ed ●
Day ● / Week ○ / Board ●

For further information and a prospectus, please contact the school.

St Christopher's School

Address: Berrow Road,
Burnham on Sea, Somerset
TA8 2NY
Telephone: 0278 782234

Head: Mrs S P Morrell-Davies

Age range: 3-13
No. of pupils: 150
Scholarships: Yes
Religion:

Fees per term
Day: £650-£1335
Weekly board: £2150-
Full board: £2150-

Boy ● / Girl ● / Co-ed ○
Day ● / Week ● / Board ●

Throughout the school a sound grounding is given in the basic subjects in a happy relaxed atmosphere where a work ethic can be developed in a Christian environment. The gradual introduction of specialist teaching allows for a broad currriculum leading to Common Entrance examinations. Music, drama and sports are encouraged. An escort service is available to all main airports. Boys 3-8

St Martin's School

Address: 22 Abbey Street,
Crewkerne, Somerset
TA18 7SL
Telephone: 0460 73265

Head: Mrs J A Murrell

Age range: 4-13
No. of pupils: 100
Scholarships:
Religion:

Fees per term
Day: -
Weekly board: -
Full board: -

Boy ○ / Girl ○ / Co-ed ●
Day ● / Week ○ / Board ○

For further information and a prospectus, please contact the school.

Taunton Junior Boys School

Address: Staplegrove Road, Taunton, Somerset TA2 6AE

Telephone:

Head: Mr A D Wood

Age range: 2-12
No. of pupils: 219
Scholarships: Yes
Religion: Non-denominational

Fees per term
Day: £850-£1640
Weekly board: £1330-£2560
Full board: £1330-£2560

Boy (●) Girl (○) Co-ed (○)
Day (●) Week (●) Board (●)

The boys' preparatory school of Taunton School.

Taunton Junior Girls School

Address: Weirfield, Taunton, Somerset TA1 1DW

Telephone: 0823 272502

Head: Mr S A M Purdom

Age range: 4-12
No. of pupils: 268
Scholarships: Yes
Religion: Non-denominational

Fees per term
Day: £395-£1640
Weekly board: £1330-£2560
Full board: £1330-£2560

Boy (○) Girl (●) Co-ed (○)
Day (●) Week (●) Board (●)

The girls' preparatory school of Taunton School.

Taunton School *

Address: Taunton, Somerset TA2 6AD

Telephone: 0823 284596

Head: Mr B B Sutton MA

Age range: 13-18
No. of pupils: 550
Scholarships: Yes
Religion: Non-denominational

Fees per term
Day: £2100-
Weekly board: £3275-
Full board: £3275-

Boy (○) Girl (○) Co-ed (●)
Day (●) Week (●) Board (●)

Taunton School celebrates 20 years of being fully co-educational this year. It is a lively school with a modern outlook; carefully and professionally arranged, it has first-class facilities. Great all-round academic and cultural strengths with a particularly distinguished record in debating and games.

Tor International School

Address: High Lam, Langport, Somerset TA10 9BY

Telephone: 0458 250427

Head: Major B G Whittall BSc(Eng) MBIM

Age range: 13-18
No. of pupils: 25
Scholarships:
Religion:

Fees per term
Day: -
Weekly board: -
Full board: -

Boy (○) Girl (○) Co-ed (●)
Day (●) Week (○) Board (●)

For further information and a prospectus, please contact the school.

Wellington *

Address: South Street, Wellington, Somerset TA21 8NT
Telephone: 0823 664511

Head: Mr A J Rogers

Age range: 10-18
No. of pupils: 838
Scholarships: Yes
Religion: Church of England

Fees per term
Day: -£3510
Weekly board: -
Full board: -£6534

Boy ○   Girl ○   Co-ed ●
Day ●   Week ○   Board ●

Wellington School has existed on its original site on the southern side of this ancient Somerset town for over 150 years, serving its community and nowadays a wider worldwide field. A Level results have been consistently pitched around 90% with 93% of last year's 6th formers entering higher education. The school boasts a fine sporting record, not only for team sports but with distinguished individuals.

Wells Cathedral Junior School

Address: 10 New Street, Wells, Somerset BA5 2LQ
Telephone: 0749 72291

Head: Mr P M Peabody

Age range: 5-11
No. of pupils: 219
Scholarships:
Religion:

Fees per term
Day: -
Weekly board: -
Full board: -

Boy ○   Girl ○   Co-ed ●
Day ●   Week ○   Board ●

For further information and a prospectus, please contact the school.

Wells Cathedral School *

Address: Wells, Somerset BA5 2ST
Telephone: 0749 672117

Head: Mr J S Baxter

Age range: 5-18
No. of pupils: 815
Scholarships: Yes
Religion: Church of England

Fees per term
Day: £689-£1444
Weekly board: -
Full board: £2147-£2457

Boy ○   Girl ○   Co-ed ●
Day ●   Week ○   Board ●

Established in the 12th century, Wells Cathedral School possess all modern facilities for independent education contained within a traditional atmosphere. The school has a national and international reputation, in particular for the excellence of its music which is fully integrated with a normal academic curriculum in which musicians and non-musicians are free to develop their individual talents.

STAFFORDSHIRE

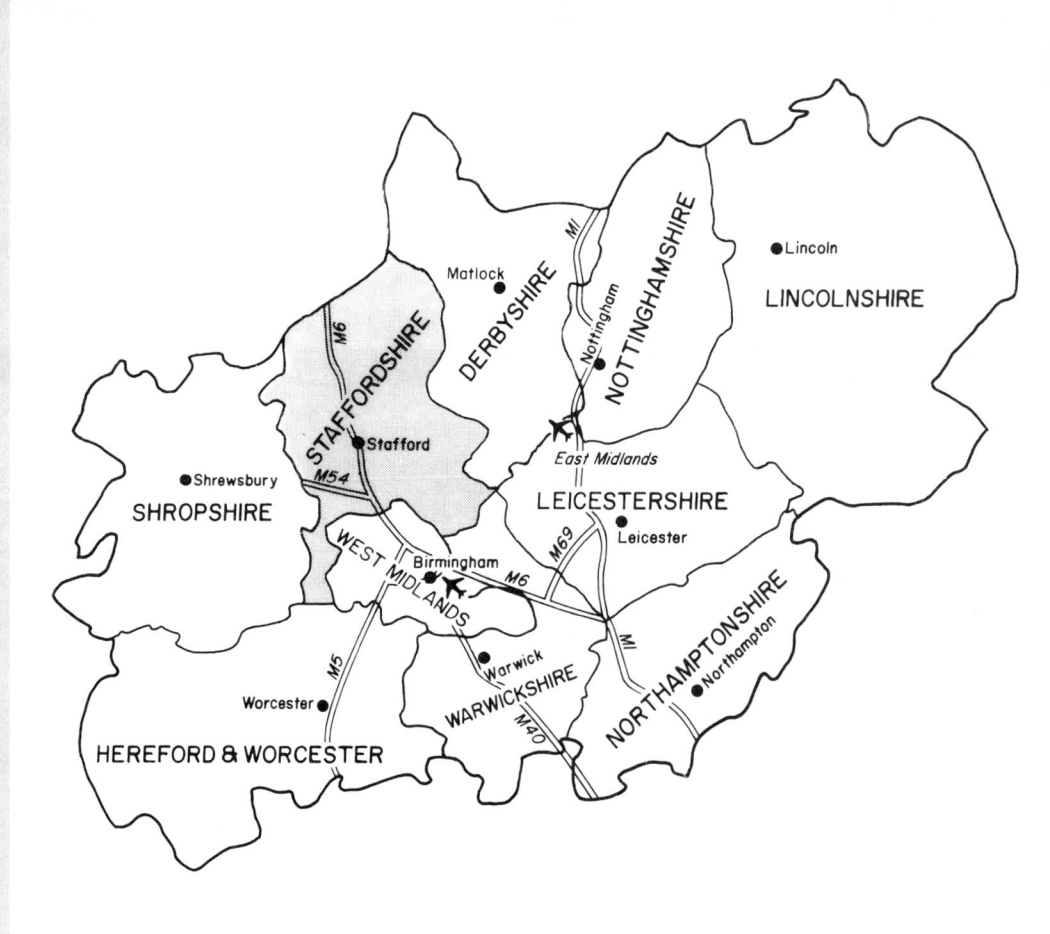

Abbotsholme School

Address: Rocester, Uttoxeter, Staffordshire ST14 5BS

Telephone: 0889 590 217

Head: Mr D J Farrant

Age range: 11-18
No. of pupils: 250
Scholarships: Yes
Religion: Non-denominational

Fees per term
Day: £2168-£2168
Weekly board: £3252-£3252
Full board: £3252-£3252

Boy / Girl / **Co-ed**
Day / **Week** / **Board**

Abbotsholme has excellent academic and practical teaching facilities and a fine record in public examinations. Most sixth formers aim for University entrance, including Oxbridge. There is a strong programme of outdoor education and traditional team games, with a wide variety of indoor activities in the new sports hall. The school is set in a beautiful country estate, including its own farm and riding stables.

Brooklands School

Address: 167 Eccleshall Road, Stafford, Staffordshire ST16 1PD

Telephone: 0785 51399

Head: Mr C T O'Donnell

Age range: 3-13
No. of pupils: 122
Scholarships: Yes
Religion: Non-denominational

Fees per term
Day: £500-£965
Weekly board: -
Full board: -

Boy / Girl / **Co-ed**
Day / Week / Board

Brooklands is an independent preparatory school attractively situated on the edge of Stafford. Classes are small and the academic progress of each child is closely supervised. Music and academic scholarships have been won on a regular basis. Brooklands is a happy and caring school with an emphasis on good manners and a regard for the needs of others.

Denstone College *

Address: Uttoxeter, Staffordshire ST14 5HN

Telephone: 0889 590484

Head: Mr H C K Carson

Age range: 11-18
No. of pupils: 290
Scholarships: Yes
Religion: Church of England

Fees per term
Day: £1575-£2279
Weekly board: -£3197
Full board: -£3197

Boy / Girl / **Co-ed**
Day / **Week** / **Board**

Denstone College is an HMC co-educational school for 11 to 18 year olds in a rural central England setup. Classes are small, and there is a good level of achievement in a wide variety of activities. Cricket, choral singing and Duke of Edinburgh Award Scheme are particularly strong. Church worship takes place daily. The house and tutorial system ensure close personal attention and the maximisation of potential.

Denstone College Preparatory School *

Address: Smallwood Manor, Uttoxeter, Staffordshire ST14 8NS

Telephone: 0889 562083

Head: Mr A C Ninham

Age range: 3-13
No. of pupils: 200
Scholarships: Yes
Religion: Church of England

Fees per term
Day: £690-£1575
Weekly board: -
Full board: £1995-£2110

Boy / Girl / **Co-ed**
Day / Week / **Board**

Smallwood Manor is co-educational, boarding and day, with small classes, enthusiastic staff and excellent facilities. It gives a Christian education, producing confident children, encouraging them to excel in music, art, games, hobbies as well as academic work. Scholarships and Government Assisted Places available. Pre-preparatory 3-8 years, preparatory 8-13 years.

Edenhurst Preparatory School

Address: Westlands Avenue, Newcastle-under-Lyme, Staffordshire ST5 2PU
Telephone: 0782 619348

Head: Mr N H F Copestick

Age range: 3-13
No. of pupils: 200
Scholarships:
Religion: Non-denominational

Fees per term
Day: £493-£1051
Weekly board: -
Full board: -

○ ○ ● Boy Girl Co-ed
● ○ ○ Day Week Board

For further information and a prospectus, please contact the school.

Howitt House School

Address: Hanbury, Burton upon Trent, Staffordshire DE13 8TG
Telephone: 0283 820236

Head: Mr M H Davis

Age range: 3-12
No. of pupils: 85
Scholarships: Yes
Religion: Christian

Fees per term
Day: £685-£685
Weekly board: -
Full board: -

○ ○ ● Boy Girl Co-ed
● ○ ○ Day Week Board

Howitt House is a primary and nursery school. It is set in pleasant countryside midway between Burton upon Trent and Uttoxeter, and unlike most day-schools has spacious grounds. Howitt House still emphasises traditional standards in classwork and behaviour, but is not afraid of innovations when they are worthwhile. The headmaster and some staff live on the estate giving a warm and friendly feel to the school.

Lichfield Cathedral School p698, p745

Address: The Palace, Lichfield, Staffordshire WS13 7LH
Telephone: 0543 263326

HeadMaster: Mr A F Walters

Age range: 4-13
No. of pupils: 216
Scholarships: Yes
Religion: Church of England

Fees per term
Day: £900-£1480
Weekly board: £1895-£1965
Full board: £2085-£2155

○ ○ ● Boy Girl Co-ed
● ● ○ Day Week Board

A first class preparatory school in magnificent surroundings. Academic and choral scholarships granted. Examinations in early March.

Lyncroft House

Address: Convent Close, St John's Road, Cannock, Staffordshire
Telephone: 0543 502388

Head: Mr M W Mash

Age range: 3-18
No. of pupils: 150
Scholarships: Yes
Religion: Church of England

Fees per term
Day: £800-£1150
Weekly board: £1512-
Full board: £2250-

○ ○ ● Boy Girl Co-ed
● ● ● Day Week Board

Emphasis placed on literacy, numeracy, good manners and effective use of leisure time in preparation for adult life. Well equipped science laboratories, IT and CDT centres. Maximum 16 pupils per class. GCSE, A levels and BTec National Diploma courses. Leisure centre within grounds.

Newcastle-under-Lyme School *

Address: Mount Pleasant, Newcastle, Staffordshire ST5 1DB
Telephone: 0782 633607

Head: Dr R M Reynolds

Age range: 8-18
No. of pupils: 1340
Scholarships: Yes
Religion: Non-denominational

Fees per term
Day: £913-£1050
Weekly board: -
Full board: -

○ ○ ● Boy Girl Co-ed
● ○ ○ Day Week Board

Newcastle-under-Lyme School has built up a strong academic reputation over the years with, on average, sixteen pupils proceeding to Oxford annually. Extra-curricular activities also have a high profile and the school has become noted for its high standards in sport, music and drama. Set in attractive grounds, the school's excellent facilities include an indoor swimming pool and computer laboratories.

School of S Mary and S Anne * p699

Address: Abbots Bromley, Rugeley, Staffordshire WS15 3BW
Telephone: 0283 840232

Head: Mr A J Grigg

Age range: 5-18
No. of pupils: 300
Scholarships: Yes
Religion: Church of England

Fees per term
Day: £1322-£2114
Weekly board: £3139-£3139
Full board: £2684-£3173

○ ● ○ Boy Girl Co-ed
● ● ● Day Week Board

Abbots Bromley is an independent boarding, weekly boarding and day school for girls, aged 5-18. First class sports facilities, sports hall, indoor pool, all weather tennis and netball courts. Music school with national reputation; tuition available in most instruments. Many extra-curricular activities including ballet, riding, gymnastics, speech and drama and Duke of Edinburgh's Award.

St Bede's School

Address: Bishton Hall, Wolseley Bridge, Stafford, Staffordshire ST17 0XN
Telephone: 0889 881277

Head: Mr A H Stafford Northcote

Age range: 3-13
No. of pupils: 170
Scholarships:
Religion: Roman Catholic

Fees per term
Day: £704-£1208
Weekly board: -
Full board: -£1627

○ ○ ● Boy Girl Co-ed
● ○ ● Day Week Board

The school offers a thorough and balanced education in a happy, family environment. All pupils are encouraged to develop fully their characters and abilities, with particular attention being paid to the individual requirements of each child. The school prides itself on an excellent academic record and sets high standards in other important activities such as drama, music, art and games.

St Dominic's Indepndent Junior School

Address: Hartshill Road, Stoke on Trent, Staffordshire ST4 7LY
Telephone: 0782 48588

Head: Mr D G Hare

Age range: 3-11
No. of pupils: 158
Scholarships:
Religion: Non-denominational

Fees per term
Day: £490-£630
Weekly board: -
Full board: -

○ ○ ● Boy Girl Co-ed
● ○ ○ Day Week Board

For further information and a prospectus, please contact the school.

St Dominic's Priory School

Address: 21 Station Road, Stone, Staffordshire ST15 8EN
Telephone: 0785 814181
Head: Sister Mary Henry

Age range: 4-18
No. of pupils: 414
Scholarships: Yes
Religion: Roman Catholic

Fees per term
Day: £742-£855
Weekly board: -
Full board: -

● Boy ● Girl ○ Co-ed
● Day ○ Week ○ Board

For further information and a prospectus, please contact the school. Boys 4-8, girls 4-18.

St Dominic's School

Address: 32 Bargate Street, Stafford, Staffordshire ST19 9BA
Telephone: 0902 850248
Head: Mrs K S Butwilowska

Age range: 2-18
No. of pupils: 505
Scholarships: Yes
Religion: All denominations

Fees per term
Day: £690-£1074
Weekly board: -
Full board: -

● Boy ● Girl ○ Co-ed
● Day ○ Week ○ Board

While we recognise the importance of examinations we believe that it is essential to create an environment where the highest spiritual, moral and cultural values combine with academic achievements.

St John's Preparatory School

Address: 28 St John Street, Lichfield, Staffordshire
Telephone: 0543 263345
Head: Ms S P DeGruchy

Age range: 3-11
No. of pupils: 70
Scholarships:
Religion: Church of England

Fees per term
Day: £350-£700
Weekly board: -
Full board: -

○ Boy ○ Girl ● Co-ed
● Day ○ Week ○ Board

St John's School is a small independent preparatory school with its own nursery department. Children are eligible for entry between the ages of 3 and 9 plus years. Pupils receive a sound basic education in small classes with the emphasis on literacy, numeracy and good manners.

St Joseph's College *

Address: Trent Vale, Sroke on Trent, Staffordshire ST4 5NT
Telephone: 0782 48008
Head: Rev Br P K Loughran

Age range: 4-18
No. of pupils:
Scholarships:
Religion: Roman Catholic

Fees per term
Day: £582-£974
Weekly board: -
Full board: -

○ Boy ○ Girl ● Co-ed
● Day ○ Week ○ Board

The college aims to provide a stimulating, relaxed environment so that pupils can enjoy their work. The college believes they should be free to develop as individuals and to this end we endeavour to help them discover their own talents. Confidence, reliability and self discipline are all of prime importance. We encourage a Christian family atmosphere of caring and sharing in order to assist spiritual end emotional growth.

Stafford Grammar School *

Address: Burton Manor,
Stafford, Staffordshire
ST18 9AT
Telephone: 0785 49752

Head: Dr J R Garrood

Age range: 11-18
No. of pupils: 183
Scholarships:
Religion:

Fees per term
Day: -
Weekly board: -
Full board: -

○ ○ ●
Boy Girl Co-ed
● ○ ○
Day Week Board

For further information and a prospectus, please contact the school.

Vernon Lodge Preparatory School and Kindergarten

Address: School Lane,
Stretton, Brewood,
Staffordshire
Telephone: 0902 850568

Head: Mrs D W Lodge

Age range: 2-11
No. of pupils: 87
Scholarships:
Religion: Non-Denominational

Fees per term
Day: £635-£763
Weekly board: -
Full board: -

● ● ○
Boy Girl Co-ed
● ○ ○
Day Week Board

Vernon Lodge is an independent day school for boys and girls aged 2 -11+. The school is set in a beautiful country garden. A wide curriculum and small classes produce excellent results to senior schools in the area. Our kindergarten has the reputation of being the best in the locality providing the children with a thorough pre-school education.

Wolstanton Preparatory School

Address: 30 Woodland
Avenue, Wolstanton,
Staffordshire ST5 8AZ
Telephone: 0782 626675

Head: Mrs E A Cooper

Age range: 3-11
No. of pupils: 70
Scholarships:
Religion:

Fees per term
Day: -
Weekly board: -
Full board: -

○ ○ ●
Boy Girl Co-ed
● ○ ○
Day Week Board

For further information and a prospectus, please contact the school.

Yarlet Hall

Address: Stafford,
Staffordshire
Telephone: 08897 240

Head: Mr R S Plant

Age range: 7-13
No. of pupils: 110
Scholarships:
Religion: Church of England

Fees per term
Day: £1560-
Weekly board: -
Full board: £1915-

● ○ ○
Boy Girl Co-ed
● ○ ●
Day Week Board

Set in open unspoilt countryside four miles north of Stafford on the A34 and two miles from the M6, Yarlet caters for a wide range of academic, sporting and practical abilities. Many boys leaving at 13+ obtain academic, music or art awards to major senior independent schools. Specialist dyslexic tuition can be provided.

SUFFOLK

Amberfield School

Address: Nacton, Ipswich, Suffolk IP10 0HL

Telephone: 0473 659265

Head: Mrs M L Amphlett-Lewis

Age range: 3-16
No. of pupils: 300
Scholarships:
Religion: Non-denominational

Fees per term
Day: £780-£1175
Weekly board: -
Full board: -

○ Boy   ○ Girl   ● Co-ed
● Day   ○ Week   ○ Board

In both junior and senior schools our aim is to meet the needs of each child as an individual. To achieve this, all classes are small and all subjects are taught by qualified and experienced staff. There is setting for most subjects after the second year in the senior school when the average class size is 15.

Barnardiston Hall Preparatory School

Address: Barnardiston, Haverhill, Suffolk CB9 7TG

Telephone: 0440 86316

Head: Lt Col K A Boulter

Age range: 2-13
No. of pupils: 162
Scholarships:
Religion: Church of England

Fees per term
Day: £830-£1007
Weekly board: £1705-
Full board: £1925-

○ Boy   ○ Girl   ● Co-ed
● Day   ● Week   ● Board

A well-established school with a good academic record based on small classes and dedicated staff. A wide range of sports - hockey at 4, Snowdon at 6. French begins at 4, computers throughout the school. Country house set in 16 acres. Follows Common Entrance syllabus. Dormitories second to none.

Briar (Independent) School

Address: 8 Gunton Cliff, Lowestoft, Suffolk NR32 4PE

Telephone: 0502 583481

Head: Miss S Butcher

Age range: 3-16
No. of pupils: 130
Scholarships:
Religion: Non-denominational

Fees per term
Day: £740-£990
Weekly board: -
Full board: -

○ Boy   ○ Girl   ● Co-ed
● Day   ○ Week   ○ Board

A family community where each individual is encouraged to achieve his full potential in a happy caring environment. Enter our nursery at age 3 and continue through to GCSE, or receive excellent preparation for entry to other schools. Special provision for children with specific learning difficulties; french by the direct method from age 4; water-sports and riding available.

Culford School * p740

Address: Bury St Edmunds, Suffolk IP28 6TX

Telephone: 0284 728615

Head: Mr J Richardson

Age range: 8-18
No. of pupils: 680
Scholarships: Yes
Religion: Methodist

Fees per term
Day: £1612-£1894
Weekly board: -
Full board: £2479-£2914

○ Boy   ○ Girl   ● Co-ed
● Day   ● Week   ● Board

Culford seeks to provide a stimulating yet orderly environment in which each child in this fully educational school can develop its potential. We start with great assets in our 400 acre park, stately home and modern boarding/teaching and sports buildings. We add thorough teaching and supportive pastoral care and are proud of the way our children develop into well educated, responsible and balanced adults.

Eversley Preparatory School

Address: Southwold, Suffolk
IP18 6AH

Telephone: 0502 723302

Head: Mr A F Bottomley

Age range: 4-14
No. of pupils: 80
Scholarships: Yes
Religion: Christian

Fees per term
Day: £475-£855
Weekly board: £1068-
Full board: -

Boy ○ Girl ○ Co-ed ●
Day ● Week ● Board ○

Eversley is a supremely happy small school taking children with a wide range of ability but achieving complete success in the appropriate leaving examinations. Discipline is firm but understanding and not repressive. A wide range of subjects and activities is offered.

Fairfield Preparatory School

Address: North Lodge,
Saxmundham, Suffolk
IP17 1AY

Telephone: 0728 602293

Head: Mr R Neve DC DMS MBIM CertEd

Age range: 2-11
No. of pupils: 50
Scholarships:
Religion: Christian

Fees per term
Day: £710-£740
Weekly board: -
Full board: -

Boy ○ Girl ○ Co-ed ●
Day ● Week ○ Board ○

From 2+ to 11+, small classes, offering a firm foundation in reading writing and numeracy, in addition to optional subjects including dance, piano, speech and drama, pottery etc. Specialist teaching for pupils with special learning difficulties. Accredited. Enquiries welcome.

Fairstead House School

Address: Fordham Road,
Newmarket, Suffolk CB8 7AA

Telephone: 0638 662318

Head: Mr D J Wedgwood

Age range: 4-11
No. of pupils: 120
Scholarships: Yes
Religion: Non-denominational

Fees per term
Day: £620-£750
Weekly board: -
Full board: -

Boy ○ Girl ○ Co-ed ●
Day ● Week ○ Board ○

Our aim is to provide a sound primary education in a happy atmosphere, at the same time preparing children for entry into one of a number of independent preparatory and secondary schools. In addition, some children return to the maintained sector. A full curriculum is offered with emphasis on a thorough grounding in the 'core' subjects.

Felixstowe College ✳

Address: Maybush Lane,
Felixstowe, Suffolk
IP11 7NQ

Telephone: 0394 284269

Head: Mrs A Woodings

Age range: 5-18
No. of pupils: 300
Scholarships: Yes
Religion: Church of England

Fees per term
Day: £680-£1878
Weekly board: -
Full board: -£3018

Boy ○ Girl ● Co-ed ○
Day ● Week ● Board ●

Felixstowe College combines good academic standards with a friendly atmosphere. Its proximity to the continent has led to educational and sporting links with Europe. Strong music, drama and dance departments. Wide range of extra-curricular activities including Duke of Edinburgh, Young Enterprise, riding, golf etc.

Finborough School

Address: The Hall, Great Finborough, Stowmarket, Suffolk IP14 3EF
Telephone: 0449 674479

Head: Dr S K Land PhD MA

Age range: 7-18
No. of pupils: 240
Scholarships: Yes
Religion: Any

Fees per term
Day: £850-£1150
Weekly board: £1250-£1620
Full board: £1774-£2278

Boy ○ Girl ○ Co-ed ●
Day ● Week ● Board ●

The school is a young and forward looking school. Classes are small, staff are qualified, fully-professional people. The school provides high standards of pastoral care in a secure and friendly environment. A wide range of clubs and activities are available and are included in fees.

Framlingham College Junior School

Address: Brandeston Hall, Brandeston, Woodridge, Suffolk IP13 7AQ

Telephone: 0728 685331
Head: Mr N Johnson

Age range: 4-13
No. of pupils: 280
Scholarships: Yes
Religion: Church of England

Fees per term
Day: £763-£1404
Weekly board: -
Full board: £2263-£2263

Boy ○ Girl ○ Co-ed ●
Day ● Week ● Board ●

This beautiful I.A.P.S. School, set in 30 acres of grounds offers a curriculum designed to meet the needs of all children from the age of four to thirteen. We have specialist teachers, well-equipped laboratories, a wide activities programme, close co-operation between school and home and excellent sports facilities. Our boarding community is based on family units in a caring and committed environment.

Framlingham College * p699

Address: Framlingham, Woodbridge, Suffolk IP13 9EY

Telephone: 0728 723789

Head: Mr J F X Miller

Age range: 4-18
No. of pupils: 700
Scholarships: Yes
Religion: Church of England

Fees per term
Day: £1300-£1706
Weekly board: -
Full board: £2095-£2658

Boy ○ Girl ○ Co-ed ●
Day ● Week ○ Board ●

Framlingham College, a co-educational school, provides excellent educational opportunity between the ages of 4-18 years. At all stages emphasis is placed upon developing the talents and abilities of the individual. A caring pastoral system, superb facilities and an extensive range of GCSE and A Level subjects are offered to our pupils together with fine sporting and cultural traditions.

Hillcroft Preparatory School

Address: Walnutree Manor, Haughley Green, Stowmarket, Suffolk IP14 3RQ
Telephone: 0449 673003

Head: Mr F Rapsey

Age range: 2-13
No. of pupils: 130
Scholarships: Yes
Religion: Non-denominational

Fees per term
Day: £320-£1200
Weekly board: £650-
Full board: -

Boy ○ Girl ○ Co-ed ●
Day ● Week ● Board ○

Individual development is harnessed to the need to co-operate. Healthy competition thrives in a family atmosphere where there is emphasis on basic subjects. We have a positive European outlook with theschool's large house in France and many visiting foreign- ers. This highlights our traditionally english cultural approach and education which gains many scholarships. Dyslexia centre with free assessment.

Ipswich High School GPDST *

Address: Wolverstone, Ipswich, Suffolk IP9 1AZ
Telephone: 0473 780201
Head: Miss V MacCuish

Age range: 4-18
No. of pupils: 620
Scholarships: Yes
Religion: Non-denominational

Fees per term
Day: £880-£1148
Weekly board: -
Full board: -

Boy ○ / Girl ● / Co-ed ○
Day ● / Week ○ / Board ○

The school stands in eighty acres with wide views over the Orwell Estuary and the surrounding parkland. There are excellent facilities for the senior and junior departments including modern laboratories, computer rooms, sports hall and theatre and extensive playing fields. Public examination results are very good and almost all sixth formers go on to university or professional training.

Ipswich Preparatory School

Address: Henley Road, Ipswich, Suffolk IP1 3SQ
Telephone: 0473 255730
Head: Mr N M Allen

Age range: 7-11
No. of pupils: 150
Scholarships:
Religion: Church of England

Fees per term
Day: £926-£987
Weekly board: -
Full board: -

Boy ● / Girl ○ / Co-ed ○
Day ● / Week ○ / Board ○

For further information and a prospectus, please contact the school.

Ipswich School *

Address: Henley Road, Ipswich, Suffolk IP1 3SG
Telephone: 0473 255313
Head: Dr J M Blatchly

Age range: 11-18
No. of pupils: 620
Scholarships: Yes
Religion: Church of England

Fees per term
Day: £1378-£1454
Weekly board: £2165-£2417
Full board: £2203-£2488

Boy ● / Girl ● / Co-ed ○
Day ● / Week ● / Board ●

At Ipswich School we aim to maintain a 600-year-old tradition of providing the best education possible and a broad training for life beyond school. A Level mean pass rate 90%. All major sports; excellent facilities. Girls accepted in sixth form.

Kesgrave Hall School

Address: Bealings Road, Kesgrove, Ipswich Suffolk IP5 7PU
Telephone: 0473 624755
Head: Mr E J Richardson

Age range: 11-18
No. of pupils: 50
Scholarships:
Religion:

Fees per term
Day: -
Weekly board: -
Full board: £5550-£5850

Boy ● / Girl ○ / Co-ed ○
Day ○ / Week ○ / Board ●

Kesgrave Hall School is for academically able boys of secondary school age, but who are emotionally or behaviourally disturbed. The school has an academic record second to none achieving on average 6 GCSE passes at C or above and 2 A level passes per 6th former.

Moreton Hall

Address: Mount Road, Bury St Edmunds, Suffolk IP32 7BJ

Telephone: 0284 753532

Head: Mr A I Varley

Age range: 2-13
No. of pupils: 140
Scholarships: Yes
Religion: Roman Catholic

Fees per term
Day: £990-£1725
Weekly board: -
Full board: -£2395

Boy ○ Girl ○ Co-ed ●
Day ● Week ○ Board ●

For further information and a prospectus, please contact the school.

Old Buckenham Hall

Address: Brettenham Park, Ipswich, Suffolk IP7 7PH

Telephone: 0449 740252

Head: Mr H D Cocke BA

Age range: 2-13
No. of pupils: 161
Scholarships: Yes
Religion: Church of England

Fees per term
Day: £850-£1800
Weekly board: £2225-
Full board: £2440-

Boy ● Girl ○ Co-ed ○
Day ● Week ● Board ●

A country house location near Bury St Edmunds in 75 acres of Suffolk countryside. There are 6 tennis courts, squash courts, golf course and heated swimming pool.

The Old Rectory School

Address: Brettenham, Ipswich, Suffolk IP7 7QR

Telephone: 0449 736404

Head: Mr M A Phillips

Age range: 7-13
No. of pupils: 45
Scholarships:
Religion: Non-denominational

Fees per term
Day: £2950-
Weekly board: £3850-
Full board: £3850-

Boy ○ Girl ○ Co-ed ●
Day ● Week ● Board ●

The Old Rectory is a fully registered specialist school approved by the National Registration Council for up to 45 boys and girls between the ages of 7-13 years who suffer from dyslexia. Children stay between one and two years before returning to mainstream schools.

Orwell Park School p700

Address: Nacton, Ipswich, Suffolk IP10 0ER

Telephone: 0473 659225

Head: Mr I H Angus

Age range: 7-13
No. of pupils: 201
Scholarships: Yes
Religion: Non-denominational

Fees per term
Day: £1795-£1995
Weekly board: £2500-£2750
Full board: £2500-£2750

Boy ● Girl ● Co-ed ●
Day ● Week ● Board ●

A full and weekly preparatory boarding school with a few day pupils. The School is set in beautiful surroundings and has outstanding facilities. There is a distinct academic tradition and emphasis is placed on self discipline and self motivation. Well qualified and enthusiastic staff teach a broad curriculum both inside and outside the classroom.

The Royal Hospital School

Address: Holbrook, Ipswich, Suffolk IP9 2KX

Telephone: 0473 328342

Head: Mr M A B Kirk MA

Age range: 11-18
No. of pupils: 620
Scholarships: Yes
Religion: Christian

Fees per term
Day: -
Weekly board: -
Full board: £1800-£2034

Co-ed / Board

All fees are subsidised by Greenwich Hospital which enables us to offer our pupils an excellent education at very reasonable cost. The School is exceptionally well equipped, the latest addition being a £1.2 million Technology extension. Sixty acres of grounds and playing fields overlooking the Stour estuary and a fleet of sailing boats provide marvellous opportunities for sport and recreation.

The Ryes School †

Address: Little Henny, Sudbury, Suffolk CO10 7EA

Telephone: 0787 374998

Principal: Mrs R Stamp

Age range: 8-16
No. of pupils: 25
Scholarships:
Religion: Non-denominational

Fees per term
Day: -
Weekly board: -
Full board: -

Co-ed / Day / Board

For details of fees, further information and a prospectus, please contact the school.

Salter's Hall School

Address: Stour Street, Sudbury, Suffolk CO10 6AX

Telephone: 0787 372789

Head: Mr W W Neimeyer

Age range: 3-11
No. of pupils: 155
Scholarships:
Religion: Non-denominational

Fees per term
Day: £435-£1120
Weekly board: -
Full board: -

Co-ed / Day

For further information and a prospectus, please contact the school.

School of Jesus and Mary

Address: Woodbridge Road, Ipswich, Suffolk IP4 4BB

Telephone: 0473 728112

Head: Mrs E A McKay

Age range: 3-16
No. of pupils: 300
Scholarships: Yes
Religion: Non-Denominational

Fees per term
Day: £790-£1170
Weekly board: -
Full board: -

Boy / Girl / Day

For further information and a prospectus, please contact the school. Boys 3-7, girls 3-16.

SUFFOLK 439

South Lee Preparatory School

Address: Nowton Road, Bury St Edmunds, Suffolk IP33 2BT

Telephone: 0284 754654

Head: Mrs R Williamson

Age range: 3-13
No. of pupils: 237
Scholarships:
Religion: Non-denominational

Fees per term
Day: £975-£1280
Weekly board: -
Full board: -

○ Boy ○ Girl ● Co-ed
● Day ○ Week ○ Board

South Lee School is an independent day school for boys and girls from toddlers through to 13 years. It provides both a stimulating and a caring environment where every child is encouraged to attain the highest academic standard of which he or she is capable. South Lee gives a sound educational base for children which prepares them for the next stage of their education so that they are offered places at the schools of their choice.

St Felix School ✻ p700

Address: Southwold, Suffolk IP18 6SD

Telephone: 0502 722175

Head: Mrs S R Campion

Age range: 11-18
No. of pupils: 270
Scholarships: Yes
Religion: Non-denominational

Fees per term
Day: £1965-
Weekly board: £3056-
Full board: £3056-

○ Boy ● Girl ○ Co-ed
● Day ● Week ● Board

Single sex girls' school which provides limitless opportunities for academic excellence (separate sciences, strong classics) and for the development of confidence, independence and a sense of adventure. Thirty five Gold Duke of Edinburgh Awards in five years. Full range of evening and weekend activities includes the traditional feminine art of flower arranging as well as more masculine pursuits of clay shooting and karate.

St George's School

Address: Southwold, Suffolk IP18 6SD

Telephone: 0502 723314

Head: Mrs W H Martin

Age range: 4-11
No. of pupils: 82
Scholarships: Yes
Religion: Non-denominational

Fees per term
Day: £657-£1091
Weekly board: £1955-£1955
Full board: £1955-£1955

○ Boy ○ Girl ● Co-ed
● Day ● Week ● Board

Saint George's School is an IAPS Preparatory School catering for day and boarding pupils. It is set in idyllic grounds close to the sea. Classes are small and all teachers are qualified. Pupils are prepared for the Common Entrance Examination. Many and varied extra-curricular activities are offered. Daily buses deliver and collect pupils from outlying towns and villages.

St Joseph's College

Address: Birkfield, Ipswich, Suffolk IP2 9DR

Telephone: 0473 690281

Head: Mr D Hennessy

Age range: 4-18
No. of pupils: 828
Scholarships: Yes
Religion:

Fees per term
Day: £883-£1356
Weekly board: £1917-£2136
Full board: £2130-£2374

● Boy ● Girl ○ Co-ed
● Day ● Week ● Board

Pupils learn to relate to all people by seeking greater understanding of them, by thinking critically about all aspects of life and seeing themselves as unique and valuable. Parents, choose a place where you are as certain as you can be that your child will be happy and so gain self-esteem. Girls 16-18.

St Joseph's Preparatory School *

Address: Oak Hill Lane,
Oakhill, Ipswich, Suffolk
IP2 9AN
Telephone: 0473 601927

Age range: 4-11
No. of pupils: 200
Scholarships:
Religion: Roman Catholic

Fees per term
Day: -
Weekly board: -
Full board: -

● ○ ○
Boy Girl Co-ed
● ○ ○
Day Week Board

Head: Mr D Evans

For further information and a prospectus, please contact the school.

Starting Points PP and Southfield Pre-Preparatory School

Address: School Lane,
Halesworth, Suffolk IP19 8BW
Telephone: 0986 874569

Age range: 2-8
No. of pupils: 60
Scholarships:
Religion: Non-denominational

Fees per term
Day: -£730
Weekly board: -
Full board: -

○ ○ ●
Boy Girl Co-ed
● ○ ○
Day Week Board

Head: Mrs J Jones

For further information and a prospectus, please contact the school.

Stoke College

Address: Stoke by Clare,
Sudbury, Suffolk CO10 8JE
Telephone: 0787 278141

Age range: 3-16
No. of pupils: 283
Scholarships:
Religion: Non-denominational

Fees per term
Day: £910-£1356
Weekly board: £1920-£2211
Full board: -

○ ○ ●
Boy Girl Co-ed
● ● ○
Day Week Board

Head: Mr J G Mitchell

The aim of the school is to provide a broad balanced and relevant curriculum within a disciplined but friendly, Christian environment. Children are taught in small classes and examination results are above national averages. In addition to a wide range of extra-curricular activites a language development unit provides support for a small number of dyslexic pupils.

Summerhill School

Address: Leiston, Suffolk
IP16 4HY
Telephone: 0728 830540

Age range: 6-16
No. of pupils: 65
Scholarships:
Religion:

Fees per term
Day: -
Weekly board: -
Full board: -

○ ○ ●
Boy Girl Co-ed
● ○ ●
Day Week Board

Head: Mrs Z S Readhead

For further information and a prospectus, please contact the school.

Woodbridge School

Address: Woodbridge, Suffolk
IP12 4JH

Telephone: 0394 385547

Head: Dr D Younger

Age range: 11-18
No. of pupils: 545
Scholarships:
Religion:

Fees per term
Day: -
Weekly board: -
Full board: -

○ Boy ○ Girl ● Co-ed
● Day ● Week ● Board

For further information and a prospectus, please contact the school.

SURREY

Aberdour

Address: Brighton Road, Burgh Heath, Tadworth, Surrey KT20 6AJ
Telephone: 0737 354119

Head: Mr A Barraclough

Age range: 3-13
No. of pupils: 250
Scholarships: Yes
Religion: Church of England

Fees per term
Day: £500-£1310
Weekly board: -
Full board: -

● Boy   ○ Girl   ○ Co-ed
● Day   ○ Week   ○ Board

Aberdour prides itself on quality of excellence in all fields. Scholarships have been won to many major senior schools: boys are encouraged in music- there is a school orchestra, concert band and choir: all usual games are taught by skilled coaches: drama, art and craft are enjoyed during school and after-school clubs. An excellent all-round and academic start in life.

Abinger Hammer Village School

Address: Hackhurst Lane, Abinger Hammer, Dorking, Surrey RH5 6SE
Telephone: 0306 730343

Head: Ms B Turner BEd

Age range: 5-8
No. of pupils: 20
Scholarships:
Religion: Christian

Fees per term
Day: -
Weekly board: -
Full board: -

○ Boy   ○ Girl   ● Co-ed
● Day   ○ Week   ○ Board

The village school which survived closure by establishing a charitable trust, there are no fees. All National Curriculum subjects are covered in a friendly atmosphere with individual attention. Children go on into the state system or private sector.

Aldro School

Shackleford, Godalming, Surrey GU8 6AS

Telephone: 0483 810266

Head: Mr I M Argyle

Age range: 8-13
No. of pupils: 194
Scholarships: Yes
Religion: Church of England

Fees per term
Day: £1900-
Weekly board: -
Full board: £2570-

● Boy   ○ Girl   ○ Co-ed
● Day   ○ Week   ● Board

Aldro stands in over 25 acres of outstanding beauty, convenient for London and airports. Boys are encouraged to develop their full potential in all spheres, led by the headmaster and his wife. Boys are prepared for leading public schools. There is a wide range of sporting and leisure activities, an active drama department, flourishing music school, cubs and scouts.

Ambleside School

Address: 1 West Drive, Cheam, Surrey SM2 7NP
Telephone: 081 642 2862

Head: Mrs L M Vaughan Stevens

Age range: 3-7
No. of pupils: 100
Scholarships:
Religion: Church of England

Fees per term
Day: £516-£810
Weekly board: -
Full board: -

○ Boy   ○ Girl   ● Co-ed
● Day   ○ Week   ○ Board

The school was founded in 1926. Our aim in education is to give pupils wide interests and a good basic knowledge, using modern methods. All pupils are encouraged to develop their talents and personality, and every pupil is given individual consideration. The School attaches great importance to sound discipline and good manners.

The American Community School Ltd p701

Address: Heywood,
Portsmouth Road, Cobham,
Surrey KT11 1BL
Telephone: 0932 867251

Head: Mr P Hlozek

Age range: 4-18
No. of pupils: 1165
Scholarships:
Religion: Non-denominational

Fees per term
Day: £3265-£3750
Weekly board: -£5415
Full board: -£6065

○ ○ ● Boy Girl Co-ed
● ● ● Day Week Board

Spacious campus near to London. Stable environment, high educational standards, happy social life for relocated youngsters. Fully accredited co-educational day school pre-kindergarten to grade 13. Full and 5-day boarding grades 7-13. Advanced Placement and International Baccalaureate programs additional to curriculum designed to promote acceptance at colleges and universities worldwide.

Amesbury Preparatory School

Address: Hazel Grove,
Hindhead, Surrey GU26 6BL
Telephone: 0428 604322

Head: Mr P R Cheater

Age range: 3-13
No. of pupils: 200
Scholarships: Yes
Religion: Church of England

Fees per term
Day: £1150-£1975
Weekly board: £2435-
Full board: -

○ ○ ● Boy Girl Co-ed
● ● ○ Day Week Board

Amesbury is a co-educational preparatory school for weekly boarders and day pupils. The grounds extend to 25 acres; facilities include the chapel, two grass tennis courts, floodlit all-weather surface (with two further courts), heated swimming pool, gymnasium, two science laboratories, art/craft/technology centre, specialist teaching rooms for all subjects. Pupils prepared for all independent senior schools.

Barfield Preparatory School

Address: Runfold, Farnham,
Surrey GU10 1PB
Telephone: 02518 2271

Head: Mr B J Hoar BA Cert Ed

Age range: 3-13
No. of pupils: 150
Scholarships:
Religion: None

Fees per term
Day: £895-£1645
Weekly board: -
Full board: -

○ ○ ● Boy Girl Co-ed
● ○ ○ Day Week Board

Barfield - situated in twelve beautiful acres, is a day preparatory school for girls and boys aged 3-13 years. Facilities are excellent, with a modern science/CDT centre and indoor heated swimming pool, together with recent developments which include six superb classrooms for Little Barfield, an art centre and special needs centre. Children, taught in small classes, thrive in a happy, stimulating atmosphere.

Barrow Hills School

Address: Roke Lane, Witley,
Godalming, Surrey GU8 5NY
Telephone: 0428 683639

Head: Fr R Barralet OFM

Age range: 4-13
No. of pupils: 145
Scholarships: Yes
Religion: Catholic

Fees per term
Day: £995-£1760
Weekly board: £2180-£2340
Full board: £2220-£2400

● ● ○ Boy Girl Co-ed
● ● ● Day Week Board

Barrow Hills is a Catholic preparatory school set in 40 acres of rural Surrey 10 miles south of Guildford and about 45 minutes by road from Heathrow and Gatwick. It is a Catholic school but non-Catholics are welcomed. All the children are encouraged to achieve their individual best through a curriculum that is demanding and yet supportive of individual needs. There is specialist support for those with learning difficulties.

Beech House School

Address: 15 Church Way, Sanderstead, Surrey CR2 0JT

Telephone: 081 660 6919

Head: Mrs M Robinson

Age range: 3-7
No. of pupils: 50
Scholarships:
Religion: None

Fees per term
Day: £410-£570
Weekly board: -
Full board: -

Co-ed / Day

Beech House provides kindergarten and preparatory education for girls and boys from 3 to 7 years. Small classes ensure each pupil individual attention from qualified and specialist staff. The school has a high standard of success in entrance examinations.

Belmont School

Address: Feldemore, Holmbury St Mary, Dorking, Surrey RH5 6LQ
Telephone: 0306 730852

Head: Mr ST C Gainer

Age range: 4-13
No. of pupils: 210
Scholarships: Yes
Religion: Church of England

Fees per term
Day: £770-£1510
Weekly board: £2245-
Full board: -

Co-ed / Day, Week

IAPS school with good boarding facilities from 7 upwards. Specialist dyslexia unit for 40 children in new purpose-built accommodation. Other facilities include sports hall, all-weather pitch, swimming pool, computer room and drama studio. Excellent academic and sporting traditions in a caring, friendly environment. 60 acres of beautiful grounds in rural Surrey.

Box Hill School

Address: Mickleham, Dorking, Surrey RH5 6EA

Telephone: 0372 373382

Head: Dr R A S Atwood

Age range: 11-18
No. of pupils: 300
Scholarships: Yes
Religion: Non-denominational

Fees per term
Day: £1885-
Weekly board: £2974-
Full board: £3035-

Co-ed / Day, Week, Board

The school stands in 40 acres of attractive grounds near London. It has a strong academic tradition but also seeks to produce a well rounded citizen not just one who is academically successful. Afternoons are used for a wide range of compulsory activities, sports, expedition work and DOE Award Scheme. Drama and music play a strong part in the life of the school, and pupils are encouraged to play musical instruments.

Bramley

Address: Chequers Lane, Walton on the Hill, Tadworth, Surrey
Telephone: 0737 812004

Head: Mrs B Johns

Age range: 3-12
No. of pupils: 110
Scholarships:
Religion: Church of England

Fees per term
Day: £430-£950
Weekly board: -
Full board: -

Girl / Day

Bramley provides a happy, caring educational environment for girls aged 3-12, in which every individual is helped to attain her highest potential. Academic success is of obvious importance, but alongside that children are encouraged to develop their own interests and talents so that they become confident, considerate members of the community.

Bretby House School

Address: 39 Woodlands Avenue, New Malden, Surrey KT3 3UL
Telephone: 081 942 5779

Age range: 3-7
No. of pupils: 130
Scholarships:
Religion: Non-denominational

Fees per term
Day: £495-£1078
Weekly board: -
Full board: -

○ Boy ○ Girl ● Co-ed
● Day ○ Week ○ Board

Head: Mrs S M Mallin

For further details and a prospectus, please contact the school.

Broomfield House School

Address: 10 Broomfield Road, Kew Gardens, Richmond, Surrey TW9 3HS
Telephone: 081 940 3884

Age range: 3-11
No. of pupils: 150
Scholarships:
Religion: Church of England

Fees per term
Day: £525-£1050
Weekly board: -
Full board: -

○ Boy ○ Girl ● Co-ed
● Day ○ Week ○ Board

Head: Mrs I O Harrow

For further details and a prospectus, please contact the school.

Bury's Court School

Address: Leigh, Reigate, Surrey RH2 8RE
Telephone: 0306 78372

Age range: 6-14
No. of pupils: 100+
Scholarships:
Religion: Christian

Fees per term
Day: £800-
Weekly board: -
Full board: -

● Boy ○ Girl ○ Co-ed
● Day ○ Week ○ Board

Head: Mr D V W White

For further information please contact the school.

Cable House School

Address: Horsell Rise, Woking, Surrey GU21 4AY
Telephone: 0483 760759

Age range: 3-11
No. of pupils: 125
Scholarships:
Religion: Non-denominational

Fees per term
Day: £840-£925
Weekly board: -
Full board: -

○ Boy ○ Girl ● Co-ed
● Day ○ Week ○ Board

Head: Mr R D G Elvidge

Cable House has an excellent academic record, which is achieved by a combination of small classes (maximum 15), enthusiastic members of staff and promotion based on ability rather than age. Every day, each child tackles number work, reading and writing before moving on to a variety of other subjects and activities. High standards of courtesy and behaviour are a particular feature of Cable House.

SURREY 447

Cambridge Tutors College p739

Address: Water Tower Hill, Croydon, Surrey

Telephone: 081 688 5284

Head: Mr D N Wilson

Age range: 16-19
No. of pupils: 250
Scholarships: Yes
Religion:

Fees per term
Day: £2097-£2332
Weekly board: -
Full board: -

○ ○ ● Boy Girl Co-ed
● ○ ○ Day Week Board

Cambridge Tutors College is situated in its own grounds only 10 minutes' walk from the town centre and East Croydon station. Teaching is in small groups and is supplemented by weekly tests and tuition in Study Skills. Accommodation is available with local families approved by the College. Courses offered: one-year GCSE; one-year, 18-month and two-year A Level.

Canbury School

Address: Kingston Hill, Kingston-upon-Thames, Surrey KT2 7LN
Telephone: 081 549 8622

Head: Mr J G Wyatt

Age range: 11-16
No. of pupils: 46
Scholarships: Yes
Religion: Non-denominational

Fees per term
Day: £688-£1375
Weekly board: -
Full board: -

○ ○ ● Boy Girl Co-ed
● ○ ○ Day Week Board

Canbury School was founded in 1982 with the aim of establishing a very small secondary school where pupils could enjoy the maximum amount of personal attention. The classes, which average 10 pupils, are taught a broad curriculum by very well qualified teachers. The school occupies a fine position on Kingston Hill with easy access to Richmond Park.

Caterham School *

Address: Harestone Valley, Caterham, Surrey CR3 6YA

Telephone: 0883 343028

Head: Mr S R Smith

Age range: 7-18
No. of pupils: 740
Scholarships: Yes
Religion: United Reformed

Fees per term
Day: £990-£1645
Weekly board: -
Full board: £2300-£3205

● ● ○ Boy Girl Co-ed
● ● ● Day Week Board

Continuity of education for boys from 7 to 18 is provided in a rural yet highly accessible setting. Girls are accepted in the sixth form. Large enough to provide a full range of academic and extra-curricular activities but small enough for every pupil to be known and to make their mark. High academic standards and a wide choice of sporting and cultural activities expand pupil horizons and fulfil their potential.

Charterhouse *

Address: Godalming, Surrey GU7 2DJ

Telephone: 0483 426796

Head: Mr P J Attenborough

Age range: 13-18
No. of pupils: 700
Scholarships: Yes
Religion: Church of England

Fees per term
Day: -
Weekly board: -
Full board: -£3855

● ● ○ Boy Girl Co-ed
○ ○ ● Day Week Board

Charterhouse seeks to continue its distinguished tradition of high standards academically and across a broad range of activities (eg intellectual, cultural, sporting). The aim of the school is to produce good citizens, intellectually curious, able to think for themselves and aware of the problems around them who have developed their individual potential and want to make the world a better place. Girtls accepted in the sixth form.

Cheswycks School

Address: Guildford Road, Frimley Green, Camberley, Surrey GU16 6PB
Telephone: 0252 835669

Heads: Mr and Mrs E Streete

Age range: 3-11
No. of pupils: 200
Scholarships:
Religion: Church of England

Fees per term
Day: -£995
Weekly board: -
Full board: -

○ ○ ● Boy Girl Co-ed
● ○ ○ Day Week Board

For further information and a prospectus, please contact the school.

Chinthurst School

Address: Tadworth Street, Tadworth, Surrey KT20 5QZ
Telephone: 0737 812011

Head: Mr T J Egan

Age range: 3-13
No. of pupils: 400
Scholarships:
Religion: Non-denominational

Fees per term
Day: £365-£1055
Weekly board: -
Full board: -

● ○ ○ Boy Girl Co-ed
● ○ ○ Day Week Board

Boys are prepared for all public schools by way of the Common Entrance or scholarships. A very experienced and well qualified staff ensure a high standard is achieved both academically and on the games field. Chinthurst has a 'family' ethos, aimed at the achievement of high academic standards allied to a purposeful and active school life within a happy environment.

City of London Freemen's School * p701

Address: Ashtead Park, Ashtead, Surrey KT21 1ET
Telephone: 0372 277933

Head: Mr D C Haywood

Age range: 8-18
No. of pupils: 680
Scholarships: Yes
Religion: Church of England

Fees per term
Day: £1278-£1713
Weekly board: £2145-£2580
Full board: £2232-£2667

○ ○ ● Boy Girl Co-ed
● ● ● Day Week Board

The HMC school, founded in 1854, originally for orphan children of Freemen. Now a fee paying school with high education standards - sending over 75% of pupils to universities each year. Twenty corporation scholarships and music awards are available annually.

Claremont Fan Court School

Address: Claremont Drive, Esher, Surrey KT10 9LY
Telephone: 0372 467841

Head: Mr J H Scott MA

Age range: 3-8
No. of pupils: 700
Scholarships: Yes
Religion: Christian Science

Fees per term:
Day: £505-£1715
Weekly board: £2615-£2725
Full board: £2615-£2725

○ ○ ● Boy Girl Co-ed
● ● ● Day Week Board

The foundation of the school rests upon a love for children and a deep appreciation of their God-given potential. The school maintains a high standard of academic expectation and achievement at all levels, but it also places importance on a friendly atmosphere in which pupils' own confidence and individuality can develop. A firm policy on Christian moral values is taken and children are encouraged to express them in daily life.

SURREY 449

Clewborough House Preparatory School

Address: Clewborough Drive, Camberley, Surrey GU15 1NX
Telephone: 0276 64799
Vice Principal: Mr R M Johnston

Age range: 3-13
No. of pupils: 250
Scholarships:
Religion: Non-denominational

Fees per term
Day: £1037-£1307
Weekly board: -
Full board: -

○ ○ ● Boy Girl Co-ed
● ○ ○ Day Week Board

Clewborough House Preparatory School has established itself as a school that encourages academic and sporting excellence. A wide variety of sporting facilities are provided, including football, netball, athletics, squash, trampolining, tennis, skiing, canoeing, adventure training, judo, archery, ballet, riding and swimming. Extra-curricular activities are available for all age groups until 6pm every evening.

Cobham Montessori Nursery School

Address: 23 Spencer Road, Cobham, Surrey
Telephone: 03068 76465
Head: Mrs S Hall

Age range: 2-5
No. of pupils: 40
Scholarships:
Religion: All

Fees per term
Day: -£385
Weekly board: -
Full board: -

○ ○ ● Boy Girl Co-ed
○ ○ ○ Day Week Board

The school was started over 30 years ago by its principal Mrs Hall and has sent children into state and private schools with reading, writing and social skills. The children learn in a happy environment of three separate halls and grass garden, with trained staff. Part-time pro-rata.

Collingwood School

Address: 3 Springfield Road, Wallington, Surrey SM6 0BD
Telephone: 081 647 4607
Head: Mr D W Sweet

Age range: 3-11
No. of pupils: 180
Scholarships:
Religion: Non-denominational

Fees per term
Day: £785-
Weekly board: -
Full board: -

○ ○ ● Boy Girl Co-ed
● ○ ○ Day Week Board

Collingwood offers a rounded education where the higher academic achievement possible for each child, an enthusiastic approach to a wide variety of sports and activities and a happy disciplined atmosphere are combined with the expectation of good manners and behaviour, and a concern for others. Children normally enter at 3, 5 or 7, but may enter at other ages.

Commonweal Lodge School

Address: Woodcote Lane, Purley, Surrey CR8 3HB
Telephone: 081 660 3179
Head: Miss J M Brown

Age range: 4-18
No. of pupils: 240
Scholarships: Yes
Religion: Non-denominational

Fees per term
Day: £416-£1299
Weekly board: -
Full board: -

○ ● ○ Boy Girl Co-ed
● ○ ○ Day Week Board

Commonweal Lodge is an independent day school for girls. It was founded in 1916 and in 1958 an educational trust was set up and Commonweal Lodge became a public school. At Commonweal our aim is to educate girls to use their individual abilities to the full. The school is non-denominational and has sound standards and values based on Christian principles.

Coniston School

Address: 22 Alma Road,
Reigate, Surrey RH2 0DH

Telephone: 0737 243370

Head: Mrs M H Harvey

Age range: 3-8
No. of pupils: 90
Scholarships:
Religion: Church of England

Fees per term
Day: £277-£806
Weekly board: -
Full board: -

● Boy ○ Girl ○ Co-ed (filled: Co-ed)
● Day ○ Week ○ Board

Coniston is a school with small classes of 16 pupils maximum in each of the senior classes, but much lower numbers for younger children. This, together with total staff commitment, ensures very high academic standards. The school also offers day/extended care from 8.30 to 5.30 for working mothers.

Coworth Park School

Address: Valley End,
Chobham, Woking, Surrey
GU24 8TE

Telephone: 0276 855707

Head: Mrs P S Middleton

Age range: 3-11 girls
No. of pupils: 150
Scholarships:
Religion: Christian

Fees per term
Day: £565-£1250
Weekly board: -
Full board: -

Boy ○ Girl ○ Co-ed ●
Day ● Week ○ Board ○

Coworth Park is an independent pre-preparatory and preparatory school for boys and girls. Founded in 1971 the school has recently moved into lovely premises at Valley End, Chobham, from their previous site in Sunningdale. The school is inter-denominational and is managed by a Board of Governors elected by parents. Classes are small and staffed by qualified and experienced teachers.

Cranleigh Preparatory School

Address: Cranleigh, Surrey
GU6 8QH

Telephone: 0483 274199

Head: Mr M R Keppie

Age range: 7-13
No. of pupils: 177
Scholarships: Yes
Religion: Church of England

Fees per term
Day: -£1895
Weekly board: -
Full board: -£2515

Boy ● Girl ○ Co-ed ○
Day ● Week ○ Board ●

The entry is by interview and a simple non-competitive test. The curriculum is broad and balanced, a blend of the traditional and the modern which has plenty in it to excite and extend. There are also various extra-curricular activities and hobbies. Substantial time is set aside each day for games and sports.

Cranleigh School ✱ p740

Address: Cranleigh, Surrey
GU6 8QQ

Telephone: 0483 273997

Head: Mr T A A Hart

Age range: 13-18
No. of pupils: 550
Scholarships: Yes
Religion: Church of England

Fees per term
Day: £2635-
Weekly board: -
Full board: £3510-

Boy ● Girl ● Co-ed ○
Day ● Week ○ Board ●

High academic aims; strong pastoral support; a busy but enjoyable life; Cranleigh's essentially boarding community encourages its members to make the most of their varied potential, to relish challenge, to be known as individuals. Facilities are excellent. Most parents live close enough to come regularly to a wide range of musical, dramatic, artistic and sporting events: to get to know us well. Girls accepted in VI form.

Cranmore School

Address: West Horsley, Surrey KT24 6AT

Telephone: 04865 4137

Head: Mr K A Cheney

Age range: 3-13
No. of pupils: 475
Scholarships:
Religion: Roman Catholic

Fees per term
Day: £400-£1290
Weekly board: -
Full board: -

● Boy ○ Girl ○ Co-ed
● Day ○ Week ○ Board

Cranmore is a Roman Catholic foundation but boys of all religious denominations are accepted and integrate harmoniously. Excellent scholarship and Common Entrance results are achieved annually. Superb facilities - attractive classrooms, computers, gymnasium, sports hall, swimming pool, music building and eight games pitches. Many extra-curricular activities. Excellent academic, sporting and music traditions.

Croham Hurst School *

Address: 79 Croham Road, South Croydon, Surrey CR2 7YN
Telephone: 081 680 3064

Head: Miss J M Shelmerdine BSc

Age range: 4-18
No. of pupils: 560
Scholarships: Yes
Religion: Non-denominational

Fees per term
Day: £600-£1260
Weekly board: -
Full board: -

○ Boy ● Girl ○ Co-ed
● Day ○ Week ○ Board

The school provides a balanced and challenging education within a caring and stimulating atmosphere. It lies on a pleasant open site and buildings include assembly hall and libraries, large science block, modern technology and computer facilities; fine art, music and sporting facilities. The curriculum is challenging and up to date and most students go on to higher education including Oxbridge.

Croydon High School GPDST *

Address: Old Farleigh Road, Selsdon, Old Croydon, Surrey CR2 8YB
Telephone: 081 651 5020

Head: Mrs P E Davies

Age range: 4-18
No. of pupils: 1050
Scholarships: Yes
Religion: Non-denominational

Fees per term
Day: £1036-£1340
Weekly board: -
Full board: -

○ Boy ● Girl ○ Co-ed
● Day ○ Week ○ Board

Croydon High School offers an excellent academic education to girls of ability from a wide range of backgrounds. As well as high academic standards there is a strong emphasis on music, drama, art and sport. We seek to develop tolerance and sensitivity towards other by the standards of conduct set within school and by serving others in the local community.

Cumnor House School

Address: 168 Pampisford Road, Croydon, Surrey CR2 6DA
Telephone: 081 660 3445

Head: Mr A A Jeans ACP M(Coll)P

Age range: 4-13
No. of pupils: 350
Scholarships: Yes
Religion: Church of England

Fees per term
Day: £1100-£1255
Weekly board: -
Full board: -

● Boy ○ Girl ○ Co-ed
● Day ○ Week ○ Board

A high standard of work is maintained throughout the school, and the school record of examination success is outstanding. The school encourages participation in a wide range of sporting activities including soccer, rugby, cricket, swimming, table tennis and athletics. Its record in this sphere is exceptional. Music and drama flourish.

Danes Hill School

Address: Leatherhead Road, Oxshott, Surrey KT22 0JG

Telephone: 0372 842509

Head: Mr R Parfitt MA, MSc

Age range: 2-13
No. of pupils: 660
Scholarships: Yes
Religion: Church of England

Fees per term
Day: £223-£1548
Weekly board: -
Full board: -

Boy ○ Girl ○ Co-ed ●
Day ● Week ○ Board ○

Danes Hill prepares children for all independent schools. A high academic record (44 scholarships in the last five years) combines happily with a strong tradition of sporting prowess. The curriculum is broad and a wide range of extra curricular activity is encouraged. The junior school is situated separately, but is within easy walking distance of the main school.

Danesfield Preparatory School

Address: Rydens Avenue, Walton-on-Thames, Surrey

Telephone: 0932 220930

Head: Mrs T C Yates

Age range: 4-11
No. of pupils: 160
Scholarships:
Religion: Non-denominational

Fees per term
Day: £450-£845
Weekly board: -
Full board: -

Boy ○ Girl ○ Co-ed ●
Day ● Week ○ Board ○

Danesfield endeavours to provide the children with the best possible opportunities for personal growth, progress in scholarship and the development of cultural appreciation and ability.

Doods Brow School

Address: 54 High Street, Nutfield, Redhill, Surrey RH1 4HQ
Telephone: 0737 823372

Head: Mrs B D Wadlow

Age range: 3-11
No. of pupils: 100
Scholarships:
Religion: Church of England

Fees per term
Day: £510-£620
Weekly board: -
Full board: -

Boy ○ Girl ○ Co-ed ●
Day ● Week ○ Board ○

The school is housed in a building of great architectural interest and has been fully modernised to present day standards. There is a modern, fully equipped gym and science room. The school is situated on the main A25 at Nutfield on a main bus route to Godstone and Redhill. Experienced and well qualified staff prepare the children for schools of their parents' choice.

Downsend

Address: 1 Leatherhead Road, Leatherhead, Surrey KT22 8TJ

Telephone: 0372 372197

Head: Mr A D White

Age range: 7-13
No. of pupils: 350
Scholarships:
Religion: Non-denominational

Fees per term
Day: £1215-
Weekly board: -
Full board: -

Boy ● Girl ○ Co-ed ○
Day ● Week ○ Board ○

Downsend is a traditional academic preparatory school and a thriving community. The school plays an important role in developing the character and personality of each boy, providing a strong academic framework, a wealth of opportunities and good facilities. Downsend boys are thus able to achieve examination success and gain confidence for future life.

Downsend Lodge (Ashtead)

Address: 22 Oakfield Road, Ashtead, Surrey KT21 2RE

Telephone: 0372 273778

Head: Mrs M R New

Age range: 2-7
No. of pupils: 100
Scholarships:
Religion: Non-denominational

Fees per term
Day: -£920
Weekly board: -
Full board: -

Boy ○ Girl ○ Co-ed ●
Day ● Week ○ Board ○

Downsend Lodge (Ashtead) prides itself in providing a happy, caring and supportive environment where each child is presented with opportunities to develop mind, body and spirit. Our aim is to encourage children to achieve their potential in all areas of the curriculum, thus preparing them for a happy and successful career in the next stage of their education.

Downsend Lodge (Epsom)

Address: 6 Norman Avenue, Epsom, Surrey KT17 3NL

Telephone: 0372 721824

Head: Mrs G Brooks

Age range: 3-7
No. of pupils: 130
Scholarships:
Religion:

Fees per term
Day: £245-£825
Weekly board: -
Full board: -

Boy ○ Girl ○ Co-ed ●
Day ● Week ○ Board ○

Downsend Lodge (Epsom) is a pre-preparatory department of Downsend Group of Schools. People make a school, although buildings and grounds certainly help, and the school is fortunate in both. It is the staff, children and the parents who are most important, and a visit to the school will demonstrate how the Headmistress and her teachers aim to do the very best for every child at Downsend Lodge (Epsom).

Downsend Lodge (Rowans)

Address: 13 Epsom Road, Leatherhead, Surrey KT22 8ST

Telephone: 0372 372123

Head: Mrs Kekwick

Age range: 3-7
No. of pupils:
Scholarships:
Religion:

Fees per term
Day: £945-£995
Weekly board: -
Full board: -

Boy ○ Girl ○ Co-ed ●
Day ● Week ○ Board ○

The main aim of the school is to provide a happy, caring environment in which the children can develop their many skills at this very important stage of their lives. Preparation is made for transfer at the age of 7 to a variety of local schools including Downsend for boys and Downsend Lodge (senior girls).

Downsend Lodge Senior Girls

Address: 1 Leatherhead Road, Leatherhead, Surrey KT22 8TJ

Telephone: 0372 362668

Head: Mrs D M Harvey

Age range: 7-13
No. of pupils: 100
Scholarships:
Religion: Christian

Fees per term
Day: £1215-£1215
Weekly board: -
Full board: -

Boy ○ Girl ● Co-ed ○
Day ● Week ○ Board ○

Downsend Lodge has a strong academic reputation and aims to provide a balanced education within which each girl is individually monitored to ensure maximum development of her potential both academically and socially. Specialist staff encourage all to take part in music, drama and dance productions and to make use of the excellent sports facilities.

Downside Preparatory School

Address: 1 Woodcote Lane, Woodcote, Purley, Surrey CR8 3HB
Telephone: 081 660 0558

Head: Mr T I Andrews

Age range: 3-14
No. of pupils: 285
Scholarships:
Religion: Church of England

Fees per term
Day: £495-£1260
Weekly board: -
Full board: -

● ○ ○
Boy Girl Co-ed
● ○ ○
Day Week Board

Downside School and Lodge is an independent boys' preparatory school, educating boys from three and a half to thirteen and a half. It has spacious grounds, a caring, qualified staff, small classes and excellent facilities. Downside has a strong musical tradition, and extra activities include computing, carpentry, chess, judo and gymnastic clubs. It is accessible from all main routes.

Drayton House School

Address: 35 Austen Road, Guildford, Surrey GU13 3MP
Telephone: 0483 504707

Head: Mrs J Tyson-Jones

Age range: 2-8
No. of pupils: 100
Scholarships:
Religion: Non-denominational

Fees per term
Day: £500-£800
Weekly board: -
Full board: -

○ ○ ●
Boy Girl Co-ed
● ○ ○
Day Week Board

For further information and a prospectus, please contact the school.

Duke of Kent School p702

Address: Ewhurst, Cranleigh, Surrey GU6 7NS
Telephone: 0483 277313

Head: Mr R K Wilson

Age range: 7-13
No. of pupils: 170
Scholarships: Yes
Religion: Church of England

Fees per term
Day: £1338-£1857
Weekly board: -
Full board: £2053-£2993

○ ○ ●
Boy Girl Co-ed
● ○ ●
Day Week Board

Duke of Kent School is a co-educational boarding school for 140 full boarders and 30 day-boarders. It is situated 10 miles from Guildford and has excellent modern facilities for science, computers, CDT, art, music and drama. Games facilities, which include a heated indoor swimming pool are extensive. High academic standards and a homely and caring atmosphere enable all children to thrive.

Dunottar School

Address: High Trees Road, Reigate, Surrey RH2 7EL
Telephone: 0737 761945

Head: Miss J Burnell

Age range: 5-18
No. of pupils: 455
Scholarships: Yes
Religion: Non-denominational

Fees per term
Day: £695-£1260
Weekly board: -
Full board: -

○ ● ○
Boy Girl Co-ed
● ○ ○
Day Week Board

Dunottar is a member of the Girls' Schools Association and ISIS. The school aims to enable each girl to reach her full potential academically and personally. Leadership qualities are strongly encouraged and the school has a flourishing sixth form. Modern facilities and a happy environment enable students to produce excellent public examination results. The school has a strong sporting and musical traditions.

Eagle House

Address: Sandhurst,
Camberley, Surrey
GU17 8PH
Telephone: 0344 772134

Age range: 7-13
No. of pupils: 200
Scholarships: Yes
Religion: Church of England

Fees per term
Day: £1870-
Weekly board: £2560-
Full board: £2560-

● ○ ○
Boy Girl Co-ed
● ● ●
Day Week Board

Head: Mr S J Carder

Eagle House is a boarding and day preparatory school for boys aged 7-13. The extensive grounds are adjacent to those of Wellington College with which the school enjoys close links. The boys are prepared for Common Entrance and Scholarship examinations at 13+ (30 awards won in the past 3 years). Long tradition of excellence in sport and the Arts.

Edgeborough School p702

Address: Frensham, Farnham,
Surrey GU10 3AH
Telephone: 025 125 2495

Age range: 3-13
No. of pupils: 190
Scholarships:
Religion: Church of England

Fees per term
Day: £450-£1800
Weekly board: £2600-
Full board: £2600-

○ ○ ●
Boy Girl Co-ed
● ● ●
Day Week Board

Head: Mr R A Jackson

Edgeborough school, set in 40 acres of beautiful woodland, is a co-educational boarding and day school which prepares children for entry to public school at 13+. A thriving pre-preparatory, opened in September 1991, and a nursery class planned for January 1993 enables the school to offer a continuous education to a high academic standard from 3 to 13, in classroom and sporting facilities suited to the demands of the 1990s.

Elmhurst Ballet School

Address: Heathcote Road,
Camberley, Surrey GU15 2EU
Telephone: 0276 65301

Age range: 9-18
No. of pupils: 265
Scholarships:
Religion: Church of England

Fees per term
Day: £1808-£2012
Weekly board: -
Full board: £2582-£2745

○ ○ ●
Boy Girl Co-ed
● ○ ●
Day Week Board

Head: Mr J Skitch BSc

Provision for academic and vocational dance, drama and musical theatre training for girls and boys aged 10-19. Accredited by the Independent Schools Joint Council, provision for GCSE and A Levels. Accredited by Council for Dance Education and Training. Major RAD and ISTD dance examinations. Boarding and day pupils. Many new buildings and studios. Excellent facilities.

Elmhurst School for Boys

Address: South Park Hill Road,
Croydon, Surrey CR2 7DW
Telephone: 081 688 0661

Age range: 4-11
No. of pupils: 243
Scholarships:
Religion: Non-denominational

Fees per term
Day: £915-£1085
Weekly board: -
Full board: -

● ○ ○
Boy Girl Co-ed
● ○ ○
Day Week Board

Heads: Mr R E Anderson, Mr B K Dighton

Elmhurst School provides a friendly, family atmosphere where boys (aged 4-11) can enjoy school, experience a wide curriculum, including computer studies, sports, drama etc. and be prepared for entry to schools such as Whitgift and Trinity. Prospective parents are welcome to visit the school and judge the atmosphere and attainments for themselves.

Emberhurst

Address: 94 Ember Lane, Esher, Surrey

Telephone: 081 398 2933

Head: Mrs S D Hunter

Age range: 3-8
No. of pupils: 45
Scholarships:
Religion: Non-denominational

Fees per term
Day: -
Weekly board: -
Full board: -

○ ○ ● Boy Girl Co-ed
● ○ ○ Day Week Board

For further details and a prospectus, please contact the school. Fees upon application.

Eothen

Address: 3 Harestone Hill, Caterham, Surrey CR3 6SG

Telephone: 0883 343386

Head: Mrs A Coutts

Age range: 3-18
No. of pupils: 300
Scholarships: Yes
Religion:

Fees per term
Day: £465-£1401
Weekly board: -
Full board: -

○ ● ○ Boy Girl Co-ed
● ○ ○ Day Week Board

Eothen is a happy place with an air of positive achievement. Foundation for this is laid in the pre-preparatory department and developed in the preparatory school. Girls move to main school at 11 and embark on a wide curriclum specialising at 14+.

Epsom College *

Address: Epsom, Surrey KT17 4JQ

Telephone: 0372 723621

Head: Mr A H Beadles

Age range: 13-18
No. of pupils: 660
Scholarships: Yes
Religion: Christian

Fees per term
Day: £2500-£2500
Weekly board: £3280-£3280
Full board: £3330-£3330

● ● ○ Boy Girl Co-ed
● ● ● Day Week Board

Epsom College has a fine site of 80 acres close to open countryside, 15 miles south of central London. The school is very well equipped with virtually every necessary facility. Pupils are expected to aim for very high academic standards and at the same time be fully involved in the life of a very active community. Most leavers go to degree courses at universities. Girls are accepted in the sixth form.

Essendene Lodge

Address: Essendene Road, Caterham, Surrey CR3 5PB

Telephone: 0883 348349

Headmistress: Mrs S A Haydock *Headmaster:* Mr J G Davies

Age range: 2-11
No. of pupils: 195
Scholarships:
Religion: Non-denominational

Fees per term
Day: £315-£650
Weekly board: -
Full board: -

○ ○ ● Boy Girl Co-ed
● ○ ○ Day Week Board

Essendene Lodge School - established in 1966 providing a broad based education for boys and girls. Low pupil to teacher ratio. Eleven classes with experienced and qualified staff including specialist teaching in some subjects. Full and varied curriculum incorporating the National Curriculum requirements with emphasis on sound foundation in basic subjects using traditional methods.

Ewell Castle School

Address: Church Street, Ewell, Epsom, Surrey KT17 2PQ

Telephone: 081 393 1413

Head: Mr R A Fewtrell

Age range: 3-18
No. of pupils: 500
Scholarships: Yes
Religion: Church of England

Fees per term
Day: £680-£1290
Weekly board: -
Full board: -

Boy ● Girl ● Co-ed ○
Day ● Week ○ Board ○

We aim at excellence over a broad field: in academic work, in games, music and drama, in extra curricular activities and in self-discipline. The small size of the school ensures individual attention and small teaching groups within a friendly working environment. A family atmosphere exists with the pastoral and academic responsibilities shared by the staff as a whole.

Feltonfleet

Address: Cobham, Surrey KT11 1DR

Telephone: 0932 862264

Head: Mr D T Cherry

Age range: 7-13
No. of pupils: 164
Scholarships:
Religion: Church of England

Fees per term
Day: £1750-
Weekly board: -
Full board: £2350-

Boy ● Girl ○ Co-ed ○
Day ● Week ○ Board ●

Feltonfleet is a traditional IAPS boys' boarding and day preparatory school accepting boys from the age of 7 to 13. Strong emphasis placed on friendly, busy community. New buildings for art, design and technology, music, computing and science and leisure centre. Excellent sporting facilities, rugby, football, hockey, cricket, scouts/cubs, athletics, sailing, riding, shooting, swimming, tennis, squash, golf and judo.

Flexlands School

Address: Station Road, Chobham, Surrey GU24 8AG

Telephone: 0276 858841

Head: Mrs S Shaw BA

Age range: 3-11
No. of pupils: 184
Scholarships:
Religion: Non-denominational

Fees per term
Day: £496-£1295
Weekly board: -
Full board: -

Boy ● Girl ● Co-ed ○
Day ● Week ○ Board ○

Flexlands is a day preparatory school. Pupils are prepared for Common Entrance and entrance examinations to a variety of independent schools. Each class has a form mistress. Specialist teachers for science, French, mathematics, English, music, art and design technology. Sports include athletics, netball, rounders, tennis and swimming. The curriculum is broad and a high standard in encouraged in all subjects.

Frensham Heights School p703, p742

Address: Rowledge, Farnham, Surrey

Telephone: 025125 2134

Head: Mr A L Pattinson

Age range: 11-18
No. of pupils: 285
Scholarships: Yes
Religion: Non-denominational

Fees per term
Day: £2265-£2265
Weekly board: £3550-£3550
Full board: £3550-£3550

Boy ○ Girl ○ Co-ed ●
Day ● Week ● Board ●

Frensham Heights represents free thinking, the open mind and good human relations. It sees the aim of education as liberation from immobilising forces so that the personality may develop as fully as possible. It is genuinely co-educational, creatively dynamic, academically excellent, providing an enlightened and liberal education for a relatively mixed-ability intake.

The German School

Address: Douglas House, Petersham Road, Richmond, Surrey TW10 7AH
Telephone: 081 948 3410

Age range: 5-19
No. of pupils: 565
Scholarships:
Religion:

Fees per term
Day: -
Weekly board: -
Full board: -

Boy ○ Girl ○ Co-ed ●
Day ● Week ○ Board ○

Head: Mr E Backhaus

For further information and a prospectus, please contact the school.

Glaisdale School

Address: 14 Arundel Road, Cheam, Sutton, Surrey SM2 7AD
Telephone: 081 642 4266

Age range: 3-11
No. of pupils: 155
Scholarships:
Religion: Non-denominational

Fees per term
Day: £520-£660
Weekly board: -
Full board: -

Boy ○ Girl ○ Co-ed ●
Day ● Week ○ Board ○

Head: Mrs H M Steel

Glaisdale School was founded in 1925 and is administered by an educational trust with a governing body. As a small school we provide a happy, stimulating and constructive environment with a family atmosphere for children aged 3 to 11. All children are expected to play as full a part in school life as possible and to contribute their own particular strengths for the good of the school community and their own personal development.

Glenesk School

Address: Ockham Road North, West Horsley, Surrey
Telephone: 04865 2329

Age range: 3-8
No. of pupils: 197
Scholarships:
Religion: Church of England

Fees per term
Day: £625-£975
Weekly board: -
Full board: -

Boy ○ Girl ○ Co-ed ●
Day ● Week ○ Board ○

Head: Mrs S P Johnson

The early years of a young life are so important and Glenesk aims to create a secure, purposeful and happy environment with high standards for children to strive towards. In this atmosphere children will develop positive attitudes to work and play, self-confidence and a respect for others.

Grantchester House School

Address: 5 Hinchley Way, Hinchley Wood, Esher, Surrey KT10 0BD
Telephone: 081 398 1157

Age range: 3-7
No. of pupils: 96
Scholarships:
Religion: Non-denominational

Fees per term
Day: £556-£944
Weekly board: -
Full board: -

Boy ○ Girl ○ Co-ed ●
Day ● Week ○ Board ○

Head: Mrs A E M Fry

We are a small private school for boys and girls and aim to educate children to a high academic standard, but at the same time, we offer a caring and happy environment. Happiness and discipline are the keynote of the school.

Greenacre Shool for Girls p704

Address: Sutton Lane, Banstead, Surrey SM7 3RA

Telephone: 0737 352114

Head: Mrs P M Wood BA

Age range: 4-18
No. of pupils: 400
Scholarships: Yes
Religion: Non-denominational

Fees per term
Day: £830-£1424
Weekly board: -
Full board: -

○ ● ○
Boy Girl Co-ed
● ○ ○
Day Week Board

Greenacre School provides a sound academic education in a happy atmosphere. All pupils are encouraged to achieve their full potential and their individual strengths are nurtured by a caring and committed teaching staff. National Curriculum guidelines are followed leading to a full range of GCSE and A Level subjects (49) in the senior school. Extra curricular activities are varied and popular.

Greenfield School

Address: Brooklyn Road, Woking, Surrey GU22 7TP

Telephone: 0483 772525

Principal: Mrs J Becker

Age range: 3-11
No. of pupils: 150
Scholarships:
Religion: Non-denominational

Fees per term
Day: £375-£636
Weekly board: -
Full board: -

○ ○ ●
Boy Girl Co-ed
● ○ ○
Day Week Board

Greenfield is an independent junior day school for girls and boys aged 3-11. The best traditional and modern teaching are used, in a happy, purposeful atmosphere. Early emphasis upon reading and number skills ensures every child benefits from the full range of National Curriculum subjects. Children are well prepared for entry into chosen senior schools. Details from the principal.

The Grove School p703

Address: Portsmouth Road, Hindhead, Surrey GU26 6BW

Telephone: 0428 605407

Head: Mr C Brooks

Age range: 5-18
No. of pupils: 340
Scholarships: Yes
Religion: Church of England

Fees per term
Day: £969-£1674
Weekly board: £2115-£2580
Full board: £2175-£2640

○ ● ○
Boy Girl Co-ed
● ● ●
Day Week Board

Situated in 50 acres of woodland, just off the A3 at Hindhead, approximately one hour from Gatwick and Heathrow airports; ten minutes from Haslemere main-line station, making travelling very easy. The school has invested heavily in new building over the last five years and all teaching is in purpose-built accommodation with small classes in all subject areas.

Guildford High School *

Address: London Road, Guildford, Surrey GU1 1SJ

Telephone: 0483 61440

Head: Mrs S H Singer

Age range: 4-18
No. of pupils: 620
Scholarships: Yes
Religion: Church of England

Fees per term
Day: £877-£1464
Weekly board: -
Full board: -

○ ● ○
Boy Girl Co-ed
● ○ ○
Day Week Board

Guildford High School is an independent day school which aims to prepare young women to meet the challenges of adult life and make a mature contribution to the community. It is committed to the concept of equal opportunities and strives to make its pupils aware of the full range of courses available to them.

Hall Grove School

Address: London Road, Bagshot, Surrey GU19 5HZ

Telephone: 0276 473059

Head: Mr A R Graham

Age range: 4-13
No. of pupils: 225
Scholarships:
Religion: Non-denominational

Fees per term
Day: £1020-£1315
Weekly board: -
Full board: -

● Boy ○ Girl ○ Co-ed
● Day ○ Week ○ Board

Hall Grove is a popular family-run day preparatory school for boys set in 35 acres. It offers excellent teaching, and in 1992 a new classroom block was opened which has greatly enhanced the facilities. The school has an impressive range of sports and activities and a strong musical tradition. Boys are prepared for Common Entrance or scholarship at 13. In 1991 eleven scholarships to senior schools were awarded.

Halstead Preparatory School

Address: Woodham Rise, Woking, Surrey GU21 4EE

Telephone: 0483 772682

Head: Mrs A Hancock

Age range: 3-11
No. of pupils: 210
Scholarships:
Religion: Christian

Fees per term
Day: £460-£1080
Weekly board: -
Full board: -

○ Boy ● Girl ○ Co-ed
● Day ○ Week ○ Board

Halstead is a day preparatory school, having a happy, friendly atmosphere with high standards in all areas. There is a well-balanced broad curriculum resulting in excellent academic achievement to senior public schools. Musical, dramatic and artistic talents are encouraged. Faciltities include gymnasium, tennis courts, science laboratory, music rooms, computers. Fully qualified caring staff.

Haslemere Preparatory School

Address: The Heights, Hill Road, Haslemere, Surrey GU27 2JP

Telephone: 0428 642350

Head: Mr A C Morrison BEd CertEd

Age range: 5-13
No. of pupils: 200
Scholarships:
Religion: Non-denominational

Fees per term
Day: £1150-£1465
Weekly board: -
Full board: -

● Boy ○ Girl ○ Co-ed
● Day ○ Week ○ Board

The aim of the school is to introduce boys to a broad education. They should work hard at their studies and also enjoy life in a happy and well-ordered community. The school is proud of its record of helping boys of all abilities to make progress, not only through academic work, but also through sporting and other activities outside the class-room.

Hawley Place School

Address: Fernhill Road, Blackwater, Camberley, Surrey GU17 9HU

Telephone: 0276 32028

Heads: Mr T G Pipe, Mrs M L Pipe

Age range: 9-16
No. of pupils: 100
Scholarships: Yes
Religion: Non-denominational

Fees per term
Day: £990-
Weekly board: -
Full board: -

○ Boy ● Girl ○ Co-ed
● Day ○ Week ○ Board

Set in an ideal learning environment of 16 acres of beautiful grounds, Hawley Place is an independent day school for girls aged 9-16. Scholarship and School Assisted Places are available. An extensive range of GCSE subjects is offered and enviably small groups ensure personal attention to needs in a friendly caring atmosphere where courtesy, kindness and consideration are fostered in all pupils.

The Hawthorns

Address: Pendell Court, Bletchingley, Surrey RH1 4QJ

Telephone: 0883 743048

Head: Mr T R Johns

Age range: 3-13
No. of pupils: 298
Scholarships:
Religion: Church of England

Fees per term
Day: £300-£1250
Weekly board: -£1815
Full board: -

Boy ○ Girl ○ Co-ed ●
Day ● Week ● Board ○

For further information and a prospectus, please contact the school. Weekly boarding for boys from 7 years.

Hazelwood School

Address: Wolfs Hill, Limpsfield, Surrey RH8 0QU

Telephone: 0883 712194

Head: Mr R D Bawtree MA

Age range: 3-13
No. of pupils: 266
Scholarships:
Religion: Church of England

Fees per term
Day: £445-£1685
Weekly board: -
Full board: -£2405

Boy ○ Girl ○ Co-ed ●
Day ● Week ○ Board ●

Hazelwood is set in grounds of outstanding beauty. The school's unrivalled facilities include a recently built 200 seat theatre, a new music school and chapel, all weather surface for cricket, netball and tennis and an indoor swimming pool. A broadly based curriculum is offered and prepares boys and girls for entry into independent senior school through the Common Entrance or scholarship examinations.

Highfield School

Address: 143 Old Woking Road, Pyrford, Surrey

Telephone: 0932 342565

Head: Miss Pelmere

Age range: 2-8
No. of pupils:
Scholarships:
Religion: Non-denominational

Fees per term
Day: £136-£768
Weekly board: -
Full board: -

Boy ○ Girl ○ Co-ed ●
Day ● Week ○ Board ○

Highfield School - system is essentially informal as compared with ordinary kindergartens - as its specific aim is to develop the child in every way; emotionally, intellectually and physically, and not solely academically. By giving the pupil's imagination and inventiveness every chance to develop, it is found that the aptitude for lessons is greatly increased, also the ability to sustain applied concentration without effort.

Hoe Bridge School

Address: Hoe Place, Old Woking Road, Woking, Surrey

Telephone: 0483 760018

Head: Mr R W K Barr

Age range: 7-13
No. of pupils: 180
Scholarships:
Religion: Non-denominational

Fees per term
Day: £1415-£1630
Weekly board: £2140-£2355
Full board: -

Boy ● Girl ○ Co-ed ○
Day ● Week ● Board ○

Hoe Bridge School and its pre-preparatory school, The Trees, are well established in the Woking area. The prime aim of the schools is the development of the individual in a happy and caring atmosphere, so that whatever their ability pupils are best prepared for their future education.

Holy Cross Preparatory School p705

Address: George Road,
Kingston upon Thames,
Surrey KT2 7NU
Telephone: 081 942 0729

Head: Mrs M K Hayes

Age range: 4-11
No. of pupils: 240
Scholarships:
Religion: Roman Catholic

Fees per term
Day: -£925
Weekly board: -
Full board: -

● ● ○
Boy Girl Co-ed
● ○ ○
Day Week Board

A Catholic independent day school for girls aged 4-11 and boys aged 4-7 offering a quality all-round education in a caring manner for children of all abilities. The school has a proven record of attainment and a high success rate in gaining placements at public, high and grammar schoools. Prospectus on request. Member of ISIS.

Homefield Preparatory School

Address: Western Road,
Sutton, Surrey SM1 2TE

Telephone: 081 642 0965

Head: Mr P R Mowbray BA (Cantab)

Age range: 4-13
No. of pupils: 260
Scholarships: Yes
Religion: Non-denominational

Fees per term
Day: £760-£1200
Weekly board: -
Full board: -

● ○ ○
Boy Girl Co-ed
● ○ ○
Day Week Board

Homefield aims to provide a sound, broadly based education attuned to contemporary needs and in line with religious ideals. The school is proud of its record in helping boys of varying abilities to aquire initiative, to build self-confidence and to develop individual talents in their academic work and in a wide range of sporting and extra-curricular activities.

Hurtwood House

Address: Holmbury St Mary,
Dorking, Surrey RH5 6NU

Telephone: 0483 277416

Head: Mr K R B Jackson

Age range: 15-18
No. of pupils: 250
Scholarships: Yes
Religion: Non-denominational

Fees per term
Day: -
Weekly board: -
Full board: £4000-£5000

○ ○ ●
Boy Girl Co-ed
○ ○ ●
Day Week Board

Fully residential, co-educational sixth form college preparing English and overseas students for GCSEs, A Levels and university entrance. Well-qualified staff, small classes and weekly assessments in each subject. Excellent examination results and 90% university entrance in 1992. Located in its own 50 acre estate. Facilities include modern classrooms and laboratories. Theatre, and all-weather sports complex.

Kew College

Address: 24/26 Cumberland
Road, Kew Gardens,
Richmond, Surrey TW9 3HQ
Telephone: 081 940 2039

Head: Mrs D Lyness

Age range: 3-11
No. of pupils: 200
Scholarships:
Religion: Non-denominational

Fees per term
Day: £400-£575
Weekly board: -
Full board: -

○ ○ ●
Boy Girl Co-ed
● ○ ○
Day Week Board

For further information and a prospectus, please contact the school.

King Edward's School Witley *

Address: Wormley,
Godalming, Surrey GU8 5SG

Telephone: 0428 682572

Head: Mr R J Fox

Age range: 11-18
No. of pupils: 520
Scholarships: Yes
Religion: Church of England

Fees per term
Day: -£1985
Weekly board: -
Full board: -£2685

Boy ○ Girl ○ Co-ed ●
Day ● Week ○ Board ●

The school provides a structured approach to co-education in a caring community, which encompasses a wide cross-section of society. There are excellent teaching and living facilities, first class academic tuition and a full range of vocational and sporting activities. There are substantial bursaries available for children whose home circumstances make boarding education a real need.

King's House School

Address: 68 King's Road,
Richmond, Surrey TW10 6ES

Telephone: 081 940 1878

Head: Mr R Armitage MA

Age range: 4-13
No. of pupils: 360
Scholarships: Yes
Religion: Church of England

Fees per term
Day: £900-£1330
Weekly board: -
Full board: -

Boy ● Girl ○ Co-ed ○
Day ● Week ○ Board ○

As well as preparing boys for the next stage in their education, the aim of the school is to lay the foundations of a boy's character, so that he may grow up to think independently. The education prepares boys for Common Entrance Examination, and in appropriate cases for scholarship examinations. Boys leave the school to go to independent schools - both day and boarding.

Kingston Grammar School

Address: 70-72 London Road,
Kingston-upon-Thames,
Surrey KT2 6PY
Telephone: 081 546 5875

Head: Mr C D Baxter MA

Age range: 10-18
No. of pupils: 584
Scholarships: Yes
Religion: Church of England

Fees per term
Day: £1495-£1570
Weekly board: -
Full board: -

Boy ○ Girl ○ Co-ed ●
Day ● Week ○ Board ○

Kingston Grammar School is fully co-educational and is conveniently situated in Kingston teon centre, drawing pupils from Surrey and South West London. The boat house and extensive playing fields are located opposite Hampton Court Plalace. High academic standards are achieved (92% pass rates at A Level and GCSE in 1991) and sport (especially hockey and rowing), music, drama and art are outstanding.

Kingswood House School

Address: 56 West Hill, Epsom,
Surrey KT19 8LF

Telephone: 0372 723590

Head: Mr M Harvey BA

Age range: 4-13
No. of pupils: 210
Scholarships: Yes
Religion: Non-denominational

Fees per term
Day: £850-£1258
Weekly board: -
Full board: -

Boy ● Girl ○ Co-ed ○
Day ● Week ○ Board ○

Every child has considerable potential. Our aim is to help your son realise this, whether in class, on the sports field, stage, in art, or music. Each boy at Kingswood House is made to feel important in his own right; his efforts are praised and his abilities are valued. We strive to produce confident, responsible, polite and caring young men.

Lalelam Lea Preparatory School

Address: 29 Peaks Hill, Purley, Surrey CR8 3JJ

Telephone: 081 660 3351

Head: Mr A C F Baseley

Age range: 4-11
No. of pupils: 120
Scholarships:
Religion: Catholic

Fees per term
Day: £670-
Weekly board: -
Full board: -

● Boy ● Girl ○ Co-ed
● Day ○ Week ○ Board

To provide a happy and stimulating learning environment based on Catholic principles and ideals. To encourage confidence, reliability and self-discipline in order that children realise their full potential.

Lanesborough School

Address: Maori Road, Guildford, Surrey GU1 2EL

Telephone: 0483 502060

Head: Mr S Deller

Age range: 4-13
No. of pupils: 287
Scholarships: Yes
Religion: Church of England

Fees per term
Day: £680-£1404
Weekly board: -
Full board: -

● Boy ○ Girl ○ Co-ed
● Day ○ Week ○ Board

Lanesborough aims to stimulate an interest in learning by encouraging the proper use of memory and developing critical and reasoning powers. It believes social, moral and spiritual considerations are of the utmost importance. Lanesborough prepares boys for entry to the Royal Grammar School at either 11 or 13 and via Common Entrance to other independnent schools. Scholarships for Cathedral Choristers.

Laverock

Address: 19 Bluehouse Lane, Oxted, Surrey RH8 0AA

Telephone: 0883 714171

Head: Mrs A C Paterson

Age range: 3-11
No. of pupils: 170
Scholarships:
Religion: Non-denominational

Fees per term
Day: £350-£955
Weekly board: -
Full board: -

○ Boy ● Girl ○ Co-ed
● Day ○ Week ○ Board

Laverock aims to provide a broad-based curriculum in a happy and secure environment. High standards are maintained and the school has a strong tradition of music, good sports record and excellent academic results. Visitors are welcome to visit the school.

Linley House School

Address: 6 Berrylands Road, Surbiton, Surrey KT5 8RA

Telephone: 081 399 4979

Head: Mrs S Dainty

Age range: 3-7
No. of pupils: 30
Scholarships:
Religion: Non-denominational

Fees per term
Day: -
Weekly board: -
Full board: -

○ Boy ○ Girl ● Co-ed
● Day ○ Week ○ Board

For further information and a prospectus, please contact the school.

Longacre School

Address: Shamley Green, Guildford, Surrey GU5 0NQ

Telephone: 0483 893225

Head: Mrs H A Clarke NFF

Age range: 3-11
No. of pupils: 160
Scholarships:
Religion: Non-denominational

Fees per term
Day: £512-£1060
Weekly board: -
Full board: -

● Boy ● Girl ○ Co-ed
● Day ○ Week ○ Board

For further information and a prospectus, please contact the school. Boys 3-8, girls 3-11.

Lyndhurst School

Address: 36 The Avenue, Camberley, Surrey GU15 3NE

Telephone: 0276 22895

Head: Mr R L Cunliffe

Age range: 3-11
No. of pupils: 194
Scholarships: Yes
Religion: Non-denominational

Fees per term
Day: £385-£1015
Weekly board: -
Full board: -

○ Boy ○ Girl ● Co-ed
● Day ○ Week ○ Board

For further information and a prospectus, please contact the school.

Lynton Preparatory School

Address: Epsom Road, Ewell, Epsom, Surrey KT17 1LJ

Telephone: 081 393 4169

Head: Mrs V M A Thorns

Age range: 4-12
No. of pupils: 170
Scholarships:
Religion:

Fees per term
Day: £500-£575
Weekly board: -
Full board: -

○ Boy ○ Girl ● Co-ed
● Day ○ Week ○ Board

We endeavour to provide a solid foundation for future education and to stimulate the desire for knowledge. We feel that the child must be secure and happy in his school life if he is to develop his physical and mental capacity to the full. We encourage a spirit of independence coupled with a sense of responsibility towards each other. Good manners, consideration and reliability are regarded as important characteristics.

Manor House School

Address: Manor House Lane, Little Bookham, Leatherhead, Surrey KT23 4EN

Telephone: 0372 458538

Head: Mrs L A Mendes

Age range: 3-16
No. of pupils: 320
Scholarships: Yes
Religion: Church of England

Fees per term
Day: £365-£1604
Weekly board: £1203-£2399
Full board: -

● Boy ● Girl ○ Co-ed
● Day ● Week ○ Board

The aim of Manor House is to provide the best possible education opportunity for each pupil. The school recognises that children develop at different rates and have individual strengths and weaknesses so we expect to cater for them and this is possible by a high ratio of teachers to pupils. The curriculum is wide and the facilities are excellent. Boys 3-8, girls 3-16.

Marymount International School p705

Address: George Road,
Kingston-upon-Thames,
Surrey KT2 7PE
Telephone: 081 949 0571

Head: Sr R Sheridan

Age range: 11-18
No. of pupils: 200
Scholarships:
Religion: Roman Catholic

Fees per term
Day: £1966-£2166
Weekly board: £3633-£3833
Full board: £3700-£3900

Boy ○ Girl ● Co-ed ○
Day ● Week ● Board ○

In beautiful landscaped grounds, Marymount combines a desire to care for and nurture its students with an emphasis on academic excellence which leads to a 98% university entrance rate. With a 10:1 student/teacher ratio and first-class facilities, the girls are helped to grow into confident and international young women. The American College Preparatory Curriculum and the Int.Baccalaureate programmes are followed.

Micklefield School

Address: 10/12 Somers Road,
Reigate, Surrey RH2 9DU
Telephone: 0737 242615

Head: Mrs C Belton BA

Age range: 2-12
No. of pupils: 320
Scholarships:
Religion: Non-denominational

Fees per term
Day: £195-£1035
Weekly board: -
Full board: -

Boy ● Girl ● Co-ed ○
Day ● Week ○ Board ○

Pupils accepted from two-and-a-half-years. Lower school co-educational, preparing boys for transfer to preparatory schools at seven. Upper school girls prepared for Common Entrance Examinations. Graduate teachers are reasponsible for much of the academic work of the older girls. Emphasis is also given to the teaching of information technology and design technology throughout the school.

Milbourne Lodge School

Address: 43 Arbrook Lane,
Esher, Surrey KT10 9EG
Telephone: 0372 462737

Head: Mr N R Hale

Age range: 8
No. of pupils: 200
Scholarships: Yes
Religion: Non-denominational

Fees per term
Day: £1300-£1350
Weekly board: -
Full board: -

Boy ○ Girl ○ Co-ed ●
Day ● Week ○ Board ○

Milbourne Lodge prepares boys from the age of 8 for Common Entrance and scholarships to independent senior schools. A few girls are taken. Since 1950, 300 scholarships and exhibitions have been won including 45 to Winchester, and some to Eton. All usual games are played and the school has its own heated swimming pool and hard tennis court.

More House School

Address: Frensham, Farnham,
Surrey GU10 3AW
Telephone: 0251 252303

Head: Mr S M Mullen

Age range: 10-16
No. of pupils: 107
Scholarships:
Religion: Roman Catholic

Fees per term
Day: £1450-
Weekly board: £2335-
Full board: £2400-

Boy ● Girl ○ Co-ed ○
Day ● Week ● Board ●

More House School is offering secondary education for boys to GCSE level. Carefully structured small classes provide an environment which encourages boys to fulfil their potential. The pupil teacher ratio is excellent and the staff committed and well-qualified. Special help is available for children with specific learning difficulties, including dyslexia. The facilities, educational, residential and recreational are excellent

Normanton School

Address: 17-21 Normanton Road, South Croydon, Surrey

Telephone: 081 688 3095

Head: Mr N G Croxford

Age range: 3-18
No. of pupils: 172
Scholarships: Yes
Religion: Christian

Fees per term
Day: £440-£1080
Weekly board: -
Full board: -

Boy ○ Girl ○ Co-ed ●
Day ● Week ○ Board ○

Normanton School offers a full and varied curriculum with a wide range of GCSE options. There is a keen involvement in sport for all ages and abilities. There are small classes throughout the school and we aim to develop the potential of each child within a caring atmosphere. Facilities are available for children with learning difficulties.

Notre Dame Preparatory School

Address: Burwood House, Cobham, Surrey KT11 1HA

Telephone: 0932 862152

Head: Sister J Lanaghan

Age range: 3-11
No. of pupils: 300
Scholarships:
Religion: Roman Catholic

Fees per term
Day: £450-£1085
Weekly board: -
Full board: -

Boy ● Girl ● Co-ed ○
Day ● Week ○ Board ○

For further information and a prospectus, please contact the school. Boys 3-7, girls 3-11.

Notre Dame School

Address: Lingfield, Surrey RH7 6PH

Telephone: 0342 832407

Head: Mrs N E Shepley B.A.

Age range: 3-18
No. of pupils: 400
Scholarships: Yes
Religion: Ecumenical

Fees per term
Day: £390-£1245
Weekly board: -
Full board: -

Boy ● Girl ● Co-ed ○
Day ● Week ○ Board ○

Notre Dame provides education for girls 3-18, and boys 3-11 and 16-18. Ecumenical school in the Christian tradition, occupying beautiful grounds on the fringe of Lingfield. Provides a wide and balanced curriculum. Teaching groups are small and there is close monitoring of pupils' progress. The school has a fine tradition of academic excellence within a caring and friendly yet disciplined environment.

Nower Lodge School

Address: Coldharbour Lane, Dorking, Surrey RH4 3BT

Telephone: 0306 882448

Head: Miss A M Pearce BEd

Age range: 3-13
No. of pupils: 120
Scholarships:
Religion: Non-denominational

Fees per term
Day: £735-£1180
Weekly board: -
Full board: -

Boy ○ Girl ○ Co-ed ●
Day ● Week ○ Board ○

Nower Lodge is a co-educational preparatory school for children aged 3-13 years. The pre-school is open all year round for 3-5 year olds. Individual teaching is the essential characteristic in the pre-preparatory department and the preparatory school has a very successful Common Entrance record. For children requiring additional help there is a special needs facility.

Oakfield School

Address: Cold Harbour Road, Pyrford, Woking, Surrey GU22 8SJ
Telephone: 0932 342465

Head: Mrs R C Brothers

Age range: 3-16
No. of pupils: 180
Scholarships: Yes
Religion: Non-denominational

Fees per term
Day: £559-£1524
Weekly board: -
Full board: -

● Boy ● Girl ○ Co-ed
● Day ○ Week ○ Board

For further information and a prospectus, please contact the school. Boys 3-11, girls 3-16.

Oakhryst Grange School

Address: 160 Stanstead Road, Caterham, Surrey CR3 6AF
Telephone: 0883 343344

Head: Mrs D F Cooper DipEd

Age range: 4-12
No. of pupils: 140
Scholarships:
Religion: Non-denominational

Fees per term
Day: £350-£800
Weekly board: -
Full board: -

● Boy ○ Girl ○ Co-ed
● Day ○ Week ○ Board

For further information and a prospectus, please contact the school.

Oakland Nursery School

Address: Palmersfield Road, Banstead, Surrey SM7 2LD
Telephone: 0737 351157

Head: Mrs M Dollimore

Age range: 3-5
No. of pupils: 60
Scholarships:
Religion:

Fees per term
Day: £190-£315
Weekly board: -
Full board: -

○ Boy ○ Girl ● Co-ed
● Day ○ Week ○ Board

The school aims to provide a sound nursery education. Classes are small to ensure individual attention and children are taught basic mathematics and reading skills. They also have ample opportunity for painting, craftwork and free play to develop creativity, in a happy, caring and stimulating environment.

Old Palace School

Address: Old Palace Road, Croydon, Surrey CR0 1AX
Telephone: 081 688 2027

Head: Miss K L Hilton

Age range: 7-18
No. of pupils: 750
Scholarships: Yes
Religion: Anglican

Fees per term
Day: £765-£1074
Weekly board: -
Full board: -

○ Boy ● Girl ○ Co-ed
● Day ○ Week ○ Board

The school is housed in the former residence of the Archbisops of Canterbury, which does much to give the school its own distinctive ethos. There have been many additions to provide accommodation for modern educational needs. The academic standard is high, the curriculum wide and the school achieves a high standard in music and drama. Much emphasis is placed on the needs of the individual and her development.

The Old Vicarage School

Address: 48 Richmond Hill, Richmond upon Thames, Surrey TW10 6QX
Telephone: 081 940 0922

Head: Miss J Reynolds

Age range: 4-11
No. of pupils: 168
Scholarships:
Religion: Non-denominational

Fees per term
Day: £995-£1210
Weekly board: -
Full board: -

Boy ○ / Girl ● / Co-ed ○
Day ● / Week ○ / Board ○

The school provides an intimate environment with a caring atmosphere conducive to learning. As well as attaining high academic standards girls build personal qualities of confidence, self reliance and respect for others, to prepare them for the challenges and opportunities of the modern world. They are prepared for entry to the London Day Schools and a variety of boarding schools.

Park Hill School

Address: 8 Queen's Road, Kingston Upon Thames, Surrey KT2 7SH
Telephone: 081 546 5496

Head: Mrs M D Christie

Age range: 3-11
No. of pupils: 122
Scholarships:
Religion: Inter-denomination

Fees per term
Day: £430-£845
Weekly board: -
Full board: -

Boy ○ / Girl ○ / Co-ed ●
Day ● / Week ○ / Board ○

For further information and a prospectus, please contact the school. Boys 3-8, girls 3-11

Parkside

Address: The Manor, Stoke D'Abernon, Cobham, Surrey KT11 3PX
Telephone: 0932 862749

Head: Mr R L Shipp

Age range: 14
No. of pupils: 4
Scholarships: Yes
Religion: Non-denominational

Fees per term
Day: £950-£1625
Weekly board: -£2460
Full board: -£2460

Boy ● / Girl ○ / Co-ed ○
Day ● / Week ● / Board ●

Parkside is a day and boarding preparatory school. Situated in a rural setting, the school is easily accessible; Gatwick and Heathrow airports are close by.

Parsons Mead School p706

Address: Ottways Lane, Ashtead, Surrey KT21 2PE
Telephone: 0372 276401

Head: Miss E B Plant

Age range: 3-18
No. of pupils: 485
Scholarships: Yes
Religion: Church of England

Fees per term
Day: £900-£1435
Weekly board: £2370-£2535
Full board: £2590-£2755

Boy ○ / Girl ● / Co-ed ○
Day ● / Week ● / Board ●

Parsons Mead boasts 12 acres of wooded gardens yet is within one mile of the M25 (Junction 9). It is small enough for the interests of the individual to be paramount, but large enough to provide a wide choice of subjects at GCSE and A Level. Public examination results are excellent. Facilities are constantly upgraded and include sports hall, pool, information technology suite and science block.

Pierrepont School

Address: Frensham, Farnham, Surrey GU10 3DN

Telephone: 0251 252110

Head: Mr N Taylor

Age range: 11-18
No. of pupils: 170
Scholarships: Yes
Religion: Non-denominational

Fees per term
Day: -£1834
Weekly board: -£2881
Full board: -£3048

○ Boy   ○ Girl   ● Co-ed
● Day   ● Week   ● Board

Pierrepont School, Frensham prides itself on its excellent facilities and on creating an environment which allows each pupil to develop to the fullest extent of their ability. Offering a wide range of academic courses, as well as sporting and cultural activities, the school strives to produce well educated young adults, able to interact easily and positively with people from a wide range of cultures and experiences.

Prior's Field

Address: Godalming, Surrey GU7 2RH

Telephone: 0483 810551

Head: Mrs J M McCallum

Age range: 11-18
No. of pupils: 250
Scholarships: Yes
Religion: Non-denominational

Fees per term
Day: £1830-
Weekly board: £2895-
Full board: £2895-

○ Boy   ● Girl   ○ Co-ed
● Day   ● Week   ● Board

Prior's Field is a small and friendly boarding/day school in a delightful rural setting within easy reach of London and airports. High academic standards, and a wide curriculum which includes theatre studies, business skills, media studies, photography, Young Enterprise etc.

The Priory School

Address: Bolters Lane, Banstead, Surrey SM7 2AJ

Telephone: 0737 354479

Head: Mr I R Chapman

Age range: 4-13
No. of pupils: 185
Scholarships:
Religion: Non-denominational

Fees per term
Day: £850-£1270
Weekly board: -
Full board: -

● Boy   ○ Girl   ○ Co-ed
● Day   ○ Week   ○ Board

For further information and a prospectus, please contact the school.

Redehall School

Address: Redehall Road, Smallfield, Horley, Surrey RH6 9QL

Telephone: 0342 842987

Head: Mrs M Scholefield

Age range: 4-12
No. of pupils: 92
Scholarships:
Religion: Non-denominational

Fees per term
Day: -£340
Weekly board: -
Full board: -

○ Boy   ○ Girl   ● Co-ed
● Day   ○ Week   ○ Board

For further information and a prospectus, please contact the school.

Reigate Grammar School *

Address: Reigate Road, Reigate, Surrey RH2 0QS

Telephone: 0737 222231

Head: Mr J G Hamlin

Age range: 10-18
No. of pupils: 850
Scholarships: Yes
Religion: Non-denominational

Fees per term
Day: £1420-
Weekly board: -
Full board: -

Boy ○ Girl ○ Co-ed ●
Day ● Week ○ Board ○

Reigate Grammar School is an independent co-educational day school for boys and girls aged from 10 to 18. The School has always been well known for its high academic standards and its vigorous programme of extra-curricular activities, especially its music, drama and games. The Headmaster, John Hamlin MA, MSc, is a member of the Headmasters' Conference.

Reigate St Mary's Preparatory and Choir School

Address: Chart Lane, Reigate, Surrey RH2 7RN

Telephone: 0737 244880

Head: Mr J A Hart

Age range: 3-13
No. of pupils: 250
Scholarships: Yes
Religion: Church of England

Fees per term
Day: -
Weekly board: -
Full board: -

Boy ● Girl ○ Co-ed ○
Day ● Week ○ Board ○

The school is set in 15 acres of parkland in the very centre of Reigate. The atmosphere is Christian and buoyant; results in public examinations are excellent. A lively programme of out of class activities and educational and sporting holidays is on offer. Fifteen choral scholarships of 50% are available.

Ripley Court School

Address: Rose Lane, Ripley, Woking, Surrey GU23 6NE

Telephone: 0483 225217

Head: Mr J W N Dudgeon MA

Age range: 4-13
No. of pupils: 272
Scholarships:
Religion: Christian

Fees per term
Day: £773-£1245
Weekly board: -
Full board: -£1912

Boy ○ Girl ○ Co-ed ●
Day ● Week ○ Board ●

Ripley Court School is a co-educational preparatory and pre-preparatory school for day children from 4 to 14, and weekly and full boarders (boys) aged 8 to 14. It is situated 25 miles from London and 25 minutes' drive from both Heathrow and Gatwick. For further information please contact the school secretary.

Rokeby School

Address: George Road, Kingston-upon-Thames, Surrey KT2 7PB
Telephone: 081 942 2247

Head: Mr R M Moody

Age range: 4-13
No. of pupils: 125
Scholarships: Yes
Religion: Non-denominational

Fees per term
Day: £1080-£1565
Weekly board: -
Full board: -

Boy ● Girl ○ Co-ed ○
Day ● Week ○ Board ○

For further information and a prospectus, please contact the school.

Rowan Preparatory School

Address: 6 Fitzalan Road, Claygate, Esher, Surrey KT10 0LX
Telephone: 0372 462627

Head: Mrs M A Rice-Jones

Age range: 3-12
No. of pupils: 297
Scholarships:
Religion: Non-denominational

Fees per term
Day: £420-£1350
Weekly board: -
Full board: -

○ ● ○
Boy Girl Co-ed
● ○ ○
Day Week Board

School has a happy working atmosphere in which Head and staff are able to build close relationships with each child, developing artistic and practical talents as well as academic potential. Pupils are encouraged to taste success and achievements of each pupil are acknowledged and praised, laying the foundation of confidence on which progress is built. Girls are prepared to Common Entrance and scholarships.

The Rowans

Address: 13 Epsom Road, Leatherhead, Surrey KT21 1RB
Telephone:

Head:

Age range:
No. of pupils:
Scholarships:
Religion:

Fees per term
Day: -
Weekly board: -
Full board: -

○ ○ ●
Boy Girl Co-ed
○ ○ ○
Day Week Board

For further information and a prospectus, please contact the school.

Royal Ballet School

Address: White Lodge, Richmond Park, Richmond, Surrey TW10 5HR
Telephone: 081 876 5547

Head: Dame M Park

Age range: 11-16
No. of pupils: 135
Scholarships:
Religion: Non-denominational

Fees per term
Day: -£3364
Weekly board: -
Full board: -£4545

○ ○ ●
Boy Girl Co-ed
● ○ ●
Day Week Board

For further information and a prospectus, please contact the school.

Royal Grammar School *

Address: High Street, Guildford, Surrey GU1 3BB
Telephone: 0483 502424

Head: Mr T M S Young

Age range: 11-18
No. of pupils: 810
Scholarships: Yes
Religion: Church of England

Fees per term
Day: £1706-£1804
Weekly board: -
Full board: -

● ○ ○
Boy Girl Co-ed
● ○ ○
Day Week Board

The RGS is known for its high academic standards; 98% of its pupils go on to university. It provides a broad, balanced curriculum in a caring environment. There is great emphasis on extra-curricular activities, with notable achievement in sport, music and drama, for example. A go-ahead school for able boys.

Royal Naval School For Girls

Address: Farnham Lane, Haslemere, Surrey GU27 1HQ
Telephone: 0428 605415
Head: Dr J L Clough

Age range: 11-18
No. of pupils: 250
Scholarships: Yes
Religion: Church of England

Fees per term
Day: -£1840
Weekly board: -
Full board: -£2760

Boy / ● Girl / Co-ed
● Day / ● Week / Board

The school occupies an estate of 60 acres. It comprises modern facilities built around two spacious Edwardian villas, Stoatley and High Rough, and the newer Kilmorey. Set in wooded and terraced grounds which are part of an area designated as of 'outstanding natural beauty', the school is within 40 minutes journey of Central London and the South Coast and less than an hours drive from Heathrow and Gatwick airports.

Royal Russell School

Address: Coombe Lane, Croydon, Surrey
Telephone: 081 657 4433
Head: Mr R D Balaam

Age range: 4-18
No. of pupils: 750
Scholarships: Yes
Religion: Church of England

Fees per term
Day: £815-£1575
Weekly board: -£2990
Full board: -£2990

Boy / Girl / ● Co-ed
● Day / ● Week / ● Board

Set in over one hundred acres of beautiful grounds in the Surrey hills, Royal Russell is one of the country's oldest established co-educational schools. The school is well known for its happy and positive atmosphere. The facilities are excellent and the examination results well above the national average.

Rydes Hill Preparatory School

Address: Aldershot Road, Guildford, Surrey GU2 6BP
Telephone: 0483 63160
Head: Miss B May BEd(Hons)

Age range: 3-11
No. of pupils: 165
Scholarships:
Religion: Roman Catholic

Fees per term
Day: £650-£1005
Weekly board: -
Full board: -

● Boy / ● Girl / Co-ed
● Day / Week / Board

Rydes Hill, which welcomes children from all denominations, has a long established tradition of helping each child attain full potential in a loving, Christian environment, where the happiness and security of the child is of paramount importance. A gently diciplined approach to work and play results in outstanding achievements at Common Entrance, and a good scholarship record. Boys 3-11, girls 3-7.

Sanderstead Junior School

Address: 29 Purley Oaks Road, Sanderstead, Croydon, Surrey CR2 0NW
Telephone: 081 660 0801
Head: Mrs A Barns

Age range: 4-12
No. of pupils: 125
Scholarships:
Religion: Non-denominational

Fees per term
Day: £535-£890
Weekly board: -
Full board: -

Boy / Girl / ● Co-ed
● Day / Week / Board

The school was established in 1906 and is a member of ISA and accredited by ISJC. Children are entered for all the prestigious senior schools and have gained an unbroken record of scholarships and awards from 1968 to 1992. Boys and girls are accepted from four to twelve years and enjoy a wide academic curriculum together with varied sports, music and computer studies.

Scaitcliffe School

Address: Bishopsgate Road, Englefield Green, Egham, Surrey TW20 0YJ
Telephone: 0784 432109

Head: Mr W A Constable

Age range: 7-13
No. of pupils: 130
Scholarships:
Religion: Church of England

Fees per term
Day: £1375-£1666
Weekly board: -£2255
Full board: -

● Boy ○ Girl ○ Co-ed
● Day ● Week ○ Board

The school is in beautiful surroundings beside Windsor Great Park, within easy reach of Heathrow and the motorway network. Boys are taught in small classes by a qualified staff. Each individual is encouraged to be active in sport, music, drama, travel and a wide range of other activities. Boarders are under the personal care of the Headmaster's wife and the housemaster.

Seaton House School

Address: 67 Banstead Road South, Sutton, Surrey SM2 5LH
Telephone: 081 642 2332

Head: Mrs E Butler

Age range: 3-11
No. of pupils: 190
Scholarships:
Religion: Non-denominational

Fees per term
Day: £395-£875
Weekly board: -
Full board: -

● Boy ● Girl ○ Co-ed
● Day ○ Week ○ Board

Seaton House is a small school with a relaxed and friendly, though disciplined atmosphere, where every child is encouraged to take part in every activity on offer. We have a broad-based curriculum with high standards, not only in academic subjects but in every area of school life. We make full use of specialist teaching from age seven. Booys 3-5, girls 3-11.

Shaftesbury Independent School

Address: Godstone Road, Purley, Surrey CR8 2AN
Telephone: 081 668 8080

Head: Mr P A B Gowlland BSc, DipTh, CertEd

Age range: 5-18
No. of pupils: 58
Scholarships: Yes
Religion: Christian

Fees per term
Day: £795-£7095
Weekly board: -
Full board: -

○ Boy ○ Girl ● Co-ed
● Day ○ Week ○ Board

Shaftesbury is a Christian foundation but welcomes children of all faiths and emphasises standards of work, discipline and morals. There is a family atmosphere: the average class size is 9 and the maximum 15, so individuals matter. Drama and badminton flourish. GCSE: 63% passed 7 or more grades A-C. A Level: 90% pass. Inspected and accredited by ISJC (ISIS).

Shrewsbury House

Address: 107 Ditton Road, Surbiton, Surrey KT6 6RL
Telephone: 081 399 3066

Head: Mr C M Ross

Age range: 7-13
No. of pupils: 235
Scholarships:
Religion: Anglican

Fees per term
Day: £1290-£1350
Weekly board: -
Full board: -

● Boy ○ Girl ○ Co-ed
● Day ○ Week ○ Board

Set in pleasant 6 acre grounds, the school provides a balanced all round education. Boys are prepared for both independent local schools and all boarding schools. In the past three years 26 scholarship awards have been won.

Sir Willim Perkin's School *

Address: Guildford Road, Chertsey, Surrey KT16 9BN

Telephone: 0932 562161

Head: Mrs A Darlow

Age range: 11-18
No. of pupils: 530
Scholarships: Yes
Religion: Non-denominational

Fees per term
Day: -£1145
Weekly board: -
Full board: -

○ Boy ● Girl ○ Co-ed
● Day ○ Week ○ Board

For further information and a prospectus, please contact the school.

St Andrew's

Address: Church Hill House, Horsell, Woking, Surrey GU21 4QW

Telephone: 0483 760943

Head: Mr D Cassell

Age range: 3-13
No. of pupils: 200
Scholarships: Yes
Religion: Church of England

Fees per term
Day: £635-£1600
Weekly board: £2215-
Full board: -

● Boy ○ Girl ○ Co-ed
● Day ● Week ○ Board

St Andrew's is an old established preparatory for boys in Horsell with its own playing fields. Modern classrooms complement the Victorian house. The school has a good scholarship record - also CE passes to a wide selection of senior schools. Flourishing art and music.

St Catherine's School

Address: Park Road, Camberley, Surrey GU15 2LL

Telephone: 0276 23511

Head: Mrs H M Burt

Age range: 3-11
No. of pupils: 160
Scholarships:
Religion: Non-denominational

Fees per term
Day: £420-£1020
Weekly board: -
Full board: -

● Boy ● Girl ○ Co-ed
● Day ○ Week ○ Board

For further information and a prospectus, please contact the school. Boys 3-5, girls 3-11.

St Catherine's School * p706, *p750*

Address: Bramley, Guildford, Surrey GU5 0DF

Telephone: 0483 893363

Head: Mr J R Palmer

Age range: 4-18
No. of pupils: 600
Scholarships: Yes
Religion: Church of England

Fees per term
Day: £1060-£1625
Weekly board: £2490-£2660
Full board: £2490-£2660

○ Boy ● Girl ○ Co-ed
● Day ● Week ● Board

Situated just outside Guildford, within convenient reach of both Heathrow and Gatwick. The school has a wide curriculum of both academic and other subjects, with strong emphasis on developing pupils' potential in any direction to the full. The school has modern facilities for the sciences, art, languages, computer studies and physical education.

St Christopher's School

Address: 6 Downs Road, Epsom, Surrey KT18 5HE

Telephone: 03727 21807

Head: Miss J Luckman

Age range: 3-8
No. of pupils: 120
Scholarships:
Religion: Non-denominational

Fees per term
Day: £390-£760
Weekly board: -
Full board: -

Boy ○ Girl ○ Co-ed ●
Day ● Week ○ Board ○

For further information and a prospectus, please contact the school.

St David's School

Address: 23 Woodcote Valley Road, Purley, Surrey CR8 3AL

Telephone: 081 660 0723

Head: Mrs L Randall

Age range: 4-11
No. of pupils: 165
Scholarships:
Religion: Church of England

Fees per term
Day: £645-£770
Weekly board: -
Full board: -

Boy ○ Girl ○ Co-ed ●
Day ● Week ○ Board ○

Small classes and individual attention enable children to obtain excellent results in all selective secondary school entrance examinations where many scholarships are won. In addition to emphasis on an academic education, St David's offers enthusiastic teaching in art, music, drama and all sporting activities. Emphasis is placed on the individual child fulfilling his or her potential in all things.

St Edmunds School

Address: Hindhead, Surrey GU26 6BH

Telephone: 0428 604808

Head: Rev A Sangster

Age range: 7-13
No. of pupils: 140
Scholarships:
Religion: Church of England

Fees per term
Day: -£1910
Weekly board: -
Full board: -£2650

Boy ● Girl ○ Co-ed ○
Day ● Week ○ Board ●

The aim of the school is to provide a first class all round education in a happy atmosphere and to bring out and develop the talents of each boy. A high standard of work and effort is required and for Common Entrance all subjects are taught. The school has a good scholarship record.

St George's College

Address: Weybridge Road, Addlestone, Surrey KT15 2QS

Telephone: 0932 854811

Head: Dr P A Johnson

Age range: 11-18
No. of pupils: 563
Scholarships: Yes
Religion: Roman Catholic

Fees per term
Day: £1760-£2025
Weekly board: -
Full board: -

Boy ● Girl ○ Co-ed ●
Day ● Week ○ Board ○

St George's College offers high quality academic standards and superb sporting facilities. A leading Catholic independent day school accepting Christians of all denominations, the college aims to fulfil the potential of every pupil. With extensive dedicated bus routes, there is a wide catchment area. Girls are accepted into the college's co-educational sixth form.

St George's School (Pierrpont Junior)

Address: Frensham, Surrey GU10 3DN

Telephone: 025 125 2006

Head: Mrs P E M Green

Age range: 2-11
No. of pupils: 60
Scholarships:
Religion: Non-denominational

Fees per term
Day: £632-£805
Weekly board: -
Full board: -

Boy ○ Girl ○ Co-ed ●
Day ● Week ○ Board ○

For further information and a prospectus, please contact the school.

St Hilary's School

Address: Holloway Hill, Godalming, Surrey GU7 1AZ

Telephone: 0483 416551

Head: Miss R E Morgan

Age range: 3-12
No. of pupils: 360
Scholarships:
Religion: Non-denominational

Fees per term
Day: £370-£1075
Weekly board: -
Full board: -

Boy ○ Girl ○ Co-ed ●
Day ● Week ○ Board ○

For further information and a prospectus, please contact the school. Boys 3-8, girls 3-12

St Ives School

Address: Three Gates Lane, Haslemere, Surrey GU27 2ES

Telephone: 0428 643734

Head: Mrs M Greenway

Age range: 4-11
No. of pupils: 140
Scholarships:
Religion: Church of England

Fees per term
Day: £1070-£1380
Weekly board: -
Full board: -

Boy ○ Girl ● Co-ed ○
Day ● Week ○ Board ○

Situated in its own spacious grounds, St Ives has a lively friendly atmosphere. A broad balanced curriculum is offered and a good pupil/teacher ratio ensures individual needs are catered for and a good record of scholarships to a wide variety of senior schools. Emphasis is placed on high standards of manners, discipline and appearance as well as academic excellence.

St John's School *

Address: Epsom Road, Leatherhead, Surrey KT22 8SP

Telephone: 0372 372021

Head: Mr D E Brown MA

Age range: 13-18
No. of pupils: 450
Scholarships: Yes
Religion: Church of England

Fees per term
Day: -
Weekly board: -
Full board: -

Boy ● Girl ○ Co-ed ○
Day ● Week ○ Board ●

For further information and a prospectus, please contact the school.

St Mary's Preparatory School

Address: Chart Lane, Reigate, Surrey RH2 7AN

Telephone: 0737 244880

Head: Mr J A Hart BA(Dunelm)

Age range: 3-13
No. of pupils: 260
Scholarships:
Religion: Church of England

Fees per term
Day: -
Weekly board: -
Full board: -

● Boy ○ Girl ○ Co-ed
● Day ○ Week ○ Board

For further information and a prospectus, please contact the school.

St Maur's School *

Address: Thames Street, Weybridge, Surrey KT13 8NL

Telephone: 0932 851411

Head: Mrs M E Dodds

Age range: 4-18
No. of pupils: 750
Scholarships: Yes
Religion: Catholic

Fees per term
Day: £645-£1850
Weekly board: -
Full board: -

○ Boy ● Girl ○ Co-ed
● Day ○ Week ○ Board

St Maur's, Weybridge, was founded in 1898 by members of a French Religious Community. Now under Lay management, it is a Christian educating community, in the Catholic traditions for students aged 4-18, sharing a Joint Co-educational Sixth Form with St George's College. A broad and balanced programme of study is followed in line with the National Curriculum, with a flourishing extra-curricular life.

St Michael's School

Address: Hoe Place, Woking, Surrey GU22 8JE

Telephone:

Head:

Age range: 3-13
No. of pupils:
Scholarships:
Religion:

Fees per term
Day: -
Weekly board: -
Full board: -

○ Boy ○ Girl ● Co-ed
● Day ○ Week ○ Board

For further information and a prospectus, please contact the school.

St Michael's School

Address: Wolf's Hill, Limpsfield, Oxted, Surrey RH8 0QR

Telephone: 0883 712311

Head: Dr M J Hustler

Age range: 3-18
No. of pupils: 154
Scholarships:
Religion: Church of England

Fees per term
Day: -
Weekly board: -
Full board: -

● Boy ● Girl ○ Co-ed
● Day ○ Week ● Board

For further information and a prospectus, please contact the school. Boys 3-8, girls 3-18.

St Teresa's Convent

Address: Grove House Junior School, Guildford Road, Leatherhead, Surrey KT24 5QA
Telephone: 0372 53456

Head: Mrs W Nash

Age range: 3-5
No. of pupils: 250
Scholarships:
Religion:

Fees per term
Day: -
Weekly board: -
Full board: -

○ ○ ● Boy Girl Co-ed
● ● ● Day Week Board

For further information and a prospectus, please contact the school.

St Teresa's Convent School

Address: Effingham Hill, Dorking, Surrey RH5 6ST
Telephone: 0372 452037

Head: Mr L Allan

Age range: 11-18
No. of pupils: 350
Scholarships: Yes
Religion: Roman Catholic

Fees per term
Day: £1480-
Weekly board: £3010-
Full board: £3010-

● ● ○ Boy Girl Co-ed
● ● ● Day Week Board

St Teresa's is a GSA independent day and boarding school for 350 girls, aged 11 to 18. With high academic standards, excellent facilities and a superb location, St Teresa's is easily accessible from the M25 (equi-distant from Gatwick and Heathrow) and the A3. Approximately 20 GCSE and A-level subjects are offered, with many extra-curricular activities (e.g. sport, drama, public speaking) encouraged.

Stanway

Address: Chichester Road, Dorking, Surrey RH4 1LR
Telephone: 0306 882151

Head: Mrs C A Belk BA(Hons)

Age range: 3-12
No. of pupils: 200
Scholarships:
Religion: Christian

Fees per term
Day: £160-£1020
Weekly board: -
Full board: -

○ ● ○ Boy Girl Co-ed
● ○ ○ Day Week Board

Stanway is a preparatory school for girls aged 3-12 and boys aged 3-8. Academic standards are high and the main subjects are taught by graduate specialists. Pupils are encouraged to be courteous and kind, and each child is treated as an individual. Stanway aims to provide a sound, all-round education in a happy, caring environment.

Staplands School

Address: Oatlands, Weybridge, Surrey
Telephone:

Head:

Age range: 3-13
No. of pupils:
Scholarships:
Religion:

Fees per term
Day: -
Weekly board: -
Full board: -

● ● ○ Boy Girl Co-ed
● ○ ● Day Week Board

For further information and a prospectus, please contact the school. Boys 3-6, girls 3-13.

Stowford College

Address: 95 Brighton Road, Sutton, Surrey

Telephone: 081 661 9444

Principal: Mr A J Hennessy

Age range: 7-19
No. of pupils: 70
Scholarships:
Religion: Non-Denominational

Fees per term
Day: £780-£1285
Weekly board: -
Full board: -

Boy ○ Girl ○ Co-ed ●
Day ● Week ○ Board ○

Stowford is one of the smaller independent schools. Single site, in an agreeable urban residential area with good public transport links. It has well equipped laboratories and art room. Rules and regulations are kept to a minimum. The school prides itself on insistence on hard work and homework in a friendly and informal atmosphere. There is a programme of help for dyslexic students.

Streete Court

Address: Rooks Nest, Godstone, Surrey RH9 8BZ

Telephone: 0883 742358

Head: Mr D N Hopkins

Age range: 3-13
No. of pupils: 150
Scholarships:
Religion: Christian

Fees per term
Day: £415-£1514
Weekly board: -
Full board: £2200-£2200

Boy ● Girl ○ Co-ed ○
Day ● Week ○ Board ●

A family-run prep and pre-prep school for boys. Set in a beautiful Georgian mansion in 24 acres of lovely grounds, the school combines excellent facilities with a friendly and happy atmosphere. The school is well located, with London Airport 40 minutes drive away and Gatwick 15 minutes.

The Study School

Address: 57 Thetford Road, New Malden, Kingston-upon-Thames, Surrey KT3 5DP
Telephone: 081 942 0754

Head: Mr J H N Hudson

Age range: 3-11
No. of pupils: 130
Scholarships:
Religion:

Fees per term
Day: -
Weekly board: -
Full board: -

Boy ○ Girl ○ Co-ed ●
Day ● Week ○ Board ○

For further information and a prospectus, please contact the school.

Surbiton High School *

Address: Surbiton Crescent, Kingston-upon-Thames, Surrey KT1 2JT
Telephone: 081 546 5245

Head: Mrs R A Thynne

Age range: 5-18
No. of pupils: 687
Scholarships:
Religion:

Fees per term
Day: -
Weekly board: -
Full board: -

Boy ● Girl ● Co-ed ○
Day ● Week ○ Board ○

For further information and a prospectus, please contact the school. Boys 5-11, girls 5-18.

Surbiton Preparatory School

Address: 3 Elmers Avenue, Kingston-upon-Thames, Surrey KT6 4SP
Telephone:

Head:

Age range: 5-11
No. of pupils: 100
Scholarships:
Religion: Church of England

Fees per term
Day: -
Weekly board: -
Full board: -

● Boy ○ Girl ○ Co-ed
● Day ○ Week ○ Board

For further information and a prospectus, please contact the school.

Sutton High School GPDST *

Address: 55 Cheam Road, Sutton, Surrey

Telephone: 081 642 0594

Head: Miss A E Cavendish

Age range: 4-18
No. of pupils: 820
Scholarships: Yes
Religion: Non-denominational

Fees per term
Day: £1036-£1340
Weekly board: -
Full board: -

○ Boy ● Girl ○ Co-ed
● Day ○ Week ○ Board

Academically selective girls' school with a lively, positive and friendly atmosphere. Importance attached to academic study and girls are encouraged to extend their talents by participation in music, drama, sports and in a variety of activities.

TASIS England American School

Address: Coldharbour Lane, Thorpe, Surrey TW20 8TE

Telephone: 0932 565252

Head: Mr L Rigg

Age range: 4-18
No. of pupils: 625
Scholarships: Yes
Religion: Non-denominational

Fees per term
Day: £2017-£2262
Weekly board: -
Full board: £3627-£3750

○ Boy ○ Girl ● Co-ed
● Day ○ Week ● Board

TASIS provides England and American education for students in grades Pre-K - 12. The school year runs from September to June, with vacations at Christmas and Easter and shorter breaks in October and February, when school trips throughout Europe are offered. The U.S. college-preparatory curriculum includes Advanced Placement courses, art, music, drama, and a complete sports program.

Tormead School *

Address: Cranley Road, Guildford, Surrey GU1 2JD

Telephone: 0483 575101

Head: Mrs H M Alleyne

Age range: 5-18
No. of pupils: 540
Scholarships: Yes
Religion: Non-denominational

Fees per term
Day: £815-£1495
Weekly board: -
Full board: -

○ Boy ● Girl ○ Co-ed
● Day ○ Week ○ Board

Tormead encourages its pupils to aim high and to develop their full potential but also emphasizes the importance of co-operating effectively and enthusiastically with others. The expertise of a stable and committed staff generates excellent academic standards. The sixth form is thriving and the majority of the girls go on to university. The school is active and successful in sport, drama, public speaking and music.

The Trees Pre-Preparatory School

Address: Hoe Place, Woking, Surrey GU22 8JE

Telephone: 0483 772194

Head: Mrs J Hall

Age range: 3-7
No. of pupils: 182
Scholarships:
Religion:

Fees per term
Day: -
Weekly board: -
Full board: -

Boy ○ Girl ○ Co-ed ●
Day ● Week ○ Board ○

For further information and a prospectus, please contact the school.

Trinity School *

Address: Shirley Park, Croydon, Surrey CR9 7AT

Telephone: 081 656 9541

Head: Mr R J Wilson

Age range: 10-18
No. of pupils: 850
Scholarships:
Religion:

Fees per term
Day: -
Weekly board: -
Full board: -

Boy ● Girl ○ Co-ed ○
Day ● Week ○ Board ○

For further information and a prospectus, please contact the school.

Unicorn

Address: 238 Kew Road, Richmond, Surrey TW9 3JX

Telephone: 081 948 3926

Head: Mrs F C Timmis

Age range: 3-11
No. of pupils: 160
Scholarships:
Religion: Non-Denominational

Fees per term
Day: £519-£1100
Weekly board: -
Full board: -

Boy ○ Girl ○ Co-ed ●
Day ● Week ○ Board ○

Unicorn is a parent-owned school founded in 1970. It is situated opposite Kew Gardens in a large Victorian house. Many of the staff are Froebel trained. Classes average 20 children. Boys and girls are prepared for entry to the London day schools and a wide variety of boarding schools.

Virginia Water Preparatory School

Address: Gorse Hill Road, Virginia Water, Surrey GU25 4AU

Telephone: 0344 843138

Head: Mrs S Winson

Age range: 3-11
No. of pupils: 115
Scholarships:
Religion: Non-denominational

Fees per term
Day: £900-£975
Weekly board: -
Full board: -

Boy ○ Girl ○ Co-ed ●
Day ● Week ○ Board ○

Founded in 1933, the school is on a private road on the Wentworth Estate. The school provides a variety of activities for the children with a background of sensible discipline and good scholastic work.

Wallop

Address: 28 Hanger Hill,
Weybridge, Surrey KT13 9YD

Telephone: 0932 852885

Head: Mr D J Parry

Age range: 4-13
No. of pupils: 185
Scholarships:
Religion: Non-denominational

Fees per term
Day: £1120-£1393
Weekly board: -
Full board: -

● Boy ● Girl ○ Co-ed
● Day ○ Week ○ Board

Wallop is a day preparatory school for boys aged 4-13 and girls aged 4-8. Facilities include a gym, large playing fields and a separate classroom block for art and computers. 1992 has seen the addition of a new library/resources room, an all weather sports area and an exhibition studio.

West Dene School

Address: 167 Brighton Road,
Purley, Surrey CR8 4HE

Telephone: 081 660 2404

Head: Mrs S M Carter

Age range: 3-9
No. of pupils: 150
Scholarships:
Religion:

Fees per term
Day: -
Weekly board: -
Full board: -

○ Boy ○ Girl ● Co-ed
● Day ○ Week ○ Board

For further information and a prospectus, please contact the school.

Westbury House School

Address: 80 Westbury Road,
New Malden, Surrey KT3 5AS

Telephone: 081 942 0754

Head: Mrs M T Morton

Age range: 3-12
No. of pupils: 185
Scholarships:
Religion:

Fees per term
Day: -
Weekly board: -
Full board: -

○ Boy ○ Girl ● Co-ed
● Day ○ Week ○ Board

For further information and a prospectus, please contact the school.

Weston Green School

Address: Weston Green Road,
Thames Ditton, Surrey
KT7 0JN
Telephone: 081 398 2778

Head: Mrs J Winser

Age range: 3-11
No. of pupils: 120
Scholarships:
Religion:

Fees per term
Day: -
Weekly board: -
Full board: -

● Boy ● Girl ○ Co-ed
● Day ○ Week ○ Board

For further information and a prospectus, please contact the school. Boys 3-8.

Westward School

Address: 47 Hersham Road, Walton-on-Thames, Surrey KT12 1LE
Telephone: 0932 220911

Head: Mrs P B Townley

Age range: 4-11
No. of pupils: 150
Scholarships:
Religion: All denominations

Fees per term
Day: £445-£765
Weekly board: -
Full board: -

○ ○ ● Boy Girl Co-ed
● ○ ○ Day Week Board

Westward is a traditional school with high academic standards. Music and drama are very important in the curriculum. Children are encouraged to take part in a wide variety of activities in order to develop their full potential. Although there is no selective entrance examination, children from Westward are frequently awarded scholarships into their senior schools.

Whitgift School *

Address: Haling Park, Croydon, Surrey CR2 6YT
Telephone: 081 688 9222

Head: Dr C A Barnett

Age range: 10-18
No. of pupils: 950
Scholarships: Yes
Religion: Church of England

Fees per term
Day: £1600-
Weekly board: -
Full board: -

● ○ ○ Boy Girl Co-ed
● ○ ○ Day Week Board

Whitgift, founded in 1596, is an independent day school, with high academic standards, for 950 boys aged 10-18, enjoying a beautiful, yet easily accessible, parkland site. Facilities are of outstanding quality, and excellent standards are achieved in sport, music, drama and other activities - large number of scholarships and bursaries available.

Winton School

Address: 205-209 Addiscomb Road, Croydon, Surrey CR0 6SP
Telephone: 081 654 1531

Head: Mr I E McFadyen

Age range: 4-18
No. of pupils: 180
Scholarships:
Religion:

Fees per term
Day: -
Weekly board: -
Full board: -

○ ○ ● Boy Girl Co-ed
● ○ ○ Day Week Board

For further information and a prospectus, please contact the school.

Wispers School

Address: High Lane, Haslemere, Surrey GU27 1AD
Telephone: 0428 643646

Head: Mr L H Beltran BA

Age range: 11-18
No. of pupils: 190
Scholarships:
Religion:

Fees per term
Day: -
Weekly board: -
Full board: -

○ ● ○ Boy Girl Co-ed
● ○ ● Day Week Board

For further information and a prospectus, please contact the school.

Woburn Hill School

Address: Weybridge Road, Addlestone, Surrey KT15 2QS

Telephone: 0932 845784

Head: Rev M D Ashcroft

Age range: 4-10
No. of pupils: 185
Scholarships:
Religion: Roman Catholic

Fees per term
Day: £890-£1345
Weekly board: -
Full board: -

● Boy   ○ Girl   ○ Co-ed
● Day   ○ Week   ○ Board

The school, encompassing its hugely successful new pre-preparatory department, offers parents a total education for their sons from 4 to 18 on the campus. The all-round education offered within the structured and well-disciplined ethos of the school, together with the active involvement of parents, provides a solid foundation for entry to the senior school, St George's College at 11+.

Woldingham

Address: Marden Park, Woldingham, Surrey CR3 7YA

Telephone: 0883 349431

Head: Dr P Dineen

Age range: 11-18
No. of pupils: 465
Scholarships:
Religion: Roman Catholic

Fees per term
Day: £1961-
Weekly board: -
Full board: £3241-

○ Boy   ● Girl   ○ Co-ed
● Day   ○ Week   ● Board

Social strengths of Woldingham include: - Committment to an internationally recognised philosophy of education that emphasises traditional values. - A consistently good record of GCSE and A level successes. - Caring but unfussy support from induction to departure (usually to a degree course in higher education). - Strong links with other Sacred Heart schools in Europe. .

Woodcote House School

Address: Snows Ride, Windlesham, Surrey GU20 6PF

Telephone: 0276 72115

Head: Mr N H K Paterson

Age range: 7-14
No. of pupils: 110
Scholarships:
Religion:

Fees per term
Day: -
Weekly board: -
Full board: -

● Boy   ○ Girl   ○ Co-ed
● Day   ○ Week   ● Board

For further information and a prospectus, please contact the school.

Yateley Manor

Address: Yateley, Camberley, Surrey GU17 7UQ

Telephone: 0252 873298

Head: Mr F G F Howard

Age range: 3-13
No. of pupils: 432
Scholarships:
Religion: Church of England

Fees per term
Day: £395-£1299
Weekly board: -
Full board: -

○ Boy   ○ Girl   ● Co-ed
● Day   ○ Week   ○ Board

Yateley Manor offers a wide and stimulating education in a warm and friendly environment so that children grow into happy, confident and fulfilled people. High academic standards are achieved within a framework of activities that develop the whole person.

Yehudi Menhuin School

Address: Stoke D'Abernon, Cobham, Surrey KT11 3QQ

Telephone: 0932 864739

Head: Mr N Chisholm

Age range: 8-18
No. of pupils: 41
Scholarships:
Religion:

Fees per term
Day: -
Weekly board: -
Full board: -

Boy ○ Girl ○ Co-ed ●
Day ○ Week ○ Board ●

For further information and a prospectus, please contact the school.

SUSSEX (EAST)

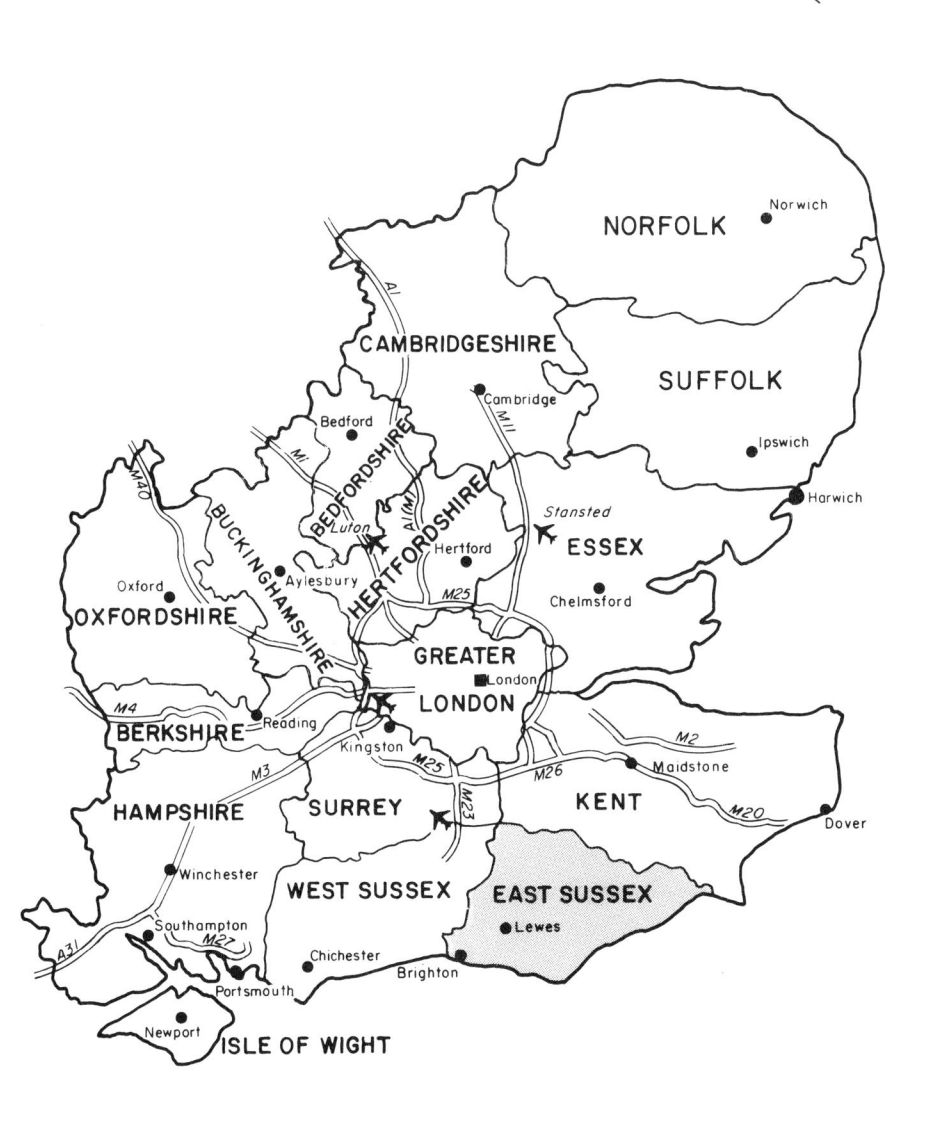

Amberley School

Address: 9 Buckhurst Road, Bexhill-on-Sea, East Sussex

Telephone: 0424 212472

Head: Mrs B A Sparks

Age range: 3-8
No. of pupils: 55
Scholarships:
Religion: Non-denominational

Fees per term
Day: £240-£350
Weekly board: -
Full board: -

Boy / Girl / **Co-ed**
Day / Week / Board

Amberley School is a long established kindergarten school which strives to encourage the joy of learning in a fairly structured setting. Small classes, usually 8-10 children, provide a good opportunity for pupils to learn the basics in education together with the full range of other subjects. Testing for the National Curriculum is undertaken at age seven.

Ashdown House School

Address: Forest Row, East Sussex RH18 5JY

Telephone: 0342 822574

Head: Mr M V C Williams MA

Age range: 8-13
No. of pupils: 171
Scholarships:
Religion: Church of England

Fees per term
Day: -
Weekly board: -
Full board: £2700-£2700

Boy / Girl / **Co-ed**
Day / Week / **Board**

Ashdown House is situated in its own grounds extending to approximately 40 acres. The school aims to provide a first class education in all subjects including games and the arts: but it attaches the greatest importance to the fostering of a warm and friendly environment in which children of widely differing abilities, talents and personalities flourish. All pupils take Common Entrance to public schools.

Barton School

Address: 67 Sedlescombe Road South, St Leonards-on-Sea, East Sussex TN38 0TJ

Telephone: 0424 436055

Head: Mrs A M Burton

Age range: 2-6
No. of pupils: 130
Scholarships:
Religion: Non-denominational

Fees per term
Day: -£616
Weekly board: -
Full board: -

Boy / Girl / **Co-ed**
Day / Week / Board

Barton has been run for over 40 years as a private school and, since 1970, as a kindergarten and nursery school by the present owners, incorporating their ideals and beliefs. The aim of Barton is to prepare children from the age of two and a half years to six to enter the local preparatory or state primary schools. The process of leaving the home environment is eased by the small classes in sympathetic hands of experienced staff.

Battle Abbey School p707

Address: Battle, East Sussex TN33 0AD

Telephone: 04246 2385

Head: Mr D J A Teall BSc

Age range: 2-18
No. of pupils: 250
Scholarships: Yes
Religion: Christian

Fees per term
Day: £940-£1710
Weekly board: £2220-£2770
Full board: £2220-£2770

Boy / Girl / **Co-ed**
Day / **Week** / **Board**

Battle Abbey is an independent school for 250 boys and girls aged from two and a half to eighteen (boarders from eight). It is situated within the historic Abbey founded by William the Conqueror. With a pupil to staff ratio of 10:1 a very high level of individual care is guaranteed. The school follows the National Curriculum, achieves excellent results and maintains high standards of conduct and social skills.

SUSSEX (EAST) 489

Bellerbys College p729

Address: 44 Cromwell Road, Hove, East Sussex BN3 3ER

Telephone: 0273 723911

Head: Mr A M Burton

Age range: 13+
No. of pupils: 250
Scholarships: Yes
Religion:

Fees per term
Day: £1740-£2330
Weekly board: -
Full board: £2500-£3528

○ ○ ● Boy Girl Co-ed
● ○ ● Day Week Board

Bellerbys College has built up a strong academic reputation since its foundation in 1959, helping students to achieve their maximum potential grades in GCSE and A level examinations through intensive teaching methods. Each year a high number of students win places at top universities to study subjects such as law, engineering, business studies, accounting and medicine. Courses commence September, January and April.

Bricklehurst Manor

Address: Stonegate, Wadhurst, East Sussex

Telephone: 0580 200448

Head: Mrs R.A. Lewis

Age range: 4-11
No. of pupils: 100
Scholarships:
Religion: Non-denominational

Fees per term
Day: £470-£1025
Weekly board: -
Full board: -

○ ○ ● Boy Girl Co-ed
● ○ ○ Day Week Board

We provide a happy environment for all our pupils so that we can help them become confident, well balanced, self disciplined, considerate individuals, aware of their wider responsibilities. We have gained a reputation for an informal family atmosphere, happy children and close, friendly relations with parents. We have excellent, modern facilities for developing each child's physical, intellectual and creative skills.

Brighton and Hove High School GPDST *

Address: The Temple, Mountpelier Road, Brighton, East Sussex BN1 3AT
Telephone: 0273 734112

Head: Miss R A Woodbridge

Age range: 4-18
No. of pupils: 720
Scholarships: Yes
Religion: Non denominational

Fees per term
Day: £880-£1148
Weekly board: -
Full board: -

○ ● ○ Boy Girl Co-ed
● ○ ○ Day Week Board

The school, founded in 1876, stands in its own grounds about 2.5 miles from the main railway station making access easy from all parts of Sussex. The selective entry take, on average, 9 GCSE's and most go on to take 3 A Levels and proceed to higher education. Music, drama and sport are all important as is the school's social service commitments.

Brighton College *

Address: Eastern Road, Brighton, East Sussex BN2 2AL
Telephone: 0273 605788

Head: Mr J D Leach

Age range: 13-18
No. of pupils: 477
Scholarships: Yes
Religion: Church of England

Fees per term
Day: £2277-
Weekly board: £3108-
Full board: £3465-

○ ○ ● Boy Girl Co-ed
● ● ● Day Week Board

The College provides a supportive and structured environment for each pupil to learn, and to discover and employ his or her special talents. The flexible mix of day and boarding pupils and of boys and girls aims to support family education. Pupils aim for the best for others and for themselves.

Brighton College Junior School

Address: Walpole Lodge, Walpole Road, Brighton, East Sussex BN2 2EU
Telephone: 0273 606845

Age range: 8+
No. of pupils: 240
Scholarships: Yes
Religion: Church of England

Fees per term
Day: £1727-
Weekly board: -
Full board: -

Boy ○ Girl ○ Co-ed ●
Day ● Week ○ Board ○

Head: Mr G Brown

The school tries to develop a full potential of each pupil, in small classes, which allow the teachers to give individual attention. The curriculum is wide and facilities very good, games and activities complement the school work.

Brighton College Pre-Preparatory School

Address: Sutherland Road, Brighton, East Sussex BN2 2EQ
Telephone: 0273 603495

Age range: 3-8
No. of pupils: 165
Scholarships: Yes
Religion: Church of England

Fees per term
Day: £388-£900
Weekly board: -
Full board: -

Boy ○ Girl ○ Co-ed ●
Day ● Week ○ Board ○

Head: Mr P A Foster

Brighton College Pre-Preparatory School offers a caring and disciplined education in a stimulating environment with constantly good academic results. Our team of dedicated teachers will give your child individual attention and a sound educational foundation. Early application essential.

Broomham School

Address: Guestling, East Sussex TN35 4LT
Telephone: 0424 814456

Age range: 5-13
No. of pupils: 115
Scholarships: Yes
Religion: None

Fees per term
Day: £600-£800
Weekly board: -
Full board: £1540-£1815

Boy ○ Girl ○ Co-ed ●
Day ● Week ○ Board ●

Head: Mr J Euer

Broomham is the junior department of Wilton House School, catering for boys and girls aged 5-13 years. We have a 50% mixture of boarders and day pupils, with a roll of approximately 115 at the junior department. The curriculum is forward looking and innovative, without discarding the elements of the traditional that are the hallmark of a good independent education.

Buckswood Grange

Address: Uckfield, East Sussex TN22 3PU
Telephone: 0825 761666

Age range: 4-16
No. of pupils: 118
Scholarships: Yes
Religion: Non-denominational

Fees per term
Day: £745-
Weekly board: £2070-
Full board: £2170-

Boy ○ Girl ○ Co-ed ●
Day ● Week ● Board ●

Principal: Mr M B Reiser

Choosing a smaller school, like Buckswood Grange, you can almost feel the benefits your child will derive. They respond to being treated as an individual, rather than as just another face. They feel that there is a genuine interest in how they are doing. They actually look forward to coming to school, because of all this, and because of the atmosphere.

SUSSEX (EAST) 491

Charters-Ancaster School

Address: Penland Road,
Bexhill-on-Sea, East Sussex
TN40 2TQ
Telephone: 0424 730499

Head: Mrs K Lewis

Age range: 3-18
No. of pupils: 375
Scholarships: Yes
Religion: Non-denominational

Fees per term
Day: £1144-
Weekly board: £2244-
Full board: £2244-

● Boy ● Girl ○ Co-ed
● Day ● Week ● Board

Charters-Ancaster School GPDST is an independent day and boarding school in Bexhill-on-Sea. The extensive grounds include tennis courts, hockey pitches and an indoor swimming pool. It offers a fine academic edcuation at modest cost. Girls are prepared for a wide range of GCSE and A level examinations. (Boys accepted from 3-8 years).

Claremont School

Address: Baldslow, St.
Leonards-on-Sea, East Sussex
TN37 7PW
Telephone: 0424 751555

Head: Mr A R Lee BA

Age range: 3-14
No. of pupils:
Scholarships:
Religion: Non-denominational

Fees per term
Day: £695-£1520
Weekly board: -£2060
Full board: -£2360

○ Boy ○ Girl ● Co-ed
● Day ● Week ● Board

Schools' curriculum is designed to ensure that children can change from the maintained system, or indeed from any other school, to the independent sector without being at any disadvantage, school aims to discover each child's strong and weak subjects. There is also a remedial class for children with specific learning difficulties.

Convent of Our Lady

Address: 116 Filsham Road, St
Leonards-on-Sea, East Sussex
TN38 0PF
Telephone: 0424 420470

Head: Miss V F Thurston

Age range: 3-16
No. of pupils: 168
Scholarships:
Religion:

Fees per term
Day: -
Weekly board: -
Full board: -

● Boy ● Girl ○ Co-ed
● Day ● Week ● Board

For further information and a prospectus, please contact the school. Boys 3-7, girls 3-16.

Deepdene School p708

Address: 195 New Church
Road, Hove, East Sussex
BN3 3ED
Telephone: 0273 418984

Head: Mrs F T Bird

Age range: 3-16
No. of pupils: 140
Scholarships:
Religion: Anglican

Fees per term
Day: £330-£1122
Weekly board: £2498-£2498
Full board: £2698-£2698

● Boy ● Girl ○ Co-ed
● Day ● Week ● Board

Deepdene is an independent school for girls aged 3-16 and boys aged 3-7 years. Throughout the school efforts are concentrated on traditional values and sound fundamentals with a strong emphasis on the '3 Rs'. French is taught formally from 7 years. Small classes and qualified staff provide quality education within Deepdene's own personal, caring environment leading to excellent standrds at GCSE.

Eastbourne College p741

Address: Eastbourne, East Sussex BN21 4JX

Telephone: 0323 37655

Head: Mr C J Saunders

Age range: 13-18
No. of pupils:
Scholarships: Yes
Religion: Church of England

Fees per term
Day: £2049-£2943
Weekly board: -
Full board: £2772-£3978

● Boy ● Girl ○ Co-ed
● Day ○ Week ● Board

Eastbourne College is situated in the residential area of a spacious and attractive Edwardian town. It enjoys considerable success in the academic, sporting, musical and dramatic spheres and a major feature of school life is the opportunity provided for pupils to gain confidence and expertise in one or more of the wide range of activities available. Girls are accepted in the sixth form.

The Fold School

Address: 201 New Church Road, Hove, East Sussex

Telephone: 0273 410901

Head: Mrs B Drake

Age range: 3-9
No. of pupils: 75
Scholarships: Yes
Religion: Church of England

Fees per term
Day: £625-£700
Weekly board: -
Full board: -

○ Boy ○ Girl ● Co-ed
● Day ○ Week ○ Board

The Fold School provides an extensive curriculum (encompassing the National Curriculum) including swimming and rural studies at our centre. Each group has twelve children who attain high academic standards. All staff are qualified for the curricular areas with which they are involved. The greatest asset of the school is the caring, family atmosphere which leads to confident, highly motivated children.

Frewen College †

Address: Northiam, East Sussex TN31 6NL

Telephone: 0797 252494

Head: Dr A B Fiddian-Green

Age range: 10-17
No. of pupils: 119
Scholarships:
Religion: Non-denominational

Fees per term
Day: -£2446
Weekly board: -
Full board: -£4892

● Boy ○ Girl ○ Co-ed
● Day ○ Week ● Board

Further information and a prospectus available on application to the school.

Greenfields School p708

Address: Priory Road, Forest Row, East Sussex RH18 5JD

Telephone: 0342 822189

Head: Mrs M I Hodkin

Age range: 3-18
No. of pupils: 200
Scholarships: Yes
Religion: Non-denominational

Fees per term
Day: £248-£1265
Weekly board: £1721-£2095
Full board: £1821-£2195

○ Boy ○ Girl ● Co-ed
● Day ● Week ● Board

Greenfields offers a wide choice of academic, creative and sporting options. This adds scope and variety to the central core of National Curriculum aligned subjects. Teaching is in small groups. Students are taught how to study, and supported self study is a feature of the senior school. We currently offer 23 GCSE subjects and 9 A level options.

Hawkhurst Court †

Address: 161 Eastern Road, Brighton, East Sussex BN2 2AG
Telephone: 0273 681484

Head: Mrs M F Hollinshead

Age range: 7-13
No. of pupils: 48
Scholarships:
Religion: Church of England

Fees per term
Day: -£2120
Weekly board: -£2515
Full board: -

○ Boy ○ Girl ● Co-ed
● Day ● Week ○ Board

The centre accepts children of average or above average intelligence with specific learning difficulties (dyslexia), or pupils experiencing difficulties with language or numeracy, who are in need of specialist teaching. The curriculum has been planned to include the relevant areas of the National Curriculum. Full use is made of the excellent facilities within Brighton College Senior and Junior Schools for various activities.

Mayfield College

Address: Mayfield, East Sussex TN20 6PL
Telephone: 0435 872041

Head: Mr D P Banister

Age range: 11-18
No. of pupils: 140
Scholarships: Yes
Religion: Roman Catholic

Fees per term
Day: -£2025
Weekly board: -£2965
Full board: -£2995

○ Boy ○ Girl ● Co-ed
● Day ● Week ● Board

The College will embark on the initial phase of co-education in September 1992 by admitting day girls at all levels. Entrance is through a short test and report. Common Entrance is also used where appropriate. The curriculum is broad at GCSE and A level, supportive of individual needs and some EFL tuition is available. Classes are small and the house and tutorial arrangements help to foster a positive family atmosphere.

Michael Hall Rudolf Steiner School

Address: Kidbrooke Park, Forest Row, East Sussex RH18 5JB
Telephone: 0342 822275

Head: Mr P Bark

Age range: 4-18
No. of pupils: 503
Scholarships:
Religion: Non-denominational

Fees per term
Day: £695-£1175
Weekly board: £2250-£2478
Full board: £2425-£2625

○ Boy ○ Girl ● Co-ed
● Day ● Week ● Board

Michael Hall is a co-educational school offering an unusually broad curriculum for pupils from pre-school to university entrance. Each child experiences the full range of creative arts subjects, scientific disciplines and practical activities. The developmental phases of children determine the curriculum. The school was founded in 1925 by teachers enthused by the work Rudolf Steiner.

Micklefield School

Address: Sutton Avenue, Seaford, East Sussex BN25 4LP
Telephone: 0323 892457

Head: Mr E Reynolds

Age range: 8-18
No. of pupils: 200
Scholarships: Yes
Religion: Non-denominational

Fees per term
Day: £1125-£1695
Weekly board: -
Full board: £1985-£2995

○ Boy ● Girl ○ Co-ed
● Day ○ Week ● Board

A small, friendly school for girls sited on the edge of a south coast seaside town. Easy rail and road access to Gatwick and London. The school prides itself on enabling the girls to reach their full potential through small classes, excellent sport and drama facilities and a strong musical tradition. Good academic record; over 95% of girls go on to higher education.

Moira House School

Address: Upper Carlisle Road, Eastbourne, East Sussex BN20 7TD
Telephone: 0323 644144

Head: Mr A R Underwood

Age range: 2-18
No. of pupils: 400
Scholarships: Yes
Religion: Non-denominational

Fees per term
Day: £898-£1928
Weekly board: -
Full board: £2862-£2986

Boy ○ Girl ● Co-ed ○
Day ● Week ○ Board ●

Our founder, Charles Ingham, was an enlightened Victorian engineer, who was determined that girls should have every opportunity to follow challenging careers fulfilling themselves as individuals in every way. He was concerned that a girl's potential should be developed by her school environment. Over 100 years later that remains our aim, even though our founder's school of 30 has grown to over 400.

The Mount School †

Address: The Mount, Wadhurst, East Sussex TN5 6PT
Telephone: 0892 782025

Head: College of Teachers

Age range: 14-21
No. of pupils: 42
Scholarships:
Religion: Christian

Fees per term
Day: -
Weekly board: -
Full board: £3978-

Boy ○ Girl ○ Co-ed ●
Day ○ Week ○ Board ●

The Mount is a therapeutic community which provides education, training and community living for adolescents with special educational needs. Emphasis is given to crafts and occupational skills.

Mowden School

Address: The Drove Way, Hove, East Sussex BN3 6LU
Telephone: 0273 503452

Head: Mr C E M Snell

Age range: 7-13
No. of pupils: 98
Scholarships:
Religion: Church of England

Fees per term
Day: -£1550
Weekly board: -£1850
Full board: -

Boy ● Girl ○ Co-ed ○
Day ● Week ● Board ○

Mowden is a preparatory school for approximately 100 boarding and day boys between the ages of 7 and 13. The Headmaster is a member of IAPS. The school, which has an excellent record of academic and sporting achievements, is situated in 7 acres of grounds on the outskirts of Brighton and Hove.

Newlands Manor School

Address: Sutton Place, Seaford, East Sussex BN25 3PL
Telephone: 0323 890309

Head: Mr B F Underwood

Age range: 13-18
No. of pupils: 250
Scholarships: Yes
Religion: Non-denominational

Fees per term
Day: £1675-
Weekly board: £2623-
Full board: £2650-

Boy ○ Girl ○ Co-ed ●
Day ○ Week ○ Board ●

The school is located in the coastal town of Seaford and is only 90 minutes away from London by train. Our aim is to treat each student as an individual and although encouraged in many activities, our main emphasis is academic. We are strongly linked to our junior school (Newlands School) and offer educational continuity for boarders from age 8 on the same campus.

Newlands Pre Preparatory School

Address: Eastbourne Road, Seaford, East Sussex BN25 4NP
Telephone: 0323 890390

Head: Mrs A Morgan ACP CertEd BEd(Hons)

Age range: 2-8
No. of pupils: 200
Scholarships: Yes
Religion: Non-denominational

Fees per term
Day: -
Weekly board: -
Full board: -

Co-ed / Day

For further information and a prospectus, please contact the school.

Newlands Preparatory School

Address: Sutton Place, Eastbourne Road, Seaford, East Sussex BN25 4NP
Telephone: 0323 890309

Head: Mr R C Clark BA MA(Ed)

Age range: 7-13
No. of pupils: 280
Scholarships: Yes
Religion: Non-denominational

Fees per term
Day: £1260-£1550
Weekly board: -
Full board: -£2350

Co-ed / Day / Board

For further information and a prospectus, please contact the school.

Northease Manor School †

Address: Rodmell, Lewes, East Sussex BN7 3EY
Telephone: 0273 472915

Head: Mr R J Dennien

Age range: 10-17
No. of pupils: 102
Scholarships:
Religion: Non-denominational

Fees per term
Day: -
Weekly board: -
Full board: -

Co-ed / Week

Details of fees, further information and a prospectus available on application to the school.

The Old Grammar School

Address: 136 High Street, Lewes, East Sussex BN7 1XS
Telephone: 0273 472634

Principal: Mr R.E. Mead

Age range: 4-18
No. of pupils: 412
Scholarships: Yes
Religion: Inter-dominational

Fees per term
Day: £681-£1141
Weekly board: -
Full board: -

Co-ed / Day

The Old Grammar School, Lewes, is an independent school offering an excellent education to boys and girls aged 4 and a half-18. Small classes taught by highly qualified staff cover a wide range of subjects and produce exceptional examination results. The school owes its success to a disciplined, hardworking atmosphere where each pupil has the chance to reach their full potential.

Roedean *p748*

Address: Brighton, East Sussex BN2 5RQ

Telephone: 0273 603181

Head: Mrs A R Longley MA

Age range: 11-18
No. of pupils: 460
Scholarships: Yes
Religion: Church of England

Fees per term
Day: £2665-
Weekly board: -
Full board: £3885-

Boy ○ | Girl ● | Co-ed ○
Day ● | Week ○ | Board ●

Roedean School is an independent girls' boarding school (for ages 11-18) which aims to provide a 'whole life' education. High academic standards with excellent music, drama and sport. First-rate new facilities for humanities, technology and performing arts. Sixth form preparing for university entrance, with a few places for day girls.

Sacred Heart School

Address: Mayfield Lane, Durgates, Wadhurst, East Sussex TN5 6DQ

Telephone: 0892 783414

Head: Mrs H Castle

Age range: 3-11
No. of pupils: 96
Scholarships:
Religion: Roman Catholic

Fees per term
Day: £200-£540
Weekly board: -
Full board: -

Boy ○ | Girl ○ | Co-ed ●
Day ● | Week ○ | Board ○

For further details and a prospectus, please contact the school.

Skippers Hill Manor Preparatory School

Address: Five Ashes, Mayfield, East Sussex TN20 6HR

Telephone: 0825 830234

Head: Mr T W Lewis

Age range: 3-13
No. of pupils: 175
Scholarships: Yes
Religion: Non-denominational

Fees per term
Day: £450-£1310
Weekly board: -
Full board: -

Boy ○ | Girl ○ | Co-ed ●
Day ● | Week ○ | Board ○

Skippers enjoys the reputation for happiness among the children and success at meeting its aims at 11+ and Common Entrance. The Headmaster encourages a forward-looking approach and in this takes a personal lead. Children are encouraged to achieve self-discipline, courtesy and the spirit of sharing. They become dynamic, competitive individuals with a firm foundation on which to build.

Spinney School †

Address: Little London, Heathfield, East Sussex TN21 0NU

Telephone:

Head:

Age range:
No. of pupils:
Scholarships:
Religion:

Fees per term
Day: -
Weekly board: -
Full board: -

Boy ○ | Girl ○ | Co-ed ○
Day ○ | Week ○ | Board ○

For further information and a prospectus, please contact the school.

St Andrew's School

Address: Meads, Eastbourne, East Sussex BN20 7RP

Telephone: 0323 733203

Head: Mr H Davies Jones

Age range: 3-13
No. of pupils: 400
Scholarships: Yes
Religion: Church of England

Fees per term
Day: £460-£1650
Weekly board: -
Full board: -£2390

Boy ○ Girl ○ Co-ed ●
Day ● Week ○ Board ●

For further information and a prospectus, please contact the school.

St Aubyns

Address: 76 High Street, Rottingdean, Brighton, East Sussex BN2 7JN
Telephone: 0273 302170

Head: Mr J A L James

Age range: 7-13
No. of pupils: 117
Scholarships: Yes
Religion: Church of England

Fees per term
Day: £1925-
Weekly board: -
Full board: £2525-

Boy ● Girl ○ Co-ed ○
Day ● Week ○ Board ●

St Aubyns is a happy and friendly school and firmly believes in the traditional values which encourage self-discipline, good manners and consideration for others. The school has an excellent academic record.

Entry is by assessment and reports. The Hampton Gervis Scholarship is held in January for entry the following September and there is the James Virgo Sports Bursary.

St Bede's School

Address: The Dicker, Upper Dicker, Hailsham, East Sussex

Telephone: 0323 843252

Head: Mr R A Perrin

Age range: 12-18
No. of pupils: 350
Scholarships: Yes
Religion:

Fees per term
Day: £2050-
Weekly board: £3300-
Full board: £3300-

Boy ○ Girl ○ Co-ed ●
Day ● Week ● Board ●

Co-educational with a roll of 350 (150 in the sixth form) St Bede's offers 28 GCSE subjects, and a comprehensive A and AS level choice. Our club activities programme has 80 weekly and 30 daily options. Set in rolling countryside, St Bede's has a wealth of facilities, but the best way is to come and see for yourself.

St Bede's School

Address: Duke's Drive, Eastbourne, East Sussex BN20 7XL
Telephone: 0323 734222

Head: Mr P Pyemont

Age range: 3-13
No. of pupils: 450
Scholarships:
Religion: Non-denominational

Fees per term
Day: £530-£1720
Weekly board: -
Full board: -£2770

Boy ○ Girl ○ Co-ed ●
Day ● Week ○ Board ●

We are conscious that we are preparing children for adulthood in the 21st century. Basic philosophies like discipline, courtesy, industry and an awareness for others will never change. Technology, expertise and leisure pursuits will. During the past decade many improvements have been made to the facilities of St Bede's. The next decade promises to be equally exciting. A new multi-purpose sports hall has just been opened.

St Christopher's

Address: 33 New Church Road, Hove, East Sussex

Telephone: 0273 735404

Head: Mr R J M Saunders MA

Age range: 4-14
No. of pupils: 230
Scholarships:
Religion: Church of England

Fees per term
Day: -£765
Weekly board: -
Full board: -

- Boy ○ Girl ○ Co-ed
- Day ○ Week ○ Board

A very strong academic boys preparatory school with plenty of emphasis on sport, music and drama.

St Giles' College

Address: 13 Silverdale Road, Eastbourne, East Sussex

Telephone:

Head:

Age range: 12-16
No. of pupils:
Scholarships:
Religion:

Fees per term
Day: -
Weekly board: -
Full board: -

○ Boy ○ Girl ● Co-ed
○ Day ○ Week ○ Board

For further information and a prospectus, please contact the school.

St Leonards-Mayfield School

Address: The Old Palace, Mayfield, East Sussex TN20 6PH

Telephone: 0435 873383

Head: Sister J Sinclair

Age range: 11-18
No. of pupils: 525
Scholarships: Yes
Religion: Roman Catholic

Fees per term
Day: £1865-
Weekly board: £2775-
Full board: £2880-

○ Boy ● Girl ○ Co-ed
● Day ● Week ● Board

St Leonards-Mayfield School values and seeks to live its Catholic Christian foundation in fostering high standards of academic, musical, sporting, dramatic and artistic achievement within a supportive and compassionate community. Central of our ethos is respect for and careful development of the unique gifts of each girl; hence, the vast majority proceed to higher education (over 80% to degree courses).

St Mary's Hall ✱ *p751*

Address: Eastern Road, Brighton, East Sussex BN2 5JF

Telephone: 0273 606061

Head: Mrs M T Broadbent

Age range: 3-18
No. of pupils: 370
Scholarships: Yes
Religion: Church of England

Fees per term
Day: £330-£1810
Weekly board: £2246-£2623
Full board: £2356-£2733

● Boy ● Girl ○ Co-ed
● Day ● Week ● Board

St Mary's Hall is a Church of England foundation combining tradition with educational development. Emphasis within the school community is on caring for individuals, courtesy and respect for others, realisation of pupils' potential, and high expectations all-round. Classes are small; teachers enthusiastic. Prospective pupils are welcome to spend a day at the school.

St Mary's School †

Address: Wrestwood Road, Bexhill-on-Sea, East Sussex TN40 2LU
Telephone: 0424 730740

Principal: Mr D Cassar MA

Age range: 5-16
No. of pupils: 90
Scholarships:
Religion: Christian

Fees per term
Day: £5160-
Weekly board: -
Full board: £7740-

○ ○ ● Boy Girl Co-ed
● ○ ● Day Week Board

A DES approved residential special school catering predominantly for children with speech and language disorders, although each one of our pupils is unique because of an overlay of other complex medical/emotional problems and associated learning difficulties. Pupils have full access to the National Curriculum, adapted into individual learning programmes, comprehensive therapy and medical support.

St Michael's Hill House Preparatory School

Address: New Town, Uckfield, East Sussex TN22 5DJ
Telephone: 0825 763874

Head: Sister Lucy

Age range: 4-11
No. of pupils: 101
Scholarships:
Religion:

Fees per term
Day: -
Weekly board: -
Full board: -

○ ○ ● Boy Girl Co-ed
● ○ ○ Day Week Board

For further information and a prospectus, please contact the school.

St Michael's Nursery School

Address: New Town, Uckfield, East Sussex TN22 5DN
Telephone: 0825 3647

Head: Sister Barbara

Age range: 2-5
No. of pupils: 160
Scholarships:
Religion:

Fees per term
Day: -
Weekly board: -
Full board: -

○ ○ ● Boy Girl Co-ed
● ○ ○ Day Week Board

For further information and a prospectus, please contact the school.

St Nicholas School

Address: Harrock House, Buxted, East Sussex
Telephone: 0825 732335

Head: Mrs J E Lee

Age range: 3-14
No. of pupils: 120
Scholarships:
Religion: Non-denominational

Fees per term
Day: £470-£1166
Weekly board: -
Full board: -

● ● ○ Boy Girl Co-ed
● ○ ○ Day Week Board

St Nicholas is a well established day school with an excellent academic aand sporting record. Children are taught in small classes with great emphasis on individual progress. There is a thriving kindergarten for three year olds. The school offers many extra-curricular activities and an optional extended day.

Temple Grove School p709

Address: Heron's Ghyll,
Uckfield, East Sussex
TN22 4DA
Telephone: 082571 2112

Age range: 3-13
No. of pupils:
Scholarships:
Religion: Church of England

Fees per term
Day: £580-£1915
Weekly board: -£2550
Full board: -£2550

○ ○ ●
Boy Girl Co-ed
● ● ●
Day Week Board

Head: Mr S P Blackmore

School is situated in 40 acres of grounds with modern facilities. School specialises in small classes and experienced, devoted staff create happy, friendly environment for children, who are well motivated and gain confidence.

Vinehall School

Address: Robertsbridge, East Sussex TN32 5JL

Telephone: 0580 880413

Age range: 4-14
No. of pupils: 300
Scholarships:
Religion:

Fees per term
Day: -
Weekly board: -
Full board: -

○ ○ ●
Boy Girl Co-ed
● ○ ●
Day Week Board

Head: Mr D C Chaplin

For further information and a prospectus, please contact the school.

Wadhurst College (Incorporating Legat Ballet School)

Address: Mayfield Lane,
Wadhurst, East Sussex TN5 6JA

Telephone: 0892 783193

Age range: 11-18
No. of pupils: 180
Scholarships: Yes
Religion: Church of England

Fees per term
Day: £1885-£1955
Weekly board: -£3045
Full board: -£3070

○ ○ ●
Boy Girl Co-ed
● ● ●
Day Week Board

Head: Miss A.M. Phillips B.ed Hons

A caring Christian, boarding and day school for girls 11-18 in beautiful Sussex countryside. Small classes, sixth form centre, dance studios, indoor swimming pool, sports hall. Strong arts department with drama and music alongside the Legat Ballet School. Vocational courses and A Levels offered to equip girls to meet the challenge of life. Entry by Common Entrance or our tests. Scholarships offered annually.

Westerleigh

Address: Hollington Park Road, St Leonards on Sea, East Sussex TN38 0SE
Telephone: 0424 421909

Age range: 2-13
No. of pupils: 190
Scholarships: Yes
Religion: Non-denominational

Fees per term
Day: £120-£1090
Weekly board: -
Full board: -

○ ○ ●
Boy Girl Co-ed
● ○ ○
Day Week Board

Head: Mrs P K Wheeler

Independent day school founded in 1907. Eleven acres in urban surroundings with well equipped class rooms and dedicated caring staff. Many artistic and academic scholarships are won to senior schools.

Wilton House School p709

Address: Catsfield Place,
Battle, East Sussex TN33 9BS

Telephone: 0424 830234

Head: Mrs F Auer

Age range: 5-18
No. of pupils: 170
Scholarships: Yes
Religion: Church of England

Fees per term
Day: £600-£1370
Weekly board: £1540-£2350
Full board: £1540-£2350

○ ○ ●
Boy Girl Co-ed
● ● ●
Day Week Board

Wilton House School incorporates 'Broomham' School for juniors and Catsfield Place for seniors. Both enjoy a lovely setting and many leisure facilities.

Winton House School

Address: 4 Dane Road, St Leonards-on-Sea, East Sussex TN38 0QU
Telephone: 0424 421909

Head: Mr D J Cole

Age range: 4-12
No. of pupils: 50
Scholarships:
Religion:

Fees per term
Day: -
Weekly board: -
Full board: -

○ ○ ●
Boy Girl Co-ed
● ○ ○
Day Week Board

For further information and a prospectus, please contact the school.

SUSSEX (WEST)

SUSSEX (WEST) 503

Ardingly College * p737

Address: Haywards Heath, West Sussex RH17 6SQ

Telephone: 0444 892577

Head: Mr J W Flecker

Age range: 6-18
No. of pupils: 600
Scholarships: Yes
Religion: Church of England

Fees per term
Day: £1680-£2740
Weekly board: -
Full board: £2240-£3450

○ ○ ● Boy Girl Co-ed
● ○ ● Day Week Board

Ardingly College is a co-educational boarding and day school for 6 to 18 year olds set in the heart of Sussex, approximately 12 miles from Gatwick Airport and 25 miles south of London. There is a single campus which is shared by the junior school of about 130 boys and 90 girls from 6 to 13, and the senior school of about 300 boys and 200 girls aged from 13 to 18.

Arundale

Address: Lower Street, Pulborough, West Sussex

Telephone: 0798 872520

Head: Miss K Lovejoy

Age range: 4-11
No. of pupils: 99
Scholarships:
Religion:

Fees per term
Day: £495-£995
Weekly board: -
Full board: -

● ● ○ Boy Girl Co-ed
● ○ ○ Day Week Board

Arundale is a day preparatory school with a friendly atmosphere that encourages every child to do their very best at all times. Girls are prepared for Common Entrance and scholarship examinations. The school offers a wide range of musical and sporting activities and regular outings to museums, theatres, field trips, etc. Emphasis is placed upon a sound educational basis, good manners, thoughtfulness and self-confidence.

Brambletye School

Address: East Grinstead, West Sussex RH19 3PD

Telephone: 0342 321004

Head: Mr D G Fowler-Watt MA (Cantab), JP

Age range: 7-13
No. of pupils: 220
Scholarships:
Religion: Church of England

Fees per term
Day: £1900-
Weekly board: -
Full board: £2600-

● ○ ○ Boy Girl Co-ed
● ○ ● Day Week Board

Brambletye is a boarding preparatory school for boys in 140 acres of beautiful grounds overlooking Ashdown Forest in Sussex. The school has a strong academic reputation and aims to give the children confidence by offering them a wide range of sporting and cultural facilities. The headmaster and wife, supported by an experienced staff, provide a warm and caring atmosphere.

Broadwater Manor School

Address: Broadwater Road, Worthing, West Sussex BN14 8HU

Telephone: 0903 201123

Head: Mr D Telfer

Age range: 2-13
No. of pupils: 400
Scholarships: Yes
Religion:

Fees per term
Day: £85-£1000
Weekly board: -
Full board: -

○ ○ ● Boy Girl Co-ed
● ○ ○ Day Week Board

The school covers the whole age range from 2-13 in three separate stages: nursery, pre-preparatory and preparatory. The curriculum includes all items necessary for successful completion of the Common Entrance examination at 13+ and also many areas desirable for a wider education such as German, information technology, design technology etc.

Burgess Hill School for Girls *

Address: Keymer Road,
Burgess Hill, West Sussex
RH15 0AQ
Telephone: 0444 241050

Headmistress: Mrs B H Webb

Age range: 4-18
No. of pupils: 532
Scholarships: Yes
Religion: Non-denominational

Fees per term
Day: £695-£1450
Weekly board: -
Full board: £2195-£2450

○ ● ○
Boy Girl Co-ed
● ● ●
Day Week Board

Burgess Hill is an independent day and boarding school for approximately 600 girls from 4-18 situated in a country town near Gatwick on the London to Brighton railway line. There is a sixth form of 60/70 and 95% go on to higher education. Most of the extensive facilities have been built over the past 10 years with an emphasis on science provision. Examination results are consistently high with regular

Christ's Hospital *

Address: Horsham, West
Sussex RH13 7YP

Telephone: 0403 211293

Head: Mr R C Poulton

Age range: 11-18
No. of pupils: 800
Scholarships:
Religion: Church of England

Fees per term
Day: -
Weekly board: -
Full board: -£3102

○ ○ ●
Boy Girl Co-ed
○ ○ ●
Day Week Board

Founded in 1552, Christ's Hospital offers a first class education in an ethos of care to those of good average ability or above who are eager to work hard and seize the opportunities offered in academic work, in music, in art and design, on games and sport of all kinds and in friendhsip and companionship. Fees according to means.

Conifers School

Address: Midhurst, West
Sussex GU29 9BG

Telephone: 073081 3243

Head: Mrs P Peel

Age range: 3-11
No. of pupils: 150
Scholarships: Yes
Religion: Non-denominational

Fees per term
Day: £450-£880
Weekly board: -
Full board: -

○ ○ ●
Boy Girl Co-ed
● ○ ○
Day Week Board

Conifers is a small, lively independent preparatory school for children of 3-11 years, preparing children for 11 plus and Common Entrance examinations. All aspects of the curriculum are covered. Children are given individual attention to develop their potential.

Convent of the Blessed Sacrament

Address: The Towers, Upper
Beeding, Steyning, West
Sussex BN44 3TF
Telephone: 0903 812185

Head: Sister M Andrew

Age range: 5-16
No. of pupils: 210
Scholarships:
Religion: Roman Catholic

Fees per term
Day: £885-£963
Weekly board: -
Full board: £1652-£1725

○ ● ○
Boy Girl Co-ed
● ○ ●
Day Week Board

The Towers, a small Roman Catholic boarding and day-school, in the healthy and beautiful setting of the South Downs, is run by a community of sisters and noted for its homely, caring atmosphere and Christian values. Twice winner of the Whitbread Prize for GCSE results, The Towers combines academic expectations with extra-curricular activities and noteworthy sporting achievements.

Copthorne School

Address: Effingham Lane, Copthorne, Crawley, West Sussex RH10 3HR
Telephone: 0342 712311

Head: Mr D Newton

Age range: 4-14
No. of pupils: 244
Scholarships: Yes
Religion: Church of England

Fees per term
Day: £890-£1630
Weekly board: £1970-£1970
Full board: -

○ Boy ○ Girl ● Co-ed
● Day ● Week ○ Board

Copthorne is a co-educational, day and weekly boarding preparatory school for children aged 4-14 years. Facilities include two science laboratories, art and design department, sports hall, theatre and music block. There are two playing fields, one with three cricket pitches and one with five football and rugby pitches, four tennis courts (one indoor), a small golf course and swimming pool.

Cottesmore School

Address: Buchan Hill, Pease Pottage, West Sussex RH11 9AU
Telephone: 0293 520648

Head: Mr M A Rogerson

Age range: 7-13
No. of pupils: 150
Scholarships: Yes
Religion: Non-denominational

Fees per term
Day: -
Weekly board: -
Full board: -£2580

○ Boy ○ Girl ● Co-ed
○ Day ○ Week ● Board

Cottesmore is a family school, which has been preparing children for the major public schools for almost a century. It is one of the few all boarding co-educational preparatory schools in the country. We are large enough to be competitive in academic standards and facilities, but small and friendly enough to allow us to respect each boy and girl as an individual.

Cumnor House School

Address: Danehill, Haywards Heath, West Sussex RH17 7HT
Telephone: 0825 790347

Head: Mr N J Milner-Golland

Age range: 4-13
No. of pupils: 192
Scholarships:
Religion: Church of England

Fees per term
Day: £790-£1975
Weekly board: -
Full board: £2445-£2575

○ Boy ○ Girl ● Co-ed
● Day ○ Week ● Board

Co-educational boarding and day school for 150 children (7-13), with pre-preparatory department (4-7) for 40 children. The school is liberal in outlook, with a fine reputation for art, music, drama and creativity, as well as for high academic achievement. There are excellent facilities for outdoor activities and many sports, which are coached to a high standard.

Dorset House School

Address: The Manor, Bury, Pulborough, West Sussex RH20 1PB
Telephone: 0798 831456

Head: Mr A L James

Age range: 5-13
No. of pupils: 100
Scholarships: Yes
Religion: Church of England

Fees per term
Day: £990-£2000
Weekly board: £2390-£2390
Full board: £2390-£2390

● Boy ○ Girl ○ Co-ed
● Day ● Week ● Board

Dorset House is situated in the beautiful Arun Valley close to the South Downs. Boys are prepared for entrance to a wide range of senior independent schools. Art and music play a large part in the curriculum of the school. Entry is by interview.

Farlington School p710

Address: Horsham, West Sussex RH12 3PN

Telephone: 0403 54967

Head: Mrs P Mawer

Age range: 9-18
No. of pupils: 280
Scholarships: Yes
Religion: Church of England

Fees per term
Day: £1600-£1730
Weekly board: £2600-£2800
Full board: £2600-£2800

Boy ○ Girl ● Co-ed ○
Day ● Week ● Board ●

Farlington is an independent day and boarding school for girls standing in 27 acres of grounds containing an all weather pitch for hockey, athletics and tennis; heated open air swimming pool; playing fields and two lakes for recreational and environmental studies. Girls are prepared for GCSE, 'A' levels and university entrance by a fully graduate staff. There is a strong tradition of music and drama in the school.

Farney Close School Ltd †

Address: Bolney Court, Bolney, Haywards Heath, West Sussex RH17 5RD

Telephone: 0444 881811

Head: Mr J R Tompson

Age range: 8-17
No. of pupils: 75
Scholarships:
Religion: Non-denominational

Fees per term
Day: -
Weekly board: -
Full board: -

Boy ○ Girl ○ Co-ed ●
Day ● Week ○ Board ●

A special school dealing with children with emotional and behavioural problems. We cater for children for whom mainstream schooling has been an unhappy experience. We offer a range of support services to children with the aim of creating a therapeutic milieu and are able to offer 52 week care to suitable clients. Pupils are offered a range of GCSE examinations with AEB Basic Skills and C&G Foundation Courses.

Firth House Preparatory School

Address: Claigmar Road, Rustington, West Sussex BN16 2NL

Telephone: 0903 784462

Head: Mr J H W Samson

Age range: 3-11
No. of pupils: 50
Scholarships:
Religion: Ecumenical

Fees per term
Day: £330-£770
Weekly board: -
Full board: -

Boy ○ Girl ○ Co-ed ●
Day ● Week ○ Board ○

Firth House is a small independent school for boys and girls from the ages of 3 to 12 years. The aim of the school is to provide a happy, homely atmosphere where the child can learn and develop as an individual. Very small classes cater for the needs of each child. The 3 Rs form the basis of the curriculum.

Fonthill Lodge School

Address: Coombe Hill Road, East Grinstead, West Sussex RH19 4LY

Telephone: 0342 321635

Head: Mrs J M Griffiths

Age range: 3-11
No. of pupils: 142
Scholarships: Yes
Religion: Non-denominational

Fees per term
Day: £451-£1205
Weekly board: -
Full board: -

Boy ● Girl ● Co-ed ○
Day ● Week ○ Board ○

An independent day school founded in 1808 where individual attention is given in small classes. High academic standards are attained, excellent facilities including well structured nursery. Boys aged 3-8 years are prepared for entry into preparatory schools. Girls aged 3-11+ are prepared for Common Entrance. Internal and external scholarships are offered to girls aged 8 years.

SUSSEX (WEST) 507

Franciscan Convent

Address: Borers Arms Road, Copthorne, West Sussex RH10 3LN
Telephone: 0342 712088

Head: Sister Attracta

Age range: 4-9
No. of pupils: 130
Scholarships:
Religion: Catholic

Fees per term
Day: £400-£500
Weekly board: -
Full board: -

○ ● ○
Boy Girl Co-ed
● ○ ○
Day Week Board

The Franciscan Convent School is an independent school for children aged four to nine years and is run by the Franciscan Missionary Sisters of Littlehampton. The religious background is Catholic and a Christian atmosphere permeates the life of the school. We aim to create a warm family atmosphere where young children will develop emotionally, socially, psychologically and in fromal learning.

Great Ballard

Address: Eartham, Chichester, West Sussex PO18 0LR
Telephone: 0243 65236

Head: Mr R E T Jennings

Age range: 3-13
No. of pupils: 166
Scholarships: Yes
Religion: Church of England

Fees per term
Day: £860-£1515
Weekly board: £2045-£2145
Full board: £2145-£2145

○ ○ ●
Boy Girl Co-ed
● ● ●
Day Week Board

Great Ballard is an IAPS co-educational day and boarding school for children from the ages of 3-13. At Great Ballard children are genuinely happy and are involved in a very wide range of activities, where their interest is constantly being stimulated. The school operates a free minibus service from Petworth, Chichester, Bognor and Littlehampton. Generous bursaries to Forces children, scholarships are awarded in February.

Great Walstead School

Address: Lindfield, Haywards Heath, West Sussex RH16 2QL
Telephone: 0444 483528

Head: Mr H J Lowries

Age range: 4-13
No. of pupils: 347
Scholarships: Yes
Religion: Non-denominational

Fees per term
Day: £620-£1640
Weekly board: -
Full board: £1995-£1995

○ ○ ●
Boy Girl Co-ed
● ○ ●
Day Week Board

Great Walstead School is set within an extensive wooded estate in the lovely Sussex countryside. The school provides a happy family atmosphere, lively Christian tradition, individual attention in small classes, a pre-prep from 4+, and the perfect environment in which to educate children in their formative years.

Handcross Park School

Address: Handcross, Haywards Heath, West Sussex RH17 6HF
Telephone: 0444 400526

Head: Mr S G I Kerruish

Age range: 2-13
No. of pupils: 272
Scholarships: Yes
Religion: Church of England

Fees per term
Day: £84-£1950
Weekly board: £2380-
Full board: £2380-

○ ○ ●
Boy Girl Co-ed
● ● ●
Day Week Board

Preparation for Scholarships and Common Entrance. All major subjects and art, music, computer studies and wide range of extra activities. Set within 50 acres of stunningly beautiful grounds and playing fields; an educational paradise for young children, Handcross Park is a very special school.

Highfield School

Address: Highfield Road, East Grinstead, West Sussex RH19 2DX
Telephone: 0342 323193

Head: Mr R Gordon-Walker

Age range: 3-11
No. of pupils: 110
Scholarships:
Religion: Non-denominational

Fees per term
Day: £225-£630
Weekly board: -
Full board: -

○ Boy ○ Girl ● Co-ed
● Day ○ Week ○ Board

Highfield gives its pupils a sound academic education in small classes, with good sports facilities. Children are prepared for entry to all independent and maintained secondary schools.

Hurstpierpoint College *

Address: Hassocks, West Sussex BN6 9JS
Telephone: 0273 833636

Head: Mr S A Watson

Age range: 7-18
No. of pupils: 550
Scholarships: Yes
Religion: Church of England

Fees per term
Day: £1400-£2550
Weekly board: -
Full board: £2150-£3185

● Boy ● Girl ○ Co-ed
● Day ○ Week ● Board

Boys only for 150 years, Hurstpierpoint is to become fully co-educational starting in the junior school from September 1993. Average GCSEs 9+ per candidate; 95% A Level pass rate; 70% to university or polytechnic. Senior and junior school share 115 acre campus with olympic sports hall, indoor heated pool and music school. New £1.5 million VIth form house, St Johns, with 80 individual bed studies opened in 1992.

Lancing College

Address: Lancing, West Sussex BN15 0RW
Telephone: 0273 452213

Head: Mr J S Woodhouse MA

Age range: 13-18
No. of pupils: 540
Scholarships: Yes
Religion: Church of England

Fees per term
Day: -£2695
Weekly board: -
Full board: -£3590

● Boy ● Girl ○ Co-ed
● Day ○ Week ● Board

Lancing College offers a broad education in a well organised Christian community. Academic standards are high with over 90% of pupils proceeding to higher education. Individual tutorial and pastoral care with good communications between staff, pupils and parents are emphasised at Lancing. Pupils are encouraged to fulfil their potential and have an excellent opportunities for performing arts, games and expeditions. Girls 16-18.

Lavant House School

Address: West Lavant, Chichester, West Sussex PO18 9AB
Telephone: 0243 527788

Head: Mrs Y G Graham

Age range: 5-18
No. of pupils: 145
Scholarships: Yes
Religion: Church of England

Fees per term
Day: £750-£1795
Weekly board: £2375-£2945
Full board: £2375-£2945

○ Boy ● Girl ○ Co-ed
● Day ● Week ● Board

Lavant House School, set in beautiful Sussex countryside, three miles from Chichester, offers a broad spectrum of subjects with equal emphasis on languages and the sciences. It has a flourishing art department and a long tradition of success at drama. The school has a heated open air swimming pool and its own riding stables, which offer full or DIY livery and horse leasing facilities.

Littlemead Grammar School

Address: Woodfield House, Oving, Chichester, West Sussex PO20 6EU
Telephone: 0243 787551

Principal: Mr I F A Bowler

Age range: 3-16
No. of pupils: 200
Scholarships:
Religion: Church of England

Fees per term
Day: £416-£1352
Weekly board: -£1902
Full board: -£2022

Boy ○ Girl ○ Co-ed ●
Day ● Week ● Board ●

The school is sub-divided into lower, middle, and upper schoools and although they have their own head and identity, care is taken to ensure a smooth transistion from one school to the next. The programmes of work are designed to meet the demands of the National Curriculum and the GCSE examination boards and to give the pupils thorough grounding in a broad range of subjects.

Mill Hill School for Deaf Children †

Address: Whitemans Green, Cuckfield, Haywards Heath, West Sussex RH17 5HX
Telephone: 0444 454000

Head: Mr J M Brown

Age range: 4-12
No. of pupils: 56
Scholarships:
Religion:

Fees per term
Day: £3146-
Weekly board: £4231-
Full board: -

Boy ● Girl ● Co-ed ●
Day ● Week ● Board ○

Special school following a natural oral/aural approach, teaching deaf children to develop listening and talking skills. Small class groups of 5 to 8 children, high level of individual support, and purpose built audiology clinic.

Northgate House School

Address: 38 North Street, Chichester, West Sussex
Telephone: 0243 784828

Head: Mrs W E Shoesmith

Age range: 4-8
No. of pupils: 86
Scholarships:
Religion: Church of England

Fees per term
Day: £100-£250
Weekly board: -
Full board: -

Boy ○ Girl ○ Co-ed ●
Day ● Week ○ Board ○

Classes are small enough for much individual attention. We endeavour to give the children a sound basic education but there are many other subjects including French, elocution, drama, art, handicraft, music, rhythm and movement, knitting, needlework, projects of all kinds and games. We have won many prizes for music, drama and elocution and several scholarships to well known schools.

Oakwood School

Address: Chichester, West Sussex PO18 9AN
Telephone: 0243 575209

Head: Mr S Whittle

Age range: 3-13
No. of pupils: 178
Scholarships: Yes
Religion: Church of England

Fees per term
Day: £375-£1515
Weekly board: £1955-£1955
Full board: £2055-£2055

Boy ○ Girl ○ Co-ed ●
Day ● Week ● Board ●

The school was founded in 1912 and is situated 2.5 miles west of Chichester. A wide range of activities is offered to enable each pupil to discover and develop his or her own particular talents. Good academic record, small classes, family atmosphere, well qualified staff.

Our Lady of Sion School

Address: Gratwicke Road, Worthing, West Sussex BN11 4BL
Telephone: 0903 204063

Head: Mr B Sexton

Age range: 3-18
No. of pupils: 500
Scholarships: Yes
Religion: Roman Catholic

Fees per term
Day: £685-£1299
Weekly board: -
Full board: -

Boy ○ Girl ○ Co-ed ●
Day ● Week ○ Board ○

Sion School is an independent co-educational day school. It offers traditional academic education at reasonable cost in a friendly, caring environment. Public examination success rates among the very best in the country. Excellent range of clubs/societies. Superb VI form scholarships (boarding can be arranged in town separately at this level).

Pennthorpe School p710

Address: Rudgwick, Horsham, West Sussex RH12 3HY
Telephone: 0403 822391

Head: Rev J E Spencer

Age range: 4-14
No. of pupils: 276
Scholarships: Yes
Religion: Church of England

Fees per term
Day: £650-£1750
Weekly board: £1920-£2250
Full board: -

Boy ○ Girl ○ Co-ed ●
Day ● Week ● Board ○

Pennthorpe is a co-educational preparatory school of 51 boarders and 210 day pupils aged between 4 and 14. We offer computing, music, art, CDT, cooking, rifle shooting, cubs and brownies; sporting activities include soccer, rugby, hockey, cricket, athletics, swimming, netball, squash, trampolining and judo. The school has its own chapel and chapel choir and regularly is invited to sing in various cathedrals.

Philpots Manor School †

Address: West Hoathly, East Grinstead, West Sussex RH19 4PR
Telephone: 0342 810268

Principal: Mr P B Ogilvy

Age range: 6-19
No. of pupils: 70
Scholarships:
Religion: Christian

Fees per term
Day: -
Weekly board: -
Full board: -

Boy ○ Girl ○ Co-ed ●
Day ○ Week ○ Board ●

The school is based on the social and educational principles of Rudolf Steiner. It was founded in 1958 to offer an education to children with special needs who have, because of their own particular difficulties, been unable to learn and develop within the setting of an ordinary school. The school provides a homely and caring environment, and offers a lively and artistic approach to both social and academic education.

PNEU School Compton

Address: 1 The Square, Compton, Chichester, West Sussex PO18 9HA
Telephone: 0705 631208

Head: Mrs O M Norton

Age range: 4-12
No. of pupils: 35
Scholarships:
Religion:

Fees per term
Day: -
Weekly board: -
Full board: -

Boy ○ Girl ○ Co-ed ●
Day ● Week ○ Board ○

For further information and a prospectus, please contact the school.

SUSSEX (WEST) 511

Prebendal School

Address: 53 West Street, Chichester, West Sussex PO19 1RT
Telephone: 0243 782026

Head: Rev G C Hall

Age range: 7-14
No. of pupils: 198
Scholarships: Yes
Religion: Church of England

Fees per term
Day: -£1488
Weekly board: -£2000
Full board: -£2052

Boy ○ Girl ○ Co-ed ●
Day ● Week ● Board ●

For further information and a prospectus, please contact the school.

Rosemead

Address: East Street, Littlehampton, West Sussex BN17 6AL
Telephone: 0903 716065

Head: Mrs H A Kingham

Age range: 3-18
No. of pupils: 245
Scholarships: Yes
Religion: Church of England

Fees per term
Day: £380-£1560
Weekly board: -
Full board: £2320-£2695

Boy ○ Girl ● Co-ed ●
Day ● Week ● Board ●

Co-ed Prep Department, Rosemead is a friendly day and boarding school, set in lovely grounds and only five minutes walk from the sea. It has excellent facilities and is within easy reach of London. It offers a rich and varied curriculum, with small class sizes giving girls personal attention and guidance. The boarding house is modern, yet comfortable, with a happy family atmosphere. Life is lived to the full at Rosemead.

S Michaels

Address: Burton Park, Petworth, West Sussex GU28 0LS
Telephone: 0798 42517

Head: Mrs L J Griffin

Age range: 11-18
No. of pupils: 142
Scholarships: Yes
Religion: Church of England

Fees per term
Day: £1980-
Weekly board: £2950-
Full board: £2950-

Boy ○ Girl ● Co-ed ○
Day ● Week ● Board ●

S Michaels is a Woodard School set in 150 acres of parkland in the Sussex Downs close to Gatwick and easily reached from London. It is a caring community with good academic standards based on a broad curriculum excelling in sport, music, drama and offering an unusually extensive activities programme.

Sandhurst Independent Preparatory School

Address: 101 Brighton Road, Worthing, West Sussex BN11 2EL
Telephone: 0903 210933

Head: Mrs C Skomski

Age range: 3-13
No. of pupils: 133
Scholarships:
Religion: Non-denominational

Fees per term
Day: £390-£450
Weekly board: -
Full board: -

Boy ○ Girl ○ Co-ed ●
Day ● Week ○ Board ○

Sandhurst is situated close to the town centre and was established in 1935. It is run by a non-profit making charitable trust. The school follows a well structured, traditional curriculum, encouraging all children to reach their full potential, academically, socially and physically. The lower school is currently expanding into newly-acquires, adjacent premises.

Seaford College

Address: Lavington Park, Petworth, West Sussex GU28 0NB
Telephone: 0798 6392
Head: Mr R C Hanniford BSc MIBiol CertEd

Age range: 11-18
No. of pupils: 300
Scholarships: Yes
Religion: Church of England

Fees per term
Day: £1880-£2095
Weekly board: -
Full board: £2580-£3010

● Boy ● Girl ○ Co-ed
● Day ○ Week ● Board

Founded at Seaford and moved to Petworth in 1946. Boys boarding 11-18 with some day places. Good academic record and we provide an all-round education. New junior house and art/CDT centre. Chapel choir with international reputation. CCF and outstanding sporting facilities and achievements. Three hundred acres of parkland. Day girls in the sixth form.

Shoreham College

Address: St Julian's Lane, Shoreham by Sea, West Sussex BN43 6YW
Telephone: 0273 592681
Head: Mr B H Mead MA(Cantab)

Age range: 4-18
No. of pupils: 270
Scholarships: Yes
Religion: Church of England

Fees per term
Day: £645-£1655
Weekly board: -
Full board: -

○ Boy ○ Girl ● Co-ed
● Day ○ Week ○ Board

This is a comparatively small day 'grammar' school where classes are small and it is therefore easier for individuals to feel recognized and for sound relationships to flourish. Boys and girls are certainly encouraged and structured to fulfil their potential academically, but we also seek to develop all-round character through active participation in cultural, sporting and other activities.

Sion School

Address: Gratwicke Road, Worthing, West Sussex BN11 4BL
Telephone: 0903 237676
Head: Mr B Sexton

Age range: 2-18
No. of pupils: 500
Scholarships: Yes
Religion: Roman Catholic

Fees per term
Day: £685-£1299
Weekly board: -
Full board: -

● Boy ● Girl ● Co-ed
● Day ○ Week ○ Board

The school has a fine academic record (88% pass at 'C' and above in GCSE - 70% of these grades 'A' and 'B' with 94% pass at A Level - 52% of these 'A' and 'B'). More importantly, it offers a friendly, caring environment of mutual respect.

Slindon College p711

Address: Slindon House, Slindon, Arundel, West Sussex
Telephone: 0243 65320
Head: Mr A C Baldwin BA

Age range: 11-18
No. of pupils: 165
Scholarships:
Religion: Non-denominational

Fees per term
Day: £1705-£2640-
Weekly board: £2640-
Full board: £2640

● Boy ● Girl ○ Co-ed
● Day ● Week ● Board

Independent boarding and day school for boys (11-18) and 6th form girls, occupying a beautiful postion on the South Downs. Facilities include swimming pool, squash courts and floodlit hardcourt. Teaching in small groups to GCSE and A Level. The special needs unit is staffed by fully qualified, experienced teachers. Activities include skateboarding, canoeing, motor vehicle club and computer studies.

Sompting Abbotts Preparatory School

Address: Sompting, Lancing, West Sussex BN15 0AZ

Telephone: 0903 235960

Head: Mr N A Sinclair

Age range: 4-13
No. of pupils: 186
Scholarships:
Religion: Church of England

Fees per term
Day: £280-£1140
Weekly board: -£1805
Full board: -

● Boy ○ Girl ○ Co-ed
● Day ● Week ○ Board

Sompting Abbotts has 30 acres of ground, with two hard tennis courts, an outdoor swimming pool and an indoor shooting range. It is on the South Downs, two and a half miles north east of Worthing. Boys are prepared for Common Entrance and scholarship to public schools. The main games played are cricket, soccer and rugby.

Southdown School

Address: Gervays Hall, Jarvis Lane, Steyning, West Sussex BN44 3GL

Telephone: 0903 814581

Head: Mrs R A Hoare

Age range: 3-8
No. of pupils: 62
Scholarships:
Religion: Non-denominational

Fees per term
Day: £200-£450
Weekly board: -
Full board: -

○ Boy ○ Girl ● Co-ed
● Day ○ Week ○ Board

For further information and a prospectus, please contact the school.

St Joseph's Dominican Convent School

Address: The Abbey, Storrington, Pulborough, West Sussex RH20 4HE

Telephone: 0903 743279

Head: Sister Loretta

Age range: 4-11
No. of pupils: 140
Scholarships:
Religion: Roman Catholic

Fees per term
Day: -
Weekly board: -
Full board: -

○ Boy ○ Girl ● Co-ed
● Day ○ Week ○ Board

For further information and a prospectus, please contact the school.

St Margeret's Convent School

Address: Convent of Mercy, Petersfield Road, Midhurst, West Sussex GU29 9JN

Telephone: 0730 813899

Head: Sister Ethelreda

Age range: 11-16
No. of pupils: 300
Scholarships:
Religion: Roman Catholic

Fees per term
Day: £650-
Weekly board: £1375-
Full board: -

○ Boy ● Girl ○ Co-ed
● Day ● Week ○ Board

The school offers a full curriculum leading to GCSE. Technology and computer studies are taught from year seven; keyboard skills from year nine. Two languages from French, Spanish and German may be followed. Individual science subjects are taught as well as single and double award modular courses. There is a 7 acre playing field. Transport from a wide area is arranged by the parents.

St Margeret's Junior School

Address: Convent of Mercy, Petersfield Road, Midhurst, West Sussex GU29 9JN
Telephone: 0730 813956

Head: Sister Joan

Age range: 3-11
No. of pupils: 400
Scholarships:
Religion: Roman Catholic

Fees per term
Day: £270-£500
Weekly board: £1225-
Full board: -

Boy ○ Girl ○ Co-ed ●
Day ● Week ● Board ○

The aim of the school is to make the children happy and to incalcate the fundamental principles of Christian living and responsibility and social values. The children are encouraged to make full use of the abilities and talents. The school enjoys an excellent teacher/pupil relationship and values highly the co-operation and involvement of parents. Most girls continue on to the senior school.

St Peter's Upper School

Address: Upper St John's Road, Burgess Hill, West Sussex RH15 8HB
Telephone: 0444 235880

Head:

Age range:
No. of pupils:
Scholarships:
Religion:

Fees per term
Day: -
Weekly board: -
Full board: -

Boy ○ Girl ○ Co-ed ○
Day ○ Week ○ Board ○

For further information and a prospectus, please contact the school.

Stoke Brunswick School

Address: Ashurst Wood, East Grinstead, West Sussex RH19 3PF
Telephone: 0342 82 2233

Head: Mr W M Ellerton

Age range: 3-13
No. of pupils: 160
Scholarships:
Religion:

Fees per term
Day: -
Weekly board: -
Full board: -

Boy ○ Girl ○ Co-ed ●
Day ● Week ● Board ○

For further information and a prospectus, please contact the school.

Tavistock & Summerhill

Address: Summerhill Lane, Haywards Heath, West Sussex RH16 1RP
Telephone: 0444 450256

Head: Mr T Locke

Age range: 4-13
No. of pupils: 180
Scholarships:
Religion: Non-denominational

Fees per term
Day: £795-£1225
Weekly board: -
Full board: -

Boy ○ Girl ○ Co-ed ●
Day ● Week ○ Board ○

We are always happy to welcome children for a trial day. Since they are most involved, it seems only fair that they should have the opportunity to experience a 'taster'. The school has resisted the temptation to outgrow its potential and it is still possible for everyone to know everyone else, so the sense of identity is very strong.

The Towers

Address: Convent of the Blessed Sacrament, Steyning, West Sussex BN44 3TF
Telephone: 0903 812185

Head: Sister M Andrew

Age range: 5-16
No. of pupils: 258
Scholarships:
Religion:

Fees per term
Day: -
Weekly board: -
Full board: -

Boy ○ Girl ● Co-ed ○
Day ● Week ● Board ●

For further information and a prospectus, please contact the school.

Westbourne House School

Address: Shopwyke, Chichester, West Sussex PO20 6BH
Telephone: 0243 782739

Head: Mr S L Rigby

Age range: 3-13
No. of pupils: 225
Scholarships:
Religion:

Fees per term
Day: -
Weekly board: -
Full board: -

Boy ● Girl ● Co-ed ○
Day ● Week ○ Board ●

For further information and a prospectus, please contact the school. Girls 3-8.

Windlesham House

Address: Washington, Pulborough, West Sussex RH20 4AY
Telephone: 0903 873207

Heads: C C & E A Malden

Age range: 7-13
No. of pupils: 350
Scholarships:
Religion: Church of England

Fees per term
Day: -
Weekly board: -
Full board: £2580-£2580

Boy ○ Girl ○ Co-ed ●
Day ○ Week ○ Board ●

School aims to help pupils enjoy their childhood without being selfish, to offer as many and wide experiences as possible, to help them learn about themselves intellectually, creatively and emotionally. All children board. Easy reach of Gatwick and Heathrow. Special care to make weekends flexible and fun. Excellent facilities: theatre, music school, chapel, design centre, squash and tennis courts, indoor pool.

Worth School

Address: Worth, Crawley, West Sussex RH10 4SD
Telephone: 0342 715911

Head: Rev S Ortiger

Age range: 9-18
No. of pupils: 410
Scholarships: Yes
Religion: Roman Catholic

Fees per term
Day: £1910-£2590
Weekly board: -
Full board: £2550-£3450

Boy ● Girl ○ Co-ed ○
Day ● Week ○ Board ●

A small, young and vigorous school, set in superb Sussex countryside, 15 minutes south of Gatwick. Run by Benedictine monks and by lay men, Worth is strong academically but also in drama, sport and voluntary service.

TYNE AND WEAR

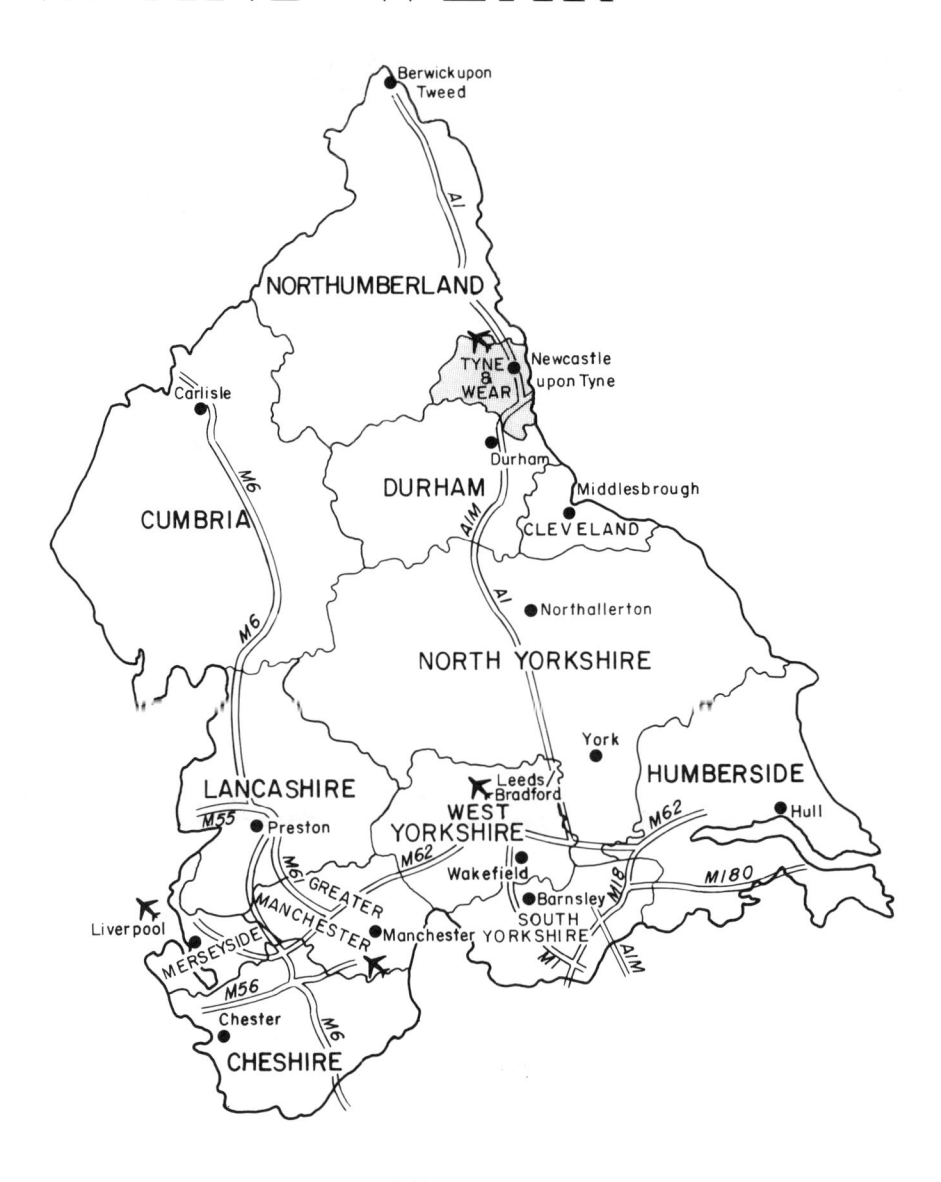

TYNE AND WEAR 517

Akhurst School

Address: The Grove, Jesmond, Newcastle upon Tyne, Tyne and Wear NE2 2PN
Telephone: 091 281 2116

Age range: 2-12
No. of pupils: 200
Scholarships:
Religion: Non-denominational

Fees per term
Day: £450-£900
Weekly board: -
Full board: -

○ ○ ● Boy Girl Co-ed
● ○ ○ Day Week Board

Principals: Mr R J Derham Mrs F M Derham

Nursery school offers an introduction to learning through play and discovery. There is a proper curriculum and children are taught in a stimulating educational environment. Learning activities are carefully planned and supervised and children are treated as individuals. Preparatory school starts at 4. Children progress smoothly and without trauma from the nursery, through the school.

Argyle House School p711

Address: 19-20 Thornhill Park, Sunderland, Tyne and Wear
Telephone: 091 510 0726

Age range: 3-16
No. of pupils: 230
Scholarships:
Religion: Non-denominational

Fees per term
Day: £480-£850
Weekly board: -
Full board: -

● ○ ○ Boy Girl Co-ed
● ○ ○ Day Week Board

Head: Mr J N Johnson

Argyle House, an independent day school for boys, offers a broad curriculum, from kindergarten to GCSE's. Pupils enjoy a wide variety of sporting and non-sporting extra-curricular activities. The school maintains excellent staffing ratios and a philosophy of caring development for each individual. Pupils are prepared for local public schools. Post-16 studies are arranged locally.

Ascham House School

Address: 30 West Avenue, Gosforth, Newcastle upon Tyne, Tyne and Wear NE3 4ES
Telephone: 091 285 1619

Age range: 4-13
No. of pupils: 270
Scholarships: Yes
Religion: Non-denominational

Fees per term
Day: £890-£920
Weekly board: -
Full board: -

● ○ ○ Boy Girl Co-ed
● ○ ○ Day Week Board

Head: Mr S H Reid

Ascham House offers a broad based approach to education in which non-academic pursuits are considered to be just as important for life as pure academic achievement. The school provides a secure, caring environment, with a happy atmosphere, in which all its pupils are encouraged to discover and then to develop their abundant talents and abilities.

Central Newcastle High School GPDST *

Address: Eskdale Terrace, Newcastle, Tyne and Wear
Telephone: 091 281 1768

Age range:
No. of pupils: 825
Scholarships: Yes
Religion: Non-denominational

Fees per term
Day: £808-£1052
Weekly board: -
Full board: -

○ ● ○ Boy Girl Co-ed
● ○ ○ Day Week Board

Head: Mrs A M Chapman

Recently the sixth form building has been re-furbished, the junior school extended and a new art school and restaurant have been added. In July 1992 the building of a spacious new music school will commence, followed by an indoor tennis court. 90% of girls are accepted each year into degree courses and of last year's leavers eleven girls were accepted at Oxford or Cambridge.

Craigievar High School

Address: 37 Roker Park Road, Sunderland, Tyne and Wear SR6 9PL
Telephone: 091 548 5468

Head: Mrs M Chadwick

Age range: 3-16
No. of pupils: 50
Scholarships:
Religion: Christian

Fees per term
Day: £300-£500
Weekly board: -
Full board: -

● Boy ● Girl ○ Co-ed
● Day ○ Week ○ Board

The school curriculum includes English language, English literature, mathematics, computer mathematics, history, geography, science and technology, French, Latin, domestic science, art and technology, RI, games, tennis (including LTA and County Championships). Ballet (exams taken through BITDA); speech and drama (prepared for exams); music (includes recorder, piano, flute, clarinet, violin).

Dame Allan's Boys' School *

Address: Fowberry Crescent, Fentham, Newcastle upon Tyne, Tyne and Wear NE4 9YJ
Telephone: 091 275 0608

Principal: Mr T A Willcocks MA

Age range: 9-18
No. of pupils: 466
Scholarships: Yes
Religion: Non-denominational

Fees per term
Day: £805-£1047
Weekly board: -
Full board: -

● Boy ○ Girl ○ Co-ed
● Day ○ Week ○ Board

At Dame Allan's we are concerned to develop to the full the talents of all our pupils. Selecting boys of high promise we encourage them to make the most of their opportunities, be they in the classroom, on the games field, in the concert hall or on the hills. The Government Assisted Places Scheme and also the Governors' Scholarships ensure that no worthy candidate is denied through lack of parental means.

Dame Allan's Girls' School *

Address: Fowberry Crescent, Fentham, Newcastle upon Tyne, Tyne and Wear NE4 9YJ
Telephone: 091 275 0708

Principal: Mr T A Willcocks MA

Age range: 9-18
No. of pupils: 454
Scholarships: Yes
Religion: Non-denominational

Fees per term
Day: £805-£1047
Weekly board: -
Full board: -

○ Boy ● Girl ○ Co-ed
● Day ○ Week ○ Board

At Dame Allan's we are concerned to develop to the full the talents of all our pupils. Selecting girls of high promise we encourage them to make the most of their opportunities educationally, culturally, morally and spiritually. The Government Assisted Places Scheme and also the Governors' Scholarships ensure that no worthy candidate is denied through lack of parental means. Our selection is based on talent not finance.

Eastcliffe Grammar School

Address: 33 The Grove, Gosforth, Newcastle upon Tyne, Tyne and Wear NE3 1NE
Telephone: 091 285 4873

Head: Mr G D Pearson

Age range: 3-18
No. of pupils: 230
Scholarships: Yes
Religion: Non-denominational

Fees per term
Day: £660-£1195
Weekly board: -
Full board: -

○ Boy ○ Girl ● Co-ed
● Day ○ Week ○ Board

Eastcliffe offers boys and girls a wide range of educational opportunities from the nursery to the sixth form in a friendly, family atmosphere. There is an emphasis on high academic standards and there are good facilities for the arts and science subjects together with PE, games and extra-curricular activities.

Fulwell Grange Day School

Address: 2 Viewforth Terrace, Fulwell, Sunderland, Tyne and Wear SR5 1PZ
Telephone: 091 548 6531

Head: Mrs E Gray

Age range: 4-16
No. of pupils: 107
Scholarships: Yes
Religion: Christian

Fees per term
Day: £470-£635
Weekly board: -
Full board: -

Boy ○ Girl ○ Co-ed ●
Day ● Week ○ Board ○

The school is an inter-denominational, independent school which caters for 120 children between the ages of 4 and 16. To assist them to develop a well-balanced character, emphasis will be laid on the importance of sound learning, firm discipline and right conduct. The curriculum will take into account the demands of the National Curriculum and the children are prepared for success in publicly recognised examinations.

Grainger Grammar School

Address: 35 Grainger Park Road, Newcastle upon Tyne, Tyne and Wear NE4 8SA
Telephone: 091 273 3426

Head: Mr N P T Staunton

Age range: 4-16
No. of pupils: 76
Scholarships: Yes
Religion: Church of England

Fees per term
Day: £560-£1000
Weekly board: -
Full board: -

Boy ○ Girl ○ Co-ed ●
Day ● Week ○ Board ○

This is a small independent day school quietly located west of Newcastle city centre. It is parent-owned through a charitable trust and aims to provide a good all-round education with strong support for each individual pupil. To achieve this class sizes are kept to a normal maximum of 15 whilst the curriculum provides the full range of subjects up to GCSE.

King's School * p712

Address: Tynemouth, North Shields, Tyne and Wear NE30 4RF
Telephone: 091 258 5995

Head: Mr W T Gillen

Age range: 4-18
No. of pupils: 900
Scholarships: Yes
Religion: Church of England

Fees per term
Day: £558-£1051
Weekly board: -
Full board: -

Boy ○ Girl ○ Co-ed ●
Day ● Week ○ Board ○

King's (HMC) Tynemouth is the North East's leading independent day school for boys and girls between 4-18 years. King's offers a broad, progressive curriculum, with emphasis on academic excellence of GCSE, AS, A and Oxbridge levels. A dedicated staff ensures individuals realise their own talents and abilities in a secure environment based on Christian principles, self discipline and pastoral care.

La Sagesse Convent High *

Address: North Jesmond, Newcastle upon Tyne, Tyne and Wear NE2 3RJ
Telephone: 091 281 3474

Head: Mrs D C Parker

Age range: 3-18
No. of pupils: 520
Scholarships: Yes
Religion: Roman Catholic

Fees per term
Day: £450-£1070
Weekly board: -
Full board: -

Boy ○ Girl ● Co-ed ○
Day ● Week ○ Board ○

La Sagesse is an independent day school for girls 3-18 years, welcoming all denominations in this traditionally Christian foundation. A caring atmosphere, small classes, careful academic monitoring lead to excellent results and happy fulfilled girls. Great value is placed on achievement outside of the classroom and the school has an excellent record in sport, art, drama and music.

Linden School

Address: 72 Station Road, Newcastle Upon Tyne, Tyne and Wear NE12 9BQ
Telephone: 091 266 2943

Head: Colonel A K Johnson

Age range: 4-11
No. of pupils: 150
Scholarships:
Religion: Non-denominational

Fees per term
Day: -£550
Weekly board: -
Full board: -

○ ○ ● Boy Girl Co-ed
● ○ ○ Day Week Board

For further information and a prospectus, please contact the school.

Musgrave School

Address: 335 Durham Road, Low Fell, Gateshead, Tyne and Wear NE9 5HA
Telephone: 091 487 6405

Head: Mrs M Maddison

Age range: 3-11
No. of pupils: 140
Scholarships:
Religion: Non-denominational

Fees per term
Day: £650-£660
Weekly board: -
Full board: -

○ ○ ● Boy Girl Co-ed
● ○ ○ Day Week Board

An independent day school for boys and girls aged 3.5 to 11 years. Founded in 1902 and upholding traditional educated standards of diligence and discipline. There is a proven scholarship and academic record. The curriculum is broad based providing grounding in basic skills in mathematics, reading and language work. There is interdisciplinary teaching in history, geography and science.

Newcastle Preparatory School

Address: 6 Eslington Road, Newcastle-upon-Tyne, Tyne and Wear NE2 4RH
Telephone: 091 281 1769

Head: Mr G Clayton

Age range: 2-13
No. of pupils: 245
Scholarships: Yes
Religion: Non-denominational

Fees per term
Day: £795-£970
Weekly board: -
Full board: -

○ ○ ● Boy Girl Co-ed
● ○ ○ Day Week Board

For further information and a prospectus, please contact the school.

The Newcastle Upon Tyne Church High * p746

Address: Tankerville Terrace, Newcastle Upon Tyne, Tyne and Wear NE2 3BA
Telephone: 091 2814306

Head: Miss P E Davies

Age range: 4-18
No. of pupils: 624
Scholarships: Yes
Religion: Church of England

Fees per term
Day: £675-£995
Weekly board: -
Full board: -

○ ● ○ Boy Girl Co-ed
● ○ ○ Day Week Board

Independent Day School for 620 girls offering sound education in a happy atmosphere. Highly qualified staff encourage development of character as well as academic attainment. External examination results are good. Excellent facilities for music, drama, art, dancing, physical education. Duke of Edinburgh Award Scheme and other activities provided. New science laboratories, separate sixth form accomodation.

Newlands

Address: 34 The Grove, Newcastle upon Tyne, Tyne and Wear NE3 1NH
Telephone: 091 285 2208

Head: Mr N R Barton

Age range: 4-13
No. of pupils: 240
Scholarships: Yes
Religion: Non-denominational

Fees per term
Day: £770-£1000
Weekly board: -
Full board: -

● Boy ○ Girl ○ Co-ed
● Day ○ Week ○ Board

Newlands is a traditional boys' preparatory school. It prepares boys for both Common Entrance and local independent day schools. The sporting and outdoor pursuits tradition is particularly strong.

Royal Grammar School *

Address: Eskdale Terrace, Newcastle-upon-Tyne, Tyne and Wear NE2 4DX
Telephone: 091 281 5711

Head: Mr A S Cox

Age range: 8-18
No. of pupils: 1129
Scholarships:
Religion: Non-denominational

Fees per term
Day: £860-£1060
Weekly board: -
Full board: -

● Boy ○ Girl ○ Co-ed
● Day ○ Week ○ Board

For further information and a prospectus, please contact the school.

St Anne's Mixed High School

Address: 52 Sunderland Road, South Shields, Tyne and Wear NE34 0SW
Telephone: 091 455 2310

Head: Mrs A B Smith

Age range: 3-16
No. of pupils: 80
Scholarships:
Religion: Non-denominational

Fees per term
Day: £280-£830
Weekly board: -
Full board: -

○ Boy ○ Girl ● Co-ed
● Day ○ Week ○ Board

A small school with classes of no more than 16 pupils. Kindergarten have an integrated morning of pre-school work, leading to reading and writing at the child's own pace. Infant work continues with the three 'Rs' plus artwork, PE and introduction of humanitites. Senior work leads to GCSE in all academic subjects. All children work at their own pace throughout the junior school.

St Anthony's Montessori School

Address: Tunstall Road, Sunderland, Tyne and Wear SR2 7JR
Telephone: 091 567 7893

Head: Sister Hilda Ward

Age range: 3-11
No. of pupils: 172
Scholarships:
Religion: Roman Catholic

Fees per term
Day: £550-£710
Weekly board: -
Full board: -

○ Boy ○ Girl ● Co-ed
● Day ○ Week ○ Board

Saint Anthony's Montessori School was founded and formally opened on September 1st 1921 by Anna Macceroni. Since then we have gradually introduced different teaching methods from those used by Dr Montessori but the essential character of the school has been retained and we still take great pride in maintaining the family atmosphere that has always been the hallmark of Montessori.

Sunderland High School

Address: Mowbray Road, Sunderland, Tyne and Wear SR2 8HY
Telephone: 091 567 4984

Head: Mrs M Thrush

Age range: 3-18
No. of pupils: 518
Scholarships: Yes
Religion: Church of England

Fees per term
Day: £680-£1183
Weekly board: -
Full board: -

Boy ○ Girl ○ Co-ed ●
Day ● Week ○ Board ○

This school has recently merged with Tonstall School to form a school with continuous education for boys and girls from age 3 to 18. In addition to the National Curriculum, the school offers french in the junior school and latin, three single sciences and a second foreign language in the senior school. In the VI form all students may pursue three A levels and a general programme to include a third foreign language.

Thornhill Park School

Address: 21 Thornhill Park, Sunderland, Tyne and Wear SR2 7LA
Telephone:

Head:

Age range: 5-19
No. of pupils:
Scholarships:
Religion:

Fees per term
Day: -
Weekly board: -
Full board: -

Boy ○ Girl ○ Co-ed ●
Day ● Week ○ Board ○

For further information and a prospectus, please contact the school.

Tonstall School

Address: TheCroft, Thornholme Road, Sunderland, Tyne and Wear SR2 7JS
Telephone: 091 567 2464

Head: Mr A R Friswell

Age range: 3-11
No. of pupils: 150
Scholarships:
Religion: Church of England

Fees per term
Day: £680-£1010
Weekly board: -
Full board: -

Boy ● Girl ○ Co-ed ○
Day ● Week ○ Board ○

Tonstall School is now part of Sunderland High School, a new co-educational school for pupils aged 3-18. Tonstall will continue as a separate school for boys aged 3-11, until the new co-educational preparatory school (to be called Tonstall House) is opened in September 1993.

Westfield School

Address: Oakfield Road, Gosforth, Newcastle upon Tyne, Tyne and Wear
Telephone: 091 285 1948

Head: Mrs M Farndale

Age range: 3-18
No. of pupils: 360
Scholarships: Yes
Religion: Christian

Fees per term
Day: £387-£1113
Weekly board: -
Full board: -

Boy ○ Girl ● Co-ed ○
Day ● Week ○ Board ○

The ethos of Westfield from the Nursery to the sixth form is based very much on the development of the individual within a broad and challenging curriculum and with a wide range of extra-curricular activities. Teaching methods are a careful blend of the traditional and the best in new ideas. Classes are kept small and parental involvement is welcomed. Examination results are excellent.

WARWICKSHIRE

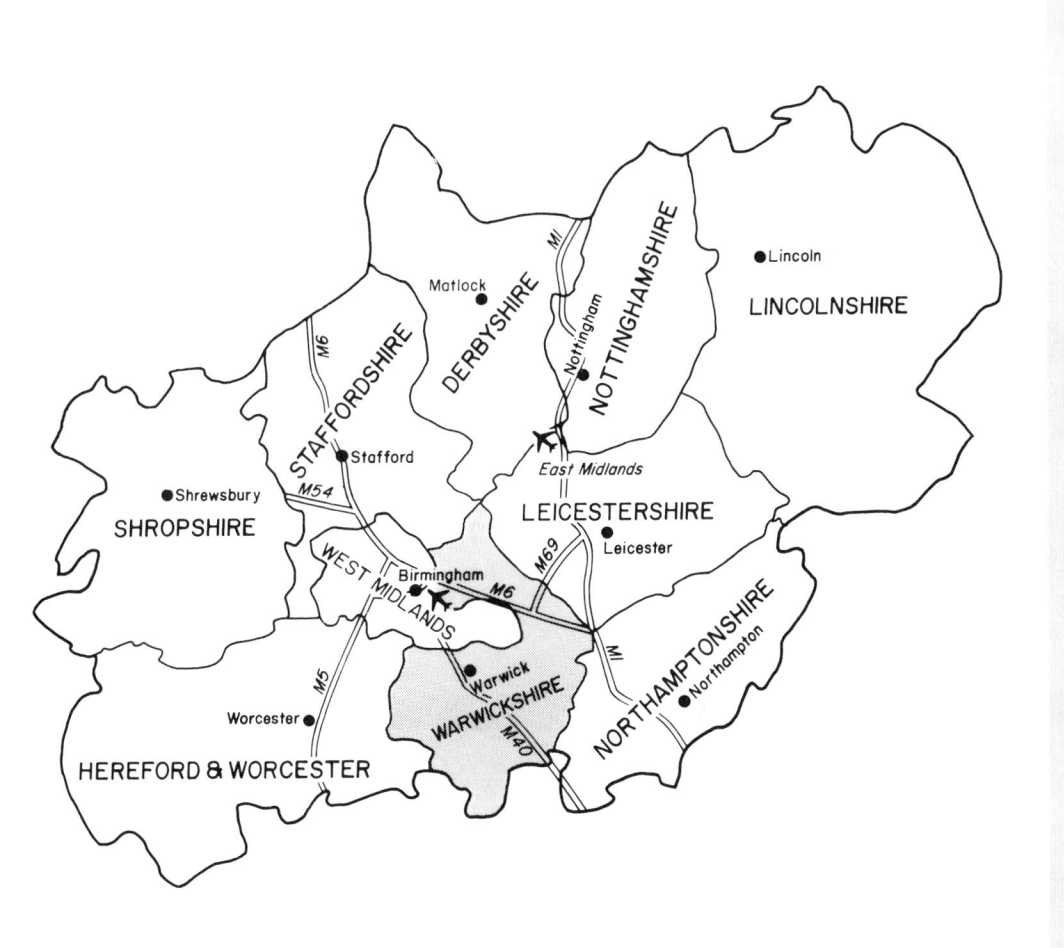

Abbotsford School

Address: Bridge Street, Kenilworth, Warwickshire CV8 1BD
Telephone: 0926 52826

Head: Mrs B Chitty

Age range: 3-11
No. of pupils: 119
Scholarships:
Religion: Non-denominational

Fees per term
Day: £285-£763
Weekly board: -
Full board: -

○ ○ ● Boy Girl Co-ed
● ○ ○ Day Week Board

A co-educational preparatory school specialising in small classes where each child receives individual attention by a caring and well-qualified staff. A recent large extension has provided many extra facilities. The National Curriculum has been adopted and the school is committed to retaining its high academic standards. Pupils are successfully prepared for examinations to independent secondary schools in the area.

Arnold Lodge School

Address: Kenilworth Road, Leamington Spa, Warwickshire CV32 5TW
Telephone: 0926 424737

Head: Mr A Reekes M A

Age range: 3-13
No. of pupils: 350
Scholarships: Yes
Religion: Non-denominational

Fees per term
Day: £1127-£1331
Weekly board: £1865-
Full board: -

○ ○ ● Boy Girl Co-ed
● ● ○ Day Week Board

Arnold Lodge is an independent preparatory school situated on the outskirts of the town and convenient to the motorway links. The school sets very high standards, with firm discipline and traditional values. It achieves scholarships to some of the best senior schools in England. Staff are experienced and dedicated, closely monitoring each individual's progress. Games, music and art are excellent.

Bilton Grange

Address: Dunchurch, Rugby, Warwickshire CV22 6QU
Telephone: 0788 810217

Head: Mr Q G Edwards

Age range: 7-13
No. of pupils: 190
Scholarships:
Religion: Church of England

Fees per term
Day: £1875-£2125
Weekly board: £2499-£2499
Full board: £2499-£2499

● ● ○ Boy Girl Co-ed
● ● ● Day Week Board

Bilton Grange, with its sister school, Homefield, caters for children from 3-13 years, on an estate of 160 acres, with wonderful modern facilities. Full or weekly boarding is available for boys and girls from age 7 to 13.

Crescent School

Address: Bawnmore Road, Bilton, Rugby, Warwickshire CV22 7QH
Telephone:

Headmaster: Mr I J Wren CertEd

Age range: 3-12
No. of pupils: 200
Scholarships:
Religion:

Fees per term
Day: -
Weekly board: -
Full board: -

○ ○ ● Boy Girl Co-ed
● ○ ○ Day Week Board

For further information and a prospectus, please contact the school.

Dunchurch-Winton Hall Preparatory School

Address: Dunchurch, Warwickshire CV22 6NG

Telephone: 0788 810205

Head: Mr D A C Marshall

Age range: 4-13
No. of pupils: 110
Scholarships: Yes
Religion: Chruch of England

Fees per term
Day: -£1445
Weekly board: -£1935
Full board: -£2055

○ ○ ● Boy Girl Co-ed
● ● ● Day Week Board

Dunchurch-Winton Hall is a traditional preparatory school standing in beautiful grounds. Emphasis is placed on the maintenance of high standards in every aspect of school life, and the ability of the staff to recognise and develop the individual interests and potential of each pupil. The school is small, with friendly and sensible discipline in a caring, family atmosphere.

Emscote Lawn School

Address: 21 Emscote Road, Warwick, Warwickshire CV34 5QD

Telephone: 0926 491961

Head: Mr J H Riley

Age range: 3-13
No. of pupils: 410
Scholarships: Yes
Religion: Non-denominational

Fees per term
Day: £626-£1235
Weekly board: -
Full board: -£1823

● ● ○ Boy Girl Co-ed
● ○ ● Day Week Board

The school is renowned for its academic excellence and has gained many scholarships over the years. We achieve these results by offering a wide syllabus inside and outside the classroom. Youngsters are prepared for their future lives by teaching them the benefits of hard work and the purpose of learning. We encourage a caring attitude and a happy atmosphere. Boys 3-13, girls 3-11.

Homefield School

Address: Bilton Grange, Dunchurch, Rugby, Warwickshire CV22 6QT

Telephone: 0788 810287

Head: Miss S J Clements

Age range: 3-11
No. of pupils: 108
Scholarships:
Religion: Church of England

Fees per term
Day: £331-£1763
Weekly board: -£2203
Full board: -£2203

● ● ○ Boy Girl Co-ed
● ● ● Day Week Board

A small friendly school which cares very much about individuals. The aim of the school is to develop potential to the full. Some facilities are shared by Bilton Grange e.g. indoor heated swimming pool, arts and craft room, science laboratory, sports hall, concert hall, music school and chapel. Homefield School accepts boys from 3-8 and girls from 3-11; Bilton Grange accepts boys from 7-13.

King's High School for Girls *

Address: Smith Street, Warwick, Warwickshire CV34 4HJ

Telephone: 0926 494485

Head: Mrs J M Anderson

Age range: 10-18
No. of pupils: 550
Scholarships: Yes
Religion: Non-denominational

Fees per term
Day: £1042-£1042
Weekly board: -
Full board: -

○ ● ○ Boy Girl Co-ed
● ○ ○ Day Week Board

Do you want your daughter to develop into an independent and confident young woman? For over a hundred years King's High School with its strong academic tradition, has encouraged girls to pursue a career and develop their own interests. The recent addition of a language centre, sports hall and facilities for design technology ensure first class resources for a first class education.

The Kingsley School *

Address: Beauchamp Hall,
Beauchamp Avenue,
Leamington Spa, Warwickshire
Telephone: 0926 425127

Age range: 3-18
No. of pupils: 587
Scholarships: Yes
Religion: Church of England

Fees per term
Day: £720-£1120
Weekly board: -
Full board: -

Boy ○ | Girl ● | Co-ed ○
Day ● | Week ○ | Board ○

Head: Mrs M A Webster

Kingsley believes in personal achievement through a well rounded education and provides an environment in which all students receive individual attention. As a result, academic achievements are impressive and girls develop into confident and capable young women. 200 students are involved in the Duke of Edinburgh Award Scheme. 1992 sees enhanced provision for the performing arts and computing.

New College

Address: 61 Kenilworth Road,
Leamington Spa,
Warwickshire CV32 6JU
Telephone: 0926 424058

Age range: 9-16
No. of pupils: 50
Scholarships:
Religion: Non-denominational

Fees per term
Day: £500-
Weekly board: -
Full board: -

Boy ○ | Girl ○ | Co-ed ●
Day ● | Week ○ | Board ○

Head: Mrs A K Atkin

For further information and a prospectus, please contact the school.

Princethorpe College

Address: Princethorpe,
Rugby, Warwickshire
CV23 9PX
Telephone: 0926 632147

Age range: 11-18
No. of pupils: 535
Scholarships: Yes
Religion: Roman Catholic

Fees per term
Day: £1095-
Weekly board: £2065-
Full board: £2190-

Boy ● | Girl ● | Co-ed ○
Day ● | Week ● | Board ●

Head: Rev A R Whelan

For further information an a prospectus, please contact the school. Girls accepted in sixth form.

Rugby School

Address: Rugby,
Warwickshire CV22 5EH

Telephone: 0788 543465

Age range: 13-18
No. of pupils: 650
Scholarships: Yes
Religion: Non-denominational

Fees per term
Day: £1370-£2275
Weekly board: -
Full board: -£3840

Boy ○ | Girl ○ | Co-ed ●
Day ● | Week ○ | Board ●

Head: Mr M B Mavor

Rugby is conveniently located, at the heart of the country, close to rail, motorways and the airport. Boys and girls enjoy a huge range of facilities within the school as well as outside, with visits abroad, outward bound course and work experience visits. The school is divided into small units thus giving the pupils a lot of individual care and attention.

St Joseph's Junior School

Address: Coventry Road,
Kenilworth, Warwickshire
CV8 2FT
Telephone: 0926 55348

Head: Mr F J Rimmer

Age range: 3-11
No. of pupils: 356
Scholarships:
Religion: Roman Catholic

Fees per term
Day: -
Weekly board: -
Full board: -

Boy ○ Girl ○ Co-ed ●
Day ● Week ○ Board ○

For further information and a prospectus, please contact the school.

St Joseph's Senior School

Address: Coventry Road,
Kenilworth, Warwickshire
CV8 2FT
Telephone: 0926 55348

Head: Mr F J Rimmer

Age range: 11-18
No. of pupils: 320
Scholarships:
Religion: Catholic

Fees per term
Day: £700-£895
Weekly board: -
Full board: -

Boy ○ Girl ● Co-ed ○
Day ● Week ○ Board ○

A full and varied curriculum is offered at all levels, with the school's chief aim being to help the girls grow up as good Christians with a true sense of values.

Stratford Preparatory School

Address: Old Town,
Stratford-upon-Avon,
Warwickshire CV37 6BG
Telephone:

Head:

Age range: 2-11
No. of pupils:
Scholarships:
Religion: Church of England

Fees per term
Day: -
Weekly board: -
Full board: -

Boy ○ Girl ○ Co-ed ●
Day ● Week ○ Board ○

For further information and a prospectus, please contact the school.

Twycross House School

Address: Twycross,
Atherstone, Warwickshire
CV9 3PL
Telephone: 0827 880651

Head: Mr R V Kirkpatrick

Age range: 8-18
No. of pupils: 260
Scholarships:
Religion: Non-denominational

Fees per term
Day: £900-£1200
Weekly board: -
Full board: -

Boy ○ Girl ○ Co-ed ●
Day ● Week ○ Board ○

A small selective school which provides an academic education leading to GCSE, 'A' level and Oxbridge examinations. Gifted children specially catered for. Small classes. Games and drama feature strongly in extra-curricular activities. Rural environment.

Warwick Preparatory School

Address: Bridge Field, Banbury Road, Warwick, Warwickshire CV34 6PL
Telephone: 0926 491545

Age range: 3-10
No. of pupils: 423
Scholarships:
Religion:

Fees per term
Day: -
Weekly board: -
Full board: -

Boy ○ Girl ○ Co-ed ●
Day ● Week ○ Board ○

Head: Miss C E Major

For further information and a prospectus, please contact the school. Boys 3-6.

Warwick School * p752

Address: Warwick, Warwickshire CV34 6PP
Telephone: 0926 492484

Age range: 7-19
No. of pupils: 982
Scholarships: Yes
Religion: Church of England

Fees per term
Day: £1187-£1346
Weekly board: -£1360
Full board: -£1550

Boy ● Girl ○ Co-ed ○
Day ● Week ● Board ●

Head: Dr P J Cheshire

Warwick is an independent boys' day and boarding school situated on land near the River Avon and the historic town of Warwick. The school has a fine record of academic success but combines this with a broad education including opportunities for sport on the 50 acre site, music, drama and wide range of activities. Most leaving pupils enter university.

Wroxall Abbey School

Address: Warwick, Warwickshire CV35 7NB
Telephone: 0926 484220

Age range: 7-18
No. of pupils: 150
Scholarships: Yes
Religion: Church of England

Fees per term
Day: £1300-£1750
Weekly board: £2370-£2870
Full board: £2700-£3000

Boy ○ Girl ● Co-ed ○
Day ● Week ● Board ●

Principal: Mrs I D M Iles

Wroxall Abbey, a gracious Warwickshire country house is the home of Wroxall Abbey School. Elegant and comfortable rooms, historic landscaped gardens, well-equipped classrooms, highly-qualified staff, all offer a wealth of opportunity to the student at every stage. Wroxall Abbey already has an international aspect and well established links with Europe.

WEST MIDLANDS

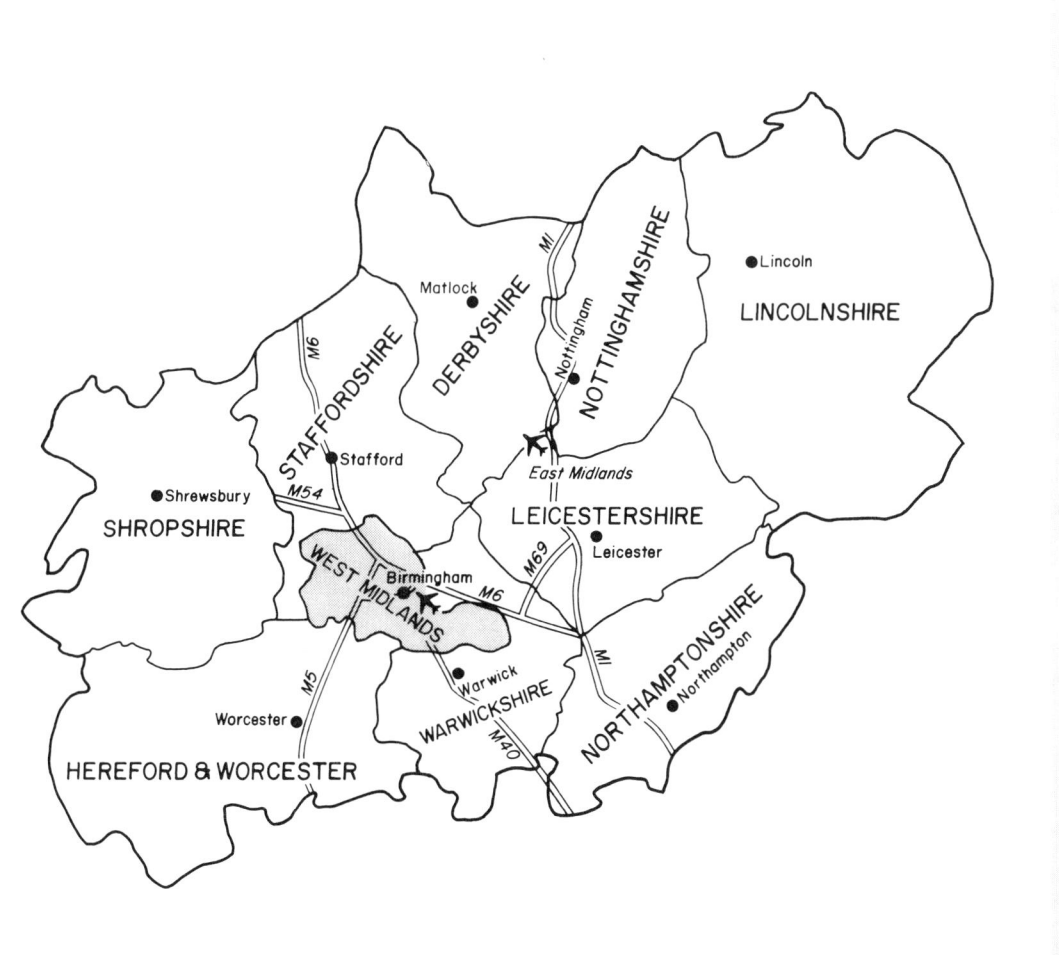

Ardenhurst School

Address: Henley-in-Arden, Solihull, West Midlands B95 6AB
Telephone: 0564 792308

Principal: Mr P S Blunt MA

Age range: 3-16
No. of pupils: 140
Scholarships: Yes
Religion: Non-denominational

Fees per term
Day: £820-£1540
Weekly board: -
Full board: -

Boy ○ Girl ○ Co-ed ●
Day ● Week ○ Board ○

Founded in 1869, Ardenhurst School is situated almost mid way between Solihull and Stratford-upon-Avon. Small classes ensure that every pupil receives personal attention and special tuition is available for children with learning difficulties. National Curriculum teaching and well established GCSE courses produce successful results. Music, art, drama and computing are taught to all.

Astwell Preparatory School

Address: 144/146 Hampstead Road, Birmingham, West Midlands B20 2QR
Telephone: 021 554 5791

Head: Mrs J Manners

Age range: 3-11
No. of pupils: 137
Scholarships:
Religion: Non-denominational

Fees per term
Day: £480-£680
Weekly board: -
Full board: -

Boy ○ Girl ○ Co-ed ●
Day ● Week ○ Board ○

Astwell Preparatory School offers a traditional approach within small classes, where courtesy, good manners and character training are an essential part of school life. Great emphasis is placed upon literacy and numeracy throughout the school while following the guidelines set out in the National Curriculum. Junior age children have weekly swimming lessons and elocution is offered as an optional extra.

Birchfield School

Address: Albrighton, Wolverhampton, West Midlands
Telephone: 0902 372534

Head: Mr A M Synge

Age range: 4-13
No. of pupils: 161
Scholarships: Yes
Religion: Non-denominational

Fees per term
Day: £845-£1315
Weekly board: £1530-
Full board: £1650-

Boy ● Girl ○ Co-ed ○
Day ● Week ● Board ●

Birchfield is a happy school in a pleasant rural location. We live and work in a fine Edwardian country house and well-designed modern buildings, all surrounded by delightful woods, gardens and playing fields. We enjoy a positive relationship with Albrighton village and have excellent communications in all directions.

The Blue Coat School

Address: Somerset Road, Edgbaston, Birmingham, West Midlands B17 0HR
Telephone: 021 454 1425

Head: Mr B P Bissel

Age range: 3-13
No. of pupils: 380
Scholarships: Yes
Religion: Church of England

Fees per term
Day: £600-£1350
Weekly board: -£2075
Full board: -£2075

Boy ○ Girl ○ Co-ed ●
Day ● Week ● Board ●

The Blue Coat School, founded in 1722, is a popular and successful IAPS preparatory school. Boarders start at 7 and are prepared via the Common Entrance Examination and scholarshipsfor entry to well-known senior independent schools throughout the UK. The school has excellent teaching and boarding facilities and a high reputation for its music, drama, art and sport.

Bremond College

Address: Leamington Road, Coventry, West Midlands CV3 6GG
Telephone: 0203 418379

Head: Miss J M Hill BEd(Hons) MSc

Age range: 3-16
No. of pupils: 50
Scholarships:
Religion: Christian

Fees per term
Day: £550-£1000
Weekly board: £1425-
Full board: £1650-

● Boy ● Girl ○ Co-ed
● Day ● Week ● Board

Bremond College is an independent school for girls (3-16) and junior boys (3-11). The building, set in pleasing grounds, is easily accessible yet near Coventry's centre. The school offers caring traditional teaching, with firm, fair discipline, from age 3 to GCSE. There are extra-curricular options for day pupils and senior girl boarders and specially supported tuition such as English as a second language.

Cheshunt School

Address: 8 Park Road, Coventry, West Midlands CV1 2LH
Telephone: 0203 221677

Head: Mrs F P Ward

Age range: 3-8
No. of pupils: 120
Scholarships:
Religion: Non-denominational

Fees per term
Day: £600-£650
Weekly board: -
Full board: -

○ Boy ○ Girl ● Co-ed
● Day ○ Week ○ Board

For further information and a prospectus, please contact the school.

Chetwynd House School

Address: 6 Streetly Lane, Sutton Coldfield, West Midlands B74 4TT
Telephone: 021 308 0332

Head: Mr W P Coldrick

Age range: 4-12
No. of pupils: 100
Scholarships:
Religion: Non-denominational

Fees per term
Day: £670-£670
Weekly board: -
Full board: -

● Boy ○ Girl ○ Co-ed
● Day ○ Week ○ Board

Chetwynd House School, founded around 1920, is a day preparatory school for boys. Pupils are prepared for the entrance examinations of the public schools (e.g. King Edward's Solihull, Bromsgrove, Oundle) and also for the local grammar schools. The most able pupils have won scholarships or exhibitions to schools such as King Edward's or Solihull School.

Coventry Preparatory School *

Address: Kenilworth Road, Coventry, West Midlands CV3 6PT
Telephone: 0203 675289

Head: Mr D Clark

Age range: 3-13
No. of pupils: 142
Scholarships:
Religion: Church of England

Fees per term
Day: £637-£931
Weekly board: -
Full board: -

● Boy ● Girl ○ Co-ed
● Day ○ Week ○ Board

The school is situated on the south side of Coventry in approximately four acres. There is an experienced and qualified staff. Pupils are prepared for entry to all independent senior schools. There is a co-educational pre-preparatory department from four and also a nursery class. Although the school currently caters only for boys from the age of eight, girls will be encouraged to come through from the pre-preparatory from 1992 onwards.

Davenport Lodge School

Address: 21 Davenport Road, Coventry, West Midlands CV5 6QA
Telephone: 0203 675051

Principal: Mrs M D Martin

Age range: 2-8
No. of pupils: 130
Scholarships:
Religion: Non-denominational

Fees per term
Day: £290-£600
Weekly board: -
Full board: -

Co-ed, Day

Davenport Lodge School has enjoyed a record of academic success for 25 years. Through nursery and pre-preparatory departments children are prepared for competitive entrance examinations to King Henry VIII and Bablake Schools. Children may attend from two and a half years part-time. The upper age limit is 8 years. A broad curriculum is offered with emphasis on basic skills. Swimming, PE, art and music are offered.

The Drive School

Address: Wrottesley Road, Wolverhampton, West Midlands WV6 8SE
Telephone: 0902 751125

Head: Mrs P M Yates

Age range: 3-7
No. of pupils: 65
Scholarships:
Religion: Non-denominational

Fees per term
Day: £520-£760
Weekly board: -
Full board: -

Co-ed, Day

The Drive School aims to provide a sound education on an efficient and up-to-date basis. We endeavour to instil into our pupils an attitude to learning and behaviour which will be of value to them when they continue their education in their senior schools and throughout their lives.

Eastbourne House School

Address: 111 Yardley Road, Acocks Green, Birmingham, West Midlands B27 6LL
Telephone: 021 706 2013

Head: Mr P Moynihan

Age range: 3-11
No. of pupils: 144
Scholarships:
Religion: Non-denominational

Fees per term
Day: £590-£679
Weekly board: -
Full board: -

Co-ed, Day

Eastbourne House is a well-established, family-run school, which provides a first-class education for its one hundred and fifty pupils, aged from three to eleven years. Situated in its own spacious grounds, the school offers a range of sports and enjoys a good record of successes in fixtures with other schools. Competition is encouraged, as are the traditional values of good manners and hard work.

Eccleston School

Address: 22 St Peters Road, Harborne, Birmingham, West Midlands B17 0AX
Telephone: 021 427 2329

Head: Mrs J R Higgit

Age range: 5-11
No. of pupils: 100
Scholarships:
Religion: Roman Catholic

Fees per term
Day: £380-£405
Weekly board: -
Full board: -

Co-ed, Day

Entry to Eccleston School is by application and interview. Children are prepared for 11+ entry to Birmingham grammar schools and for entry to private schools in the area.

Edgbaston Church of England College for Girls * p712

Address: 31 Calthorpe Road, Birmingham, West Midlands B15 1RX
Telephone: 021 454 1392

Head: Mrs A P R Varley-Tipton

Age range: 3-18
No. of pupils: 420
Scholarships: Yes
Religion: Church of England

Fees per term
Day: £781-£1276
Weekly board: -
Full board: -

○ ● ○
Boy Girl Co-ed
● ○ ○
Day Week Board

The college, founded in 1886, is situated in a central site with extensive grounds. A complete education meeting National Curriculum requirements is provided from kindergarten to sixth form. Expeditions and field trips complement studies. Extra-curricular activities including sport, music, drama, debating and the Duke of Edinburgh Award Scheme give girls the opportunity to extend their horizon.

Edgbaston College

Address: 249 Bristol Road, Edgbaston, Birmingham, West Midlands B5 7UH
Telephone: 021 472 1034

Head: Father A W D Ledwich

Age range: 2-18
No. of pupils:
Scholarships: Yes
Religion: Christian

Fees per term
Day: £755-£1375
Weekly board: -
Full board: -

○ ○ ●
Boy Girl Co-ed
● ○ ○
Day Week Board

The school educates the whole child, academically, physically, socially and spiritually. Pupils are encouraged to engage in a wide range of interests. Many extra-curricular activities are available, and the school has a specialist emphasis on the performing arts. Full academic education begins in the Motessori Nursery from the age of 2. The middle school prepares for our own entrance to the high school at 13.

Edgbaston High School for Girls

Address: Westbourne Road, Edgbaston, Birmingham, West Midlands B15 3TS
Telephone: 021 454 5831

Head: Mrs S J Horsman

Age range: 3-18
No. of pupils: 875
Scholarships: Yes
Religion: Non-denominational

Fees per term
Day: £497-£1275
Weekly board: -
Full board: -

○ ● ○
Boy Girl Co-ed
● ○ ○
Day Week Board

Edgbaston High aims to provide a balanced, intellectual, cultural, physical and sporting education for girls aged three and a half to eighteen so that each may develop her individual gifts to the full and become a useful, concerned member of society. With this in mind girls are prepared for public examinations, entry to further and higher education and for their chosen careers.

Elmfield Rudolf Steiner School

Address: 14 Love Lane, Stourbridge, West Midlands DY8 2EA
Telephone: 0384 394633

Head: Chairman of the College of Teachers

Age range: 3-17
No. of pupils: 282
Scholarships:
Religion: Non-denominational

Fees per term
Day: £440-£920
Weekly board: -
Full board: -

○ ○ ●
Boy Girl Co-ed
● ○ ○
Day Week Board

Rudolf Steiner Schools recognise the inner development of the child and seek to nourish it with appropriate experiences at each stage, through a wide-ranging curriculum. They foster the child's experience of rhythm through a balance of artistic, practical and intellectual work in the day, and the celebration of the seasons during the year.

Eversfield Preparatory School

Address: Warwick Road, Solihull, West Midlands B91 1AT
Telephone: 021 705 0354

Head: Mr K Barnes

Age range: 3-13
No. of pupils: 210
Scholarships: Yes
Religion: Christian

Fees per term
Day: £545-£1261
Weekly board: -
Full board: -

Boy ● Girl ● Co-ed ○
Day ● Week ○ Board ○

A day preparatory school for boys situated close to the centre of Solihull and set in five acres of playing fields. Eversfield offers a full, well balanced education. Excellent facilities, modern equipment and dedicated staff, combine with well-established teaching methods to achieve high academic standards. A caring, Christian environment enables the pupils to develop good personal qualities and fulfil their potential.

Haden Hill School

Address: 154 Barrs Road, Cradley Heath, Warley, West Midlands B64 7EX
Telephone: 0384 69318

Principal: Mrs B M Simons

Age range: 3-11
No. of pupils: 180
Scholarships:
Religion:

Fees per term
Day: £725-£949
Weekly board: -
Full board: -

Boy ○ Girl ○ Co-ed ●
Day ● Week ○ Board ○

Haden Hill School was founded in 1945 and consists of three departments, kindergarten, infants and junior. Pleasantly situated the school is easily accessible from the south-west of Birmingham. Haden Hill is justly proud of the happy, caring and busy atmosphere enabling each child's self-confidence to fully develop. Pupils attain high degrees of competence culminating in outstanding examination successes.

Hallfield School

Address: 48 Church Road, Edgbaston, Birmingham, West Midlands B15 3SJ
Telephone: 021 454 1496

Head: Mr J G Cringle

Age range: 4-13
No. of pupils: 400
Scholarships:
Religion: Christian

Fees per term
Day: £810-£1190
Weekly board: -
Full board: -

Boy ○ Girl ○ Co-ed ○
Day ● Week ○ Board ○

Hallfield School, founded in 1879, has occupied its present 20 acre site since 1936. Essentially an academic school, Hallfield has always catered for a broad range of ability. There is an excellent record of academic achievement. Competitive sport is encouraged, as are music, drama and extra-curricular activities. Our aim is to provide a wide range of educational opportunity in a happy, structured environment.

Highclare School

Address: 241 Birmingham Road, Sutton Coldfield, West Midlands B72 1EA
Telephone: 021 354 1882

Head: Mrs C A Hanson BSc

Age range: 3-18
No. of pupils: 365
Scholarships: Yes
Religion: Non-denominational

Fees per term
Day: £545-£1085
Weekly board: -
Full board: -

Boy ○ Girl ● Co-ed ○
Day ● Week ○ Board ○

At Highclare School the academic, pastoral and social welfare of the pupils is fundamental to all planning. The headmistress and fully qualified staff know every pupil well and encourage them to achieve their full potential. Academic excellence is achieved and applauded, but the contribution made by pupils whose talents lie in other spheres is also valued. A wide range of subjects is offered at both GCSE and A Level.

Holy Child *

Address: Sir Harry's Road, Edgbaston, Birmingham, West Midlands B15 2UR
Telephone: 021 440 4103

Head: Miss J M Johnson

Age range: 3-18
No. of pupils: 350
Scholarships: Yes
Religion: Roman Catholic

Fees per term
Day: £834-£1289
Weekly board: £2295-
Full board: -

○ ● ●
Boy Girl Co-ed
● ● ○
Day Week Board

We provide Christian education with a European dimension. The curriculum fosters pursuit of excellence - academic, aesthetic and athletic - so as to develop the fullest potential of each pupil. As a community of faith recognising that only 60% of pupils are Catholic, we aim to prepare pupils for their lives as members of the wider British and European Community. Co-educational 3-11, girls 11-18.

Honeybourne School

Address: 621 Fox Hollies Road, Birmingham, West Midlands B28 9DW
Telephone: 021 777 3778

Head: Mrs J A Hillstead

Age range: 2-7
No. of pupils: 60
Scholarships:
Religion: Non-denominational

Fees per term
Day: £450-£450
Weekly board: -
Full board: -

○ ○ ●
Boy Girl Co-ed
● ○ ○
Day Week Board

Honeybourne School is a co-educational kindergarten for boys and girls aged between 2 and 7 years. The teaching uses the insights of the National Curriculum as a firm basis. Our aim is to combine a child's natural curiosity with the training, discipline and stimulation of a will to learn. The school aims to provide the best possible education to each pupil whatever their ability.

Hydesville Tower School

Address: 25 Broadway North, Walsall, Birmingham, West Midlands WS1 2QG
Telephone: 0922 24374

Head: Mr T D Farrell

Age range: 3-16
No. of pupils: 360
Scholarships:
Religion: Non-denominational

Fees per term
Day: £530-£1260
Weekly board: -
Full board: -

○ ○ ●
Boy Girl Co-ed
● ○ ○
Day Week Board

While small enough to ensure no-one is overlooked we are large enough to pursue high standards. Excellent examination results at all stages are complemented by our high reputation for music and drama. There is also a full range of games activities as well, supporting the Hydesville claim 'To provide a broad education for all in structured and caring surroundings.'

King Edward VI High School for Girls *

Address: Edgbaston Park Road, Birmingham, West Midlands B15 2UB
Telephone: 021 472 1834

Head: Miss E W Evans

Age range: 11-18
No. of pupils: 544
Scholarships: Yes
Religion: Non-denominational

Fees per term
Day: £1223-
Weekly board: -
Full board: -

○ ● ○
Boy Girl Co-ed
● ○ ○
Day Week Board

Founded in 1883, the school moved to its present site in Edgbaston in 1940. Purpose built and well equipped it enjoys good teaching and high academic achievement. Most leavers go on to degree courses. Character development is considered equally important. Cultural, spiritual and aesthetic awareness are nurtured and opportunities abound for sport, music, community service and other practical pursuits.

King Edward's School *

Address: Edgbaston Park Road, Birmingham, West Midlands B15 2UA
Telephone: 021 472 1672

Age range: 11-18
No. of pupils: 845
Scholarships: Yes
Religion: Church of England

Fees per term
Day: -£1328
Weekly board: -
Full board: -

Boy ●   Girl ○   Co-ed ○
Day ●   Week ○   Board ○

Chief Master: Mr H R Wright

For further information and a prospectus, please contact the school.

King Henry VIII School

Address: Warwick Road, Coventry, West Midlands CV3 6AQ
Telephone: 0203 675050

Age range: 11-18
No. of pupils: 834
Scholarships: Yes
Religion: Christian

Fees per term
Day: £1056-£1056
Weekly board: -
Full board: -

Boy ○   Girl ○   Co-ed ●
Day ●   Week ○   Board ○

Head: Mr G R James

King Henry VIII is part of the Coventry School Foundation and one of the leading co-educational schools in the country. Examination results at all levels are outstanding, but the school is equally proud of its achievements in sport, music and drama. The recently completed science block can have few equals anywhere. Scholarships, bursaries and Government assisted places are available subject to status.

Kingsley Preparatory School

Address: 53 Hanbury Road, Dorridge, Solihull, West Midlands B93 8DW
Telephone: 0564 774144

Age range: 3-11
No. of pupils: 40
Scholarships:
Religion: Non-denominational

Fees per term
Day: £300-£700
Weekly board: -
Full board: -

Boy ○   Girl ○   Co-ed ●
Day ●   Week ○   Board ○

Head: Mrs J A Scott

Established in 1950 the School operates from purpose built classrooms with adjoining playing fields. Highly qualified staff, excellent equipment and specialist teachers in elocution, music, dancing, swimming and karate. Every provision is made for boys and girls aged 3-11 years. to develop individually in a happy and challenging environment. The result is mature pupils with high academic standards.

Kingswood School

Address: St James Place, Shirley, Solihull, West Midlands
Telephone: 021 744 7883

Age range: 3-13
No. of pupils: 105
Scholarships:
Religion:

Fees per term
Day: £330-£850
Weekly board: -
Full board: -

Boy ○   Girl ○   Co-ed ●
Day ●   Week ○   Board ○

Head: Mr P Callaghan

The School provides each pupil with a full and sound education in a happy and disciplined atmosphere by encouraging healthy and positive attitudes towards learning and the acquisition of skills and knowledge whilst maintaining traditional values. The school has a good record of examination results from a well-balanced curriculum.

Mayfield Preparatory School

Address: Sutton Road, Walsall, West Midlands WS1 2PD

Telephone: 0922 24107

Head: Mrs C M Jones

Age range: 3-11
No. of pupils: 195
Scholarships:
Religion: Non-denominational

Fees per term
Day: £585-£785
Weekly board: -
Full board: -

○ ○ ● Boy Girl Co-ed
● ○ ○ Day Week Board

For further information and a prospectus, please contact the school.

Newbridge Preparatory School

Address: 51 Newbridge Crescent, Wolverhampton, West Midlands WV6 0LH
Telephone: 0902 751088

Head: Miss M J Coulter

Age range: 3-11
No. of pupils: 133
Scholarships:
Religion: Non-denominational

Fees per term
Day: £675-£1025
Weekly board: -
Full board: -

● ● ○ Boy Girl Co-ed
● ○ ○ Day Week Board

For further information and a prospectus, please contact the school. Boys 3-7

Norfolk House School

Address: 4 Norfolk Road, Edgbaston, Birmingham, West Midlands B15 3PS
Telephone: 021 454 7021

Head: Mrs A Harding

Age range: 3-11
No. of pupils: 140
Scholarships:
Religion: Non-denominational

Fees per term
Day: £370-£695
Weekly board: -
Full board: -

○ ○ ● Boy Girl Co-ed
● ○ ○ Day Week Board

For further information and a prospectus, please contact the school.

Old Swinford Hospital School p713

Address: Stourbridge, West Midlands DY8 1QX

Telephone: 0384 370025

Head: Mr C F R Potter

Age range: 11-18
No. of pupils: 540
Scholarships: Yes
Religion: Church of England

Fees per term
Day: -
Weekly board: £1060-
Full board: £1060-

● ○ ○ Boy Girl Co-ed
● ● ● Day Week Board

One of the first grant maintained schools, draws pupils from all over British Isles. Strong sixth form, with individual study bedrooms for all sixth form boarders. Four new boarding houses built over the last few years. Parents only pay for boarding fees, education costs free. School situated on edge of town with playing fields on site. Close to motorway system.

Parkdale Independent School

Address: Tettenhall Road, Wolverhampton, West Midlands WV1 4TE
Telephone: 0902 23467

Age range: 2-11
No. of pupils: 65
Scholarships:
Religion: Methodist

Fees per term
Day: £175-£495
Weekly board: -
Full board: -

Co-ed / Day

Head: Mrs J Startin

Parkdale provides a homely, happy atmosphere in which our children thrive. In the nursery they learn to listen and to extend their vocabulary which in turn leads to the joy of early reading and writing followed quickly by number work. In the infants and juniors they continue to grow, enjoying a wide range of activities both indoor and outdoor.

Pattison College

Address: 86-90 Binley Road, Coventry, West Midlands CV3 1FQ
Telephone: 0203 455031

Age range: 3-16
No. of pupils: 160
Scholarships:
Religion: Non-denominational

Fees per term
Day: £455-£792
Weekly board: -£1477
Full board: -£1507

Co-ed / Day / Week / Board

Head: Miss B Pattison

For further information and a prospectus, please contact the school.

Rathvilly

Address: 119 Bunbury Road, Northfield, Birmingham, West Midlands B31 2NB
Telephone: 021 475 1509

Age range: 3-11
No. of pupils: 120
Scholarships:
Religion: Church of England

Fees per term
Day: £512-£746
Weekly board: -
Full board: -

Co-ed / Day

Head: Mr A G Dowell-Lee

Rathvilly is an independent day school for boys and girls, aged 3-11 years. Set in pleasant grounds in a quiet residential area, we have served Northfield for the best part of 100 years. There is a warm, family atmosphere in the school, where we aim to educate boys and girls of every ability to their potential.

Rosslyn School

Address: 1597 Stratford Road, Hall Green, Birmingham, West Midlands B28 9JB
Telephone: 021 744 2743

Age range: 3-11
No. of pupils: 140
Scholarships:
Religion: Non-denominational

Fees per term
Day: £385-£510
Weekly board: -
Full board: -

Co-ed / Day

Head: Mrs J Taylor

For further information and a prospectus, please contact the school.

Royal Wolverhampton School

Address: Penn Road, Wolverhampton, West Midlands WV3 0EG
Telephone: 0902 341230

Head: Mr P Gorringe MA

Age range: 2-18
No. of pupils: 600
Scholarships: Yes
Religion: Anglican

Fees per term
Day: £690-£1510
Weekly board: £1800-£2360
Full board: £2040-£2640

○ Boy ○ Girl ● Co-ed
● Day ● Week ● Board

The Royal Wolverhampton School offers fully co-educational education from two and half years in the nursery to university entry at 18. Classes are small (usually less than 20). Facilities are constantly improved with a new design, technology and art centre opened in 1990, four new laboratories in 1991, and a new dining room in 1992. The computer suite has been uprated to 30 stations.

Ruckleigh School

Address: 17 Lode Lane, Solihull, West Midlands B91 2AB
Telephone: 021 705 2773

Head: Mr D N Carr-Smith

Age range: 3-11
No. of pupils: 265
Scholarships:
Religion: Non-denominational

Fees per term
Day: £231-£1123
Weekly board: -
Full board: -

○ Boy ○ Girl ● Co-ed
● Day ○ Week ○ Board

Ruckleigh is offering education to boys and girls between the ages of four and eleven with a pre-school department catering for children from the age of three. Pupils are guided into habits of clear thinking, self-reliance and courtesy. Sound practical judgement, sensitivity towards the needs of others and a willingness at all times to 'have a go' are qualities which the school seeks to promote.

Saint Martin's

Address: Brueton Avenue, Solihull, West Midlands B91 3EN
Telephone: 021 705 1265

Head: Mrs S J Williams

Age range: 3-18
No. of pupils: 500
Scholarships: Yes
Religion: Non-denominational

Fees per term
Day: £772-£1314
Weekly board: -
Full board: -

○ Boy ● Girl ○ Co-ed
● Day ○ Week ○ Board

Saint Martin's is a day school for girls aged 3-18. The school is situated in 20 acres of attractive grounds and playing fields, offers a varied and well-balanced education, broadly in line with the National Curriculum; there are, however, many opportunities to develop strengths in creative, aesthetic and practical subjects. A wide range of subjects is offered at GCSE and A level and most girls go on to some form of HE.

The Shrubbery School

Address: Walmley Ash Road, Walmley, Sutton Coldfield, West Midlands B76 8HY
Telephone: 021 351 1582

Head: Miss J M Rankin

Age range: 3-12
No. of pupils: 270
Scholarships:
Religion:

Fees per term
Day: -
Weekly board: -
Full board: -

○ Boy ○ Girl ● Co-ed
● Day ○ Week ○ Board

For further information and a prospectus, please contact the school.

Solihull School * p750

Address: Warwick Road, Solihull, West Midlands B93 8DX
Telephone: 021 705 4273

Head: Mr A Lee

Age range: 7-18
No. of pupils: 1000
Scholarships: Yes
Religion: Church of England

Fees per term
Day: £803-£1156
Weekly board: -
Full board: -

● Boy ● Girl ○ Co-ed
● Day ○ Week ○ Board

Solihull School maintains high academic standards alongside an impressive range of achievements and activities in music, games, and outdoor pursuits. Buildings have been modernised in recent years to accommodate new educational requirements. A strong sense of community is fostered by four separate sections for different age-groups, the House system and close links with the locality and families.

St Paul's Convent

Address: 88 Lichfield Road, Sutton Coldfield, West Midlands B74 2SY
Telephone: 021 355 8205

Head: Sister Maureen Marston

Age range: 3-12
No. of pupils: 130
Scholarships:
Religion:

Fees per term
Day: -
Weekly board: -
Full board: -

○ Boy ○ Girl ● Co-ed
● Day ○ Week ○ Board

For further information and a prospectus, please contact the school. Boys 4-8, girls 3-12.

St Paul's School

Address: Hertford Street, Balsall Heath, Birmingham, West Midlands B12 8NJ
Telephone:

Head:

Age range: 11+
No. of pupils:
Scholarships:
Religion:

Fees per term
Day: -
Weekly board: -
Full board: -

○ Boy ○ Girl ● Co-ed
○ Day ○ Week ○ Board

For further information and a prospectus, please contact the school.

Stoke Lodge School

Address: Lodge Road, Coventry, West Midlands CV3 1FU
Telephone: 0203 455479

Head: Mrs R Hemsley

Age range: 3-12
No. of pupils: 70
Scholarships:
Religion:

Fees per term
Day: -
Weekly board: -
Full board: -

○ Boy ○ Girl ● Co-ed
● Day ○ Week ○ Board

For further information and a prospectus, please contact the school.

Tettenhall College

Address: Wolverhampton, West Midlands WV6 8QX

Telephone:

Head: Mr W J Dale

Age range: 7-18
No. of pupils: 460
Scholarships: Yes
Religion: Non-denominational

Fees per term
Day: £1300-£1620
Weekly board: -
Full board: £2160-£2635

Boy ○ Girl ○ Co-ed ●
Day ● Week ○ Board ●

Set in 33 acres of well wooded grounds, the school lays stress on academic standards and seeks to give sound instruction within a clear framework of discipline. Special talents and extra-curricular activities are very much encouraged and coaching is offered in a variety of games. Buses provide transport for many day pupils and the school is within reach of the railway station and Birmingham Airport.

West House School

Address: 24 St James's Road, Edgbaston, Birmingham, West Midlands B15 2NX
Telephone: 021 440 4097

Head: Mr G K Duce

Age range: 3-13
No. of pupils: 243
Scholarships:
Religion:

Fees per term
Day: -
Weekly board: -
Full board: -

Boy ● Girl ○ Co-ed ○
Day ● Week ● Board ○

For further information and a prospectus, please contact the school.

Wolverhampton Grammar School *

Address: Compton Road, Wolverhampton, West Midlands WV3 9RB
Telephone: 0902 712004

Head: Mr B ST J Trafford

Age range: 11-18
No. of pupils: 654
Scholarships: Yes
Religion: Non-denominational

Fees per term
Day: £1276-
Weekly board: -
Full board: -

Boy ○ Girl ○ Co-ed ●
Day ● Week ○ Board ○

Founded in 1512 and now co-educational, Wolverhampton Grammar School sets demanding academic standards for its intelligent, highly motivated pupils. The traditional, caring ethos encourages self-reliance and individuality. Achievement and co-operation flourish outside the classroom, too: regular competitive success in sport (a Far East cricket tour in 1992).

Wylde Green College

Address: 245 Birmingham Road, Sutton Coldfield, West Midlands B72 1EA
Telephone: 021 354 1505

Head: Mr P J Burd

Age range: 3-16
No. of pupils: 200
Scholarships:
Religion: Non-Denominational

Fees per term
Day: £625-£1035
Weekly board: -
Full board: -

Boy ● Girl ○ Co-ed ○
Day ● Week ○ Board ○

Wylde Green College has been family run since its foundation in 1922. Small, well disciplined classes offer a broad traditional education up to GCSE level. Boys are prepared for entrance examinations to other schools at 11, and sporting activities take place on the school's 13 acre sports' ground.

WILTSHIRE

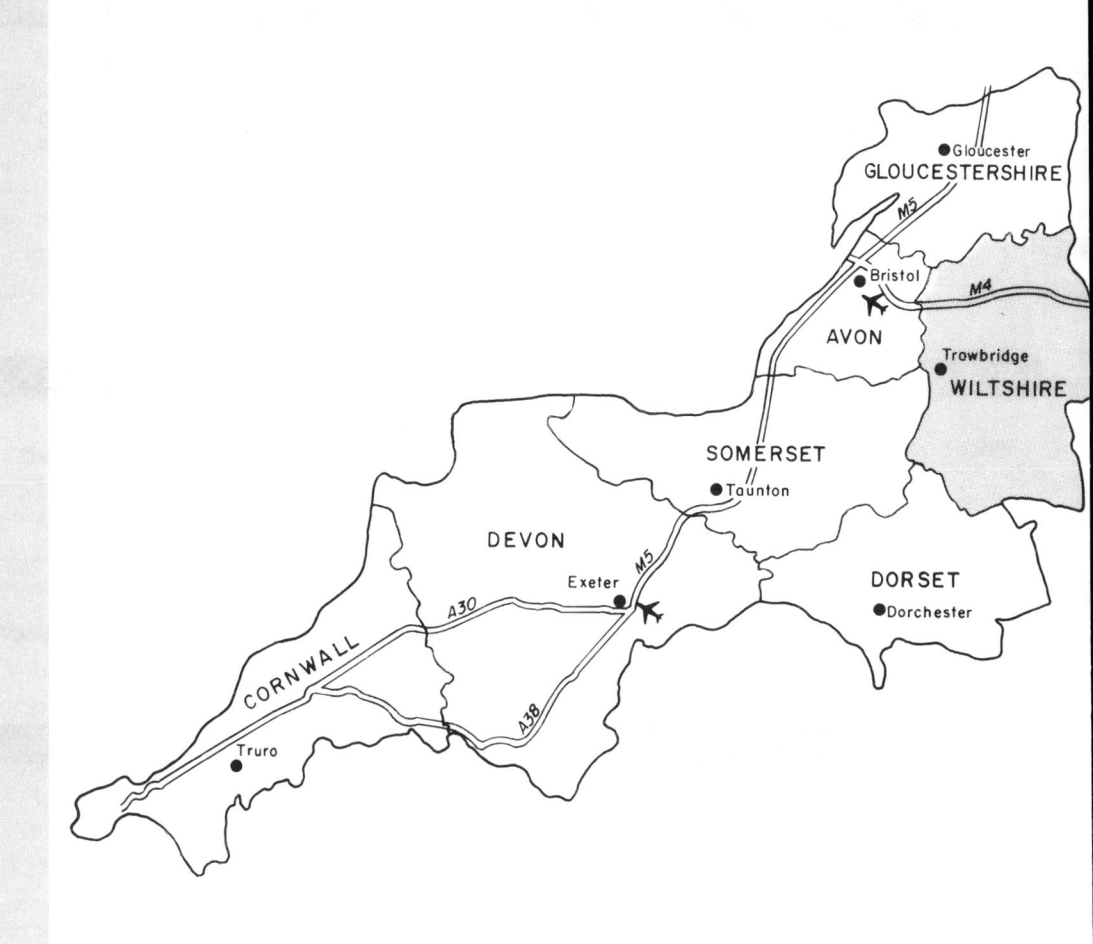

Chafyn Grove School

Address: Bourne Avenue, Salisbury, Wiltshire SP1 1LR

Telephone: 0722 33423

Head: Mr M J F Andrews

Age range: 4-13
No. of pupils: 230
Scholarships: Yes
Religion: Church of England

Fees per term
Day: £795-£1700
Weekly board: £2280-£2280
Full board: £2280-£2280

Boy ○ Girl ○ Co-ed ●
Day ● Week ● Board ●

Chafyn Grove School, established in 1876, is a thriving, purpose built, Christian foundation. It aims to produce confident, responsible, caring young people who have had the privilege of enjoying the broadest educational opportunities and experience. Its facilities include eleven acres of playing fields, a new sports hall, squash and tennis courts, magnificent arts centre, libraries and refurbished boarding accommodation.

Dauntsey's School *

Address: West Lavington, Devizes, Wiltshire SN10 4HE

Telephone: 0380 818441

Head: Mr C R Evans MA

Age range: 11-18
No. of pupils: 620
Scholarships: Yes
Religion: Non-denominational

Fees per term
Day: £1928-
Weekly board: -
Full board: £3115-

Boy ○ Girl ○ Co-ed ●
Day ● Week ○ Board ●

A fully co-educational boarding and day school with high academic standards and a wide range of sporting, musical and other extra-curricular activities. A happy and purposeful place, family orientated: 45% of pupils have a sibling at the school. Assisted Places and scholarships available.

Flambeaux Montessori School

Address: 18 Burford Road, Salisbury, Wiltshire SP2 8AN

Telephone: 0722 322179

Head: Mrs N M Brinn

Age range: 2-5
No. of pupils: 90
Scholarships:
Religion: Non-denominational

Fees per term
Day: -
Weekly board: -
Full board: -

Boy ○ Girl ○ Co-ed ●
Day ● Week ○ Board ○

Fees on application. For further information and a prospectus, please contact the school.

The Godolphin School *

Address: Milford Hill, Salisbury, Wiltshire SP1 2RA

Telephone: 0722 333059

Head: Mrs H A Fender

Age range: 11-18
No. of pupils: 350
Scholarships: Yes
Religion: Church of England

Fees per term
Day: £1885-
Weekly board: -
Full board: £3175-

Boy ○ Girl ● Co-ed ○
Day ● Week ○ Board ●

A happy school with an excellent academic record (95% pass rate at A level). Strong emphasis on responsibility, self confidence and thoughtfulness for others. Eighty in sixth form. Good facilities for science and technology, art, music and sport. Scholarships (including sixth form and music awards) available annually. Assisted places. Preparatory department for day girls aged 7-11 opens September 1993.

Grittleton House School

Address: Grittleton,
Chippenham, Wiltshire
SN14 6AP
Telephone: 0249 782434

Head: Mr P Moore

Age range: 3-16
No. of pupils: 280
Scholarships: Yes
Religion: Non-denominational

Fees per term
Day: £510-£980
Weekly board: -
Full board: -

Boy ○ Girl ○ Co-ed ●
Day ● Week ○ Board ○

Grittleton House School is a co-educational day school for children between the ages of 3 to 16. Small classes. Firm sensible discipline. Computer department. Traditional teaching allied with National Curriculum. Well equipped academic and sports facilities. Entrance by interview. Bursaries and scholarships available. Transport from most areas available.

Hawtreys

Address: Savernake Forest,
Marlborough, Wiltshire
SN8 3BA
Telephone: 0672 870331

Head: Mr G F Fenner

Age range: 7-13
No. of pupils: 120
Scholarships: Yes
Religion: Church of England

Fees per term
Day: -£1890
Weekly board: -
Full board: -£2835

Boy ● Girl ○ Co-ed ○
Day ● Week ○ Board ●

Hawtreys prepares the boys for all the leading public schools and a high standard of work is achieved without recourse to cramming. The scholarship list is good, while special attention is given to those boys to whom learning does not come easily. The curriculum is very broad and the school has good academic and sport facilities.

Heywood Preparatory School

Address: The Priory, Corsham,
Wiltshire SN13 0AP

Telephone: 0249 713379

Head: Mr H Sivil

Age range: 3-11
No. of pupils: 207
Scholarships:
Religion: Non-denominational

Fees per term
Day: £595-£720
Weekly board: -
Full board: -

Boy ○ Girl ○ Co-ed ●
Day ● Week ○ Board ○

For further information and a prospectus, please contact the school.

Kingsbury Hill House p714

Address: Kingsbury Street,
Marlborough, Wiltshire
SN8 1JA
Telephone: 0672 512680

Headmaster: Mr M Innes-Williams

Age range: 3-13
No. of pupils: 95
Scholarships:
Religion: Christian

Fees per term
Day: £700-£1100
Weekly board: -
Full board: -

Boy ○ Girl ○ Co-ed ●
Day ● Week ○ Board ○

The school maintains a fine academic tradition, but also believes that loyalty, a sense of fair play, and good manners are just as important as academic achievement. The school provides a broad curriculum so that each pupil receives a sound and balanced start to their education. A pupil/teacher ratio of less than 10 ensures that all pupils work at their own pace.

La Retraite School

Address: Campbell Road, Salisbury, Wiltshire SP1 3BQ

Telephone: 0722 333094

Head: Mrs M P Paisey

Age range: 3-18
No. of pupils: 260
Scholarships: Yes
Religion: Roman Catholic

Fees per term
Day: £715-£1280
Weekly board: -
Full board: -

Boy ○ Girl ○ Co-ed ●
Day ● Week ○ Board ○

For further information and a prospectus, please contact the school. Boys 3-7, girls 3-18.

Leaden Hall School

Address: 70 The Close, Salisbury, Wiltshire SP1 2EP

Telephone: 0722 334700

Head: Mrs D Watkins BAHons

Age range: 4-11
No. of pupils: 194
Scholarships:
Religion: Christian

Fees per term
Day: £650-£800
Weekly board: -£1235
Full board: -£1475

Boy ○ Girl ● Co-ed ○
Day ● Week ● Board ●

The aim of the school is to ensure that every child should develop in body, mind and character in a happy environment, to give the children a sound general education in preparation for their future schools and to encourage individual talent whenever possible. The staff are well qualified. Classes are kept to reasonable numbers and when more individual attention is required, small tutorial groups are arranged.

Marlborough College

Address: Marlborough, Wiltshire SN8 1PA

Telephone: 0672 515511

Head Mr D R Cope

Age range: 13-18
No. of pupils: 850
Scholarships: Yes
Religion: Church of England

Fees per term
Day: -
Weekly board: -
Full board: £2816-£3755

Boy ○ Girl ○ Co-ed ●
Day ○ Week ○ Board ●

Marlbrough: a co-educational boarding school, one hour west of London on the edge of a market town. 23 A level courses, 18 GCSEs, over 30 sports, more than 40 clubs and societies. Busy seven days a week. Entry at 13 and 16. Academic, art and music scholarships. Particular emphasis on individual care, with one pastoral tutor for every 8 children.

The Mill School

Address: Potterne, Devizes, Wiltshire SN10 5TE

Telephone: 0380 723011

Head: Mr J Eman

Age range: 4-11
No. of pupils: 61
Scholarships:
Religion: Non-denominational

Fees per term
Day: £850-£1265
Weekly board: -
Full board: -

Boy ○ Girl ○ Co-ed ●
Day ● Week ○ Board ○

For further information and a prospectus, please contact the school.

Northaw School

Address: West Tytherley, Salisbury, Wiltshire SP5 1NH

Telephone: 0980 862345

Head: Mr P E J Thwaites

Age range: 4-14
No. of pupils: 177
Scholarships:
Religion: Church of England

Fees per term
Day: £830-£1745
Weekly board: £2340-
Full board: £2340-

○ Boy ○ Girl ● Co-ed
● Day ● Week ● Board

Northaw places particular importance on the happiness of all its pupils and likes to maintain close contact with parents. By creating as many educational opportunities as possible, and by encouraging the children to take these opportunities, we offer each child every chance of success at his or her own level.

The Old Ride School

Address: Bath Road, Bradford-on-Avon, Wiltshire BA15 2PD
Telephone:

Head:

Age range: 4-13
No. of pupils: 122
Scholarships:
Religion: Church of England

Fees per term
Day: -
Weekly board: -
Full board: -

● Boy ○ Girl ○ Co-ed
● Day ○ Week ● Board

For further information and a prospectus, please contact the school.

Pinewood School

Address: Bourton, Swindon, Wiltshire SN6 8HZ

Telephone: 0793 782205

Head: Mr H G C Boddington

Age range: 7-13
No. of pupils: 142
Scholarships: Yes
Religion: Church of England

Fees per term
Day: £1675-£1740
Weekly board: -
Full board: -£2310

○ Boy ○ Girl ● Co-ed
● Day ○ Week ● Board

For further information and a prospectus, please contact the school.

Prior Park Preparatory School

Address: Calcutt Street, Cricklade, Wiltshire SN6 6BB

Telephone: 0793 750275

Head: Mr J E Bogie

Age range: 7-13
No. of pupils: 210
Scholarships:
Religion: Roman Catholic

Fees per term
Day: -£1455
Weekly board: -
Full board: -£2079

○ Boy ○ Girl ● Co-ed
● Day ○ Week ● Board

Prior Park Preparatory School is an independent school, accepting boarders and day pupils from the age of 8-13+ and preparing them for Common Entrance and scholarship to public schools. The school seeks to provide a happy and caring atmosphere in which children may develop and be able to progress to their public schools as confident and committed youngsters.

Salisbury Cathedral School

Address: Holmwood House, 26 The Close, Salisbury, Wiltshire SP1 2EJ
Telephone: 0722 335037

Head: Mrs M A A Nicols

Age range: 4-8
No. of pupils: 71
Scholarships:
Religion: Church of England

Fees per term
Day: £720-£870
Weekly board: -
Full board: -

Boy ○ Girl ○ Co-ed ●
Day ● Week ○ Board ○

We are a small, caring pre-preparatory school. There are approximately 80 pupils aged 4-8 equally divided between the sexes. Good manners, respect for one's peers and help for those less fortunate, social awareness, some knowledge of national and international affairs are all activities encouraged. Our academic standards are high and the National Curriculum is implemented from the age of 5.

Salisbury Cathedral School p714

Address: The Old Palace, 1 The Close, Salisbury, Wiltshire SN1 2EU
Telephone: 0722 322652

Head: Mr C J A Helyer

Age range: 4-13
No. of pupils: 305
Scholarships: Yes
Religion: Church of England

Fees per term
Day: £850-£1653
Weekly board: -
Full board: £2209-

Boy ○ Girl ○ Co-ed ●
Day ● Week ○ Board ●

Salisbury Cathedral School is an independent, co-educational, boarding and day, pre-preparatory, preparatory and choir school for boys and girls aged 4 to 13. The grounds extend to 27 acres within the beautiful Cathedral Close. Children are prepared for Common Entrance and 11+ grammar school entry. Substantial choral scholarships available.

Sandroyd School

Address: Rushmore House, Tollard Royal, Salisbury, Wiltshire SP5 5QD
Telephone: 0725 516264

Head: Mr D J Cann

Age range: 7-13
No. of pupils: 150
Scholarships: Yes
Religion: Church of England

Fees per term
Day: -
Weekly board: -
Full board: -£2475

Boy ● Girl ○ Co-ed ○
Day ○ Week ○ Board ●

An all-boarding boys preparatory school of a traditional family character. Sandroyd is set in a uniquely beautiful park. Boys can enjoy the care and up to date teaching of an excellent staff.

St Andrew Day School

Address: Ogbourne St Andrew, Marlborough, Wiltshire SN8 1SB
Telephone: 0672 84291

Head: Miss S Platt

Age range: 3-11
No. of pupils: 40
Scholarships:
Religion: Non-denominational

Fees per term
Day: £610-£995
Weekly board: -
Full board: -

Boy ○ Girl ○ Co-ed ●
Day ● Week ○ Board ○

For further information and a prospectus, please contact the school.

St Francis School

Address: Marlborough Road, Pewsey, Wiltshire SN9 5NT

Telephone: 0672 63228

Head: Mr A J G Collier

Age range: 3-13
No. of pupils: 175
Scholarships:
Religion: Christian

Fees per term
Day: £330-£1150
Weekly board: -
Full board: -

Boy ○ Girl ○ Co-ed ●
Day ● Week ○ Board ○

Founded in 1941 as a nursery and, now a trust, we have expanded to two classes per year under 12 and will take 12/13 year olds from 1994. Two fine houses with 17 acres provide first class teaching and games facilities and a new multi-purpose hall is planned. Small classes and caring qualified teachers produce a happy family atmosphere and impressive results.

St Mary's School

Address: Calne, Wiltshire SN11 0DE

Telephone: 0249 815899

Head: Miss D H Burns

Age range: 11-18
No. of pupils: 315
Scholarships: Yes
Religion: Church of England

Fees per term
Day: -£1990
Weekly board: -
Full board: -£3350

Boy ○ Girl ● Co-ed ○
Day ● Week ○ Board ●

St Mary's School, which is set in attractive grounds of 25 acres on the edge of Calne, is an independent boarding and day school for 320 girls, most of whom go on to Universities or Colleges of Higher Education. The girls enjoy excellent facilities and a wide variety of extra-curricular activities are available. A one-third Entrance Scholarship, together with a limited number of bursaries are available each year.

Stonar

Address: Cottles Park, Atworth, Melksham, Wiltshire

Telephone: 0225 702309

Head: Mrs S Hopkinson

Age range: 4-18
No. of pupils: 552
Scholarships: Yes
Religion: Church of England

Fees per term
Day: £850-£1590
Weekly board: £2630-£2870
Full board: -

Boy ○ Girl ● Co-ed ○
Day ● Week ● Board ●

A delightful rural location, 9 miles from Bath, with easy access to mainline stations and M4. Current facilities include indoor swimming pool, covering Riding School (BHSA Centre), purpose-built Music School, Sixth Form and Junior School. Full range of subjects taught to GCSE A Level and university entrance. Entry requirements and procedures: School's own examination at 9+-13+.

Stourbridge House

Address: Castle Street, Mere, Warminster, Wiltshire BA12 6JQ

Telephone: 0747 880165

Head: Mrs E Coward

Age range: 4-8
No. of pupils: 60
Scholarships:
Religion: Church of England

Fees per term
Day: £630-£670
Weekly board: -
Full board: -

Boy ○ Girl ○ Co-ed ●
Day ● Week ○ Board ○

We are a small, friendly school with a well established and caring staff, providing the ideal environment to give your child the best possible start to school life. The aim of the school is to provide a sound and systematic education for all children, enabling each one to realise his/her full potential. The curriculum is carefully prepared to keep in line with the new National Curriculum.

The Tanwood School

Address: 46-48 Bath Road,
Swindon, Wiltshire

Telephone:

Head:

Age range: 3-5
No. of pupils:
Scholarships:
Religion: Church of England

Fees per term
Day: -
Weekly board: -
Full board: -

Boy ○ Girl ○ Co-ed ●
Day ● Week ○ Board ○

For further information and a prospectus, please contact the school.

Warminster School

Address: Church Street,
Warminster, Wiltshire BA12 8PJ

Telephone: 0985 213038

Head: Mr T D Holgate

Age range: 5-18
No. of pupils: 490
Scholarships: Yes
Religion: Church of England

Fees per term
Day: £1180-£1470
Weekly board: £2245-£2445
Full board: £2245-£2445

Boy ○ Girl ○ Co-ed ●
Day ● Week ● Board ●

Warminster School is a fully co-educational day and boarding school for 490 pupils aged 5-18. It offers a rare opportunity to educate the whole family together, and provides a caring environment and small class sizes, enabling a high level of individual attention.

YORKSHIRE (NORTH)

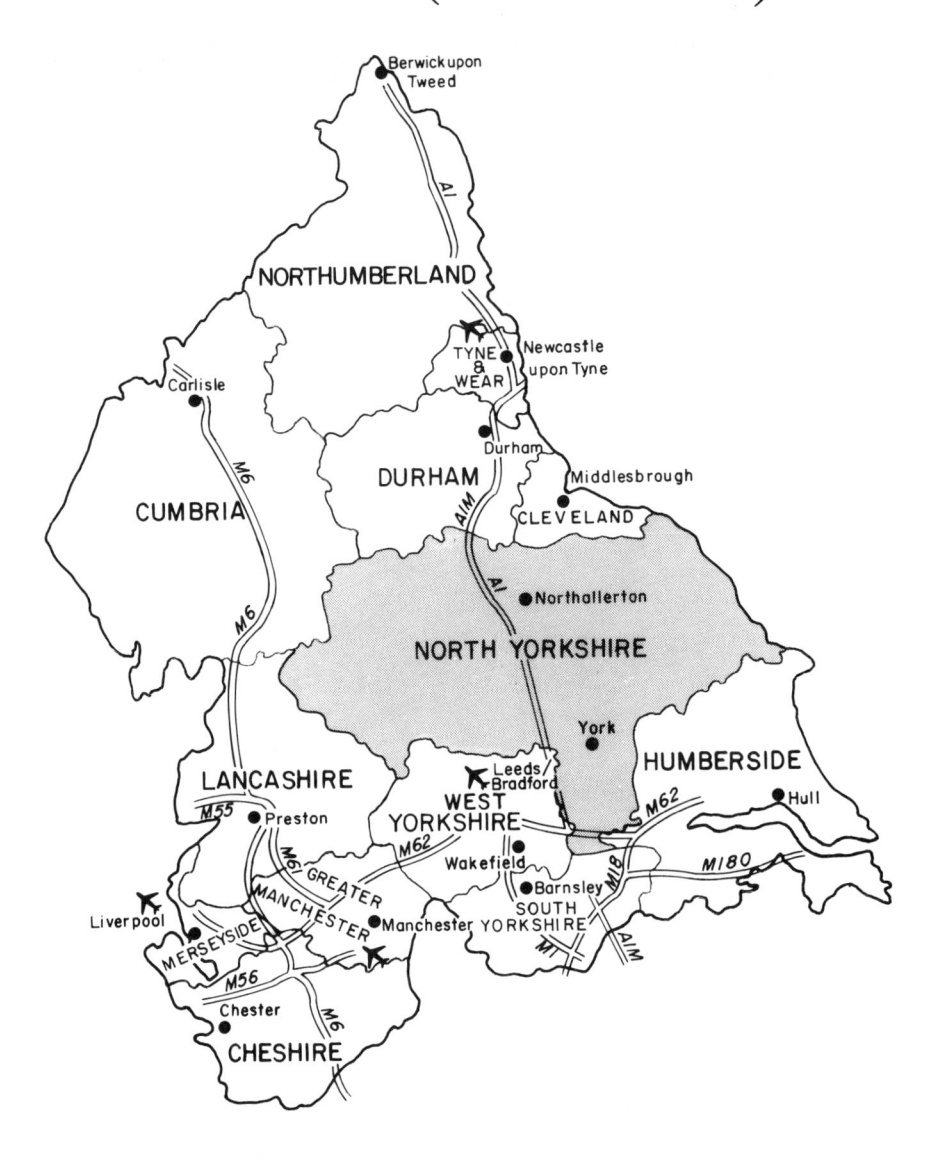

YORKSHIRE (NORTH) 551

Ampleforth College p715

Address: York, North Yorkshire YO6 4ER

Telephone: 04393 224

Age range: 10-18
No. of pupils: 630
Scholarships: Yes
Religion: Roman Catholic

Fees per term
Day: £2250-£2850
Weekly board: -
Full board: £2750-£3450

● Boy ○ Girl ○ Co-ed
○ Day ○ Week ● Board

Head: Rev G F L Chamberlain OSB MA

Monks have been educating boys for centuries, their proven success comes from the Christian faith which penetrates the whole community. Every boy shares in this family spirit, each boy is challenged to develop his potential according to his talents, helped by excellent academic teaching, and a full programme of extra-curricular activities. The house system gives each boy the support of a small community.

Ampleforth Preparatory School

Address: Gilling Castle, Gilling East York, North Yorkshire YO6 4HP

Telephone: 04393 238

Age range:
No. of pupils:
Scholarships:
Religion: Roman Catholic

Fees per term
Day: £1930-
Weekly board: £2485-
Full board: £2485-

● Boy ○ Girl ○ Co-ed
● Day ● Week ● Board

Head: Mr G J Sasse MA

Governed by Benedictine monks, Gilling Castle offers a challenging curriculum, excellent facilities (including golf course, sports hall, heated swimming pool) and a high staffing ratio. Christian values and a friendly, family atmosphere are found within a wonderful, historic setting amidst the peace of security of the Ampleforth estate. Ampleforth College is across the valley with the North York Moors nearby.

Ashville College *

Address: Harrogate, North Yorkshire HG2 9JR

Telephone: 0423 566358

Age range: 7-18
No. of pupils: 680
Scholarships: Yes
Religion: Methodist

Fees per term
Day: £1233-£1433
Weekly board: -
Full board: £2469-£2669

○ Boy ○ Girl ● Co-ed
● Day ● Week ● Board

Head: Mr M H Crosby

Independent, ex Direct-Grant, co-ed day and boarding school. On the edge of Harrogate close to both Leeds and Bradford and within half an hour of the Yorkshire Dales, with good road, air and rail links.

Forty acres of land: superb facilities, including music and drama centre, sports hall and purpose built boarding accommodation.

Assumption School

Address: Reeth Road, Richmond, North Yorkshire DL10 4EP

Telephone: 0748 822117

Age range: 4-16
No. of pupils: 130
Scholarships:
Religion: Roman Catholic

Fees per term
Day: £591-£1491
Weekly board: £1974-£2448
Full board: £1991-£2466

○ Boy ● Girl ○ Co-ed
● Day ● Week ● Board

Head: Mrs V E Fisher

Founded in 1850 for Roman Catholic girls from the UK and abroad, our small classes encourage high academic achievement and artistic and musical development. We offer personal attention for pupils with special needs either very able or with learning problems. Secure, friendly boarding environment with a variety of activities organised for the weekends.

Aysgarth Preparatory School

Address: Bedale, North Yorkshire DL8 1TF

Telephone: 0677 50240

Head: Mr J C Hodgkinson

Age range: 8-13
No. of pupils: 100
Scholarships:
Religion: Church of England

Fees per term
Day: -£1690
Weekly board: -£2415
Full board: -£2415

Boy ● Girl ○ Co-ed ○
Day ● Week ● Board ●

The boys are prepared in small classes for the Common Entrance and scholarship examinations to a broad spread of senior schools. Parents are kept well informed of academic progress. The teaching covers the requirements of the National Curriculum. Music and drama flourish, as do many other activities. IT is taught on modern computers. There is a strong record in sport, especially in soccer, rugby and cricket.

Ayton School

Address: High Green, Great Ayton, North Yorkshire TS9 6BN
Telephone: 0642 722141

Head: Mr D G Cook

Age range: 4-18
No. of pupils: 165
Scholarships: Yes
Religion: Quaker

Fees per term
Day: £680-£1285
Weekly board: £2305-£2445
Full board: £2655-£2775

Boy ○ Girl ○ Co-ed ●
Day ● Week ● Board ●

Ayton School combines the advantages of the small school with the opportunities of the large. It is particularly well endowed and pupils enjoy excellent facilities and a high degree of personal attention. It is beautifully situated in 60 acres of magnificent grounds virtually in the shadow of the northern escarpment of the North York Moors - yet major road, rail and air connections are close at hand.

Bairnswood Preparatory School

Address: Lady Edith's Park, Scarborough, North Yorkshire YO12 5PB
Telephone: 0723 363100

Head: Mrs A Johnstone

Age range: 3-6
No. of pupils: 50
Scholarships:
Religion: Non-denominational

Fees per term
Day: £355-£355
Weekly board: -
Full board: -

Boy ○ Girl ○ Co-ed ●
Day ● Week ○ Board ○

Bairnswood School develops an all round confidence in your children. It has a reputation for its friendly caring atmosphere which has proved ideal for a standard of learning and attainment at the infant age. The aim of the school is to develop your child's abilities to the full by providing a wide all round education with fully qualified teaching staff.

Belmont-Birklands

Address: 68 Kent Road, Harrogate, North Yorkshire HG1 2NH
Telephone: 0423 502465

Head: Miss V Arthur

Age range: 2-11
No. of pupils: 169
Scholarships:
Religion: Non-denominational

Fees per term
Day: £585-£725
Weekly board: -
Full board: -

Boy ● Girl ● Co-ed ○
Day ● Week ○ Board ○

Small and friendly, Belmont-Birklands stands in pleasant grounds in a quiet residential area. Small classes ensure individual attention to pupils. The timetable broadly follows the National Curriculum, with French starting at seven years. Well qualified staff foster good work habits, a positive attitude, self-motivation and commitment to achieving one's best. Entrance is by interview and informal assessment.

Bootham School *

Address: York, North Yorkshire YO3 7BU

Telephone: 0904 623261

Head: Mr I M Small

Age range: 11-18
No. of pupils: 370
Scholarships: Yes
Religion: Quaker

Fees per term
Day: -£1839
Weekly board: -£2860
Full board: -£2860

○ ○ ● Boy Girl Co-ed
● ● ● Day Week Board

One of England's Quaker schools where care for individual pupils is of paramount importance. A lively community where outstanding facilities provide for an extensive range of extra-curricular activities in a friendly atmosphere. All pupils take nine or ten GCSE's and over 80% of sixth form leavers go on to degree courses at universities and polytechnics.

Brackenfield School

Address: 128 Duchy Road, Harrogate, North Yorkshire HG1 2HE

Telephone: 0423 508558

Head: Mrs M Sutcliffe

Age range: 3-11
No. of pupils: 170
Scholarships:
Religion: Non-denominational

Fees per term
Day: £362-£743
Weekly board: -
Full board: -

○ ○ ● Boy Girl Co-ed
● ○ ○ Day Week Board

Brackenfield School is a nursery and preparatory school for boys and girls from three to eleven years. It is situated on the edge of the town overlooking open countryside. The school, which is staffed by qualified teachers, offers a broad curriculum incorporating a balance of traditional and child-centred teaching and prepares the children for entrance examinations to senior schools.

Bramcote School

Address: Filey Road, Scarborough, North Yorkshire

Telephone: 0723 373086

Head: Mr J R Gerrard

Age range: 8-13
No. of pupils: 96
Scholarships:
Religion: Church of England

Fees per term
Day: -
Weekly board: -
Full board: £2190-£2190

● ○ ○ Boy Girl Co-ed
○ ○ ● Day Week Board

Bramcote is a boy's boarding preparatory school, situated close to sea, woodland and theatre on Scarborough South Cliff and offering good food, friendly atmosphere, a dedicated and energetic staff, an exceptional range of evening, weekend and holiday activity and a good record of entrance or scholarship to major senior schools throughout the country.

Catteral Hall

Address: Catteral Hall, Settle, North Yorkshire BD24 0DG

Telephone: 0729 822527

Head: Mr M A J Streule

Age range: 8-13
No. of pupils: 150
Scholarships: Yes
Religion: Church of England

Fees per term
Day: £1773-£1908
Weekly board: -
Full board: £2655-£2850

○ ○ ● Boy Girl Co-ed
● ○ ● Day Week Board

Founded in 1512-magnificent Dales setting-close to motorway and rail networks. Boarding and day education for 450 boys and girls aged 8-13 years. Generous scholarships and assisted places scheme. Catteral is a self-contained unit within Giggleswick School sharing many facilties including the swimming pool and chapel but having its own classrooms, sports hall and the new music school and science room.

Clifton Preparatory School

Address: 13 The Avenue, Clifton, York, North Yorkshire YO3 6AS
Telephone: 0904 623716

Age range: 4-11
No. of pupils: 115
Scholarships:
Religion: Non-denominational

Fees per term
Day: £585-£675
Weekly board: -
Full board: -

Boy ○ Girl ○ Co-ed ●
Day ● Week ○ Board ○

Head: Mrs B Appleby

The school offers an excellent education based on traditional methods and aims in a friendly, happy atmosphere. Besides giving excellent grounding in English and mathematics; science, history, geography, languages, RE, art, music and PE are considered of the highest importance and are an integral part of the school time table. Extra-curricular activities include drama workshop, speech and drama, fencing, dancing, gym.

Cundall Manor School

Address: Helperby, York, North Yorkshire YO6 2RW
Telephone: 0423 360200

Age range: 4-13
No. of pupils: 185
Scholarships:
Religion: Church of England

Fees per term
Day: £950-£1423
Weekly board: -
Full board: -£2082

Boy ○ Girl ○ Co-ed ●
Day ● Week ○ Board ●

Head: Mr J F Napier

The school aims to create a secure and happy environment in which children can grow in confidence and ability. There is a healthy balance between work and play, and while children are expected to work hard and do their best, they are also given the opportunity to enjoy a wide range of activities. The classes are small and pupils benefit from individual attention.

Fyling Hall School

Address: Robin Hoods Bay, North Yorkshire YO22 4QD
Telephone: 0947 880261

Age range: 5-18
No. of pupils: 250
Scholarships: Yes
Religion: Non-denominational

Fees per term
Day: £670-£725
Weekly board: -
Full board: £1550-£1660

Boy ○ Girl ○ Co-ed ●
Day ● Week ○ Board ●

Principal: Mrs C White

The school, founded in 1923, is situated in beautiful countryside where children may safely enjoy much freedom. The aim of the school is to provide a natural atmosphere for growth and not to impose any special view of life and learning. Value is placed on good manners and consideration for others. The academic standards are high with a wide curriculum and small classes.

Giggleswick School * p715

Address: Settle, North Yorkshire BD24 0DE
Telephone: 0729 823545

Age range: 13-18
No. of pupils: 300
Scholarships: Yes
Religion: Church of England

Fees per term
Day: £2312-
Weekly board: -
Full board: £3487-

Boy ○ Girl ○ Co-ed ●
Day ● Week ○ Board ●

Head: Mr M A P Hobson

Founded in 1512--magnificent Dales setting--close to motorway and rail networks. Boarding and day education for 450 boys and girls aged 13-18 years. Generous scholarships and assisted places scheme. Excellent academic results. Strong tradition of sport, outdoor pursuits, art, drama and music. First class facilities and comfortable modern accommodation.

YORKSHRE (NORTH) 555

Grosvenor House School

Address: Swarcliffe Hall, Birstwith, Harrogate, North Yorkshire HG3 3TG
Telephone: 0423 771029

Head: Mr G J Raspin

Age range: 3-13
No. of pupils: 186
Scholarships: Yes
Religion: Non-denominational

Fees per term
Day: £390-£1150
Weekly board: -
Full board: -£1920

Boy ● Girl ○ Co-ed ○
Day ● Week ○ Board ●

The school is in a delightful country situation six miles from Harrogate in Nidderdale. Amongst the many facilities available are extensive playing fields, a heated indoor swimming pool, gymnasium/theatre, modern art and science blocks, music, and fishing in the river Nidd. Boys are prepared for entrance to a wide range of senior schools.

Harrogate Ladies College ✱

Address: Clarence Drive, Harrogate, North Yorkshire HG1 2QG
Telephone: 0423 504543

Head: Mrs J C Lawrence

Age range: 10-18
No. of pupils: 400
Scholarships: Yes
Religion: Church of England

Fees per term
Day: £1810-
Weekly board: -
Full board: £2695-

Boy ○ Girl ● Co-ed ○
Day ● Week ○ Board ●

Independent girls' school, 100 years old in 1993 offers an excellent all-round education with academic bias. Extensive programme of activities in music, field study, sport, art and design and computing. Beautiful situation with very good road, rail and air communication. 400 students, aged 10-18, 110 in sixth form. Mainly full boarding, residential accommodation and care to a high standard.

Harrogate Tutorial College Limited

Address: 2 The Oval, Harrogate, North Yorkshire HG2 9BA
Telephone: 0423 501041

Head: Mr K W Pollard

Age range: 15-19
No. of pupils: 100
Scholarships: Yes
Religion:

Fees per term
Day: £700-£1900
Weekly board: -
Full board: -

Boy ○ Girl ○ Co-ed ●
Day ● Week ● Board ○

Harrogate Tutorial College is a small, fully accredited college, located close to the centre of the most attractive spa town in the North. Classes are small, average 4 students; the teachers highly qualified and sympathetic. A wide range of subjects can be taken at A level and GCSE in one and two year courses, retakes, Easter and Summer revision courses.

Howsham Hall

Address: York, North Yorkshire YO6 7PJ
Telephone: 065 381 374

Head: Mr S J Knock

Age range: 5-14
No. of pupils: 75
Scholarships: Yes
Religion: Church of England

Fees per term
Day: £400-£1070
Weekly board: -
Full board: £1500-

Boy ● Girl ○ Co-ed ○
Day ● Week ○ Board ●

Howsham is a family run school and as such provides an ideal and happy community in which boys can settle down to a way of life away from home. Children are guided rather than moulded and individuality is maintained with a Christian education stressing tolerance and kindness. Pupils are escorted to and from London and the airports each term.

The Minster School

Address: Deangate, York, North Yorkshire YO1 2JA

Telephone: 0904 625217

Head: Mr R Shephard

Age range: 4-13
No. of pupils: 150
Scholarships: Yes
Religion: Church of England

Fees per term
Day: £410-£1130
Weekly board: -
Full board: -

Boy ○ Girl ○ Co-ed ●
Day ● Week ○ Board ○

Founded originally in 627 to educate the singing boys at York Minster, the Minster School is arguably the oldest educational establishment in the north of England. Nowadays it is a co-educational preparatory school with a pre-preparatory department standing next to the Minster, opposite the south transept. The choristers (20 boys) recieve a scholarship from the Dean and Chapter. The school has an enviable reputation.

The Mount School *

Address: Dalton Terrace, York, North Yorkshire YO2 4DD

Telephone: 0904 622275

Head: Miss B J Windle

Age range: 11-18
No. of pupils: 290
Scholarships: Yes
Religion: Quaker

Fees per term
Day: £2010-
Weekly board: £3020-
Full board: £3020-

Boy ○ Girl ● Co-ed ○
Day ○ Week ● Board ●

The Mount School, set in the historic City of York offers girls sound academic standards combined with Quaker values. Equal care is given to the development of academic and all round talents to achieve a poised and confident individual, capable of playing her part in the challenging world we live in.

Pocklington School * p747

Address: West Green, Pocklington, York, North Yorkshire YO4 2NJ

Telephone: 0759 303125

Head: Mr J N D Gray

Age range: 7-18
No. of pupils: 719
Scholarships: Yes
Religion: Church of England

Fees per term
Day: £1141-£1374
Weekly board: -
Full board: £2521-

Boy ○ Girl ○ Co-ed ●
Day ● Week ○ Board ●

A co-educational boarding and day school, with a reputation for academic success. The School has also been recognised as being innovative in the field of Art and Technical Design, winning numerous national awards. Emphasis is placed on both cultural and sporting activities for all students. Excellent facilities and a happy atmosphere.

Queen Ethelburga's College p716

Address: Thorpe Underwood Hall, Ouseburn, York, North Yorkshire

Telephone: 0423 331480

Head: Mrs J M Town

Age range: 2-18
No. of pupils: 320
Scholarships: Yes
Religion: Church of England

Fees per term
Day: £685-£1595
Weekly board: £2275-£2475
Full board: £2275-£2475

Boy ○ Girl ● Co-ed ○
Day ● Week ● Board ●

Set in 100 acre estate between York and Harrrogate, girls are prepared for GCSE and A Level examinations with full careers advice. Small classes ensure individual attention and new boarding accommodation is under the direction of caring staff. Purpose built facilities include science block, music and drama centre, computer and business area, health and leisure, art and design and home economic units.

Queen Margaret's School

Address: Esrick Park, York, North Yorkshire YO4 6EU

Telephone: 0904 728261

Head: Dr G Chapman

Age range: 11-18
No. of pupils: 360
Scholarships: Yes
Religion: Church of England

Fees per term
Day: -£1890
Weekly board: -
Full board: -£2980

Boy ○ · Girl ● · Co-ed ○
Day ● · Week ○ · Board ●

Queen Margaret's provides a happy blend of ancient and modern. Set in a charming park at Esrick, south of York, the house exudes a warmth to all comers. Girls join at 11, 12, 13 and 16 from a variety of backgrounds and links are fostered with Europe and beyond. Best boarding school A Level results north of Peterborough. Outstanding games and forging ahead in IT, design, art.

Queen Mary's School

Address: Baldersby Park, Topcliffe, Thirsk, North Yorkshire YO7 3BZ
Telephone: 0845 577425

Joint-Heads: Mr P Belward, Mrs M F Belward

Age range: 4-16
No. of pupils: 230
Scholarships: Yes
Religion: Church of England

Fees per term
Day: £590-£1640
Weekly board: -
Full board: £2290-£2620

Boy ● · Girl ● · Co-ed ○
Day ● · Week ○ · Board ●

The school is situated at Baldersby Park, a beautiful mansion in 40 acres of grounds. High academic standards are consistently achieved. There is an outstanding music department, run by a full time director, assistant and fifteen peripatetic staff. Strong emphasis on physical education and drama. Optimum personality development firmly founded on Christian principles is the main aim of the school.

Read School p717

Address: Drax, Selby, North Yorkshire YO8 8NL

Telephone: 0757 618248

Head: Mr A J Saddler

Age range: 5-18
No. of pupils: 240
Scholarships: Yes
Religion: Church of England

Fees per term
Day: £765-£1060
Weekly board: £1830-£2010
Full board: £1950-£2150

Boy ● · Girl ● · Co-ed ○
Day ● · Week ● · Board ●

Founded in 1667, Read School provides for day boys and day girls 5-18, and for boarding (full and weekly) boys 8-18. The Headmaster is a member of ISAI and BSA. Pupils are prepared for GCSE and A Levels in a wide range of subjects. Staffing ratios are generous, particularly in the classes being prepared for public examinations.

Red House School

Address: Moor Monkton, York, North Yorkshire YO5 8JQ
Telephone: 0904 83256

Head: Major A V Gordon

Age range: 3-13
No. of pupils: 50
Scholarships: Yes
Religion: Church of England

Fees per term
Day: £500-£1350
Weekly board: -
Full board: -£1975

Boy ○ · Girl ○ · Co-ed ●
Day ● · Week ○ · Board ●

For further information and a prospectus, please contact the school.

Ripon Cathedral Choir

Address: Whitcliffe Lane, Ripon, North Yorkshire HG4 2LA
Telephone: 0765 602134

Head: Mr R H Moore

Age range: 4-13
No. of pupils: 120
Scholarships: Yes
Religion: Church of England

Fees per term
Day: £955-£1340
Weekly board: £1700-
Full board: £1835-

Boy ○ Girl ○ Co-ed ●
Day ● Week ● Board ●

In a pleasant position on the edge of Ripon, the school aims to give children a first class academic education in a friendly atmosphere. There are excellent facilities for sport and music.

Scarborough College *

Address: Filey Road, Scarborough, North Yorkshire YO11 3BA
Telephone: 0723 360620

Head: Dr D S Hempsall MA PhD

Age range: 11-18
No. of pupils: 45
Scholarships:
Religion: Non-denominational

Fees per term
Day: -£1540
Weekly board: -
Full board: -£2840

Boy ○ Girl ○ Co-ed ●
Day ● Week ○ Board ●

Scarborough College seeks to achieve the fullest possible personal development of each boy and girl. Every pupil is exposed to a wide range of experiences and opportunities. The highest standards of which the individual is capable are expected in all aspects of life so that the young men and women who leave the college possess both confidence and integrity. The environment is friendly and caring.

Scarborough College Junior School

Address: Lisvane, Sandybed Lane, Scarborough, North Yorkshire YO12 5LJ
Telephone: 0723 361595

Head: Mr P M Greenfield

Age range: 3-11
No. of pupils: 171
Scholarships:
Religion: Non-denominational

Fees per term
Day: £712-£1066
Weekly board: -
Full board: -£2025

Boy ○ Girl ○ Co-ed ●
Day ● Week ○ Board ●

For further information and a prospectus, please contact the school.

St Andrew's Preparatory School

Address: West Royd, Castle Howard Road, Malton, North Yorkshire YO17 0AY
Telephone: 0653 695232

Head: Mrs J M Yates

Age range: 4-11
No. of pupils: 70
Scholarships:
Religion: Non-denominational

Fees per term
Day: £446-£660
Weekly board: -
Full board: -

Boy ○ Girl ○ Co-ed ●
Day ● Week ○ Board ○

For further information and a prospectus, please contact the school.

St Hilda's School

Address: Sneaton Castle, Whitby, North Yorkshire YO21 3QN
Telephone: 0947 600051

Head: Sister Janet Elizabeth OHP

Age range: 4-18
No. of pupils: 215
Scholarships: Yes
Religion: Church of England

Fees per term
Day: £695-£1295
Weekly board: £1950-£2350
Full board: £2000-£2400

Boy ○   Girl ○   Co-ed ●
Day ●   Week ●   Board ●

The school is kept small on principle so that each pupil can be known and treated as an individual. Pastoral care is a priority, with staff available to advise on academic, personal and career matters. We expect high standards of behaviour and consideration towards others and try to lead students towards responsible citizenship in today's world.

St Martin's School

Address: Kirkdale Manor, Nawton, York, North Yorkshire YO6 5UA
Telephone: 0439 71215

Head: Mr M J Jones

Age range: 7-13
No. of pupils: 110
Scholarships:
Religion:

Fees per term
Day: -
Weekly board: -
Full board: -

Boy ○   Girl ○   Co-ed ●
Day ●   Week ●   Board ●

For further information and a prospectus, please contact the school.

St Olav's School

Address: Clifton, York, North Yorkshire YO3 6AB
Telephone: 0904 623269

Head: Mr T Muryne

Age range: 8-13
No. of pupils: 300
Scholarships:
Religion:

Fees per term
Day: -
Weekly board: -
Full board: -

Boy ○   Girl ○   Co-ed ●
Day ●   Week ○   Board ●

For further information and a prospectus, please contact the school.

St Peter's School *

Address: Clifton, York, North Yorkshire YO3 6AB
Telephone:

Head: Mr R N Pittman

Age range: 13-18
No. of pupils: 480
Scholarships:
Religion:

Fees per term
Day: -
Weekly board: -
Full board: -

Boy ○   Girl ○   Co-ed ●
Day ●   Week ○   Board ●

For further information and a prospectus, please contact the school.

Terrington Hall Preparatory School

Address: Terrington, York, North Yorkshire YO6 4PR

Telephone: 0653 84227

Head: Mr J D Gray BA

Age range: 4-13
No. of pupils: 101
Scholarships: Yes
Religion: Non-denominational

Fees per term
Day: £600-£1400
Weekly board: £2050-
Full board: £2050-

○ ○ ● Boy Girl Co-ed
● ● ● Day Week Board

Terrington House is situated in beautiful countryside close to Castle Howard and some 15 miles from the city of York. Terrington prepares pupils for all the leading independent schools. With a teacher/pupil ratio of 1:10 every child has the opportunity to achieve his or her academic potential. Music, art and drama form an important part of the curriculum. The school has excellent facilities.

Tregelles

Address: Dalton Terrace, York, North Yorkshire YO2 4DD

Telephone: 0904 622275

Head of Department: Mrs L Atkinson

Age range: 5-11
No. of pupils: 35
Scholarships:
Religion: Quaker

Fees per term
Day: £860-£1140
Weekly board: -
Full board: -

○ ○ ● Boy Girl Co-ed
● ○ ○ Day Week Board

Tregelles, the growing Junior Department of the Mount School, shares with it the Quaker ethos of openess to all and attention to the individual in a warm family atmosphere. Opened in September 1991 the co-educational school for day boys and girls is growing well. Enquiries for all ages are welcome.

Woodleigh School Langton

Address: Langton Hall, Malton, North Yorkshire YO17 9QN

Telephone: 065 385 215

Head: Mr D M England

Age range: 7-13
No. of pupils: 50
Scholarships: Yes
Religion: Church of England

Fees per term
Day: £1200-£1200
Weekly board: £1840-£1840
Full board: £1840-£1840

○ ○ ● Boy Girl Co-ed
● ● ● Day Week Board

Teaching in small classes of up to 12 children allows for close individual attention at all times. The young and enthusiastic staff generate a positive and stimulating environment in which the children develop academically, culturally and socially.

York College for Girls

Address: 62 Petergate, York, North Yorkshire YO1 2HZ

Telephone: 0904 646421

Head: Mrs J L Clare

Age range: 3-18
No. of pupils: 326
Scholarships:
Religion:

Fees per term
Day: -
Weekly board: -
Full board: -

● ● ○ Boy Girl Co-ed
● ○ ○ Day Week Board

For further information and a prospectus, please contact the school. Boys 3-8 only.

YORKSHIRE (SOUTH)

Ashdell Preparatory

Address: 266 Fulwood Road, Sheffield, South Yorkshire S10 3BL
Telephone: 0742 663835

Head: Mrs J Upton

Age range: 4-11
No. of pupils: 135
Scholarships:
Religion: Non-denominational

Fees per term
Day: £1040-£1160
Weekly board: -
Full board: -

○ ● ○
Boy Girl Co-ed

● ○ ○
Day Week Board

This small academic school provides an opportunity for pupils of above average ability to discover their talents by tasting a wide variety of experiences. The teaching of basic subjects is carefully structured and class size is small. The school day proceeds at a brisk pace and includes French, Latin, music, ballet, drama plus science in the new science laboratory.

Birkdale School

Address: Oakholme Road, Sheffield, South Yorkshire S10 3DH
Telephone: 0742 668408

Head: Revd M D A Hepworth

Age range: 4-18
No. of pupils: 750
Scholarships: Yes
Religion: Non-denominational

Fees per term
Day: £860-£1310
Weekly board: -
Full board: -

● ○ ○
Boy Girl Co-ed

● ○ ○
Day Week Board

Birkdale has developed in recent years to give Sheffield and South Yorkshire a day school which provides a first class edcuation for boys from 4 to university entrance. Separate preparatory (4-11) and senior schools, strong academic tradition. Full range of academic subjects to GCSE and A Level. Wide choice of extra-curricualr activities.

Brantwood Independent School for Girls

Address: 1 Kenwood Bank, Sheffield, South Yorkshire S7 1NV
Telephone: 0742 581747

Head: Mrs E M Swynnerton

Age range: 4-17
No. of pupils: 200
Scholarships:
Religion:

Fees per term
Day: £792-£890
Weekly board: -
Full board: -

○ ● ○
Boy Girl Co-ed

● ○ ○
Day Week Board

Brantwood is an independent day school for girls. Founded over 80 years ago, the school provides a friendly, caring and stimulating environment where all girls are ancouraged to reach their maximum academic potential. The school provides small class sizes and has extensive facilities. Individual attention for all pupils is of major importance and traditional teaching values are combined with a progressive curriculum.

Hill House Preparatory School

Address: Rutland Street, Doncaster, South Yorkshire DN1 2TD
Telephone: 0302 323565

Head: Mr A P Cruickshan

Age range: 3-13
No. of pupils: 250
Scholarships:
Religion: Non-denominational

Fees per term
Day: £810-£1220
Weekly board: -
Full board: -

○ ○ ●
Boy Girl Co-ed

● ○ ○
Day Week Board

Much thought is given to the preparation of our children for the transition from the lower to upper school at 8 years. Children are prepared for Common Entrance Examinations at 13+ and also work closely with the National Curriculum. Music, art, drama and sport play an important part in the life of the school.

Montessori School

Address: Sheffield, South Yorkshire NP5 3XP

Telephone: 07742 580035

Principal:

Age range:
No. of pupils:
Scholarships:
Religion:

Fees per term
Day: -
Weekly board: -
Full board: -

○ Boy ○ Girl ○ Co-ed
○ Day ○ Week ○ Board

For further information and a prospectus, please contact the school.

Mount St Mary's College *

Address: Spinkhill, Sheffield, South Yorkshire S31 9YL

Telephone: 0246 433388

Head: Mr P B Fisher MA

Age range: 13-18
No. of pupils: 325
Scholarships: Yes
Religion: Roman Catholic

Fees per term
Day: £1807-
Weekly board: £2475-
Full board: £2675-

○ Boy ○ Girl ● Co-ed
● Day ● Week ● Board

Mount St Mary's (HMC) is a co-educational Jesuit College which takes boarders and day pupils. It is a Catholic school but other denominations are welcomed. The curriculum is traditionally academic, sport, drama and music are very strong, and the underlying philosophy is to prepare young people for the service of others.

Mylnhurst Convent School

Address: Button Hill, Ecclesall, Sheffield, South Yorkshire S11 9HJ

Telephone: 0742 361411

Head: Mrs P Fuller

Age range: 3-11
No. of pupils: 170
Scholarships:
Religion: Roman Catholic

Fees per term
Day: £575-£790
Weekly board: -
Full board: -

○ Boy ○ Girl ● Co-ed
● Day ○ Week ○ Board

Independent Roman Catholic day school for boys and girls, aged 3-11 years, with a well equipped nursery department. Children of other faiths are welcomed. The sports facilities include playing fields, gymnasium and indoor swimming pool. Computer, drama and music facilities. French is taught throughout the junior school. Pupils are prepared for Common Entrance and scholarship examinations.

Rudston Preparatory School

Address: 59/63 Broom Road, Rotherham, South Yorkshire S60 2SW

Telephone: 0709 364291

Head: Mrs A W Cartner

Age range: 4-11
No. of pupils: 165
Scholarships:
Religion: Non-denominational

Fees per term
Day: £595-£625
Weekly board: -
Full board: -

○ Boy ○ Girl ● Co-ed
● Day ○ Week ○ Board

For further information and a prospectus, please contact the school.

Sheffield High School *

Address: 10 Rutland Park,
Sheffield, South Yorkshire
S10 2PE
Telephone: 0742 660324

Head: Mrs M A Houston MA

Age range: 4-18
No. of pupils: 757
Scholarships: Yes
Religion: Non-denominational

Fees per term
Day: £880-£1148
Weekly board: -
Full board: -

○ ● ○
Boy Girl Co-ed
● ○ ○
Day Week Board

For further information and a prospectus, please contact the school.

St Mary's School

Address: 65 Bawtry Road,
Doncaster, South Yorkshire
DN4 7AD
Telephone: 0302 535926

Head: Mr J Hall

Age range: 4-16
No. of pupils: 167
Scholarships:
Religion:

Fees per term
Day: -
Weekly board: -
Full board: -

○ ● ○
Boy Girl Co-ed
● ○ ○
Day Week Board

For further information and a prospectus, please contact the school.

Story House School

Address: 134 Barnsley Road,
Wath-upon-Dearne, South Yorkshire
Telephone:

Head:

Age range: 4-19
No. of pupils:
Scholarships:
Religion:

Fees per term
Day: -
Weekly board: -
Full board: -

○ ○ ●
Boy Girl Co-ed
○ ○ ○
Day Week Board

For further information and a prospectus, please contact the school.

Sycamore Hall Preparatory School

Address: 1 Hall Flat Lane,
Balby, Doncaster, South Yorkshire DN4 8PT
Telephone: 0302 856800

Head: Miss J Spencer

Age range: 4-12
No. of pupils: 56
Scholarships:
Religion:

Fees per term
Day: -
Weekly board: -
Full board: -

○ ○ ●
Boy Girl Co-ed
● ○ ○
Day Week Board

For further information and a prospectus, please contact the school.

Westbourne Preparatory School

Address: 50-54 Westbourne Road, Sheffield, South Yorkshire S10 2QQ
Telephone: 0742 660374

Head: Mr C R Wilmshurst

Age range: 4-13
No. of pupils: 170
Scholarships:
Religion:

Fees per term
Day: -
Weekly board: -
Full board: -

● Boy ○ Girl ○ Co-ed
● Day ○ Week ○ Board

For further information and a prospectus, please contact the school.

YORKSHIRE (WEST)

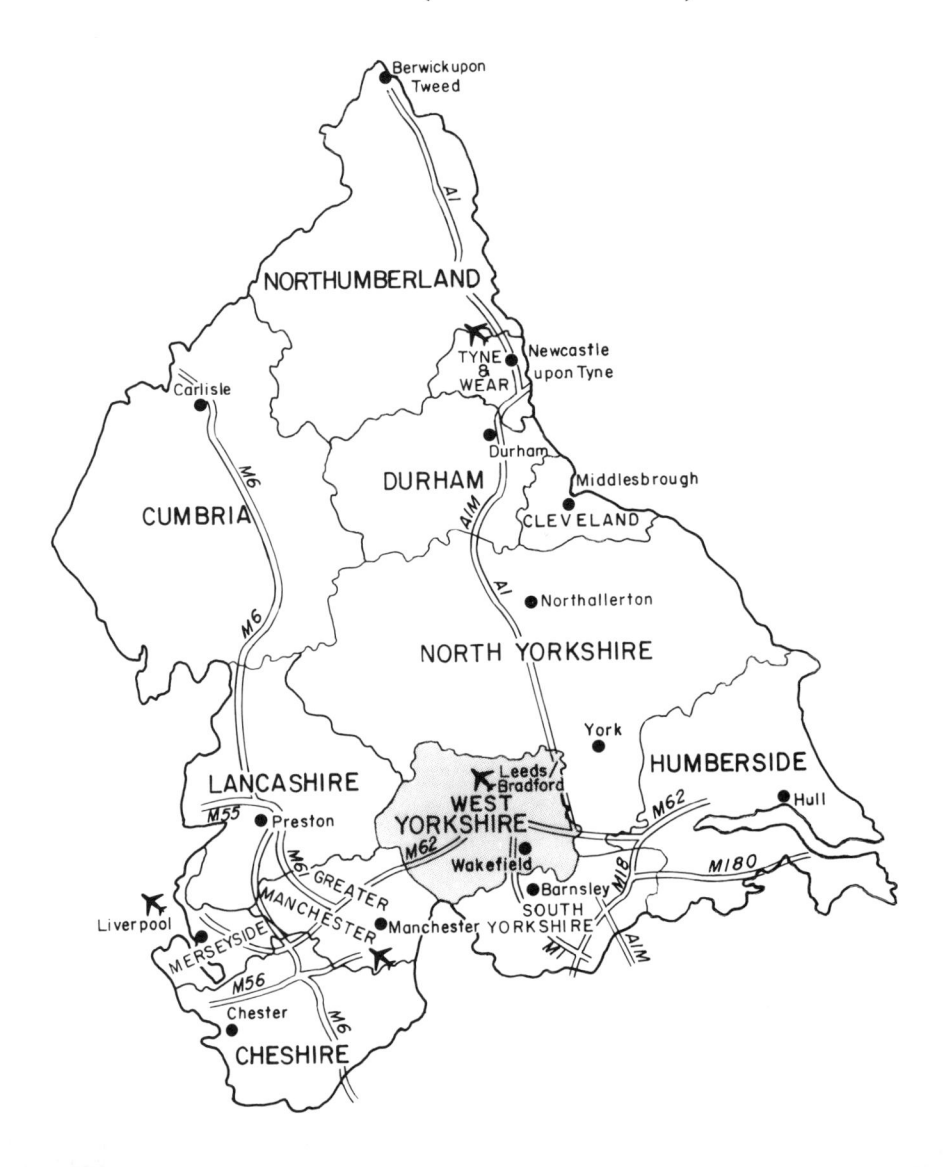

Ackworth School * p737

Address: Ackworth,
Pontefract, West Yorkshire
WF7 7LT
Telephone: 0977 611401

Age range: 7-18
No. of pupils: 510
Scholarships: Yes
Religion: Quaker

Fees per term
Day: £827-£1525
Weekly board: -
Full board: -£2677

Boy ○ Girl ○ Co-ed ●
Day ● Week ● Board ●

Head: Mr D S Harris

Over recent years Ackworth has earned itself the reputation for high academic results at both A and GCSE Levels. Underlying the academic rigour is a belief in the importance and worth of each individual and the value of an education that goes beyond the narrowly scholastic. The atmosphere is busy and purposeful, friendly and welcoming.

Batley Grammar *

Address: Carlinghow Hill,
Batley, West Yorkshire
WF17 0AD
Telephone: 0924 474980

Age range: 11-18
No. of pupils: 607
Scholarships: Yes
Religion: Non-denominational

Fees per term
Day: £1034-
Weekly board: -
Full board: -

Boy ● Girl ● Co-ed ○
Day ● Week ○ Board ○

Head: Mr C S Parker

Batley Grammar School encourages its pupils to high academic achievement across a wide curriculum within a disciplined and caring environment. There are many opportunities open to pupils for involvement in sporting, outdoor and other extra-curricular activities. Via the above combination we hope to develop both their intellect and character to meet the increasing challenge of the world beyond school.

Beech House Preparatory School

Address: 52 Headingley Lane,
Leeds, West Yorkshire
LS6 2BW
Telephone: 0532 789893

Age range: 3-11
No. of pupils: 116
Scholarships:
Religion: Non-denominational

Fees per term
Day: £800-£1004
Weekly board: -
Full board: -

Boy ○ Girl ○ Co-ed ●
Day ● Week ○ Board ○

Head: Mrs A C Newman BEd(Hons) AdvDipEd

For further information and a prospectus, please contact the school.

Bradford Girls' Grammar School *

Address: Squire Lane,
Bradford, West Yorkshire
BD9 6RB
Telephone: 0274 545395

Age range: 4-18
No. of pupils: 900
Scholarships: Yes
Religion: Non-denominational

Fees per term
Day: £854-£1200
Weekly board: -
Full board: -

Boy ● Girl ● Co-ed ○
Day ● Week ○ Board ○

Head: Mrs L J Warrington

The aims and objectives are academic excellence and the development of social consciousness and conscience. The school offers a broad and balanced curriculum for girls aged 4-18 and boys aged 4-8. Children are admitted at 4 by interview, at 9, 11, 12 and 13 by examination and direct entry in the sixth form is dependent upon interview and GCSE results.

Bradford Grammar School *

Address: Keighley Road,
Bradford, West Yorkshire
BD9 4JP
Telephone: 0274 542492

Age range: 8-18
No. of pupils: 1165
Scholarships:
Religion: Non-denominational

Fees per term
Day: £947-£1187
Weekly board: -
Full board: -

● Boy ○ Girl ● Co-ed
● Day ○ Week ○ Board

Head: Mr D A G Smith

Bradford Grammar School is an old established grammar school which has existed since Tudor times. 85% of leavers go on to higher education of whom a significant number go to the universities of Oxford and Cambridge. The school curriculum ranges from classics to economics and electronic systems, and foreign languages, including Russian and Japanese, are a significant part of the curriculum.

Bronte House School

Address: Apperley Bridge,
Bradford, West Yorkshire
BD10 0PA
Telephone: 0532 502811

Age range: 7-11
No. of pupils: 160
Scholarships: Yes
Religion: Methodist

Fees per term
Day: £1325-
Weekly board: £2220-
Full board: £2220-

○ Boy ○ Girl ● Co-ed
● Day ● Week ● Board

Head: Mr F F Watson

An IAPS day and boarding school, combining traditional values with good modern practice. National Curriculum and three European languages. Additional emphasis on music and sport.

Pre-preparatory department to open in 1994. The preparatory school of Woodhouse Grove

Cliff School

Address: St John's Lodge,
2 Leeds Road, Wakefield, West
Yorkshire WF1 3JT
Telephone: 0924 373597

Age range: 3-11
No. of pupils: 175
Scholarships:
Religion: Non-denominational

Fees per term
Day: -£705
Weekly board: -
Full board: -

● Boy ● Girl ○ Co-ed
● Day ○ Week ○ Board

Head: Mr E J C Wallace BEd MA

Cliff School is small, friendly and caring with a strong academic tradition and great stress is placed on the social and moral development of the child. The size of the school and the family atmosphere means that children are offered very personal attention; this, coupled with the courtesy engendered in the children leads to the vast majority gaining places at other independent schools. Boys from 3-9 years.

The Froebelian School

Address: Clarence Road,
Horsforth, Leeds, West
Yorkshire LS18 4LB
Telephone: 0532 583047

Age range: 3-11
No. of pupils: 192
Scholarships:
Religion: Non-denominational

Fees per term
Day: £458-£690
Weekly board: -
Full board: -

○ Boy ○ Girl ● Co-ed
● Day ○ Week ○ Board

Head: Mr J Tranmer

The Froebelian School will celebrate its eightieth anniversary in 1993 with the opening of a new adventure challenge area. Tradition and a commitment to excellence are the hallmarks of a school which enjoys an unrivalled reputation locally. Most pupils gain scholarships or places at the prestigious independent schools at age 11.

Fulneck Boys' School

Address: Pudsey, West Yorkshire LS28 8DT

Telephone: 0532 571864

Head: Mr I D Cleland

Age range: 7-18
No. of pupils: 335
Scholarships:
Religion: Moravian

Fees per term
Day: £1113-£1337
Weekly board: £1861-£2288
Full board: £2102-£2591

● Boy ○ Girl ○ Co-ed
● Day ● Week ● Board

Fulneck Boys' School is part of The Fulneck School Foundation and shares a lovely valley site with its sister school. There is one boarding house and a joint (co-educational) sixth form. The curriculum is rich and broad and there is also provision for special needs

Fulneck Girls' School

Address: Fulneck, Pudsey, West Yorkshire LS28 8DS

Telephone: 0532 362214

Head: Mrs B A Heppell

Age range: 3-18
No. of pupils: 416
Scholarships: Yes
Religion: Moravian

Fees per term
Day: £495-£1250
Weekly board: £1955-£2200
Full board: £2105-£2350

○ Boy ● Girl ○ Co-ed
● Day ● Week ● Board

The school is an 18th Century Moravian Foundation open to pupils of all faiths and backgrounds. Set in beautiful surroundings yet close to motorways and airport. Providing a traditional academic education based on Christian values with a wide range of sporting and musical activities; there is a joint sixth form with Fulneck Boys' School. Two scholarships at 11+ are awarded for academic excellence.

Gateways

Address: Harewood, Leeds, West Yorkshire LS17 9LE

Telephone: 0532 886345

Head: Miss L M Brown

Age range: 4-18
No. of pupils: 360
Scholarships: Yes
Religion: Non-denominational

Fees per term
Day: £670-£1030
Weekly board: -
Full board: -

○ Boy ● Girl ○ Co-ed
● Day ○ Week ○ Board

Close to Leeds, the school enjoys rural and urban amenities. Broad curriculum leads to A Level and beyond. Individual care develops confidence and ambition to aim high. Choirs, teams, expeditions, orchestra, clubs and drama develop life long leisure and sporting interests.

Ghyll Royd School

Address: Grove Road, Ilkley, West Yorkshire LS29 9QE

Telephone: 0943 607657

Head: Mrs E Shepherd

Age range: 3-11
No. of pupils: 115
Scholarships:
Religion: Christian

Fees per term
Day: £305-£895
Weekly board: -
Full board: -

● Boy ○ Girl ○ Co-ed
● Day ○ Week ○ Board

Ghyll Royd expects total effort in class and in games. Boys are prepared for competitive entry to grammar, other independent and maintained schools. Sport includes athletics, badminton, cricket, cross-country, football, hockey, rugby, swimming, short- and lawn tennis. The school is privately owned and has provided a sound education to the boys of Ilkley and district for over 100 years.

Gleddings School

Address: Birdcage Lane,
Halifax, West Yorkshire
HX3 0JB
Telephone: 0422 354605

Age range: 3-11
No. of pupils: 140
Scholarships:
Religion: Non-denominational

Fees per term
Day: £430-£720
Weekly board: -
Full board: -

Boy ○ Girl ○ Co-ed ●
Day ● Week ○ Board ○

Head: Mrs I M Brearly

The aim, throughout the school, is that each child may recieve the maximum amount of individual tuition from experienced and qualified staff. The emphasis is on formal teaching but the children are also encouraged to study freely and independently. Pupils are given as broad a based education as is possible in preparation for entrance examinations for other schools.

Heathfield Rishworth School

Address: Oldham Road,
Rishworth, Selby Bridge, West
Yorkshire HX6 4QF
Telephone: 0422 823564

Age range: 4-11
No. of pupils: 150
Scholarships: Yes
Religion: Church of England

Fees per term
Day: £715-£1315
Weekly board: -
Full board: -£2545

Boy ○ Girl ○ Co-ed ●
Day ● Week ○ Board ●

Head: Mr P J Searle

The children are taught a general course by class teachers. Mainly traditional teaching methods are employed, with the basic academic disciplines such as spelling and arithmetical tables receiving proper emphasis. The curriculum is broad and varied. Heathfield is well equipped and pupils have access to computers and many other facilities.

Hipperholme Grammar School *

Address: Bramley Lane,
Hipperholme, Halifax, West
Yorkshire HX3 8JE
Telephone: 0422 202256

Age range: 11-18
No. of pupils: 380
Scholarships: Yes
Religion: Christian

Fees per term
Day: £960-
Weekly board: -
Full board: -

Boy ○ Girl ○ Co-ed ●
Day ● Week ○ Board ○

Head: Mr C C Robinson

Founded in 1648 for local boys, the school now serves a large area of Calderdale Kirklees and Bradford. It is small enough for all to be involved and noticed yet large enough to offer a full range of GCSE's and A Levels. Recent developments include a sports hall and Technology Centre.

Inglebrook

Address: Northgate Close,
Pontefract, West Yorkshire
WF8 1HJ
Telephone: 0977 700120

Age range: 3-11
No. of pupils: 250
Scholarships:
Religion: Christian

Fees per term
Day: £475-£504
Weekly board: -
Full board: -

Boy ○ Girl ○ Co-ed ●
Day ● Week ○ Board ○

Head: Mrs J S Bellamy

Inglebrook caters for boys and girls from 3-11. The pre-schoolers attend part-time initially, moving on to full time at age 4. We have a caring family atmosphere and encourage our pupils to live up to our motto of 'Striving for Excellence.'

YORKSHIRE (WEST) 571

Kays' College

Address: New North Road, Huddersfield, West Yorkshire HD1 5NE
Telephone: 0484 531835

Head: Mrs E J Jackson

Age range: 9-16
No. of pupils: 110
Scholarships: Yes
Religion: Non-denominational

Fees per term
Day: £665-£875
Weekly board: -
Full board: -

○ Boy ○ Girl ● Co-ed
● Day ○ Week ○ Board

For further information and a prospectus, please contact the school.

Keighley Preparatory School

Address: West Cliffe, Skipton Road, Keighley, West Yorkshire BD21 2TA
Telephone: 0535 602773

Head: Mr A M Russel

Age range: 4-11
No. of pupils: 100
Scholarships:
Religion: Non-denominational

Fees per term
Day: £640-
Weekly board: -
Full board: -

○ Boy ○ Girl ● Co-ed
● Day ○ Week ○ Board

For further information and a prospectus, please contact the school.

Leeds Girls' High School *

Address: Headingley Lane, Leeds, West Yorkshire LS6 1BN
Telephone: 0532 744000

Head: Miss P A R Randall

Age range: 3-18
No. of pupils: 980
Scholarships: Yes
Religion: Non-denominational

Fees per term
Day: £651-£1274
Weekly board: -
Full board: -

● Boy ● Girl ○ Co-ed
● Day ○ Week ○ Board

High academic standards are maintained amidst a happy and stimulating environment in which each individual is valued. There is a wide range of extra-curricular activities. Facilities include 10 science laboratories, a computer room with 32 work stations, a music and drama centre and modern sports complex with indoor swimming pool. Junior boys are accepted in the school.

Leeds Grammar School *

Address: Moorland Road, Leeds, West Yorkshire LS6 1AN
Telephone: 0532 433417

Head: Mr B W Collins

Age range: 7-18
No. of pupils: 1144
Scholarships: Yes
Religion: Non-denominational

Fees per term
Day: £1052-£1277
Weekly board: -
Full board: -

● Boy ○ Girl ○ Co-ed
● Day ○ Week ○ Board

Academically, we have a consistently high level of examination sucess. In order to achieve this we recognise the importance of the care of the individual because we believe that boys will only develop if they are happy and self confident. Our teaching staff exhibit great commitment and this coupled with first class facilities provide our boys with the environment in which they can flourish.

Licensed Victuallers' School p717

Address: Clevedon House, Ben Rhydding, Ilkley, West Yorkshire LS29 8BJ
Telephone: 0943 608515

Head: Mr I A Mullins

Age range: 3-16
No. of pupils: 210
Scholarships: Yes
Religion: Non-denominational

Fees per term
Day: £350-£1205
Weekly board: £925-£2185
Full board: £925-£2185

Boy ○ Girl ○ Co-ed ●
Day ● Week ● Board ●

The Licensed Victuallers' School is a co-educational school offering day and boarding for pupils aged 7-16. The school also caters for day pupils aged 3-7 in the nursery and infant departments. The school boasts a superb site with developing facilities. A new sports complex has recently been completed. Outdoor pursuits are a key feature of the school.

Malsis

Address: Cross Hills, West Yorkshire BD20 8DT
Telephone: 0535 633027

Head: Mr J D C Clark

Age range: 7-13
No. of pupils: 185
Scholarships:
Religion: Church of Egnland

Fees per term
Day: -
Weekly board: -
Full board: £2350-

Boy ● Girl ○ Co-ed ○
Day ○ Week ○ Board ●

A boys' preparatory school in delightful countryside on the Yorkshire/Lancashire border. The staff/pupil ratio is less than 1:10. Forty scholarships have been won in the last five years. There is a special needs unit. Music, drama, art, design technology, information technology, sport and outdoor pursuits are central to school life. Malsis is an educational trust.

Moorlands School

Address: Foxhill, Leeds, West Yorkshire LS16 5PF
Telephone: 0532 785286

Head: Mr N H Woolnough

Age range: 3-13
No. of pupils: 190
Scholarships: Yes
Religion: Non-denominational

Fees per term
Day: £468-£1050
Weekly board: -
Full board: -

Boy ○ Girl ○ Co-ed ●
Day ● Week ○ Board ○

Founded in 1898, the school has a graduate and experienced staff of 18 and consists of children who live in the city of Leeds and neighbourhood. Pupils are prepared for independent senior and grammar schools by means of CEE. and other entry examinations. Over the last 10 years 20 scholarships have been gained and over 250 pupils successfully prepared for senior schools.

Muslim Girls School

Address: Ryan Street, Bradford, West Yorkshire BD5 7DQ
Telephone: 0274 734693

Head: Mrs N A Mirza

Age range: 11-18
No. of pupils: 120
Scholarships:
Religion: Muslim

Fees per term
Day: -£500
Weekly board: -
Full board: -

Boy ○ Girl ○ Co-ed ●
Day ● Week ○ Board ○

For further information and a prospectus, please contact the school.

Netherleigh School

Address: Lynton Drive,
Heaton, Bradford, West
Yorkshire BD9 5JH
Telephone: 0274 543162

Age range: 3-8
No. of pupils: 76
Scholarships:
Religion: Non-denominational

Fees per term
Day: £325-£560
Weekly board: -
Full board: -

Boy / Girl / **Co-ed**
Day / Week / Board

Head: Mr P Nelson

For further information and a prospectus, please contact the school.

North Leeds and St Edmunds Hall Preparatory School

Address: Gledhow Lane,
Leeds, West Yorkshire LS8 1RT
Telephone: 0532 668005

Age range: 3-11
No. of pupils: 245
Scholarships: Yes
Religion: Non-denominational

Fees per term
Day: £315-£765
Weekly board: -
Full board: -

Boy / Girl / **Co-ed**
Day / Week / Board

Head: Mr J E W Lynch

The school is situated in the pleasant suburb of Roundhay. Its aims are to provide a happy and hard-working environment in which the children can reach their full potential. Pupils are prepared for entry to independent senior schools

Queen Elizabeth Grammar School (Junior Section)

Address: 156 Northgate,
Wakefield, West Yorkshire
WF1 3QY
Telephone: 0924 373943

Age range: 7-11
No. of pupils: 250
Scholarships: Yes
Religion: Non-denominational

Fees per term
Day: £873-£910
Weekly board: -
Full board: -

Boy / Girl / Co-ed
Day / Week / Board

Head: Mr M Bisset

The school was founded in 1591 and is a member of IAPS. The school offers bursaries. There is a wide curriculum, and strong accent is put on sports. Many extra-curricular activities are available such as: choir, computer club, drama and music, as well as sailing. The school has also an indoor swimming pool.

Queen Elizabeth Grammar School *

Address: 154 Northgate,
Wakefield, West Yorkshire
WF1 3QY
Telephone: 0924 373943

Age range: 11-18
No. of pupils: 750
Scholarships: Yes
Religion: Non-denominational

Fees per term
Day: £1221-£1221
Weekly board: -
Full board: -

Boy / Girl / Co-ed
Day / Week / Board

Head: Mr R P Mardling

Queen Elizabeth is a boys school founded in 1591. It is a member of HMC and has a long tradition of high standard education. There are both scholarships and bursaries available and these are awarded each year to most deserving pupils. The school also caters for certain disabilities - please contact the headmaster for details.

Richmond House School

Address: 170 Otley Road,
Leeds, West Yorkshire
LS16 5LG
Telephone: 0532 752670

Head: Mrs E E Cleland

Age range: 3-11
No. of pupils: 296
Scholarships:
Religion: Christian

Fees per term
Day: £629-£972
Weekly board: -
Full board: -

Co-ed, Day

The school is situated in two Victorain houses with a wide range of other buildings which together include a library, practical rooms for art, science, design and technology, music, information technology and a gymnasium, thus enabling a wide and varied curriculum. The school has a distinguished academic record and aims to develop individual potential, encourage self discipline and widen childrens' horizons.

Rishworth School

Address: Ripponden, West Yorkshire HX6 4QA

Telephone: 0422 822217

Head: Mr M J Elford BSc

Age range: 3-18
No. of pupils: 630
Scholarships: Yes
Religion: Church of England

Fees per term
Day: £715-£1430
Weekly board: -
Full board: £2545-£2765

Co-ed, Day, Week, Board

Co-educational day and boarding (from 11) school for those aged between 4 and 18 years. Set in a beautiful Pennine valley, the school caters for 630 pupils with 100 in the sixth form. Full preparation for GCSE, A Level and university entrance is provided. Some scholarships and bursaries are available.

Rosemeade

Address: 12 Bank End Lane,
Almondbury, Huddersfield,
West Yorkshire HD5 8ES
Telephone: 0484 421076

Head: Miss H M Hebblethwaite

Age range: 3-11
No. of pupils: 90
Scholarships:
Religion: Non-denominational

Fees per term
Day: £600-£600
Weekly board: -
Full board: -

Co-ed, Day

Rosemeade is a small, family school offering a sound education to boys and girls from the age of 3.5 years to 11. Our aim is to develop each child to his or her maximum potential in a caring atmosphere, to think independently and to be courteous in their dealings with others.

Rossefield School

Address: Parsons Road,
Heaton, Bradford, West
Yorkshire BD9 4AY
Telephone: 0274 543549

Head: Mr P Nelson

Age range: 4-11
No. of pupils: 242
Scholarships:
Religion: Non-denominational

Fees per term
Day: £342-£615
Weekly board: -
Full board: -

Co-ed, Day

For further information and a prospectus, please contact the school.

YORKSHIRE (WEST) 575

Shaw House School

Address: 150/2 Wilmer Road, Bradford, West Yorkshire BD9 4AH
Telephone: 0274 496299

Head: Mrs J B Eccles

Age range: 9-16
No. of pupils: 90+
Scholarships:
Religion: Non-denominational

Fees per term
Day: £725-£850
Weekly board: -
Full board: -

● Boy ● Girl ○ Co-ed
● Day ○ Week ○ Board

This is a small, friendly school offering a full range of subjects up to GCSE Level. Pupils may sit up to 11 subjects. Many extra-curricular activities including Duke of Edinburgh Award. Science and IT are very strong, also music and drama. Very small classes. Visits welcome at any time by prior arrangement. Excellent results.

Silcoates School *

Address: Wrenthorpe, Wakefield, West Yorkshire WF2 0PD
Telephone: 0924 291614

Head: Mr A T Spillane

Age range: 7-18
No. of pupils: 560
Scholarships: Yes
Religion: United Reformed

Fees per term
Day: £998-£1580
Weekly board: -
Full board: -

○ Boy ○ Girl ● Co-ed
● Day ○ Week ○ Board

Silcoates was founded in 1820 for the sons of ministers and missionaries in the Congregational Church. While it retains strong links with the original church (now the United Reformed Church), the school welcomes boys and girls of all denominations and faiths. The school is situated in 55 acres of grounds, a mile outside Wakefield and within easy reach of the M1 and M62.

St Agnes' PNEU School

Address: 25 Burton Crescent, Headingley, Leeds, West Yorkshire LS6 4DN
Telephone: 0532 786722

Head: Mrs J P Corfield

Age range: 3-9
No. of pupils: 45
Scholarships:
Religion: Church of England

Fees per term
Day: £585-£788
Weekly board: -
Full board: -

● Boy ● Girl ○ Co-ed
● Day ○ Week ○ Board

St Agnes' School is one of the PNEU schools founded by Charlotte Mason in the 1880s. It has kept pace with modern trends but still reflects the founder's ideas that education should be rigorous but enjoyable and caring and that parents should play an active part. There is a wide curriculum based on self expression in reading and writing. Boys 3-8, girls 3-9.

St David's School

Address: Royds Mount, Marsh, Huddersfield, West Yorkshire HD1 4QX
Telephone: 0484 424549

Head: Mr B Marxham

Age range: 3-16
No. of pupils: 350
Scholarships:
Religion: Non-denominational

Fees per term
Day: £455-£950
Weekly board: -
Full board: -

○ Boy ○ Girl ● Co-ed
● Day ○ Week ○ Board

For further information and a prospectus, please contact the school.

St Hilda's School

Address: Dovecote Lane, Horbury, Wakefield, West Yorkshire WF4 6BB
Telephone: 0924 260706

Head: Mrs A R Mackenzie

Age range: 3-11
No. of pupils: 133
Scholarships:
Religion: Non-denominational

Fees per term
Day: -£745
Weekly board: -
Full board: -

For further information and a prospectus, please contact the school. Boys 3-7, girls 3-11.

St Joseph's School

Address: Cunliffe Road, Bradford, West Yorkshire BD8 7AP
Telephone:

Head: Miss M C Flair

Age range: 13-19
No. of pupils: 710
Scholarships:
Religion: Roman Catholic

Fees per term
Day: -
Weekly board: -
Full board: -

For further information and a prospectus, please contact the school.

Wakefield Girls' High School

Address: Wentworth Street, Wakefield, West Yorkshire WF1 2QS
Telephone: 0924 372490

Head: Mrs P A Langham

Age range: 4-18
No. of pupils: 1000
Scholarships: Yes
Religion: Unaffiliated

Fees per term
Day: £777-£1113
Weekly board: -
Full board: -

The school occupies an extensive site in a conservation area near the centre of Wakefield. A steady programme of building and the acquisition of nearby property have enabled the school to anticipate and meet the needs of succeeding generations of pupils. The science and technology centre was opened in 1990 and contains classrooms, suites of specialist facilities with resource and preparatory areas, design, technology etc.

Wakefield Independent School

Address: Chapelthorpe Hall, Church Lane, Wakefield, West Yorkshire WF4 3JB
Telephone: 0924 258857

Head: Mrs M Milner BSc(Hons)

Age range: 4-16
No. of pupils: 200
Scholarships:
Religion: Non-denominational

Fees per term
Day: £525-£735
Weekly board: -
Full board: -

Founded in 1980, Wakefield Independent School is firmly established with a proven record of success. The emphasis of the school is to provide a traditional balanced education, sufficiently progressive to bring out the best in every pupil. There is a friendly community spirit throughout the school and an air of cheerful hard work pervades the classrooms.

YORKSHIRE (WEST) 577

Wakefield Tutorial School

Address: Commercial Street,
Morley, West Yorkshire
LS27 8HY
Telephone: 0532 534033

Head: Mr R Favell

Age range: 4-11
No. of pupils: 80
Scholarships:
Religion: Christian

Fees per term
Day: £400-£450
Weekly board: -
Full board: -

○ ○ ●
Boy Girl Co-ed
● ○ ○
Day Week Board

Founded in 1937 the school aims to provide a progressive and balanced type of education which will help to develop an active mind and a sound character.

Westville House School

Address: 9 Westville Road,
Ilkley, West Yorkshire LS29 9AJ
Telephone: 0943 608053

Head: Dr M B Tait MA, DPhil(Oxon), ARCO

Age range: 3-13
No. of pupils: 85
Scholarships: Yes
Religion: Christian

Fees per term
Day: £395-£750
Weekly board: -
Full board: -

○ ○ ●
Boy Girl Co-ed
● ○ ○
Day Week Board

Westville's classes are restricted to a maximum of fifteen. This allows us to combine the highest academic standards with a happy family atmosphere. There is a wide range of sporting, musical and other extra-curricular activities. The flourishing parents' committee organises social and fund-raising events. Two scholarships are offered annually.

Woodhouse Grove School *

Address: Apperley Bridge,
Bradford, West Yorkshire
Telephone: 0532 502477

Head: Mr D W Welsh

Age range: 7-18
No. of pupils: 730
Scholarships: Yes
Religion: Methodist

Fees per term
Day: £1310-£1525
Weekly board: -
Full board: £2200-£2550

○ ○ ●
Boy Girl Co-ed
● ● ●
Day Week Board

Entry to the Preparatory School, Bronte House at age 7, and to the main school at 11, 13 and Sixth Form. Both schools are situated in spacious, well-kept grounds within easy reach of Bradford and Leeds. Music and art awards available. Sport is played to a high competitive level.

Zakaria Muslim Girls' High School

Address: 111 Warwick Road,
Batley, West Yorkshire
WF17 6AJ
Telephone:

Head:

Age range: 11-16
No. of pupils:
Scholarships:
Religion:

Fees per term
Day: -
Weekly board: -
Full board: -

○ ● ○
Boy Girl Co-ed
● ○ ○
Day Week Board

For further information and a prospectus, please contact the school.

CLWYD

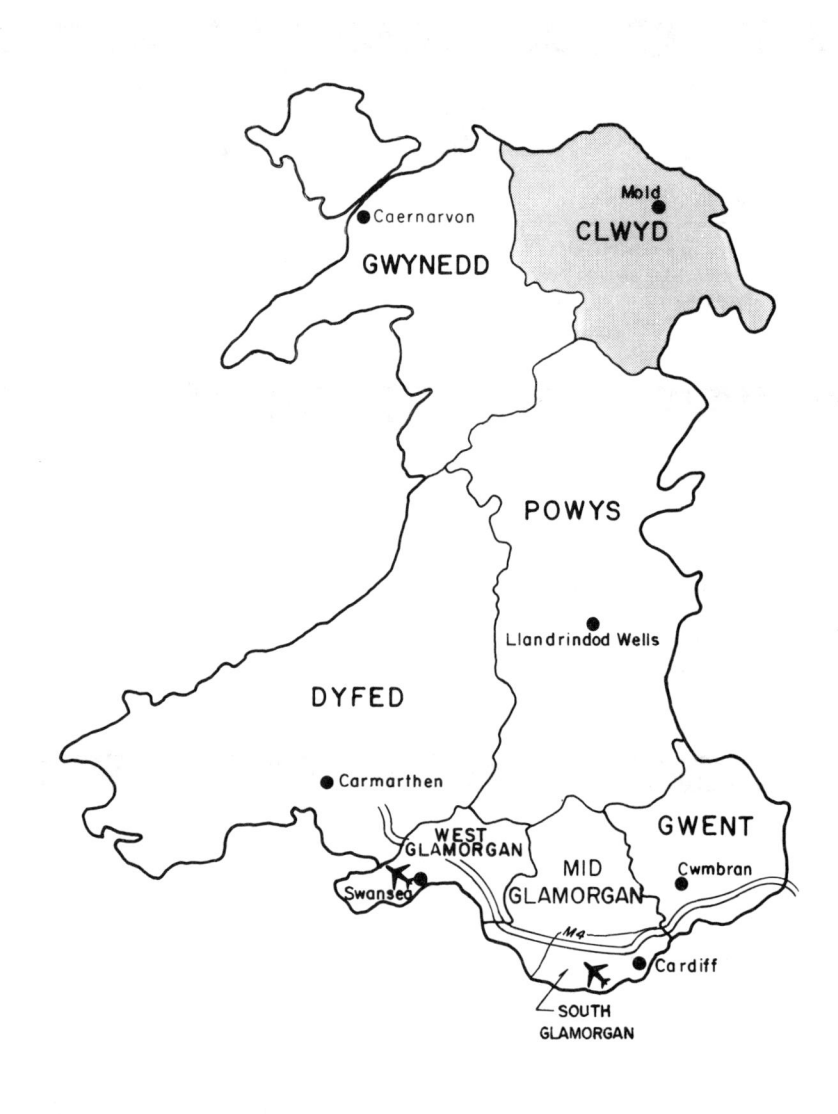

CLWYD 579

Arden School

Address: Llanfair D C,
Wrexham Road, Ruthin,
Clwyd LL15 2RT
Telephone: 0824 702833

Head: Mrs S Grace

Age range: 3-11
No. of pupils: 72
Scholarships:
Religion: Non-denominational

Fees per term
Day: £600-
Weekly board: -
Full board: -

○ ○ ● Boy Girl Co-ed
● ○ ○ Day Week Board

A co-educational preparatory school for boys and girls aged 3-11 years. The school is based in a large Victorian house set in beautiful mature grounds which afford ample facilities for all sporting activites. The school's reputation has been firmly founded on its academic success which is largely achieved by the installation of traditional educational and social aims and values.

Fairholme Preparatory

Address: The Mount, Mount Road, St Asaph, Clwyd

Telephone: 0745 583505

Head: Mrs M M Cashman

Age range: 3-11
No. of pupils: 140
Scholarships:
Religion: Christian

Fees per term
Day: £325-£550
Weekly board: -
Full board: -

○ ○ ● Boy Girl Co-ed
● ○ ○ Day Week Board

A Christian, academic and disciplined education is provided and high standards are expected from the pupils in their behaviour and personal relationships. Every effort is made to make children eager to learn, confident and articulate with enquiring minds and good study skills. They are encouraged to become aware of other people's needs and to develop their own abilities to the full in a friendly caring atmosphere.

Howell's School *

Address: Denbigh, Clwyd LL16 3EN

Telephone: 0745 813631

Head: Mrs M Steel

Age range: 2-18
No. of pupils: 350
Scholarships: Yes
Religion: Anglican

Fees per term
Day: £753-£1935
Weekly board: -
Full board: -£2990

○ ● ○ Boy Girl Co-ed
● ○ ● Day Week Board

For further information and a prospectus, please contact the school.

Lindisfarne College

Address: Wynnstay Hall,
Ruabon, Wrexham, Clwyd
LL14 6LD
Telephone: 0978 810407

Head: Mr K Morgan

Age range: 5-18
No. of pupils: 200
Scholarships: Yes
Religion: Christian

Fees per term
Day: £700-£1667
Weekly board: -
Full board: -£3109

○ ○ ● Boy Girl Co-ed
● ○ ● Day Week Board

Lindisfarne offers a broad curriculum for pupils from the age of four to university entrance level. The exceptionally low staff/pupil ratio allows the full academic, aesthetic, spiritual and physical potential of each child to be developed fully. Our pupils enjoy close individual support from their personal tutor.

Lyndon School

Address: Grosvenor Road, Colwyn Bay, Clwyd LL29 7YF

Telephone: 0492 532347

Head: Mrs A Ashworth

Age range: 3-11
No. of pupils: 114
Scholarships:
Religion: Church in Wales

Fees per term
Day: £630-£805
Weekly board: -
Full board: -

○ Boy ○ Girl ● Co-ed
● Day ○ Week ○ Board

For further information and a prospectus, please contact the school.

Northgate Preparatory School

Address: Russell Road, Rhyl, Clwyd LL18 3DD

Telephone: 0745 342510

Head: Mr P G Orton

Age range: 4-11
No. of pupils: 80
Scholarships:
Religion: Non-denominational

Fees per term
Day: £425-£475
Weekly board: -
Full board: -

○ Boy ○ Girl ● Co-ed
● Day ○ Week ○ Board

The school was established in 1977 and is a member of ISAI. The school has a wide curriculum and a number of extra-curricular activities such as bell-ringing, chess, computer club and drama circle.

There are also some Welsh language classes available.

Penrhos College * p718, p747

Address: Colwyn Bay, Clwyd LL28 4DA

Telephone: 0492 530333

Head: Mr N C Peacock

Age range: 11-18
No. of pupils: 260
Scholarships: Yes
Religion: Non-denominational

Fees per term
Day: £1795-£1920
Weekly board: £2480-£2805
Full board: £2480-£2805

○ Boy ● Girl ○ Co-ed
● Day ● Week ● Board

Penrhos College is a forward looking, friendly, boarding and day school for girls. Seaside location. Strong academically with consistently good results. Intensive courses in France and Germany are integral parts of language curriculum. We offer a unique extra-curricular programme designed to broaden horizons and develop the confidence that brings success.

Penrhos College Junior School p719

Address: Oak Drive, Colwyn Bay, Clwyd LL29 7YW

Telephone: 0492 530170

Head: Mr R G Dell MA(Oxon)

Age range: 2-11
No. of pupils: 130
Scholarships:
Religion: Non-denominational

Fees per term
Day: £520-£1190
Weekly board: £1830-£2065
Full board: £1830-£2065

○ Boy ○ Girl ● Co-ed
● Day ● Week ● Board

Penrhos Junior School combines a family atmosphere with high academic standards. Small groups and specialist teaching. Encourgement of creativity and enquiring minds. Stress on three Rs as foundation for all other activities. Regular projects, day and overnight study trips, ballet, judo, skiing, orienteering, etc. Most activities included in fees. Overlooks the sea and stands in extensive grounds.

Ruthin School

Address: Ruthin, Clwyd LL15 1EE

Telephone: 0824 702543

Head: Mr F R Ullmann MA

Age range: 6-18
No. of pupils: 223
Scholarships: Yes
Religion: Non-denominational

Fees per term
Day: £650-£1945
Weekly board: £1895-£2295
Full board: £1895-£2825

○ ○ ● Boy Girl Co-ed
● ● ● Day Week Board

The school is within an easy reach from motorway and rail network and only one hour's drive from Manchester Airport. In junior school literacy and numeracy are central to the curriculum with regular assessments for each child. In senior school, each pupil has a housemaster, and progress is discussed on a one-to-one basis. Guidance and support are always available.

Rydal * p720, p748

Address: Colwyn Bay, Clwyd LL29 7BT

Telephone: 0492 530155

Head: Mr N W Thorne

Age range: 7-18
No. of pupils: 600
Scholarships: Yes
Religion: Methodist

Fees per term
Day: £686-£2137
Weekly board: -
Full board: £1223-£2811

○ ○ ● Boy Girl Co-ed
● ○ ● Day Week Board

Rydal, with preparatory and senior sctions on the same campus, and an integrated syllabus, offers continuity throughout Key Stages 2, 3 and 4 (7 to 18 years). The school shares an inspiring coastal and mountain environment with the convenience of dual carriageway access to Chester, Manchester and the motorway network. Rydal is fully co-educational for both boarding and day pupils.

Rydal Preparatory School

Address: Pwyllycrochan, Colwyn Bay, Clwyd LL29 7BP

Telephone: 0492 530381

Head: Mr D A Armstrong BSc

Age range: 7-13
No. of pupils: 246
Scholarships: Yes
Religion: Methodist

Fees per term
Day: £686-£1857
Weekly board: -
Full board: £1223-£2442

○ ○ ● Boy Girl Co-ed
● ○ ● Day Week Board

For further information and a prospectus, please contact the school.

St Brigid's School

Address: Plas-yn-Green, Denbigh, Clwyd Ll16 4BS

Telephone:

Head:

Age range: 4-18
No. of pupils:
Scholarships:
Religion:

Fees per term
Day: -
Weekly board: -
Full board: -

○ ○ ● Boy Girl Co-ed
● ● ○ Day Week Board

For further information and a prospectus, please contact the school. Boys 4-11, girls 4-18

DYFED

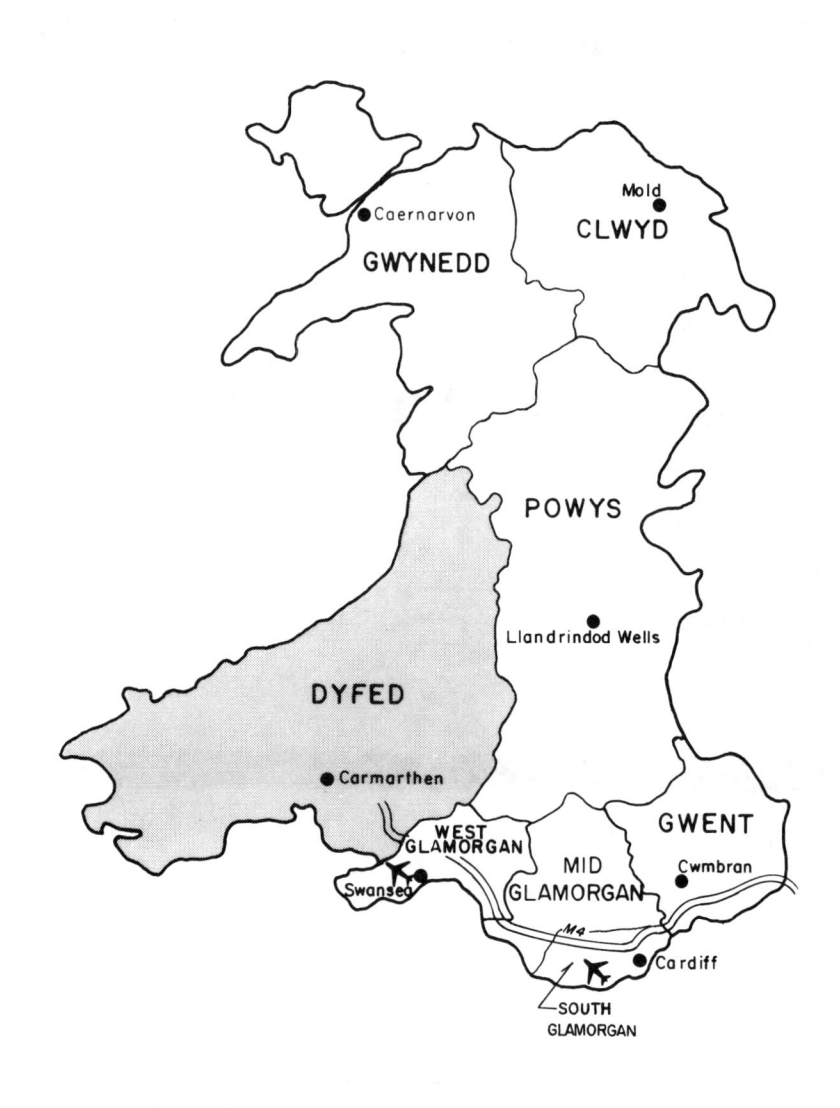

Haylett Grange PNEU School

Address: Haverfordwest, Dyfed SA62 4LA

Telephone: 0437 762472

Head: Mrs J M Sharp

Age range: 2-11
No. of pupils: 150
Scholarships:
Religion: Non-denominational

Fees per term
Day: £300-£400
Weekly board: -
Full board: -

Boy ○ Girl ○ Co-ed ●
Day ● Week ○ Board ○

The school is set in well kept grounds and surrounded by fields on the outskirts of Haverfordwest. We follow a wide programme of subjects. As our classes are small, each child can reach their full potential and take art in all school activities. Games, swimming and gymnastics form an integral part of the day.

Llandovery College *

Address: Llandovery, Dyfed SA20 0EG

Telephone: 0550 20315

Head: Dr C E Evans

Age range: 11-18
No. of pupils: 230
Scholarships: Yes
Religion: Church in Wales

Fees per term
Day: £1560-£1753
Weekly board: £2277-£2687
Full board: £2277-£2687

Boy ○ Girl ○ Co-ed ●
Day ● Week ● Board ●

A fully co-educational Headmasters' Conference member, offering boarding, weekly boarding and day education. Small classes, excellent facilities, including a new sports centre and Apple computer network means every pupil is fully extended. Over 75% proceed to higher education. A full curriculum including business computer studies and department of sports science. Welsh a language option.

Nant-Y-Cwm Steiner School

Address: Llanycefn, Clunderwen, Dyfed SA66 7QJ

Telephone: 0437 563640

Head: College of Teachers

Age range: 4-14
No. of pupils: 87
Scholarships:
Religion: Christian

Fees per term
Day: -
Weekly board: -
Full board: -

Boy ○ Girl ○ Co-ed ●
Day ● Week ○ Board ○

Nant-Y-Cwm, situated in rural west Wales, is part of the world Steiner School movement, which strives to educate the whole child as a human being endowed with body, soul and spirit. Nant-Y-Cwm offers a balance of academic and artistic activities and emphasises individual development. Children leave at 14 to take GCSEs at either local schools or Steiner boarding schools. No set fees, but a contribution system operates.

Netherwood School

Address: Saundersfoot, Dyfed SA69 9BE

Telephone: 0834 811057

Head: Mr F W Edwards

Age range: 3-16
No. of pupils: 180
Scholarships: Yes
Religion: Non-denominational

Fees per term
Day: £520-£845
Weekly board: £1340-£1540
Full board: £1600-£1800

Boy ○ Girl ○ Co-ed ●
Day ● Week ● Board ●

Netherwood stands in beautiful grounds in the midst of pine trees, three quarters of a mile from the sea. Pupils are prepared for 12 GCSE subjects. Entrance by interview before 11 years and examination after. Music, dancing and riding are optional. Sea bathing during the summer term. Games include rugby, soccer, cricket, athletics, judo, swimming, hockey, rounders, basketball and netball.

St Michael's School

Address: Bryn, Llanelli, Dyfed SA14 9TU

Telephone: 0554 820325

Age range: 7-18
No. of pupils: 300
Scholarships: Yes
Religion: Non-denominational

Fees per term
Day: £755-£880
Weekly board: -
Full board: -

Boy ○ Girl ○ Co-ed ●
Day ● Week ○ Board ○

Head: Mr J R Vaughan Evans BA(Hons) CertEd

With small classes and a traditional approach to learning most children have a far better chance of developing their potential. The emphasis is on a caring, sympathetic approach within the framework of sensible discipline and good standards of behaviour.

GWENT

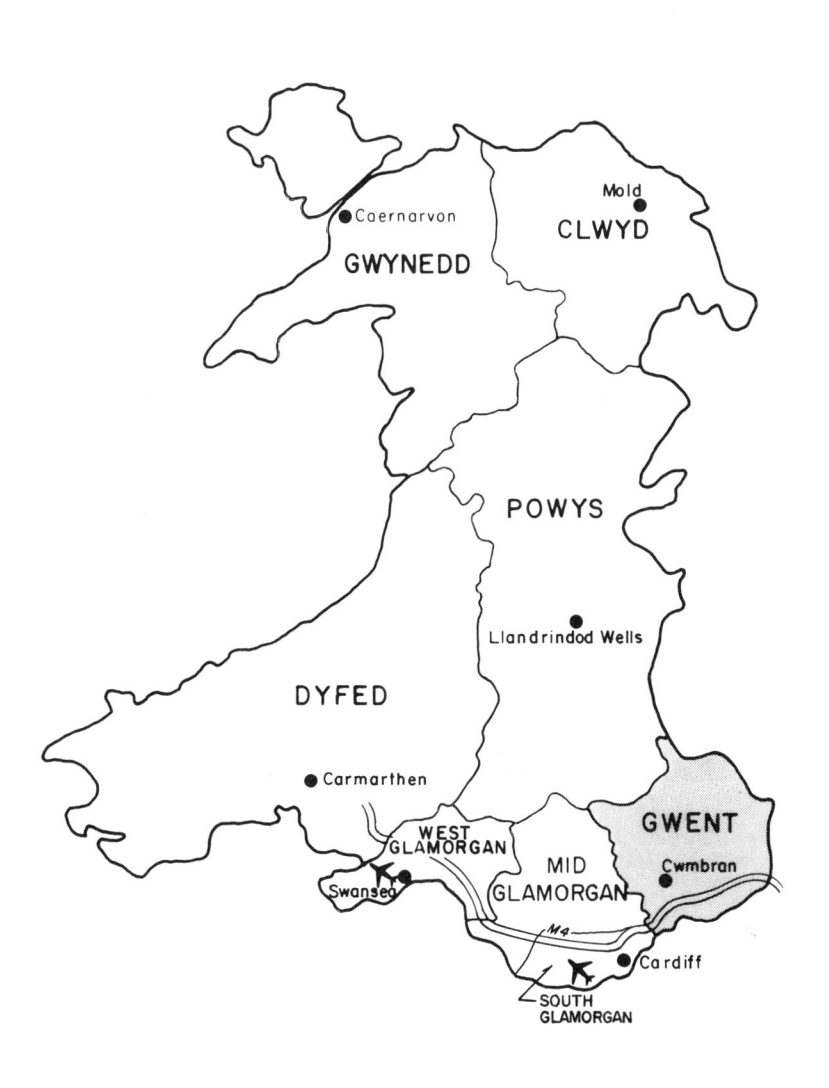

Agincourt School

Address: Dixton Lane, Dixton, Monmouth, Gwent NP5 3SJ
Telephone: 0600 713970
Head: Mrs F M Newman

Age range: 3-11
No. of pupils: 70
Scholarships:
Religion: Non-denominational

Fees per term
Day: £340-£640
Weekly board: -
Full board: -

Boy ○ Girl ○ Co-ed ●
Day ● Week ○ Board ○

Agincourt School is a family school catering for children from 3 to 11+. The school has a record of: academic success; high standards in art and music; enthusiastic sport; careful remedial teaching where required. Parent co-operation plays a large part in the continuing success of the school.

Haberdashers' Monmouth School for Girls *

Address: Hereford Road, Monmouth, Gwent NP5 3XT
Telephone: 0600 714214
Head: Mrs D L Newman BA

Age range: 7-18
No. of pupils: 635
Scholarships: Yes
Religion:

Fees per term
Day: £960-£1277
Weekly board: £2004-£2321
Full board: £2004-£2321

Boy ○ Girl ● Co-ed ○
Day ● Week ● Board ●

High academic standards and achievements with ample scope also for creative arts: drama, music and design workshops. Situated in historic town in Wye Valley. Extensive grounds: playing fields, covered swimming pool, sports hall on site. Sixth form scholarship. Examination for entry at eleven. The preparatory department (Inglefield House) has separate entry.

Monmouth School *

Address: Monmouth, Gwent NP5 3XP
Telephone: 0600 713143
Head: Mr R D Lane

Age range: 11-18
No. of pupils: 540
Scholarships: Yes
Religion: Church of England

Fees per term
Day: £1476-£1476
Weekly board: £2458-£2458
Full board: £2458-£2458

Boy ● Girl ○ Co-ed ○
Day ● Week ● Board ●

A school of the Haberdashers' Company situated in the beautiful Wye Valley. Entry at 11+, 13+ and post GCSE. Scholarships, bursaries and assisted places available. The school has strong academic and sporting traditions, with modern facilities for music, arts, science and technology. Numerous extra-curricular activities include drama, debating and Duke of Edinburgh Awards.

Rougemont School

Address: Kingshill, Stow Hill, Newport, Gwent NP9 4EA
Telephone: 0633 211813
Head: Mr G Sims BA

Age range: 3-18
No. of pupils: 535
Scholarships: Yes
Religion:

Fees per term
Day: £860-£1248
Weekly board: -
Full board: -

Boy ○ Girl ○ Co-ed ●
Day ● Week ○ Board ○

The school has a caring family atmosphere with small class sizes. This has led to some outstanding achievements with a recent Financial Times survey placing Rougemont 38th out of 500 independent schools based on A Level results. The junior school (aged 7-10) will be moving to our new 50 acre site at Llantarnam Hall in September 1992.

GWENT 587

Seddon House School

Address: Dingestow Court, Dingestow, Monmouth, Gwent NP5 4YD
Telephone: 0600 83353

Head: Mrs L S Keywood

Age range: 4-8
No. of pupils: 43
Scholarships:
Religion: Non-denominational

Fees per term
Day: -
Weekly board: -
Full board: -

○ ○ ●
Boy Girl Co-ed
● ○ ○
Day Week Board

For fees, further information and a prospectus, please contact the school.

St John's-on-the-Hill

Address: Tutshill, Chepstow, Gwent

Telephone: 0291 622045

Head: Mr J Quash

Age range: 2-13
No. of pupils: 194
Scholarships: Yes
Religion: Non-denominational

Fees per term
Day: £460-£1508
Weekly board: £2040-
Full board: £2040-

○ ○ ●
Boy Girl Co-ed
● ● ●
Day Week Board

St John's is a co-educational, boarding and day school set in 6.5 acres of grounds within two miles of the Severn Bridge and the M4/M5 Motorway systems. There are around 200 children in the school ranging from the age of 2 (in the nursery) to 13+. The school has a dedicated and well-qualified staff, small classes and a happy, caring atmosphere.

Troy School †

Address: Troy House, Monmouth, Gwent

Telephone:

Head:

Age range: 10-17
No. of pupils:
Scholarships:
Religion:

Fees per term
Day: -
Weekly board: -
Full board: -

○ ○ ○
Boy Girl Co-ed
○ ○ ●
Day Week Board

A boarding school for maladjusted pupils, for further information and a prospectus, please contact the school.

GWYNEDD

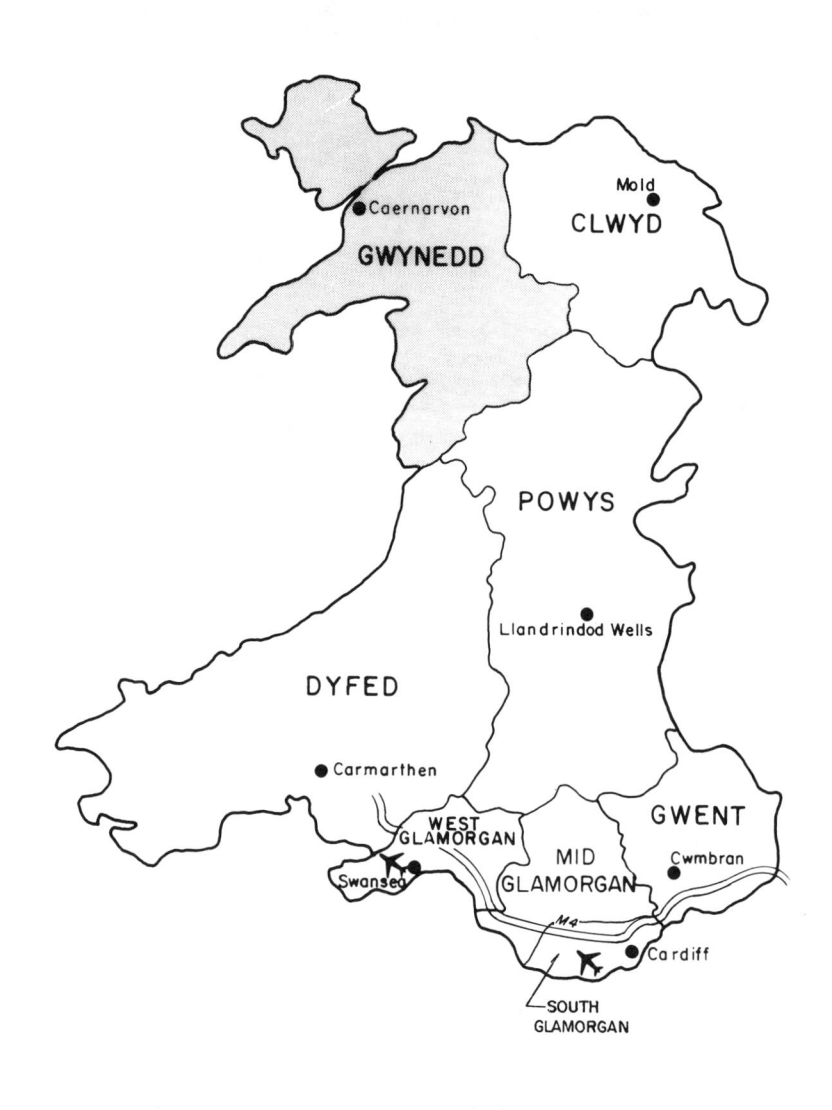

Hillgrove School

Address: Ffriddoedd Road, Bangor, Gwynedd LL57 2TW

Telephone: 0248 353568

Heads: Mr & Mrs J G J Porter

Age range: 3-16
No. of pupils: 160
Scholarships:
Religion: Non-denominational

Fees per term
Day: £496-£790
Weekly board: -
Full board: -

Boy ○ Girl ○ Co-ed ●
Day ● Week ○ Board ○

The School is able to integrate new children into the school at virtually any time during the school year, and to offer the indivdual attention needed to ensure that there is minimal setback in educational progress. This can be of especial value where parents are seconded or posted to the North Wales area at short notice. Apart from well qualified staff, Hillgrove has also invested in up-to-date teaching facilities.

Indefatigable School

Address: Plas Llanfair, Llanfairpwll, Anglesey, Gwynedd LL61 6NT

Telephone: 0248 714338

Head: Mr P D White

Age range: 11-16
No. of pupils: 136
Scholarships: Yes
Religion: Church of England

Fees per term
Day: -
Weekly board: -
Full board: -£2250

Boy ● Girl ○ Co-ed ○
Day ○ Week ○ Board ●

Indefatigable School is ideal for a boy who wishes to work and play hard. The curriculum is broad and sporting activities exceptionally wide ranging. Over the last three years an extensive modernisation and building programme has provided educational, boarding and sporting facilities of the highest standards. Fees are subsidised and bursaries are available.

Snowdonia Steiner School

Address: Tan-Yr-Allt, Tremadog, Gwynedd LL49 9RG

Telephone: 0766 512068

Head: The Management Group

Age range: 4-14
No. of pupils: 70
Scholarships:
Religion: Christian

Fees per term
Day: £262-£575
Weekly board: -
Full board: -

Boy ○ Girl ○ Co-ed ●
Day ● Week ○ Board ○

Education in a Rudolf Steiner (Waldorf) school recognises the inner development of the child, seeks to nourish it with appropriate experiences at each stage through a wide ranging curriculum, that treats all subjects as inter-dependent, so that science, art and craft weave a meaningful whole with the whole human being as the focus.

St David's College

Address: Llandudno, Gwynedd

Telephone: 0492 875974

Head: Mr W G Seymour

Age range: 11-18
No. of pupils: 215
Scholarships: Yes
Religion: Non-denominational

Fees per term
Day: £1750-£1750
Weekly board: £2710-£2710
Full board: £2710-£2710

Boy ● Girl ○ Co-ed ○
Day ● Week ● Board ●

St David's is spectacularly situated on the edge of Snowdonia and provides a broad curriculum to deliver education in its widest sense. Small classes and sound discipline ensure high academic attainment. We are renowned for our wide range and high standard of outdoor pursuits in addition to the traditional range of sports and extra-curricular activities.

St Gerard's School Trust

Address: Ffriddoedd Road, Bangor, Gwynedd LL57 2EL

Telephone: 0248 351656

Head: Miss A Parkinson

Age range: 4-18
No. of pupils: 330
Scholarships:
Religion: Roman Catholic

Fees per term
Day: £545-£790
Weekly board: -
Full board: -

Boy / Girl / **Co-ed**
Day / Week / Board

St Gerard's is a small school standing in its own grounds. It is a Catholic, co-educational day school, welcoming also pupils of other faiths. The curriculum is a comprehensive one and academic achievements are significantly above the national average. A friendly atmosphere prevails in which self-discipline and respect for others is fostered.

Tower House School

Address: Barmouth, Gwynned LL42 1RF

Telephone: 0341 280127

Head: Mrs J Pugh

Age range: 4-17
No. of pupils: 147
Scholarships:
Religion:

Fees per term
Day: -
Weekly board: -
Full board: -

Boy / Girl / **Co-ed**
Day / Week / Board

For further information and a prospectus, please contact the school.

Treffos Independent School

Address: Llansadwrn, Anglesey, Gwynedd LL59 5DC

Telephone: 0248 712322

Head: Dr S Humphreys

Age range: 3-11
No. of pupils: 100
Scholarships:
Religion: Church of England

Fees per term
Day: £595-
Weekly board: -
Full board: -

Boy / Girl / **Co-ed**
Day / Week / Board

Treffos, located in a beautiful country house set in 8 acres of lawn and woodland, is the only independent school in Anglesey. The school pursues a broad curriculum and seeks to develop the talents and potential of all pupils so that they have a strong foundation on which to build at the secondary stage. Welsh is taught as a second language.

MID GLAMORGAN

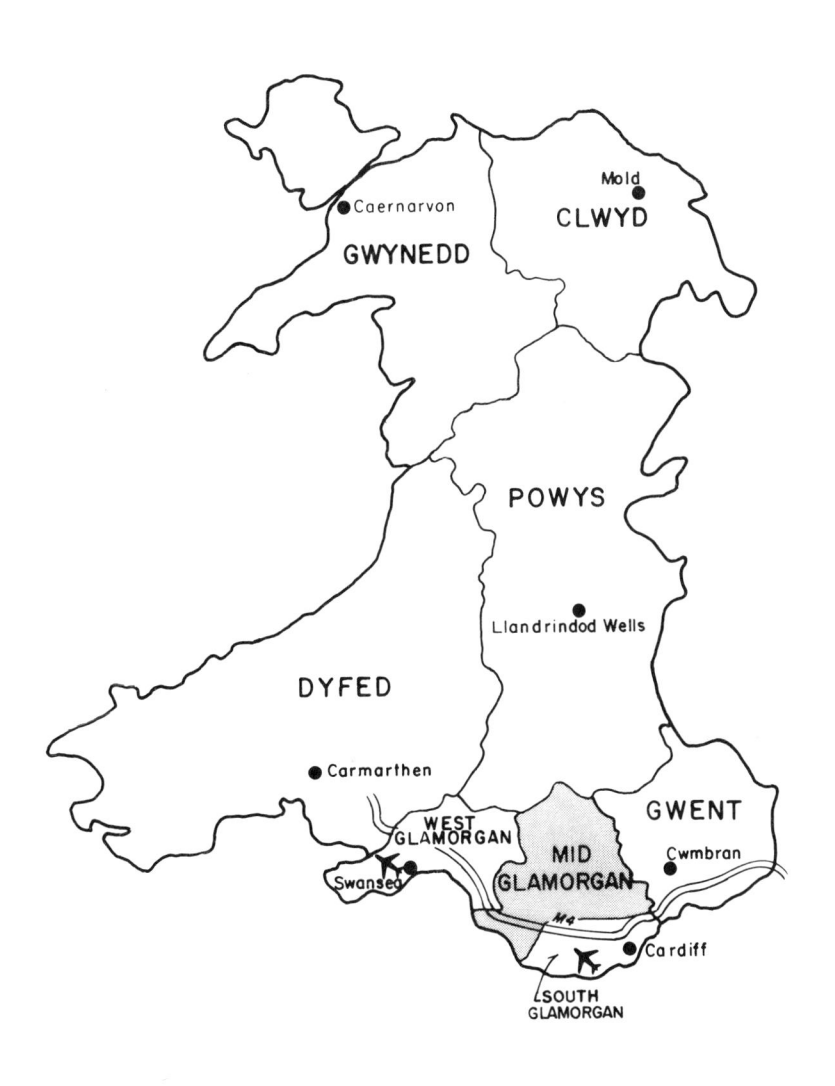

Craig-Y-Parc School †

Address: Pentrych, Cardiff, Mid Glamorgan CF4 8NB

Telephone: 0222 890397

Head: Mrs H Fowler

Age range: 3-16
No. of pupils: 45
Scholarships:
Religion: Non-denominational

Fees per term
Day: -
Weekly board: -
Full board: -

○ Boy ○ Girl ● Co-ed
● Day ● Week ● Board

The school is run by the Spastic Society, for further details and fees please contact the school.

St Clares Convent School

Address: Newton, Porthcawl, Mid Glamorgan CF36 5NR.

Telephone: 0656 782509

Head: Miss A Jarrett

Age range: 4-18
No. of pupils: 450
Scholarships: Yes
Religion: Roman Catholic

Fees per term
Day: £570-£950
Weekly board: -
Full board: -

○ Boy ○ Girl ● Co-ed
● Day ○ Week ○ Board

For further information and a prospectus, please contact the school.

St John's School

Address: Newtown, Porthcawl, Mid Glamorgan

Telephone: 0656 783404

Head: Mr A J Hughes

Age range: 3-13
No. of pupils: 180
Scholarships:
Religion:

Fees per term
Day: £795-£1085
Weekly board: £1665-£1665
Full board: £1845-£1845

○ Boy ○ Girl ● Co-ed
● Day ● Week ● Board

A flourishing family-sized school with a lively atmosphere.

Wynclif Christian School

Address: Wyndham Street, Machen, Mid-Glamorgan

Telephone:

Head:

Age range: 3-10
No. of pupils:
Scholarships:
Religion:

Fees per term
Day: -
Weekly board: -
Full board: -

○ Boy ○ Girl ● Co-ed
● Day ○ Week ○ Board

For further information and a prospectus, please contact the school.

POWYS

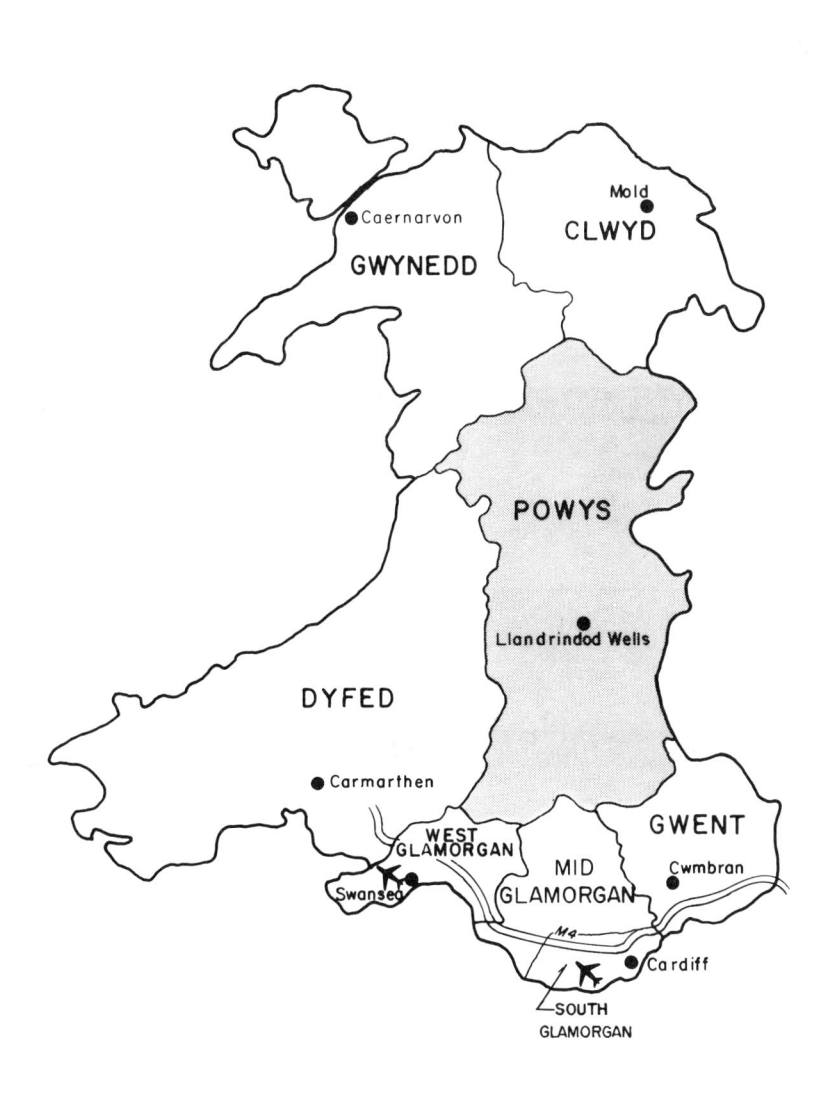

Christ College *

Address: Brecon, Powys LD3 8AG

Telephone: 0874 623359

Head: Mr S W Hockey

Age range: 11-18
No. of pupils: 360
Scholarships: Yes
Religion: Anglican

Fees per term
Day: £2055-£2055
Weekly board: -
Full board: £2712-£2712

● Boy ● Girl ○ Co-ed
● Day ○ Week ● Board

Christ College is a small school situated in an area of outstanding beauty within the Brecon Beacons National Park. Staffing ratio of 1:9, average class size 12. Extremely wide range of extra-curricular activities. Academic results at GCSE and A Level, as well as sporting records and music, are very notable indeed. Boys 11-18, girls 16-18.

Powis College

Address: Brookland Hall, Welshpool, Powys SY21 9BU

Telephone: 0938 552326

Head: Mr M J Hutchinson

Age range: 9-17
No. of pupils: 40
Scholarships:
Religion: Church of England

Fees per term
Day: -
Weekly board: -
Full board: -

○ Boy ○ Girl ● Co-ed
● Day ○ Week ● Board

For fees, further information and a prospectus, please contact the school.

St David's Ursuline Convent School

Address: Brecon, Powys LD3 7DN

Telephone: 0874 622080

Head: Sr Anne Conway

Age range: 7-18
No. of pupils: 180
Scholarships: Yes
Religion: Roman Catholic

Fees per term
Day: -
Weekly board: -
Full board: -

● Boy ● Girl ○ Co-ed
● Day ○ Week ● Board

For fees, further information and a prospectus, please contact the school. Boys 7-11, girls 7-18

St Mary's RC-Aided Primary School

Address: Newtown, Powys

Telephone:

Principal

Age range: 4-11
No. of pupils:
Scholarships:
Religion:

Fees per term
Day: -
Weekly board: -
Full board: -

○ Boy ○ Girl ● Co-ed
● Day ○ Week ○ Board

For further information and a prospectus, please contact the school.

Tregynon Hall School †

Address: Tregynon, Newtown, Powys SY16 3PG

Telephone:

Principal:

Age range: 9-18
No. of pupils: 24
Scholarships:
Religion:

Fees per term
Day: -
Weekly board: -
Full board: -

● Boy ○ Girl ○ Co-ed
● Day ○ Week ● Board

For further information and a prospectus, please contact the school.

SOUTH GLAMORGAN

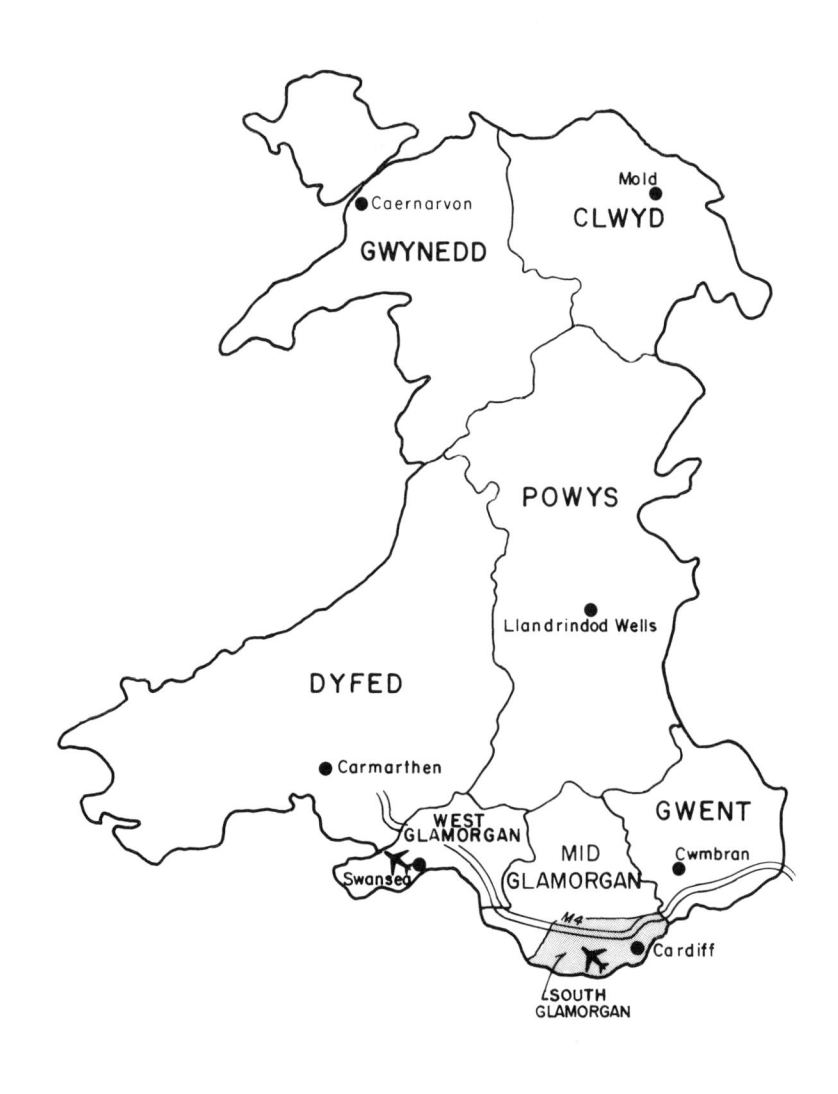

The Cathedral School

Address: Llandaff, South Glamorgan CF5 2YH

Telephone: 0222 563179

Head: Mr J C Knapp

Age range: 4-13
No. of pupils: 375
Scholarships: Yes
Religion: Non-denominational

Fees per term
Day: £875-£1285
Weekly board: -
Full board: -£2000

Boy ○ Girl ○ Co-ed ●
Day ● Week ○ Board ●

A member of the Western Division Woodard Corporation, of IAPS, ISIS and the CSA, a co-educational school in 15 acres of parkland. Pupils aged 4-13, with boarding pupils from the age of 7. The average size of classes is 15 with a staff-pupil ratio of 1-12. In the last five years we have gained 80 academic, music and art awards to independent secondary schools.

Elm Tree House

Address: 27 Palace Road, Llandaff, Cardiff, South Glamorgan CF5 2AG
Telephone: 0222 563386

Headmistress: Mrs C M L Thomas

Age range: 3-11
No. of pupils: 140
Scholarships:
Religion: Non-denominational

Fees per term
Day: £675-£755
Weekly board: -
Full board: -

Boy ○ Girl ● Co-ed ●
Day ● Week ○ Board ○

Elm Tree House School was founded in 1922. It is a small school, with a caring, stimulating and lively environment. The encouraging guidance of the staff helps the children to appreciate the joy of learning and the understanding of themselves and their abilities. Small classes, allow the staff to give maximum amount of attention to each child, affording excellent results into senior schools.

Headlands School †

Address: Paget Place, Penarth, South Glamorgan CF6 1YY

Telephone: 0222 709771

Head: Mr P Caradice

Age range: 11-16
No. of pupils: 40
Scholarships:
Religion: Methodist

Fees per term
Day: -
Weekly board: -
Full board: -

Boy ○ Girl ○ Co-ed ●
Day ● Week ○ Board ●

Headlands is a special school for children with severe social, emotional and educational problems offering education and child care of the highest quality. Class groups are small (approximately 5-6) with the emphasis on remediation, but also with opportunities for external examinations. Living accommodation is in small, off-campus units, with specific therapeutic aims.

Howell's School *

Address: Cardiff Road, Llandaff, Cardiff, South Glamorgan CF5 2YD
Telephone: 0222 562019

Head: Mrs J Fitz

Age range: 4-18
No. of pupils: 680
Scholarships: Yes
Religion: Non-denominational

Fees per term
Day: £880-£1148
Weekly board: £2413-
Full board: £2413-

Boy ○ Girl ● Co-ed ○
Day ● Week ○ Board ○

Howell's School, Llandaff, an academically selective independent school for 684 girls aged 5-18, is a member of GPDST. The school offers an exciting and stimulating learning environment, a caring comunity, a broad and balanced curriculum with an extensive range of extra-curricular activities. Facilities include a sixth form complex, a music house, seven science laboratories, computer rooms and lots more.

Kings College

Address: Wordsworth Avenue, Roath, Cardiff, South Glamorgan CF2 1AR
Telephone: 0222 482854

Age range: 3-16
No. of pupils: 210
Scholarships: Yes
Religion: Non-denominational

Fees per term
Day: £600-£950
Weekly board: -
Full board: -

Boy ○ Girl ○ Co-ed ●
Day ● Week ○ Board ○

Head: Mr R N Griffin BA BEd

Kings College is an independent non-denominational school offering an academic education to boys and girls aged 3-16. The school has achieved chartered status under the Mensa scheme which identifies those schools with proven success in the education of children of high intelligence. The school prides itself on its high standards of individual attention and pastoral care.

Lamorna School

Address: 15 Church Road, Whitchurch, Cardiff, South Glamorgan CF4 2DX
Telephone: 0222 623015

Age range: 2-11
No. of pupils: 100
Scholarships:
Religion: Non-denominational

Fees per term
Day: £450-£680
Weekly board: -
Full board: -

Boy ○ Girl ○ Co-ed ●
Day ● Week ○ Board ○

Head: Mrs R M Evans

For further information and a prospectus, please contact the school.

Monkton House Educational Trust

Address: 19 The Parade, Cardiff, South Glamorgan CF2 3UA
Telephone: 0222 483130

Age range: 11-18
No. of pupils: 170
Scholarships: Yes
Religion: Non-denominational

Fees per term
Day: £1104-£1158
Weekly board: -
Full board: -

Boy ○ Girl ○ Co-ed ●
Day ● Week ○ Board ○

Head: Mr T Cox

Monkton School and College have a proven track record of success in preparing students for GCSE and A Level examinations. Pupils of all ethnic and religious backgrounds are welcomed and attitudes of respect and self-discipline are actively encouraged. The school and college boast specialist teaching facilities for art, science, technology and computing. The teaching staff are highly qualified and widely experienced.

Monkton Junior School

Address: Clive Hall, Clive Road, Llandaff, South Glamorgan CF5 1GN
Telephone: 0222 388445

Age range: 3-11
No. of pupils: 120
Scholarships:
Religion: Multi-faith

Fees per term
Day: £638-£907
Weekly board: -
Full board: -

Boy ○ Girl ○ Co-ed ●
Day ● Week ○ Board ○

Head: Mr P Cox

Monkton Junior School offers a warm, friendly and disciplined society in which the pupils can develop intellectually and socially. Great importance is attached to academic progress and development of awareness and concern for other people and each other. The small class numbers involved allow a family atmosphere to develop. Close co-ordination with the senior school ensures continuity of education.

New College School

Address: Bute Terrace, Cardiff, South Glamorgan CF1 2TS

Telephone: 0222 463355

Head: Mr W Hoole

Age range: 5-16
No. of pupils: 140
Scholarships: Yes
Religion: Christian

Fees per term
Day: £730-£1525
Weekly board: -
Full board: -

Boy ○ Girl ○ Co-ed ●
Day ● Week ○ Board ○

The school has been conceived as bringing together, in a convenient place, the best that can be offered in the name of Education as we near the 21st Century. The school is in search of academic excellence and will allow no pupil to neglect either his academic and moral growth or his artistic and physical development. The school accepts any pupil who has a reasonable hope of achieving academic success.

Our Lady's Convent School

Address: The Walk, Cardiff, South Glamorgan CF2 3AG

Telephone: 0222 490907

Head: Sister Mary Antoinetta Toomey BEd MPhil

Age range: 3-16
No. of pupils: 234
Scholarships: Yes
Religion: Roman Catholic

Fees per term
Day: £595-£780
Weekly board: -
Full board: -

Boy ● Girl ● Co-ed ○
Day ● Week ○ Board ○

A sound general education with thorough training in basic subjects and skills. Opportunities for developing talent in art and craft, music, sport and drama. French is taught throughout the school. BDA trained teacher for pupils with special needs. Before and after school care facility. Excellent GCSE results are consistently achieved in a caring environment. Boys 3-8, girls 3-16.

St Illtyd's High School

Address: Cardiff, South Glamorgan CF3 8XQ

Telephone:

Head: Mr P A Gamble

Age range: 11-16
No. of pupils: 720
Scholarships:
Religion: Roman Catholic

Fees per term
Day: -
Weekly board: -
Full board: -

Boy ○ Girl ○ Co-ed ●
Day ● Week ○ Board ○

For further information and a prospectus, please contact the school.

St John's College

Address: Greenway Road, Cardiff, South Glamorgan CF3 8QR

Telephone: 0222 778936

Head: Dr D J Neville

Age range: 3-18
No. of pupils: 430
Scholarships: Yes
Religion: Roman Catholic

Fees per term
Day: £635-£820
Weekly board: -
Full board: -

Boy ○ Girl ○ Co-ed ●
Day ● Week ○ Board ○

For further information and a prospectus, please contact the school.

St Joseph's Convent School

Address: North Road, Cardiff, South Glamorgan CF4 3BL

Telephone: 0222 621491

Head: Sr Michael O'Driscoll

Age range: 3-11
No. of pupils: 120
Scholarships:
Religion: Roman Catholic

Fees per term
Day: -£585
Weekly board: -
Full board: -

Co-ed / Day

For further information and a prospectus, please contact the school.

Westbourne Primary School

Address: 12 Victoria Road, Penarth, South Glamorgan

Telephone:

Head:

Age range: 5-8
No. of pupils:
Scholarships:
Religion:

Fees per term
Day: -
Weekly board: -
Full board: -

Co-ed / Day

For further information and a prospectus, please contact the school.

Westbourne Schools

Address: 4 Hickman Road, Penarth, South Glamorgan

Telephone: 0222 707861

Head: Mr A J Bentley-Taylor

Age range: 3-16
No. of pupils: 208
Scholarships: Yes
Religion: Non-denominational

Fees per term
Day: £625-£1225
Weekly board: -
Full board: -

Co-ed / Day

Founded in 1896 in the small seaside town of Penarth, educating boys and girls 3-16 years. A well qualified and experienced staff work closely with the Headmaster to produce a caring and disciplined context. Excellent academic results. A wide range of sports facilities.

WEST GLAMORGAN

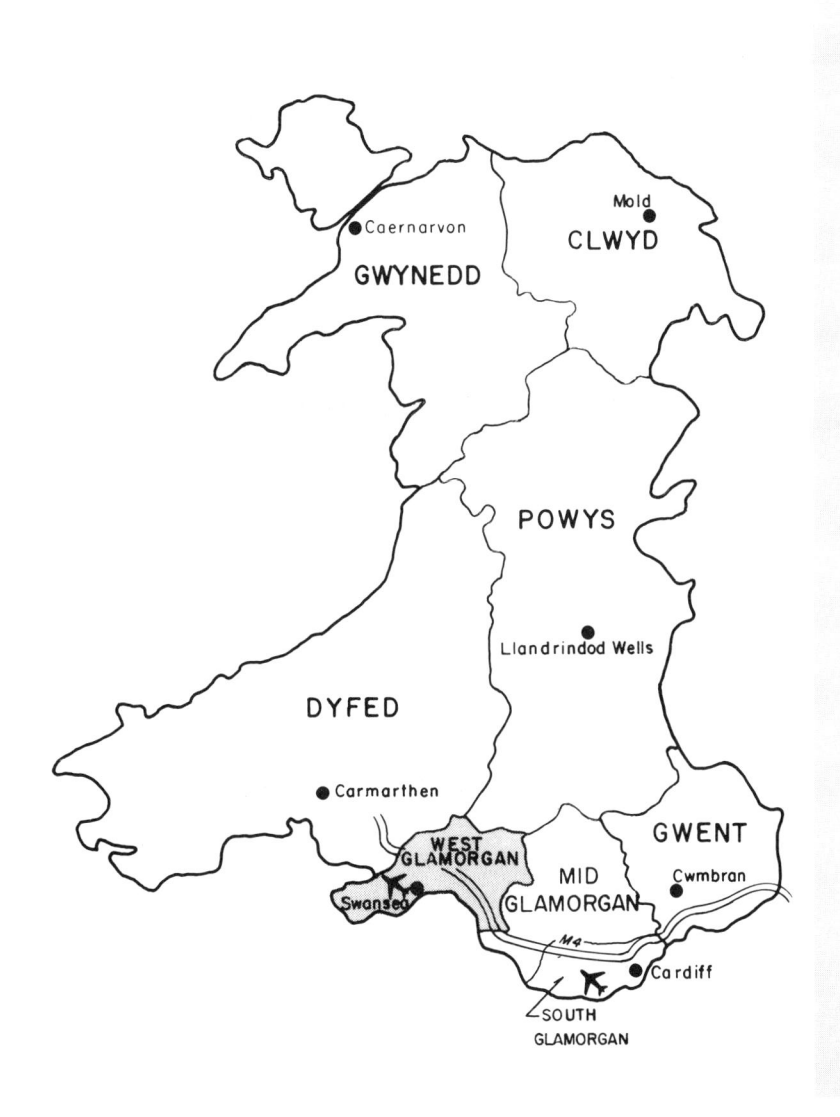

Craig-Y-Nos School

Address: Clyne Common, Bishopston, Swansea, West Glamorgan
Telephone: 044 128 4288

Head: Mr G W Fursland

Age range: 2-11
No. of pupils: 115
Scholarships:
Religion: Non-denominational

Fees per term
Day: £515-£695
Weekly board: -
Full board: -

○ ○ ●
Boy Girl Co-ed
● ○ ○
Day Week Board

An independent school in which pupils can achieve their potential and prepare themselves for secondary education in a pleasant, friendly atmosphere in a rural location, with an emphasis on individual needs.

Dumbarton House School

Address: Bryn-Y-Mor Hill, Swansea, West Glamorgan SA1 4QT
Telephone: 0792 472613

Heads: Mr A Thomas, Miss J Thomas

Age range: 2-16
No. of pupils: 200
Scholarships:
Religion: Non-denominational

Fees per term
Day: £450-£750
Weekly board: £1250-£1450
Full board: -

○ ○ ●
Boy Girl Co-ed
● ● ○
Day Week Board

The special aim of the school, is to prepare children for life, helping them to develop sound character and ensuring they are thoroughly grounded in all the usual subjects. In this school they are introduced into a community small enough to offer maximum individual attention and yet large enough for them to learn self discipline, responsibility, loyalty and initiative.

Emmanuel School

Address: Derwen Fawr, Sketty, Swansea, West Glamorgan SA2 8EB
Telephone: 0792 204035

Head: Mr G R Lippett BSc

Age range: 4-18
No. of pupils: 114
Scholarships: Yes
Religion: Non-denominational

Fees per term
Day: £520-£750
Weekly board: -
Full board: -

○ ○ ●
Boy Girl Co-ed
● ○ ○
Day Week Board

Emmanuel School is a branch of the Bible College of Wales and was founded in 1933. It offers education to day pupils from the locality. Its aim is to give a sound education for mind and body combined with the development of individual character and Christian standards. It follows the National Curriculum and enters pupils for GCSE and A Level with the MEG and WJEC examinations boards.

Ffynone House School

Address: 36 St James Crescent, Swansea, West Glamorgan SA1 6DR
Telephone: 0792 464967

Head: Mr J R Thomas BSc DipEd

Age range: 8-18
No. of pupils: 170
Scholarships: Yes
Religion: Church of England

Fees per term
Day: £760-£1100
Weekly board: -
Full board: -

○ ○ ●
Boy Girl Co-ed
● ○ ○
Day Week Board

For further information and a prospectus, please contact the school.

Oakleigh House School

Address: 38 Penlan Crescent, Uplands, Swansea, West Glamorgan
Telephone: 0792 298537

Head: Mrs H Evans

Age range: 4-11
No. of pupils: 184
Scholarships:
Religion: Non-denominational

Fees per term
Day: £605-£665
Weekly board: -
Full board: -

○ ○ ● Boy Girl Co-ed
● ○ ○ Day Week Board

Has a caring atmosphere and aims for high academic standards within a framework of firm discipline. Emphasis is placed on music and drama. The school choir has recently sung at the Royal Festival Hall and senior girls won the British Naturalists' Association Ward Cup 1991. The school has twice received a School's Curriculum Award for high standards and community links.

Stella Maris Primary School

Address: Easton Crescent, Swansea, West Glamorgan
Telephone:

Head:

Age range: 2-11
No. of pupils:
Scholarships:
Religion:

Fees per term
Day: -
Weekly board: -
Full board: -

○ ○ ● Boy Girl Co-ed
● ○ ○ Day Week Board

For further information and a prospectus, please contact the school.

BORDERS

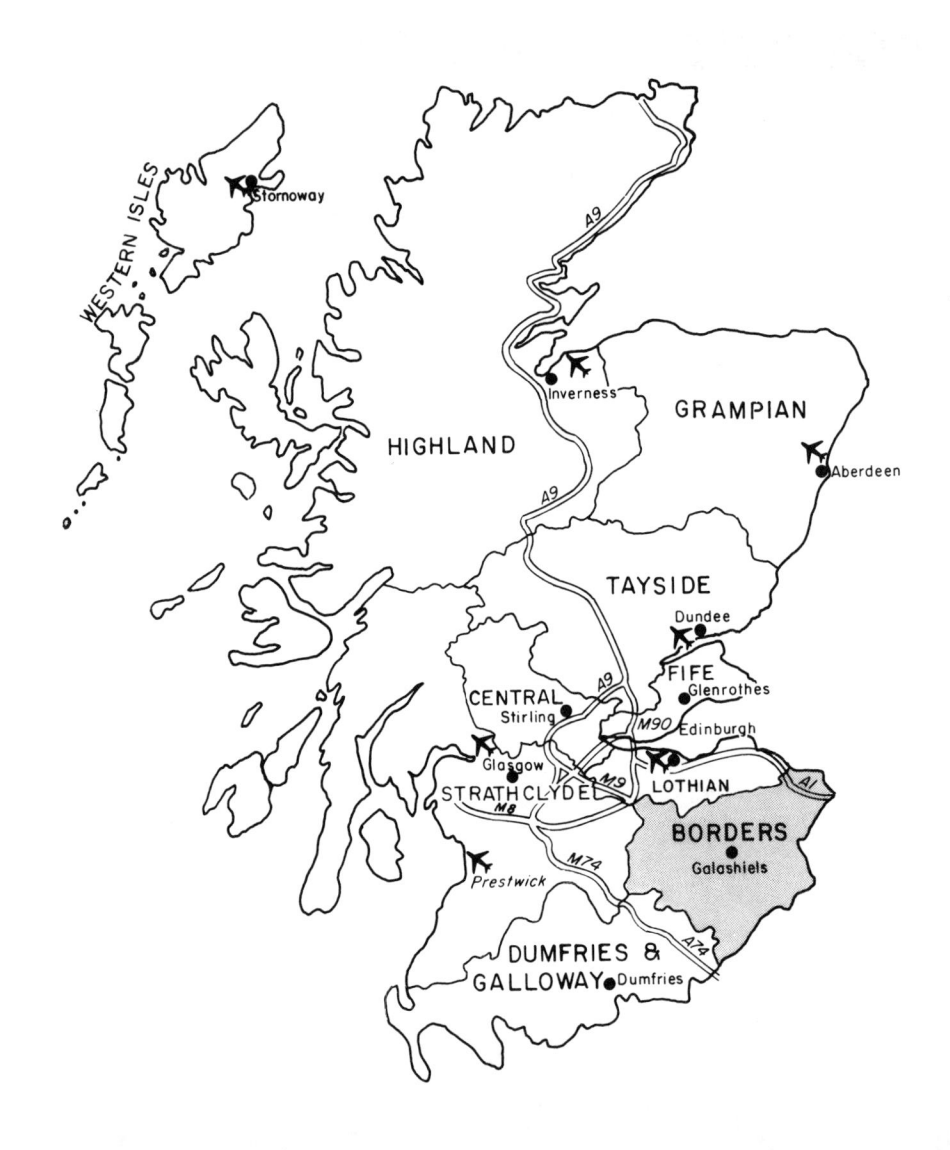

St Mary's School *

Address: Abbey Park, Melrose,
Borders TD6 9LN

Telephone:

Head: Mr R M Common MA

Age range: 4-13
No. of pupils: 90
Scholarships:
Religion:

Fees per term
Day: -
Weekly board: -
Full board: -

○ Boy ○ Girl ● Co-ed
● Day ○ Week ● Board

For further information and a prospectus, please contact the school.

CENTRAL

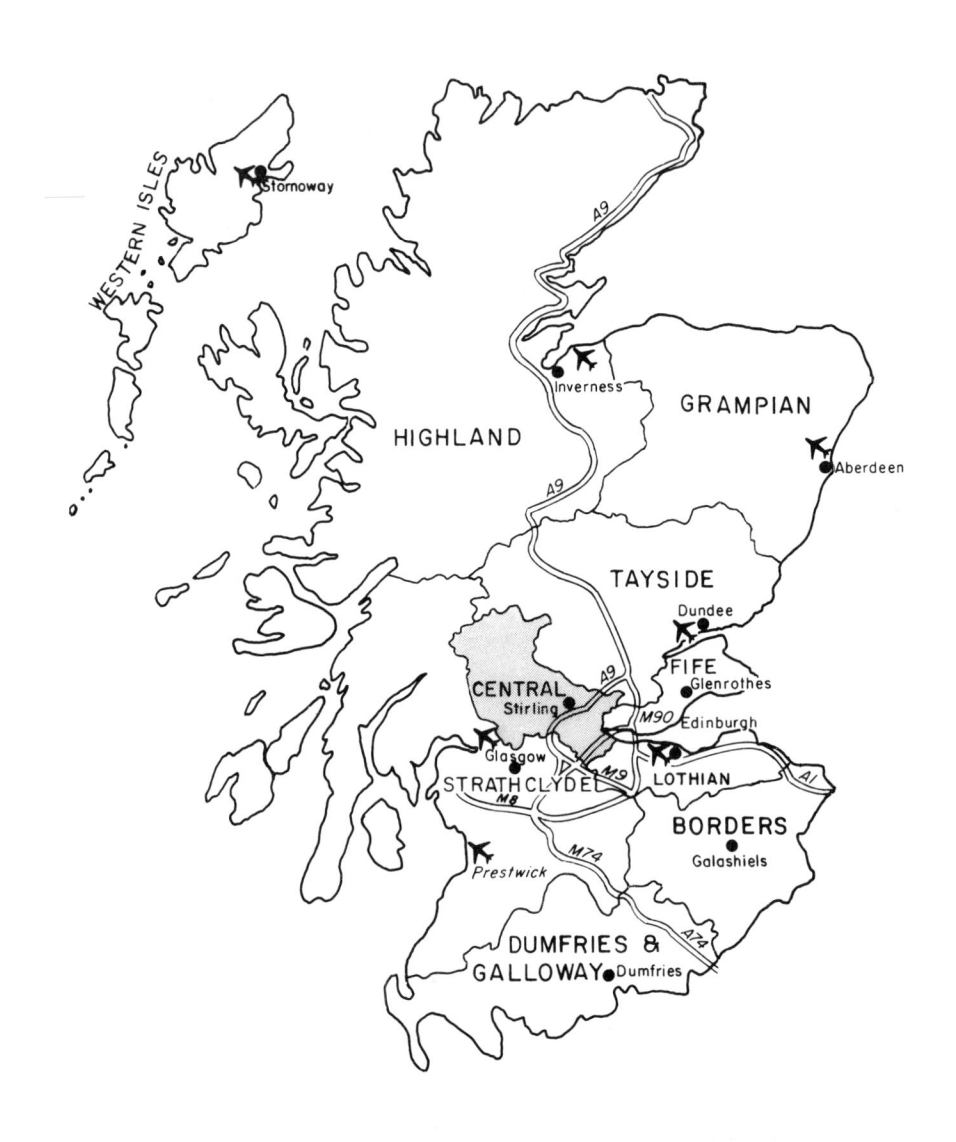

Beaconhurst Grange School *

Address: 52 Kenilworth Road, Bridge of Allan, Central FK9 4RR
Telephone: 0786 832146

Head: Mr R Clegg

Age range: 3-14
No. of pupils: 235
Scholarships: Yes
Religion: Non-denominational

Fees per term
Day: £820-£1245
Weekly board: -
Full board: -

Boy ○ Girl ○ Co-ed ●
Day ● Week ○ Board ○

Beaconhurst aims to provide a broadly based education within a happy but disciplined atmosphere. In September 1991 a senior department was opened which will offer a full course of secondary education through to university entrance by 1996. There is a wide range of sporting and other leisure activities to encourage pupils to develop worthwhile leisure time interests; these include choir, orchestra, brownies, cubs and handcrafts.

Dollar Academy *

Address: Dollar, Central FK14 7DU
Telephone: 0259 42511

Rector: Mr L Harrison

Age range: 5-18
No. of pupils: 1130
Scholarships: Yes
Religion: Church of Scotland

Fees per term
Day: £894-£1183
Weekly board: £2196-£2485
Full board: £2334-£2623

Boy ○ Girl ○ Co-ed ●
Day ● Week ● Board ●

Dollar Academy is situated in its extensive grounds in Central Scotland. Co-educational since its foundation (1820), Dollar combines strong local roots with international awareness. Boys and girls from five to university standard at eighteen experience: a powerful academic preparation; a rich sporting, artisitic and musical life; an exposure to a range of languages; a tradition of courtesy and friendliness.

Snowden School †

Address: 31 Spittal Street, Stirling, Central FT8 1DU
Telephone: 0786 473449

Head: Mr A W MacIntyre BSc

Age range: 11-16
No. of pupils: 18
Scholarships:
Religion: Non-denominational

Fees per term
Day: -
Weekly board: -
Full board: -

Boy ○ Girl ● Co-ed ○
Day ○ Week ○ Board ●

For fees, further information and a prospectus, please contact the school.

DUMFRIES AND GALLOWAY

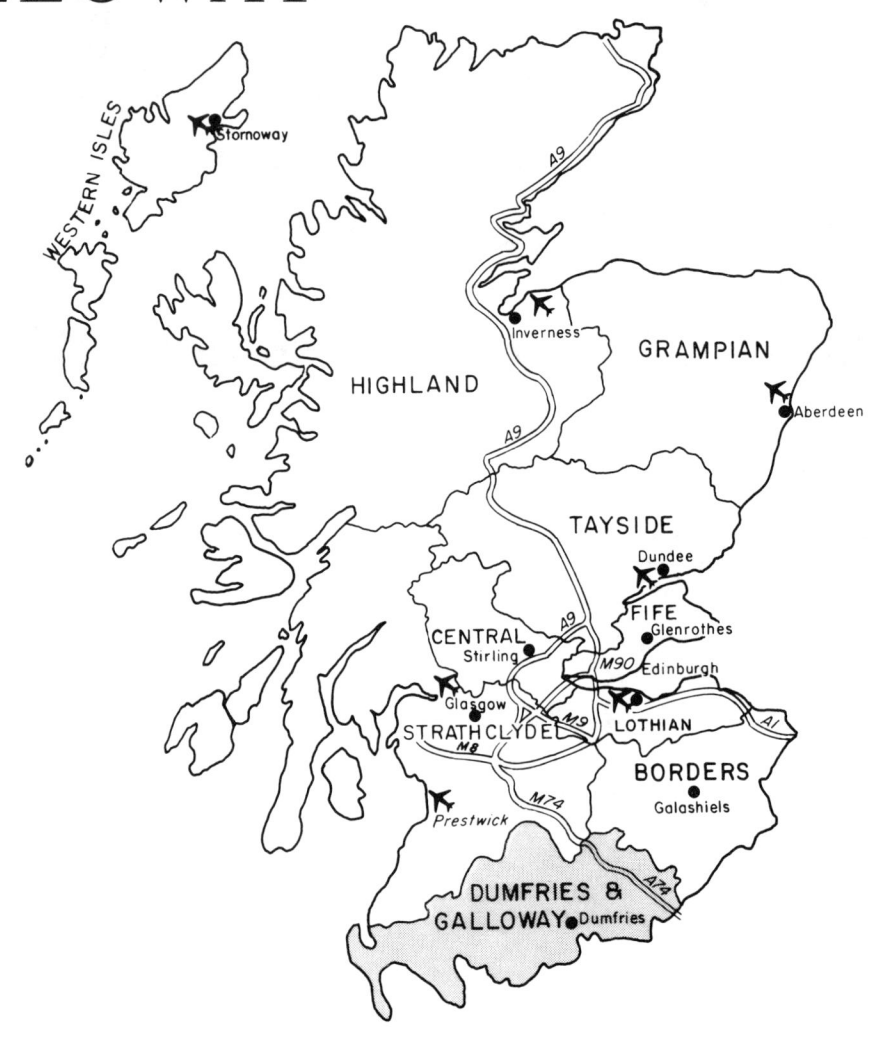

Crawfordton House School *

Address: Moniaive, Thornhill, Dumfries and Galloway DG3 4HG
Telephone: 084 82212

Head: Mr D M Argyle

Age range: 5-14
No. of pupils: 65
Scholarships: Yes
Religion: Non-denominational

Fees per term
Day: £595-
Weekly board: £2490-
Full board: £2540-

Boy ○ Girl ○ Co-ed ●
Day ● Week ● Board ●

Crawfordton's pupils enjoy a delightful country setting. With a chapel, domestic science room, carpentry workshop, squash court, swimming pool, golf course, fishing loch, sailing loch, tennis courts, activities are diverse. The teacher pupil ratio of 1:9 helps the tradition of academic excellence maintained by the committed, qualified staff. Individual tutors, a homely atmosphere and good food all nurture growing children.

Kilquhanity House *

Address: Castle Douglas, Dumfries and Galloway DG7 3DG
Telephone: 055 665 242

Head: Mr J Aitkenhead MA MEd

Age range: 5-17
No. of pupils: 50
Scholarships: Yes
Religion: Non-denominational

Fees per term
Day: -£2200
Weekly board: -
Full board: -£4000

Boy ○ Girl ○ Co-ed ●
Day ● Week ○ Board ●

Kilquhanity House was founded in a spirit of idealism in 1940. Inspired by the work of A S Neill it continues as a creative, radical, international school for half a hundred boys and girls 5-14 years. All the arts and crafts generously promoted as the very stuff of education along with sound approach to the three Rs. Dyslexic pupils welcomed. Assisted Places available.

Merton Hall School †

Address: Newtown Stewart, Dumfries and Galloway DG8 6QL
Telephone: 0671 2447

Heads: Mr P Richards, Mrs E Richards

Age range: 5-16
No. of pupils: 17
Scholarships:
Religion: Non-denominational

Fees per term
Day: -
Weekly board: -
Full board: -

Boy ○ Girl ○ Co-ed ●
Day ○ Week ○ Board ●

Details of fees, further information and a prospectus available on application to the school.

St Joseph's College

Address: Craigs Road, Dumfries, Dumfries and Galloway DG1 3DB
Telephone:

Head:

Age range: 12-18
No. of pupils: 700
Scholarships:
Religion: Roman Catholic

Fees per term
Day: -
Weekly board: -
Full board: -

Boy ○ Girl ○ Co-ed ●
Day ● Week ○ Board ○

For further information and a prospectus, please contact the school.

Woodlands School

Address: Corsbie Road,
Newton Stewart, Dumfries
and Galloway DG8 6QL
Telephone:

Head:

Age range: 10-17
No. of pupils: 42
Scholarships:
Religion:

Fees per term
Day: -
Weekly board: -
Full board: -

Boy ○ Girl ○ Co-ed ●
Day ○ Week ○ Board ●

For further information and a prospectus, please contact the school.

FIFE

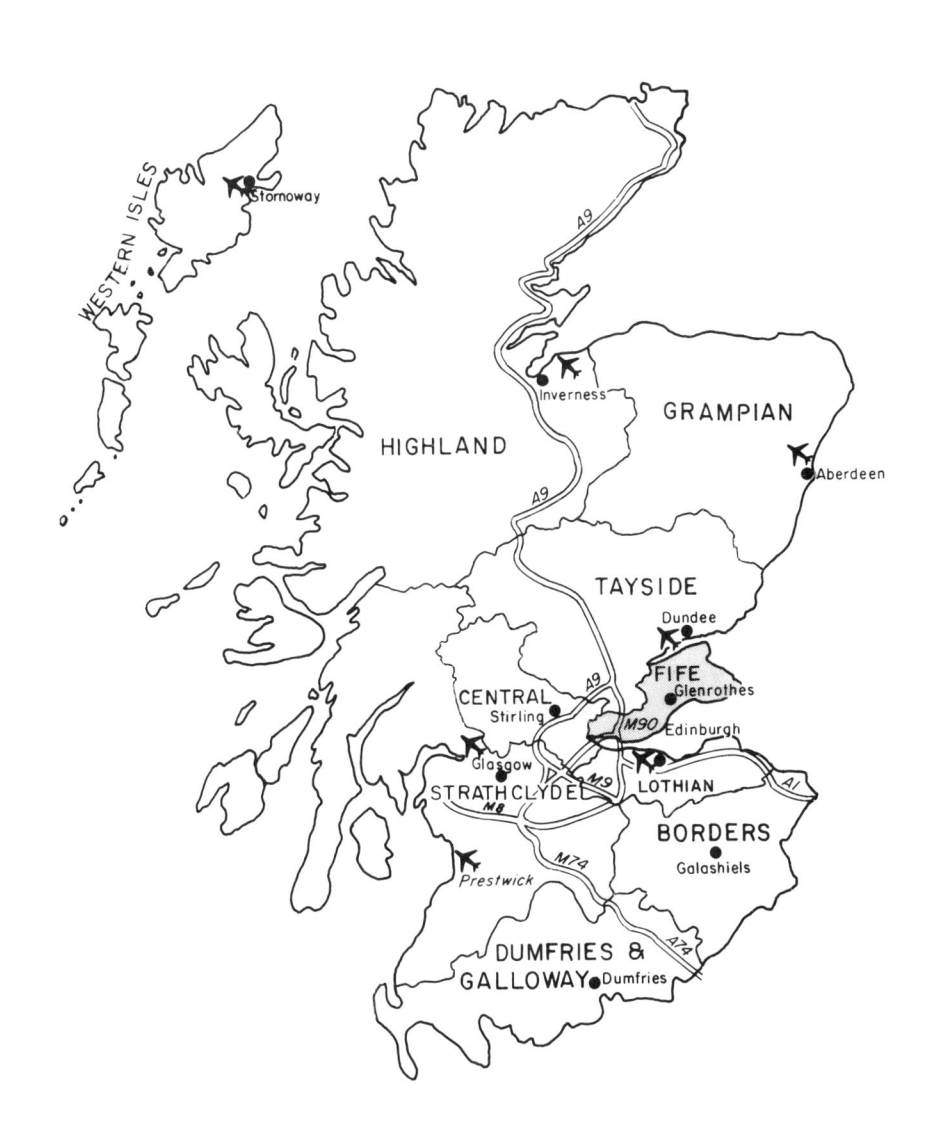

Falkland House School †

Address: Falkland Estate, Falkland, Fife KY7 7AE

Telephone: 0337 57268

Head: Mr T Swan BA(Hons)

Age range: 11-16
No. of pupils: 42
Scholarships:
Religion: Non-denominational

Fees per term
Day: -£7583
Weekly board: -
Full board: -

● Boy ○ Girl ○ Co-ed
○ Day ○ Week ● Board

The school provides for boys aged 11-16 years experiencing emotional and behavioural difficulties. The curriculum is intended to articulate with mainstream educational provision, leading to presentation for Standard Grade and SCOTVEC awards in the third and fourth years. Great emphasis is placed on creating a supportive milieu for the children and their families, utilizing the services of a child psychiatrist.

Hillside School †

Address: Aberdour, Fife KY3 0RH

Telephone: 0383 860731

Principal: Mr D Harvey

Age range: 11-16
No. of pupils: 58
Scholarships:
Religion: Non-denominational

Fees per term
Day: -
Weekly board: -
Full board: -

● Boy ○ Girl ○ Co-ed
● Day ○ Week ● Board

For fees, further information and a prospectus, please contact the school.

Inchkeith School

Address: Balgownie House, Culross, Fife KY12 8JJ

Telephone: 0383 880330

Head: Mrs J M Poustie

Age range: 3-11
No. of pupils: 64
Scholarships:
Religion: Non-denominational

Fees per term
Day: £328-£546
Weekly board: -
Full board: -

○ Boy ○ Girl ● Co-ed
● Day ○ Week ○ Board

As a small primary and nursery school with traditional values, Inchkeith aims to provide a thorough grounding in the basic skills of reading, writing and arithmetic. Notwithstanding size and traditions, the school's broad curriculum includes French, computer studies, art, dance and sport. Children develop to the full in a caring environment and small classes ensure each child gets plenty of attention.

New Park School *

Address: 98 Hepburn Gardens, St Andrews, Fife KY16 9LN

Telephone: 0334 72017

Head: Mr M J E Wareham

Age range: 3-13
No. of pupils: 130
Scholarships: Yes
Religion: Non-denominational

Fees per term
Day: £250-£1335
Weekly board: £2125-
Full board: £2445-

○ Boy ○ Girl ● Co-ed
● Day ● Week ● Board

New Park is a co-educational preparatory school of 130 pupils on the edge of the attractive university town of St Andrews. An excellent academic record is allied to a successful sports programme, varied and inventive arts, and outstanding drama. Extensive camping, hill-walking and skiing take advantage of its location close to the Cairngorms. Day and boarding places are available.

Seaview Private School

Address: 102 Loughborough Road, Kirkcaldy, Fife KY1 3DD

Telephone: 0592 52244

Head: Mrs E Mason

Age range: 3-11
No. of pupils: 65
Scholarships:
Religion: Non-denominational

Fees per term
Day: £275-£625
Weekly board: -
Full board: -

Boy ○ Girl ○ Co-ed ●
Day ● Week ○ Board ○

For further information and a prospectus, please contact the school.

St Leonards School *

Address: St Andrews, Fife KY16 9QU

Telephone: 0334 72126

Head: Mrs L E James

Age range: 12-18
No. of pupils: 270
Scholarships: Yes
Religion: Non-denominational

Fees per term
Day: £1875-
Weekly board: -
Full board: £3550-

Boy ○ Girl ● Co-ed ○
Day ● Week ○ Board ●

St Leonards is bold and ambitious on what it offers. Academic standards are high and first rate opportunities exist in respect of sport, music, art & design and drama. The emphasis is upon individuality and confidence and the pastoral care is exceptionally good. Girls live in small house communities which are conducive to friendship. Career advice encourages realistic ambition.

Starley Hall School

Address: Aberdour Road, Burntisland, Fife KY3 0AG

Telephone:

Head:

Age range:
No. of pupils:
Scholarships:
Religion:

Fees per term
Day: -
Weekly board: -
Full board: -

Boy ○ Girl ○ Co-ed ○
Day ○ Week ○ Board ○

For further information and a prospectus, please contact the school.

GRAMPIAN

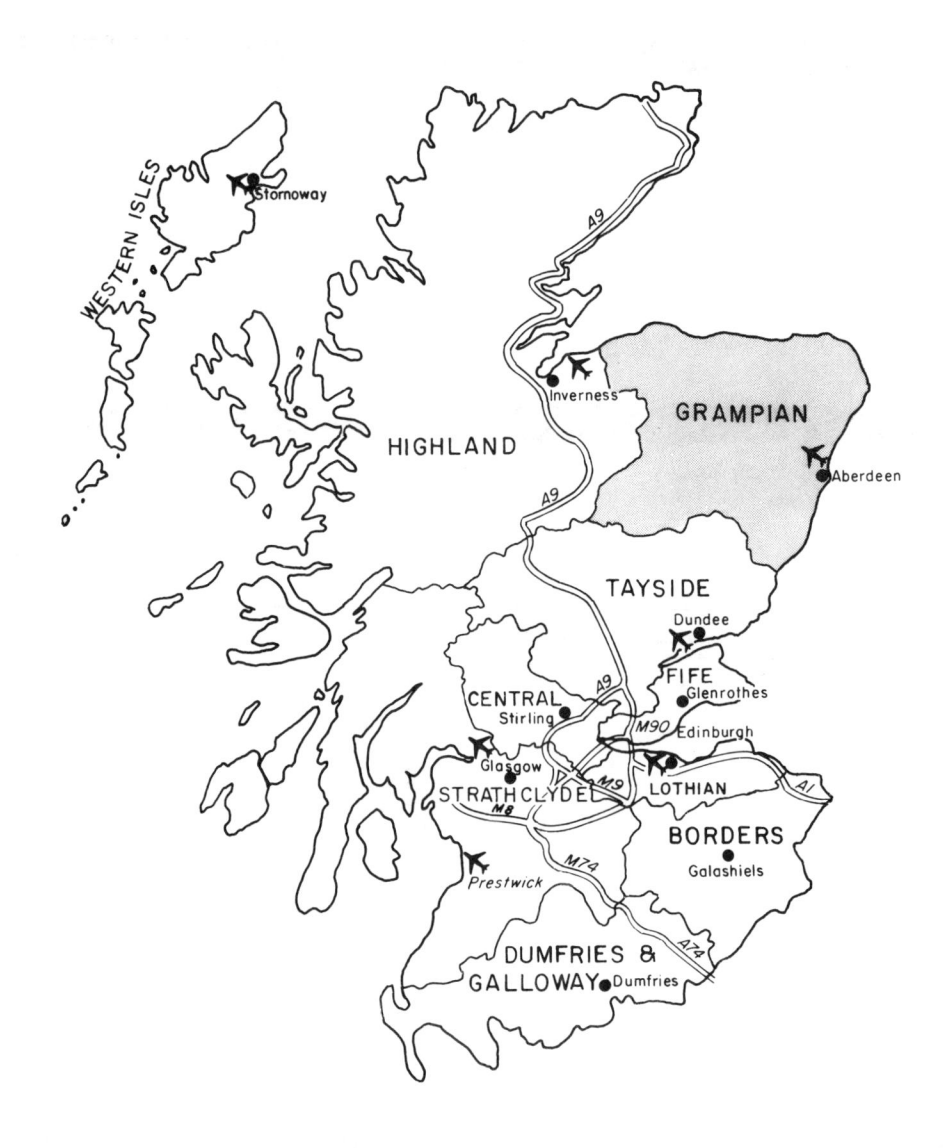

GRAMPIAN 615

Aberdeen Waldorf School

Address: 111 Gallowgate, Aberdeen, Grampian AB1 1BU
Telephone: 0224 646111

Age range: 4-18
No. of pupils: 135
Scholarships:
Religion: Non-denominational

Fees per term
Day: £440-£1000
Weekly board: -
Full board: -

Boy ○ Girl ○ Co-ed ●
Day ● Week ○ Board ○

Head: Chairman College of Teachers

The Aberdeen Waldorf School was begun in 1977 by a group of parents desiring Waldorf education for their children. The pioneering initiative of these parents and their 7 children has grown into the present school of 135 children. The Aberdeen Waldorf School is still young, but ready to start on a new phase of life. With the active involvement of all parents, teachers and friends loyal to Waldorf education.

Aberlour House *

Address: Aberlour, Grampian AB38 9LJ
Telephone: 0340 871267

Age range: 8-13
No. of pupils: 120
Scholarships: Yes
Religion: Non-denominational

Fees per term
Day: £1700-
Weekly board: -
Full board: £2485-

Boy ○ Girl ○ Co-ed ●
Day ○ Week ○ Board ●

Head: Mr J W Caithness

Aberlour House occupies a fine late Georgian country house surrounded by parkland, situated between Aberlour and Craigellachie in Strathspey, 20 miles from Gordonstoun. All members of staff are properly qualified and most are graduates. The school has a good record of academic, music and art scholarships. Physical activities include rugby, hockey, netball, rounders, tennis, athletics and riding.

Albyn School for Girls *

Address: 17/23 Queen's Raod, Aberdeen, Grampian AB9 2PA
Telephone: 0224 322408

Age range: 3-18
No. of pupils: 450
Scholarships: Yes
Religion: Non-affiliated

Fees per term
Day: £255-£1215
Weekly board: £1050-£1685
Full board: £1050-£1685

Boy ○ Girl ● Co-ed ○
Day ● Week ● Board ●

Head: Miss N H Smith

Albyn School accepts girls from age 3 - 18, and boys in the nursery. A scottish curriculum is followed leading to 'S' grade/'H' grade and CSYS examinations. Music, art, debating and a wide range of sports are included in both the curriculum and in extra-curricular activities with many girls reaching district and national standards.

American School in Aberdeen

Address: Graigton Road, Cults, Aberdeen, Grampian AB1 9QD
Telephone: 0224 868927

Age range: 5-18
No. of pupils: 360
Scholarships:
Religion: Non-denominational

Fees per term
Day: -
Weekly board: -
Full board: -

Boy ○ Girl ○ Co-ed ●
Day ● Week ○ Board ○

Head: Mr J C Thomas

The mission of ASA is to provide an education equal to or better than that provided by an excellent private or public school in suburban United States. The curriculum centres around a college preparation agenda with extra-curricular emphasis being placed upon travel and the students' better understanding of the United Kingdom and neighbouring nations. Annual fee of £7,300 for all ages.

Blairmore *

Address: Glass, Huntley, Grampian AB5 4XH

Telephone: 0466 85200

Head: Mr D P Hepburn

Age range: 8-13
No. of pupils: 53
Scholarships: Yes
Religion: Non-denominational

Fees per term
Day: £1475-
Weekly board: -
Full board: £2500-

Boy ○ Girl ○ Co-ed ●
Day ● Week ○ Board ●

Blairmore School is set in beautiful countryside in the Deveron Valley. A happy relaxed family environment encourages high academic and sporting standards. Music, art and drama along with outdoor pursuits ensure a wide choice of leisure activities. Golf and skiing are school specialities.

Camphill-Rudolf Steiner-Schools †

Address: Central Office, Murtle Estate, Bieldside, Aberdeen, Grampian AB1 9EP

Telephone: 0224 867935

Head: Joint Co-ordinators

Age range: 5-19
No. of pupils: 154
Scholarships:
Religion: Non-denominational

Fees per term
Day: -
Weekly board: -
Full board: -

Boy ○ Girl ○ Co-ed ●
Day ○ Week ○ Board ●

The Camphill Schools are devoted to the care and education of children and young people with multiple disabilities and emotional disturbances: e.g. a blind child who is autistic, a deprived child who is mentally handicapped, a spastic child who is maladjusted. The recognition of the individuality of a child in the keynote of Camphill's work. The fees range from £1482 to £3578 per quarter, and are for a 38 week year.

Glen Morven Preparatory School

Address: Ballogie, Aboyne, Grampian AB34 5DP

Telephone: 0339 886765

Head: Mrs K White

Age range: 4-12
No. of pupils: 30
Scholarships:
Religion:

Fees per term
Day: £685-
Weekly board: -
Full board: -

Boy ○ Girl ○ Co-ed ●
Day ● Week ○ Board ○

A small independent registered preparatory school situated in Royal Deeside. The school provides education for boys and girls from 4 to 12 years.

Gordonstoun School *

Address: Elgin, Grampian IV30 2RF

Telephone: 0343 830445

Head: Mr MCSR Pyper

Age range: 13-18
No. of pupils: 465
Scholarships: Yes
Religion: Non-denominational

Fees per term
Day: £2290-
Weekly board: -
Full board: £3550-

Boy ○ Girl ○ Co-ed ●
Day ● Week ○ Board ●

Gordonstoun places emphasis on both the best academic qualifications and on development of personal qualities through the encouragement of the cultural, physical, social and spiritual faculties of every boy and girl. The school provides an environment of unparalleled facility and opportunity for all. Also international summer school courses offering EFL, adventure, sports and computers.

Lathallan School

Address: Montrose, Grampian DD10 0HN

Telephone: 0561 62220

Head: Mr P D De Iongh

Age range: 5-13
No. of pupils: 72
Scholarships: Yes
Religion: Christian

Fees per term
Day: £990-£1554
Weekly board: -£2435
Full board: -£2495

○ ○ ● Boy Girl Co-ed
● ● ● Day Week Board

A vigorous and happy school set in magnificent surroundings on Kincardineshire coast. Prepares children for all major senior independent schools. Splendid facilities, team games, small classes, high standards, pipe band.

Linn Moor Residential Special School †

Address: Petercutler, Grampian AB1 0PY

Telephone: 0224 732246

Head: Mr H Mulford

Age range: 5-18
No. of pupils: 30
Scholarships:
Religion: Non-denominational

Fees per term
Day: -
Weekly board: -
Full board: -

○ ○ ● Boy Girl Co-ed
○ ○ ● Day Week Board

School for children with various disabilities. For further details please contact the headmaster.

Moray Steiner School

Address: Clovenside Road, Forres, Grampian IV36 0RD

Telephone: 0309 676300

Head: Board of Directors

Age range: 3-14
No. of pupils: 75
Scholarships:
Religion: Non-denominational

Fees per term
Day: -
Weekly board: -
Full board: -

○ ○ ● Boy Girl Co-ed
● ○ ○ Day Week Board

Contribution according to means. For further information and a prospectus, please contact the school.

Robert Gordon's College *

Address: Schoolhill, Aberdeen, Grampian AB9 1FE

Telephone: 0224 646346

Head: Mr G A Allan

Age range: 5-18
No. of pupils: 1260
Scholarships: Yes
Religion: Non-denominational

Fees per term
Day: £720-£1108
Weekly board: -
Full board: -£2408

○ ○ ● Boy Girl Co-ed
● ○ ● Day Week Board

For further information and a prospectus, please contact the school.

Rosebrae Pre-Preparatory School and Nursery

Address: Rosehaugh Farm, Elgin, Grampian IV30 3YW

Telephone: 0343 544841

Head: Mrs C Bell

Age range: 2-10
No. of pupils: 60
Scholarships:
Religion: Non-denominational

Fees per term
Day: £281-£732
Weekly board: -
Full board: -

Boy ○ Girl ○ Co-ed ●
Day ● Week ○ Board ○

For further information and a prospectus, please contact the school.

St Margaret's School for Girls *

Address: 17 Albyn Place, Aberdeen, Grampian

Telephone: 0224 584466

Head: Miss L M Ogilvie

Age range: 3-18
No. of pupils: 409
Scholarships: Yes
Religion: Non-denominational

Fees per term
Day: -
Weekly board: -
Full board: -

Boy ○ Girl ● Co-ed ○
Day ● Week ○ Board ○

Founded in 1846, St Margaret's provides an integrated education from nursery to sixth form. It is a school small enough to care about the individual but large enough to provide a full and varied curriculum.

Girls are prepared for living and working in the 21st century and encouraged to assume repsonsibility whilst showing courtesy and self-discipline at all times.

Total Oil Marine's French School

Address: Crawpeel Road, Altens, Aberdeen, Grampian AB9 1HT

Telephone: 0224 645545

Head: M Le Bresne

Age range: 5-16
No. of pupils: 95
Scholarships:
Religion:

Fees per term
Day: -
Weekly board: -
Full board: -

Boy ○ Girl ○ Co-ed ●
Day ● Week ○ Board ○

For further information and a prospectus, please contact the school.

HIGHLAND

Fort Augustus Abbey School * p721

Address: Fort Augustus, Highlands PH32 4DB

Telephone: 0320 6232

Head: Rev E Delepine OSB

Age range: 11-18
No. of pupils: 70
Scholarships: Yes
Religion: Roman Catholic

Fees per term
Day: £1696-£1701
Weekly board: £2378-£2502
Full board: £2478-£2602

Boy ● Girl ● Co-ed ○
Day ● Week ● Board ●

Small 'family' school on the shores of Loch Ness, virtually individual tuition. Scottish examination system, but English examinations on request. Usual games plus sailing and canoeing on Loch Ness.

Assisted places. Reductions for service personnel. Day girls only.

Raddery School †

Address: Fortrose, Highland IV10 8SN

Telephone: 0381 20271

Head: Mr D Dean OBE

Age range: 9-16
No. of pupils: 39
Scholarships:
Religion: Non-denominational

Fees per term
Day: -
Weekly board: -
Full board: -£9115

Boy ○ Girl ○ Co-ed ●
Day ○ Week ○ Board ●

Further information and a prospectus available on application to the school.

LOTHIAN

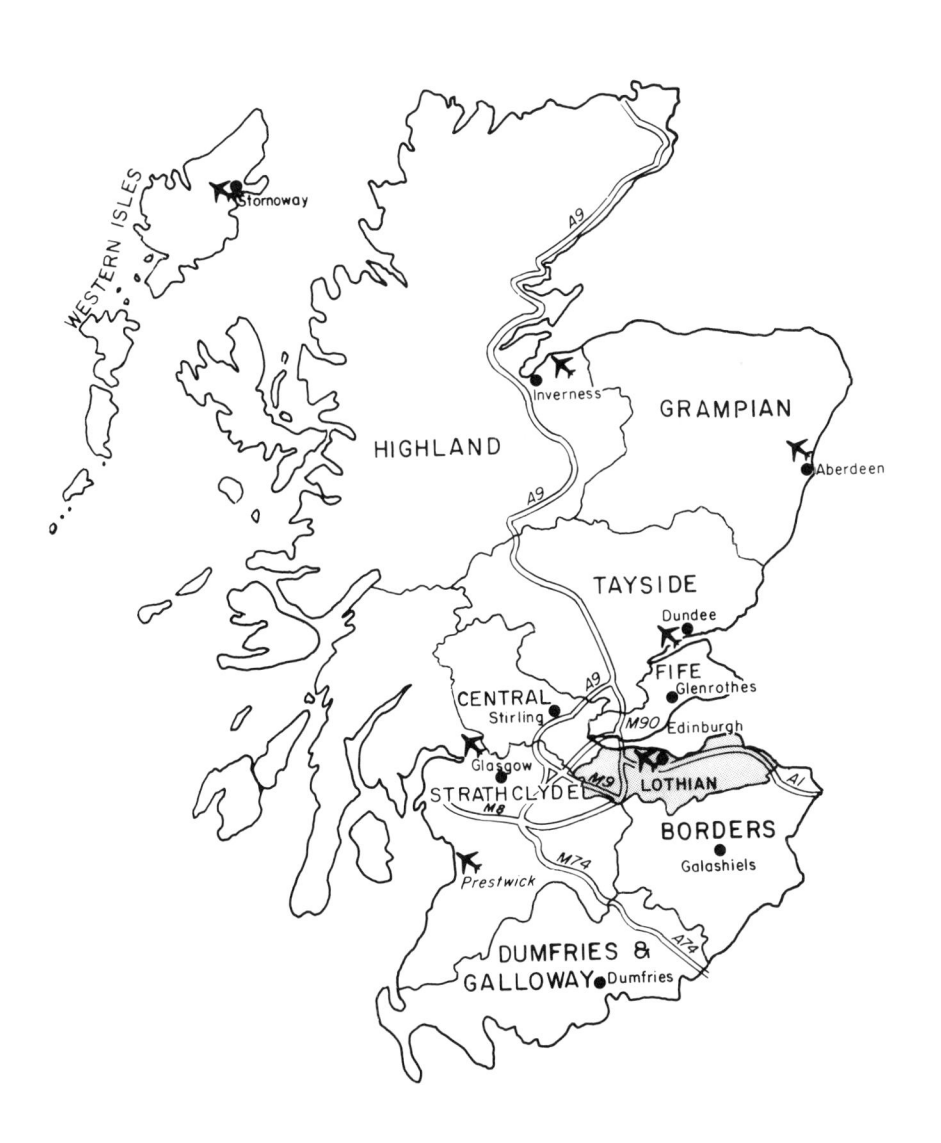

Basil Paterson College p728

Address: 22/23 Abercromby Place, Edinburgh, Lothian EH3 6QE
Telephone: 031 556 7695

Head: Mr R McKenzie

Age range: 17+
No. of pupils: 90
Scholarships:
Religion:

Fees per term
Day: £748-£2288
Weekly board: -
Full board: -

○ ○ ● Boy Girl Co-ed
● ○ ○ Day Week Board

For more than sixty years, Basil Paterson has provided education and training for students from Britain and throughout the world. Our success is based on the highest academic standards and attention to student's individual needs. The college has three schools: School of Academic Studies, School of Secretarial and Business Studies and the School of English for Foreign Students.

Belhaven Hill School *

Address: Dunbar, Lothian EH42 1NN

Telephone: 0368 62785

Head: Mr I M Osborne

Age range: 8-13
No. of pupils: 90
Scholarships:
Religion: Christian

Fees per term
Day: £2475-
Weekly board: £2450-
Full board: £2650-

● ○ ○ Boy Girl Co-ed
● ● ● Day Week Board

For further information please apply to the headmaster for the school prospectus.

Cargilfield *

Address: 37 Barton Avenue West, Edinburgh, Lothian EH4 6HU
Telephone: 031 336 2207

Head: Mr A J S Bateman

Age range: 3-13
No. of pupils: 189
Scholarships:
Religion: Non-denominational

Fees per term
Day: £415-£1835
Weekly board: £2575-
Full board: £2575-

○ ○ ● Boy Girl Co-ed
● ● ● Day Week Board

Cargilfield is a purpose built boarding (and day) school on the edge of Edinburgh (airport - 15 mins). There are 110 children (68 boarders) in the upper school with excellent academic facilities and strong games, music and activities programmes. Visitors are always welcome.

Clifton Hall School *

Address: Newbridge, Edinburgh, Lothian EH28 8LQ
Telephone: 031 333 1359

Head: Mr M A M Adams

Age range: 3-14
No. of pupils: 145
Scholarships: Yes
Religion: Non-denominational

Fees per term
Day: £815-£1600
Weekly board: -£2650
Full board: -£2650

○ ○ ● Boy Girl Co-ed
● ● ● Day Week Board

Clifton Hall School is a small, friendly preparatory school with day and boarding facilities in a magnificent house and country grounds only 20 miles west of Edinburgh. Entry is by interview. Pupils are prepared for the best Scottish and English independent schools by providing good teaching in small classes, balanced with a wide range of other activities. Prospectus sent by return.

The Compass School

Address: West Road, Haddington, Lothian EH41 3RD
Telephone: 0620 822642

Head: Miss C R Budge

Age range: 4-11
No. of pupils: 103
Scholarships:
Religion: Non-denominational

Fees per term
Day: £450-£925
Weekly board: -
Full board: -

Boy ○ Girl ○ Co-ed ●
Day ● Week ○ Board ○

The Compass School is situated on the edge of Haddington overlooking the Lammermuir Hills. The children are taught in small classes with considerable individual attention. Emphasis is laid on the development of the child as an individual, encouraging the progression of knowledge, skills and confidence. The school has a family atmosphere with good relations between staff and parents.

Daniel Stewart's & Melville College *

Address: Queensferry Road, Edinburgh, Lothian EH4 3EZ
Telephone: 031 332 7925

Head: Mr P J F Tobin MA

Age range: 12-18
No. of pupils: 780
Scholarships: Yes
Religion: Non-denominational

Fees per term
Day: £3936-£3666
Weekly board: -
Full board: £7116-

Boy ● Girl ○ Co-ed ○
Day ● Week ○ Board ○

This Edinburgh Merchant Company School is situated in impressive buildings close to the centre of the city. It is 'twinned' with its sister school, The Mary Erskine School for Girls, and the two schools share the same junior school and are administered by the same principal and governing council. The school prides itself on its academic record, on the range and quality of extra-curricular programme and its pastoral provision for boys.

Dunedin School †

Address: 5 Gilmerton Road, Edinburgh, Lothian EH16 5TV
Telephone: 031 664 1328

Head: Co-operative of Teachers

Age range: 7-16
No. of pupils: 50
Scholarships:
Religion: Non-denominational

Fees per term
Day: -
Weekly board: -
Full board: -

Boy ○ Girl ○ Co-ed ●
Day ● Week ○ Board ○

Fees, further information and a prospectus available on application to the school.

The Edinburgh Academy * p742

Address: Henderson Row, Edinburgh, Lothian EH3 5BL
Telephone: 031 556 4603

Head: Mr A J D Rees

Age range: 3-18
No. of pupils: 920
Scholarships: Yes
Religion: Non-denominational

Fees per term
Day: £680-£1415
Weekly board: £2513-£2948
Full board: £2560-£2995

Boy ● Girl ● Co-ed ○
Day ● Week ● Board ●

The Edinburgh Academy offers a capital education. It is concerned to achieve the best for its pupils, boys or sixth form girls, day or boarding. A careful balance is maintained between the demands of the changing curriculum and the wide range of musical, sporting, artistic and creative activities which are available. Easy access by rail (Waverley) and air (Turnhouse).

Edinburgh Tutorial College

Address: 29 Chester Street, Edinburgh, Lothian

Telephone: 031 225 9888

Head: Mr A W Morris

Age range: 16-19
No. of pupils: 40
Scholarships:
Religion: Non-denominational

Fees per term
Day: £1400-
Weekly board: £2776-£2988
Full board: £2776-£2988

Boy ○ Girl ○ Co-ed ●
Day ● Week ● Board ●

The Edinburgh Tutorial College (ETC) was founded by A W Morris BSc MInstP in 1973. The college stands in Chester Street in the West End area of the New Town. ETC offers the full range of GCSE, Standard Grade, Higher and A Level courses. The college has its own residential accommodation, Douglas House, which is situated only two minutes walk away from the college.

Fettes College *

Address: Carrington Road, Edinburgh, Lothian EH4 1QX

Telephone: 031 332 2281

Head: Mr M T Thyne MA

Age range: 10-18
No. of pupils: 430
Scholarships: Yes
Religion: Non-denominational

Fees per term
Day: £1565-£2475
Weekly board: -
Full board: £2510-£3685

Boy ○ Girl ○ Co-ed ●
Day ● Week ○ Board ●

Fettes College was founded in 1870. One of the distinctive features of our history has been the attention to every pupil. Discipline is firm and caring and is based on mutual respect. Academic excellence is given a high priority. The curriculum is broad and well-rounded. The school also aims for a high standard in sports and games.

Fettes Junior School

Address: Carrington Road, Edinburgh, Lothian EH4 1QX

Telephone: 031 332 2976

Head: Mr M Thyne

Age range: 10-13
No. of pupils: 90
Scholarships: Yes
Religion: Christian

Fees per term
Day: -
Weekly board: -
Full board: -

Boy ○ Girl ○ Co-ed ●
Day ● Week ○ Board ●

Nearly all junior school pupils will qualify for entry to the senior school to which there is a strong tradition of success in winning both academic and music scholarships. All subjects are taught in small classes and the staff are concerned to help pupils develop secure intellectual, social and emotional foundations. Fees on application.

George Heriot's School *

Address: Lauriston Place, Edinburgh, Lothian EH3 9EQ

Telephone: 031 229 7263

Head: Mr K P Pearson MA

Age range: 3-18
No. of pupils: 1480
Scholarships: Yes
Religion: Non-denominational

Fees per term
Day: £596-£1140
Weekly board: -
Full board: -

Boy ○ Girl ○ Co-ed ●
Day ● Week ○ Board ○

The school has long enjoyed a reputation for academic excellence, and we strive to help pupils to attain the highest possible level of competence. In the same spirit, every pupil is encouraged to participate in an extensive array of extra-curricular activities. We value sporting achievement, particularly in team games, and we encourage activity in art, music and design.

George Watson's College *

Address: Colinton Road,
Edinburgh, Lothian EH10 5EG

Telephone: 031 447 7931

Head: Mr F E Gerstenberg

Age range: 4-18
No. of pupils: 2100
Scholarships: Yes
Religion: Non-denominational

Fees per term
Day: £250-£1210
Weekly board: -
Full board: £2410-£2410

Boy ○ Girl ○ Co-ed ●
Day ● Week ● Board ●

George Watson's College is a family school which provides high academic standards combined with a strong caring atmosphere. Extra-curricular provision very wide, music particularly strong. Entry to universities 30% to English, 70% to Scottish. Boarding provision for 11-18 year olds.

Loretto Junior School

Address: North Esk Lodge,
Musselburgh, Lothian
EH21 6JA
Telephone: 031 665 2628

Head: Mr D P Clark

Age range: 8-13
No. of pupils: 80
Scholarships: Yes
Religion: Non-denominational

Fees per term
Day: £1740-
Weekly board: £2510-
Full board: £2610-

Boy ● Girl ○ Co-ed ○
Day ● Week ● Board ●

This traditional preparatory school enjoys first class facilities for sport, leisure and study on its own campus, but pupils have access to the many outstanding features of the upper school including swimming pool, sports hall and the chapel.

Loretto School * p722

Address: Musselburgh,
Lothian EH21 7RE

Telephone: 031 665 2567

Head: Rev N W Drummond

Age range: 13-18
No. of pupils: 301
Scholarships: Yes
Religion: Ecumenical

Fees per term
Day: -£2143
Weekly board: -
Full board: -£3215

Boy ● Girl ● Co-ed ○
Day ● Week ○ Board ●

Loretto, the longest established boarding school in Scotland, is also the smallest. It remains our policy to take no more than 300 pupils in the upper school (265 boys and 35 sixth form girls) and 100 nippers in the junior school. A school of this size allows small classes; each pupil is known by everyone and feels part of the community. It is also large enough to offer a wide range of academic, artistic, musical and sporting activities.

Mary Erskine & Stewart's Melville Junior School

Address: Queensferry Road,
Edinburgh, Lothian EH4 3EZ

Telephone: 031 332 0888

Head: Mr B Lewis BA

Age range: 3-12
No. of pupils: 1135
Scholarships: Yes
Religion: Non-denominational

Fees per term
Day: £480-£1006
Weekly board: -
Full board: £2066-

Boy ○ Girl ○ Co-ed ●
Day ● Week ○ Board ●

We provide a caring but disciplined environment in which each child is treated as an individual, expected to have the highest standards and encouraged to participate in all aspects of school life. We believe in hard work but this belief is tempered with the ability to smile and we take pride in seeing our children develop into happy, confident and well-motivated pupils in a totally co-educational environment until the age of 12.

The Mary Erskine School *

Address: Ravelstone Dykes, Edinburgh, Lothian EH4 3NT

Telephone: 031 337 2391

Head: Mr P F J Tobin MA

Age range: 12-18
No. of pupils: 616
Scholarships: Yes
Religion: Non-denominational

Fees per term
Day: £1222-£1312
Weekly board: -
Full board: £2372-

Girl · Day · Board

This Edinburgh Merchant Company School is situated in 40 acres of parkland within two miles of the city centre. It is 'twinned' with Daniel Stewart's & Melville College for Boys, and the two schools share the same junior school and are administered by the same principal and governing council. The school prides itself on academic record, on the range and quality of extra-curricular programme and its pastoral provision for girls.

Merchiston Castle School *

Address: Colinton, Edinburgh, Lothian EH13 0PU

Telephone: 031 441 1722

Head: Mr D M Spauforth

Age range: 11-18
No. of pupils: 380
Scholarships: Yes
Religion: Non-denominational

Fees per term
Day: £1860-£2200
Weekly board: -
Full board: £2730-£3400

Boy · Day · Board

The school endeavours to develop to the full the academic potential of each pupil, to give him a thorough grounding in the basic skills and traditional subjects and then to foster particular talents to enable him to move on, well prepared, to the next stage of his life, whether it be university or direct entry to a career. The academic curriculum is very broad.

Murrayfield Kindergarten School

Address: 76 Murrayfield Gardens, Edinburgh, Lothian EH12 6DQ

Telephone: 031 337 3663

Head: Mrs C M Irving

Age range: 2-5
No. of pupils: 23
Scholarships:
Religion: Non-denominational

Fees per term
Day: -£245
Weekly board: -
Full board: -

Co-ed · Day

Murrayfield Kindergarten School has an experienced staff and small classes. We prepare children for pre-preparatory schools in a disciplined and friendly environment. Children are encouraged to care for others whilst developing their own personalities.

Oxenfoord Castle School *

Address: Pathead, Lothian EH37 5UD

Telephone: 0875 320241

Head: Miss M Carmichael

Age range: 8-18
No. of pupils: 84
Scholarships: Yes
Religion: Non-denominational

Fees per term
Day: £1175-£1765
Weekly board: -
Full board: £2530-£3390

Girl · Day · Board

For further information and a prospectus, please contact the school.

Rudolf Steiner School of Edinburgh *

Address: 38 Colinton Road, Edinburgh, Lothian EH10 5BT
Telephone: 031 337 3410
Head: Chairman of the College of Teachers
Age range: 3-18
No. of pupils: 240
Scholarships:
Religion: Non-denominational
Fees per term
Day: £550-£1125
Weekly board: -
Full board: -

Boy ○ | Girl ○ | Co-ed ●
Day ● | Week ○ | Board ○

Steiner education aims to integrate the personality in terms of thoughts, feelings and will. Through this education the child can develop a feeling for the freedom and integrity of other people, a sense of security in life with the ability to contribute socially and develop a deep interest in the world and needs of others.

St Denis & Cranley School for Girls *

Address: Ettrick Road, Edinburgh, Lothian EH10 5BJ
Telephone: 031 229 1500
Head: Mrs J M Monro
Age range: 3-18
No. of pupils: 220
Scholarships: Yes
Religion: Non-denominational
Fees per term
Day: £665-£1325
Weekly board: -
Full board: £2005-£2665

Boy ○ | Girl ● | Co-ed ○
Day ● | Week ● | Board ●

St Denis & Cranley provides the education and broader experience to prepare girls to become good citizens and to lead a fully satisfying life. The school aims to enable each girl to develop her full potential-intellectual, physical, artistic and spiritual. High standards, courtesy and good manners are encouraged as well as the respect for others and self discipline.

St George's School for Girls p722

Address: Garscube Terrace, Edinburgh, Lothian EH12 6BG
Telephone: 031 332 4575
Head: Mrs J G Scott
Age range: 5-18
No. of pupils: 859
Scholarships:
Religion: Non-denominational
Fees per term
Day: -
Weekly board: -
Full board: -

Boy ○ | Girl ○ | Co-ed ○
Day ○ | Week ○ | Board ○

Urban situation; splendid 11 acre site surrounded by playing fields; excellent facilities; music centre (1990), centenary sports hall (1989), art centre (1985); outstanding academic tradition encourages girls to be self reliant while gaining in confidence as they discover and develop their own talents within an active, stimulating, caring environment.

St Margaret's Edinburgh *

Address: East Suffolk Road, Edinburgh, Lothian EH16 5PJ
Telephone: 031 668 1986
Head: Mrs M J Cameron
Age range: 3-8
No. of pupils: 800
Scholarships: Yes
Religion: Non-denominational
Fees per term
Day: £634-£1117
Weekly board: £2217-£2291
Full board: £2217-£2291

Boy ○ | Girl ● | Co-ed ○
Day ● | Week ● | Board ●

St Margaret's is renowned for its happy, caring atmosphere, where children are treated as individuals. At the same time praise and encouragement lead to excellent examination results. Science and technology are particularly strong in the school, but art, music and a wide range of sporting activities all flourish.

St Mary's Music School

Address: Manor Place, Edinburgh, Lothian EH3 7EB

Telephone: 031 220 1664

Principal:

Age range: 7-18
No. of pupils:
Scholarships:
Religion:

Fees per term
Day: -
Weekly board: -
Full board: -

○ Boy   ○ Girl   ● Co-ed
○ Day   ○ Week   ● Board

For further information and a prospectus, please contact the school.

St Serf's School

Address: 5 Wester Coates Gardens, Edinburgh, Lothian EH12 5LT

Telephone: 031 337 1015

Head: Mrs B E Clapp

Age range: 5-18
No. of pupils: 240
Scholarships: Yes
Religion: Non-denominational

Fees per term
Day: £290-£360
Weekly board: -
Full board: -

○ Boy   ○ Girl   ● Co-ed
● Day   ○ Week   ○ Board

St Serf's is a small co-educational school with a very happy atmosphere. The emphasis is on encouragement and the aim is to see that each pupil fulfils their potential.

Wellington School

Address: Peebles Road, Penicuik, Lothian EH26 8PT

Telephone:

Head:

Age range: 12-16
No. of pupils:
Scholarships:
Religion:

Fees per term
Day: -
Weekly board: -
Full board: -

● Boy   ○ Girl   ○ Co-ed
● Day   ○ Week   ● Board

For further information and a prospectus, please contact the school.

Westerlea School for Spastic Children †

Address: 22 Corstophine Road, Edinburgh, Lothian EH12 6HP

Telephone:

Head:

Age range: 3-18
No. of pupils:
Scholarships:
Religion:

Fees per term
Day: -
Weekly board: -
Full board: -

○ Boy   ○ Girl   ● Co-ed
● Day   ○ Week   ○ Board

For further information and a prospectus, please contact the school.

STRATHCLYDE

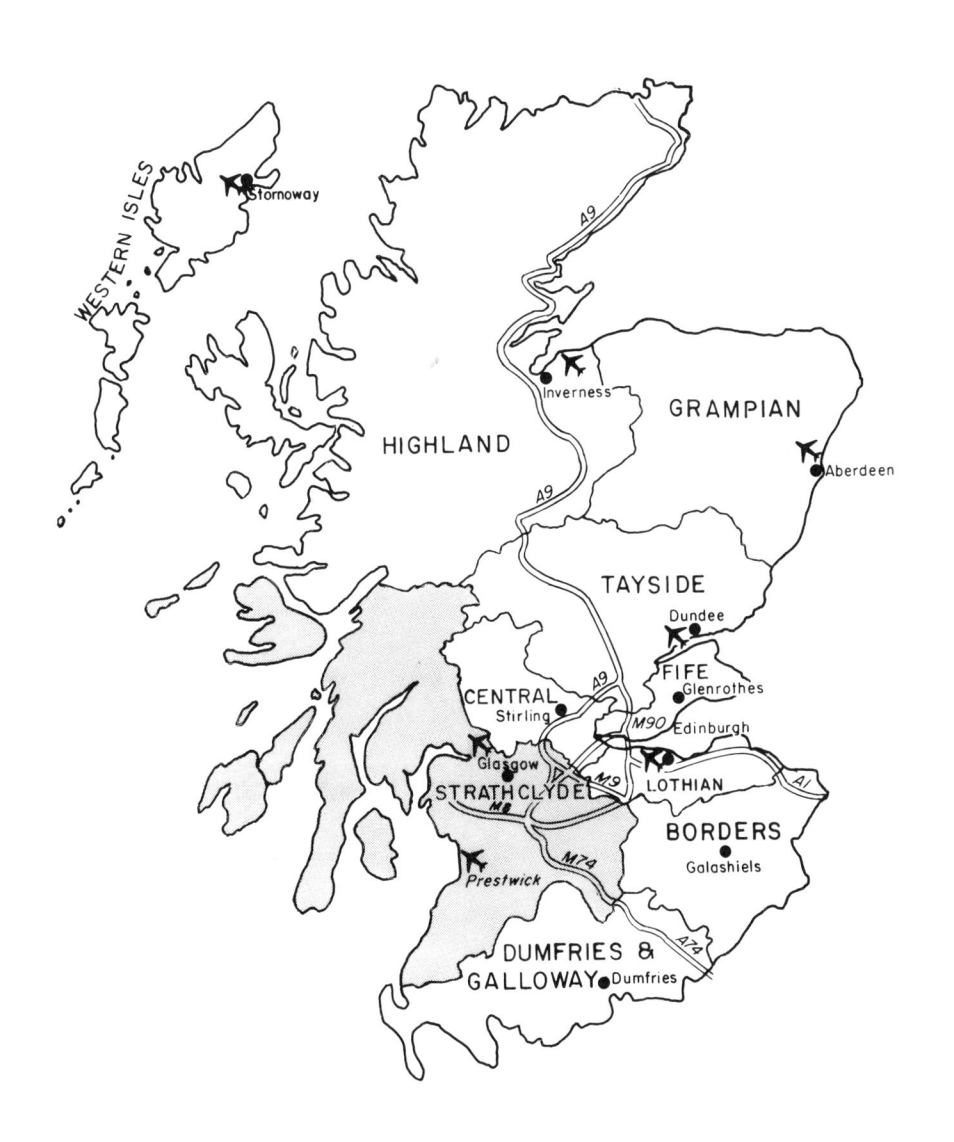

Atholl Preparatory School

Address: Mugdock Road, Milngavie, Strathclyde G62 8NP
Telephone: 041 956 3758

Age range: 3-9
No. of pupils: 78
Scholarships:
Religion: Non-denominational

Fees per term
Day: £345-£600
Weekly board: -
Full board: -

Boy ○ Girl ○ Co-ed ●
Day ● Week ○ Board ○

Head: Mrs S Windebank

Established in 1925, Atholl Preparatory School is an independent co-educational school located in pleasant rural surroundings to the north west of Glasgow. Its aim is to provide pupils with a sound basic education in a small friendly community thus negating the need to travel to city schools at an early age.

Ballikinrain School †

Address: Balfron by Glasgow, Glasgow, Strathclyde G63 0LL
Telephone: 0360 40645

Age range: 8-16
No. of pupils: 50
Scholarships:
Religion: Non-denominational

Fees per term
Day: -
Weekly board: -
Full board: -

Boy ● Girl ○ Co-ed ○
Day ○ Week ○ Board ●

Head: Mr D H Denholm

For fees, further information and a prospectus, please contact the school.

Belmont House School *

Address: Sandringham Avenue, Newton Mearns, Strathclyde G77 5DU
Telephone: 041 639 2922

Age range: 4-18
No. of pupils: 390
Scholarships:
Religion: Non-denominational

Fees per term
Day: £235-£1100
Weekly board: -
Full board: -

Boy ● Girl ○ Co-ed ○
Day ● Week ○ Board ○

Head: Mr J Mercer

It is the aim of the school to maintain the tradition of Belmont House as a happy, caring, purposeful and disciplined community; to provide courses of study and extra-curricular activities which will allow pupils to develop fully in mind, body and spirit; to encourage in pupils integrity, self discipline and self reliance; to provide pupils with adequate vocational, curricular and personal guidance.

Craigholme School *

Address: 72 St Andrews Drive, Glasgow, Strathclyde G41 4HS
Telephone: 041 427 0375

Age range: 3-18
No. of pupils: 514
Scholarships:
Religion: Non-denominational

Fees per term
Day: £260-£1045
Weekly board: -
Full board: -

Boy ○ Girl ● Co-ed ○
Day ● Week ○ Board ○

Head: Mrs G R Burt

Craigholme School provides an excellent academic education, a happy, disciplined environment and wide extra-curricular activities for girls from the age of three to eighteen years. There are superb sports facilities near the school. Situated in one of Glasgow's most pleasant suburbs, Craigholme is close to the city centre motorway and rail links.

Dairsie House School

Address: 54 Newlands Road, Glasgow, Strathclyde G43 2JG

Telephone: 041 632 0736

Head: Mrs J W Penman

Age range: 3-9
No. of pupils: 111
Scholarships:
Religion: Non-denominational

Fees per term
Day: £460-£787
Weekly board: -
Full board: -

Boy ○ Girl ○ Co-ed ●
Day ● Week ○ Board ○

Here at Dairsie House School we combine traditional standards with modern teaching methods. This results in what is virtually 100% success rate in placing children in suitable independent schools when their preparatory education here is complete.

Drumley House *

Address: Mossblown, Ayr, Strathclyde KA6 5AT

Telephone: 0292 520340

Head: Mr C F Robinson

Age range: 3-13
No. of pupils: 130
Scholarships: Yes
Religion:

Fees per term
Day: £350-£1460
Weekly board: £1835-£1960
Full board: -

Boy ○ Girl ○ Co-ed ●
Day ● Week ● Board ○

Founded in 1960, Drumley House offers to boys and girls between the ages of 3 and 13 an environment in which they can seek to fulfil their academic potential and discover and develop their other abilities and talents.

Fernhill School *

Address: Fernbrae Avenue, Burnside, Rutherglen, Strathclyde G73 4SG
Telephone: 041 634 2674

Head: Mrs L M McLay

Age range: 5-18
No. of pupils: 305
Scholarships:
Religion: Roman Catholic

Fees per term
Day: £790-£865
Weekly board: -
Full board: -

Boy ● Girl ● Co-ed ○
Day ● Week ○ Board ○

Fernhill School, established in 1972, is a Catholic independent school for girls 5-18 and boys 5-11, managed by a board of governors. The school has both a primary and a secondary department, fully equipped with modern classrooms and laboratories. The aims of the school are to provide an academic education of a high standard and to help the children to develop their potential in a secure and pleasant atmosphere.

Gask House School

Address: 28 Colston Drive, Bishopriggs, Glasgow, Strathclyde G64 2AZ
Telephone: 041 772 4708

Principal: Miss V P Henderson

Age range: 3-11
No. of pupils: 160
Scholarships:
Religion:

Fees per term
Day: -
Weekly board: -
Full board: -

Boy ○ Girl ○ Co-ed ●
Day ● Week ○ Board ○

For further information and a prospectus, please contact the school.

The Glasgow Academy

Address: Colebrook Street, Glasgow, Strathclyde G12 8HE
Telephone: 041 334 8558
Rector: Mr C W Turner

Age range: 4-18
No. of pupils: 900
Scholarships: Yes
Religion: Church of Scotland

Fees per term
Day: £815-£1265
Weekly board: -
Full board: -

Boy ○ Girl ○ Co-ed ●
Day ● Week ○ Board ○

For almost 150 years, the name 'Glasgow Academy' has been synonymous with academic and sporting success in the city which it serves. Its merger with Westbourne School for Girls in 1991 has resulted in a caring, family school in which academic traditions are maintained by an excellent staff which is also committed to providing a wide range of extra-curricular activities.

Hamilton College *

Address: Bothwell Road, Hamilton, Strathclyde ML3 6AA
Telephone: 0698 282 700
Head: Mr S J Mitchell MA

Age range: 4-18
No. of pupils: 780
Scholarships: Yes
Religion: Non-denominational

Fees per term
Day: £525-£710
Weekly board: -
Full board: -

Boy ○ Girl ○ Co-ed ●
Day ● Week ○ Board ○

This young school has grown dramatically to its present full capacity of 780. It stresses academic excellence in the Scottish tradition, high quality of conduct and welcomes children of all faiths and backgrounds, fostering a family atmosphere. Including 17 acre grounds, fine assembly hall, swimming pool, sports and dining hall, gymnasia and libraries, it enjoys a strategic location in picturesque greenery.

The High School of Glasgow *

Address: 637 Crow Road, Glasgow, Strathclyde G13 1PL
Telephone: 041 954 9628
Head: Mr R G Easton

Age range: 3-18
No. of pupils: 951
Scholarships: Yes
Religion: Non-denominational

Fees per term
Day: £460-£1130
Weekly board: -
Full board: -

Boy ○ Girl ○ Co-ed ●
Day ● Week ○ Board ○

Housed in modern purpose-built premises, the school provides a happy, caring and ordered community in which pupils are encouraged to develop a sense of responsibility and a concern for others and to pursue excellence. Academic standards are exceptionally high, but emphasis is placed on an all-round education and a very wide range of extra-curricualr opportunities is available.

Hutchesons' Grammar School *

Address: 21 Barton Road, Glasgow, Strathclyde G41 4NW
Telephone: 041 423 2933
Head: Mr D R Ward

Age range: 5-18
No. of pupils: 1687
Scholarships: Yes
Religion: Non-denominational

Fees per term
Day: £900-£1053
Weekly board: -
Full board: -

Boy ○ Girl ○ Co-ed ●
Day ● Week ○ Board ○

Hutchesons' seeks to take advantage of its size to offer a wide variety of choices to its pupils - both academic and extra-curricular - while proudly preserving its academic record.

Keil School * p723

Address: Helenslee Road, Dumbarton, Strathclyde G82 4AL
Telephone: 0389 62003

Head: Mr C H Tongue

Age range: 10-18
No. of pupils: 224
Scholarships: Yes
Religion: Non-denominational

Fees per term
Day: £1294-£1509
Weekly board: £2647-£2694
Full board: £2647-£2694

Boy ○ Girl ○ Co-ed ●
Day ● Week ● Board ●

The pursuit of academic excellence together with character development through a wide range of games and activities forms the basis of school life. With its rural location on the banks of the Clyde, it offers easy access by road, rail or air, Glasgow Airport being only 10 miles away. Since August 1989, girls have been admitted at all levels.

Kelvinside Academy *

Address: 33 Kirklee Road, Glasgow, Strathclyde G12 0SW
Telephone: 041 357 3376

Head: Mr J H Duff

Age range: 4-18
No. of pupils: 650
Scholarships: Yes
Religion: Non-denominational

Fees per term
Day: £690-£1295
Weekly board: -
Full board: -

Boy ● Girl ○ Co-ed ○
Day ● Week ○ Board ○

Kelvinside Academy is the leading boys-only independent school in the west of Scotland, providing all boys with an excellent opportunity to reach their full potential. The school has an outstanding academic record, and is equally prominent in the arts and sport. Emphasis is placed on the relaxed, friendly yet disciplined atmosphere.

Laurel Bank School *

Address: 4 Lilybank Terrace, Glasgow, Strathclyde G12 8RX
Telephone: 041 339 9127

Head: Miss L G Egginton

Age range: 5-18
No. of pupils: 410
Scholarships: Yes
Religion: Non-denominational

Fees per term
Day: £744-£1242
Weekly board: -
Full board: -

Boy ○ Girl ● Co-ed ○
Day ● Week ○ Board ○

A day school which draws girls from all over Glasgow. Strong emphasis on academic excellence and individual achievement. Small classes backed up with innovative use of technology. Girls mostly go to a wide range of university courses. Music, sport, travel and other extra-curricular activities highly encouraged.

Lomond School * p723

Address: 10 Stafford Street, Helensburgh, Strathclyde G84 9JX
Telephone: 0436 72476

Head: Mr A D MacDonald

Age range: 3-18
No. of pupils: 540
Scholarships: Yes
Religion: Non-denominational

Fees per term
Day: £340-£1180
Weekly board: £1380-
Full board: £1470-

Boy ○ Girl ○ Co-ed ●
Day ● Week ● Board ●

Lomond is a day and boarding co-educational school of 540 pupils. The average class size is 15 (maximum of 20). Examinations sat are SCE 'S' and 'H' grade and GCE 'A' level. There is a very extensive extra-curricular programme. Major sports are hockey, rugby, athletics and cricket. Assisted Places Scheme, service bursaries, traditional music and academic scholarships.

Park Lodge School *

Address: 17 Charlotte Street, Helensburgh, Strathclyde G84 7EY
Telephone: 0436 73008

Head: Mrs E S Durward

Age range: 2-12
No. of pupils: 114
Scholarships: Yes
Religion: Non-denominational

Fees per term
Day: £310-£770
Weekly board: -
Full board: -

Boy ○ Girl ○ Co-ed ●
Day ● Week ○ Board ○

Park Lodge School is a small, friendly community within which pupils realise full potential, each working at an individual ability level. Classes are kept as small as possible (average ten pupils) and the academic standard is high. This is essentially a forward looking school but with a firm belief in the traditional values of good manners and discipline.

The Park School *

Address: 25 Lynedoch Street, Glasgow, Strathclyde G3 6EX
Telephone: 041 332 0426

Head: Mrs M E Myatt

Age range: 3-18
No. of pupils: 400
Scholarships:
Religion:

Fees per term
Day: £351-£1065
Weekly board: -
Full board: -

Boy ○ Girl ● Co-ed ○
Day ● Week ○ Board ○

The Park School has provided education for girls since 1880. It has an excellent record of success in public examinations, but, despite the emphasis on academic achievement we aim to develop the whole child. The family atmosphere, small teaching sets, wide programme of extra-curricular activities and, above all, a highly qualified and caring staff enable each girl to achieve her full potential.

Red Brae Residential School †

Address: 24 Alloway Road, Maybole, Strathclyde KA19 8AA
Telephone: 0655 83104

Head: Dr Dalrymple

Age range: 12-16
No. of pupils: 30
Scholarships:
Religion: Non-denominational

Fees per term
Day: -
Weekly board: -
Full board: -

Boy ● Girl ○ Co-ed ○
Day ● Week ○ Board ●

For details of fees, further information and a prospectus, please contact the school.

Southannan School †

Address: Fairlie, Largs, Strathclyde KA29 0EF
Telephone:

Head:

Age range:
No. of pupils:
Scholarships:
Religion:

Fees per term
Day: -
Weekly board: -
Full board: -

Boy ○ Girl ○ Co-ed ○
Day ○ Week ○ Board ○

For further information and a prospectus, please contact the school.

Springbank School

Address: c/o The YMCA, Westcoates Road, Cambuslang, Strathclyde G72
Telephone: 041 647 6647

Head: Mrs M Russell

Age range: 3-9
No. of pupils: 50
Scholarships:
Religion: Non-denominational

Fees per term
Day: £190-£385
Weekly board: -
Full board: -

○ Boy ○ Girl ● Co-ed
● Day ○ Week ○ Board

For further information and a prospectus, please contact the school.

St Aloysius' College *

Address: 45 Hill Street, Glasgow, Strathclyde G3 6RJ
Telephone: 041 332 3190

Head: Rev J W Hanvey DPhil

Age range: 8-18
No. of pupils: 1100
Scholarships: Yes
Religion: Roman Catholic

Fees per term
Day: £930-
Weekly board: -
Full board: -

○ Boy ○ Girl ● Co-ed
● Day ○ Week ○ Board

For further information and a prospectus, please contact the school.

St Columba's School *

Address: Duchal Road, Kilmacolm, Strathclyde PA13 4AU
Telephone: 0505 87 2238

Head: Mr A H Livingstone

Age range: 4-18
No. of pupils: 572
Scholarships:
Religion: Non-denominational

Fees per term
Day: £285-£1125
Weekly board: -
Full board: -

○ Boy ○ Girl ● Co-ed
● Day ○ Week ○ Board

St Columba's is a non-denominational co-educational school with a roll of 570 of which 340 are in the senior department. It has an excellent academic reputation but additionally encourages the development of the individual through participation in sport, music and drama. Kilmacolm is a most attractive small village, approximately 20 miles from Glasgow in a rural setting.

St Francis Primary - Merrylee

Address: Broom Road, Newlands, Glasgow, Strathclyde
Telephone: 041 637 0740

Head: Mrs J McGreal

Age range: 3-11
No. of pupils: 120
Scholarships:
Religion: Roman Catholic

Fees per term
Day: £600-
Weekly board: -
Full board: -

○ Boy ○ Girl ● Co-ed
● Day ○ Week ○ Board

St Francis - Merrylee is set in lovely secluded grounds and conveniently situated in the south side of Glasgow, and has a fully qualified and caring teaching staff who have the experience and ability to develop your child's capabilities to the full. Pupils are prepared for external examinations.

St Phillip's School

Address: Plains, Airdrie, Strathclyde ML6 7SF

Telephone:

Head:

Age range:
No. of pupils:
Scholarships:
Religion:

Fees per term
Day: -
Weekly board: -
Full board: -

● ○ ○
Boy Girl Co-ed
● ○ ○
Day Week Board

For further information and a prospectus, please contact the school.

St Ronan's Preparatory School

Address: 202 Nithsdale Road, Glasgow, Strathclyde G41 5EV

Telephone: 041 423 1938

Head: Mrs K Kemmet

Age range: 3-9
No. of pupils: 145
Scholarships:
Religion:

Fees per term
Day: -
Weekly board: -
Full board: -

○ ○ ●
Boy Girl Co-ed
● ○ ○
Day Week Board

For further information and a prospectus, please contact the school.

Wellington School *

Address: Carleton Tuttets, Ayr, Strathclyde KA7 2XH

Telephone: 0292 269321

Head: Mrs D A Gardner

Age range: 3-18
No. of pupils: 500
Scholarships:
Religion:

Fees per term
Day: -
Weekly board: -
Full board: -

○ ● ○
Boy Girl Co-ed
● ● ●
Day Week Board

For further information and a prospectus, please contact the school.

Westbourne School for Girls *

Address: 1 Winton Drive, Glasgow, Strathclyde G12 0PY

Telephone: 041 339 6006

Head: Mr J N Cross

Age range: 2-18
No. of pupils: 300
Scholarships:
Religion:

Fees per term
Day: -
Weekly board: -
Full board: -

○ ● ○
Boy Girl Co-ed
● ○ ○
Day Week Board

For further information and a prospectus, please contact the school.

TAYSIDE

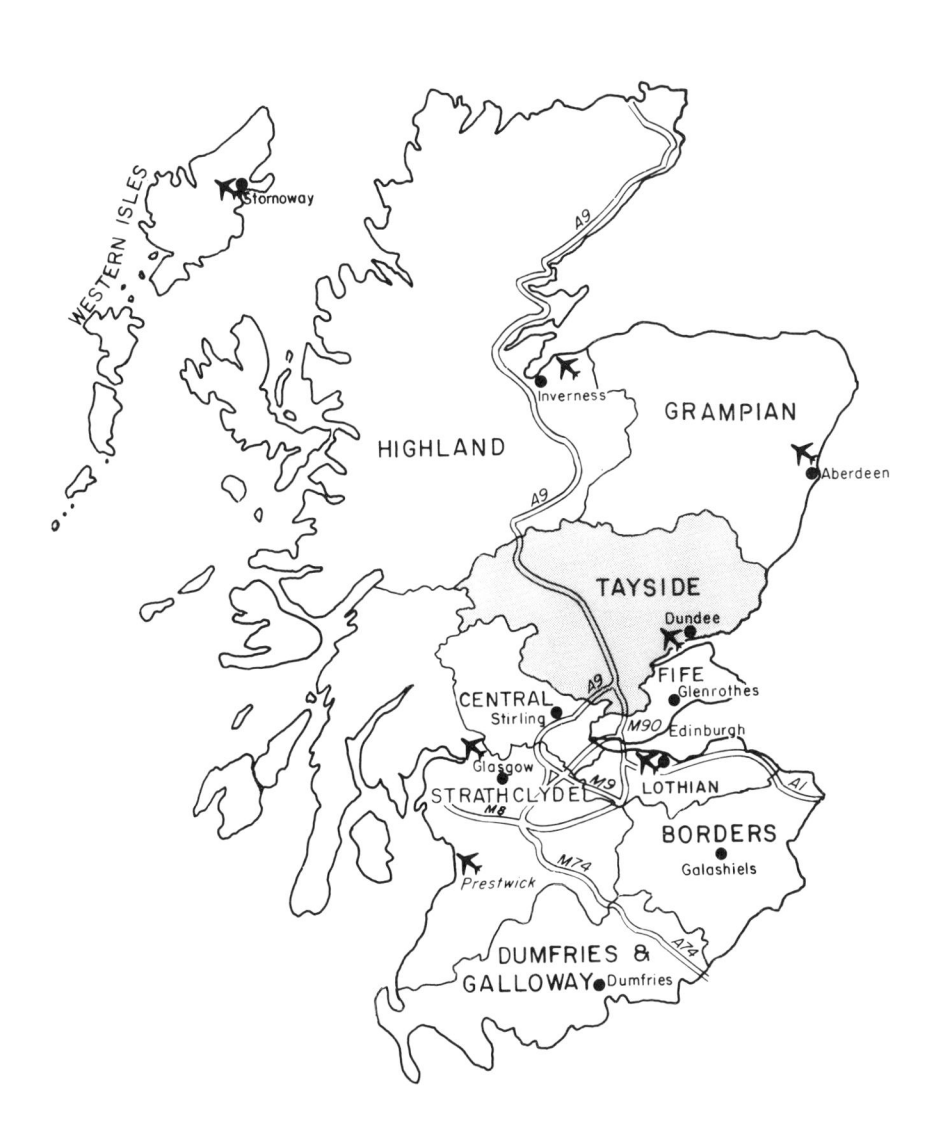

Ardvreck School *

Address: Crieff, Tayside
PH7 4EX

Telephone: 0764 4920

Head: Mr J R Bridgeland

Age range: 5-13
No. of pupils: 150
Scholarships: Yes
Religion: Church of England

Fees per term
Day: £1400-£1400
Weekly board: -
Full board: £2300-£2300

○ ○ ● Boy Girl Co-ed
○ ○ ● Day Week Board

Ardvreck is a well-equipped, full boarding preparatory school situated on the edge of Crieff. The school aims to keep all the children happy and busy. The school has an enviable academic, sporting and musical reputation. The staff, who are all professionally qualified, live on the school premises.

Balnacraig School †

Address: Fairmount Terrace, Perth, Tayside PH2 7AR

Telephone: 0738 36456

Head: Mr E Matthew

Age range: 12-16
No. of pupils: 24
Scholarships:
Religion: Non-denominational

Fees per term
Day: -
Weekly board: -
Full board: -

○ ○ ● Boy Girl Co-ed
○ ○ ● Day Week Board

Balnacraig is a co-educational residential school for 24 adolescents. It attempts to effect meaningful change in the young people's lives, many of whom are troubled and troublesome. The emphasis is very much on self esteem and achievement, all pupils are encouraged to sit Standard Grade examinations, Scot-vec modules and short courses.

Butterstone School *

Address: Arthurstone, Meigle, Blairgowrie, Tayside
PH12 8QY
Telephone: 08284 528

Head: Mr C G Syers-Gibson

Age range: 5-13
No. of pupils: 47
Scholarships:
Religion: Church of Scotland

Fees per term
Day: -£1610
Weekly board: -
Full board: -£2515

○ ● ○ Boy Girl Co-ed
● ○ ● Day Week Board

Butterstone School, which recently moved to new premises in lovely rural surroundings in central Perthshire, is the only girls preparatory school entirely independent of a senior school. There is a strong family atmosphere, and examination results are very good. Extra-curricular activities include dancing, riding, skiing, cooking, flower-arranging as well as the usual games.

Craigclowan *

Address: Edinburgh Road, Perth, Tayside PH2 8PS

Telephone: 0738 26310

Headmaster: Mr M E Beale

Age range: 3-13
No. of pupils: 192
Scholarships: Yes
Religion: Non-denominational

Fees per term
Day: £1155-£1155
Weekly board: -
Full board: -

○ ○ ● Boy Girl Co-ed
● ○ ○ Day Week Board

Craigclowan prepares children for Common Entrance and scholarship to a wide variety of schools in Scotland and England. In the past year children have entered Dundee High, St Leonards, Kilgraston, Strathallan, Glenalmond, Fettes, Loretto, Eton, Rugby, Sherborne, Downe House, St Mary's Ascot, Millfield and Haileybury. We also have a wide variety of extra-curricular activities and small classes.

Croftinloan School *

Address: Pitlochry, Tayside

Telephone: 0796 472057

Head: Mr N J Heuvel

Age range: 8-13
No. of pupils: 98
Scholarships: Yes
Religion: Non-denominational

Fees per term
Day: -£1810
Weekly board: -
Full board: -£2450

Boy ○ | Girl ○ | Co-ed ●
Day ● | Week ○ | Board ●

Croftinloan is a family-based Christian co-educational boarding school in the heart of beautiful Perthshire. Children are prepared for scholarship and entrance examinations to all secondary independent schools. Music, drama, crafts and all traditional games provide a fully rounded education in a caring environment.

Glenalmond College * p724

Address: Glenalmond, Perth, Tayside PH1 3RY

Telephone: 0738 88442

Head: Mr I Templeton

Age range: 12-18
No. of pupils: 300
Scholarships: Yes
Religion: Episcopalian

Fees per term
Day: £2200-
Weekly board: -
Full board: £3300-

Boy ○ | Girl ○ | Co-ed ●
Day ● | Week ○ | Board ●

On the edge of the Grampians, the college offers a friendly and secure rural environment with easy access to several cities. A wide range of outdoor activities includes fishing, golf, skiing, shooting, hillwalking and ice climbing. Modern sixth form girls' house. Choice of Highers or A levels in sixth form.

High School of Dundee *

Address: PO Box 16, Euclid Crescent, Dundee, Tayside DD1 9BP

Telephone: 0382 202921

Head: Mr R Nimmo OBE

Age range: 5-18
No. of pupils: 1136
Scholarships: Yes
Religion: Non-denominational

Fees per term
Day: £762-£1127
Weekly board: -
Full board: -

Boy ○ | Girl ○ | Co-ed ●
Day ● | Week ○ | Board ○

The High School of Dundee is a predominantly academic school. Each year the vast majority of pupils go on to university or to other forms of further education. High standards in academic fields are, of course, only part of a wider purpose; there is a wide range of out-of-school activities, many carried to high levels of achievement, and a strong corporate life-both essential to the education of the whole pupil.

Kilgraston School * p724

Address: Convent of the Sacred Heart, Bridge of Earn, Tayside PH2 9BQ

Telephone: 0738 812257

Head: Sr B F Farquharson

Age range: 8-18
No. of pupils: 280
Scholarships:
Religion: Roman Catholic

Fees per term
Day: £1300-£1435
Weekly board: £2465-£2720
Full board: £2465-£2720

Boy ○ | Girl ● | Co-ed ○
Day ● | Week ● | Board ●

Kilgraston is a Catholic foundation run by the International Society of the Sacred Heart. We aim to educate each individual to develop her talents and personality as fully as possible. Staff, parents and pupils work together to form a truly educational and vibrant community. Academic standards are excellent, and a very wide curriculum is available. Extra-curricular activities are diverse and ambitious.

Morrison's Academy * p725

Address: Crieff, Tayside
PH7 3AN

Telephone: 0764 3885

Head: Mr H A Ashmall

Age range: 5-18
No. of pupils: 700
Scholarships: Yes
Religion: All religions

Fees per term
Day: £748-£1054
Weekly board: -
Full board: £2620-£2918

Boy ○ Girl ○ Co-ed ●
Day ● Week ○ Board ●

Founded in 1860 this HMC school makes good use of its beautiful Perthshire situation in developing clubs and societies to complement the academic work leading to Scottish highers and Oxford and Cambridge A Levels.

The New School

Address: Butterstone, Dunkeld, Tayside PH8 0HJ

Telephone:

Head: Miss C G Syers-Gibson

Age range: 5-13
No. of pupils:
Scholarships:
Religion:

Fees per term
Day: -
Weekly board: -
Full board: -

Boy ○ Girl ● Co-ed ○
Day ● Week ○ Board ●

For further information and a propsectus, please contact the school.

Ochil Tower Rudolf Steiner School †

Address: Auchterarder, Tayside PH3 1AD

Telephone: 0764 62363

Head: Mr J M Surcamp

Age range: 6-18
No. of pupils: 34
Scholarships:
Religion: Christian

Fees per term
Day: -
Weekly board: -
Full board: -

Boy ○ Girl ○ Co-ed ●
Day ● Week ○ Board ●

Children are referred to Ochil Tower from all parts of Scotland and beyond by Education or Social Work Departments in consultation with the parents. Whether socially, mentally, or physically handicapped, they find here a suitable setting in which they may come to terms with themselves and their environment. Experience has shown that children gain most when they are admitted at an early age.

Queen Victoria School

Address: Dunblane, Tayside FK15 0JY

Telephone: 0786 822288

Head: Mr J D Hankinson MA

Age range: 10-18
No. of pupils: 255
Scholarships:
Religion: Non-denominational

Fees per term
Day: -
Weekly board: -
Full board: -

Boy ● Girl ○ Co-ed ○
Day ○ Week ○ Board ●

A boarding school for the sons of Scottish servicemen, Queen Victoria School is funded by the Ministry of Defence and boys come from a wide range of home backgrounds. Classes of 20 boys are of a wide ability range. There is ample opportunity for extra-curricular activities and hobbies. Older boys have the facility for private study, good teaching and excellent resources.

Rannoch School ✱

Address: Rannoch, by Pitlochry, Perth, Tayside PH17 2QQ
Telephone: 0882 632332

Head: Mr M Barratt

Age range: 10-18
No. of pupils: 290
Scholarships: Yes
Religion: Non-denominational

Fees per term
Day: £1795-£1795
Weekly board: -
Full board: £2830-£3070

○ ○ ● Boy Girl Co-ed
● ○ ● Day Week Board

Rannoch School in its magnificent Highland setting encourages every boy and girl to develop their own talents and to foster in all a sense of adventure, self-reliance and responsibility to the community. These qualities are much in demand in the Duke of Edinburgh's Award Scheme where the school has an outstanding record. Rannoch pupils have now gained over 400 Gold Awards.

Strathallan School ✱

Address: Forgandenny, Perth, Tayside PH2 9EG
Telephone: 0728 812546

Head: Mr C D Pighills

Age range: 10-18
No. of pupils: 480
Scholarships:
Religion:

Fees per term
Day: -
Weekly board: -
Full board: -

○ ○ ● Boy Girl Co-ed
○ ○ ● Day Week Board

For further information and a prospectus, please contact the school.

Trinity School

Address: 16 Bath Street, Broughton Ferry, Dundee, Tayside DD5 2BY
Telephone:

Head:

Age range: 5-9
No. of pupils:
Scholarships:
Religion:

Fees per term
Day: -
Weekly board: -
Full board: -

○ ○ ● Boy Girl Co-ed
● ○ ○ Day Week Board

For further information and a prospectus, please contact the school.

NORTHERN IRELAND

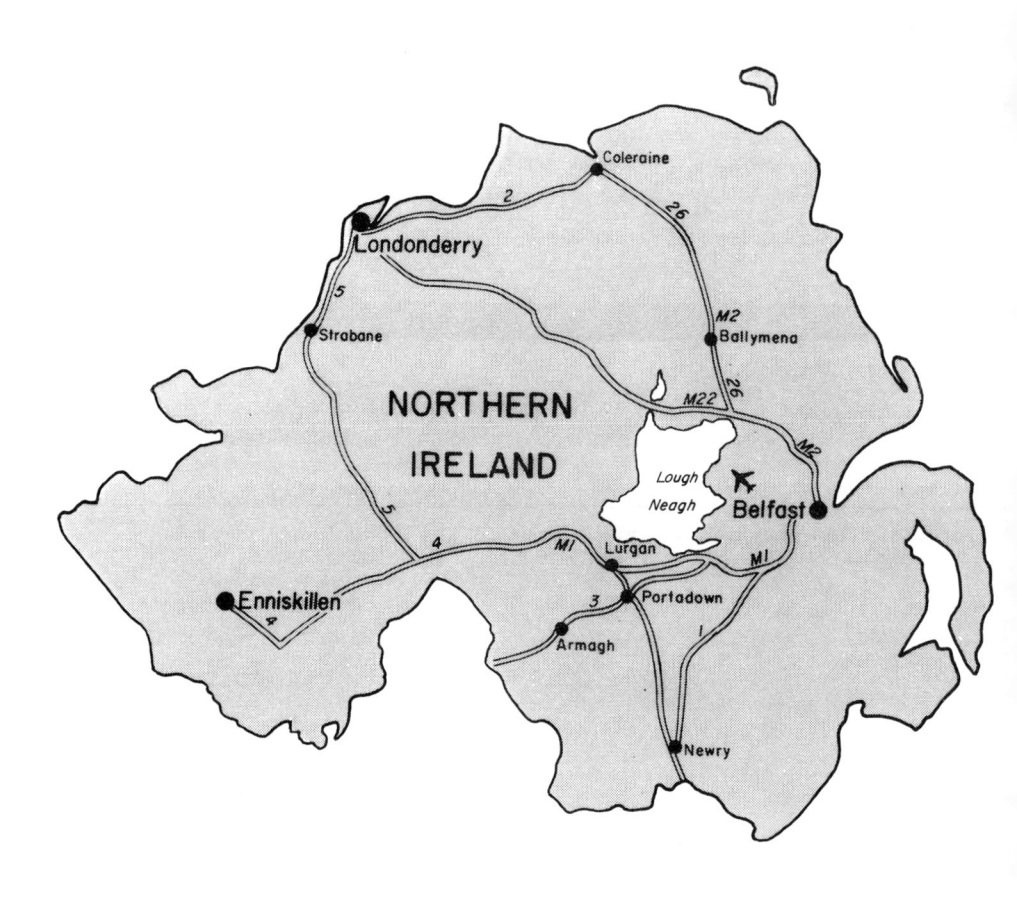

Bangor Grammar School

Address: 13 College Avenue, Bangor, Co Down

Telephone: 0247 473734

Head: Mr T W Patton

Age range: 11-13
No. of pupils: 900
Scholarships: Yes
Religion: Non-denominational

Fees per term
Day: £56-
Weekly board: -
Full board: -

● Boy ○ Girl ○ Co-ed
● Day ○ Week ○ Board

Bangor Grammar School is a voluntary grammar school with its own independent Board of Governors. Its first aim is academic excellence supported by the broader education of the 'whole man'. The school provides a wide range of extra-curricular activity and has a particularly high reputation in music, drama and debating. It has enjoyed an outstanding record of success in sport over the last decade.

Belfast Royal Academy

Address: 7 Cliftonville Road, Belfast, Co Antrim BT14 6JL

Telephone: 0232 740423

Head: Mr W M Sillery

Age range: 4-18
No. of pupils: 1617
Scholarships:
Religion: Non-denominational

Fees per term
Day: £400-£800
Weekly board: -
Full board: -

○ Boy ○ Girl ● Co-ed
● Day ○ Week ○ Board

Belfast Royal Academy, founded in 1785, is the oldest school in the city and is now a non-denominational co-educational, voluntary, day grammar school listed among the public schools of the United Kingdom: the headmaster is a member of the Headmasters' Conference. The management is vested in a Board of Governors, on which parents and teachers are represented.

Cabin Hill School

Address: 562-594 Upper Newtownards Road, Knock, Belfast, Co Antrim BT4 3HJ
Telephone: 0232 653368

Head: Mr C A I Dyer MA PGCE

Age range: 4-13
No. of pupils: 450
Scholarships: Yes
Religion: Non-denominational

Fees per term
Day: £467-£800
Weekly board: -
Full board: £1867-£1867

● Boy ○ Girl ○ Co-ed
● Day ○ Week ● Board

For further information and a prospectus, please contact the school.

Campbell College

Address: Belmont Road, Belfast, Co Antrim BT4 2ND

Telephone: 0232 763076

Head: Dr R J I Pollock BSc

Age range: 11-18
No. of pupils: 616
Scholarships: Yes
Religion: Non-denominational

Fees per term
Day: £1316-£1316
Weekly board: £2550-£2550
Full board: £2650-£2650

● Boy ○ Girl ○ Co-ed
● Day ○ Week ● Board

Campbell College was founded in 1894 under the will of Henry James Campbell, of Lorne, Craigavad. Although the college receives a limited amount of grant aid, in structure and management it is an indepedent school with a board of governors and with the headmaster who is a member of the Headmasters' Conference. It was incorporated by Royal Charter in 1951.

Coleraine Academical Institution

Address: Castle Rock Road, Coleraine, Co Londonderry BT51 3LA
Telephone: 0265 44331

Age range: 11-19
No. of pupils: 850
Scholarships:
Religion:

Fees per term
Day: -
Weekly board: £950-£950
Full board: £950-£950

● Boy ○ Girl ○ Co-ed
○ Day ● Week ● Board

Head: Mr R S Forsythe

Coleraine Academical Institution is a voluntary grammar school which encourages each boy to develop his academic potential as fully as possible, and at the same time open up wider issues through the avenues of sport and extra-curricular interest.

Foyle and Londonderry College

Address: Duncreggan, Londonderry, BT48 0AW
Telephone: 0504 269321

Age range: 4-18
No. of pupils: 910
Scholarships:
Religion: Non-denominational

Fees per term
Day: £700-
Weekly board: -
Full board: -

○ Boy ○ Girl ● Co-ed
● Day ○ Week ○ Board

Head: Mr H W Gillespie

This voluntary grammar school was founded in 1617 by a Master of the Merchant Taylors' Company. Set in over 30 acres on the west bank of the Foyle it prepares pupils for GCSE and A Levels and has a small Oxbridge entry. Strongest departments are mathematics, computing, English, music; emphasis on sport, Duke of Edingburgh Award Scheme and extra-curricular activities.

Friend's School Lisburn

Address: 6 Magheralave Road, Lisburn, Co Antrim BT28 3BH
Telephone: 0846 662156

Age range: 4-18
No. of pupils: 1050
Scholarships:
Religion: Quaker

Fees per term
Day: -£2002
Weekly board: -£2632
Full board: -£2732

○ Boy ○ Girl ● Co-ed
● Day ● Week ● Board

Head: Mr J T Green

Friend's School is a co-educational voluntary grammar school with boarding and preparatory departments. It is a Quaker foundation but caters for all sections of the community and draws from overseas as well as Northern Ireland. The school provides first-rate education up to A level and scholarship standard. It has also a fine reputation in games and extra-curricular activities.

Hunterhouse College p726

Address: Finaghy, Belfast, Co Antrim BT10 0LE
Telephone: 0232 612293

Age range: 5-18
No. of pupils: 720
Scholarships: Yes
Religion: Non-denominational

Fees per term
Day: -£716
Weekly board: £830-£1546
Full board: £830-£1546

○ Boy ● Girl ○ Co-ed
● Day ● Week ● Board

Head: Miss D E M Hunter

Long established grammar school with preparatory department situated in beautiful 37 acre wooded estate. School buildings, high standard, purpose built. Main boarding house a former Linen Mansion. Emphasis on breadth of education, academic excellence and personal development. Most girls take degree courses or equivalent, including Oxbridge. A happy school with wide extra-curricular involvement.

Methodist College Belfast

Address: 1 Malone Road,
Belfast, Co Antrim BT9 6BY

Telephone: 0232 669558

Head: Mr T W Mulryne

Age range: 4-18
No. of pupils: 2200
Scholarships: Yes
Religion: Methodist

Fees per term
Day: £95-£2316
Weekly board: £2745-£5016
Full board: £2745-£5016

Boy / Girl / Co-ed (Co-ed)
Day / Week / Board (all)

The Methodist College is a voluntary grammar school with two preparatory departments. The main points of entry are at 11+ (assessed on academic ability) and at 16+ (on GCSE results). There are about 200 boarders, and the sixth form is about 550 in number, to whom 22 A-level subjects are offered. Music, sport and drama are especially strong in a very wide range of extra-curricular activities.

Portora Royal School

Address: Enniskillen, County
Fermanagh BT74 7HA

Telephone: 0365 322658

Head: Mr R L Bennett BA DipEd

Age range: 11-18
No. of pupils: 409
Scholarships:
Religion: Non-denominational

Fees per term
Day: -£2502
Weekly board: -
Full board: -£2601

Boy / Girl / Co-ed (Boy)
Day / Week / Board (Day, Board)

The tuition fees are not paid by European Nationals. For further information and a prospectus, please contact the school.

Rockport

Address: Craigavad,
Holywood, Co Down
BT18 0DD
Telephone: 0232 428372

Head: Mr G Broad

Age range: 3-13
No. of pupils: 195
Scholarships: Yes
Religion: Non-denominational

Fees per term
Day: £562-£1155
Weekly board: -£1735
Full board: -£1735

Boy / Girl / Co-ed (Co-ed)
Day / Week / Board (all)

Rockport, set in beautiful surroundings overlooking Belfast Lough is an independent preparatory school for boys and girls aged 3-13. Pupils are prepared for transfer at 11 if they are staying in Northern Ireland and going to grammar schools, or for transfer at 13 to senior independent schools in England, Scotland and the Republic of Ireland. Complementing the academic side, pupils enjoy the challenge of sport every day.

Royal Belfast Academical Institution

Address: College Square East,
Belfast, Co Antrim BT1 6DL

Telephone: 0232 240461

Principal: Mr R M Ridley MA

Age range: 5-18
No. of pupils: 961
Scholarships: Yes
Religion: Non-denominational

Fees per term
Day: £110-£230
Weekly board: -
Full board: -

Boy / Girl / Co-ed (Boy)
Day / Week / Board (Day)

For further information and a prospectus, please contact the headmaster.

Royal School

Address: College Hill, Armagh, BT61 9DH

Telephone: 0861 522807

Head: Mr T Duncan MA BSC

Age range: 4-18
No. of pupils: 655
Scholarships:
Religion: Church of Ireland

Fees per term
Day: £950-£2600
Weekly board: £2960-£4610
Full board: £4750-£5450

Boy ○ Girl ○ Co-ed ●
Day ● Week ● Board ●

For further information and a prospectus, please contact the school.

The Royal School

Address: Dungannon, Co Tyrone BT71 6AP

Telephone: 08687 22710

Head: Mr P D Hewitt

Age range: 4-19
No. of pupils: 650
Scholarships: Yes
Religion: Non-denominational

Fees per term
Day: £985-£2510
Weekly board: -£5230
Full board: -£5230

Boy ○ Girl ○ Co-ed ●
Day ● Week ● Board ●

The Royal School Dungannon is the second oldest school in Ireland. Its 40 acre grounds lie in a peaceful and beautiful rural setting. Known as a centre of academic and sporting excellence, with 85% proceeding to British universities annually, the boarding department is extremely popular with overseas pupils because of this and the warmth of reception and friendliness given to them.

St Columb's College

Address: Londonderry

Telephone:

Head:

Age range: 11-18
No. of pupils:
Scholarships:
Religion: Roman Catholic

Fees per term
Day: -
Weekly board: -
Full board: -

Boy ● Girl ○ Co-ed ○
Day ● Week ○ Board ○

For further information and a prospectus, please contact the school.

St Malachy's College

Address: 36 Antrim Road, Belfast

Telephone:

Head:

Age range: 11-19
No. of pupils:
Scholarships:
Religion: Roman Catholic

Fees per term
Day: -
Weekly board: -
Full board: -

Boy ● Girl ○ Co-ed ○
Day ● Week ○ Board ○

For further information and a prospectus, please contact the school.

St Mary's Christian Brothers Grammar School.

Address: Glen Road, Belfast, County Antrim BT11 8NR

Telephone: 0232 615321

Head: Rev Br D Gleeson

Age range: 11-18
No. of pupils: 1112
Scholarships:
Religion: Roman Catholic

Fees per term
Day: -
Weekly board: -
Full board: -

● Boy ○ Girl ○ Co-ed
● Day ○ Week ○ Board

For further information and a prospectus, please contact the school.

Victoria College

Address: Cranmore Park, Belfast, Co Antrim BT9 6JA

Telephone: 0232 662506

Head: Dr C J Higginson

Age range: 4-18
No. of pupils: 795
Scholarships:
Religion:

Fees per term
Day: -
Weekly board: -
Full board: -

○ Boy ● Girl ○ Co-ed
● Day ○ Week ● Board

For further information and a prospectus, please contact the college.

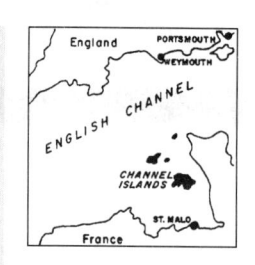

CHANNEL ISLANDS

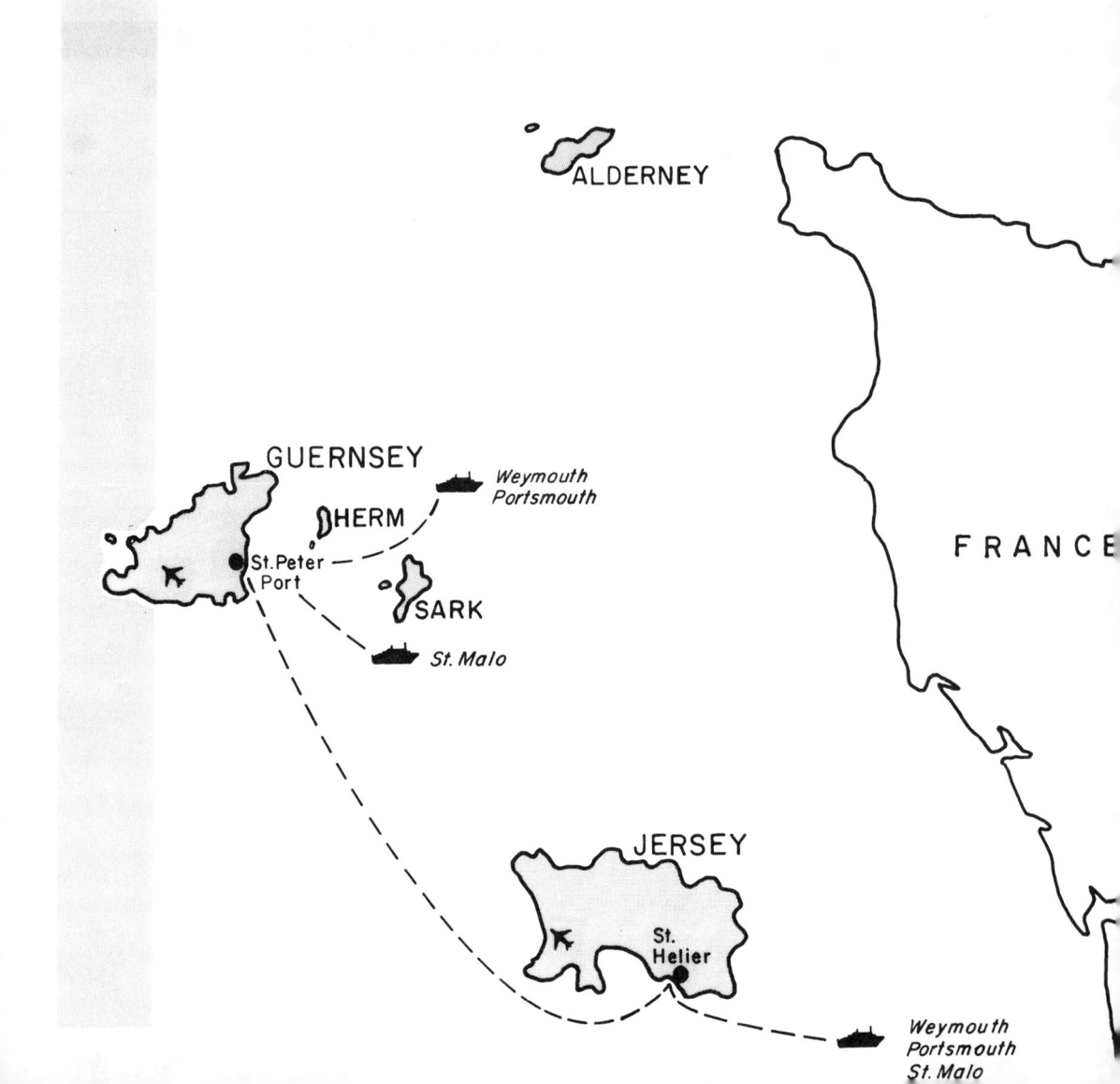

CHANNEL ISLANDS 649

Convent of Mercy

Address: Cordier Hill, St Peter Port, Guernsey

Telephone: 0481 720729

Head: Sister Carmel

Age range: 3-7
No. of pupils: 120
Scholarships:
Religion: Roman Catholic

Fees per term
Day: -£350
Weekly board: -
Full board: -

○ ○ ● Boy Girl Co-ed
● ○ ○ Day Week Board

For further information and a prospectus, please contact the school.

Elizabeth College

Address: Guernsey

Telephone: 0481 726544

Head: Mr J H F Doulton

Age range: 11-18
No. of pupils: 550
Scholarships: Yes
Religion: Church of England

Fees per term
Day: £700-£700
Weekly board: -
Full board: £1825-£1825

● ○ ○ Boy Girl Co-ed
● ○ ● Day Week Board

The college is a traditional day and boarding school. Despite being on an island a full programme of sport etc. is maintained and links with the mainland are close. Boarders are welcome from the UK or elsewhere. Regular flights run to all principal UK airports.

Jersey College School for Girls

Address: La Pouquelaye, St Helier, Jersey JE2 3ZN

Telephone: 0534 31543

Head: Mr I C Stevenson BSc

Age range: 5-18
No. of pupils: 820
Scholarships:
Religion:

Fees per term
Day: £483-£520
Weekly board: -
Full board: -

○ ● ○ Boy Girl Co-ed
● ○ ○ Day Week Board

The preparatory school (5-10) takes boys up to the age of 7 who then go to Victoria College Preparatory. Entry to the senior school (11-18) by examination in the previous February. The sixth form has a linked time-table with Victoria College giving a wide choice of subjects.

The Ladies' College

Address: Les Gravées, St Peter Port, Guernsey

Telephone: 0481 721602

Head: Miss M Macdonald

Age range: 3-18
No. of pupils: 562
Scholarships:
Religion: Christian

Fees per term
Day: £630-£630
Weekly board: -
Full board: -

● ● ○ Boy Girl Co-ed
● ○ ○ Day Week Board

Situated above the main town, the senior school, built in 1965, contains a large library, lecture theatre, gymnasium and a spacious hall with fully-equipped stage. The lower school and sports facilities are housed within the pleasant grounds. The aims of the college are to provide the best of the traditional, laying a secure foundation in the basics, and to encourage the pursuit of excellence. Boys 3-7 years.

St George's Preparatory School

Address: Le Hague Manor, St Peter, Jersey JE3 7DB
Telephone: 0534 481593
Head: Mr T Clare

Age range: 3-13
No. of pupils: 80
Scholarships:
Religion: Non-denominational

Fees per term
Day: £540-£1300
Weekly board: -
Full board: -

Boy ○ Girl ○ Co-ed ●
Day ● Week ○ Board ○

For further information and a prospectus, please contact the school.

St Michael's Preparatory School

Address: St Saviour, Jersey
Telephone:
Head:

Age range: 5-13
No. of pupils:
Scholarships:
Religion:

Fees per term
Day: -
Weekly board: -
Full board: -

Boy ○ Girl ○ Co-ed ●
Day ● Week ○ Board ●

For further information and a prospectus, please contact the school.

Victoria College

Address: Mont Millais, St Helier, Jersey
Telephone: 0534 37591
Headmaster: Mr J Hydes

Age range: 11-18
No. of pupils: 673
Scholarships:
Religion:

Fees per term
Day: £520-
Weekly board: £1950-
Full board: £2525-

Boy ● Girl ○ Co-ed ○
Day ● Week ● Board ●

Victoria College is beautifully situated overlooking St Helier. A school with a long record of academic success, offering a broad curriculum in GCSE, A Level, sport, culture and activities. The large majority of leavers go on to English universities and polytechnics.

Victoria College Preparatory

Address: Pleasant Street, St Helier, Jersey JE2 4RR
Telephone: 0534 23468
Head: Mr J H Hibbs

Age range: 7-11
No. of pupils: 290
Scholarships: Yes
Religion: Church of England

Fees per term
Day: £573-
Weekly board: -
Full board: -

Boy ● Girl ○ Co-ed ○
Day ● Week ○ Board ○

Victoria College Preparatory School is housed in fine buildings in the grounds of Victoria College overlooking St Helier. There is a staff of experienced and well qualified teachers with specialists in music, art, PE, French and science. The boys enter the preparatory department at 7 and normally pass on to Victoria College at the age of 11+.

ISLE OF MAN

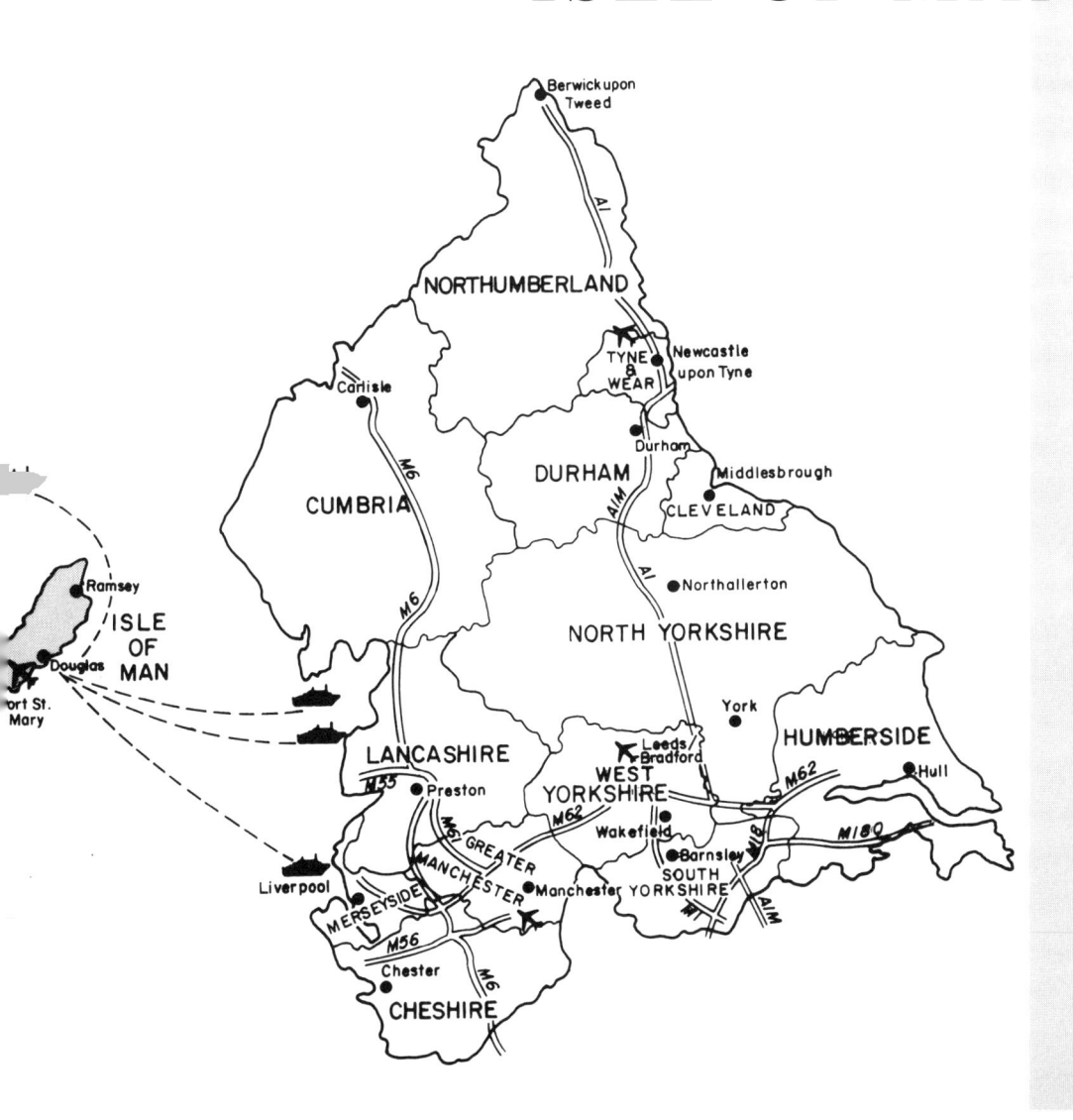

Buchan School

Address: Castletown, Isle of Man

Telephone: 0624 822526

Head: Mr B D Head MA

Age range: 3-13
No. of pupils: 340
Scholarships: Yes
Religion: Non-denominational

Fees per term
Day: £1130-£1600
Weekly board: -
Full board: -£2500

● Co-ed
● Day
● Board

As the preparatory school for King William's College, to which pupils are guaranteed progression, we cater for day children and boarders from UK and overseas. The Isle of Man has an impressive record as a safe and friendly environment for children, and the school possesses a range of impressive facilities near the magnificent mediaeval castle and harbour of historic Castletown.

King William's College

Address: Castletown, Isle of Man

Telephone: 0624 822551

Head: Mr S A Westley

Age range: 4-18
No. of pupils: 610
Scholarships: Yes
Religion: Church of England

Fees per term
Day: £1130-£2250
Weekly board: -
Full board: £2500-£3150

● Co-ed
● Day
● Board

King William's College with its preparatory school, Buchan School, is situated in the south of the Isle of Man adjacent to Ronaldsay Airport in a remarkably attractive and safe location. Academic standards are high; there is a full extra-curricular programme with a comprehensive pastoral system.

BEDFORD HIGH SCHOOL

At Bedford High School excellent standards are combined with courses which reflect the latest developments in education. The school occupies a central site in Bedford easily accessible by road and rail, convenient for Gatwick, Heathrow and Stansted Airports.

The Junior School in its modern setting provides the ideal foundation for life at the High School, offering a wide range of subjects in line with and beyond the requirements of the national curriculum. As it is closely linked, both physically and academically, with the Senior School, girls are able to progress happily and confidently to the next stage of their education.

In addition to the 21 subjects offered at GCSE, there are many extra-curricular activities and 20 sport options available. The school provides tuition in most orchestral instruments and there is a fine organ in the Main Hall. Students are able to participate with other schools in choral, orchestral and dramatic productions. Pastoral care, service to the community and the spiritual side of life are of importance to us, emphasis being on the balanced development of the individual.

The school has a thriving Sixth Form where students can choose from our 26 A-level and a number of A/S-level subjects, as well as a specially designed Business Course. Ninety per cent of our students go on to further education at Universities, Polytechnics or Colleges of Further Education. Careers guidance begins with the 13-year-olds and the girls receive counselling throughout all the major decision-making stages of their education.

Boarding is available from the age of 11. There are approximately 100 boarders in two houses, Wimborne Grange (11 to 15) and the Quantocks (16 to 18).

Main entry ages are 7, 8, 9, 11, 13 and 16, but applications at other ages will be considered if there are vacancies. The school offers Government Assisted Places and its own Bursaries.

For further details, a copy of the school prospectus and current fees, apply to the Headmistress:

Mrs. D. M. Willis, B.A.(Hons.) London, A.K.C.

**Bedford High School
Bromham Road
Bedford MK40 2BS
Telephone: (0234) 360221
Fax: (0234) 353552**

DOUAI SCHOOL
(Pronounced "DOW-EE")

Founded in Paris in 1615 by English Benedictine monks, the school moved to Douai, in northern France, before settling finally at Woolhampton, near Reading, in 1903.

Set in 150 acres of glorious Berkshire countryside, yet within minutes of the M4 and the towns of Reading, Newbury and Basingstoke, Douai boasts an enviable location. Central London and Gatwick are one hour away and Heathrow 45 minutes.

Although the majority of pupils are Roman Catholics, the school welcomes Christians of other denominations. Similarly, most pupils currently board, but we have growing number of day pupils. The School is becoming co-educational in 1993.

The school is small enough to have a family atmosphere and it maintains a tradition of good order and sound discipline. Although Douai is rooted in traditions which have stood the test of time, nevertherless we are flexible enough to meet changing demands and to look to the future. The staff comprises qualified and exerienced laymen and women and in 1991 a new Board of Governors was brought in to advise the Abbot and Community in the running of the school. In partnership with parents the expressed aims of Douai are:

★ to develop the academic potential of each pupil successfully and enjoyably;
★ to foster mature, caring behaviour and high standards;
★ to develop talents and skills whether physical, artistic, technical or social;
★ to nurture in each young person the growth of religious faith and spiritual understanding.

Douai School, Upper Woolhampton, Reading, Berkshire RG7 5TH   Telephone: 0734 713114

THE LICENSED VICTUALLERS' SCHOOL

Fully coeducational, ages 5-18

The Licensed Victuallers' School was founded in London in 1803 and has benefited from royal patronage since the accession of William IV. The School moved to a new site at Ascot in 1989, where it occupies purpose-built accommodation for some 700 day and boarding pupils. The new buildings have been constructed to an extremely high standard, and include a theatre, music school, chapel, sports halls and swimming pool, in addition to classrooms, laboratories, common rooms and boarding houses. The landscaped and wooded site also contains games fields.

Main entries are at five, seven, 11 and 16 by reports and interview. Boarding (weekly and full) from seven.

Enquiries should be made to the Headmaster at the address below

**The Licensed Victuallers' School
London Road
Ascot
Berks SL5 8DR
Telephone: (0344) 882770**

ST. ANDREW'S SCHOOL

I.A.P.S. Boys' and Girls' Preparatory School. Pre-Prep Department 4½-7½ years.

The School is set in 54 acres of magnificent woodlands and playing fields, but is only 10 minutes away from Junction 12 of the M4.

The curriculum is geared towards providing a broad education, and the modern, technology-related subjects sit happily by their more traditional counterparts. Class sizes are kept to approximately 18.

The School is a trust controlled by a Board of Governors, whose Chairman is P. P. Sanders-Rose, Esq.

Headmaster: R. J. Acheson, M.A., Ph.D.

Number of Pupils: 260.

Fees: Boarders £2,365 a term (inclusive). Day Pupils £1,695 a term.

Station: Pangbourne

St. Andrew's School
Buckhold
Pangbourne
Reading RG8 8QA
Telephone: 0734 744276

DAVENIES SCHOOL

Davenies occupies a superb eight-acre site in the heart of Beaconsfield, a delightful market town in rural South Buckinghamshire.

The school was founded in 1940 and has grown to accommodate some 170 boys between four and 13. The last five years have seen a major redevelopment programme to include a new classroom block, science laboratory, sports hall, 20-metre swimming pool, pavilion with changing and showering facilities and fully refurbished rooms for Music, Information Technology and Design Technology.

At Davenies great stress is laid on encouragement, enthusiasm and a happy family atmosphere. We aim to satisfy children's natural curiosity and desire for knowledge by making learning enjoyable, and by giving all our pupils plenty of scope to express themselves and develop mind, body and spirit to the full. All the traditional values are important here – hard work, hard play, courtesy, honesty and a sense of responsibility are all encouraged and expected.

Boys follow a course which combines the requirements of the National Curriculum with the more broadly based preparatory school mix of subjects. Davenies mainly prepares boys for Scholarship and Common Entrance examinations to all Independent School, but it is also possible for boys to proceed to the local Bucks. grammar schools through selection at either 12+ or 13+.

Headmaster: J. Roger Jones, B.Ed.(Oxon)

Davenies School, Station Road, Beaconsfield, Bucks. HP9 1AA. Tel: (0494) 674169. Fax: (0494) 681170

LADYMEDE

Girls' Preparatory and co-educational Pre-preparatory School situated in beautiful countryside. The interest of the staff is to provide a happy family atmosphere and first-class education, 11+, 12+ CE, in small classes.

Swimming is available throughout the year.

Escorted transport to and from London and airports.

Number of pupils: 130.

Pre-preparatory department for boys and girls age 3-8.

Day and boarding Preparatory School for girls aged 7-12½.

Weekly boarding welcome.

Prospectus, fees and all details from School Secretary.

Headmistress:
Mrs. P. A. Hollis, Dip.Ed.

Ladymede
Little Kimble
Aylesbury
Buckinghamshire HP17 0XP
Telephone: 08444 6154

Maltman's Green School

Maltman's Green is a Day and Boarding Preparatory School for girls aged 4-13.

It is our aim to encourage individual talents and develop skills which will prepare each pupil for successful entry to the right Senior School and lay the foundations for continued success. We measure this success in terms of confidence, achievement and fulfilment and we seek to provide the happy and secure environment which stimulates such growth.

A large, specialist teaching staff guarantees small classes with individual attention and we cover a broad curriculum, offering German and Spanish in addition, and with particular emphasis on design and information technology and computer studies. Music plays an important part and strong emphasis is placed on sport, especially swimming and tennis. Our gymnastics record is outstanding, both nationally and internationally.

The school is an attractive combination of 17th-century Malthouse and modern purpose-built buildings; there is a continuous development programme to ensure that the girls are equipped to meet the challenges of the 21st century.

Situated in 11 acres of countryside just outside Gerrards Cross, the school is within easy reach of London, close to the M1, M4 and M40 and a short journey from Heathrow, Gatwick, Stansted and Luton airports.

Girls may board from the age of seven and we have recently introduced weekly boarding. A bus service to and from London may be in operation in September 1993.

Maltman's Lane, Gerrards Cross, Bucks. SL9 8RR   Tel: (0753) 883022   Fax: (0753) 891237

PETERBOROUGH HIGH SCHOOL

Peterborough High School is an independent day and boarding school for girls aged 4-18 years and for boys aged 4-8 years.

The school is attractively situated close to the centre of the city of Peterborough, easily accessible by road and rail.

The High School has a very good academic record. Girls are prepared for GCSE, A-level and University entrance.

There are purpose-built classrooms, Science Laboratories, an Art Studio and Home Economics block.

Extensive out-of-school activities include Music, Drama, foreign visits, the Duke of Edinburgh Award scheme and numerous sporting activities.

Visitors are most welcome.

(Founded 1895)

A Girls' School of the Woodard Corporation.

Further particulars and prospectus may be obtained from:

**The Admissions Secretary
Peterborough High School
Westwood House
Thorpe Road
Peterborough PE3 6JF
Telephone: 0733 343357**

ABBEY GATE COLLEGE

An 11-18 Coeducational Day School of 300 pupils

The College is set in beautiful surroundings less than three miles from Chester City Centre.

★ Strong Sixth Form.
★ Outstanding academic results (87% at A-level).
★ The only coeducational independent secondary day school in the area.
★ Outstanding music department: Chapel Choir, College Choir and Dance Band.
★ Wide range of extra-curricular activities includes Duke of Edinburgh Award.
★ Scholarships and Bursaries at 11+ and in the Sixth Form.

For further details and prospectus, please contact:

**The Admissions Secretary
Abbey Gate College
Saighton Grange
Saighton
Chester CH3 6EG
Telephone: (0244) 332077**

ABBEY GATE SCHOOL

Foundation

The School was started in 1910 in Abbey Square, having a strong Christian foundation and association with the Cathedral.

The School is privileged to have its Harvest Festivals and Carol Services in the Cathedral.

Members of other religions or of none are welcomed, also other nationalities, thus adding to the stature of the School.

**Abbey Gate School
Victoria Road
Chester CH2 2AY
Telephone: 0244 380552**

TREMOUGH CONVENT SCHOOL

Tremough Convent School is an Independent Weekly Boarding and Day School for Girls from 3 to 18 years, and Day Boys from 3 to 11 years. The School is set in over 70 acres of beautiful grounds about four miles from Falmouth in Cornwall.

In September 1993 the School will be celebrating 50 years of its foundation by the Community of The Daughters of the Cross. Tremough is a Catholic School with over one-third Catholic pupils and the rest from other denominations.

Teaching is in accordance with the National Curriculum and the School offers a wide range of Arts and Science subjects to GCSE and GCE A-level. There are strong Art, Music and Drama Departments. Tremough is proud of its sporting achievements and has excellent facilities including an indoor, heated swimming pool and all-weather tennis courts.

A Prospectus and further details may be obtained from the Headmistress, Sister Maria.

**Tremough Convent School
Penryn
Cornwall TR10 9EZ
Telephone: 0326 372226**

ST. ANNE'S SCHOOL FOR GIRLS

THE Lake District National Park is an outstanding environment for a school. St. Anne's has over 80 acres of land together with lake frontage. Established in 1863, St. Anne's is a member of the G.B.S.A., the G.S.A. and Round Square Conference Schools.

The School is international in outlook, and there are approximately 400 girls aged 3-18, the majority of whom are boarders. The Senior and Junior Departments are strongly linked, giving a continuous and progressive education. Girls are prepared for the Arts or Science side of University Scholarship and Entrance Exams, and for G.C.E. A-level and G.C.S.E. Music, Art and Drama play an important part in the life of the School and optional activities include Sailing, Canoeing, Fell-walking, Camping, Swimming, Ballet, Riding and Driving Instruction. The School emphasises Voluntary Service and girls are encouraged to take on responsibility through the School Council.

St. Anne's is within easy reach of the M6, major rail links and Manchester Airport. Escorts are arranged to and from major rail terminals and there is a 24-hour service for those who have to fly abroad.

Entry: Girls are accepted into the Junior Department at any stage. Entry into the Senior School is at 11+ and 13+ or by direct entry into the Sixth Form. In special circumstances girls are occasionally accepted at other times. For further details, particulars of entry and fees, please write to:

**The Headmaster, M. P. Hawkins, M.A.
St. Anne's School for Girls, Windermere
Tel: Windermere (05394) 46164**

(See also page 750)

ST. ELPHIN'S

St. Elphin's School was founded in 1844 and is one of the oldest independent English Public Schools for Girls. It is a school in which there is a happy, friendly atmosphere, sensible discipline, good academic results and many extra-curricular activities.

The School buildings stand in extensive grounds and include specialist teaching rooms, Science laboratories, Art and Technology rooms, Gymnasium, recently refurbished music wing with practice rooms, an Assembly Hall, and Sixth-Form Houses with study bedrooms. The School Chapel stands close to the main buildings. There are hockey pitches, tennis and netball courts in the grounds.

Residence—There are four Houses in the Senior School with boarders and day girls in each. Sixth-Form boarders are housed in purpose-built accommodation with study bedrooms; girls aged 11-13 and 14-16 have their own sleeping areas and Junior boarders are in separate accommodation. Day girls are fully integrated into the life of the School.

Pupils receive preparation for the GCSE, A-level (J.M.B. and London Board) and for university and college entrance.

Fees—Senior boarders £2,949, Senior day girls £1,717 per term. Special fee rate for clergy and service daughters.

Up to 20 scholarships awarded annually, following examinations in January.

All particulars and prospectus may be obtained on application to the Headmaster.

Headmaster: A. P. C. Pollard, B.A., P.G.CE.

Church of England School. (Founded 1844)

**St. Elphin's
Darley Dale
Matlock
Derbyshire DE4 2HA**

ST. MARGARET'S SCHOOL

ST. MARGARET'S is an Independent Day School for 460 girls (95 in sixth form; weekly boarding facilities in separate accommodation).

A well-qualified staff prepares pupils for a wide range of Advanced level G.C.Es (26 subjects available). Co-ed approach in sixth form with Exeter School (H.M.C.).

The School is convenient to the City Centre and is equipped with modern laboratories and rooms for Home Economics, Art and Word-Processing, as well as all the usual facilities.

Special emphasis is given to Music and Drama, and Music Scholarships are available from 11+ upwards. Government Assisted Places are available at 11+ and 12+.

Academic bursaries for able sixth-form entrants.

Girls are encouraged to participate in a wide range of extra-curricular activities including Duke of Edinburgh Scheme, C.C.F. and Field Trips overseas. Young Enterprise, Christian Union, three Orchestras, Wind Band, Jazz Bands.

Please send for prospectus for full details

Woodard Schools (Western Division) Ltd.
MAGDALEN ROAD, EXETER, DEVON
Telephone: 73197

Headmistress:
Mrs. J. M. Giddings, B.A.Hons.(Durham)

STELLA MARIS SCHOOL
(including the Junior Department, St. Joseph's)

Stella Maris provides high educational standards in a caring environment.

It is a Christian school with committed, well-qualified staff. Laboratories and classrooms are well-equipped, and sports facilities include a heated, indoor swimming pool.

Drama, Art, Music and outdoor activities flourish throughout the school.

Senior Entrance Examination:
Saturday 16 January, 1993 at 9.15am.

Scholarships for girls of good academic ability are awarded annually.

Independent Day and Boarding School
Day: Girls 3-18; Boys 3-11
Boarding: Girls 8-18

For details, contact the Headmaster
Stella Maris School
Bideford
North Devon EX39 2PW
Telephone: (0237) 472208

TALBOT HEATH SCHOOL

FOUNDED 1886
GSA

For over 100 years we have provided high-quality education for pupils from Bournemouth and far beyond; day girls form the majority, but we also offer accommodation for full-, weekly- or short-term boarders. Though an Anglican school, we cherish the diversity of our students' religious and social backgrounds; our paramount aims are the growth of altruistic personal values and high achievement across a whole spectrum of activities.

Academic standards are excellent, and pupils receive careful individual guidance about subject and career choices. Our highly-qualified specialist staff are committed to their students' overall development and welfare; we value the caring, co-operative atmosphere within the school.

Pupils are encouraged to extend their interests through an impressive range of extra-curricular activities; we constantly seek to forge links between the school and the wider world, to prepare students for the global workplace of the 21st century.

For Sport and Music we offer extensive up-to-date facilities, and are proud of our girls' numerous successes at local and national levels of competition.

Entry is at 7+ (Juniors) and 11+ (Main School) by successful examination.

Scholarships, Assisted Places and Bursaries are available.

Please come and visit us and/or send for a prospectus to the Head Mistress:

Talbot Heath, Rothesay Road
Bournemouth BH4 9NJ
Telephone: (0202) 761 881

CROWSTONE SCHOOLS

Aims:
The choice of school in the Independent sector can be a perplexing and worrying task for parents. Academic success, staff qualifications, the curriculum and ethos, are all areas of school life which are of vital importance to parents. At *Crowstone Schools* these areas are not left to chance. Considerable thought and effort is put into providing an education which is a thorough preparation for life. It is our desire, not only to produce the highest possible achievement from each individual child in our care, but also to provide a happy atmosphere in which to develop the learning years. We are equally concerned in providing extra stimulus for those children of high ability, as we are in providing extra help and guidance for children with learning difficulties.

Perhaps the most important feature of our approach is the attention we can give to individuals. We aim to discover and develop the talents and strengths of each pupil and also help them redress areas of weakness.

The School:
Crowstone Schools are Independent Day Schools for boys and girls between the ages of three and 16 years. It consists of Pre-School, Infant, Junior and Senior departments to G.C.S.E. (at the newly opened *Sutton School,* Rochford).

The School was founded by Mrs. R. H. Watkins and Miss J. H. Watkins in 1946. Mr. J. P. Thayer (Teacher's Certificate, University of London) became the Headmaster and Proprietor, along with Mrs. S. G. Thayer, in September 1980.

The *Westcliff School* is situated at the south-eastern corner of the Chalkwell Hall Estate, a short distance from Westcliff Station. The school has large, bright, airy classrooms, recently re-equipped with a variety of new textbooks and reading books. Facilities include a hard surface playground, a playing field (*other specialised sports facilities in the area are sometimes used*), Music and Movement. P.E. and Indoor Games are organised in a newly built and well-equipped School Hall.

Crowstone Schools
121/123 Crowstone Road
Westcliff-on-Sea
Essex SS0 8LH

Telephone: 0702 346758

ST. HILDA'S SCHOOL

In addition to the General Certificate of Secondary Education pupils are prepared for examinations with the Royal Society of Arts, the Imperial Society of Teachers of Dancing, the Guildhall School of Music, the Associated Board of the Royal School of Music, Speech and Drama, and the London Academy of Music and Dramatic Art.

A large staff of qualified teachers gives a favourable staff : pupil ratio which ensures more personal teaching with caring general supervision.

The School also offers extensive facilities for sport and physical education which include gymnastics, netball, volleyball, rounders, tennis, swimming, cross-country running and athletics.

Day School for Girls from 3 to 16 years.

For full particulars and Prospectus, please apply to the School.

Principal:
Mrs. V. M. Tunnicliffe
University of London Teacher's Diploma

St. Hilda's School
15 Imperial Avenue
Westcliff-on-Sea
Essex SS0 8NE

Telephone:
Southend-on-Sea (0702) 344542

ST. MARY'S SCHOOL

Established in 1908, St. Mary's is a day school for 600 girls.

In the Junior School girls are admitted from the age of four. Opportunity is provided for each girl to develop her personality and academic potential as fully as possible.

The Senior School offers a full academic curriculum for girls aged 11 to 16 years. Participation in a wide range of cultural and physical activities is encouraged in addition to the formal curriculum. There is an entrance examination for girls who wish to join the School.

The main School buildings face South. The grounds contain a heated swimming pool and three hard courts, and there is a fully-equipped gymnasium.

The Lower School, at Comrie House, Stanway, is set in extensive grounds and has two hard tennis courts and its own gymnasium.

Girls are prepared for the Common Entrance Examination to Public Schools at 11+, and for the G.C.S.E.

Principal: Mrs. G. M. G. Mouser, M.Phil.

**St. Mary's School
Lexden Road
Colchester CO3 3RB**
and
**Comrie House
Stanway
Telephone: 0206 572544**

BEAUDESERT PARK SCHOOL

The School is an Educational Trust. The Staff consists of 16 full-time teaching staff and eight music staff. All the staff take a personal interest in the children's welfare and good manners. Classes are small and pupils are given individual attention in streamed classes.

The School stands high up in the Cotswolds in its own grounds of 30 acres and adjoins Minchinhampton Golf Course.

Over the last 10 years there have been many additions to the academic, cultural and sporting facilities to enable us to accommodate the extra pupils and extend their interests. An indoor swimming pool and enlarged technology department opened last year.

Activities include cricket, soccer, rugger, hockey, tennis, swimming, golf, archery, badminton, netball, dancing, judo, rifle shooting and hill walking and over a dozen Societies and Clubs meet each week.

Over 200 Scholarships have been gained to the leading Public Schools.

Number of pupils: 242 (including Pre-Prep. Dept.)
Fees: Boarders £2,495, Day £1,835,
 under-10 £1,630,
 Pre-Prep. Dept. £915-£1,150
 inclusive of all but optional extras

Headmaster: J. C. P. Keyte, M.A.
Assistant Headmaster: M. J. Stevens, Cert.Ed.

**Beaudesert Park School, Minchinhampton
Gloucestershire GL6 9AF
Tel: Stroud (0453) 832072. Station: Stroud**

THE JUNIOR SCHOOL CHELTENHAM COLLEGE

The Junior School is a boys' Preparatory School from seven to 13 boarding and day. Girls and boys are being admitted into a new Pre-Prep Department which opens in September 1993. By 1996 the Junior will have girls at all stages up to the age of 11 years. The final two years of the Junior will remain boys only, in preparation for transfer to Cheltenham College or other Public Schools at 13.

The Junior enjoys very fine facilities indeed. The school is set in a secluded parkland setting in the heart of the dignified Regency town of Cheltenham.

The Junior School is totally self-contained and provides an extremely high level of teaching with a very wide range of sporting, musical, athletic and aesthetic activities. In addition The Junior is also privileged to share Cheltenham College's six-lane 25m swimming pool, all-weather pitches, science laboratories and magnificent College Chapel.

The new Pre-Prep (rising five to rising seven) and Lower School (seven to nine) are contained in their own building. In Middle School (nine to 11) more specialist teachers are introduced to the children. In the final two years of The Junior the boys are prepared for Common Entrance and Scholarship Entrance to Cheltenham College and other Public Schools.

The staff of 30 fully qualified teachers are dedicated to bringing out the very best in each individual child. A well-developed tutorial system ensures that every child's progress is monitored closely so that the best possible benefits from our academic and extra-curricular package can be fully enjoyed by every pupil.

The Junior is particularly keen on sport, music, art and technology. There are special rooms and buildings, including a fine Music School, to accommodate the appropriate facilities to ensure that these subjects are taught to the highest possible level alongside the more traditional academic subjects.

On the boarding side a resident married Housemaster, assisted by resident tutors and three matrons, looks after the boys in a home-from-home atmosphere. A full programme of activities is arranged for the boarders. They particularly enjoy the school lake, the adventure playground and the play barn.

Regular meetings are arranged between home and school so that parents are kept fully briefed on their children's progress. The Headmaster is happy to meet parents by appointment during term or holiday time.

265 Pupils: 75 Boarders; 190 Day.
Boarding fees £2,375-£2,575.
Day fees £1,795-£1,995.

Headmaster:
N. I. Archdale, B.Ed(Bristol), M.Ed(Edinburgh).

Cheltenham College, Thirlestaine Road, Cheltenham   Tel: 0242 522697

SELWYN SCHOOL

Selwyn School is Gloucester's leading independent school for girls from 3 to 18 (and for boys 3 to 11). It has seen rapid growth in numbers and facilities since 1990. A major development programme has been undertaken including the provision of a new Junior Department for boys and girls aged 3 to 11, Food Technology suite, an Orchestral and other Music rooms, a resited and expanded library, enhanced P.E. and Drama facilities and the provision of other senior classrooms.

The Junior Department puts a high priority on teaching the fundamentals. In the middle school there is a modern and broad curriculum for girls aged 11-14, an extensive range of GCSE subjects with strong representation of Science and a choice of currently 20 A-levels. The intellectual intake of the school has always been broad but it has an excellent academic reputation, with record GCSE pass rates of over 80% A-C grade passes achieved in the last two years. Tutorial-based teaching is in small groups in the lively and expanding Sixth Form.

Selwyn is, above all, small and friendly, looking at individual needs of each child academically, socially and personally. Classes are small and never over 18. Over 30 extra-curricular activities are normally offered. Drama has an exceptional reputation and Music is popular.

The school is traditional in its emphasis on good manners and a concern for others. These values are fostered in every way and furthermore in the girls' senior school every encouragement is given to leadership, initiative, independence, self-reliance and a pride in femininity.

Most students are day pupils often brought in by coach from Swindon, Cheltenham, Stroud, Ross, Lydney, Cirencester, Tewkesbury and Gloucester but, in Taylor House, Selwyn has excellent, very friendly boarding facilities providing study bedroom accommodation for girls of 14 and over. Weekly boarding is very popular. A very full programme exists for boarders at weekends and during the week. Children board from the age of nine. A small number of overseas students are personally under the care of an expert team who look after welfare and educational needs, led by the Co-ordinator for Overseas Students, to provide them with an individual programme of study. There is a Special Needs Department in the school, run by two specialist teachers, for small numbers of children with dyslexia or related conditions.

Scholarships are available every October at 7+, 11+, 13+ and 16+. Music, Drama and P.E. scholarships are awarded every summer.

Set in beautiful and extensive parkland on the edge of Gloucester, Selwyn School is an ideal environment in which to grow and learn. We strongly believe that *happy children make successful adults.* We are a school dedicated at senior level to the needs of girls and look to the future in preparing them for tomorrow's world. Prospectus and other details sent on request.

Selwyn School, Matson House, Gloucester GL4 9DY   Telephone: 0452 305663

WESTONBIRT SCHOOL

Westonbirt is set in glorious countryside, yet is within easy reach of Bristol, Bath and Cheltenham, the M4 and M5. Day girls join the 260 boarders in many of the extra-curricular activities.

Westonbirt caters for the good all-rounder who will excel and enjoy the many opportunities available. Academic ability ranges from the very bright to the average and most girls take at least nine GCSEs and later three A-levels, with the majority continuing on to some form of further education. A wonderful new Art, Design and Technology building opened in September 1992 and new Science Laboratories will be ready in September 1993.

For further information, write or telephone:

**The Registrar
Westonbirt School
Tetbury
Gloucestershire GL8 8QG**

Telephone: Westonbirt (0666) 880333

Wynstones School

A Rudolf Steiner School

An Education for Life

Set in 25 acres, Wynstones School is in the lea of the Cotswolds, near Gloucester. The School Farm is close by.

The school is a Charitable Trust, administered by parents and some of the teachers. There is no headmaster – the teachers carry the responsibility together for the educational direction of the school.

From kindergarten to University entrance age there are about 300 pupils. Children receive individual attention and get to know the teachers and all those in their age groups well, making for strong friendships and a social cohesion which is rare.

Wynstones is part of a world-wide network – more than 500-strong and growing. Common to them all is Rudolf Steiner's approach: to awaken the potential of each child and to nourish the whole personality. Thus the arts and practical work are taken as seriously as the academic.

At the heart of all education is a simple principle: **people learn by doing.** If we are healthy we continue to learn all our lives. When Wynstones' pupils leave with their A-levels and GCSEs they are ready to continue their education for life.

**Wynstones School
Whaddon
Gloucester GL4 0UF
Telephone: 0452 522475
Fax: 0452 525667**

NORTH FORELAND LODGE

North Foreland Lodge was founded in 1909 in Kent and moved to Hampshire in 1947. The school is set in 90 acres of parkland with easy access to M4, M3, Heathrow, Gatwick and London (Waterloo 55 minutes).

Entry at 11+ or 12+ – School's own Assessment Day and interview followed by Common Entrance. Entry to Sixth Form is based on GCSE results plus interview. The school aims to provide a balanced education and to encourage each girl to achieve her full potential, not only in the academic field, but also in sport, art and music. The staff : pupil ratio is 1 : 9. All girls follow a common core curriculum for the first three years which includes all basic subjects, including three Sciences, IT, CDT, Latin, Modern Languages. At 14+ girls take five compulsory subjects for GCSE plus 3-5 options. A-levels are offered in most GCSE subjects plus Economics/Business Studies, Politics, Sociology. In addition girls can study for the RSA Clait Diploma.

Most girls continue on into further education: about 75% go to University and others to Polytechnic, Art College etc.

The school has a large area of playing fields and tennis courts, a swimming pool and a new sports hall. Other new facilities include a language laboratory, two teaching wings and science laboratories. All girls are encouraged to join a wide range of clubs and societies.

North Foreland Lodge, Sherfield-on-Loddon Basingstoke, Hampshire RG27 0HT
Tel: Basingstoke (0256) 882431

ST BENEDICT'S CONVENT SCHOOL

ACCREDITED BY THE INDEPENDENT SCHOOLS ASSOCIATION
(ASSISTED BY BOARD OF GOVERNORS)

Girls, Boarding and Day School 4-16
Boys, Day 4-9, Nursery Class 3-4

Pupils prepared for GCSE
Associated Board Music
Royal Academy of Dancing examinations
Fully qualified caring staff

While academic standards are high the aim of the school is to allow pupils to attain their full potential

All denominations welcomed

Two Bursaries available of up to half tuition fees

Contact:
School Secretary
St. Benedict's Convent, Penton Lodge
Andover, Hants

Telephone:
Weyhill (0264) 772291

SCHOOL PROFILES — Hampshire

ST. NICHOLAS' SCHOOL

A Public Day School for Girls and for Pre-Preparatory School Boys.

There are three Houses and a new well-equipped Science Block.

In the Senior House girls of 12 years upwards are prepared for G.C.S.E., A- and Scholarship-level and for entrance to Universities and Colleges of Higher Education. Boys are prepared for Preparatory School.

Children of 4½ to seven attend the Kindergarten department.

Entry at 11+ by Common Entrance Examinations.

The religious teaching is that of the Church of England and early morning monthly Communion Services are held in the School Chapel.

Games and Gym are in the charge of a fully-qualified Staff and gymnasts enjoy the facilities of a modern Gymnasium.

Art, Needlework, Music and Drama are included in the Timetable.

There is a wide range of optional extras including Typing, Fencing, Dancing, Riding, Piano, Wind, String and Brass Instruments.

School Societies offer opportunities for furthering individual interests: Guides, Brownies, Dance Club, Gym Club, Badminton Club, Riding Club, Choirs and Orchestra (Junior and Senior).

(G.B.G.S.A.)

Educational Trust Ltd.

Principal:
Mrs. L. G. Smith, B.A.(Hons) P.GC.E.

St. Nicholas' School
Fleet
Hampshire GU13 8JT

ST. SWITHUN'S SCHOOL

St. Swithun's School is an Independent Boarding and Day School for Girls aged 11-18 years with a separate Junior School for Girls aged 3-11 years and Boys up to the age of 8 years.

The School was founded in 1884 in the city of Winchester and moved in 1931 to its present fine site on the Downs to the east of the city, about a mile from its centre.

The majority of girls enter the Senior School between the ages of 11 and 13 years, but girls are accepted at other ages, including the Sixth Form, subject to satisfactory tests.

A flexible, broadly-based academic education is offered, enabling girls to develop their potential.

The School grows and flourishes in a way appropriate to the present day, but it is glad to be very firmly rooted in its traditions and the fine things in its past. In attitude it largely reflects the changes and relaxations to be found in any modern institution or community and, within a framework of easier discipline, there really is a remarkably friendly and relaxed atmosphere in the School.

Headmistress: Miss Joan Jefferson B.A.

St. Swithun's School
Winchester
Hants. SO21 1HA
Telephone: 0962 861316

(See also page 751)

WYKEHAM HOUSE SCHOOL
FAREHAM

We endeavour to produce girls who are confident, have strong convictions and who are capable of contributing to the community in a clear-thinking and positive way.

The curriculum aims to maintain standards and yet recognises the need to keep apace of educational developments and modern teaching techniques. The girls have every opportunity to develop their scientific knowledge and information technology skills as well as their talents in more traditional subjects.

Wykeham House has many areas of excellence, not least the strong sense of community fostered by staff and parent contact.

Please telephone the school if you want to see us in action.

**Wykeham House School
East Street
Fareham
Hants PO16 0BW**

Telephone: 0329 280178

Fax: 0329 823964

THE ABBEY COLLEGE

The Abbey College is a well-established international boarding school, co-educational, taking students from the age of 12 years upwards.

Located on the southern slopes of the beautiful Malvern Hills, set in 70 acres of its own grounds, the College offers a full range of academic leisure and sporting amenities and prepares candidates for a wide range of GCSE and A-level subjects. The College is also involved in special University Access Programmes with a number of U.K. and European Institutions.

Admission is by entrance test and school report, plus interview where possible. Parents and potential students are welcome to visit the College at any time by appointment.

Boarding is arranged in eight separate houses, each under the supervision of a resident member of staff.

For a prospectus and/or appointment please contact the Registrar at the address below.

Principal:
Mr. Robin Bellerby, M.A., B.Sc., Grad.Cert.Ed., F.B.I.M., F.B.I.S.

**The Abbey College
253 Wells Road
Malvern Wells
Worcestershire WR14 4JF**

Tel: 0684 892300

Fax: 0684 892757

HOME FROM SCHOOL

WHAT DOES YOUR CHILD DO AT THE END OF A SCHOOL DAY?

*Do they have someone to welcome them home?
Do they have friends around them? Do they have leisure activities to enjoy?
Do they have prep. to do for the next day? Do they have time to themselves?
Do they have to take their turn with helping in the house?*

RNIB NEW COLLEGE WORCESTER

Offers all these to
VISUALLY IMPAIRED YOUNGSTERS
As well as
ACADEMIC EDUCATION

Principal: Revd. B. R. Manthrop. Tel: 0905 763933

ABBOT'S HILL SCHOOL

A Foundation For Achievement

(Girls 11-16)

— Day, boarding or weekly boarding
— A new Science and Technology Block
— Small classes/high staff : pupil ratio

— Wide range of extra-curricular activities
— Strong sports and music department
— Easy access from M1, M25 and airports
— 70 acres of parkland

For further information or prospectus, please contact:

**The School Secretary
Abbot's Hill School
Bunkers Lane
Hemel Hempstead
Herts. HP3 8RP**

**Telephone: (0442) 240333
Fax: (0442) 69981**

THE JUNIOR SCHOOL
BISHOP'S STORTFORD COLLEGE

The school offers an all-round education in a friendly and caring environment. Boys are prepared for Common Entrance and for Senior Schools Scholarships by a qualified staff of 20 full-time and three part-time teachers. Maths is setted from the age of eight, French taught from the age of nine and setted later with English and Latin; there are three streams in each of the final three years. No class is larger than 22 and the average class size is 16. A close eye is kept on national reforms in education and the curriculum constantly updated to take account of best practice. As well as the usual subjects, Information and Design Technology, European Affairs, Drama and Music are all taught within the timetable.

The boarding house is under the supervision of a Housemaster and his wife with the assistance of four resident staff and a number of visiting House Tutors. The accommodation has recently been refurbished to provide light, airy and homely surroundings.

The Junior School enjoys first-rate facilities, including a purpose-built building, incorporating classrooms, library and craft room, designed for the particular needs of seven- to nine-year-old boys.

About 90% of leavers choose to proceed to our Senior School (13-18 years, HMC, boarding and day, with an A-level pass rate well over 90% in each of the last four years), in which a place is guaranteed subject to good academic progress and behaviour.

**The Junior School
Bishop's Stortford College
Maze Green
Bishop's Stortford
Herts CM23 2PH**
Telephone: 0279 653616
Fax: 0279 755865

CONVENT OF ST. FRANCIS DE SALES
Our Lady of Light Independent Day Schools

The Convent of St. Francis de Sales is an independent day school set in spacious, attractive grounds, close to the centre of Tring with views over open countryside. It is situated on the bus route within easy access of Aylesbury, Hemel Hempstead, Dunstable, Luton and Chesham. The School caters for children from the ages of 2½ to 17 years in two adjacent purpose-built schools. Girls 2½-17. Boys 2½-11.

Whilst a pleasant working environment is an important asset, education is concerned with people. Through the dedication, commitment and encouragement of the Sisters and Staff the Convent ensures each individual pupil experiences the pleasures and rewards of achievement. Our students are encouraged to be hard-working, active and self-disciplined.

At the same time, within the Christian environment they develop an understanding of the needs for others and so grow into caring adults.

Curriculum:
The School course includes Religious Knowledge, English Language and Literature, Mathematics, Geography, Art, Domestic Science, Physics, Chemistry, Biology, French, German, History, Needlework, Class Singing, Music, Computer Studies and Typing.

Examinations:
Pupils are prepared for G.C.S.E. Examinations and also for examinations in Music Theory and Pianoforte of the Associated Board and examinations of the Pitman Institute.

Admission Requirements:
Average and above average ability and achievement. Some exceptions can be made for the child with slight learning difficulties providing that he or she is willing and eager to work. A personal interview is given and children over the age of eight are required to sit an entrance examination.

**The Convent of St. Francis de Sales
Aylesbury Road, Tring, Herts HP23 4DL**
Telephone: 0442 822315

Edge Grove Preparatory School

A traditional boarding and day school for boys aged 7-13 years, Edge Grove believes that children acquire self-confidence and self-discipline in a happy atmosphere which they can identify with home and places emphasis on consideration and good manners. There is an excellent Common Entrance record, and one leaver in six gains a Public School scholarship; with 11 forms of 15 pupils, success is attributed to good teaching by a highly qualified and dedicated staff. Music is strong and sport has a high profile, but there is an awareness that not everyone is a natural games player and sport for the less able must be made fun.

Excellent facilities include a chapel, music school, art block, new science and technology wing and recently constructed assault course; the grounds provide eight playing fields, croquet lawns, a swimming pool, natural woodland and a boating lake which is a bird sanctuary. An extensive extra-curricular programme offers brass band, computers, model-making and roller-skating and the school has its own cub pack. Expedition training takes place in Devon and Scotland and there are international football and cricket tours in addition to skiing in the French Alps and a French Canals trip. There are term-time exchanges with schools from France, Spain and Luxembourg.

Set in 25 acres of countryside, Edge Grove lies 15 miles north-west of Central London, close to the M1, A1 and M25 and less than 45 minutes from Heathrow, Stansted and Gatwick airports.

Administered by a Board of Governors it offers full boarding, weekly boarding and day places, and provides a bus service.

PUBLIC SCHOOL PLACES GAINED
1985 – 1992

Harrow	46	Felsted	4
Aldenham	37	King's Canterbury	4
Eton	21	Merchant Taylor's	4
Haileybury	16	Radley	4
Uppingham	11	St. Alban's	3
Oundle	10	Mill Hill	3
Shrewsbury	6	Marlborough	2
Millfield	5	Sherborne	2
Rugby	5	Shiplake	2
Bradfield	4	Stoneyhurst	2
Charterhouse	4	Tonbridge	2

One place each at: Bishop's Stortford – Blundell's – Canford – Cranleigh – Culford – Douai – Gordonstoun – Gresham's – Haberdasher's Aske's – King Edward's, Whitley – King's, Bruton – King's, Ely – Monkton Coombe – Oakham – Pangbourne – Rannoch – Repton – St. David's – St. Paul's – St. George's – The Leys – Warwick – Wellington – West Buckland – Winchester.

SCHOLARSHIPS GAINED
1985 – 1992

Eton	7	Radley	2
Aldenham	6	Shrewsbury	2
Haileybury	5	Uppingham	2
Harrow	3	Bishop's Stortford	1
Rugby	3	Millfield	1
Felsted	2	Repton	1
King's, Canterbury	2	The Leys	1
Oundle	2	Tonbridge	1

Aldenham, Hertfordshire WD2 8BL   Tel: 0923 855724   Fax: 0923 859920

Headmaster: Mr. K. J. Waterfield, Cert.Ed.

EGERTON-ROTHESAY SCHOOL

Egerton-Rothesay School is a co-educational day school for children aged 2½ to 18 years.

In the 11 years since the present principals took over, the pupil roll has increased from 92 to 652 by popular demand.

Classes are small enough for teachers to give each child sufficient attention to effect academic, social and emotional progress. In the senior school pastoral care is administered through a house system.

A full-time Chartered Psychologist on our staff ensures progress for the child with specific learning difficulties and for the especially gifted child there is a combination of a stimulating environment for academic prowess with social balance and integration within the peer group.

The School is run on Christian principles which is reflected in the total ethos of the whole School. Children from all cultural backgrounds are welcomed.

Principals: J. R. Adkins, B.Sc.(Hons), P.G.C.E. and F. H. Adkins, S.R.N., S.C.M.

**Egerton-Rothesay School
(Lower School)
3-7 Charles Street, Berkhamsted
Herts HP4 3DG
Telephone: Berkhamsted (0442) 866305**

**Egerton-Rothesay School
(Middle and Upper Schools)
Durrants Lane, Berkhamsted
Herts HP4 3UJ
Telephone: Berkhamsted (0442) 865275**

HOW MANY TREES DID THE WORLD LOSE TO PRODUCE THIS PUBLICATION?

The answer may surprise you . . . none.

Because, for every one tree that is cut down to make paper, at least two are planted.

If **you** have any concern or query about the production of paper and its effect on the environment, please write to or call:

**THE PULP AND PAPER INFORMATION CENTRE
Papermakers House, Rivenhall Road
Swindon SN5 7BE.
Tel: (0793) 886086**

Paper, naturally.

RICKMANSWORTH MASONIC SCHOOL

The Rickmansworth Masonic School is set in over 300 acres of parkland less than a mile from the M25. This gives access to airports and the other major motorway networks of the United Kingdom. The whole site is set among the beautiful backslopes of the Chiltern Hills. It is easily accessible and yet rural in outlook

Founded originally for the daughters of Freemasons, the School is now a charitable educational trust offering all the advantages of independent education to a wide range of girls. The spirit of the original foundation is honoured by the very generous provision of bursaries and scholarships available at 7, 11 and 16 years of age.

There are 650 girls in school of whom over 300 are boarders. The ethos is essentially that of a boarding school into which the day girl population is integrated. There are well-appointed comfortable houses combining dormitories for younger girls and shared and single study bedroom accommodation for older pupils. Housemistresses, who are members of the teaching staff, are assisted in their care of the girls by House Tutors, Matrons and Assistant Matrons.

Junior girls, aged 7 to 11, are taught and housed in a separate area of school with their own specialist staff and facilities.

Most girls stay on to the Sixth Form and every year a few newcomers join at this stage. The majority of the 130 sixth-formers go on to take university degrees or other higher education courses. Business and secretarial courses are also available in the Sixth Form and a few go straight into business and commercial careers.

Teaching facilities are of a very high standard with excellent laboratories and good specialist areas for all departments. There is an attractive circular library and a fine chapel. Sporting facilities include a heated indoor pool, 18 tennis courts and superb playing fields; work will begin very soon on a new sports hall.

In addition to school games, riding, sailing, aerobics and fencing are all popular. The Duke of Edinburgh Award Scheme, Brownie and Guide units all flourish and there is a very wide range of clubs and societies. The School has a strong music and drama tradition with major productions every year.

A recent Social Services report concluded: "We observed a warm, caring environment, where girls are enabled to take full advantage of their many opportunities. We consider the Rickmansworth Masonic School for Girls to be a school where girls flourish as their individual needs are sensitively met."

Rickmansworth Masonic School, Rickmansworth, Herts WD3 4HF   Telephone: 0923 773168

ST. CHRISTOPHER SCHOOL

Curriculum: The core areas of the National Curriculum are covered, with all pupils continuing with Physics, Chemistry and Biology to Double Certificate Level at the GCSE. Foreign languages have a strongly practical emphasis, with all pupils paying at least two visits to our exchange schools in France and/or Germany in years II, III and IV. The creative arts and technology are particularly encouraged and the facilities are available and staffed at weekends. Internationalist and green values are encouraged.

Entry: Entry for boarders is usually at age 11 with some joining at nine and others at 13. Decisions are made in the light of interview, school reports and informal tests usually conducted on the day of interview. We look for an ability to respond to the spirit and opportunities of St. Christopher. Direct entrants to the Sixth Form have to show the ability to follow a 3A/AS-level programme. The School provides for children of average to outstanding ability, aiming to help everyone achieve their full potential.

Range of fees as at 1.6.92:
Day £634-£1,860, Boarders £2,628-£3,284
Sixth Form: Day £1,860, Boarders £3,284
The average amount required to cover educational extras is £30 a term plus any public exam fees.
Examinations offered: GCSE (MEG, NEG, SEG), GCE A and A/S-levels (O & C, JMB, AEB London) in 16 subjects.

Destination and career prospects of leavers:
Almost all leavers go on to a course in further or higher education, ranging from Universities (regularly including Oxbridge) to courses in engineering, business, the applied and performing arts and vocations like nursing and social work.

Academic and leisure facilities: The School has all the usual specialist rooms and science laboratories, with particularly fine Theatre, Music and Arts Centres added in recent years. As one of the pilot schools of Education 2000 it has pioneered major developments in information technology and two computer networks link the library and all the teaching areas. We complement academic study with learning through experience. There is a strong emphasis on Outdoor Pursuits (with all pupils learning to canoe, sail and rock-climb), on service to the community and on self-government, through which pupils learn both how to put forward their own ideas and listen to those of others.

Values: The School is an unusually tolerant community, recognising and caring for all as individuals. There is no compulsory worship so people of different religions and of none feel equally at home. There is a significant period of silence in every assembly. The diet is vegetarian.

Long-term aims: St. Christopher is noted for its success in developing life-long self-confidence. The School is informal (there is no uniform and all children and adults are called by their first names); at the same time it is purposeful and challenging of mind, body and spirit. We aim for our young people to develop an effective competence, a social conscience, moral courage, a sense of initiative, the capacity for friendship and a true zest for life.

Headmaster: Colin Reid, MA (since 1981).

School foundation: 1915. Member of GBA.

Coeducational Boarding and Day School.

Non-denominational.

Age range of pupils: 2½ to 18. Boarders from 7. Two-thirds of the senior school are boarders.

No. of students enrolled as at 1.6.92.
Junior School: 97 Boys, 63 Girls
Senior School: 186 Boys, 161 Girls.
Sixth Form: 37 Boys, 46 Girls.

**St. Christopher School, Letchworth
Herts. SG6 3JZ
Tel: 0462 679301. Fax: 0462 481578**

ST. FRANCIS' COLLEGE

INDEPENDENT BOARDING AND DAY SCHOOL FOR GIRLS
G.B.G.S.A., G.S.A.

Kindergarten/Preparatory 3½-11; Senior 11-18.

* We prepare your daughter for life in the 1990s with a curriculum which is strongly academic and also broadly based.

* Extensive Science facilities include five modern laboratories and 20 computers.

* We have excellent facilities for Sport, Drama and Music, including a 600-seat theatre, heated indoor swimming pool and a 12-room music wing.

Tuition fees range from £595 per term in the Kindergarten School to £1,450 per term in the Senior School. Girls are admitted at all ages subject to satisfactory entrance requirements and availability of places.

Please send for a copy of our Prospectus to:
Mrs. J. Frith, G.R.S.M., Headmistress

St. Francis' College
Letchworth
Herts

Telephone:
Letchworth (0462) 670511

St Martha's Senior School

Religious denomination: Roman Catholic

Type: Independent Girl's Day School.

Age range: 11-18.

No. of pupils enrolled as at 1.5.91:
Seniors: 300. Girls, *Sixth Form:* 25

Fees per annum: Day £2,550

(Founded 1947)

Curriculum: The School is divided into two clases per year. During the first three years pupils follow a basic course in academic and craft subjects, including computer studies and CDT. During the third year girls, in consultation with staff and parents, choose the course for which they are best suited.

English Language, English Literature, French, Mathematics and Science are compulsory subjects to GCSE level. There are 15 further subjects from which choice may be made for GCSE.

There is an expanding Sixth Form and a wide range of courses available. Sixth-Form girls are given every opportunity to become responsible adults. They have their own common and study rooms and are taught in small tutorials.

There is a lively careers department under the guidance of a senior member of staff. A wide range of information is available, and the School holds Careers Conventions from time to time.
Entry requirements: the School holds its own entrance examination in the spring term before entry.

Head: Sister M Cecile Archer, BA(Hons), (PGCE) (Member of Congregation of St Martha)

St Martha's Senior School
Camlet Way
Hadley
Barnet
Hertfordshire EN5 5PX

Telephone: (081) 449 6889

BEDGEBURY SCHOOL

BEDGEBURY is an independent school for 430 girls aged 3 to 18 and their very little brothers (300 boarders). It offers a wide range of GCSE subjects and over 29 A-levels ranging from Double Mathematics and Greek to Communication Studies and Interior Design in the superb new Arts Centre.

The Lower School in Hawkhurst caters for girls aged 3 to 12 and boys aged 3 to 8 years; the Upper School in Bedgebury Park prepares 13- to 18-year-olds for GCSE, A-levels, University entrance and Oxbridge.

Sixth-Form courses include Agriculture, Child Care, CDT, Ceramics, Design and Fashion, Computing, Photography, Music and Theatre Studies, and the British Horse Society AI and AII examinations. There is a full Secretarial and Business Studies Course (to RSA Stage III). The new Boarding House provides single study bedrooms with washing facilities for 60 Sixth-Form girls.

Bedgebury is situated in 250 acres of beautiful parkland estates in the Weald of Kent with a first-class riding centre (BHS Grade 5) with 50 horses and ponies. The Lower School, in the village of Hawkhurst, has grounds of about 25 acres at Lillesden House: the Pre-preparatory Department and Kindergarten are close by in Collingwood House.

The whole school offers excellent facilities for sports. Outdoor pursuits, including Golf, Sailing, Canoeing, Rock Climbing, Abseiling – and Flying – are available at Upper School.

Visitors are welome by appointment. We believe in looking at each candidate for entry individually, as a person, not just as a writer of examination papers. We therefore invite each candidate to spend a night in the school before taking tests and joining lessons during the school day. This is a reflection of our attitude to all the girls in our care: each is considered in relation to her own gifts and needs. Scholarship examinations are held each Spring.

Apply to the Registrar for details and a prospectus.

Headmistress:
Mrs. M. E. A. Kaye, M.A.(Oxon)

Upper School & Registry
Bedgebury School
Bedgebury Park
Goudhurst
Cranbrook
Kent TN17 2SH
Telephone: (0580) 211221

Registry telephone: (0580) 211954
Fax: (0580) 212252
Telex: 957565 CBJ AG

(See also page 738)

COBHAM HALL

One of Britain's leading girls' schools, Cobham Hall has 250 girls 11-18 years, mainly full/weekly boarding, with a few day girls. A strong Sixth Form, with 91% in 1992 going on to higher education; equally strong in sciences and arts, with much excellent teaching and a full-time careers adviser. A new multi-purpose sports centre and indoor swimming pool. An EFL centre offering overseas students intensive language teaching. In 1992 65 girls represent 27 counties worldwide. This international, interdenominational school is a member of the Round Square Conference, which links 25 schools around the world, providing many and varied exchange opportunities.

Founded in 1962, this beautiful 16th-century historic house, in grounds of 150 acres, was the former house of the Earls of Darnley. Situated 25 miles from central London, close to the M25 with easy access to Gatwick and Heathrow airports (transport arranged).

This friendly school produces confident, articulate young women, prepared for the 21st century; a strong believer in the virtues of single-sex education, everyone is expected to get involved with plenty of drama, music, sport, and charity work; extras include riding, fencing, golf, scuba-diving, sailing, Duke of Edinburgh, and Young Enterprise; and, as one second-year said, "Cobham lets you be your own person" and, from a Sixth-Former, "Cobham doesn't mould you into a particular type, every girl is different, bringing out the best in each of us."

Cobham Hall, Cobham, Kent DA12 3BL
Telephone: (0474) 823371
Fax: (0474) 822995

FARRINGTONS SCHOOL

* 500 places for day girls (3-18) and full and weekly boarders (7-18).
* Excellent academic results from a broad ability intake. In 1992 88% University entry and 82% A–C GCSE passes.
* High teacher : pupil ratio.
* A One-Year Sixth-Form Business Course which equips girls with a true working knowledge of the commercial world and a recognised set of vocational qualifications.
* Excellent pastoral care and a strong sense of caring and community. Our day girls may arrive from 7.30 am and stay until 6 pm or later to help working parents.
* Situated in 25 acres of parkland with extensive sports grounds, swimming pool and large, new sports hall.
* Excellent rail and road links. Proximity to London's airports. (20 minutes from Central London.)
* Busy, cheerful Junior School sharing Senior School site.
* Full day kindergarten sessions.

Methodist Foundation.

Headmistress: Mrs. B. J. Stock, B.A.(Hons)

Please contact the Registrar for further details.

Farringtons School
Chislehurst
Kent BR7 6LR
Telephone: 081-467 0256

(See also page 742)

KING'S SCHOOL
ROCHESTER

King's School, Rochester, is an independent coeducational day and boarding school. We have Pre-Preparatory, Preparatory and Senior Schools which cater for pupils between the ages of four and 18. We are able to take boy boarding pupils between the ages of nine and 18.

Here, at King's, we do believe very firmly in the virtue of academic excellence, but we realise that its achievement will not be universal; hence, we seek to establish in which direction an individual pupil's particular talents lie. We do this not only by close monitoring of performance inside and outside the classroom, but also by providing a wide range of new experiences and ideas for individuals to consider through involvement in music, art and drama, clubs and societies, a wide range of sporting activities through travel at home and abroad, through lectures and formal and informal discussion.

We believe in a strong distinction between right and wrong, compassion for others, self-discipline and the pursuit of excellence. We seek a mastery of the processes by which knowledge can be acquired and a maturity and sympathy gained from exposure to the mainstreams of intellectual thought, both classical and modern. We aim not only to provide our pupils with adequate qualifications for their entry into the wider world, but also the means for the mastery of the process of mind which will enable them to cope with the world about them and the ethical integrity by which they can govern their lives.

We are open to new ideas in technology, science and the arts, whilst holding fast to that which is good in tradition. We aim to cultivate creativity, flexibility and confidence, and this within a Christian context.

**King's School
Satis House, Boley Hill
Rochester, Kent ME1 1TE
Telephone: 0634 843913**

STRATFORD HOUSE SCHOOL

Stratford House aims to develop fully the academic and practical student by providing a wide curriculum and small groups. We are noted for our ability to build confidence and provide a caring environment.

The Junior School, while independent in its approach, is able to share the many facilities of the Senior School, including the laboratories, Music department, sports hall and swimming pool.

Opportunities are available to take a wider range of subjects than the National Curriculum at G.C.S.E., and in the Sixth Form, Business Courses provide a firm foundation for careers in industry, whilst a pass rate at A-Level of between 95% and 100% means that girls enter all major universities and professions including Music, Drama and Art.

Situated beside Bickley station and close to major bus routes, the School caters for girls from three to 18 with entry at all ages by appropriate test, interview and report.

**Stratford House School
Bickley
Kent BR1 2EB
Telephone: 081-467 3580**

CASTERTON SCHOOL

Set amidst delightful rural scenery one mile from the charming Market Town of Kirkby Lonsdale, Casterton is a boarding and day school for girls aged 8-18. It has first-class facilities and an outstanding academic record and is widely recognised as one of the leading girls' boarding schools in the country.

Casterton was founded in 1823 and is one of the oldest girls' schools. It is ideally situated to promote a secure environment which gives both peace to study and the stimulus for wider activities beyond the classroom. Full use is made of the splendid location and of the school's proximity to the Lake District and the Yorkshire Dales.

Access to the school is by excellent road and rail links and by air through Manchester Airport. A comprehensive escort system operates for girls travelling by rail or air.

The younger girls live in Brontë House, named after the Brontë sisters who were at the school in the 1820s. They have access to all of the Senior School facilities and an exciting programme of activities operates every weekend. Between the ages of 12 and 16 girls join one of the five Senior Boarding Houses. The Houses are all small and friendly with dormitories varying in size from four beds to single study bedrooms. There are four separate, highly individual Sixth-Form Houses. All have been recently modernised to provide single or double study bedroom accommodation for every girl. There is greater freedom at this stage in order to prepare girls for future working or University life. They spend their free time in their Houses and may cook for themselves at weekends. Sixth-Formers do, however, play an active part in the organisation and care of the younger girls.

All girls are prepared for nine GCSE subjects and a high proportion of girls remain at Casterton for their A-level studies. Most Casterton girls go on to University or other Higher Education Courses. Examination results have been consistently outstanding with 95% pass rates regularly achieved at both GCSE and A-level.

Casterton offers a wide choice of extra-curricular activities. Hockey, Netball, Lacrosse, Tennis and Rounders are played, there is an indoor heated swimming pool and the school has its own riding stables. Most girls take part in the Duke of Edinburgh's Award Scheme where full use is made of the school's unique environment.

Casterton has strong traditions in Music, Drama and Art. It is particularly proud of its new Creative Arts Centre. An exceptionally high standard is achieved in all branches of Fine Art, and an Artist in Residence is on hand to ensure that the Centre is open throughout the weekend.

The school has, from its foundation, been closely linked with the Church of England, but girls of other denominations and faiths are welcomed and encouraged to make a positive contribution to the religious life of the school. There is a resident Chaplain and the School has its own church which is shared with the local community.

Entrance examinations are conducted in January/February and the School is in the Assisted Places Scheme. Academic and Music Scholarships are available.

For further information and a copy of the school's prospectus, please write or telephone to the Headmaster's Secretary:

**Casterton School
Kirkby Lonsdale, Carnforth
Lancs LA6 2SG
Telephone: (05242) 71202
Fax: (05242) 71146**

Emmanuel Christian School

The school was founded in 1979 and is independent, co-educational and caters for children from 3½ years old through to a wide range of courses for GCSE.

There is a warm, friendly atmosphere in the school, where the aim is to educate young people of every ability in the highest principles of Christian morality and behaviour, self-discipline, individual responsibility and personal integrity.

Children through to 14 years work for a part of the day in study booths where work is individually tailored to the child's needs and abilities. The student also spends time in conventional classroom situations which build upon what has been learned in private study.

Students are encouraged and trained to take responsibility for their learning by setting daily achievable goals. Through controls and motivation they are able to advance to their highest potential.

Biblical truths permeate the instruction and scholars benefit from academic excellence and awareness of right and wrong. The result is greater academic achievement.

Your are welcome to come and look around our school to see for yourself and to discuss any questions you may have, or ask for a Prospectus.

For further information, contact:

Miss J. Ingham BSc(Hons) **Mrs. P. Derry B.Ed.**
Head of Upper School **Head of Lower School**
Elm Street
Fleetwood FY7 6TJ

Telephone: (0253) 770646

LEICESTER HIGH SCHOOL FOR GIRLS

Leicester High School is a well-established day school for girls situated in pleasant grounds on the south side of the city. Founded in 1906 as Portland House School, it now comprises a Junior Department of 120 girls (3-9 years) and a Senior Department of 310 girls (10-18) sited on the same campus.

The school offers an academic education of a high standard, while being a friendly community where an emphasis is placed on honesty, integrity and respect for the views of others.

Class size is kept small so that there is every opportunity for each girl to achieve her full potential while developing the self-confidence and self-discipline to help in her future.

The Headmistress is responsible for both junior and senior departments. There is a well-qualified staff of 32 full-time, 15 part-time and several peripatetic music staff. The school is renowned for both its academic excellence and sporting achievements. At the moment 19 subjects are offered at GCSE level and 17 subjects at A-level.

The facilities of the school have been systematically improved over the past 10 years to provide excellent laboratories, a well-fitted computer room with Archimedes network and a new sports hall. Future projects include the provision of a new classroom block and a new music/drama school.

The school is a Trust with a Board of Governors. It is in membership of the GBGSA and the Headmistress belongs to the GSA.

454 London Road, Leicester LE2 2PP   Tel: (0533) 705338

Nevill Holt School

The School was founded in 1868 and has been on its present site since 1920. It is situated on a beautiful estate midway between Uppingham and Market Harborough.

Nevill Holt provides a full and well-rounded education in order to enable both boys and girls to pass into their Senior Schools at 13+ through Common Entrance or Scholarship examinations.

Sport includes Rugby, Hockey, Cricket, Netball, Rounders, Tennis, Athletics and Swimming. It is also possible to learn golf, archery, canoeing, riding and pistol and clay pigeon shooting. We have over 20 acres of playing fields.

There is also an RSCM choir, an orchestra and jazz band and music appreciation is taught throughout the School. The Art Department includes a display gallery. Other facilities include carpentry shop, theatre and computer centre.

The aim of the School is to enable EVERY boy and girl to produce the best of which they are capable, both in the classroom as well as in all other spheres of school life, firm in the belief that every pupil has a talent at which to shine.

Each evening there are Clubs and Societies offering a wide variety of activities for the boarders. The pupils' general health, pastoral care and welfare are closely watched. The Headmaster's wife is a nurse and is also responsible for the catering side.

Headmaster: C. M. Woolley, B.A., Dip.Ed., F.R.G.S., F.R.S.A.

The Hall, Nevill Holt, Market Harborough, Leicestershire LE16 8EG   Tel: 085-883 234

Oakham School

Oakham School was founded in 1584 by Robert Johnson, Archdeacon of Leicester. It is now a co-educational boarding and day school (HMC) of 1,000 pupils of whom 300 are in the VIth form.

■ BUILDINGS

completed since 1984
❏ Queen Elizabeth Theatre ❏ Music School ❏ Computer Centre ❏ Biology Laboratories ❏ The Barraclough (Dining Hall) ❏ Boarding and Day Houses ❏ Rifle range ❏ Classrooms for Mathematics, History and English

Proposed Development
Library and Resource Centre

■ THE ARTS
❏ Plays and Musicals ❏ Symphony Orchestra ❏ Chamber Orchestra ❏ Concert Band ❏ Big Band ❏ Choirs ❏ Art & Design Centre

■ EXPEDITIONS
in 1992: ❏ Explorers to Zambia ❏ Biologists to Madagascar ❏ Musicians to Zimbabwe ❏ Rugby players to Australia

■ SPORTS include:
❏ Rugby Football ❏ Soccer ❏ Golf
❏ Cricket ❏ Hockey ❏ Tennis
❏ Athletics ❏ Swimming ❏ Shooting
❏ Squash ❏ Netball ❏ Sailing
❏ Badminton ❏ Basketball

■ 21 YEARS experience
of Co-education and its proximity to London and Midland airports make Oakham well suited to families living abroad

---

For a prospectus, or further information please contact:
The Registrar, Chapel Close, Oakham, Rutland LE15 6DT. Tel. (0572) 722487

BELMONT SCHOOL

Belmont School, situated in the heart of the Mill Hill conservation area of North-West London, is a well-established independent preparatory school for boys. Founded 80 years ago in the Regency mansion that bore its name, Belmont was later merged with Mill Hill School (H.M.C.) which it has served as a Junior School. The two establishments share the same governors and financial administration as well as certain sports facilities, but the Master of Belmont (Mr. J. R. Hawkins, B.A., Cert. Ed.) is autonomously responsible for running the Prep. School.

Most boys progress from Belmont to Mill Hill at the age of 13 by way of interview and report, with Common Entrance exams used for setting purposes only, once a boy is accepted. But an equally successful pass rate is achieved by the minority of boys whose parents have selected alternative senior schools.

Belmont is ready to meet modern teaching needs with its Computer Room, Maths Room and two Science Laboratories, in addition to its Art Room, D.T. Room and a Library that is uniquely well staffed and equipped by junior school standards.

Rugby, Soccer and Cricket are the major sports, but many minor sports and activities also flourish. There is a strong music tradition, as evidenced by two choirs, an orchestra and a wind band.

**The Ridgeway
Mill Hill
London NW7 4ED
Telephone: 081-959 1431
Fax: 081-906 4828**

Clifton Lodge (Founded 1979)

Religious denomination: Christian

Clifton Lodge is a school that stands for standards: standards of proper behaviour and all that that embraces in attitudes to others and standards of personal achievement of any sort, and we believe that boys want to be a success in life. This they can only obtain by hard work, confidence in their own ability and a properly disciplined approach, whatever the activity. Clifton Lodge seeks at all times to impart these values.

The school is geared to give much individual attention, with boys being able to work at their own level, enabling them to realise their own potential.

The curriculum is based on the need to prepare boys for entry to Public School at 13+ through the Common Entrance Examination, Public School Scholarships or other equivalent examinations, and Clifton Lodge is justifiably proud of its excellent record of success in these. Whereas this provides the core of the academic programme, nevertheless we consider it essential to educate all pupils as broadly as possible and much time is also given to Music, Sport and Drama, these avenues providing boys with valuable opportunities to develop further talents and to build up their self-confidence.

The school is of Chrisian denomination and the daily assembly, attended by the whole community, is based around these ideals.

We believe that the combination of these values, the emphasis put on self-discipline, and the healthy encouragement to achieve success both within and without the classroom, are essential ingredients for any boy's future happiness and fulfilment in life.

Head: D. A. P. Blumlein, BA

9 Florence Road, Ealing, London W5 3TU   Telephone: (081) 579 3662

DEVONSHIRE HOUSE PREPARATORY AND PRE-PREPARATORY SCHOOL

Devonshire House School is situated in the heart of Hampstead. The School provides education of high quality for both boys and girls, both to nurture ability in the traditional subjects and to foster a variety of talents so that every individual child can enjoy school and reach his or her full potential.

The School seeks to achieve high academic standards whilst developing enthusiasm and initiative throughout a wide range of interests. It is considered essential to encourage pupils to develop their own individual personalities and a good sense of personal responsibility. Devonshire House provides education for those whose parents wish their children to have the advantage of outstanding education in the early years of their schooling. The School places particular importance on high standards and on individual attention for each child.

The main School provides for children from five to 13 years of age. The pre-preparatory School provides for the needs of younger children, generally from three years of age, giving care and attention and providing a sound preparation for school.

Devonshire House is situated at the crest of the hill running into Hampstead Village. The fine School buildings are set in charming grounds and walled gardens.

If you would like to have a copy of the School's prospectus, or would like to visit Devonshire House, do please let us know.

Principal:
M. W. Loveridge

**69 Fitzjohn's Avenue
Hampstead
London NW3 6PB**

Telephone: 071-435 1916

Girls' Public Day School Trust

* The largest group of independent schools in the UK.

* 18,000 pupils in 26 schools.

* High academic standards. Moderate fees.

* Founded 1872 – Scholarships and Assisted Places at most schools.

For details of the Trust's schools in:

Bath, Bexhill (also boarders), Birkenhead, Blackheath, Brighton, Bromley, Cardiff, Croydon, Ealing, Ipswich, Kensington, Liverpool, Newcastle, Norwich, Nottingham, Oxford, Pinner, Portsmouth, Putney, Sheffield, Shrewsbury, South Hampstead, Streatham, Sutton, Sydenham, Wimbledon,

contact the Trust Office:

**26 Queen Anne's Gate
London SW1H 9AN
Telephone: 071-222 9595**

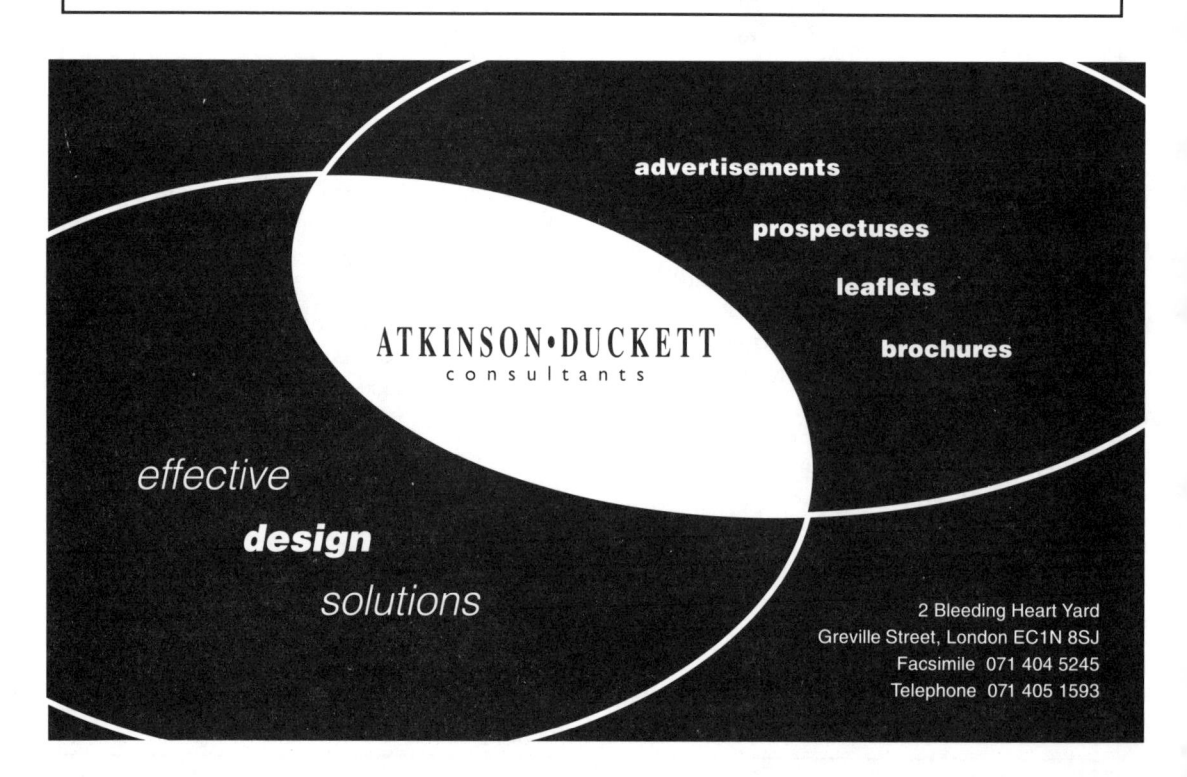

ATKINSON•DUCKETT
consultants

effective design solutions

advertisements
prospectuses
leaflets
brochures

2 Bleeding Heart Yard
Greville Street, London EC1N 8SJ
Facsimile 071 404 5245
Telephone 071 405 1593

HILL HOUSE
INTERNATIONAL JUNIOR SCHOOL

Hill House was founded in 1951 and is fully co-educational, taking boys and girls from 3 to 14. It is an international school not only because it operates in two countries, England and Switzerland, but because half the places in the school are given to English boys and girls and half to non-English boys and girls.

The Four Principles

The school works on four principles. In order of priority they are:-

1. Safety of the boy and girl.
2. Happiness at work and games.
3. Good manners and discipline.
4. Preparation for the next school.

Curriculum

The curriculum is English, boys and girls being prepared not only for entry into English public schools but also schools overseas. The main subjects in which a boy and girl should have at least one lesson each day are: English, Maths, Science, French. The supporting subjects requiring fewer lessons are: Geography, History, Biology, Latin, Divinity, Music, Art, Carpentry, Computer Programming and, for girls, Ballet.

At a normal English preparatory school the boys play soccer, rugger and cricket with some athletics and swimming. Hill House has boys and girls from many countries and the policy is not to specialise but to teach all the boys and girls the basic principles of all games.

Swiss Annexe

Hill House has always had a permanent annex in Switzerland.

The house in Glion was purpose built. The dormitory with French Oak on the walls, it's ceiling of polished Finnish Pine and it's view overlooking from a height of 2,500 ft. over the largest lake in Europe to the snow-capped mountains of Grammont and the 11,000 ft. Dents du Midi is unique.

The courses in Switzerland are optional and parent's pay no extra fees. The school pays the air fares, all expenses at Glion, including laundry, excursions, ski-lifts and provides skis, ski-boots, climbing-boots anoraks etc.

HILL HOUSE
INTERNATIONAL JUNIOR SCHOOL
Hans Place
London SW1X 0EP
Tel (071) 584 1331

Co-educational • Day • Ages 3-14
1,050 pupils (57% boys)
Fees: (1992-93) £3,400-4,600
Head: Col. Stuart Townend, OBE, MA (Oxon)

KENSINGTON PARK

(INCORPORATING DIXON AND WOLFE)

Kensington Park is a co-educational school providing an academic curriculum to GCSE level. It offers a unique and very successful educational option: tutorial-type education combined with the social and pastoral benefits of a school.

Because of its small size (60 pupils), the School is able to respond sympathetically and effectively to the needs of individual students. We can cater for students who have lost ground in other schools because of ill health, relocation, or other circumstances. Our small class sizes and tutorial style also enable us to provide the attention that children with Specific Learning Difficulties need if they are to achieve their best. We take care to promote a positive atmosphere where pupils and teachers work supportively together.

- ♦ A friendly, carefully organised school community
- ♦ Average class size of eight students
- ♦ Well qualified and experienced staff
- ♦ Full range of GCSE subjects
- ♦ Short, intensive working day (10.00-4.00) which promotes concentration of effort and efficient learning
- ♦ Supervised homework sessions before and after school (9.15-10.00 and 3.00-4.00)
- ♦ Flexible approach to individual needs
- ♦ Specialist help for pupils with specific learning difficulties
- ♦ Central London location

A small co-educational school to GCSE level with a commitment to care and attention

Kensington Park
11 Pembridge Square
London W2 4ED
Telephone: 071-221 5748   Fax: 071-792 0730

LATYMER UPPER SCHOOL

Independent Boys' Day School, HMC

Prep 8-11 years, Main School 11-18 years

- Latymer Upper School is an active, caring, friendly school for clever and ambitious boys, suiting parents who value both independence of thought and academic success.

- The school is well-resourced, has good facilities, and strong pastoral care.

- A wide-ranging extra-curricular programme in Sport, Music, Drama, and many clubs and societies, as well as exchanges, tours, work experience and other trips.

- Applications for 1994 Entrance Examinations at 8+, 9+ and 11+, should register by 11 December 1993. Sixth-Form entry is also possible.

- We invite you to obtain our prospectus, or visit the school on one of our open days in the autumn.

For more details contact the Registrar
Latymer Upper School
King Street
Hammersmith W6 9LR
Telephone: 081-741 1851

MILL HILL SCHOOL

Founded 1807.

Independent Boys' Boarding, Flexi-Boarding and Day School, Girls in the Sixth Form.

Curriculum: Pupils enter the School at 13 and take GCSEs three years later. A boy studies a wide range of subjects in the first year so that GCSE choices are based on experience. The 'core' subjects are separately setted.

In the Sixth Form, pupils take three, or sometimes four A-levels. Suitable candidates are prepared for entry to Oxford or Cambridge, including STEP and S-level. Normally over 75% of Sixth-Formers go on to Higher Education, thanks to an A-level pass rate of over 90%.

Entry requirements, procedures and Scholarships: The 13+ entry is by the Entrance Scholarship or Common Entrance Examination or our own assessments. Girls (and some boys) enter the Sixth Form, where provisional acceptance is dependent on GCSE forecasts, interviews and the previous school's testimonial. Government Assisted Places are available for 13-year-olds and Sixth Formers. The School offers up to 12 academic and music scholarships annually.

Academic facilities: Teachers have their own specialist classrooms. The teacher\pupil ratio of 1 : 10 means that set sizes are favourable. Lower school sets average 18, Sixth Form sets average 10. The central library is well stocked and departments have their own resource bases.

The Computer Centre has 24 Acorn Archimedes computers, networked with Filestore and Level 4. Sixteen IBM, 36 BBC Micro and 20 Laptop computers are distributed throughout the various departments for more specialist use and as teaching aids. The Business Education and Information Technology Centre has 32 Apple Mackintosh Computers, six laser printers and two scanners. This facility is available to all pupils and is utilised by all departments.

The Music School has 10 teaching and practice rooms, and a Recital Hall and a computerised recording studio. Almost any instrument may be learned and vocal theory and practice studied. The Choir and Orchestra, Chamber Orchestra, Wind Band and Jazz Groups perform in concerts throughout the year. Drama is also a high-profile activity.

Extra-curricular activities include a Community Service Group, the Duke of Edinburgh Award Scheme and a Combined (Army and Navy) Cadet Force. Pupils also have ample opportunities to utilise the outstanding facilities for Art, Pottery, Design and Technology. A wide range of societies caters for a variety of interests.

Sports, games and leisure facilities: The School is situated in the Green Belt on the edge of London with 120 acres of parkland. The generous playing fields are matched by a Sports Hall, providing indoor facilities, two swimming pools, squash courts, Eton fives courts, an all-weather pitch and an indoor range. Mill Hill is proud of its strong tradition in its major sports (Rugby, Hockey and Cricket); competitive excellence is highly valued and the coaching skills are exceptional.

Pastoral Care: New pupils are allocated to one of nine Houses, five of which are Boarding. A House Master is the first link between parents and the School in any matter relating to welfare and progress. Each pupil also has an academic Tutor and close links with parents are maintained through regular meetings and full reports.

For further information, please contact:
Mr. C. R. Kelly, Director of Admissions.

Mill Hill School
The Ridgeway, Mill Hill
London NW7 1QS

Montessori College & Nursery

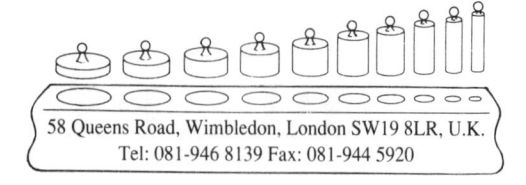

58 Queens Road, Wimbledon, London SW19 8LR, U.K.
Tel: 081-946 8139 Fax: 081-944 5920

The Montessori College, Wimbledon, offers a Foundation Course and a Correspondence Course for the training of Montessori Teachers. The College, a Charter Member of MACTE (Montessori Accreditation Council for Teacher Education) and a consortium of independent colleges across the U.S.A., was awarded full international accreditation status for the Foundation Course on 24 May 1992. MACTE is the governing body for Montessori. Our students, in addition to the College Diploma, can obtain, subject to certain MACTE requirements, an internationally recognised Montessori Diploma. Students can take full advantage of international career opportunities with the possibility of doing the teaching practice requirements in the U.S.A. Our Employment Agency will help students, when qualified, to find positions.

Montessori teaching is not simply a method of teaching but more an attitude of mind. Although Montessori teaching is structured it allows the children to be free to develop at their own pace within the prepared environment. It is essential for our student teachers to have love, respect and understanding of young children.

The College is central, and has excellent facilities. Attention is given on an individual basis and this approach to the Courses enables the students to achieve the high standard we demand for the College Diploma(s). The College is registered with the Inland Revenue for tax relief on Vocational Training. Currently the tax relief is 25% on the fees.

THE MOUNT SCHOOL

Founded in 1925 and situated in Mill Hill village on the edge of the Green Belt, but easily reached from North and North-West London, the Mount offers a wide range of GCSE and A-level subjects in a caring and supportive environment. The classes are small, giving maximum opportunity for individual attention. Entrance is normally by examination and interview at 7+, 11+ and 13+ and also at sixth-form level by interview. Places are sometimes available at other age groups. English for overseas students and as a second language is offered. The school has good facilities for Art, CDT, Music, Theatre Studies, Information Technology, Business Studies and a variety of sports.

Four modern languages are offered and the school has a strong science tradition. A tutorial system and careers guidance is an integral part of the school's pastoral care. The school grounds consist of five acres within the Green Belt, which are attractively arranged with tennis and netball courts, hockey pitch and a large, well-equipped gymnasium containing a badminton court. Good use is made of opportunities offered in London theatres and art galleries, and regular school journeys are arranged at home and abroad.

The school is served by the Northern Line at Mill Hill East, British Rail at Mill Hill Broadway and the 240 and 221 bus routes.

A Charitable Company

The Mount School
Milespit Hill
London NW7 2RX
Telephone: 081-959 3403
Fax: 081-959 1503

ST. PHILIP'S SCHOOL

(Established 1934)

A Roman Catholic day preparatory school conveniently situated in Kensington (close to Gloucester Road Underground Station).

Boys from seven to 13 years are prepared for Common Entrance and Scholarship level entrance to public schools.

Size of classes is small.

Excellent facilities for games.

St. Philip's is accredited by the Mensa Foundation for Gifted Children

Please apply to the Headmaster for further details and prospectus

**St. Philip's School
6 Wetherby Place
London SW7 4NE
Telephone: 071-373 3944**

SYDENHAM HIGH SCHOOL
G.P.D.S.T.

Opened in 1887, the school occupies a pleasant five-and-a-half-acre site, well served by public transport complemented by school coaches. This provides easy access to girls from a wide catchment area.

Sydenham High School retains a good balance between the traditional values it embodies and the best of current educational thinking. The school fosters a strong sense of individual achievement providing a broad, balanced education that fosters confidence through success.

There are 490 pupils in the Senior School, 97 in the Sixth Form. The Junior Department, which takes girls aged from 4 to 11, has 225 pupils.

The school is an attractive blend of Victorian buildings and modern purpose-built accommodation, providing excellent facilities for science, technology and the arts. A separate Sixth-Form centre allows the senior girls independence whilst they remain a valued, integral part of the school community.

Careers guidance is prominent in the pastoral programme. Most students proceed to degree courses; others begin vocational training when they leave school.

A wide variety of sport is played, either at school or at the nearby national stadium at Crystal Palace. A new sports hall, expected to be completed by May 1993, will add to the facilities.

Music and drama are vital elements of the school education programme. Over a third all pupils learn instruments in school and play in the school orchestras, wind and string ensembles or jazz group. Middle school and senior choirs perform regularly. Plays and concerts are popular and inspiring extra-curricular activities.

A happy, lively school, we aim to ensure that each individual achieves her potential and develops her natural talent.

**Sydenham High School, G.P.D.S.T.
19 Westwood Hill, London SE26 6BL
Telephone: 081-778 8737 Senior School
            081-778 9558 Junior House**

BRIDGEWATER SCHOOL
(Founded in 1950)

Religious denomination: non-denominational. Member of ISIA and ISIS.

Throughout the age range all children receive a balanced curriculum in line with the recommendations of the National Curriculum. Up to age 11, the school is one-form entry but, in seniors, two forms are admitted of equal ability.

Throughout the school, the maximum size of any class is 25. Computer Studies and Technology are an integral part of the curriculum. In Years 2 and 5 option groups have even smaller numbers in order to give pupils as much individual attention as possible. Setting is introduced gradually from Year 2 upwards and careers advice is given from Year 3 in order that a wise choice of subjects is made for GCSE. All pupils study nine subjects to this level, core subjects being English, English Literature, Mathematics, French and Dual Award Science. The A groups study three separate Sciences at GCSE. A wide range of A-levels is available.

Entry to Prep is by interview and appropriate written tests. For Seniors, tests are set in English and Mathematics, together with a Verbal Reasoning test.

Examinations offered – GCSE, NEA, SEG, JMB.

A variety of clubs and societies exists in which pupils partake after school hours, including an annual drama/musical production. Each year visits to France and Germany are organised and pupils are encouraged to go on these at least once to further their study of foreign languages.

Headmaster: Dr. B. J. Blundell, B.Sc., M.Sc., Ph.D.

Co-educational Day School aged 3-18.
Number of pupils enrolled at 1.1.93: 405.
Fees per annum: £1,985 - £3,500.

Bridgewater School
Drywood Hall
Worsley Road
Worsley
Manchester M28 4WQ
Telephone: 061-794 1463

The Purcell School

The only Specialist Music School in Greater London. Outstanding musical opportunities and training, together with an excellent academic education up to A-level in small classes.

All orchestral instruments, keyboard, composition, voice, media music. Orchestral and choral training. Regular performing opportunities include major London concert halls and overseas tours.

Talented children aged eight to 18 years are selected by musical audition throughout the year and can be funded by the DES, bursaries and other awards. The school is coeducational and has approximately 150 pupils, day and boarding.

Patron: HRH The Prince of Wales

President: Simon Rattle

For information and Prospectus please contact:

The Registrar
The Purcell School
Mount Park Road
Harrow-on-the-Hill
Middlesex HA1 3JS

Tel: 081-422 1284

Fax: 081-423 0526

RIDDLESWORTH HALL

Riddlesworth is a fine country house set in 32 acres of parkland. A happy, caring atmosphere, high educational standards and excellent facilities contribute to our success in preparing girls for Common Entrance and Scholarship examinations to senior schools. A wide range of activities and clubs is offered. Self-reliance, self-discipline and tolerance are encouraged and good manners are expected.

(Member of Allied Schools IAPS and ISIS)

Chairman: A. R. Buxton, Esq.

Headmistress: Miss S. A. Smith, B.A.(Hons.)

PREPARATORY SCHOOL FOR GIRLS AGED 7-13 YEARS

FULL BOARDING – WEEKLY BOARDING – DAY PUPILS

PRE-PREPARATORY DEPARTMENT FOR BOYS AND GIRLS AGED 4-7 YEARS

**Riddlesworth Hall
Diss
Norfolk IP22 2TA
Telephone:
095-381 246** for prospectus/appointment

Cokethorpe
SCHOOL
Witney, Oxfordshire

**AN INDEPENDENT SCHOOL FOR
BOYS AND GIRLS
Age 11 – 18
Day and Boarding**

Small classes with an excellent selection of academic courses and a wide range of extra-curricular activities.

A well-developed House and tutorial system provides academic and pastoral support.

Pupils leave Cokethorpe equipped for a wide variety of careers or further education at University or Polytechnic.

Daily buses from the surrounding area

Admission by Assessment and Interview

For further information contact:
**The Headmaster's Secretary
Cokethorpe School, Witney
Oxon OX8 7PU
Telephone: 0993 703921**

HEADINGTON SCHOOL

OXFORD OX3 7TD

Junior children with computer

Front of school building

Visitors to Headington often remark on the happy atmosphere of the school, where the girls, both day and boarders, lead a very full and busy life.

There is a sound academic tradition and the majority of the sixth form continue to degree courses. The school gives much guidance on different career possibilities to senior girls, with career talks, interviews, videos and films, and work experience and shadowing.

Every girl in the school can enter the extra-curricular activities of her choice. There are many different musical groups, with orchestras, choirs, chamber groups and an operatic production every year. There are thriving drama societies, all the usual sports, and girls can also join the Duke of Edinburgh's Award scheme and a wide variety of clubs and societies.

The 210 boarders live in four houses, one of which is a sixth-form house, in the school's 22 acres of parkland and have many outings and organised activities at weekends. Fifth- and sixth-form girls have a sensible amount of freedom. Many of our parents have overseas postings and we are well experienced in looking after girls whose families are far away.

Headington is most fortunate in being within the university town of Oxford, which means that an exceptionally wide variety of extra subjects can be offered, following the National Curriculum. Girls can learn almost any musical instrument and a very wide variety of languages as extra subjects, and the school seldom fails to meet a request for tuition in a language or an instrument.

The Junior School is small and happy. It follows a normal primary curriculum and the pupils receive a firm grounding in the basic skills. The atmosphere is uncompetitive and much emphasis is laid on care and concern for others.

Fees: Junior School (188 pupils aged 4-11).
£540-£818 a term.
Senior Day Girls (325 aged 11-18).
£1,313 a term.
Senior Boarders (210 aged 11-18).
£2,573 a term.

The prospectus and annual report give full details. Visitors to the school are always most welcome.

A member of the G.S.A. and ISIS

Telephone: Oxford (0865) 62711
Admissions: Oxford (0865) 741968
Fax: (0865) 60268

KINGHAM HILL SCHOOL

Kingham Hill School was founded in 1886 by Charles Edward Baring Young to provide a boarding education for those whose family circumstances made residential schooling desirable. The Trust, established by the Founder, administers the school and its sister foundation, Oak Hill Theological College.

Set in a beautiful 60-acre site in the heart of the Cotswolds between Chipping Norton and Stow-on-the-Wold, the school offers a full and rounded education to boys and girls aged 11-18. There are seven separate boarding houses each run by a husband and wife team. The restriction on numbers in each house to 35 children allows for a warm and friendly atmosphere.

The school is justifiably proud of its ability to meet the ever-changing needs of the British education system. Examples of this are the computer department and the purpose-built design and technology centre, along with our adherence to the national curriculum and development of asessments and records of achievement.

Class sizes are kept small and each pupil has an academic tutor to guide them through their progress. While the atmosphere is caring, we also aim to stretch pupils so that they reach their potential in all that they do. A full range of GCSE and A-level courses are available, and for those with specific learning difficulties there is a very successful specialised unit that gives the additional support that they need. The facilities throughout the school are excellent and the staff have all the equipment they need to make learning interesting.

As well as the traditional team games (rugby, soccer, hockey, cricket) the school runs successful basketball teams and has its own tennis courts, covered heated swimming pool, gymnasium, shooting range and assault course. In addition, skiing, squash and riding have strong minority followings. Once a week pupils participate in other extramural activities such as Scouts, the Duke of Edinburgh Award scheme, or the CCF, which has Army, RAF and Commando sections. These provide the opportunity for leadership training and outdoor activities, including parachuting.

There are opportunities for artistic pursuits, and the Music School and Art Department are popular centres. The school has an orchestra, and the choir regularly sings at such venues as Tewkesbury Abbey. Being equidistant from Oxford, Stratford and Cheltenham means that quality plays and concerts are always within reach.

Kingham Hill has remained true to its origins in that the sole criterion for awarding the hundred or so bursaries that are on offer is boarding need, not academic ability. The natural consequence of this policy is that the school has a broad social and academic mix, which we believe is a natural and healthy environment in which to grow up.

We aim to maintain the Christian tradition established by the Founder. The Chapel and the voluntary Christian groups play an important part in the life of the school.

KINGHAM HILL SCHOOL
KINGHAM
CHIPPING NORTON
OXON OX7 6TH
Telephone: 0608 658999
Fax: 0608 658658

WYCHWOOD SCHOOL

★ Large and fully qualified staff
★ Half a mile from City centre
★ Duke of Edinburgh Award Scheme
★ Small school — very happy atmosphere

Results   1991 100% A-level (A-C 45%)
          1991 91% GCSE (A-C)

Established 1897

★ Girls, 11-18
★ Independent Boarding and Day School
★ GCSE, university and Oxbridge entrance
★ Girls accepted directly into sixth form
★ Secretarial Skills course available combined with A-levels

**Wychwood School
74 Banbury Road
Oxford OX2 6JR
Telephone: (0865) 57976**

EDINGTON SCHOOL (I.A.P.S.)

A coeducational junior school for DYSLEXIC children aged 8-13.

Depending on the severity of the problem, pupils will follow a multi-sensory programme, specifically designed to meet their needs and overcome their language difficulties. Gradually the children should start to realise their educational potential and discover themselves.

The reading, spelling, writing and maths skills are taught by trained and sympathetic staff, and it is hoped with their help the children will develop the all-important self-confidence, self-respect, self-discipline and individuality which they are earnestly seeking.

To supplement these important skills, the Junior School follows a traditional prep school programme, which is also geared to each pupil's language level and ability.

A full games programme is also followed and an adventure holiday and skiing trip is annually undertaken.

Continuity for such children is paramount and thus SHAPWICK SENIOR SCHOOL (see page 00) is possibly the natural progression. The majority of our pupils leave us in their 13th year to follow a G.C.S.E. curriculum at the Senior School, or to other schools recommended by the Headmaster.

Coeducational (Boarding and Day)
Ages: 8-13
Number of pupils: 100
Number of boarders: 65
Fees: Boarding £8,802; Day £5,748

Headmaster: G. L. Nickerson, Cert.Ed.(Manchester Univ.)

Prospectus from the Secretary:
**Edington School
Mark Road, Burtle
Bridgwater
Somerset TA7 8NJ
Telephone: Bridgwater (0278) 722012**

MILLFIELD

MILLFIELD is a coeducational Boarding/Day School, a member of G.B.A., with approximately 1,200 pupils and 170 members of staff. These numbers allow relatively small classes and considerable timetable flexibility and subject choice (for instance 30 subjects at G.C.E. A-level and 40 subjects at G.C.S.E. are offered); and there is also the opportunity to choose from among more than 40 extra-curricular activities.

Whilst appropriate educational provision is made both for those who are gifted and for those who suffer from dyslexia or other learning difficulties, the majority fit happily between these two extremes and clear their academic hurdles in step with their contemporaries.

It may help parents to know that over 180 pupils annually gain entry to degree courses, including about 25 successful Oxford and Cambridge applicants; each year 20-30 pupils gain international recognition in a variety of sports.

Traditional discipline exists alongside both traditional teaching methods and the use of closed-circuit television and other modern aids. The work of both the Language Development Unit and the English as a Second Language Department is internationally recognised.

A significant number of bursaries is available, on a competitive basis, for those who show both attainment and high potential in academic, sporting or artistic fields. Formal academic, art and music scholarships are also available.

EDGARLEY HALL, I.A.P.S., prepares boys and girls aged eight to 13½ for Common Entrance Examination and scholarships for entry to Millfield and other independent schools. The teaching methods, tutor-to-pupil ratio and facilities are very similar to those at Millfield. There are approximately 500 pupils and 60 members of staff. Scholarship examinations are held in November.

Prospectus, school video and further details concerning applications for admission are available from the Tutor for Admissions at Millfield or from the Headmaster at Edgarley Hall.

**Millfield
Street
Somerset
Tel: Street 42291**

Headmaster:
Christopher S. Martin, M.A.

**Edgarley Hall
Glastonbury
Somerset
Tel: Glastonbury 32446**

Headmaster:
Richard Smyth, M.A.

(See also page 746)

SHAPWICK SCHOOL

A senior school for dyslexic boys and girls aged 13-17.

Shapwick School is a flourishing school of 100 students, providing a sympathetic and purposeful learning environment for dyslexics whose achievements have been handicapped by problems in written communication and arithmetic. All students follow a full curriculum taught by subject specialists who are trained and experienced in dyslexia. The school aims to achieve the maximum possible G.C.S.E. results for each student without sacrificing the fullness of a broad education. We provide an environment where students gain confidence and self-respect.

The school has a full range of specialist rooms, including Biology, Chemistry and Physics laboratories, Computing Room, Library, Design Centre, Sports Hall and Fitness Room. Keyboarding, Word processing Skills and Study Skills are also taught.

The academic timetable is supported by a very full programme of visits, speakers, field trips, ski trips, Art trips, rugby tours, games, inter-school matches, Duke of Edinburgh Award Scheme and a wide variety of club activities.

Students aged 13-17

Number on roll: 99

Number of boarders: 84

Fees: Boarding, £9,444
Day, £5,948

Joint Headmasters:
D. C. Walker, B.A.(Hons), Cert.Ed.
J. P. Whittock, Cert.Ed.

Prospectus from:
**The Secretary
Shapwick School
Shapwick Manor
Shapwick
Bridgwater
Somerset TA7 9NJ
Tel: Ashcott (0458) 210384**

LICHFIELD CATHEDRAL SCHOOL

Day and boarding places.

Academic and Choral Scholarships.

Further information from the Head Master.

A first-class preparatory school education in management surroundings for boys and girls between the ages of four and 13+.

**Lichfield Cathedral School
The Palace
Lichfield
Staffordshire WS13 7LH
Tel: Lichfield (0543) 263326**

(See also page 745)

SCHOOL OF S. MARY AND S. ANNE

A Woodard Church of England School. 300 girls 5-18 years with 70 in Sixth-Form.

Day, Weekly Boarding and Boarding.

* A family school where traditional values are important.

* A dynamic school looking to the 1990s with confidence.

* A school where academic success is part of a rounded education — with excellent facilities for Music, Sport, Art and a wide range of extra-curricular activities.

* Scholarships, Bursaries, Assisted Places.

School of S. Mary and S. Anne
Abbots Bromley
Nr. Rugeley
Staffordshire WS15 3BW
Telephone: (0283) 840 232/225
Fax: (0283) 840 988

Framlingham College

Expectations, Breadth, Community, and the Individual

Coeducational Boarding and Day School:
4-13 years/13-18 years.
Framlingham College and its Junior School, Brandeston Hall, offer all pupils the opportunity of a full and varied educational programme from reception through to university entrance. The schools enjoy beautiful Suffolk locations and excellent communications with London, the South-East and the Midlands. Our superb academic, cultural and sporting facilities are being constantly developed to ensure our pupils are prepared for the new and exciting challenges of the future. Great emphasis is placed on nurturing the individual and collective talents of all pupils, whilst maintaining a strong sense of community and responsibility for the welfare of others.

The Junior School, Brandeston Hall (260 pupils, including pre-prep), is well known for its friendly and happy atmosphere. Pupils are taught in small classes and are prepared for transfer to the College at 13 years. A balanced games and activity programme is seen as an important part of the day and boarding pupil's life.

At Framlingham College (430 pupils — sixth form 150) a wide range of academic options is available at GCSE and Advanced Level, along with some more innovative courses in the sixth form.

Each pupil's development is carefully guided within an open and supportive pastoral care structure. The College enjoys fine sporting traditions in both boys' and girls' games. An excellent reputation for the arts is maintained by encouraging a practical involvement in this area..

For further details and a copy of the prospectus, please contact the Headmaster: Mr. J. F. X. Miller
Framlingham College, Framlingham, Woodbridge, Suffolk IP13 9EY
Telephone: (0728) 723789. Fax: (0728) 724546

ORWELL PARK SCHOOL

Orwell Park, a coeducational preparatory school, is situated in a Georgian-style mansion set in 80 acres of parkland with glorious views over the Orwell river. The School has a distinct academic tradition and the generous staff:pupil ratio of 1:8 enables a very broad curriculum to be offered to all boys and girls. Pupils are prepared for Common Entrance and Scholarship entry to their senior schools, and Orwell Park feeds its students into over 20 different schools every year.

Our facilities are unrivalled and are used extensively, both for formal lessons and to support the huge variety of extra-curricular activities offered. There are bright classrooms with audio-visual equipment, an assembly hall, a music department with over 40 practice rooms, squash courts, sports hall and stage, games room, swimming pool, tennis courts, nine-hole golf course, shooting gallery and observatory. The new technology block comprises three science laboratories, rooms for art, ceramics, photography, design and technology, home economics, electronics and radio, a library and resources room.

The tutor system provides individual support for our pupils throughout their time with us and children's tutors monitor their tutees' progress carefully and liaise closely with parents. Parents are encouraged to play a positive role in their children's education and be closely involved with the School.

Prospective parents are always most welcome to visit the Orwell Park.

A prospectus and full details of the School may be obtained from the Registrar, Mrs. Margaret Angus.

Headmaster: I. H. Angus, M.A., H.Dip.Ed.

**Orwell Park School
Nacton
Ipswich
Suffolk IP10 0ER**

Telephone: (0473) 659225

Fax: (0473) 659822

ST. FELIX SCHOOL

St. Felix School, which celebrates its centenary in 1997, stands in 75 acres of broad campus near the seaside town of Southwold, in Suffolk. Its spacious boarding houses were purpose built, mostly in the early part of this century. Its own Preparatory School, Saint George's, stands in separate grounds adjoining St. Felix.

Girls are prepared for GCSE, A-level and University entrance. The extensive curriculum is finely balanced with a decided leaning towards traditional subjects like Classics and separate Sciences, supported by modern ones like Technology and Design. Twenty subjects are available to A-level. There is strong emphasis on careers guidance, from the third year on. The School makes special provision for gifted children.

Facilities include exceptionally well-equipped Science laboratories; new Technology block, Music wing, Art and Design studios; extensive computer network. There are swimming and diving pools; squash courts, gymnasium, playing fields.

There is a wide range of weekend and evening activities, societies and clubs – among them riding, shooting, karate; debating, drama, modern dance, flower arranging. Thirty-five St. Felix girls have attained Gold Duke of Edinburgh Awards in the last five years. The School is noted for its music.

We believe strongly in the value of single sex education for girls; academically our results reflect the advantages of girls-only schools. We have 100% pass rate in A-level Science and Modern Languages in 1992; 82% of our Mathematics and Science results combined were A/B grades. Equally important, our girls are given every encouragement and opportunity to develop confidence, independence and a sense of adventure.

St. Felix School, Southwold, Suffolk IP18 6SD.   **Telephone: 0502 722175.**   **Fax: 0502 722641.**

World class education in an English setting

- Two superbly-equipped schools in stately settings, close to London
- Pre-kindergarten to Grade 13 program
- Co-ed boarding for Grades 7 to 13
- International Baccalaureate Diploma for worldwide University access
- American High School Diploma

For further information please contact:
American Community Schools, England

The Information Office,
American Community Schools,
'Heywood', Portsmouth Road, Cobham,
SURREY KT11 1BL, ENGLAND.
Tel: 0932 867251   Fax: 0932 860379
Telex: 886645 ACS G

CITY OF LONDON FREEMEN'S SCHOOL

THIS H.M.C. day and boarding coeducational school is for pupils aged eight to 18. Founded in 1854 at Brixton for orphan children of Freemen, it was moved to Ashtead in 1926 and began to admit fee-paying pupils. It now has about 680 on roll, 300 of whom are under 13, and a Sixth Form of 120+ sending 75% plus to universities annually. There are about 80 in the Boarding Houses, including weekly boarders who comprise half that total.

Admission:
The main entry is by selection based on examinations and school reports at 8+, also by Common Entrance (or school examinations) at 13+, and by G.C.S.E. results to the Sixth Form.

Scholarships:
Five Government Assisted Places. Twenty valuable Corporation Scholarships at 8+/13+/16+, and Music Awards at 13+ are available annually.

For prospectus and further details apply to the Admission Secretary.

**City of London Freemen's School
Ashtead Park
Surrey KT21 1ET**

Tel: Ashtead (0372) 277933

DUKE OF KENT SCHOOL

The Duke of Kent School is a coeducational preparatory school for 150 full boarders and 30 day-boarders (115 boys, 65 girls) aged between seven and 13 years. The school is magnificently situated in a wooded area of exceptional beauty between Guildford and Cranleigh, within easy reach of central London, Gatwick and Heathrow.

The school aims to provide a stable, ordered, caring and, above all, happy environment, in which each child is given the opportunity to discover and develop, as far as possible, his or her own skills. Every child is good at something and success in an activity, which may at first sight seem relatively unimportant, often produces the confidence necessary for success in later life.

The curriculum is broad and all the children benefit from the excellent purpose-built facilities which are available for Science, CDT, Computing, Art and Drama. The Music Department, which is particularly strong, has its own main teaching room and a suite of nine individual teaching/practice rooms. The provision for games is equally good.

There is a heated indoor swimming pool, a games hall, tennis courts and extensive outdoor playing areas which have been imaginatively laid out within the 40-acre site.

Considerable emphasis is laid on pastoral care and each child is the special responsibility of one of six Pastoral Tutors. These Tutors all live on the site as do many other members of staff. This high adult and family presence enables the creation of an exceptionally caring and happy atmosphere which is immediately obvious to all who visit.

**Duke of Kent School
Ewhurst, Cranleigh
Surrey GU6 7NS
Telephone: Cranleigh (0483) 277313**

EDGEBOROUGH

Edgeborough Photo: Roger Smeeton

Edgeborough is a coeducational Preparatory School for boarders and day children, set in 40 acres of beautiful Surrey woodland, two miles south of Farnham. Based on a Christian philosophy, the school looks to provide a broad academic and sporting curriculum to prepare children for entry into Public School at 13+.

The Nursery and Pre-Preparatory Departments form an independent unit, enabling children from the ages of three to seven to develop in a secure, yet stimulating, environment, with access to all the School's facilities.

Entry into the main school is usually by an assessment at the age of seven; streaming begins at nine. All major subjects are covered in the curriculum, with French available from four and Latin at nine. Music, Art, Pottery and Design Technology are all taught by specialists in purpose-built premises. At 11 a scholarship stream is available for those aiming for awards.

The main sports played are rugby, soccer, netball, hockey, cricket and athletics, but every child has the opportunity to take part in squash, tennis, basketball, riding, sailing and gymnastics. The school has spacious playing fields, a sports hall, hard surface play area and an outdoor heated swimming pool.

Boarding at Edgeborough is available at any age, but is encouraged from the age of 11.

Boarders are free to go out on Saturdays and Sundays after fulfilling school commitments, but there is always a wide range of activities provided by the staff.

Edgeborough's strength is its warm, family atmosphere, in which children can flourish.

Edgeborough, Frensham, Surrey GU10 3AH   Tel: (0252) 792495

FRENSHAM HEIGHTS SCHOOL
H.M.C.

Coeducational boarding and day school of 285 pupils aged 11-18.

Very high entry to degree courses; wide range of exam subjects.

Good discipline based on good relationships. Staff : pupil ratio 1 : 8.

No religious affiliation. Liberal values. Boarders may go home at weekends.

The annual ENTRANCE EXAMINATIONS are to be held in January 1993

Prospective Parents' Days held twice a term.

Please telephone the Headmaster's Secretary, Sue Rickard, for further information and a prospectus.
Frensham (025 125) 2134

Headmaster:
A. L. PATTINSON, M.A.(Oxon.), Cert.Ed.

**Frensham Heights School
Rowledge
Farnham
Surrey**

(See also page 742)

THE GROVE SCHOOL

The Grove School is an Independent Public Boarding and Day School for Girls with Pre-Preparatory, Preparatory and Senior Departments, taking girls from rising five to 18.

The Grove School offers an integrated 8-16 curriculum with the needs of GCSE in mind. Girls joining the Preparatory Department (8-10+) have automatic right of transfer to the Senior School at 11+.

The Grove School offers specialist teaching throughout the 8-16 age range and has a strong commitment to languages, science and technology. The National Curriculum is accepted in its entirety, although many other optional subjects are also on offer.

All subjects are available at Advanced Level within the Sixth Form. All girls complete a Diploma Course in Information Technology and a minimum of nine GCSE subjects.

The Grove is a very special place. We are proud of our girls and constantly strive to improve the quality of what we can offer them. Our motto is 'Girls first'. Come and visit us for an informal discussion and tour of the School. You will receive a warm welcome.

Headmaster: Colin Brooks, BA(Hons), AdDipEd, CertEd, FRGS, FRMetS

For further details and a prospectus, please contact the Headmaster's Personal Assistant.

**The Grove School
Hindhead
Surrey GU26 6BW**

Telephone: 0428 605407

GREENACRE SCHOOL FOR GIRLS

Fides et Opera

Pre-preparatory class for girls of three and four years.
Preparatory School for girls five to 10+.
Senior School for girls 11 to 18.

Greenacre aims to provide a sound education in happy surroundings. Throughout the school individuals matter and there is a caring, supportive atmosphere underlying the very active community life.

The girls benefit from the continuity of method obtained from the close links between the different sections of the school and the interest and care given to each pupil.

Day girls are received from the age of four+ into the Preparatory Department. The requirements of the National Curriculum are incorporated into the broad general education leading to GCSE and Advanced level in the Senior School. A balance is maintained between modern ideas and the best of traditional practice. High standards of courtesy and behaviour are expected.

A wide range of subjects is offered in the Sixth Form and the well-established tutorial system helps provide a bridge between school and University and College courses to which girls proceed at 18+. Sixth-Form scholarships are awarded on the results of examinations held in December each year.

Art, Drama and Music are encouraged and there are good facilities for sports, including a heated, covered swimming pool. The position of the school at the edge of the Green Belt on the North Downs provides a pleasant, healthy environment, while the close proximity of London enables full use to be made of theatres, concerts and specialist lectures.

Scholarships (half tuition fees) for Sixth-Form entrants and 11+ pupils by examinations held in December and January, respectively.

The Headmistress is always pleased to meet parents.

Girls' Public School (Day and Boarding)
GSA and GBGSA

400 Pupils

Headmistress:
Mrs. P. M. Wood, B.A.

Greenacre School for Girls
Sutton Lane
Banstead
Surrey SM7 3RA

Telephone:
Burgh Heath (0737) 352114

HOLY CROSS PREPARATORY SCHOOL

IN CRUCE SALUS

A Catholic Independent Day School for Girls aged 4-11+ and Boys aged 4-7 offering a quality all-round education in a caring manner for children of all abilities.

The school has a proven record of attainment and a high success rate in gaining placements at Public, High and Grammar Schools.

The school is set in eight picturesque acres on a private estate on Kingston Hill (off the A3).

Prospectus on request.

Member of ISIS.

Head: Mrs. K. HAYES

Type: INDEPENDENT DAY SCHOOL

Age range: 4-11

No. of Pupils enrolled as at 1/9/91
12 Boys and 228 Girls

Fees per annum: £2,775

**Holy Cross Preparatory School
George Road
Kingston upon Thames
Surrey KT2 7NU**

Telephone: 081-942 0729

MARYMOUNT INTERNATIONAL SCHOOL

For excellence in education

- Day and boarding school for 200 girls aged 11-18 years
- International Baccalaureate Programme
- American College Preparatory Curriculum
- 98% university entrance rate
- In excess of 40 nationalities represented
- Domestic and foreign travel an integral part of the educational programme

For further information apply to:
The Admissions Office
Marymount International School, George Road,
Kingston upon Thames, Surrey KT2 7PE, England
Tel: 081-949 0571   Fax: 081-336 2485

PARSONS MEAD

Parsons Mead is an independent public day and boarding school for girls controlled by a Board of Governors under an Educational Trust. The original building, now the boarding house, still retains its character of a big, private house, standing in a large garden and facing south. The School is situated close to the M25 motorway which provides easy access to Heathrow and Gatwick Airports. There are separate modern, purpose-built classrooms, a laboratory block, Art Room, Computer Room, Home Economics and Textile Rooms, a Music block and a Sixth Form unit. Within the 12 acres of grounds are playing fields, five hard courts, a swimming pool and a sports hall.

The aim of the curriculum is to provide a sound, broadly-based education up to the G.C.S.E., followed by a two-year Advanced Level course in preparation for entry to university and to professional training courses. Alternatively a one-year, general course may be taken in the Sixth Form, in which cultural and practical subjects are emphasised. Sixth Formers are taught in small tutorial groups to ensure the maximum of individual attention. Senior boarders are provided with study bedrooms. Girls are accepted into the school for Sixth Form courses as well as into the main school.

(Founded 1897)
Member G.B.G.S.A. and G.S.A.

180 Junior girls 3+ to 11 years.
260 Senior girls 11 to 18 years.
including places for 55 boarders from eight to 18 years.

Head Mistress: Miss E. B. Plant, B.A.

Parsons Mead
Ashtead
Surrey KT21 2PE
Telephone: Ashtead 276401

ST. CATHERINE'S SCHOOL

St. Catherine's School is a Church of England Independent Day and Boarding School for Girls, founded in 1885. The School is a Member of G.S.A. and I.A.P.S.

Situated three miles south of Guildford off the main Horsham Road (A281), we are within convenient reach of Heathrow and Gatwick, and transport to and from the airports is arranged for girls travelling abroad.

Boarders are accepted from the age of nine-plus to 18 years and day girls from four to 18. Weekly boarders are also accepted.

Entry to the School from the age of seven is by Entrance Examination, held in January. Early registration is advised.

11+ Entrance Scholarships are available, together with Internal Scholarships at Fifth-Form level to assist with A-level courses.

Assisted places available at 11, 12 and Sixth-Form level.

The girls are prepared for G.C.S.E. and A-level examinations and for entry to the Universities. There are good modern facilities for the Sciences, Art, Languages, Computer Studies and Physical Education. There is a wide range of extra subjects and girls can take external examinations in Music, Speech and Drama, and Dancing. During their last two years girls are housed in a separate Sixth-Form Unit and in the New Centenary Building.

Whilst the emphasis is on academic subjects, the school's aim is to enable a girl to develop her potential in any direction to the full.

For a Prospectus, apply to the Headmaster, who will be pleased to see parents by appointment.

Headmaster: J. R. Palmer, BSc.

St. Catherine's School
Bramley
Guildford
Surrey
Telephone: Guildford 893363

(See also page 750)

BATTLE ABBEY SCHOOL

The School is big enough to encourage healthy competition and to develop the social skills and awareness of others learnt by being part of a lively community, but it is small enough to have many of the attributes of a large family. The Headmaster and his wife live within the main school building, as do the Senior Master and his wife, ensuring caring supervision of the pupils' welfare at all times.

Teaching classes are small throughout the school, allowing individual attention and the opportunity for all pupils to achieve their maximum potential. The curriculum is based on the National Curriculum and a highly qualified staff, using modern methods and equipment, prepares pupils for maximum success in GCSE, A-level and University Entrance examinations. For those spending only one year in the Sixth Form there is a popular course, 'Education for the Nineties', in which both practical and cultural interests are developed.

The School has extensive sports fields: every age group has time-tabled games lessons each week. Music and drama also have an important place in the curriculum; there is at least one major production every year.

At Battle Abbey, the filling of leisure time is no problem; there are ample opportunities for developing skills and hobbies. Private coaching is available in many subjects including riding, sailing and instrumental music. Activity groups, which are a regular feature of weekends, sample a wide variety of pursuits, and there are frequent visits to theatres, art galleries and other places of interest. Those who wish to do so may join Cubs, Brownies, Scouts or Guides.

The School is privileged to occupy one of the most famous historical sites in the world, that of the 1066 Battle of Hastings. The main school building, with its assembly hall, common rooms, dining-room and library, is the 15th-century Abbot's House belonging to the Abbey of St. Martin founded by the Conqueror himself. It has been beautifully preserved and modernised, and is typical of the School's happy blend of traditional values with up-to-date facilities.

Grouped around this building are well-equipped specialist rooms including laboratories and cumputer areas. The Preparatory and Kindergarten pupils have their own separate classrooms and plenty of space for safe play. The dormitories are bright and cheerful, many having magnificent views over the surrounding contryside. The Sixth-Form pupils have study-bedrooms in another very comfortable house within the school grounds.

Battle is only 57 miles from London, on the main railway line to Hastings. Gatwick, Heathrow, and the Channel Ports are within easy reach. There is accompanied travel to and from London at the beginning and end of each term and half-term.

The School believes strongly in the principal of partnership between school and home. Parents may visit at any time and be assured of a warm welcome.

Further details may be obtained from the School Secretary. If you can visit the School, please make an appointment to do so. Try to come in term-time, if possible, when you will be able to see Battle Abbey at its best, alive and in action.

Fees:

	Boarding:	Day:
Pre-Preparatory forms	–	£ 940 per term
Preparatory forms:	£2,220 per term	£1,270 per term
Senior forms I & II:	£2,560 per term	£1,600 per term
Senior forms III & above:	£2,770 per term	£1,710 per term

There is a 12% bursary for serving members of Her Majesty's Forces

An Independent Co-educational School for 200 boys and girls between the ages of four and 18, who may be full boarders, weekly boarders or day pupils. The school is administered by B.A.S. (School) Ltd., a registered charity.

Chairman of the Governors:
Colonel M. W. Henry, MBE
Headmaster:
D. J. A. Teall, Esq., BSc(Newcastle)

**Battle Abbey School
East Sussex TN33 0AD
Tel: Battle (04246) 2385**

Deepdene School. Successful education through smaller classes

Deepdene School is an independent school for girls aged 3 – 16 and boys aged 3 – 7.

An essential feature of the Deepdene approach is to provide the appropriate educational environment for each individual pupil. Small classes are the school's trademark, ensuring that each pupil receives the attention they need and deserve.

Throughout the school efforts are concentrated on traditional values and sound fundamentals, with a strong emphasis on the three R's. The creative, performing arts and music play an important role, and French is taught formally from the age of 7.

Deepdene's staff are highly qualified and enjoy teaching in small classes where they can devote time to each pupil and monitor individual progress. The New Way Reading and SPMG Maths Schemes are begun in our Nursery Classes and continue throughout the Junior School.

From the ages of 11 – 14 timetables offer a broad based educational foundation incorporating the core subjects set down in the National Curriculum guidelines.

When choosing their GCSE subjects at 14+, pupils are individually counselled ensuring an appropriate selection of subjects is pursued that will stimulate and interest each pupil and lead to examination success. Intensive English language lessons are available for pupils who initially have insufficient English for academic study.

Deepdene School can help to acheive your child's potential in a traditional, caring and encouraging environment.

Deepdene School, 195 New Church Road, Hove, East Sussex BN3 4ED. Telephone 0273 418984

GREENFIELDS SCHOOL

This coeducational, non-denominational school, with 200 pupils from 3 to 18, caters for a wide range of ability. Teaching is in small groups. Students are taught how to study and supported self-study is a feature of Senior School. Primarily a day school, a growing number of older students stay in boarding houses near by.

A wide academic and sporting curriculum enables students to take up subjects that interest them, like photography, ceramics or astronomy, and develop their individual talents. We have a high pass rate in GCSE and A-level examinations. Twenty-three subjects are currently offered and more are planned.

Scholarships are awarded for all-round ability, sport and music. Greenfields has a very-well-endowed music department and lively drama department. Cultural outings and community projects extend interests and responsibilities.

Situated on the edge of the Ashdown Forest, the school lies in 11 acres of woodland, one mile from the A22. Trains run from London to East Grinstead, three miles away: Gatwick Airport is a 20-minute car ride, bringing the school within reach of families from all over the United Kingdom and abroad.

Principal: Margaret Hodkin, BA(Hons)(Lond).
Deputy Principal: Mark McQuade, MA(Oxon).

Founded 1981

**Greenfields School
Priory Road
Forest Row
East Sussex RH18 5JD
Telephone: (0342) 822189 and 822845**

TEMPLE GROVE SCHOOL

Co-ed Prep School, Boarding and Day 7½.-13; also Co-ed Pre-Prep, Day 3-7½. CE.

Temple Grove is an IAPS Preparatory School situated in 40 acres of grounds and providing up-to-date facilities, which include a hard, all-weather playing surface, indoor gym, golf course and rifle range, heated swimming pool and computer room.

The school specialises in small classes and has an excellent well-qualified and devoted staff who are experienced in instilling confidence and motivation among the children in a happy, friendly environment.

For a prospectus and further information please apply to the Headmaster at the address below or telephone:

Nutley 2112 (STD code 082 571).

Fax: Nutley 3432.

Temple Grove School
Heron's Ghyll
Uckfield
East Sussex

WILTON HOUSE SCHOOL

Co-educational Boarding and Day School

Small classes, Remedial and individual tuition arranged when required

- Computer Workshop
- Swimming Pools
- Tennis Courts
- Games Field and Horse Riding
- Escort Services to and from Airports

Established since 1954

Head Office and Senior School:
Catsfield Place
Battle
GCSE and A-levels
13-18 years

Junior School:
Broomham
Guestling
Hastings
5-13 years

Apply: The Principal at Head Office

Wilton House School
Battle
Hastings
East Sussex TN33 9BS
Telephone: 0424 830234

FARLINGTON SCHOOL

Farlington is an Independent Day and Boarding School for 280 girls from nine to 18 years, standing in 27 acres of grounds containing two small Lakes, Playing Fields, Hard Tennis Courts, a Heated Outdoor Swimming Pool and a Multi-Purpose All-Weather Pitch.

A fully-qualified Staff prepares girls for the G.C.S.E., A-Levels and University entrance. There is a strong tradition of MUSIC and DRAMA in the School. Outings are arranged to plays, concerts, etc.; parties are taken abroad and groups go on Field Courses. There is excellent careers advice and links with industry. The School successfully participates in the Young Enterprise Scheme and the Duke of Edinburgh Awards Scheme.

Prospectus on application to the Headmistress.

Founded in 1896, the School is an Educational Trust.

Headmistress:
Mrs. Trina Mawer, B.A.

Horsham
West Sussex RH12 3PN
Telephone: (0403) 254967

PENNTHORPE SCHOOL

Pennthorpe, which is an Educational Trust, is situated in 14 acres of ground on the Surrey/Sussex border. The school, which is coeducational and accepts children from the age of four upwards, prepares boys and girls for Scholarships and Common Entrance to a wide range of Public Schools. A wide range of activities is offered to enable each pupil to discover and exercise their talents. These include music, including instrumental and choral training (the Chapel choir singing regularly in various cathedrals), drama, under professional direction, cooking, Cubs, Brownies, rifle shooting, and debating. Sporting activities include Soccer, Rugby, Hockey, Cricket, Athletics, Cross-country, Swimming, Badminton, Netball, Tennis, Squash, Trampolining and Judo. The school has its own Chapel, Library, Sports Hall, swimming pool, CDT Dept and Music rooms. The school seeks to provide a homely and stable environment in which the values of reliability, consideration for others, good manners and self-discipline are stressed.

Chairman of the Governors: Mr. R. Masding
Headmaster: Rev. J. E. Spencer, BA(Bristol)
Number of Pupils: 51 Boarders, 201 Day Pupils
Fees: Weekly Boarders £1,920-£2,250 per term
Day Pupils £650-£1,750 per term

Pennthorpe School
Rudgwick
Horsham
West Sussex RH12 3HJ

Tel: Rudgwick (0403) 822391
Fax: (0403) 822438

SLINDON COLLEGE

Slindon College is a small, independent boarding and day school with approximately 165 boys, with day girls admitted to the Sixth Form. An excellent staff : pupil ratio means that classes are small, so the school is well able to fulfil its major aim: to cater for the particular needs of all pupils and help them achieve their potential. Thus some will pursue their studies here through to A-level and on to university while others will succeed in different, less academic, but no less important areas. We seek to provide a caring environment, and to promote an enthusiasm for learning.

There are three boarding houses, each staffed by a Housemaster and a Housetutor and there are two full-time Matrons to look after the well-being of the pupils.

The National Curriculum is followed. A One-Year Course, or A-levels, are offered to Sixth-Formers.

Slindon has an excellent Special Needs department with four fully qualified and experienced teachers.

Facilities include a heated swimming pool, squash courts and floodlit hard courts. A full range of activities is offered, including skateboarding, motor vehicle maintenance, canoeing, golf and computer studies.

Slindon is close to the main London Victoria railway line, and the College is experienced with pupils whose parents are overseas.

It is intended that when pupils leave Slindon College they will be ready to face the challenges of adult life with tolerance, confidence and maturity.

Slindon College, Slindon House, Slindon, Arundel West Sussex BN18 0RH. Tel: (0243) 65320

ARGYLE HOUSE SCHOOL

Argyle House School has, for more than a century, provided independent education for boys in the Sunderland area, academic success and caring for the individual development.

Small classes in the Primary School are taught a broad curriculum, with emphasis on core skills in English and Mathematics, within a happy and exciting atmosphere.

Senior School optimises this foundation to achieve outstanding academic results and develop mature, responsible citizens.

There is a wide variety of extra-curricular activities including many sports, chess, computer clubs and the Duke of Edinburgh Award Scheme.

**Argyle House School
19/20 Thornhill Park
Tunstall Road
Sunderland SR2 7LA
Tyne & Wear**

Tel: (091) 510 0726 (School)

KING'S SCHOOL

Founded in 1860, King's is proud of its history of academic success through a wide curriculum to G.C.S.E., AS, A and Oxbridge levels. Academic results are excellent. This year 45% of A-level candidates achieved A and B grades with an average UCCA score of 20.2, securing King's place in National League tables. Ninety per cent of the Upper Sixth-formers gained places at universities, including Oxford and Cambridge.

A dedicated staff and small classes working within a secure environment ensure the development of each individual's talents and abilities. The School also encourages physical and social awareness in its boys and girls. Sport, literature, and the Arts play an integral part in the life of the School, as do links with industry and the local community.

King's has a full range of playing fields, as well as a fully equipped gymnasium and weights room, two field study centres, newly opened CDT and Art Rooms, Computer Labs, Business/Economic Suites, Drama Studio, Food Technology and Science Laboratories. A continuing development plan provides excellent facilities with which to prepare boys and girls to meet the demands of the modern world.

The School is proud of its 'open door' policy allowing parents access to staff at any time of the school day. The Parents' Association is very active.

**King's School
Huntington Place
Tynemouth
Tyne & Wear NE30 4RF
Telephone: 091-258 5995**

EDGBASTON COLLEGE

Edgbaston College, recently awarded the MENSA Charter, has been providing first-class education since 1889. Its 10 acres of grounds and Regency house provide a peaceful working environment which is only 10 minutes' drive from Birmingham City Centre. Four school buses bring pupils from all sides of the City. A late service and holiday activity scheme are provided.

The College is split into four sections: Montessori Kindergarten, Pre-Prep, Middle and High Schools. Entry is by test/interview as appropriate. There are generous bursaries for those who achieve good results at 11+. The National Curriculum is observed but the Edgbaston College Curriculum is generally more demanding at each stage than the Government guidelines. Progress is measured regularly. A wide range of GCSE and A-level subjects is offered, with teaching undertaken in small groups by highly qualified and experienced staff. BTEC courses have also been introduced into the Sixth Form, where students enjoy countless opportunities to gain experience in the workplace.

The College also recruits young people from other European countries to study A-level, BTEC and Foundation courses for entry into British universities.

There are well-established departments in English as a Foreign Language and Dyslexia.

Edgbaston College has strong traditions in Music and Drama. Approximately 50% of pupils play a musical instrument. There are several major play productions each year, some of which take place at the Lyttleton Theatre in Birmingham. There are regular theatre visits and workshops.

The College offers a wide range of sports and competes with remarkable success in fixtures organised both regionally and nationally.

A high standard of discipline and unselfish courtesy is combined with care for the well-being of each pupil. A strongly Christian atmosphere pervades an active and happy school.

If you would like to visit, please contact our Registrar, Mrs. Groom

Edgbaston College, 249 Bristol Road, Birmingham B5 7UH. Telephone: 021-472 1034

OLD SWINFORD HOSPITAL SCHOOL STOURBRIDGE
Founded 1667

Full Boarding Fees £1,060 per term

The School is grant maintained, so no tuition fees are payable.
540 boys aged 11-18, mainly boarders.
170 in the Sixth Form.
Traditional academic education to University entrance.
'A' levels including Business Studies, Computer Science, Design, Archaeology and Electronics.

Entry at 11, 13 or Sixth Form.
Academic Scholarships and Bursaries
Weekly boarding available

Study bedrooms for all Sixth Formers. Four new Boarding Houses and new Technology Centre. Wide range of out-of-school activities including Cadet Force, indoor Rifle Range, Squash Courts, a floodlit all-weather playing surface and a Climbing Wall.

If we may send you a prospectus or you would like to visit the school, please phone the Admissions Secretary or write to:

OLD SWINFORD HOSPITAL SCHOOL
Stourbridge, West Midlands, DY8 1QX.
Tel: Stourbridge 370025

KINGSBURY HILL HOUSE SCHOOL

The school maintains a fine academic tradition, but also believes that loyalty, a sense of fair play, and good manners, are just as important as academic achievement. The school provides a broad curriculum so that each pupil receives a sound and balanced start to their education. A pupil : teacher ratio of less than 10 ensures that all pupils work at their own pace.

Further details from:

**Kingsbury Hill House School
Kingsbury Street
Marlborough
Wilts SN8 1JA**

Tel: 0672 512680

SALISBURY CATHEDRAL SCHOOL

The Cathedral School is a co-educational preparatory school set in 25 acres of grounds in the Cathedral Close.

The curriculum aims to balance academic achievement with music, sport, drama and technology in a family environment.

Each year a number of academic and music scholarships are won by pupils moving on to senior schools.

Entry to local grammar schools is also available through 11-plus and 13-plus examinations.

To complement the boys' choir, which has sung in the Cathedral for 900 years, a girls' Cathedral choir has now been formed.

Entry into the school is by assessment and report, and into the choir by assessment and voice trial.

Substantial choral scholarships are available.

Co-educational pre-preparatory education is available from four to seven years old.

For further details contact:
**The Registrar, The Cathedral School
1 The Close, Salisbury SP1 2EQ
Telephone: 0722 322652**

SCHOOL PROFILES — Yorkshire, North 715

AMPLEFORTH
PREPARATORY SCHOOL
GILLING CASTLE

R.C., I.A.P.S.

**BOYS 8 - 13 YEARS
DAY AND BOARDING PLACES**

- Challenging curriculum
- Christian values
- Governed by Benedictine monks
- Friendly atmosphere
- Heated indoor pool
- Golf course and sports hall
- Beautiful historic setting
- High teacher/pupil ratio

Headmaster: Graham Sasse (M.A. Oxon)

**Ampleforth Preparatory School
Gilling Castle
Gilling East
York YO6 4HP · UK
Telephone: (04393) 238**

Giggleswick

Founded in 1512, Giggleswick School lies in magnificent Dales scenery, only an hour away from Leeds, Manchester and the Lakes. Its green-domed Chapel is a notable landmark

The Senior School and Catteral Hall, its Preparatory School, provide first-class, all-round education for about 450 boys and girls between the ages of 8 and 18.

Academic achievements are high and about 80% of pupils go on to degree courses. There is an extensive extra-curricular programme with excellent facilities for games and outdoor pursuits. The school enjoys an outstanding reputation for music, drama and art, and prides itself in being a busy, happy community.

Pupils enjoy a high quality of facilities and accommodation. A million-pound refurbishment of the boys' Houses will be completed this November. Other recent developments include the Dutton Sixth Form Centre, girls' accommodation and Catteral Hall's Music School and Science Room.

We believe a boarding school allows all boys and girls the scope to develop their individual skills and personalities so they can acquire the self-confidence, qualifications and values necessary to meet the challenges of adult life.

We are proud of our school – please come and visit us and see it for yourself by contacting . . . Peter Hobson, M.A., Headmaster,

Giggleswick School, Settle, North Yorkshire BD24 0DE   Tel: (0729) 823545   Fax: (0729) 824187

Queen Ethelburga's College

Queen Ethelburga's College relocated from Harrogate, in 1991, to Thorpe Underwood, a 100-acre estate between Harrogate and York. Set in the heart of the countryside, Thorpe Underwood Hall is free from traffic congestion and pollution yet easily accessible from the A1, M1 and M62 motorways. The new bypass from Harrogate affords ready access from Wharfedale and North Leeds and its surrounding areas, whilst major railway stations and the airports of Leeds/Bradford, Manchester and Newcastle are close to hand. The countryside around the College provides a wealth of material for geography fieldwork, and the local history of Fountains Abbey, Aldborough and the City of York combines with Thorpe Underwood's own literary history (both Anne and Branwell Brontë taught at the old Thorpe Green Hall) to provide a stimulating framework for study.

The College has benefited from the spending of over £6,000,000 on new facilities and the quality of the technical equipment shows the level of commitment the College has towards educating its pupils for the career opportunities of the 21st century.

Both girls and boys share a happy, balanced and creative atmosphere in the Junior Department, where National curriculum guidelines are both met and exceeded in certain areas.

From 11 years old the College retains its single-sex status and educates girls only up to the age of 18. A happy, purposeful atmosphere is created by highly qualified enthusiastic staff who motivate girls to make the most of their abilities.

A full range of GCSE and A-level subjects is offered and the College also offers several vocational courses including Business Studies and Office Practice.

There has always been a strong sporting tradition at Queen Ethelburga's which resulted in the first lacrosse team touring the USA last season, the first-ever Yorkshire team to do so. The College has also excelled in the number of Gold Awards for the past two years in the Duke of Edinburgh Award scheme and a wealth of other sporting activities is offered including tennis, netball, swimming, cross-country, canoeing, rock-climbing, badminton and fencing and its own equestrian centre.

There is no doubt that Queen Ethelburga's will continue to grow in its new surroundings where old traditions meet new requirements. It will, nevertheless, remain a place where everyone is an individual.

**Queen Ethelburga's College
Thorpe Underwood Hall
Ouseburn
York YO5 9SZ
Telephone: 0423 331480
Fax: 0423 331007**

Principal: Mrs. J. M. Town BA(Oxon)

READ SCHOOL, DRAX

Independent Day School for Boys and Girls 4-18
Boarding School for Boys 8-18

- Easy access to A1, M62 and M18
- Continuity of education from four to 18 in small teaching groups
- A caring, yet traditional, disciplined environment

- Full curriculum to GCSE and A-level
- Good teacher : pupil ratio and small classes
- Excellent reputation in rugby, hockey, athletics and cricket
- Wide range of extra-curricular activities
- Transport available for Day Pupils
- Long-established – founded 1667
- Admissions considered at any age
- Good academic record and university entrance
- Superb new pre-preparatory department
- Playing fields adjacent and heated swimming pool
- Flourishing Cadet Force – Army and RAF sections. Plus D of E

Head:
A. J. Saddler, M.A., Jesus College, Cambridge

For further details and prospectus please contact the Headmaster's Secretary:
**Read School
Drax, Selby
North Yorkshire YO8 8NL
Telephone: SELBY (0757) 618248**

LICENSED VICTUALLERS' SCHOOL

Boys: 3-16+
Boarding: 37 Day 101 *Staff:* Full-time 16
Girls: 3-16+
Boarding: 24 Day 38   Part-time 5

Religious affiliation: Non-denominational.
Entry requirements: Interview and/or examination.

The Licensed Victuallers' School is a coeducational School offering Day and Boarding places from seven to 16+ with additional day places in the Nursery and Infant departments in the age range three to seven. The provision of Infant, Junior and Senior departments on the same site facilitates the establishment of continuity of education, in small groups, from an early age through to GCSE.

The School aims to provide a happy, caring environment in which children can achieve their full potential and acquire self-confidence and an enthusiasm for work. It seeks to develop and encourage the different talents that each pupil possesses and challenges them to do their best at all times.
The School commands panoramic views of Wharfedale and Ilkley Moor and is ideally located for adventure training and Duke of Edinburgh Award activity work. Outdoor pursuits is a key feature of work at the School.

Recent developments include refurbished Library, Science Laboratory, Art Room, Home Economics room, a heated indoor swimming pool and a new sports complex.

The main sports are Soccer, Rugby, Hockey and Cricket for boys and Netball, Hockey and Rounders for girls. Coaching is also given in swimming, athletics, badminton, tennis and golf, and the School has its own small none-hole golf course in the grounds.

There is a wide range of clubs and societies in which all children are encouraged to participate.

Head: I. A. Mullins, B.Ed(Hons), M.Sc., M.B.I.M.

**Clevedon House
Ben Rhydding
Ilkley
West Yorkshire LS29 8BJ
Telephone: (0943) 608515**

Penrhos College
COLWYN BAY
Founded 1880

Headmaster: Mr. Nigel C. Peacock, M.A.(Cantab.)
Telephone: 0492 530333
Fax: 0492 533198

PENRHOS COLLEGE exists to provide education for children. It is a boarding and day school of about 300 girls aged 11-18. There is a Junior department for 3- to 11-year-olds to which day boys are welcome.

The school combines the traditional virtues of academic excellence, hard work and good discipline with a forward looking and friendly approach. Situated in 18 acres beside the sea it has not only a well-qualified staff but excellent facilities including six laboratories, library, textile and cookery rooms, music wing with 18 practice rooms, gym, art room, activity centre, geography room, audio-visual room, lecture theatre, Chapel, CDT workshop, two squash courts, five tennis courts and a 25m indoor swimming pool. The well-equipped sanatorium is run by an SRN who has a full-time assistant. The Upper VI House is intended to be a stepping stone between school and College. The girls have their own kitchen where they can make their own breakfast and weekend meals if they wish.

We believe that education extends far beyond the walls of the classroom and there is a comprehensive programme of more than 25 evening activities (ranging from Ballet to Welding). Riding is popular. A full-time director of extra-curricular activities runs climbing, walking, canoeing and sailing expeditions every weekend. We are an RYA centre. Service to others is important too. Recently we built an adventure playground for local children and the girls crew an auxiliary rescue boat in co-ordination with the local coastguard. The sixth form annually give a holiday to handicapped children.

Normal entry is at age 11 and girls are prepared first for G.C.S.E. and then for A-levels. The sixth form is large and flourishing and about 55% of the girls proceed to degree courses. Virtually all go on to some form of higher education. The school participates in H.M. Government's Assisted Places Scheme and there are generous bursaries for daughters of service personnel and daughters of Old Penrhosians.

Five Scholarships are awarded annually (value 50% current fee). The Isa Clarke French Scholarship (£1,200 per annum), two Science Scholarships and a Music Scholarship (value 50% current fee) are available for girls entering the sixth form.

The Secretary to the Headmaster will be pleased to send a prospectus on request.

(See also pages 719 and 747)

Penrhos College Junior School
Oak Drive, Colwyn Bay
Headmaster: Mr. Richard Dell, M.A.(Oxon.)
Telephone: 0492 530170

Penrhos Junior exists to provide education for children. It combines a family atmosphere with high academic standards: bringing out the very best from children of all abilities. 'Atmosphere' is everything, and the children learn within a beautiful environment that is both natural and happy.

Boarding is run on a 'home' basis, with matrons acting as 'mums'. The highest standards of behaviour are fostered, whilst at the same time there is no doubting that Penrhos Junior is the children's term-time home. There are regular week-end outings involving a whole range of activities from picnics and treasure hunts to swimming and theatres. There are also such sessions as orienteering and skiing during the week.

The sound and outward looking educational programme lays stress on the three 'Rs' as the foundation for all other activities. Regular projects and the running of their Houses, together with day and overnight study trips both within Snowdonia and further afield, allow the children to put into practice what they have learnt.

The needs of each child are catered for within small teaching groups, with class-based teaching in infants giving way to specialist teaching for the older children. Everything is done to encourage creativity and an enquiring mind within a properly ordered and well-mannered environment. Full use is made of the extensive resources provided by Penrhos College. As well as the usual subjects, the broad curriculum includes Laboratory Science, Computers, French, Art, Music and the full range of games, swimming and gymnastics.

Penrhos Junior overlooks the sea and stands in its own extensive grounds of gardens and woods.

Pupils are prepared for Entrance and Scholarship Examinations to Penrhos College and other leading Public Schools.

Girls attend as boarders or day pupils; boys as day pupils only.

The Headmaster will be pleased to send a prospectus on request.

(See also pages 718 and 747)

RYDAL

Member of HMC and IAPS

Colwyn Bay
Clwyd
LL29 7BT
Tel: 0492-530155

Rydal is one of the top Independent Schools in the North-West, a reputation which has been earned by consistently good exam results, and a genuine concern for the education and welfare of each individual pupil. The School, with its Methodist foundation, is guided by Christian values, and visitors are immediately struck by the warm, friendly and supportive atmosphere which pervades the whole School.

The School is fortunate in its environment. The campus lies on rising ground close to the centre of Colwyn Bay amongst leafy avenues, with plenty of open spaces and a fine view over the sea to the North, particularly from the Prep School. Steeply rising woodland forms a natural boundary to the south, yet, in spite of the general air of being 'out of town', the station is less than 10 minutes' walk, and the A55 Expressway within a couple of hundred metres.

With the sea on the doorstep, and the mountains of Snowdonia in the back garden, Rydal is particularly popular with families who like 'The Great Outdoors'. Many boarders live in the Cheshire/Shropshire/Wirral/Merseyside area, and the School's flexible approach to weekend 'exeats' offers a regular opportunity for parents and children to go walking together in the hills, or to sail, or simply to enjoy what North Wales has to offer. And the new A55 Expressway gets you to Chester and the motorways in 40 minutes.

Girls and boys normally enter the School at ages 7, 11, 13 or 16, and there is a smooth transition from the Junior section in the Preparatory School into the Senior School at around age 13. With the two sections of the School on the same campus, shared facilities, and an integrated curriculum, this transition could not be more natural. The School is committed to the National Curriculum as a minimum level of attainment, but with the extended learning opportunities which are offered by a boarding school, parents can expect more demanding intellectual, social and physical development targets.

Classes are small – particularly at the very top and bottom where individual attention is most important. The teaching staff are well-qualified, experienced and, above all, dedicated – working at Rydal is very much a 'way of life'. The facilities are good, as you would expect – well-equipped classrooms and labs, including a modern IT facility, a Music School, a CDT Centre, extensive playing fields, and indoor heated pool and gymnasium, squash courts, a hard-play area and two impressive Assembly Halls which are also used for some of the high-quality dance and drama produced by the School.

Day pupils are an important part of the School. They maintain that all-important link between School and Community, which is of particular benefit to boarders. And the benefits of a boarding school which, by its very nature, provides round-the-clock educational opportunities, are a particular attraction for many local parents.

We believe that your child will come as close to attaining his or her full potential at Rydal as they would at any school in the land. For some, this will mean Oxbridge Scholarships – for others, more worldly achievements. But each will find challenge and encouragement matched to their needs.

(See also page 748)

EXCELLENCE IN EDUCATION

FORT AUGUSTUS ABBEY SCHOOL

- Independent RC boarding secondary school for boys. Weekly boarders and day pupils accepted.
- Other denominations welcome.
- SCE Standard Grade, Higher Grade and CSYS COURSES; A-levels.

- Small classes and family atmosphere.
- Highland setting on shores of Loch Ness, outdoor pursuits, canoeing, etc.
- Run by Benedictine monks and lay staff.
- CCF and considerable Service connections.
- Reduction for Service families.

Apply to the Headmaster

Fort Augustus Abbey School
Fort Augustus
Inverness-shire
PH32 4DB
Telephone: 0320 6232
Fax: 0320 6218

LORETTO

Loretto, the longest established Independent Boarding School in Scotland, is also the smallest. It remains our policy to take no more than 300 pupils in the Upper School (260 boys and 40 Sixth-Form girls) and 80 Nippers in the Junior School.

A school of this size allows small classes; each pupil is known by everyone and feels part of the community in which much emphasis is placed on the maintenance of Christian values and standards. The School is also large enough to offer a very wide range of Academic and Music Scholarships, Exhibitions and Bursaries, particularly as many of them are open to boys in the Junior School from age eight onwards and continue throughout their time at Loretto.

For further details please contact:
The Reverend Norman W. Drummond,
Headmaster
Loretto
Musselburgh
Near Edinburgh EH21 7RE

Telephone: 031-665 5003
Facsimile: 031-653 2773

ST. GEORGE'S SCHOOL FOR GIRLS

GSA 850 Girls 5-18: 150 in Sixth Form 95 Boarders from age nine.

Close to the West End, built in its own playing fields. Excellent facilities, including new purpose-built Art, Music and Sports Centres. Academically outstanding.

Broad, modern curriculum leading to GCSE SCE Higher, GCE A-level and Oxbridge entrance.

Fees:
   Tuition from £670 to £1,280 per term
   Boarding £1,230 per term

Plus Fabric Fee of £35 per term at all stages.

Participates in the Assisted Places Scheme.

Prospectus available from
The Headmistress
St. George's School for Girls
Garscube Terrace
Edinburgh EH12 6BG

Telephone: 031-332 4575
Fax: 031-315 2035

KEIL SCHOOL
(Founded 1915)

Religious denomination: Church of Scotland
Member of: SHMIS, GBA, HAS, SHA
Curriculum: Broad-based curriculum prepares candidates for Scottish O Grades, S Grades and Highers and also A-levels. Particular strengths include Science and Technology.
Entry requirements: Entry is by a combination of testing, interview and school report. Main Entrance/Bursary examination is in February.
Examinations offered: Scottish Examination Board: O Grades, S Grades and Highers.
University of London Examination Board: A-levels.
Academic and sports facilities: The pursuit of academic excellence together with character development, through a wide range of games and activities, forms the basis of School life. With its rural location on the banks of the Clyde, it offers easy access by road, rail or air, Glasgow Airport being only 10 miles away. Since August 1989, girls have been admitted at all levels.
Head: Mr. Christopher H. Tongue, MA(Cantab).
Type: Coeducational Boarding and Day.
Age range: 10-18.
Number of Pupils enrolled as at 1.9.92:
  Junior: 52 Boys   34 Girls
  Senior: 63 Boys   23 Girls
  Sixth Form: 45 Boys   15 Girls
Fees per annum at 1.9.92:
Day: £3,882-£4,527; Boarding: £7,941-£8,082

Keil School, Helenslee Road, Dumbarton G82 4AL
Tel: (0389) 62003   Fax: (0389) 64267

Lomond School

Lomond is a co-educational school of 540 pupils situated 25 miles north-west of Glasgow in the beautiful town of Helensburgh. Catering for pupils aged from three to 18, and for boarders as well as day pupils, it both serves and is part of the local community.

Academically, the school has an excellent reputation. Ninety-two per cent of leavers obtain three or more Highers and proceed to College or University education, but there is also help given to those that require it via the medium of Learning Support and English as a Foreign Language tuition. The examinations sat are SCE S and H grades and GCE A-level.

Whilst keeping in touch with new ideas, the school also demands the highest standards of good work, manners, honesty and self-discipline in the belief that these traditional values will produce young men and women of integrity and worth to the community.

There is a very extensive extra-curricular programme in which every pupil is expected to participate. Major sports are hockey, rugby, athletics and cricket and there is a major outdoor education programme. Sixth-formers participate in a week's Outward Bound course and the school hosts the 'Lomond Challenge' – a national inter-schools triathlon – to provide the sort of challenge that is the cornerstone of confidence building.

Art, Drama and Music are very strong strands and a special feature is the Traditional Music Scholarship which has given Lomond an international reputation in this area.

Lomond participates in the Assisted Places Scheme, offers Service Bursaries and Traditional Music and Academic Scholarships.

Lomond School
10 Stafford Street
Helensburgh
Dunbartonshire G84 9JX
Tel: (0436) 72476
Fax: (0436) 78320

724 SCHOOL PROFILES — Tayside

GLENALMOND COLLEGE

Glenalmond College occupies a position in the heart of Scotland, on its own 290-acre estate amid the glorious scenery of the Grampians; a setting which provides a unique quality of life. Close to the city of Perth, it is about an hour from Scotland's major airports, where pupils can always be met. There are both day and boarding pupils, with boys from 12 to 18 and girls in the Sixth Form. A bus service tailored to day pupils' requirements operates from Perth and Crieff.

Glenalmond has a strong tradition of academic success, and A-levels and Scottish 'Highers' are both offered. A recently built technology centre provides superb facilities for engineering and design work, and the school has links with business and industry. Music at Glenalmond too is renowned for its excellence, with more than a third of pupils playing at least one instrument. The other creative arts flourish in an Art School and 400-seat theatre. With its own golf course, artificial ski-slope and salmon river in the grounds, the range and quality of outdoor activities are unrivalled.

Glenalmond benefits from being an independent rural community, which is a centre not only for staff and pupils, but for parents and friends of the College. At the same time, it looks outwards with frequent visits to theatres, concerts, exhibitions and sporting events, as well as being involved in the local community through service to the sick and elderly, local schools and relief organisations.

Headmaster: I. G. Templeton, Esq., M.A., B.Ed.

**Glenalmond College
Perth PH1 3RY
Telephone: 0738 88 205**

KILGRASTON SCHOOL

GSA Independent Boarding and Day School for Girls 8-18 years.

A VIBRANT AND OUTWARD LOOKING SCHOOL

Kilgraston School in Perthshire, Scotland, is a medium-sized (280) girls' boarding and day school. It has excellent academic standards in a wide range of subjects at SCE Standard and Higher Grade, Sixth-Year Studies and GCE A-level. Presentations are also made in Speech and Drama (LAMDA), and the well-equipped Music Department encourages group and individual talent.

The school has modern and extensive sporting facilities, and the Duke of Edinburgh's Award Scheme promotes a variety of interests, as well as expeditions to the nearby hills.

Academic, Art and Music Scholarships are awarded at all levels including Sixth-Form.

The School participates in the Assisted Places Scheme.

Prospectus from:

**The Headmistress
Kilgraston School
Convent of the Sacred Heart
Bridge of Earn
Perthshire PH2 9BQ
Telephone: 0738 812257**

MORRISON'S ACADEMY

Founded in 1860 this HMC school prepares day and boarding pupils for the Scottish Examination Board's papers as well as Oxford and Cambridge A-levels. Pupils are enrolled at all stages, from Primary 1 to Secondary 6, with boarding available from eight years.

Set in the heart of beautiful Perthshire the school complements its sound, academic teaching with provision for art, drama, music and sport, both within the curriculum and in the 34 clubs and societies.

The school participates in the Government's Assisted Places Scheme and some additional financial help may be available for boarding.

Further information is available from
**The Director of Admissions
Morrison's Academy
Crieff
Perthshire PH7 3AN
Scotland
Telephone: 0764 3885**

HUNTERHOUSE COLLEGE

Opened in 1987 on the amalgamation of two of Northern Ireland's most respected grammar schools for girls, Princess Gardens and Ashleigh House, Hunterhouse College made an immediate impact through academic achievement and national awards for technology, science, public speaking and music. It is situated in 37 acres of wooded parkland in a residential area near Queen's University.

This is a happy school where individual talents and interests are nurtured and community spirit is fostered by giving girls responsibility and opportunity for leadership. Hunterhouse College is noted for its breadth of educational provision. Teaching is by highly qualified, experienced staff, many of whom sit on GCSE/A-level subject panels or are engaged in public examining. Students enter universities throughout the United Kingdom and beyond and a pleasing number secure First-Class Honours degrees.

Over 20 clubs and societies meet weekly outside school hours and many girls are involved in voluntary work in the local community. Music and Drama are important and Sports facilities are excellent, with girls regularly selected for Ulster teams up to Commonwealth Games level. The Careers Department is recognised as being one of the best in Northern Ireland. The College draws its pupils from all over Northern Ireland as well as the U.K., Far East, the Americas and Africa. Regular exchanges take place with schools in France, Germany and Eire.

School buildings are modern, fully equipped and regularly updated. Boarding accommodation consists of three houses, all on The Campus, one listed as of architectural interest. The Upper Sixth have their own separate Lodge with student-type accommodation.

Hunterhouse College, Finaghy, Belfast BT10 0LE   Tel: 0232 612293

AIGLON COLLEGE

The School stands in the resort of Chesières (1,200m) in the Swiss Alps, an hour and a half from Geneva airport. There are 6 senior boarding houses and a separate Junior School for 50 boys and girls, language and science laboratories, art and music studios, three libraries, two playing fields, tennis courts and a modern gymnasium. The School also has access to an indoor sports centre, swimming pools, skating rink and extensive ski slopes.

The academic programme prepares students for admission to universities and colleges in the UK, US, Europe and Canada. A full range of GCSEs and A-levels (Oxford Board) are taken (including all major European languages), as well as US College Board examinations (SAT, ACH). The School has an excellent record of success in public examinations and university placement.

Aiglon's aim is to turn out boys and girls of integrity who know how to cope with adversity and are aware of their responsibilities to the community. Academic study is complemented by a high degree of pastoral care and a challenging programme of sports and outdoor activities including skiing and mountain expeditions.

Admission is through the school's entrance tests or the Common Entrance Examinations and a small number of places is also available in the Lower Sixth for candidates with good GCSE qualifications.

Language summer school courses are held during July and August for ages 10-16.

Fees: (incl. a fixed charge to cover most extras)
as at 1.9.92 are: under-13s: SFr 40,650 per annum
over-13s: SFr 46,635 per annum

Headmaster: Philip Parsons MA (Cantab.)

Member of:
HMC, ECIS, COBISEC, AVDEP, ADISR, RSC, ISIS

**1885 Chesières-Villars, Switzerland
Tel: 71 25 - 35 27 21   Fax: 41 25 - 35 28 11
Telex: 456211 ACOL CH**

Basil Paterson College

Basil Paterson College occupies a spacious 19th-century building in Edinburgh's famous Georgian New Town, five minutes from the heart of the city centre. The College is known worldwide for its high educational standards and for its friendly, caring atmosphere. Its three schools combine to offer a unique range of courses for students from Britain and overseas: School of Academic Studies; School of Secretarial and Business Studies; and the School of English.

The School of Academic Studies offers a wide range of courses in preparation for SCE, GCE and GCSE examinations. Permanent staff of mature, qualified and experienced teachers, who are specialists in their fields, conduct small classes, thus allowing students individual attention. Student advisers are present to monitor progress, offer advice and assist with academic and personal matters. The School is appropriate for students who have outgrown the restrictions of school life, who have had to change schools, or who want to obtain qualifications some time after leaving secondary education. The School is accredited by the British Accreditation Council.

The School of Academic Studies can combine courses with the School of Secretarial and Business Studies. Established in 1893, it is renowned for the quality of its tuition and its success in placing students in satisfying and well-paid jobs. The School prepares women and men of all ages and backgrounds for successful careers in the business world.

For further information contact:
**Basil Paterson College
Dugdale-McAdam House
22/23 Abercromby Place
Edinburgh EH3 6QE
Tel: 031-556 7695   Fax: 031-557 8503**

BOSWORTH TUTORIAL COLLEGE

Bosworth Tutorial College overlooks parkland in the centre of Northampton, a thriving market town, just one hour from London.

Bosworth is a fully residential College, taking approximately 70 students and preparing them for a very wide range of G.C.S.E. and A-level examinations. Courses run over one or two years. Small group tuition is intensive, with supervised prep and Saturday morning tests. Students benefit from personal attention and respond positively to the tutorial system, which encourages self-confidence and a mature approach to study. Every student's progress is carefully monitored by their Personal Tutor, who gives regular interviews enabling all work to be checked and recent performances frankly assessed. Guidance and assistance is given with careers and University applications.

Residential accommodation is within the College or at nearby College houses where students are looked after by full-time wardens. Some older students, however, prefer to live with local families. The College organises a full programme of social, sporting events and weekend excursions.

What makes us so special?
There are certainly, at first glance, plenty of colleges offering courses such as ours, but here we offer something much more than just classroom teaching. We address ourselves to the whole person. It is not an easy world to grow up in today and we pride ourselves on our concern for our students. We have, over the years, helped many students whose previous school careers have not been conspicuously successful.

Bosworth Tutors, 9, 10, 11 & 12 St. Georges's Avenue, Northampton NN2 6JA   Tel: (0604) 619988

Bellerbys College
INDEPENDENT SIXTH FORM EDUCATION

Students come to Bellerbys College to achieve their maximum potential grades in A Level and GCSE exams. The College specialises in helping students to win places at university and since its formation in 1959 (as Davies's College, Hove) it has built up a strong academic reputation, regularly placing a high number of students (around 85% annually) on honours degree courses in subjects such as Law, Accounting, Engineering, Business Studies and Medicine.

Our first consideration is the development of individual abilities, skills and knowledge through personal tuition in small classes (average 8 students). This method of intensive tuition, in a friendly and enjoyable learning environment, enables students to fulfil their true potential in public examinations.

Bellerbys College has two campuses in Sussex, the main campus being located in Hove with a smaller campus in Hastings. Both are situated in quiet residential areas close to the amenities of the town centre. The largest group of students is from the UK but an international atmosphere prevails as the College also welcomes students from many countries around the world. Between them the two campuses cater for around 300 students.

The College offers full **A Level** programmes with enrolments in September, January and April. The largest intake is September and most students are able to complete three A Levels in one year, the majority attaining high grades through our intensive teaching methods.

GCSE courses are also offered in a wide range of subjects, with enrolments in September each year.

Resit courses for one term and one year also commence in September and each year the College runs specialist **Easter Revision** courses for both GCSEs and A Levels.

The College offers its own boarding accommodation (supervised by residential College staff) in Hove as well as accommodation options with local families in both Hove and Hastings. A full sporting and social programme is also offered to students on a optional basis.

Every year the College offers a limited number of bursaries and scholarships for students of outstanding academic ability.

Bellerbys College is accredited by the BAC and is a member of the Conference for Independent Further Education (CIFE).

Please write or telephone for a copy of our prospectus and video or to arrange an informal interview.

Bellerbys College
44 Cromwell Road
Hove, East Sussex
BN3 3ER
Telephone (0273) 723911
Fax (0273) 28445

CAMBRIDGE SEMINARS

An independent sixth-form college offering over 40 subjects at A-level and GCSE.

★ Accelerated retake courses
★ Full one- and two-year programmes
★ Easter and summer revision courses

The College combines a relaxed and friendly atmosphere with an excellent reputation for academic success.

Cambridge Seminars is recognised as efficient by the British Accreditation Council.

For more information contact:
Cambridge Seminars
4 Hawthorn Way
Cambridge CB4 1AX
Telephone: 0223 313464
Fax: 0223 355352

CAMPANA FINISHING SCHOOL

Telephone: 0252 727111
Fax: 0252 712011

Courses in: English as a foreign language, Secretarial/Business Studies, Cordon Bleu Cookery, Full programme of excursions

THE FLOWER SCHOOL

Telephone: 0252 734477
Fax: 0252 712011

20-week Floristry/Business Diploma Course

15-week Floristry Certificate Course

4-week Foundation Course/Day Courses

Residential schools situated in Grade II Listed building in 75-acre park.
One-hour journey to London and only 45 minutes to both Heathrow and Gatwick airports

Moor Park House, Moor Park Lane, Farnham, Surrey GU9 8EN, England

CHERWELL TUTORS

Oxford **CIFE**

GCSE AND A-LEVELS

Cherwell Tutors accepts students to be prepared for the GCSE and Advanced level exams. Emphasis is placed upon preparation by experienced staff under close personal supervision in a mature and friendly environment. Select accommodation in Hall of Residence or with family.

Excellent academic facilities.

One-term and one-year retake Courses.

Prospectus from:
**The Secretary
CHERWELL TUTORS
Greyfriars
Paradise Street
Oxford
Telephone:
Oxford (0865) 242670 and 246119**

EASTBOURNE COLLEGE of FOOD and FASHION

Established in 1907.

Residential College for young ladies from 16-25 superbly situated next to the seafront.

Excellent facilities and a highly qualified and experienced staff.

Study for a professional, practical one year Diploma in:
Cordon Bleu Cookery
Catering and Restaurant Management
Fashion
Child Care
New! One-year Career Cooks Course

Secretarial Studies, Flower Artistry, Interior Design and Wine Appreciation form part of the curriculum.

GCSE and A-level retakes possible.

Careers Guidance given.

Extensive opportunities for sport and leisure.

Also: One-term Intensive Cordon Bleu Certificate

'Ideal in Your Gap Year'

Courses commence January, April and September.

Recognised by:
The British Accreditation Council.

Write or telephone for a Prospectus:
**The Principal
Eastbourne College of Food and Fashion
1 Silverdale Road
Eastbourne BN20 7AA
Telephone: (0323) 30851**

Inchbald School of Design

The Inchbald School runs courses in all aspects of the History and practice of Interior and Garden Design, lasting from three days to three years.

DIPLOMA COURSES

- Environmental Design — 3 year Master Diploma
- Environmental Design — 2 year Higher Diploma
- Interior Design — 2 year Higher Diploma
- Design History/Garden Design — 2 year Higher Diploma
- Interior Design — 1 year Diploma
- Garden Design — 1 year Diploma
- Art & Design History — 1 year Diploma

CERTIFICATE COURSES

Environmental Design — Commencement Dates
- Personalised Study Programmes — 1 year — September/January/April

Interior Design
- Design & Decoration — 10 wks — September/January/April

Garden Design
- Garden & Landscape Design Principles — 10 wks — September
- Intermediate Garden Design — 10 wks — January
- Advanced Garden Design — 10 wks — April

Art & Design History
- Foundation in European Art & Design — 10 wks — September
- Development of Design 1700-c. 1830 — 10 wks — January
- Design in the Industrial Age c. 1830-1990 — 10 wks — April

SHORT COURSES

Foundation Studies — Commencement Dates
- Design & Drawing Foundation — 6 wks — July

Interior Design
- Interior Visual: Advanced — 3 wks — August
- Interior Visual: Intermediate — 2 wks — March
- Interior Design Drawing — 2 wks — September
- Business Management for Interior Designers — 5 days — July
- Design of Furniture and Built-in Fitments — 5 days — February
- Design in Period Property — 5 days — September
- Colour in Design — 5 days — November
- Computer Aided Design — 3 days — February/April/June/July/September

Garden Design
- Garden Design Drawing — 3 wks — September
- Business Management for Garden Designers — 2 wks — June
- Colour in Design — 5 days — November
- Computer Aided Design — 3 days — February/April/June/July/September

Art & Design History
- Design in Period Property — 5 days — September

PART TIME COURSE
- Garden Design — 10 wks — September/April

A prospectus is available on request:
The Secretary
Inchbald School of Design (IS)
7 Eaton Gate, London SW1W 9BA, England - Telephone 071 730 5508/6969
32 Eccleston Square, London SW1V 1PB, England - Telephone 071-630 9011/2/3

IRWIN COLLEGE

IRWIN COLLEGE is a coeducational independent tutorial college. It offers one-year and two-year GCSE and A-level courses in a wide range of subjects with tutorials in small groups, whose average size never exceeds six students. Detailed attention is paid to each student's academic progress, social development and personal needs. Many students thus thrive and succeed at IRWIN after being unable to do so in any other type of school.

The emphasis of IRWIN'S large staff – all graduate specialists – is on regularly assessed written work and concentration on examination techniques. Private study is supervised and regular examinations are set to monitor each student's progress. The combination of pastoral concern with an emphasis on hard work in a warm, friendly environment has produced impressive academic results: in our A-level retake course from 1990 to 1991 the overall pass rate was 80% and the average improvement was of two grades per subject.

Every student at IRWIN has a Personal Tutor who helps with personal and social problems and regularly checks that each student's work is up to date, up to standard, well organised and well presented. This regular contact ensures a high level of individual attention, which has become the College's hallmark.

IRWIN enjoys a fairly relaxed atmosphere outside the hours of study. There is no uniform or prefect system, but in return all students are expected to be conscientious, courteous and co-operative.

Sporting events and social activities are organised regularly. IRWIN COLLEGE provides academic and career counselling as required.

Accommodation: Boarding facilities at IRWIN consist of three houses, which provide comfortable accommodation with meals, and are supervised by a residential warden.

IRWIN is well placed for easy access by train, motorway and air.

Accreditation: IRWIN is recognised as efficient by the BACIFHE and is a member of CIFE.

Irwin College, 164 London Road, Leicester LE2 1ND   Tel: 0533 552648

LINCOLNSHIRE COLLEGE OF AGRICULTURE AND HORTICULTURE
Your College of the Countryside

FULL-TIME COURSES
AGRICULTURE
BTEC Higher National Diploma in Agriculture
BTEC National Diploma in Agriculture
BTEC National Diploma in Poultry Management
BTEC National Diploma in Arable Mechanisation
BTEC National Diploma in Agricultural Merchanting
BTEC National Diploma in European Agriculture Production & Marketing
BTEC Higher National Certificate in Specialist Vegetable Production
BTEC First Diploma in Agriculture
BTEC First Diploma in Poultry
NEB Advanced National Certificate in Agriculture
NEB Advanced National Certificate in Agricultural Merchanting
NEB Advanced National Certificate in Poultry
NEB National Certificate in Agriculture
NEB National Certificate in Poultry
NEB Advanced National Certificate in Gamekeeping
College Diploma in Tropical Poultry
College Certificate in Gamekeeping

HORTICULTURE
BTEC National Diploma in Floristry
BTEC National Diploma in Forestry (1993)
BTEC National Diploma in Horticulture
BTEC First Diploma in Horticulture
BTEC First Diploma in Floristry
BTEC First Diploma in Forestry
BTEC Higher National Diploma in Horticulture
BTEC Higher National Diploma in Floristry (1993)
NEB National Certificate in Horticulture (Conservation)
NEB National Certicate in Horticulture (Landscape Construction)
NEB National Certificate in Horticulture (Arboriculture)
NEB National Certificate in Forestry
Certificate Course in General Horticulture
General Horticulture for the Visually Impaired
Practical Skills in Land Based Industries (for students with learning difficulties)

ENGINEERING AND MECHANISATION
BTEC Higher National Certificate in Agricultural Engineering
BTEC Higher National Diploma in Agricultural Engineering
BTEC First Diploma in Agricultural Engineering
Diploma in Advanced Tractor & Machinery Repairs (16 weeks)
BTEC National Diploma in Arable Mechanisation
BTEC National Diploma in Agricultural Engineering

RURAL BUSINESS MANAGEMENT
Diploma in Rural Business Management
BTEC First Diploma in Rural Leisure Studies
BTEC National Diploma in Rural Leisure Management
BTEC Higher National Diploma in Business Studies
BTEC National Diploma in Business Studies (options in Agriculture, Equine Studies, Tourism)
BTEC First Diploma in Business Studies
NEB National Certificate for Farm Secretaries

RURAL ACTIVITIES
BTEC Higher National Diploma in Food Technology (1993)
BTEC National Diploma in Horse Studies
BTEC National Diploma in Food Technology (1993)
BTEC First Diploma in Horse Studies
BTEC First Diploma in Food Technology
NEB Advanced National Certificate in Equine Business Management
BTEC First Diploma in Small Animal Care
NEB National Certificate in Management of Horses
NEB National Certificate in Animal Care (Kennel & Cattery Management)
BTEC Higher National Diploma in Horse Studies

For career advice or course details, please ring Student Services' 24-hour Hotline **0400 73038** *or write to:*

Student Services
Lincolnshire College of Agriculture & Horticulture
Caythorpe Court, Caythorpe
Grantham, Lincs. NG32 3EP
Telephone: 0400 72521

LINCOLNSHIRE COUNTY COUNCIL

THE NORLAND COLLEGE

The Norland College, founded in 1892, prepares students of 18 years and over for the examinations of the National Nursery Examination Board and those who successfully complete the course (including a nine-month post with a private family) are awarded the Norland Diploma and Badge.

All applicants with the minimum academic requirements (English Language and at least two other subjects at G.C.S.E. at Grades A, B, C or equivalent) are interviewed at the College and successful candidates are accepted for training. New entrants commence training in January and September each year. During the 24-month residential course students receive instruction and practical experience with babies and children up to eight years of age in Nursery Schools and classes, Infant Schools, the Norland Day-Care Units and our unique residential nursery, known as The Children's Hotel. This includes secondment to selected hospitals. Lectures are given throughout training by an experienced and fully qualified staff on all aspects of general care, health development and the management of children, education, literature, art, craft, music and home economics. The comprehensive nature of the Norland Training ensures that all students are well qualified to work as nursery nurses in every possible branch of the profession, including private homes, day and residential nurseries, hospitals and schools. The demand for Norland Nurses always exceeds supply and the College Registry secures employment in private families in the U.K. and abroad.

Affiliated to the Association of Nursery Training Colleges.

Principal: Mrs. Louise E. Davis, M.Phil., S.R.N.

For fees and full particulars please apply to the Admissions Secretary.

**The Norland College
Denford Park, Hungerford
Berkshire RG17 0PQ
Telephone: 0488 682252
Fax: 0488 685212**

THE ST. JAMES'S SECRETARIAL COLLEGE

Founded in 1912 and located in a pleasant, residential section of Kensington, The St. James's Secretarial College is the oldest in London. This BAC accredited college offers a very flexible programme of courses including a Nine-Month Executive Secretarial Diploma Course, Six-Month Certificate Course and Three-Month Intensive Course. Options are offered in Journalism and Public Relations as well as Commercial Language instruction in French, German, Italian and Spanish. A member of FRES, the college actively seeks to place students in suitable positions at the end of their training. For those who do not live in London, accommodation in supervised hostels can be arranged.

Principal: Mrs. G. M. Hewetson

Fees per term as at 1.9.92: £2,100 (including VAT). 25% tax relief on term's fees for NVQ qualifications.

**The St. James's Secretarial College
4 Wetherby Gardens
London SW5 0JN
Tel: 071-373 3852
Fax: 071-370 3303**

UNIVERSITY OF DUBLIN
Trinity College

The College offers a wide range of courses for primary degrees in Arts, the Sciences and professional subjects. There are also interesting opportunities for post-graduate work leading to higher degrees.

For information on requirements for admission to undergraduate courses enquiries should be addressed to the Admissions Officer. The Dean of Graduate Studies advises on work for higher degrees but initially correspondence should be addressed to the Graduate Admissions Office. Teachers interested in the Higher Diploma in Education may address enquiries to the Registrar of the Department of Teacher Education.

The College maintains a full-time careers and appointments service to undergraduates and graduates. The Careers and Appointments Officer will welcome enquiries from School Principals concerning immediate or future staffing problems.

University of Dublin
Trinity College
Dublin 2

Telephone: 772941

Fax: 722853

ABINGDON SCHOOL

ENTRANCE awards for 13-year-old candidates are offered in May of each year. These will normally consist of one to the value of a full tuition fee and others to the value of ½, ¼ and ⅛. In addition, one music scholarship worth ½ of the tuition fee, and one of ¼, together with exhibitions covering the cost of intrumental tuition in up to two instruments and singing, and one art and design scholarship worth ¼ of the tuition fee, are awarded annually.

Two boarding scholarships, value ½ of the combined tuition and boarding fee, may be awarded annually.

Abingdon is a member of the Government's Assisted Places Scheme, and offers 11 places at 11 years old, four at 13 and up to five Sixth-Form places. Assistance is also available for three boarding candidates per year.

Further details may be had from:

**The Admissions Secretary
Abingdon School
Oxfordshire OX14 1DE**

ALLEYN'S SCHOOL, DULWICH

The following awards are offered each year:

1. **11-year-old entry.**
   Up to 14 scholarships worth half the full fee will be awarded: these scholarships will remain at the same proportion of full fees or will increase by 10% per year, whichever is the lesser figure, during the career of the pupil at the school. Where a pupil is prevented by financial circumstances from taking up a scholarship, further help may be granted, but this will be dependent on a full declaration of parent's income. Some of the holders of these awards will be designated Saddlers' Scholars, in recognition of the support given by the Livery company to the school.
   At least one of these scholarships will be awarded to a pupil showing special aptitude in music.
   Twenty-five Assisted Places are also available under the Government's scheme; in special circumstances, the school may be able to award its own bursaries.

2. **13-year-old entry.**
   One scholarship, worth half the full fee, will be awarded to a candidate of sufficient merit; a Coates' scholarship, nominal value £100 per annum, will always be awarded and this will be augmented as necessary. Five Assisted Places are available under the Government scheme. A Music scholarship may be awarded at this level.

3. **Sixth-form entry.**
   One scholarship worth half the full fee will be awarded to an external candidate of sufficient academic merit.
   A Wolfson Foundation Bursary will be awarded each year to a suitable candidate who would not otherwise be able to undertake a sixth-form education. Five Assisted Places are available under the Government scheme.

The award of scholarships at 11, 13 and 16 will be by examination in late January.

Further particulars from the Headmaster, to whom application forms should be sent by 1 January.

**Alleyn's School
Townley Road
London SE22 8SU
Telephone: 081-693 3422**

ACKWORTH SCHOOL

Academic Scholarships of up to 50% are available to those entering the school in 1st, 2nd, 3rd and Lower 6th years. For the three junior forms awards are made on the results of the entrance tests which are held in the February of the year of entry.

For those entering the Lower 6th to study for a two-year Advanced level course, awards are made on the basis of interview and reports made by the Head of the previous school, in addition to GCSE results.

Music Scholarships are also awarded up to 50% of fees on the basis of an audition.

Art Scholarships: up to 25% of fees are also offered to those with outstanding talent on the basis of a morning art session and portfolio.

Further details can be obtained from
The Head, Ackworth School, Ackworth Pontefract, West Yorkshire WF7 7LT
Tel: (0977) 611401

ARDINGLY COLLEGE
SUSSEX

ACADEMIC, Music, Art, C.D.T., Drama and Sports Scholarships are available for boys and girls (boarding and day) at both the 13+ and the sixth-form stages. Ashdown Awards for those with all-round talent are available at the 13+ stage.

The competitions for sixth-form Academic and Music Scholarships are held in November. Up to five awards, each of which may be worth up to 50% of fees p.a., are available in each field. The examination for Academic Scholarships at the 13+ stage is held in the Summer Term and that for Music Scholarships at the 13+ stage in the Lent Term. Up to 10 academic awards may be made, their value depending on the merit shown by the candidates in the examination. Up to eight Music Awards may be made, including six which may be worth 50% of fees p.a. Two of these six are open, two are reserved for orchestral string players and two are closed awards for choristers attending schools in membership of the Choir Schools Association. An Organ Scholarship is available at either stage and two Choral Scholarships for sixth-form boys: these awards may be worth up to 33% of basic fees p.a.

The competitions for Art, Drama and Sports Scholarships, at both 13+ and sixth-form stages, take place in the Lent Term. Two awards are available for both Art and Drama. Art awards may be worth 50% of fees p.a. and Drama awards 25% of fees p.a. Up to 10 Sports awards may be made, their value depending on sporting ability shown, but between 10% and 50% of basic fees p.a. This amount may then be increased according to a candidate's score in Common Entrance, Ardingly's own entrance papers or GCSE.

Closed awards worth 15% of the fees p.a. are available for (a) Children of Clergy, (b) Children of Serving Members of HM Forces, (c) Children of former members of Ardingly College, and (d) a member of Ardingly College Junior School.

Two Weald Scholarships, worth 20% and 15% of fees p.a., are awarded annually on Common Entrance results to boys and girls from preparatory schools in Sussex, Surrey and Kent, registered for first-choice entry to Ardingly College.

In conjunction with Ardingly College Junior School, five Government-Assisted Places are available each year for 11+ entrants.

In all cases, when awards are not enough to enable pupils to take up places offered, supplementary bursaries may be available and may bring remission up to the value of full fees.

Age limits: over 15 and under 17 and over 12 and under 14 on 1 September of the year of examination.

Further particulars from the Registrar

**Ardingly College
Haywards Heath
West Sussex RH17 6SQ**

Telephone: Ardingly (0444) 892577

BEDALES, Petersfield GU32 2DG
(Co-educational)

SCHOLARSHIPS – A number of general Scholarships of up to half of the school fees p.a. in value, according to the financial needs of parents. As well as all-round academic ability, achievement in Art and Music is recognised in the awarding of general Scholarships. There are also certain special scholarships available in particular subjects, e.g. Music (up to half fees) and Science.

BEDGEBURY SCHOOL

11+ and 13+ Academic, Art and Music Scholarships. Sixth-Form Academic, Art, Music, Fashion and Sport Scholarships.

Various awards each Spring up to one-third day fees, together with De Noailles Trust Bursaries for daughters of Church of England clergy.

Bedgebury School
Bedgebury Park
Goudhurst, Cranbrook
Kent TN17 2SH
Telephone: (0580) 211221/211954

(See also page 677)

BLOXHAM SCHOOL

Entrance Scholarship 1993: W/C 3 May.
SCHOLARSHIPS: Raymond Scholarships and John Schuster Scholarships to the value of 50% of fees. There are other Scholarships, and also Exhibitions and Chapel Centenary Bursaries. Music and Art Scholarships may be up to half of fees. Candidates should normally be under 14 on 1 September in the year of entry. There are also Sir Lawrence Robson Scholarships for boys and girls entering the Sixth Form at age 16. All the above awards (except Raymond Scholarships) are open to day/boarders and all awards may be augmented up to 100% of fees after assessment of the means of parents.

Further particulars from the Headmaster:
**Bloxham School
Nr. Banbury
Oxon. OX15 4PE**

BRENTWOOD SCHOOL

Three BOARDING SCHOLARSHIPS for boys under 14 and a limited number of Bursaries.
Six Foundation Scholarships and three Music Scholarships for boys at 11; two Foundation Scholarships and one for Music for girls at 11, 18 Assisted Places at 11.
Five Assisted places and an Art Scholarship for Sixth-Formers; Colonel Laurie Award for sons of Servicemen.

Particulars from the Headmaster

**Brentwood School
Ingrave Road
Brentwood
Essex CM15 8AS
Telephone: (0277) 212271**

BRUTON SCHOOL FOR GIRLS

11+ entry — THREE OPEN SCHOLARSHIPS 75%, 40% and 30% of the tuition fees, with one Scholarship 50% of tuition fees for a daughter of a former pupil.
13+ entry — ONE EXHIBITION 15% of tuition fees.
Sixth Form entry — ONE SCHOLARSHIP 50% of tuition fees.

Government Assisted places offered at 11+ and 16+.

**Sunny Hill, Bruton
Somerset BA10 0NT
Telephone: 0749 812277**
Independent Public School

CAMBRIDGE TUTORS COLLEGE

Full Scholarships. One or two full scholarships may be awarded each year. These scholarships are normally reserved for overseas students who are refugees or for home students with unusual family hardship, who have also shown good academic potential.

A-level Scholarships. A number are awarded each year on the basis of GCSE/O-level grades. These grant up to 50% reduction in fees for students with six or more A grades or the equivalent overseas qualifications.

Bursaries. Bursaries may be awarded to deserving cases (e.g. on the sudden death of a parent, redundancy of a breadwinner or severe family hardship). These will normally offer a 25% reduction in fees.

Further details from:
**The Principal, Cambridge Tutors College
Water Tower Hill, Croydon, Surrey CR0 5SX
Tel: 081-688 5284**

CANFORD SCHOOL

Scholarships up to 50% of fees may be supplemented by Bursaries; all indexed so value remains constant throughout scholar's school career.
SIXTH FORM: At least **FOUR SCHOLARSHIPS** (Academic and Music) for boys and girls entering each September.
13+ OPEN SCHOLARSHIPS: Up to eight Scholarships.
ROYAL NAVAL SCHOLARSHIP: 20% of fees for a son of a serving Naval Officer.
MUSIC: Up to four Scholarships. Each award carries free tuition on two instruments.
ART: One Scholarship of 20% or possible two of 10%.
Bursaries for sons of Church of England Clergymen will be offered in 1993.
Particulars: **Registrar, Canford School
Wimborne, Dorset BH21 3AD. Tel: (0202) 841254**

CHEADLE HULME SCHOOL

ONE OR MORE NIEL PEARSON OR SCHOOL SCHOLARSHIPS OF EITHER 50% or 25% of TUITION FEES (1992 Tuition Fee £3,660) offered to candidates for entry into the Sixth Form who show outstanding promise in Music, Drama or the Arts.

(Day, Co-Ed)

Particulars may be obtained from:
**The Registrar
Cheadle Hulme School
Claremont Road
Cheadle Hulme, Cheadle
Cheshire SK8 6EF**

THE CHELTENHAM LADIES' COLLEGE

Major and Minor Academic and Music Scholarships awarded at 11, 12 and 13+ entry. Up to half the annual fees.

Academic, Music and Art Scholarships awarded to Sixth-Form entrants. Up to half the annual fees.

Principal: Miss E. Castle

**The Cheltenham Ladies' College
Bayshill Road
Cheltenham GL50 3EP
Telephone: 0242 520691**

CRANLEIGH SCHOOL
SURREY

Scholarships at 13: **Academic/Art** (May examination): four half-fee Scholarships, eight others up to one-quarter fees which may include one for special ability in Mathematics. Closed Awards for sons of: Commissioned Officers on active list of RN, Army or RAF, C of E Clergy, members of public services. One quarter-fee Scholarship may be for Art. **Music** (February examination): one or two Scholarships of half fees, two up to one-quarter fees; all include free tuition.

For boys/girls entering at **Sixth-Form** level (November examination): up to six **Academic,** two **Music** Scholarships of one-quarter fees.

Further details from Admissions Secretary, Cranleigh School, Surrey GU6 8QQ.

CULFORD SCHOOL

A NUMBER of Scholarships are awarded each year at 13+. The School offers a limited number of Assisted Places at 11+ (boarders) and 13+ (day).

Candidates should take common Entrance or the School's own Entrance Examination in February and the Scholarship papers in March.

For prospectus and particulars apply to the Headmaster.

**Culford School
Bury St. Edmunds
Suffolk IP28 6TX**

DOVER COLLEGE

An examination takes place each year for ENTRANCE (13+ and Sixth Form) SCHOLARSHIPS AND EXHIBITIONS for boys and girls, with bursaries up to full fees in value, awarded for academic ability.
One or more ASTOR AWARDS, up to £3,500 p.a., are awarded annually for boys and girls with a good Common Entrance pass and exceptionally good preparatory school record.

At least one MUSIC SCHOLARSHIP (vocal or instrumental), up to £3,000 p.a., with free musical tuition, is offered annually.
At least one ART SCHOLARSHIP, up to £3,500 p.a., is offered annually.
Sixth form scholarships in Modern Languages, Maths and Economics are available.

Further particulars may be had on application to the Headmaster.
Dover College, Dover, Kent

DOWNE HOUSE

Downe House is a boarding school for 470 girls with a small number of day girls, 11-18 years. The School has an excellent academic record and offers a wealth of additional activities; 90% go on to higher education from a Sixth Form of 120. Excellent Sixth-Form facilities.

SCHOLARSHIPS
One Downe House Open Scholarship for girls under 12 years to the value of half the fees p.a.
Minor Scholarship for girls under 12 years to the value of one-third the fees p.a.
One Downe house Open Scholarship for girls under 13 years to the value of half the fees p.a.
Minor Scholarship for girls under 13 years to the value of one-third the fees p.a.
The Olive Willis Open Scholarship for girls under 14 years to the value of two-thirds of the fees p.a.
Open Exhibitions for girls under 14 years.
Open Music Scholarship for girls under 13 years to the value of half the fees pa. and free tuition in two instruments.

Candidates should be under the qualifying age on the following 1 September.

Two Sixth-Form Scholarships to the value of full fees p.a.
Open Music Scholarship for girls entering the Sixth Form to the value of half the fees p.a. and free tuition in two instruments.

Five Assisted Places a year are available to 11- and 12-year-olds.

Further details may be obtained from:

**The Registrar
Downe House
Cold Ash
Newbury
Berks. RG16 9JJ
Telephone: (0635) 200286**

DURHAM SCHOOL

A GENEROUS range of Academic, Music and Art Scholarships are available.

Each year, five or six King's Scholarships are open to boys under 14 on 1 September. These are worth up to half fees for a boarder or a day boy and can be increased to full fees in case of need.

Further Academic Exhibitions, Music and Art Scholarships and Exhibitions are also awarded, both to those aged 13 and to those aged 11.

Burkitt Scholarships are awarded to entrants to the Sixth Form and can be won by both boys and girls. The competitions for all the awards take place in late-February or early-March.

Clerical Bursaries may be awarded to the sons of Church of England clergy, and Assisted Places were awarded for the first time in 1989.

Further particulars may be obtained from:
The Headmaster, Durham School, Durham DH1 4SZ

EASTBOURNE COLLEGE

AN examination for entrance scholarships and exhibitions will be held in May. Two Scholarships of 75% of school fees; two scholarships of 50% of school fees; one scholarship of 33⅓% of school fees; one scholarship of 25% of school fees and two exhibitions of 15% of school fees are offered. Music scholarships and Art scholarships to the value of two-thirds of school fees are also offered.

THE EDINBURGH ACADEMY

SIX A. L. F. Smith Scholarships are offered each year to candidates (aged 9-12 or 16-17) of sufficient merit who are not already attending the Academy. One is reserved for candidates from State Primary 7 Classes. Their value is not less than a half of the tuition Fees, plus a quarter of the Boarding Fees where relevant, and rises at need to three-quarters of the total Fees. They may also be awarded for Music or Art.

Pupils are prepared for G.C.S.E. in the full range of subjects, and most proceed via Higher and/or A-levels to higher education. A number regularly win places at Oxford and Cambridge.

The Art and Science Departments are particularly strong, and Business Studies is available to A-level. Greek and Russian are among the languages taught.

There is a growing VIth Form entry of boys and girls, both day and boarding.

The Entrance Examination is held in February

FARRINGTONS SCHOOL

Up to four awards are offered at 11 years. These may vary in value dependent upon the ability of the candidate at examination and interview.

Music Scholarship
One award of full-term day fees is made to a girl in the form of an organ scholarship. (Details from Registrar.)

Music awards are also given to girls already in the school which pay varying amounts towards tuition/instruments.

**Farringtons School
Chislehurst
Kent BR7 6LR
Telephone: 081-467 0256**

(See also page 678)

FOREST SCHOOL

Forest Junior School – Boys 7-12
Forest Girls' School – 11-18
Forest Senior School – Boys 13-18

* 7+ Scholarships of one-third fees tenable for four years
* 11+ – 13 full Scholarships (shared boys and girls)
* Two Music Scholarships of half tuition fees
* Four Sixth-Form Scholarships
* 21 Assisted Places at 11+
* Five Assisted Places at 16+

* Bursarial awards may be considered for Sixth-Form students
* Two Boarding Scholarships are awarded of up to half boarding fees to boys at 11 or 13

H.M.C., I.A.P.S., G.B.A.; Day and Boarding
Warden: A. G. Boggis, M.A.
Headmaster of the Junior School: R. T. Cryer, M.Ed.
Headmistress of the Girls' School: Mrs. C. Y. Daly, B.Sc.
Director of the Senior School: Dr. C. Barker, B.Sc., Ph.D.

Forest School, Nr. Snaresbrook, London E17 3PY.   Telephone: 081-520 1744

FRENSHAM HEIGHTS SCHOOL

This coeducational boarding and day school of 285 pupils aged 11-18 offers a friendly atmosphere and excellent academic results. Wide curriculum, staff : pupil ratio of 1 : 8, high university entry, equality of the sexes.

Scholarships and bursaries at Headmaster's descretion related to parental need.

**Frensham Heights School
Rowledge
Farnham
Surrey
Telephone: 025 125 2134**

(See also page 703)

GRENVILLE COLLEGE

Ten entrance scholarships, ranging from three-quarters to one-quarter of the total annual fees, are offered on the basis of good results in the Common Entrance Examinations of February and June, and in our own entrance tests of February at the age of 10-12.

Full details from the Admissions Secretary

**Grenville College
Bideford
Devon EX39 3JR
Telephone: 0237 472212**

HAILEYBURY

About 10 Entrance Scholarships or Exhibitions, up to a possible value of a half-fees place, are offered for competition each year. There are also some specially endowed Scholarships which become available from time to time, and there are up to five awards in Music (of which one Scholarship of half fees may be increased by a bursary to full fees in the case of demonstrable financial need) and three in Art. The Academic examination is held in May, and the Music and Art examinations in February, and Sixth-Form Scholarship examinations in November.

Further particulars from the Registrar.

**Haileybury
Hertford SG13 7NU
Telephone: 0992 463353**

HARROW SCHOOL

ENTRANCE SCHOLARSHIPS examination in February for boys under 14 on 1 July. Approximately 15 Scholarships and Exhibitions are offered annually, ranging in value from £100 to half of the fees.
A percentage of the remaining fee may be remitted in cases of need and having regard to the Scholar's ability. Music and Art Scholarships are offered annually; Music Scholarships of half fees are also supplementable. Particulars are available from the Head Master's Secretary the preceding October.
A candidate not in need of financial assistance may compete for election to an honorary award.

**Harrow School
Harrow
Middlesex**

HEADINGTON SCHOOL, OXFORD OX3 7TD

Two academic scholarships awarded annually following the Common Entrance Examination, one for half the day fees at 11+ and one for half the boarding fees at 12 or 13+. One half boarding fees sixth form entry scholarship.

Pupils who have been entered for Headington and who obtained very high marks in the Common Entrance Examination are invited to the School for interviews and tests for the scholarship.

Open to girls of 11, 12 or 13+.

**Telephone: Oxford (0865) 62711
Admissions: Oxford (0865) 741968
Fax: (0865) 60268**

KING'S COLLEGE SCHOOL

Up to 15 Scholarships will be awarded of values up to 50% of the full tuition fee. One or more awards may be made to boys who show outstanding ability as classical or modern linguists.

The number of Scholarships awarded in any year will vary according to the quality of the Candidates. One or more Music Scholarships of up to the value of half-fees is awarded to a boy or boys of high musical ability.

Candidates must be under 14 years of age on the first day of September of he year in which they sit the examination.

Further information may be obtained from the Head Master

Kings's College School
Wimbledon Common, London SW19 4TT

THE KING'S SCHOOL

Entrance Scholarships and Exhibitions are awarded in the Summer Term. Awards may be made to candidates showing exceptional promise in Art or Music. The value of an award may range up to 50% of the appropriate current fees for both internal and external candidates.

Junior School Awards are for the two final years of the Common Entrance course. Middle School Awards are tenable until the completion of the GCSE course. Sixth Form Awards are available for the two years of the GCE A-level course.

All Choristers of Ely Cathedral are members of the Junior School. Choral Scholarships, valued at up to two-thirds of the appropriate Junior School fees, are awarded to all Choristers. An annual voice trial for selection of Choristers is held each year. Bursaries worth one-third of the appropriate fee are available to ex-Choristers who proceed directly to the Middle School.

For full particulars apply to

The Headmaster
The King's School
Ely
Cambs. CB7 4DB

THE KING'S SCHOOL

King's and Queen's Scholarships on the Foundation Scholarships and Exhibitions; 14-18 awards offered annually, some reserved in the first instance for music; value – scholarships one-half to one-third tuition fees; for boarders there will be additional support towards boarding fees. Exhibitions value £850, preference given to sons of clergy. All awards supplemented from Bursary funds in cases of need.

Choristers' Scholarships for entry to the Cathedral Choir. Inclusive boarding fee (Sept. 1992) £7,953 per annum. Day £4,752.

For particulars and prospectus apply to
Dr. J. M. Moore, Headmaster.

The King's School
Worcester WR1 2LH

LAWNSIDE SCHOOL

Two Academic Scholarships offered in any one year at 11+, 12+ or 13+.

One Art and one Music Scholarship, plus one sixth form Scholarship, also offered annually.

All scholarships to value of 33% of fees.

Examined at Lawnside in March.

Lawnside School
Great Malvern WR14 3AJ

LICHFIELD CATHEDRAL SCHOOL

Choral Scholarships worth 50/60% of the value of school fees are awarded to boys elected to the Cathedral Choir. Voice trials are held annually. This year January 29 for September entry. Academic Scholarships are now offered. Examinations take place in early March. Some Bursaries are also available for the children of Clergy.

For further details, please contact the Head Master.

Lichfield Cathedral School
Lichfield
Staffordshire WS13 7LH
Telephone: (0543) 263326

(See also page 698)

MALVERN COLLEGE

SCHOLARSHIPS AT MALVERN 1993

THE Porch Memorial Award, consisting of a scholarship of 50% of the fees which may be increased by a means-tested bursary to a total of 75% of the fees, is offered to a candidate of outstanding ability. Up to 20 other academic awards are offered. They range from Scholarships of up to 50% of the fees to Exhibitions of lesser value. Music Awards of up to 50% of the fees and one Art Scholarship of up to 30% of the fees are also offered. There are also two Art Exhibitions of lesser value. Scholarships, but not Exhibitions, are linked to the fees and are increased automatically each time the fees are increased.

Candidates for Scholarships must be under 14 years of age on 1 June 1993, but there is no age limit on Exhibitions. Entries must be received three weeks before the examination.

A Sixth-Form Scholarship is also available.

Entry forms may be obtained from Preparatory Schools or from:
The Headmaster, Malvern College
Malvern
Worcestershire WR14 3DF

Scholarships are also available at the age of 11 at Hillstone School, tenable for the first two years at Hillstone and then for five years at Malviern College.

For further detail, contact:
The Headmaster, Hillstone School
Abbey Road
Malvern
Worcester WR14 3HF

MILLFIELD (BOYS AND GIRLS)

A large number of scholarships (academic, art and music) will be awarded each year

For further particulars write to: **The Tutor for Admissions**
Millfield
Street
Somerset BA16 0YD

(See also page 697)

MILLFIELD (GIRLS)

A large number of scholarships (academic, art and music) will be awarded each year

For further particulars write to: **The Tutor for Admissions**
Millfield
Street
Somerset BA16 0YD

(See also page 697)

MILTON ABBEY SCHOOL
BOARDING AND DAY SCHOOL FOR 260 BOYS

SIXTH-FORM SCHOLARSHIPS
Two (value up to full fees) scholarships for entry to Sixth Form in September 1993. Interviews and examinations at the school on Wednesday, 3.02.93. Candidates should be under 17 on 1.09.93.

ENTRY SCHOLARSHIPS
Up to eight Open Scholarships (value 75%-25% of fees), including awards for Art and Music, for candidates under 14 on 1.08.93.

Milton Abbey, Blandford Forum, Dorset DT11 0BZ.

For academic awards, preliminary examination at current school in February, '93, leading to selection for main examination at Milton Abbey in May 1993. Art and Music candidates examined at Milton Abbey in February.

Closing date for entries: 1 February 1993.

Awards may be supplemented by Bursaries in cases of need.

For full details apply to the Headmaster.

Telephone: 0258 880484.   Fax: 0258 881194

THE NEWCASTLE UPON TYNE CHURCH HIGH SCHOOL

HIGH SCHOOL for Girls with Church foundation. Entrance Scholarships and Exhibitions are offered at 11+, and for girls already in school at 16+. Government Assisted Places at 11+.
Special tuition terms for Clergy daughters.

Headmistress:
Miss P. E. Davies, M.A.(Leeds)

Newcastle upon Tyne
Church High School
Tankerville Terrace
Newcastle upon Tyne NE2 3BA

THE ORATORY SCHOOL
Roman Catholic School

ACADEMIC awards, including major scholarships, scholarships and exhibitions, are made annually on the results of an examination held in May.
Awards are of varying values, not exceeding half-fees.
Awards are given also in Music and Art.

Particulars from:
THE HEADMASTER

**The Oratory School
Woodcote
Nr. Reading RG8 0PJ**

PANGBOURNE COLLEGE

FOUR scholarships for half fees

(Academic, Art, Music, All-Rounder)

Additional Exhibitions between 10% and 25% fees

Further particulars can be obtained from the Headmaster

PENRHOS COLLEGE

Five Entrance Scholarships of approximately 50% of the current fees are offered annually. Papers are set for girls who on 1 September after the examination will be 11, 12 and 13 years old, respectively. Two of the Scholarships are reserved for girls attending the primary school of a Local Education Authority, one Scholarship may be awarded to the daughter or granddaughter of an old Penrhosian. Particulars may be obtained from the Secretary.

**Penrhos Junior School
Colwyn Bay**
A Scholarship to Penrhos College is offered annually for competition among girls at Penrhos College Junior School. (See also pages 718 and 719)

POCKLINGTON SCHOOL

SCHOLARSHIPS and EXHIBITIONS awarded annually to boys or girls through Common Entrance at 13+; or through our School Entrance Examination 13+ or 11+. Sixth Form Scholarships available. For particulars of these, Bursaries and the Government's Assisted Places Scheme, apply to the Headmaster.

**West Green, Pocklington
York YO4 2NJ
Telephone: 0759 303125**

REPTON SCHOOL

UP to nine Scholarships and up to nine Exhibitions may be awarded as a result of examination in May. The value of Scholarships will vary between a maximum of 50% of the fees for a Major one and 20% of the fees for a Minor one. The value of Exhibitions will be 10% of the fees. Up to six Music awards (maximum value 50% of the fees): examination in February. An Art Scholarship is, and an Exhibition may be, offered, whose value will depend on our estimate of the candidate's potential in the examination in May. Music awards are open to candidates who wish to join the School at the Sixth-Form stage.

Further particulars from:
**The Headmaster
Repton School
Repton, Derby DE6 6FH**

ROEDEAN

Independent Girls' Boarding School for ages 11-18.

(Day and Boarding places offered in the Sixth Form)

SCHOLARSHIP EXAMINATIONS

Scholarships are offered to girls under 14 years of age on 1 September of year of entry and to girls entering the Sixth Form who show outstanding academic, musical or artistic potential.

Scholarships will normally be worth one-half of the fees. The value of all awards is index-linked to increases in school fees throughout the duration of the award. In exceptional circumstances, further finance, by way of a Bursary, may also be available. Junior Scholarship Examinations take place in January and the Sixth-Form Scholarships in November.

For full details and a prospectus please apply to:

**The Admissions Secretary
Roedean School
Brighton
East Sussex BN2 5RQ**

Telephone: 0273 603181

Fax: 0273 676722

RYDAL

AS many as 10 Scholarships and Exhibitions of up to 50% fees per annum in value will be offered by examination in May. One or two will be reserved for Music or Art. Candidates must be under 14 on 1 September.

Three valuable Scholarships are also offered to boys and girls entering directly into the Sixth Form.

Headmaster: N. W. Thorne, M.Sc., B.Ed. (Senior)
D. A. Armstrong, B.Sc. (Preparatory)

Particulars and Prospectus from the Headmaster's Secretary.

**Rydal School
Colwyn Bay, Clwyd LL29 7BT
Tel: 0492 530155**

(See also page 720)

Sevenoaks School

Scholarships 1993:

Over FIFTY Awards available at: 11+ (Junior School), 13+ (Middle School) and Sixth Form.

For: Outstanding academic ability.
Music.
All-round qualities (outstanding ability in sport may be taken into account). These Pipemakers' Scholarships are available only to day and boarding boys and girls entering at 13+, and to boarding boys and girls at 16+. Candidates proposing to study for the International Baccalaureate in the Sixth Form.

Major Scholarships are normally to the value of half of the day fee.
Minor Scholarships are normally to the value of one-third of the day fee.
Foundation Scholarships are normally to the value of £1,000 p.a.
Music Scholarships are of the same value as Academic Scholarships plus free music tuition.

Pipemakers' Awards are to the value of at least £1,200 p.a.
A number of Bursaries are also available (not least to supplement Major or Minor Scholarships).

Dates of Examinations for entry in September 1993:
Sixth Form 14 November 1992.
Junior (11+) 11 January 1993.
Music 24 and 25 February 1993.
Senior (13+) 1, 2 and 3 March 1993.

Applications should be made to the Sixth Form Admissions Tutor for Sixth Form Awards (by early October 1992), and to the Registrar for Music (by end-December 1992), 11+ (by end-November 1992) and 13+ Awards (by end-January 1993).

**Sevenoaks School
High Street
Sevenoaks
Kent TN13 1HU**
Telephone: (0732) 455133 Fax: (0732) 456143

SHEBBEAR COLLEGE

SCHOLARSHIPS of up to half fees are awarded each year following 11+ entrance examination in February.

Scholarships for 13+ entrants following own examination or C.E. — Awards to Sixth Form on recommendation and interview.

**Shebbear College
Shebbear
Devon EX21 5HJ**

SHERBORNE SCHOOL FOR GIRLS

SIX academic Scholarships and two Exhibitions are offered annually as the result of examination and interview; in addition there are two Scholarships offered for oustanding promise in music.

Dates of examinations: Sixth-Form Scholarship in November; others in January and February.

Winners of academic or music awards are offered emoluments related to the current fees.

Fees: On application

Headmistress: MISS JUNE M. TAYLOR, B.Sc.

**Sherborne School for Girls
Sherborne
Dorset DT9 3QN**

SOLIHULL SCHOOL
GIRLS IN SIXTH FORM ONLY

SEVEN free places covering full tuition fees and at least ELEVEN other Scholarships or Exhibitions are available at 11.

Examination in January, Government-assisted places also available, applies to 11+ and Sixth Form only. Scholarships worth 75% and 50% of tuition fees are available at 13, plus two Exhibitions worth 30%. Examinations in April.

Music: ONE free place and ONE other Scholarship (half-fees) for 11- to 13-year-olds, and a half-fee award for the Sixth Form.

Other Sixth Form Scholarships include the Ansell (full-fees) for Mathematics and Science; the Bushell (half-fees) for any other subject; Design and Technology (half-fees) and Art (half-fees).

Full details available from:
The Headmaster, Solihull School, Warwick Road Solihull, W. Midlands B91 3DJ. Tel: 021-705 4273

ST. ANNE'S SCHOOL, WINDERMERE

SCHOLARSHIPS. The majority of Scholarships are awarded at 11+, 13+, others at Sixth-Form level. Details of these Academic, Music, Art and Drama Scholarships and Awards will be given on request.

(See also page 659)

ST. CATHERINE'S SCHOOL

Church of England School for Girls (Day and Weekly Boarding).

11+ Entrance Scholarships are awarded annually by competitive examination. Sixth Form scholarships also available.

Member of G.S.A. and I.A.P.S.

Particulars from School Secretary.

**St. Catherine's School
Bramley
Guildford**

(See also page 706)

ST. CLARE'S, OXFORD

SCHOLARSHIP examinations for the International Baccalaureate Course are held on the first Saturday in March. Closing date for applications 17 February. Two major scholarships (full tuition and boarding) and up to six minor scholarships (full or part tuition) are offered. The I.B. course, acceptable to all British and many other universities worldwide, is ideal for the talented post-GCSE student who would find A-levels too narrow.

Enquiries to: Miss Jo Dewar (ISUK)

**St. Clare's
139 Banbury Road
Oxford OX2 7AL
Tel: (0865) 52031   Fax: (0865) 310002**

ST. MARY'S HALL, BRIGHTON

SCHOLARSHIPS are awarded each year on the results of examinations held in January to girls aged 11+, 12+, or 13+ by the September of their year of entry. The Award is for at least 25% of the fees but may be increased in special cases of ability or financial need.

A Music Scholarship and Sixth-Form Scholarships are also awarded and details are available on request. In addition, there are bursaries reserved for Daughters of the Clergy and Armed Forces of up to 75% of the fees.

ST. SWITHUN'S SCHOOL

SCHOLARSHIPS, BURSARIES AND ASSISTED PLACES

Scholarships are offered on a competitive basis for both Boarders and Day Girls. The examinations are held in January/February (December for entry to the Sixth Form) and awards take effect from the following September. The Major Scholarship is two-thirds of the fees. Other Scholarships offering an annual reduction of up to 50% of the fees are also awarded. Music Scholarships cover Music tuition fees only and the School is able to offer two Assisted Places at Sixth Form level for Day Girl places.

**St. Swithun's School
Winchester
Hants. SO21 1HA
Telephone: 0962 861316**

(See also page 668)

SUTTON VALENCE SCHOOL

FOUNDATION Scholarships (up to two-thirds fees), Exhibitions and Music and Art Scholarships may be awarded at 11+, 13+ and into the Sixth Form.

Five Assisted Places are available at Sixth-Form level, and 10 at 11+/13+.

**Sutton Valence School
Sutton Valence
Maidstone
Kent ME17 3HL
Telephone: (0622) 842281**

TONBRIDGE SCHOOL

SCHOLARSHIPS for boys under 14 on 1 June.

Academic	One Ainslie Scholarship worth up to full fees. Up to 20 Scholarships and Exhibitions worth up to half fees.
Music	Up to six Scholarships and Exhibitions worth up to half fees.
Art	Up to four Scholarships and Exhibitions worth up to half fees.

Any Scholarship or Exhibition awarded may be supplemented by a bursary in cases of need.

Further details from The Admissions Secretary

**Tonbridge School
Tonbridge
Kent TN9 1JP**

UPPINGHAM SCHOOL, Leics.

AT LEAST 20 Scholarships and Exhibitions to the value of a half to one-tenth of the fees are awarded annually, if suitable candidates present themselves. These include Music Scholarships and Exhibitions worth up to half fees and Sixth Form Scholarships worth up to two-thirds of the fees.

Scholarships are also offered for Art and CDT.

WALHAMPTON SCHOOL

A number of academic entry Scholarships are awarded each Spring term.

Candidates must be over seven and under 10 on the following 1 September.

There is a Bursary fund, and application to it is welcome.

**Walhampton School
Lymington
Hampshire SO41 5ZG**

WARWICK SCHOOL

H.M.C.: Independent/Assisted Places (at 11+, 12+, 13+, 16+). Up to 10 SCHOLARSHIPS valued at up to half fees are awarded on the results of the entrance examination at 11+ each year. At least four more SCHOLARSHIPS valued at up to half-fee remission are available to be awarded on the results of the 13+ entrance examination each year. At least two more SCHOLARSHIPS valued at two-fifths fee remission are awarded on the results of the Sixth Form Scholarship examination. A Bursary may be awarded to increase the value of any award where need is shown.

Fees: Tuition and board: £7,641-£8,688, Day Boys Tuition: £3,561-£4,038.
Headmaster: Dr. P. J. Cheshire, London University.

WEST BUCKLAND SCHOOL

Scholarships are awarded at the following ages: at seven, for entry to Langholme, our Prep. School; at 11 and 13 for entry to the senior school and at 16 for entry to the sixth form.

Scholarships are valued from 20% to 50% of fees (day or boarding).

Other assistance may be provided in case of need.

Government Assisted Places are available for entrants at 11 and 13 and to the sixth form.

Details and registration forms from the Headmaster:

**West Buckland School
Barnstaple
Devon EX32 0SX
Telephone: (0598) 760281**

INDEX

A

Abberley Hall, Worcester, Hereford and Worcester		196
The Abbey College, Malvern Wells, Hereford and Worcester	**669,**	196
Abbey Gate College, Chester, Cheshire	**657,**	89
Abbey Gate School, Chester, Cheshire	**658,**	89
The Abbey School ✻, Reading, Berkshire		55
The Abbey School, Westgate-on-Sea, Kent		233
The Abbey School, Tewkesbury, Gloucestershire		167
Abbey School, Glastonbury, Somerset		418
The Abbey School, Torquay, Devon		120
Abbots Hill School, Hemel Hempstead, Hertfordshire	**670,**	209
Abbotsford School, Kenilworth, Warwickshire		524
Abbotsholme School, Uttoxeter, Staffordshire		427
Abercorn Place School, London		281
Aberdeen Waldorf School, Aberdeen, Grampian		615
Aberdour, Tadworth, Surrey		443
Aberlour House ✻, Aberlour, Grampian		615
Abingdon School ✻, Abingdon, Oxfordshire	736,	397
Abinger Hammer Village School, Dorking, Surrey		443
Ackworth School ✻, Pontefract, West Yorkshire	737,	567
Acton Reynald, Shrewsbury, Shropshire		410
Adams Grammar School, Newport, Shropshire		410
Adcote School, Shrewsbury, Shropshire		410
Agincourt School, Monmouth, Gwent		586
Airthrie School with Hillfield Dyslexia Trust, Cheltenham, Gloucestershire		167
Akeley Wood Junior School, Milton Keynes, Buckinghamshire		74
Akeley Wood School, Buckingham, Buckinghamshire		74
Akhurst School, Newcastle upon Tyne, Tyne and Wear		517
Akiva School, London		281
Aldwickbury School, Harpenden, Hertfordshire		209
The Albany College, London		281
Albyn School for Girls ✻, Aberdeen, Grampian		615
Aldenham School ✻, Elstree, Hertfordshire		209
Aldro School, Godalming, Surrey		443
The Alice Ottley School ✻, Upper Tything, Hereford and Worcester		196
All Hallows, Shepton Mallet, Somerset		418
Allendale Preparatory School, London		281
Alleyn Court Preparatory School, Westcliff-on-Sea, Essex		151
Alleyn's School ✻, London	736,	282
Allhallows School, Lyme Regis, Dorset		136
Alpha Preparatory School, Harrow, Middlesex		359
Altrincham Preparatory School for Boys, Altrincham, Cheshire		89
Amberfield School, Ipswich, Suffolk		433
Amberleigh Preparatory School, Chorlton-cum-Hardy, Manchester		341
Amberley House, Bristol, Avon		36
Amberley School, Bexhill-on-Sea, East Sussex		488
Ambleside School, Cheam, Surrey		443
The American Community School Ltd, Cobham, Surrey	**701,**	444
The American Community School Ltd, Hillingdon, Middlesex		359
American School in Aberdeen, Aberdeen, Grampian		615
The American School in London, London		282
Amesbury Preparatory School, Hindhead, Surrey		444
Ampleforth College, York, North Yorkshire	**715,**	551
Ampleforth Preparatory School, York, North Yorkshire		551
Annemount School, London		282
Arden School, Ruthin, Clwyd		579
Ardenhurst School, Solihull, West Midlands		530
Ardingly College ✻, Haywards Heath, West Sussex	737,	503
Ardvreck School ✻, Crieff, Tayside		638
Argyle House School Sunderland, Tyne and Wear	**711,**	517
Arnold House School, London		282
Arnold Lodge School, Leamington Spa, Warwickshire		524

Entry	Page
Arnold School ✻, Blackpool, Lancashire	258
The Arts Educational London Schools, Chiswick, London	283
The Arts Educational School, Tring, Hertfordshire	209
Arundale, Pulborough, West Sussex	503
Ascham House School, Newcastle upon Tyne, Tyne and Wear	517
Ash Lea School, Eccles, Manchester	341
Ashbourne Independent School, London	283
Ashbourne PNEU School, Ashbourne, Derbyshire	115
Ashbrooke House Preparatory School, Weston-super-Mare, Avon	36
Ashdell Preparatory, Sheffield, South Yorkshire	562
Ashdown House School, Forest Row, East Sussex	488
Ashfold, Aylesbury, Buckinghamshire	74
Ashford School ✻, Ashford, Kent	233
Ashton House School, Isleworth, Middlesex	359
Ashville College ✻, Harrogate, North Yorkshire	551
Assumption School, Richmond, North Yorkshire	551
Astwell Preparatory School, Birmingham, West Midlands	530
Athelstan House School, Hampton, Middlesex	359
The Atherley School, Southampton, Hampshire	177
Atherton House, Liverpool, Merseyside	349
Atholl Preparatory School, Milngavie, Strathclyde	630
Atholl School, Pinner, Middlesex	360
Audley House School, Bicester, Oxfordshire	397
Austin Friars School ✻, Carlisle, Cumbria	111
Avalon School, Wirral, Merseyside	349
Avon House, Woodford Green, Essex	151
Avonlea School, Ringwood, Hampshire	177
Aymestrey School, Worcester, Hereford and Worcester	196
Ayscoughfee Hall School, Spalding, Lincolnshire	276
Aysgarth Preparatory School, Bedale, North Yorkshire	552
Ayton School, Great Ayton, North Yorkshire	552

B

Entry	Page
Babington House School, Chiselhurst, Kent	233
Badminton Junior School, Bristol, Avon	36
Badminton, Bristol, Avon	36
Bairnswood Preparatory School, Scarborough, North Yorkshire	552
Ballikinrain School ✝, Glasgow, Strathclyde	630
Balnacraig School ✝, Perth, Tayside	638
Bancroft's ✻, Woodford Green, Essex	151
Bangor Grammar School, Bangor, Co Down	643
Barbara Speake Stage School, East Acton, London	283
Barfield Preparatory School, Farnham, Surrey	444
Barlborough Hall School, Chesterfield, Derbyshire	115
The Barn School, Ware, Hertfordshire	210
Barnard Castle School ✻, Barnard Castle, Co Durham	148
Barnardiston Hall Preparatory School, Haverhill, Suffolk	433
Barrow Hills School, Godalming, Surrey	444
Barton School, St Leonards-on-Sea, East Sussex	488
Basil Paterson College, Edinburgh, Lothian	**728,** 622
Bassett House School, London	283
Baston School, Bromley, Kent	233
Bath High School ✻, Bath, Avon	37
Batley Grammar ✻, Batley, West Yorkshire	567
Battersea Montessori Schools, London	284
Battle Abbey School, Battle, East Sussex	**707,** 488
Beachborough, Brackley, Northamptonshire	379
Beacon House School, Ealing, London	284
The Beacon School and Winterbourn, Amersham, Buckinghamshire	74
Beaconhurst Grange School ✻, Bridge of Allan, Central	607
Bearwood College, Wokingham, Berkshire	55
Beaudesert Park, Minchinhampton, Gloucestershire	**663,** 167
Bedales School ✻, Petersfield, Hampshire	738, 177
Bedford High School ✻, Bedford, Bedfordshire	**653,** 50
Bedford Modern School ✻, Bedford, Bedfordshire	50
Bedford Preparatory School, Bedford, Bedfordshire	50
Bedford School ✻, Bedford, Bedfordshire	50
Bedgebury School Goudhurst, Kent	738, **677,** *234*

School	Page
Bedstone College, Bucknell, Shropshire	410
Beech Hall School, Macclesfield, Cheshire	89
Beech House Preparatory School, Leeds, West Yorkshire	567
Beech House School, Sanderstead, Surrey	445
Beech House School, Rochdale, Lancashire	25
Beechwood Park School, St Albans, Hertfordshire	210
Beechwood School Sacred Heart, Tunbridge Wells, Kent	234
Beehive Preparatory School, Ilford, Essex	151
Beehive School, Taunton, Somerset	418
Beeston Hall School, Cromer, Norfolk	371
Belfast Royal Academy, Belfast, Co Antrim	643
Belhaven Hill School *, Dunbar, Lothian	622
Bell House School, Brentwood, Essex	152
Bellan House, Oswestry, Shropshire	411
Bellerbys College Hove, East Sussex	729, 489
Belmont Abbey School, Hereford, Hereford and Worcester	197
Belmont House School *, Newton Mearns, Strathclyde	630
Belmont School Mill Hill, London	684, 284
Belmont School, Dorking, Surrey	445
Belmont-Birklands, Harrogate, North Yorkshire	552
The Belvedere School, GPDST*, Liverpool, Merseyside	349
Bembridge School, Isle of Wight	230
Bendarroch School, Ottery St. Mary, Devon	120
Benenden School, Cranbrook, Kent	234
Bentham School, Lancaster, Lancashire	258
Berkhampstead School, Cheltenham, Gloucestershire	167
Berkhamsted School *, Berkhamsted, Hertfordshire	210
Berkhamsted School for Girls *, Berkhamsted, Hertfordshire	210
Bethany, Cranbrook, Kent	234
Bickley Park School, Bromley, Kent	235
Bickley Parva School, Bromley, Kent	235
Bilton Grange, Rugby, Warwickshire	524
Birchfield School, Wolverhampton, West Midlands	530
Birkdale School, Sheffield, South Yorkshire	562
Birkenhead High School, G.P.D.S.T. *, Birkenhead, Merseyside	349
Birkenhead School *, Birkenhead, Merseyside	350
Bishop Challoner School, Bromley, Kent	235
Bishop's Stortford College *, Bishop's Stortford, Hertfordshire	211
Bishop's Stortford College Junior School, Bishop's Stortford, Hertfordshire	671, 211
Blackheath High School GPDST *, Blackheath, London	284
Blairmore *, Huntley, Grampian	616
Bloomsbury College, London	285
Bloxham School *, Banbury, Oxfordshire	738, 397
The Blue Coat School, Birmingham, West Midlands	530
Blundell's School, Tiverton, Devon	120
Bolton School (Boy's Division) *, Bolton, Lancashire	258
Bolton School (Girls School) *, Bolton, Lancashire	259
Bootham School *, York, North Yorkshire	553
Boundary Oak School, Fareham, Hampshire	177
Bow School, Durham, Co. Durham	148
Bowbrook House School, Pershore, Hereford and Worcester	197
Bowbrook School, Kidderminster, Hereford and Worcester	197
Bowden Preparatory School, Altrincham, Cheshire	90
Box Hill School, Dorking, Surrey	445
Brabyns School, Stockport, Cheshire	90
Brackenfield School, Harrogate, North Yorkshire	553
Bracknell Montessori School, Bracknell, Berkshire	55
Bracondale School, Norwich, Norfolk	371
Bradfield College *, Reading, Berkshire	55
Bradford Girls' Grammar School *, Bradford, West Yorkshire	567
Bradford Grammar School *, Bradford, West Yorkshire	568
Braeside School, Buckhurst Hill, Essex	152
Bramble Wood School, Orpington, Kent	235
Brambletye School, East Grinstead, West Sussex	503
Bramcote School, Scarborough, North Yorkshire	553
Bramcote School, Retford, Nottinghamshire	388
Bramdean Independent Preparatory and Grammar School, Exeter, Devon	120
Bramley, Chequers Lane, Tadworth, Surrey	445

Bramwood Preparatory School, Eccles, Manchester		341
Brantwood Independent School for Girls, Sheffield, South Yorkshire		562
Breaside Preparatory School, Bromley, Kent		236
Bredon School, Tewkesbury, Gloucestershire		168
Bremond College, Coventry, West Midlands		531
Brentwood School ✻, Brentwood, Essex	738,	152
Bretby House School, New Malden, Surrey		446
Briar (Independent) School, Lowestoft, Suffolk		433
Bricklehurst Manor, Wadhurst, East Sussex		489
Bridgewater School, Worsley, Manchester	**692,**	341
Brigg Preparatory School, Brigg, Humberside		227
Brighthelmston School, Southport, Merseyside		350
Brightlands School, Newnham-on-Severn, Gloucestershire		168
Brighton and Hove High School GPDST ✻, Brighton, East Sussex		489
Brighton College ✻, Brighton, East Sussex		489
Brighton College Junior School, Brighton, East Sussex		490
Brighton College Pre-Preparatory School, Brighton, East Sussex		490
The Brigidine School, Windsor, Berkshire		56
Bristol Cathedral School ✻, Bristol, Avon		37
Bristol Grammar School ✻, Bristol, Avon		37
Bristol Waldorf School, Bristol, Avon		37
Broadgate School, Nottingham, Nottinghamshire		388
Broadmead School, Luton, Bedfordshire		51
Broadwater Manor School, Worthing, West Sussex		503
Brockhurst, Hermitage, Newbury, Berkshire		56
Brocksford Hall, Doveridge, Derbyshire		115
Bromley High School GPDST ✻, Bromley, Kent		236
Bromsgrove Lower School, Bromsgrove, Hereford and Worcester		197
Bromsgrove Pre-Preparatory School, Bromsgrove, Hereford and Worcester		198
Bromsgrove School ✻, Bromsgrove, Hereford and Worcester		198
Bronte House School, Bradford, West Yorkshire		568
Bronte, Gravesend, Kent		236
Brooke Priory, Rutland, Leicestershire		269
Brooklands School, Stafford, Staffordshire		427
Broomfield House School, Richmond, Surrey		446
Broomham School, Guestling, East Sussex		490
Broomwood Hall Preparatory School, London		285
Bruern Abbey School, Oxford, Oxfordshire		397
Bruton School for Girls ✻, Bruton, Somerset	739,	418
Bryanston School, Blandford, Dorset		136
Bryony, Gillingham, Kent		236
Buchan School, Castletown, Isle of Man		652
Buckfast Abbey School, Buckfastleigh, Devon		121
Buckholme Towers School, Poole, Dorset		136
Buckingham College Lower School, Kenton, Middlesex		360
Buckingham College Senior School, Harrow, Middlesex		360
Buckswood Grange, Uckfield, East Sussex		490
Burgess Hill School for Girls ✻, Burgess Hill, West Sussex		504
Bury Catholic Preparatory School, Bury, Lancashire		259
Bury Grammar School (Girls) ✻, Bury, Lancashire		259
Bury Grammar School ✻, Bury, Lancashire		259
Bury Lawn School, Milton Keynes, Buckinghamshire		75
Bury's Court School, Reigate, Surrey		446
Bushey Place School, Aylsham, Norfolk		371
Butterstone School ✻, Blairgowrie, Tayside		638
Buxlow Preparatory School, Wembley, Middlesex		360

C

Cabin Hill School, Belfast, Co Antrim		643
Cable House School, Woking, Surrey		446
Caius House School, Urmston, Manchester		342
Calder House School †, London		285
Caldicott School, Farnham Royal, Buckinghamshire		75
Cambridge Centre for Sixth Form Studies, Cambridge, Cambridgeshire		83
Cambridge Tutors College, Croydon, Surrey	739,	447
Cameron House, Chelsea, London		285
Campbell College, Belfast, Co Antrim		643
Camphill-Rudolf Steiner-Schools †, Aberdeen, Grampian		616

School		Page
Canbury School, Kingston-upon-Thames, Surrey		447
Canford School ✻, Wimborne, Dorset	739,	1367
Cannock School, Orpington, Kent		237
Cargilfield ✻, Edinburgh, Lothian		622
Carleton House Preparatory School, Liverpool, Merseyside		350
Carmel College ✻, Mongewell Park, Wallingford, Oxfordshire		398
The Carrdus School, Banbury, Oxfordshire		398
Casterton School ✻, Carnforth, Lancashire	**680,**	260
Castle Court Preparatory, Wimborne, Dorset		137
Castle House, Newport, Shropshire		411
Caterham School ✻, Caterham, Surrey		447
The Cathedral School, Llandaff, South Glamorgan		597
The Cathedral School, Lincoln, Lincolnshire		276
Catteral Hall, Settle, North Yorkshire		553
The Cavendish School, Camden, London		286
Cawston College, Norwich, Norfolk		371
Central Newcastle High School GPDST ✻, Newcastle, Tyne and Wear		517
Chafyn Grove School, Salisbury, Wiltshire		543
Channing School, Highgate, London		286
Chard School, Chard, Somerset		419
Charterhouse ✻, Godalming, Surrey		447
The Charterhouse Square School, London		286
Charters-Ancaster School, Bexhill-on-Sea, East Sussex		491
Chartfield School, Westgate-on-Sea, Kent		237
Cheadle Hulme School ✻, Cheadle Hulme, Cheshire	739,	90
Cheadle Preparatory School, Cheadle, Cheshire		90
Cheam School, Newbury, Berkshire		56
The Chelsea Kindergarten, London		286
The Chelsea Nursery School, London		287
Cheltenham College Junior School, Cheltenham, Gloucestershire	**664,**	168
Cheltenham College, Cheltenham, Gloucestershire		168
The Cheltenham Ladies' College ✻, Cheltenham, Gloucestershire	740,	169
Cherwell Tutors, Oxford, Oxfordshire	**731,**	398
Chesham Preparatory School, Chesham, Buckinghamshire		75
Cheshunt School, Coventry, West Midlands		531
Cheswycks School, Camberley, Surrey		448
Chetham's School of Music, Long Millgate, Manchester		342
Chetwynd House School, Sutton Coldfield, West Midlands		531
Chigwell School ✻, Chigwell, Essex		152
The Children's House Montessori Nursery School, London		287
Childscourt School †, Lattiford House, Wincanton, Somerset		419
Chiltern House School, Thame, Oxfordshire		398
Chilton Cantelo School, Yeovil, Somerset		419
Chinthurst School, Tadworth, Surrey		448
Chiswick and Bedford Park Preparatory School, Bedford Park, London		287
Chorcliffe School, Chorley, Lancashire		260
The Chorister School, Durham, Co Durham		148
Christ Church Cathedral School, Oxford, Oxfordshire		399
Christ College ✻, Brecon, Powys		594
Christ's College, Blackheath, London		287
Christ's Hospital ✻, Horsham, West Sussex		504
Christian Fellowship School, Liverpool, Merseyside		350
Churcher's College ✻, Petersfield, Hampshire		178
City of London Freemen's School ✻, Ashtead, Surrey	**701,**	448
City of London School ✻, London		288
City of London School for Girls ✻, The Barbican, London		288
Claires Court School, Maidenhead, Berkshire		56
Claremont Fan Court School, Esher, Surrey		448
Claremont School, St. Leonards-on-Sea, East Sussex		491
Clark's Grammar School, Bristol, Avon		38
Clayesmore Preparatory School, Blandford, Dorset		137
Clayesmore, Blandford Forum, Dorset		137
Cleve House School, Bristol, Avon		38
Clevelands Preparatory School, Bolton, Lancashire		260
Clewborough House Preparatory School, Camberley, Surrey		449
Cliff School, Wakefield, West Yorkshire		568
Clifton College ✻, Bristol, Avon		38
Clifton College Preparatory School, Bristol, Avon		38

School	Page
Clifton Hall School ✳, Edinburgh, Lothian	622
Clifton High School for Girls ✳, Bristol, Avon	39
Clifton Lodge Boys Preparatory School, Ealing, London	**684,** 288
Clifton Preparatory School, York, North Yorkshire	554
Cobham Hall, Cobham, Kent	**678,** 237
Cobham Montessori Nursery School, Cobham, Surrey	449
Cokethorpe, Witney, Oxfordshire	**693,** 399
Colchester Boys' High School, Colchester, Essex	153
Coleraine Academical Institution, Coleraine, Co Londonderry	644
Colf's School ✳, London	288
College St Pierre, Leigh-on-Sea, Essex	153
Collingham, London	289
Collingwood School, Wallington, Surrey	449
Colston's Colegiate Lower School, Bristol, Avon	39
Colston's Collegiate School ✳, Bristol, Avon	39
Colston's Girls' School ✳, Bristol, Avon	39
Combe Bank School, Sevenoaks, Kent	237
Commonweal Lodge School, Purley, Surrey	449
The Compass School, Haddington, Lothian	623
Concord College, Shrewsbury, Shropshire	411
Coney Hill School and Nash House †, Bromley, Kent	238
Conifers School, Midhurst, West Sussex	504
Coniston School, Reigate, Surrey	450
Connaught House School, London	289
Convent of Mercy, St Peter Port, Guernsey	649
Convent of Our Lady of Providence School, Alton, Hampshire	178
Convent of Our Lady, St Leonards-on-Sea, East Sussex	491
Convent of St Francis de Sales, Tring, Hertfordshire	**671,** 211
Convent of the Blessed Sacrament, Steyning, West Sussex	504
Convent of the Sacred Heart, Swaffam, Norfolk	372
Convent Preparatory School, Gravesend, Kent	238
Convent Primary School, Rochdale, Lancashire	260
Conway School, Boston, Lincolnshire	276
Coopersale Hall School, Epping, Essex	153
Copthorne School, Crawley, West Sussex	505
Corfton Hill Educational Establishment †, Ealing, London	289
Cothill House, Abingdon, Oxfordshire	399
Cotsbrook Community †, Shifnal, Shropshire	411
Cotswold Chine Home School †, Stroud, Gloucestershire	169
Cotswold House School, Woodthorpe, Nottinghamshire	388
Cottesmore School, Pease Pottage, West Sussex	505
Coventry Preparatory School ✳, Coventry, West Midlands	531
Coworth Park School, Woking, Surrey	450
Coxlease School †, Lyndhurst, Hampshire	178
Craig-Y-Nos School, Swansea, West Glamorgan	602
Craig-Y-Parc School †, Cardiff, Mid Glamorgan	592
Craigclowan ✳, Perth, Tayside	638
Craigholme School ✳, Glasgow, Strathclyde	630
Craigievar High School, Sunderland, Tyne and Wear	518
Cranbrook College, Ilford, Essex	153
Cranbrook School, Cranbrook, Kent	238
Cranford House School, Wallingford, Oxfordshire	399
Cranleigh School ✳, Cranleigh, Surrey	*740,* 450
Cranmore School, West Horsley, Surrey	451
Cransley School, Northwich, Cheshire	91
Crawfordton House School ✳, Thornhill, Dumfries and Galloway	609
Crescent School, Oxford, Oxfordshire	400
Crescent School, Rugby, Warwickshire	524
Croft House School, Hexham, Northumberland	385
Croft House School, Blandford, Dorset	137
Croftdown School, Great Malvern, Hereford and Worcester	198
Croftinloan School ✳, Pitlochry, Tayside	639
Croham Hurst School ✳, South Croydon, Surrey	451
Crosfields, Reading, Berkshire	57
Crown House, High Wycombe, Buckinghamshire	75
Crowstone School, Westcliff-on-Sea, Essex	**662,** 154
Croydon High School GPDST ✳, Old Croydon, Surrey	451
Culcheth Hall School, Altrincham, Cheshire	91

Culford School ✳, Bury St Edmunds, Suffolk	740,	433
Cumnor House School, Croydon, Surrey		451
Cumnor House School, Haywards Heath, West Sussex		505
Cundall Manor School, York, North Yorkshire		554

D

Dagfa House School, Beeston, Nottinghamshire		388
Daiglen School, Buckhurst Hill, Essex		154
Dair House School Trust Ltd., Slough, Buckinghamshire		76
Dairsie House School, Glasgow, Strathclyde		631
Dallington, London		289
Dame Alice Harpur ✳, Bedford, Bedfordshire		51
Dame Allan's Boys' School ✳, Newcastle upon Tyne, Tyne and Wear		518
Dame Allan's Girls' School ✳, Newcastle upon Tyne, Tyne and Wear		518
Dame Johane Bradbury's School, Saffron Walden, Essex		154
Danes Hill School, Oxshott, Surrey		452
Danesfield Preparatory School, Walton-on-Thames, Surrey		452
Daneshill School, Basingstoke, Hampshire		178
Daniel Stewart's & Melville College ✳, Edinburgh, Lothian		623
Dauntsey's School ✳, Devizes, Wiltshire		543
Davenies School, Beaconsfield, Buckinghamshire	**655,**	76
Davenport Lodge School, Coventry, West Midlands		532
Dean Close Junior School, Cheltenham, Gloucestershire		169
Dean Close School, Cheltenham, Gloucestershire		169
Dean Grange Preparatory School, Huntingdon, Cambridgeshire		83
Deepdene School, Hove, East Sussex	**708,**	491
Denmead, Hampton, Middlesex		361
Denstone College ✳, Uttoxeter, Staffordshire		427
Denstone College Preparatory School ✳, Uttoxeter, Staffordshire		427
Derby High School ✳, Derby, Derbyshire		115
Derwent Lodge, Tunbridge Wells, Kent		238
Devonshire House Preparatory and Pre-Preparatory School, Hampstead, London	**685,**	290
Dewlish House, Bournemouth, Dorset		138
Ditcham Park School, Petersfield, Hampshire		179
Dodderhill, Droitwich, Hereford and Worcester		198
Dollar Academy ✳, Dollar, Central		607
Dolphin School, Reading, Berkshire		57
The Dolphin School, Exmouth, Devon		121
Doods Brow School, Redhill, Surrey		452
Dorchester Preparatory School, Dorchester, Dorset		138
The Dormer House PNEU School, Moreton-in-Marsh, Gloucestershire		170
Dorset House School, Pulborough, West Sussex		505
Douai School ✳, Reading, Berkshire	**654,**	57
Dover College ✳, Dover, Kent	740,	239
Dover College Preparatory School, Folkestone, Kent		239
Downe House ✳, Newbury, Berkshire	741,	57
The Downs School, Malvern, Hereford and Worcester		199
The Downs School, Bristol, Avon		40
Downsend Lodge (Ashtead), Ashtead, Surrey		453
Downsend Lodge (Epsom), Epsom, Surrey		453
Downsend Lodge (Rowans), Leatherhead, Surrey		453
Downsend Lodge Senior Girls, Leatherhead, Surrey		453
Downsend, Leatherhead, Surrey		452
Downside Preparatory School, Purley, Surrey		454
Downside School, Bath, Avon		40
Dr Rolfe's Montessori School, London		290
Dragon School, Oxford, Oxfordshire		400
Drayton House School, Guildford, Surrey		454
The Drive School, Wolverhampton, West Midlands		532
Drumley House ✳, Ayr, Strathclyde		631
Duchy Grammar, Tregye, Truro, Cornwall		106
Duke of Kent School, Cranleigh, Surrey	**702,**	454
Duke of York's Royal Military School, Dover, Kent		239
Dulwich College ✳, Dulwich, London		290
Dulwich College Preparatory School, London		290
Dulwich College Preparatory School, Cranbrook, Kent		239
Dumbarton House School, Swansea, West Glamorgan		602

E

School	Page refs
Dumpton School, Wimborne, Dorset	138
Dunchurch-Winton Hall Preparatory School, Dunchurch, Warwickshire	525
Duncombe School, Hertford, Hertfordshire	211
Dunedin School †, Edinburgh, Lothian	623
Dunhurst School, Petersfield, Hampshire	179
Dunottar School, Reigate, Surrey	454
Durham High School, Durham, Co Durham	148
Durham School *, Durham, Co Durham	741, 149
Durlston Court School, Barton on Sea, Hampshire	179
Durston House, Ealing, London	291
Eagle House, Camberley, Surrey	455
Ealing College Upper School, Ealing, London	291
The Ealing Dean Anglo-French School, Ealing, London	291
East Court School †, Ramsgate, Kent	240
Eastbourne College, Eastbourne, East Sussex	741, 492
Eastbourne House School, Birmingham, West Midlands	532
Eastcliffe Grammar School, Newcastle upon Tyne, Tyne and Wear	518
Eastcourt Independent School, Goodmayes, Essex	154
Eaton House School, London	291
Eaton Square Nursery & Pre-Preparatory School, London	292
Eccles Hall School, Norwich, Norfolk	372
Eccleston School, Birmingham, West Midlands	532
Eden Park School, Beckenham, Kent	240
Edenhurst Preparatory School, Newcastle-under-Lyme, Staffordshire	428
Edgarley Hall (Millfield Junior School), Glastonbury, Somerset	419
Edgbaston Church of England College for Girls *, Birmingham, West Midlands	712, 533
Edgbaston College, Birmingham, West Midlands	533
Edgbaston High School for Girls, Birmingham, West Midlands	533
Edge Grove Preparatory School for Boys, Aldenham, Hertfordshire	672, 212
Edgeborough School, Farnham, Surrey	702, 455
Edgehill College *, Bideford, Devon	121
Edgehill School, Newark, Nottinghamshire	389
The Edinburgh Academy *, Edinburgh, Lothian	742, 623
Edinburgh House School, New Milton, Hampshire	179
Edinburgh Tutorial College, Edinburgh, Lothian	624
Edington †, Bridgewater, Somerset	696, 420
Egerton-Rothesay School, Berkhamsted, Hertfordshire	672, 212
Elizabeth College, Guernsey	649
Ellesmere College *, Ellesmere, Shropshire	412
Elliot Clark School, Liverpool, Merseyside	351
Elliott Park School, Sheppey, Kent	240
Elm Green Preparatory School, Chelmsford, Essex	155
Elm Grove School, Exeter, Devon	121
Elm Tree House, Cardiff, South Glamorgan	597
Elmfield Rudolf Steiner School, Stourbridge, West Midlands	533
Elmhurst Ballet School, Camberley, Surrey	455
Elmhurst School for Boys, Croydon, Surrey	455
The Elms School, Malvern, Hereford and Worcester	199
Elmslie Girls' School, Blackpool, Lancashire	261
Elmwood Montessori School, London	292
Elstree School, Reading, Berkshire	58
Eltham College, London	292
Emanuel School *, London	292
Emberhurst, Esher, Surrey	456
Embley Park School, Romsey, Hampshire	180
Emmanuel Christian School, Fleetwood, Lancashire	681, 261
Emmanuel School, Swansea, West Glamorgan	602
Emscote Lawn School, Warwick, Warwickshire	525
Eothen, Caterham, Surrey	456
Epsom College *, Epsom, Surrey	456
Essendene Lodge, Caterham, Surrey	456
Eton College, Windsor, Berkshire	58
Eton End PNEU, Slough, Berkshire	58
Eton House School, Southend-on-Sea, Essex	155
Eversfield Preparatory School, Solihull, West Midlands	534

Eversley Preparatory School, Southwold, Suffolk		434
Ewell Castle School, Ewell, Epsom, Surrey		457
Exeter Cathedral School, Exeter, Devon		122
Exeter Preparatory School, Exeter, Devon		122
Exeter School ✳, Exeter, Devon		122
Eylesden Court Preparatory School, Maidstone, Kent		240

F

Fairfield PNEU School, Bristol, Avon		40
Fairfield Preparatory School, Saxmundham, Suffolk		434
Fairfield School, Loughborough, Leicestershire		269
Fairholme Preparatory, St Asaph, Clwyd		579
Fairley House School †, London		293
Fairstead House School, Newmarket, Suffolk		434
Falcon Manor School, Towcester, Northamptonshire		379
The Falcons Pre-Preparatory School, Chiswick, London		293
Falkland House School †, Falkland, Fife		612
Falkland St Gabriel's, Newbury, Berkshire		58
Falkner House Girls' Preparatory School, London		293
Farleigh School, Andover, Hampshire		180
Farlington School, Horsham, West Sussex	**710,**	506
Farnborough Hill ✳, Farnborough, Hampshire		180
Farney Close School Ltd †, Haywards Heath, West Sussex		506
Farringtons School, Chislehurst, Kent	*742,* **678,**	241
Farrowdale House, Oldham, Manchester		342
Felixstowe College ✳, Felixstowe, Suffolk		434
Felsted Preparatory School, Dunmow, Essex		155
Felsted School ✳, Dunmow, Essex		155
Feltonfleet, Cobham, Surrey		457
Ferndale School, Faringdon, Oxfordshire		400
Fernhill Manor School, New Milton, Hampshire		180
Fernhill School ✳, Rutherglen, Strathclyde		631
Fettes College ✳, Edinburgh, Lothian		624
Fettes Junior School, Edinburgh, Lothian		624
Ffynone House School, Swansea, West Glamorgan		602
Finborough School, Stowmarket, Suffolk		435
Finton House School, London		293
The Firs School, Chester, Cheshire		91
Firth House Preparatory School, Rustington, West Sussex		506
Flambeaux Montessori School, Salisbury, Wiltshire		543
Fleetwood Preparatory School, Fleetwood, Lancashire		261
Fletewood School, Plymouth, Devon		122
Flexlands School, Chobham, Surrey		457
The Fold School, Hove, East Sussex		492
Fonthill Lodge School, East Grinstead, West Sussex		506
Forest Girls' School, Snaresbrook, London		294
Forest Junior School, Snaresbrook, London	*742,*	294
Forest Park School, Sale, Cheshire		91
Forest School, Timperley, Cheshire		92
Forest Senior School ✳, Snaresbrook, London	*742,*	294
Forres School, Swanage, Dorset		138
Fort Augustus Abbey School ✳, Fort Augustus, Highlands	**721,**	620
Fosse Bank Preparatory School, Tonbridge, Kent		241
Fosse Way School, Leicester, Leicestershire		269
Foxley PNEU School, Reading, Berkshire		59
Foyle and Londonderry College, Duncreggan, Londonderry,		644
Framlingham College ✳, Woodbridge, Suffolk	**699,**	435
Framlingham College Junior School ,		435
Framlingham College Junior School , Woodbridge, Suffolk		435
Francis Holland School ✳, London		294
Franciscan Convent, Copthorne, West Sussex		507
The French Institute, London		295
Frensham Heights School, Farnham, Surrey	*742,* **703,**	457
Frewen College †, Northiam, East Sussex		492
Friar Gate House School, Derby, Derbyshire		116
Friars School, Ashford, Kent		241
Friend's School Lisburn, Lisburn, Co Antrim		644
Friends' School ✳, Saffron Walden, Essex		156

The Froebelian School, Leeds, West Yorkshire — 568
Fulneck Boys' School, Pudsey, West Yorkshire — 569
Fulneck Girls' School, Pudsey, West Yorkshire — 569
Fulwell Grange Day School, Sunderland, Tyne and Wear — 519
Fyling Hall School, Robin Hoods Bay, North Yorkshire — 554

G

Gad's Hill School, Higham-by-Rochester, Kent — 241
Garden House School, London — 295
Gask House School, Glasgow, Strathclyde — 631
Gatehouse School, Bethnal Green, London — 295
Gateway School, Great Missenden, Buckinghamshire — 76
Gateways, Leeds, West Yorkshire — 569
Gayhurst School, Gerrards Cross, Buckinghamshire — 76
George Heriot's School ✻, Edinburgh, Lothian — 624
George Watson's College ✻, Edinburgh, Lothian — 625
The German School, Richmond, Surrey — 458
Ghyll Royd School, Ilkley, West Yorkshire — 569
Gidea Park College, Romford, Essex — 156
Giggleswick School ✻, Settle, North Yorkshire — **715,** 554
Glaisdale School, Sutton, Surrey — 458
The Glasgow Academy, Glasgow, Strathclyde — 632
Glebe House School, Hunstanton, Norfolk — 372
Glebe House School, Rochdale, Lancashire — 261
Gleddings School, Halifax, West Yorkshire — 570
Glen Morven Preparatory School, Aboyne, Grampian — 616
Glenalmond College ✻, Perth, Tayside — **724,** 639
Glenarm College, Ilford, Essex — 156
Glendower School, London — 295
Glenesk School, West Horsley, Surrey — 458
Glenhurst School, Havant, Hampshire — 181
Glenn Preparatory School, Leicester, Leicestershire — 269
The Godolphin and Latymer School ✻, Hammersmith, London — 296
The Godolphin School ✻, Salisbury, Wiltshire — 543
Godstowe School, High Wycombe, Buckinghamshire — 77
Golders Hill School, Barnet, London — 296
Goodwyn School, Mill Hill, London — 296
Gordonstoun School ✻, Elgin, Grampian — 616
Gosfield School, Halstead, Essex — 156
Grace Dieu Manor School, Coalville, Leicestershire — 270
Gracefield Preparatory School, Bristol, Avon — 40
Grainger Grammar School, Newcastle upon Tyne, Tyne and Wear — 519
Gramercy Hall School, Brixham, Devon — 123
Grange Park Preparatory School, Enfield, London — 296
The Grange School, Northwich, Cheshire — 92
Grangewood Hall School †, Wimborne, Dorset — 139
Grantchester House School, Esher, Surrey — 458
The Granville School, Sevenoaks, Kent — 242
Grasscroft Independent School, Oldham, Manchester — 342
Great Ballard, Chichester, West Sussex — 507
Great Beginnings Montessori School, London — 297
Great Houghton Preparatory School, Northampton, Northamptonshire — 379
Great Walstead School, Haywards Heath, West Sussex — 507
Green Hill School, Evesham, Hereford and Worcester — 199
Greenacre Shool for Girls, Banstead, Surrey — **704,** 459
Greenbank School, Cheadle, Cheshire — 92
Greenfield School, Woking, Surrey — 459
Greenfields School, Forest Row, East Sussex — **708,** 492
Greenhayes School for Boys, — 242
Greenhayes School for Boys, West Wickham, Kent — 242
Greenholme School, Nottingham, Nottinghamshire — 389
The Gregg School, Southampton, Hampshire — 181
Grenville College, Bideford, Devon — *743,* 123
Gresham's Preparatory School, Holt, Norfolk — 372
Gresham's School ✻, Holt, Norfolk — 373
The Grey House School, Hartley Wintney, Hampshire — 181
Greycotes School, Oxford, Oxfordshire — 400
Greylands Preparatory School, Paignton, Devon — 123

Grittleton House School, Chippenham, Wiltshire SN14 6AP		544
Grosvenor House School, Edwalton, Nottinghamshire		389
Grosvenor House School, Harrogate, North Yorkshire		555
The Grove School, Hindhead, Surrey	**703,**	459
Guildford High School ✳, Guildford, Surrey		459
Gyosei International School UK, Milton Keynes, Buckinghamshire		77

H

The Haberdashers' Aske's School ✳, Elstree, Hertfordshire		212
Haberdashers' Aske's School for Girls ✳, Elstree, Hertfordshire		212
Haberdashers' Monmouth School for Girls ✳, Monmouth, Gwent		586
Haddon Dene School, Broadstairs, Kent		242
Haden Hill School, Warley, West Midlands		534
Haileybury ✳, Hertford, Hertfordshire	*743,*	213
Haileybury Junior School, Windsor, Berkshire		59
Hale Preparatory School, Altrincham, Cheshire		92
Hall Grove School, Bagshot, Surrey		460
The Hall, London		297
The Hall, Winscombe, Avon		41
Hallfield School, Birmingham, West Midlands		534
Halliford School, Shepperton, Middlesex		361
Halstead Preparatory School, Woking, Surrey		460
Hamilton College ✳, Hamilton, Strathclyde		632
Hammond School, Chester, Cheshire		93
Hampden Manor, Great Missenden, Buckinghamshire		77
The Hampshire School (Kensington Gardens), London		297
The Hampshire School (Knightsbridge), London		297
Hampstead Hill Pre-Preparatory and Nursery School, London		298
Hampton School ✳, Hampton, Middlesex		361
Handcross Park School, Haywards Heath, West Sussex		507
Handel House Preparatory School, Gainsborough, Lincolnshire		276
Hanford School, Blandford Forum, Dorset		139
Harecroft Hall, Gosforth Seascale, Cumbria		111
Harenc Preparatory School, Footscray, Kent		242
Haresfoot School, Berkhamsted, Hertfordshire		213
Haresfoot Senior School, Berkhamsted, Hertfordshire		213
Harrogate Ladies College ✳, Harrogate, North Yorkshire		555
Harrogate Tutorial College Limited, Harrogate, North Yorkshire		555
Harrow School, Harrow on the Hill, Middlesex	*743,*	361
Harvington School, Ealing, London		298
Haslemere Preparatory School, Haslemere, Surrey		460
Hatherop Castle School, Cirencester, Gloucestershire		170
Hawforth Lodge School, Worcester, Hereford and Worcester		199
Hawkhurst Court †, Brighton, East Sussex		493
Hawley Place School, Camberley, Surrey		460
The Hawthorns, Bletchingley, Surrey		461
Hawtreys, Marlborough, Wiltshire		544
Haylett Grange PNEU School, Haverfordwest, Dyfed		583
Hazel Hurst Preparatory School, Mapperley, Nottinghamshire		389
Hazelhurst School For Girls, Wimbledon, London		298
Hazelwood School, Limpsfield, Surrey		461
Headington School ✳, Oxford, Oxfordshire	*743,* **694,**	401
Headlands School †, Penarth, South Glamorgan		597
Heath Mount School, Hertford, Hertfordshire		213
Heathcote School, Chelmsford, Essex		157
Heatherton House School, Amersham, Buckinghamshire		77
Heathfield Rishworth School, Selby Bridge, West Yorkshire		570
Heathfield School, Ascot, Berkshire		59
Heathfield School, Blackburn, Lancashire		262
Heathfield School, Kidderminster, Hereford and Worcester		200
Heathfield School, Pinner, Middlesex		362
Heathlands Preparatory School, Grantham, Lincolnshire		277
The Hellenic College of London, London		298
Hemdean House School, Reading, Berkshire		59
Hendon Preparatory School, Hendon, London		299
The Hereford Cathedral Junior School, Hereford, Hereford and Worcester		200
Hereford Cathedral School ✳, Hereford, Hereford and Worcester		200
Hereford Waldorf School, Hereford, Hereford and Worcester		200

School		Page
Hereward House School, London		299
Herington House School, Brentwood, Essex		157
Herries School, Cookham Dean, Berkshire		60
Hethersett Old Hall School, Norwich, Norfolk		373
Heywood Preparatory School, Corsham, Wiltshire		544
High March, Beaconsfield, Buckinghamshire		78
High School of Dundee *, Dundee, Tayside		639
The High School of Glasgow *, Glasgow, Strathclyde		632
Highclare School, Sutton Coldfield, West Midlands		534
Highfield PNEU School, Maidenhead, Berkshire		60
Highfield Priory School, Preston, Lancashire		262
Highfield School, Highgate, London		299
Highfield School, Pyrford, Surrey		461
Highfield School, Wandsworth Common, London		299
Highfield School, Birkenhead, Merseyside		351
Highfield School, East Grinstead, West Sussex		508
Highfield School, Liphook, Hampshire		181
Highfields School, Newark, Nottinghamshire		390
Highgate Junior School, London		300
Highgate School, London		300
Highlands School, Henly-on-Thames, Oxfordshire		401
The Highlands School, Reading, Berkshire		60
Hilden Grange School, Tonbridge, Kent		243
Hilden Oaks School, Tonbridge, Kent		243
Hill House International Junior School, London	**687,**	300
Hill House Preparatory School, Doncaster, South Yorkshire		562
The Hill School, Westerham, Kent		243
Hillcrest Grammar School, Stockport, Cheshire		93
Hillcroft Preparatory School, Stowmarket, Suffolk		435
Hillgrove School, Bangor, Gwynedd		589
Hillside School †, Aberdour, Fife		612
Hipperholme Grammar School *, Halifax, West Yorkshire		570
Hoe Bridge School, Woking, Surrey		461
Holland House School, Edgware, Middlesex		362
Hollington School, Ashford, Kent		243
Holly Bank School, Chester, Cheshire		93
Hollygirt School, Nottingham, Nottinghamshire		390
Holme Grange School, Wokingham, Berkshire		60
Holme Park Preparatory School, Kendal, Cumbria		111
Holmewood House, Tunbridge Wells, Kent		244
Holmwood House School, Colchester, Essex		157
Holy Child *, Birmingham, West Midlands		535
Holy Cross Convent, Chalfont St Peter, Buckinghamshire		78
Holy Cross Junior School, Portsmouth, Hampshire		182
Holy Cross Preparatory School, Kingston upon Thames, Surrey	**705,**	462
Holy Trinity Convent School, Bromley, Kent		244
Holy Trinity School, Kidderminster, Hereford and Worcester		201
Homefield Preparatory School, Sutton, Surrey		462
Homefield School, Rugby, Warwickshire		525
Homefield School, Christchurch, Dorset		139
Homewood Independent, St Albans, Hertfordshire		214
Honeybourne School, Birmingham, West Midlands		535
Hopelands, Stonehouse, Gloucestershire		170
Hordle House School, Lymington, Hampshire		182
Hornsby House School, London		300
Horris Hill, Newtown, Newbury, Berkshire		61
Howell's School *, Cardiff, South Glamorgan		597
Howell's School *, Denbigh, Clwyd		579
Howitt House School, Burton upon Trent, Staffordshire		428
Howsham Hall, York, North Yorkshire		555
Hull High School for Girls, Kingston-upon-Hull, Humberside		227
Hulme Grammar School for Boys *, Oldham, Manchester		343
The Hulme Grammar School for Girls, Oldham, Manchester		343
Hulme Hall Schools Junior Section, Stockport, Cheshire		94
Hulme Hall Schools, Stockport, Cheshire		93
Hunter Hall School, Penrith, Cumbria		111
Hunterhouse College, Belfast, Co Antrim	**726,**	644
Hurlingham Private School, Putney, London		301

	Hurst Lodge School, Sunningdale, Berkshire	61
	Hurstpierpoint College ✳, Hassocks, West Sussex	508
	Hurtwood House, Dorking, Surrey	462
	Hurworth House School, Darlington, Co Durham	149
	Hutchesons' Grammar School ✳, Glasgow, Strathclyde	632
	Huyton College, Liverpool, Merseyside	351
	Hydesville Tower School, Birmingham, West Midlands	535
	Hyland House, 896 Forest Road, Walthamstow, London	301
	Hylton Pre-Preparatory School, Exeter, Devon	123
	Hymers College ✳, Hull, Humberside	227
I	Ibstock Place School, Roehampton, London	301
	Ilford Usuline High School, Ilford, Essex	157
	Inchkeith School, Culross, Fife	612
	Indefatigable School, Anglesey, Gwynedd	589
	Inglebrook, Pontefract, West Yorkshire	570
	Ingleside PNEU School, Cirencester, Gloucestershire	170
	Inhurst House School, Basingstoke, Hampshire	182
	Innellan House, Pinner, Middlesex	362
	International School of London, London	301
	Ipswich High School GPDST ✳, Ipswich, Suffolk	436
	Ipswich Preparatory School, Ipswich, Suffolk	436
	Ipswich School ✳, Ipswich, Suffolk	436
	Islamia Primary School, London	302
	Islamic College, London	302
	Italia Conti Academy of Theatre Arts, London	302
J	Jack and Jill School, Hampton, Middlesex	362
	Jacques Hall Foundation, Manningtree, Essex	158
	James Allen's Girls' School ✳, London	302
	James Allen's Preparatory School, London	303
	Jersey College School for Girls, St Helier, Jersey	649
	Jewish High School for Girls, Salford, Manchester	343
	Jewish Preparatory School, London	303
	The John Loughborough School, Tottenham, London	303
	The John Lyon School ✳, Harrow, Middlesex	363
	Josca's Preparatory School, Abingdon, Oxfordshire	401
K	Kays' College, Huddersfield, West Yorkshire	571
	Keble Preparatory School, London	303
	Keighley Preparatory School, Keighley, West Yorkshire	571
	Keil School ✳, Dumbarton, Strathclyde	**723,** 633
	Kelly College, Tavistock, Devon	124
	Kelvinside Academy ✳, Glasgow, Strathclyde	633
	Kenley Montessori School, Notting Hill, London	304
	Kensington Park, London	**688,** 304
	Kensington Preparatory School For Girls, Kensington, London	304
	Kent College ✳, Canterbury, Kent	244
	Kent College Junior School, Pembury, Kent	245
	Kent College, Pembury, Kent	244
	Kerem House, London	304
	Kerem School, London	305
	Kesgrave Hall School †, Ipswich Suffolk	436
	Kew College, Richmond, Surrey	462
	Kilgraston School ✳, Bridge of Earn, Tayside	**724,** 639
	Kilquhanity House ✳, Castle Douglas, Dumfries and Galloway	609
	Kimbolton School ✳, Huntingdon, Cambridgeshire	83
	The King Alfred School, London	305
	King Edward VI High School for Girls ✳, Birmingham, West Midlands	535
	King Edward VI School ✳, Southampton, Hampshire	182
	King Edward VII School ✳, Lytham, Lancashire	262
	King Edward's Junior School, Bath, Avon	41
	King Edward's School ✳, Birmingham, West Midlands	536
	King Edward's School ✳, Bath, Avon	41
	King Edward's School Witley ✳, Godalming, Surrey	463

The King Fahad Academy, London			305
King Henry VIII School, Coventry, West Midlands			536
King William's College, Castletown, Isle of Man			652
King's College School ✻, Wimbledon Common, London		744,	305
King's College School, Cambridge, Cambridgeshire			83
King's College, Taunton, Somerset			420
King's Hall School, Taunton, Somerset			420
King's High School for Girls ✻, Warwick, Warwickshire			525
King's House School, Richmond, Surrey			463
King's School ✻, North Shields, Tyne and Wear		**712,**	519
The King's School ✻, Worcester, Hereford and Worcester		744,	201
The King's School ✻, Macclesfield, Cheshire			94
The King's School ✻, Chester, Cheshire			94
The King's School, Ely, Cambridgeshire		744,	84
King's School Bruton Junior ✻, Yeovil, Somerset			421
King's School Bruton, Bruton, Somerset			420
King's School Rochester ✻, Rochester, Kent		**679,**	245
The King's School, Canterbury, Kent CT1 2ES			245
The King's School, Gloucester, Gloucestershire			171
Kingham Hill School, Chipping Norton, Oxfordshire		**695,**	401
Kings College Junior School, Wimbledon Common, London			306
Kings College, Cardiff, South Glamorgan			598
Kingsbridge Preparatory School, Kingsbridge, Devon			124
Kingsbury Hill House, Marlborough, Wiltshire		**714,**	544
Kingscote Pre-preparatory School, Gerrards Cross, Buckinghamshire			78
Kingshott School, Hitchin, Hertfordshire			214
Kingsland Grange Junior School, Shrewsbury, Shropshire			412
Kingsland Grange, Shrewsbury, Shropshire			412
Kingsley Preparatory School, Solihull, West Midlands			536
The Kingsley School ✻, Leamington Spa, Warwickshire			526
Kingsmead School, Hoylake, Merseyside			351
Kingston Grammar School, Kingston-upon-Thames, Surrey			463
Kingston Vale Montessori School, Kingston Vale, London			306
Kingswood Day Preparatory School, Bath, Avon			41
Kingswood House School, Epsom, Surrey			463
Kingswood School ✻, Bath, Avon			42
Kingswood School, Southport, Mersyside			352
Kingswood School, Solihull, West Midlands			536
Kinloss School, Worcester, Hereford and Worcester			201
Kirkham Grammar School ✻, Preston, Lancashire			262
Kirkstone House School, Peterborough, Cambridgeshire			84
Kitebrook House School, Moreton-in-Marsh, Gloucestershire			171
Knighton House School, Blandford, Dorset			139
The Knightsbridge and Chelsea Kindergarten, Knightsbridge, London			306
The Knoll School, Kidderminster, Hereford and Worcester			201
Knowle Court, Tunbridge Wells, Kent			245

L

La Retraite School, Salisbury, Wiltshire			545
La Sagesse Convent High ✻, Newcastle upon Tyne, Tyne and Wear			519
La Sagesse Convent School, Romsey, Hampshire			183
Ladbrooke Square Montessori School, London			306
The Ladies' College, St Peter Port, Guernsey			649
Lady Barn House School, Cheadle, Cheshire			94
Lady Eden's School, London			307
The Lady Eleanor Holles ✻, Hampton, Middlesex			363
Ladymede, Aylesbury, Buckinghamshire		**656,**	78
Lalelam Lea Preparatory School, Purley, Surrey			464
Lambrook School, Bracknell, Berkshire			61
Lammas School, Sutton-in-Ashfield, Nottinghamshire			390
Lamorna School, Cardiff, South Glamorgan			598
Lancaster House School, Weston-super-Mare, Avon			42
Lancing College, Lancing, West Sussex			508
Landry School, Ingatestone, Essex			158
Lanesborough School, Guildford, Surrey			464
Langley Manor School, Slough, Berkshire			61
Langley Preparatory School, Norwich, Norfolk			373
Langley School, Norwich, Norfolk			373

Lathallan School, Montrose, Grampian		617
Latymer Upper *, Hammersmith, London	**688,**	307
Laurel Bank School *, Glasgow, Strathclyde		633
Lavant House School, Chichester, West Sussex		508
Laverock, Oxted, Surrey		464
Lawnside School, Great Malvern, Hereford and Worcester	745,	202
Lawrence House School, Lytham St. Annes, Lancashire		263
Laxton Junior School, Oundle, Northamptonshire		379
Laxton School *, Oundle, Northamptonshire		380
Lea House School, Kidderminster, Hereford and Worcester		202
Leaden Hall School, Salisbury, Wiltshire		545
Leeds Girls' High School *, Leeds, West Yorkshire		571
Leeds Grammar School *, Leeds, West Yorkshire		571
Leicester Grammar School, Leicester, Leicestershire		270
Leicester High School Charitable Trust Limited, Leicester, Leicestershire	**682,**	270
Leighton Park School *, Reading, Berkshire		62
The Leys *, Cambridge, Cambridgeshire		84
Licensed Victuallers' School, Ascot, Berkshire	**654,**	62
Licensed Victuallers' School, Ilkley, West Yorkshire	**717,**	572
Lichfield Cathedral School, Lichfield, Staffordshire	745, **698,**	428
Lilliput Nursery School, Fulham, London		307
Lime House School, Carlisle, Cumbria		112
Linden School, Newcastle Upon Tyne, Tyne and Wear		520
Lindisfarne College, Wrexham, Clwyd		579
Linley House School, Surbiton, Surrey		464
Linn Moor Residential Special School †, Petercutler, Grampian		617
The Little Folks Lab, Stevenage, Hertfordshire		214
Littlegarth School, Colchester, Essex		158
Littlemead Grammar School, Chichester, West Sussex		509
Liverpool College *, Liverpool, Merseyside		352
Llandovery College *, Llandovery, Dyfed		583
Lochinver House School, Potters Bar, Hertfordshire		214
Lockers Park School, Hemel Hempstead, Hertfordshire		215
The Loddon †, Basingstoke, Hampshire		183
Lomond School *, Helensburgh, Strathclyde	**723,**	633
London Montessori Centre Ltd., London		307
Long Close, Slough, Berkshire		62
Longacre Preparatory School, Bingham, Nottinghamshire		390
Longacre School, Guildford, Surrey		465
Longridge Towers School, Berwick upon Tweed, Northumberland		385
Lord Wandsworth College *, Basingstoke, Hampshire		183
Lord's College, Bolton, Lancashire		263
Loreto Convent Grammar School *, Altrincham, Cheshire		95
Loretto Junior School, Musselburgh, Lothian		625
Loretto School *, Musselburgh, Lothian	**722,**	625
Lorne House School, East Retford, Nottinghamshire		391
Loughborough Grammar School *, Loughborough, Leicestershire		270
Loughborough High School *, Loughborough, Leicestershire		271
Loyola Preparatory School, Buckhurst Hill, Essex		158
Lubavitch House Grammar School for Boys, East Finchley, London		308
Lubavitch House Primary School, London		308
Luckley Oakfield School, Wokingham, Berkshire		62
Lucton School, Leominster, Hereford and Worcester		202
Ludgrove School, Wokingham, Berkshire		63
Lycee Francais Charles De Gaulle, London		308
Lyncroft House, Cannock, Staffordshire		428
Lyndale, St Albans, Hertfordshire		215
Lyndhurst House Preparatory School, Hampstead, London		308
Lyndhurst School, Camberley, Surrey		465
Lyndon School, Colwyn Bay, Clwyd		580
Lynton Preparatory School, Scunthorpe, Humberside		227
Lynton Preparatory School, Epsom, Surrey		465
Lyonsdown School, New Barnet, Hertfordshire		215

M

School		Page
Macclesfield Preparatory School, Macclesfield, Cheshire		95
Madingley School, Cambridge, Cambridgeshire		84
Magdalen College School ✳, Oxford, Oxfordshire		402
Maidenhead College for Girls, Maidenhead, Berkshire		63
Maidwell Hall, Northampton, Northamptonshire		380
Maldon Court Preparatory School, Maldon, Essex		159
The Mall School, Twickenham, Middlesex		363
Malsis, Cross Hills, West Yorkshire		572
Maltman's Green Preparatory School for Girls, Gerrards Cross, Bucks	**656,**	79
Malvern College ✳, Malvern, Hereford and Worcester	745,	202
Malvern Girls' College, Great Malvern, Hereford and Worcester		203
Manchester Grammar School ✳, Manchester		343
Manchester High School for Girls ✳, Manchester		344
Manchester Jewish Grammar School, Prestwich, Manchester		344
Mander Portman Woodward School, Clifton, Avon		42
Manor House School, Hanwell, London		309
Manor House School, Leatherhead, Surrey		465
Manor House School, Ashby-de-la-Zouch, Leicestershire		271
Manor House School, Honiton, Devon		124
The Manor Preparatory School, Abingdon, Oxfordshire		402
Margaret Allen Preparatory School, Hereford, Hereford and Worcester		203
Margaret May Schools Ltd., Sevenoaks, Kent		246
Margaret McMillan Nursery School, Plymouth, Devon		124
Maria Montessori Children's House, London		309
Marist Convent Junior School, London		309
Marist Convent Nursery School, Ottery St Mary, Devon		125
Marist Convent Senior School ✳, Ascot, Berkshire		63
Marist Convent Senior School, London		309
Marland School †, Torrington, Devon		125
Marlborough College, Marlborough, Wiltshire		545
Marlborough House School, Cranbrook, Kent		246
Marlin Montessori School, Berkhamsted, Hertfordshire		21
Mary Erskine & Stewart's Melville Junior School, Edinburgh, Lothian		625
The Mary Erskine School ✳, Edinburgh, Lothian		626
Mary Hare Grammar School for the Deaf †, Newbury, Berkshire		63
Marycourt School, Gosport, Hampshire		183
Marymount Convent School, Wallesey, Merseyside		352
Marymount International School, Kingston-upon-Thames, Surrey	**705,**	466
Mayfield College, Mayfield, East Sussex		493
Mayfield Preparatory School, Walsall, West Midlands		537
Mayfield School, Alton, Hampshire		184
Maynard School ✳, Exeter, Devon		125
Maypole House, Horncastle, Lincolnshire		277
Mayville High School, Southsea, Hampshire		184
McKee School of Education, Dance, Drama, Liverpool, Merseyside		352
The Mead School, Tunbridge Wells, Kent		246
Meoncross Pre-school, Fareham, Hampshire		184
Meoncross School (Infant & Junior Department), Fareham, Hampshire		184
Meoncross Senior School, Fareham, Hampshire		185
Merchant Taylor's School ✳, Northwood, Middlesex		363
Merchant Taylors' School ✳, Liverpool, Merseyside		353
Merchant Taylors' School for Girls ✳, Liverpool, Merseyside		353
Merchiston Castle School ✳, Edinburgh, Lothian		626
Merlin School, Wandsworth, London		310
Merton Court Preparatory School, Sidcup, Kent		246
Merton Hall School †, Newtown Stewart, Dumfries and Galloway		609
Merton House School, Chester, Cheshire		95
Methodist College Belfast, Belfast, Co Antrim		645
Michael Hall Rudolf Steiner School, Forest Row, East Sussex		493
Michael House School, Heanor, Derbyshire		116
Micklefield School, Reigate, Surrey		466
Micklefield School, Seaford, East Sussex		493
Milbourne Lodge School, Esher, Surrey		466
Milestone College, London		310
Mill Hill School ✳, Mill Hill, London	**689,**	310
Mill Hill School for Deaf Children †, Haywards Heath, West Sussex		509
Mill Hill School, Middlesborough, Cleveland		103
The Mill School, Devizes, Wiltshire		545

Millbrook House School, Abingdon, Oxfordshire		402
Millfield, Street, Somerset	746, **697,**	421
Milton Abbey School, Blandford Form, Dorset	746,	140
Milton Keynes Preparatory School, Milton Keynes, Buckinghamshire		79
The Minster School, York, North Yorkshire		556
Miss Morley's Nursery School, London		310
Moffats, Bewdly, Hereford and Worcester		203
Moira House School, Eastbourne, East Sussex		494
Monkton Combe Junior School, Bath, Avon		42
Monkton Combe School *, Bath, Avon		43
Monkton House Educational Trust, Cardiff, South Glamorgan		598
Monkton Junior School, Llandaff, South Glamorgan		598
Monmouth School *, Monmouth, Gwent		586
Montessori 3-5 Nursery Wimbledon, Wimbledon, London	**690,**	311
Montessori School, Sheffield, South Yorkshire		563
Montessori St Nicholas School, Kensington, London		311
Moor Allerton, West Didsbury, Manchester		344
Moor Park School, Ludlow, Shropshire		412
Moorland School, Clitheroe, Lancashire		263
Moorlands School, Leeds, West Yorkshire		572
Moorlands School, Luton, Bedfordshire		51
Moray Steiner School, Forres, Grampian		617
More House School, Farnham, Surrey		466
More House, London		311
Moreton End School, Harpenden, Hertfordshire		216
Moreton Hall, Bury St Edmunds, Suffolk		437
Moreton Hall, Oswestry, Shropshire		413
Moreton House School, Petersfield, Hampshire		185
Morrison's Academy *, Crieff, Tayside	**725,**	640
Mostyn House, Wirral, Merseyside		353
Motcombe Grange School, Shaftsbury, Dorset		140
Moulsford Preparatory School, Wallingford, Oxfordshire		402
Mount Carmel School *, Alderley Edge, Cheshire		95
Mount Day Nursery and Preparatory School, Nottingham, Nottinghamshire		391
Mount House, Tavistock, Devon		125
The Mount School †, Wadhurst, East Sussex		494
The Mount School *, York, North Yorkshire		556
Mount School, Mill Hill, London	**690,**	311
Mount School, Bromsgrove, Hereford and Worcester		203
Mount St Mary's College *, Sheffield, South Yorkshire		563
Mount St Mary's Convent School, Exeter, Devon		126
Mountford House School, Nottingham, Nottinghamshire		391
Mowden Hall School, Stocksfield, Northumberland		385
Mowden School, Hove, East Sussex		494
Moyles Court School, Ringwood, Hampshire		185
Murrayfield Kindergarten School, Edinburgh, Lothian		626
Musgrave School, Gateshead, Tyne and Wear		520
Muslim Girls School, Bradford, West Yorkshire		572
Mylnhurst Convent School, Sheffield, South Yorkshire		563

N

Nant-Y-Cwm Steiner School, Clunderwen, Dyfed		583
Nativity School, Sittingbourne, Kent		247
Nethercliffe School, Winchester, Hampshire		185
Netherleigh School, Bradford, West Yorkshire		573
Netherton Hall †, Colyton, Devon		126
Netherwood School, Saundersfoot, Dyfed		583
Nevill Holt, Market Harborough, Leicestershire	**682,**	271
New Barns School †, Toddington, Gloucestershire		171
New Beacon School, Sevenoaks, Kent		247
New College School, Cardiff, South Glamorgan		599
New College School, Oxford, Oxfordshire		403
New College, Leamington Spa, Warwickshire		526
New Hall School, Chelmsford, Essex		159
New Park School *, St Andrews, Fife		612
The New School, Dunkeld, Tayside		640
Newbold School, Bracknell, Berkshire		64
Newborough School, Liverpool, Merseyside		353

Newbridge Preparatory School, Wolverhampton, West Midlands		537
Newcastle Preparatory School, Newcastle-upon-Tyne, Tyne and Wear		520
The Newcastle Upon Tyne Church High *, Newcastle Upon Tyne, Tyne and Wear	746,	520
Newcastle-under-Lyme School *, Newcastle, Staffordshire		429
Newell House School, Sherborne, Dorset		140
Newland House School, Twickenham, Middlesex		364
Newlands Manor School, Seaford, East Sussex		494
Newlands Pre Preparatory School, Seaford, East Sussex		495
Newlands Preparatory School, Seaford, East Sussex		495
Newlands, Newcastle upon Tyne, Tyne and Wear		521
Nightingale Montessori School Beck Kindergartens Ltd., London		312
Norfolk House School, London		312
Norfolk House School, Birmingham, West Midlands		537
Norland Place School, Kensington, London		312
Norman House Preparatory School, New Moston, Manchester		344
Normanhurst School, Chingford, London		31
Normanton School, South Croydon, Surrey		467
Normanton School, Buxton, Derbyshire		116
North Cestrian Grammar, Altrincham, Cheshire		96
North Foreland Ladge, Basingstoke, Hampshire	**667,**	186
North Leeds and St Edmunds Hall Preparatory School, Leeds, West Yorkshire		573
North London Collegiate School, Edgeware, Middlesex		364
Northampton High School *, Hardinstone, Northamptonshire		380
Northaw School, Salisbury, Wiltshire		546
Northbourne Park School, Deal, Kent		247
Northbridge House Junior School, London		313
Northbridge House Senior School, London		313
Northcliffe School, Southampton, Hampshire		186
Northease Manor School †, Lewes, East Sussex		495
Northfield School, Watford, Hertfordshire		216
Northgate House School, Chichester, West Sussex		509
Northgate Preparatory School, Rhyl, Clwyd		580
Northwood College, Northwood, Middlesex		364
Northwood Preparatory School, Rickmansworth, Hertfordshire		216
The Norwegian School, Wimbledon, London		313
Norwich High School for Girls GPDST *, Norwich, Norfolk		374
Norwich School *, Norwich, Norfolk		374
Notre Dame Preparatory School, Norwich, Norfolk		374
Notre Dame Preparatory School, Cobham, Surrey		467
Notre Dame School, Lingfield, Surrey		467
Notting Hill and Ealing High School, GPDST *, London		313
Nottingham High School *, Nottingham, Nottinghamshire		391
Nottingham High School for Girls, GPDST *, Nottingham, Nottinghamshire		392
Nower Lodge School, Dorking, Surrey		467
Nugent House School †, Wigan, Lancashire		263
Nunnykirk Hall School †, Morpeth, Northumberland		385

O

Oak Hill First School, Bristol, Avon		43
Oakfield Preparatory School, Dulwich, London		314
Oakfield School, Woking, Surrey		468
Oakham School *, Oakham, Leicestershire	**683,**	271
Oakhill College, Whalley, Lancashire		264
Oakhryst Grange School, Caterham, Surrey		468
Oakland Nursery School, Banstead, Surrey		468
Oaklands Preparatory School, Chorlton, Manchester		345
Oaklands School, Loughton, Essex		159
Oakleigh House School, Swansea, West Glamorgan		603
Oakley Hall, Cirencester, Gloucestershire		171
Oakwood School, Chichester, West Sussex		509
Ochil Tower Rudolf Steiner School †, Auchterarder, Tayside		640
Ockbrook School, Derby, Derbyshire		116
Old Buckenham Hall, Ipswich, Suffolk		437
The Old Grammar School, Lewes, East Sussex		495
The Old Hall, Wellington, Telford, Shropshire		413
The Old Malthouse, Swanage, Dorset		140

Old Palace School, Croydon, Surrey		468
The Old Rectory School, Ipswich, Suffolk		437
The Old Ride School, Bradford-on-Avon, Wiltshire		546
Old Swinford Hospital School, Stourbridge, West Midlands	**713,**	537
The Old Vicarage School, Richmond upon Thames, Surrey		469
The Oratory Preparatory School, Reading, Berkshire	*747,*	64
The Oratory School, Reading, Berkshire		64
Orchard School (Nursery Department), Retford, Nottinghamshire		392
Orchard School, South Leverton, Retford, Nottinghamshire		392
Oriel Bank High School, Stockport, Manchester		345
Orley Farm School, Harrow, Middlesex		364
Orwell Park School, Ipswich, Suffolk	**700,**	437
Oswestry Junior School, Oswestry, Shropshire		413
Oswestry School, Oswestry, Shropshire		413
Oswestry School, Oswestry, Shropshire		414
Oundle School, Oundle, Northamptonshire		380
Our Lady of Sion School, Worthing, West Sussex		510
Our Lady's Convent High School, Alnwick, Northumberland		386
Our Lady's Convent Junior School, Abingdon, Oxfordshire		403
Our Lady's Convent School, Cardiff, South Glamorgan		599
Our Lady's Convent School, Loughborough, Leicestershire		272
Our Lady's Convent School, Kettering, Northamptonshire		381
Our Lady's Convent Senior School, Abingdon, Oxfordshire		403
Overndale School, Bristol, Avon		43
Oxenfoord Castle School ✻, Pathead, Lothian		626
Oxford High School GPDST ✻, Oxford, Oxfordshire		403
Oxford House, Colchester, Essex		159

P

Packwood Haugh School, Shrewsbury, Shropshire		414
Padworth College, Reading, Berkshire		64
Paint Pots Montessori School, Newton Road, London		314
Palmers Green High School, Hoppers Road, London,		314
Pangbourne College ✻, Pangbourne, Berkshire	*747,*	65
Papplewick, Ascot, Berkshire		65
The Paragon Hill School, London		315
The Paragon Hill School, Hampstead, London		314
The Paragon School, Bath, Avon		43
Parayhouse School †, Chelsea, London		315
Pardes House School Ltd, London		315
Park Hill School, Kingston Upon Thames, Surrey		469
Park Lodge School ✻, Helensburgh, Strathclyde		634
The Park School ✻, Glasgow, Strathclyde		634
Park School for Girls, Ilford, Essex		160
The Park School, Bath, Avon		44
The Park School, Yeovil, Somerset		421
Parkdale Independent School, Wolverhampton, West Midlands		538
Parkside Preparatory School, Leighton Buzzard, Bedfordshire		52
Parkside, Cobham, Surrey		469
Parsons Mead School, Ashtead, Surrey	**706,**	469
Pattison College, Coventry, West Midlands		538
Pembridge Hall School, London		315
Pennthorpe School, Horsham, West Sussex	**710,**	510
Penrhos College ✻, Colwyn Bay, Clwyd	*747,* **718,**	580
Penrhos College Junior School, Colwyn Bay, Clwyd	**719,**	580
Perrott Hill, Crewkerne, Somerset		421
Perry Court Rudolf Steiner School, Canterbury, Kent		247
The Perse ✻, Cambridge, Cambridgeshire		85
The Perse School for Girls ✻, Cambridge, Cambridgeshire		85
Pershore House School, Wirral, Merseyside		354
Peterborough and St Margaret's High School for Girls, Harrow, Middlesex		365
Peterborough High School, Peterborough, Cambridgeshire	**657,**	85
Philpots Manor School †, East Grinstead, West Sussex		510
Pierrepont School, Farnham, Surrey		470
The Pilgrim's School, Winchester, Hampshire		186
Pinewood School, Swindon, Wiltshire		546
Pipers Corner School, High Wycombe, Buckinghamshire		79
Plymouth College ✻, Plymouth, Devon		126

Plymouth College Preparatory School, Plymouth, Devon		126
PNEU School Compton, Chichester, West Sussex		510
PNEU School, Nottingham, Nottinghamshire		392
PNEU School, Uppingham, Leicestershire		272
PNEU School, Loughborough, Leicestershire		272
Pocklington School *, York, North Yorkshire	747,	556
The Pointer School, Blackheath, London		316
Polam House School *, Darlington, Co Durham		149
Polam School, Bedford, Bedfordshire		52
Polwhele House Pre-Preparatory School, Truro, Cornwall		106
Polwhele House Preparatory School, Truro, Cornwall		106
Port Regis, Shaftesbury, Dorset		141
Portland House School, Leicester, Leicestershire		272
Portora Royal School, Enniskillen, County Fermanagh		645
The Portsmouth Grammar School *, Portsmouth, Hampshire		186
Portsmouth High School *, Southsea, Hampshire		187
Potterspury Lodge School, Towcester, Northamptonshire		381
Powis College, Welshpool, Powys		594
Pownhall Hall School, Wilmslow, Cheshire		96
The Pre-Preparatory School, Wimbledon, London		316
Prebendal School, Chichester, West Sussex		511
Prenton Preparatory School, Birkenhead, Merseyside		354
The Preparatory School, Newbury, Berkshire		65
The Preparatory School, Congleton, Cheshire		96
Presentation College, Reading, Berkshire		65
Presentation of Mary Convent School, Exeter, Devon		127
Prestfelde, Shrewsbury, Shropshire		414
Prince's Mead School, Winchester, Hampshire		187
The Princess Helena College, Hitchin, Hertfordshire		216
Princethorpe College, Rugby, Warwickshire		526
Prior Park College, Bath, Avon		44
Prior Park Preparatory School, Cricklade, Wiltshire		546
Prior's Court Preparatory, Newbury, Berkshire		66
Prior's Field, Godalming, Surrey		470
Priory College, Stamford, Lincolnshire		277
Priory Preparatory School, Stamford, Lincolnshire		277
The Priory School, Banstead, Surrey		470
The Purcell School, Harrow on the Hill, Middlesex	**692,**	365
Putney High School *, London		316
Putney Park School, Putney, London		316

Q

Quainton Hall, Harrow, Middlesex	365
Quantock School, Bridgwater, Somerset	422
Queen Anne's School, Reading, Berkshire	66
Queen Elizabeth Grammar School (Junior Section), Wakefield, West Yorkshire	573
Queen Elizabeth Grammar School *, Wakefield, West Yorkshire	573
Queen Elizabeth Hospital *, Bristol, Avon	44
Queen Elizabeth's Grammar School *, Blackburn, Lancashire	264
Queen Ethelburga's College, York, North Yorkshire **716,**	556
Queen Margaret's School, York, North Yorkshire	557
Queen Mary School *, Lytham, Lancashire	264
Queen Mary's School, Thirsk, North Yorkshire	557
Queen Victoria School, Dunblane, Tayside	640
Queen's College *, London	317
Queen's Park School †, Oswestry, Shropshire	414
The Queen's School *, Chester, Cheshire	96
Queens College *, Taunton, Somerset	422
Queens College Junior School, Taunton, Somerset	422
Queens College Pre-Preparatory School, Taunton, Somerset	422
Queens' Gate School, London SW7 5LE	317
Queensland Preparatory School, Westcliffe-on-Sea, Essex	160
Queenswood, Shepherd's Way, Hatfield, Hertfordshire	217
Querns School, Cirencester, Gloucestershire	172
Quinton House School, Northampton, Northamptonshire	381

R

Raddery School †, Fortrose, Highland		620
Radlett Preparatory School, Radlett, Hertfordshire		217
Radley College, Abingdon, Oxfordhsire		404
Rainbow Montessori School, Highgate, London		317
Rainbow Montessori School, London		317
Ramillies Hall, Cheadle Hulme, Cheshire		97
Ranby House, Retford, Nottinghamshire		393
Rannoch School ✳, Perth, Tayside		641
Raphael, Romford, Essex		160
Ratcliffe College ✳, Ratcliffe on the Wreake, Leicestershire		273
Rathvilly, Birmingham, West Midlands		538
Ravenscourt Theatre School, London		318
Ravenstone House, Marble Arch, London		318
Read School, Selby, North Yorkshire	**717,**	557
Reading Blue Coat School, Sonning-on-Thames, Berkshire		66
Reading School, Reading, Berkshire		66
Red Brae Residential School †, Maybole, Strathclyde		634
Red House School, Stockton on Tees, Cleveland		103
Red House School, York, North Yorkshire		557
The Red Maids' School ✳, Bristol, Avon		44
Redcliffe School, London		318
Reddiford School, Pinner, Middlesex		365
Redehall School, Horley, Surrey		470
Redland High School ✳, Bristol, Avon		45
Reigate Grammar School ✳, Reigate, Surrey		471
Reigate St Mary's Preparatory and Choir School, Reigate, Surrey		471
Rendcomb College ✳, Cirencester, Gloucestershire		172
Repton Preparatory, Milton, Derbyshire		117
Repton School ✳, Repton, Derbyshire	748,	117
Richard Pate School, Gloucester, Gloucestershire		172
Richmond House School, Leeds, West Yorkshire		574
Rickmansworth Masonic School, Rickmansworth, Hertfordshire	**674,**	217
Rickmansworth PNEU School, Rickmansworth, Hertfordshire		217
Riddlesworth Hall, Diss, Norfolk	**693,**	374
The Ridge House School, Newbury, Berkshire		67
Ridgeway School (Claires Court Junior School), Maidenhead Thicket, Berkshire		67
Ringwood Waldorf School, Ringwood, Hampshire		187
Ripley Court School, Woking, Surrey		471
Ripon Cathedral Choir, Ripon, North Yorkshire		558
Rishworth School, Rippondon, West Yorkshire		574
The River School, Worcester, Hereford and Worcester		204
Riverside School, Milnthorpe, Cumbria		112
Riverston School, Lee Green, London		318
RNIB New College †, Worcester, Hereford and Worcester	**670,**	204
Robert Gordon's College ✳, Aberdeen, Grampian		617
The Roche School, Wandsworth, London		319
Rockport, Holywood, Co Down		645
Rockwood School, Andover, Hampshire		187
Rodney School, Newark, Nottinghamshire		393
Roedean, Brighton, East Sussex	748,	496
Rokeby School, Kingston-upon-Thames, Surrey		471
Rookesbury Park School, Wickham, Hampshire		188
Rose Hill School, Tunbridge Wells, Kent		248
Rose Hill, Wotton-under-Edge, Gloucestershire		172
The Rose Montessori School, London		319
Rosebrae Pre-Preparatory School and Nursery, Elgin, Grampian		618
Rosecroft Preparatory School, Didsbury, Manchester		345
Roselyon School, Par, Cornwall		106
Rosemead Preparatory School, Dulwich, London		319
Rosemead, Littlehampton, West Sussex		511
Rosemeade, Huddersfield, West Yorkshire		574
Rossall Pre-Preparatory School, Fleetwood, Lancashire		264
Rossall Preparatory School, Fleetwood, Lancashire		265
Rossall School ✳, Fleetwood, Lancashire		265
Rossefield School, Bradford, West Yorkshire		574
Rossholme School, Highbridge, Somerset		423
Rosslyn School, Birmingham, West Midlands		538

Rougemont School, Newport, Gwent	586
Rowan Preparatory School, Esher, Surrey	472
The Rowans, Leatherhead, Surrey	472
Rowens School, Wimbledon, London	319
Roxeth Mead School, Harrow, Middlesex	366
Royal Ballet School, Richmond, Surrey	472
Royal Belfast Academical Institution, Belfast, Co Antrim	645
Royal Caledonian Schools, Watford, Hertfordshire	218
Royal Grammar School *, Newcastle-upon-Tyne, Tyne and Wear	521
Royal Grammar School *, Guildford, Surrey	472
Royal Grammar School *, Worcester, Hereford and Worcester	204
The Royal Hospital School, Ipswich, Suffolk	438
Royal Naval School For Girls, Haslemere, Surrey	473
Royal Russell School, Croydon, Surrey	473
Royal School, Hampstead, London	320
Royal School, Armagh, Co Armagh	646
The Royal School, Dungannon, Co Tyrone	646
The Royal School, Bath, Avon	45
Royal Wolverhampton School, Wolverhampton, West Midlands	539
Ruckleigh School, Solihull, West Midlands	539
Rudolf Steiner School of Edinburgh *, Edinburgh, Lothian	627
Rudolf Steiner School, Dartington, Devon	127
Rudolf Steiner School, Kings Langley, Hertfordshire	218
Rudston Preparatory School, Rotherham, South Yorkshire	563
Rugby School, Rugby, Warwickshire	526
Runnymede Preparatory School, Liverpool, Merseyside	354
Runton and Sutherland School, Cromer, Norfolk	375
Rupert House School, Henley-on-Thames, Oxfordshire	404
Rushmoor Independent School, Farnborough, Hampshire	188
Rushmoor School, Bedford, Bedfordshire	52
Rushmore Independent Nursery School, Farnborough, Hampshire	188
Russell House, Sevenoaks, Kent	248
Ruthin School, Ruthin, Clwyd	581
Rydal *, Colwyn Bay, Clwyd	748, **720,** 581
Rydal Preparatory School, Colwyn Bay, Clwyd	581
Rydal School, Clevedon, Avon	45
Ryde *, Ryde, Isle of Wight	230
Rydes Hill Preparatory School, Guildford, Surrey	473
Rye St Antony, Pullen's Lane, Oxford, Oxfordshire	404
The Ryes School †, Sudbury, Suffolk	438
The Ryleys, Alderley Edge, Cheshire	97

S

S Helen and S Katherine, Abingdon, Oxfordshire	404
S Hillary's School, Alderley Edge, Cheshire	97
S Michaels, Petworth, West Sussex	511
Sackville, Hildenborough, Kent	248
Sacred Heart Preparatory, Bristol, Avon	45
Sacred Heart School, Wadhurst, East Sussex	496
Saint Martin's, Solihull, West Midlands	539
Salcombe Preparatory School, Southgate, London	320
Salesian College *, Farnborough, Hampshire	188
Salisbury Cathedral School, Salisbury, Wiltshire	**714,** 547
Salisbury Cathedral School, Salisbury, Wiltshire	547
Salter's Hall School, Sudbury, Suffolk	438
Salterford House, Calverton, Nottinghamshire	393
Sancton Wood School, Cambridge, Cambridgeshire	85
Sandbach School, Sandbach, Cheshire	97
Sanderstead Junior School, Croydon, Surrey	473
Sandhurst Independent Preparatory School, Worthing, West Sussex	511
Sandle Manor, Fordingbridge, Hampshire	189
Sandroyd School, Salisbury, Wiltshire	547
Sands School, Greylands, Ashburton, Devon	127
Sarum Hall School, Camden, London	320
Saville House School, Mansfield Woodhouse, Nottinghamshire	393
Scaitcliffe School, Egham, Surrey	474
Scarborough College *, Scarborough, North Yorkshire	558
Scarborough College Junior School, Scarborough, North Yorkshire	558

School	Page refs
Scarisbrick Hall School, Ormskirk, Lancashire	265
School of Jesus and Mary, Ipswich, Suffolk	438
School of S Mary and S Anne ✻, Rugeley, Staffordshire	**699,** 429
The School of St Clare, Polwithen, Penzance, Cornwall	107
Seafield School, Fareham, Hampshire	189
Seaford College, Petworth, West Sussex	512
Seaton House School, Sutton, Surrey	474
Seaview Private School, Kirkcaldy, Fife	613
Sedbergh School ✻, Sedbergh, Cumbria	112
Seddon House School, Monmouth, Gwent	587
Selwyn, Gloucester, Gloucestershire	**665,** 173
Sevenoaks Preparatory School, Sevenoaks, Kent	248
Sevenoaks School ✻, Sevenoaks, Kent	749, 249
Shaftesbury Independent School, Purley, Surrey	474
Shapwick School, Bridgwater, Somerset	**698,** 423
Shaw House School, Bradford, West Yorkshire	575
Shebbear College, Shebbear, Devon	749, 127
Sheffield High School ✻, Sheffield, South Yorkshire	564
The Sheila Bruce Community Arts Establishment, Hartlepool, Cleveland	103
Sheiling School Camphill Community, Bristol, Avon	46
The Sheiling School, Ringwood, Hampshire	189
The Shepherd's Bush Day Nursery, London	320
Sherborne House School, Chandlers' Ford, Hampshire	189
Sherborne Preparatory School, Sherborne, Dorset	141
Sherborne School for Girls, Sherborne, Dorset	749, 141
Sherborne School, Sherborne, Dorset	141
Shernold School, Maidstone, Kent	249
Sherrardswood School, Welwyn Garden City, Hertfordshire	218
Shiplake College, Henley-on-Thames, Oxfordshire	405
Shobrooke House School, Crediton, Devon	128
Shoreham College, Shoreham by Sea, West Sussex	512
Shotton Hall School †, Shrewsbury, Shropshire	415
Shrewsbury High School ✻, Shrewsbury, Shropshire	415
Shrewsbury House, Surbiton, Surrey	474
Shrewsbury School, Shrewsbury, Shropshire	415
The Shrubbery School, Sutton Coldfield, West Midlands	539
Sibford School, Banbury, Oxfordshire	405
Sibton Park Girls' Preparatory School, Folkestone, Kent	249
Sidcot School, Winscombe, Avon	46
Silchester House School, Maidenhead, Berkshire	67
Silcoates School ✻, Wakefield, West Yorkshire	575
Silfield School, Kings Lynn, Norfolk	375
Silverhill School, Winterbourne, Bristol, Avon	46
Sinclair House School, Fulham, London	321
Sion School, Worthing, West Sussex	512
Sir Roger Manwood's, Sandwich, Kent	249
Sir Willim Perkin's School ✻, Chertsey, Surrey	475
Skippers Hill Manor Preparatory School, Mayfield, East Sussex	496
Slindon College, Arundel, West Sussex	**711,** 512
Snaresbrook College, South Woodford, London	321
Snowden School †, Stirling, Central	607
Snowdonia Steiner School, Tremadog, Gwynedd	589
Solefield, Sevenoaks, Kent	250
Solihull School ✻, Solihull, West Midlands	750, 540
Somerleaze Preparatory School, Leominster, Hereford and Worcester	204
Somerville School, London	321
Sompting Abbotts Preparatory School, Lancing, West Sussex	513
South Hamstead High School, London	321
South Lee Preparatory School, Bury St Edmunds, Suffolk	439
South Lodge School, Baldock, Hertfordshire	218
Southannan School †, Largs, Strathclyde	634
Southdown School, Steyning, West Sussex	513
Southfields School, Sale, Cheshire	98
Spinney School †, Heathfield, East Sussex	496
Spratton Hall School, Northampton, Northamptonshire	381
Spring Grove School, Ashford, Kent	250
Springbank School, Cambuslang, Strathclyde	635
Springfield PNEU, Ongar, Essex	160

The Squirrel School, Oxford, Oxfordshire		405
St Agnes' PNEU School, Leeds, West Yorkshire		575
St Albans High School for Girls ✻, St Albans, Hertfordshire		219
St Albans School ✻, St Albans, Hertfordshire		219
St Aldates College, Oxford, Oxfordshire		405
St Aloysius' College ✻, Glasgow, Strathclyde		635
St Ambrose College ✻, Altrincham, Cheshire		98
St Andrew Day School, Marlborough, Wiltshire		547
St Andrew's Boys' Preparatory School, North Harrow, Middlesex		366
St Andrew's Independent Montessori Preparatory School, Bushey, Hertfordshire		219
St Andrew's Preparatory School, Edenbridge, Kent		250
St Andrew's Preparatory School, Malton, North Yorkshire		558
St Andrew's School, Harrow, Middlesex		366
St Andrew's School, Reading, Berkshire	**655,**	67
St Andrew's School, Rochester, Kent		250
St Andrew's School, Bedford, Bedfordshire		52
St Andrew's School, Eastbourne, East Sussex		497
St Andrew's School, Wantage, Oxfordshire		406
St Andrew's Senior Girls School, Harrow, Middlesex		366
St Andrew's, Woking, Surrey		475
St Angelo Preparatory School, Ealing, London		322
St Anne's College Grammar School and Junior School, Lytham St Annes, Lancashire		265
St Anne's High School, Bishop Aukland, Durham		149
St Anne's Mixed High School, South Shields, Tyne and Wear		521
St Anne's School, Chelmsford, Essex		161
St Anne's, Lee-on-the-Solent, Hampshire		190
St Annes School for Girls, Windermere, Cumbria	750, **659,**	112
St Anselm's College ✻, Birkenhead, Merseyside		354
St Anselm's School, Bakewell, Derbyshire		117
St Anthony's Convent Preparatory School, Sherborne, Dorset		142
St Anthony's Convent School, Cinderford, Gloucestershire		173
St Anthony's Montessori School, Sunderland, Tyne and Wear		521
St Anthony's School, Camden, London		322
St Antony's-Leweston School, Sherborne, Dorset		142
St Aubyn's (Woodford Green) School Ltd, Woodford Green, Essex		161
St Aubyn's School, Tiverton, Devon		128
St Aubyns, Brighton, East Sussex		497
St Audrey's Convent, Wisbech, Cambridgeshire		86
St Augustine's College, Westgate on Sea, Kent		251
St Augustine's Priory, Ealing, London		32
St Bede's College ✻, Manchester		345
St Bede's College Preparatory School, Manchester		346
St Bede's School, Stafford, Staffordshire		429
St Bede's School, Eastbourne, East Sussex		497
St Bede's School, Hailsham, East Sussex		497
St Bees School ✻, St Bees, Cumbria		113
St Benedict's Convent School, Andover, Hampshire	**667,**	190
St Benedict's Junior School, Ealing, London		323
St Benedict's School ✻, London		323
St Bernard's Preparatory School, Slough, Berkshire		68
St Bernard's School, Newton Abbot, Devon		128
St Brandon's School, Clevedon, Avon		46
St Bride's School, Macclesfield, Cheshire		98
St Brigid's School, Denbigh, Clwyd		581
St Catherine's Preparatory School, Stockport, Cheshire		98
St Catherine's School ✻, Guildford, Surrey	750, **706,**	475
St Catherine's School, Twickenham, Middlesex		367
St Catherine's School, Camberley, Surrey		475
St Cedd's School, Chelmsford, Essex		161
St Christina's Roman Catholic Preparatory School, Regents Park, London		323
St Christopher School, Letchworth, Hertfordshire	**675,**	219
St Christopher's School †, Bristol, Avon		476
St Christopher's School, Radlett, Hertfordshire		220
St Christopher's School, London		323
St Christopher's School, Beckenham, Kent		251
St Christopher's School, Epsom, Surrey		476

School		Page
St Christopher's School, Wembley, Middlesex		367
St Christopher's School, Burnham on Sea, Somerset		423
St Christopher's School, Norwich, Norfolk		375
St Christopher's, Hove, East Sussex		498
St Clare's, Oxford, Oxfordshire	750,	406
St Clares Convent School, Porthcawl, Mid Glamorgan		592
St Clotilde's School, Lechlade, Gloucestershire		173
St Columb's College, Londonderry		646
St Columba's College, St Albans, Hertfordshire		220
St Columba's School ✶, Kilmacolm, Strathclyde		635
St Crispin's, Leicester, Leicestershire		273
St David's College, Llandudno, Gwynedd		589
St David's College, West Wickham, Kent		251
St David's Junior School, Ashford, Middlesex		367
St David's School, Purley, Surrey		476
St David's School, Ashford, Middlesex		367
St David's School, Huddersfield, West Yorkshire		575
St David's Ursuline Convent School, Brecon, Powys		594
St Denis & Cranley School for Girls ✶, Edinburgh, Lothian		627
St Dominic's College, Harrow, Middlesex		368
St Dominic's Independent Junior School, Stoke on Trent, Staffordshire		429
St Dominic's Priory School, Stone, Staffordshire		430
St Dominic's School, Stafford, Staffordshire		430
St Dunstan's Abbey, Plymouth, Devon		128
St Dunstan's Abbey, Plymouth, Devon		12
St Dunstan's College ✶, Catford, London		324
St Edmund's College ✶, Ware, Hertfordshire		220
St Edmund's School, Canterbury,		251
St Edmunds School, Hindhead, Surrey		476
St Edward's College ✶, Liverpool, Merseyside		355
St Edward's School, Reading, Berkshire		68
St Edward's School, Cheltenham, Gloucestershire		173
St Edward's School, Oxford, Oxfordshire		406
St Elphin's School, Matlock, Derbyshire	**659,**	117
St Faith's School, Ash, Kent		252
St Faith's School, Cambridge, Cambridgeshire		86
St Felix School ✶, Southwold, Suffolk	**700,**	439
St Francis Primary - Merrylee, Glasgow, Strathclyde		635
St Francis School, Pewsey, Wiltshire		548
St Francis' College, Letchworth, Hertfordshire	**676,**	220
St Gabriel's School, Newbury, Berkshire		68
St Genevieve's Convent, Dorchester, Dorset		142
St George's College, Addlestone, Surrey		476
St George's Preparatory School, St Peter, Jersey		650
St George's School (Pierrepont Junior), Frensham, Surrey		477
St George's School for Girls, Edinburgh, Lothian	**722,**	627
St George's School, Dunstable, Bedfordshire		53
St George's School, Ascot, Berkshire		68
St George's School, Southwold, Suffolk		439
St George's School, Windsor, Berkshire		69
St Gerard's School Trust, Bangor, Gwynedd		590
St Giles' College, Eastbourne, East Sussex		498
St Godric's College, Hampstead, London		324
St Helen's College, Hillingdon, Middlesex		368
St Helen's School ✶, Northwood, Middlesex		368
St Hilary's School, Godalming, Surrey		477
St Hilda's School, Westcliffe-on-Sea, Essex	**662,**	161
St Hilda's School, Harpenden, Hertfordshire		221
St Hilda's School, Wakefield, West Yorkshire		576
St Hilda's School, Bushey, Hertfordshire		221
St Hilda's School, Whitby, North Yorkshire		559
St Hugh's Preparatory School, Ware, Hertfordshire		221
St Hugh's School, Faringdon, Oxfordshire		406
St Hugh's School, Woodhall Spa, Lincolnshire		278
St Illtyd's High School, Cardiff, South Glamorgan		599
St Ives School, Haslemere, Surrey		477
St James Independent School for Boys, London		324
St James Independent School for Boys, London		324

School	Page
St James Independent School for Girls, London	325
St James Independent School for Girls, London	325
St James' and The Abbey School, Great Malvern, Hereford and Worcester	205
St James' School, Grimsby, Humberside	228
St John's Beaumont, Old Windsor, Berkshire	69
St John's College *, Portsmouth, Hampshire	190
St John's College School, Cambridge, Cambridgeshire	86
St John's College, Cardiff, South Glamorgan	599
St John's Preparatory School, Lichfield, Staffordshire	430
St John's Preparatory School, Potters Bar, Hertfordshire	221
St John's Priory School, Banbury, Oxfordshire	407
St John's School *, Leatherhead, Surrey	477
St John's School, Porthcawl, Mid Glamorgan	592
St John's School, Northwood, Middlesex	368
St John's School, Billericay, Essex	162
St John's Wood, St John's Wood, London	325
St John's-on-the-Hill, Chepstow, Gwent	587
St Johns School, Sidmouth, Devon	129
St Joseph's Academy, Lewisham, London	325
St Joseph's College *, Stoke on Trent, Staffordshire	430
St Joseph's College, Ipswich, Suffolk	439
St Joseph's College, Dumfries, Dumfries and Galloway	609
St Joseph's Convent Preparatory School, Reading, Berkshire	69
St Joseph's Convent School *, Reading, Berkshire	69
St Joseph's Convent School, Chesterfield, Derbyshire	118
St Joseph's Convent School, Broadstairs, Kent	252
St Joseph's Convent School, Wanstead, London	326
St Joseph's Convent School, Cardiff, South Glamorgan	600
St Joseph's Convent School, Burnley, Lancashire	266
St Joseph's Convent, Barnet, London	326
St Joseph's Dominican Convent School, Pulborough, West Sussex	513
St Joseph's Junior School, Kenilworth, Warwickshire	527
St Joseph's Preparatory School *, Ipswich, Suffolk	440
St Joseph's Roman Catholic School, Bideford, Devon	129
St Joseph's School, Nottingham, Nottinghamshire	394
St Joseph's School, Bradford, West Yorkshire	576
St Joseph's School, Nympsfield, Gloucestershire	174
St Joseph's School, Launceston, Cornwall	107
St Joseph's School, Hertingfordbury, Hertfordshire	222
St Joseph's School, Lincoln, Lincolnshire	278
St Joseph's Senior School, Kenilworth, Warwickshire	527
St Lawrence College *, Ramsgate, Kent	252
St Lawrence College Junior School, Ramsgate, Kent	252
St Leonards School *, St Andrews, Fife	613
St Leonards-Mayfield School, Mayfield, East Sussex	498
St Luke's School †, Teignmouth, Devon	129
St Malachy's College, Belfast, Co Antrim	646
St Margaret's Edinburgh *, Edinburgh, Lothian	627
St Margaret's Exeter *, Exeter, Devon	660, 130
St Margaret's Preparatory School, Gosfield, Essex	162
St Margaret's School *, Bushey, Hertfordshire	222
St Margaret's School for Girls *, Aberdeen, Grampian	618
St Margeret's Convent School, Midhurst, West Sussex	513
St Margeret's Junior School, Midhurst, West Sussex	514
St Margeret's School, London	326
St Martha's Junior School, Barnet, Hertfordshire	222
St Martha's Senior School, Barnet, Hertfordshire	676, 222
St Martin's Preparatory School,Grimsby, Humberside	228
St Martin's School, Crewkerne, Somerset	423
St Martin's School, Barnet, London	326
St Martin's School, Northwood, Middlesex	369
St Martin's School, York, North Yorkshire	559
St Martins', Bournemouth, Dorset	142
St Mary's Catholic School, Bishops Stortford, Hertfordshire	223
St Mary's Christian Brothers Grammar School, Belfast, County Antrim	647
St Mary's College *, Crosby, Merseyside	355
St Mary's College, Southampton, Hampshire	190
St Mary's College, Twickenham, Middlesex	369

St Mary's Convent School, Worcester, Hereford and Worcester		205
St Mary's Convent School, Folkestone, Kent		253
St Mary's Convent, Camden, London		327
St Mary's Hall *, Brighton, East Sussex	*751,*	498
St Mary's Hall, Stonyhurst, Lancashire		266
St Mary's Hare Park School, Romford, Essex		162
St Mary's Music School, Edinburgh, Lothian		628
St Mary's Preparatory School, Reigate, Surrey		478
St Mary's RC-Aided Primary School, Newtown, Powys		594
St Mary's School †, Bexhill-on-Sea, East Sussex		499
St Mary's School *, Melrose, Borders		605
St Mary's School *, Cambridge, Cambridgeshire		86
St Mary's School, Colchester, Essex	**663,**	162
St Mary's School, Henley-on-Thames, Oxfordshire		407
St Mary's School, Lincoln, Lincolnshire		278
St Mary's School, Doncaster, South Yorkshire		56
St Mary's School, Ascot, Berkshire		70
St Mary's School, Calne, Wiltshire		548
St Mary's School, Shaftesbury, Dorset		143
St Mary's School, Wantage, Oxfordshire		407
St Mary's, Gerrards Cross, Bucks		79
St Matthews Preparatory School, Northampton, Northamptonshire		382
St Maur's School *, Weybridge, Surrey		478
St Michael's - Kelly College Junior School, Tavistock, Devon		130
St Michael's College, Tenbury Wells, Hereford and Worcester		205
St Michael's Hill House Preparatory School, Uckfield, East Sussex		499
St Michael's Nursery School, Uckfield, East Sussex		499
St Michael's Preparatory School, St Saviour, Jersey		650
St Michael's School, Leigh-on-Sea, Essex		163
St Michael's School, Llanelli, Dyfed		584
St Michael's School, Woking, Surrey		478
St Michael's School, Barnstaple, Devon		130
St Michael's School, Oxted, Surrey		478
St Michaels Preparatory School, Sevenoaks, Kent		253
St Michaels School PNEU, Tavistock, Devon		130
St Monica's, Poole, Dorset		143
St Neot's School, Basingstoke, Hampshire		191
St Nicholas House, Hemel Hempstead, Hertfordshire		223
St Nicholas Nursery and Preparatory, Folkestone, Kent		253
St Nicholas Preparatory and Kindergarten School, North Walsham, Norfolk		375
St Nicholas School, Buxted, East Sussex		499
St Nicholas's School, Fleet, Hampshire	**668,**	191
St Nicholas, Old Harlow, Essex		163
St Olav's School, York, North Yorkshire		559
St Olave's Preparatory School, Greenwich, London		327
St Paul's Cathedral Choir School, London		327
St Paul's Convent, Sutton Coldfield, West Midlands		540
St Paul's Girls' Preparatory School, Hammersmith and Fulham, London		327
St Paul's Girls' School, Hammersmith and Fulham,		328
St Paul's Preparatory School, Barnes, London		328
St Paul's Primary Independent School, Leicester, Leicestershire		273
St Paul's School *, Barnes, London		328
St Paul's School, Birmingham, West Midlands		540
St Peter and St Paul's School, Chesterfield, Derbyshire		118
St Peter's Independent School, Northampton, Northamptonshire		382
St Peter's Preparatory School, Congleton, Cheshire		99
St Peter's School *, York, North Yorkshire		559
St Peter's School, Kettering, Northamptonshire		382
St Peter's School, Bournemouth, Dorset		143
St Peter's School, Lympstone, Devon		131
St Peter's Upper School, Burgess Hill, West Sussex		514
St Petroc's School, Bude, Cornwall		107
St Philip's, London	**691,**	328
St Phillip's Priory New School, Chelmsford, Essex		163
St Phillip's School, Airdrie, Strathclyde		636
St Philomena's School, Frinton-on-Sea, Essex		163
St Piran's, Maidenhead, Berkshire		70
St Pius X Preparatory School, Preston, Lancashire		266

School	Ref	Page
St Richard's, Bromyard, Hereford and Worcester		205
St Ronan's Preparatory School, Glasgow, Strathclyde		636
St Ronan's School, Bridport, Dorset		143
St Ronans, Hawkhurst, Kent TN18 5DJ		253
St Serf's School, Edinburgh, Lothian		628
St Swithun's Junior School, Winchester, Hampshire		191
St Swithun's School *, Winchester, Hampshire	*751,* **668,**	191
St Teresa's Catholic School, Princes Risborough, Buckinghamshire		80
St Teresa's Convent School, Dorking, Surrey		479
St Teresa's Convent, Leatherhead, Surrey		479
St Therese Presentation Convent, Ryde, Isle of Wight		230
St Thomas Garnet's School, Bournemouth, Dorset		144
St Thomas More's School, Totnes, Devon		131
St Ursula's High School, Bristol, Avon		47
St Vedast Independent School for Boys, Camden, London		329
St Wilfrid's Junior School, Exeter, Devon		131
St Wilfrid's School, Exeter, Devon		131
St Winefride's, Shrewsbury, Shropshire		415
St Winifrid's School, Southampton, Hampshire		192
St Wyburn School, Southport, Merseyside		355
St Wystan's, Derby, Derbyshire		118
Stafford Grammar School *, Stafford, Staffordshire		431
Staines Preparatory School Trust, Staines, Middlesex		369
Stamford High School *, Stamford, Lincolnshire		278
Stamford School *, Stamford, Lincolnshire		279
Stanborough School, Watford, Hertfordshire		223
Stanbridge Earls School, Romsey, Hampshire		192
Stancliffe Hall, Matlock, Derbyshire		118
Stanley House School, Aldershot, Hampshire		192
Stanway, Dorking, Surrey		479
Staplands School, Weybridge, Surrey		479
Starley Hall School, Burntisland, Fife		61
Starting Points PP and Southfield Pre-Preparatory School, Halesworth, Suffolk		440
Steatham House School, Great Crosby, Merseyside		355
Stella Maris Junior School, Stockport, Cheshire		99
Stella Maris Primary School, Swansea, West Glamorgan		603
Stella Maris School, Bideford, Devon	**660,**	132
Stockport Grammar School *,Stockport, Cheshire		99
Stoke Brunswick School, East Grinstead, West Sussex		514
Stoke College, Sudbury, Suffolk		440
Stoke Lodge School, Coventry, West Midlands		540
Stonar, Melksham, Wiltshire		548
Stonefield House School, Lincoln, Lincolnshire		279
Stonelands School of Dance and Drama, Dawlish, Devon		132
Stonely Grange School, Huntingdon, Cambridgeshire		87
Stoneygate School, Leicester, Leicestershire		273
Stonyhurst College *, Stonyhurst, Lancashire		266
Stoodley Knowle Convent School, Torquay, Devon		132
Stormont, Potters Bar, Hertfordshire		223
Story House School, Wath-upon-Dearne, South Yorkshire		564
Stourbridge House, Warminster, Wiltshire		548
Stover School, Newton Abbot, Devon		132
Stowe School *, Buckingham, Buckinghamshire		80
Stowford College, Sutton, Surrey		480
Stratford House, Bromley, Kent	**679,**	254
Stratford Preparatory School, Stratford-upon-Avon, Warwickshire		527
Strathallan School *, Perth, Tayside		641
Streatham Hill and Clapham High School *, London		329
Streatham Modern School, London		329
Streete Court, Godstone, Surrey		480
Stretton House PNEU School, Knutsford, Cheshire		99
The Stroud School, Romsey, Hampshire		192
Stubbington House, Ascot, Berkshire		70
The Study Preparatory School, Wimbledon Common, London		329
The Study School, Kingston-upon-Thames, Surrey		480
Summer Fields School, Oxford, Oxfordshire		407
Summerhill School, Leiston, Suffolk		440

Sunderland High School, Sunderland, Tyne and Wear		522
Sunfield †, Stourbridge, Hereford and Worcester		206
Sunningdale, Sunningdale, Berkshire		70
Sunninghill Preparatory School, Dorchester, Dorset		144
Sunnybank Preparatory School, Burnley, Lancashire		267
Sunnymede School, Southport, Merseyside		356
Sunnyside School, Worcester, Hereford and Worcester		206
Sunrise Independent, Maidstone, Kent		254
Surbiton High School ✲, Kingston-upon-Thames, Surrey		480
Surbiton Preparatory School, Kingston-upon-Thames, Surrey		481
Sussex House Preparatory School, Kensington and Chelsea, London		330
Sutherland House School, Cromer, Norfolk		376
Sutherlands School, Leighton Buzzard, Bedfordshire		53
Sutton High School GPDST ✲, Sutton, Surrey		481
Sutton Valence School ✲, Maidstone, Kent	751,	254
Swanbourne House, Swanbourne, Milton Keynes, Buckinghamshire		80
Sycamore Hall Preparatory School, Doncaster, South Yorkshire		564
Syddal Park School, Stockport, Cheshire		100
Sydenham High School GPDST ✲, London	**691,**	330
Sylvia Young Theatre School, Marylebone, London		330

T

Tabley House School, Knutsford, Cheshire		100
Talbot Heath School ✲, Bournemouth, Dorset	**661,**	144
Talbot House Preparatory School, Bournemouth, Dorset		144
Talmud Torah School, London		330
The Tanwood School, Swindon, Wiltshire		549
TASIS England American School, Thorpe, Surrey		481
Taunton Junior Boys School, Taunton, Somerset		424
Taunton Junior Girls School, Taunton, Somerset		424
Taunton School ✲, Taunton, Somerset		424
Taverham Hall, Norwich, Norfolk		376
Tavistock & Summerhill, Haywards Heath, West Sussex		514
Teesside High School ✲, Stockton-on-Tees, Cleveland		103
Temple Grove School, Uckfield, East Sussex	**709,**	500
Terra Nova School, Holmes Chapel, Cheshire		100
Terrington Hall Preparatory School, York, North Yorkshire		560
Tettenhall College, Wolverhampton, West Midlands		541
Thetford Grammar School, Thetford, Norfolk		376
Thomas's Preparatory School, Battersea, London		331
Thomas's Preparatory School, Kensington, London		331
Thornhill Park School, Sunderland, Tyne and Wear		522
Thornlow Junior School, Weymouth, Dorset		145
Thornlow Senior School, Weymouth, Dorset		145
Thornton College, Milton Keynes, Buckinghamshire		80
Thorpe Hall School, Thorpe Bay, Essex		164
Thorpe House School, Norwich, Norfolk		376
Thorpe House School, Gerrards Cross, Buckinghamshire		81
Toad Hall Nursery School, Kennington, London		331
Tockington Manor, Bristol, Avon		47
Tonbridge School ✲, Tonbridge, Kent	751,	254
Tonstall School, Sunderland, Tyne and Wear		522
Tor International School, Langport, Somerset		424
Tormead School ✲, Guildford, Surrey		481
Torwood House School, Bristol, Avon		47
Total Oil Marine's French School, Aberdeen, Grampian		618
Tower College, Rainhill, Merseyside		356
Tower Dene Preparatory School, Southport, Merseyside		356
Tower House School, Barmouth, Gwynned		590
Tower House School, Paignton, Devon		133
Tower House, London		331
The Towers, Steyning, West Sussex		515
Town Close House Preparatory School, Norwich, Norfolk		377
The Trees Pre-Preparatory School, Woking, Surrey		482
Treffos Independent School, Anglesey, Gwynedd		590
Tregelles, York, North Yorkshire		560
Tregynon Hall School †, Newtown, Powys		595
Treliske School, Truro, Cornwall		107

781

U

Tremore Christian School, Bodmin, Cornwall	108
Tremough Convent School, Penryn, Cornwall	**658,** 108
Trengweath School †, Plymouth, Devon	133
Trent College ✻, Long Eaton, Nottinghamshire	394
Trescol Vean, Truro, Cornwall	108
Trinity Catholic High School, Redbridge, London	332
Trinity School ✻, Croydon, Surrey	482
Trinity School, Dundee, Tayside	641
Trinity School, Teignmouth, Devon	133
Troy School †, Monmouth, Gwent	587
Truro High School for Girls ✻, Truro, Cornwall	108
Truro School ✻, Truro, Cornwall	109
Tudor Hall, Banbury, Oxfordshire	40
Twice Times Montessori Nursery School, South Park, London	332
Twickenham Preparatory School, Hampton, Middlesex	369
Twycross House School, Atherstone, Warwickshire	527
Twyford School, Winchester, Hampshire	193

U

Underhill Preparatory School, Maidstone, Kent	255
Unicorn, Richmond, Surrey	482
University College School ✻, Hampstead, London	332
University College School Junior Branch, London	332
Upfield Preparatory School Ltd, Stroud, Gloucestershire	174
Uplands School, Poole, Dorset	145
Upper Chine School, Shanklin, Isle of Wight	230
Upper Tooting Independent High School, London	333
Uppingham, Uppingham, Leicestershire	752, 274
Upton Hall Convent School ✻, Wirral, Merseyside	356
Upton House School, Windsor, Berkshire	71
The Urdang Academy of Ballet, London	333
Ursuline Convent Preparatory School, Wimbledon, London	333
Ursuline Convent School ✻, Westgate-on-Sea, Kent	255
Ursuline High School ✻, Ilford, London	333
Ursuline Preparatory School, Brentwood, Essex	164

V

The Vale School, Aylesbury, Buckinghamshire	81
The Vale, London	334
Vernon Holme, Canterbury, Kent	255
Vernon Lodge Preparatory School and Kindergarten, Brewood, Staffordshire	431
Victoria College Preparatory, St Helier, Jersey	650
Victoria College, Belfast, Co Antrim	647
Victoria College, St Helier, Jersey	650
Victoria School for Physically Handicapped Children †, Poole, Dorset	145
The Village School, London	334
Vinehall School, Robertsbridge, East Sussex	500
Virginia Water Preparatory School, Virginia Water, Surrey	482
Virgo Fidelis Convent, Upper Norwood, London	334
Vita et Pax Convent School, Southgate, London	334

W

Wadhurst College, Wadhurst, East Sussex	500
Wakefield Girls' High School, Wakefield, West Yorkshire	576
Wakefield Independent School, Wakefield, West Yorkshire	576
Wakefield Tutorial School, Morley, West Yorkshire	577
Waldorf School of South West London, London	335
Walhampton School, Lymington, Hampshire	752, 193
Wallop, Weybridge, Surrey	483
Walmsley House School, Bedford, Bedfordshire	53
Walthamstow Hall ✻, Sevenoaks, Kent	255
Warminster School, Warminster, Wiltshire	549
Warwick Preparatory School, Warwick, Warwickshire	528
Warwick School ✻, Warwick, Warwickshire	752, *528*
Waterside School, Bishop's Stortford, Hertfordshire	224
Watford Grammar School, Watford, Hertfordshire	224
Waverley School, Crowthorne, Berkshire	71
Welbeck College, Worksop, Nottinghamshire	394

Wellesley House, Broadstairs, Kent		256
Wellingborough School ✻, Wellingborough, Northamptonshire		382
Wellington ✻, Wellington, Somerset		425
Wellington College ✻, Crowthorne, Berkshire		71
Wellington School ✻, Ayr, Strathclyde		636
Wellington School, Wirral, Merseyside		357
Wellington School, Penicuik, Lothian		628
Wellow House School, Newark, Nottinghamshire		394
Wells Cathedral Junior School, Wells, Somerset		425
Wells Cathedral School ✻, Wells, Somserset		425
Wells House School, Malvern Wells, Hereford and Worcester		206
Welsh School of London, London		335
Wentworth Milton Mount, Bournemouth, Dorset		146
Werneth Private Preparatory School, Oldham, Manchester		346
West Bridgford School, Nottingham, Nottinghamshire		395
West Buckland School ✻, Barnstaple, Devon	752,	133
West Dene School, Purley, Surrey		483
West Downs School, Winchester, Hampshire		193
West Heath School, Sevenoaks, Kent		256
West Hill Park, Fareham, Hampshire		193
West House School, Birmingham, West Midlands		541
West Lodge School Ltd, Sidcup, Kent		256
Westbourne House School, Chichester, West Sussex		515
Westbourne Preparatory School, Sheffield, South Yorkshire		565
Westbourne Primary School, Penarth, South Glamorgan		600
Westbourne School for Girls ✻, Glasgow, Strathclyde		636
Westbourne School, Wallasey, Merseyside		357
Westbourne Schools, Penarth, South Glamorgan		600
Westbrook Hay School, Hemel Hempstead, Hertfordshire		224
Westbury House School, New Malden, Surrey		483
Westerlea School for Spastic Children †, Edinburgh, Lothian		628
Westerleigh, Hollington Park Road, St Leonards on Sea, East Sussex		500
Western College Preparatory School, Plymouth, Devon		134
Westfield School, Newcastle upon Tyne, Tyne and Wear		522
Westholme ✻, Blackburn, Lancashire		267
Westminster Abbey Choir School, London		335
Westminster Cathedral Choir School, London		335
Westminster School ✻, London		336
Westminster Tutors, London		336
Westminster Under School, London		336
Westmont School, Newport, Isle of Wight		231
Weston Favell School, Northampton, Northamptonshire		383
Weston Green School, Thames Ditton, Surrey		483
Westonbirt School, Tetbury, Gloucestershire	666,	174
Westville House School, Ilkley, West Yorkshire		577
Westward School, Walton-on-Thames, Surrey		484
Westwing School, Bristol, Avon		48
Westwood School, Bushey, Hertfordshire		224
White House School, Whitchurch, Shropshire		416
White House School, Seaton, Devon		134
White House School, Stamford, Lincolnshire		279
White House, Wokingham, Berkshire		71
Whitefield Preparatory School, Whitefield, Manchester		346
Whitford Hall School, Bromsgrove, Hereford and Worcester		206
Whitgift School ✻, Croydon, Surrey		484
Whittingham School, London		336
Wicken Park School, Milton Keynes, Buckinghamshire		81
Widford Lodge, Chelmsford, Essex		164
William Hulme's Grammar School ✻, Manchester		346
The William Skurr School, Rochdale, Manchester		267
Willington School, Wimbledon, London		337
Willoughby Hall School, Hampstead, London		337
Wilmslow Preparatory School, Wilmslow, Cheshire		100
Wilton House School, Battle, East Sussex	709,	501
Wimbledon College Preparatory School, Wimbledon, London		337
Wimbledon Common Preparatory School, Merton, London		337
Wimbledon High School GPDST ✻, Wimbledon, London		338
Wimbledon Park Montessori School, Wimbledon, London		338

Winbury School, Maidenhead, Berkshire	72
Winchester College ✸, Winchester, Hampshire	194
Winchester House School, Brackley, Northamptonshire	383
Windlesham House, Pulborough, West Sussex	515
Winterfold House School, Kidderminster, Hereford and Worcester	207
Winton House School, St Leonards-on-Sea, East Sussex	501
Winton School, Croydon, Surrey	484
Wisbech Grammar School ✸, Wisbech, Cambridgeshire	87
Wispers School, Haslemere, Surrey	484
Witham Hall School, Bourne, Lincolnshire	279
Withington Girls' School ✸, Fallowfield, Manchester	347
Woburn Hill School, Addlestone, Surrey	485
Wolborough Hill School, Newton Abbot, Devon	134
Woldingham, Woldingham, Surrey	485
Wolstanton Preparatory School, Wolstanton, Staffordshire	431
Wolverhampton Grammar School ✸, Wolverhampton, West Midlands	541
Wood Dene School, Norwich, Norfolk	377
Wood Tutorial College, Camden, London	338
Woodbank Grammar School, Leicester, Leicestershire	274
Woodbridge School, Woodbridge, Suffolk	441
Woodcote House School, Windlesham, Surrey	485
Woodcroft School †, Loughton, Essex	164
Woodford Green Preparatory School, Woodford Green, Essex	165
Woodhill Preparatory School, Southampton, Hampshire	194
Woodhill School, Chandlers Ford, Hampshire	194
Woodhouse Grove School ✸, Bradford, West Yorkshire	577
Woodlands School, Preston, Lancashire	267
Woodlands School, Newton Stewart, Dumfries and Galloway	610
Woodleigh School Langton, Malton, North Yorkshire	560
Woodsford House School †, Dorchester, Dorset	146
Woodside Park School, London	338
Worksop College ✸, Worksop, Nottinghamshire	395
Worth School, Crawley, West Sussex	515
Wrekin College ✸, Telford, Shropshire	416
Wroxall Abbey School, Warwick, Warwickshire	528
Wychwood School, Oxford, Oxfordshire	**696,** 408
Wycliffe College Junior School ✸, Stonehouse, Gloucestershire	174
Wycombe Abbey School, High Wycombe, Buckinghamshire	81
Wykeham House, Fareham, Hampshire	**669,** 194
Wylde Green College, Sutton Coldfield, West Midlands	541
Wynclif Christian School, Machen, Mid-Glamorgan	592
Wynstones, Gloucester, Gloucestershire	**666,** 175

Y

Yardley Court, Tonbridge, Kent	256
Yarlet Hall, Stafford, Staffordshire	431
Yarm School, Yarm, Cleveland	104
Yateley Manor, Camberley, Surrey	485
Yehudi Menhuin School, Cobham, Surrey	486
Yesodey Hatorah Jewish School, London	339
Yetev Lev Day School for Boys, London	339
York College for Girls, York, North Yorkshire	560
York House School, Rickmansworth, Hertfordshire	225
Yorston Lodge, Knutsford, Cheshire	101
Young England Kindergarten, London	339

Z

Zakaria Muslim Girls' High School, Batley, West Yorkshire	577